SEXUAL VARIANCE IN
SOCIETY AND HISTORY

VERN L. BULLOUGH

SEXUAL VARIANCE IN SOCIETY AND HISTORY

A WILEY-INTERSCIENCE PUBLICATION

JOHN WILEY & SONS, New York • London • Sydney • Toronto

Library of Congress Cataloging in Publication Data:

Bullough, Vern L
  Sexual variance in society and history.

  "A Wiley-Interscience publication."
  Includes bibliographical references and indexes.
    1. Sex customs—History. 2. Sexual deviation—History.
I. Title. [DNLM: 1. Sex behavior—History.
2. Sex deviation—History. 3. Attitude—History.

WM11.1 B938s]
HQ12.B84   301.41'79   75-38911
ISBN 0-471-12080-4

Printed in the United States of America
10 9 8 7 6 5 4 3 2 1

To Reed Erickson, without whose help this book never would have been written.

PREFACE

Everyone knows that sex has existed throughout history, since children have continued to be born, although the vast majority of history books seem to imply that offspring just happen. Historians have often reported the existence of mistresses, mentioned prostitutes, and made clear the needs of kings and other rulers to beget male heirs, but until recently they rarely mentioned homosexuality, neglected topics such as contraception, and in fact generally ignored sex, even though it has to be regarded as one of the major, if not the most important, forces, in shaping history.

This reluctance of "professional" historians to examine sexual topics to the degree they look at other aspects of human behavior has often perpetuated misconceptions, because other investigators, most not particularly qualified to deal with historical materials, have skimmed the surface of sexual history and perpetuated exaggerated and inaccurate beliefs. During my researches I have run across statements that masturbation did not exist until the eighteenth century, that homosexuality caused the fall of the Roman Empire, and that the nineteenth century was a period of pristine sexual purity. Many similar claims come to mind, some so obviously inaccurate that I have not cited their authors, to avoid embarrassing those still writing today. Theories have been built on historical assumptions about sexuality without any effort to determine the accuracy of the historical data.[1]

Still, for those willing to dig into the records and sources, all kinds of data are available. I have gathered some of this information and furnished a history of some aspects of human sexuality. The word *some* is used advisedly, for I have concentrated on a history of attitudes toward sex and their relationship to certain forms of stigmatized sexual behavior, primarily homosexuality, but also to other forms of sexual behavior often lumped with it in the past, including masturbation, transvestism, transsexualism, and bestiality. I have also included information about other aspects of sexual behavior, such as celibacy, incest, rape, adultery, eunuchism, pornography, phallicism, sadism, masochism, and fetishism, but the emphasis has not been on these topics, and they have been included to supplement the main theme. Generally I have ignored prostitution, since I have written on this elsewhere.[2] Contraception is mentioned only occasionally, since other historians have made first-rate studies of this.[3] Marriage and family have also been dealt with only cursorily, because to discuss these topics in detail would have lengthened the book greatly. Moreover, some recent studies are available on these topics.[4]

This being a study of sexual attitudes, I have avoided identifying individuals as engaging in homosexual or other forms of stigmatized sexual behavior unless strong evidence indicates they did so or they were widely believed by their contemporaries to have done so, and even then they are mentioned only when identifying them permits insights into societal attitudes. I have, however, occasionally taken notice of intimate same-sex friendships, not because this necessarily indicates a homoerotic relationship, but because such attachments give an insight into societal opinion. So, for that matter, do the relationships society permits with the opposite sex. For this reason I have included material on male–female relationships and on generalized attitudes toward women. Though I have not subscribed to any theory about what causes individuals to adopt stigmatized sexual behavior, I have looked at some of the variables that seem important, including not only those mentioned already but also opportunities for contact with the opposite sex, the attitudes of a society toward sex, and the punishments imposed on those violating societal sexual norms.

The book concentrates on Western Culture, although there are also views of other cultures for perspective on the Western viewpoint. Though I am a historian, and this is a historical work, I have written to several different audiences: to the nonhistorian who might find the historical overview helpful in his or her own research; to the interested general reader; and to the nonspecialist historian, that is, a nonspecialist in some of these areas. Hence, I have used English translations of source materials and relied most heavily in the footnotes on scholarly material in English. This has sometimes led me to cite an English translation of a French translation of an Arabic original, but in those languages I can read I have checked the original, and for languages, such as Arabic, that I do not read I have had others check the translations. Often, however, there simply are no translations, and then and only then have I cited a work in the original language. Occasionally there is a work of such importance that, even though it is in a foreign language, the reader should know it exists. In these cases I have so indicated.

To provide a background for the nonspecialist, I have also given a brief introduction to the time period or culture surveyed. For those desiring more information it would be wise to consult general textbooks and their bibliographies.[5] For reasons of space as well as the interests of the nonspecialist reader, I have confined myself to offering suggestions for further reading rather than a comprehensive bibliography. Those interested in pursuing the topic should look at the footnotes. In addition I, along with several colleagues, have prepared an extensive listing of more than 10,000 items dealing with various forms of stigmatized sexual behavior that will be published separately.[6]

One of the richest sources of information about sexual behavior is found in religious writings. Early peoples and cultures usually made assumptions about the nature of creation, the need for reproduction, and the importance of the sex act that exercised great influence long after their original basis had been discarded. As new religious concepts replaced older ones, the original assumptions were often kept unchanged or were slightly modified and put in a new garb, probably because the prohibitions involved were so deeply engrained in a society. Thus Western assumptions about sexuality, first formulated by the Greeks, if not before, were given new impetus by the early Christian Fathers, reaffirmed by the Protestant reformers, and accepted by the scientific community of the eighteenth, nineteenth, and even twentieth centuries with little basic change. The Chinese, starting with different assumptions, had an equally persistent tradition, and this is true of most other cultures. Once accepted within a religious or theological framework, sexual attitudes were reinforced by law codes punishing those deviating from accepted norms. Usually this was then followed by an attempt to find philosophical or scientific justification for aspects of sexual behavior sanctioned by religion and law and reasons why those disapproved by religion and law should be prohibited.

Obviously there were always countertrends within a culture, for example, the Jewish tradition in Western culture as opposed to the Greek tradition, and sometimes one interpretation would seem dominant whereas at other periods slight variations would be more acceptable. Western culture, as compared with some other cultures, has generally been hostile to sexual expression, and hence, I have labeled it a sex-negative culture. Western man's hostility has sometimes been so great that there has often been a fear of sex; in this case the term *man* refers to males, since women as a group have said very little about sex and much of the male hostility to sex has been directed to the female.[7]

Some periods have repressed overt sexuality more than others, whereas some have been more accepting of variant forms of heterosexuality and more condemnatory of homosexuality. Regardless of such slight modifications, Western culture, and for that matter almost all other cultures and societies, have emphasized progeny, the need to provide an heir to look after the parents in their old age, to take care of the necessary rituals when they were dead, to keep the family going, and to perform a variety of other functions. Few societies have ever tolerated exclusive homosexuality, except for a few special individuals, although several have tolerated bisexuality.

Since the emphasis on progeny has been so great, it leads to speculation about what the present population crisis and the deemphasis on procreation will do to sexual mores. Most societies have also had a double standard in sexual behavior, greater latitude being permitted the male than the female. Undoubtedly this was due to the female's ability to bear children, and though there were some partially effective contraceptives, most women engaging in sexual intercourse regularly probably became pregnant unless they were sterile, either from gonorrhea or from natural causes. Because this no longer need be the case, a woman is probably freer than ever before to express her sexuality, and the consequences of this assault on the double standard might well be changes in the sexual mores. In fact, for the numerous reasons mentioned in this book, there has been a growing challenge to the traditional Western attitudes toward sex.

A major purpose of this book is to explain the reasons for this assault, for I believe sexuality is defined within a cultural setting and depends greatly on socialization. Thus, in spite of official attitudes, sexual behavior has often contained massive contradictions. For example, many societies that condemned homosexuality had institutions socializing individuals into homoerotic relationships. A good example was the English public school system of the nineteenth century,[8] particularly as the attitudes developed there were enforced by other societal factors. Undoubtedly, many people were aware of these contradictions but held the institutions that might have encouraged homosexuality or other forms of "stigmatized" sexuality to be valuable enough to tolerate for other reasons. There are many other ambiguities about sex in Western culture, for on the surface Western culture appears to have made absolute prohibitions against certain sexual practices whereas in reality few of them have ever been absolute.

This is why it is important to examine the creative writers of the past. Though the religious, legal, philosophical, and scientific literature dealing with sex gives vast information about sexual attitudes, particularly about official attitudes, a different picture is often available in the writings of the poet, the novelist, the dramatist, and the diarist, and in the writings of those who observed different cultures, preserved their letters, or composed their autobiographies. Unfortunately, as we approach the modern period, the amount of such material becomes overwhelming, far beyond the capacity of any one person to examine. Inevitably this means that this study is by no means exhaustive; a vast mine of materials remains to be exhumed by other investigators. As investigation proceeds, more and brighter light will be focused on the subjects discussed here as well as on aspects of sexual behavior more or less ignored here. Still, before detailed monographic studies can be done, it is essential to point out what is known and what is not known, where work has been done and where work needs to be done. By giving an overview of the forest of information about sexuality, I hope to make it easier for others to examine in detail a particular tree or even a branch of a tree.

Ultimately no historical study can be definitive for any length of time, and this is particularly true of this phase of study in sexuality. Anyone investigating the history of sexuality eventually realizes that even the so-called sexual radicals of the past were very much prisoners of their own unexamined assumptions and often ended perpetuating an old mythology in a new form. This realization necessitates some words of caution to the reader, for it must become obvious that I am the victim of the same cultural prison. To avoid some of these dangers, I have not adopted any theory about sexuality, whether Freudian, Marxian, or Augustinian, but have accepted sexuality as a biological fact and described what past attitudes have been, in the process examining their contradictions. My judgments are not, however, value free, since I have assumed that social and cultural beliefs are important in explaining why societies and peoples differ. I have accepted the notion that no form of sexuality is against nature, and although I find some expressions of sexuality more distasteful than others, I have tried to avoid condemnation. Occasionally my bias must appear evident, namely that sex is personal, something to be enjoyed as long as those involved engage in it of their own free will. It is my hope that readers will come away from this book with a better understanding of what human sexuality is as well as a realization of the wealth of material history offers on the subject. A major obstacle to understanding our own sexuality is realizing we are prisoners of past societal attitudes toward sex.

Research for this book was supported by the Erickson Educational Foundation, Baton Rouge, Louisiana, and the book itself is dedicated to Reed Erickson, founder and president of the foundation. Several friends and colleagues have helped me in this study. Most obvious is my wife Bonnie, a professional herself, who has read and commented on the book through its many stages of development. My friend and fellow medical historian John Burnham has also read the entire manuscript and made many helpful suggestions. Other friends and colleagues have given me the benefit of their scholarship or expertise on particular chapters or sections, including S. V. Fulkerson, Thomas Africa, Thomas Parker, Allen Dirrim, Roger Rogahn, Martha Voght, Joseph Chen, Shiva Bajpai, Joseph Breslin, Ezel Shaw, David Sanderlin, Barbara Fleming, John Broesamle, Nora Weckler, Lee Matsunaga, Charles Kaplan, Robert ap Roberts, Ashley Montagu, Dorr Legg, Don Slater, Virginia

Prince, Gamel Ramedi, John Money, Arlene Wolinski, Ira Pauley, Alex Runciman, and Richard Smith. I also want to thank the librarians in the various countries in which I did research, particularly in England, Scotland, France, Germany, Spain, Italy, Egypt, India, and Japan. Special thanks are also due to the librarians at California State University, Northridge, who helped me track down obscure references. Also helpful were the librarians at the University of California, Los Angeles, whose collection proved useful. Special thanks should be given to my students, most particularly to Carol Ruyf, who served as my assistant during part of the research. Several typists helped prepare versions of manuscript, including Joy Thornbury, Margaret Ball, Selma Rosen, Mary Alvarez, and Ann Welling. The final manuscript was typed by Jane Metzler and Nancy Meadows. Helen Myers, Margaret Moe, and James Bullough helped me prepare the index. I also want to thank Eric Valentine of Wiley-Interscience for his faith in pushing ahead with a decision to publish this work. Special thanks are due to W. R. Mobley for helping to put the manuscript in readable English and to Mrs. Valda Aldzeris and Sally Fliess for seeing it through production.

VERN L. BULLOUGH

Department of History
California State University
Northridge, California
October 1975

NOTES

1. See Vern L. Bullough, "Sex in History: A Virgin Field," *The Journal of Sex Research,* VIII (1972), pp. 101–116.

2. My original study of this, *The History of Prostitution* (New Hyde Park, N.Y.: University Books, 1964) was my first tentative effort in the field of sexual history. Since that time my studies have progressed, and the prostitution study has been rewritten and will soon be republished.

3. The pioneering study was by Norman E. Himes, *Medical History of Contraception,* originally published in 1936 but republished (New York: Schocken Books, 1970). Also important is John T. Noonan, Jr., *Contraception* (Cambridge, Mass.: Belknap Press, Harvard University Press, 1966).

4. See Bernard I. Murstein, *Love, Sex, and Marriage Through the Ages* (New York: Springer, 1974). For a recent study of rape see Susan Brownmiller, *Against Our Will: Men, Women, and Rape* (New York: Simon and Schuster, 1975).

5. See, for example, my own text, Vern L. Bullough, *Man in Western Civilization* (New York: Holt, Rinehart, and Winston, 1970).

6. Vern L. Bullough, Dorr Legg, Barry Elcano, et al., *A Bibliography of Homosexuality, Transvestism, and Other Stigmatized Sexual Behavior* (New York: Garland Publishers, 1976).

7.   See Vern L. Bullough, *The Surbordinate Sex* (Urbana, Ill.: University of Illinois, 1973).

8.   For some indication of this see *Sexual Heretics,* an anthology edited by Brian Reade (New York: Coward-McCann, 1970), and Timothy d'Arch Smith, *Love in Earnest* (London: Routledge & Kegan Paul, 1970). There is an excellent essay on the subject by Noël Gilroy, Lord Annan, entitled, "The Rise of the Cult of Homosexuality," to be included in a series of essays, *The Victorian Counter Culture,* Willie D. Reader, ed.

CONTENTS

SEXUAL VARIANCE IN SOCIETY AND HISTORY

PART ONE

THE BACKGROUND

1
THE BACKGROUND

In this age of science, few areas of human behavior remain so much a part of mythology and so full of misinformation as the study of sexual behavior. Though sex has been both glorified and condemned throughout history, only in recent decades has it become the subject of scientific investigation. Most of the pioneer investigators of sexuality were physicians: only gradually and much later did psychologists, sociologists, anthropologists, biologists, physiologists, lawyers, and various others begin to contribute different points of view. The historians have, however, remained strangely silent. This silence has continued, even though many early pioneering studies of sex relied heavily on historical and cross-cultural data to show the variety of human conduct. This book is an attempt to examine past societal attitudes, to look at what societies have considered deviant sexuality, to compare and contrast Eastern and Western societies, to trace the sources of Western concepts, and to indicate how many of the assumptions of the past still influence our sexual attitudes and behavior today.

Unfortunately, whereas we know sexual activity has been a constant factor in history, it is an aspect of human behavior about which we know almost nothing. Mostly all we know is what society has thought about sex. We know what activities were against the law, the sexual mores that religion sanctioned or philosophy attempted to establish, and the assumptions medical or scientific writers made, but only rarely what people actually did. Much of our portrayal of actual sexuality comes from literature or art. Moreover some forms of sexual behavior are more likely to be recorded than others. For example, we have far more information about the extent of prostitution in most societies than we do about homosexuality, in large part because prostitution was tolerated, if not encouraged, and homosexuality was usually condemned. Some societies or periods seem obsessed with certain kinds of sexual activity, whereas others totally ignored these kinds and concentrated on others.

In part, it seems, toleration depended on the sexual assumptions of the society itself, although no past society had the same understanding or knowledge about the sexual process we have. The base for many of these assumptions often appears in the creation myths, usually involving the earth and the sky. Western culture in general is built on an old assumption that the earth is female, mother earth, and the sky is male, the heavenly father; this deeply engrained mythological assumption has served as the norm for sexual relations with the male on top, the female underneath. Some cultures have considered the earth as male and the sky as female, accepting the woman-superior position as natural, whereas others have looked elsewhere for symbols of maleness and femaleness.

In simple biological terms, sexual behavior can be defined as the activity that makes fertilization and reproduction possible. Though asexual reproduction takes place in some lower forms of plant and animal life, sexual reproduction is the general rule among higher plants and animals. In fact, sexual reproduction makes possible the genetic changes that make each of us unique. Sex in man is, however, much more than an animal function. This has been emphasized by the association of sex with magical and mystical rituals from before recorded history. Male circumcision today is a carryover of these ancient rituals, whose meaning has been lost.

People long ago recognized that sexual intercourse not only results in offspring, a miracle in itself, but also is a great source of pleasure. Conversely, sexual dysfunction was a source of frustration. Impotence and frigidity are known to have existed before the twentieth century, and there have probably always been males who ejaculated prematurely or females who failed to achieve orgasm. Expertise in the art of lovemaking can, moreover, be taught. One thing marriage counselors are called on to do is teach some couples how to have sexual intercourse. Even when couples know the basic techniques, they often express interest in becoming more proficient, and we have vast numbers of drawings, paintings, and sculptures from the past that have served this purpose. Since the invention of writing, there have also been uncounted numbers of manuals purporting to teach the art of love. These early manuals, whether Greek, Indian, Chinese, or other, indicate considerable experimentation in the sexual act. Nonetheless, in spite of their description of foreplay, positions, or other sexual data, they also indicate a lack of understanding of what actually takes place in the sexual act.

In Western culture (and others as well) one of the more obvious sources of information has been the observation of sexual reproduction in animals. This should not be surprising, for sex in animals is usually fairly obvious. On the other hand, Western culture has more or less ignored sexual activity among plants, perhaps because it is not so obvious. Invariably in Western culture, flowering plants have been regarded as symbols of chastity and coupling animals as symbols of concupiscence. There have even been religious groups, such as the medieval Cathars (also known as the Albigensians), who forbade their adherents to eat any product of sexual union but permitted them to eat vegetables and fruits, as well as fish, because they believed these did not result from sexual union.

The most influential author in Western culture on sexual activity among animals has been Aristotle, the fourth-century B.C. Greek philosopher. His *History of Animals, Parts of Animals,* and *Generation of Animals* can be regarded as the foundation not only of Western zoology but also of Western sexology. So great was his influence that the most widely used sex manual in the English-speaking world from the seventeenth through the nineteenth century was known as *Aristotle's Masterpiece,* although only fragments of the information and misinformation it served can be traced to Aristotle.[1]

Aristotle classified animals into three groups: those that reproduced (1) by sexual means, (2) by asexual means, and (3) by spontaneous generation. This last category included a number of lower animals, such as fleas, mosquitoes, and flies, which he held were produced out of putrefying substances. Among the shellfishes he tried to differentiate those that reproduced through bud formation from those that came from self-generation. He held, for example, that the hermit crab grew spontaneously out of the soil and slime and found its way into untenanted shells, shifting to ever larger shells as it grew. His favorite example of spontaneous generation was the eel. As proof he pointed out that no eel had ever been found supplied with either milt or spawn, nor when it was cut open, was it possible to see any passages for spawn or eggs. As further evidence, he reported that eels appeared after a fall of rain, even where the standing pools had been drained and the mud dredged. On the other hand, they never appeared in stagnant pools, even in times of drought. This led him to conclude that eels were derived from the "earth's guts" and grew spontaneously in mud on sustenance from rainwater.

In spite of such assumptions, Aristotle, or those on whom he relied for information, often proved to be insightful observers of reproduction. One of his most remarkable observations was the mating of the octopus. He wrote that in mating the two octopi swam about, intertwining mouths and tentacles until they fitted closely together. Then

> The octopus rests its so-called head against the ground and spreads abroad its tentacles, the other sex fits into the outspreading of these tentacles, and the two sexes then bring their suckers into mutual connexion.
>
> Some assert that the male has a kind of penis in one of his tentacles, the one in which are the largest suckers; and they further assert that the organ is tendinous in character, growing attached right up to the middle of the tentacle, and that the latter enables it to enter the nostril or funnel of the female.[2]

This is a more or less accurate description of mating in which the male uses his hectostylus (a tentacle serving as the arm of procreation) to remove a semen cartridge from his own mantle and then places it in the female's. Because Aristotle's observations were such a mixture of masterful insight and popular superstition, there was a reluctance to challenge his beliefs in spontaneous generation. It seems obvious that not until the concept of spontaneous generation was laid to rest would we fully understand the importance of sexuality.

One of the earliest challengers of spontaneous generation was Francesco Redi, a seventeenth-century Italian. Redi filled a number of vessels with fresh meat, cheese, and other substances subject to decay. He wrapped some of these containers tightly with gauze and left others uncovered. All were placed where they would receive the hot sun and become putrescent. Later, when Redi examined them, he found the unsealed vessels swarming with maggots but the closed ones not. On closer examination he found tiny eggs clinging to the gauze of the covered vessels and concluded these eggs had been deposited by blowflies attracted by the odor of decay. In effect Redi had proved maggots were not born from putrescent material but came from fly eggs.

Though Redi demonstrated the source of maggots, he was unwilling to mount a frontal assault on the spontaneous generation, perhaps because the theology of the time supported that belief, because of the necessity of explaining human parasites. According to general Christian teachings, Adam and Eve had lived happily in Paradise before their expulsion, but it was difficult to explain how they could have lived so happily if they had been plagued by tapeworms, roundworms, or other parasites. Not until Louis Pasteur's discovery in the nineteenth century that fermentation is due to the existence of minute organisms was the theory of spontaneous generation laid to rest.

It was still necessary, however, to explain how organisms reproduced and increased. The first realization that plants and lower forms of life might reproduce sexually is usually attributed to the Englishman Nehemiah Grew. In his *Anatomy of Plants,* published in 1685, he stated that the flowers of plants were their sexual organs, stamens the male organs, pollen the male seed, and pistils the female organs. Since the flowers encompassed elements of both sexes, Grew held that plants were hermaphrodites. This belief, at least for some plants, was challenged by his German contemporary Rudolf Jakob Camerarius in his 1694 essay *Letter on the Sex Life of Plants*. Camerarius had observed that a fruit-bearing mulberry tree near where there was no pollen-bearing mulberry tree produced only empty, sterile seedvessels. This led him to conclude there might well be male and female plants. To test his hypothesis, he began experimenting with a plant popularly known as Dog's Mercury, which he had observed in two different variations. Some of the plants had only stamens in their flowers but bore no seeds or fruits, and others, lacking stamens in the flowers, bore fruit. Isolating the fruit-bearing from the pollen-producing plants, he demonstrated that, whereas seed vessels still appeared on the former, they were sterile.

But how did fertilization take place? In the eighteenth century J. G. Kolreuter pointed out the importance of wind, insects, and the movement of the stamen in fertilization through his study of the hibiscus. He also demonstrated that crossing was successful only when it took place between related individuals, that is, within the same species. Continuing and expanding on this research was another German, Christian Konrad Sprengel, who published *The Newly Revealed Mystery of Nature in the Structure and Fertilization of Flowers* in 1795. Convinced that God had put everything in nature for a purpose, Sprengel set out to determine what useful purposes the different parts and properties of flowers had been created to serve. He concluded that color in flowers was to attract insects and that certain colors attracted certain insect forms. He then observed that the flower was adapted not only to the general conditions of its own life but also to those of the insects visiting it. He found that, whereas some flowers appeared to be hermaphrodites and have both stamen and pistil, a differential development cycle made it impossible for the flower to be fertilized by its own pollen. Instead, fertilization was by pollen conveyed by insects from other flowers. This led him to philosophize that nature did not desire a flower to be fertilized by its own pollen. It was in part the work of Sprengel that led Charles Darwin to the importance of sexual selection in evolution.[3]

Real understanding of fertilization had to await the discovery of the cell, achieved independently in the nineteenth century by Matthias Jakob Schleiden and Theodor Schwann. In 1838 Schleiden had concluded from microscopic observations that plants were an aggregate of individual, self-contained organic molecules. Still uncertain of what he had discovered, he discussed it with a friend, Theodor Schwann, who reported he had seen similar structures in animal membranes. Their discovery resulted in the foundation of cytology, the study of the structure and function of cells.

One of their early discoveries was that unicellular organisms could also reproduce sexually. Though one-celled organisms normally reproduce by budding and division, a process allowing for tremendous population growth but also resulting in extreme inbreeding, other means are also available, perhaps as a way to lessen the dangers of inbreeding. Periodically cells go through processes described as autogamy, conjugation, and copulation. And some forms of life alternate between sexual and asexual propagation, as does plasmodium, the agent causing malaria. In man, the plasmodia reproduce by dividing, but in the intestine of the mosquito they reproduce sexually.

If man had difficulty in fully understanding the importance of sexual reproduction in lesser forms of life, he also labored under severe handicaps in trying to explain how conception takes place in his own species. Some investigators have held that ancient man believed the male played no part in conception but that instead, through some magical means, ancestral spirits in the form of living germs found their ways into the maternal body. In the nineteenth century, in fact, some theorists of societal evolution classified the stages of man's cultural development into ascending stages from anarchy, to matriarchy, to patriarchy, claiming that patriarchy, the highest stage, began when man discovered he was in fact responsible for the miracle of birth. Such a theory of the evolutionary nature of society, as well as the discovery of the male's importance in procreation, is only a hypothesis, and no consensus exists among investigators about when and if such a momentous discovery took place in history. It is true that figurines with female characteristics such as hips and mammary glands considerably exaggerated are one of the most common surviving representations of the paleolithic period, and this might well indicate a worship of the generative power of the female, but it might also indicate that ancient men were artists who enjoyed portraying or observing the opposite sex, much as men do today. The *Playboy* centerfold, for example, is not necessarily indicative of the worship of the female; it might well serve a less exalted purpose.[4] Once the male recognized his importance, if he had ever doubted it, he tended to claim the male element was more important than the female.

Much of our Western cultural notions about conception and sexual reproduction can also be traced to the Greeks, and again Aristotle is a key figure. Aristotle is responsible for setting the Western belief in the importance of the male principle in reproduction, although he did grant that the female supplied the matter for shaping.

> If, then, the male stands for the effective and active, and the female, considered as female, for the passive, it follows that what the female would contribute to the semen of the male would not be semen but material for semen to work upon.[5]

Some historians of science have considered Aristotle's views of conception a forward step over some of his predecessors, because he at least recognized that the female supplied the necessary substance for the formation of the embryo, and this meant the female was something more than a mere vessel to carry a man's children, a belief advocated by some earlier writers.[6]

If the only alternative to Aristotle in Greek thinking was a complete denial of the female's importance in conception, he would represent an advance, but other Greek writers assigned much more importance to the female, though they tended to be overshadowed by him. The writer of the Hippocratic work on *Generation,* contemporary with Aristotle, held that two seeds were involved in conception, the male, equated with semen, and the female, described as vaginal secretion.[7] The second-century medical writer Galen also held the two-seed doctrine, claiming both the male and female seeds had coagulative power and receptive capacity for coagulation but that one was stronger in the male and the other in the female.

Though some later writers also adopted the two-seed doctrine, the generally accepted view came to be that of the Arabic medical writer Avicenna, who wrote in the early part of the eleventh century and was a key transmitter of Aristotelian ideas to medieval Europe. Avicenna modified Aristotle somewhat in comparing the process of generation to the manufacture of cheese. The male agent was equivalent to the clotting agent of milk and the female "sperm" to the coagulum. Just as the starting point of the clotting was in the rennet, so the starting point of the clot that was to become "man" was in the male semen.[8] Avicenna's concept was adopted by St. Albertus Magnus in the thirteenth century. Though St. Albert mentioned female semen, he made it clear that it could be called semen only in an equivocal sense and that the male contributed the essential material for generation.[9] In this he was supported by the greatest of the medieval scientific theologians St. Thomas Aquinas, his pupil, who believed that the female generative power was imperfect as compared with the male and since:

> In the arts the inferior art gives a disposition to the matter to which the higher art gives the form . . . so also the generative power of the female prepares the matter, which is then fashioned by the active power of the male.[10]

Better understanding of the process depended on more effective knowledge of the human body. In this the anatomical work of Andreas Vesalius in the sixteenth century proved important, as did the more specialized studies on female anatomy by Gabriele Falloppio, his younger contemporary. Falloppio described the clitoris as well as the tubes that bear his name. Falloppio was also important in male anatomy, since he described the *arteria profunda* of the penis, which helps explain why it becomes erect. There were still, however, errors about female anatomy that remained a part of popular misconceptions. One was the belief that an inactive uterus caused hysteria.

One of the earliest references to this belief was by Plato. In his *Timaeus* the womb is described as having an existence almost independent from the woman. It was an

> indwelling creature desirous of child-bearing. [When] it remains barren too long after puberty, it is distressed and sorely disturbed, and straying about in the body and cutting off the passages of the breath, it impedes respiration and brings the sufferer into extreme anguish and provokes all manners of diseases besides.[11]

Most ancient writers, including Soranus of Ephesus, the second-century writer on gynecology, rejected such notions. He held that, though the uterus appeared similar to an animal to some writers, it was not. He believed the misunderstanding arose because the uterus had characteristics similar to those of an animal, including a sense of touch causing it to be contracted by cooling agents and relaxed by relaxing ones.[12] Much less cautious in his description of the uterus was the second-century writer Aretaeus of Cappadocia, who reported that:

> In the middle of the flanks of women lies the womb, a female viscus, closely resembling an animal; for it is moved of itself hither and thither in the flanks, also upwards in a direct line to below the cartilage of the thorax, and also obliquely to the right or to the left, either to the liver or spleen; and it likewise is subject to prolapsus downwards, and, in a word, it is altogether erratic.[13]

In contrast Galen, opposing the theory of the wandering womb, held that anyone experienced in anatomy would recognize that the uterus could not jump over the stomach to touch the diaphragm.[14] Nevertheless, he as well as others, assumed that the womb desired to be pregnant and that the only solution for female complaints was intercourse and pregnancy. He wrote that woman had a secretion similar to the male semen that was produced in the uterus and that retention of this substance led to the spoiling and corruption of the blood, which in turn led to a cooling of the body and eventually to an irritation of the nerves, producing hysteria. Galen felt the solution for women unable to conceive or have regular intercourse was masturbation. He described what happened when one of his woman patients applied warm substances to her pudenda and used digital manipulation:

> Following the warmth of the remedies and arising from the touch of the genital organs required by the treatment there followed twitchings accompanied at the same time by pain and pleasure after which she emitted turbid and abundant sperm. Thus it seems to me that the retention of sperm impregnated with evil essences had—in causing damage throughout the body—a much greater power than that of the retention of the menses.[15]

In spite of advances in anatomical study there was still considerable misunderstanding of women's physiology. The first effective challenge to the male's importance in reproduction came from William Harvey, whose *Anatomical Exercitations Concerning the Generation of Living Creatures* was published in Latin in 1651 and translated into English under the same title in 1653. Harvey, perhaps best known for his demonstration of the circulation of the blood, devoted much of his life to studying generation. He gathered a wide variety of observations on reproduction in all types of animals, but primarily his attention was centered on the day-to-day development of the chick embryo and on his dissection of the uteri of deer at various stages during mating and pregnancy. Believing his research had disproved the ideas of Aristotle and to a lesser extent those of Galen, he emphasized the importance of the egg in generation. Some indication of this importance had earlier been advanced by Hieronymus Fabricus ab Aquapendente (1537–1639), a student of Falloppio, [16] but it was Harvey who pushed the oviparous theory to its logical conclusion. Harvey could find no evidence that the seminal mass of the cock entered into or even touched the eggs during their formation within the hen. He did find that for a time a hen could continue producing fertile eggs after all detectable traces of semen had vanished from her body. To Harvey this seemed to offer solid evidence that the contribution of the cock's semen to generation was indirect and incorporeal; it simply conferred a certain fecundity on the hen and then played no further role in the actual generation of the egg or the chick. Once endowed with this fecundity, the hen could entirely on her own produce fertile eggs, which would give rise to chicks resembling both herself and the cock. In explaining this principle of fecundity Harvey fell back on an analogy with the spread of disease by contagion, whereby exposure to a sick individual could engender within a second individual an internal principle that subsequently reproduced in him the same specific disease. In the same way, the principle of fecundity was transmitted. Furthermore, Harvey said that the role of parents is to produce, not a chick, but a fertile egg that subsequently gave rise to a chick through its own innate powers. He believed he had demonstrated this by his dissection of deer in the royal deer park, for he observed it was some time after the male semen had disappeared from the body of the female and after a period in which the uterus was otherwise empty that the first evidence of conception appeared. This led him to formulate his famous dictum that "an egg is the common primordium of all animals," which meant in effect that the role of the parents in generation was indirect; they produced a fertile egg, or conceptus, or seed, and subsequently this produced a new animal or plant through an innate vegetative power.[17]

The Harveian view was summarized somewhat later by the Swedish biologist Carl Linnaeus as *Vivum omne ex ovo*—or everything living comes from the egg. Other researchers came forth with supporting conclusions, particularly Marcello Malpighi, whose study of the embryo in hen's eggs was published in 1672. At about the same time Reynier de Graaf, observing the changes taking place in rabbit's ovaries in the first days after fertilization, concluded that similar changes probably took place in the human female.

The growing tide of the ovists ran, however, into a roadblock in the studies of Anton van Leeuwenhoek (1632–1723), the Dutch microscopist, whose microscopic observations were not equaled until the nineteenth century. Johan Ham, a medical student, to confirm his observation of little creatures in it, brought Leeuwenhoek a glass bottle containing the semen of a man who had suffered from nocturnal emissions. Leeuwenhoek confirmed their existence but noted these little creatures were different from other *animalcula* he had observed, being distinguished by their round bodies with tails five or six times as long as their bodies. He reported they made swimming movements like an eel's. After first observing them he put them aside to look at again, but a few hours later, he found they were no longer moving although still clearly recognizable. To make certain these *animalcula* were not the result of any sickness, Leeuwenhoek and Ham examined the semen of healthy males and observed the same kind of creatures. They estimated there must be a thousand or more in the space of a grain of sand. When different observations were made under different conditions, it was found that the *animalcula* died within 24 hours if kept in cold temperature but survived several days if kept in warmed conditions. Leeuwenhoek called these creatures spermatozoa. Almost immediately after the results of his discoveries were published in the proceedings of the British Royal Society in 1678, all kinds of findings were being reported. One observer reported seeing a minature horse in the semen of a horse, and another, a miniature donkey in the semen of a donkey. Still others distinguished male and female sperm. Some even believed they saw male and female sperm copulating and then giving birth to little sperm. The effect, in spite of some of the ludicrous tales, was to reassert, at least in many minds, the male's supremacy.

Closely associated with this was the growth of preformationism, usually associated with Jan Swammerdam, another seventeenth-century Dutchman and a pioneer investigator of insects, who had been studying insect metamorphosis. Having hardened the chrysalis with alcohol, he had observed the butterfly folded and perfectly formed within the cocoon. This caused him to believe the butterfly had been hidden or masked in the caterpillar, and from this it was not too great a step to regard the egg in a similar light. Each butterfly in each cocoon must contain eggs within it, which in their turn must contain butterflies, which in their turn must contain eggs, and so on. He soon extended his theory to man, arguing there was no generation but only propagation, the growth of parts. Thus all men were contained in the organs of Adam and Eve, and when their stock of eggs was finished, the human race would cease. Some argued the male held all the seeds, and others, the female.

Complete understanding of fertilization did not come until near the end of the nineteenth century, although the mammalian egg had been discovered in 1827. In higher animals the actual moment of fertilization was first observed among sea urchins by Oscar Hertwig in 1875. The Mediterranean sea urchins provided an almost unique opportunity for such observations, since the eggs are transparent, occur in large numbers, and develop rapidly. Under such conditions it was fairly easy for Hertwig to observe the coming together of two nuclei in the egg, this leading him to surmise he had observed fertilization. Not until 4 years later did Herman Fol actually observe the spermatozoon penetrate an egg.

Further light on sexual reproduction was shed by Edouard Van Beneden, who found that sexual reproduction entailed a reduction of the number of chromosomes in each cell of fertility to half what it normally was. Thus fertilization finally came to be understood as the joining of two half sets of chromosomes to form one full set. From these observations in easily studied animals it was not too difficult to surmise and eventually to prove that a similar phenomenon takes place in human beings, although the ova in the human female were not observed until the twentieth century.[18]

Fertilization is only one aspect of understanding sex. With the discovery of chromosomes in 1873 by Anton Schneider, Walter Flemming, Otto Butschli, and others, there had been considerable investigation into the actual nature of femaleness and maleness. For a time studies of human sexuality were handicapped by an erroneous counting of human chromosomes, but with the discovery of J. H. Tijio and A. Levan that there are 46 chromosomes in the human cell instead of the 48 previously hypothesized, there has been rapid advancement.[19]

In the 1960s it was found that sexuality was not quite the two-sided affair we once thought it was. Since chromosomes had first been discovered it had been assumed that sex was determined by the sex-determining chromosomes labeled X and Y. Two X chromosomes (XX) in the egg fertilized by the sperm led to the birth of a female, and an X chromosome plus a Y (XY) led to birth of a male. The matter proved somewhat more complicated, for it now seems that among the viable genetic possibilities are not only XX and XY but also X, XXX, XXY, and XYY. There is also a condition known as mosaicism in which some of the cells (not all) of a given individual have either a supernumerary or a missing chromosome. As far as can be determined at present, a single Y combination is not viable, although a single Y chromosome in any combination of X's will cause the embryo to differentiate as a male unless other biochemical factors intervene to inhibit masculinity.

When there is a single X chromosome, a condition known as Turner's syndrome (45,X), the person is characterized by a female body type, but the ovaries are either nonfunctional or have degenerated entirely. This ovarian deficiency prevents the child from developing normally at puberty and also has a growth-hindering effect, since such individuals seldom grow as tall as 5 feet. Many individuals also have other congenital organ defects coupled with a strong likelihood of intellectual disabilities. Fortunately, if the condition is diagnosed early enough, the individual can be helped by administration of estrogen, the female sex hormone, although even after treatment the individual remains somewhat shorter than average and is sterile.

The person with the XXX condition develops as a normal female body type, although her fertility may be diminished, and there is a greater probability of mental retardation. XXY individuals have what is known as Klinefelter's syndrome. Their penises are usually small, the testes in the adults are shrunken, and the output of testicular androgen is so low as to result in female breast formation, although there are variations from individual to individual. The XYY body type is male, abnormally tall, and usually sterile or suffers from genital anomalies. It is now believed that certain behavior disorders might be more apt to occur with this genetic inheritance, although the case for this has not been fully demonstrated.[20]

Even when there is a normal chromosomal pattern, other things can occur that influence sex development *in utero*. We now believe that the male gonads (the testes) begin to develop about the 6th week if the child is to be a male, but the ovarian differentiation does not come until the 12th week if the child is to be a female. Experiments on animals show that, if the embryonic gonads are removed before the sexual anatomy is formed, then the embryo differentiates as a female, regardless of cellular sex. This seems to imply that, to be masculine, it is necessary to add something. Once the testes of the fetus begin to develop, they secrete a müllerian-inhibiting substance, so called because it suppresses all further development of the primitive müllerian ducts that form the uterus, fallopian tubes, and upper segment of the vagina. If for some reason this substance fails to be secreted in a genetically male embryo, a boy is born with a uterus and fallopian tubes in addition to normal internal and external male organs. The male organs are normal except for cryptorchidism (undescended testicles).[21]

In addition to secreting the müllerian-inhibiting substance, the testes release testosterone, the male sex hormone, which promotes the proliferation of the wolffian ducts to form the internal male reproductive structure. Later, by circulating in the blood, the testosterone reaches the embryonic sexual organs, effecting their development. The genital tubercle becomes a penis instead of a clitoris, and the skin folds wrap around the penis on both sides of the genital slit and fuse in the midline, forming the urethal tube and foreskin, in place of the bilateral labia minora and the clitoral hood. The outer swelling on either side of the genital slit fuses in the midline to form the scrotum and receive the testes instead of remaining in place as the bilateral labia majora of the female.

If testosterone is added to the bloodstream of a genetic female fetus during a critical period in development, a girl will be born with either a grossly enlarged clitoris or, in rare instances, a normal-looking penis with an empty scrotum. In human beings such masculinization occurs in the fetus through an abnormal functioning of the adrenal cortex. It may also occur if the pregnant mother has a tumor inducing her to produce male hormones or if she has any other condition causing a large number of male hormones to be present. For a brief period in recent history the condition was much more common than it statistically ought to have been, because the synthetic pregnancy-saving hormone progestin led to masculinization of the fetus.

Embryologically the external organs are the last stage of sexual development to be completed. This means it is not uncommon for the external genitalia to be left unfinished, neither fully masculinized nor feminized. Since the unfinished state of either sex looks remarkably like that of the other in infants,[22] this has caused great difficulties with infant sexual identification in the past. In countries and cultures that value having a male child, doubtful cases tended to be assigned to the male category, and this assignment caused considerable trauma in many individuals on reaching puberty. Even today in countries such as Egypt, where a male child is so prized, a number of "boys" undergo trauma when they begin to menstruate. Fortunately, most of the human race has no genetic or other complications in their biological sexual development, but sex role and sexual behavior also entail a number of cultural and socializing factors that were not fully explored even in the 1970s. No information yet fully explains why males are attracted to females and females to males. Why do women differ not only in their anatomy but also in their behavior from males? In general we have usually assumed this was the way things were meant to be, that males were designed to respond to females and females to males. But if this is the case, why do we have people who respond only to individuals of their own sex, others who find sexual satisfaction with nonhuman creatures, and others who get sexual satisfaction from objects?

Plato, perhaps somewhat facetiously, proposed an answer for the different love objects of man in his *Symposium*. One participant in the *Symposium*, Aristophanes, stated there had originally been three kinds of human beings: males, females, and hermaphrodites, all of whom had four arms, four legs, and two faces on opposite sides of one head. These creatures moved by whirling over and over with legs stuck straight out. Originally the males were the offspring of the sun, and the females, of the earth, but the hermaphrodites were offspring of the moon and partook of both. These early individuals were of such great strength and vigor they soon began to conspire against the gods, and the gods, following the advice of Zeus, decided to lessen their strength and ability by slicing them in two. Their skin was pulled together like a purse and tied

with a string, this resulting in their having a navel, but even though the individuals could navigate well on two legs and their one face served adequately,
each creature longed for union with the part from which it had been severed.

All the women who are sections of the woman have no great fancy for men; they
are inclined rather to women, and of this stock are the she-minions. Men who are
sections of the male pursue the masculine, and so long as their boyhood lasts they
show themselves to be slices of the male by making friends with men and delighting
to lie with them and to be clasped in men's embraces; these are the finest boys and
striplings, for they have the most manly nature. Some say they are shameless creatures, but falsely; for their behavior is due not to shamelessness but to daring,
manliness, and virility, since they are quick to welcome their like. Sure evidence of
this is the fact that on reaching maturity these alone prove in a public career to be
men. So when they come to man's estate they are boy-lovers, and have no natural
interest in wiving and getting children, but only do these things under stress of
custom; they are quite contented to live together unwedded all their days. A man of
this sort is at any rate born to be a lover of boys or the willing mate of a man,
eagerly greeting his own kind. Well, when one of them—whether he be a boy-lover
or a lover of any other sort—happens on his own particular half, and two of them
are wondrously thrilled with affection and intimacy and love, and are hardly to be
induced to leave each other's side for a single moment. These are they who
continue together throughout life, though they could not even say what they would
have of one another . . .[23]

Even though heterosexual coitus seems to be the prevalent sexual behavior
for the majority of adults in all human societies, societies themselves differ
about what sexual behavior will be tolerated. In the past, even those cultures
that accepted or tolerated other sexual behaviors were biased in favor of copulation between males and females, because it was necessary for the perpetuation
of the family or the tribe, not only in this world but also in the next. Once an
individual had performed his or her duty, other forms of sexuality were
allowed, or even a few individuals were exempted from reproducing.

Clellan S. Ford and Frank A. Beach attempted a statistical survey of sexual
behavior in primitive societies. They found that, in 49 of the 76 societies
examined, some homosexual activity was considered normal and socially acceptable, at least for certain members of the community.[24] Different levels of
toleration or acceptance are reported for almost all other forms of sexual behavior. Even within more sophisticated societies, such as the United States,
where certain sexual behaviors were severely disapproved and the practitioners
often punished, Kinsey and his collaborators found wide variations. In their
male survey, Kinsey, Pomeroy, and Martin concluded that 37 percent of the
postpubertal males in our society had had at least one homosexual contact
resulting in orgasm and that, for men who had not married before the age of
35, the incidence rose to 50 percent. Some 4 percent of the adult white males

were reported to be exclusively homosexual.[25] Incidences for the females were much lower. Some 19 percent of the women had had homosexual contacts by age 40, and 28 percent had reported homosexual arousal. From 2 to 6 percent of the unmarried females in the Kinsey sample but less than 1 percent of the married females had been more or less exclusively homosexual.[26] Yet the United States officially disapproved homosexuality.

How much this differentiation in sex preference is due to socialization and how much to other factors is as yet unknown. Closely allied with sex preference is sex or gender role. These are the characteristic patterns of thought and action distinguishing women from men, boys from girls. Anthropologists have long attempted to point out that what we regard as masculine activity in some societies is defined as feminine in others and vice versa. Increasingly, we have become conscious that male and female patterns of sexual orientation and behavior, what the sociologists call sex role, are attributable in large part to acquired learning.

Some of the more significant studies of individuals in this area have been carried out at The Johns Hopkins University by John Money and Joan and John Hamson on hermaphrodites. Their hermaphroditic patients were examined and classified in regard to the usual criteria of sex assignment, gonadal sex, hormonal sex, chromosomal sex, and internal and external genitalia. In the 20 patients in whom a contradiction was found between gonadal sex and sex of rearing, 17 disclosed themselves in a gender role concordant with their rearing. Of 27 patients whose hormonal functioning and secondary sexual body morphology contradicted their sex of rearing, 4 became ambivalent with respect to gender role as male or female, but 23 established gender roles consistent with their sex of rearing.[27] As far as chromosonal sex was determined, all 20 patients whose chromosomal sex differed from their assigned sex, it was found that the gender role and sexual orientation were in accordance with socially assigned sex and rearing. In 22 of 25 individuals the gender role agreed with the assigned sex and rearing and was not in accord with the predominant male or female internal accessory structure. Where sex of rearing was contradictory to the sex of the external genitalia, 23 of 25 individuals had been able to come to terms with their anomalous appearance and establish a gender role consistent with their assigned sex and rearing.[28] In effect only 8 of the 131 comparisons (6 percent) did not show concordance of assigned sex and gender role.

> In the light of hermaphroditic evidence, it is no longer possible to attribute psychologic maleness or femaleness to chromosomal, gonadal or hormonal origins, nor to morphological sex differences of either the internal accessory reproductive organs or the external gentalia . . . From the sum total of hermaphroditic evidence the conclusion that emerges is that sexual behavior and orientation as male or female does not have an innate, instinctive basis. In place of a theory of instinctive masculinity or femininity which is innate, the evidence of hermaphroditism lends

support to a conception that psychologically, sexuality is undifferentiated at birth and that it becomes differentiated as masculine or feminine in the course of the various experiences of growing up.[29]

More recently Money extended his research to individuals not classed as pseudohermaphrodites but who for some reason have deliberately been reared in a sex different from the one to which they should have anatomically been assigned.[30]

Though such studies did not fully negate the concept of inherent sexuality, they did indicate how much the traditional views of sex behavior are culturally based. It seems that an individual's sexual behavior is not neutral or without direction at birth but that sexual predisposition is only one potential factor in setting one's life patterns. Obviously, in sexuality the human being is extremely flexible, his behavior a composite of prenatal and postnatal influences.[31] Among the postnatal influences are various situations affecting the individual, such as family setting and peer group, but also important are general social and cultural factors, and this book is aimed at examining both social and cultural determinants in forming sexual behavior.

Societal and cultural determinants are particularly important in looking at what has been defined as sexually deviant behavior. In simple dictionary terms, to deviate is to stray, as from a standard or a topic, or in terms of an individual, a deviate is one who differs considerably from the average or departs from the norms of society. Deviation then in sociological terms is culturally and socially defined, and deviant sexual behavior is anything a society says it is. Deviation in a sense is implicit in the idea of society, for no matter what the measure of moral rectitude, deviation will occur. The sociologist Emile Durkheim wrote that, even in a society of saints where crimes, at least what we regard as crimes, would be unknown, faults appearing venial to us would create the same scandal an ordinary offense does in our society, and individuals committing such acts would be regarded as deviant.[32] In effect, societies set norms of conduct for their members, assign social roles, and attempt to enforce these rules. A breach of this order is called social deviance, the organization of society almost by definition implying deviance. Howard Becker put it simply when he stated that "social groups create deviance by making the rules whose infraction constitutes deviance, and by applying these rules to particular people and labeling them as outsiders."[33] A deviant person is one stigmatized by society, and deviant behavior is whatever people label deviant. Thus, in dealing with what societies stigmatized as sexual deviance in the past, we should look at how societies attempted to set the norms of sexual standards, for only by so doing can we understand why they regarded certain activities as deviant.

Closely allied to the labeling of conduct or individual as deviant is the appearance of subcultures of deviants. These groupings serve a dual function. On the one hand involvement in the subculture facilitates access to an immersion in deviant roles that "members" either feel a need for or find pleasurable or desirable, and on the other hand the subculture serves a protective or defensive function, shielding individuals from the negative attitudes of outsiders. In the process it often also inculcates the values of the group into the individual.

In a historical study of sex, it is comparatively easy to determine what a society regarded as deviant sexuality, for this appears in the legal codes, in the religious and theological literature, and often in scientific or philosophic writing. It is not always possible, however, to understand why such conduct was regarded as deviant, although this study attempts to do so.

Even more difficult is to examine the deviants themselves, either in groups or as individuals, since for the most part all we know is what the society said about them and not always what they did. In a particular culture what constitutes deviation differs not only from time to time or within different segments but also from one individual to another.

There is also the problem that the stated norms of society might not be the actual norms. A society might say, for example, that it does not believe in premarital intercourse, but in actuality it is accepted by a significant portion of that society. Even though societies in the past might not have fully understood the nature of sexuality (do we?), all had strong positive and negative sanctions for different aspects of sexual behavior. Some emphasized chastity and tolerated intercourse only in a marriage relationship with procreation specifically in mind, others had a double standard in which almost everything was tolerated for the male but not for the female, and still others tolerated, if not encouraged, almost any sexual activity, there being all kinds of variation in between. In general Western culture has inclined more to the first type of generalized society than to the second or third, and the reasons why this was the case still have implications for today. It is hoped that this study will enable us to understand our own sexuality.

NOTES

1. Vern L. Bullough, "An Early American Sex Manual, or Aristotle Who?" *Early American Literature*, VII (1973), pp. 236–247.

2. Aristotle, *History of Animals*, V, 6 (541b), translated by D'Arcy Wentworth Thompson in *The Works of Aristotle*, J. A. Smith and W. D. Ross, eds., Vol. 4 (Oxford, England: Clarendon Press, 1910).

3. Much of the material in this section comes from Herbert Wendt's *The Sex Life of the Animals*, translated from the German by Richard and Clara Winston (New York: Simon and Schuster, 1912). See also various histories of biology, such as the popular one by Eric Nordenskold, *The History of Biology*, translated by Leonard Bucknall Eyre (reprinted, New York: Tudor Publishing Company, n.d.). Biographical sketches of the various individuals can be found in *The Dic-*

tionary of Scientific Biography (New York: Scribner's, 1970, in progress), although for some unaccountable reason Camerarius has been relegated to a not yet published supplement.

4.   I have developed some of these ideas at greater length in Vern L. Bullough, *The Subordinate Sex* (Urbana, Ill.: University of Illinois, 1973), pp. 6–15.

5.   Aristotle, *Generation of Animals,* 729A, 25–34, translated by A. L. Peck (London: William Heinemann, 1953).

6.   See, for example, Joseph Needham, *A History of Embryology* (New York: Abelard-Schuman, 1959), pp. 43–44.

7.   See Hippocrates, *On Intercourse and Pregnancy,* a translation of *On Semen and On the Development of the Child* by T. U. H. Ellinger (New York: Henry Schuman, 1952), Chap. 1, pp. 21 ff.

8.   Avicenna, *Canon of Medicine,* translated by O. Cameron Gruner (London: Luzak and Company, 1930), I, 196, p. 23.

9.   Albertus Magnus, *De animalibus libri XXVI,* Hermann Studler, ed. (Munster: *Beitrage zur Geschichte des Mittelalters,* Vols. 15 and 16, 1916–1920, 2 vols.), lib. IX, tract 2, cap. 3, pp. 714 ff; lib. XV, tract 2, caps. 4–11, pp. 1026 ff.

10.   St. Thomas Aquinas, *Summa Theologica* (New York: Benziner Brothers, 1947), Part III, question 32, "De conceptione Christi quod activum principium," iv.

11.   Plato, *Timaeus,* 91C, translated by R. G. Bury, ed. (London: William Heinemann, 1961).

12.   Soranus, *Gynecology,* I, 3, viii, translated by Owsei Temkin (Baltimore: Johns Hopkins Press, 1956), p. 9.

13.   Aretaeus, *The Extant Works of Aretaeus the Cappadocian,* translated by Francis Adams, ed. (London: Sydenham Society, 1856), II, xi, pp. 285–287.

14.   See Ilza Veith, *Hysteria: The History of a Disease* (Chicago: University of Chicago Press, 1965), pp. 39 ff, for ancient beliefs on the subject. Her work is the best work in English on the subject.

15.   Henri Cresbron, *Histoire critique de l'hysterie* (Paris: Asslin Houzean, 1909), p. 44. See Galen, *De locia affectis,* VI (Venice, 1586) 2:39.

16.   See Howard B. Adelmann, *Embryological Treatises of Hieronymus Fabricus of Aquapendente* (Ithaca, N.Y.: Cornell University Press, 1967, 2 vols.), for a discussion of this.

17.   See Arthur W. Meyer, *An Analysis of the De generatione animalium of William Harvey* (Stanford, Calif.: Stanford University Press, 1936); Howard B. Adelmann, *op. cit.,* pp. 113–121; and Elizabeth B. Gasking, *Investigations into Generation,* 1651–1828 (Baltimore: Johns Hopkins Press, 1967), pp. 16–36.

18.   See Joseph Needham, *A History of Embryology* (New York: Abelard-Schuman, 1959); Clifford Dobell, *Antony van Leeuwenhoek and His "Little Animals"* (reprinted, New York: Russell & Russell, 1958); and F. J. Cole, *Early Theories of Sexual Generation* (Oxford, England: Clarendon Press, 1930). For an account written in the eighteenth century, see Pierre Louis Moreau de Maupertius, *The Earthly Venus,* translated from the *Venus Physique* by Simone Brangier Boas with notes and introduction by George Boas (New York: Johnson Reprint Corp., 1966).

19.   J. H. Tijio and A. Levan, "The Chromosome Number of Man," *Hereditas,* XLII (1956), pp. 1–6. For background to this discovery, see Malcolm Jay Kottler, "From 48 to 46: Cytological technique, Preconception and the Counting of Human Chromosomes," *Bulletin of the History of Medicine,* XLVIII (1974), pp. 465–502.

20.   For a more nearly complete discussion of this see John Money and Anke A. Ehrhardt, *Man & Woman Boy & Girl* (Baltimore: Johns Hopkins Press, 1972), pp. 23–33. See also H. F. Klinefelter, I. C. Reifenstin, and F. Albright, *Journal of Clinical Endocrinology,* II (1942), p. 615.

21. Money and Ehrhardt, *op. cit.*, pp. 6–7.

22. See John Money, *Sex Errors of the Body* (Baltimore: Johns Hopkins Press, 1968), p. 41.

23. Plato, *Symposium,* 191E–192D, translated by W. R. M. Lamb (London: William Hein-emann, 1932).

24. Clellan S. Ford and Frank A. Beach, *Patterns of Sexual Behavior* (New York: Harper, 1951), p. 130.

25. Alfred C. Kinsey, Wardell B. Pomeroy, and Clyde E. Martin, *Sexual Behavior in the Human Male* (Philadelphia: W. B. Saunders, 1948), pp. 650–651.

26. Alfred C. Kinsey, Wardell B. Pomeroy, Clyde E. Martin, Paul H. Gebhard, et al., *Sexual Behavior in the Human Female* (Philadelphia: W. B. Saunders, 1953), pp. 475–475, 487–489.

27. John Money, J. G. Hampson, and J. L. Hampson, "An Examination of Some Basic Sexual Concepts: The Evidence of Human Hermaphroditism," *Bulletin Johns Hopkins Hospital,* XCVII (1955), pp. 301–319.

28. J. L. Hampson and J. G. Hampson, "The Ontogenesis of Sexual Behavior in Man," in W. C. Young, ed., *Sex and Internal Secretions,* 3rd ed. (Baltimore: Williams and Wilkins, 1961), pp. 1401–1432.

29. Money, Hampson, and Hampson, *op. cit.*

30. Money and Ehrhardt, *op. cit ,* passim.

31. For a good survey of the literature with some critical questions, see Milton Diamond, "A Critical Evaluation of the Ontogeny of Human Sexual Behavior," *The Quarterly Review of Biology,* XL (1965), pp. 147–175.

32. Emile Durkheim, *The Rules of Sociological Method* (New York: Free Press of Glencoe, 1938), pp. 68–69.

33. Howard S. Becker, *The Outsiders* (New York: Free Press of Glencoe, 1963), p. 9.

2
CULTURE AND SEXUALITY

Among the richest sources of data for any cross-cultural or cross-historical study of human activity are the reports on "primitive" and other societies gathered by various observers over the past several hundred years. The very richness of this treasure trove of data poses difficulty however, for it is surrounded by booby traps, and frequently the treasure turns out to be fool's gold. Nowhere is this more true than in sexual behavior. Part of the difficulty is that many of the reports on which we can base assumptions about sexual behavior reflect the conscious and unconscious biases of the observers, few of them trained anthropologists. Until fairly recently, information about primitive and other societies was gathered and reported by missionaries, trappers, prospectors, or businessmen. Even when the professional anthropologist entered the field, there were and are the questions of how much of what he or she observed had been influenced by the presence of an outside observer and of how much the society itself had been affected by Western culture. At times also the professional anthropologist was not as precise in his or her observations as we would have liked, many showing a reluctance to deal with the more intimate details of sexual life. Often, too, the professional ethnographer depended on a selected informant for his data, and occasionally these data have not been accurate. A good example is found in the Tibetan reports of Prince Peter of Greece, who achieved professional recognition for his studies. The prince reported there were no prostitutes in Tibet. He recognized, however, that since the Tibetans believed tobacco was grown with the aid of the menstrual flow of prostitutes, they could not be entirely ignorant of such practices. He explained this discrepancy by stating the Tibetans must have received this belief from outside of Tibet, for he could see no prostitutes.[1] Other contemporary observers reported widescale prostitution. Prostitutes were said to accompany the caravans and were numerous around most army garrisons. It was, moreover, common for Tibetan men to use a prostitute as an act of bravado, either to boast about their abilities to friends or to indicate they were rich.[2] One observer even compiled a price list for prostitutes.[3] The point is that outside observers, even professionals, can often be misled and overlook customs and practices different from their own.

In the most nearly comprehensive survey yet undertaken of the observations of sexual behavior in various cultures, Clellan S. Ford and Frank A. Beach concluded there was such a wide variation among peoples and cultures that no one society could be regarded as "representative" of the human race.[4] Though they found many cross-cultural similarities, they also found a number of differences. Some societies condoned and encouraged the sexual impulses of children, but others forbade and punished such behavior. Different societies have held widely different rules and attitudes about masturbation, but, regardless of whether the attitude was approval or condemnation, at least some adults in all or nearly all societies appear to have masturbated. Though a number of societies reported bestiality, many such references were found only in their folklore and were not observed in everyday life. Homosexual behavior was not found predominant among adults in any of the societies, although some homosexual behavior took place in a significant proportion.

> The apparent universality of this form of sexual activity might be due to some equally widespread social influence that tends to force a portion of every group into homosexual alliance. Certain social factors probably do incline certain individuals toward homosexuality, but the phenomenon cannot be understood solely in such .terms.[5]

About 190 cultural groups or peoples were included in the survey, although some were the subject of more detailed observations than others. Information was derived primarily from the Human Relations Area Files, Inc., formerly known as the Yale Cross-Cultural Survey. This compilation, catalogued both by subject matter and geographic area, is based on thousands of books, articles, and reports describing peoples by a variety of reporters and observers ranging from casual travelers to professional ethnographers. Though the summaries of Ford and Beach are invaluable, they reflect the biases of the compilers of their sources material, and the nature of these sources causes difficulty to investigators of sexual behavior.

A good illustration appears in the findings concerning homosexuality. Ford and Beach found references to homosexuality in some 76 societies. In 49 (64 percent), homosexuality was considered normal and socially acceptable, at least for certain members of the community. In the other 27 (36 percent), homosexual activity among adults was reported to be totally absent, rare, or carried on only in secrecy.[6] Because no reference to homosexuality, either positive or negative, was reported for the majority of societies, these were excluded from the statistics. Does the absence of either positive or negative statements about homosexuality mean it was unknown in the majority of societies or simply that the informants neglected mentioning the subject? The answer would seem to incline more toward the latter explanation, but if so, even the accuracy of the observations might be questioned, since the investigators reporting it were looking for proof of its existence.

Another problem is what constitutes homosexual activity. Balinese society, for example, was classified by Ford and Beach among the 36 percent minority where homosexual activity was rare, absent, or carried on only in secret. Yet the crossing of sex roles is common among the Balinese, their religion placing a high valuation on the hermaphroditic figure of Syng Hyang Toenggal, also known as the Solitary or Tijinitja. Tijinitja, according to Balinese cosmology, represents the time before the gods, before the separation of male from female. Thus Tijinitja is thought of as both husband and wife.[7] Obviously, the cross-dressing associated with the god represents transvestite conduct, but is it homosexuality? Probably Ford and Beach were correct in not classifying this activity as homosexual, but then why did they classify the cross-dressing among the *berdache* as homosexuality?[8] Can the classification in the one case be any more justified than in the other?

In one sense the argument over classification represents nit-picking, but in another it constitutes an essential problem for anyone engaged in a cross-cultural study of sexual activity. This is because, as research progresses, we become more precise in our definitions. New categories such as transvestism and transsexualism have been established that earlier were subsumed under the same category as homosexuality. Unfortunately, our historical and anthropological data are not usually detailed or precise enough to indicate into which category an individual should fall. The most workable and practical solution often is to avoid diagnosing a sexual condition outside the culture in which it existed; even when the data are sufficient to permit some preliminary classifying, definitive assignment in terms of current scholarship can be misleading if not actually erroneous.

These limitations and difficulties being remembered, the ethnographic data still make it possible to look at situations or conditions encouraging sexual activities regarded as deviant by Western society. Obviously, differing societal attitudes or practices or social conditions encourage different sexual responses.

One important variable is the availability of partners of the opposite sex. Tied in with this are factors such as polygamy, the age at which marriage is permitted, concepts about chastity, and attitudes about sex itself—both male and female. During the formative years sexually segregated institutions seem to encourage a different sexual response than sexually integrated institutions. The degree to which certain sex or role activities are forbidden is important, as is the ability of a society to institutionalize man's sexual activity. Child-rearing practices and status role concepts are also significant. In short, there are numerous variables, some of which might appear more important than others as this study progresses. Some can, however, be easily illustrated from the data about contemporary primitives.

Granted the sexual nature of men and women, it seems likely that, if there is a paucity of sexual partners of the opposite sex, then either individuals would be more likely to turn to members of the same sex or sexual activity between members of the same sex would at least encounter less hostility. We know, for example, that more homosexuality exists in prisons than outside. Donald Clemmer's study of prison cultures found that about 40 percent of his convict population had had some homosexual activity, but only 10 percent had engaged in such activity before they went to jail[9] That other researchers tend to agree with these figures[10] implies that many individuals turn to homosexuality when no other sex partner is available. Similar findings emerge from the anthropological data. Henri Junod's classic study of the Thonga (Bathonga) tribe of Mozambique reported widespread homosexuality among the individuals brought to Johannesburg to work the mines and then confined to all-male camps. In 1915 a colleague of Junod observed what he thought were a large number of native women in the camps. Further investigation found they were

> not women: They were *tinkhentshana,* boys who have placed on their chests the breasts of women carved in wood, and who are going to the dance in order to play the part of women. To-night when they return to their dormitories, their "husbands" will have to give them 10 (shillings), and only on that condition will the *tinkhentshana* remove their breasts and comply with the desire of their "husbands."[11]

It was also found that earlier colonies of prostitutes had lived near the compound but had been driven away by the authorities. Junod said, however, that the Thongas had not frequented the prostitutes in great numbers, because of the fear of venereal disease, but instead they preferred homosexual relations. It became more or less standard practice within the compound for the native supervisor and his assistants to look over each new gang of workers and select those who might assume the women's role. Those consenting to become *tinkhentshana* received special work assignments and only rarely had to work underground in the mines. Actual marriage ceremonies sometimes took place between the inhabitants of the camp.

Junod believed that this homosexual activity had been brought on by confinement and that the Thonga in their native villages disapproved of such practices. On the other hand, Junod, a missionary, was upset because the immense majority of the natives did not consider their homosexual conduct a sin. His solution for "fighting" the evil was to secure separate dormitories where a "certain number of boys can find a refuge against contamination." One of his colleagues also recommended that the curtains enclosing beds be removed, that the beds be fixed so that they did not touch each other, that electric lights be installed to illuminate the dormitories at night, and that a watch be kept.[12]

A somewhat similar separation of the sexes took place in New Guinea, where native workers were brought into towns or sent out on plantations. The informant in New Guinea was, however, much less judgmental in the description of such activities than Junod.

> Such behavior, though sometimes condemned as foolish, calls forth no moral indignation, for the local opinion is that everyone is entitled to the kind of pleasure which be prefers, and many persons freely admit personal acquaintance with similar practices while away working for Europeans. Women are seldom available on the larger plantations and in the towns, and the older labourers, already accustomed to indulgence, are forced to take youths as lovers instead. A boy's behind is said to be a not unsatisfactory substitute, though everyone from Wogeo prefers the real thing, and is thankful on his return to go back to it. "It is like the tinned meat they give us on the goldfields," said one informant. "We like it quite well, but once home again we gladly eat pork and fish once more and never think of buying it from visiting schooners." Even bond-friends, who wander about together with arms entwined, are said to have no wish to make homosexual experiments. They may engage in mutual masturbation for a short time, it was agreed, but not after the greater attractions of normal intercourse are fully appreciated.[13]

Separation from the opposite sex can, however, be voluntary as well as involuntary. Monasticism is an example of voluntary segregation, homosexuality having been reported in some monastic institutions. A 1963 observer stated

> The monasteries in Tibet . . . have . . . a very strong reputation for male homosexuality, and jokes about master–novice relations are often made along these lines. George N. Patterson assured me that in Kham, interviewing patients medically in the course of his work, he was often called upon to treat monks for venereal disease of the anus, fistulas and other ailments, which were admittedly the result of homosexual contact, and which the people who came to him for medicine made no attempt to dissimulate.[14]

Perhaps it was a fear of homosexuality that led authorities in medieval Christian monasteries to keep a light burning and to issue regulations forbidding more than one monk to sleep in the same bed.

Even when sexual partners are present, access might be denied because of various cultural prohibitions. Among the Azande people in the Eastern Sudan area of central Africa, much of the male population between 25 and 35 was reported in 1932 to be organized into *vura* or groups of men denied access to women. During this period in their lives they were supposed to fight for the chief or, in the absence of war, work on his land. Boys were, however, available, many of the men bringing boys with them; these boys were sometimes spoken of as women and were even addressed as such. Within the *aparanga,* where the *vura* lived, the boys behaved as women did within the Azande culture; that is, they ate out of sight of other men, performed numerous female tasks such as serving meals, and went to bed with their "husbands." The custom was accepted as a substitute for the normal heterosexual union forbidden during this period.[15]

Widespread polygamy also curtails the availability of partners of the opposite sex. Because it was the older and wealthier males who were most likely to have large polygamous households, fewer brides were available for the young men. In such societies other forms of sexual behavior were often tolerated, perhaps to avoid a challenge to the prerogatives of the powerful polygamous ruling class. Since the wife in a polygamous household, particularly a very large one, might not have much access to her husband, it was perhaps inevitable that the greatest amount of female homosexuality or other erotic practice has been observed in polygamous societies. Though Ford and Beach found that females were less likely to engage in homosexual relations than males (only 17 of their societies reported such activities),[16] the figures are open to even more challenge than those on the males, because the overwhelming majority of observers have been men who faced greater difficulties in getting information about the sexual activities of women than of men. In polygamous societies, however, female homosexuality was either more obvious, or the informants were more willing to talk about it, or the investigator, suspecting its existence, displayed more persistence in uncovering it.

Regardless of the reason, a number of observers have claimed that the "starved sexuality" of women in large polygamous households found an outlet in homosexuality.[17] Nadel, reporting widespread female homosexuality among the Nupe in Nigeria, stated on the other hand that homosexuality among men did not seem to occur. Often, however, male and female homosexuality coexisted in polygamous societies. Among the Azande the monopoly of wives among the rich and powerful led to the toleration not only of male homosexual practices but of female as well, although it was still more hidden than the male.[18] Autoerotic practices were also widespread. In the larger harems, Azande women fashioned phalli of bananas, manioc, or sweet potato roots, in spite of the fact that if their husbands had caught them using such devices they would have been expelled from his household. Among the lower status groupings of polygamous wives, possession of a dildo resulted in a public beating.[19] More overtly lesbian practices have been reported in other areas where large-scale polygamy was or is common.[20]

If the anthropological data are correct, it also appears that homosexuality and other sexual activities were regarded with greater tolerance in societies where several variables were present, namely where marriage was delayed until late in life, female chastity was prized, marriage fees were expensive, housing difficulties existed, or other factors were present that made contact with members of the opposite sex difficult. Such conditions are now present in much of Africa and other parts of the underdeveloped world where rural men are moving into the cities to earn a better living and leaving their women behind in the village. Among the Wolof in Senegambia, for example, homosexuality has reportedly increased as womanless men have concentrated in the ports and big trade centers. Many of the Wolof men in such situations dress as women, and these *gor-digen* ("men–women") have found themselves much in demand, even though the Muslim society of the area disapproves of them and refuses them religous burial.[21] It has been postulated that the rapid influx into the city by the Wolof has been encouraged by the severe restrictions on heterosexual and homosexual relations in the village. In the cities the prohibitions for women still exist but are relaxed for men. In part of Indonesia, even in the 1950s, among the Makassar, where contact with women was extremely difficult for the young male and contact with male relatives or *kampong* fellows was equally prohibited, a number of young men left their villages to seek their fortune as male prostitutes in the marketplace. Here there was a flourishing market for homosexual prostitution because the girls were so repressed about sex in their childhoods that their frigidity carried over into adulthood.[22]

Among the Aranda in Central Australia early in this century, a man who was fully initiated but not yet married took a boy of 10 or 12 years of age to live with him as his wife until the man became eligible to marry a woman. The practice was tolerated because of the great difficulties in finding a suitable wife in the required strict class lines, a difficulty compounded by the polygamy of the older man.[23] Similar practices for young boys were tolerated among the Lau in the Fiji Islands. The young Lau boy could not play in mixed groups or in adult ones, and he was also excluded from normal masculine activites.

> He is thwarted and he suffers from feelings of inferiority, becomes self-conscious, awkward, silent and retiring. His plight is highly amusing to the community, especially the young women and swaggering initiated youths who amuse themselves by ridiculing and spurning him. The only emotional outlets for boys of this age is in masturbation or homosexual relations with other *pilos* (prepuberty boys).[24]

In many societies, homosexuality was acceptable only in certain age groups and not in others. Among the Ngonde, in the 1950s, for example, where boys were confined to boys' villages, homosexual activities were tolerated from the age of 10 to the time the boy was married. When a boy slept with his friend, sexual activity was permissible, provided it was voluntary; the only crime was to force sex upon another boy. Married men could not, however, sleep together, since such activity was a mark of adolescence.[25] Observers reported a lack of homosexual activity among Ngonde girls, mainly because the girls were married young and quickly became pregnant. Instead, female homosexuality was more likely to exist among the older wives of the chiefs and other polygamists, being tolerated because the older women received relatively little attention from the polygamous husbands. Undoubtedly, one reason for the acceptance of homosexuality among young men was that there were no available wives for them.[26]

Among the Tusi and Hutu classes of the Rundi area of East Africa, any heterosexual activity for girls before marriage was strictly prohibited and severely punished. After marriage, however, women could engage in sexual activities not only with their husbands but also with other privileged partners.[27] In fact, the Rundi believed that, once the heterosexual activity of an individual had begun, he could legitimately expect to enjoy intercourse as frequently as possible. Before marriage Rundi girls were encouraged to masturbate, on the assumption that this made them more fit for marriage. They rubbed their labia with roots of plants and trees and tried to extend them by friction so that they would protrude, become yellow, and attain extraordinary size and length. The purpose of such activities was not, however, so much to obtain pleasure as to make themselves more acceptable for marriage. They believed that a man would not marry a girl who did not have distorted labia, considered by them a sign of sexual attractiveness. After marriage, females were expected to abstain from this manipulation.[28]

Attitudes toward sexual conduct are also influenced by the attitudes each sex has toward the other. Among the Malay, where female chastity was valued and early marriage for a girl encouraged, if only to protect her virtue, the result was very close friendships, usually between relatives of the same sex.[29] This was coupled with a rigid double standard in which wives were expected to tolerate their husband's infidelities but the husband had a right to kill his wife's seducer on the spot, at least if he found him in his house.[30] One result of such strict prohibition against sex, which went so far as to make some parts of the body shameful, was an increase in exhibitionism.

> In the extreme of anger and contempt, the worst form of insult that one can offer to any Malay of the opposite sex is purposely to uncover to him or her the private parts and calling his or her attention to the exhibits. Such an action amounts to

saying to him or her: "That face of yours is equivalent in dignity to this shameful part of mine."[31]

Friendly interaction between the sexes, at least in public, was difficult, if not impossible. In public dances, plays, and other events where female characters were called for, men usually assumed women's parts. In the so-called *Myong* shows, the female impersonation was so successful that Malay youths have been known to fall in love with the male actresses.[32]

Among the Gond of Central India, sex was not a sin provided relations were with the right people at the right time, in the right place, and in the right way. In the segregated communal dwelling (*ghotul*) where the young people lived there was freedom of sex, and in the boy's *ghotul* they played with each other's genitals, rode each other in imitation of the normal sex act, and were often taught to massage the legs of their elders. In contrast, marriage put limits on sexual activity, although male and female transvestism was still permissible. For example, men put on women's jackets when they went in a prophetic trance before a god, and at the bigger clan festivals the mediums danced and gestulated dressed in their rather "incongruous" women's blouses. Much more common, however, was women's dressing as men, particularly before a hunt. During one stage in the marriage ceremony the bride was also dressed as a male, along with other girls, and her husband was supposed to pick her out from the group. In both cases the cross-dressing was strictly ceremonial, although its original meaning has been lost. In the marriage ceremony it is postulated that the cross-dressing might have had something to do with fertility, begetting a male heir, transferring the pains of childbirth, or averting danger from the evil eye.[33]

A society's views on sex also influenced its concept of deviation. Among the Manus of New Guinea, for example, Margaret Mead reported that married women were believed to suffer pain in intercourse until they had borne a child, and even then they were still supposed to regard sex as a wearisome abomination. In fact, it was believed that women welcomed children because it gave their husbands a new interest and diverted their concentration from sexual activity. One women expressed the thought by saying that

"That house is good in which there are two children, one to sleep with the husband on one side of the house, one to sleep with the wife on the other. Then husband and wife do not sleep together."[34]

Margaret Mead stated that, since the spirits were not concerned with any aspect of sex not involving heterosexual activity by the Manus women, other types of sex behavior escaped the stigma of sin, although all sex activity was shameful.

In societies where women and men were not seen together or could appear in mixed company only under carefully controlled conditions, the need for companionship and entertainment was often served either by professional outcasts such as prostitutes or by men who acted the part of women. Some of these men–women were true transvestites, others were homosexuals, and for others the line was somewhat blurred. In Kashmir, for example, no sexual activity was recognized or tolerated for women before marriage.[35] There was also a rigid double standard and more or less strict separation of the sexes. Transvestism was fairly common, many of the femal impersonators being young boys who tossed back their waist-long hair and smiled until

the audience looks as though it will appreciate the vulgar lyrics which have now replaced some of those long known, they start to sing and sometimes act them. At other times, the artistes are paid to improvise some jive set at a villager whose own people, maybe those he employs, fear themselves to tell the truth.

Some of these boys continued to play to the full the female role all through their lives. One impersonator with a falsetto voice, I quite imagined to be a rather attractive girl, was backed by an orchestra of one drum, a shahnai and a raba, she started a kind of shimmy-shuffle dance on the river bank by the side of our houseboat. After a while . . . the girl's movements speeded up the tempo, and she started twirling round and round high kicking in a kind of Can-Can. . . . The boatmen were by then shrieking with laughter, the reason for which I could not understand. . . . Then the old manji . . . observed, "You see sahib, not even these eunuch men can dance like a girl!"[36]

Among the Siwans of the Libyan desert, where segregation of the sexes, had been traditionally enforced, homosexual conduct among men was accepted. One informant said "All normal Siwan men and boys practice sodomy." The investigator, Walter Cline, reported that his informant, after questioning some 60 Siwan men, found that 59 had engaged in homosexual activity. Among the Siwans the accepted homosexual relationship was between a man and a boy but not between adult men or between two young boys.[37] Another investigator claimed that the Siwans were more pleased at the birth of boys than girls:

The source of their pleasure lies in the fact that the bringing up of a boy costs very little whereas the girl needs ornaments, clothing, and stains. Moreover the boy is a very fruitful source of profit for the father, not for the work he does, but because he is hired by his father to another man to be used as a catamite. Sometimes two men exchange their sons. If they are asked about this, they are not ashamed to mention it.[38]

Some societies institutionalized homosexuality, transvestism, or other variants of sexual behavior by allowing those who for some reason could not

accept their required sex role to change it. This was most evident in the so-
called *berdache* or *bardash*. These two similar terms, one probably derived
from the Spanish *bardajo* or *bardaja* ("kept boy") and the other from the
French *Bardache* or Italian *bardaccia* ("catamite"), originally probably meant
male prostitute. Some have also traced the term to an Arabic corruption of a
Persian word that then passed into Spanish, Italian, French, and eventually
English. Still another explanation comes from the word *burdash*, an article of
men's clothing described as an effeminate sash worn around the waist, a lace
collar, or a tie. Regardless of its origin, the term as commonly found in anthropological literature describes the social institution reported by explorers in
many of the Indian societies of North America. By extension, the term was
later applied to similar institutions occurring elsewhere, particularly in Siberia
and other parts of Asia. Some writers have also applied it to the male temple
prostitutes of India, Sumeria, and elsewhere, or to various historical
phenomena such as the transvestite medieval mummers. There were, however,
real differences among the institutions so described; some of the individuals so
labeled could be called homosexuals, others could more easily be regarded as
transvestites, and others as transsexuals.[39]

One of the earliest, if not the earliest, references to the existence of such
groups among the American Indians appears in the writings of Pietro Martire
(Peter Martyr) D'Anghiere (1455–1526). whose *De orbe nove* covers Spanish
explorations in America at the beginning of the sixteenth century. In 1513
Vasco Balboa encountered and defeated a group of natives while crossing the
Isthmus of Panama. His troops then went on to capture the house of the king,
which was

> infected with most abominable and unnatural lechery. For he (Balboa) found the
> king's brother and many other young men in women's apparel, smooth and effem-
> inately decked, which by the report of such as dwelt about him, he abused with
> preposterous Venus. Of these about the number of forty, he commanded to be given
> for a prey to his dogs. . . . When the people had heard of the severe punishment
> which our man had executed upon that filthy kind of men, they resorted to them . . .
> by violence bringing with them all such as they knew to be infected with that
> pestilence, spitting in their faces and crying out to our men to take revenge of them
> and rid them out of the world from among men as contagious beasts. This stinking
> abomination had not yet entered among the people, but was exercized only by the
> noble men and gentlemen. But the people lifting up their hands and eyes toward
> heaven gave tokens that god was greviously offended with such vile deeds.[40]

How much Peter Martyr was carried away by his own prejudices is at least debatable, for another chronicler dealt with the incident in somewhat different
terms:

> Either from their effeminate dress or from the accusations of their enemies, the

Spaniards were induced to consider them guilty of unnatural crimes, and in their abhorrence and disgust, gave them to be torn to pieces by the blood hounds.[41]

Some *berdaches,* at least in their institutionalized form, as among the Chukchee of northeastern Asia, accepted a role reversal because of some extraordinary dream or vision:

Transformation takes place by the command of the *ke'let* (spirits) usually at the critical age of early youth when shamanistic inspiration first manifests itself. It is, however, much dreaded by the youthful adepts; and in most of these cases in which I spoke of the young shamans preferring death to obedience to the call of the 'spirits,' there was connected with the call a reference to change of sex. There are, however, various degrees of transformation of this kind.

In the first stage, the person subjected to it personages the woman only in the manner of braiding and arranging the hair of the head. . . . The second stage is marked by the adoption of female dress, which is also practiced either for shamanistic or for medico-magical purposes. It does not imply complete change of sex. . . . The third stage of transformation is more complete. A young man who is undergoing it leaves off all pursuits and manners of his sex, and takes up those of a woman. He throws away the rifle and the lance, the lasso of the reindeer herdsman, and the harpoon of the seal-hunter, and takes up the needle and the skin-scraper. He learns the use of these quickly because the 'spirits' are helping him all the time. Even his pronunciation changes from the male to the female mode. At the same time his body alters, if not in its outward appearance, at least in its faculties and forces. He loses masculine strength, fleetness of foot in the race, endurance in wrestling, and acquires instead the helplessness of a woman. Even his physical character changes. The transformed person loses his brute courage and fighting spirit, and becomes shy of strangers, even fond of small talk and nursing small children. Generally speaking, he becomes a woman with the appearance of a man.[42]

Among the Lapps the shaman or *nosi'da* journeyed to the other world in a trance and on certain occasions had to wear female apparel and bear a woman's name.[43] Among the Illinois and Dakota Indians of the American plains early observers reported individuals compelled to wear women's clothes and always consulted by the councils because their special way of living had given them incomparable insights.[44]

Berdaches, among the Ojibwa, abandoned their own sex and adopted the other, but they were

never ridiculed or despised by the men on account of their new costumes, but are, on the contrary, respected as saints, or being in some degree inspired by the *Manitou,* yet, in other respect, they are merely considered as women and are never allowed the privileges refused the latter.[45]

A. L. Kroeber, in his report on the Yurok Indians of California, stated that

> One in several hundred Yurok men, on the average, preferred the life and dress of a woman, and was called *wergern*. This frame of mind, which appears to have a congenital or psychological basis well recognized by the psychiatrist, was not combatted, but socially recognized by the Indians of California—in fact, probably by all the tribes of the continent north of Mexico. Only among the advanced peoples of that region did the law frown upon transvestites. The Yurok explanation of the phenomenon is that such males were impelled by the desire to become shamans. This is certainly not true, since men shamans were not unknown. It is a fact, however, that all the *wergern* seem to have been shamans and esteemed as such—a fact that illuminates the Yurok institution of shamanism. The *wergern* usually manifested the first symptoms of his proclivities by beginning to weave baskets. Soon he donned women's clothing and pounded acorns.[46]

The *berdache* attracted the attention of many early observers, and there was considerable misunderstanding. Some early theorizers such as Edward Carpenter, believing all *berdaches* were shamans, made them into primitive geniuses, the archetype homosexual, and thereby implied all homosexuals were geniuses.[47] Others, more hostile to any sexual deviation, went to the opposite extreme, dismissing them as perverts and psychotics. Only a few actually studied them, and even then there was a curious reticence to speak about their sexual activity. Mrs. Matilda Coxe Stevenson, one of the better early observers of life in the pueblo, gave a fairly detailed description of the phenomenon among the Zuni Indians and then added, "There is a side to the lives of these men which must remain untold. They never marry women, and it is understood that they seldom have any relations with them."[48] In some societies the *berdaches* seem to have married other males, and in others they seem to have performed women's work and tasks and yet to have fathered children. Among the Papago Indians of Arizona, where a man lived and worked among the women, one of the women informants indicated:

> Our husbands used to tease us girls. "How do we know these children running around the house belong to us? We are away in the mountains all the time and in the fields. It is Shining Evening (the berdache) who is with the women." Then they would laugh and say to the babies, "Run along, over there is your daddy. . . ."[49]

Usually, however, if a man chose to live among women, he had to forsake sexual activity with them, or otherwise he would have been in great trouble with their husbands. Among the Iban of Borneo the *manang* or "village doctor" not only assumed woman's attire and adopted woman's ways after receiving the supernatural command but also was castrated. Following the castration the *manang* gave a feast, after which he was treated in every respect like a woman and occupied himself in feminine pursuits.

His chief aim in life is to copy female manners and habits so accurately as to be un-
distinguishable from other women, and the more nearly he succeeds in this the
more highly he is thought of.[50]

The *manang* often took a husband, and the couple were permitted to adopt
children. Among the Mohave, some females took the part of males, and males,
of females. George Devereux, who studied these people in the 1930's, reported
they had so changed their sexual identity in their own minds that, when they
described their anatomy, they used the terms suitable to their adopted sex, not
to their own biological sex.[51]

Among the Makassar in Indonesia, people were divided into men, women,
and *kawe kawe,* or "it" people. The male *kawe kawe* were accepted by their
female peers as women, but sexual contact with them was forbidden. If any
sexual activity took place, the male *kawe kawe* would suffer expulsion to the
men's group, where it was believed he would not be emotionally comfortable.
Many of the male *kawe kawe,* once outside the women's group, behaved as
men, although they usually carried things and did other tasks in the women's
way. The female *kawe kawe* usually lived with the women but did men's work,
and in their performance of their other tasks such as carrying burdens, they
acted as men, carrying things with a yoke over the shoulders instead of on the
head.[52] The Makassar also had an institutionalized transvestite group known
as the *bissu,* whose sexual orientation was heterosexual. In the past, the *bissu*
were kept at various princely courts, where they took care of the ornaments and
performed certain rituals while dressing and behaving as women. During the
twentieth century they, along with most of the courts, have more or less disappeared. In the few areas where they do live, many are married and live with
their wives and children and in daily life dress and act as men. When certain
rituals are performed, however, they dress and act as females.[53] Some *bissu* are,
however, recognized as having a homosexual orientation. One observer believed
that homosexuality might have been tolerated among the Makassar, because
there were prohibitions against contacts between boys and girls, and the only
acceptable sexual outlet for young boys was in homosexuality, but girls were
denied this sexual expression.[54]

That cross-dressing may have represented a loss of status for the male is indicated by reports of the Lepcha peoples in the Sikkim Himalayas, where sex
has been described as the people's sole recreation "and the common topic of
conversation on practically every occasion."[55] Here a "girl will dress up in
men's clothes as a joke, but it would be considered rather shameful for a grown
man to dress up as a women, though young boys occasionally do so in play."[56]
This in spite of the fact that the Lepcha had relatively fluid or open sex role
boundaries and did not recognize any inherent temperamental differences
between the sexes.

This concept of status loss might well explain why such conduct was permissible for men who had lost status and not so permissible for women, who then would have gained male status. A similar association of clothing with sex role seems to have formed the basis for much of Western hostility to male transvestism.[57]

In some societies, in fact, it is difficult to ascertain with any certainty whether the *berdache* assumed the woman's guise to escape the burden of being a man or whether it was woman's work itself that attracted him. Among the Papago Indians the male transvestite was a common figure. When the war trophies were hung up, the *berdache* might dance around it with a bow, taunting, "See what you are reduced to! The men will not look at you, but I can shoot you."[58] Some of the *berdaches* among the Papago Indians took husbands, but others did not. The man–woman got along well with the women, since on food-gathering expeditions with them he did not get as tired as they, and he was usually an expert potter and basket maker. The men also accepted him–her, since he joked with them, giving them obscene nicknames, far bolder than those bestowed by women. A woman informant reported to an ethnologist that the man–woman

> was so strong! She did not get tired grinding corn as I did, so sometimes she did it for me. That was something my husband could never do even though he was kind. It would look too bad for a man to grind corn. I found the man-woman very convenient . . . when I was tired she carried my baby for me. No man could do that; it would not be right.[59]

Among the Isneg on the Philippines, there was a strict sexual division of labor, and no member of the opposite sex would normally dare to encroach upon these customary divisions. Those who did were regarded as deviant, including the *táyyén* and the *takowáń*. The *táyyén*

> do not know how to handle a hatchet, while, on the other hand, they use a woman's *iko*-knife as easily as if it were a tool specifically their own; even in their gait, they take over everything that is characteristic of women. The *takowáń* dress like women and perform all kinds of work usually done by the latter: they plant, weed, and pound rice as well as the most experienced members of the fair sex.[60]

In such sex-differentiated societies, outside forces such as colonial administrators unconsciously added to the confusion about sex roles. When the Americans occupied the Philippines, they tended to teach home economics to the girls and gardening to the boys, but many of the Philippine tribal groups regarded gardening as mainly a female activity, and only the *"bayutes"* ("men-women") would garden or do other feminine tasks.[61]

Specific forms of sexual behavior were also encouraged in some societies to preserve an effective civil servant class unable to challenge the power of the rulers. The Korean kings, for example, were surrounded by palace eunuchs acquired as boys from poor families to serve in the royal service. In theory they were given the best education possible so that they might be a restrained and dispassionate influence on the monarch. This theory was not always practiced, some being described as "illiterate parasites" devoted primarily to enriching themselves. Many eunuchs married and carried on a continuum of eunuch families by adopting castrated boys.[62]

Among the Mossi in the Western Sudan the chief was traditionally surrounded by a veritable army of *soroné* ("pages"), *samande* ("bodyguards"), *ourkima* ("grooms") and *jussaba* ("eunuchs").[63] The chief eunuch was guardian of the king's wives and could have not legitimate heirs. Rich and important cantons were entrusted to eunuchs, because upon their death their fortunes reverted to the king, and the eunuch appointed to replace him would have to establish his own fortune.[64] The *soroné* were young boys, usually between 7 and 15 years of age and the firstborn of all men to whom the chief gave a wife. The firstborn daughters of such marriages were given in marriage by the chief to recruit further *soroné*. These pages wore their hair like women, and also, like women, they wore heavy copper bracelets on their wrists; they also served as women in other ways. While the pages were serving, they were required to abstain from intimate contact with women and were tested on this each year by having to look into a gourd of water. From their reflection it was determined whether or not they were "free of stain."[65]

In other societies, variant sexual behavior was associated with certain specific ceremonies. Among the Big Nambas in the New Hebrides homosexuality was intimately bound up with the rites of circumcision. Every father of a boy about to be circumcised sought a special companion or guardian for his son. The guardian acted as the boy's husband before circumcision, but for 30 days after there was no sexual contact. Then there were homosexual relations until the boy assumed his bark-belt, the sign of manhood, and could take a boy lover himself. The natives believed such customs were necessary to make the boy's penis grow strong.[66]

The Ashanti believed sex preference was due to the soul or spirit of the individual. The *sunsum* ("the soul personality") of the men was heavy or aggressive, but that of the women was light or receptive, although such things could become somewhat confused; a woman with a "heavy" *sunsum* was very extroverted or had homosexual tendencies, and she was

> referred to as *obaa banyin* (female man). Her masculine tendencies may also be indicated by adding *banyin* (male) to her day name, such as "Ama banyin." Similarly, males with "light" sunsum are the cowards, sexual deviants, or those of retarded mentality who usually stay around the house in the company of women.[67]

Other societies tried to explain homosexuality in terms of causal factors. Among the Lepchas, homosexual conduct was explained as being caused by eating the flesh of an uncastrated pig. Normally the Lepchas castrated all domesticated boars at 3 or 4 months of age, lest they become savage or wander away into the forest, but there was another reason, since "if a man should happen to eat the flesh of an uncastrated pig he would therefore commit sodomy."

> Sodomy is strongly anti-social—it is called *nam-toak*, an act producing a year of disaster, the term which is also applied to incest—and an extremely embarrassing subject, one of the very few people don't like discussing. There is one man in the village, Takneum *youm*, who has twice sodomized people when he was drunk and the victim asleep. In the second case, which occurred recently, the victim was old Lharibu Chujen, himself a grandfather; he was not angry at the indignity offered and did not claim the recompense of a pig and five rupees and ceremonial cleansing by a Mun to which he was entitled.[68]

A sodomite who risked the year of disaster was thought to be not responsible for his acts, and no disgust was shown for Takneum *youmi,* although people avoided sleeping near him when he was drunk. In contrast, the Lepchas believed that other people could eat uncastrated pig without evil results and that the eating of wild boars implied no danger. Interestingly, women could eat uncastrated domesticated boars without ill effects, and, of course, both men and women could eat wild ones.

The Bhils (Nimar district of India) on the other hand believed heterosexual relations were sacred, "being limited only to and between the married couple," and "the relations are not for pleasure only but for a higher purpose." Some premarital sex took place, but this became a crime if the parties were not accepted as bride and groom. In spite of such strict control, masturbation was practiced, as were bestiality and homosexual activities. The informant reported that homosexuality was not common "but when nothing is available why not that?"[69] Since all sexual contact outside marriage was a crime in the eyes of the Bhils, and even suicides were committed to atone for violations of the sex norms, homosexuality in many ways was more preferable than some other sexual acts.

The ethnographic data so far sampled come from a variety of time periods and represent a range of societies. The specifics of human activity have not been emphasized but rather the conditions in societies that might have led to greater or lesser toleration of certain forms of sexual behavior. A considerable amount of data has, however, been gathered in a specific historical context that throws light not only on sex attitudes of some other cultures but also on those of the Western observers, namely, the observations made by the sixteenth-century European conquerors of Central and South America. At times the precision and detail are often missing, but even though much of the sexual activity is categorized as abominable sin, [70] it is still occasionally possible to distinguish homosexuality, bestiality, and various other kinds of nonprocreative sex often included under this rubric.[71]

One civilization described in some detail by the conquerors was that of the Incas, which extended down the Pacific coast from Colombia to Chile and inland to the Andes. Inca society was rigidly stratified. The king was of divine origin, the Son of the Sun, and was married to another person of divine origin, his sister, although he also had other wives selected from the virgins in the Temple of the Sun. In the temples priests, under the vow of chastity, performed sacrifices, sometimes of human beings. There were also virgin girls who prepared *chicha*, an alcoholic beverage obtained by the fermentation of maize, and who also wove the Inca ruler's clothing from alpaca wool. Because the Incas lacked a system of writing, our information comes primarily from reports by the Spanish conquerors.

As to sexual mores, the Incas were attempting to assert greater state control over sexual practices. This appears in the several collections of pre-Columbian Inca laws, the most nearly complete of which was probably that made by the Jesuit P. Valera (about 1594). Suggesting strong efforts to assert state control is a law stipulating that a husband who killed his wife without catching her in the act of adultery could be executed; even if he killed her in the actual act, he could be exiled. On the other hand, if he denounced her and her companion to the authorities, she would be executed. Probably earlier it had been permissible for a husband to execute his own wife, but the Incas were attempting to change this. Rape of a virgin was punishable by death unless the man married the girl. Rape of married women could be punished by execution, and rape of young girls called for flogging and exile. There were also several prohibitions against incest. Sexual intercourse between father and daughter, mother and son, or brother and sister could be punished by the death penalty for both parties, though if one party had been a more or less unwilling participant, his or her life would be spared. Intercourse with other levels of kinship, such as between an uncle and a niece or between cousins, could also evoke the death penalty or, at the minimum, flogging and imprisonment. Anal intercourse and bestiality were punished by hanging.[72] Similar legal restrictions were reported by Fernandez de Piedrahita,[73] Huaman Poma de Ayala,[74] and Torquemada.[75] There were, however, class differences and exceptions. Marriage between blood relations was a privilege of the nobility, and at times brother–sister marriages were the norm among certain classes. There were also geographical variations. The chronicler Cieza de León, for example, pointed out that, though the Incas themselves did not engage in homosexual relations, the practice was institutionalized in the highlands.

> In this kingdom of Peru, the public fame among all the natives is that the abominable sin was practiced in some of the villages of the district of Pueblo Viejo, as well as in other lands where there were evil people, as in the rest of the world. I shall record a great virtue in these Incas; for, being lords with such freedom, and with no one to whom to give an account, besides being able to take their pleasure with

women, night and day, and enjoy themselves as their fancies dictated, it has never been alleged, or even hinted, that any of them committed the above crime. On the contrary, they abhorred those who were guilty of it, looking upon them as vile wretches for glorying in such filthy conduct. Not only were they free from such vices in their own persons, but they would not permit anyone who was guilty of such practices to remain in the royal houses or palaces. I believe, also, and I have heard it related, that even if it came to their knowledge that anyone had committed an offence of that kind, they punished it with such severity that it was known to all. . . . With the exception of Puerto Viejo, sinners of this class were unknown throughout Peru, except that, as in the case in all countries, there may be eight or ten here and there who do the evil secretly. Those who were kept as priests in the temples, with whom it was rumored that the lords joined in company on days of festivity, did not meditate the committing of such sin, but only the offering of sacrifice to the demon. If the Incas, by chance, had some knowledge of such proceedings in the temple they may have ignored them, thinking that it was enough if they ordered that the Sun and their other gods should be worshipped in all parts, without considering it necessary to prohibit other ancient customs and religions, to abandon which would have been as bad as death itself, to those who were born in their practice.[76]

Cieza de León believed that homosexual intercourse in the temples represented a symbolic sacrifice to the devil. It took place on feast days, at which time chieftains and other men of rank engaged in intercourse with men dressed in women's clothes in the temple. According to tradition, the practice had been introduced into the highlands by a race of giants who had neither women of their own nor any use for local women. Cieza de León's chronicle is full of instances of homosexuality, almost an area-by-area listing. No other history is quite so replete with details, although his account is confirmed in general by Agustin de Zárate, his contemporary.[77]

Regardless of class or area, sexual activity was accepted as a normal function by the peoples of Latin America. Moreover, because parents and children were thrown together in most acts of their daily lives—eating, sleeping, and working together—and there was little privacy, children early learned about sex. Perhaps for this reason, a child was regarded as an adult at puberty. Polygamy existed only among the high officials or local chiefs, although in theory a man could have as many wives as he could support. Virginity was institutionalized in the Chosen Women, specially chosen young girls attached to the rituals associated with the religion of the sun. Wherever there were Sun Temples there were convents of Chosen Women. Usually, their dwelling place was fairly inaccessible, out of reach of ordinary man. It has been estimated that, at any one time, there were as many as 15,000 Chosen Women, but not all remained perpetual virgins. Those not directly connected with the rituals were taken in royal concubinage or as wives by famous generals. Later, if they still remained unmarried, the older Chosen Women became instructors and guardians for the newly arrived recruits. A group of these women, quartered at Caxas in the Sun Temple in northern Peru, were raped by Spanish soldiers at the onset of their conquest of Peru. They forced 500 Virgins of the Sun out into the plaza, and then, while crossbowmen kept off any Indians, the soldiers engaged in intercourse until satiated; then exhausted and tired, they continued the conquest. The Incas regarded the Spanish behavior as barbaric.[78]

Included within the Inca empire were the Chimú, who had taken over an earlier Mochica civilization almost intact. Although the Chimú and the Mochica worhshipped the sun, as did the Inca, their principal god was the moon, and they sacrificed children in its honor. Though neither the Chimú nor Mochica were literate, we know a great deal about them from their surviving pottery, many depicting sexual scenes. Most of the pottery dates from before 1000 A.D. and represents Mochica rather than Chimú, but we know the Chimú continued to hold many of the same ideas. Because the potters were women, we also get some impression about how women felt about the sexual act; if the facial grimaces are representative of their attitude, it appears that they did not share the male's pleasure in the act. The male is usually depicted as deriving pleasure and the female as registering displeasure or even revulsion, at best indifference. Similarly, the male is portrayed as richly dressed and wearing fine jewelry, whereas the woman lacks ornamentation. She was regarded as submissive and beneath the male, although it was also part of her duty to entice men to engage in sex. Much of this pottery has been collected by the Larco family, on whose property some of the first finds were made, and is preserved in the Rafael Larco Herrera Museum in Peru. The pottery is not the only pictorial representation of intercourse known to have existed among the peoples of Peru, but it has survived in the largest quantity. Some of the earlier representations of homosexual intercourse, including one in gold, were destroyed by the Spanish.[79] In the archaeological specimens taken from grave sites by the Larco family and reproduced in a volume by Rafael Larco Hoyle, the erotic statistics are rounded off as follows: 24 percent are of the penis; 4 percent, of the vulva; 11 percent, of the missionary position in coitus; 5 percent, of male masturbation; 31 percent, of heterosexual anal intercourse; 3 percent, of homosexual anal intercourse; 1 percent, of homosexual manipulation between women; 14 percent, of fellatio (mostly heterosexual, cunnilingus); and 6 percent, of bestiality of both men and women with various animals. The representations of the penis consist mostly of drinking vessels designed so that the user was forced to drink from the penis. Those attempting to drink from the top of the cup found themselves squirted by the penis. The same design held true for the vessels portraying the vulva, so that there was a symbolic cunnilingus even if only fellatio is pictured on the pottery itself. Why the emphasis was on the one form of oral–genital contact and not on the other is difficult to explain. It might well be that the Mochicas did not think the female pudenda deserving of their attention, although they regarded the tongue and lips as erotically sensitive areas.[80] Even more difficult to explain is the focus on anal intercourse, whether heterosexual or homosexual. Larco Hoyle claimed that it served as a way to avoid pregnancy, but he offered no evidence to support this belief.[81] Undoubtedly, in some cases this was true, but it seems doubtful this would be the case on such a massive scale. Larco Hoyle has also argued that a chief purpose of the erotic pottery was to warn people of the dangers of sexual excesses. As evidence he advanced the fact that many of those engaged in what he considered abnormal sexual relations showed body mutilations or were portrayed as skeletal forms, as if to imply that excessive sexuality would cause one to waste away.[82] In this, however, he ignored the facts that nose and lip mutilations were ritualistic operations having no connection with sexual activities and that skeletal forms also had symbolic meaning. An alternative explanation is that anal intercourse was engaged in by temple virgins to allow them to have sex without losing their virtue, but this also has to remain a hypothesis.[83] Perhaps the most logical explanation is that the Mochicas saw nothing evil in most forms of sexual activity, and the males at least delighted in engaging in several types of sexual activity. They did have certain taboos, such as cunnilingus, and in no case is there a portrayal of sex between an adult and a minor, but in general sex was regarded as a creative force pervading all aspects of nature. Though the Mochica culture had declined by the time of Inca domination, their successors, the Chimú, continued many of the same ideas. Since this was the case, it is no wonder that the Incas and later the Spanish had such difficulty in imposing their more restrictive sexual views.

A second major civilized area was in Central America and the Yucatán peninsula, where the Maya were culturally dominant at the time of the Spanish conquest, although no longer as powerful as they once had been. The religious centers of the Maya were characterized by temples built on stepped pyramids, which in a few instances contain burials. They identified their gods with the natural phenomena controlling the agricultural cycle. The world had been created by Huab. His son Itzammá was the lord of heaven, and Ixchel, his wife, was the goddess of floods, pregnancy, and medical matters. The Maya had a sophisticated numbering system and hieroglyphic writing, although only a little has been deciphered.[84]

The law code as published by the Spanish conquerers was in many ways similar to that of the Incas. An adulterous woman could be executed, as could her paramour if she was of royal blood, and among the lower classes a husband could repudiate her. Simple fornication called for a fine varying according to social class. A young man who had intercourse with a virgin had to marry her. Rape was usually punished by the death penalty, but if rape was attempted and not completed, the individual could be made a slave. Male homosexuality was also against the law, but it is not clear what the punishment was.[85]

Young men lived apart from their families, sleeping with each other. In spite of this, the Spanish reported little homosexual activity but instead accused the young men of bringing prostitutes to their quarters. Marriageable age was 14 for girls and 18 for men. A man could not marry a women having the same surname. Marriages were arranged by a professional matchmaker. Though the female form appears infrequently in Mayan art, there are numerous depictions of the nude male, many protrayed with erect phalli. This is particularly true in the Puuc region of the Yucatán, the site of the ancient city of Uxmal. Most Spanish observers emphasized the Maya were not homosexually inclined. Diego de Landa (about 1570) wrote he had not heard of the "nefarious sin" in Yucatán as he had in other parts of the Indies.[86] Other Spaniards, such as Caspar Antonio Chi, confirm the testimony.[87] In contrast, other reporters, such as Bernal Díaz del Castillo, claimed the Maya, committed sodomy, although his observations seem to be based on Mayan statuary in Guatemala rather than actual observation.[88] Torquemada, the Franciscan chronicler, also wrote that, despite a law prohibiting the "bestial vice," such vices had been introduced by a devil named Chin, who had induced the Maya Indians of Vera Paz, Guatemala, to practice sodomy by claiming sodomy was not a sin but an action of the gods. Thus encouraged, many parents started giving a boy to their sons to use as a woman.[89] Others also reported widespread homosexuality. From the contradictory reports, it seems homosexuality was practiced more among some of the Maya than others and by some of the peoples closely associated with the Maya but not by others. Where it did exist, it was often institutionalized through the *berdache*.

The group about whom we have the most information are the Aztecs of Mexico, who, building on the cultural achievements of the Toltecs, dominated much of central Mexico. Their religion was initially centered around the cult of Huitzilopochtli, symbolizing the sun, reborn every day, who had to be sustained by human blood. Their rituals included sacrifices of prisoners or other victims. Other gods of conquered peoples were gradually incorporated, including such deified priests as Quetzalcoatl and Tezcatlipoca. The universe was believed to have been created by Tonacatecuhtli, the male god, and Tonacacihuatl, the female principle. The Aztecs had a pictographic system of writing and a sophisticated numbering system. Their cities were large, Tenochtitlan, the capital, built on Lake Texcoco, having a population estimated at around 200,000. Included in the city were some 25 pyramids with temples at the top, the largest of which was the great pyramid of Huitzilopochtli.[90]

The Aztecs appear to have been polygamous, practicing widespread concu-

binage and prostitution. A wife's function being to bear children, she could be
cast out if she failed to do so. A divorced woman could remarry, but a widow
had to marry a brother of her deceased husband or one of his clansmen. A boy
reached marriage age at 20 and a girl at 16; marriage was arranged with the
consent of the two participants, provided a priest considered the two harmonious.[91] There were strong incest prohibitions. A father and daughter who had
intercourse were to be strangled, as were brothers and sisters. Women engaged
in homosexual activities were to be strangled. Not only was the adulterous
woman stoned to death, but so was her paramour.[92] Rape of a virgin was
punished by death. Male homosexuality was also given the death penalty, as
was transvestism by either the male or the female.[93] The Franciscan Friar
Sahagún described the male homosexuals he observed in rather hostile terms:

> The sodomite is an effeminate, a defilement, a corruption, filth; a taster of filth,
> revolting, perverse, full of affliction. He deserves laughter, ridicule, mockery; he is
> detestable, nauseating, disgusting. He makes one acutely sick. Womanish, playing
> the part of a woman, he merits being committed to flames, burned, consumed by
> fire, he burns; he is consumed by fire. He talks like a woman, he takes the part of a
> woman.[94]

This is, of course, a Spaniard speaking, but there is considerable evidence
that the Aztec himself was restrictive in his sexuality. An Aztec father was said
to have advised his son:

> *Do not throw yourself upon women*
> *like the dog which throws itself upon food.*
> *Be not like the dog*
> *when he is given food or drink*
> *giving yourself up to women before the time comes.*
>
> *Even though you may long for women,*
> *hold back, hold back with your heart*
> *until you are a grown man, strong and robust.*
> *Look at the maguey plant.*
> *If it is open before it has grown*
> *and its liquid is taken out,*
> *it has no substance.*
> *It does not produce liquid; it is useless.*
> *Before it is opened*
> *to withdraw its water,*
> *it should be allowed to grow and attain full size.*
> *Then its sweet water is removed*
> *all in good time.*

This is how you must act;
before you know woman
you must grow and be a complete man.
And then you will be ready for marriage;
you will beget children of good stature,
healthy, agile, and comely.[95]

Francisco Guerra, in his study of aberrant behavior among pre-Columbian Americans, found that all kinds of sexual behavior were reported, along with cannibalism, human sacrifice, and drug addiction. Anal intercourse with both heterosexual and homosexual partners was widespread among most of the Indian cultures. Homosexuality itself was often institutionalized in the *berdache.* Bestiality was most common in Peru, but it became part of the manual of confession for both South and Central American Indians, indicating the concern of the priests about this "sin" among their parishioners. Masturbation was probably lumped with the abominable sin, although its extent is now hard to determine because of the lack of definition by the Spanish observers. There were a number of incest taboos, but these were conditioned by class status and varied from area to area. Adultery, particularly by the female, was heavily penalized, since all the Indian cultures had a double standard. Among certain classes and groups female adultery was punished by the death penalty. Prostitution for the most part was reported as a marginal problem, although we know it existed on various levels among the Aztecs, the Mayas, and the Incas. Homosexual prostitution was also reported in some areas of Central America.[96] Many cultures also had rigid menstrual taboos.

In short, pre-Columbian Americans, like the other peoples reported on in the ethnographic data, engaged in a wide variety of sexual activities, including many condemned by Western culture. Several variables seem to be operative, including emphasis on female chastity, marriage prohibitions, housing difficulties, sexual segregation, and general attitudes toward sex itself. These and other variables will be surveyed in succeeding chapters as we examine how Western attitudes were formed and modified.

NOTES

1. Prince Peter of Greece, "Tibetan, Toda, and Tiya Polyandry: A Report on Field Investigations," New York Academy of Sciences, *Transactions,* ser. 2, X (1948), p. 217.

2. Geoffrey Gorer, *Himalayan Village: An Account of the Lepchas of Sikkim* (London: Michael Joseph, 1938), p. 331.

3. William O. Douglas, *Beyond the High Himalayas* (Garden City, N.Y.: Doubleday, 1953), p. 183.

4.   Clellan S. Ford and Frank A. Beach, *Patterns of Sexual Behavior* (New York: Harper, 1951), p. 250.

5.   *Ibid.*, p. 257.

6.   *Ibid.*, pp. 129–130.

7.   Jane Belo, *Bali: Rangda and Barong, American Ethnological Society Monograph* No. 16 (1949), p. 58.

8.   Ford and Beach, *op. cit.*, p. 130.

9.   Donald Clemmer, *The Prison Community* (New York: Holt, Rinehart, and Winston, 1958).

10.   See, for example, Joseph E. Fishman, *Sex in Prison* (New York: National Library Press, 1934): Robert Lindner, "Sex in Prison," *Complex,* VI (1951), pp. 5–20; and the two Kinsey reports, *Sexual Behavior in the Human Male* (Philadelphia: W. B. Saunders, 1948) and *Sexual Behavior in the Human Female* (Philadelphia: W. B. Saunders, 1953).

11.   Henri A. Junod, *The Life of a South African Tribe* (London: Macmillan, 1927), 2 vols. p. 493.

12.   *Ibid.*, p. 494.

13.   H. Ian Hogbin, "Puberty to Marriage, A Study of the Sexual Life of the Native of Wogeo, New Guinea," *Oceania,* XVI (1946), pp. 205–206.

14.   Prince Peter, *A Study of Polyandry* (The Hague: Mouton and Company, 1963), p. 458.

15.   Charles Gabriel and Brenda Z. Seligman, *Pagan Tribes of the Nilotic Sudan* (London: George Routledge, 1932), pp. 506–507.

16.   Ford and Beach, *op. cit.*, p. 133.

17.   Seigfried Frederick Nadel, *A Black Byzantium: The Kingdom of Nupe in Nigeria* (London: Oxford University Press, 1942), p. 152.

18.   Albert de Graer, *L'Art de guerir chez les Azandex* (Brussels: Goemaere, 1929), p. 362.

19.   Edward Evans Pritchard, *Witchcraft, Oracles and Magic Among the Azande* (Oxford, England: Clarendon Press, 1937), pp. 56–57; C. R. Lagae, "Les Azande ou Niam-Niam," *Bibliotheque-Congo,* XVIII (1926), p. 16; and P. H. Larken, "An Account of the Zande," *Sudan Notes and Records,* IX (1926), p. 24; XIII (1930), p. 103.

20.   Gustave E. Hulstaert, "Les Marriage des Nkundo," Institut royal colonial Belge, section des sciences morales et politiques, *Memoires,* I (1938), pp. 86–87.

21.   Geoffrey Gorer, *African Dances* (London: Faber and Faber, 1935), p. 36.

22.   H. T. Chabot, *Verwantschap, standen Sexe in Zuid Celebes* (Groningen, Netherlands; Djakarta, Indonesia: J. B. Wolters, 1950), pp. 210, 315; Raymond Kennedy, *Field Notes on Indonesia: South Celebes* (unpublished, Human Relations Area Files, 1953), pp. 117, 213–214.

23.   Carl Strehlow, "Das soziale Leben der Aranda und Loritja," *Veröffentlichungen aus dem städtischen Völker-Museum,* I, 4–1 (1913), p. 98.

24.   Laura Thompson, "Fijian Frontier," *Studies of the Pacific,* IV (1960), p. 44.

25.   Monica Wilson, *Good Company: A Study of Nyakyusa Age-Villages* (London: Oxford University Press, 1957), pp. 88, 126, 196–197.

26.   Monica Wilson, *Communal Rituals of the Nyakyusa* (London: Oxford University Press, 1959), p. 197.

27.   Jacques J. Maquet, *The Promise of Inequality in Ruanda* (London: Oxford University Press, 1961), p.77.

28.   Hans Meyer, *Die Barundi* (Leipzig: Otto Spamer, 1916), p. 174.

29. Rosemary Firth, *Housekeeping among Malay Peasants* (London: School of Economics and Political Science, 1943), p. 32; Zainal-'Abidin bin Ahmad, "Malay Manners and Etiquette," *Journal of the Malay Branch of the Royal Asiatic Society*, XXIII (1950), pp. 43–74, 80.

30. J. Rigby, *Papers on Malay Subjects: Law, II: The Ninety-Nine Laws of Perak* (Kuala Lumpur: Federated Malay States Government Press, 1929), pp. 53–54.

31. Ahmad, *op. cit.*, pp. 67–68.

32. J. D. Vaughan, "Notes on the Malay of Pinang and Province Wellesley," *The Journal of the Indian Archipelago and Eastern Asia*, n.s., II, 2 (1957), p. 134.

33. Verrier Elwin, *The Muria and their Ghotul* (Bombay, India: Geoffrey Cumberledge, 1947), pp. 445, 41, 655.

34. Margaret Mead, *Growing Up in New Guinea* (New York: William Morrow, 1930), pp. 165–166.

35. Jivanji Jamshedji Modi, "The Pundits of Kashmir," *The Journal of the Anthropological Society of Bombay*, X (1913–1916), p. 476.

36. Pearce Gervis, *This is Kashmir* (London: Cassell and Company, 1954) p. 278.

37. Walter Cline, "Notes on the People of Siwan and El Garah in the Libyan Desert," *General Series on Anthropology*, No. 4 (Menasha, Wis.: George Banta Publishing Company, 1936), passim.

38. Mahmud Mohammad 'Abd Allah, "Siwan Customs," *Harvard African Studies*, I (1917), p. 7.

39. Dorr Legg, "The Berdache and Theories of Sexual Inversion," *One Institute Quarterly*, II, 2 (1959), p. 60. See also Arno Karlen, *Sexuality and Homosexuality* (New York: W. W. Norton, 1971), pp. 463–465.

40. Peter Martyr, (Pietro Martire d'Anghiere), *The Decades of The New Worlds or West India . . .* (1516) in *The First Three English Books on America*, Edward Arber, ed. (Edinburgh: Turnbull and Spears, Printers, 1885), p. 138.

41. Antonio de Herrern y Tordesillas, *Historia general de los hechos de los Castellanos en las isla y tierra firme del Mar Oceano* (1601), in *Voyages and Discoveries of the Companions of Columbus*, Washington Irving, ed. (reprinted New York: Rimington and Hooper, 1929), p. 195.

42. Waldemar Bogores, *The Chukchee, Memoirs of the American Museum of Natural History*, XI (1904, 2 vols.), pp. 449–451.

43. Gustorm Gjessing, *Changing Lapps: A Study in Culture Relations in Northernmost Norway* (London: London School of Economics, 1954), p. 26.

44. W. J. Hoffman, *The Mide'wiwin or "Grand Medicine Society" of the Ojibwa* (Washington, D.C.: U.S. Bureau of Ethnology, 1891), p. 153.

45. W. Vernon Kinietz, *Chippewa Village: The Story of Katikitegon* (Bloomfield Hills, Mich.: Cranbrook Institute of Science, Bulletin 25 (1947), p. 156.

46. A. L. Kroeber, *Handbooks of the Indians of California*, Bureau of American Ethnology, Report No. 78 (1925), p. 46.

47. Edward Carpenter, *Intermediate Types among Primitive Folk* (New York: Mitchell Kennerly, 1914).

48. Matilda Coxe Stevenson, *The Zuni Indians*, Bureau of Ethnology, Report No. 23 (1901–1902), pp. 37–38.

49. Ruth Murray Underhill, *Social Organization of the Papago Indians*, Columbia University Contributions to Anthropology, XXX (1939), pp. 186–187.

50. H. Ling Roth, "The Native of Borneo," *The Journal of the Anthropological Institute of Great Britain and Ireland,* XXI (1892), p. 119.

51. George Devereux, "Institutionalized Homosexuality of the Mohave Indians," *Human Biology,* IX (1937), pp. 498–527, reprinted *The Problem of Homosexuality in Modern Society,* Henry Ruitenbeck, ed. (New York: Dutton, 1963).

52. H. T. Chabot, *op. cit.,* pp. 205–208, 213, 214.

53. *Ibid.,* pp. 209–210.

54. Raymond Kennedy, *op. cit.,* p. 117.

55. John Morris, *Living with Lepchas: A Book about the Sikkim Himalayas* (London: William Heinemann, 1938), p. 290.

56. Geoffrey Gorer, *Himalayan Village,* p. 279.

57. Vern Bullough, "Transvestites in the Middle Ages, a Sociological Analysis," *American Journal of Sociology,* LXXIX (1974) pp. 1381–1394.

58. Ruth Murray Underhill, *op. cit.,* pp. 186–187.

59. Ruth Murray Underhill, *The Autobiography of a Papago Woman,* American Anthropological Association, *Memoirs,* XLVI (1936), pp. 39, 44.

60. Morice Vanoverbergh, *The Isneg Farmer,* Catholic Anthropological Conference, *Publications,* III, 4 (1941), p. 285.

61. Donn V. Hart, *The Philippine Plaza Complex,* Yale University Southeast Asia Studies, Cultural Report Series, No. 3 (1955), p. 24; and Donn V. Hart, *Barrio Caticugan: A Visayan Filipino Community* (unpublished doctoral dissertation, Syracuse University, 1954), p. 415.

62. Cornelius Osgood, *The Koreans and Their Culture* (New York: Ronald Press, 1951), p. 146.

63. Louis Tauxier, *Le Noir du Soudan, pays Mossi et Gouronsi documents et analyses* (Paris: Emile Larose, 1912), p. 108.

64. A. A. Delobsom, *L'Empire du Mogho-Naba* (Paris: Les Editions Domat-Montcrestien, 1932), p. 3.

65. Louis Tauxier, *Le Noir de Yatenga: Mossis—Nioniossés—Samos—Yarsés—SilmiMossis—Peuls* (Paris: Emile Larose, 1917), p. 108.

66. John Layard, *Stone Men of Malekula* (London: Chatto and Windus, 1942), pp. 486–488.

67. James Boy Christenson, *Double Descent among the Fanti,* Human Relations Area Files (1954), p. 92.

68. Geoffrey Gorer, *Himalayan Village,* p. 102.

69. T. B. Naik, *The Bhils: A Study* (Delhi, India: Bharatiya Adimjati Sevak Sangh, 1956), pp. 231–232.

70. Pedro de Cieza de León, *The Second Part of the Cronicle of Peru,* translated by Clements R. Markham, ed. (London: Hakluyt Society, 2nd ser., N. 68, 1883), pp. 78–79.

71. See Francisco Guerra, *The Pre-Columbian Mind* (London: Seminar Press, 1971), pp. 43–44. Guerra's book is invaluable.

72. [Blás Valera], "Relación de las costumbres antiguas de los naturales del Piru," in *Biblioteca de authores espanōles,* CCIX (1968), 151–190, esp. 177–180. There is an English translation of the laws in Guerra, *op. cit.,* pp. 34–37.

73. Lucas Fernandez de Piedrahita, *Historia general de las conquistas del Nuevo Reyno de Granada* (Amberes: Juan Bautista Verdussen, 1688), Part 1, Book 2, Chap. 5, pp. 45–48. English translation by Guerra, *op. cit.,* p. 34.

74. Felipe Huaman Poma de Ayala, *Nueva corónica y buen gobierno* (Paris: Institut d'Ethnologie, 1936), pp. 182–193. There is an English summary of the laws in Guerra, *op. cit.*, pp. 38–39.

75. Juan de Torquemada, *I^a–III^a Parte de los veynte y un libros rituales y Monarchia Indiana con el origen y guerras de la Indias Occidentales* (Sevilla, Spain: Mathias Clavijo, 1615). There is an English summary in Guerra, *op. cit.*, p. 37.

76. Pedro de Cieza de León, *op. cit.*, pp. 78–79. For another English version, see Pedro de Cieza de León, *The Incas*, translated by Harriet de Onis (Norman, Okla.: University of Oklahoma Press, 1959). The first part of his chronicle was published in 1553, the second part in 1880.

77. Agustin de Zárate, *Historie del descubrimiento y conquista del Peru . . .* (Anvers [Antwerp]: Martin Nucio, 1555). Part of this is summarized in Guerra.

78. For what it is worth, most of the popular surveys of Inca culture include similar information. See, for example, G. H. S. Bushnell, *Peru* (New York: Praeger, 1957); Victor W. Von Hagen, *Realm of the Incas* (New York: Praeger, 1957); Hans Dietrick Disselhoff, *Daily Life in Ancient Peru*, translated by Alisa Jaffa (New York: McGraw-Hill, 1967). See also Louis Baudin, *A Socialist Empire: The Incas of Peru*, translated by Katherine Woods (Princeton, N. J. Van Nostrand Company, 1961).

79. Guerra, *op. cit.*, p. 255.

80. Rafael Larco Hoyle, *Checan: Essay on Erotic Elements in Peruvian Art* (Geneva: Nagel Publishers, 1965), passim.

81. *Ibid.*, p. 112.

82. *Ibid.*, pp. 87–88.

83. Guerra, *op. cit.*, p. 258.

84. There are a number of popular histories of the Maya on which this section relies. See Victor W. Von Hagen, *World of the Maya* (New York: New American Library, 1960); G. W. Brainder, *The Maya Civilization* (Los Angeles: The Southwest Museum, 1954); S. G. Morley, *The Ancient Maya* (Palo Alto, Calif.: Stanford University Press, 1946); J. E. S. Thompson, *The Rise and Fall of Maya Civilization* (Norman, Okla: The University of Oklahoma Press, 1954); and R. Redfield, *The Folk Culture of Yucatán* (Chicago: University of Chicago Press, 1941).

85. Juan de Torquemada, *op. cit.*, Book 12, Chaps. 8, 9, 10, 11, 12, in Vol. 2, pp. 417–428. English translation in Guerra, *op. cit.*, pp. 31–33.

86. Diego de Landa, *Relación des chosse de Yucatán*, translated by Abbé Brasseur de Bourbourg, ed. (Paris: Arthus Bertrand, 1864), Chap. 30, p. 178. See also *Landa's Relación de las cosas de Yucatán*, translated by Alfred M. Tozzer, ed. (Cambridge, Mass.: Peabody Museum, 1941).

87. Gaspar Antonio Chi, "Relación sobre las costumbres de los Indios," in *Landa's Relación de las cosas de Yucátan*, pp. 230–232.

88. Bernal Díaz del Castillo, *Historia verdadera de la conquista de la Nueva-España* (Madrid: Imprenta del Reyno, 1632), Chaps. 2 and 51, translated by Guerra, *op. cit.*, p. 123.

89. Torquemada, *op. cit.*, Book 12, Chap. 11, in Vol. 1, p. 422, translated by Guerra, *op. cit.*, pp. 172–173.

90. This description is drawn from several popular histories of Aztec culture such as G. C. Vaillant, *The Aztecs of Mexico* (reprinted, London: Penguin Books, 1950); Miguel León-Portilla, *Aztec Thought and Culture*, translated Jack Emory Davis (Norman, Okla.: University of Oklahoma Press, 1963); Frederick A. Peterson, *Ancient Mexico* (New York: Capricorn Press, 1962); Victor W. Von Hagen, *The Aztec: Man and Tribe* (New York: New American Library, 1958). See also Miguel León-Portilla, *Pre-Columbian Literatures of Mexico*, translated by Grace Lobanov (Norman, Okla.: University of Oklahoma Press, 1969).

91.   See Adolph F. Bandelier, *On the Social Organization and Mode of Government of the Ancient Mexicans,* (Cambridge, Mass.: Peabody Museum of American Archaeology and Ethnology, *Report* No. 12, 1880), II, pp. 557–699.

92.   Bartolomé de las Casas, *Apologética historia de las Indias,* M. Serano y Sanz ed. (Madrid: M. Bailly-Bailliere e hijos, 1909), Chap. 215, pp. 562–563. There is an English translation in Guerra, *op. cit.,* pp. 22–23.

93.   Jerónimo de Mendieta, *Historia eclesiastica Indiana* (Mexico City: F. Diaz de León y S. White, 1870), Book 2, Chap. 29, pp. 136–138.

94.   This is the translation of Bernardino de Sahagún by Guerra, *op. cit.* p. 26.

95.   This is the translation by Miguel León-Portilla in *Aztec Thought and Culture,* pp. 149–150.

96.   See Guerra, *op. cit.,* pp. 259–263.

3

THE SOURCES OF
WESTERN ATTITUDES

Written history began with the appearance of cities about 5000 years ago, some of the earliest and most important being those in the river valleys of the Near East (sometimes called the Middle East), particularly in the area from modern Egypt to modern Iraq. Here we first know the names of peoples, cities, gods, and enemies; we have narrations of events and collections of myths; and we first have insights into mankind's ways of thought and living going beyond what we can reconstruct from the physical remains of a civilization. Since the attitudes of these early early peoples affected others throughout the Near East and helped form our culture, their sexual attitudes become important for understanding not only them but ourselves.

The earliest builders of the Mesopotamian culture were the Sumerians, a people of uncertain origin who, by the beginning of the third millennium (3000 B.C.), had established an extraordinarily well-integrated civilization. The Sumerians were soon challenged by newcomers, and throughout the early history of Mesopotamia fresh waves of migrants appeared; Semitic-speaking peoples such as the Amorites and Assyrians came up the Euphrates Valley from the Arabian and Syrian deserts, and Indo-European peoples such as the Mitanni came over the mountains from the Caucasus region to the north. Inevitably, both the peoples and their culture were modified. In spite of these changes, one can speak of an ancient Mesopotamian civilization having considerable continuity in ideas, attitudes, and institutions from approximately 3000 to 300 B.C., and even later a handful of priestly families in Babylon kept the old tradition alive until the first century A.D.

A chief source of information about the attitudes of these peoples is the law codes, which give the official attitudes, although these might not reflect reality. The earliest collections of Sumerian laws come from Ur-Nammu in the Third Dynasty of Ur (about 2110 B.C.) and Lipit-Ishtar of Isin (about 1925 B.C.). Neither code is preserved completely; their great importance lies in their influence on later laws. In the Semitic dialects the first surviving law code is that of the town of Eshnunna, from about 1800 B.C., although the best known is that of Hammurabi (about 1700 B.C.). Still another collection dates from 1100 B.C., when the Assyrians were in control; most surviving portions of this code deal with the legal position and rights and duties of women.

As these law codes are examined, several generalizations come to mind. First, the laws seem to avoid stating any general principles, such as a wide-ranging prohibition against stealing or killing. Instead the laws usually spell out the fixed circumstances or precise details of the deeds they prohibit. From this it might be assumed the laws were not intended as a comprehensive set of rules for society but instead were based on a fixed body of accepted norms. If so, then they were designed to deal with particular incidents wherein growth and change of society gave rise to circumstances for which no traditional ruling existed. It might well have been that the growing complexity of urban life demanded that traditional rural customs be modified.

Second, the laws demonstrate the growth of a legal tradition. Once incorporated in a code, a given law was apt to turn up in later codes, even though it might no longer have been pertinent to the community concerned. Only occasionally were old laws brought up to date or worded in a more explicit fashion.

The third and perhaps most perplexing factor is that the laws do not seem to have been observed in all cases or at all times. It is certain, for example, that two contracting parties were free to disregard the law if they wished. This was made easier because there was almost no machinery to ensure the laws' being observed. In effect, it seems everyone knew the basic norms of social interaction, without a need to put everything into writing. Everyone was regarded as a guardian of standards, although spheres of influence were different: rulers over cities, elders over districts or quarters of cities, and parents over children.[1]

The peoples of the Tigris–Euphrates river valley had a much different outlook than modern men and women, most obviously on the connection between morals and magic, there being no distinction between the morally right and the ritually proper. The god was just as angry with the ritually impure food as with the oppressing of the widow and the orphan. His anger in most cases could be appeased more easily with a ritual offering than with a vow to reform.

Women were basically property, many of the attitudes toward sexual activity coming from this assumption. Adultery was not a sin against morality but a trespass against the husband's property. A husband had freedom to fornicate, but a wife could be put to death for the same thing. Free women, as distinguished from slave women, were inviolable and guarded; a man employing a married woman not closely related to him was in difficulty. A man caught fornicating with an adulterous woman could be castrated or put to death, and the woman could be executed or have her nose cut off. Offenses with unmarried free women were treated differently from those with married women because there was no husband. If the offender had a wife, she was given to the father of the victim to serve as a prostitute, and the offender was compelled to marry his victim. If he lacked a wife, he had to pay money to the girl's father as well as marry her, although the father might accept money and refuse to give him his daughter. In any case, the payment was for damaging property and lessening the girl's value. Marriage was for procreation, not companionship. The wife's first duty was to raise her children; a sterile marriage was grounds for divorce. The mother, particularly of sons, was accorded special protection. The man who divorced the mother of his sons or took another wife was committing a culpable act. Her childbearing responsibilities were emphasized by penalties to anyone injuring a woman sufficiently to cause a miscarriage and also by the statutes against abortion.

Whereas prostitution was accepted and widely practiced,[2] none of the early law codes have prohibitions against homosexuality, although there might be a reference to male prostitution in paragraph 187 of the Code of Hammurabi. This paragraph states the adopted sons of eunuchs and hierodules could not be reclaimed by their natural parents. *Hierodule,* a Greek term with no particular sexual meaning used in translations for the general category temple servant, has frequently been equated with homosexuality, but this is a misreading. Although in some instances the hierodules might have served as either male or female prostitutes, this was not invariably the case. Homosexuals were not necessarily priests, and priests were not necessarily homosexuals, and, moreover, the ancient Mesopotamians apparently had different sexual attitudes than we do.[3] Male prostitutes served Ishtar at the temple at Erech and other places and were literally called men "whose manhood Ishtar has changed into womanhood."[4]

Later Middle Assyrian law tablets contain more specific references to homosexual activity. Though these laws date from the late twelfth century, B.C. They are believed to be copies or extensions of earlier laws going back at least to the fifteenth century. In Assyrian laws unproved allegations of homosexual conduct were classified as libelous, similar to unproved allegations about an individual's wife. In fact, the provisions about homosexuality follow a provision similar to that of adultery.

18:   If a seignior said to his neighbor either in private or in a brawl, "People have lain repeatedly with your wife; I will prosecute (her) myself," since he is not able to prosecute (her and) did not prosecute (her), they shall flog that seignior forty (times) with staves (and) he shall do the work of the king for one full month; they shall castrate him and he shall pay one talent of lead.

19:   If a seignior started a rumor against his neighbor in private, saying, "People have lain repeatedly with him," or said to him in a brawl in the presence of (other) people, "People have laid repeatedly with you: I will prosecute you," since he is not able to prosecute (him and) did not prosecute (him), they shall flog that seignior fifty (times) with staves (and) he shall do the work of the king for one full month; they shall castrate him and he shall also pay one talent of lead.[5]

These suggest that, in certain cases, to call someone a homosexual was to slander his character, and slander had become an offense against the state. Since allegations of homosexuality had earlier not been regarded as slander, at least in the law codes, it is possible that a change in attitude toward homosexual intercourse had taken place, a possibility also suggested by another statute:

20:   If a seignior lay with his neighbor, when they have prosecuted him (and) convicted him, they shall lie with him (and) turn him into a eunuch.

G. R. Driver, an authority on the Assyrian laws, believed there might have been a change in attitude toward sodomy from an earlier period. He also felt he had detected a similar change in attitudes among the Hebrews between the preexilic and postexilic times.[6] There is little other evidence that a change took place and much that it did not. Even the legal prohibitions can be interpreted in different ways; a slanderous charge of homosexuality or homosexual activity may have been taken seriously only when the victim stood in a specially close relationship to the offender, and not in other cases. Since the law does not mention other homosexual activities, we cannot assume they were prohibited. In fact, in most cases the forbidden activities are mentioned in some detail, for example, the prohibitions against incest:

189:   If a man violates his own mother, it is a capital crime. If a man violates his daughter, it is a capital crime. If a man violates his son, it is a capital crime.

In a polygamous society, and at least certain groups in Babylonian society were polygamous, there are various levels of incest, not only between a man (or a boy) and his mother, but also between him and his various stepmothers. The law covered such situations:

190:   . . . if a man violates his stepmother, there shall be no punishment (but) if his father is living, it is a capital crime.

Another example of the detailed activities with which the law concerned itself is a series of laws on bestiality, with different laws for cattle, sheep, and pigs, although all read more or less the same.

187:   If a man does evil with a head of cattle, it is a capital crime and he shall be killed. They bring him to the king's court. Whether the king orders him killed or whether the king spares his life, he must not appeal to the king.

All we can conclude from the legal evidence is that some types of sexual activity (incest and bestiality) were illegal and that homosexuality, under certain conditions, was disapproved.

Babylonian society, even in its sex laws, was male oriented, the male organ being regarded as the key to conception.

8:   If a woman has crushed a seignior's testicle in a brawl, they shall cut off one finger of hers, and if the other testicle has become affected along with it by catching the infection even though a physician has bound (it) up, or she has crushed the other testicle in the brawl, they shall tear out both her (eyes).

There is no similar reference to a woman's sexual organs. Instead, the concern is with involuntary abortion, destruction of a fetus, or the lessening of a woman's property value through adultery or fornication.

Sex was accepted as a fact of life, with no need for disguise. The original Sumerian signs for male and female, for example, were merely simplified representations of the sexual parts; a married person was portrayed by a juxtaposition of the two. In religion, the sexuality most often appears in the figure of the female goddess Inanna (later known as Ishtar), who personified love and procreation. Human sexual activity was equated with the fertility of nature, and in the new year festival a priest and priestess engaged in intercourse as a means of securing fertility for the state.[7] At least one love charm has survived from early in Babylonian history,[8] but much of our information about sex is from later source materials.

One of the best sources of information on sexual practices, Tablet 104 of the *Summa Alua,* describes the sexual activities of human beings, in some detail,[9] but supplementing this are numerous pictorial and graphic representations of sexual activities. We have clay models of female sexual parts and stone models of erect penises, most of them found on the sites of temples to Ishtar. There are also numerous carved and pictorial representations of couples having intercourse in various ways. A number of terra-cotta models portray the couple in bed having intercourse, and others show a couple having intercourse in the standing position, usually *per anum.* In some models, both individuals are male, a clear indication of the existence and acceptance of homosexuality.[10]

This acceptance appears as late as the sixth century B.C. in the astrological tests dealing with potency and lovemaking. The region of Libra, for example, is said to be good for the love of a man for a woman; Pisces, for the love of a woman for a man; and Scorpio, for the love of a man for a man.[11] Left out is the love of a woman for a woman, but since the sources are mostly male written and women were certainly considered subordinate if not inferior to the male, this was perhaps inevitable.

The male's importance in sex is further indicated in the surviving collection of potency tests—incantations ostensibly recited by a woman and directed toward a man to stimulate him to lovemaking. When a man found it difficult to gain an erection, he was advised to rub his penis (or have it rubbed) with a special pūru-oil mixed with pulverized, magnetic iron particles, perhaps to provide additional friction.[12] Though the majority of incantations are incomplete, their meaning seems directed more toward heterosexual than homosexual intercourse, but the imagery varies considerably:

Let a horse (make love to me [?])[13]

Or

(Let his penis be a stick of martu-wood [?])

(Let it strike the) anus of the woman . . .[14]

Anal intercourse was widely practiced in Mesopotamia, there being no evidence it was taboo. The "entu-priestess" perhaps permitted it to avoid pregnancy, but whatever the reason, it was accepted between men and women, and so there would have been little reason to prohibit it between males. In fact, the potency incantations often included statements such as "if a man has anal intercourse with his male companion."[15] In spite of the laws prohibiting various forms of sexual intercourse, as between man and animals, the only comdemnatory attitude in the potency incantations is toward ritual uncleanliness, and not toward any sexual act. There is no evidence that any sexual act was considered immoral or illegal.[16]

The Sumerians believed the universe was governed by divine laws, rules, and regulations, known as me. A list of 100 of these me was compiled by an ancient Sumerian poet, and some 68 survive, although many are only bare words without any descriptive meaning hinting of their real significance. Scattered among the words describing institutions such as lordship or kingship, priestly offices of "divine lady" or ishib, ritualistic paraphernalia such as exalted scepter or exalted shrine, and mental and emotional attitudes encompassed in terms like truth, there are five terms with sexual connotation. Two, intercourse and *prostitution,* deal with sexual activity, and three are descriptive terms meaning eunuch or "effeminate" men. The inclusion of these terms seems to imply that sexual activity and sexual role, like all other aspects of human society or cultural traits, are based on divine prescription.[17]

Further evidence for this statement comes from Sumerian mythology. According to the *Enuma Elish,* man had been created by Enki (later known as Marduk) from the blood of Kingu, the husband of the goddess Tiamat, from whose body, after she had been slain by Enki, the earth and heavens were formed. Apparently, there were six different types of humanity, although only two can be deciphered in the listing, the barren woman and the sexless, sometimes translated as eunuch.[18] In the earliest versions the person translated as a eunuch is said to lack both male and female sexual organs and might be better described by the term *epicene* than eunuch; in later versions the description is not quite so clear. One justification for the creation of the epicene appears in an early Babylonian story recounting the descent of Ishtar (or Inanna) into the nether world. The story tells how Ishtar was rescued from her sister Ereskigal, queen of the underworld, by Asushunamir (Asushu-Namir), whose sexless or effeminate nature made him immune to the "great enchantment" of Queen Ereskigal. Ereskigal thereupon cursed him with a fate "not to be forgotten through eternity."

> *The food of the city's* gutters *shall be thy food,*
> *The* sewers *of the city shall be thy drink.*
> *The shadow of the wall shall be thy station,*
> *The threshold shall be thy habitation,*
> *The besotted and thirsty shall smite thy cheek.*[19]

Just how much this curse justified a hostility toward effeminate men is unclear, although, since Asushunamir had helped save Ishtar, such creatures could be judged to serve a useful purpose.

As important as the *Enuma Elish* in setting attitudes is the second of the great Babylonian epics, the story of Gilgamesh.[20] In outline the story is a series of dreams by Gilgamesh recounting the flood that destroyed all of mankind who did not find refuge in the ark. The story has as one of its important themes the friendship between the two heroes of the epic, Gilgamesh and Enkidu, but whether the story implies only a powerful friendship between two men or whether it has more overt homosexual connections is a matter of opinion.[21]

Some semimythological evidence for transvestism has been preserved in the Greek writer Diodorus Siculus. According to Diodorus, Sardanapalus, an Assyrian ruler whom we cannot identify, spent his time in his palace, unseen by his subjects, dressed in women's apparel and surrounded by his concubines. Eventually, when his conduct became known to some of his key nobles, they led a revolt against him. Finding his throne threatened, Sardanapalus threw aside his feminine finery and showed his mettle as a warrior. Though he twice defeated the rebels, he could not put down the revolution. Finally he retreated to Nineveh, which, after a 2-year siege, was ready to surrender. Sardanapalus then collected his treasury, wives, and concubines, and placing them on an immense pile he had constructed, set everything on fire, destroying himself and them.[22] Modern writers believe the whole narrative might well be a myth, although there are parallels with the reign of the historical king Asurbanipal, who was defeated by the Medes, Chaldeans, and others in the seventh century B.C.

In short, the Tigris–Euphrates civilizations could not be regarded as particularly hostile to sexuality, for a wide variety of sexual activities was tolerated. Nonetheless, the Assyrian phase seemed to be less tolerant of sexual deviation than other periods. The need for procreation was emphasized, and those, such as eunuchs or homosexual priests, who could not have children were encouraged to adopt them. The people of the area, or at least the sources describing their activities, are primarily male centered, and while we know that close friendships between males were encouraged, we know very little about female friendships. Probably close friendships between women were discouraged, since the activities of women were so restricted. The purpose of marriage was procreation, not companionship, and a wife was a valuable piece of property. Sex was a source of pleasure for men, although a dependency on women could weaken men, preventing them from realizing their full potentiality.[23]

Somewhat different in outlook and accomplishments were the residents of ancient Egypt, though in sexual attitudes they were as tolerant as the Babylonians. Nudity was common until the thirteenth century B.C. (the XIXth Dynasty), but it did not make the Egyptians any less conscious of sex distinctions. Preserved among the illustrations in various early tombs of nobles are portraits of their inhabitants looking with considerable pleasure on youthful, near-nude dancing girls and girl musicians. This same acceptance of sex appears in the temple paintings, where the gods are depicted in various sex acts. There are also numerous phallic idols, as well as incantations and rituals, whose purpose was to restore virile force to the dead man in the next world. Buried with him were statuettes of his concubines, on whom he could symbolically test his restored potency. The acceptance of the sexual nature of man is also evident in the hieroglyphic writing, where the symbol for intercourse simply combined the symbol for pudenda with that for penis.

What restrictions existed on sexual activities, such as the condemnation of female adultery, were justified, not in moral terms, but as necessary for preserving public order or because they resulted in ritual impurity. This would be the case with the prohibitions against sexual intercourse in sacred places or the taboos against visiting such places after intercourse without first undergoing purification. This concern with ritual purity probably explains why the Egyptians prohibited homosexual intercourse in Memphis and two other administrative districts,[24] and not elsewhere. Menstruating women were also regarded as impure and unclean.

Like almost all other recorded civilizations 'Egypt was essentially a man-centered culture. Thus, most of our information about sex is given from the male point of view, comparatively little information being available about female sex life. Unlike most other peoples in the Western cultural tradition, the Egyptians, held, for at least part of their history, that the proper position for intercourse was with the female on top, the so-called woman-superior position which coincided with a reversal of the positions of the gods. In Egyptian mythology the earth was a male deity and the sky a female one, and the earth god Geb is usually pictured as lying beneath his spouse Nut, the sky goddess.[25]

Generally, the Egyptians were monogamous, although the kings and powerful nobles could have more than one wife. Ramses II (13th century B.C.) had five or six Great Wives, numerous concubines, and more than 100 children. The laws made a clear distinction between a concubine and a wife, and a bachelor could technically keep a concubine without being married. Adultery by a woman was cause for divorce and could be punished by burning at the stake, but a married male was permitted other sexual partners. A husband could divorce a wife more or less at his convenience, provided he paid her compensation, but no such freedom was given the woman. If a couple failed to have children, they could jointly acquire a young female slave to act as a sexual proxy for the wife, and any children she bore would be legitimated and emancipated at the husband's death. Lifelong celibacy was discouraged, although at some periods in Egyptian history the priestesses devoted to Amun were virgins. Girls usually married young, probably at 12 or 13, and their husbands were not much more than 15 or 16 as a rule, although among the upper classes marriage for men might not take place until 20. Sexual relations probably took place from the time males began to feel the urge, because slave girls were available in all the wealthier households and were probably unable to resist the advances of the lord or his growing sons.[26]

The Egyptian male was often circumcised. Herodotus, the Greek historian, believing the Egyptians were the first to circumcise, claimed that all other cultures had adopted the custom from them.[27] Whether they were the first or not is difficult to determine, but we know that circumcision took place very early in Egyptian history. Several of the earliest tombs (mastabas) contain representations of circumcised workmen, and literary references include statements about a child who was at that age when his "sex organ has still not been unbound," interpreted as a reference to circumcision. We also have two portrayals of the operation. The earliest scene, often reproduced, dates from the VIth Dynasty of the Old Kingdom.[28] A later illustration appears in the temple of Khonsu

(XXIst Dynasty) at Thebes (Luxor). The upper part of this second relief has been destroyed, but enough has been preserved to permit a reconstruction of the operation.[29]

How widespread circumcision was is debatable. Herodotus claimed the Egyptians accepted the operation as a way of keeping clean; he wrote they felt it was better to be clean than comely.[30] In spite of this statement, it seems to have been more of a religious ritual than a medical or health practice. This is indicated by the fact that later, when the Romans had occupied Egypt, they tried to discourage circumcision on the grounds it was a barbaric custom but were unsuccessful because certain religious acts required the participating officials to be circumcised.[31] Giving further emphasis to the religious overtones of the act was its being performed by priests and not by physicians. The official performing the operation was, in fact, called the "circumcising priest."[32]

An interesting autobiographical account of circumcision has been preserved:

> I was one beloved of his father, favored of his mother, whom his brothers and sisters loved. When I was circumcised, together with one hundred and twenty men, there was none thereof who hit out, there was none thereof who was hit, there was none thereof who scratched, there was none thereof who was scratched.[33]

What the last part of the inscription means is not clear. The original editor was apparently not certain that all of it referred to circumcision and translated the last phrase to read that the writer had never "abused anyone." Generally, however, it is taken to mean that the writer considered it remarkable that in such a large group no one reacted violently. The fact that such large numbers were circumcised together is a further indication of the religious character of the act, a characteristic still existing in its description in modern Egyptian Arabic, where it is called *tahara* ("purification"), as against the term *el khitan* ("circumcision") applied in other Arabic countries.

Girls were also circumcised in ancient Egypt, as they still are in parts of modern Egypt, but it is difficult to state when the custom started. Strabo, the first-century B.C. Greek geographer, stated on two different occasions that the Jews followed the Egyptian custom of circumcising girls,[34] but from other evidence it seems that female circumcision among Jews was rare. This might lead one to argue that, since the Jews practiced male but not female circumcision, the latter began only after the exodus. Unfortunately, the state of preservation of the mummies does not allow any definite conclusion, and no illustrations deal with female circumcision in the same way as the male's is portrayed. Female circumcision, sometimes called excision, entails the resection or "cutting out" of the clitoris and labia minora, or at least parts of them. The effect of the more drastic operation was to make a female orgasm all but impossible and to deny any erotic stimulation in the genital area. The operation is still widespread in the Near East today, and in Nubia, (and elsewhere) it is sometimes combined with infibulation (the fastening of the foreskin of the labia majora) to prevent copulation.

One Egyptian custom not widely adopted by surrounding peoples was the marriage of brothers and sisters. This incestuous custom had the sanction of the gods, for Isis had married her brother Osiris, and Nephthys her brother Seth. In as much as the pharaoh was an incarnation of the deity on earth, he could be expected to follow the divine custom, although there is considerable debate about how common these marriages were. Professor Jaroslav Cerny concluded that the term *sister* had come to mean wife and lover, rather than sibling of the same mother and father. In his study of some 490 marriages in the XXIInd Dynasty, he found that only two could be taken as between brother and sister, and these could be debated, although marriages of half-brothers and sisters were very probably more common. Not until Greek times, in the reign of the Ptolemies, did it become a rule for a pharaoh to marry his sister. This custom may have been adopted from the Persians rather than carried over from ancient Egypt.[35] In the Greek–Egyptian city of Arsinoe, it has been estimated that two-thirds of the marriages recorded during the second century A.D. were between brothers and sisters.[36] The Greek historians, tolerant about other sexual practices in the countries they visited or wrote about, were somewhat hostile to these incestuous marriages. Diodorus Siculus, for example, called them "contrary to the general custom of mankind."[37] There have been some examinations of the genetic effects of these intermarriages, particularly during the Hellenistic period. The Greek Ptolemies provide a particularly interesting example, for the first four kings were products of nonconsanguineous marriages, and from the time of Ptolemy V to Ptolemy XV, marriage with the sister was the rule. Marc Armand Ruffer could find no differences between the two groups of Ptolemies in anything measurable statistically; the average age at death of both groups, not counting those murdered, was 65 years.[38]

The penis was greatly admired by the ancient Egyptians. The god Min, for example, is usually pictured as a thin figure, standing rigidly at attention, with his right arm bent at the elbow and raised over his head and his left arm under his robe holding the divine phallus, huge and stiff in his hand. The vagina, at least throughout much of early Egyptian history, was not so positively regarded, although it was thought that a woman might succumb to hysteria if the womb remained barren long after puberty.[39] Later, in the Graeco–Roman Egypt, the womb is given more importance, particularly in the alchemical treatises. The cosmos was seen as made up of male and female genitalia operating inside a womb that was thus fertilized.[40]

References to masturbation occur in the Pyramid Texts of the Vth and VIth Dynasties (third millennium B.C.).[41] Most indicative of the Egyptian attitude is the so-called Shabaka stone, which, though it dates from the Pharaoh Shabaka

(7th century B.C.), is believed to refer to an earlier time and said to be a transcription of ancient records ordered by Shabaka. Several scholars have worked on the translation, the references to masturbation occuring in lines 54–56.

> Now the heart and the tongue have power over all (the other) members, on account of the fact that one is in every body, (and) the other is in every mouth of all the gods, of all men, all cattle, all reptiles, and (all else) that lives—the one conceiving, (and) the other decreeing that which is willed. His (Ptah's) Ennead of Atum indeed came into being through the semen and the fingers of Atum. But the Ennead (of Ptah) is the teeth and lips in this mouth, which pronounced the name of all things, from whom came forth Shu and Tefnet who created the Ennead.[42]

Though it is difficult to follow the logic of the comparison in all its parts, Ptah's Ennead (a group of gods) is equated as teeth and lips with the semen and hands of Atum, and Atum's Ennead is the product of his semen and hands (that is, masturbation). No condemnation is implied in Atum's creative act of masturbation, although Ptah's act of creation, which resulted from pronouncing the name of the thing, is held to be superior, since knowledge of the name connotes power above and beyond that of mere sexual orgasm.

There are other references to masturbation in the Pyramid Texts:

> Atum became as one who masturbates in Heliopolis. He put his phallus in his hand to excite desire. The son and daughter were born, the brother and the sister, Shu and Tefnet.[43]

From this it seems that the Egyptians felt they had proof the male element was the most important and assumed in biological terms that the male factor in generation was decisive. Sometimes the female was not even necessary, as the fourth-century B.C. Papyrus Bremner–Rhind stated:

> When I had come into being, being (itself) came into being . . . I planned in my own heart, and there came into being a multitude of forms of beings, the forms of children and the forms of their children. I was the one who copulated with my fist, I masturbated my hand. Then I spewed with my own mouth; I spat out what was Shu, and sputtered out what was Tefnet . . .[44]

In some ways the Egyptians might be regarded as an anal erotic people. There was, for example, a specialist known as "the shepherd of the anus." Though it has been suggested that this title was only a poetic appellation for the enema makers who inserted fluids into the pharaoh's rectum, this subordinate situation does not accord with the pompous titles usually accompanying this euphemism. The enema's importance to the Egyptians is evident from their belief that it had been invented by the god Thoth, the chief of the healing gods. At times Thoth is represented as a monkey, but generally, as an ibis or as a man with the head of an ibis surmounted by the solar disc and the lunar crescent. Perhaps from this symbolism the purpose of the curved beak of the ibis was thought to be to enable the bird to clean its anus regularly.[45]

Both the anus and the vagina were subject to fumigation. The Egyptians prescribed that the woman stand over hot charcoals on which an ibis of wax had been placed and allow the fumes to enter her vulva. This, they believed, would cause the womb to go back to its proper place.[46] In a recipe for fumigation of the anus heated bricks were used. The Berlin papyrus recommended that seven bricks be heated and then cold drugs be poured over them while the patient was held over the fumes.[47] Apparently, piles, fissures, and "turning out" of the anus (prolapse) were frequent, large sections of the medical papyri being devoted to the subject.[48] One such prescription in the Papyrus Ebers stated:

> For a dislocation of the hinder part: myrrh, frankincense, rush-nut from the garden, mhtt from the shore, celery, coriander, oil, salt, are boiled together, applied in seed wool and put in the hinder part.[49]

Suppositories were used in the treatment of ills of both the rectum and the vagina, and seemingly, there was not a liquid, from oil to milk to beer, that the Egyptians did not try to absorb through the rectum.[50]

A similar variety of substances was used to prevent conception. One of the earliest was crocodile dung, but honey and resinous gums made from acacia shrubs were some other substances inserted into the vagina. A woman was urged to drink numerous concoctions to avoid pregnancy, most of them not particularly effective. Probably both honey and acacia gum tampons were effective to some extent, since honey would lessen the motility of the sperm, while the acacia gum would produce a lactic acid, an effective spermaticide. The crocodile dung, except esthetically, would not prove an effective contraceptive, for its slight alkalinity would tend to neutralize vaginal acidity and promote rather than inhibit fertilization. In later recipes, elephant dung, probably somewhat more effective as a chemical contraceptive,[51] was used.

Some Egyptians are believed to have practiced ovariotomy, removal of the ovaries, although the mortality rate must have been fairly high. The second-century Greek writer Athenaeus, attributing the operation to the ancient Lydians, said that Adramyttes, their king, was the first man who ever spayed women and used female eunuchs instead of male eunuchs.[52] The reasons for this dangerous operation are not clear, but it might have been to prevent conception.[53]

Anal intercourse, both heterosexual and homosexual, was common. Evidence of possible homosexual leanings is evident in the story of Pepi II, a pharaoh of the Old Kingdom, who was apparently enamored of one of his generals.[54] Various initiation ceremonies, such as that pictured in Papyrus Number 10018 in the British Museum, have strong overtones of homosexuality. Unfortunately, we lack the type of law codes for Egypt that exist for the Tigris–Euphrates area. The negative confessions found in the *Book of the Dead* might, however, represent what society considered shortcomings if not crimes, and this evidence can be supplemented by the positive attitudes found in the wisdom literature. Various declarations of innocence in the *Book of the Dead* indicate at least some form of "homosexual" activity was unacceptable.

> *I have not done that which the gods abominate.*
> *I have not defamed a slave to his superior . . .*
> *I have not killed . . .*
> *I have not had sexual relations with a boy.*
> *I have not defiled myself.*[55]

Or

> *O* Wamemti-serpent, *who comes forth from the place of judgment,*
> *I have not committed adultery*
> *(actually had sexual relations with the wife of another man)*
> *O* Maa-Intef, *who comes forth from the Temple of Min,*
> *I have not defiled myself . . .*
> *O His-Face-Behind-Him, who comes forth from* Tep-het-djat,
> *I have not been perverted;*
> *I have not had sexual relations with a boy.*[56]

Pederasty, at least in these cases, was equated with adultery and other things the gods abominated. But how did the Egyptians regard homosexual relationships between adults?

Here the Egyptian materials are plentiful enough to permit some theorizing. Adult homosexual intercourse is not so much condemned as frowned upon, at least for the passive partner, perhaps because it implied submissive behavior.[57] The relationship between anal intercourse among males and submissiveness appears most clearly in the legendary story of Seth and Horus, whose struggle against each other constitutes a central theme in the religious literature of ancient Egypt. Of the various versions of the homosexual incident, a Middle Kingdom papyrus from Kahun is the earliest and longest.

The Majesty of Seth said to the Majesty of Horus, "How beautiful are thy buttocks! How flourishing (?) . . ." The Majesty of Horus said, "Wait that I may tell it . . . to their palace." The Majesty of Horus said to his mother Isis . . . "Seth desires (?) to have intercourse with me." And she said to him, "Take care, do not approach him for that; when he mentions it to thee a second time, say thou to him, 'It is altogether too difficult for me because of (my) nature (?), since thou art too heavy for me; my strength will not be equal to thine,' thou shalt say to him. Then, when he shall have given thee strength, do thou place thy fingers between thy buttocks. Lo, it will give . . . Lo, he will enjoy it exceedingly (?) . . . this seed which has come forth from his generative organ without letting the sun see it . . ."[58]

Horus, following the advice of Isis, caught the semen Seth ejaculated in his hands, and when Seth was not looking, threw it into a nearby stream. Later, when he reported this to Isis, she ordered him to produce semen of his own and give it to her. When he did, she spread it on a piece of lettuce, which she then fed to Seth. Later, when Seth had boasted to the gods about how he had vanquished Horus in a sexual act, Horus denied it, and the gods, to settle the argument between them, summoned the seeds of both. The seed of Seth replied to the gods from the depths of the water where Horus had thrown it, while the seed of Horus issued forth from the forehead of Seth in the shape of a golden disc. It was evident then that Seth was not to be believed, and one of the gods, Thoth, seized the golden disc from the head of Seth and placed it on his own head as an ornament. In a sense the text can be interpreted symbolically as the birth of Thoth as the moon god, who in other sources is called the "son of the two lords, who came forth from the lock of hair."[59]

What is the significance of this homosexual incident? Some interpreters have claimed that the story signifies the ignominy dealt to the conquered by the conquerer and that anal intercourse was an outrage reserved for the vanquished. There are difficulties with this explanation, for no stigma is attached to the birth of Thoth as a moon god from this alleged homosexual liaison. Moreover, Seth is not the ultimate conquerer, even though he was the dominant figure in the sexual act; instead Horus, the god who allegedly submitted, turned out victorious. Still, it seems clear that anal intercourse was regarded as a mark of ignominy for the passive partner, and if it was not abominated as an expression of triumph by the enemy, it had shameful connotations.

Some other evidence supports the belief that anal penetration was a sign of submission. It is said of Shu and Tefnet, two other Egyptian gods, that "their abomination is for the hand of god to fall on them, and for the shade of the god to abuse them sexually. His seed shall not enter into them."[60] Later, a coffin text includes the statement that "Re has no power over me, for I am he who takes away his breath. Atum has no power over me, for I copulate between his buttocks."[61] The implications seem to be that Re and Atum could be rendered powerless simply by being the submissive partner in anal intercourse. Does this offer a justification for the belief that Egyptians performed anal intercourse on their defeated enemies? The supposition is there, but conclusive proof is lacking. One investigator concluded that, though "we have unmistakable evidence of the belief that such a practice existed," there is no proof "of its actual performance" in Egypt.[62]

We do know that the phalli of the defeated enemy were prized and that it was not unusual to amputate the penis of those defeated. The pharaoh Merneptah in the XIXth Dynasty, for example, listed among the booty taken after the defeat of an invading Libyan army a total of 6359 uncircumcised phalli, plus the phalli of the children of the chiefs, brothers of the priests, and others.[63] From such cases it would seem almost natural that the penis was regarded as very important and that its loss or anything believed to weaken masculinity, such as submitting to anal intercourse, might be regarded as a sign of loss of status. We know also that to call a man womanly was to be scornful of him, and it seems logical that to put the man to sexual use in place of a woman could only imply a greater indignity.[64]

Such a conclusion must remain a conjecture. All we can state from the evidence is that, though anal intercourse was known and practiced by the Egyptians, when it took place between two men, it was not viewed with great public favor, and if a man and a young boy were involved, it was more strongly condemned. It might be that, as in the Tigris–Euphrates Valley, homosexual activities were regarded with more hostility later in the civilization than earlier. In early Egyptian history, for example, Seth is not regarded with any particular ill will, but by the XXIInd Dynasty he has entered a period of decline. By the tenth century B.C., his statues were being broken and his features smashed with a hammer. Ultimately, he was removed from the Egyptian pantheon and made a god of the unclean. In contrast, Thoth, product of the union of two males, never seems to have suffered such ostracism; in fact he became much more important later than he had been earlier. In Greek mythology he is known as Hermes.

Cross-dressing was also known in ancient Egypt, the best example being a female rather than a male, the famous Hatshepsut, the XVIIIth Dynasty (15th century B.C.) pharaoh who was a woman. Hatshepsut, the daughter of Thutmose I and his Great Wife, was married to her half-brother Thutmose II to legitimate his claim, something perhaps necessary, since he was the son of a lesser wife. When Thutmose II died after a short rule, Hatshepsut was married to Thutmose III, another half-brother. Apparently, neither Thutmose II nor Thutmose III was of an age to rule, or at least initially they lacked the ability to do so, since Hatshepsut acted as the real ruler for a time, and in this she had the support of the rich temple of Amun. She built magnificent monuments in honor of Amun, notably one at Deir el Bahari (near Luxor), where the queen's reign was commemorated. In her statues and pictures she is usually pictured in male attire, including the beard symbolic of royalty. On her death, Thutmose III tried to obliterate her memory, and later the Amun-hating Amenhotep IV tried to complete the task by removing all references to the god. Whether Hatshepsut was a transvestite or assumed the role as a necessity for her rule is debatable. Some have argued that in fact she was a transvestite or perhaps even a transsexual, since she is pictured with a boy's sex organs, although the pronouns accompanying the text are feminine, making it clear she was also a woman.[65] If she was a transvestite,[66] she is one of the few about whom we have information.

Bestiality was also known in ancient Egypt, its prevalence possibly related to the Egyptian gods' being usually represented with human bodies and animal heads. Herodotus mentioned the veneration of the goat and reported a goat's having intercourse with a woman in the name of Mendes.[67] This so-called "Buck of Mendes" later became a source of amorous amusement for Plutarch and other Roman writers, as well as more modern ones such as Rabelais and Voltaire. Other animal–human sexual contacts are occasionally portrayed on the tombs, and the dragomen today are usually willing to point them out if requested.

Herodotus is also the source of another unverified bit of gossip about necrophilia in ancient Egypt.

> The wives of men of rank are not given to be embalmed immediately after death, nor indeed are any of the more beautiful and valued women. It is not until they have been dead three or four days that they are carried to the embalmers. This is done to prevent the embalmers having intercourse with them. It is said that once a man was detected in the act with a woman newly dead and denounced by his fellow-workers.[68]

How much should be made of this reference is unclear. He records only one actual incident and though such practices must have occurred occasionally, there is no documentation for the frequency Herodotus implies.

Increasingly, in late Egyptian history, sexual conduct and morality seem equated, but their standards were not ours. In general, the Egyptians held virtue profitable, since if one behaved amicably toward his god, his king, his equal, and even his inferiors, he would receive health, long life, and honor on earth in exchange. As to sex life, the need for producing children was stressed, and this accomplished, other sexual activities were allowed, provided they did not take advantage of others. All sexual activities, from bestiality to anal intercourse to oral–genital contacts are portrayed in the various tomb pictures, and though the Egyptians might have disapproved some activities more than others, their society seemed to be fairly permissive sexually.

This permissive attitude in both the Tigris–Euphrates and the Nile valleys was challenged by the conquering Persians in the sixth century B.C. In general, the Persians were magnanimous conquerers; they did not burn down cities, ravage, plunder, or massacre, nor did they arrogate to themselves all the privileges usually accorded to the victorious. They honored the gods and customs of the peoples they conquered, allowing them considerable autonomy in their affairs. Still the Persians influenced the peoples they conquered, and the ideas and attitudes about sex associated with their Zoroastrian religion had an effect on the later attitudes of the people in the area and probably influenced Greek thinking, for the Greeks under Alexander the Great took over the Persian Empire.

Zoroastrianism was based on the teachings of Zoroaster, an almost legendary Iranian who may have lived about 600 B.C. Before Zoroaster, the Persians, like many other ancient pagans, worshipped numerous gods, widely different although each had both good and evil characteristics. In contrast, Zoroaster classified all gods into two groups, the good and the evil (demons); he then logically recommended that men serve the good ones. Usually this Zoroastrian dualism is expressed as the contrast between light and darkness, each striving for mastery. Man's purpose was to work for the better cause, and what this constituted was the essence of his teachings.

As to sex, Zoroaster and later advocates stood for controlling and regulating bodily desires, but not for suppressing and killing them. Man could serve righteousness and assail wickedness only with a sound body; essential to this was the maintenance of life in this generation and in future ones. Only when the flesh gained victory over the spirit, as in the wicked, did the body become a burden to the soul. This occurred when an individual lived solely for his body, when he feasted his eyes on the vices of the flesh and became a willing slave to bodily passions. Thus, the righteous man regulated his body in conformity with the higher desires of the soul. Sex was necessary because it was man's duty to procreate, but all aspects of sexual activity detracting from this purpose were to be condemned and prohibited. This meant celibacy was not a virtue, for every Zoroastrian was to marry and rear a family. Homosexuality, masturbation, and any other sexual activity not leading to procreation were condemned, as was intercourse with courtesans and prostitutes. Adultery and polygamy were also condemned, but some groups adopting Zoroastrianism did advocate polygamy and even the sharing of wives. Though Zoroaster did not particularly advocate it, the Persians apparently tolerated and encouraged marriages between parents and children and between brothers and sisters.[69] This might well have had an effect on the Ptolemies in Egypt.

Sexual desires were typified by Jeh, the Primeval Whore, who had mixed the seed of the wicked with that of the good, instead of keeping them apart. Her evil influence over man was indicated by menses of women, and inevitably, Jeh was the demoness of menstruation. She was also the patron of all prostitutes, who brought the evil sexual impulses out of man.[70] Because Jeh was such a powerful demon, women, during their menses, were regarded as particularly dangerous. They were made to retire to a secluded part of the house, staying away from every object that might be polluted by their touch, lest they defile them by contact. Their food was served from a distance so that they would not touch the utensils. Even their look defiled a consecrated object, just as their touch polluted it, and their proximity to a holy place of worship desecrated it.[71]

Of the sins of lust the most heinous was intercourse not leading to procreation, and the man who engaged in intercourse with another man was committing a more serious sin than a person who slayed a righteous man.[72] Even an involuntary emission of a male seed was a grievous sin, and if a man did so voluntarily without procreation in mind, there was no atonement.[73] The Zoroastrian prohibitions were not, however, designed to ensure chastity, and there was no concern with this as such; childbearing was regarded as essential.

In sum, the Western tradition as established in the ancient Near East was a mixed one, but increasingly, it came to be more restrictive, more hostile toward all forms of sex not leading to procreation. With the Persians, a restrictive sexual life came to be regarded as necessary for salvation and the good life, and the Persian correlation of sexual morality with religious salvation came to have great influence on the West, first through its effect on the Jews and the Greeks and ultimately through the adoption of similar ideas by the early Christians.

NOTES

1. W. G. Lambert, "Morals in Ancient Mesopotamia," Van Het Vooraziatisch-Egyptisch Genootschap, ex Oriente lux, *Jaarbericht,* XV (1957–1958), pp. 184–196.

2. This description is taken from the various law codes. The standard collection in English is that edited by G. R. Driver and John C. Miles, *The Assyrian Laws* (Oxford, England: Clarendon Press, 1955). There are also translations of some of the codes by J. J. Finkelstein, S. N. Kramer, Albrecht Goetz, and Theophile J. Meek, in *Ancient Near Eastern Texts,* James B. Pritchard, ed. (Princeton, N. J.: Princeton University Press, 1955). Reuven Yaron, *The Laws of Eshnunna* (Jerusalem: Hebrew University, 1969), has a comprehensive discussion of these particular laws. There are several other editions, particularly of the Code of Hammurabi.

3. Robert D. Biggs, *ŠÁ.ZI.GA: Ancient Mesopotamian Potency Incantations* in *Texts From Cuneiform Sources,* II (1967), p. 1.

4. Lambert, *op. cit.,* p. 195. See also Edward Westermarck, *The History of Human Marriage,* 5th ed. (New York: Allerton Books, 1922, 3 vols.), Vol. 1, p. 225; Robert Briffault, *The Mothers* (London: George Allen & Unwin, 1927, 3 vols.), Vol. 2, pp. 207–208.

5. For a translation, see T. J. Meek in *Ancient Near East Texts,* pp. 180–197.

6. G. R. Driver and John C. Miles, *op. cit.,* p. 71

7. S. N. Kramer, "Cuneiform Studies and the History of Literature: The Sumerian Sacred Marriage Texts," *American Philosophical Society Proceedings,* No. 107 (1963), pp. 485–510. See also S. N. Kramer in *Ancient Near Eastern Texts,* pp. 637–645.

8.   Edited by A. Falkenstein, "Sumerische religiose Texte," *Zeitschrift für Assyriologie,* LVI, pp. 113–129.

9.   This tablet is published in the *Cuneiform Texts from Babylonian Tablets in the British Museum,* XXXIX, pp. 44–46, but the only translation of it that I know, that by A. Boissier, *Revue Semitique,* I (1893), pp. 171 ff., left out the key passages because of their realistic descriptions.

10.   See, for example, Charlotte Ziegler, *Die Terrakotten von Werka* (Berlin: Verlag. Gebr. Mann, 1962), p. 55; and H. W. F. Saggs, *The Greatness That Was Babylon* (London: Sidgwick and Jackson, 1962), p. 51C.

11.   Robert D. Biggs, *op. cit.,* p. 5.

12.   *Ibid.,* p. 2.

13.   *Ibid.,* p. 21, No. 5, line 16.

14.   *Ibid.,* p. 25, No. 8, lines 14–15.

15.   *Ibid.,* p. 41, n. 28. There are several references in the potency formulas to anal intercourse, and it is not always evident that they refer to intercourse with women.

16.   *Ibid.,* p. 1, n. 6.

17.   Samuel Noah Kramer, *History Begins at Sumer* (Garden City, N.Y.: Doubleday, 1959), pp. 99→100. The first edition was called *From the Tablets of Sumer* (Indian Hills, Colo.: Falcon's Wing Press, 1956).

18.   Samuel Noah Kramer, *Sumerian Mythology* (revised, New York: Harper, 1961), p. 71.

19.   Translated by Samuel Noah Kramer in *The Ancient Near East,* James B. Pritchard, ed. (Princeton, N.J.: Princeton University Press, 1958), pp. 80–85.

20.   Several translations exist. The pertinent portions can be found in S. N. Kramer, *Ancient Near Eastern Texts,* pp. 40–72. See also A. Heidel, *The Gilgamesh Epic and Old Testament Parallels* (Chicago: University of Chicago, 1946); and R. Campbell Thompson, *The Epic of Gilgamesh* (London: Luzak and Company, 1928).

21.   For some discussion, see A. Leo Oppenheim, *The Interpretation of Dreams in the Ancient Near East,* American Philosophical Society, *Transactions,* XLVI (1956). See also Vern L. Bullough, *"Attitudes Toward Deviant Sex in Ancient Mesopotamia,"* VII (August 1971), *Journal of Sex Research,* pp. 184–203.

22.   Diodorus Siculus, *History,* II, 21, translated by C. H. Oldfather, ed. (London: William Heinemann, 1933).

23.   See the section in the Gilgamesh epic where Gilgamesh sends a prostitute to tame Enkidu by having sex with him. Only after this is Gilgamesh able to defeat him. Heidel, *op. cit.,* tablet 1, col. iv, p. 22, leaves the section in Latin. A readily available version of this section can, however, be found in H. W. F. Saggs, *op. cit.,* p. 372.

24.   *A Dictionary of Egyptian Civilization,* Georges Posener, ed. (London: Methuen and Company, 1962), p. 279B.

25.   S. G. F. Brandon, *Creation Legends of the Ancient Near East* (London: Hodder and Stoughton, 1963), pp. 28–29. See, for example, the representations of the impregnation of Isis by the dead Osiris, *Histoire generale des religions,* M. Groce et R. Mortier, eds. (Paris: A. Quillet, 1947–1952, 5 vols.), Vol. 1, p. 242.

26.   Alfred Wiedemann, *Das alte Aegypten* (Heidelberg: C. Winter, 1920), p. 74; Adolf Erman, *The Ancient Egyptians,* translated by Aylward M. Blackman (revised, New York: Harper & Row, 1966), p. 60, No. 12; W. Flanders Petrie, *Social Life in Ancient Egypt* (Boston: Houghton Mifflin, 1923), p. 109.

27. Herodotus, *Persian Wars*, II, 26, 104, translated by A. D. Godley, ed. (London: William Heinemann, 1921).

28. Henry E. Sigerist, *A History of Medicine* (New York: Oxford University Press, 1951), Vol. 1; fig. 58 reproduces it.

29. Paul Ghalioungui, *Magic and Medical Science in Ancient Egypt* (London: Hodder and Stoughton, 1963), p. 97; fig. 9 reproduces this.

30. Herodotus, *op. cit.*, II, 37.

31. For a general survey and analysis of the sources on circumcision, see G. Foucart in *Encyclopedia of Religions and Ethics*, James Hastings, ed. (New York: 1890–1921, 12 vols.), Vol. 2, pp. 670–677.

32. Jean Capart, *Une rue de tombeaux a Saggarah* (Brussels: Vromant, 1897), II, Pl. XLVI; and Walter Wreszinski, *Atlas zur altägyptischen Kulturgeschichte*, III (Leipzig: J. C. Hinrichs, 1936), pp. 25–26.

33. An easily available translation is by John A. Wilson in *Ancient Near Eastern Texts*, p. 326. The stella, now in the Oriental Institute at the University of Chicago, was transcribed by Dows Dunham, *Naga-ed-Dér Stelae of the First Intermediate Period* (London: published for the Boston Museum of Fine Arts by Oxford University Press, 1937), p. xxxii, No. 84, pp. 102–104. Dunham believed it dated from the early part of the first intermediate period in the third millennium.

34. Strabo, *Geography*, XVII, 5, and XVI, 37, translated by H. L. Jones, ed. (London: William Heinemann, 1954–1961, 8 vols.).

35. J. Cerny, "Consanguineous Marriage in Pharaonic Egypt," *Journal of Egyptian Archaeology*, XL (1954), pp. 23 ff.

36. Adolf Erman, *Aegypten and Aegyptisches Leben in Altertum,* new edition by H. Ranke (Tübingen, Germany: Mohr, 1923), p. 180.

37. Diodorus Siculus, *Bibliotheca historica*, I, 27, 1, translated by C. H. Oldfather, et al eds. (London: William Heinemann, 1921).

38. Marc Armand Ruffer, *Proceedings of the Royal Society of Medicine,* Section on the History of Medicine, XII (1919), pp. 145–190. The study was reprinted in *Studies in the Paleopathology of Egypt* (Chicago: 1921), pp. 322–356.

39. Ilza Veith, *Hysteria: The History of a Disease* (Chicago: University of Chicago Press, 1965), p. 7.

40. For a discussion of the subject, see Jack Lindsay, *The Origins of Alchemy in Graeco–Roman Egypt* (New York: Barnes and Noble, 1970), pp. 288–289, and passim.

41. Samuel A. B. Mercer, *The Pyramid Texts* (New York: Longmans, Green and Company, 1952, 4 vols.), Vol. 1, p. 206; Vol. 3, p. 621.

42. See K. Sethe, Dramatische Texte zu altaegyptischen Mysterienspielen, I, "Das Denkmal mephitischler Theologie der Schabokstein des Britischen Museum," in *Untersuchungen zur Geschichte und Altertumskund Aegyptens* Band X, (Leipzig: 1928), pp. 55 ff.; H. Junker, *Der Götterlehre vom Memphis* (Schabka-Inschrift), *Abhandlunger der Preussischen Akademie der Wissenschafter*, No. 23 (1939), pp. 45–54; and Brandon, *op. cit.*, pp. 34–35.

43. Mercer, *op. cit.*, Vol. 1, p. 206.

44. Brandon, *op. cit.*, p. 24.

45. This is the belief reported in Pliny, *Natural History*, VIII, 27, translated by H. Rackham, W. H. S. Jones, and D. E. Eichholz, eds. (London: William Heinemann, 1947–1963, 10 vols.).

46. *The Papyrus Ebers, the Greatest Egyptian Medical Document,* translated by B. Ebbell (Copenhagen: Levin & Munksgaard, 1937), pp. 108–109.

47. See W. Wreszinski, "Der grosse medizinische Papyrus des Berliner Museums (Papyrus Berlin 3038)," *Die Medizin der alten Aegypter* (Leipzig: J. C. Hinrichs, 1909), Vol. 1, p. 60.

48. *Le Papyrus medical Chester Beatty,* Frans Jonckheere, ed., *La Medicine Egyptienne,* No. 2, (Brussels: Foundation Egyptologique Reine Elisabeth, 1947) and *Papyrus Ebers.*

49. *Papyrus Ebers,* p. 32.

50. *Chester Beatty,* Jonckheere, pp. 70 ff.

51. For a discussion of this, see Norman Himes, *Medical History of Contraception* (reprinted, New York: Schocken Brooks, 1970), pp. 59–66.

52. Athenaeus, *Deipnosophistae,* XII, 515e, translated by C. B. Gulick, ed. (London: William Heinemann, 1951–1963, 1 vol.).

53. Francis Adams, *The Seven Books of Paulus Aegineta* (London: Sydenham Society, 1844–1857, 3 vols.), Vol. 1, p. 612.

54. *A Dictionary of Egyptian Civilization,* p. 260.

55. This was translated into English by John A. Wilson in *Ancient Near Eastern Texts,* p. 34.

56. *Ibid.,* p. 35.

57. For a somewhat more lengthy discussion of this, see Vern L. Bullough, "Homosexuality as Submissive Behavior: Example from Mythology," *The Journal of Sex Research,* IX (1973), pp. 283–288. For some of the theoretical assumptions, see A. H. Maslow, "Love in Self-Actualizing People," and "Self-esteem (Dominance-Feeling) and Sexuality in Women," reprinted in *Sexual Behavior and Personality Characteristics,* Manfred F. Martino, ed. (New York: Citadel Press, 1963); and A. H. Maslow, H. Rand, and S. Newman, "Some Parallels between Sexual Dominance Behavior of Infra-Human Primates and the Fantasies of Patients in Psychotherapy," in *Sexual Behavior and Personality Characteristics.* See also Hugo Beigel, "The Meaning of Coital Postures," in *Sexual Behavior and Personality Characteristics;* Abraham Kardiner and Lionel Ovesey, *The Mark of Oppression* (New York: Meridian Books, 1962); and Lionel Ovesey, *Homosexuality and Pseudohomosexuality* (New York: Science House, 1969).

58. The best discussion of this is by J. Gwyn Griffiths, *The Conflict of Horus and Seth* (Chicago: Argonaut Publishers, 1969). This quotation comes from p. 42. The gaps in the quotation are due to difficulties in the manuscript.

59. *Ibid.,* pp. 43 and 21. Willem Pleyte and F. Rossi, *Papyrus de Turin* (Leiden, Netherlands: E. J. Brill, 1869–1876), p. 74.

60. Hermann Kees, "Ein alter Götterhymnus als Begleittext zur Opfertafel," *Zeitschrift fur ägyptische Sprache und Altertumskunde,* LVII (1922), p. 110; and also LX (1925).

61. Adrian de Buck, *The Egyptian Coffin Texts* (Chicago: University of Chicago, 1935–1956, 6 vols.), Vol. 6, pp. 258d–g.

62. Alan H. Gardiner, *Hieratic Papyri in the British Museum. Third Series: Chester Beatty Gift* (London: British Museum 1935, 2 vols.), No. 1, p. 22, n. 2; and Griffiths, *op. cit.,* p. 44.

63. James Henry Breasted, *Ancient Records of Egypt* (reprinted, New York: Russell and Russell, 1962, 5 vols.), Vol. 3, 588, p. 248.

64. *Griffiths, op. cit.,* p. 44, n. 3.

65. Breasted, *op. cit.,* Vol. 2, 187, p. 76, n. c.; 202, p. 81, n. h.

66. Edward L. Margetts, "The Masculine Character of Hatshepsut, Queen of Egypt," *Bulletin of the History of Medicine,* XXV (1951), pp. 559 ff.

67. Herodotus, *op. cit.,* II, 46.

68. *Ibid.,* II, 89

69. Jacques Duchesne-Guillemin, *Symbols and Values in Zoroastrianism* (New York: Harper & Row, 1966), pp. 149–150.

70. Manekji Nusservanji Dhalla, *Zoroastrian Theology* (reprinted, New York: AMS Press, 1972), pp. 267–268.

71. *Venidad,* XVI, 1–18, in the *Zend-Avesta,* translated by James Darmesteter, in *Sacred Books of the East,* F. Max Müller, ed., Vol. 4 (reprinted, Delhi, India: Motilala Banarsidass, 1965), pp. 181–185.

72. *Dînâ-Î Maînôg-Î Khirad,* XXXVI, 1–33, translated by E. W. West, in *Pahlavi Texts,* Part 3, in *Sacred Books of the East,* F. Max Müller, ed., Vol. 24 (reprinted, Delhi, India: Motilala Banarsidass, 1965), p. 71; and *Sad Dar,* IX, 1–7, translated by E. W. West, in *Pahlavi Texts,* Part 3 pp. 267–268.

73. *Venidad,* VIII, v. 26–27.

4

THE JEWISH CONTRIBUTION

More directly influential in forming Western sexual attitudes than any other African and Asian peoples of the Middle East were the ancient Hebrews, the founders of Judaism, a religion that gave birth to both Christianity and Islam. Politically and militarily the ancient Hebrew state was never particularly important, and for only a comparatively brief period was there a viable Jewish state; instead, their genius and ability were concentrated in developing religious beliefs that preserved an identity during periods of exile, occupation, and repression. Judaism came to be a religion of laws, founded on the teachings of Moses. The believer was to regulate his conduct in light of God's commandments; failure to do so brought divine disfavor on the community. This meant the individual's hopes and expectations lay with the perpetuation of an orderly, organized society and with the continuation of future generations. Men could not serve themselves without also considering the community.

In light of the patchwork history of independence, defeat, occupation, exile, and threatened assimilation, the Jewish sexual attitude predictably varied with time, place, and individual spokesman, but in general it stressed social control of sexual activity. Judaism placed a negative value on sexual behavior outside the marital bed and considered the primary purpose of sex to be procreation, best exemplified in the Biblical injunction, "Be fruitful and multiply."[1]

Nevertheless, the Jews always recognized that sex was more than a duty and that there was an inherent pleasure in the act.

Earliest Judaism, that of the preexilic period (before 600 B.C.), had only a simple code of sex behavior equating certain sexual activities with immorality. In the postexilic period and until the destruction of Jerusalem by the Romans in 70 A.D., sex seems to have been an all-pervading concern. During this period, man was conceived of as a weak, helpless creature, heir to inborn evil tendencies, his greatest weakness being the desire for sexual pleasures. This urge for sexual satisfaction made man a helpless victim in the hands of Satan. Inevitably, a rigid code of sex morality developed in which even casual social contact was regarded with suspicion and condemned as immoral. Some segments of the Jewish community felt celibacy essential, and even the most liberal segments drew up strictures and rules about sex.

In the succeeding Talmudic period, coinciding with the first few centuries of the Christian era, there was again more permissiveness and a tendency toward greater sophistication about sex. The rabbis of this period denied the flesh was essentially evil; instead, they insisted on the legitimate pleasures of sex, particularly within marriage. During this period the performance of the marital act on Friday night came to be a religious duty.[2] Later, in the Middle Ages, the sexual standards again became more restrictive, although there were always sectarian variations and individual differences.[3]

In retrospect, the second period, following the return from exile, the period of greatest sexual repression, appears to be most important to understanding Western culture, for the attitudes were those incorporated in Christianity, although other factors were also at work in establishing the Christian hostility to sex.

The most logical explanation for the changes in attitude seems to lie with the Jewish attitudes toward themselves. When Judaism seemed threatened, when the Jews, both as a group and as individuals, were insecure, their sexual attitude was the most repressive. When there was a greater feeling of security, attitudes were more tolerant. During the postexilic period, for example, many Jews regarded assimilation as a threat. One way of preventing this was to establish rigid barriers between believers and nonbelievers, to distinguish sexually between what a Jew did and what a non-Jew did, and to obstruct the path of any intermingling as through intermarriage. When the pressure of assimilation declined, the Jewish sexual attitude became somewhat more relaxed, only to be tightened later, in the face of Christian hostility.

The change in attitudes should not, however, be overemphasized; it was more one of degree than of kind. Regardless of period, Judaism remained a male-oriented religion, in which considerable ambiguity was expressed toward women. Woman was to assist man, to serve him, and marriage was a symbol of man's need for companionship. Still, the difficulty with woman as a companion was that she was often troublesome. In the Jewish scriptural tradition women seem to have had the more constant and aggressive sexual drive. It was Eve who led Adam astray,[4] although not until the Christian period was the eating of the fruit equated with sexual knowledge.[5] Lot's daughter plied him with liquor and then went to bed with him so that they might have children.[6] Potiphar's wife tried to seduce Joseph,[7] and when she failed, she accused him of trying to rape her. Rachel and Leah bargained for the sexual rights of their husband Jacob.[8] Delilah was the cause of Samson's downfall.[9] The term *Jezebel,* the name of Ahab's wife, has become a perjorative term in English, because the Biblical writers state that she led her husband to worship Baal.[10] So insatiable was women's need for sex that one way a husband was allowed to punish an errant wife was to deny her the pleasure of sexual relations.[11] Man was so often a willing victim of women's enticement that the Talmudic literature later prohibited men and women from meeting except under rigidly prescribed conditions.[12]

The scriptures recognized this sexuality of women by insisting the duty of their husbands was to satisfy them. As the King James version put it:

> When a man hath taken a new wife, he shall not go out to war, neither shall he be charged with any business; but he shall be free at home one year, and shall cheer up his wife which he hath taken.[13]

Or

> And what man is there that hath betrothed a wife, and hath not taken her? Let him go and return to his house lest he die in the battle, and another man take her.[14]

The Talmudic writers stipulated that a man was not to marry more than four wives, to ensure his ability to distribute his sexual favors equally. In any case, each wife was to be ensured of having intercourse with her husband at least once a month.[15] In intercourse women were supposed to achieve orgasm; according to several passages in the Talmud, the best way a man could be certain of begetting a son was to bring his wife to orgasm before he himself achieved it.

This recognition of sexuality was accompanied by strictures about promiscuity. Traditionally, sexual morality was protected by an emphasis on early marriage, as soon after puberty as possible, although it was recognized that a boy of 9 years of age was capable of a sex act, as was a girl of 3 years.[16] In the scriptures, marriage at about age 15 seems to have been the rule for males, and females were at least betrothed, if not married, at even younger ages. Eighteen was considered a maximal age for young men, and a man who continued to put off marriage might be called to account before the elders of the community. The aim of Hebrew society was to have every eligible person married. There was no place in society for the single person, and widows and widowers were to be re-married quickly if possible. No one was supposed to be left for a prolonged period without a mate of the opposite sex.[17]

Within marriage there was considerable sexual freedom, although there were several attempts to regulate sexual mores, in part, at least, for ritualistic reasons. One of the taboos dealt with menstruating women, regarded as unclean.

> And if a man shall lie with a woman having her sickness, and shall uncover her nakedness; he hath discovered her fountain, and she hath uncovered the fountain of her blood: and both of them shall be cut off from their people.[18]

Menstruating women were regarded as unclean for 7 days, and everything they "lieth upon," "sitteth upon," or "toucheth" was also regarded as unclean.

> And if any man lie with her at all, and her flowers be upon him, he shall be unclean seven days; and all the bed whereon he lieth shall be unclean.[19]

Later in Judaism this period of uncleanliness was terminated by undergoing the *mikwa,* the traditional ritual bath still required of Orthodox Jews.

As long as ritual purity was observed, however, Jewish men were supposed to follow the scriptural injunction to see that their wives' "conjugal rights" were not diminished.[20] Talmudic writers went to great lengths to specify the minimal obligations in sex, although factors such as strength and occupation were to be taken into account. Gentlemen of leisure were to have intercourse every night. Laborers employed in their city of residence were to engage in sex twice weekly, but if they had to travel to another city for work, once a week sufficed. Donkey drivers were to have intercourse once a week; camel drivers, once in 30 days; sailors, once in 6 months; and scholars, once a week, customarily on Friday night.[21] A man was to continue to engage in intercourse with his wife even when she was barren.[22]

Though we know little about the actual technique of coitus practiced by the ancient Hebrews, there were relatively few prohibitions about the manner or postures of intercourse. Some rabbinical authorities recommended coitus be performed rapidly with a minimum of foreplay, but others were much more liberal. Sexual relations were permitted during pregnancy and nursing. In general, if the Song of Songs and Proverbs are any indication, the Jews were tolerant toward sexual activity between males and females, as long as penetration took place. Jewish law never indicted sexual relations between unmarried persons, although virginity in a bride was highly prized. Children born either in or out of wedlock were normally regarded as legitimate. Those classed as illegitimate were the offspring of unions impermissible in marriage, such as from incest or adultery, or from a union of a member of a priestly caste and a divorcée.[23]

Sex information was probably passed on from parents to children or acquired from one's peers, and sex investigation was considered a legitimate scholarly investigation, as demonstrated by the Talmudic story about Rabbi Kahana:

> Rav Kahana once went in and hid under Rab's bed. He heard him chatting (with his wife) and joking and doing as he required. He said to him (from under the bed): "One would think that (you) had never tasted of this dish before!" (Rab) said to him: "Kahan, is that you there? Get out! It's rude!" Then (Kahana) replied: "It is a matter of the Torah, and I need to learn."[24]

Toleration of sexuality did not, however, include the deposit of semen anywhere else than in the female vagina. A major source of contamination from men was an emission of semen, voluntarily or otherwise:

> And if a man's seed of copulation go out from him, then he shall wash all his flesh in water, and be unclean until the evening. And every garment, and every skin, whereupon is the seed of copulation, shall be washed with water, and be unclean until the evening.[25]

To become ritually pure after such emissions, a short period of continence was normally required,[26] though sometimes the punishment was more severe, as in the story of Onan.

> *And Er, Judah's first born, was wicked in the sight of the Lord;*
> *and the Lord slew him.*
> *And Judah said unto Onan, Go in unto thy brother's wife,*
> *and marry her, and raise up the seed to thy brother.*
> *And Onan knew that the seed should not be his;*
> *and it came to pass, when he went in unto his brother's wife,*
> *that he spilled it on the ground,*
> *lest that he should give seed to his brother.*
> *And the thing which he did displeased the Lord;*
> *wherefore he slew him also.*[27]

Though this story has often been regarded as a prohibition against masturbation, the act described is coitus interruptus; the punishment seems to be not so much for spilling the seed as for refusal to obey the levirate requirement that Onan take his brother's wife as his own. Still onanism and masturbation have often been used synonymously in Western culture. Later in the Talmud masturbation is rigidly interdicted; one Talmudic writer went so far as to regard masturbation as a crime deserving the death penalty. In fact, it is possible that the prohibition forbidding a man to hold his penis even while urinating, except for a married man whose wife was readily available for intercourse, resulted from a fear of loss of semen.[28]

Why the loss of semen was so feared is unclear. It might be that a loss implied the failure of the male's duty to procreate and replenish the earth. If this was so, the commandment was interpreted as applying only to men;[29] thus it was permissible for women to use contraceptive measures, and women were allowed to insert *mokh* (a spongy substance) into their vaginas to hinder conception.[30] This difference in treatment of men and women emphasizes that the ancient Hebrews regarded the male semen as the key to conception. The women supplied nothing of themselves to the new being except a receptacle providing a suitable environment for growth.[31] Moreover, since intercourse, even under the most desirable conditions, did not always lead to pregnancy, procreation could not be justified as the sole purpose of sexual relations. Thus, a man was to have regular intercourse with his wife, even after the menopause, since, after all, God had made Sarah, the wife of Abraham, pregnant late in life, and as long as a man channeled his seed in the correct way, it was always possible for God to work miracles. The danger was in diverting the male seed to avoid the possibilities of pregnancy.

This male-oriented emphasis is a dominant theme of Jewish writing about sex, although occasionally prohibitions are directed against women. One prohibition deals with bestiality.

> And if a woman approach unto any beast, and lie down thereto, thou shalt kill the woman, and the beast they shall surely be put to death; their blood shall be upon them.[32]

Talmudic writers, fearful that a woman denied a proper male partner might be tempted to engage in animal contacts, went so far as to prohibit a widow from keeping a pet dog.[33] Fear of female sexuality probably also led to the prohibitions against widows' acquiring a slave.[34] In general, however, the ancient Hebrew writers assumed a woman's sexuality could be satisfied with a husband, and only occasionally were alternative forms of sexual expression mentioned. With their male-oriented view of sexuality and penetration, they also assumed that women could do little among themselves. Thus, although lesbianism is occasionally equated with harlotry, few prohibitions were put on the private association of one woman with another, and the subject of homosexual intercourse between women is generally ignored.[35]

Cross-dressing was condemned, both male and female:

> The woman shall not wear that which pertaineth unto a man, neither shall a man put on a woman's garment; for all that do so are abomination unto the Lord thy God.[36]

This prohibition was not, however, so much against the sexual overtones in transvestism as against the pagan practices in which the goddess Atargatis was worshipped by men and women dressed in the clothing of the opposite sex.[37] Still, there was some concern with the sexual overtones of transvestism, for men were enjoined from using cosmetics, from wearing brightly colored garments, from donning jewelry or ornaments associated with women, and from shaving the hair on the hidden parts of their bodies. Women were to keep their hair long and men were to keep their hair short.

An intriguingly ambiguous reference dealing with the scandal and moral evils associated with idolatry appears in the Wisdom of Solomon, an apocryphal work written in Greek in the first century B.C. and included in the Catholic Douay Version of the scriptures.[38] The problem with the reference is that we are not sure what the Greek term *geneseōs enallagē* means.[39] It has often been translated as "change of kind" or "change of sex," but what does this mean? We know that simulated sex changes were a feature of many fertility cults,[40] and this might well be what the passage refers to, since it concerns idolatry. On the other hand, it might not even have any sexual connotation but instead refer to attempts by some Jews to eliminate the distinctions between themselves and non-Jews. If it does refer to any simulated sex change, then transvestism might occasionally have been practiced in spite of prohibitions. In fact, cross-dressing was probably more frequent than seems likely from its prohibitions. It was even encouraged when the motive was innocent or when it was necessary to preserve honor, as when a woman traveled in disguise in an all-male caravan.[41] It might well be that the Biblical prohibition started as an effort to combat pagan practices and only later acquired sexually erotic overtones.

Like other Middle Eastern peoples, the Jews were impressed with the generative power of the male phallus. A castrated person was despised. The Bible specified that:

> He that is wounded in the stones, or hath his privy member cut off, shall not enter into the congregation of the Lord.[42]

A castrated animal was not acceptable as an offering upon the altar, although, like most things in the Bible, there are ambiguities, and in some cases eunuchs were not cut off from their congregations.[43] Like the Egyptians, the Jews considered phalli as suitable war trophies, and when the young David slew some 200 Philistines, he:

> brought their foreskins, and they gave them in full tale to the king, that he might be the king's son-in-law. And Saul gave him Michal his daughter.[44]

Phalli of the Jews themselves were to be protected, and women, as in other parts of the Near East, were forbidden to injure a man's testicles under any conditions.

Tied in with this emphasis on the phallus was circumcision. The custom dated from very ancient times, as is evident from the fact that flint stones were ceremonially required in the operation.[45] Tradition ascribed its introduction to the covenant Abraham had made with God:

> And God said unto Abraham, Thou shalt keep my covenant therefore,
> thou, and thy seed after thee in their generations.
> This is my covenant, which ye shall keep, between me and you and
> thy seed after thee: every man child among you shall be
> circumcised.
> And ye shall circumcise the flesh of your foreskin: and it shall
> be a token of the covenant betwixt me and you.
> And he that is eight days old shall be circumcised among you, every
> man child in your generations, he that is born in the house, or
> bought with money of any stranger, which is not of thy seed.
> He that is born in thy house, and he that is bought with thy money,
> must needs be circumcised: and my covenant shall be in your flesh
> for an everlasting covenant.
> And the uncircumcised man child whose flesh of his foreskin is not
> circumcised, that soul shall be cut off from his people, he hath
> broken my covenant.[46]

This only further highlights the male orientation of the Jewish scriptures. Males made the covenant, not the women, and this emphasis carried over into other aspects of sexual relations. Adultery, for example, existed in Jewish law, but it applied only to the sex relations of a married woman with a man other than her husband, not to a married man. Adultery was punishable by the death penalty.[47]

One of the most obvious indications of the subordinate status of women in the Jewish tradition is the treatment of rape, most notably in the Talmud, where it is stressed that, since the initial moral resentment of the woman may gradually turn into an inward instinctual consent, it is next to impossible for a woman to be raped.[48] Though the sons of Jacob killed Shechem for raping their sister Dinah, Jacob condemned them for it.[49] The case of Tamar, the daughter of David, and his son Ammon,[50] is less rape than incest, and incest was considered one of the crimes a Jew was not to commit, even under threat of death.[51] Rape in wartime was not considered rape at all, a more or less standard practice for the Hebrew soldiers being to ravish the women captured in war.[52] Some attempts to ameliorate such practices appear in the Bible, but the custom was never fully condemned nor abolished.[53]

No such ambiguity existed toward overt homosexual practices, although it is not clear whether the condemnations date from early in Hebrew history or were later inserts. It seems logical that sexual acts between two males would be condemned, for a man was both wasting his seed and committing a ritual impurity, but the Jewish reaction to homosexuality is more severe than simple condemnation, and this has led to considerable speculation about the reasons. The earliest mention of homosexuality in the Bible is in that portion of the Holiness Code preserved in Leviticus: "Thou shalt not lie with mankind, as with womankind: it is abomination."[54] This is later amplified:

> If a man also lie with mankind, as he lieth with a woman, both of them have committed an abomination: they shall surely be put to death; and their blood shall be upon them.[55]

At one time the Holiness Code was regarded as dating from the period of the exile, but scholars today do not necessarily agree. Part of the difficulty is that many of the other references to homosexuality in the Bible equate it with cult prostitution of the pagans.[56] This is the case of the reference in the Code of Deuteronomy, believed to date from the seventh century B.C.: "There shall be no whore of the daughters of Israel, nor a sodomite of the sons of Israel."[57]

Other references seem to give further attention to the association of homosexuality with paganism.[58] Some writers have also believed that the Jewish hostility to nudity[59] is a veiled fear of homosexuality[60] and that only such an equation could account for the reaction of Noah in cursing his son Ham for not covering his nakedness.[61] One investigator summed up:

> It is clear that incest was regarded as a grave offense, but apparently it was not as serious as uncovering the nakedness of a father, uncle or brother. In other words, male homosexuality within a family was most heinous.[62]

It is not so much what the scriptures say about homosexuality that has dominated Western thinking on the subject as what later commentators have read into the scriptures. This is particularly true of the story of Sodom, from which we get the term *sodomy*. According to the Biblical account, Jehovah had vowed to destroy Sodom and other cities of the plain because of their wickedness, but when Abraham protested such an act would destroy the innocent with the guilty, God promised not to destroy them if he could find 10 good men. Two angels were sent to the cities to seek out good and virtuous people; in Sodom they met Lot, who invited them into his house. While they were there, the male inhabitants of the city gathered around calling upon Lot to bring out his guests so that they might "know them."[63] The Hebrew word *yādha* (to know) can be interpreted in the sexual sense to mean intercourse or in the social sense of becoming acquainted.[64] Which meaning was intended by the Biblical writers? Giving some impetus to the social interpretation was the reaction of Lot, who refused to bring out his guests but instead offered his two daughters.

> Behold now, I have two daughters which have not known man; let me, I pray you, bring them out unto you, and do ye to them as is good in your eyes: only unto these men do nothing; for therefore came they under the shadow of my roof.[65]

When the crowd persisted in their demands to know the strangers, they were struck blind. The next morning, Lot and his family left the city on the advice of the angels after being warned not to look back. When Lot's wife did so, she was turned to salt.

The whole story seems to be a hodgepodge of remembered fact and legend. From archaeological, geological, and literary evidence, we know there was a great disaster, perhaps an earthquake, that destroyed several cities (or villages) of the plain around 1900 B.C. These areas now lie under the southern part of the Dead Sea.[66] The sexual aspects of the story seem, however, to be a much later addition, probably inserted, as Derrick Sherwin Bailey has argued, as part of an anti-Greek campaign in Palestine.[67] If this is the case, the sexual connotation coincided with the postexilic period of the Second Commonwealth, when Judaism was under stress from outside influences.

Giving support to the belief of a late insertion is that no Biblical condemnations of homosexuality refer to Sodom, nor more importantly, do any of the Biblical references to Sodom explain what crimes the residents were guilty of. Occasionally a passage in Deuteronomy referring to dogs or male prostitutes has been translated to read Sodomite, but this is not justified by the original text.[68] Still another passage in Deuteronomy mentions Sodom, Gomorrah, Admah, and Zeboim as the cities destroyed, but the reasons are not given,[69] nor are they given in the other references to Sodom and Gomorrah.[70] It might be that the Genesis account of Sodom is a combination of several stories, since a similar story is related in Judges about Gibeah.[71] The residents of Gibeah were not, however, destroyed by any catastrophe but instead were defeated in battle by the rest of an enraged Israel, and all but 600 males were destroyed. Still, they were not cursed, since it was from these survivors that Boaz, David, Solomon, and Jesus were said to be descended.[72]

When the Bible does spell out the sins for which Sodom was destroyed, they are listed as pride, unwillingness to aid the poor and needy, haughtiness, and the doing of abominable things.[73] Though the last might refer to sexual activities, their greatest sin was pride and contentment and ignoring the needy. None of these sins was regarded as unforgivable, for the Lord promised to restore Sodom to its former estate.[74] Not until the Palestinian *Pseudepigrapha,* the noncanonical Jewish books composed between 200 B.C. and 200 A.D., are the sexual sins of Sodom emphasized. In the *Book of Jubilees,* written about 135–

105 B.C., there are some three references to Sodom. One passage is as ambiguous as the Genesis account toward sex,[75] but the other two introduce a new theme:

> . . . the Lord executed his judgments on Sodom, and Gomorrah, and Zeboim, and all the region of the Jordan, and He burned them with fire and brimstone, and destroyed them until this day, even as I have declared unto thee all their works, that they are wicked and sinners exceedingly, and that they defile themselves and commit fornication in their flesh, and work uncleanness on the earth. And in like manner, God will execute judgment on the places where they have done according to the uncleanness of the Sodomites, like unto the judgment of Sodom.[76]

And Abraham told his sons and grandsons:

> of the judgment of the giants, and judgment of the Sodomites, how they had been judged on account of their wickedness, and had died on account of their fornication, and uncleanness, and mutual corruption through fornication.

> *And guard yourself from all fornication and uncleanness,*
> *And from all pollution of sin,*
> *Lest ye make our name a curse*
> *And your whole life a hissing,*
>
> *And all your sons to be destroyed by the sword,*
> *And ye become accursed like Sodom,*
> *And all your remnant as the sons of Gomorrah.[77]*

Here the story of Sodom and Gomorrah clearly has sexual connotations, although, since the judgment of the giants is mentioned and this is also associated with sexual sins, it is not so much homosexuality as sexual license and promiscuity that is condemned.[78]

The *Testament of Naphtali,* included in the *Testaments of the Twelve Patriarchs* written at the end of the second century B.C., cautions readers not to become "as Sodom, which changed the order of nature. In like manner the Watchers also changed the order of their nature, whom the Lord cursed at the flood."[79] Though homosexuality later, as a result of Greek concepts, came to be equated with the sin against nature, it is not certain that this reference is to homosexuality, for the Watchers, with whom the residents of Sodom are compared, were nonhuman creatures who had intercourse with an incompatible order of beings, namely, the daughters of men.

There are several other references to the story of Sodom, each somewhat ambiguous, but the sin of Sodom seems increasingly to be associated with homosexuality.[80] By the time Philo Judaeus, a Hellenized Egyptian Jew, wrote at the end of the first century A.D., the homosexual meaning had become clear. He wrote that the men of Sodom ignored

the law of nature, and applied themselves to deep drinking of strong liquor and dainty feeding and forbidden forms of intercourse. Not only in their mad lust for women did they violate the marriage of their neighbors, but also men mounted males without respect for sex nature which the active partner shares with the passive; and so when they tried to beget children they were discovered to be incapable of any but a sterile seed. Yet the discovery availed them not, so much stronger was the force of lust which mastered them. Then, as little by little they accustomed those who were by nature men to submit to play the part of women, they saddled them with the formidable curse of a female disease. For not only did they emasculate their bodies by luxury and voluptousness, but they worked a further degeneration in their souls and, so far as in them lay, were corrupting the whole of mankind.[81]

From this brief examination of the Sodom story, it seems that Sodom in general stood for whatever the ancient Hebrews regarded as wicked and that, while some of these forms of wickedness, such as pride, inhospitality, or neglect of God, remained constant, others came to the fore as the Jews came into contact with other groups. The increasing hostility to homosexuality probably developed because the Jews associated it with the Greeks, and the Palestinian Jews felt particularly threatened by the spread of Greek culture and influence. The result was a circular process. Their antagonism to the Greeks could most easily be expressed in an antagonism to homosexuality, and for this reason there was an increasing concern with homosexuality.[82]

Before the threat of assimilation to Greek ideas and culture led to such overt condemnation of homosexuality, the Jews may have occasionally tolerated some homosexual relationships. Some commentators, not all homosexuals, have read tacit approval of homosexual relationships into the stories of David and Jonathan and Ruth and Naomi. David had much to gain by an intimate friendship with Jonathan, the son of Saul,[83] and the Biblical description that David's love of Jonathan passed "the love of woman,"[84] as well as Saul's reaction to this friendship, gives some support to the belief in a possibly homosexual relationship. Whether it had sexual overtones or not, it seems safe to say that the two were very intimate friends. Similarly, the story of Ruth and Naomi has been interpreted by some to imply a lesbian relationship. Even today, we view the relationship as ideal for lovers, as is evident from the incorporation of part of the passage of Ruth's devotion to Naomi in the marriage ceremony:

Intreat me not to leave thee, or to return from following after thee: for whither thou goest, I will go; and whither thou lodgest, I will lodge; thy people shall be my people, and thy God my God.

Where thou diest, will I die, and there will I be buried: the Lord do so to me, and more also, if aught but death part thee and me.[85]

Jeanette Foster, who believed in the homosexual potential of the relationship, argued that, since Ruth had been married for some 10 years when she was widowed, her devotion to Naomi could not be regarded as the simple clinging of a bereaved adolescent to her husband's mother. Since there were good prospects for a husband in Moab if Ruth chose to remain there, but instead she went back to her mother-in-law's people, the relationship could at least allow some speculation about a homosexual bond,[86] although close friendships are not necessarily homosexual.

Wainwright Churchill claimed that only among Judaism and Zoroastrianism was there an "all encompassing denunciation of homosexual relations" among the people of antiquity,[87] but in light of what has already been said, the statement seems to be an oversimplification for the Jews. Among the Hebrews, the denunciations seem to be not so much against homosexuality as such as against the idolatry associated with it, or they spring from fears of assimilation. There is no evidence that the Jews mounted a large-scale campaign against it. Probably male homosexual acts were penalized because they did not result in procreation[88] and, hence, ran afoul of the law. It is even possible that some forms of homosexual intercourse might have been punished by death, although there is no record of this sentence's ever having been carried out.[89] The Talmud distinguishes between wanton homosexual transgression, which might merit the death sentence, and homosexual acts that were inadvertent and rendered the offender liable only to a sin offering. Whenever there was doubt whether the act had occurred, it was stipulated that a suspensive guilt offering be made.[90] For homosexual acts committed upon one asleep or upon a minor by one of full age, the innocent parties were not to suffer any punishment.[91] Some rabbis held that a boy could not be accountable for a homosexual act until he was 13; others, until he was 9; and others were not so lenient.[92]

In summary, ancient Judaism set certain norms for sexual relationships. Sexual intercourse between a man and wife was encouraged, the begetting of children being the nominal purpose. Homosexuality, bestiality, transvestism, and even masturbation were reproved, at least for men; it is not clear that the prohibitions applied to women in all cases. Though these attitudes exercised great influence on Christianity, they were only part of the tradition that passed into Western Europe through Christianity.

NOTES

1. Genesis, 1:28. All Biblical quotations are from the King James Version, although in all cases I have consulted other versions, particularly that published by the Jewish Publication Society of America, and various scholarly versions.

2. Raphael Patai, *The Hebrew Goddess* (New York: Ktav Publishing House, 1968), p. 247.

3.   Louis M. Epstein, *Sex Laws and Customs in Judaism* (New York: Bloch Publishing Company, 1948), pp. 3–24.

4.   Genesis, 3:1–6.

5.   St. Augustine argued that the sin of Adam was transmitted from parents to their children throughout all generations by the sexual act. St. Augustine, *De nuptiis et concupiscentia ad valerium libri duo*, 1, 5, 6–8, 9, in *Patrologiae Latinae*, J. P. Migne, ed. (Paris: Garnier Fratres, 1844–1864), XLII, pp. 209–319; or in the *Corpus scriptorum ecclesiastorum Latinorum* (Vienna: C. Geroldi filium, 1866 ff.), XLIV, pp. 413–474; also *Sermones*, 51, in Migne, *op. cit.*, XXXVIII; and *De Genesi ad litteram libri duodecim*, 9, 10, 16 ff, in Migne, *op. cit.*, XXVIII, i, pp. 3–435; or *Corpus scriptorum ecclesiastorum Latinorum*, XXXIV, pp. 245–286. Augustine's views were affirmed in the Council of Carthage, 418, and Second Council of Orange, 529.

6.   Genesis, 19:30–38.

7.   Genesis, 39:7–18.

8.   Genesis, 30:1–24.

9.   Judges, 16:4–20.

10.   I Kings, 16:31–33; 18:13,19; 19:1,2; 21:5–25; II Kings, 9:7, 10, 22, 30, 36–37.

11.   II Samuel, 6:20–23.

12.   Epstein, *op. cit.*, pp. 68–131.

13.   Deuteronomy, 24:5.

14.   Deuteronomy, 20:7.

15.   Yebamoth, 44a, translated by Israel W. Slotki, in the *Babylonian Talmud*, Isidore Epstein, ed. (London: Soninco Press, 1936, 2 vols.).

16.   Abodah Zarah, 179, translated by A. Mishcon and A. Cohen, in the *Babylonian Talmud*, Isidore Epstein, ed. (London: Soncino Press, 1935).

17.   David Mace, *Hebrew Marriage* (London: Epworth Press, 1953), pp. 143–144.

18.   Leviticus, 20:18.

19.   Leviticus, 15:19–24.

20.   Exodus, 21:10.

21.   Ketuboth, 5:6, in the Mishnah, translated by Herbert Danby (London: Oxford University Press, 1933).

22.   Epstein, *op. cit.*, p. 145.

23.   Mace, *op. cit.*, pp. 210–211.

24.   Berakoth, 62a, translated by Maurice Simon, in the *Babylonian Talmud*, I. Epstein, ed. (reprinted, London: Soncino Press, 1965).

25.   Leviticus, 15:16–18.

26.   Exodus, 19:14–15.

27.   Genesis, 38:7–10.

28.   Niddah, 13a, translated into English by Israel W. Slotki, in the *Babylonian Talmud*, I. Epstein, ed. (London: Soncino Press, 1948).

29.   Norman E. Himes, *Medical History of Contraception* (reprinted, New York: Schocken Books, 1970), pp. 72–75.

30.   Yebamoth, 12b, 100b; Ketuboth, 39a; Niddah, 45a; and others.

31.   Mace, *op. cit.*, pp. 206–207.

32.   Leviticus, 20:16.

33.   Abodah Zarah, 22b.

34. Baba Mezia, 71a, translated into English by Salis Daiches and H. Freeman, in *Babylonian Talmud,* I. Epstein, ed. (London: Soncino Press, 1935).

35. Epstein, *op. cit.,* p. 138.

36. Deuteronomy, 22:5.

37. S. R. Driver, *A Critical and Exegetical Comment on Deuteronomy,* 3rd ed. (reprinted, Edinburgh: T. & T. Clark, 1951), pp. 250–251.

38. *Wisdom of Solomon,* 14:22f. In addition to the Douay Version, see the *Apocrypha and Pseudepigrapha of the Old Testament in English,* R. H. Charles, ed. (Oxford, England: Clarendon Press, 1913, 2 vols.). Volume 1 has the *Apocrypha,* Volume 2 the *Pseudepigrapha.*

39. For a discussion of this, see Derrick Sherwin Bailey, *Homosexuality and the Western Christian Tradition* (London: Longmans, Green and Company, 1955), pp. 45–48.

40. L. R. Farnell, *The Cults of the Greek States* (Oxford, England: Clarendon Press, 1896 ff.), V, pp. 160–161.

41. Epstein, *op. cit.,* pp. 64–67.

42. Deuteronomy, 23:1.

43. Isaiah, 56:3–5.

44. I Samuel, 18:27.

45. Exodus, 4:25; and Joshua, 5:2.

46. Genesis, 17:9–14.

47. Leviticus, 20:10.

48. Kethuboth, 51b, translated by Israel W. Slotki, in the *Babylonian Talmud,* I. Epstein, ed. (London: Soncino Press, 1936, 2 vols.).

49. Genesis, 34:1–31.

50. II Samuel, 13:1–39.

51. Leviticus, 10:17; 21:11; see also Mace, *op. cit.,* pp. 150–164.

52. Judges, 21:16 ff.

53. Deuteronomy, 22:10–14.

54. Leviticus, 18:22.

55. Leviticus, 21:13.

56. Driver, *op. cit.,* pp. 264–265. It is possible that some forms of male prostitution were also practiced in the temple at Jerusalem for a brief period. See Johannes Pedersen, *Israel,* pp. 470–471, part 4 (London: Oxford University Press, 1926–1947, 4 parts in 2 vols.).

57. Deuteronomy, 23:17.

58. I Kings, 14:24; 15:12; 22:46; and possibly II Kings, 23:7; Job, 36:14; and Hosea, 4:14.

59. Genesis, 9:21–27; Leviticus, 21:11, 21.

60. Cuthbert A. Simpson, in his exegesis on *Genesis, The Interpreter's Bible* (New York: Abingdon Press, 1952), Vol. 1, p. 556.

61. Genesis, 9:22–24.

62. George W. Henry, *All the Sexes* (New York, Holt, Rinehart, and Winston, 1955), p. 502.

63. Genesis, 19:1–11.

64. See G. A. Barton, "Sodomy," *Encyclopedia of Religion and Ethics,* James Hastings, ed. (New York: Scribner's, 1928, 13 vols.), Vol. 11, pp. 672–674.

65. Genesis, 19:8.

66. Jack Finegan, *Light from the Ancient Past: The Archaeological Background of the Hebrew–Christian Religion* (Princeton, N.J.: Princeton University Press, 1946), p. 126; and J. Penrose

Harland, "Sodom and Gomorrah," *The Biblical Archaelogist,* VI (1943), p. 3; and also V (1942), p. 2.

67. Bailey, *op. cit.,* pp. 1–28.

68. Deuteronomy, 23:18.

69. Deuteronomy, 29:23.

70. Genesis, 19:248–228; Deuteronomy, 32:32.

71. Judges, 20:16–30.

72. Robert W. Wood, "Homosexual Behavior in the Bible," *One Institute Quarterly,* V (No. 16, 1962), pp. 12–13.

73. Ezekiel, 16:49–50. "Behold, this was the iniquity of thy sister Sodom: pride, fullness of bread, and prosperous ease. . . . And they were haughty, and committed abominations before me: therefore I took them away as I saw good." The word *abomination (tō ebhāh)* might suggest a homosexual act, but its conventional meaning is worshipping of idols or idolatry. Since idolatry in the Jewish mind was equated with sacred prostitution, it might indirectly refer to homosexuality. Other references to Sodom also mention the general corruption but do not carry sexual overtones: Isaiah, 1:9–10; 3:9; Jeremiah, 23:14; Lamentations, 4:6.

74. Ezekiel, 16:53, 55.

75. Jubilees, 13:17 (see Charles, *op. cit.,* Vol. 2).

76. Jubilees, 16:5–6.

77. Jubilees, 20:5–6.

78. Bailey, *op. cit.,* pp. 12–13.

79. Testament of Naphtali, 3:4–5.

80. Bailey, *op. cit.,* pp. 22–23.

81. Philo Judaeus, *On Abraham,* XXVI, 134–136, translated by F. H. Colson (London: William Heinemann, 1959–1962), Vol. 6 of the Loeb Classical Library edition.

82. Bailey, *op. cit.,* p. 27.

83. R. W. Wood, *Christ and the Homosexual* (New York: Vantage Press, n.d.), pp. 140–141.

84. II Samuel, 1:26.

85. Ruth, 1:16–17.

86. Jeanette H. Foster, *Sex Variant Women in Literature* (London: Frederick Muller, 1958), pp. 22–23.

87. Wainwright Churchill, *Homosexual Behavior among Males* (New York: Hawthorn Books, 1967), p. 76.

88. John Addington Symonds, *A Problem in Modern Ethics* (London: privately printed, 1896), p. 6, argued that male homosexual acts were probably penalized in the interests of population, of the necessity to procreate.

89. For various types of crimes in ancient Judaism, see W. H. Bennett, "Crimes and Punishments (Hebrew)," in Hastings, *op. cit.,* Vol. 4, p. 281. Bennett breaks down the crimes into religious crimes, offenses against the state, sexual offenses (bestiality, incest, sodomy, prostitution), offenses against property (including adultery and rape), offenses against the person, and offenses against the family. Later, in the Talmud, it is possible homosexual intercourse was punished by stoning: Sanhedrin, vii. 4 in the Mishnah, and Sanhedrin, 54a, translated by Jacob Schacter and H. Freeman in the *Babylonian Talmud,* I. Epstein, ed. (London: Soncino Press, 1935, 2 vols.).

90. Kerithoth, 1:1–2, Mishnah.

91. *Ibid.,* ii. 6.

92. Sanhedrin, 54a–55a, *op. cit.*

PART TWO

THE EUROPEAN INHERITANCE

5

THE CONTRADICTORY
CONTRIBUTION OF THE GREEKS

Though the residents of the ancient Middle East exercised a strong influence on traditional Western sexual attitudes, particularly through Judaism, the Greeks were much more important. As with the Middle Eastern heritage, however, only certain aspects of Greek thinking were incorporated in Christian attitudes, others being largely ignored. Within classical Greece itself, sexual attitudes varied from group to group, ranging from sexual abstinence at one extreme to almost complete promiscuity on the other. Christian culture tended to select aspects of the Greek tradition emphasizing asceticism, but enough information survives about other aspects to give a radically different picture of Greek attitudes than usual with other peoples, particularly of homosexuality, a sexual behavior widely practiced among the Greeks. The Greeks also attempted to arrive at scientific, or at least naturalistic, explanations for sexual behavior, these explanations, particularly those advanced by Aristotle and his successors, dominating Western thinking until the twentieth century, although often based on innaccurate data and erroneous assumptions.

Since the source material is so varied and so much a part of the Western cultural tradition, more information has been published on Greek sexual life than on that of almost any other peoples.[1] Unfortunately, because the research has usually been isolated from the main line of Greek scholarship, the available

93

information has not entered the generalized surveys or even the scholarly monographs. Whereas it is easy to claim that this failure to deal with the sexual life of the Greeks, except by a few specialists or advocates, has been due to our inherent prudishness, this answer seems far too simplistic. Rather the answer seems to be the way we regard the Greeks as the source of much of what is good in our culture. We tend to regard them as the originators of our literature, history, philosphy, and science, portraying them as almost perfect mortals. This exaggerated view has discouraged considering them as people whose culture and sexual attitudes were quite different from our own. Because the Western Christian tradition came to be hostile toward homosexuality, we generally ignored this aspect of Greek culture. Even well into the twentieth century the American essayist and writer John Jay Chapman expressed horror when he found that the Greek mind was "abnormal."

> By why had I not found this out before? Because the books and essays on Plato which I had been reading were either accommodated to the Greek psychology or else they were accommodated to modern Miss Nancyism—and, by the way, the two agree very sociably."[2]

Concerned with Greek homosexuality, Chapman believed these sexual vices had been introduced by the Greeks, who passed them on to Italy, and then they took root through the whole Roman Empire. "They spread like fungi that survive in the depth of a tangled forest."[3]

Until we have come to terms with both the normal and "abnormal" sexuality of the Greeks, we ignore the fact that, even in Western culture, attitudes toward sex other than those espoused by the dominant culture of today are possible. A thesis of this book is that one of the influential factors in setting sexual outlooks is the attitude toward the opposite sex, and since in the male-oriented history of the past the opposite sex has almost invariably been women, the views on women become crucial. Though the Greek stance on women varied from Homeric times to the early Christian period, in general a woman was clearly subordinate to the male, useful for having children, but not as a companion. In Homeric times women enjoyed considerable social freedom within their husband's house or domain, but their position depended entirely on their husband's success as a warrior and his ability to maintain his family's independence in a jealously competitive world where failure brought slavery or starvation or both. Later in Greek history, at least in Athens, the upper classes retained some features of this heroic pattern, although women of the lower classes obviously had a somewhat different role in both periods.

As the democratic revolution developed in Athens in the sixth and fifth centuries B.C., some of the aristocracy's freedom to acquire wives and concubines or to regard whom they would as their heir was restricted.[4] This restriction did not allow women any more freedom, but it did protect them as wives and mothers. Even after the Peloponnesian War (late fifth century B.C.), when there was a general democratization of defeated Athens, it was of such overriding importance that not a breath of suspicion should fall on young girls or young wives that they were protected far beyond what modern society would regard as reasonable. For example, one ancient Greek writer praised his sister and his niece because they had lived in the women's quarter of the house "with so much concern for their modesty that they were embarrassed even to be seen by their male relatives."[5] Xenophon (about 400 B.C.), in his treatise on domestic management, wrote that the ideal bride had lived under strict supervision before her marriage.

> Seeing, hearing and saying as little as possible . . . she knew no more than how, when given wool, to turn out a cloak, and had seen only how spinning is given out to the maids . . . in control of her appetite . . . she had been excellently trained, and this sort of training is, in my opinion, the most important to man and woman alike."[6]

A wife did not go out to dinner with her husband and in general was excluded from eating with her husband when he was entertaining male visitors.[7]

The civic necessity for female virginity ensured that girls were married very young, probably at 14, though some Athenian writers thought it should be more like the 18 to 20 years of age it was said to be in Sparta. The husband's being usually much older than his wife led to a serious age gap, leaving them little in common. Perhaps for this reason Aristotle, in his discussion of friendship, did not consider the relationship of husband and wife at all.[8] In fact, more paternalism than partnership was hinted in the normal married relationship.

Woman's purpose was to bear children, particularly sons, children being thought essential. Aristotle, for example, began his treatise on *Politics*[9] by dividing the communities into their smallest parts, namely the family (*oikos*), composed of the male, the female, and the servant. The servant by definition could be the plow ox for the poor or the human slave for the richer. According to Aristotle, the family unit would soon increase in size, because the male and female elements have a natural instinct to procreate, and with the appearance of the fourth element, children, the family was a true *oikos*.[10] A true family was to be considered a living organism requiring renewal every generation to be alive and supporting its living members' need for good and its deceased members' need for the performance of cult rituals. A childless family was visibly dying, and so in effect, a child, particularly a male child, was essential to perpetuate the organism. If a man had only female children, it was customary to arrange for the girls to be married to their nearest agnatic relative (a father's brother, that is the girl's uncle), to reestablish the family in the next generation. Men without natural heirs could also adopt sons, but the adopted son could not fully inherit until he himself had begotten a son and registered him in the family of his adoptive father.[11]

An American sociologist, Philip E. Slater, has argued that the strong denigration of women in Greek literature was due to patriarchal delusion. He held that the rejection of the females was little more than an attempt by the males to deny the influence of the female and reject her influence over the Greek male child and that in reality the Greek woman, denied access to power outside the home, exercised control over the family from within.

> The Greek male's contempt for women was not only compatible with, but also indissolubly bound to, an intense fear of them, and to an underlying suspicion of male inferiority. Why else would such extreme measures be necessary? Customs such as the rule that a woman should not be older than her husband, or of higher social status, or more educated, or paid the same as a male for the same work, or be in a position of authority—betray an assumption that males are incapable of competing with females on an equal basis; the cards must first be stacked, the female given a handicap. Otherwise, it is felt, the male would simply be swallowed up, evaporate, lose his identity altogether.[12]

This mother-dominant, father-avoidant culture inevitably, in Slater's opinion, led to male homosexuality.

Several difficulties oppose accepting Slater's correlation of the fear of women with homosexuality, although this is not to deny that his thesis has some validity. One difficulty is simply that ancient Greece was not twentieth-century Western culture. The mother in Greek society was not the key figure she is in much of middle-class Western society, sacrificing herself and her independence to further her children's development, although undoubtedly this sometimes happened. Instead the most influential figure in reasonably well-off Greek families (the group with which Slater is most concerned), was the "nanny," who was usually also a slave.[13] Moreover, girl children, from the moment of their births, were regarded and treated as inferior to boys, a condition of which young boys became conscious, if only because their slave nannies emphasized it to secure their own status. This makes it seem doubtful that the combination of a doting "nanny" and the concept of superiority of the male so engrained in the young male would have led to the anxieties Slater feels existed. Instead, the disdain males felt for females might well have encouraged homosexual outlets— since few women could have been true companions.

Another difficulty with accepting Slater's theorizing is that he bases his conceptions on the work of Karen Horney. Horney, a disciple of Sigmund Freud, disagreed with her teacher on the universality of penis envy. Freud taught that females hold great feelings of inferiority over their lack of male genitalia, and the males, conscious of their possession, fear women, who want to castrate them. In short, the narcissistic rejection of the female by the male is liberally mingled with fear and disdain.[14] On the contrary, Horney held that the male's attempts to find a penis in a female is an attempt to deny the existence of the intrinsically "sinister" female genitalia, which represents a fear of maternal envelopment. She claimed that male homosexuals, for example, dream of falling into a pit, sailing a boat in a narrow channel, and being sucked into a whirlpool, finding themselves in a cellar full of "uncanny, blood-stained plants and animals," or of being lured to death by a female. To overcome this dread of the female genitalia, Horney believed that men develop two techniques, disparagement and idealization. By the first, the male reassures himself there is nothing to be feared from so poor and inadequate a creature, and by the second, that there is nothing to fear from so saintly a being.[15] Slater found Greek mythology full of Horney's symbolism about female genitalia. To support further the application of this thesis to Greece, Slater pointed to the misogyny of most Greek literature and to the Greeks' tendency to marry barely pubescent girls and to encourage their women, and only their women, to practice depilation of all body hair. Inevitably also the mature, maternal women were the most feared and most dangerous in Greek literature.[16] But why adopt the concept of the sinister female genitalia instead of the penis envy theory of Freud to explain ancient Greece? In fact, does either explain the Greeks? The difficulty with applying any such theoretical concept to Greece is that the data are conflicting, and different outlooks were dominant at different time periods. Slater would agree that stances change but held that the increasing misogyny was due to a transition from a matriarchy to a patriarchy, a debatable concept in itself.[17]

Slater would also tie in the development of homosexuality with other changes in Greek society, mainly the change from a rural to an urban environment. As Greek society moved from the rural society pictured in Homer to the urban society we associate with fifth-century Athens, the husband absented himself more and more from the home while the woman became more imprisoned within the household. This resulted, he claimed, in the breakdown of the extended-family system and threw an emotional burden on the nuclear family it was not equipped to handle. As ties of blood weakened, there was no corresponding strengthening of the marital bond to fill the gap, and the tensions between the sexes were simply accentuated. The strain on the family was further highlighted by the rising youth culture, represented in Greek literature by the sophists in the fifth century. Thus, to ease the tensions put on them and society, the Athenian males turned to the source of their own pathology, pederasty and misogyny.[18] Pederasty and misogyny are not, however, necessarily the opposite sides of the same coin, although it seems to follow that, when the female is condemned, the male is exalted. On the other hand, if the female is exalted too highly, males tend to turn to each other also. Overlooked in such explanations are the socialization and acculturation patterns that have to be considered to explain the development of the Greek attitudes. From present evidence, it seems to be much too simple to explain either homosexuality or misogyny in Slater's terms. Rather, a whole series of variables must be considered.

One such variable is the Greek acceptance of pleasure. The Greek ideal recognized the dependence of man on the world of the senses, although accepting certain gifts of fortune as necessary to self-development. Of these, the chief was economic security sufficient to guard a person against sordid cares, health to ensure physical excellence, and children to support and protect an individual in his or her old age. Aristotle's definition of the happy man was one whose activity accorded with perfect virtue and who was adequately furnished with external goods, not just for a short time, but for a complete or perfect lifetime.[19] With a solid basis of external goods behind him, the Greek then felt free to play; the Greeks have been called the "first people" in the world to play, and they played on a grand scale.[20] All over Greece there were religious festivals, men going to them at Olympia, Delphi, Corinth, and Nemea, not so much to honor the gods as to witness the heroic contests of chosen athletes.

Cheerful enjoyment of life (hedone), particularly the joys of love, was one thing the Greeks most sought to achieve. Apart from a few individual exceptions, the Greeks recognized the pleasure of sensuous enjoyments. Even the gods sought such pleasure, often for the benefit of mankind. In the *Iliad*, for example, Hera is reported to have charmed her husband to help the Greeks in their fight with the Trojans.[21] One part of the *Iliad* has been called a "hymn of the omnipotent rights of sensuality,"[22] and Greek literature in general is full of numerous instances of sensuous pleasure.[23]

Nevertheless, sensuous pleasure and marital duties were not the same thing. As a fourth-century orator put it:

> We resort to courtesans for our pleasures, keep concubines to look after our daily needs and marry wives to give us legitimate children and be the faithful guardians of our domestic hearths.[24]

Xenophon has Socrates say:

> Surely you do not suppose that lust provokes men to beget children, when the streets are full of people who will satisfy the appetites, as are the brothels? No, it is clear that we select for wives the women who will bear us the best children, and then we marry them to raise a family.[25]

Several writers, in fact, cautioned their readers against having oversexed wives.[26] This cautionary warning might have resulted from a fear that a sexually demanding wife would curtail the extracurricular activities of her husband or also that she might be more inclined to commit adultery, female adultery being a threat to survival of the family. A sexually demanding wife might also become pregnant too frequently, something the Greeks tried to avoid, since they favored family limitation. Both Plato and Aristotle, for example, favored a stationary population for the Greek city–state. Some population control was exercised by having men marry comparatively late, but there were also various recommended methods for avoiding pregnancy, including douching with urine, inserting oil or lead ointment in the vagina, and coitus interruptus.[27] Abortion and infanticide were also practiced, although generally infanticide by exposure was used only for infants born out of wedlock to slave girls, courtesans, or prostitutes, or through other forms of extralegal sexual intercourse.[28]

In general, however, the Greeks might be labeled a sex-positive culture, few aspects of sex being ritually prohibited. Menstruation was considered a normal bodily function, important in procreation, no required purification ceremony being associated with it.[29] Masturbation was regarded as a natural substitute for men lacking opportunity for sexual intercourse, considerable reference to it appearing in the extant literature.[30] References to female masturbation are fewer, but this is largely due to the literature's being almost entirely written by males. We do know, however, that the Greeks had constructed instruments known as "self satisfiers" to aid females in masturbation and perhaps in intercourse.[31] Premarital and extramarital relations were tolerated for the male and even often encouraged.

As to reproduction, the Greeks believed the male element most important. The semen supplied the form, the female supplying the matter fit for shaping. "If, then, the male stands for the effective and active, and the female, considered as female, for the passive, it follows that what the female would contribute to the semen of the male would not be semen but material for the semen to work upon."[32] This is the view of Aristotle, and as indicated earlier, became the dominant view. Aristotle at least recognized that the female supplied the substance needed for the growth of the embryo, which he identified with the menstrual blood. This is still far short of the views of the water of the Hippocratic work, *On generation,* wherein the doctrine of two seeds was advanced, the female seed identified as vaginal secretion.[33] Unfortunately, Galen, the dominant influence on later generations, adopted the views of Aristotle.[34]

The Greeks emphasized the body, a good body being the necessary correlative of a good soul.[35] The guiding ideal of Greek education was expressed in a word—*kalokagathia*—"being a man both beautiful and good." "Good" signified the moral aspect, having social and worldly implications, and "beautiful" implied physical beauty along with an aura of eroticism. The training of the body became the training of the soul, exemplified in the various pan-Hellenic games and in the surviving remnants of Greek sculpture. Most perfect was the grace of harmonious motion in naked men and youth, and from 720

B.C. onwards, runners and other contestants appeared in the nude. The penis was not regarded as a "shameful" part of the body to be hidden but as something that should arouse awe and pious adoration because it held the power of propagation. Inevitably, the Greeks, at least when ever clothing was felt unnecessary, burdensome, or impossible, went over to complete nakedness. The Greek word *gymnasion* comes from *gymnos* meaning naked or clad in a tunic. The Greeks were, however, contradictory, keeping their gymnasia free from women, even excluding them as spectators from athletic events.[36] Sparta differed in this prohibition from other Greek states, young girls being allowed to do gymnastic exercises, although whether they wore a light covering or went naked is not clear. Later Roman authors assumed the Spartan girls went without clothing. Plutarch, for example, stated that Spartan girls not only exercised in the nude but also did so before the eyes of young men so that young men might be encouraged to marry them.[37]

The phallus itself was a religious symbol having special properties enabling it to break the spell of the evil eye—the evil eye became so enchanted and fascinated by the sight of a phallus that it ignored everything else. Phalli were painted or imitated in plastic art wherever the evil eye was thought to be especially feared. Representations of the penis, sometimes colossal, were found on houses, on gates, in public places, on implements in daily use, on dress and ornaments, and in fact almost everywhere. Special phalli were designed to be carried by a handle, and others were designed with claws and wings. There were also amulets in the form of the female pudenda, but these were much scarcer, undoubtedly because the Greeks ascribed greater power to the man, and his genitals would, therefore, have greater power in averting the evil eye. Instead of representing the actual female pudenda on amulets, it was most often suggested by symbolism, usually in the guise of the fig.[38] The phallus was also used in certain religious ceremonies, such as those of the cult of Dionysus. During the period of the Athenian empire, various colonies were required to send phalli to the great Dionysia at Athens; there is an extant account from Delos of a gigantic phallus prepared for this festival at a cost of 43 drachmas.[39]

The Greek idea of beauty was, of course, masculine rather than feminine. In Greek art, particularly in vase paintings, boys and youths are portrayed far more frequently and with much greater attention to detail than girls are. Even the most erotic of females, such as the legendary Sirens, are portrayed as almost boyish looking in the early paintings. Inscriptions referring to beautiful boys appear on a large number of vases, but those devoted to girls are comparatively rare.[40] Though later in Greek history the female figure is represented somewhat more effectively in art, the woman is usually not nude but draped.

These ideas of male beauty reflected the Greek idea of the most desirable love or sex object. A seventh-century B.C. inscription from the temple of Apollo Carneius on the island of Thera (Sanotrin) in the Aegean reads: "invoking the

Delphic Apollo, I, Crimon, here copulated with a boy, son of Bathycles."[41] Numerous examples of similar inscriptions survive, all following a common formula: "Here X copulated with Y," both names being given in the masculine, one in the nominative and the other in the dative case. A number of vases with the inscription reading "the boy is beautiful" known as "kalós vases" have survived; they were gifts from male lovers to beloved boys. These vases often portray adult males with erect phalli, but the young boys seem to be without phallic attributes.[42]

Contrariwise, homosexual activity is also described at different times in terms that mean "dishonor," "to outrage," "to commit a shameful act," "to carry out infamous conduct," "to be full of impurity," or "to have despicable habits."[43] In Athens homosexual intercourse was strictly regulated by law;[44] in some cases, it was a crime. Boys still at school, for example, were protected against sexual assaults by law.[45] Male prostitution was also disapproved. Adult male citizens who had been male prostitutes or were still prostitutes suffered from some diminution of their civil rights,[46] and procurers of boys for sexual purposes were liable to punishment.[47] Sexual activity between two older men was technically legal but not approved, even if one partner was a noncitizen.[48] In general sexual relations between members of the same sex who were citizens does not appear to have been legal except in Elis. Even in Crete and Sparta, where there was more or less open acceptance of such relations, any violation of an *ephebe* (young man) and any sort of carnal relationship were forbidden and were, theoretically, punishable offenses.[49]

Why the apparent contradiction regarding homosexuality? Some scholars have gone so far as to argue that the Greek talk of boy love was pure idealism with no carnal activity involved. Such a statement ignores, however, the vast evidence pointing to actual sexual relations. Thorkil Vanggaard has argued that the laws, instead of trying to prevent sexual activity, were put on the books because the Greeks attached such great importance to homosexual relations that they wanted to limit the conditions under which people could engage in it. They thus prohibited slaves from having sexual intercourse with free boys; prevented slaves from rubbing boys with oil, a prelude to a pederastic relationship; and in general tried to elevate the relationship by limiting it to free men and to free adolescents.[50] To support his view, he quotes Plutarch's statement that Solon, the great sixth-century lawgiver of Athens, placed pederasty "in the category of what was honorable and worthy, thus in a way prompting the worthy to that which he forbade the unworthy."[51]

The answer seems, however, simpler. The Greeks tolerated (and perhaps encouraged) homosexual relationships as long as they did not threaten the *oikos* ("family"). Thus exclusive homosexuality was discouraged, because it was essential that a man marry and have children. Homosexual prostitution for citizens was discouraged, because this degraded a free man, just as it did a free woman, and threatened the family. Procuring a boy still in school also threatened the family. What kind of homosexuality was permissible? Solon, the lawgiver, poet, and perhaps also a pederast, speaks in some surviving verses about loving a "lad in the flower of youth, bewitched by thighs and by sweet lips."[52] It was just this type of relationship that was acceptable. From the surviving evidence, it seems that the submissive role in a homosexual love affair was tolerated (perhaps encouraged) for a brief period in the young man's life, from the time he had his hair cut (about 16) through his military training and for a brief period thereafter until he was fully accepted as a citizen.[53] Then he was supposed to assume a heterosexual lifestyle, marry, and beget children. Later in life he was supposed to take a young adolescent under his protective custody, and the cycle was repeated.

The Greek word *paiderasty* (anglicized as pederasty) is derived from *pais,* "a boy," and *erastēs,* "a lover," and in its ideal sense denoted the spiritual and sensual affection felt by an adult for a boy who had reached puberty. It is impossible to indicate the number of homosexuals in Greek society or to estimate how many of the homosexual relationships went from idealized affection to actual sex. All we can do is look at the nature of love and speculate how this might have affected homosexuality. Plato in his *Symposium* put the case for homosexual love very effectively:

Thus Love is by various authorities allowed to be of most venerable standing; and as most venerable, he is the cause of all our highest blessings. I for my part am at a loss to say what greater blessing a man can have in earliest youth than an honorable lover, or a lover than an honorable favorite. For the guiding principle we would choose for all our days, if we are minded to live a comely life, cannot be acquired either by kinship of office or wealth or anything so well as by Love. What shall I call this power? The shame that we feel for shameful things, and ambition for what is noble, without which it is impossible for city or person to perform any high and noble deeds. Let me then say that if a man in love should be detected in some shameful act or in a cowardly submission to shameful treatment at another's hands, would not feel half so much distressed at anyone observing it, whether father or comrade or anyone in the world, as when his favorite did; and in the self-same way we see how the beloved is especially ashamed before his lovers when he is observed to be about shameful business. So that if we could somewise contrive to have a city or an army composed of lovers and their favorites (as at Thebes), they could not be better citizens of their country than by thus refraining from all that is base in a mutual rivalry for honor; and such men as these, when fighting side by side, one might almost consider able to make even a little band victorious over all the world. For a man in love would surely choose to have all the rest of his host rather than his favorite see him forsaking his station or flinging away his arms; sooner than this, he would prefer to die many deaths: while, as for leaving his favorite in the lurch, or not succouring him in his peril, no man is such a craven that Love's own influence cannot inspire him with valour that makes him equal to the bravest born, and without doubt what Homer calls a "fury inspired" by a god in certain heroes is the effect produced on Love's peculiar power.[54]

If Plato represents one aspect of Greek thought, it seems that at least certain segments in Greek society found the most characteristic and noble form of love in the passionate friendship between men, or more precisely between the adult male and an adolescent one. The perfect lover for the adult was a male between 15 and 19. Sexual intimacy in itself was not the intent of the ideal, but to claim that sexual relations never resulted is to overlook the historical evidence and man's biological and psychological nature. Both the Jews[55] and the Romans[56] believed that pederastic love and athletic nudity were the distinguishing marks of Hellenism, the life style in which the Greeks contrasted most sharply with non-Greeks.[57]

Why did the Greeks accept homosexuality as natural? Elsewhere in this book it is reported that Plato had one of the participants in his *Symposium* explain that mankind had originally been different and in fact had been composed of individuals with four legs and four arms whom the gods had divided into two people. Some of these double people had, however, been composed of both male and female elements, and after they had been separated, they spent their lives trying to get back together. Thus homosexual as much as heterosexual love was part of nature's plan.[58] Aristotle offered a somewhat more scientific answer:

Why is it that some persons find pleasure in submitting to sexual intercourse, and some take pleasure in performing the active part, and others do not? . . . (if a man) has a superfluity of semen, it all collects there (in the region of the fundament); and so, when desire comes upon him, the part in which it is collected desires friction. This desire may be due to diet or to the imagination, When desire is stirred from any cause, the breath collects and secretion of this kind flows to its natural place. If the secretion be thin and full of air, when the breath finds its way out the desire ceases (just as the erection in boys and other persons sometimes ceases without the discharge of any moisture); and the same thing happens if the moisture dries up. But if neither of these things occurs, the desires continue till the one or the other of them take place. But those who are effeminate by nature are so constituted that little or no semen is secreted where it is secreted by those who are in a natural state, but it collects in this part of the body. The reason of this is that they are unnaturally constituted; for, though male, they are in a condition in which this part of them is necessarily incapacitated. Now incapacity may involve either complete destruction or else perversion; the former, however, is impossible, for it would involve a man becoming a woman. They must therefore become perverted and aim at something other than the discharge of semen. The result is that they suffer from unsatisfied desires, like women; for the moisture is scanty and has not enough force to find its way out and quickly cools. When it finds its way to the fundament only, there is a desire to submit to sexual intercourse; but if it settles both there and in the sexual organs, there is a desire both for performing and submitting to the sexual act, and the desire for one or other is greater as more semen is present in either part. This condition is sometimes the result of habit; for men take a pleasure in whatever they are accustomed to do, and emit the semen accordingly. They therefore desire to do the acts by which pleasure and the emission of semen are produced, and habit becomes more and more a second nature. For this reason those who have been accustomed to submit to sexual intercourse about the age of puberty and not before, because recollection of the past presents itself to them during the act of copulation and with the recollection the idea of pleasure, desire to take a passive part owing to habit, as though it were natural to them to do so; frequent repetition, however, and habit become a second nature. All this is more likely to occur in the case of one who is both lustful and effeminate.[59]

From this rather matter-of-fact explanation, it seems that homosexuality was fairly widespread in Greece at the time of Aristotle and accepted for at least some people as suitable to their nature. Unlike the ancient Middle East, where references to homosexuality appear very early in the history of the people and only later is it described with some hostility, in Greece there is little evidence for the early existence of homosexuality and much for its later appearance. There is, for example, no direct mention of homosexual love in Homer, although there may be hints in Homer's references to Zeus and Ganymede[60] or to Achilles and Patroclus.[61] Either the oral epic originated in an age in which the Greek concept of pederasty had not developed[62] or Homer decided to ignore a well-known institution of his day. Probably the answer is more the former than the latter, although some of the relationships seem to be described more in the language of passion than friendship.[63]

Despite the lack of direct references to homosexuality in Homer, there are numerous references in other accounts of Greek mythology of loves between persons of the same sex, such as Zeus and Ganymede, Heracles and Iolaus (or Hylas), and Apollo and Hyacinth, to claim that it was tolerated, if not institutionalized, fairly early in Greek thought. Jane Harrison, an earlier investigator of Greek religion, complained that the Olympian gods were so detached from their roots in the rich soil of popular religion and everyday magic that they often appear to us as remote, two-dimensional, trivial figures.[64] In spite of the justification of such criticism, this bloodless collection of images still had deep social–psychological significance. This is because the Olympian deities received a partial transfusion from the emotional concerns of the civilized Greeks, who used them as a child uses play-therapy materials–reading their own inner preoccupations into them.

The story of Orpheus, best known for his love of Eurydice, also has symbolic meaning for homosexuality. According to the Latin poet Ovid, a late source (first century B.C.), when Orpheus returned to his Thracian mountain home after his failure to rescue Eurydice from the underworld, he rejected all love of woman, to demonstrate his faithfulness to his wife. He did not, however, remain celibate but instead turned to the love of boys, since these love affairs could not be regarded as lessening his wedded faithfulness. Not only did be become devoted to pederasty, but also his songs glorify boys.[65] Similar themes of homosexual affairs of the Gods appear much earlier, as early as the Greek lyric poets of the late seventh and early sixth centuries B.C.

Some nineteenth-century scholars, intrigued by the increasing references to homosexuality, believed a change in Greek attitudes was brought about by the migration of the Dorians into the Greek peninsula in the eleventh century B.C.[66] Though the Dorians might well have practiced homosexuality, the problem then becomes explaining why the Dorians were any more in favor of homosexuality than the other migrants to the Greek peninsula. The English historian and scholar of homosexuality John Addington Symonds believed that the Dorians were more inclined to homosexuality because they entered Greece in warrior bands, and

> Fighting and foraging in company, sharing the same wayside board and heathstrewn bed, rallying to the comrade's voice in outset, these men learned the meanings of the words *Philētēr* (lover) and *Parastatēs* (comrade). To be loved was honorable, for it implied being worthy to be died for. To love was glorious, since it pledged the lover to self-sacrifice in case of need. In these conditions the paiderastic passion may well have combined manly virtue with carnal appetite, adding such romantic sentiment as some stern men reserve within their hearts for women.[67]

Whether homosexuality was more widespread among the Dorians than among other Greeks is impossible to prove, although the most Dorian states, Crete and Sparta, were obviously tolerant of it. So, however, were the Ionian Athenians, and other Greeks. It might well be that the military society of the early Greeks originally tolerated, if not encouraged, homosexual love,[68] but would the roving bands of Greeks be any more homosexually inclined than the later Celtic, German, or Scandinavian migrants into Europe? It might be that all such bands have homoerotic tendencies. Werner Cohn has argued that in certain groups, such as adolescents, and in certain activities, such as hunting, fishing, or fighting, the social process becomes charismatic rather than stratified. In a charismatic relationship, there is a tendency toward equality, a lack of systematized allocation of privilege or rank, and acceptance of a free-flowing camaraderie resulting in homosexual, though not necessarily erotic, relationships. This relationship is distinguished from those in socially stratified societies, which emphasize hierarchical differences rather than similarities and exert strong control over potential friends and mates of youths regardless of class.[69] But even if this descriptive dichotomy has some value, the question remains how and why adolescent companionship between persons of the same sex became institutionalized into homosexuality as it existed among the Greeks.

Lionel Tiger, in his study of male bonding, deliberately ignored homoerotic behavior, although he felt there might be analytic and practical profit in seeing male homosexuality as a specific feature of the more general phenomenon of male bonding.[70] But the formalized bonding patterns in the Greek world, as exemplified by the men's clubs with fixed articles of association, reached a height after the death of Alexander the Great in the later fourth century, during the Hellenistic monarchies, and long after we have the most evidence for the existence of homosexuality.[71] Perhaps rather than attempt to find such bonding patterns in private clubs, a better solution might be to regard the Greek city itself as a men's club, the whole organization of the city–state encouraging close and intimate relationships between males.[72] Plato in a sense gave some validity to this idea by arguing that the most formidable army in the world would be one composed of lovers, inspiring one another to deeds of heroism and sacrifice.[73] This ideal, if it was an ideal, was perhaps realized in the fourth century in the elite fighting corps at Thebes formed by Gorgidas known as the Sacred Band and consisting of 300 men traditionally grouped as pairs of lovers. The band, admired throughout the Greek world, was responsible for the brief period of military supremacy of Thebes.[74] A similar corps was later formed by the Carthaginians, perhaps in imitation of the Thebans. This homosexual interaction in the military forces may be an important factor in the modern buddy system encouraged in the American army, but little research has been done on the subject.[75]

A somewhat different form of institutionalized personal homosexual relationship was seemingly established by both the Spartans and the classical Cretans, both dominated by the Dorian Greeks. Sparta and Crete were conservative, almost fossilized states where past or primitive attitudes were still likely to be in evidence when history was written. Nonetheless, part of the difficulty in reconstructing the place of homosexuality in these states is that the information we have, particularly about Sparta, seems influenced more by mythology than reality, a mythology encouraged by Athens. As members of the Athenian upper classes became more and more dissatisfied with the developing democracy of Athens in the fifth century B.C., their admiration for conservative Sparta increased. Sparta's reputation grew even stronger in the fourth century, when it defeated the Athenian empire, even though Athens appeared initially to be far stronger. Not until the Thebans defeated the Spartans in 371 did disillusion with Sparta catch up with the mythology, this defeat being soon followed by the breakup of the Spartan system. Even after this defeat there was little questioning of the Spartan system's efficacy but rather a tendency to blame its decline on its degeneracy from the high ideals of its mythical constitution giver Lycurgus. The main source of information about the reforms of Lycurgus is

Plutarch, who wrote in the first century A.D. and whose accuracy is doubtful; his explanation seems to be more philosophical theorizing than genuine research.

In a sense, it is unimportant what the real Sparta was like, for it was the Plutarchian and other propagandistic descriptions of its constitution that most Athenians believed in and that have been preserved. According to Plutarch, in Sparta, as well as in Crete and elsewhere, it was the custom for an adolescent male between 12 and 16 to pair with an honorable man of his own tribe. In such situations the older man was known as *erastēs* ("wooer") during the courtship and *philētōr* ("lover") after the relationship had been publicly recognized. In Sparta the term *eispenēlas* ("inspirer") was also commonly used. The boy was called *erōmenos* ("beloved") or more commonly in Sparta *aïtas* ("hearer" or "listener"). Man and boy were to stay together, sometimes even sharing a bed, but sexual play was officially forbidden.[76] The original purpose of the adult companion was to teach the boy by precept and example how to behave and how to cope with various situations. The Spartans regarded these unions as conjugal,[77] the man being held responsible to his tribe for the conduct of his youthful charge until the boy had gone beyond the age at which such unions were usually ended, that is, when beard and body hair developed. Plutarch stated that the Spartans punished the older lover of a boy if the boy screamed from pain in the battle.[78] Aelian claimed that the *ephors*, the executive council of Sparta, also punished boys who refused to find an adult protector.[79]

The geographer Strabo (64 B.C.–21 A.D.) embroiders the account of such relationships in his description of Crete, writing that each young man was the victim of a veritable abduction by his older patron, although it was carried out with the connivance of those around him. The abducted boy was introduced into the men's club by his abductor, and then he and his friend left for a 2 months' holiday in the country, celebrating their union with banquets and hunting. When this "honeymoon" ended, the young man returned and was solemnly feted. His patron lover gave him a suit of armor and other gifts, and the boy became the shield bearer for his adult sponsor, learning from him what the noble life entailed before being accepted as an adult and taking the place of honor in the choirs and gymnasia. Strabo emphasized the high social rank required of both participants, claiming the purpose was to bring about "valor and good education."[80]

This ritual may have represented an initiation and integration into the male community, and the sex acts that might or might not have taken place may have served as a way of transmitting warlike virtue from one generation to another generation of males in a rather brutal, material way.[81] Whether this was so is disputable, but there is a strong correlation of the ceremony with that of marriage. According to Plutarch, in Sparta a girl was carried off by her would-be husband, and then the bride, disguised as a boy by having her hair cut off by her bridesmaids and wearing men's clothes, was left alone to be secretly visited by her husband after he had dined at the mess with his male comrades. After penetrating the bride, the bridegroom returned to his barracks to spend the night. In fact, the married couple were able to snatch only brief interludes of intimacy together until the bridegroom was 30 years old.[82] Marriage for the Spartans was, however, compulsory, and persistent bachelors were punished by the loss of their citizenship rights.[83] Similar descriptions of the marriage ceremony survive from Gortyn, on Crete, the town Plato believed to be the Cretan community with the highest reputation.[84]

Within the military system, pederasty was linked with valor and courage and said to be justified by the gods.[85] The older man was expected always to make an effort to stand out in the eyes of his beloved, and the younger man likewise was to show himself worthy of his lover by emulating his example.[86] It was perhaps inevitable that there would be rivalry for the love of a desirable boy, Greek history recording a number of crimes involving such competition. Heroic deeds were, moreover, performed in the name of love. Several tyrants were assassinated and several revolts were said to have been fomented as a result of unhappy love affairs. Plutarch, in explaining why so many lovers took issue with the tyrants over beautiful, well-born youths, stated that:

> they had at first no quarrel with their tyrants, though they say that these were acting like drunkards and disfiguring the state, but when tyrants tried to seduce their beloved, they spared not even their own lives in defending their loves, holy, as it were, and inviolable shrines.[87]

To document this, at least one dedicated researcher has compiled a list of cases where pederastic love led to attempts to take the lives of tyrants, some of them successful.[88] As a result an institution that might once have had military value became associated with the cause of freedom, and the deeds of famous lovers were admired and set before the young for their respect and imitation.

Adding to the acceptance of homosexuality was the institutionalization of pederasty within the educational system. According to Plato, the purpose of homosexual love was to "educate."[89] The Greek educational system was a closed masculine society excluding women. In fact, they were excluded not only physically but also ideologically, for the purpose of education was to inculcate manliness, the characteristics most associated with the masculine sex. To Socrates, for example, love represented an aspiration toward a higher perfection, an ideal of excellence, and he was most concerned with inculcating certain values into the young male by having him emulate a suitable adult. Education, after the primary grades, implied an intimate relationship, a personal union between a young man and an elder who was at once his model, guide, and initiator—a relationship on which the fire of passion smoldered and burned. The admiration of the younger partner for the older and the need and desire of the older to gain the admiration and affection of the younger were believed to be the stimulus for the best type of education, since it aroused ardent and active involvement. Thus the object of love, in Plato's terms, was to procreate and beget the sphere of the "beautiful."[90] Idealized love was distinguished from sensual desire, the opposite of true love. Moreover, the Greeks showed little toleration for adults who took the passive role in any homoerotic relationship. Still, the love relationship entailed the teaching of the young, an attitude of docility and veneration by the young being encouraged.

The relationship between the adult and the adolescent boy was maintained by daily association, personal contact and example, intimate conversations, a sharing in more or less common life, and the gradual initiation of the younger into the social activities of the older men—the club, the gymnasium, and the banquet. In this education, the family was more or less ignored. The mother was in the background; her duty was to look after the babies and supervise the training of girls, but at age 7, boys were removed from her hand. The father, at least those belonging to the aristocracy, the group on which most of our information is based, was a citizen and a man of politics. Fathers paid little attention to their own male children but instead left their upbringing to an adult male whose relationship as lover of the son was a "union far closer" than what bound parents to children.[91] Public opinion, and in some cases even the law, held the lover morally responsible for the development of his beloved. Pederasty came to be considered the most beautiful, the most perfect form of education.[92]

It was best when the tutor could choose his own pupil. This attitude helps explain why the Greeks, as well as other peoples of antiquity, tended to look down on the teacher who made a business of teaching, offering his learning to any customer who came along. Rather, the communication of knowledge was to be reserved for those worthy of receiving it. This was the ideal, and as an ideal, carnal relations held no part. The object was to bring the young man along until he could attain the same civic and personal virtue as the teacher; it was not hostile to marriage but supplemented it.

Reality often differed from the ideal, but the boy who gave himself up for money or any other kind of payment was the object of reproach. The playwright Aristophanes reported that poets were never weary of recalling the good old times when a boy, as a reward for favors, was satisfied with a little bird, or even a ball to play with, or such similar trifles,[93] and he implied that this was no longer the case. Sometimes it is difficult to tell whether there were actual carnal relationships between the teachers and the students, but Greek literature is full of tales of homoerotic passion. Socrates stands preeminent in this respect, but he is not an isolated example. Plato was the lover of Alexis of Dion, and for three generations the position of head of the academy he founded passed from lover to beloved. Such relationships were not confined to the followers of Plato. Aristotle was the lover of his pupil Hermias, whom he immortalized in a hymn. The same relationship is found between poets, artists, and scholars: Euripides, the playwright, was the lover of the tragic poet Agathon; the sculptor Phidias, the lover of his pupil Agoracritus of Pharos; the physician Theomedon, the lover of the astronomer Eudoxus of Cnidus.[94]

Such love could be much more than friendly admiration, as is evident from the following dialogue of the second-century A.D. satirist Lucian:

Drosis.	In any case, I'm dying of love. But Dromo said that Aristaenetus is the sort who's fond of boys, and by pretending to teach them, keeps company with the handsomest youths, and has now got Cleinias on his own, and spins him tales, promising of all things that he will make him like a god. Besides that, he is reading with him amorous discourses addressed by the old philosophers to their pupils, and is all wrapped up in the lad. Dromo threatened he'd tell Cleinias' father as well.
Chelidonoion.	You ought to have greased his palm properly!
Drosis.	I have done that, but he is mine without that, for he is violently in love with that man of mine, Nebris.
Chelidonoion.	If that is so, be of good courage, Everything will turn out as you wish. I think I will also write on the wall of the Cermaicus [a special meeting place of lovers of boys] where his father is in the habit of walking, in large letters: "Aristaenetus is corrupting Cleinias," so that I may support Dromo's accusation.
Drosis.	But how will you write that without anyone seeing you?
Chelidonoion.	By night, Drosis, with a lump of charcoal.
Drosis.	Good luck to you. If you help me to fight, I still hope to get the better of that windbag Aristaenetus.[95]

In lyric poetry, the most direct expression we have of the personal state of mind and feeling of the ancient Greeks, homosexual love occupied a major place. Unfortunately, only small fragments of the lyric poets have survived. Among the earliest are some fragments of Theognis of Megara, who lived and wrote in the sixth century B.C. Some 158 lines of the surviving fragments are devoted to the poet's favorite, Cyrnus, and though some have argued that these lines are apocryphal or derive from a later data, there is no questioning that his elegies included not only fatherly advice to his young friend but also the plaintive laments of a lover for him.[96] Pindar, regarded as the greatest of all Greek lyric poets, recounts his love in his Ode to Zenkorates; tradition has it that he died in the arms of his lover Theoxenus, whom the gods have given him as the most beautiful thing in the world.[97] Of the 30 idylls preserved under the name of Theocritus, who lived about 310–245 B.C., no fewer than 8 are exclusively devoted to the love of youths, and there are many others.[98] One chief source is the so-called *Palatine Anthology,* poems of some 320 different authors collected in the tenth century A.D. by Constantinus Cephalās. Constantine's anthology contained poems from as early as the seventh century B.C. up to his own time. The twelfth book of the anthology, almost exclusively devoted to the love of youths, includes 258 epigrams, that is, short elegiac poems, for a total of 1300 lines. The poems in this section were attributed by Constantine to Straton, a second-century A.D. writer, but in addition there are numerous other poems devoted to homosexual love.[99]

It seems logical that if males in Greek societies formed a close, autonomous fellowship, then women must of necessity have been confined to activities with others of their own sex. Women were, however, far more restricted than men, being confined to the women's quarters of the house, with little opportunity to meet and visit with women not of their own family. Thus, though the Greeks, in theory, should have been as tolerant of female homosexuality as they were of the male variety, we have far less information about the existence of such relationships. One of the few examples we have is Sappho of Lesbos (about the sixth century B.C.). Only fragments of her work survive, and little is known about her, except that she was the head of a school for girls in Mytilene in Lesbos. The school was dedicated to Aphrodite and the Muses, and the education probably took the form of a religious fellowship, wherein, under the direction of a mistress, young girls were fashioned to conform to an ideal of feminine beauty and wisdom. The pupils were taught dancing, the playing of musical instruments, and singing. From the surviving references, the school seems to have concentrated on the passive and subordinate aspects of womanhood rather than encourage feminine independence. Charm and coquetry seem to have played a major part in the curriculum; among the surviving sayings are one warning girls not to act proud when they were looking for a husband and one condemning a woman who did not even know how "to lift her skirt to show her ankles."[100]

Several of the surviving fragments of Sappho's poems imply feeling and intimacy with other women, Sappho having often been identified as a homosexual. Her birthplace at Mytilene in Lesbos has led to female homosexuals' being called lesbians, and at various times in history the term *sapphic* or *sapphist* has also been applied to women erotically attached to other women. In spite of this popular assumption, even in ancient times there were doubts about whether Sappho's love implied carnal activity, and there still remains a group of scholars who maintain she was a woman of absolute virtue.[101] Some have even gone so far as to claim there were two Sapphos, to account for the contradictions in her life, including her suicide (recorded by Ovid) over her rejection by her handsome young (male) lover.[102] The only way for the modern reader to arrive at the true Sappho is through the fragmentary remains of her poems, where, in spite of marriage and motherhood, opportunities for a second husband, and a number of conventional verses, her love ideal is female.[103] In addition to Sappho, the names of two other principals of female schools are known, Andromeda and Gorge, but the Greeks never held woman's education to be important, except where it led to moral poise, better hygiene, and a knowledge of the domestic arts.[104]

In Greek literature, the terms used to refer to female homosexuality include *tribad*, meaning "to rub," *hetairistria* and *dihestairistria*. Both of the latter terms are derived from *hetaira*, referring to prostitutes. The Greek writer Lucian, in his *Dialogues of Courtesans*, implied an association of lesbianism with prostitution, and in his account of Megille, he included a discussion of female homosexuality.[105] Plutarch also observed that female homosexuality was frequent, at least in Sparta,[106] but there are only occasional literary references, perhaps because there are almost no women writers from the Greek period. The male writers generally ignored the subject, as they did most of women's activities. Licht, in his study of Greek sexual mores, often equated female homosexuality with masturbation or use of artificial phalluses, but neither of these activities is particularly homosexual.[107] Female homosexuality probably existed in Greece, but like the Greek women themselves, was rarely mentioned. It was permitted, provided it did not threaten the *oikos*.

As the legal evidence already cited shows, homosexual prostitution existed in Greece, as did heterosexual, although there were more attempts to circumscribe it. Solon is reported to have said that homosexual prostitution was to be feared, because anyone who sold his body for money would also sacrifice the common interests of the state without giving much thought to what he was doing.[108] No matter how much the Greeks might have approved of a relationship between a man and a youth that rested on mutual liking, they rejected it if the boy sold himself for money. Aristophanes has a line in one of his plays about boys doing such things, "not for their lovers, but for money's sake. Not the better sort, but the sodomites; for the better sort do not ask for money."[109] Another writer complained:

> Woe is me! Why in tears again and so woe-begone, my lad? Tell me plainly; don't give me pain; what do you want? You hold out the hollow of your hand to me. I am done for! You are begging perhaps for payment; and where did you learn that? You no longer love slices of seed-cake and sweet sesame and nuts to play at shots with, but already your mind is set on gain. May he who taught you perish! What a boy of mine he has spoilt![110]

We know that sexual partners not only were bought for money for an occasional act of intercourse but also could be hired for longer periods by contract. In Athens, and probably in other major towns, there were houses in which boys and youths were to be had along with girls for money.[111] Many inmates of

such houses had been prisoners of war who had been sold into slavery. Phaedo
of Elis, with whom Socrates held his famous final dialogue before being executed, had been captured in the war between Elis and Sparta and then sold to a
possessor of a "public" house in Athens. It was there Socrates had made his acquaintance and then induced one of his well-to-do disciples to purchase Phaedo
as a gift for him.[112] Free youths might also have spent some time in such
houses, although this was condemned.[113] Both male and female prostitutes not
only could be visited in the public houses but also could be taken by their patrons to their homes.[114]

Cross-dressing was known to the Greeks, playing a part both in the real and
in the mythological world of the gods. In the real world, most of the reported
cases of cross-dressing involved males impersonating females, and in the
mythological world it often involved a change of sex and was more from female
to male, unlike more recent cases of actual sex change, which have been more
male to female.[115] It might be that the few cases of recorded sex changes in the
ancient world, probably pseudohermaphrodites, were from female to male and
also that, since the males were a much higher status sex, masculine writers
would regard it as unthinkable that any male would want to be a female, except for a masquerade.

The term *hermaphroditism* is an amalgam of the names of the god Hermes
and Aphrodite; Hermaphrodite was an offspring of a love affair of the gods and
represented both the male and female elements. Another offspring of Aphrodite, this time with Dionysus, yielded Priapus, an ugly child with enormous
genitals. In spite of these mythological accounts of sexual abnormalities, the
ancients were usually fearful of any abnormal formation of the generative
organs. Hermaphrodites, as well as other grossly abnormal infants, were
usually destroyed at birth. Still, a few cases probably managed to pass the birth
inspection and were more likely to be reared as female than male, because girl
children were reared under more sheltered conditions and it was easier to pass
off a doubtful child as a girl than a boy, fewer demands being put on girls.
Thus the sex changes might understandably be from female to male.

In Greek mythology the most famous case of sex change is the soothsayer Tiresias, born a boy, changed into a woman, and then back into a man. According to one version, Tiresias witnessed two serpents in the act of coupling,
whereupon both snakes attacked him. When he killed the female snake by hitting it with his staff, he was immediately turned into a woman and later became a celebrated harlot. This, in a sense, parallels the case of so many male-
to-female transsexuals of today, who, in an effort to prove their new-found female sexuality, often go through a period of promiscuity. After some 7 years as
a woman, Tiresias happened to be passing the same spot where she had seen
the snakes coupling and once again saw the same thing. When the snakes attacked her this time, she killed the male snake and thus was restored to

manhood. Once Tiresias had regained his manhood, he became involved as an umpire in a dispute between Hera and Zeus. Hera had reproached Zeus for his numerous infidelities. Zeus, while admitting them, defended himself by saying that it did not matter, because women enjoyed sex so much more than men. Hera, in denying this, turned to Tiresias to settle the heated dispute with her husband. From his experience as a member of both sexes he replied:

> *If the parts of love pleasure be counted as ten,*
> *Thrice three go to women, one only to men.*

Hera was so exasperated by the decision that she blinded Tiresias, but Zeus compensated him with inward sight and a life extended to seven generations.[116]

The story of Leucippus has both transvestite and transsexual variations. In the transsexual version, Lampros, a citizen of Phaestos, told his pregnant wife Galatea that he would not rear a child unless it was a boy. A girl was born, but Galatea, unwilling to expose her, dressed the baby as a boy, giving it the masculine name of Leucippus. When the child's sex could no longer be easily concealed, Galatea sought the goddess Leto to change its sex. The goddess granted the wish. This event was commemorated by a feast called *ekdysia,* the divestment, a term later adopted to describe a striptease artist. It became the custom for the bride, before her nuptials took place, to sleep beside an image of Leucippe, the feminine form of Leucippus.[117]

It was apparently widely believed by the Greeks that, if women had had their choice, they would have been born men. One piece of evidence for this is the story of Caenis, daughter of the king of Lapithae. Poseidon, in return for sexual favors from Caenis, promised to fulfill any wish she might make. Caenis requested that she become a man invulnerable to wounds.[118]

It seems that women were more likely to suffer from their transvestite experiences than males, perhaps as punishment for daring to be as strong as the male. Procris, according to legend, had been rejected by her husband Cephalus, supposedly because she had been untrue to him, although in reality her lover had been her husband in disguise. In disgrace she fled to Crete, where she met Diana, goddess of the hunt, who, touched by the misfortunes of Procris, gave her a javelin that always found its target and a dog from which no wild beast could escape. Then, disguised as a boy, she returned to the mainland, where she challenged and surpassed her husband. Cephalus tried to purchase the dog and javelin, but Procris refused, even after he had promised her–him a share of his kingdom. Finally, after much pleading, Procris agreed, if Cephalus would do to her that which "boys are wont to grant." Cephalus, eager to please, took the "young boy" to his bedchamber, whereupon Procris took off her tunic and revealed herself as a woman and his wife.[119] The story did not end happily, however, since Procris was later accidentally killed by her husband.

The Greeks were also intrigued by the customs of people they encountered, although it is not always clear whether the customs they reported were as others saw them. Herodotus, reported that among the Scythians were people known as *Enarëes,* who dressed as females and had the gift of divination, of fortelling the future.[120] He explained that these men were descendants of those who had been cursed with the "feminine disease" by Aphrodite for pillaging her temple at Ascalon in Palestine.[121] One of the contributors to the Hippocratic corpus called such individuals *Anarieīs,* claiming they were honored by the Scythians because they were believed to have elements of divinity. The writer reported that these men were impotent, did woman's work, and spoke like women, but nonetheless other men prostrated themselves before them for fear the gods might similarly punish them. The Hippocratic writer rejected the supernatural explanation of Herodotus, claiming the condition was due to the Scythians always being on horseback. This caused many men to become temporarily impotent, and if the impotency continued, the men believed they had committed a sin against the gods; to expiate it they put on women's clothing and devoted themselves to feminine occupations. He also reported that the illness usually attacked only the most powerful and richest men, who then became powerful shamans.[122] Aristotle described the disease as hereditary among the Scythian kings,[123] and both writers emphasize that the *Enarëes* were respected as well as feared.

Transvestite shamans were not recorded in classical Greece, but wearing the clothes of the opposite sex often assumed magical connotations, particularly in marriage ceremonies. In Sparta, for example, it was the custom for the young bride's head to be shaved by the woman in charge of her, who then dressed her in male clothing. The bride then lay on the bed alone until her husband came secretly to her.[124] She was not to resume her place among the women until she was pregnant. At Argos, the bride wore a false beard on the wedding night,[125] and in Cos the husband put on the dress of a woman to receive his new bride.[126]

Cross-dressing was deemed a loss of status for men in many cases. Plutarch reported that the Lycians wore women's clothing while in mourning, to remind them to cut short the kind of lamentations in which women alone should indulge.[127] This threatened loss of status could be tolerated if the aim was laudable, such as courting a girl who might otherwise have been unattainable, or if the alternatives to the impersonation were considered more socially undesirable than the disguise itself. There are several illustrations for each of these suppositions. Hymenaeus, a youth from Argive, disguised himself as a girl to follow the young Athenian maid he loved, and during his disguise, when both he and his beloved were captured by pirates, he was able to assert his "superior" masculine strength and save her.[128] Leucippus, the transsexual already mentioned, fell in love with fair Daphne, who hated men and wanted to be a virgin. Only by disguising himself as a girl was he able to gain her confidence, although when he was discovered he was killed.[129] There are other variants of this story.[130] Disguise was also permissible if it permitted one to capture or defeat an enemy. Solon defeated the Megarians by disguising part of his troops as women and infiltrating the city.[131] Transvestism was also justified on the stage, where males played the female roles, because the alternative would have been to have women portray themselves, to exhibit themselves in public, something that no decent woman would do.

Each year in Sparta men dressed as women marched in a procession to Mount Taygetos. Herodotus explained the custom derived from an incident in the history of Sparta when the Minyae, the descendants begotten by the fabled Argonauts and the women of Lemnos whom they had visited, settled near Sparta. The Spartans, angered over what they felt was the growing insolence of Minyae, seized the men, imprisoning them in Sparta to await execution. While their husbands were awaiting execution at sundown, their womenfolk were allowed to visit them, and they exchanged clothes with their husbands, who walked away as women, leaving their wives behind in prison. When the Spartans discovered what had happened, they allowed the women to go free as a reward for their bravery and ingenuity.[132] Supposedly, it was this incident that was commemorated by a procession to Mount Taygetos, the place where the Minyae had presumably taken refuge. Others have argued that this romantic story was nothing more than a pseudohistorical explanation for a past initiation ceremony involving cross-dressing that had lost its meaning and forced the Spartans to invent another story.[133]

But if this is the case, why would an initiation ceremony involve the changing of clothes? One investigator has claimed:

> The symbolism of initiation corresponds to the sense of an essential opposition between the male essence, personified in the community of young men, and the female element. So it is not uncommon for novices, at the beginning of the initiation rites, to put on clothing resembling that worn by women, and for the culmination of the ceremonies to be the donning of the masculine garb.[134]

Or similarly:

> The practice of disguise and of exchange of clothing from one sex to the other expresses a symbolism inspired by the same preoccupation. The feminine principle in the candidate is affirmed in the initiation at the very moment when he is about to cast it aside.[135]

It is also possible that clothing was exchanged in such ceremonies to deceive the malignant powers, the evil eye, whose hostility was to be particularly feared at such critical times.[136]

Cross-dressing was often a part of the various festivals associated with the god Dionysus. The prevalence of transvestite episodes has been explained as based on a legend that Dionysus had been reared as a girl by King Atham (or Orhoemnus) and his Queen Ino.[137] He was also reported to have impersonated a girl at various stages of his career, including an appearance to the three daughters of Minya, who refused to acknowledge him.[138] In Egypt at the beginning of the fourth century B.C. men arrayed themselves as women in the Dionysian procession, and this apparently continued down to the first century.[139] Other gods and goddesses also encouraged cross-dressing. At the feast devoted to Hera at Samos, men donned long white robes sweeping the ground, their hair encased in golden nets, and adorned with feminine bracelets and necklaces.[140] In the month of Hermaios, the Argives celebrated this *Hybristika festival* by having women dress as men and men as women. In Plutarch's time it was said that this custom commemorated the heroism of the poetess Telesilla, who at the beginning of the fifth century B.C. had put herself at the head of an army of women to defend Argos against Cleomenes, king of Sparta, who was laying seige to it.[141] This again is a pseudohistorical explanation probably invented after the real meaning was lost. In fact, the very name of the feast suggests a carnival rather than a patriotic ceremony

In Amathus on the island of Cyprus, where a male–female divinity was worshipped, as part of the ceremonies each year a young boy pretended to lie in childbed and imitated the pains of labor. The god, called Aphroditos, had a female body shape and clothing but a beard and penis. At sacrifices men wore female clothing and women wore male clothing.[142]

The ubiquity of such festivals might well indicate that the Greeks, who drew such strict barriers between the sex roles and assigned such a confined role as a model for women, needed periods in which the barriers were removed. Some of the ancients themselves recognized some such need. A good example is Philostratus, who, describing the rituals involved in such festivals, said that the image or the person impersonating the god was accompanied by a numerous train in which girls mingled with men because the festival allowed "women to act the part of men, and men to put on women's clothing and play the woman."[143] The ubiquity of such festivals is indicated by a chance remark of Artemidorus in his *Interpretation of Dreams*. He held that, whereas the best omen in a dream was for a person to see himself dressed in his usual clothes, it was not harmful for a man to be seen in a varicolored garment or a woman's garment, provided the dream seemed to take place during a feast or festival.[144] Another indication of the widespread nature of such cross-dressing is the survival of at least 15 vases depicting bearded figures in women's clothing, all seemingly bent on pleasure. Some of the individuals appear to be men in women's clothes, and others are women wearing false beards.[145]

Several legendary heroes also had a transvestite episode in their career. Achilles, a hero of the Trojan War, was believed by the later Greeks to have

lived part of his life as a girl. This was because his mother Thetis, worrying
that he might be killed in the expedition against Troy, sent him to Lycomedus
in Scyros, where, disguised as a girl, he went into hiding. The Greeks, anxious
to have Achilles fight for them, sent out various individuals to trace him.
Odysseus finally tracked him to Scyros but was unable to distinguish him from
the other girls until he hit on a strategem for exposing him. Disguised as a
merchant, Odysseus was allowed entrance to the women's quarters, where he
placed a pile of gifts including jewels, girdles, embroidered dresses, a shield,
and a sword for the girls to examine. When one of them took the shield and
sword, Odysseus knew he had found his man.[146]

Heracles (Hercules in Latin) is another hero who donned feminine garb, in
this case as a sign of humiliation and degradation. He dressed himself in the
clothing of Queen Omphale. Though her girdle was much too small for his
waist, his shoulders split the sleeves of her gown, and the ties of her sandals
were too short to cross his instep, the god Pan tried to seduce him, whereupon
Heracles kicked him across the room. Thereafter Pan was so suspicious of
clothing that he would have nothing to do with clothes.[147] As with Achilles
there are numerous versions of Heracles as a transvestite, some picturing him
surrounded by girls, spinning wool, and being scolded when his fingers crushed
the spindle.

Theseus also, according to tradition, passed as a woman when he first arrived in Athens. In fact, he appeared so effeminate that, when he passed the
temple of Apollo, a group of workers, mistaking him for a girl, demanded to
know why he was allowed to go about unescorted. Theseus did not bother to
reply but instead, after unyoking the oxen from a nearby cart, tossed one of
them up in the air[148] and then proceeded on his way. Is there any significance
in these stories beyond simple cross-dressing? One authority has claimed that,
since Achilles, Heracles, and Theseus were the three males most successful in
dealing with the Amazons, these legendary women who acted as men, the point
of the stories might be to emphasize that only a man who is able to pass as a
women can deal with a woman who carries the weapons of a man.[149] This
seems rather farfetched. Rather, it is possible that the Greeks, recognizing that
within each man there are some feminine elements, just as there are masculine
ones within each woman, chose to stress this dual nature of men through their
strongest and greatest heroes. It was perhaps this same factor that encouraged
the worship of the bisexual Aphroditos on Cyprus. Several other deities in
ancient times seem to have also hesitated between the two sexes, including
Pales, Pomo–Pomona, and Tellumon–Tellurus–Tellus, but why they did so is
still not clear.[150] It was to the legend of the Cyprian Aphrodite, Venus castina
in Latin, that C. J. Bulliet dedicated his history of transvestism.[151]

The necessity for a man to recognize his femininity appears in the character
of Agathon in Aristophanes' *Thesmophoriazusae,* who is portrayed as dressing

in women's clothes. When questioned, Agathon stated:

> *I chose my dress to suit my poesy*
> *A poet, sir, must needs adapt his ways*
> *To the high thoughts which animate his soul.*
> *And when he sings of women, he assumes*
> *A woman's garb, and dons a woman's habit.*[152]

Aristophanes also has some fun with his transvestite comedy *Ecclesiazusae,* in which women dress as men to attend all male meetings of the Athenian assembly, where they wrest control of the state by outvoting the men.[153]

Masochism and sadism were part of some of the religious ceremonies, and self-mutilation occasionally took place.[154] Bestiality is seldom mentioned in Greek classical writing but does occur in some of the fables and romances. Zeus approached Leda as a swan, Persephone as a snake. Pasiphaë fell in love with a bull and had intercourse with it; the fruit of this union was the legendary Minotaur, half man, half ox.[155]

In summary, the Greeks accepted and cultivated the human body, deemed sex a source of pleasure, had a double standard, and tolerated most sexual activity, as long as it did not threaten the survival of the family. They had rigidly circumscribed roles, but occasional crossing of roles was permitted in religious festivals and on other occasions through cross-dressing. The theater also allowed some males to impersonate women for longer periods. Homosexuality was widespread and accepted. The Greek military ideal had early emphasized the importance of close male friendships, these having been further encouraged by the low status of women in society. This had also thrown women more upon their own resources for companionship. The Greek educational system institutionalized these homosexual relations, and though the pederastic relationship was in theory Platonic, ideal and reality were often quite different, as the Greeks themselves recognized. Many of the heroic models for the Greeks tended to have had homosexual experiences, and these justified actual homosexual practices. At any rate, pedophilia came to be associated with the Greeks, and part of the Hebrew and the later Christian attitudes can be interpreted as a reaction to Greek attitudes toward homosexuality. There was, however, still another trend in Greek thought, the ascetic, asexual trend, which the later Christians emphasized, and this will be discussed in a later chapter.

NOTES

1. A very early study of Greek sex life was that by M. H. E. Meier in the 3rd sec., Vol. 9 of *Encyclopädie der Wissenschaften und Künsten,* J. S. Ersch and J. G. Gruber, eds. (Leipzig: Brockhaus, 1837), pp. 149–188. I have not seen the original, but it was translated into French and

amplified with a number of literary and historical passages as well as footnotes by L. R. de Pogey-Castries under the title of *Histoire de l'amour Grec dans l'antiquité* (Paris: Guy le Prat, 1952). The work is cited in this chapter as Pogey-Castries. Another study was that of Hans Licht, *Sexual Life in Ancient Greece* (London: Routledge and Kegan Paul, 1932). Licht was a pseudonym for Paul Brandt, and the English edition is a kind of bowdlerized translation of Brandt's *Sittengeschichte Griechenlands*. Other studies of importance include W. K. Lacey, *The Family in Classical Greece* (London: Thames and Hudson, 1968); J. A. Symonds, *A Problem in Greek Ethics* (privately printed, 1901); Rudolf Beyer, *Fabulae Graecae quatenus quave aetate puerorum amore commutatae sint* (Ph.D. dissertation, University of Leipzig, 1910); Philip E. Slater, *The Glory of Hera: Greek Mythology and Greek Family* (Boston: Beacon Press, 1968); Robert Flacelliere, *Love in Ancient Greece,* translated by James Cleugh (New York: Crown Publishers, 1962); J. Z. Eglinton, *Greek Love* (New York: Oliver Layton Press, 1964). This last book, which deals with pedophilia, has only one chapter on Greece.

2. John Jay Chapman, *Lucian, Plato, and Greek Morals* (Boston: Houghton Mifflin, 1931), p. 120.

3. *Ibid.*

4. Lacey, *op. cit.,* pp. 24–25, 151–176.

5. Lysias, *Orationes,* III, 6, translated by W. R. M. Lamb (London: William Heinemann, 1957), III, 6.

6. Xenophon, *Oeconomicus,* VII, 5–6, translated by E. C. Marchant (London: William Heinemann, 1953).

7. Isaeus, *Speeches,* III, 13–14, William Wyse, ed. (Hildesheim Germany: George Olms, 1967); and Lysias, I, 22.

8. Aristotle, *Nichomachean Ethics,* VIII, 10, 4–12, 8 (1160B–1162A), translated by H. Rackham (London: William Heinemann, 1934).

9. Aristotle, *Politics,* I, 1, 306 (1252A–B), translated by H. Rackham (London: William Heinemann, 1944).

10. Aristotle, *Politics,* I, 2, 1 (1253B).

11. Lacey, *op. cit.,* pp. 24–25.

12. Philip E. Slater, *op. cit.,* p. 8.

13. H. I. Marrou, *A History of Education in Antiquity,* translated by George Lamb (New York: Sheed and Ward, 1956), p. 142.

14. Sigmund Freud, "The Taboo of Virginity," in *Collected Papers,* translated by Joan Riviere (reprinted, New York: Basic Books, 1959, 5 vols.), Vol. 4, p. 226; and "Some Physical Consequences of the Anatomical Distinction between the Sexes," *op. cit.,* Vol. 5, pp. 186–197.

15. Karen Horney, "The Dream of Woman," *International Journal of Psychoanalysis,* XIII (1932), pp. 348–360.

16. Slater, *op. cit.,* p. 12.

17. Vern L. Bullough, *The Subordinate Sex* (Urbana, Ill.: University of Illinois, 1973), pp. 6–11.

18. Slater, *op. cit.,* pp. 724–774.

19. Aristotle, *Magna moralia,* I, ii–iv (1183B–1185B), translated by G. Cyril Armstrong (London: William Heinemann, 1962).

20. Edith Hamilton, *The Greek Way* (New York: W. W. Norton, 1942), p. 31.

21. *Iliad,* XIV, 153–361, translated by A. T. Murray (London: William Heinemann, 1960, 2 vols.).

22.   Licht, *op. cit.*, p. 8, gave this appellation to parts of the 14th book.

23.   See, for example, *ibid.*, pp. 9–17.

24.   Demosthenes, *Against Neaera,* translated by A. T. Murray, ed. (London: William Heinemann, 1939–1958).

25.   Xenophon, *Memorabilia,* II, 2,4, translated by E. C. Marchant (London: William Heinemann, 1953).

26.   See, for example, Xenophon, in the reference cited above, and Aristotle, *Historia animalium,* VII, 1 (581B), translated by D'Arcy Wentworth Thompson (Oxford, England: Clarendon Press, 1962); and Aristotle, *Politics,* VII, xiv, 5 (1335A).

27.   Norman E. Himes, *Medical History of Contraception* (reprinted, New York: Schocken Books, 1970), pp. 79–82.

28.   Licht, *op. cit.*, pp. 314 ff.

29.   Flacelliere, *op. cit.*, p. 118.

30.   Licht, *op. cit.*, p. 314, has the references.

31.   *Ibid.*, pp. 314–315.

32.   Aristotle, *Generation of Animals,* 729A, 25–34, translated by A. L. Peck (London: William Heinemann, 1953).

33.   T. U. H. Ellinger, *Hippocrates on Intercourse and Pregnancy* (New York: Abelard-Schuman, 1953); Joseph Needham, *A History of Embryology,* 2nd ed., (revised, New York: Abelard-Schuman, 1959), pp. 31–37.

34.   Needham, *op. cit.*, pp. 69–74.

35.   G. Lowes Dickinson, *The Greek View of Life* (New York: Doubleday, Page and Company, 1918), pp. 137–142.

36.   At least this is implied by Pausanias, *Description of Greece,* VI, xx, 9, translated by W. H. S. Jones (London: William Heinemann, 1959). See also Licht, *op. cit.*, pp. 93–94.

37.   Plutarch, *Lycurgus* XV, 1, in *Plutarch's Lives,* translated by Bernadotte Perrin (London: William Heinemann, 1959).

38.   Licht, *op. cit.*, pp. 369–370.

39.   *Ibid.*, p. 122. See also *Corpus inscriptionum Graecarum,* Augusta Boeckh, ed. (Berlin: ex officina academica 1815–1877), II, p. 321.

40.   Licht, *op. cit.*, p. 427; Lacey, *op. cit.*, p. 157: and Kenneth Clarke, *The Nude,* Bollingen Series, 35, 2 (Princeton, N.J.: Princeton University Press, 1956).

41.   Johann Friedrich Hiller von Gärtringen, *Thera* (Berlin: G. Reimer, 1895–1902), Vol. 3, pp. 67 ff., and *Inscriptiones Graecae* (Berlin: 1873–1939) Vol. 12, pp. 3, 537.

42.   Thorkil Vanggaard, *Phallos: A Symbol and Its History in the Male World* (London: Jonathan Cape, 1972), pp. 23–24.

43.   Pogey-Castries, *op. cit.*, pp. 176, 307–308.

44.   For a discussion of the law, see Pogey-Castries, *op. cit.*, pp. 281–291.

45.   Aeschines, *Timarchus,* 6–12, translated by Charles Darwin Adams (London: William Heinemann, 1911).

46.   *Ibid.*, 19–20. Adult Athenians who acted as prostitutes or panderers were excluded from all offices in public life, administrative, judicial, and diplomatic, and were even forbidden to address the assembly. This presumably explains some of the insults in Aristophanes' plays leveled at orators. See Lacey, *op. cit.*, pp. 303–304, n. 42.

47.   Aeschines, *Timarchus,* 13–14. Boys who were prostituted by their parents or guardians are

said to have been freed from the normal obligation to maintain their aged parents or guardians; the guilty parent or guardian was also liable to be treated as a panderer and punished, as was the person who paid money for the use of the boy. Aeschines, *Timarchus,* 15–17.

48. *Ibid.,* 21, 28, 29, 30, 32, 119, 138, 158.

49. Pogey-Castries, *op. cit.,* pp. 284–290, has collected the references. See also Xenophon, *Lacedaemonians,* 2, 12–13, translated by E. C. Marchant (London: William Heinemann, 1956); Plutarch, *Pelopidas,* 19, *Lives;* Strabo, *Geography,* X, 4, 19–21 (483), translated by Horace Leonard Jones (London: William Heinemann, 1944).

50. Vanggaard, *op. cit.,* p. 26.

51. Plutarch, *Solon,* I, 3, *Lives.*

52. Plutarch, *The Dialogue on Love,* in Vol. IX of the *Moralia,* 751C, translated by F. C. Babbitt, W. C. Helmhold, P. H. de Lacey, E. L. Minar, et al., eds. (London: William Heinemann, 1927–1969).

53. Lacey, *op. cit.,* p. 158. See also Cicero, *De republica,* IV, 4, translated by Clinton W. Keyes (London: William Heinemann, 1961); and Plutarch, *Amatoriae narrationes,* 773–774, in *Moralia,* Vol. X, translated by Harold North Fowler (London: William Heinemann, 1960).

54. Plato, *Symposium,* 178C, translated by W. R. M. Lamb (London: William Heinemann, 1953).

55. II Maccabees, IV, 9–16. See also the chapter on the Jews.

56. Cicero, *Tusculan Disputations,* IV, 70, translated by V. E. King (London: William Heinemann, 1960).

57. See Herodotus, *History,* I, 135, translated by A. D. Godley (London: William Heinemann, 1946); and Lucian, *Amores,* 35, translated by M. D. Macleod (London: William Heinemann, 1967).

58. Plato, *Symposium,* 1913E–192D.

59. Aristotle, *Problemata,* IV, 26 (879B–880A), translated by E. S. Forster in Vol. 7, *The Works of Aristotle,* W. D. Ross, ed. (Oxford, England: Clarendon Press, 1927).

60. Homer, *Iliad,* XX, 231 ff; V, 266.

61. *Ibid.,* XVIII, 22–34, 80–83; XXIII, 93–101, 211–225; XXIV, 3–12.

62. This is the conclusion of several writers, including J. Z. Eglinton, *op. cit.,* p. 231; and H. I. Marrou, *op. cit.,* p. 27.

63. Erotic connotations have been read into the passages by John Addington Symonds, *Studies of the Greek Poets* (New York: Harper, 1879), Vol. 1, p. 95; and André Gide, *Corydon* (New York: Farrar, Straus, and Company, 1950), pp. 132–133. Some of the ancient writers also regarded such passages as indicating carnal passion. See, for example, Aeschylus, *Myrmidones,* fragments, 64, 65, 66, translated by Hugh Lloyd-Jones (London: William Heinemann, 1963); and Lucian, *Amores,* 54. See also Licht, *op. cit.,* p. 450.

64. Jane Harrison, *Themis: A Study of the Social Origins of Greek Religion* (reprinted, New Hyde Park, N.Y.: University Books, 1962), pp. 445–479. This study was first published in 1912.

65. Ovid, *Metamorphoses,* X, 86–119, translated by Frank J. Miller, ed. (reprinted, London: William Heinemann, 1966). There are others: Licht, *op. cit.,* pp. 463–468.

66. See K. O. Müller, *Die Dorier,* Vols. 2 and 3 of *Geschicten hellenischer stämme und stadte* (Breslau: J. Max 1820–1824, 3 vols.), Vol. 2, pp. 289–298; and E. E. Bethe, "Die Dorische Knabenliebe, ihre Ethik und ihre Idee," *Rheinisches Museum für Philologie,* LXII (1907), pp. 438–457.

67. John Addington Symonds, *A Problem in Greek Ethics* (privately printed, 1901), pp. 16–17.

68. Marrou, *op. cit.*, p. 27.

69. Werner Cohn, "Social Stratification and the Charismatic," *Midwestern Sociologist,* XXI (1948), pp. ,1 ff.

70. Lionel Tiger, *Men in Groups* (London: Thomas Nelson, 1969), p. 216.

71. M. Cary and T. J. Haarhoff, *Life and Thought in the Greek World* (London: Methuen, 1940), p. 151.

72. Ernest Barker, *Greek Political Theory* (London: Methuen, 1964), p. 218.

73. Plato, *Symposium,* 178C; see also Xenophon, *Symposium,* VIII, 32, translated by O. J. Todd (London: William Heinemann, 1932); and Plutarch, *The Dialogue on Love,* 761–763, translated by W. C. Helmbold in Vol. IX of *Moralia* (London: William Heinemann, 1961).

74. Plutarch, *Pelopidas,* 18.

75. Harold Laswell, *Psychopathology and Politics* (New York: Viking Press, 1960), p. 178.

76. Licht, *op. cit.,* pp. 414–415; and Eglinton, *op. cit.,* pp. 244–245.

77. Xenophon, *Lacedaemonians,* 2, 12–13.

78. Plutarch, *Lycurgus,* 18.

79. Aelian, *Varia historia,* III, ii, Rudolph Hercher, ed. (Leipzig: Teubner, 1864).

80. Strabo, *Geography,* X, 19 21 (483).

81. See Bethe, *op. cit.,* fn. 51. This thesis was severely criticized by A. Semenov, "Zur Dorischen Knabenliebe," *Philologus,* N.F. XXIV (1911), pp. 146–150. For a list of references on the debate, see Marrou, *op. cit.,* p. 367, n. 10.

82. Plutarch, *Lycurgus,* XV, 3–5. See also Lacey, *op. cit.,* pp. 197–204.

83. Plutarch, *Lycurgus,* XV, 1–2.

84. Plato, *Laws,* 708A, translated by R. G. Bury, ed. (London: William Heinemann, 1926). See also Lacey, *op. cit.,* pp. 211–212; and R. F. Willetts, *Aristocratic Society in Ancient Crete* (London: Routledge and Kegan Paul, 1955), pp. 3–6.

85. For a catalogue of Greek myths of love affairs between the Gods and their respective boyfriends, see Beyer, *op. cit.*

86. Plato, *Phaedrus,* 239AB, translated by Harold North Fowler (London: William Heinemann, 1953); Plato, *Symposium,* 178C, 192CD; Xenophon, *Symposium,* VIII, 26; and Plutarch, *Amatorius,* 760–763.

87. Plutarch, *Amatoriae,* 760C.

88. Pogey-Castries, *op. cit.,* pp. 160–168.

89. Plato, *Symposium,* 209C.

90. *Ibid.,* 207BC.

91. *Ibid.,* 209C.

92. Xenophon, *Lacedaemonians,* 2, 13.

93. Aristophanes, *Plutus,* 153, Benjamin Bickley Rogers, ed. (London: George Bell, 1907).

94. Much of this discussion is based on Marrou, *op. cit.,* pp. 30–33; and on Pogey-Castries, *op. cit.,* pp. 80–95 and 235–274.

95. Lucian, *Dialogues of Courtesans,* 10, based on the translation by M. D. Macleod (London: William Heinemann, 1961).

96. See T. F. Lucas, *Greek Poetry for Everyman* (Boston: Beacon Press, 1951), pp. 248–254; and Alistair Sutherland and Patrick Anderson, *Eros: An Anthology of Friendship* (London: Anthony Blond, 1961), pp. 35–36. For a more scholarly version, see *Lyra Graeca,* translated by J. M. Edmonds, ed. (London: William Heinemann, 1934), Vol. 1.

97. Pindar, *Odes, Pythia* 6, translated by Richard Lattimore (Chicago: University of Chicago Press, 1947), pp. 74–75. Pindar can also be found in the Loeb Classical Library.

98. See Sutherland and Anderson, *op. cit.*, pp. 29–73; Pogey-Castries, *op. cit.*, pp. 273–274. The poets with references to homoerotic love would include Solon, Phanocles, Anacreon, Pindar, and Alcaeus, among others.

99. See the *Greek Anthology*, translated by W. R. Paton, ed. (London: William Heinemann, 1918–1920, 5 vols.).

100. See the various fragments of Sappho's poems in *Lyra Graeca*, Vol. 1. There is another English translation by Willis Barnstone, *Sappho* (New York: New York University Press, 1965).

101. See U. von Wilamowitz-Mollendorf, *Sappho und Simonides* (Berlin: Weidmann, 1913); T. Reinach, *Alcée et Sapho* (Paris: Societe d'edition, "Les belles lettres," 1937); and especially Jeanette H. Foster, *Sex Variant Women in Literature* (London: Frederick Muller, 1958).

102. Ovid, *Heroides,* Epistle 15, Sappho to Phaon, translated by Grant Showerman, ed. (London: William Heinemann, 1958).

103. In this I agree with Foster, *op. cit.*, pp. 20–21. One reason her verses were destroyed was that others held to this same belief.

104. Marrou, *op. cit.*, pp. 34–35.

105. Lucian, *Dialogues of Courtesans*, V (289–292).

106. Plutarch, *Lycurgus*, 18.

107. Licht, *op. cit.*, pp. 316–328.

108. Aeschines, *Timarchus*, 13, 22, 30, 137–138.

109. Aristophanes, *Plutus*, 153.

110. *Greek Anthology*, XII, 212.

111. For a discussion of prostitution, see Pogey-Castries, *op. cit.*, pp. 96–105. See also Licht, *op. cit.*, pp. 316–328.

112. Diogenes Laertius, "Phaedo," II, 9, in *Lives of Eminent Philosophers*, translated by R. D. Hicks, ed. (London: William Heinemann, 1950).

113. Aeschines, *Timarchus*, 40.

114. *Ibid.,* 40–42.

115. Robert J. Stoller, *Sex and Gender* (New York: Science House, 1968), pp. 195–197.

116. Ovid, *Metamorphoses,* III, 315–338; Hyginus, *Fabula,* LXXV, in *The Myths of Hyginus,* translated by Mary Grant, ed. (Lawrence, Kans.: University of Kanses Press, 1960); Apollodorous, *The Library,* III, vi, 6–7, translated by Sir James G. Frazer, ed. (London: William Heinemann, 1921). Frazer gives several citations in his footnotes to this incident, as well as discussion of the tradition that it was unlucky to see snakes coupling.

117. Antoninus Liberalis, *Metamorphoses,* cap. XVII, Edgar Martin, ed. (Leipzig: Teubner, 1896). See also Marie Delcourt, *Hermaphrodite: Myths and Rites of the Bisexual Figure in Classical Antiquity,* translated from the French by Jennifer Nicholson (London: Studio Books, 1956), pp. 60–66. Professor Delcourt is invaluable on this subject.

118. Ovid, *Metamorphoses,* XII, 458–531, and Hyginus, *Fabula,* XIV.

119. Hyginus, *Fabula,* XCVI, CLXXXIX; Ovid, *Metamorphoses,* VII, 685–865; Antoninus Liberalis, *Metamorphoses,* cap. XLI.

120. Herodotus, *History,* IV, 67.

121. *Ibid.,* I, 105.

122. Hippocrates, *Of the Airs,* XXII, in *Collected Works,* translated by W. H. S. Jones, ed. (London: William Heinemann, 1923).

123. Aristotle, *Nichomachean Ethics*, VII, 7 (1150b). See also Karl Meuli, "Scythica," *Hermes*, LXX (1935), pp. 121–176; and George Dumézil, "Les 'Enarées' scythiques et la grossesse du Narte Hamye," *Latomus*, V (1946), pp. 249–255.

124. Plutarch, *Lycurgus*, XV, 3.

125. Plutarch, *Virtue of Women*, IV (245) in *Moralia*, translated by Frank Cole Babbitt, ed. (London: William Heinemann, 1931 ff.). This is at least one interpretation of this rather obscure passage.

126. Plutarch, *Quaestiones Graecae*, 58, in Vol. IV of the *Moralia*.

127. Plutarch, *A Letter of Condolence to Appolonius*, 22 (112F) In Vol. II of the *Moralia*. This is repeated by Valerius Maximus, *Factorum et dictorum memorabilium*, II, vi, 13, Carolus Kempf, ed. (Leipzig: Teubner, 1888).

128. In another version of the story, Hymenaeus is said to have vanished or died on his own wedding night. The wedding song of Hymenaeus can be found in Catullus, *Carmina*, LXII, LXIII, translated by F. W. Cornish, ed. (revised, London: William Heinemann, 1962).

129. Pausanius, *Descriptions of Greece*, VIII, 20, 3–4; Parthenius, *Love Romances*, 15, translated by Stephen Gaselee, ed. (reprinted, London: William Heinemann, 1962).

130. For a variant version, see Hyginus, *Fabula*, XCX, pp. 146–147.

131. Plutarch, *Solon*, VIII, 4–6.

132. Herodotus, *History*, IV, 145–146.

133. George Dumézil, *Crime des Lemniennes* (Paris: P. Geuthner, 1924), pp. 51–54; and Delcourt, *op. cit.*, p. 81.

134. Henri Jeanmaire, *Coiroir et couretes* (Lille: Bibliotheque universitaire, 1939), p. 153. The translation is essentially that made by Delcourt, *op. cit.*, p. 5.

135. Jeanmaire, *op. cit.*, p. 321; and Delcourt, *op. cit.*, p. 6.

136. Jeanmaire, *op. cit.*, p. 352.

137. Euripides, *Bacchanals*, translated by Arthur S. Way, ed. (London: William Heinemann, 1919); Diodorus Siculus, *History*, II, 62, translated by C. H. Oldfather, ed. (London: William Heinemann, 1933). For a hostile account of some of the rituals, see Clement of Alexandria, *Exhortation to the Greeks*, translated by G. W. Butterworth (London: William Heinemann, 1953).

138. Ovid, *Metamorphoses*, IV, 399–415, tells part of the story. For the rest, see Antoninus Liberalis, *Metamorphoses*, cap. x; Plutarch, *Questiones Graecae*, 38; and various other sources.

139. Philostratus, *Apollonius of Tyana*, IV, xxi, translated by F. C. Conybeare, ed. (reprinted, London: William Heinemann, 1948).

140. Athenaeus, *The Deipnosophists*, XII, 525e–f, translated by Charles Burton Gulick, ed. (London: William Heinemann, 1937).

141. Plutarch, *Virtue of Women*, IV (245).

142. Plutarch, *Theseus*, 20, 304, translated by Bernadotte Perrin, ed. (London: William Heinemann, 1959); and Macrobius, *Saturnalia*, III, viii, 2, translated by Percival Vaughn Davies (New York: Columbia University Press, 1969).

143. Philostratus, *Imagines*, I, ii, 9–10, translated by Arthur Fairbanks, ed. (London: William Heinemann, 1931).

144. Artemidorus Daldiani, *Onirocriticon*, II, 3, 8, Rudolph Hercher, ed. (Leipzig: Teubner, 1864), II, 3, 8.

145. Delcourt, *op. cit.*, p. 12.

146. Ovid, *Metamorphoses*, XIII, 162–180; Hyginus, *Fabula*, CXVI; Apollodorus, *The Li-*

brary, II, xiii, 8; Statius, *Achilleis,* lines 560–674, translated by J. H. Mozley, ed. (London: William Heinemann, 1931).

147.   Ovid, *Heroides,* IX, 57–120; Ovid, *Fasti,* II, 303–358, translated by Sir James C. Frazer, ed. (reprinted, London: William Heinemann, 1959); Lucian, *Dialogue of the Gods,* 15 (13), translated by M. D. Macleod, ed. (London: William Heinemann, 1961); Plutarch, *Whether an Old Man Should Engage in Public Affairs,* 785E–F, in Vol. X of *Moralia.*

148.   Pausanias, *Description of Greece,* I, xix, 1–2.

149.   Delcourt, *op. cit.,* pp. 10–11.

150.   *Ibid.,* pp. 27–29; and Lewis R. Farnell, *The Cults of the Greek States* (Oxford, England: Clarendon Press, 1896–1909, 5 vols.), Vol. 2, pp. 628, 755.

151.   C. J. Bulliet, *Venus castina* (reprinted, New York: Bonanza Books, 1956). The original edition was published in 1928.

152.   Aristophanes, *The Thesmophoriazusae,* 147–152, translated by Benjamin Bickley Rogers, ed. (reprinted, London: William Heinemann, 1955).

153.   Aristophanes, *The Ecclesiazusae,* translated by Benjamin Bickley Rogers, ed. (reprinted, London: William Heinemann, 1955).

154.   Licht, *op. cit.,* pp. 503–504.

155.   Ovid, *Artis amatoriae,* II, 24, translated by J. H. Mozley, ed. (London: William Heinemann, 1962).

6

ROMAN MYTHOLOGY AND REALITY

Roman writers, particularly after Rome had come to exercise control over the Mediterranean basin, liked to look back to the primitive origins of Rome, a subject about which they had little accurate information. As the Romans became captivated by the Greek way of life and increasingly adopted Greek ideas and customs, they idealized their past, more and more fearful that they had forsaken the higher standards of their heroic Roman ancestors. Nostalgically, they pictured Rome as a village where every Roman male had been a simple, honest, hardworking citizen who only reluctantly took up the weapons of war and then happily laid them aside as soon as the crisis was over. It was pictured as a time when the moral integrity of every Roman wife was above reproach, children did not question their father's decisions, and adults piously remembered their ancestors. The rules of behavior were signified by *gravitas,* a sense of dignity and responsibility; *pietas,* loyal, respectful feelings toward the established order; and *mos maiorum,* the power of the father over the household. Since this fictionalized view of the idealized past came to be believed by vast numbers of later Romans, the Romans in retrospect manifested ambivalent feelings toward the realities of power and the enjoyment of life. They gloried in the rewards of conquest, for this was an indication that their way had been right, but at the same time they tried to justify their imperialistic ventures as only defensive actions; they rejoiced in physical pleasures but exaggerated the resultant decline in morals; they were proud of their material success but felt a need to return to the virtues of the mythical past.

Exemplifying these attitudes was the historian Livy (died 17 A.D.), who took as his mission the recording of the great Roman achievements, so that future generations might learn from the examples of noble conduct and virtuous action of these early Romans, the rightful sovereigns of the world. Livy believed no other people in history had preserved their integrity and honor over such a long time, although he was worried that the Romans of his own time were beginning to debase the noble heritage of their ancestors. He wrote:

> I hope everyone will pay keen attention to the moral life of earlier times, to the personalities and principles of the men responsible at home and in the field for the foundation and growth of the empire, and will appreciate the subsequent decline in discipline and in moral standards, the collapse and disintegration of morality down to the present day. For we have now reached a point where our degeneracy is intolerable—and so are the measures by which alone it can be reformed.[1]

Livy hoped that those who read of the old virtues would forsake their pursuit of the petty pleasures of life and once again live as the great Romans had lived. Understandably, with such an attitude, it is difficult to reconstruct an accurate picture of Roman sexual life, because with such a more or less official attitude, charges of sexual deviance were a standard way of darkening the character of individuals whom the propagandizers disliked or who threatened the establishment of which they were a part. Officially, all good Romans were morally upright, heterosexual, abstemious individuals, and only the less worthy citizens or rulers were labeled sexually deviant; in their descriptions of such individuals the Romans exhibited a tabloid mentality,[2] always pointing out sexual peccadilloes, real or imagined. Such exposés were reserved for the prominent and the aristocrats; we know very little about the ordinary person.

As the wealth of empire streamed into the city, Rome became a state with great social and economic inequalities. The aristocracy, in spite of their longing for the "virtuous life" of the past, had little understanding of what a simple life entailed or how the vast majority of people lived. This is evident in Seneca's (died 65 A.D.) description of a "pastoral" trip.

> My friend Maximus and I have been spending a most happy period of two days, taking with us very few slaves—one carriage load—and no paraphernalia except what we wore on our persons. The mattress lies on the ground, and I upon the mattress. There are two rugs—one to spread beneath us and one to cover us. Nothing could have been subtracted from our luncheon; it took not more than an hour to prepare . . .[3]

A simple luncheon taking only an hour to prepare and a camping trip including one carriage load of slaves was a life far different from that of the average Roman.

Cicero (died 43 B.C.) manifested in a different way the outlook of the Roman establishment toward themselves:

> But when with a rational spirit you have surveyed the whole field, there is no social relation among them all more close, none more dear than that which links each one of us with our country. Parents are dear; dear are children, relatives, friends; but one native land embraces all our loves; and who that is true would hesitate to give his live for her . . .[4]

The model of the Roman patriot to the conservative writers of a later generation was the elder Cato (died 149 B.C.), who earned his greatest fame as Censor when he attempted to reestablish what he believed were the values of early Rome. He found it necessary, of course, to attack contemporary immorality, which he equated with the growing influence of Greek literature and philosophy on Roman cultural life.[5]

This is not to imply that the Romans were ascetics in sex; rather, sex was accepted as one of the pleasures of life, at least for the male. As Cicero stated:

> If there is anyone who thinks that young men should be forbidden affairs even with courtesans, he is doubtless eminently austere (I cannot deny it) but his view is contrary not only to the license of this age, but also to the custom and concessions of our ancestors. For when was this not a common practice? When was it blamed? When was it forbidden? When, in fact, was it that what is allowed was not allowed?[6]

Women, on the other hand, were supposed to remain virtuous. In this the paragon was Lucretia, who killed herself after being raped by her kinsman Tarquinus Superbus. According to Livy, Lucretia would have killed herself rather than submit, but Tarquinus had threatened to kill not only her but a male slave as well and to leave both bodies naked in her bedroom to prove to the world she had been caught by her kinsman in the act of adultery. When Tarquinus rode off the next day, Lucretia summoned home her husband Collatinus from the front lines, and after telling him what had happened and why she had submitted, she enjoined him to avenge her dishonor and then stabbed herself to death, the only suitable ending for a wife who had disgraced her husband.[7]

Latin has a rich vocabulary dealing with the physical nature of sexual relationships.[8] Such terms as *cunnilingus, fellatio, tribadism, masturbation,* and *prostitute,* as used by the Romans, have continued to be used in our own time. Some Latin terms were, however, dropped in favor of Greek ones by later generations. The term *phallus,* for example, was borrowed by the Romans from the Greek, and this term rather than the Latin *fascinum* has entered into

English. In a sense, this is unfortunate, because this term, from which we get the word *fascinate,* more truly indicates the magical powers associated with the penis, the Romans, like the Greeks, using the phallus to ward off the evil eye. So potent was the symbol that, according to Pliny (died 79 A.D.), little children wore images of phalli around their necks as protection.[9] Phalli were also set up above the doors of shops, attached to the triumphal chariot of a general, and put on the city gates to ensure good luck. Such images not only guaranteed sexual happiness but also expelled general unhappiness by "fascinating" or drawing the attention of the gods. Phallic amulets have survived in quantities.[10] Juvenal (died about 130 A.D.) mentions some made into drinking glasses,[11] and Petronius (died 66 A.D.) wrote that even pastries were made in phallic forms.[12]

Priapus, the god of fertility, whose symbol was the phallus, had probably been imported from Asia Minor, but included in the ceremonies associated with his worship were vestiges of earlier Roman practices originally associated with the god Mutinus Titinus. Priapus was often portrayed as a giant phallus, his statues being found in many Roman gardens. Horace, mentioning such a figure in the garden of his patron Maecenas, has the image state:

> *I was once, long ago, the trunk of a wild fig tree.*
> *The wood was no good, so a carpenter wracked his brains*
> *As to whether he ought to turn me into a stool*
> *Or into Priapus . . . So I'm god,*
> *And scare hell out of thieves and birds.*[13]

It became the custom to inscribe short, humorous poems or epigrams on the statues of the god. Some 80 of these epigrams survive from the reign of the Emperor Augustus, collected under the title of *Priapeia.*[14]

The female pudendum was also revered as a symbol of the generative power. Emblematically, the female was usually represented by a shell or *concha veneris,* and in fact the cowrie shell had long been used to indicate the female, perhaps because the ancients thought it resembled the female pudenda.[15] But symbolism was one thing and reality another; in spite of the various symbolic reproductions of the generative organs, the Romans regarded actual nakedness in adults as obscene. In fact, the very term *pudenda* means "shameful parts," derived from the verb *pudeo,* "to make or be ashamed." Even when the Greek influence was at its height the Romans still reproved public nudity.

Masturbation is also a Latin word, but there is some disagreement about its original meaning. In the past it was generally accepted that the word was formed from a combination of the Latin word *manus* ("hand") with the verb *stupro,* meaning "to defile." This derivation implies that the Romans regarded masturbation as an act of defilement and gives an emotional, derogatory connotation to the activity not readily apparent in the Latin sources. Hence, it is possible that the word was formed by combining *manus,* not with *stupro,* but instead with the verb *turbo,* meaning "to agitate or disturb." Thus *masturbation* simply meant "to agitate by hand," no connotation of defilement being implied. The matter must remain only conjecture, for the Romans associated the left hand with masturbation, and the Latin for "left," *sinister,* has achieved the connotation of evil. Even in Roman times, left-handedness had the connotation of being improper, although how much this was due to association with masturbation is unclear. The epigrammist Martial (died about 104 A.D.) makes numerous references to masturbation and left-handedness,[16] often in a rather degrading context:

> Ponticus, you never enter a woman, but use your left hand as a mistress to Venus; do you think this is nothing? It is wrong-doing, believe me, indeed one so great that your own mind hardly grasps it. To be sure, Horatius copulated only once to beget triplets, Mars only once to get chaste Ilia with twins. Neither could have done it if by masturbation they had entrusted their dirty joys to their hand. You had better believe that Nature herself says to you, "What you are losing between your fingers, Ponticus, is a human being."[17]

Elsewhere he calls his left hand a Ganymede to serve him, a reference to masturbation as an alternative of anal intercourse.[18]

Not surprisingly, there were strong links between sexuality and religion going beyond the gods of fertility, although some of the Eastern cults with strong sexual overtones had originally had some difficulty in becoming established in Rome. The Bacchanalia, the Roman version of the Dionysian cult,[19] at first ran into opposition, although the opposition probably was not to the sexual connotations but rather to Roman fears that the festival served as a screen for a hidden conspiracy. Even more opposition was expressed to the cult of *Magna Mater,* introduced to Rome during the second Punic War (end of the third century B.C.), the opposition being strong enough to prevent Roman citizens from becoming priests. The prohibition was due to the cult's requiring its priests to be castrated,[20] something the Romans regarded with horror. The emasculation was in imitation of Attis, who, in a frenzy, had castrated himself, died, and then risen again. Later Romans were allowed to become priests of the cult, but even as late as the second century A.D., Roman writers regarded the priests as lewd and degenerate men who gratified their gross lusts with strong young peasants.[21] Fauna, known as the *Bona Dea,* or "good goddess," was worshipped exclusively by women; it was believed that in a yearly ceremony, the women engaged in sexual acts with each other and with young men.[22] Other Roman religions carried various sexual connotations, although sex itself was probably not any more or less important in Roman religion than in other ancient religions or, for that matter, in our own.[23]

Though the Romans, like the Greeks, were essentially male oriented, women had a different place in Rome than in Greece, and this might have had some influence on sexual attitudes. At no time did the Roman woman live in the semioriental seclusion in which Greek women did, but still, she was clearly under the control of the male, whether her father, husband, or brothers. Until fairly late in Roman history women even lacked individual names in the proper sense, taking family names, such as Claudia, Julia, Cornelia, and Lucretia, and sisters often had the same name, distinguished from one another by the terms *elder* or *younger,* and so forth. As riches flowed into Rome from the booty of empire, the well-to-do Romans took to making their wives and daughters visible signs of their wealth by adorning them with costly clothing and jewelry. Women took eagerly to the supports of beauty that wealth put within their reach, cosmetics becoming a necessity. In the process the woman, hitherto little more than a chaste and discreet housewife and mother, began to show a somewhat independent personality. A few women even attempted to assert themselves, to be independent of the male circle so dominating their lives.

In a sense, there was a changing relationship between the sexes, but the most visible result was a denunciation of women by those male writers who believed the only true state of existence and ideology was masculine.[24] This denunciation has led some commentators on Roman history to argue that "homosexuality among males undoubtedly increased in Rome along with the emancipation of women, and such may also be the case in our own culture."[25] This is a false correlation, because Roman women were never particularly emancipated, and though they had somewhat more freedom to appear in public than their Greek sisters, their role was conceived primarily in terms of the family, helping their men to be happy and content, and bearing and nurturing the next generation of men. Women were supposed to subordinate their feelings to those of men, and a woman could do little outside the family. As in Greece, women were even excluded from playing female parts on the stage. The male actors assumed the female role by donning wigs and, eventually, masks. Though this gave a role in society for men with transvestite tendencies, it did little for women. Later, when some women did enact some of the comedy roles, they did so at the expense of their reputations, for an actress was more or less synonymous with prostitute. About the only way a woman could earn a living outside marriage was as a prostitute, and here she would have had to compete with the slaves, who were being prostituted by their masters.

The one area in which the women most acceptably could express their emotions was as spectators in the ampitheaters, and here thcy may have achieved the greatest semblance of equality with the males. M. I. Finley has claimed that "women relished the horrible brutality" of the gladiatorial shows and of the martyrodoms with the "same fierce joy" as the men. "Gladiators became the pin-ups for Roman women, especially in the upper classes. And at the very top, the women became, metaphorically, gladiators themselves."[26] Because women were forbidden to assume power openly, it is perhaps understandable that the imperial women in the first and second centuries of the modern era revealed a ferocity in the backstairs struggles for power seldom equaled. Being unable to struggle for the throne themselves, they displayed their frustrated energy by claiming power for their sons, brothers, and lovers, and almost any tactic was justified. In spite of this, it seems clear that the majority of Roman women accepted their lot, more or less content to love their husbands, bear their children, and keep house; when they did rebel, they often did so with violence and with a great deal of sexual overtones.

Both sexes and all classes seemed to relish watching cruelty as perpetuated in the arena, although the stories of mass Christian martyrdoms have been grossly exaggerated. This Roman receptivity to watching cruelty fits in with the hypotheses of the early psychoanalyst Wilhelm Stekel, who, in his *Sadism and Masochism,* called cruelty "the expression of hatred and the will to power."[27] He implied there is no cruelty not tinged with sexual pleasures, and the Roman experience might well support Stekel's hypothesis. The Romans recognized in themselves the need to dominate. Virgil (died 19 B.C.), in his *Aeneid,* a national epic specifically designed to celebrate the origin and growth of the Roman Empire, put the matter diplomatically by having Anchises foretell the task of the yet unborn Roman people: "Remember thou, O Roman, to rule the nations with thy sway—these shall be thine arts—to crown peace with Law, to spare the humbled, and to tame in war the proud."[28] The Romans never shrank from taking the steps deemed necessary for their mastery and development of a world empire. Later, when they had the empire, it is possible that when "this will to power had no further end in view, it was compelled to turn against itself to its enslaved subjects; or else it was aimlessly dissipated in the constantly intensified thrills of the circus with the combats of wild beasts and human beings."[29] Seemingly at times, causing pain to others became a necessity, and the Romans punished with great cruelty. Flogging was a standard preliminary to execution. Death in such cases was almost a liberation.[30] The sadistic emperor Caligula is reported to have urged the public executioners to strike so that the condemned could feel they were dying.[31]

Roman citizens themselves were exempt from flogging and had the right to appeal a death sentence,[32] but the non-Romans were not exempt and had no such appeal. The exception was a Roman soldier who demonstrated cowardice in the face of the enemy.[33] Even the Roman ways of execution were designed to prolong agony. Crucifixion was the usual form of execution for slaves, but it was not confined to them. Before being put upon the cross, the condemned man was beaten, but there were all kinds of additional torture. Seneca described several ways in which crucifixion took place, since crosses were not

> of a single kind, but differently contributed by different peoples. Some hang their
> victims with heads toward the ground, some impale their private parts, others
> stretch out their arms on a fork-shaped gibbet; I see cords, I see scourges, and for
> each separate limb and each joint there is a separate engine of torture.[34]

Other forms of execution included burning alive; being tied in a sack with snakes, dogs, and other animals; and being tossed into a river or from a high place.[35] Death penalties could also be carried out in the arena; during the first centuries of the modern era these "ceremonial executions" took place most frequently. Even during the Republic, however, a criminal could be executed by being torn to pieces by wild beasts. At the end of the third century B.C., for example, Scipio Africanus, the conqueror of Carthage, threw foreign deserters to the wild beasts at the public shows he produced in Rome. Lucius Paulus, after his victory over Perseus of Macedon in the second century B.C., ordered his victims to be laid out and trampled by elephants.[36] Under the Emperor Augustus, execution by being thrown to wild beasts became a statutory punishment.

There is, however, a distinction between the punishment of condemned criminals and the gladiatorial games in the arena. These were not necessarily regarded as a punishment for criminals. According to one tradition, the Romans had inherited the custom of gladiatorial fights from the Etruscans, who had put on such shows not only at festivals and in theaters but also during banquets. The Greek writer Athenaeus, in the third century A.D., stated that the Romans often invited

> their friends to dinner, not merely for other entertainment, but that they might wit-
> ness two or three pairs of contestants in gladiatorial combat; on these occasions
> when finished with dining and drinking, they called in the gladiators. No sooner
> did one have his throat cut than the masters applauded with delight at this.

There were limits on who could fight duels, Athenaeus stating that once a Roman had

> provided in his will that his most beautiful wives, acquired by purchase, should
> engage in duels; still another directed that young boys, his favorites, should do the
> same. But the provision was in fact disregarded, for the people would not tolerate
> this outrage, but declared the will void.[37]

According to another account, the first gladiatorial show in Rome was sponsored by Marcus and Decimus Brutus in 265 B.C. to honor their father at his funeral ceremony.[38] The two accounts are not necessarily contradictory, for it might have been that the Etruscan funeral custom had not been transplanted to Rome until the third century. From that time onward, the custom grew in popularity as greater and greater sums of money were spent on such shows. In 174 B.C. some 74 men fought for 3 days in honor of the funeral of the father of Titus Flamininus.[39]

In late Republican times, large numbers of gladiators were retained by private persons, so much so that their numbers came to be regarded as a danger to peace and order. The danger became real when Spartacus escaped from a private school of gladiators at Capua and led the so-called slave revolt of 73 B.C. Cicero, in one of his letters, mentioned a school at Capua where a thousand gladiators underwent training.[40] By the end of the Republican period, the state had taken formal recognition of the gladiatorial shows by issuing regulations for them. These regulations had been brought on by senatorial fear of Julius Caesar, whose plans to import gladiators so terrified his political enemies that they managed to get laws passed limiting the number of gladiators a private individual could keep in Rome.[41] Even with these regulations Caesar sponsored some 320 pairs of gladiators.[42]

Obviously, gladiatorial shows were a source of public favor, and this could not be ignored by the Roman rulers from Augustus on, who undertook the sponsorship of games. The fighters were usually prisoners of war or criminals who had been sentenced to the arena or had chosen the arena in a desperate hope of bettering their condition. Cicero reported that

> a gladiatorial show is apt to seem cruel and brutal to some eyes, and I incline to think that it is so, as now conducted. But in the days when it was criminals who crossed swords in the death struggle, there could be no better schooling against pain and death.[43]

Tacitus (died about 117 A.D.), one of our main sources of information for the early empire in spite of his bias, condemned the Emperor Tiberius, to whom he was extremely hostile, for his repugnance to gladiatorial fights, even though Tacitus also felt repugnance toward those who received too much pleasure in observing the slaughter.[44] In a classic study of Roman morals, Ludwig Friedländer observed that the increasingly

> bloodthirsty combats and magnificent scenery failed to excite the dulled nerves of the mob, aristocratic or vulgar; only things absolutely exotic, unnatural, or nonsensical ticked their jaded senses. Domitian gave gladiatorial combats and animal hunts by night, and the swords reflected lamps and candelabra. In the December festival of 88 he set dwarfs and women fighting. . . . Thus in the course of centuries from small beginnings the gladiatorial games had become an immense institution. The accommodation for spectators correspondingly increased. . . . The first real amphitheater in Rome was built by Caesar in 46 B.C. of wood; a stone

one built by Statilius Taurus in 20 B.C. was probably burned at Nero's fire; Nero even built a wooden one on the Campus Marius. Only at about 90 A.D. was the Colosseum of the Flavians finished.[45]

Other cities quickly followed suit, and prostitutes flocked to such areas. Isidore of Seville, a Christian writer of the late sixth century, who cannot be regarded as an unbiased witness, stated that the theater and brothel were identical, for after the games were over, prostitutes were everywhere.[46] Though this might be dismissed simply as the prostitutes' going where the crowds were, there are too many other references to sexual activity to deny a connection between the activities in the arena and sexual arousal.[47]

The popularity of the arena, as well as the orgiastic excesses periodically cropping up, are one of the marks distinguishing the Romans from the Greeks. To conquer and rule the Mediterranean world, the Romans had to demonstrate a great deal of self-discipline, but the conquest gave them tremendous power that caused a breakdown of the discipline, and when their discipline broke, the Romans seemed to try to outdo each other in excess. Though the luxury of Rome might not seem like much to citizens of the richer countries of the world today, it impressed their contemporaries. They were able to import delicacies from all over the known world, and with their hosts of slaves waiting on every movement in town and country houses, the richer Romans managed to establish a reputation for luxurious living that echoes until today. Their wealth seemed so great because the poor were so poor and there were such gross inequalities. In the last years of the Republic, Lucullus, Caesar, Pompey, Scaurus, Crassus, and others built huge fortunes, some of which were expended for political purposes and some for luxurious living. Lucullus established such a reputation for what Thorsten Veblen later called "conspicuous consumption" that the Lucullan banquet has endured as a cliché to the present.

When wealth was combined with tremendous political power, as it was with the advent of the emperors, there was almost no limit to the excesses. This was particularly true of individuals who came to power, or were designated for power, at a very early age, for it was next to impossible for a servant or teacher to discipline a child who in a few years might be regarded as a god. Parents who might have intervened were busy elsewhere. Instead of enforcing discipline, servants and slaves often tried to ingratiate themselves with the young infants who would be their rulers by catering to every whim, by introducing them to activities and customs that might later give them an edge over other retainers. These emperors, particularly Caligula and Nero, achieved a reputation for wastefulness and self-indulgence still unmatched. Caligula, for example, is said to have delighted in attempting to do what others deemed impossible. One of his projects was to erect buildings in the sea during a storm; during one day he squandered the tribute of three provinces (10 million sesterces). Nero was almost his equal.[48] These emperors were the exception rather than the rule, but the difficulty with all emperors was that, if they took it in their minds to do something, there was almost no way, short of assassination, that they could be prevented from using their great power and wealth to accomplish what they wanted. Inevitably, some of the Roman rulers achieved a reputation for licentiousness or cruelty seldom matched.

This tendency to extremes among the rulers should be kept in mind in any examination of deviant sexuality, for it was more or less the same emperors (Caligula, Nero, and others of a similar personality pattern) who were accused of the most flamboyant and extreme forms of erotic activity. Whether they engaged in all the sexual activities attributed to them might well be questioned but is of no importance in the long run in a study of sexual attitudes. If the Romans equated certain deviant sexual acts with a hated emperor, it indicates not only how they regarded the emperor but also what they considered extremes in sexual activity.

The Greek attitudes toward homosexuality have been in part attributed to the camaraderie of men at arms. The Romans were soldiers, too, and their military training required greater cooperation and interdependence than the Greek system did, because the legions were more coordinated units, but this did not lead to the acceptance of homosexuality seen in the Greek world. In fact, the Romans generally tended to regard both nudity and homosexuality as something of which the Greeks should be ashamed rather than proud.[49] *Suidas*, the Greek lexicon or encyclopedia compiled long after the fall of Rome in the tenth century A.D., included a statement that the non-Roman inhabitants of Italy had been the inventors of pederasty and that the Etruscans, Samnites, and Messalians bore equal responsibility with the Greek of southern Italy for encouraging its practice.[50] Edward Gibbon also exempted the Romans from originally practicing homosexuality, claiming instead that the "primitive" Romans had only been "infected" with this "odious vice" by the example of the Etruscans and Greeks.[51] Neither statement can be corroborated by the evidence, although the first mention of homosexual activity does not occur until the fourth century B.C., when a citizen was accused of engaging in a homosexual affair with a slave.[52] There are other reported incidents in which the attitude is hostile, so much so that in some cases the death penalty was considered justified.[53]

At the end of the third century B.C., the Tribune C. Scantinus was charged before the people's assembly (*comitia tributa*) with having made an indecent proposal to a young boy.[54] Supposedly as a result of this charge, the *Lex Scantinia* or *Scantina* was said to have been passed to repress homosexuality, though scholars are not now certain there ever was such a law. Part of the difficulty is that laws were usually named after the person introducing them, and the obvious similarity of the law's title to the accused Tribune Scantinus makes its existence rather doubtful, for it is hard to imagine that the tribune introduced a law resulting in his own prosecution.[55] It might be that the references in Cicero[56] and other sources to such a law indicate the action taken against Scantinus rather than the passage of a law. Homosexual intercourse, was, however, punished in the *Lex Julia de adulteriis,* part of the moral reform legislation passed under the Emperor Augustus after he came to power at the end of the first century B.C. In these laws, homosexual intercourse was defined as *stuprum,* defilement, dishonor, or violation, as was a liaison with a free unmarried girl or widow, unless the woman was a registered prostitute or a recognized concubine. The purpose of the law, part of a series, was to ensure that men between 25 and 60 marry and father children.[57] Anyone found guilty of *stuprum* was subject to a fine, although later legislation provided for other penalties.[58]

Because the Augustan legislation coincided with the increasing influence of the Greeks, it is possible that, just as the Romans adopted Greek artists, poets, and men of letters, so they might also have practiced pederasty and homosexuality more widely than before. Basically, however, all indices of Roman standards show that Roman men maintained their interest in women, and not in either young boys or older men.[59] Though homosexual affairs have been imputed to various figures in the last century of the Republic (first century B.C.), it was not until the appearance of the Caesars that homosexuality received significant attention from the Roman writers themselves. This leads to considerable hesitation in accepting earlier accusations, if only because so many of the writers making them were hostile to the individuals involved and might have charged them with homosexuality because they knew such allegations would be received unfavorably by their readers. Caesar, for example, is said to have had an affair with King Nicomedes of Bithynia, and his troops supposedly sang:

> All the Gauls did Caesar vanquish,
> Nicomedes vanquished him;
> Lo! now Caesar rides in triumph,
> Victor over all the Gauls
> Nicomedes does not triumph,
> Who subdued the conqueror.[60]

Another contemporary of Caesar is alleged to have called him the husband of all women and wife of all men.[61] Inevitably, those associated with Caesar were reported to have had homosexual inclinations,[62] including Octavian (later the Emperor Augustus), alleged to have prostituted himself to Caesar in return for becoming his heir. Augustus was, however, viewed favorably by most of the writers of the time, and so Suetonius, who mentioned the charge in his collection of scandalous anecdotes, quickly dismissed it, saying these slanderous charges could easily be refuted by the "purity of life" practiced by Augustus.[63] In short, homosexual activity was believed to be true about those the Roman writers disliked and regarded as false when it concerned individuals the writers respected.

The political implications of such charges appear most readily in the case of the Emperor Tiberius, painted by several Roman writers as a drunken, obscene, debauched, indulgent old man, acting with monstrous and revolting lust in every way that a "depraved imagination could suggest." Whereas most modern historians agree that Tiberius might have become mentally ill in the last 6 years of his life, they believe that his portrait, at least as painted by Tacitus, was politically motivated.[64] Adding to the public legend of sexual deviation was his isolation on the island of Capri, which encouraged speculation about what he could be doing there. This public gossip, reported by Suetonius, has left us the picture of an old degenerate swimming in a grotto, surrounded by lascivious boys swimming alongside and nibbling at him like little fishes beside an old shark.[65] Since the account goes counter to what we know about Tiberius during most of his active life, it might well be another incident of blackening the reputation of a person by attributing deviant sexual behavior to him.

Not so easy to dismiss are the stories surrounding Tiberius' successor, Gaius Caesar Germanicus, better known as Caligula, an autocratic tyrant who became increasingly cruel and sadistic as the unrest grew around him. All sorts of sexually connected activities are attributed to him. He is said to have worn women's clothes in public, appearing as Venus but still retaining some semblance of masculinity by wearing a golden beard.[66] Claudius, his successor, allegedly kept favorite freedmen and eunuchs but is best remembered for being cuckolded by his wives. He was succeeded to the throne by the 17-year-old Nero, who, when under the influence of his mother and advisers, ruled fairly effectively but later made his name synonymous with vain, egotistic, and childish rule. Though twice married, Nero was also interested in members of his own sex, engaging in practices he had supposedly been taught by his tutor Seneca. The scandal-mongering Suetonius summed up:

> Besides abusing freeborn boys and seducing married women, he debauched the vestal virgin Rubria. The freedwoman Acte he all but made his lawful wife, after bribing some ex-consuls to perjure themselves by swearing that she was of royal birth. He castrated the boy Sporus and actually tried to make a woman of him; and he married him with all the usual ceremonies, including a dowry and a bridal veil, and took him to his house attended by a great throng, and treated him as his wife. And the witty jest that someone made is still current, that it would have been well for the world if Nero's father Domitius had had that kind of wife. This Sporus, decked out with the finery of the empresses and riding in a litter, he took with him to the assizes and marts of Greece, and later at Rome through the Street of the

Images, fondly kissing him from time to time. That he even desired illicit relations with his own mother, and was kept from it by her enemies, who feared that such a relationship might give the reckless and insolent woman too great influence, was notorious, especially after he added to his concubines a courtesan who was said to look very like Agrippa [his mother]. Even before that, so they say, whenever he rode in a litter with his mother, he had incestuous relations with her, which were betrayed by the stains on his clothing.

He so prostituted his own chastity that after defiling almost every part of his body, he at last devised a kind of game, in which covered with the skin of some wild animal, he was let loose from a cage and attacked the private parts of men and women, who were bound to stakes, and when he had sated his mad lust, was dispatched by his freedman Doryphorus; for he was even married to this man in the same way that he himself had married Sporus, going so far as to imitate the cries and lamentations of a maiden being deflowered.[67]

This list is a good catalogue of the sexual activities that Suetonius, at least, regarded as immoral, although whether Nero engaged in all of them can only be left to the imagination.

In the struggle for power following the assassination of Nero in 68 B.C., four men contested for the throne before Vespasian established his claim in 69 B.C. One contestant was Otho, nicknamed *Pathicus* by the satirist Juvenal,[68] a term translated as "one who submits to unnatural lust." Other, more friendly sources represent him as having an effeminate and dandified appearance. Yet, despite his appearance and the Roman hostility to homosexuality, Otho is usually portrayed rather favorably in most accounts, perhaps because it was believed he took his own life to prevent the killing of more soldiers in the battle for succession. Though he was apparently a rather incapable and profligate person, his suicide made him a hero to the Republicans, who thought he had intended to restore the Republic, and there was an attempt to whitewash his character[69] and to downplay allegations of homosexuality.

Obviously, Caligula and Nero were emotionally disturbed individuals; their behavior is no more typical of homosexuality than it is of heterosexuality. Fearful that such conduct might be labeled as an example of homosexuality, some scholars have gone to extremes. J. Z. Eglinton, for example, in his defense of "Greek love," stated that he could fill pages and pages with scandalous anecdotes about the Caesars and their boyfriends, but that, with the exception of the Emperor Hadrian, they had all perverted "true" boy love.[70] Wainwright Churchill is somewhat more subtle but expresses similar views.[71] This selective labeling of certain kinds of conduct as true homosexual love and other variations as perversions is as judgmental as labeling all homosexual activity as perversion. Both Nero and Caligula might well have been bisexual rather than exclusively heterosexual, but the issue is really the extremism they represent in their pursuit of sensuous pleasure, an extremism on which their great power imposed no limits.

Much more in the idealized tradition of homosexual love was the Emperor Hadrian and his male concubine Antinoüs. Nonetheless, even Hadrian went to imperial excess when Antinoüs died in Egypt. He honored him and their love by building a city where he had died, naming it after Antinoüs and placing statues and busts of Antinoüs in almost every major city in the Empire.[72] Many of these busts have survived and now form part of collections in museums such as the Louvre, the Vatican, the National Museum of Naples, and classical museums in cities such as Florence and Berlin. A French archaeological team excavating the city of Antinoöpolis found mummies of priests dedicated to the deified Antinoüs, who became a sort of second Osiris and was believed by his disciples to have arisen from the dead.[73]

One of the most enigmatic and perhaps tragic figures in the whole list of emperors was Elagabalus, who succeeded to the throne as a 14-year-old boy in 218 A.D. He was described as a particularly beautiful boy, and he might well have been a transvestite or perhaps even a transsexual. Elagabalus detested Roman clothes, which he said were made of cheap wool, and refused to wear anything but silk. His grandmother Julia worried about his costume for fear the Romans might think it "more suitable for a woman than a man." Her worries were perhaps justified, since Elagabalus was said to have requested castration so that he could be a true woman. After 4 years of rule he was deposed and murdered by the military.[74] In fact, with the exception of Hadrian and the much-maligned Tiberius, all the emperors accused of rampant sexual excesses were eliminated after comparatively short periods of rule.

Even if the accounts of imperial homosexuality are exaggerated, it was obviously difficult for the Romans to enforce any prohibitions against homosexuality. We also know, for example, that male prostitutes were available to serve the sexual demands of at least a segment of the population.[75] Some of the very rich even had seraglios of boys, called *paedagogia*. Pupils in these alleged schools were designated by caressing terms such as "delicate" or "delicious" boys. Most of the youths in these houses and in the houses of prostitution were slaves, imported by slave merchants to sell to any buyer with money. Though the *paedagogia* served primarily as a diversion for the masters, not all such diversion was sexual, several boys becoming known for their wit. Some of the boys were adopted as heirs by their masters or left a fortune.[76] In at least one case, an unnamed Roman ordered his boys to be killed upon his death, but state officials intervened to prohibit this funeral massacre.[77] In one of his numerous references to homosexuality Martial described a house of prostitution in which both boys and girls were kept:

Whenever you have passed the threshold of a placarded cubicle, whether it be a boy or a girl who has smiled on you, you are not satisfied with a door and a curtain and a bolt, and you require that greater secrecy should be provided for you. If there be any suspicion of the smallest chink it is plastered up, as also the eyelets that are bored by a mischievous needle. No one is of modesty so tender and so anxious as Catharus, the pedicat, poker of either boys or women.[78]

The most common term used by Romans to refer to an adult male homosexual was *cinaedus* (originally meaning "unchaste" or "lewd"), a term that can still be made out on the walls at Pompeii attached to two male names, one in the possessive case. And several surviving wall paintings deal with male homosexual intercourse.[79] Another term used by the Romans was *paedicator* or *paedico*,[80] derived from the Greek *paiderasty*. Similarly, the term *catamite* came from the Latinized name of Ganymede, who had been carried off by Zeus. *Pathic*, another term applied to homosexuals, was also derived from the Greek, this time *pathikos*, a word meaning "passive."[81] The Romans also used the term *subactor*, meaning "to subjugate" or "to work," to describe the passive partner in a homosexual relationship.[82] The term *corvus* was equated with *fellatio*,[83] another Latin term, though technically *corvus* meant "raven." Its application to sexual activities derived from the popular belief that ravens copulated with their mouths.[84] Most such terms were restricted to males engaged in homosexual activity, although *pathicus* was also applied to females.[85] More commonly, females were described by the term *tribas*, borrowed from the Greek, meaning "rubbing together."[86] Lesbianism and sapphism were not terms the Romans normally applied to woman homosexuals, although the *Suidas* later defined *lesbianize* as "to defile the mouth."

The widespread use of Latinized Greek terms indicates how much the Romans, consciously or unconsciously, associated homosexuality with Greece and how it became a matter of popular discussion only after the Greek influence had been strongly felt in Rome. Though the Romans might have attempted to punish homosexual intercourse between free men (or free women), no such prohibition existed for sexual relations between slaves or prostitutes.[87] This raises the questions of how much the Roman law reflected the reality of sexual practices in Rome and why the Romans might have been reluctant to enforce their sexual laws.

Standards of taste or law were profoundly influenced not only by the Romans' conservativism but also by social class. Some laws were directed only at specified social classes, as for example, a law of Augustus prohibiting senators from contracting legal marriages with any woman who was or ever had been an actress, although no such prohibition was applied to other classes of Roman citizens. This law was based on an older Roman custom, but exceptions were always allowed, provided the proper procedures were followed. Undoubtedly, a number of similar laws were simply ignored. For example, soldiers in the legions (unlike their officers) were prohibited from marrying during the period of service, set at 20 years under Augustus and later raised to 25 years. Though the law was not repealed until 197 A.D., we know that soldiers went on marrying and rearing families, for their tombstones are full of references to loving wives and children. Obviously, the soldiers could not have acted so clandestinely in such large numbers without the connivance of Roman officials, who were not so stupid as to have been ignorant of what was taking place. Rather, it appears the Romans merely insisted on the formal unlawfulness of the relationship and then made and constantly revised regulations for the unavoidable confusion about inheritance, the status of the children, and the rights of all the parties involved once the soldier had been discharged. Still, the official discouragement of marriage among soldiers might well have encouraged prostitution, including homosexual prostitution, near army camps. How much homosexuality existed among the soldiers must remain conjecture, for neither poets nor historians nor philosophers concerned themselves with the ordinary soldier or, for that matter, with the poorer peasantry or with the tens of thousands of urban dwellers crowded in the slumlike apartments the Romans called *insulae*.

Some indication that homosexuality might not have been as widespread as the sources indicate appears in some of the medical literature. Since medical and scientific knowledge was more or less common to the educated classes and not necessarily confined to the professional medical practitioners,[88] explanations in such works were aimed at the literate Romans and probably not only reflected Roman attitudes but also influenced them. One of the best descriptions of the medical causes of homosexuality was by Soranus, a Greek physician who lived in the first half of the second century A.D., whose works on acute and chronic diseases have been preserved in an abbreviated Latin translation by Caelius Aurelianus. Included in the discussion of chronic diseases is a brief chapter on effeminate men (*subactors*) or *pathics*.

People find it hard to believe that effeminate men or pathics [Greek *malthacoe*] really exist. The fact is that, though the practices of such persons are unnatural to human beings, lust overcomes modesty and puts to shameful use parts intended for other functions. That is, in the case of certain individuals, there is no limit to their desire and no hope of satisfying it; and they cannot be content with their own lot, the lot which divine providence had marked out for them in assigning definite functions to the parts of the body. They even adopt the dress, walk, and other characteristics of women. Now this condition is different from a bodily disease; it is rather an affliction of a diseased mind. Indeed, often out of passion and in rare cases out of respect for certain persons to whom they are beholden, these pathics suddenly change their character and for a while try to give proof of their virility. But since they are not aware of their limitations, they are again the victims of excesses, subjecting their virility to too great a strain and consequently involving themselves in worse vices. And it is our opinion that these persons suffer no impairment of sensation. For, as Soranus says, this affliction comes from a corrupt and debased mind. Indeed, the victims of this malady may be compared to the women who are called *tribades* because they pursue both kinds of love. These women are more eager to lie with women than with men; in fact, they pursue women with almost masculine jealousy, and when they are freed or temporarily relieved of their passion . . . They rush, as if victims of continual intoxication, to new forms of lust, and sustained by this disgraceful mode of life, they rejoice in the abuse of their sexual powers.

Soranus held that no bodily treatment could be applied to overcome the disease, for the mind rather than the body had been affected. To support his case he quoted what others had said about the possibility of curing the disease. The Greek Parmenides, he reported, held that people were born as homosexuals because of the circumstances at their conception and were not truly of one sex or the other. Others had held that the disease was inherited, passed on by the seed, and physicians holding this view believed the blame should have been placed on the human race rather than on any individual, because once man had incurred such defects, he retained them. Unlike other hereditary diseases, moreover, this one became stronger as the body grew older, causing a hideous and ever-increasing lust. This was because in the

years when the body is still strong and can perform the normal functions of love, the sexual desire (of these persons) assumes a dual aspect, in which the soul is excited sometimes while playing a passive role and sometimes while playing an active role. But in the case of old men who have lost their virile powers, all their sexual desire is turned in the opposite direction and consequently exerts a stronger demand for the feminine role in love. In fact, many infer that this is a reason why boys too are victims of this affliction. For, like old men, they do not possess virile powers; that is, they have not yet attained those powers which have already deserted the aged.[89]

Though homosexuality became more or less tolerated in Rome, there were basic differences between Roman attitude and the Greeks'. In Greece, *paiderasty* played an important part in the educational process and was highly idealized. Contrariwise, the Romans would have none of the subtleties associated with the Greek ideas about love, and during much of the Republican period it was in disfavor. When either homosexuality became more common or discussion of it became more open, the homosexual love object was almost always a slave. There is little of the idealization of homosexuality in Latin literature that there is in Greek literature, and when this does appear, it seems to be more plagiarism of Greek ideas than a reflection of Roman attitudes.[90]

Favorable references to homoerotic love occur in Virgil, Horace, Catullus, and Tibullus, and as a result, all four have been labeled as homosexual. Obviously, other writers discussed the subject, but there is less debate about their sexual orientation. Though Virgil has been claimed as a boy lover by some,[91] his poetry dealing with homosexuality seems imitative of Greek models rather than indicating anything from his own experience. In the ninth book of the *Aeneid*,[92] Virgil tells of heroic deaths of the lovers Nisus and Euralus, but this seems to be included in the poem mainly to replicate the relationship of Achilles and Patroclus in Homer's *Iliad*. A second reference appears in Virgil's *Ecologues*, which is in imitation of the Greek poet Theocritus, and again it is questionable whether it expresses a personal sentiment of Virgil's about Corydon's love for Alexis or whether it is an attempt to demonstrate that Latin poetry can rival Greek both in metrical skill and in subject matter.[93] Still, the account has proved deeply moving to many homosexuals, André Gide, for example, entitling his philosophic defense of homosexuality after Corydon.[94]

Horace provides a somewhat different case, for in one of his epodes he implies he is attracted to both boys and girls, and if the poetic meter has not altered his meaning, he claims his love of boys surpasses even that of girls.[95] Some doubt has been raised because, although his works are full of the names of his mistresses, they mention the names of only two boys, Lyciscus and Ligurinus.[96] Horace's favorable references to homosexuality might have been due, not to any homoerotic inclination of the author, but to the homosexuality of his patron and sponsor Maecenas, the trusted counselor of Augustus and a prominent patron of literature, who sponsored both Horace and Virgil. It is likely that, when the patron is homosexual, his clients might write favorably about boy love. It is also possible that both Horace and Virgil were homosexuals and that attempts by some to denigrate the homosexual references in their writings are part of the conspiracy of silence surrounding homosexuality for so long. The reader will have to judge for himself or herself.

Catullus (died 54 b.c.) is a much less debatable case. He was clearly bisexual. His great love was for the beautiful and aristocratic Clodia, this adulterous affair being marked by infidelity on her part, by rifts and reconciliations, and finally, by explosion and rupture. We have a more or less complete account of it in his poems to Lesbia, the literary name he used for Clodia. Only after breaking with Clodia did Catullus take up with Juventius, a beautiful boy from an illustrious Roman family. This affair proved almost as stormy as that with Lesbia–Clodia since, unfortunately for Catullus, Juventius did not fully reciprocate the poet's love and preferred others.[97]

Albius Tibullus (died 19 b.c.), the fourth of the group, referred to homosexual love in his poems dealing with advice from Priapus,[98] but most particularly in his laments over the inconstancy and willful perversity of Marathus, who seemed to be especially difficult to get along with.[99] There are also numerous references to homosexuality in Plautus,[100] Juvenal,[101] Martial,[102] and in *Satyricon* of Petronius.[103] This last work, which has survived only in fragments, offers the nearest approach to a defense of homosexuality existing in classical Latin literature. How much the *Satyricon* approaches the reality of post-Augustan society is a matter of considerable debate.

Seemingly, the view it gives of certain segments of Roman life might well be true, but that segment was a tiny minority.

Probably more typical of the majority view is Ovid, who has deservedly earned an erotic reputation but who remains rather unfavorable on boy love because both participants do not equally consummate.[104] His *Ars amoris* has been called the Roman equivalent of a modern American sex manual, [105] and if Ovid with his Greek orientation viewed homosexual love with disfavor, we have to conclude that either homosexual love was not of major concern to most Romans or that Ovid felt it would detract from his essentially heterosexual message. Nevertheless, it is difficult to explain why Juvenal felt compelled to warn parents about the dangers of having a handsome son, unless homosexuality was not regarded as a danger by some.

> A handsome son keeps his parents in constant fear and misery; so rarely do modesty and good looks go together. For though his home be rough and simple, and have taught him ways as pure as those of the ancient Sabines, and though Nature besides with kindly hand have lavishly gifted him with a pure mind and a cheek mantling with modest blood . . . he will not be allowed to become a man. The lavish wickedness of some seducer will tempt the boy's own parents: such trust can be placed in money! No misshapen youth was ever unsexed by a cruel tyrant in his castle; never did Nero have a bandy-legged or scrofulous favorite, or one that was hump-backed or pot-bellied![106]

Though Juvenal also recounts the heterosexual dangers awaiting such a boy, such as the wrath of a husband with whose wife he commits adultery, the dangers of homosexual enticement lead the list. Juvenal was, however, a natural pessimist hostile to homosexuality and even more hostile to women.

Lesbianism, as evidenced from the preceding discussion, was something the Romans knew existed, but they paid little attention to it. Martial mentions the subject, devoting an epigram to the lesbian Bassa, who had never been intimate with men but who was always surrounded by women. He implied that, though she lacked a penis, her *"cunnus"* was able to satisfy another woman. He stated she had become a prodigy worthy of the Theban riddle, because "here, where no man is, there was adultery!"[107] He also mentions Philaenis, who does not suck but "guzzles" on girl's middles and who believes that to "lick a 'cunnum'" is desireable.[108] Juvenal's sixth *Satire,* dealing with the rituals associated with Bona Dea, includes lesbian incidents, [109] and there are several incidents in Lucian's *Dialogues of Courtesans,*[110] as well as others,[111] but we have no account by women themselves, all accounts being by men and generally more hostile to female homosexuality than to male.

Greek mythological stories about sex change and sex impersonation were incorporated in Roman mythology, and, in fact, Latin writers are often the main source for stories about the gods and their relationships with human beings. There is little original Roman mythology about impersonation. An exception is the Roman god Vertumnus, the god of the changing year. He loved Pomona, goddess of fruit trees, but Pomona refused to have anything to do with him; to overcome her opposition, he adopted various disguises, finally achieving success as an old woman.[112] Some Romans took the possibility of sex change seriously. Pliny, a popularizer of both scientific and pseudoscientific ideas, wrote in the first century A.D.:

> Transformation of females into males is not an idle story. We find in the Annals that in the consulship of Publius Licinius Crassus and Gaius Cassius Longinus [171 B.C.], a girl at Casinum was changed into a boy under the observation of the parents, and at the order of the augurs was conveyed to a desert island. Licinius Macianus has recorded that he personally saw at Agros a man named Arescon who had been given the name of Arescusa and had actually married a husband, and then had grown a beard and developed masculine attributes and taken a wife; and that he had also seen a boy with the same record at Smyrna. I myself saw in Africa a person who had turned into a male on the day of marriage to a husband; this was Lucius Constitus, a citizen of Thysdritium.[113]

This account suggests some of the hostility with which pseudohermaphrodites or person with endocrine dysfunctions were regarded, although only the earliest case had been exiled. Elsewhere, Pliny reported that two hermaphrodites were drowned at birth so that no one would perish by being defiled by their blood.[114] As late as 90 B.C. a woman reported to be changing into a man had been burned alive.[115]

Transvestism was somewhat less threatening and, as indicated earlier, Caligula, Nero, and Elagabalus allegedly sometimes impersonated women. Nero also wanted to make his slave Sporus into a woman, and Elagabalus requested surgery for himself. The stage allowed an outlet for professional impersonators, for as a general rule women were not allowed on the stage.[116] During the reign of the Emperor Domitian, at the end of the first century A.D., an actor named Paris, noted for his impersonations of nymphs and goddesses, is said to have attracted the attention of the emperor. Juvenal bitterly attacked Paris, as well as Bathyllus and Urbicus, who were also professional impersonators.[117] The Bona Dea feast, where lesbian practices were reported, also encouraged female impersonation, although the ceremony must have changed between the time of Julius Caesar and Juvenal. Caesar, in fact, became involved in a political scandal over female impersonation during the festival. His wife Pompeia is supposed to have entered into a intrigue with Clodius Pulcher to slip Clodius into the house in female disguise during the celebration of the Bona Dea rites, at which no man was supposed to be present. Clodius was detected and exposed, although he was eventually acquitted of having committed a sacrilege. In spite of the acquittal, Caesar divorced Pompeia with the famous statement that the wife of a Caesar must be above suspicion.[118]

Juvenal later reported, however, that, during the Bona Dea festival, young men dressed in the flimsiest of female garments and wearing hoods were introduced into the ceremony so that sexual orgies could take place.[119] Undoubtedly, Juvenal, in his usual fashion, is exaggerating, but there might be some truth in his account. Juvenal also alleged that a number of men dressed in women's clothes and often went about in the company of women. He claimed that, though other males regarded them as harmless, many females consulted them about marriage and divorce and learned lascivious ideas and notions from them. He cautioned husbands to beware because:

> That teacher is not always what he seems: true, he darkens his eyes and dresses like a women, but adultery is his design. Mistrust him the more for his show of effeminacy; he is a valiant mattress-knight; there Triphallus drops the mask of Thais. Whom are you fooling? Not me; play this farce to those who cannot pierce the masquerade. I wager you every inch a man; do you own it, or must we wring the truth out of the maid servants? I know well the advice and warnings of my old friends: "Put on a lock and keep your wife indoors." Yes, but who is to ward the warders? They get paid in kind for holding their tongues as to their young lady's escapades; participation seals their lips. The wily wife arranges accordingly . . . [120]

Again Juvenal is probably magnifying one incident into a vast condemnation of homosexuals, transvestites, and women, all of whom he delighted in condemning. According to Juvenal, women would do anything for sex; he alleged that numbers of them submitted themselves to asses if no man was available to satisfy them.[121] Lucius Apuleius' allegorical story of a man changed into an ass also tells how an ass could also satisy women,[122] but the reality in such accounts is difficult to detect.

Even though the Romans accepted the sexual nature of mankind, they preferred that the sexual urges be directed into heterosexual channels. They recognized that children were the natural result of sexual intercourse but were not averse to using contraceptives, a number of prescriptions and devices being available, and thus indicating that sex was regarded as a source of pleasure. Most of the contraceptives probably proved useless, although some, such as pessaries made with cedar gum or soft wool, might well have been effective.[123] Knowledge of contraceptives was disseminated by medical writers, such as Soranus, who devoted a section of his book on gynecology to them.[124] Contraceptives and abortifacients were not to be used to eliminate families altogether, the Roman ideal always remaining the dedicated father and mother of their mythical history. Though their wealth and power often led Romans to extremes of indulgence, they never quite accepted what they regarded as "deviant" sexuality, in spite of Greek influence. They even felt guilty about extremes in heterosexual indulgence and kept trying to make the morals of reality correspond with what they believed had once been the case.

Why were the Romans so reluctant to accept homosexuality in the same way that the Greeks did? The key might well be that the Roman view of education was different from the Greeks', this difference tending to keep the Romans feeling guilty about any sexual deviation or even any open display of sexual excess, even though they knew these existed. Throughout Roman history, education was regarded as the way to implant respect for ancestors' customs, most Romans feeling the best place to educate children was at home under family control. Even during the height of the Empire, when the custom of educating children together in schools had become well established, the Romans continued to discuss the advantages and disadvantages of family versus school, large numbers continuing to hold that the home was better.[125] The Romans always believed it was the duty of the mother rather than of a slave or others to take major responsibility for early childhood education.[126] Even in the most powerful families the mother was expected to stay at home and be, as it were, a servant to her children, in spite of the vast number of slaves during the height of Roman power. Under such a system, the mother's influence lasted a lifetime.[127]

The upper-class boy child, from the age of 7 onward ceased, as he did in Greece, to be entirely in the hands of women, but in Rome he came under his father's supervision, the father being regarded as the male child's true teacher. Even when professional teachers became somewhat more common, it was emphasized that these teachers were to behave as though they were the child's father,[128] and not his lover.[129] Education is Rome concentrated on training a child for adult tasks. Girls remained at home with their mothers, learning women's tasks; even the wife of Augustus brought up her granddaughters in this fashion.[130] Boys, likewise, went with their fathers, among the aristocrats even attending the Senate meetings,[131] to learn precepts and examples from their fathers.[132] Though such training was not possible for the nonaristocratic boy, it still remained the ideal. Most Roman fathers took their job as teacher of their sons with a strong sense of duty. There is, for instance, an excellent account of the care that Cato the Censor took over his son's education.[133] Cato, in today's terms, would be called a reactionary politician, but as a politician he was also very conscious of the publicity value of his activities. This indicates that he thought his efforts would strike a strong responsive chord in the hearts and minds of the electorate. H. I. Marrou attempted to sum up what he felt were the guiding principles in Roman education. He wrote that:

> The essential thing was the development of the child's or the young man's conscience, the inculcation of a rigid system of moral values, reliable reflexes, a particular way of life—it was the old city ideal, and meant sacrifice, renunciation, and absolute devotion to the community, the State.

> The striking feature about the Roman ideal is that it was never questioned; neither in the tradition nor in the corporate memory is there the slightest trace of any rival

that the city-ideal had to overcome before it could establish itself. . . . The Roman
hero, whatever his name . . . was the man who, by his courage or wisdom, and in
the face of great difficulties, saved his country when it was in danger—a very different person from the wild and imaginative Homeric hero.[134]

A child was always supposed to express gratitude and reverence to his parents,
even after he was an adult, and the parents were supposed to set a proper
example for him or her.[135] This Roman ideal, emphasized by Juvenal, even at
his most bitter, enabled the scandal-mongering gossip columnists of Rome to
point out continually the failings of their leaders. Peccadilloes and sexual
activities were exaggerated to remind Romans of the need to maintain the old
traditions that had brought them the power to rule the world.

Though the Romans went to Athens to study and attended lectures by Greek
philosophers, they never accepted all the Greek practices. They considered
Greek physical education a type of play, disliking its emphasis on performance
and competition. Rather, they wanted the Greeks to act like the Romans: the
Latin term *ludus* meant not only "a game" but "training," moral as well as
physical, and training was to be directed toward a desired end, not simple competition. Greek sport was based on the pure athletics of the *palaestra* and the
stadium, but the Romans viewed sports as entertainment, preferring the circus
and amphitheater.[136]

Beneath the scandalous conduct and rampant sexuality described by the
writers of the first and second centuries A.D., a strong ascetic trend remained
among the Romans. This is most evident in the growth and influence of
Stoicism, which had both political and moral connotations. Stoicism gave a
philosophical, some would say religious, foundation to those aristocrats who
opposed emperors who tried to rule without or against the Senate. Stoicism
taught that to be virtuous was to live in harmony with reason and that this was
the only good. The man who lived the Stoic ideal knew that pain and death
were not the evils others thought them to be; he knew that pleasure was not a
good, and he was not to be influenced by prejudice or by favor, and thus he
could be brave, continent, and just. These Stoic ideals increasingly came to
dominate Rome and had a great influence on Christian attitudes. Tied in with
this was the growth of neo-Platonism, based on the writings of Plotinus, who
urged abstinence from all carnal pleasures, even fron sexual intercourse. He
held that the purifying virtues that turn a man from sensuality were higher
than the social virtues, which only restrained lust to meet social needs; still
higher were the spiritual values, but highest of all were the ideal virtues, which
gave man the power to see God. Every human act deserving to be called virtuous was in some way a purification of the soul; to lapse into carnal love was
a sin. In sum, beneath the outward sexuality of the early Roman empire lay a
Roman ascetic who was trying to emerge, and it was this aspect of Roman (and

Greek) thought that dominated Christian thought and that is discussed in a later chapter.

In spite of some of their excesses, the Romans remained essentially a very moralistic people willing to accept rather bawdy humor[137] but emphasizing the importance of marriage and children and hostile to certain sexual behaviors regarded as deviant. Stoicism and neo-Platonism came to be more influential among the aristocratic writers, the strongest statements and denunciations of Roman sexuality being derived from this group. In retrospect, much of the reported behavior was probably exaggerated, since only rarely was any sexual behavior outside heterosexual relations officially condoned by the Romans, with the possible exception of the sadistic spectacles in the arena. Though several works composed in the first centuries B.C. and A.D. seem to have homosexual connotations, a general denunciation of such "immorality" is a constant theme of Roman literature. Homosexuality tended, in particular, to be regarded as a deviation, and though the Romans might well have tolerated it as beyond an individual's control, they never romanticized it or philosophized about it. It could be that the very narrowness and restrictiveness of the Roman ideal meant that, when individuals broke with the norms, they went overboard. Unfortunately, their exaggerated descriptions and hostility to what they regarded as sexual deviance have misled the casual reader into thinking the Romans accepted such practices. The magnification of these excesses has continued to this day. A college textbook writer recently stated:

> The civilization of the Roman empire was vitiated by homosexuality from its earliest days. A question, uncomfortable to our contemporary lax moralists, may be raised: Is not the common practice of homosexuality a fundamental debilitating factor in any civilization where it is extensively practiced, as it is a wasting spiritual disease in the individual? It is worth considering that another great and flourishing civilization, the medieval Arabic, where homosexuality was also widespread, similarly underwent a sudden malaise and breakdown. Is there some moral psychological causation, resulting from the social effects of homosexuality that has been ignored?[138]

The author of this paragraph has adopted a deplorably narrow view of history; moreover, by implication he labels every homosexual a sick person and homosexuality itself a threat to civilization. Roman society was never vitiated by homosexuality, and though we know little of the sex behavior of the masses, the Roman ideal never fully accepted homosexuality or any other kind of variant sex. The fruits of conquest, the influx of slaves, and the general luxuriousness possible in Rome might temporarily have modified the Roman behavior, but the Romans never ceased to assert their ideals. Even when the old laws and customs were violated, the Romans continued to pretend that these old mores were valid. In fact, as the growth of Stoicism, neo-Platonism, and, eventually, Christianity seemed to indicate, the Romans became ever more rigid in what they regarded as permissible conduct. Historians will have to look elsewhere than alleged weakness caused by homosexuality or sexual excess for the fall of Rome. It was the Roman concept of the correct code of sexual conduct that passed into the Christian world of the West, and not that of the Greeks, which was far more tolerant and less guilt laden.

NOTES

1. Livy, *Ab urbe condita libri,* Introduction, 9, translated by B. O. Foster, Evan T. Sage, and F. G. Moore, eds. (London: William Heinemann, 1936).

2. Crane Brinton, *A History of Western Morals* (New York: Harcourt, Brace, Jovanovich, 1959), p. 113.

3. Seneca, *Epistolae morales,* LXXXVII, 2, translated by Richard M. Gummere, ed. (London: William Heinemann, 1920).

4. Cicero, *De officis,* I, 17 (57), translated by Walter Miller, ed. (London: William Heinemann, 1951).

5. Plutarch, "Cato Major," 22–23, and passim in *Lives,* translated by Bernadotte Perrin, ed. (reprinted, London: William Heinemann, 1959).

6. Cicero, *Pro caelio,* XX, 48, translated by R. Gardner, ed. (reprinted, London: William Heinemann, 1965).

7. *Livy,* I, 57–60.

8. Otto Kiefer, *Sexual Life in Ancient Rome* (London: Routledge and Kegan Paul, 1934), p. 56.

9. Pliny, *Natural History,* XXVIII, vii, 39, translated by W. H. S. Jones, ed. (reprinted, London: William Heinemann, 1963).

10. Some of them are pictured in *Roma amor,* Jean Marcade, ed. (Geneva: Nagel Publishers, 1965). See also Kiefer, *op. cit.;* and Ove Brusendorff and Poul Henningsen, *A History of Eroticism* (New York: Lyle Stuart, 1963), Vol. 1.

11. Juvenal, *Satires,* II, 95, translated by G. C. Ramsay (reprinted, London: William Heinemann, 1957).

12. Petronius, *Satyricon,* translated by William Arrowsmith (Ann Arbor, Mich.: University of Michigan Press, 1959), p. 58. For those using the standard edition of Petronius, which lacks the flair of Arrowsmith's version, the reference can be found in par. 60.

13. Horace, *Satires,* I, 8, translated by Smith Palmer Bovie (Chicago: University of Chicago Press, 1959).

14. See *The Priapeia: An Anthology of Poems on Priapus,* translated by Mitchell S. Buck (privately printed, 1937). See also R. S. Bradford, "Priapaea and the Virgilian Appendix," American Philosophical Association, *Transactions,* LII (1921). Several of the poems are translated by Jack Lindsay, *Ribaldry of Ancient Rome* (New York: Frederick Unger, 1965).

15. At the end of the eighteenth century Sir William Hamilton noticed these phallic amulets and cowrie shells and corresponded about them to Sir Joseph Banks. This led Richard Payne Knight, a wealthy collector of antiquities, to write, in 1786, his *A Discourse on the Worship of Priapus.* This has often been reprinted and is still in print. It includes several illustrations. The female pudenda

was also known colloquially by Latin terms that could be translated as "the field," "the ring," "the furrow," "the cavern," "the conch-shell," "the little boat," "the pit," "the garden," "the between-thighs," "the swine," "the slit," "the hole," "the precipice," "the trench," "the sheath," "the vulva," "veretrum" ("private parts"), and more technically, as *cysthos* and the *cunnus*. The imagery used for the male included "the catapault," "the tail," "the stem," "the parcel," "the column," "the pole," "the lance with balls," "the amulet," "the pike," "the hanger," "the nerve," "the virile sign," "the stake," "the penis," "the stopper," "the phallus," "the javelin," "the tree," "the shaft," "the mover," "the specter," "the bull," "the dart," "the beam," "the ploughshare," the *mutinus* (another name for Priapus), and the *verpa*, among others.

16. For a collection of various classical references to masturbation, particularly Latin ones, see Frederick Charles Forberg, *De figuris veneris*, a book often reprinted; among the editions was one in New York (Medical Press of New York, 1964). Forberg collected reference to sexual intercourse, masturbation, oral–genital contacts, bestiality, and so on. His fourth chapter deals with masturbation.

17. Martial, *Epigrams*, IX, xli, translated by Walter C. A. Ker, ed. (London: William Heinemann, 1968). I have translated it slightly differently.

18. *Ibid.*, II, 43.

19. *Livy*, XXXIX, ix–xiv.

20. *Ibid.*, XXIX, x, xiv.

21. Lucius Apuleius, *Metamorphoses*, VIII, 24–29, translated by S. Gaselee, ed. (reprinted, London: William Heinemann, 1958).

22. Juvenal, *Satires*, 306–345.

23. See the survey in Keifer, *op. cit.*, pp. 108–133.

24. For a discussion of this, along with citations, see Vern L. Bullough, *The Subordinate Sex: A History of Attitudes Toward Women* (Urbana, Ill.: University of Illinois Press, 1973), pp. 77–96. Such a denunciation would fit into the thesis expounded by Mathilde and Mathias Vaerting, *The Dominant Sex: A Study in the Sociology of Sex Differentiation*, translated by Eden and Cedar Paul (New York: George H. Doran, 1923). They held that, as the relationship between the sexes changed, women's actions would be donounced by those who know only a masculine state. In reality, however, the change was not that great, and I do not generally subscribe to the thesis of the Vaerting book.

25. See Wainwright Churchill, *Homosexual Behavior among Males* (New York: Hawthorn Books, 1967), p. 148.

26. M. I. Finley, *Aspects of Antiquity* (New York: Viking Press, 1968), p. 141.

27. Wilhelm Stekel, *Sadism and Masochism: The psychology of Hatred and Cruelty*, translated by Louis Brink (New York: Liveright, 1929, 2 vols.), Vol. 1, pp.31–32.

28. Virgil, *Aeneid*, VI, 851–852, translated by H. Rushton Fairclough, ed. (reprinted, London: William Heinemann, 1960).

29. Kiefer, *op. cit.*, p. 67.

30. The historian Sallust quotes Caesar as saying that death was a liberation when it took place in misfortune and grief. Sallust, *The War with Cataline*, li, 20, translated by J. C. Rolfe, ed. (reprinted, London: William Heinemann, 1960).

31. Suetonius, "Gaius Caligula," XXX in *De vita Caesarum*, translated by John C. Rolfe, ed. (reprinted, London: William Heinemann, 1951).

32. Cicero, *De re publica*, II, 31, translated by Clinton W. Keyes, ed. (reprinted, London: William Heinemann, 1961).

33. See, for example, *Livy,* II, 31.

34. Seneca, *De consolatione ad Marciam,* XX, 3, in *Moral Essays,* translated by John W. Basore, ed. (reprinted, London: William Heinemann, 1951), XX, 3.

35. Kiefer, *op. cit.,* pp. 85–86.

36. Valerius Maximus, *Factorum et dictorum memorabilium,* II, vii, 13–14, Carl Kempf, ed. (Leipzig: Teubner, 1888).

37. Athenaeus, *The Deipnosophists,* 153c, translated by Charles Carl Kempf, ed. (reprinted, London: William Heinemann, 1957).

38. *Livy* XVI (*periocha*).

39. See for example *Livy,* XXII, xxx, 15–17; XXXI, xl, 4–6; XXXIX, xlvi, 2; XLI, xxvii, 11.

40. Cicero, *Letters to Atticus,* VII, 14, translated by D. R. Shackleton Bailey, ed. (London: William Heinemann, 1965–1970).

41. *Suetonius,* "Julius," X, 2.

42. *Plutarch,* "Caesar," V, 5.

43. Cicero, *Tusculan Disputations,* II, xvii, 41, translated by J. E. King, ed. (reprinted, London: William Heinemann, 1960).

44. Tacitus, *Annals,* I, 75–76, translated by John Jackson, ed. (reprinted, London: William Heinemann, 1956).

45. Ludwig Friedländer, *Roman Life and Manners under the Early Empire,* translated by J. H. Freese and Leonard A. Magnus (reprinted, New York: Barnes and Noble, 1965), Vol. 2, p. 43.

46. Isidore, *Etymologiarum sive originum,* XVIII, 42, W. M. Lindsay, ed. (reprinted, Oxford, England: Clarendon Press, 1957).

47. See, for example, Julius Rosenbaum, *The Plague of Lust* (reprinted, New York: Frederick Publications, 1955), p. 97; and Vern L. Bullough, *The History of Prostitution* (New Hyde Park, N.Y.: University Books, 1964); as well as Ovid, *Ars amoris,* I, 99 ff., translated by J. H. Mozley, ed. (reprinted, London: William Heinemann, 1962).

48. For a lengthy discussion of luxury in Rome and its effect, see Friedländer, *op. cit.,* Vol.2, Top. 131–230.

49. For examples of this attitude, see, for example, Cicero, *Tusculan Disputations,* IV, xxxiii (70), who held that shame began with stripping of men's bodies openly. Other references would include Pliny, *Natural History,* VX, v (19). The list could go on.

50. *Suidas,* "Thamyris," Ada Adler, ed. (Leipzig: Teubner, 1928–1935).

51. Edward Gibbon, *The Decline and Fall of the Roman Empire,* James Bury, ed. (reprinted, New York: Heritage Press, 1946), p. 1475. This appears under his discussion of Roman law.

52. *Valerius Maximus,* VI, i, 9.

53. *Suidas,* "Caius Laetorius"; *Valerius Maximus,* VI, cap. 1; Dionysius Halicarnassus, *Roman Antiquities,* XVI, iv, 2, translated by Ernest Cary, ed. (reprinted, London: William Heinemann, 1950); *Livy,* VIII, xxviii, 1–8, XXXIX, xlii, 5–12; and Polybius, *The Histories,* VI, xxxvii, 9, translated by W. R. Paton ed. (reprinted, London: William Heinemann, 1960).

54. *Valerius Maximus,* VI, cap. i, 7.

55. See, for example, *Harper's Dictionary of Classical Literature and Antiquities,* Harry Thurston Peck, ed. (first published in 1896 and reprinted, New York: Cooper Square Publishers, 1963), pp. 945–946.

56. Cicero, *Epistulae ad familiares,* VIII, 12, 3, translated by W. Glynn Williams, ed. (reprinted, London: William Heinemann, 1958).

57. For details of the Augustan moral legislation, see Hugh Last, "The Social Policy of Augustus," *Cambridge Ancient History* (New York: Macmillan, 1934), Vol. 10, esp. pp. 451–455.

58. Polybius, *The Histories*, VI, xxxvii, 9; *Sciptores historiae Augustae*, "Severus Alexander," XXIV, translated by David Magie, ed. (reprinted, London: William Heinemann, 1953). Alexander attempted to suppress male prostitution but, after opposition, merely taxed it. It was later abolished, *ibid.*, XXXIX, 2. Clement of Alexandria, *Paedagogus*, III, iii, 23, translated by Simon P. Wood (New York: Fathers of the Church, 1954), p. 218, said that the Romans condemned to the mines anyone guilty of allowing his body to be used in a feminine manner. Sextus Empiricus, *Outlines of Pyrrhonism*, I, 152, III, 199, translated by R. G. Bury, ed. (reprinted, London: William Heinemann, 1955), indicated that homosexual intercourse was forbidden. In the *Institutes*, 5th ed., IV, xviii, 3, translated by J. B. Moyle, ed. (Oxford, England: Clarendon Press, 1913), it is stated that the penalty for persons who engaged in criminal intercourse with those of their own sex was death by provisions of the *Lex Julia* passed under Augustus. This is doubtful, although the death penalty might later have been provided. See also *Valerius Maximus*, VI, i, 3.

59. L. R. Pogey-Castries, *Histoire de l'amour Grec dans l'antiquité* (Paris: Guy le Prat, 1952), p. 185.

60. *Suetonius*, "Julius," XLIV, 4.

61. *Ibid.*, LII, 3.

62. Josephus, *Antiquities of the Jews*, XV, 2, translated by William Whiston (Philadelphia: J. Grigg, 1833), reports Anthony's making advances to Aristobulus.

63. *Suetonius*, "Augustus," LXXI.

64. The treatment of Tiberius by Tacitus has been much discussed. See, for example, T. S. Jerome, *Aspects of the Study of Roman History* (reprinted, New York: Capricorn Books, 1962), pp. 319–380; F. B. Marsh, *The Reign of Tiberius* (reprinted New York: Barnes and Noble, 1959); and Ronald Syme, *Tacitus* (Oxford, England: Clarendon Press, 2 vols.), Vol. 1, pp. 420–434. See also Gregorio Maranon, *Tiberius: The Resentful Caesar* (New York: Duell, Sloan and Pearce, 1956).

65. *Suetonius*, "Tiberius," XLIII.

66. *Suetonius*, "Gaius Caligula," XXXVI; and Dio Cassius, *Roman History*, LIX, ii, translated by Ernest Cary, ed. (reprinted, London: William Heinemann, 1955).

67. *Suetonius*, "Nero," XVIII–XXIX; *Dio Cassius*, LXII, xvii. There are similar references in *Juvenal* and *Tacitus*.

68. *Juvenal*, II, 99.

69. *Suetonius*, "Otho," X–XI, and, for his character, XII.

70. J. Z. Eglinton, *Greek Love* (New York: Oliver Layton Press, 1964), pp. 278–279.

71. Churchill, *op. cit.*, pp. 142–154.

72. *Scriptores historiae Augustae*, "Hadrian," XIV; *Dio Cassius*, LXIX, ii, "Sextus Aurelius Victor," *Liber de Caesaribus*, xiv, F. Pichlmayr, ed. (Leipzig: Teubner, 1911).

73. Kiefer, *op. cit.*, pp. 336–341. For a fictionalized account, see the novel by Margaret Yourcenar, *Hadrian's Memoirs* (New York: Farrar, Straus & Young, 1954).

74. Herodian, *History of the Roman Empire*, V, ii, 9; and V, v, 3–5, viii, 1–2, translated by Edward C. Echols (Berkeley, Calif.: University of California Press, 1959).

75. There are several references to this in Martial, *Epigrams*, I, 9; XI, 45. There was even a tax on prostitutes imposed originally by Caligula *(Suetonius*, "Caligula," XL), and though male prostitutes are not specially mentioned in this reference, they apparently were included, as later

references indicate. See *Sciptores historiae Augustae,* "Severus Alexander," XXIV, XXXIX, 2; and perhaps *Suetonius,* "Nero," XXVIII–XXIX; Tacitus, *Annals,* XV, xxxvii; and Justin Martyr, *Apology,* translated by Thomas B. Falls (New York: Christian Heritage, 1948), I. See also Pogey-Castries, *op. cit.*

76. This might have been the case of the adopted son who was mourned by Statius, *Silvae,* V, 5, translated by J. H. Mozley, ed. (reprinted, London: William Heinemann, 1961). See also Seneca, *De constantia,* XI, 3, in *Moral Essays.*

77. *Athenaeus,* IV, 154a.

78. *Martial,* XI, xlv.

79. *Roma amor* and other collections of Roman erotic art include such illustrations.

80. See *Suetonius,* "Julius," XLIX, 1; Catullus, *Carmen,* XVI, 2, XX, 4, translated by F. W. Cornish, ed. (reprinted, London: William Heinemann, 1966); *Martial,* I, xcii, 14; VI, xxxiii, 1; VII, lxvii, 1; XI, civ., 6, 17; XII, lxxxv, 1; XVI, ii, XX, iv.

81. *Catullus,* XVI, ii; *Juvenal,* II, 99.

82. *Scriptores historiae Augustae,* "Commodus," III, 6; "Elagabalus," V, 5.

83. *Juvenal,* II, 63; *Martial,* XIV, lxxiv.

84. Pliny, *Natural History,* X, xv, 32.

85. For the Latin references, see Priapeia in *Catulli, Tibulli, Propertii Carmina . . . et Priapeia,* 25, 41, and 76, Lucian Mueller, ed. (Leipzig: Teubner, 1885).

86. *Martial,* VII, lxvii, 1; VII, lxx, 1; and Caelius Aurelianus, *Tardarum passionum,* edited and translated as part of *On Acute Diseases and on Chronic Diseases,* IV, 9, 132, (Chicago: University of Chicago Press, 1950).

87. *Martial,* III, lxxi, and XI, lxxxviii, gives some examples of the types of activity that took place. Apparently, the male Roman homosexuals were both oral and anal in their activities. See also the collection of references in Forberg, *op. cit.,* passim.

88. See Vern L. Bullough, *The Development of Medicine as a Profession* (Basel, Switzerland: Karger, 1966), for a discussion of this point.

89. Caelius Aurelianus, *On Acute Diseases and on Chronic Diseases,* IV, 9, 131–137.

90. Pogey-Castries, *op. cit.,* p. 185.

91. This belief is based on the biography of him by the grammarian Aelius Donatus, who included it in his preface to the commentary on the works of Virgil. See Donatus, *Vita Vergilianae,* Colin Hardie, ed. (Oxford, England: Clarendon Press, 1966), pp. 6–18. There is little contemporary evidence, although *Martial,* VII, lvi, 12, mentions the beautiful Alexis.

92. Virgil, *Aeneid,* Book IX.

93. Virgil, *Ecologues,* II, translated by H. Rushton Fairclough, ed. (reprinted, London: William Heinemann, 1960).

94. André Gide, *Corydon* (New York: Farrar, Straus, and Company, 1950).

95. Horace, *Satires,* I, 2, 11, 113 ff.

96. Horace, *Epodes,* XI; and *Odes,* IV, 1 and 10, translated by C. E. Bennett, ed. (reprinted, London: William Heinemann, 1960).

97. *Catullus,* XV, XXIV, XLVIII, LXXXI, XCIX.

98. Albius Tibullus, *Elegies,* I, iv, 16, 39–40, 53–60, translated by J. P. Postgate, ed. (reprinted, London: William Heinemann, 1966).

99. *Ibid.,* I, iv, 81–84; viii, 49, and ix.

100. Plautus, *Asinaria,* 703 (II, iii, 103). *Captivi,* 867 (IV, iii, 87); *Mostellaria,* 847 (III, ll,

159); *Pseudolus,* 785 (III, i, 16); 1180 (IV, vii, 79); 1189 (IV, vii, 87), in *Comediae,* W. M. Lindsay, ed. (reprinted, Oxford, England: Clarendon Press, 1959).

101. Juvenal, *Satires,* II and IX.

102. *Martial,* passim. See, for example, the various citations in this chapter.

103. See particularly the Arrowsmith translation of the *Satyricon, op. cit.*

104. Ovid, *Ars amoris,* II.

105. This comparison was made by *Newsweek,* August 24, 1970, p. 40.

106. *Juvenal,* X, 295–309.

107. *Martial,* I, xc.

108. *Ibid.,* VII, lxvii.

109. *Juvenal,* VI.

110. Lucian, *Dialogues of Courtesans,* translated by M. D. MacLeod, ed. (London: William Heinemann, 1961).

111. See the brief discussion by Jeanette H. Foster, *Sex Variant Women in Literature* (London: Frederick Muller, 1958); anf Forberg, *op. cit.,*

112. Ovid, *Metamorphoses,* XIV, 623–697, translated by Frank J. Miller, ed. (reprinted, London: William Heinemann, 1966).

113. Pliny, *Natural History,* VII, iv.

114. *Ibid.,*XXXI, 12; XXVII, 37.

115. Diodorus Siculus, *Histories,* XXXII, 12, translated by C. H. Oldfather, ed. (London: William Heinemann, 1933).

116. For a discussion of the *magodist* and some of the roles of the female impersonators, see Athenaeus, *Deipnosophists,* XIV, 621 f.

117. *Juvenal,* VI, 60–82; VII, 79–97.

118. *Suetonius,* "Julius," 74.

119. *Juvenal,* VI, 314–351.

120. This is an insert in the Loeb edition of *Juvenal,* VI, following line 365. The 34 lines were discovered in 1899 by E. O. Einstedt in a Bodleian MS (*Canonicianus* 41) and were identified as being written by Juvenal. It cannot be found in all editions.

121. *Juvenal,* VI, 333–334. This is not translated in the Loeb edition.

122. Lucius Apuleius, *Metamorphoses or the Golden Ass.*

123. See Norman E. Himes, *Medical History of Contraception* (reprinted, New York: Schocken Books, 1970), pp. 82–101.

124. Soranus, *Gynecology,* Book 1, Chap. 19, (60–65), translated by Owsei Temkin, ed. (Baltimore: Johns Hopkins Press, 1956).

125. Quintillian, *Institutio oratoris,* II, ii, 1–9, translated by H. E. Butter, ed. (reprinted, London: William Heinemann, 1958).

126. Tacitus, *Dialogus de oratoribus,* XVIII, translated by William Peterson Smith, ed. (reprinted, London: William Heinemann, 1956).

127. A good example of the influence of the mother and of how the Romans were supposed to regard their mother is in Livy's story of the mother of Coriolanus, *Livy,* II, xl, 5–9.

128. *Quintillian,* II, ii, 1–9.

129. Plutarch, *Quaestiones Romanae,* 272c, in *Plutarch's Moralia,* translated by Frank Cole Babbitt, ed. (reprinted, London: William Heinemann, 1962).

130. *Suetonius,* "Augustus," LXIV.

131. Aulus Gellius, *Attic Nights,* I, xxiii, 4–5, translated by John C. Rolfe, ed. (reprinted, London: William Heinemann, 1954).

132. Pliny, *Epistles,* VIII, xiv, 4–5.

133. *Plutarch,* "Cato Maior," xx.

134. H. I. Marrou, *A History of Education in Antiquity,* translated by George Lamb (New York: Sheed and Ward, 1956), pp. 234–235.

135. *Juvenal,* XIV, 38–58.

136. See E. Norman Gardiner, *Athletics of the Ancient World* (Oxford, England: Clarendon Press, 1965), pp. 117–119.

137. See, for example, Lindsay, *op. cit.*

138. Norman F. Cantor, *Medieval History: The Life and Death of a Civilization* (New York: Macmillan, 1963), p. 31. Edward Gibbon, the eighteenth-century historian of the Roman Empire, had stated, in one of his footnotes, that of the "first fifteen emperors, Claudius was the only one whose taste in love was entirely correct," and later he has a brief discussion of homosexuality, but he never went as far as Cantor, whose charges seem to be made from whole cloth. Gibbon, *op. cit.*, p. 59, fn. 26, and p. 1475. The discussion of homosexuality appears chiefly in his discussion of Roman law, Chap. 44. As indicated, it was mostly in the first century A.D., at the height of the Empire, that homosexuality was portrayed somewhat favorably, and most of the references before and after are hostile.

7

CLASSICAL SOURCES
OF CHRISTIAN HOSTILITY TO SEX

Early Christians, at least as represented by the evangelical and patristic writers, sought to attain perfection through renunciation of the world and subjugation of the body. To attain this, every means was to be employed from fasting to solitude, including prayer, mortification of the flesh, and above all, sexual continence. All Christians were expected to meet a minimal level of spiritual achievement, but those desiring to achieve a higher life standard were expected, at least in practice, to abstain from coitus and even from all association with members of the opposite sex.

This emphasis on sexual asceticism did not originate with the early Christians but represented a strong countercurrent within the classical world to the more sexually positive tradition already discussed.[1] In this sense the negative sexuality in Christianity is derived more from paganism than from Judaism, the emphasis on celibacy coming more from Greek philosophy than from the Gospel writers.[2] So influential have these sex-negative attitudes of the pre-Christian philosophers been that, consciously or unconsciously, they still today determine much of Western sexual thinking. Emil Brunner, one of the most influential theologians of the twentieth century, held that a major task for the scholar of today was to oppose what he described as the false non-Christian views of marriage and sex based on Hellenistic thinking.[3] Morton S. Enslin put the matter succinctly: "Christianity did not make the world ascetic; rather the world in which Christianity found itself strove to make Christianity ascetic."[4]

Though an ascetic tradition can be traced to the beginnings of Greek history, asceticism became more powerful during the Hellenistic period, after the death of Alexander the Great in 323 B.C. By that time the old beliefs in the Olympian gods were no longer tenable to the more sophisticated, and the growing power of Rome and the political failure of the Greek world disenchanted many. In their search for certainty in a troubled world, the Greeks turned to otherworldly answers and to asceticism. This group of ascetic thinkers encouraged man to forget he was flesh and to regard himself as a separate soul lost and imprisoned in a body. When this spirit–flesh dichotomy infiltrated Christianity, it broke down the psychosomatic unity characteristic of the Old Testament view of man. According to some scholars, these intellectual carryovers sterilized the Christian sense "of creation, perverted its confession of evil, and limited its hopes to total reconciliation to the horizons of a narrowed and bloodless spiritualism."[5]

The early sources for these Greek concepts are still not clear, because so many of the earliest references are shrouded in myth and legend. As far as we can now tell, the concepts were derived from cults centered around the god Dionysus and the legendary Orpheus, although the sources about Orpheus have long been a subject of confusion. Traditionally, the legend of Orpheus recounts how he had set out for the underworld to bring his wife Eurydice back from the dead. During his visit he so charmed Hades that the god permitted Eurydice to return to the world of the living, provided Orpheus not look back until he had regained the surface. When Orpheus was unable to avoid stealing a backward glance, Eurydice was returned to the underworld. This story about Orpheus was later incorporated in the Orphic mysteries, although its significance in the cult is not clear. There are other legends about Orpheus. Some of the ancient writers stated he was later killed by Zeus for divulging the secrets of the gods. Another version, rejected by most ancients, carried homosexual overtones. In this version, Orpheus had loved Eurydice so passionately that, when he lost her the second time, he foreswore womankind altogether and introduced pederasty to Greece. This rejection of womankind so angered some of the female adherents of Dionysus that they tore him to pieces in a frenzy of passion.[6] Other accounts have him torn apart by the Maenads, women inspired by the ecstatic frenzy we believe was part of the Dionysian festival. All that we can state for certain is that Orpheus became a cult hero, a singer, a prophet, and a teacher, bringing with him a new religion to replace the old. It is as a magical musician with power over all the wild, untamed animals that he most often appears in the sarcophagi and on the surviving wall paintings. He either modified and rearranged, or was credited with modifying and rearranging, the

Bacchic rites centered around Dionysus, a god who had started out as a Thracian deity of vegetation, particularly of the vine and its product, wine.

The cardinal belief of the Orphic religion was the possibility of attaining immortality, an achievement requiring purity not only in ritual but also as a way of life.[7] Key to the doctrine of purity was a belief that the soul was undergoing punishment for sin and that the body was an enclosure or prison in which the soul had been incarcerated.[8] Though this belief was justified by a rather primitive theology, it must have served a strong need for large numbers of people, since, in spite of more sophisticated explanations, the emphasis on asceticism and celibacy remained.

In the beginning, according to the Orphic teaching, which adopted and modified the theogony of Homer and Hesiod, there had been only night. Eventually, a silver egg containing Eros (also called *Phanes* or *Erekapios*) had formed in the divine ether and began to grow until it burst, whereupon it separated into two elements, Heaven (*Uranos*) and Earth (*Ge*). These two elements copulated and gave birth to Cronos and other Titans. Cronos became the father of Rhea, Demeter, Hades, Poseidon, and Zeus, among other gods. Zeus eventually swallowed up his own father, thereby encompassing all creation, and then created another world, the present world. He copulated with Persephone, who gave birth to Dionysus, to whom Zeus gave dominion over the world. Before Dionysus could assume control, he was killed, cooked, and eaten by the Titans, although his heart had been salvaged by Athena. When Zeus discovered what had happened, he burned the Titans to ashes with his thunderbolts, and then, after eating the heart of Dionysus, he engaged in intercourse with Semele, giving birth once again to Dionysus. From the ashes of the Titans, Zeus fashioned man, an act interpreted to mean that his new creation contained something of the divine, derived from the remnants of Dionysus, and something of the opposite, coming from the Titans.[9] This was the basis of the Orphic belief that man had a twofold nature: good and evil.

To achieve his potential for divinity, man had to cherish and cultivate the divine (Dionysian) and purge away the evil (Titanic) elements in nature. Man's purpose on earth was to suppress the evil and achieve the good by periodic rituals, whose nature is unknown to us today, and by living an Orphic life.[10] Those following the Orphic way would achieve immortality in the next world, where life was pictured as a banquet of the holy, or, to translate the concept literally, a "carousal," perhaps influenced by the Dionysian association with wine. The unjust, those failing to live an Orphic life, would be punished.

Though the Orphic mysteries were never officially incorporated in the state religion of classical Greece, Orphism enjoyed a great vogue and came to exercise considerable influence on the Pythagoreans, Plato, and later Greek philosophical movements. From these sources dualism entered Christianity.

Today we know little of what actually constituted the "Orphic life" other than the tradition that the true believer abstained from eating meat (based in part on a belief in the transmigration of souls); was prohibited from wearing woolen clothing in holy places; practiced a general asceticism, including sexual abstinence; and tried to live an upright moral life. We believe that the Orphics advocated sexual abstinence because they regarded sexual intercourse as polluting. The Orphics regarded life as a conflict between the "higher" and "lower" nature of man, this representing a rather radical departure in Greek thought. Most Greek religious teachers and oral prophets continued to teach that the difference between virtue and vice was not one of kind but rather of degree and direction. From this viewpoint, any activity kept within bounds was good; only when it got out of hand and tried to usurp a larger share of an individual's life than was warranted did it become an evil. Sin then was not primarily an aberration of the will but an error of intellectual judgment that could be corrected. This view was, however, rejected by some Greek thinkers and by the bulk of the early Christians, who adopted instead the Orphic idea of the conflict of the body and the soul and viewed life as an escape from the bondage of the flesh.

From the Orphics we can trace this dualism to Pythagoras, a semimythical individual who lived in the sixth century B.C. Pythagoras adopted and modified the Orphic doctrine into an ecumenical movement encompassing Persian and Indian concepts. He created a celibate brotherhood with economic, religious, and political implications, whose object was the moral regeneration of society. In the struggle between the aristocratic and democratic movements so common in Greece in the sixth century, the Pythagoreans allied with the aristocratic party, which meant that, when the aristocratic governments were overthrown in the middle of the fifth century B.C., the Pythagoreans entered a period of decline as a political and economic movement but survived as a religious cult for several more centuries. Like the Orphics, the Pythagoreans incorporated much of Greek mythology into their belief structure, and Pythagoras himself had been closely associated with Delphi, traditionally the sacred place of Greece. The name *Pythagoras* means, in fact, "the mouthpiece of Delphi."

From what can be reconstructed of the teachings of Pythagoras, it seems he believed the universe was ultimately divisible into two opposing principles, one described as Unlimited Breath, the other as Limit. The famous Pythagorean teachings that all things are Numbers was concerned with the nature and operations of Limit. The opposition of Limit to the Unlimited was reflected in the opposition of light to darkness, odd to even, one to many, right to left, male to female, resting to moving, straight to curved, good to bad, square to oblong, and better to worse. Limit, light, odd, and male were right, and the Unlimited, darkness, even, and female were wrong, or at least, one set was superior, the other inferior.[11] The grouping of the female with the inferior had important implications, in attitudes toward both women and sex.

The soul, the higher principle, was imprisoned in the mortal body as the dead were in a tomb. The body itself was governed by evil passions, the indwelling Furies, and it was important that men not be the slaves of their bodies. Rather, man could escape the domination of flesh by achieving a *katharsis*, which required the observance of certain taboos so that men could improve and save their souls. Sexual consummation was considered to be the prime pandering to the indwelling Furies, and every passion, every symbol relating to this had to be repudiated. This belief had some rather ludicrous implications. For example, according to tradition, Pythagoras was killed because he refused to cross a bean field in his flight, either because (1) he believed that beans represented human testicles or (2) because the odor of decaying beans was similar to that of sperm or (3) because he thought that sprouting beans resembled the female genitals.[12] Ancient writers differed among these three explanations, but the point to emphasize is that sex was involved.

Apparently, Pythagoras himself did not advocate total abstinence. Rather, he is reported to have advised his followers to leave sexual pleasures for the winter and to abstain in the summer. He also taught that intercourse "was less harmful in autumn and spring," but qualified this by adding that, even under the best of circumstances, intercourse was harmful and not conducive to health. When asked when a man should consort with a woman, Pythagoras is said to have replied, "When you want to lose the strength you have."[13] Some of his later disciples went further in their condemnation of sex. In the fifth century B.C. Empedocles denounced all sexual intercourse. Empedocles might well have been an isolated extreme within the Pythagorean tradition, but his denunciation seems logical in light of the Pythagorean assumptions. Arguing from the statements of Empedocles as well as the logic of the Pythagorean position, one modern investigator, E. R. Dodds, has claimed that sexual asceticism not only originated in Greece but also was carried "by a Greek mind to its extreme theoretical limit."[14]

The most influential transmitter of some of the Pythagorean ideas was Plato, who rejected much of the cultic aspects while elevating and refining the philosophical ideals. Plato expressed contempt for those who taught or believed that God could be persuaded or bribed to confer blessed immortality on an initiate merely because he performed special ceremonials, sacraments, and rituals; because he accepted certain doctrines or revelations; or even because he adopted a way of life involving ascetic renunciation. Nonetheless, he believed that the moral law was fixed and immutable, that our fate depended on our actions during life, and that each of us, by achieving a life of virtue could rise above his Titanic nature and gain immortality.

Like the Orphics and the Pythagoreans, Plato was a dualist, although he called his two universal principles Ideas and Matter, which he equated with the intelligible and sensible worlds, respectively. Ideas were eternal and immutable, present always and everywhere, self-identical, self-existent, absolute, separate, simple, and without beginning or end. They were complete, perfect existence without taint of sense or imagery, invisible, accessible only to the mind. Most commentators on Plato (following Aristotle) had considered Plato's Ideas (or Forms) as metaphysical principles existing in and for themselves apart from the sensible world and possessing the incorporeal yet quasisubstantial being commonly attributed by Christian theologians to deity. Christianity, in fact, adopted so many of the Platonic concepts that Justin Martyr, an early Christian Father, never tired of reiterating that Plato must have been versed in Christian prophecy, for he was a Christian before Jesus had appeared. Plato appealed greatly to the early Christians; his teachings, or rather their neo-Platonic interpretations, were the dominant force in early Christian thought, as can be seen in the next chapter.

Plato argued that matter or the material world of sensible objects might exist but only so far as these caught and retained the likeness of the Idea; in any case they were always imperfect imitations. Thus Plato, perhaps influenced by Pythagoras, taught that the soul, an immaterial agent, was superior to the body and was hindered by the body in its performance of the higher, psychic functions of human life. Reality had two components for Plato, the changeable world of bodies, which man could know through sense perception, and the Ideal, the timeless essence or universal realities. Only the world of Ideas contained the ultimate realities from which the world of sensible things had been patterned. This real world could not be known through the senses but only through the *nous,* the mind or soul, which knew because it was the essence of the divine being and had existed before the body. Though the soul had been born with true knowledge, the encrustation of bodily cares and interests made it difficult to recall the truth, which was innately and subconsciously present. Sense perception might aid the soul in reminiscence, but only by using intuitive thought, by clearing the mind of all bodily concerns, and by probing ever deeper (by the Socratic method of questions and answers) might it be possible to provide the necessary stimuli for recollection.

Plato conceived of love in dualistic terms, sacred and profane, the one occupied with the mind and character of the beloved, the other with the body. Only through the higher love, the nonphysical, could true happiness be found. To reach this highest form, there was a step-by-step progression starting with the body of the beloved, then physical loveliness in general, followed by a contemplation of the beauties of the mind and soul, and finally, the pure Form or essence of loveliness in itself, absolute, separate, simple, and everlasting, which without diminution or increase or change, was imparted to the ever-growing and continually perishing beauties of all things.[15] Plato compared the two types of love to a charioteer driving two winged steeds, one of which (true love) was a thoroughbred, gentle and eager to bear its driver upward into the presence of the ideal, while the other (physical love) was vicious and refractory, forever bolting in pursuit of physical satisfaction. The discipline of love lay in training the unruly steed to run in harmony with its thoroughbred mate, and if the charioteer proved successful, the team would carry the lover and beloved away from the world of sense to the vision of absolute loveliness that alone made them truly lovely and lovable in each other's eyes. Love, to Plato, became then the mutual attainment of the self-mastery that cured the disease of physical craving.[16] By this explanation physical love must be inferior to true love, whether homosexual or heterosexual. In his mind, copulation lowered a man to the frenzied passions characteristic of beasts, and he relegated sexual desire to the lowest element of the psyche.[17]

Plato was not alone in emphasizing that the true state of goodness was devoid of physical sexual activity. Democritus (fifth century B.C.) attempted to construct a reasoned ethic based on his concept of the atomistic nature of the universe. Though there is only the flimsiest evidence from which to reconstruct his moral theory, he seems to have believed that enjoyment was the end naturally sought by all mankind, while pain was to be avoided. Democritus held, however, that not all pleasures were equally good. the pleasures of the senses were short-lived and agitating and led in the long run to surfeit and pain. They were not nearly so desirable as the calm, enduring, painless pleasures of the mind. This meant that virtue, for Democritus, was essentially the exercise of intelligence, and because sexual activity tended to interfere with the pleasures of the mind, he disapproved of it. He is reported to have said that the brave man was the one who overcame "not only his enemies but his pleasures." There were some men who were "masters of cities but slaves to women." He thought the ultimate disgrace for a man was to be ruled by a woman.

> Those who derive their pleasures from their bellies—overstepping due measure in eating or drinking or making love—find that they are brief and only last as long as they are eating and drinking, whereas the pains are many. They have a perpetual desire for the same things, and once men get what they desire, the pleasure passes quickly, and there is nothing good in them but a brief enjoyment and then they want the same things again.

This was true whether excess was present or not, for the transience of such pleasures was inherent in their very nature. To base one's life on them was to build on sand, for the pleasures of the body could not last. In the end, Democritus adopted a dualistic explanation of the soul, concluding that the man choosing the "good of the soul" made a more divine choice and the one choosing the good of the body made "a mortal choice." The beauty of the body was merely animal appeal unless intelligence was also present, and men could not be happy by virtue of their bodies or possessions but only by virtue of right living and fullness of understanding.[18]

Epicurus, the fourth-century B.C. disciple of Democritus as well as the founder of the influential Epicurean school of philosophy, was even more specific in his condemnation of sex. He held that "sexual intercourse never benefitted any man," and argued that the pleasant life could not result from "sexual intercourse with women."[19] The Epicurean school continued as an influential philosophical movement into Roman times, when its best known commentator was Carus Lucretius (98–54 B.C.). Lucretius went so far as to assert that sexual desire was a sickness and that neither homosexual nor heterosexual intercourse could cure it. He concluded that the wise man would avoid the "madness" altogether, for it could not in any case be used as a means of reaching the ideal, unruffled life.[20]

The Cynics, a somewhat less influential school than the Epicureans but also dating from the fourth century B.C., held similar ideas. The most notorious adherent of the Cynic school was Diogenes (fourth century B.C.), reputed to have spent his life living in a tub and walking the streets by daylight, lantern in hand, looking for someone worthy to be called an honest man. Diogenes, seeking to reduce man's desires and appetites to those indispensable to life, attempted to renounce all those imposed by civilization. He praised those who refrained from marriage[21]; when asked what the right time for marriage was, he quipped, "For young men, not yet; for old men, never."[22] Diogenes was not necessarily an advocate of celibacy; he condemned marriage, not because sex led men into lust, but rather because marriage was such a burden. He is, nonetheless, a representative of a strong countercurrent in Greek and Roman thought to the emphasis put on marriage and family by society and an example of the strong undercurrent of hostility to sexuality.

Zeno (340–265 B.C.), the founder of Stoicism, patterned his personal life after that of the Cynics[23] but occasionally modified their teachings, for he recognized that man had to live in a material environment. This led him to argue that instincts and emotions were not necessarily antagonistic to right living, provided they were kept in submission to the ruling principle. Salvation was reserved to the sage alone; this left the rest of humanity almost entirely in a state of total depravity, utter folly, and complete unhappiness. Man's only consolation was that there were degrees of virtue and of vice, and men could progress from total depravity to perfect virtue. Attempts at moral improvement were then a virtue.

Sex, to the Stoics, was not bad in itself, since reproduction was not merely of the body but of the soul. The ruling principle of the universe projected itself into the organs of reproduction, just as it did into those of the senses, and the resultant seed was a divine thing, a fragment of a sort of soul plasm torn from the spirits of our ancestors. Reason was not, however, present in the embryo but developed only after birth. In this sense man was like an animal, but what ultimately distinguished him from animals, whose impulses were governed only by desire and aversion, was man's ability to govern himself by reason.[24]

Anything threatening reason had to be closely watched. Immoderation in bodily activities was irrational, because it made man dependent on his own body.[25] The Stoic watchwords were nature, virtue, decorum, and freedom from excess. Marriage was recognized, but passion in marriage was suspect, because the only justification for marriage was propagation of the race. The first-century A.D. Stoic teacher Musonius Rufus went so far as to teach that marital intercourse was permissible only if the purpose was procreative. Intercourse for pleasure within the confines of marriage was reprehensible. Since homosexual activities were for pleasure alone, not for reproduction, they too were condemned and classed as unnatural.[26] Seneca, the first-century A.D. Stoic rhetorician and statesman, was cited by St. Jerome as claiming that a

> wise man ought to love his wife with judgment, not affection. Let him control his impulses and not be borne headlong into copulation. Nothing is fouler than to love a wife like an adulteress. Certainly those who say that they united themselves to wives to produce children for the sake of the state and the human race ought, at any rate, to imitate the beasts, and when their wife's belly swells not destroy the offspring. Let them show themselves to their wives not as lovers, but as husbands.[27]

This was an argument not only for restraint in the marital bed but also against birth control and abortion.

How great an influence did these philosophical concepts have on everyday attitudes? From the previous discussions of sexual life in Greece and Rome, it seems that initially they had very little. For the most part, they seem to be intellectual discussions of the select few, not designed for the masses and not yet institutionalized either in religion or in law. Indirectly, however, their influence was growing. By the first century A.D. they were being reflected in some of the medical writings. In the *De medicina*, Celsus wrote:

> Sexual intercourse neither should be avidly desired, nor should it be feared very much. Rarely performed, it revives the bodies, performed frequently it weakens. However, since nature, and not number should be considered in frequency with consideration of age and the body, sexual union is recognized as not harmful when it is followed by neither apathy nor pain.[28]

Celsus seems to be a moderate, working within the learned tradition. Increasingly, however, the ascetic ideals were becoming more and more involved in the religious teachings of the time, the religious writers carrying these philosophical doctrines to the masses. Undoubtedly, vast numbers of people ignored the sexual implications of these religious teachings, but increasingly, sexual asceticism came to be regarded as an ideal. In trying to direct public opinion into certain channels, the theologians of the time found it easier to concentrate on some aspects of sex than others, emphasizing the good of sex within marriage while condemning it outside marriage. Inevitably then, they would condemn homosexuality and any other sexual activities not leading to procreation, being much more severe in this condemnation than the pagan philosophers.

The historian has to attempt to answer still another question, namely, how much do the ideas about sex that have come down to us reflect the personal prejudice of the writers transmitting this heritage? Whereas no definite answer can be given, it is perhaps surprising how many of the early philosophers were unmarried, including Heraclitus, Plato, Epicurus, and Epictetus. It might well be that the prejudice against the flesh and against the female sex owes as much to their own ascetic, misogynistic outlooks as to any other reason. At any rate, their prejudices must have had considerable implications for their assumptions about the ideal life style.[29]

By the first century B.C., the center of philosophical speculation had shifted to Alexandria in Egypt; here the philosophical attitudes came to exercise great influence on the religious outlook that in turn so affected Christianity. Particularly influential in this respect was Philo, an Alexandrian Jew born in the last quarter of the first century B.C. As a Jew, Philo accepted the Jewish concept of the divine command to procreate and replenish the earth. From this belief it followed that marriage was blameless and worthy of high praise, but Philo, heavily influenced by the ascetic philosophies of his time, held that sex in marriage could be justified only if the goal of the husband and wife was the procreation of legitimate children for the perpetuation of the race. In short, sexual intercourse should take place only when there was hope for legitimate offspring. Philo described as mere pleasure lovers those who mated with their wives, not to beget children, but like "pigs or goats" in quest of sexual enjoyment.[30] His hostility to sex without possibility of progeny led him to state that those who mated with barren women were worthy of reproach, for in their seeking after mere pleasure, "they destroyed the procreative germs with deliberative purpose."[31] Predictably, all other kinds of nonprocreative sex, including homosexuality, were condemned by those adopting Philo's reasoning.

Like Plato and others, Philo thought of sex in dualistic terms. The highest nature of man was asexual, in imitation of God, and only the irrational part of the soul contained the categories of male and female and existed in the realm of the sexual. Philo argued that the original sin of Adam and Eve had been the result of sexual desires, the desire for bodily pleasures, and that such pleasures were the "beginnings of wrongs and violation of the law."[32] Philo believed that, for the sake of sex, mankind had exchanged a life of immortality and bliss for one of mortality and wretchedness.

Since Philo associated the fall of man in the Garden of Eden with sex, and males usually equated sex with women, Philo could logically and easily blame woman. Femaleness, for him, represented sense perception, the created world, and maleness represented the rational soul. Progress meant giving up the female gender, the material, passive, corporeal, and sense perceptible, for the male, active, rational, and incorporeal, more akin to mind and thought.[33] Women could do this best by remaining virgins,[34] the words *virgin, virginity,* and *every-virginal* occurring continually in Philo's more positive references to women.

Since anything passive or sense perceptible was wrong, Philo particularly abhorred male homosexuality. He regarded the male homosexual as enslaved to irrational passion and infected with the female disease.

> In former days the very mention of it was a great disgrace, but now it is a matter of boasting not only to the active but to the passive partners, who habituate themselves to endure the disease of effemination, let both body and soul run to waste, and leave no ember of their male sex-nature to smoulder. . . . These persons are rightly judged worthy of death by those who obey the law, which ordains that the man–woman who debases the sterling coin of nature should perish unavenged. . . . And the lover of such may be assured that he is the subject of the same penalty.

One of Philo's objections was that the homosexual person was like a bad husbandman in letting

> the deep-soiled and fruitful fields lie sterile, by taking steps to keep them from bearing, while he spends his labour night and day on soil from which no growth at all can be expected.

For him homosexuality was a blatant contradiction of man as he should be, for the homosexual was not guided by the sovereign, active, masculine mind. Though the soul or mind of man must become passive in relationship to God, for a man to become effeminate or womanish in his relations with society, and particularly within the sexual sphere, was wrong and had to be totally rejected.[35] He had nothing to say about female homosexuals as such.

Philo's hostility to homosexuality was also associated with his hostility to sexual pleasure in general. This is most obvious in his justification of circumcision, which he regarded as one way of excising the "pleasures" that bewitched the mind.

> For since among the lower lure of pleasure the palm is held by the mating of man and woman, the legislators thought good to dock the organ which ministers to such intercourse, thus making circumcision the figure of the excision of excessive and superfluous pleasure, not only of one pleasure but of all the other pleasures signified by one, and that the most imperious."[36]

Philo himself seems to have had no immediate disciples of any note and no direct influence on the Jews of his time, but he had considerable influence on Christianity. More immediately influential were those philosophers collectively known as the neo-Pythagoreans and neo-Platonists. The neo-Pythagoreans, while harking back to the original distinction drawn by the ancient Pythagoreans about the good and the divine and the evil and the earthly, were also strongly influenced by Plato, Aristotle, and the Stoics. In fact, from the first, Plato probably exerted as much influence as Pythagoras, and as this influence grew, neo-Pythagoreanism was modified into neo-Platonism.

In general, the neo-Pythagoreans believed that the soul was essentially in harmony with the immaterial and immortal and that the world and the flesh were enemies of the spirit. Redemption thus became a flight of the soul from the fetters of the body and senses. Though they did not necessarily advocate celibacy, they insisted that sexual relations not be motivated by the prompting of nature but only by a regard for propagating the species. A neo-Pythagorean treatise usually, although erroneously, attributed to Ocellus Lucanus and known as early as the first century B.C., contained the statement that "we have intercourse not for pleasure but for the purpose of procreation." The treatise insisted that sexual organs were given to man for the "maintenance of the species," and not for sensual pleasures.[37] In the first century A.D., Plutarch, strongly influenced by Pythagorean teachings, applauded philosophers who abstained from wine and love for a year "to honor God by their continence."[38]

Numenius of Apamea, a second-century A.D. writer, is an example of a writer able to incorporate both the philosophical and religious teachings into his system. Attempting to trace the teachings of Pythagoras and Plato to their original sources, he believed that both were interpreters of an earlier wisdom that he found in the teachings of the Brahmins, the Magi, the Egyptians, and the Jews, particularly Moses, whom he considered the twin of Plato. With Numenius, dualism reached an extreme. God, representing good, the ideal, or the Monad of the Pythagoreans, was so high and so remote that He was out of contact with the world as we know it and in fact had nothing whatever to do with its creation. Instead, the universe had been the work of a "Second God," derived from and inferior to the supreme Deity, and the universe itself could be called a "Third God." Thus, there were really three Gods, the Father, the Creative Agent generated by Him, and the Created World. The Second and Third Gods had a dual nature, since both contained matter and spirit, and matter for Numenius represented the evil principle opposed to the divine soul. He did not, however, consider the activities of the body to be evil in themselves but only when such activities ceased to be governed by reason and fell victim to the irrational, evil material world. Salvation represented an escape from corporeal and sensible existence, a reabsorption of the soul into its divine source. This was eventually accomplished by means of a series of reincarnations, but in the meantime it was necessary for man to cultivate his reason, to commune with God. Individual salvation consisted in the abandonment of sexual activity; this act of renunciation liberated the soul from passion and thereby led to mystical ecstasy.[39]

The amalgamation of religion and philosophic thought becomes even more apparent in the pupils of Ammonius Saccas, most particularly, Plotinus. Ammonius had been born a Christian but later rejected Christianity in favor of the ancient Greek religions. We know very little of his teachings, although he was held in great veneration by his students, particularly Plotinus, who must be regarded as his greatest, but also by Origen, the Christian theologian, and by Longinus, an important figure in both philosophy and literature. Ammonius tried to keep his philosophy secret, but his pupils published portions of it, and in view of his influence on Plotinus, he is regarded as one of the founders of neo-Platonism, a dominant force in the intellectual development of Christianity.

Plotinus lived and wrote during the third century A.D. After studying in Alexandria, he moved to Rome, where he had great influence on the Emperor Gallienus and his wife, the Empress Salonina. Plotinus was a religious mystic, and Plotinism or neo-Platonism is a theocentric form of thought. Porphyry, the pupil and biographer of Plotinus, recounted how four times, while in a state of ecstasy, Plotinus was made one with God. Plotinus is also said to have been so ashamed of his body that he considered his parentage and birthplace of no importance. His mysticism and piety were dependent on reason and intellectual balance, so much so that Plotinus refused to affiliate himself with any organized worship, on the grounds that the gods must come to him, and not vice versa. He differed from Plato in his greater stress on religious and mystical orientation, going so far as to insist that the nature of the Real was attainable only in a state of mystical ecstasy from which the last trace of not only sensible but also intelligible experience had been erased. He believed there was no personal immortality; rather, the goal of human life was to merge with the universal spirit. The path of redemption was long and gradual, taking aeons of reincarnation to traverse. In the end the soul was to be united with the divine in an indescribable ecstasy. Before that happened, it was necessary to prepare for the flight by long and rigorous discipline, both moral and intellectual. Without long and careful training, the soul would not be strong enough to attain the heights on which redemption dwells or to bear the splendors of the beatific vision there revealed.[40]

The first step to redemption was to try to attain perfection in the practice of ordinary social and practical virtues. Though eventually the world was to be renounced, that still did not absolve an individual from upright and noble participation in worldly affairs and honest, generous, and friendly relations with one's fellowmen.[41] The body and its needs were not to be despised and suppressed; rather, they had to be disciplined in such a way that they did not distract the soul from the contemplation of higher things.[42] The core of human virtue was in detachment from worldly goods (that is, evil), an indifference that put an individual out of reach of the caresses and stings of material life. Once this "apathy" from the material had been attained, the soul was free to turn its attention toward the intelligible world, to identify with the path toward Divine Reason in which truth was to be found.[43] By implication it was necessary to become indifferent to sex. This indifference becomes clearer in the writings of Porphyry, the pupil of Plotinus, who, besides writing a biography of his teacher and editing Plotinus' writings known as the *Enneads,* wrote treatises in his own right. In his *On Abstinence,* Porphyry condemned any kind of pleasure as sinful, including horseracing, theatergoing, dancing, eating meat, and, of course, sexual intercourse under any condition.[44]

In this setting of ascetic thinking Christianity was born and thrived. Though the Christians never quite adopted absolute celibacy, since there was such strong Biblical justification for marriage, they solved their conflict by recognizing marriage as a good but claiming celibacy as a higher good. Through this concept of the good versus the better, the Church Fathers managed to uphold the superiority of the virgin state and the higher merit of continence without yielding to the thoroughgoing dualism that would have denounced marriage as an evil. Nevertheless, many early Christian formulators regarded matrimony as a concession to the inordinate desires of fallen humanity, a refuge for those weaker souls who could not bear the discipline of celibacy. As might be expected, much of the patristic literature dealing with sexual matters emphasized the importance of celibacy over marriage and of widowhood over digamy (remarriage after the death of the first partner).

NOTES

1. Several pioneering studies of these Greek influences on Christianity were made in the nineteenth century. Perhaps most influential was Adolf Harnack, *Lehrbuch der Dogmengeschichte,* first published in 1886 and translated into English by Neil Buchanan under the title of *The History of Dogma* (Boston: Roberts Brothers, 1895–1903). There is also a one-volume summary of the work made by Harnack himself entitled *Outlines of the History of Dogma,* first published in English in 1893 and often republished since (Boston: Beacon Press, 1957). Also important was Edwin Hatch, *The Influence of Greek Ideas on Christianity,* first delivered as the Hibbert Lectures in 1888. This has also been republished with a new introduction and an invaluable bibliography by Frederick C. Grant (New York: Harper, 1957). Greek influences on Christian asceticism were studied by a number of early scholars, including Joseph Ward Swain, *The Hellenic Origins of Christian Asceticism* (New York: privately printed, 1916), a Ph.D. thesis at Columbia University.

2. See Swain, *op. cit.,* passim, and more recently, Johannes Leipoldt, *Griechische Philosophie und Früchristliche Askese* (Berlin: Akademia Verlag, 1961), pp. 31 ff., 60 ff.

3. Emil Brunner, *The Divine Imperative* (Philadelphia: Westminster Press, 1947), p. 364.

4. Morton S. Enslin, *The Ethics of Paul* (New York: Harper, 1930), p. 180.

5. Paul Ricoeur, "Wonder, Eroticism and Enigma," *Cross Currents*, XIV (1964), p. 135.

6. See Jane Harrison, *Prolegomena to the Study of Greek Religion* (reprinted, New York: Meridian Books, 1955), p. 460, n. 1.

7. *Ibid.*, Chaps. 9, 10, 11. There has been considerable scholarly research into the Orphic mysteries since Professor Harrison first wrote, but her work still serves as a starting point for the source materials on Orphism. Her specific interpretations have, however, been challenged.

8. Plato, *Cratyllus,* 400C, translated by H. N. Fowler, ed., (London: William Heinemann, 1953).

9. See Martin P. Nilsson, *A History of Greek Religion* (New York: W. W. Norton, 1964), pp. 214–217; and W. K. C. Guthrie, *The Greeks and Their Gods* (Boston: Beacon Press, 1950), pp. 318–320.

10. Guthrie, *op. cit.,* p. 311.

11. Aristotle, *Metaphysics,* Book 1, Vols. 3–7, (986A), translated by Hugh Tredennick, ed. (London: William Heinemann, 1936).

12. Hippolytus, *Refutations of All Heresies,* I, cap. ii, in Vol. 5, *The Ante Nicene Fathers,* translated by Alexander Roberts and James Donaldson, eds.; A. Cleveland Coxe, American ed. (reprinted, Grand Rapids, Mich., Eerdmans Publishing Company, 1961).

13. Diogenes Laertius, *Lives of Eminent Philosophers,* VIII, cap. 1, translated by R. D. Hicks, ed. (London: William Heinemann, 1950).

14. E. R. Dodds, *The Greeks and the Irrational* (Boston: Beacon Press, 1957), p. 155.

15. Plato, *Symposium,* 211B, translated by W. R. M. Lamb, ed. (London: William Heinemann, 1953).

16. Plato, *Phaedrus,* 246–247, translated by Harold North Fowler, ed. (London: William Heinemann, 1953).

17. *Ibid.,* 250–253.

18. The quotations appear in J. M. Robinson, *An Introduction to Early Greek Philosophy* (Boston: Houghton Mifflin, 1968), pp. 227–230.

19. *Diogenes Laertius,* X, cap. 1, 118, 132.

20. Lucretius, *De rerum natura,* IV, 1052–1120, translated by W. H. Rouse, ed. (London: William Heinemann, 1959).

21. *Diogenes Laertius,* VI, cap. 2, 29.

22. M. I. Finley, *Aspects of Antiquity* (New York: Viking Press, 1968), p. 94.

23. *Diogenes Laertius,* VI, cap. 6.

24. A good explanation of this appears in Epictetus, *Discourses,* translated by W. A. Oldfather, ed. (London: William Heinemann, 1956, 1959, 2 vols.).

25. *Ibid., Encheiridion,* 41.

26. A. C. Van Geytenbeck, *Musonius Rufus and Greek Diatribe,* translated by B. L. Hijamans, Jr. (Assen, Netherlands: Van Gorcum & Company, 1963), pp. 71–77.

27. Seneca, *Fragments,* in Vol. 3 of *Opera,* Frederich G. Haase, ed. (Leipzig: Teubner, 1853), No. 85. The passage is found in St. Jerome, *Against Jovinian* (1:30), and Haase claims the passage came from a lost treatise on marriage, *De matrimonio.*

28. Celsus, *De medicina,* I, 1.4, translated by W. G. Spencer, ed. (London: William Heinemann, 1935–1938).

29. See William E. Phipps, *Was Jesus Married?* (New York: Harper and Row, 1970), p. 124.

30.   Philo, *On the Special Laws* (*De specialibus legibus*), III, 113, translated by F. H. Colson, ed. (London: William Heinemann, 1958).

31.   *Ibid.*, III, 34–36.

32.   Philo, *On the Creation,* 69–70, 151, 162, translated by F. H. Colson and G. H. Whittaker, eds. (London: William Heinemann, 1963); Philo, *Questions and Answers on Genesis,* I, 40, translated by Ralph Marcus, ed. (London: William Heinemann, 1961).

33.   Richard A. Baer, Jr., *Philo's Use of the Categories Male and Female* (Leiden, Netherlands: E. J. Brill, 1970), p. 46.

34.   *Ibid.,* p. 51.

35.   Philo, *On the Special Laws,* III, vii (37–42); and Baer, *op. cit.,* p. 58.

36.   Philo, *On the Special Laws,* I, ii (9).

37.   Ocellus Lucanus, *De universi natura,* sec. 44, text and commentary by Richard Harder (Berlin: Weidmannsche, 1926), pp. 121–126.

38.   Plutarch, *On the Control of Anger,* 464b, Vol. 6 of *Moralia,* translated by W. C. Helmbold, ed. (London: William Heinemann, 1939).

39.   K. S. Guthrie, *Numenius of Apamea* (London: George Bell and Sons, 1917), p. 133.

40.   Plotinus, *The Enneads,* V, 3: par. 1–9; I, 6: par. 9, translated by Stephen MacKenna, ed., revised by B. S. Page (London: Faber and Faber, 1956).

41.   *Ibid.,* I, 3: par 6; 4: par 1.

42.   *Ibid.,* I, 4: par 1.

43.   *Ibid.,* I, 3: par 1; V, 9: par 1.

44.   Porphyry, *Abstinence from Animal Food,* I, 45; IV, 8, 20, translated from the Greek by Thomas Taylor (London: Thomas Rodd, 1823). There are many other references in Porphyry.

8

EARLY CHRISTIANITY:
A SEX-NEGATIVE RELIGION

Jesus himself said very little about sex except as it dealt with divorce and re-marriage. St. Matthew reported that in the Sermon on the Mount Jesus had said:

It hath been said, "Whoever shall put away his wife, let him give her a writing of divorcement";
But I say unto you, That whoever shall put away his wife, saving for the cause of fornication, causeth her to commit adultery; and whoever shall marry her that is divorced committeth adultery.[1]

Matthew later has Jesus make his meaning somewhat more explicit:

Pharisees also came unto him, tempting him and saying unto him, "Is it lawful for a man to put away his wife for every cause?"
And he answered and said unto them. "Have ye not read that he which made them at the beginning made them male and female,
And said, 'For this cause shall a man leave father and mother, and shall cleave to his wife: and they twain shall be one flesh?'
Wherefore they are no more twain, but one flesh. What therefore God hath joined together, let no man put asunder."

They say unto him, "Why did Moses then command to give a writing of divorcements, and to put her away?"

He saith unto them, "Moses because of the hardness of your hearts suffered you to put away your wives: but from the beginning it was not so. And I say unto you, Whosoever shall put away his wife, except it be for fornication, and shall marry another, committeth adultery; and who-so marrieth her which is put away doth commit adultery."[2]

St. Mark reported Jesus as going even further and forbidding divorce or remarriage not only to the husband but also to the wife:

And he saith unto them, "Whosoever shall put away his wife, and marry another, committeth adultery against her. And if a woman shall put away her husband, and be married to another, she committeth adultery."[3]

The disciples, after hearing Jesus expound on the matter, wondered whether it might be better simply to remain unmarried. Jesus replied:

All men cannot receive this saying, save they to whom it is given. For there are some eunuchs, which were born so from their mother's womb; and there are some eunuchs which were made eunuchs of men; and there be eunuchs which have made themselves eunuchs for the kingdom of heaven's sake. He that is able to receive it, let him receive it.[4]

Although the statement is ambiguous, it might well be interpreted to mean that service to God demanded a self-imposed continence. Occasionally, however, it was interpreted literally. Origen (died about 251–254), for example, castrated himself.[5] Others did the same, but by the fourth century such acts of self-mutilation were forbidden by Church Councils.[6] The majority of Church Fathers felt that self-castration had not been intended by Jesus, but rather, self-imposed continence.

Part of the difficulty with determining scriptural attitudes toward sex is that so many of the references seem ambiguous, as, for example, the statement by St. Luke that a man must hate his own wife and children to be a disciple of Jesus.[7] Should this be interpreted literally? Even then the meaning is unclear. Some light is shed by other Gospel writers' tendency to use a term translatable as "leave" rather than "hate"[8]; this might mean that a man is supposed to sacrifice everything for the sake of salvation. Both readings could, however, be interpreted to state that a man not having a wife and child should neither take a wife nor have children, an interpretation giving scriptural support to a trend toward asceticism already strongly pronounced in pagan thought. Further ambiguity arises in a description of the second coming, a time when, according to Jesus, there would be trouble for pregnant women: "Woe unto them that are with child, and to them that give suck in those days."[9] This might simply be interpreted to mean that pregnant women or women with infants would suffer more general distress or perhaps be too encumbered with earthly concerns to respond properly to the occasion. It has also, however, been interpreted as a divine condemnation of pregnant and lactating women, a condition that could result only from sexual activity. Jesus also said that lust itself was as evil as adultery: "Every one that looketh on a woman to lust after her hath committed adultery with her already in his heart."[10]

St. Paul built his interpretation of the proper sexual conduct for Christians from these somewhat contradictory statements of Jesus, and his own statements are often no less ambiguous. St. Paul advocated the higher good of celibacy[11] but also pointed out that, if a man did marry, he owed certain respect to his wife. Some Biblical commentators, anxious to defend Paul from charges of misogyny, have gone so far as to claim that he established an ethic of mutual obligation, and they cite the admonition in I Corinthians as evidence.

> Now concerning the things whereof ye wrote unto me: It is good for a man not to touch a woman. Nevertheless, to avoid fornication, let every man have his own wife, and let every woman have her own husband. Let the husband render unto the wife due benevolence: and likewise also the wife unto the husband. . . . For I would that all men were even as I myself. But every man hath his proper gift of God, one after this manner, and another after that. I say therefore to the unmarried and widows, It is good for them if they abide even as I. But if they cannot contain, let them marry: for it is better to marry than to burn.[12]

In spite of claims to the contrary, this passage still seems to establish marriage as little more than a reluctant concession to human frailty; though St. Paul does not make marriage sinful, he believed that married people have "trouble in the flesh" and are overly concerned with worldly things.[13] Nevertheless, St. Paul recognized marriage and went so far as to state that forbidding a person to marry was a heresy.[14]

Because early Christianity was not a unified religion, it would be a mistake to regard Paul's references to sex as a systematic or comprehensive treatment of sexual matters. There is no such treatment in the Christian Scriptures; rather, there are only answers to particular problems on which St. Paul or others were requested to comment. Some of the early Christians apparently believed that the "day of the Lord" was at hand[15] and thought they could live in idleness and perhaps even in sexual promiscuity while awaiting this blessed event.[16] Upset by this St. Paul took care to caution the Thessalonians that the time of the second coming was not known; in the interval they were to obey the will of God and try to attain sanctity in sexual matters, abstaining from fornication:

> That every one of you should know how to possess his vessel in sanctification and honour: Not in the lust of concupiscence, even as the Gentiles which know not God . . .[17]

As one who held that celibacy was a higher good than marriage, St. Paul tended to look down on women. As a man he felt it was woman's fault that men were sexually aroused. He gave unprecedented emphasis to the sin of Adam and Eve, owing in part to his belief that, without the Fall, there would have been no need for redemption by Jesus. His own misogynistic tendencies easily led him to place the major guilt on Eve, and from this he could develop the doctrine of the strict subjugation of women.

> Let the women learn in silence with all subjection. But I suffer not a woman to teach, nor to usurp authority over the man, but to be in silence. For Adam was first formed, then Eve. And Adam was not deceived, but the woman being deceived was in the transgression. Notwithstanding she shall be saved in childbearing, if they continue in faith and charity and holiness with sobriety.[18]

Women were to keep silent in the churches; if they wanted to learn anything, they were supposed to "ask their husbands at home: for it is a shame for women to speak in the church."[19] Other passages make it clear that the early Christians felt a wife was to be subject to her husband:

> Wives, submit yourselves unto your husbands, as it is fit in the lord. Husbands love your wives, and be not bitter against them.[20]

> Wives, submit yourselves unto your own husbands, as unto the Lord. For the husband is the head of the wife, even as Christ is the head of the Church: and he is the saviour of the body. Therefore as the church is subject unto Christ, so let the wives be to their own husbands in every thing. Husbands, love your wives, even as Christ also loved the church, and himself for it.[21]

> Likewise, ye wives, be in subjection to your own husbands; that, if any obey not the word, they also may without the word be won by the conversation of the wives.[22]

St. Paul, interpreting women's long hair as the natural sign of their need to be covered, insisted that they do so as a sign of subjection because:

> . . . A man indeed ought not to cover his head, forasmuch as he is the image and glory of God: but the woman is the glory of man. For the man is not of the woman: but the woman of the man. Neither was the man created for the woman; but the woman for the man.[23]

Women were also to veil themselves because of the "angels," those mysterious "sons of God" mentioned in Genesis (6:2–6) who fell in love with mortal women and begot on them children so wicked they provoked God to send the flood.[24] St. Paul evidently interpreted this story as proof that women's seductive powers were so great that they caused even angels to sin.

The most extreme misogynistic statement in the New Testament is not, however, found in the writings of St. Paul but in Revelations, whose author saw the procession of the redeemed as a company of virgins who "were not defiled with women."[25] This phrase is difficult to explain, for it apparently contradicts the statement in Hebrews that says "Let marriage be had in honour among all."[26] All we can state with any certainty is that the New Testament writers were ambiguous about both women and marital sex. In contrast, in other areas of sexual behavior they were both clear and forthright. Adultery, fornication, homosexuality, and perhaps even masturbation were condemned.

> But now I have written unto you not to keep company, if any man that is called a brother be a fornicator, or covetous, or an idolater, or a railer, or a drunkard, or an extortioner; with such an one know not to eat.[27]

> Know ye not that the unrighteous shall not inherit the kingdom of God? Be not deceived: neither fornicators, nor idolaters, nor adulterers, nor effeminate, nor abusers of themselves with mankind, Nor thieves, nor covetous, nor drunkard, nor revilers, nor extortioners, shall inherit the kingdom of God.[28]

Translators of the Bible have wrestled with various terms to describe homosexuality. The passage just quoted from the King James Version uses two terms, "effeminate" and "abusers of themselves," to translate, respectively, the Greek terms *malakoi* and *arsenokoitai* (Latin *molles* and *masculorum concubitores*). These words tend to distinguish males who engage passively from those who engage actively in homosexual acts. Derrick Sherwin Bailey has gone to considerable effort to demonstrate that this meant the compilers distinguished between homosexuality and homosexual acts and that the man who might be a homosexual but not engage in homosexual acts was not to be regarded as the sinner the various translations have labeled him.[29] This might well be the case, but one difficulty with his interpretation is that the writers of the scriptures might not have realized there were homosexuals who did not engage in homosexual practices, something that seemingly has been recognized only with the advent of modern psychology. Even if they made this distinction in their own minds, they probably would have felt that the emotional state of being a nonpracticing homosexual would have been the same as the person who lusted after a woman to commit adultery.

Two other passages in the New Testament also quite clearly deal with homosexuality.

> Knowing this, that the law is not made for a righteous man, but for the lawless and disobedient, for the ungodly and for sinners, for the unholy and profane, for murderers of fathers and murderers of mothers, for manslayers,

For whoremongers, for them that *defile themselves with mankind,* for menstealers, for liars, for perjured persons, and if there be any other thing that is contrary to sound doctrine.[30]

For this cause God gave them up into vile affections: for even their women did change the natural use into that which is against nature:

And likewise also the men, leaving the natural use of woman, burned in their lust one toward another; men with men working that which is unseemly, and receiving in themselves that recompense of their error which was meet.[31]

The term in the first passage, taken from 1 Timothy, is again *arsenokoitai.* The more ambiguous passage, however, is the second, taken from Romans, for it is not clear whether this refers to female as well as male homosexuality. It might well be that St. Paul's purpose was to illustrate the moral corruption of the heathens by showing how their women encouraged heterosexual perversion while the men went further and resorted to homosexual practice. Part of the difficulty in interpretation is due to some of the early Christian writers' holding that woman's subordination to man required her to assume a subordinate position in intercourse. If such an interpretation was held by St. Paul, who clearly believed women to be subordinate, the passage on women might refer simply to what the apostle regarded as abnormal coital positions. Even if this was the case, however, it would have implications for female homosexuality, for at least one of the female participants would usually be going contrary to the Pauline interpretation of natural positions by taking a superordinate position in the sex act. At any rate, this doubtful passage is the only possibly specific reference to female homosexuality in the Bible.

Other passages in the Bible might, however, have some reference to homosexuality in general. Various authorities have so regarded two passages in Revelations:

But the fearful, and unbelieving, and the *abominable,* and murderers, and whoremongers, and sorcerers, and idolaters, and all liars, shall have their part in the lake which burneth with fire and brimstone: which is the second death.[32]

For without are *dogs,* and sorcerers, and whoremongers, and murderers, and idolators, and whosoever loveth and maketh a lie.[33]

Both the terms *abominable* (*ebdelugmenoi*) and *dog* (*kunes*) have sometimes been interpreted to mean the same as the "monstrous and unnatural vices of heathendom." Bailey argues convincingly that this was not the writer's intention.[34] Nonetheless, whether the references were or were not intended to refer to homosexuality is beside the point. In the long run what matters is, not what the original writer's intention might have been, but how the passages were interpreted by later readers. In retrospect, it seems clear these passages were often interpreted as a condemnation of homosexuality, and they have often been cited as additional Biblical references to reinforce the condemnation of those whose sexual tastes were regarded as sinful.

One other passage in the New Testament has also been interpreted as a condemnation of homosexuality:

> . . . the things which are done by them in secret it is a shame even to speak of.[35]

Bailey again argues that, though the statement could apply to a homosexual act, there is no indication that this was the authors' intention. The difficulty with this as well as other of Bailey's explanations is simply that he is too much a scholar of the Bible, and while he can argue that the original intent had nothing to do with homosexuality, this does not mean that other readers did not read a condemnation of homosexuality into them. Though many of the preachers condemning homosexuality on the basis of such passages were not Biblical scholars, they nonetheless influenced many people's attitudes in the past as well as today.

Bailey seems, in general, to be somewhat defensive of the Christian position on sex. He argued, for example, that Biblical writers did not show the same vindictive horror of homosexuality that the Zoroastrians did, but this is an interpretation. The Christians disapproved of any nonprocreative sex. Bailey also held that the dominant stance of the New Testament writers had been influenced by the ethical considerations of the Jews, who had condemned homosexual acts between males (or perhaps only anal intercourse) as typical expressions of heathenism that must be renounced by the Jews. This is much too simple an explanation, although Philo Judaeus and Josephus, the two Jewish writers active at about the time the Christian Scriptures were being compiled, did equate homosexuality with the sins of Sodom.

Philo described the inhabitants of Sodom in a passage owing little to Genesis but undoubtedly reflecting the current Jewish (and Christian) outlooks:

> The land of the Sodomites . . . was brimful of innumerable iniquities, particularly such as arise from gluttony and lewdness . . . Not only in their mad lust for women did they violate the marriages of their neighbors, but also men mounted males without respect for the sex nature which the active partner shares with the passive: and so when they tried to beget children they were discovered to be incapable of any but a sterile seed. Yet the discovery availed them not, so much stronger was the force of lust which mastered them. Then as little by little they accustomed those who were by nature men to submit to play the part of women, they saddled them with the formidable curse of a female disease. For not only did they emasculate

their bodies by luxury and voluptuousness, but they worked a further degeneration in their souls and, so far as in them lay, were corrupting the whole of mankind.[36]

Josephus (died 96 A.D.) presented a similar view in his discussion of the Sodomites:

But the Sodomites, on seeing these young men (the angels) of remarkably fair appearances . . . were bent only on violence and outrage to their youthful beauty.[37]

On the other hand, the contemporary Rabbinical literature does not reflect a similar equation of the sin of Sodom with homosexuality. In this sense either Philo and Josephus were unusual or these passages were later emendations. Increasingly, the Christians rather than the Jews looked for a sexual connotation in the sins of Sodom. In fact, with their growing advocacy of asceticism, the Christians focused on celibacy and continence and invariably downgraded sex of any kind.

Part of this hostility to sex was due to Christianity's not developing in isolation; the ascetic and philosophical concepts of paganism discussed earlier influenced not only Christianity but also its rivals, particularly Gnosticism. Because Christianity was competing with Gnosticism as well as other redemptive cults, it was greatly influenced by what its rivals said or taught. In fact, within any particular Christian community, the degree of sexual repression depended on the practice of Christianity's leading rivals; sexual concepts ranged from permitting copulation if motivated by a desire for children to an outright demand for celibacy for all church members. At times, it seems that the early Christians tried to gain status, if not adherents, by outdoing the pagan rivals at ascetic practices. Galen (second century A.D.) observed that the Christian community in Rome included men and women who, like the philosophers, refrained from "cohabitating all through their lives."[38]

Gnosticism, like Christianity, represented a syncretism of various religious and philosophical movements prevailing during the first few centuries of the modern era. It was both pre-Christian and Christian, independent of Christianity and dependent on it. Much of the New Testament might well have been written in a reaction to the influence of Gnosticism; the earliest sources we possess for Gnostic teachings are the writings of the early Church Fathers, who militantly opposed the movement. Gnosticism had, however, many strands; in some areas it demonstrated greater affinities with ancient Egyptian concepts, in others with Babylonian, and in others with Persian, but all varieties of Gnosticism included elements from all these sources as well as from Greek philosophy.

Central to Gnostic speculation was the conception of dualistic worlds, one evil and material, the other good and spiritual, which had such a dominant hold on certain elements of pagan thought. According to the Gnostics, man had elements of both the good and the evil; his purpose on earth was to seek redemption. The Gnostics claimed to possess a saving *gnosis* or "knowledge" secretly revealed to their predecessors (some alleged to be the disciples of Jesus) and transmitted to others by the initiates alone. This knowledge concerned the supreme God, superior to the Creator, known only to them because, as spiritual beings, they had emanated from Him. Recognition of Him and of themselves would save them so that after death they would escape this alien world for the world of their Creator. In the meantime, their spirits had been temporarily imprisoned in fleshy bodies. The key to salvation was to free the body from its bondage. Such a doctrine led, of course, to a stringent asceticism, for the best way a true Gnostic could express his or her alienation from merely human existence was by adopting an ascetic life, and most particularly, by abstaining from sex. One recent investigator has labeled Gnosticism a special mixture of "Christian theology and sexual morality,"[39] but there were also Gnostics who attempted to show their indifference to the pleasures of life by rejecting sexual asceticism. Instead, they argued either that human actions were not subject to moral law or that actions usually considered sinful were not so for true believers. In either case, the Church Fathers expended large amounts of their time and effort in trying to deal with the Gnostics.

The Gnostics looked to various teachers, including Simon, Menander, Saturninus, Marcion, Valentinus, and Basilides. Some regarded themselves as Christians, although the Christian Gnostics believed Jesus had merely seemed to possess an earthly body and had not really been born of woman. The competition with what became orthodox Christianity is evident from the fact that, according to the New Testament, Simon Magus, a Gnostic teacher, was preaching in Samaria when St. Peter met him.[40] In Revelations there is a fierce denunciation of the Nicolaites,[41] the followers of Nicolas, viewed by later Christians as a Gnostic. One of the most important Gnostic leaders was Marcion, a church reformer who, after being excommunicated by the Church in Rome in 144 A.D., set up a competing organization and hierarchy. Clement of Alexandria (second century A.D.) wrote that the Marcionites regarded nature as evil because it was created out of evil matter, and since they did not wish to fill the world with other evil matter, they abstained from marriage.[42] Marcion taught that the Highest God, the Father of Jesus, was good, while the Creator-God of the Jews was merely just. According to Marcion, Jesus came as a life-giving spirit to manifest a new revelation as well as a new way of life. Unfortunately, he claimed, the message of Jesus had not been written down at first, and when it finally had been committed to writing, it had been distorted by false apostles under the spell of Judaism. Only Paul and Luke had understood the true gospel, but errors had been introduced into their teaching, errors that Marcion eliminated to restore the authentic non-Jewish gospel. Sex was associated with evil by Marcion, as were reproduction and growth. He was accused by some Christians of denying the very birth of Jesus so that he might not have to admit that Jesus had the flesh of man.[43] Marcion portrayed Jesus as descending from heaven as a fully formed adult without undergoing birth, boyhood, or temptation.[44] Marcion not only refrained from sexual relations with women but also prohibited marriage for all his followers.[45] He limited the sacraments of baptism and eucharist to virgins, widows, and those married couples who together had agreed to "repudiate the fruit of their marriage."[46]

Sharing the ascetic antisexual outlook of Marcion was another Gnostic leader, Julius Cassianus, who taught that men became most like beasts when they practiced sexual intercourse.[47] In fact, Cassianus taught that Jesus had been sent to this earth to save men from copulating. In a work entitled *De continentia* (*Concerning Celibacy*) Cassianus was said to have written:

> Let no one say that because we have these parts, that the female body is shaped this way and the male that way, the one to receive, the other to give seed, sexual intercourse is allowed by God. For if this arrangement had been made by God, to whom we seek to attain, he would not have pronounced the eunuchs blessed (Matthew 19:12); nor would the prophet have said that they are "not a fruitless tree," (Isaiah 56:3–4), using the tree as an illustration of the man who chooses to emasculate himself of any such notion.[48]

Cassianus and other ascetics based part of their antagonism to sex on a Fifth Gospel, *The Gospel According to the Egyptians*. Clement of Alexandria, who wrote in the second century and from whom we learn the most about this work, does not denounce it as apocryphal and goes to some pains to provide an exegesis for the texts that the Gnostics used to disparage marriage. Clement cited several passages from the gospel used by the Gnostics, most of which dealt with the sayings of Jesus to Salomé. On one fragment, Salomé asked Jesus, "How long shall men die?" Jesus answered her, "As long as you women bear children." This answer was taken by the Christian Gnostic writers as an implicit injunction to defeat death by ceasing from procreation.[49]

In a second text, Jesus stated: "I came to destroy the works of the female." Gnostic interpreters said that by *female* Jesus meant "desire," and by *works*, "birth and corruption,"[50] and this was interpreted to mean that there should be no more conception. A third saying had Salomé ask when these things about which she asked would be known. Jesus replied: "When you trample on the gown of shame, and when the two become one, and the male female, and the female male." The Gnostic Cassinaus held that this supported the ideal of eunuchism, "freed from the coupling of members."[51] Salomé is also reported to have said: "I would have done better had I never given birth to a child." Jesus replied: "Eat of every plant, but eat not of that which has bitterness to it," a passage interpreted by the Gnostics as a recommendation of celibacy.[52]

Though Clement and other Church Fathers denounced the Gnostic interpretations, these still exercised great influence on Christian belief, particularly through the influence of Justin Martyr. Justin had a high opinion of the value of philosophy and went so far as to state that philosophy was "the greatest possession and most honourable before God," and that it had been "truly holy men who bestowed attention on philosophy."[53] After studying at Alexandria under neo-Pythagorean teachers, he had become converted to Christianity. Though he insisted that Christianity was the "supreme and one true philosophy," his teachings on examination give only a Christian overlay to "the common moral philosophy of the day embraced by multitudes of his contemporaries."[54] Justin thought of salvation as man's own achievement, since man could choose right or wrong. He pointed to the virtuous lives of Christians, with which he contrasted the lives of their heathen contemporaries. He described approvingly a Christian youth who asked surgeons to emasculate him as a protection for bodily purity. Justin also pointed with pride to those Christians who renounced marriage to live in perfect continence.[55] His devotion to the neo-Platonic ethic, which associated virtue with sexual abstinence, was such that he could not think of Mary as sexually conceiving Jesus. Instead, he argued that Mary had been undefiled and conceived as a virgin, and he made her the antitype of Eve, with whom he associated sexual intercourse.[56] Justin taught that Christians either married for the purpose of bringing up children or abstained from marriage and were completely continent.[57] Marriage was not, however, a license for sexual activity. Clement of Alexandria had emphasized that a man who married:

> for the sake of begetting children must practice continence so that it is not desire he feels for his wife, whom he ought to love, and that he may beget children with a chaste and controlled will.[58]

The Christian ideal might be explained as to experience no desire at all.[59] Clearly, even though marriage had been instituted by God for the generation of children, it was a concession to the inordinate desires of fallen humanity and a refuge for those weaker souls who could not bear the discipline of celibacy.

Most of the Church Fathers were bachelors, but even those, such as Tertullian, who were married tended to denigrate marriage. Tertullian later felt such deep remorse over his lapse into matrimony that he joined the Montanists, a heretical Christian sect even harsher in its attitude toward sexual relations than the more orthodox Christians. In his *Letters to His Wife,* he writes as if there was no sexual element at all in marriage and, in fact, argues that celibacy was much to be preferred.[60] Tertullian was not the only Father to become a heretic. Tatian, a disciple of Justin Martyr, became a Gnostic ascetic after his teacher's martyrdom. He became the leader of a group known as the Encratites, the "self-controlled," a group believing that marriage was corruption and prohibiting sexual intercourse, intoxicants, and meats.[61] Tatian taught that sexual intercourse had been invented by the Devil, and thus anyone attempting to be married was trying to do the impossible by serving two masters, God and the Devil.[62] In his *Diatessaron,* Tatian argued that Adam rather than God had established marriage. He also argued that Jesus was separate from the material world of the flesh.[63] The Encratites group continued to produce works after Tatian's death, holding that marital relations were sordid and abominable. They referred to wedlock as a "polluted and foul way of life" and urged the true believers to replace the tree of carnal appetite with the tree of the cross. Those about to wed were counseled to abandon "filthy intercourse."[64] Tatian's greatest influence was on the Syrian Church, which apparently never considered him a heretic. The extent of his influence there is evident from the fact that a modern authority, Arthur Vööbus, can argue that all the available sources about the Syrian Christian Church of the third century were unanimous in their testimony that the fundamental conception around which the Christian belief centered was the doctrine that the Christian life was "unthinkable outside the bounds of virginity."[65]

Unavoidably, with such sexual attitudes, the Gnostics had a low opinion of women, whom they associated with sex. In the Gnostic Gospel of Thomas

> Simon Peter said to them, "Let Mary go forth among us, for women are not worthy of the life." Jesus said, "See, I will lead her that I may make her male, so that she may become a living spirit like you males. For every woman who makes herself male shall enter the kingdom of heaven."[66]

In effect, women could be saved only by becoming men or, at least, asexual creatures.

Gnosticism included, however, an antinomian strain holding it was impossible for any human act to be sinful for true believers. This Gnostic position is usually traced to Nicolas, one of the first deacons ordained by the Christian Apostles. His teachings drew the condemnation of the writer of Revelations in a passage cited earlier, but all we know about him is based on later sources open to question. There seems to be general agreement, however, that Nicolas had a very beautiful wife and that he gave a highly licentious interpretation to certain precepts about holding the flesh in contempt.[67]

Carpocrates and his son Epiphanes, who became leaders of a faction within the early Christian church, cited the example of Nicolas as one to follow. They allegedly taught that women were to be regarded as common property and that members could have intercourse as they wanted and with whom they wanted.[68] Other Gnostics were accused of regarding sexual intercourse as a sacred religious mystery, whose knowledge and practice would bring them to the kingdom of God. They derived their belief from a scriptural work that has not come down to us but that included the following passage:

> All things were one, but as it seemed good to its unity not to be alone, an inspiration came from it, it had intercourse with it, and it made the beloved.[69]

Another group of Gnostics, following Prodicus, regarded themselves as Lords of the Sabbath, that is, royal sons not bound by law and free to go nude, commit adultery, and engage in other sexual activities.[70] Still another group, the followers of Basilides, believed they could not sin, because of their perfection; they were accused of living lewd lives by the Church Fathers.[71]

How far can the sources about the Gnostics be trusted? Should we suspect that the accusations against many of the heretics were true or merely imagined by critics? The question is serious and cannot be answered with any authority, for several pagan writers, namely, Tacitus and Pliny, attributed the same excesses to Christians.[72] That the Christian writers on whom we depend do not always agree gives further caution to any generalization. Much of our information about the Gnostic sexual practices comes from Clement of Alexandria, but Irenaeus and Tertullian give contradictory information. Irenaeus, for example, a native of Smyrna who became a priest at Lyons, attributed teachings to Basilides and Valentinus that Clement ascribed only to followers, who, he alleged, had misinterpreted them. The reliability of Irenaeus on such matters has, in fact, become the subject of scholarly dispute.[73] It does not matter, however, what the Gnostics actually taught, for it was what the Christians believed they taught or said they taught that influenced the orthodox Christian position. According to Irenaeus, Saturninus and Basilides taught that the practice of all lust was a matter of indifference, and at the same time they claimed that "marriage and generation" were from Satan.[74] Valentinus, likewise, was said to have held that the spiritual man, the true Gnostic, was not bound by the moral law governing "animal men." This was because the spiritual man, initiated into perfect knowledge of God, had freedom from law and could not sin, because he could never be corrupted. The followers of Valentinus were accused of committing fornication and adultery, seducing the women they instructed, and, while pretending to live together as brothers and sisters, impregnating the sisters.[75] Irenaeus claimed that the Valentinians went so far as to state that whosoever being in this world does not so love a woman "as to obtain possession of her, is not of the truth, nor shall he attain to the truth."[76] This featuring of copulation was allegedly linked with the religious belief that the emission of seed by the spiritual man hastened the coming of the *Pleroma,* that is, the fullness of the divine hierarchy of the aeons.[77]

By the end of the second century Gnosticism was generally regarded as a distorted expression of Christianity. The organizational ability of the more orthodox Christians had begun to win the battle against them. By insisting on the importance of the community as opposed to the individual and by emphasizing its scriptural antecedents while yet incorporating pagan philosophy, Christianity succeeded in overcoming Gnosticism. In the process, however, the Christian Church became thoroughly Hellenized, its sexual attitudes seeming to have been influenced more by the ascetic Gnostics than by the more earthly Jews. The extent of the Gnostic influence is evident from the fact that one of their most avid opponents, Tertullian, stopped just short of condemning intercourse even in marriage and actually seemed to be uncertain why God had ever permitted such an act.[78] The *Second Epistle of Clement,* erroneously believed to have been written by Clement, Bishop of Rome, also wrestled with the problem. The writer of this epistle attempted to explain a statement by Jesus (probably apocryphal) that his kingdom would come, "When the two become one, and the outside as the inside, and the male with the female neither male nor female." The pseudo-Clement interpreted this to mean that when a "brother sees a sister he should have no thought of her as a female nor she of him as male."[79]

Even though continence was desirable, Christians were cautioned not to boast of their virtue, since, as Ignatius of Antioch said, boasting or publicity about such virtues could only lead to destruction. Christians who chose to remain continent were, however, allowed to inform their bishop.[80] The hostility with which some of the early Christians viewed sex is indicated by the apparent fact that only unmarried Christians could be baptized into the early Christian Church in Syria.[81] There were also bishops, such as Pinytos of Gnossus in Crete, who advocated compulsory continence.[82] In general, however, it appears that, within the main Christian tradition, such a rigorous ethic was not followed, if only because it was advocated by many ascetic-minded Gnostics, a group regarded by the Church Fathers as heretical and whose extremes were, therefore, to be avoided. Many Christians were not particularly happy about this, for the great appeal of Gnosticism lay in their only carrying to logical conclusions what many orthodox Christians seemed to want to believe.

The general temper of the times, whether Gnostic or Christian, favored continence, as evidenced by Soranus of Ephesus, probably the most renowned medical writer of the second century. Soranus believed that permanent virginity was most healthful, since:

> Even among dumb animals we see that those females are stronger which are prevented from having intercourse. And among women we see that those who, on account of regulations and service to the gods, have renounced intercourse and those who have been kept in virginity as ordained by law are less susceptible to disease. If, on the other hand, they have menstrual difficulties and become fat and ill-proportioned, this comes about because of idleness and inactivity of their bodies. . . . Consequently permanent virginity is healthful, in males and females alike; nevertheless, intercourse seems consistent with the general principle of nature

according to which both sexes (for the sake) of continuity (have to ensure) the succession of living beings.[83]

Sexual asceticism continued to exercise a hold over the Christian mind. Gregory of Nyssa, in the fourth century, dismissed marriage as a sad tragedy.[84] St.
Jerome (died 420 A.D.) emphasized its inconveniences and tribulations[85] and
summarized his views in an oft-quoted passage:

> I praise marriage and wedlock, but I do so because they produce virgins for me. I
> gather roses from thorns, gold from the earth, and pearl from the shell.[86]

St. Ambrose (died 397 A.D.) called marriage a "galling burden"[87] urging all
those contemplating matrimony to think about the bondage and servitude into
which wedded love degenerated.[88] In sum, the Fathers argued with monotonous
regularity that the wedded state was not as good as the single. Though marriage was not quite evil, it could only count as thirtyfold compared with the
sixtyfold of widowhood and the hundredfold of virginity.[89]

There was internal opposition to this cult of virginity, but the works of the
three most vocal defenders of marriage—Jovian, Helvidius, and Vigilantius—
have not survived, and their positions are known only through their opponents,
particularly St. Jerome, who took great pains to refute them. St. Jerome was,
however, careful to point out that he did not condemn wedlock, although he
admitted he had difficulty in understanding why most people would want to be
married.[90] With this somewhat cavalier dismissal of their arguments, celibacy
carried the day. It became a common practice among many Christian groups to
forbid marriage after ordination to the priesthood, although there was at first
general agreement that a man might be married before ordination. Inevitably,
there was an attempt to suggest that matrimonial cohabitation disqualified a
person for priestly ministration. The Council of Nicaea specifically rejected an
absolute rule of clerical celibacy,[91] but later Councils, particularly the Council
of Trullo in the seventh century, turned to the subject again. By the fifth
century, in fact, the Western Christian Church tended to hold that bishops,
presbyters, deacons, and others employed before the alter were to refrain from
coitus, although there were mitigating circumstances that might allow for exception.[92] The Eastern Christian Church never adopted such a position.

The growing difference between the Western and Eastern positions on celibacy and sex seems to be due more to the influence of St. Augustine (died 430
A.D.) than to any other factor. The Christian Church might have become less
hostile to sex if it had not been threatened once again by the appearance of a
rival, which led to renewed emphasis on the ascetic ideas of sex. St. Augustine
opposed this new rival, Manichaeanism, although he himself had once been a
believer. Manichaeanism was based on the teachings of the prophet Mani
(216–277 A.D.), who had lived and been crucified in southern Babylonia. His

religion incorporated various aspects of Gnostic, Christian, Zoroastrian, and Greek philosophy, and before his death, it had become influential in Egypt, Palestine, and Rome, and from there it spread to Asia Minor, Greece, Illyria, Italy, and North Africa. Manichaeanism had a canonical scripture (the seven books of Mani), claimed to be a universal religion, and had a hierarchy and apostles. In a sense, it had all the weapons of Christianity. Like Muhammad later, Mani taught that he was the last prophet in a chain of revelation. Like Christianity it was a missionary faith. Manichaeanism was a dualistic religion combining science, philosophy, and religion into a new synthesis. Although claiming the authority of revelation, the Manichaeans paid the highest deference to reason. Following the Zoroastrian and Mithraic cosmology, the universe was divided into two pantheistic portions, the kingdoms of Light and Darkness, which were in juxtaposition, each reaching out into infinity. Light and Darkness were both eternal and uncreated power in everlasting opposition and conflict, although the God of Light was alone able to know the future. Eventually, Light would overcome Darkness, but the ultimate victory depended, not on the defeat of Darkness, but on the withdrawal of Light.

Originally, the two realms had existed without intermingling, but history began when the Prince of Darkness, attracted by the splendor of the Light, invaded the Kingdom of Light. He was met by an evocation of the Father, Primordial Man, a supernatural being of Light. In the duel of Primordial Man and his sons with the King of Darkness and his sons, the forces of Light were vanquished and then devoured by their opponents, just as had happened to Dionysus and the Titans. The result was that Light was imprisoned. The God of Light evoked the Living Spirit, or Demiurge, to rescue Primordial Man, but elements of Light still remained within the sons of the King of Darkness. The God of Light then sent forth His Word, or the Living Spirit, into the universe to create this earth, the moon, the sun, the planets, and the 12 elements or creative eons, using the carcasses of some of the defeated sons of Darkness, that is, Archons, as material. The light for the sun and moon came from the entrapped light within the Archons.

The creation of man appeared somewhat differently in various versions. In one, man had been created by the Prince of Darkness from the offspring of his Archons and thereby retained the light derived from the light once within the sons of Darkness. In another version, the Father, or the God of Light, took pity on the light still imprisoned in the defeated Archons. He sent an androgynous messenger, known as the Virgin of the Lights, who appeared to the male Archons as a girl, to the female Archons as a boy. His beautiful appearance so aroused the coucupiscence of the Archons that they responded by emitting the light they had absorbed. At the same time the light was released, the "sin" was also released. The sins of the male Archons fell to the ground and became plants; the aborted fetuses of the females became animals. Adam and Eve were the result of a union between a son and daughter of the Prince of Darkness, who still retained some light, and thus Adam and Eve had both light and darkness. Adam had, however, more light than Eve. Again woman was regarded as inferior. Both Adam and Eve, recognizing their miserable fate, begged for help from the higher eons. The God of Light thereupon sent Jesus, the Incarnate Word, to warn Adam that Eve was the tool of Darkness, and Adam rejected her blandishments. Eve instead copulated with the earth Archon and gave birth to Cain, Abel, and two daughters, who married each other. Abel's wife soon became pregnant, but Abel, knowing he had not cohabited with his own wife, accused Cain of adultery, and Cain, in a rage, slew his brother and then married the widow. To offset the loss of Abel, the earth Archon taught Eve witchcraft, by which she seduced Adam, so that he became her husband and begot Seth, who was so filled with light elements that the Archon conspired with Eve to destroy him. Adam managed to foil them by taking the child away. In due time the God of Light again sent His Word, the Christ, this time to accomplish the redemption of the Elect.

Procreation, to the Manichaeans, since it kept the light imprisoned, was an evil act. The purpose of man was to gain the light, and light could be released by eating bread, vegetables, or fruit containing seeds. The release of light could also be affected or impeded by sexual actions, since the seed of man also contained light. Those entering the Manichaean religion were supposed to have tamed concupiscence as well as covetousness and refused to eat flesh, drink wine, or have marital intercourse.

The human race was, however, divided into three classes. The first were the Adepts—the Elect who renounced private property, practiced celibacy, observed strict vegetarianism, and never engaged in trade. The second were the Auditors, men and women of good will who could not contain themselves and who must, therefore, earn money, own property, eat flesh and marry, and would ultimately earn high rewards by serving and supporting the Elect in this life. Finally, there were the completely sensual members of society, totally lost in wickedness, who rejected the gospel of Mani. At death the Elect went directly to the Paradise of Light; the Auditors spent a period of purification in purgatory; and the wicked were doomed to eternal and irrevocable suffering in the three Manichaean hells. The bodies of all returned to the dust from whence they came.

The soul of God was constantly being freed from its physical fetters in the natural process of growth and death; but through the act of procreation the spirit was also continually encumbered in the dregs of creation. Sexual intercourse between male and female chained the soul to Satan and denied its progress into the Kingdom of Light. Thus the Manichaeans regarded marriage as a sin and procreation as the defiling birth of the divine substance. Sexual sin consisted not only in the overt act of sex but also in the impulse; marriage was no greater offense than the desire to marry. Within the hierarchy of membership, however, marriage was a sin only for the Elect. The Auditors were permitted to follow their natural inclinations, since Christ was the truth, the light, and the way, and no man was to be forced to do what he could not do.[93]

Since the Manichaeans believed that procreation continued the imprisonment of the light contained in the seed, their opponents charged them with engaging in sexual intercourse without procreative purpose, including coitus interruptus and anal intercourse. The Elect themselves were charged with engaging in a ritual in which they ate human semen to free part of the God of Light still imprisoned in their seed. Augustine mentioned this second charge several times but usually indicated that the Manichaeans claimed such a practice was followed only by heretical Manichaeans.[94] The Manichaeans were, of course, accused of homosexuality, because the androgynous Virgin of the Lights had caused the Archons to emit the light they had absorbed. Since any way of encouraging emission of semen without pregnancy might be viewed with favor, or at least their opponents so believed, such a charge is understandable. Even though the Manichaeans permitted their Auditors to marry, they advised them to avoid procreation or to try to abstain so that they might become members of the Elect. In the meantime they cautioned the Auditors to avoid pregnancy and devoted some energy to trying to figure a safe period within the menstrual cycle.

St. Augustine was an adherent of the Manichaean cause for some 11 years but never reached the Elect stage, in part because of his difficulties with sex. He remained an Auditor, living with a mistress and growing more and more uncomfortable about his inability to control his lustful desires. His own ambiguity about the matter is evident from his constant prayer: "Give me chastity, and continency, but do not give it yet."[95] Augustine's mother, though tolerating her son's concubine, and even his son by her, Adeoatus, wanted Augustine to become a Christian and to enter into marriage. Reluctantly, he arrived at the conclusion that the only way his venereal desires could be satisfied was through marriage.[96] For reasons that are unclear, he never considered marrying his mistress (probably she was not of the correct social class) but instead became engaged to a girl who was not yet of age (12 was the legal minimum, 14 was the custom) and sent away his mistress and son. While waiting to be married, however, Augustine found that he still could not refrain from sex and took a temporary mistress. At this juncture he went through a crisis of conscience that ended in his converting to Christianity and adopting a life of celibacy. Triggering the crisis was his reading of a passage in Romans:

> Not in rioting and drunkedness, not in chambering and wantonness, not in strife and envying; but put ye on the Lord Jesus Christ, and make not provision for the flesh, to fulfill the lusts thereof.[97]

Augustine interpreted this as a call to celibacy. Conversion came to mean to him the rejection of sexual intercourse.

> So thou convertedst me unto thyself, as that I sought now no more after a wife, nor any other hopes in this world.[98]

Once he accepted continence as the most desirable model for life, St. Augustine became particularly offended by the act of coitus. He wrote that he knew nothing that brought "the manly mind down from the heights than a woman's caresses and that joining of bodies without which one cannot have a wife."[99] He was upset that generation could not be accomplished without what he felt was a certain amount of bestial movement[100] and violent, lustful desires.[101] Sexual lust, he came to feel, was an inevitable result of the expulsion of Adam and Eve from the Garden of Eden. While in Paradise the two had been able to control their genitals, which had been obedient to the dictates of their will and never stirred except at their behest.[102] He believed that Adam and Eve had not engaged in sexual intercourse before their expulsion, although if they had chosen to do so, they could have managed the affair without lascivious heat or unseemly passion.[103]

Once they had fallen from Paradise, they became conscious of the new impulse generated by their act of rebellion, and this drove them to an insatiable quest for self-satisfaction.[104] Augustine termed this impulse *concupiscence* or *lust,* and it was through this that the genitals lost the docility of innocence and were no longer amenable to the will. Inevitably, Adam and Eve had felt shame over their desires, a shame causing them to cover their nakedness by sewing fig leaves together to make aprons concealing their genitals. Concupiscence was, however, still displayed through the sexual impulses, which proved stronger and less tractable than other passions and could be satisfied only through an orgasm engulfing the rational faculties in violent, sensual excitement. Though coitus must be regarded as a good, since it came from God, every concrete act of intercourse was evil, with the result that every child could literally be said to have been conceived in the sin of its parents.[105] Venereal desire, since it had been implanted by God for encouraging the increase of mankind, must be regarded as blameless, but the same desire corrupted by concupiscence was to be regarded as shameful and sinful. Because generation could not occur unless the carnal union of husband and wife was motivated by the stimulus of lust, it must, therefore, be a sin.[106] Did this make marriage an evil in itself? Augustine tried to distinguish between matrimony and sexual intercourse, but his answers were rather contradictory. He concluded that concupiscence could not take away the good of marriage and that marriage mitigated somewhat the evil of concupiscence. "We ought not to condemn marriage because of the evil of lust, nor must we praise lust because of the good of marriage,"[107] although marriage managed to transform coitus from a satisfaction of lust to a necessary duty.[108]

When the act was employed for human generation, it lost some of its inherent sinfulness,[109] though it still remained the channel by which the guilt of concupiscence was transmitted from parents to children. This guilt could be removed only by a baptismal regeneration, even though the impulse of lust and sense of sexual shame still remained.[110] St. Augustine concluded that marriage guarded wanton marital indulgence from the grave sinfulness of fornication or adultery and that, even though nupital embraces were not always intentionally destined for procreation, the sin resulting from this was only venial, provided there was no attempt to frustrate the natural consequences of coitus.[111] All intercourse between the unmarried was condemned by Augustine, although he held that true wedlock could exist without a ceremony.[112] In short, Augustine concluded that the only justification of sexual intercourse was for procreation by a husband and wife.[113] Celibacy was the highest good, and intercourse in itself was only an animal lust, but in marriage, and only in marriage, it was justified, because of the need for procreation. Marital intercourse could be either good or evil, and it was only through procreation that the evil became good. All other kinds of intercourse were evil.

Predictably, with such attitudes, the Church Fathers condemned any forms of sex not leading to procreation, all of which were regarded as deviant and unnatural. Condemnation of homosexuality appeared very early in the development of Christianity. In the *Didache,* a second-century manual of church life and morals, there is a list of sexual sins generally based on the Ten Commandments but extended to include pederasty and abortion.[114] The same condemnation appears in the *Epistle of Barnabas,* dating from about 130 A.D.[115] The *Apostolic Constitutions,* composed in the fourth century, held that Christians abhorred all "unlawful mixtures" and regarded them as wicked and impious.[116] St. John Chrysostom (died 407) was particularly vehement in denouncing homosexual activities as unnatural.[117] He condemned sodomy as an unpardonable insult to nature and regarded tribadism as even more disgraceful, since women were supposed to have more shame than men. He spoke out against the pederasts who came to church to look with lustful curiosity on the youths in the congregation.[118] Homosexual activities were regarded as more sinful and destructive than simple fornication because they jeopardized humanity by deflecting the sexual organs from their primary protective purpose and sowed disharmony and strife between men and women, who no longer would be impelled by their physical desires to live together peaceably. Fornication, though lawless, was at least regarded as natural, while sodomy and lesbianism were not. St. Augustine contended that homosexual practices were not only lustful acts but also transgressions of the command to love God and one's neighbor. These shameful acts, which he equated with those committed in Sodom, were to be detested and punished wherever they were found, for God had not made man to use each other in this way.[119] Fellatio and other sexual activities were also condemned.[120]

In their struggle with their sensual desires, many early Christians withdrew from the world and went off into the desert to meditate and contemplate, but even here they were troubled by sex. One of the earliest had been St. Anthony (died about 356) of Egypt. Originally, the withdrawal had been an individual act, but as more and more men sought sanctuary, it was necessary to make rules to help maintain a lifetime resolution. St. Pachomus was the first to do so, founding some nine monasteries for men and two for women in the fourth century. The early monasteries still stressed the isolation of the individual monk or nun, though the groups periodically came together for a common meal, but the fact that many of the monks and nuns were young and had sexual desires soon led to a need to deal with sex. St. Basil, a fourth-century theologian and organizer of monasticism, was particularly conscious of homosexuality. He warned the young in either mind or body to:

> Fly from intimate association with comrades of your own age and run away from them as from fire. The enemy has indeed set many aflame through such means and consigned them down into that loathsome pit of the five cities (Genesis 1:19, Deuteronomy 29:23) on the pretext of spiritual love. . . . At meals take a seat far away from your young brother; in lying down to rest, let not your garments be neighbor to his; rather, have an elderly brother lying between you. When a young brother converses with you or is opposite you in choir, make your response with your head bowed lest per chance by gazing fixedly into his face, the seed of desire be implanted in you by the wicked sower and you reap sheaves of corruption and ruin. At home or in a place where there is no witness of your actions, be not found in his company under the pretext of meditation on the Divine Word or for any other excuse, even the most urgent need.[121]

St. Augustine, who drew up rules for an order of nuns, wrote in a similar manner:

> The love between you, however, ought not to be earthly but spiritual, for the things which shameless women do even to other women in low jokes and games are to be avoided, not only by widows and chaste handmaids of Christ, living under a holy rule of life, but also entirely by married women and maidens destined for marriage.[122]

As a general rule, however, homosexuality is never discussed extensively, and is referred to only incidentally.

The Fathers left no doubt, however, of their basic hostility. Sodomists were among the persons to be debarred from baptism and admission as catechumens for instruction in the faith. The Council of Elvira (305–306), held in southern Spain, included a canon forbidding the admission of *stupratores puerorum* to Holy Communion, even if they were at death's door. Later, at the Council of Ancyra in Asia Minor (314 A.D.), two canons were passed penalizing persons termed *alogeusamenoi,* those guilty of shamelessly offensive conduct, which can be interpreted to mean homosexuality.[123] Gregory of Nyssa laid down the principle that he "who is guilty of unseemliness with males" will be under the same discipline as adulterers.[124] He justified his classification of sodomists with adulterers in that both crimes involve not only sexual lust but also treachery and wrong against someone else. Both, in turn, merit a double penalty as compared with simple fornication.[125] St. Basil held that adulterers as well as sodomists and bestialists should be excluded from the sacrament for 15 years and fornicators for only 7 years.[126] Gregory also imposed a somewhat less rigorous penalty stating explicitly that discretion was to be used in imposing the penance.[127]

In general, the attitude of the Eastern Christians seemed to be less hostile than the Western. Basil and other Eastern Fathers regarded sodomy as a grave sin, but no worse than adultery, bestiality, fornication by a monk or nun, and some types of incest. Basil treated it much more leniently than murder, divination, conjuration, and incest with a sister, all requiring a 20-year penance, and nothing like apostasy, which required exclusion from Communion until the hour of death. In fact, sodomy was not much worse than simple fornication. St. Gregory's code was even less harsh than that of Basil. It was the Western Church, perhaps influenced by St. Augustine, that tended to regard the sexual activities as much more serious.

Christianity must be classed as a sex-negative religion. As to sex itself, since the time of the Orphics there had been a strong philosophical and religious tradition arguing for the evilness of sexual intercourse and tolerating it only in marriage for procreation. The ordinary citizen in the classical world never adopted such extremes but restricted sex for women to that found in the marriage relationship while allowing men to have intercourse with wives, concubines, and prostitutes. The Jews of the Old Testament espoused a similar position, although they were more hostile to homosexuality than the Greeks or Romans. There were, however, some strong antinomians who held that intercourse in all possible ways was not only permissible for anyone but also mandatory for salvation. The bulk of the Church Fathers tolerated intercourse only in marriage and only for procreation but preferred virginity and celibacy. The strict Manichaeans as well as other pagan writers held that intercourse was never permissible, and though many Christian writers flirted with this idea, it was ultimately rejected as an absolute requirement for all Christians. Christians were, in spirit, if not always in practice, ascetics, and justifying sexual intercourse only in terms of progeny meant that any kind of sex not leading to reproduction had to be condemned. It also meant that, even when pregnancy resulted, sex was not something to be enjoyed. The Church Fathers regarded sex as at best something to be tolerated, an evil whose only good was in procreation. Western attitudes have been dominated by their concepts ever since.

NOTES

1. Matthew 5:31–32. All citations are from the Revised Standard Version (King James) unless otherwise stated. This version is used since it has had such strong influence on English speaking peoples.

2. Matthew 19:3–9.

3. Mark 10:11–12.

4. Matthew 19:11–12.

5. Eusebius, *Ecclesiastical History*, VI, viii, translated by Kirsopp Lake, ed. (London: William Heinemann, 1926).

6. See the discussion in Derrick Sherwin Bailey, *Sexual Relation in Christian Thought* (New York: Harper, 1959), p. 72, fn. 11.

7. Luke 14:26.

8. Matthew 10:37, 19:29; Mark 10:29.

9. Mark 3:17; Luke 21:23.

10. Matthew 5:28.

11. I Corinthians 7:1.

12. I Corinthians 7:1–12.

13. I Corinthians 7:28, 32–34.

14. I Timothy 4:3.

15. II Thessalonians 2:2.

16. See Robert M. Grant, *Augustus to Constantine: The Thrust of the Christian Movement into The Roman World* (New York: Harper & Row, 1970), p. 69.

17. I Thessalonians 4:3–5.

18. I Timothy 1:11–15.

19. I Corinthians 14:34–36.

20. Colossians 3:18–19.

21. Ephesians 5:22–25.

22. I Peter 3:1.

23. I Corinthians 11:4–9.

24. I Corinthians 11:10.

25. Revelations 14:4.

26. Hebrews 13:4.

27. I Corinthians 5:11.

28. I Corinthians 6:9–10.

29. Derrick Sherwin Bailey, *Homosexuality and the Western Christian Tradition* (New York: Longmans, Green and Company 1955), pp. 38–39.

30. I Timothy 1:9–10. (Italics mine.)

31. Romans 1:26–27.

32. Revelations 21:8. (Italics mine.)

33. Revelations 22:15. (Italics mine.)

34. Bailey, *Homosexuality and the Western Christian Tradition*, pp. 43–45.

35. Ephesians 5:12.

36. Philo, *De Abrahamo*, XXVI, translated by F. H. Colson, ed. (London: William Heinemann, 1935), pp. 134–146.

37. Josephus, *Jewish Antiquities*, I, 200, translated by H. St. J. Thackeray, ed. (London: William Heinemann, 1930).

38. R. Walzer, *Galen on Jews and Christians* (London: Oxford University Press, 1949), p. 65.

39. John T. Noonan, Jr., *Contraception: A History of Its Treatment by Catholic Theologians and Canonists* (Cambridge, Mass.: Harvard University Press, 1966), p. 58.

40. Acts 8:9–24.

41. Revelations 2:6, 14–15.

42. Clement, *Stromata*, III, cap. 3 (12), in Vol. 2, *The Ante Nicene Fathers* Alexander Roberts and James Donaldson, eds. (American edition A. Cleveland Coke, ed., reprinted Grand Rapids, Mich., W. B. Eerdmans, 1966). In this particular edition of Clement the editors hesitated to translate this section because of its sexual overtones. There is, however, an English translation of the third book in John F. L. Oulton and Henry Chadwick, *Alexandrian Christianity* (Philadelphia: Westminster Press, 1954). Times do change.

43. Tertullian, *On the Flesh of Christ*, cap. I, in Vol. 3, *The Ante Nicene Fathers*.

44. Tertullian, *Against Marcion*, IV, cap. vii, in Vol. 3, *The Ante Nicene Fathers*.

45. *Ibid.*, V. cap. vii.

46. *Ibid.*, IV, cap. xxxiv.

47. Clement, *Stromata*, III, cap. 17 (102).

48. *Ibid.*, III, cap. 13 (91).

49. *Ibid.*, III, cap. 9 (64).

50. *Ibid.*, III, cap. 9 (63).

51. *Ibid.*, III, cap. 13 (92–93).

52. *Ibid.*, III, cap. 9 (66).

53. Justin Martyr, *Dialogue with Trypho*, cap. ii, in Vol. 1, *The Ante Nicene Fathers*.

54. Arthur C. McGiffert, *A History of Christian Thought* (New York: Scribner's, 1932, 2 vols.), Vol. 1, p. 100.

55. Justin Martyr, *Apology*, I, cap. 29, in Vol. 1, *The Ante Nicene Fathers*.

56. Justin Martyr, *Dialogue with Trypho*, 100; also Erwin R. Goodenough, *The Theology of Justin Martyr* (reprinted, Amsterdam, Netherlands: Philo Press, 1923), pp. 181–182, 235–239.

57. Justin Martyr, *Apology*, I, xxix. See also Noonan, *op. cit.*

58. Clement, *Stromata*, II, vii.

59. See Athenagoras, *A Plea for Christians*, Chaps. 32–34, in Vol. 2, *The Ante Nicene Fathers*.

60. Tertullian, *To His Wife*, I, ii–iii, in Vol. 4, *The Ante Nicene Fathers*.

61. Eusebius, *Ecclesiastical History*, IV, cap. 29; Irenaeus, *Against Heresies*, I, cap. 28, in Vol. 1, *The Ante Nicene Fathers*.

62. Clement, *Stromata*, III, cap. 12 (81).

63. William E. Phipps, *Was Jesus Married?* (New York: Harper and Row, 1970) p. 133.

64. *Acts and Martyrdom of Andrew*, in Vol. 8, *The Ante Nicene Fathers*, p. 512; and *Acts of Thomas*, in Vol. 8, *The Ante Nicene Fathers*, p. 537.

65. Arthur Vööbus, *History of Asceticism in the Syrian Orient* (Louvain: Corpus scriptorum Christianorum Orientalium, 1958), Vol. 1, p. 69. This work is in English.

66. The gospel can be found in various editions, but the one from which this is quoted is in an

appendix in Jean Doresse, *The Secret Books of the Egyptian Gnostics,* translated by Philip Mairet (London: Hollis and Carter, 1960), *Gospel of Thomas,* V. 22.

67.   Doresse, *op. cit.,* pp. 13–14.

68.   Clement, *Stromata,* III, cap. 2 (5–8), cap. 4 (25–26).

69.   *Ibid.,* III, cap. 4 (29).

70.   *Ibid.,* III, cap. 4 (30); Oulton and Chadwick, *op. cit.,* p. 30.

71.   *Ibid.,* III, cap. 1 (3).

72.   Pliny, *Epistles,* X, 96, translated by William Melmoth, ed. (London: William Heinemann, 1953); and Tacitus, *Annals,* XV, 44, translated by John Jackson, ed. (London: William Heinemann, 1937).

73.   See, for example, G. Quispel, "The Original Doctrine of Valentine," *Vigiliae Christianae,* I (1947), 44; Oulton and Chadwick, *op. cit.,* p. 30; Noonan *op. cit.,* pp. 65–66.

74.   Irenaeus, *Against Heresies,* I, 24, 2.

75.   *Ibid.,* I, 6, 3.

76.   *Ibid.,* I, 6, 4.

77.   *Ibid.*

78   Tertullian, *On Monogamy,* cap. 3, in Vol. 4, *The Ante Nicene Fathers.*

79.   *The Second Epistle of Clement,* cap. 12, in Vol. 7, *The Ante Nicene Fathers.*

80.   Ignatius, *Epistle to Polycarp,* cap. 5, in Vol. 1, *The Ante Nicene Fathers.*

81.   See the discussion by A. Vööbus, *Celibacy, a Requirement for Admission to Baptism in the Early Christian Church* (Stockholm: Estonian Theological Society in Exile, 1951). This work is in English.

82.   Eusebius, *Ecclesiastical History,* IV, 23, 7–8.

83.   Soranus, *Gynecology,* I, vii (32), translated by Owsei Temkin (Baltimore: Johns Hopkins Press, 1956).

84.   Saint Gregory of Nyssa, *On Virginity,* translated by Virginia Woods Callahan, in Vol. 58 of *The Fathers of the Church* (Washington D.C.: The Catholic University of America, 1948f).

85.   St. Jerome, *Against Helvidius,* 21–22, translated by John N. Hritza, Vol. 53, *The Fathers of the Church;* and St. Jerome, *Letters,* xxii, 2, translated by Charles Christopher Mierow, ed., in Vol. 33, *Ancient Christian Writers* (Westminster: The Newman Press, 1963). See also Jerome, *Lettres,* translated by Jerome Labourt, ed. (Paris: Société les belles lettres, 1949 ff), xlvii; and *Select Letters,* LIV, 4, translated by F. A. Wright, ed. (London: William Heinemann, 1933).

86.   Jerome, *Select Letters,* XXII, 20.

87.   St. Ambrose, *De vidius,* cap. XIII, xxxi; and *De virginitate,* I, cap. 6, in Vol. 7, *Omnia opera,* D. A. B. Caillau, ed. (Paris: Paul Mellier, 1844).

88.   St. Ambrose, *De vidius,* cap. XV, lxxxviii; and cap. XI, lxix.

89.   Bailey, *Sexual Relation in Christian Thought,* p. 24.

90.   St. Jerome, *Contre Jovinien, contre Vigilantius,* in *Oeuvres de Saint Jerome,* M. B. de-Matougues, ed. (Paris: Soulte de pantheon litteraire, 1841); and *Against Helvidius.*

91.   Sozomen, *Ecclesiastical History,* I, xxiii, translated by Edward Walford (London: Henry G. Bohn, 1855); and Socrates, *Ecclesiastical History,* I, xi (London: Henry G. Bohn, 1904).

92.   Bailey, *Sexual Relation in Christian Thought,* p. 30.

93.   See Henri-Charles Puech, *Le Manicheisme* (Paris: Civilisations du sud [S. AEP], 1949). The various writings of St. Augustine are the best extant source for the teachings of Mani, but also invaluable is the *Fihrist, or Register of the Sciences of Muhammad ibn Ishaq ibn al-Nadim,* writ-

ten in the tenth century in Arabic. It was edited and translated by Bayard Dodge under the title of *The Fihrist of al-Nadim* (New York: Columbia University Press, 1970, 2 vols.). See also Noonan, *op. cit.*, pp. 107–130.

94. St. Augustine, *The Way of Life of the Manichaeans* (*De moribus Manichaeorum*), XVIII (65–66), translated by Donald A. Gallagher and Idella J. Gallagher, in Vol. 56 *The Fathers of the Church*.

95. St. Augustine, *Confessions*, VIII, vii, translated by William Watts, ed. (London: William Heinemann, 1919).

96. *Ibid.*, VI, xii; and also St. Augustine, *The Happy Life* (*De beata vita*), I (4), translated by Ludwig Schopp, ed., in Vol. 1, *The Fathers of the Church*.

97. Romans, 13:13–14.

98. St. Augustine, *Confessions*, VIII, xii.

99. St. Augustine, *Concerning the Nature of Good*, cap. xvii, translated by A. H. Newman, in Whitney J. Oates, ed., *Basic Writings of St. Augustine* (New York: Random House, 1948), p. 455.

100. St. Augustine, *De gratia Christi, et de peccato originali contra Pelagium* cap. 43, xxxviii, translated by Marcus Dodd in Vol. 2, *The Works of St. Augustine* (Edinburgh: T. & T. Clark, 1885).

101. St. Augustine, *City of God*, XIV, 26, translated by Demetrius B. Zema and Gerald G. Walsh, *The Fathers of the Church*.

102. *Ibid.*, XIV, 17, 19.

103. *Ibid.*, XIV, 26; also 23, 24; St. Augustine, *De nuptiis et concupiscentia*, II, cap. 14 (v), translated by Marcus Dodd, in Vol. 2, *The Works of St. Augustine*.

104. Bailey, *Sexual Relation in Christian Thought*, p. 54.

105. St. Augustine, *De peccatorium meritis et remissione*, cap. 57 (XXIX), translated by Marcus Dodd, in Vol. 4, *The Works of St. Augustine*.

106. St. Augustine, *De nuptiis et concupiscentia*, I, cap. 4 (iii).

107. *Ibid.*, I, cap. 8 (vii).

108. *Ibid.*, I, cap. 9 (viii).

109. St. Augustine, *De bono conjugali*, X, 10, in Vol. 40, J. P. Migne, *Patrologiae Latina* (Paris: Garnier fratres, 1887); and St. Augustine, *Sermones*, CCCLI, iii (5) in Vol. 39, Migne, *Patrologiae Latina*.

110. St. Augustine, *Against Two Letters of the Pelagians*, I, cap. 27 (xiii), cap. 30 (xv), in Vol. 15, *The Works of St. Augustine*.

111. St. Augustine, *De nuptiis et concupiscentia*, I, 17 (xv).

112. St. Augustine, *De bono conjugali*, V.

113. St. Augustine, *Soliloquies*, I, 10 (17), translated by Thomas F. Gilligan in Vol. 1, *The Fathers of the Church*.

114. *Didache or Teachings of the Twelve Apostles*, cap. II, in Vol. 7, *The Ante Nicene Fathers*.

115. *Epistles of Barnabas*, cap. xix, in Vol. 1, *The Ante Nicene Fathers*.

116. *Constitutions of the Holy Apostles*, VI, xi, and xxvii, in Vol. 7, *The Ante Nicene Fathers*; and also the anonymous poem, "A Strain of Sodom," in Vol. 4, *The Ante Nicene Fathers*, pp. 129–132.

117. St. John Chrysostom, *Commentaire sur l'epitre aux Romans*, IV, in Vol. 10, *Oeuvres*, translated by M. Jeannin, ed. (Nantes: L. Juerun, 1866); and *Commentaire sur l'epitre a Tite*, IV, in Vol. 11, *Oeuvres*.

118.   St. John Chrysostom, *Commentaire sur l'evangile selon S. Matthieu,* LXXXIII, 3, in Vol. 8, *Oeuvres.*

119.   St. Augustine, *Confessions,* III, viii.

120.   *Epistle of Barnabas,* x.

121.   St. Basil, *De renuntiatione saeculi (On the Renunciation of the World),* translated by Sister M. Monica Wagner in Vol. 9, *The Fathers of the Church,* pp. 23–24.

122.   St. Augustine, *Epistle,* ccxi, in *Letters,* translated by Wilfrid Parsons, *The Fathers of the Church.*

123.   Bailey, *Homosexuality and the Western Christian Tradition,* pp. 87–88.

124.   Gregory of Nyssa, *Epistle,* ccxvii, can. 62 in Vol. 67, Migne, *Patrologiae Latina.*

125.   *Ibid.,* Epistle Canonica, 4.

126.   St. Basil, *The Letters,* ccxvii; *To Amphilochius,* 57–75, translated by Roy J. de Ferrari, ed. (London: William Heinemann, 1930).

127.   St. Gregory of Nyssa, *Epistle canonica,* 4.

PART THREE

ATTITUDES TOWARD SEX
IN THE NON-WESTERN WORLD

9

ISLAM: A SEX-POSITIVE RELIGION

Islam could be classed as a sex-positive religion. Though it held many positions in common with Judaism and Christianity, and many characters in the Bible appear in the Koran,[1] Islamic laws relating to marriage, divorce, fornication, and other aspects of sexual behavior are derived more from pre-Islamic Arabic attitudes than from the Judeo–Christian tradition. Moreover, the Greek ascetic attitudes about sex were at first not particularly strong in Islam, although they later had some effect. The key to Islamic outlooks on sex, as on so many other things, is the teachings of the Prophet Muhammad, who, true to the Arabic tradition, regarded sex as a good rather than an evil aspect of life. This still holds true today.

H. R. P. Dickson, a recorder of Arab customs and mores, reported in the 1930s that it was

> no exaggeration to say that sexual intercourse is loved by the ordinary Arab above all pleasures in the world. It is the one great pleasure common to rich and poor alike, and the one moment of forgetfulness in his daily round of troubles that Badawin or townsmen can enjoy. Men and women equally love the act, which is said to keep men young, "just like riding a mare."[2]

In this attitude the Arabs were simply reflecting the teachings of Muhammad. A nineteenth-century Muslim writer summarized Islamic attitudes.

Coition is one of the causes of the preservation of health. Let him among you who is in a condition for having sufficient copulation marry: marriage gives moderation of the gaze and more obligatorily turns one away from incest and adultery.[3]

Before Muhammad, the Arabs were a male-centered tribal people practicing polygamy, circumcision, and occasional infanticide, whose customs and gods were being undermined by outside forces, including Christianity and Judaism. Though the Prophet modified, changed, abolished, and reformed many traditional Arabic customs and beliefs, the Muslim Arabs remained a male-centered, polygamous society in which women were regarded as inferior to men. Muhammad, regarded by Islam as the last and greatest of the prophets of Allah, was born in Mecca about 570 A.D. and died there in 632 A.D.

Until shortly before his birth, the Arabs lacked a written language, although they were not lacking in literature. The first great age of Arabic poetry dates from about 100 years before the birth of Muhammad. The reverence the Arabs felt for these poems is indicated by their reciting and memorizing them and transmitting them to succeeding generations until they were ultimately recorded during the second and third centuries of the Muslim era. A group of these poems is known as the *Mu-allaqat,* literally the "Hung-Up" or "Suspended Poems," so called because, according to tradition, they were so highly regarded they were hung in the *Ka'ba,* the Muslim holy of holies.

The poems, highly stylized, with involved, complex, and elaborate meters, usually begin with an expression of yearning for a vanished happiness in love and ultimately end glorifying the poet or his tribe, the poems' real object. The oldest and most famous of the *Mu-allaqat* poets is Imra' al-Quais, whose description of female beauty, in spite of the difficulties of putting it into English prose, still conveys something of the meaning it held and still holds in Arabic.

I twisted her side-tresses to me, and she leaned over me; slender-waisted she was, and tenderly plump her ankles, shapely and taut her belly, white-fleshed, not the least flabby, polished the lie of her breast-bones, smooth as a burnished mirror. She turns away, to show a soft cheek, and wards me off with the glance of a wild deer of Wajra, a shy gazelle with its fawn; she shows me a throat like the throat of an antelope, not ungainly when she lifts it upward, neither naked of ornament; she shows me her thick black tresses, a dark embellishment clustering down her back like bunches of a laden date-tree—twisted upwards meanwhile are the locks that ring her brow, the knots cunningly lost in the plaited and loosened strands; she shows me a waist slender and slight as a camel's nose rein, and a smooth shank like the reed of a watered bent papyrus . . .[4]

This erotic symbolism of pre-Islamic Arabic literature was carried over into Islam, where it acted as a major influence in forming Islamic sexual attitudes.[5]

Muhammad, though a prophet, was also a man of his time, and he has often appeared to prudish Western observers as the incarnation of sensuality and sexuality. So great was the Christian antagonism to Islam that Muhammad was regarded as the prince of darkness, the devil incarnate, and Islam has traditionally been regarded as the great enemy of Christianity.[6] Edward Gibbon, the great eighteenth-century historian, no admirer of Christianity, still expressed shock at Muhammad, claiming the Prophet had indulged all

> the appetites of man and abused the claims of a prophet. A special revelation dispensed him from the laws which he had imposed on his nation; the female sex without reserve was abandoned to his desires; and this singular prerogative excited the envy, rather than the scandal, the veneration, rather than the envy of the devout Musulmans . . .[7]

Only in recent years have Western scholars been able to view Muhammad objectively, but some biographers still appear defensive about his sexuality. One twentieth-century biographer wrote:

> No doubt the trait of Mohammad's character most offensive to the Christian Occident is his sensuality. His lack of moderation and control in this sphere appears worse to us because the common-sense Christian morality, being an heir of the ancient asceticism, is based on an exaggerated idea of the sinfulness of the sexual instinct. Offences in this sense are often regarded as the sin in an absolute and real sense. . . . Undoubtedly a prophet who declares that women and children belong to the enticements of worldly life, and who nevertheless accumulates a harem of nine wives, in addition to various slave women, is a strange phenomenon when regarded from the standpoint of morality. This situation is not improved by the fact that up to Khadijah's (his first wife) death, that is, until Mohammad was fifty years old, he was content with one wife. At the height of his career, when he was already an aging man, he gave free reign to his sensual impulses.[8]

Even historians of sex have difficulty viewing the Prophet. Richard Lewinsohn, for example, in his popularized history of sexual customs, believed that Muhammad went through a "second youth" in his middle fifties, and "sex acquired over him a mastery which it retained to the end of his own days."[9]

Though there is no question that Muhammad regarded sexual intercourse as one of the joys of life, there is considerable doubt that he was as virile as some have pictured him. Part of the difficulty is that Arabic folktales continually feature male virility, and the virility of Muhammad himself probably became embroidered with folklore. In the *Thousand Nights and A Night,* for example, a much-admired character managed to possess 40 women 30 times each in one night. Obviously, this was physiologically unlikely, if not impossible, although the unmythical King Ibn Saud of Saudi Arabia, a twentieth-century ruler, true to Arab tradition, claimed to have married 400 women during his life and to have never seen the face of any of them.[10] Many of Saud's wives were Bedouin brides whom he married for a night or two and then divorced, but his vast numbers of children might suggest that he spent much of his leisure time in bed.

Another difficulty with accepting the stories about Muhammad's sexual prowess is that he seems an unlikely candidate for such a sensuous portrait. He did not marry until he was 25; then his wife, Khadījah, was some 15 years older than he. He remained faithful to her until she died, whereupon he went into deep mourning. Muhammad was married a second time only at the urging of his companions, to a young girl of 6 or 7, Ā'ishah, who brought her dolls with her. In view of her age, there was at first no question of sex, although Arabic tradition has Muhammad finally consummating the marriage when Ā'ishah was 9 or 10,[11] in accordance with traditional Arabic practices.

Later Muhammad had a number of wives, but he took many of them for political reasons, formalizing through marriage alliances of support with various tribal leaders. Several of his later wives were widows, this kind of marriage providing the women with social security in their old age. Tradition has it that Muhammad generally tried to apportion his time equally with his wives, sleeping with each in rotation. Since only one of his later wives, the Coptic Marya, gave birth to any children, and she had only one son, Ibrahim, it is possible to conclude that most of the Prophet's wives were past the childbearing age, or they all had continual miscarriages, or the Prophet was troubled by impotence, had become sterile, or perhaps had his mind on other activities.

Nevertheless, the stories about Muhammad's sexual life remain, the story most often cited to indicate his intense sexuality being his affair with Zainab, although modern scholars disagree about the correct interpretation. Zainab (or Zaynab), Muhammad's cousin, at the Prophet's urging, was married against her will to Muhammad's adopted son and ex-slave Zaid. Pleased with the marriage, Muhammad, continued to visit his son, and on one such visit was met at the door by Zainab, dressed in the garment that Arab women were accustomed to wear inside the house but that was not to be seen by anyone other than their male relatives and husband. When he saw her, Muhammad, aroused, went away without entering, repeating: "Praise be Allah who changeth the hearts of men." The unhappy Zainab took this to mean there was a possibility of being elevated to the position of wife of the Prophet, a position she had always wanted. She badgered her husband until he went to Muhammad, volunteering to divorce her if the Prophet would marry her. Zaid was, however, Muhammad's adopted son, and by custom and Koranic law, a father could not marry his son's wife, or vice versa, since such a practice was regarded as incest. To resolve the matter Muhammad received a revelation:

and it becometh not a believing man or a believing woman, when Allah and his messengers have decided an affair (for them), that they should (after that) claim any say in their affair; and whoso is rebellious to Allah and His messenger, he verily goeth astray in error manifest. And when thou saidst unto him on whom Allah hath conferred favour and thou hast conferred favour; Keep thy wife to thyself, and fear Allah, and thou didst hide in thy mind that which Allah was to bring to light, and thou didst fear mankind whereas Allah had a better right that thou shouldst fear him. So when Zaid had performed the necessary formality (of divorce) from her, We gave her unto thee in marriage, so that (henceforth) there may be no sin for believers in respect of wives of their adopted sons, when the latter have performed the necessary formality (of release) from them. The commandment of Allah must be fulfilled.[12]

None of Muhammad's contemporaries are reported as being upset by his behavior in this incident, although Muslim scholars have been careful to acquit the Prophet of committing incest. In fact, they emphasize that the point of the revelation was not the sexuality of Muhammad but the fact that, in Islam, adopted sons would not be considered blood sons, as they had been among the pre-Islamic Arabs. Still other commentators argue that Muhammad took this action to demonstrate that a woman's own preferences were to be considered in arranging any marriage.[13]

Matters are not, however, quite so simple, and there must have been considerable shock over the Prophet's actions, since Ā'ishah, Muhammad's second wife and the source of many of the sayings and traditions surrounding him, used this incident to demonstrate that Muhammad had never suppressed any revelation he received. She argued that, if he had ever tried to do so, he surely would have repressed this one. She is also said to have remarked that "truly thy Lord makes haste to do thy pleasure."

Muhammad also had other fortuitous revelations to answer various personal crises, some of which also had sexual overtones. One series of verses in the Koran is usually regarded as a special revelation to the Prophet to enable him to deal with the jealousies of his wives. According to one interpretation, Hafṣah, one of Muhammad's wives, found him with his wife Marya, a Coptic Egyptian girl given him by the ruler of Egypt, on a day he was supposed to visit Ā'ishah. She immediately condemned Muhammad for playing favorites and violating his own rules. Muhammad, supposedly to pacify Hafṣah, swore that he would have nothing more to do with Marya on that day and promised to revert to his traditional order of visitation if Hafṣah would say nothing to Ā'ishah. Hafṣah, evidently still fuming at this departure from routine, was not appeased by his promise and told Ā'ishah and the other wives what Muhammad had done. When he discovered this, he was so furious with his other wives that, as punishment, he spent a whole month with Marya. The *sura* justifying his conduct is worth quoting at some length:

Why bannest thou that which Allah hath made lawful for thee, seeking to please thy wives? And Allah is Forgiving, Merciful. Allah hath made lawful for you (Muslims) absolution from your oaths (of such a kind), and Allah is your Protector. He is the Knower, the Wise. When the Prophet confided a fact unto one of his wives and when she afterward divulged it and Allah apprised him thereof, he made known (to her) part thereof and passed over part. And when he told it her she said: Who hath told thee? He said: The Knower the Aware hath told me.

If ye twain turn unto Allah repentant, (ye have cause to do so) for your hearts desired (the ban); and if ye aid one another against him (Muhammad) then lo! Allah, even He, is his protecting Friend, and Gabriel and the righteous among the believers; and furthermore the angels are his helpers. It may happen that his Lord, if he divorce you, will give him in your stead wives better than you, submissive (to Allah), believing, pious, penitent, inclined to fasting, widows and maids.[14]

Not all of Muhammad's specific revelations were designed to protect the male against the female. Some were supportive of women; particulary noteworthy are the verses dealing with Ā'ishah. Part of the problem was that Ā'ishah grew into a happy, fun-loving woman, not at all the sort of wife that Westerners would predict for a prophet. Another difficulty was that, though Muhammad later married several other wives (the limitation of four did not apply to him), Ā'ishah remained his favorite and often accompanied him on his campaigns. Usually, on such campaigns, Ā'ishah observed *purdah* and, as a proper Arab matron, was carried in a heavily curtained litter so that no other man might gaze on the wife of the Prophet.

On one occasion, however, Ā'ishah vanished from her litter and was nowhere to be found when the caravan stopped for the night. The next morning she arrived accompanied by a handsome young soldier; the gossips had a field day, imputing all sorts of indiscretions to her. She reported that, during an earlier rest stop, she had gone to perform her ablutions, but after returning to the *howdah,* she found she had left some of her jewelry behind. Without thinking to tell anyone, she had gone back to retrieve it, but before she returned, the expedition had moved on. She had then waited for someone to come back and rescue her, and soon after, her gallant young soldier had appeared. Few of Muhammad's followers believed her story, and various derogatory rumors about her character circulated around the camp. Muhammad, after hearing her abused for 3 days, thundered against her accusers:

Why did they not produce four witnesses? Since they produce not witnesses, they verily are liars in the sight of Allah. Had it not been for the grace of Allah and His mercy unto you in the world and the Hereafter an awful doom had overtaken you for that whereof ye murmured. When ye welcomed it with your tongues, and uttered with your mouths that whereof ye had no knowledge, ye counted it a trifle. In the sight of Allah it is very great.[15]

In effect, to accuse a woman of adultery, it was necessary to produce four witnesses, something not likely to happen very often. Without four witnesses such an accusation amounted to slander, a crime, and the gossip quickly ceased. Ā'ishah never, however, forgave those who failed to accept her innocence, among whom was Ali, Muhammad's son-in-law and, eventually, one of his successors. Her hatred was so great that, when Ali was ruling, Ā'ishah conspired to bring about his downfall as well as that of his family. The result was the murder of Ali's two sons Ḥassān and Ḥusayn and the ultimate division of Islam into two major camps. While the incident was still fresh, the principal parties concerned in the spread of gossip against her were punished with 80 lashes for false accusation.

With the sexual tradition of the pre-Islamic Arabs and the personality of Muhammad as important factors, Islam inevitably proved much more accepting of sex than Christianity and less willing to challenge existing sexual tradition in newly conquered areas. The difference between the Koran and the Bible appears early in the story of creation. In the Koran, Allah is said to have created man not only from dust and earth but also from drops of semen and congealed blood.[16] With the recognition that God had semen, Islam could easily regard sex as a good. Whereas Christianity considered celibacy as the highest good, Islam accepted marriage as the highest good, ordained by God.

> He created for you helpmeets from yourselves that ye might find rest in them, and He ordained between you love and mercy. Lo, herein indeed are portents for folk who reflect.[17]

> He hath made for you pairs of yourselves, and of the cattle also pairs, whereby he multiplieth you. Naught is His likeness; and He is the Hearer, the Seer.[18]

Muhammad was so opposed to celibacy that he held marriage was incumbent on all who possessed the ability.[19] Whereas Christianity recognized marriage as acceptable for those who could not live the celibate life, Islam accepted polygamy for those who could not be monogamous.

> . . . Marry of the women, who seem good to you, two or three or four; and if ye fear that ye cannot do justice (to so many) then one (only) or (the captives) that your right hand possess. Thus it is more likely that ye will not do injustice.[20]

Regardless of how many wives a man had, he was cautioned to treat them with kindness and warned not to beat them or abuse them, since a virtuous wife was man's best treasure.[21]

These verses were all written from the male point of view, Islam being clearly a male-oriented religion. Women were recognized as sexual companions for the male, and pious Muslims could praise Allah for having created woman in all her beauty, for having formed her body with all the charms that awakened desire, for having made her hair so silky, and for having made the precious curves of her breast. Though both men and women went to Paradise, the pictures of Paradise are aimed more at masculine than feminine wish fulfillment. The good Muslim would, for example, enjoy the society of ever-virgin *houris*, dark-eyed damsels with swelling breasts and shy, retiring glances, as well as that of eternal boys. Paradise for either sex is material; its inhabitants clad in the richest raiment, reposing on luxurious couches, enjoying exquisite food, drinking from gold and silver vessels, smelling heavenly scents, and quaffing celestial wine.[22]

On earth, Muhammad taught that men

> are in charge of women, because Allah hath made the one of them to excel the other, and because they spend of their property (for the support of women). So good women are the obedient, guarding in secret that which Allah hath guarded. As for those from whom ye fear rebellion, admonish them and banish them to beds apart, and scourge them. Then if they obey you, seek not a way against them . . .[23]

Women were seen as erotic creatures continually giving trouble to man. Thus, later Muslim tradition held that, whereas many a man had reached perfection, only two or three women in all of history had,[24] although a few women, such as the Prophet's first wife Khadījah, had been outstanding.[25] Since women were to be subordinate to men, Muhammad advised believing women to

> lower their gaze and be modest, and to display of their adornment only that which is apparent, and to draw their veils over their bosoms, and not to reveal their adornment save to their own husbands or fathers or husband's fathers, or their sons or their husband's sons, or their brothers or their brothers' sons or sisters' sons, or their women, or their slaves, or male attendants who lack vigour, or children who know naught of women's nakedness. And let them not stamp their feet so as to reveal what they hide of their adornment.[26]

When male visitors visited their homes, women were advised to stay behind a curtain so that their guest could remain purer in heart and the woman herself remain pure.[27] Women were allowed to speak freely only with their male kinsmen, their own women, or slaves, but when they went out of their homes, they were to draw their cloaks close around them so that they would not be recognized or annoyed.[28] Traditionally, this provision has been interpreted to justify the veiling of women, although the origins of the custom are much debated among scholars.

Nudity was discouraged in Islam. The Koran states:

> Say to the believers that they cast down their looks and guard their privy parts. . . . And say to the believing women that they cast down their looks and guard their

privy parts and display not their ornaments, except those of them that are external; and let them pull their veils over the opening of their chemises at their bosoms and not display their ornaments to their husbands or their fathers.[29]

Later, Islamic law required men to keep their genitals covered; they were not supposed to view or touch any part of another man's nakedness from the knees to the navel. Men were also not to look at strange women, except in the face, which was veiled, the hand, or the foot.[30] Until almost this century the law was interpreted literally, and no respectable Muslim male wore the occidental garb of short coat and close-fitting trousers, because they were regarded as indecently exposing the genitals. The whole body of a free woman was, in fact, regarded as pudendal, and no part of her was to be seen except by her husband or close kin.[31]

Since God had created men superior to women, women were to be subject to their nearest male relative, husband, father, or brother, whose right over them was regarded in the same way as a man's right over other property. In Islamic tradition the wife's honor was in the hands of her husband, whose business was to see it was not violated. She was meant to be guarded, and if he failed in his duty, it was not necessarily her fault if she strayed. Few legal sanctions enforced the subservience of a wife to her husband, but within a tribe this was accepted as the normal and honorable way of life. If a man from another tribe seduced a married woman, he committed no unlawful or dishonorable act; poets, in fact, constantly boasted of their stolen loves.[32]

Intercourse in the Koran was a good, religious deed. As the Koran stated:

Your women are a tilth (field) for you (to cultivate) so go to your tilth as ye will, and send (good deeds) before you for your souls, and fear Allah, and know that ye will (one day) meet Him. Give glad tidings to believers (O Muhammad).[33]

Muslim men, however, were cautioned to seek women out for:

honest wedlock, not debauchery. And those of whom ye seek content (by marrying them) give unto them their portions as a duty. And there is no sin for you in what ye do by mutual agreement after the duty (hath been done). Lo! Allah is ever Knowing, Wise. And whoso is not able to marry free, believing women, let them marry from the believing maids whom your right hands possess. Allah knoweth best (concerning) your faith.[34]

Women, nevertheless, had rights; in this respect Muhammad was a reformer of old Arabic customs. Women retained their right to their dowry,[35] wives were to be treated equally, and it was forbidden to turn away from one, leaving her in suspense.[36] This has usually been interpreted to mean that coitus interruptus and other forms of birth control were not to be practiced without the woman's consent. Similarly, anal intercourse or oral–genital contact was not permitted without her consent. Other commentators hold, however, that these are not absolute guarantees to wives, for Muhammad also stated that a wife was to be cultivated in any way that a man wanted to do so.

Muhammad did stipulate that wives and daughters were to inherit, although a male child's portion was to be twice that of a female's.[37] Wives could also leave legacies,[38] and a man was not to inherit a woman's estate against her will.[39] Divorced wives were allowed to keep their dowries, and a former husband was not allowed to impede their remarriage.[40] Widows who had been in mourning for 4 months and 10 days could remarry.[41] No legal age was set by Muhammad for marriage, and quite young children could be married (witness Ā'ishah). A girl was not, however, to be handed over to her husband until she was fit for marital congress, and a man who had intercourse with a girl before her menses was subject to punishment.[41] Marriage (nikāḥ) literally means "sexual intercourse," although it is used in the Koran to mean "contract."[42] If there was doubt about a girl's youth, two matrons were appointed to examine her and report on her physical preparedness. Usually, a girl was married at 12 or 13, and a girl of 19 was regarded as an old maid. In most cases the bridegroom was older than the bride.[43]

The detailed explanation of the rights and obligations of women in the Koran had greater force in Islam than a similar statement made in the Bible might have in Christendom. This is because Islam, from its inception, was not only a religion but also a state, the religious community being coextensive with the social community. This unity allowed little room for the division between the spiritual and the secular so evident in many Christian states. Muhammad was at one and the same time a prophet and a ruler, and his successors, the caliphs, were both popes and emperors. The Koran then was not only a divine transcript of a heavenly archetype but also a basic law code for all the faithful.

As the growing Arabic Empire found itself in need of a legal system to deal with the problems of political power, it turned to the Koran, for Islam implied submission to the will of God, and the Koran was the word of God. The study of the Koran, interpreting its sometimes confusing meanings and applying them to everyday life, became the tasks of early Islamic scholars, who were more in the tradition of lawyers than of theologians. Since the Koran was not always clear, it was supplemented by the knowledge of the practices of the early Islamic community in Medina or the personal practices of the Prophet himself. These were called the Hadīth, literally, "the tradition." Whenever an issue—religious, political, or cultural—arose, each party sought to find authority for its view in some word or decision of the Prophet or his companions, whether such words were real or fictitious. Because Islam was early divided into factions, there were soon conflicting traditions. To resolve these conflicts, the scholars tried to find verification, and verification of the perfect Hadīths consisted of two parts: the names of the persons who had handed on the substance of the tradition and the text of the tradition. By the time these

procedures had been developed, there were 600,000 different and often conflicting *hadīths*. Some six different collections of *hadīths* are generally regarded as
canonical.

The *Hadīth* holds a place in Islam similar to the Talmud in the Jewish community, and even seemingly trivial questions, such as the proper way of cutting
a watermelon before eating it or of cleaning the teeth with a toothpick, or the
correct position for a bowel movement, became the subject of *hadīth* literature.
The legal system of the Arabs came to be based on this tradition as well as on
the Koran, but this also proved inadequate as new conditions arose. To meet
this challenge new rules were developed based on analogy, deduction, or
general consent. Here also, different interpretations arose among the Muslims,
four schools of thought being recognized as orthodox: the liberal Iraq school,
which insisted on juridical speculation; the more conservative Medina school,
which attached special importance to the *hadīth*; the Shafi-ite school, which accepted speculation but with specific limitations; and the Hānbalite school,
which represented an uncompromising adherence to the letter of the *Hadīth*. In
addition, there is a major division of Islam known as the Shi-ites, whose
adherents accept only the Koran, although, since the Shi-ites also accept the
absolute authority and judgment of the infallible imams as well as of all
descendants of Ali (the son-in-law of Muhammad, husband of Fatimah) about
what the Koran might mean,[44] they also have a *hadīth*—it is just different from
the Sunni one.

The conflicting traditions make it difficult to generalize about the sexual attitudes of Islam, but they also make it possible periodically to update Islamic
attitudes. For example, when authorities in Egypt began, in the early 1960s, to
contemplate initiating birth control programs, they turned to the learned
sheikhs at al-Azhar University, who determined that the Prophet himself had
practiced birth control, and so there could be no religious objection to such a
program. The *Shari'ah* or "Way," the Arabic term for legal system, is seen as
an all-embracing way that should ideally govern all phases of Islamic life. But
Islamic lawyers grant Muslim rulers the right of suspending application of
certain portions of the public law and of substituting secular law, particularly
as far as criminal punishment is concerned. This does not, however, revoke or
abolish Divine Law; it only means that Divine Law is not enforced, because,
for temporal reasons, it is not, or was not at that time and place, feasible to do
so.

As to morals in general, the chief virtue in Islam seems to be to avoid
excess.[45] Liberality without profuseness, kindness to orphans and the poor
without waste, faithfulness to engagements, patience and endurance, obedience
to those in authority, and limitations of sexual indulgence to legal wives and
concubines are specifically mentioned as examples of virtue. Good works do
away with sins and make the doer righteous. Allah is, however, merciful and
forgiving and will put away the guilt of the worst actions and reward the best

actions of those who believe. For most sins involving sex the various commentators hold that a single punishment should answer for all previous repetitions of the act. This is because the punishment is seen as a way to deter people from perpetrating things Allah has forbidden, and if it could not be prevented by one punishment, there is little evidence that multiple punishments would do any good. The matter then becomes something between God and the individual.[46]

Traditionally, Islamic scholars regard all heterosexual intercourse between persons not in a state of legal matrimony or concubinage as a sin. Such intercourse (zinā') includes adultery, fornication, and sodomy. The Koran has several warnings against zinā' and, in keeping with Jewish and Christian ideas, generally represents premarital and extramarital chastity as a mark of the believer.[47] Those found guilty of certain types of zinā' were to be punished with 100 lashes, and the unchaste were to marry only the unchaste or idolaters.[48] The Caliph Umar (reigned, 634–644 A.D.) is said to have held that Muhammad had urged the stoning of the guilty couples in adultery, and this appears in a hadīth, but it seems more an interpolation than an original practice.[49] Muhammad's condemnation of zinā', in fact, is not so severe as it might first appear, because, in practice, there were modifications. For example, though the Koran stipulates that women found guilty of adultery and fornication were to be locked in their houses until they died,[50] it required four witnesses to convict, and the accuser failing to bring four witnesses was himself punished with 80 lashes.[51] In practice, this meant it was almost impossible to convict, unless the couple was exceedingly indiscreet or discovered by an angry husband, who was allowed to avoid this requirement:

> And those who cast imputations on their wives and have no witnesses except themselves, then the testimony of one of them shall be to testify four times that, by Allah, he is of those who speak the truth; and the fifth testimony shall be that the curse of Allah shall be on him if he be of those who lie. And it shall avert the punishment from her if she bears testimony four times that, by Allah, he is of those who lie; and the fifth that the wrath of God shall be on her if he be of those who speak the truth.[52]

Women cast out by their husbands under such conditions came to be regarded as fallen women. If the husband killed the guilty couple in flagrante delicto, he was not liable to punishment. A wife had, however, little recourse against her unfaithful husband, for Islam, like Christianity, had a double standard. In fact the whole concept of zinā' often seems to be concerned more with a violation of property, such as a wife or concubine, than with particularly evil conduct.

Also like the Christians, Muhammad recognized that lust itself was a sin:

> The adultery of the eye is to look with an eye of desire on the wife of another; and the adultery of the tongue is to utter what is forbidden.[53]

When a man committed adultery, Muhammad held that his faith had left him, but that, if the sinner returned to the path of right, his faith would return to him.[54] Not all cases of *zinā'* were treated equally; in some cases no blame was attached, particularly when *Shubha,* or only a resemblance to a criminal action, and not a real criminal action, took place. Intercourse in an invalid marriage was not *zinā'* unless the marriage itself was with a prohibited relation; intercourse with a woman who the man erroneously thought was his wife or slave was not *zinā',* nor was intercourse with a slave of whom he was joint proprietor. Inevitably, all the exceptions are written from a male point of view.

This same attitude is evident in the justification of polygamy. Though Muhammad was undoubtedly a reformer by his insistence that every wife had a legal personality, he quite clearly regarded the female as inferior to the male. But whether monogamy or polygamy has prevailed in a particular Islamic country or period has been a matter, not so much of faith or morals, as of social, sexual, or economic convenience. Muhammad himself married several wives, sometimes calculated as 14 in all, and several prominent early rulers of Islam also had more than four, in part because the Koranic prescription of four is not as clear-cut as it appears. Moreover, whereas the number of wives might be clearly limited, the number of concubines is not. The essential difference between concubinage and marriage was that marriage could take place only with a free woman, but concubines were slaves. To marry a slave it was necessary that she be emancipated. Concubines were not, however, to be selected from married women unless they were captives.[55]

Divorce, at least for the male, was easily arranged in Islam. If a husband divorced his wife before he consummated the marriage, he had to pay only half of the marriage fee agreed upon.[56] A man could divorce a wife twice and take her back once. Before he could marry her a third time, however, she had to be married and divorced from another husband. After a divorce a woman was to wait for three successive menses before she left her divorced husband's house, to be certain she was not pregnant, and if it was mutually agreeable, she could even remain in her former husband's house after divorce. When she was sent away, the husband had to restore her dowry. If, however, it was the woman who had persuaded her husband to divorce her, the husband could claim part of her dowry.[57] Intercourse was not to be resumed after a divorce until after a 2-month fast or the feeding of 60 needy ones.[58] A wife was permitted to divorce her husband, but only under certain specified conditions, including his sexual incapacity.[59]

Islam also provided for a somewhat easier way than divorce of circulating marriage partners, through the *Mut'a,* marriages arranged for a limited time. Such short-term marriages existed among the Arabs before Muhammad, and some scholars have also found justification for them in the Koran.

> Lawful unto you are all beyond those mentioned, so that ye seek them with your wealth in honest wedlock, not debauchery. And those of whom ye seek content (by

marrying them), give unto them their portions as a duty. And there is no sin for you in what ye do by mutual agreement after the duty (hath been done).[60]

Commentators who cite this passage as justifying *Mut'a* add the words "for a definite period" at the end of the passage. Generally, this reading does not appear among the Sunni Muslims, but it is adopted by the Shi-ites. The effect is a sort of legalized prostitution but without the onus of prostitution and with the advantage of recognizing the children of such unions as legitimate. Several stipulated conditions had to be met before *Mut'a* could take place, including an agreed length of the marriage, the size of the dowry (which could be as little as a few pennies or a handful of corn), and a recognition that the woman had no claim on the man after the agreement had expired. In general, modern Islamic legal opinion has been strongly opposed to *Mut'a* contracts, and the legal systems do not recognize it. Many prostitutes still, however, enter into these temporary relationships, and of those who do, most refuse to accept more than one engagement a night.[61] In spite of official hostility, *Mut'a* marriages are still often concluded, although to make them legal, nothing specifically is said of a time limit in the marriage contract, for this would make them invalid. Rather, the time limit is agreed to by the parties.[62]

Various rules of sexual hygiene are stipulated in the Koran or in the *Hadīth*. During menstruation (*hayz*) women are regarded as ritually impure. Almost all books of Islamic theology contain a chapter devoted to treatment of women during their menses; a menstruating woman is forbidden to touch the Koran, repeat a verse from it, or enter a mosque.[63] Men are prohibited from engaging in intercourse with a woman during her menses until she has cleansed herself.

And when they have purified themselves, then go into them as Allah hath enjoined upon you. Truly Allah loveth those who turn unto him and loveth those who have a care for cleanness.[64]

The ablutions required for a menstruating woman were the same as those required after intercourse (*jimā*), after any discharge of semen through masturbation or nocturnal emission (*ihtilam*), and after childbirth (*nifās*). All these ablutions (*ghusl*) were regarded as major ones and required the believer to wash all over, making certain that the water reached every portion of his or her body and every hair of the head. An accidental touching of the skin of a person of the opposite sex (other than a wife or relative) required that a minor ablution (*wudū'*) be performed that entailed the washing of the face, of the hands up to the elbow, and of the feet to the ankles and the rubbing of the head. If water was not available, the devout were authorized to use clear soil.[65]

A sign of a true Muslim is circumcision, although circumcision (*khitān* for males, *khāfd* for females) is not mentioned in the Koran at all. It was practiced by the Arabs before Muhammad, and he apparently adopted it without comment, although there is some disagreement about whether it is indispensable. Most Muslims, nonetheless, regard male circumcision as an essential act of the faith. Much more debatable is female circumcision, although it also is found in Islamic lands from India to Morocco.[66] Rules for circumcision vary, but al-Nawawi, in his commentary on *Tahara* (or "purity"), states:

> As regards males it is obligatory to cut off the whole skin which covers the glans, so that this latter is wholly denudated. As regards females, it is obligatory to cut off a small part of the skin in the highest part of the genitals.[67]

Describing the operation in somewhat greater detail as it existed in the nineteenth century was the English traveler and sexologist Richard Burton:

> The Muslims use a stick as a probe passed round between glans and prepuce to ascertain the extent of the frenum and that there is no abnormal adhesion. The foreskin is then drawn forward and fixed by the forceps, a fork of two bamboo splints, five or six inches long by a quarter thick, or in some cases an iron like our compasses. This is tied tightly over the foreskin so as to exclude about an inch and a half of the prepuce above and three quarters below. A single stroke of the razor drawn directly downwards removes the skin. The slight bleeding is stopped by burnt rags or ashes and healed with cerates, pledgets, and fumigations. The Moslem circumcision does not prevent skin retracting.[68]

Male circumcision is carried out with a great deal of public ceremony, but female circumcision, where it exists, is usually done in private. It is not prescribed by the Koran, and where it is practiced, it is probably a pre-Islamic carryover. In some groups a needle and thread is stuck through the top of a young girl's clitoris, which is then pulled down and cut off as far as it protrudes. In other groups only the exposed tip is cut off. In some societies, particularly in southern Egypt and the Sudan, it has been customary to do more drastic circumcisions and to cut off the labia minora and, at times, even the labia majora. In Egypt, under the late Gamal Abdul Nasser, there was considerable discussion over the abolition of female circumcision, since it had been condemned by a United Nations Committee as a torture and laceration to girls. The Sudan also has been interested in abolishing the practice and has passed some legislation to that effect.

In Muslim countries one of the contradictions inherent in female circumcision, an operation that excises the clitoris, is that the Muslims believe and teach that the clitoris is the source and wellspring of all female passion. This implies that clitoral excision is a more or less deliberate attempt to make women less sensuous and is, therefore, contrary to the Koran. One Sudanese who justified the practice claimed that the

> circumcision of women releases them from their bondage to sex, and enables them to fulfill their real destiny, as mothers. The clitoris is the basis for female mastur-

bation; such masturbation is common in a hot climate; the spiritual basis of masturbation is fantasy; in fantasy a woman broods on sexual images; such brooding inevitably leads a woman to spiritual infidelity, since she commits adultery in her heart, and this is the first step to physical infidelity, which is the breaker of homes.[69]

Apparently, partial excision of the clitoris does not entirely remove sexual feeling, but it does leave the woman much slower to respond, requiring her to take a great deal of time to reach orgasm. This has often led women to encourage their husbands to use hashish and other intoxicants to slow down their performance.[70] Radical excision, as practiced in some parts of the Islamic world (as well as elsewhere), leaves women with virtually, no ability to reach orgasm.

Masturbation in itself is not particularly condemned in Islamic countries, although in some of the *Hadīths* it is reported Muhammad held that the masturbator was cursed and that people who played with their sexual organs were tortured by God. The Koran is more or less silent, although commentators who condemn it quote the following:

And let those who cannot find a match keep chaste til Allah give them independence by His grace . . .[71]

Other commentators justify it as necessary to alleviate excessive lust but try to limit its practice.

Who practices it to alleviate his overexcessive lust which occupies totally his heart and he is single and has no woman I hope that he would be excused and no punishment would be inflicted upon him, but he who practices it to arouse himself sexually is deemed a sinner.[72]

The learned Abū-Hanīfa (about 700–767) is said to have permitted the use of a silken cloth to rub the member in case of emergency.[73] Various terms are used to describe the practice, including *khadkhada* ("jolting"); *ferrek* or *firk,* "stroking or churning"; *bil eed,* "with the hand"; *sekh,* "rubbing"; and other terms. The multiplicity of the terms indicates it was widespread. It was much more desirable, however, if ejaculation could come without the rubbing, particularly through a wet dream. One writer on sexology has quoted an Arab authority as follows:

Emissions of spermatozoa in nocturnal pollution or at the sight of a strange and beautiful woman are not held shameful but commendable. The Jinn have power over the body at night; in the day, man is worthy if his system would sacrifice in honor of beauty. And these occurrences, so common, do not violate the fast or Ramadan as must willful acts like drinking and eating, deliberate swallowing of saliva, masturbation, and carnal copulation.[74]

Some of the contradictory statements about masturbation are perhaps due to its being occasionally confused with homosexuality, particularly with oral–genital contacts.[75] On this subject Islam also has a somewhat ambiguous attitude.

Muhammad taught that the child's sex depended on which parent's seed, the husband's or wife's, was the stronger. He held that the vaginal secretion (*ma al-mar'ah*) was similar to the semen (*ma'ar-rajul*) and that whichever was dominant determined not only the sex but also the characteristic of the child.[76] This belief had important implications for the attitudes of a father toward his children, since it would seem that male children would indicate that the man dominated the woman, and sons would be more desirable than daughters, if only to prove the father's masculinity. Apparently also, Arab physicians, like their Greek predecessors, taught that women were colder and moister than men.[77] It was thus necessary to arouse the woman for intercourse, and a good Muslim indulged in some foreplay. Al-Kindi, a ninth-century Arabic medical writer, gives some prescriptions to incite women for intercourse,[78] such prescriptions being widespread in the Islamic world.

Technically, no specific punishment for homosexual conduct is mentioned in the Koran, although the story of Lot and the sins of Sodom and Gomorrah, in Islam as in Christianity, is equated with man's lusting after men instead of women. The Muslim condemnation is not so severe as the Christian, the terms describing the evilness of such conduct inviting ambiguity. For example, the residents of Sodom and Gomorrah are described in one passage as committing excesses, in a second passage as transgressing, and in still another as committing an abominable thing.

> Lo! ye come with lust unto men instead of women. Nay, but ye are wanton [*musrif*] folk.[79]

> What! Of all creatures do ye come unto the males, and leave the wives your Lord created for you? Nay, but you are people who transgress [*ādūna*].[80]

> And Lot! (Remember) when he said unto his folk (inhabitants of Sodom): "Will ye commit abomination [*fahishah*] such as no creatures ever did before you."[81]

There are other passages.[82] It is clear that the Koran looked with disfavor on homosexual conduct, but what the punishment was to be is a matter of some debate, for the differing terms imply different degrees of sin. A person who does things to excess (*musrif*), who passes his life in follies and merrymaking, utterly heedless of the signs of God, rouses God's hatred[83] but is not necessarily punished by man. Transgression (*Mu tadi*), from which root *ādūna* is derived, is usually equated with breaking the sabbath and various ritual observances of the religion,[84] a not particularly heinous crime. Other abominations, besides sodomy, are marrying a woman whom one's father had married,[85] fornication itself,[86] and adultery.[87] Most of these other "abominable" actions have specific punishment, but sodomy does not, although it is acting against God's will (*fasiq*).[88] It is also evident from reading the Koran that the destruction of Sodom and Gomorrah (not mentioned by name in the Koran) was not used by Islamic commentators for an absolute condemnation of sodomy (*liwātah*), as it was by the later Biblical commentators, but rather, as an example of the power of God.[89] The only possible punishment mentioned in the Koran is in the rather ambiguous verses following those previously cited dealing with adultery and requiring four witnesses to convict women for lewd conduct.

> And as for the two of you who are guilty thereof, punish them both. And if they repent and improve, then let them be. Lo! Allah is relenting, merciful.[90]

Unfortunately, not all commentators agree on the reading of this passage, since even though the verses use the masculine gender, it is not clear that the participants referred to are both male.[91] The nature of the punishment is also in dispute, since it seems to be less than the criminal punishment normally reserved for fornication. Some have held that the act in question requires only slight punishment, little more than a chastisement, and others, that it requires more severe reproof. If the passages are interpreted as applying to homosexual acts, note that penitence on the part of the guilty can relieve them of any punishment. The jurist al-Shāfi'i held that God had prohibited usury, adultery, homicide, theft, the drinking of wine, and other things of that sort, from which He had obligated men to abstain.[92] Nowhere in this list, however, is sodomy or any other kind of homosexual activity mentioned. Adultery, the only sex crime listed, is more a violation of a property right than an actual sex crime, and though it might be equated with *zinā'*, it is at least debatable whether any homosexual activity could be included under this rubric.[93]

Because of such ambiguous prohibitions homosexuality has usually been pictured as widespread in Islam. A nineteenth-century *Dictionary of Islam* stated: "The prevalence of this vice amongst Muhammadans is but too well known."[94] Sir Richard Burton, best known for his translation of the *Book of the Thousand Nights and a Night*, appended an essay to his translation of this collection of stories to account for the widespread acceptance of homosexuality. Though his essay is filled with misinformation as well as misunderstanding, and his conclusions would be unacceptable to most scholars in the field today,[95] Burton brought the subject out into the open, and any discussion of homosexuality in Islam has to begin where he left off.

Burton had become interested in homosexuality at least as early as 1845, when, as a young Army officer in Karachi, he was requested by his commander, Sir Charles Namier, to investigate rumors about homosexual brothels. Burton's detailed report on three brothels included such odd tidbits as the fact that boys were valued above eunuchs because the "scrotum of the unmutilated boy could be used as a kind of bridle for directing the movements of the animal." Sir Charles Namier, after closing the brothels, put the report in his secret file, where it lay more or less forgotten until some enemies of Burton forwarded it to his superiors in India. Here it caused considerable commotion, in part because of a belief that Burton himself must have engaged in homosexual practices. As a result there was a recommendation that Burton be dismissed from the service. This was never done, but Burton soon went on leave of absence and never returned to active duty. Not until 1884 did he manage to write on the subject for publication; the result was the section on pederasty in the Terminal Essays.[96]

Burton held there was a Sotadic zone starting at the Atlantic Ocean, bounded by latitude 43° to 30°, and spreading eastward until it reached Indochina, where it broadened to include China, Japan, Turkistan, the South Sea Islands, and the pre-Columbian inhabitants of the Americas. Within this zone he held that homosexuality was popular and endemic, regarded as no worse than a "mere peccadillo," whereas people to the north and south of the limits practiced it only sporadically amid the opprobrium of their fellows, who as a rule, were "physically incapable of performing the operation and look upon it with the liveliest disgust." The reason homosexuality was so widespread in these zones was that this is where the greatest blending of masculine and feminine temperaments took place. How seriously Burton took his own thesis is debatable, for much of the essay is devoted to summarizing homosexual activities outside his Sotadic zone. He does mention the Egyptians, Turks, Syrians, and Persians and documents incidents of homosexuality in the *Thousand Nights and A Night,* but other than this, very little of his essay actually deals with Islamic peoples.

Though no reputable scholar would today hold homosexuality to be geographical or climatic, many peoples and cultures, including Islam, have been far more tolerant of homosexual activities than Christianity has. This is due to cultural and social differences rather than geographical location. T. E. Lawrence, another commentator on Middle Eastern sex customs, had a different explanation than Burton:

> In the Mediterranean, woman's influence and supposed purpose were made cogent by an understanding in which she was accorded the physical world in simplicity, unchallenged, like the poor in spirit. Yet this same agreement, by denying equality of sex, made love, companionship and friendliness impossible between man and woman. Woman became a machine for muscular exercise, while man's psychic side

could be slaked only amongst his peers. Whence arose these partnerships of man and man, to supply human nature with more than the contact of flesh and flesh.[97]

To put it simply, Islam had put itself in a dilemma. It allowed polygamy and concubinage, which, in light of known sex ratios, often meant that there were not enough women for every man to have a wife. In addition, it strictly segregated men and women, making it difficult to establish any positive relationship between the sexes. All social life for men was spent in the company of other men. Even in marriage a wife was not necessarily a companion but a person whose job it was to produce children. Outside marriage, fornication and adultery were regarded with at least as much severity as homosexuality, and prostitution, though tolerated, was viewed with disfavor. Yet sex generally was regarded as a good and as pleasurable. With such contradictory attitudes homosexuality became a viable alternative for many, and even heterosexuals regarded it as a possibility.

An indication of this last attitude appears in the *Qābūs-nāma* (*Mirror for Princes*) of Kai Kā'ūs ibn Iskandar, composed in 1082 (475 in the Islamic calendar) as a guide for his eldest son. In a chapter entitled "On Taking One's Pleasure," he cautioned his son not to indulge in sexual intercourse indiscriminately, for it was only the beast who indulged every time the thought occurred to him. Man, for his part, should select the proper season, if only to preserve a distinction between himself and beasts.

> As between women and youths, do not confine your inclinations to either sex; thus you may find enjoyment from both kinds without either of the two becoming inimical to you. Furthermore, if, as I have said, excessive copulation is harmful, (complete) abstention also has its dangers. When you do it, let it be in accordance with appetite and not as a matter of course, so that it may have as little effect as possible.

He further advised his son to let his desires in the summer

> incline towards youth and during the winter towards women. But on this topic it is requisite that one's discourse should be brief, lest it engender appetite.[98]

Though Iskandar is not necessarily typical of Islamic views, the attitudes he expresses indicate a far greater tolerance in Islamic countries of the time than in contemporary Christian ones.

With such attitudes it is not to be wondered that Islamic literature often includes references to homosexual conduct, although these are not necessarily favorable. In the *Nights* Burton divided the homosexual incidents into three categories:

> The first is the funny form, as the unseemly practical joke of masterful Queen Budur and the not less hardy jest of the slave princess Zumurrud. The second is in

the grimmest and most earnest phase of the perversion, for instance where Abu Nowas debauches the three youths. In the third form it is wisely and learnedly discussed, to be severely blamed, by the Shaykhah or Reverend Woman.[99]

Queen Budur, in the example cited by Burton, found herself separated from her husband, Kamar al-Zaman. To protect her virtue during his absence she donned his clothes and, in disguise, found herself made king of a country. Eventually, she managed to locate her husband, had him brought to her kingdom, and then, still disguised as a man, tried to persuade him to go to bed with her. This aspect of the story is missing in some of the translations, but Burton's version has the merit of being unexpurgated. In trying to persuade her husband to go to bed with her, the transvestite Queen Budur argued that

The penis smooth and round was made with anus best to match it; Had it been made for cunnus' sake, it had been formed like a hatchet.

After reciting several similar verses, Kamar al-Zaman was reluctantly persuaded to submit to her embraces. Once in bed he quickly discovered that the king did not have a "tool like the tools of men," whereupon he realized that he was sleeping with his own wife.[100]

A similar tale was told about the slave girl Zumurrud, who had lost contact with her lover Ali Shar. Disguised as a man, she too became sultan of a territory, and when she found her lover had entered her city seeking her out, she had him brought to her. In Burton's translation

When the people heard of her sending for Ali Shar, they marveled thereat and each man thought his thought and said his say; but one among them declared, "At all events the King is in love with this young man, and tomorrow he will make him generalisimo of the army."

When Ali Shar appeared before her, Zumurrud, still clothed as a man, ordered him to rub her feet, then her calves, and finally, to proceed higher. Ali Shar hesitated, but Zumurrud insisted, saying:

Durst thou disobey me? It shall be an ill omened night for thee! Nay, but it behooveth thee to do my bidding and I will make thee my minion and appoint thee one of my Emirs.

Ali Shar was ordered to take off his trousers, to lie on his face, or as an alternative, to lose his head. He did as ordered, and as the investigation proceeded, soon discovered the truth.[101]

Neither of these stories exalts homosexuality, and in fact, both indicate that the heroes were reluctant to do as ordered. Nevertheless, they obeyed, since to do so was the lesser of two evils. The results of being a successful lover also appear indirectly in the story of Zumurrud, where it was implied that, since Ali Shar had attracted the attention of the king, he would become a general. This might well be an echo of the mameluke period, when the slave (*mameluke* means "owned") who became the favorite of a ruling Sultan could expect to advance rapidly.

The various stories in the *Nights* might also, however, be interpreted to mean that respectable people did not engage in homosexuality. This interpretation seems most obvious in the story of Aladin, whose father, fearing the evil eye, had kept his son in a cellar until he was nearly grown. When Aladin finally escaped, he managed to convince his father who was also the consul of the merchants, to take him along to his place of business. When the various merchants first saw the adolescent boy with their consul, they thought their leader must have become a pederast:

See thou yonder boy behind the consul of the merchants; verily, we thought well of him, but he is, like the leek, grey of head and green of heart.[102]

So upset were the merchants at this behavior that they threatened to remove their consul for keeping a mameluke, until he explained that he was not keeping the boy for lewd purposes but rather that Aladin was his son who would inherit from him.

Included among the various stories in the *Nights* are several accounts of Abu Nawas (Hasan ibn Hāni), regarded as one of the great poets of Islam during the Abbasid period. Abu Nawas was a known homosexual, whose poetry portrays pleasure as the supreme business of life, and nothing, including religious scruples, should be permitted to stand in its way. He urged his readers not to shrink from any excess, inasmuch as Divine mercy is greater than all the sins of which a man is capable:

Accumulate as many sins thou canst:
The Lord is ready to relax His ire.
When the day comes, forgiveness thou wilt find
Before a mighty King and gracious Sire,
And gnaw thy fingers, all that joy regretting
Which thou didst leave thro' terror of Hell-fire![103]

He became a part of the court of Harun al-Raschīd, and he appeared in this capacity in the *Nights*. Though brilliant, Abu Nawas was rather eccentric, his behavior often getting him into trouble with caliph, who not only threatened him with death but also actually imprisoned him on several occasions. In spite of these difficulties, the poet managed to outlive both Harun and his son Amin, and in his old age he repented somewhat because "the Devil was sick, the Devil a monk would be." During one of his terms in prison he addressed a poem to the Grand Vizier Fadl:

> *Fadl, who has taught and trained me up to goodness*
> *(And goodness is but habit), thee I praise.*
> *Now hath vice fled and virtue me revisits,*
> *and I have turned to chaste and pious ways.*[104]

Abu Nawas (which means "father of the lock of hair," a title derived from his two locks of hair hanging down to his shoulders) made little effort to disguise his homosexuality. In one story in the *Nights*, he set out to find a boy to spend the night with but instead found three handsome and beardless youths whom he propositioned:

> *Steer ye with your steps to none but me*
> *Who hath a mine of luxury—*
> *Old wine that shines with brightest blue*
> *Made by the monk in monastery;*
> *And mutton-meat the toothsomest*
> *And birds of all variety.*
> *Then eat of these and drink of those*
> *Old wines that bring you jollity:*
> *And have each other, turn by turn*
> *Shampooing this my tool you see.*[105]

The youths, in return for all the rewards he promised them, agreed to play the part of women for him. After eating, drinking, and making merry, they appealed to Abu Nawas to decide which of them was the handsomest of face and shapeliest of form. Abu Nawas, unable to decide, became drunker and drunker, kissing first one then another, while lying with the third. His revelry was interrupted by the caliph, who, as a show of disfavor, appointed him *kazi* (judge) of pimps and panderers. Instead of being upset at this, Abu Nawas rejoiced, passing the most pleasurable of nights. When the unrepentant poet appeared in court the next day, Harun ordered him stripped of his clothes, put a saddle on his back and a crupper under his rump, and led him to the harem, where the women might mock him before he was beheaded. But Abu Nawas made so many jokes about his predicament that Harun was unable to carry through his sentence. When someone asked Abu Nawas why he was saddled in such a way, he responded that he had given

the caliph a present of the best of my poetry and he presented me, in return, with the best of his raiment.[106]

In still another story in which Abu Nawas played a part, the caliph, enamored of a girl, sent some of his servants to find Abu Nawas so that he could compose some verses for the girl. The servants found the poet in a tavern, unable to leave because of debts to the owner incurred from an affair he had had with another of his beardless young lovers. Before paying Abu Nawas' debts, the chamberlain demanded to see the boy from whom he had pledged himself. After examining the boy and hearing some of Abu Nawas' verses composed for the occasion, the chamberlain agreed that Abu Nawas had fallen into debt for a worthy cause and agreed to ransom him.[107]

Considerably more earthy in its discussion of homosexual affairs is the debate between the learned woman Sitt al-Masha'ikh and a member of her audience. This story is similar to the debate reported by the Roman poet Lucian between a homosexual and a woman on which kind of sexual companion is best. Sitt al-Masha'ikh, while lecturing to a crowd of students from behind a curtain, as was suitable for a woman, noticed that one of the learned men in attendance seemed to be more interested in observing her young brother than in listening to what she was saying. She questioned the scholar about whether he was one of those who gave "men the preference over women." He replied in the affirmative, justifying his actions by stating that Allah had made the male more worthy than the female. Sitt al-Masha' ikh agreed that the Koran had stated the superiority of the male, but she held this did not prove that men or boys were to be preferred to women in sexual intercourse. Her opponent replied that youths were also superior to women in this respect and quoted Muhammad himself as stating:

> Stay not thy gaze upon the beardless, for in them is a momentary eye glance at the black-eyed girls of Paradise.

He then quoted some verses from Abu Nawas to the effect that boys were to be preferred to women since

> *The least of him is the being free*
> *From monthly courses and pregnancy.*

He also recited other verses as justification for his desires:

> *O tribe that loves the cheeks of boys, take fill*
> *Of joys in Paradise shall ne'er be found.*

Sitt al-Masha'ikh was unimpressed with the words of poets, refusing to let their words serve in judgment, particularly since those he called on were sodomites, catamites, and offenders against religion. Though the poet had also claimed Muhammad as his guide, she held that he had ignored the intent of the Prophet's meaning, for he had also said: "The things I hold dearest of the things of your world are three: women and perfume and solace of my eyes in prayer." Moreover, the pederasts were illogical, for if they really held masculinity to be so superior, they would love grey beards as much as young boys, and they manifestly did not. Finally, she pointed out the distastefulness of sodomy:

> Men's turning unto the bums of boys is bumptious:
> Whose love noble women show their own noblesse.
> How many goodly wights have slept the night, enjoying
> Buttocks of boys, and woke at morn in foulest mess;
> Their garments stained by safflower, which is yellow merde;
> Their shame proclaiming, showing colour of distress.
> Who can deny the charge, when so betrayed are they
> That e'en by daylight shows the dung upon their dress?
> What contrast wi' the man, who slept a gladsome night
> By Houri maid for glance a mere enchantress
> He rises of her borrowing wholesome bonny scent;
> That fills the house with whiffs of perfumed goodliness.
> No boy deserved place by side of her to hold;
> Canst even aloes-wood with what fills pool of cess.[108]

With this graphic description the woman was considered to have the best of the arguments. In general, however, the tales in the *Nights* cannot be considered as either hostile or favorable to male homosexuality. Male homosexual activities were instead a part of life, and though they might be distasteful to some, they existed. This was not the case with female homosexuality.

> Now this accursed old woman was a witch of the witches, past mistress in sorcery and deception; wanton and wily deboshed and deceptious; with foul breath, red eyelids, yellow cheeks, dull brown face, eyes bleared, mangy body, hair grizzled, back humped, skin withered and want and nostrils which ever ran.[109]

The woman, Zat-al-Dawahi, so described, had acquired the various magical arts and then had finally settled down with her son, King Hardub, to play with the virgins in his court. She was so enamored of lesbianism (*Sahākah*, literally, "rubbing") that she could not exist. Thus

> If any damsel pleased her, she was wont to teach her the art of rubbing clitoris against clitoris and would anoint her with saffron (regarded as an aphrodisiac) till she fainted away for excess of volupty. Whoso obeyed her she was wont to favour and make her son incline towards her; but whoso repelled her she would contrive to destroy.

The woman was loathed by the various princesses, who disliked her because of

the smell from her armpit, the stench of her fizzles more fetid than carrion, and the roughness of her hide coarser than palm fibre.[110]

The existence of a double standard, even in homosexual affairs for men and women, is also indicated in the tale of Lady Budur and her husband Jubayr bin Umayr. Jubayr once observed Lady Budur with her handmaiden and was so upset at this that he left. Lady Budur in her defense stated:

I was sitting one day whilst my handmaid here combed my hair. When she had made an end of combing it, she plaited my tresses, and my beauty and loveliness charmed her; so she bent over and kissed my cheek. At that moment he came in unawares, and seeing the girl kiss my cheek, straightways turned away in anger, vowing eternal separation and repeating these two couplets,

> "If another share in the thing I love,
> I abandon my love and live lorn of life.
> My beloved is worthless if aught she will,
> Save that which her lover doth most approve."[111]

In another tale there is reference to an old woman, Shawahi, who helps Hassan of Bassorah and his wife escape from the homosexual clutches of Queen Nur'al Huda.[112] Perhaps the most famous lesbian in Arabic tradition was Hind, the daughter of al-Hasan, who lived in the pre-Islamic era. She fell in love with the wife of al-Nuaman ibn al-Munzir, the king of Hira, and their mutual devotion was the subject of favorable commet by several poets.[113]

Anal intercourse is accepted in Islam; there is a popular old Arabic saying that a woman is "apt for two tricks," usually taken to mean that both vaginal and anal intercourse are possible.[114] The various legal authorities in Islam hold that *azil* (anal intercourse) in marriage was dependent on the wife's permission, because she had as much right to satisfaction as her husband, and anal intercourse might result in frustration instead of relief. No such consent was required of a slave.[115] Since this was the case, it would seem that similar freedom would be allowed in intercourse with males. There might be some difficulty with those interpreters of the Koran who have held that the only correct position for intercourse is with the male on top, a necessary indication of female inferiority. There is even an old saying, "Cursed be he who maketh woman Heaven and himself earth," which would apply to the passive partner in any act of anal intercourse between males. Most commentators hold, however, that no position in intercourse has been forbidden in Islam, and it is this interpretation on which homosexuals rely. In fact, since the right to determine whether to produce children lies with the husband and wife, many commentators would argue that, if both decide to forego this, anything is lawful as long as they eventually do have children.[116] This would include genital-oral contacts or acts of mutual masturbation, regarded more leniently than passive sodomy. Under this interpretation, exclusive homosexuality might be condemned, because no children would result, but something less than exclusive homosexuality would be permitted.

If we assume that homosexuality is more likely to exist in societies in which rigid sex barriers are drawn, it would seem that homosexuality would be less prevalent among the Bedouins than among the more settled communities in the Arab world. This is because the Bedouin children of both sexes play together, and, though social distance between the two sexes exist, it is much more difficult to establish *purdah* in a tent than in a house, especially when the community is nomadic. Superficially, this seems to be the case, and homosexuality is reported to occur less frequently among the Bedouins than among city dwellers.[117] Even here, however, Islamic people are much more tolerant of homosexual affairs than Western Christian society is, although Middle Eastern people in general do no like overt public displays of love, whether homosexual or heterosexual.[118] But what constitutes a public display is relative. One nineteenth-century visitor reported that the Ka⁴ba in Mecca was the scene of "such indecencies and criminal acts" that he could not mention them and stated that such conduct resulted in nothing more than a laugh or slight reprimand from the passing spectators.[119] How much such descriptions depended on the moral indignation of the Western observer, who condemned elsewhere what he ignored in his own society, is perhaps debatable. It is clear, nonetheless, that Muslims accept and tolerate many sexual activities that the West has traditionally condemned.

The conflict of Islamic values evident in the acceptance of male homosexuality is also apparent in the harem. Scholars today do not agree about when the harem system and the seclusion of women first came to exercise such great influence in Islam, but all agree it developed fairly early in Islamic history. The origins might be in Persia, for many interpreters of the Koran were men who originated in Persia, a land where women had long been secluded. By the time of Hārūn al-Rashid, a century and a half after the death of the Prophet, seclusion was fully established—so well institutionalized, in fact, that pious visitors were shocked when they came to lands where there was free social intercourse between men and women.[120]

It seems obvious that large numbers of women could not be concentrated together in *purdah* without some kind of sexual acitivity among them. The individual Muslim powerful and rich enough to have a harem had to choose between having it, tolerating some form of female homosexuality, or practicing monogamy. The powerful usually chose to keep the harem and to police them with eunuchs, which led to another contradiction, for Islamic tradition forbade making a person a eunuch. To get around this prohibition and to meet the demand there was a widespread slave trade in eunuchs castrated before they arrived in an Islamic country or castrated by Christians (as they were in Egypt).[121]

There were several degrees of eunuchs. The most highly prized were those whose penis and testicles had been amputated (*sendelee* or *sandali*, that is "clean shaven"); they were comparatively rare because of the death rate caused by hemorrhage and infection. Usually, the amputation was done with a single stroke of the razor, the wound instantly cauterized with boiling ghee, and the victim planted in a steaming, fresh dungheap. A second type had the penis itself removed (called *ebter* or "tailless one"), but this type was also rare, since the mortality would be almost as great. Most common was the *ghezee* ("stoned"), who had his testicles removed, damaged, or tied. If castration took place after puberty, a eunuch might still retain his virile powers; there are several stories about eunuchs in the *Nights*, particularly of the latter type, who were said to satisfy women without impregnating them.[122] Eunuchs were so highly prized that they were given as slaves to various mosques. Burckhardt, in his description of the Great Mosque at Mecca, reported that 40 eunuchs acting as guards had been presented to the mosque when young by the pasha and other great nobles. Many of the older eunuchs were married and had slaves of their own.[123]

Bestiality was also tolerated in Islam. A commentator stated that, though copulation with beasts was to be abhorred, it was different from *zinā,'* that is adultery or fornication, because men can have no reason for desiring carnal connection with brutes, and a person does so either because he is depraved or because he must prevent himself from committing a greater crime. If discovered, the animal was to be destroyed and the owner reimbursed, but if the animal was of an eatable species, it could be eaten.[124] There are several tales of bestiality in the *Nights,* two cases involving women. In both cases the women were discovered copulating with animals, one with a bear, the other with an ape. In the first case, the woman was killed, but in the second, her discoverer, a butcher, decided to marry the women. Try as he would, however, he was unable to satisfy his wife until he examined her closely and found worms in her vagina. The removal of the worms cured her. Such a diagnosis fitted in with a standard Middle Eastern belief that nymphomania was caused by worms in the vagina.[125] Among some nomads, having intercourse with cattle is still regarded as part of the growing-up process of males, although it is often acknowledged with groans and cursing.[126] Burton, ever observant, described natives copulating with female crocodiles, a feat regarded as an indication that one would rise to rank and riches. Though the crocodile is dangerous, once the female was on her back, she was almost helpless, and the natives demonstrated their prowess in this position.[127]

Excess in apparel and extravagance in dress were specifically reproved in the Koran.[128] Muhammad also regarded certain things as suitable only to the woman and not to the man, and vice versa. Men, were, for example, prohibited from wearing silk, gold, and silver ornaments, and any ring but a signet ring, but women wore all these things.[129] In spite of such prohibitions, transvestism, especially among males, was common and occasionally institutionalized. In Egypt, for example, it was customary for a boy about to be circumcised to be dressed in girl's clothes before the ceremony.[130] Even today, in Egypt and many other Middle Eastern countries, it is not unusual to dress boys as girls so that the boy can avoid the evil eye, which is more attracted to the male than the female. These customs might be regarded as not prohibited, since children, rather than adults, observe them. But numerous adults also cross-dressed.

Al-Bukhāri, the famous ninth-century commentator on the Koran, devotes an entire section to "men who wish to resemble women, and women who wish to resemble men." Such men were called *mukhannathūn* and women were called *mutarajjulat*.[131] As usual, in any discussion of sex, little information is available about women cross-dressers, although there are numerous references to male transvestites. Many of these transvestites were male singers who imitated women in their clothing and external appearance, painted their hands with henna, had their hair combed and braided, and wore loose, brightly colored women's clothes. They were performer–entertainers who sang accompanied by drums and probably by castanets as well. Like the male impersonators who used to act the female parts in Western dramatic productions because women were forbidden on the stage, these transvestites were tolerated because they allowed the Muslims to keep women in *purdah* while they acted the women's roles in public.

In some areas these female impersonators were called *khāwal*, "dancers," a term by which they were still known in nineteenth-century Egypt. These were favored by people, described by Lane, who thought it indecent for the female to expose herself in public:

> They are Muslims and natives of Egypt. As they personate women, their dances are exactly of the same description as those of the ghawazee; and are, in like manner, accompanied by the sounds of castanets; but, as if to prevent their being thought to be really females, their dress is suited to their unnatural profession; being partly male, and partly female: it chiefly consists of a tight vest, a girdle, and a kind of petticoat. Their general appearance, however, is more feminine than masculine: they suffer the hair of the head to grow long, and generally braid it, in the manner of the women; their hair on the face, when it begins to grow they pluck out; and they imitate the women also in applying kohl and henna to their eyes and hands. In the streets, when not engaged in dancing, they often even veil their faces; not from shame, but merely to affect the manners of women. . . . There is, in Cairo, another class of male dancers, young men and boys, whose performances,

dress, and general appearance are almost exactly similar to those of the khäwals; but who are distinguished by a different appelation, which is 'Gink;' a term that is Turkish, and has a vulgar signification which aptly expresses their character . . .[132]

Obviously, it was difficult for Lane, a nineteenth-century, sexually inhibited Englishman, to bring himself to describe any sexual acts; the best he can do is hint at the idea of men's prostituting themselves to other men.

In addition to the *ghawazi* (or *ghawazee*) and *gink* there were also the *mohabbazin,* who performed in public places or in the houses of the wealthy, at festivals preceding weddings, and at circumcisions. Boys in female garb formed a part of the rich men's harems in Afghanistan, at least down to the nineteenth century. Sir Richard Burton reported that

> the Afghans are commercial travellers on a large scale and each caravan is accompanied by a number of boys and lads almost in women's attire, with kohl'd eyes and rouged cheeks, long tresses and hennaed fingers and toes, riding luxuriously in *Kajawas* or camel-panniers: they are called *Kuch-i safari* or travelling wives and the husbands trudge patiently by their sides.[133]

In some of these cases it is difficult to distinguish transvestism from homosexuality, but there was also a kind of psychic transvestism that would almost approach what is called transsexualism today. This occurred among the dervishes, those members of a Muslim religious order who took vows of poverty and austerity and lived in monasteries or wandered about as holy men. One of the aims of the dervish was to become the perfect man, one who had realized his essential oneness with the Divine Being, in whose likeness he had been made. This experience was the foundation of the Sufi theosophy and was possible only to those who were the elect. These became *awliya,* plural of *wali,* a word meaning "near." The *wali* or "saint" was the popular type of perfect man and implied nothing less than Divine illumination, immediate vision and knowledge of things unseen and unknown, the overwhelming glory of the "One True Light." The purpose of the Path or Sufi discipline was to predispose and prepare the disciple to receive this incalculable gift. Among some sects of dervish the protégé becomes a female saint, *waliyeh,* and sits "among the women," because he was for the "moment changed into a woman." This was because saintliness and femininity were regarded as somewhat related, since

> the woman is considered in many instances holy, as being the mother of mankind, carrying no arms, and often suffering beating, baking the bread, entering the oven

—all of which were proper conduct of a *wali* or saint.[134] Not all orders of dervishes emphasized this state, nor did they equate God with both male and female. Still, when the Sufi poet Ibun al-Fārid wishes to express the transformation of the soul in his poetry, he refers to it with the feminine pronoun. The feminine is also used to denote the Universal Self.

> *Until then I had been enamoured of her, but when I*
> *renounced my desire, she desired me for herself*
> *and loved me,*
> *And I became a beloved, nay, one loving himself:*
> *this is not like what I said before, that my soul*
> *is my beloved.*
> *Through her I went forth from myself to her and came*
> *not back to myself: one like me does not hold the*
> *doctrine of return.*[135]

It might appear almost impossible at first impression for mysticism to engrave itself on the legal system of the Koran with its detailed ritual and formality, but from the time of Muhammad himself, some have set aside the literal meaning of the words of the Prophet for a supposed mystic or spiritual interpretation. In its mysticism Islam tends to approach the Gnostics in their dualism, and in a sense this dualism had as great an influence on Islamic mysticism as it had on Christianity. Key to Islamic mysticism is the belief that the soul existed before the body and was confined within it as in a cage. Death was, therefore, the ultimate object of the Sufi, for death allowed the soul to return home to the bosom of divinity. Human life was a journey (*safar*), and the seeker after God was a traveler in life. The perfect man was the one who had fully comprehended the law, the doctrine, and the truth and had been endowed with four things in perfection: good words, good deeds, good principles, and sciences. He should also have the four additional characteristics of renunciation, retirement, contentment, and leisure to contemplate. The aim of the Sufi mystic was to lose his own identity, his individuality.

Some Sufis believed there was no real difference between good and evil, for all had been reduced to Unity, and God was the real author of the acts of mankind. Abu Sa'īd, when asked what is evil, answered "evil is thou," and when questioned what the worst evil was, replied "thou when thou knowest it not."[136] There were obvious divergences of opinions among the Sufis, and some of them, particularly the group known as the *Malamatis* ("Reproached") deliberately acted in such a way as to incur blame, compounding virtues with vice, and vice with virtues. Another sect of Sufis called the *Mūhābīyah* ("Revered") maintained a community of property and women. Others refused to hold themselves in the least responsible for sins committed by the body, which they regarded as only the miserable robe of humanity encircling the pure in spirit; they seem similar to the antinomian movements in early Christianity.

A Western critic of Sufism has said the result of the Sufi denial of the indi-

vidual was pantheism, and pantheism in turn led to the destruction of a moral
law:

> If God be in all, and man's apparent individuality a delusion of the perceptive
> faculty, there exists no will which can act, no conscience which can reprove or ap-
> plaud. The individual is but a momentary seeming; he comes and goes like the
> "snow flake on the river; a moment seen, then gone forever." To reproach such an
> ephemeral creature for being the slave of its passions, is to chide the thistledown for
> yielding to the violence of the wind. Muhammadans have not been slow to discover
> these consequences. Thousands of reckless and profligate spirits have entered the
> order of the derweshes to enjoy the license thereby obtained. Their affectation of
> piety is simply a cloak for the practice of sensuality; their emancipation from the
> ritual of Islam involves a liberation also from its moral restraints. And thus a
> movement, animated at its outset by a high and lofty purpose, has degenerated into
> a fruitful source of ill.[137]

How much this criticism reflects traditional Western hostility is debatable, although there seems to be sexual ambiguity in much of the Sufi poetry, and
poetry has been defined as the essence of Sufi mysticism. For example, it was
not unusual for a poet to describe his mistress under the attributes of the opposite sex, lest he offend the prudery of Muslim feelings. At times this prudery
grew so·strong that open allusion to women was frowned on and at times even
prevented the poet from indicating that his beloved was a female. This is
evident in the great Islamic mystical poet Ibn al-Farid (1182–1235) of Cairo.
His *Diwan* deals with Divine Reality, the Beloved whom the poet addressed
and celebrated under many names, both male and female. Though his poetry
cannot fully be understood without an understanding of Islamic mysticism, its
popularity is probably due as much to its erotic content as to anything else.
Much of it can be interpreted in a homosexual sense, and though this was not
necessarily his intention, the confusion of gender in mystical expression undoubtedly had some influence on the attitudes of the ordinary Muslim:

> *Feign rapture, if thou be*
> *Not rapt indeed, and let thine eye range free:*
> *Mine, with tears overflowing, cannot range.*
> *Ask the Gazelle that counches in this valley,*
> *Knows he my heart, its passions and distress?*
> *Delighted with his beauty's pride to dally,*
> *He recks not of my love's abasedness.*
> *My dead self be his ransom! 'Tis no giving;*
> *I am all his, dead or living.* [138]

> *Though he be gone, mine every limb behold him*
> *In every charm and grace and loveliness:*
> *In music of the lute and flowing reed*

Mingled in consort with melodious airs;
And in green hollows where in cool of eye
Gazelles roam browsing, or at break of morn;
And where the gathered clouds let fall their rain
Upon a flowery carpet woven of blooms;
And where at dawn with softly-trailing skirts
The zephyr brings to me his balm most sweet;
And when kisses from the flagon's mouth
I suck wine-dew beneath a pleasant shade.[139]

Increasingly, the dualism inherent in Zoroastrianism, Gnosticism, and Manichaeanism exercised influence on the Sufi mystics, with corresponding ambiguity about the sexual urges.[140] Some of these ambiguities appeared in Islamic medical and scientific writings about sex, most notably in those of Abu-Bakr Muhammad ibn Zakarīya' (865–925 A.D.), usually known as Rhazes. Rhazes condemned passionate love as a calamity and rated the sexual appetite as the foulest and most disgusting from the viewpoint of the rational soul, for him the true measure of man. It was also the appetite that was not necessary to the survival of the individual.[241]

Islam, which accepted sex as a positive good, at the same time relegated women to the status of inferior beings, and as it became more puritanical after the twelfth century, even prohibited erotic references to them, an act that probably encouraged homosexuality. Stanley Lane-Pool has gone so far as to claim that the degradation of women was the fatal blot on Islam. Though this is an exaggeration, numerous sayings indicate a basic hostility to the "weaker" sex:

I have not left any calamity more detrimental to mankind than women.

A bad omen is found in a women, a house, or a horse.

Look to your actions and abstain from the world and from women, for verily the first sin which the children of Israel committed was on account of Women.

There are, it is true, some countersayings:

The world and all things in it are valuable, but more valuable than all is a virtuous woman.

Nevertheless, the effect was not quite the same, for a virtuous woman was one seen only by her husband and male relatives.

God will reward the Muslim who, having beheld the beauties of a woman, shuts his eyes

Do not visit the houses of men when they are absent from their homes, for the devil circulates within you like the blood in your veins. It was said "O Prophet in your veins also." He replied, "My veins also. But God has given me power over the devil and I am free from wickedness."

Some teachers went so far as to advise that

Two women must not sit together, because the one may describe the other to her husband, so that you might say the husband has seen her himself.[142]

The good woman was one who was shut off from society. As Iskandar wrote about daughters:

If you have a daughter, entrust her to kindly nurses and give her a good nature. When she grows up, entrust her to a preceptor so that she shall learn the provisions of sacred law and the essential religious duties. But do not teach her to read and write; that is a great calamity. Once she is grown up, do your utmost to give her in marriage; it were best for a girl not to come into existence, but being born she had better be married or buried . . . as long as she is in your house, treat your daughter with compassion.[143]

In effect, women, even though sexually provocative, were more or less withdrawn from male society and could neither be seen nor discussed openly. Although reality often differed from theory, and there were exceptions, by the twelfth century it was even considered somewhat indecent to refer to women in poems. Inevitably, men sought companionship among their male friends, and such companionship often had sexual implications, because the Koran did not specifically forbid homosexuality, and in practice the Muslims regarded it as a lesser evil than adultery and no worse than fornication. The purpose of marriage in Islam was primarily to have children, although this did not mean that sex was not to be enjoyed. Women were little more than property, always under the control of a male relative. They were not be seen by males other than their close relatives. With *purdah,* polygamy, concubinage, and the harem, there was both a shortage of women and a lack of opportunity for many men to become acquainted with the opposite sex. The result was the toleration, if not acceptance, of homosexuality. Even when Islam prohibited some forms of conduct, such as wearing the clothes of the opposite sex, the prohibition was not strictly observed, because it conflicted with more dearly held value, namely, the exclusion of women. Islam, moreover, emphasized tolerance, and believers who strayed were never entirely regarded as lost souls, provided they repented. In sum, homosexuality seems a natural outgrowth of a sex-positive, sexually segregating religion, in which women had little status or value.

NOTES

1. For the Christian and Jewish background of Islam, see Richard Bell, *The Origin of Islam in Its Christian Environment* (reprinted, London: Frank Cass & Company, 1968); and Charles Cutler Torrey, *The Jewish Foundation of Islam* (reprinted, New York: Ktav Publishing House, 1967).

2. H. R. P. Dickson, *The Arab of the Desert: A Glimpse into Badawin Life in Sau'di Arabia* (London: George Allen and Unwin, 1949), p. 162. The different spelling of Bedouin in the quotation represents a difficulty in translating Arabic terms that appears throughout this chapter. Arabic has no written vowels, and in the past there was no universally recognized standard, correct way to spell Arabic words. Today there is general agreement, at least among Western scholars, but quotations come from books written at different times.

3. Omer Haleby, *El Ktab or the Sex Laws of Mohammed,* translated by A. F. Niemoeller (Girard, Kans.: Haldeman–Julius, 1949), p. 10 (Chap. 2: "Concerning Natural Cohabitation"). Niemoeller's translation is not from the Arabic but from a French version made by Paul de Regia. Haleby wrote in the nineteenth century.

4. Translated by A. J. Arberry in *Arabic Poetry: A Primer for Students* (Cambridge, England: Cambridge University Press, 1965), pp. 13–14.

5. For a continuation of love theories, see Lois Anita Giffon, *Theory of Profane Love among the Arabs* (New York: New York University Press, 1971).

6. See, for example, R. W. Southern, *Western Views of Islam in the Middle Ages* (Cambridge, Mass.: Harvard University Press, 1962).

7. Edward Gibbon, *The History of the Decline and Fall of the Roman Empire,* J. B. Bury, ed. (reprinted, New York: Heritage Press, 1946), pp. 1766–1767. For those using other editions the description comes from Chap. 50.

8. Tor Andrae, *Mohammed: The Man and His Faith,* translated from the German by Theophil Menzel (reprinted, New York: Harper and Row, 1960), pp. 187–188.

9. Richard Lewinsohn, *A History of Sexual Customs* (New York: Harper, 1958), pp. 103–104.

10. At least this is what Ibn Saud told H. R. P. Dickson, *op. cit.,* p. 162.

11. Abu abd Allah Muhammad ibn al-Bukhari, *Sahih,* translated from the Arabic by Muhammad Asad (Lahore, West Pakistan: Awafat Publications, 1938f.), LI, xx (Vol. 5, 198–200). Only Vol. 5 has been translated.

12. Koran, XXXIII (The Clans), 36–37. There are various translations of the Koran into English, none of them official, since it is forbidden to translate it. In this section most of the translations have been taken from that of Mohammed Marmaduke Pickthall because it is now fairly widely distributed (New York: New American Library, 1953), although in some cases other versions are used because they seem better able to express the original Arabic.

13. W. Montgomery Watt, *Muhammad at Medina* (Oxford, England: Clarendon Press, 1956, pp. 330–331; and Andrae, *op. cit.,* pp. 152–154.

14. Koran, LXVI (Banning), 1–5.

15. Koran, XXIV (Light), 13–15.

16. Koran, XXII (The Pilgrimage), 5; XXIII (The Believers), 14.

17. Koran XXX (The Romans), 21.

18. Koran, XLII (Counsel), 11.

19. *The Sayings of Muhammad,* collected and translated by Allama Sir Abdullah al-Mamum al-Suhrawardy (London: John Murray, 1941), No. 297, p. 95.

20. Koran, IV (Women), 3.

21. *The Sayings of Muhammad,* Nos. 411–418, pp. 115–116.

22. There are numerous descriptions of Paradise in the Koran, but the above is based on XXXVI (The Poets), 55; XLVII (Muhammad), 16–17; LXXVI (Time or Man), 11–22; LXXVII (Emissaries), 31–37; LXXXIII (Defrauding), 21–28; and LXXXVIII (The Overwhelming), 8–16. The eternal boys are mentioned in LXXVI (Time or Man), 11–22; the ever-virgin nymphys, in LVI (The Event), 22–24; and LXXVII (Emissaries), 31–37; young virgins (boys and girls) who have never been deflowered by man and spirit in LVI (The Event), 15–22. The women of Paradise have been created by a special creation that has preserved their virginity, LV (The Beneficent), 72, and they are secluded in pavilions.

23. Koran, IV (Women), 34.

24. Bukhari, *op. cit.,* L. xxxiii, Vol. 5, p. 98.

25. *Ibid.,* L. liii, Vol. 5, p. 128.

26. Koran, XXIV (Light), 31.

27. Koran, XXXIII (The Clans), 53.

28. *Ibid.,* 59.

29. Koran, XXIV (Light), 30.

30. Ali ibn Abu Bakr, Burhan al-Din, al-Marghīnānī, *The Hedaya or Guide: A Commentary on the Mussulman Laws,* translated by Charles Hamilton, preface and index by Standish Grove Grady, ed. (reprinted, Lahore, West Pakistan: Premier Book House, 1957, 4 vols. in 1), Vol. 4, pp. 598–599; or Book 44, sec. 4. The book was composed in the twelfth century.

31. Reuben Levy, *The Social Structure of Islam* (Cambridge, England: University Press, 1957), p. 126.

32. *Ibid.,* p. 94; W. Robertson Smith, *Kinship and Marriage in Early Arabia* (reprinted, Boston: Beacon Press, n.d.) pp. 171–175. Koran, IV (Women), 24 forbade intercourse with all married women except captives.

33. Koran, II (The Cow), 223.

34. Koran, IV (The Women), 24–25.

35. Koran, IV (The Women), 4.

36. *Ibid.,* 129.

37. *Ibid.,* 11.

38. *Ibid.,* 12.

39. *Ibid.,* 23. Pickthall's translation is not clear on this point; in his version the verse is numbered 19.

40. Koran, II (The Cow), 231–232.

41. *Ibid.,* 234.

42. Ali ibn Abu-Bakr, *op. cit.,* Vol. 2, p. 186, Book 7, Chap. 2.

43. Levy, *op. cit.,* p. 17.

44. See H. Lammens, *Islam: Belief and Institutions,* translated by E. Denison Ross (reprinted, London: Frank Cass & Company, 1968); and Joseph Schacht, *An Introduction to Islamic Law* (Oxford, England: Clarendon Press, 1964).

45. Dwight Donaldson, *Studies in Muslim Ethics* (London: SPCK, 1963), p. 122.

46. Marghīnānī, *op. cit.,* Vol. 2, p. 202; or Book 7, Chap. 5.

47. Koran, XVII (Children of Israel), 32; XXV, (the Criterion), 68; XXXIII (The Clans), 30.

48. Koran, XXIV (Light), 2–3.

49. See Muhammad ibn Idris al-Shafti'ī, *Risala,* translated by Majid Khaddwu under the title *Islamic Jurisprudence* (Baltimore: Johns Hopkins Press, 1961), Chap. 6, 122–127, pp. 137–140; Chap. 9, 230–232, pp. 197–199.

50. Koran, IV (Women), 19.

51. Koran, XXIV (Light), 4.

52. *Ibid.,* 6–9.

53. *Sayings of Muhammed,* No. 15, p. 52. In No. 17, p. 52, he seems to imply that every eye that looks with desire on a woman commits adultery.

54. *Ibid.,* No. 14, p. 52.

55. Koran, LXX (The Ascending Stairway), 29–31; XIII (The Believers), 5–7; IV (The Women), 3, 24f or, in some, 28f.

56. Koran, II (The Cow), 237; XXXIII (The Clans), 49.

57. Koran, II (The Cow), 226–232; LXV (Divorce), 1–7.

58. Koran, LVIII (She That Disputeth), 4.

59. Levy, *op. cit.,* pp. 123–124.

60. Koran, IV (Women), 24.

61. Vern L. Bullough, *History of Prostitution* (New York: University Books, 1964), p. 87.

62. See Levy, *op. cit.,* pp. 115–117; W. Heffening, "Mut'a" in *Shorter Encyclopaedia of Islam,* H. A. R. Gibb and J. H. Kramers, eds. (Ithaca, N. Y.: Cornell University Press, 1953).

63. See, for example, Shafti'ī, *op. cit.,* Chap. 15, 718–740, pp. 333–334. See also Schacht, *op. cit.,* p. 163.

64. Koran, II (The Cow), 222.

65. Koran, IV (The Women), 43; V (The Table Spread), 6.

66. Levy, *op. cit.,* p. 252.

67. Cited by A. J. Wensinck, "Khitān" in *Shorter Encyclopaedia of Islam,* pp. 254–255.

68. See the *Book of the Thousand Nights and a Night,* translated and annotated by Richard F. Burton (reprinted, New York: Heritage Press, 1934, 6 vols. in 3), pp. 1830–1831. This is one of Burton's typical footnotes.

69. Quoted by George Allgrove, *Love in the East* (London: Anthony Gibbs & Phillips, 1962), pp. 128–129.

70. During my stay in Egypt it was widely mentioned that one of the reasons Nasser was interested in abolishing female circumcision was to curtail the illicit drug traffic.

71. Koran, XXIV (Light), 33.

72. Makhluf, *Fatawa Shareia (Legal Decisions),* (Cairo: 1965), p. 117 (in Arabic).

73. Imadu al-Din al-Kitab al-Isfahani, *Muhadarat al-Udabaa (Lectures of Men of Letters)* (Cairo, n.d.n.p.), II, p. 15. This is regarded as a prohibited book in most Arabic countries and is replete with references to sexual topics. I have the Arabic original, but as far as I know, it is untranslated. Al-Isfahani lived in the twelfth century and is to be distinguished from the tenth-century poet Abu al-Faragal-Isfahani.

74. Quoted by Allen Edwardes, *The Jewel in the Lotus* (New York: Julian Press, 1960), p. 107. I have been unable to verify his source.

75. This confusion appears in Omer Haleby, *op. cit.,* p. 22, par. 12. The translation calls it buccal onanism.

76. Bukhari, *op. cit.,* LI, xxvii, in Vol. 5, 241–243, and n. 3, p. 242.

77. Avicenna, *Canon of Medicine,* translated by Mazhar H. Shah, ed. (Karachi, West Pakistan: Naveed Clinic, 1966), Book 1, Chap. 4, ii, p. 35. Only Book 1 is translated by Shah.

78. See Al-Kindi, *The Medical Formulatory of Arābādhīn or Al-Kindi,* translated by Martin Levey (Madison, Wis.: University of Wisconsin Press, 1966), formulatory Nos. 146, 188, 226; pp. 158, 190, 220.

79. Koran, VII (The Heights), 81.

80. Koran, XXVI (The Poets), 165–168.

81. Koran, VII (The Heights), 80.

82. Koran, XII (Joseph), 77–78; and XXIX (The Spider), 28–29.

83. Toshihiko Izutsu, *Ethico-Religious Concepts in the Qur-an* (Montreal: McGill University Press, 1966), 174–177.

84. *Ibid.,* pp. 172–174.

85. Koran, IV (Women), 22.

86. Koran, XII (Joseph), 24.

87. Koran, XVII (The Children of Israel), 32.

88. The term *fisq* is equated with sodomy in Koran XXIX (The Spider), 33–34.

89. Marghīnānī, *op. cit.,* Book 7, Chap. 2, Vol. 2, pp. 184–185.

90. Koran, IV (Women), 16.

91. Shafti'ī, *op. cit.,* Chap. 2, 32, p. 81.

92. Schacht, *op, cit.,* p. 178.

93. See Robert Roberts, *The Social Laws of the Qoran* (London: Williams and Norgets, 1925), p. 16, for a brief discussion; and Ali ibn Abu Bakr, *op. cit.,* Book 7, Chap. 2, Vol. 2, pp. 184–185.

94. Thomas Patrick Hughes, *A Dictionary of Islam* (reprinted, Clifton, N. J.: Reference Book Publishers, Inc., 1965), article "Sodom," p. 601. The book had originally been published in the nineteenth century.

95. The essay entitled "Pederasty" is one of the terminal essays in his edition. See *The Book of the Thousand Nights and a Night,* translated and annotated by Richard F. Burton (reprinted, New York: Heritage Press, 1934, 6 vols. in 3, sec. D., pp. 3748–3782. The essay has often been reprinted and can also be found in *Homosexuality: A Cross Cultural Approach,* Donald Webster Cory, ed. (New York: Julian Press, 1956).

96. For a discussion of this, see Fawn M. Brodie, *The Devil Drives: A Life of Sir Richard Burton* (New York: W. W. Norton, 1967), pp. 66ff.

97. T. E. Lawrence, *Seven Pillars of Wisdom* (reprinted, Garden City, N.Y.: Doubleday, Doran and Company, 1937), pp. 508–509.

98. Kai Kā'ūs ibn Iskandar, *A Mirror for Princes (The Qabus Nama),* translated from the Persian by Reuben Levy (London: The Cresset Press, 1951), Chap. 15, pp. 77–78.

99. In the terminal essay. I have used Burton's spellings in this section.

100. Burton, *op. cit.,* "The Tale of Kamar al Zamamn," 216th Night, II, 1150–1152.

101. *Ibid.,* "The Tale of Ali Shar and Zumurrud," 326th Night, III, 1475.

102. *Ibid.,* "The Tale of Ali al-Din Abu al Shamat," 251st Night, II, 1257.

103. Quoted by Reynold A. Nicholson, *A Literary History of the Arabs,* (reprinted, Cambridge, England: University Press, 1966), p. 295.

104. *Ibid.,* p. 293.

105.   Burton, *op. cit.*, "The Tale of Abu Nowas with the Three Boys," 382nd Night, II, 1641.

106.   *Ibid.*, 383rd Night, III, 1644.

107.   *Ibid.*, "The Tale of Harn al-Rashid and the Damsel," 339th Night, III, 1511–1512.

108.   *Ibid.*, "The Man's Dispute with the Learned Woman," 420th to 423rd Night, II, 1720 to 1728.

109.   *Ibid.*, "King Omar bin'al-Nu'uman and his Sons," 93rd Night, II, 698.

110.   *Ibid.*, 698–699.

111.   *Ibid.*, "The Tale of Jubayr bin Umayr and Lady Budur," 329th Night, III, 1483–1484.

112.   *Ibid.*, "The Tale of Hasan of Bassorah," 825th Night, V. 2904.

113.   Al Isfahani, *op. cit.*, II, 124. (In Arabic).

114.   Burton, *op. cit.*, "The Man's Dispute with the Learned Woman," 423rd Night, III, 1727.

115.   Marghīnānī, *op. cit.*, Book 2, Chap. 4 Vol, 1. p

116.   In fact there is considerable discussion of sexual positions in *The Perfumed Garden* of Shaykh Nefzawi, a sixteenth century work translated by Richard Burton (reprinted, New York: Castle Books, 1964).

117.   This is noted by Wilfred Thesiger, *Arabian Sands* (New York: Dutton, 1959), p. 110; and earlier by J. L. Burckhardt, *Travels in Arabia* (reprinted, London: Frank Cass and Company, 1968), p. 198. The original edition was printed in 1831.

118.   Raphael Patai, *Sex and Family in the Bible* (Garden City, N. Y.: Doubleday, 1959), pp. 175–176.

119.   J. L. Burckhardt, *op. cit.*, p. 150.

120.   Levy, *op. cit.*, p. 127.

121.   J. L. Burckhardt, *Travels in Nubia*, (2d. ed., London: John Murray 1822), p. 294–296.

122.   See Burton, *op. cit.*, "Uns al Wujud and the Wazir's Daughter," 376th Night, III, 1613; and others.

123.   J. L. Burckhardt, *Travels in Arabia*, pp. 158–159.

124.   Marghīnānī, *op. cit.*, Book 7, Chap. 2, Vol. 2, p. 185.

125.   Burton, *op. cit.*, "The Tale of the Warden and the Butcher: His Adventure with the Lady and the Bear," 353rd to 355th Night, III, 1556–1559; and "The King's Daughter and the Ape," 355th to 357th Night, III, 1560–1562.

126.   Patai, *op. cit.*, pp. 176–178.

127.   Burton, *op. cit.*, Notes, p. 1567.

128.   Koran, VII (The Heights), 25.

129.   Marghīnānī, *op. cit.*, Book 54, sec. 2, Vol. 4, p. 597.

130.   W. E. Lane, *Manners and Customs of the Modern Egyptians* (reprinted, London: Everyman's Library, 1963), p. 511. This is essentially the text of the 1860 edition.

131.   Bukhari, *op. cit.*, VII:159. This section is not translated and is available only in Arabic, to my knowledge.

132.   Lane, *op. cit.*, pp. 388–389.

133.   Burton, *op. cit.*, Terminal Essay, passim.

134.   Philip J. Baldensperger, "Orders of Holy Men in Palestine," *Palestine Exploration Fund Quarterly Statement* (1894), p. 38. See also Frederick J. Bliss, *The Religions of Modern Syria and Palestine* (New York: C. Scribner's Sons, 1912), p. 254; and Patai, *op. cit.*, p. 173.

135.   Translated by Reynold Alleyne Nicholson, *Studies in Islamic Mysticism* (Cambridge, England: University Press, 1921), p. 217.

136.   *Ibid.,* p. 53.

137.   Major Durie Osborn, *Islam under the Khalifs of Baghdad,* p. 112, quoted by Hughes, *A Dictionary of Islam,* pp. 620–621.

138.   Nicholson, *Studies in Islamic Mysticism,* p. 170. He translated several odes.

139.   *Ibid.,* p. 176.

140.   Jacques Duchesne-Guillemin, *Symbols and Values in Zoroastrianism* (New York: Harper and Row, 1966), pp. 157–162.

141.   See Rhazes, *The Spiritual Physick of Rhazes,* translated by A. J. Arberry (London: John Murray, 1950); and Giffen, *op. cit.,* pp. 141–142.

142.   All of these are quoted by Hughes, *Encyclopedia of Islam,* pp. 678–679.

143.   Kai Kā'ūs ibn Iskandar, *op. cit.,* Chap. 27, p. 125.

10

SEX IN THE INDIAN SUBCONTINENT

Hinduism, the traditional religion of the Indian subcontinent and one of the oldest major religions in the modern world, might be classed as even more sex positive than Islam. Hindu mythology, in fact, taught that the literature of love and sex was of divine origin, derived from a collection of all knowledge compiled in some 100,000 chapters by Prājapati, the supreme god, creator of heaven and earth. This compilation had originally been divided into three parts, *dharma,* "right living or righteousness"; *artha,* "the acquisition of wealth and power"; and *kāma,* "the pursuit of pleasure," particularly sexual pleasure. Each eventually reached mankind through a series of condensations. Manu, the mythical Hindu lawgiver, gave mankind a summary of those aspects dealing with *dharma* in his code, and Brihaspati and Śukra passed on information dealing with *artha.* The transmission of *kāma* went through a much more complicated process but eventually reached mankind in some 500 chapters compiled by the sage Śvetaketu. Because this proved much too lengthy for man to digest, it was condensed into 300 chapters by Śaṅkha and further condensed into 150 chapters by Bābhravya. These chapters were, in turn, taken up and elaborated by seven authorities of the Kingdom of Magadha, an early historical kingdom in northern India.[1] Finally, the sage Vātsyāyana put them into the form, the *Kāmasūtra,* in which they have survived. The *Kāmasūtra* covers most aspects of human courtship and mating, the book forming the basis for most of the later writing on the subject by peoples of the Indian subcontinent. Vātsyāyana's authority was so greatly admired and his book so widely read that he came to be considered a *Rishi* ("inspired sage") by the Hindus, and the *Kāmasūtra*, a revelation of the gods.

A number of other sex manuals have also survived. Chronologically next in line is the *Kuṭṭāni-mata* or "*Lessons of a Prostitute*," written by Dāmodaragupta in the eighth century, and surviving only in fragments. Similar in tone is the *Samaya-mātṛikā* or the "*Prostitute's Breviary*," written by Kshemendra (990–1065), called the Voltaire of India by some Westerners. More widely read is the *Rati-rahasya* ("*The Mysteries of Passion*"), by Koka Paṇḍita, dating from about the twelfth century, a handbook on lovemaking and sexual intercourse with a classification of female types, methods of intercourse, postures of sex, and so forth. Somewhat similar is the *Pañchaśāyaka*, the "*Five Arrows*," written by Jyotirīśa in the fourteenth century. Next to the *Kāmasūtra,* the treatise best known to Western readers is the *Ananga Ranga*, "*Theater of the Love God*," written by Kalyāṇamalla in the fifteenth century and based primarily on the *Kāmasūtra* and the *Rati-rahasya*. Because its author was a Hindu in the employ of a Muslim nobleman, knowledge of its contents soon spread throughout the Islamic world, and it was translated into the languages of many of the countries held by the Muslims. Other sex manuals include the *Ngara-sarvasva*, or the "*Complete Citizen*," by Padmaśri (fourteenth century); the *Rati-mañjarī*, or the "*Blossoms of Love*," by Jayadeva (about 1370); and *Rati-ratna-pradīpkā*, "*Love Jewel Lamp*," by Devaraja (about 1400). In addition there are hundreds of lesser manuals, many quite crude, found in the various Indian vernaculars as well as in Sanskrit, and many commentaries on the *Kāmasūtra* and the *Rati-rahasya*.[2]

The number of erotic classics suggests that the peoples of the Indian subcontinent did not hold the fear of sex that some of their Western counterparts did. Strong approval of sex appears early in Hindu history. The *Vedas*, the primary scriptures of Hinduism, which Hindus believe have existed since time itself began, put creation in sexual terms:

> *In the beginning there was desire,*
> *Which was the primal germ of the mind:*
> *The sages searching in their hearts with wisdom,*
> *found in non-existence the king of existence.*[3]

The *Atharva Veda*, the fourth of the Hindu *Vedas*, and primarily a collection of magical formulations, includes many devoted to casting spells, making incantations, or fashioning charms to help or hinder lovemaking. There are charms to achieve success in love, spells to recover virility or to give birth to sons, and incantations to allow a lover to steal unnoticed into the home of his beloved. There are also harmful spells to make a man impotent, to keep a woman rival a spinster, and so forth. In general these formularies seem to reflect a solid core of pre-Aryan and non-Aryan tradition. The explicitness of some can be conveyed by quoting a spell devised to deprive a man of his virility:

1.   As the best of plants thou are reputed, O herb: turn this man for me today into a eunuch that wears his hair dressed!

2.   Turn him into a eunuch that wears his hair dressed, and into one that wears a hood! Then Indra with a pair of stones shall break his testicles both.

3.   O eunuch, into a eunuch thee I have turned; O castrate, into a castrate thee I have turned; O weakling into a weakling thee I have turned! A hood upon his head, and a hair net do we place.

4.   The two canals, fashioned by the gods, in which man's power rests, in thy testicles . . . I break them with a club.

5.   As women break reeds for a mattress with a stone, thus do I break thy member.[4]

Hinduism was not without sex prohibitions, some appearing in the Code of Manu, the first systematic treatment of Hindu law, dating from about the first century A.D.

A man who has committed a bestial crime, or an unnatural crime with a female, or has had intercourse in water, or with a menstruating woman, shall perform a *Sāmtapana Krikkhra*.[5]

He who has had sexual intercourse with sisters by the same mother, with the wives of a friend, or of a son, with unmarried maidens, and with females of the lowest caste shall perform the penance, prescribed for the violation of a Guru's bed.[6]

A twice-born man who commits an unnatural offence with a male, or has intercourse with a female in a cart drawn by oxen, in water, or in the day-time, shall bathe, dressed in his clothes.[7]

He who violates an unwilling maiden shall instantly suffer corporal punishment; but a man who enjoys a willing maiden shall not suffer corporal punishment, if his (caste be) the same (as hers).

From a maiden who makes advances to a (man of) high (caste), he shall not take any fine; but her, who courts a (man of) low caste, let him force to live confined in her house.[8]

A damsel who pollutes (another) damsel must be fined two hundred (*panas*), pay the double of her (nuptial) fee, and receive ten (lashes with a) rod. But a woman who pollutes a damsel shall instantly have (her head) shaved or two fingers cut off, and be made to ride (through the town) on a donkey.[9]

For in this world there is nothing so detrimental to long life as criminal conversation with another man's wife.[10]

Adultery was regarded as serious by the Hindus, but most of the listed prohibitions are directed, not so much against the sexual act in question, as against the crossing of caste or class lines. Even when sexual acts are forbidden, it is more because they involve ceremonial impurities than because they are evil in themselves, and the impurities could be removed by undergoing the necessary ablutions.

Although the Code of Manu has had the effect of law throughout much of Indian history, interpretations of the law have varied because of the wide range of cultural and doctrinal belief inherent in Hinduism. This very diversity makes it difficult to single out any view of sexuality as official, since Hinduism lacks a common creed or set of dogmas or practice and has no universally acceptable canon, no organized church as such, and no uniformity of worship. The religion itself could best be defined as a medley of faiths linked to some degree by the same pantheon. There are hundreds of sects, and within most, numerous splinter groups are based on a particular deity, guru, trait, or tenet held sacred. Obviously, within such a multitude of sects, sexual attitudes vary widely, and every generalization has exceptions.

Still, Hinduism has a world view, accepted by most Hindus, that developed between the fourth century B.C. and the fourth century A.D. The sources of this view appear earliest and most readily in the *Māhabhārata* and the *Rāmāyana*, the great epic poems compiled during this time. A common denominator among Hindus is a belief in the supreme Spirit, envisioned in metaphysical speculation as a single all-powerful God, the ultimate principle or Brahman or Absolute Being, who alone is real. This Spirit, manifested for mankind anthropomorphically by beings brought into existence through His emergence, is usually represented by a trio of Gods, Brahmā (with a long *a* and masculine to distinguish him from Brahman, the neuter and the ultimate), Vishnu, and Śiva. These three supervise worldly affairs, meting out rewards and punishments. Brahmā, who brought into existence the three worlds—heaven, earth, and the nether regions—created gods or lesser divinities, earth and nature spirits, demons, ogres, and man. Śiva embodies God as the final dissolver or destroyer, the personification of the disintegrative tendencies of the cosmos as well as of regeneration and sexuality. Male and female organs of generation are often used as his symbol. He is also the god of asceticism. Vishnu is the loving protector and preserver, the savior of mankind, and destroyer of evil. Beneath this Trinity are a number of lesser powers representing the forces of both good and evil. Good forces or *devas* are led by Indra, lord of clouds, and associated with him are Agni ("fire"), Varuna ("water"), Sūrya ("sun"), and Kāma ("passion"). These gods live in Indra's heaven, slightly below the Paradise of Brahmā and Vishnu. Dancing girls and musicians also live in this heaven and its majestic court full of boundless bliss. From this place the *devas* issue forth from time to time to intervene in human affairs. Demons, the exact opposite of the *devas,* take vicious pleasure in vexing or annoying the gods as well as virtuous men.

Below the gods and demons are men themselves. A man is born, dies, then is born again, and if he acts well, does his duty, and works ceaselessly for good, he follows what was known as the path of *dharma* or "righteousness." This ensures him that at each succeeding birth he will start at a stage more favorable than in his previous existence until, by sheer goodness of character, he qualifies for *Brahmā-lôka* (the "world of Brahmā") and is accounted a god. For those who achieve this state, there is no return to the human condition. Instead, they proceed from one level of illumination to ever higher levels until, finally wrapt with inexpressible bliss, they are absorbed into the supreme Spirit. The reverse of this process is illustrated by the fate of the demons, since, if a man lapses from the path of right living, his second state is always worse than the first until, if his crimes are sufficiently great, he becomes a demon. This status gives him increased capacity for evil and lessens his chances of ultimate salvation. Some Hindu writers feel that such individuals are eventually consigned to the lowest or seventh level of Hell, where they are burned, flayed, and tormented until the end of time. They have no hope of reincarnation and lie in a state of perpetual pain until Brahmā and all the worlds are comsumed in the final cataclysm.

The ultimate ends of men—salvation, bliss, knowledge, and pleasure—can be achieved by following any number of different paths or *mārga,* which vary according to the cult, creed, sect, and system. Such a variety is necessary because men differ in special abilities and competencies. Some adopt the method of good works, others perform the necessary rituals and sacrifices or follow certain ascetic principles, and others make idols and build and consecrate temples. There is a nonaction method through the cultivation of the passive virtues, and the way of neutrality through indifference to action, whether good or bad. Logic and reasoning furnish an alternate way, as do love, adoration, and devotion to duty. Usually, no single path (*mārga*) is all sufficient, a blending of two or more being regarded as essential. Faith is balanced with works, devotion with ritual, and so forth. Different sects adopt or encourage different ways, and a number of these have importance in any study of sexuality.

The most celebrated deity of the Hindu pantheon is Krishna, worshipped as an independent god in his own right but also as the eighth incarnation of Vishṇu, who assumed the form of Krishṇa to destroy the tyrant Kaṁsa. Krishṇa is particularly noted for his interest and devotion to the female sex, according to tradition having some 16,108 wives, each of whom gave him 10 sons and a daughter. Though the early references to him emphasize the destruction of Kaṁsa, the emphasis in much of the later literature is more on Krishṇa's interest in women and his physical desires. He is often portrayed in an amorous posture or state.[11]

Krishṇa's favorite was Rhādhā, the loveliest of all the milkmaids, whose love for him was so all-consuming that she ignored her family honor and disregarded her husband. In effect, in spite of the Code of Manu, Krishṇa is pictured as an adulterer. Until the fourteenth century, Hindu poets usually portrayed Rādhā as Krishṇa's mistress, not his wife, and delighted in describing their stormy adulterous liaison. Since that time, there has been an attempt to portray Krishṇa as conforming to more conventional mores, and in this effort Rādhā has been described as wife rather than mistress.[12]

Probably, as W. G. Archer has argued, the adventures of Krishṇa should not be taken to represent the actual conduct of men but rather the repressed romantic longings of males in a society where romance was nonexistent, where women were secluded, and where there was such great emphasis on female chastity.[13] Moreover, Krishṇa's love for Rādhā soon became something more than a simple affair of adultery, if that is all it signified originally, coming to be regarded as an allegorical tale designed to impress the ordinary believer. In the allegorical sense, Rādhā was the soul and Krishṇa was God. Rādhās's sexual passion for Krishṇa symbolized the soul's intense longing for God, and her willingness to commit adultery expressed the utter priority that must be accorded to love for God. Allegory or not, if ultimate union could be symbolized by sexual passion, then sex must have been recognized as a good in Hindu society. Sexual symbolism was, in fact, often used to impress the believer.

> As a man when in the embrace of his beloved wife knows nothing without or within, so the person when in the embrace of the intelligent self knows nothing without or within. That, verily is his form in which his desire is fulfilled, in which the self is his desire, in which he is without desire, free from any sorrow.[14]

In spite of the allegorical interpretations, poets used the story to highlight the nature of physical love. Particularly influential in this respect was an earlier Jayadeva, a twelfth-century Bengali poet, whose *Gitā-govinda* ("*Song of the Cowherd*") was extremely influential. This poem is concerned with the estrangement of Rādhā and Krishṇa and recounts how Krishṇa, in his efforts to humble Rādhā, turned to other cowgirls. This rejection led Rādhā to mourn her fate to a friend and to renew her efforts to attract Kṛishṇa:

> *O make him enjoy me, my friend, that Kṛishṇa so fickle,*
> *I who am shy like a girl on her way to the first of her trysts of love,*
> *He who is charming with flattering words, I who am tender*
> *In speech and smiling, he on whose hip the garment lies loosely worn.*
>
> *O make him enjoy me, my friend, that Kṛishṇa so fickle . . .*[15]

The poem proceeds for several stanzas in a similar vein until, eventually, Kṛishṇa is persuaded to return and they make love.

> *Their love play grown great was very delightful, the love play where*
> *thrills were a hindrance to firm embraces,*
> *Where their helpless closing of eyes was a hindrance to longing looks*
> *at each other, and their secret talk to their drinking of other's*
> *nectar of lips, and where the skill of their love was hindered*
> *by boundless delight.*
>
> *She loved as never before throughout the course of the conflict of love,*
> *to win, lying over his beautiful body, to triumph over her lover;*
> *And so through taking the active part her thighs grew lifeless and*
> *languid her vine-like arms, and her heart beat fast, and her*
> *eyes grew heavy and closed.*[16]

Jayadeva's poem had a major influence on Indian poetic development. There are imitators of the poem and its theme in most of the Indian vernaculars, and so admired was the poem that, either in its original or variant versions, it came to be regarded as a part of the devotional worship in certain Hindu temples. Some of the imitators of Jayadeva went to greater lengths than he did to emphasize the sensuousness of the sexual scenes, subjecting every incident of the lovemaking to detailed analysis. Some poets tried to think and feel themselves into Rādhā's mind, to describe the exquisite sensations of awakening love in a young girl about to become a woman, and others imagined they were Krishna being stirred by the glimpses of Rādhā's glowing femaleness.[17]

With the examples of the Gods before them, the Hindus could give much freer reign to feelings of sensuality and sexuality than the Christians of the West. Sex remained, however, private, the delicacies of the art of love confined to the bedchamber. As in the West, sex was for procreation, but it could also be engaged in for pleasure, for power, and even for magical purposes. Whereas little attention is given, in the various sex manuals, to sex for procreation, considerable attention is given to the other purposes of sex, particularly to pleasure.[18] Pleasure is, however, defined primarily from a male rather than a female point of view. Women are portrayed as voluptuous creatures who are fair game for the more predatory male, this attitude also appearing in the handbooks devoted to *Strītantra,* literally, the "female lore." The *Strītantra* concern themselves with different kinds of females, particularly, with women as an instrument for man's passion and a vessel for his seed. They also deal with female functions.

The handbooks emphasize that sexual desire in women depends on several things, including her education, experience, physical type, and the stimuli necessary to arouse her. This last is regarded as under the male's control; he is supposed to acquire a thorough knowledge of woman's erogenous zones—the breasts, nipples, nape of the neck, folds of the buttocks, labia, and clitoris. Different types of women have different sensitive areas to be explored, including the lobe of the ear, the middle of the palm, the navel, the anus, or the arch of the foot. Stimulation of the *madanāḍi* (literally, "passion pulse areas") helps not only to bring about orgasm but also ensures the birth of a son. The *nāḍi* most frequently praised in the Sanskrit literature are the *jaghana* ("buttock") or the *bhasad* ("devourer"), that is, the whole area of the female pudenda, including the buttocks and the anus (*guda*), which was regarded as a particular area of delight. Graphic descriptions of the rear parts of various legendary beauties are found in the classics as well as in the various vernaculars.[19]

The main area of ecstasy in the female was the *yoni* ("holder"), in a narrow sense the vulva, but in a broader sense it also included the *bhaga* ("pubic hair"); the *vedha* (or "breach," the opening or cleft of the labia); and the *garbha* ("womb"). The *yoni* was believed to have a life of its own, being regarded as a sacred area, a pad of pleasure, an occult region worthy of reverence, and a symbol of the cosmic mysteries. It is described as the abode of pleasure, the source of great bliss, and the delight of delights and is said to have been created specifically as honey to attract the male organ. It is likened to the second mouth of the creator, and it continually sends out a silent command to man to come and sip. It is the chief ruler of the universe, for it brings men in all walks of life under its control and subjection.[20]

The penis is called the *linga,* and like the *yoni* it was also the object of veneration. The *Svādiṣthāna,* the *chakra* ("center") connected with the excitation of male sexual feelings, is situated at the root of the *medhra* ("penis"). The *mushka* ("testes"), the *chakra* of time, disclose the mystery of the *yoni* place. Semen, called *bindu,* is particularly sacred. Men also have erotic areas like women, especially the *guda* (anus).[21]

In the sexual handbooks lovemaking is often referred to as a refined form of combat. The man attacks, the woman resists, and by the subtle interplay of advance and retreat, assault and defense, desires are mutually built up. But love is different from war in that the final result is a delightful victory for both parties. Women are aroused by a show of strength, men by a show of resistance. At the height of passion, consciousness is enhanced by intensive stimulation, often through sadistic acts, because the senses have become so dulled to the unpleasantness of pain that they find sharp delight in it. During this combat (*prahaṇana*) it is possible to bite, scratch, pull the hair of the partner, and beat or slap with the palm of the hand, the back of the hand, the side of the hand, a half-open fist, or a closed fist on the shoulders, back, bosom, and buttocks.[22] The partners are cautioned to avoid becoming too violent because neither the giving nor receiving partner is always aware of the severity of the blows. Various kinds of love marks (*kāmāṅka*) are described, in two major categories—those made with the fingernails and those with the teeth. Nail marks are described as shaped like a crescent, circle, lotus, tiger's claw, and so forth, and teeth marks are described as elephant tusk, broken cloud, and so forth. If a man make a certain kind of mark on the woman, she was supposed to counter with another kind.[23]

Lovemaking was also accompanied by vocal sounds, *sītkṛita*, varying from a slow expulsion of breath through clenched teeth to sounds compared to the neighing of a horse, from a deep sigh to a snore, from the hushing of a baby to a berry falling into a pond. The various kinds of sobbing, cooing, moaning, humming, hissing, clucking, bellowing, and roaring required the well-matched partners to respond with appropriate sounds or actions. Occasionally there were also verbal exclamations such as "I am dying," or "I can endure no more."[24] Moreover, the handbooks describe numerous postures for sexual intercourse, usually divided into precoital ones (*āliṅgana*) and those actually adopted during intercourse (*bandhana*). There are as many as 16 different precoital positions, dependent on whether the couple is standing, sitting, or lying down. The climbing tree position requires the woman to place one of her feet on the foot of the man, entwine her other leg around his thigh, wrap one arm around his back, and put the other on the shoulder as if she was climbing him in order to get a kiss. When a man places his breasts between the breasts of a woman and presses her to him, it is called the "embrace of the breasts," and so on. Different manuals give slightly different names or variations to the positions.[25]

When the couple engages in intercourse itself, they are faced with choosing from a number of different positions. Vātsyāyana described some 84 different postures, if minor variations are included, but one of his commentators listed 729 variations. Not all these variations could be performed by a single couple, some being highly dependent on physical peculiarities of the individual or of the genitalia. Postures are often named after animals, such as the cow, mule, donkey, cat, dog, tiger, and frog, and couples are encouraged to imitate the sounds of these animals to enhance enjoyment. When a woman stands on her hands and feet like a four-footed animal and her lover mounts her like a bull, it is called the congress of the cow, and with slight variations it becomes the congress of the goat, deer, ass, cat, tiger, elephant, and so forth. In general the positions are divided into categories according to the postures involved: standing, leaning against a pillar, sitting, half reclining, reclining, flexed, extended, face to face, front to back, lateral or sideways, astride, upside down, and reverse. Movements accompanying the postures are described as being like a pair of tongs, spinning the top, biting the board, churning the milk, sparrow playing, swinging, squeezing, and so on. In the spinning of the top, the woman is on top during coitus and spins around like a wheel. Vātsyāyana emphasized that this motion could be acquired only by practice. In the same position, when the woman squeezes the *linga* in her *yoni* and keeps it there for a long time, she is acting like a pair of tongs. All orifices were used in intercourse; there are descriptions for engaging in anal intercourse, called the "lower congress," and for oral–genital sex, called *Auparishtaka* or *"mouth congress."*[26]

It was a common Hindu belief that women enjoy sex much more than men, women being held to be much more sexual, as is emphasized in the story of Bhaṅgāsvana, recorded in the *Mahābhārata*. Bhaṅgāsvana was a powerful king, a literal tiger among men, whose life remained incomplete because he was unable to beget sons. Finally, in desperation, he performed a special sacrifice that guaranteed him sons, but he so angered the god Indra that Indra resolved to punish the impious king. Not until after 100 sons has been born to the king was Indra able to take his revenge. Then Indra's opportunity came when Bhaṅgāsvana lost his way on a hunting trip. Indra further confused the king by leading him farther and farther from his companions until he reached the shores of a magic lake, where he stopped to bathe. When he emerged from the waters, Bhaṅgāsvana was no longer a male but a female. Returning to her kingdom but unable to rule because she was a woman, she fled to the forest to live as a companion to a hermit. As a woman she soon bore the hermit as many sons as she had begotten as a man. When her sons were grown, she sent them back to her former kingdom to rule jointly with their brothers, but Indra, ever observant and still angry, felt that the ex-king had not suffered enough for the impiety involved in making the sacrifice. In his anger, Indra set the two groups of brothers fighting each other until all were killed. The calamitous death of all her sons set the ex-king to weeping and wailing. Indra came upon her in this condition and disclosed the reasons for such horrible punishments. The woman's repentance so moved Indra that he forgave her. Then he asked the woman which of the sets of sons she would choose to have live again if she had the choice, those she had mothered or those he had fathered. The ex-king replied that she would prefer the sons she had borne as a woman because the woman "cherishes a more tender love" than the man and it was for her mother's love that she wanted these sons. Indra not only granted the wish but also went further and restored both sets of sons. The god, by now curious, then asked the ex-king whether she would prefer to remain a woman or to become a man once again. She chose to remain a woman because:

> The woman has in union with man always the greater joy, that is why . . . I choose
> to be a woman. I feel greater pleasure in love as a woman, that is the truth, best
> among the gods. I am content with existence as a woman.[27]

Similar stories convey the same message. Ila, who was both a man and a woman during alternate months, spent his–her time as a woman in sexual pleasures and her–his time as a man in pious ways and thoughts.[28] In the companion epic, the *Rāmāyaṇa*, the insatiability of women in love appears in the story of the woman who sexually exhausted her husband as well as the ascetic who had taken her away from him.[29] The same theme is expressed in the Indian proverb stating that woman's power in eating is twice as great as a man's, her cunning or bashfulness four times as great, her decisions or boldness six times as great, and her impetuosity or delight in love eight times as great.[30] It was widely believed that, without sexual enjoyment, a woman would pine and ache. Love was thus a tonic for woman, although it also had noble meaning, for it filled her whole being, made her steadfast and faithful, and, as it grew ever deeper, strongly mingled with the altruistic.

Whereas sex was for pleasure, children, particularly sons, were ultimately supposed to result. A husband and wife

> *With sons and daughters by their side,*
>   *they enjoy the full span of life,*
>   *both decked with ornaments of gold.*
> *Inviting them to joys, offering wealth,*
>   *they worship together for immortality,*
>   *and united, through mutual love,*
>   *do honour to the Devas.*[31]

> *Let you two here, be not parted,*
>   *enjoy the full length of life,*
> *sporting with your sons and grandsons,*
>   *rejoicing in your own abode.*

> *May Prajāpti bring forth children of us, may*
>   *Aryaman unite us together till old age,*
> *Not inauspicious, enter thou thy husband's house,*
>   *be gracious to our bipeds and our quadrupeds.*

> . . . . .

> *Make her, thou bounteous Indra,*
>   *a good mother of sons; grant her*

good fortune; give her ten sons
and make her husband the eleventh.[32]

The bridegroom, in discussing marriage with the bride, stated:

I am song, thou are verse,
I am Heaven, thou art Earth.
We two together shall live here
becoming the parents of children.[33]

Sex also had mystical or magical reasons. In its profound, esoteric sense the *yoni* was the sacred field in which the seed of all creatures was planted and nourished. It was the emblem of the ultimate, the keeper of the great mysteries, and the sacrificial altar. The hips and haunches were the sacrificial grounds, the mons veneris the altar, the pubic hair the grass, and sexual intercourse itself a higher form of worship. Such statements are repeated in various forms in the *Upanishads*:

> Woman, verily. O Gautama, is the sacrificial fire; of this the sexual organ is the fuel, what invites is the smoke, the vulva is the flame, what is done inside is the coals, the pleasures the sparks. In this fire the gods offer (the libation of) semen; from this offering arises the foetus.[34]

Sexual symbolism was particularly useful in conveying philosophical concepts.

> He who dwells in the semen, is other than the semen, whom the semen does not know, whose body the semen is, who controls the semen from within, that is your self, the inner controller, the immortal. He is never seen but is the seer, he is never heard but is the hearer. He is never perceived, but is the perceiver. He is never thought but is the thinker. There is no other seer but he, there is no other hearer but he, there is no other perceiver but he, there is no other thinker but he. He is your self, the inner controller, the immortal.[35]

> The Great Brahman is a womb for me, in which I cast the seed. From that, O descendant of Bharata! is the birth of all things. Of the bodies, O son of Kunti! which are born from all wombs, the (main) womb is the great Brahman, and I (am) the father, the giver of the seed. Goodness, passion, darkness, these qualities born from nature.[36]

The sex act became a psychospiritual communion. The rich, deep fulfillment of love between a man and a woman was a condition of happiness so natural, so simple, yet so real that it was the best of all earthly conditions. Inevitably, it was also employed by the mystics as a symbol of divine communion in its transcendent and esoteric meaning. Sex was a way of revealing to man the hidden truth of the universe. Through sex it was possible to obtain *mukti* ("redemption") through *bhukti* ("pleasure"). Copulation itself could bring about *siddhi* ("supernatural power"), but only if the practitioner had transcended the carnal state of sexual activity and risen above passion.

In this mystical sex the male and female symbolized the dichotomy existing in the absolute between Śiva and Śakti, Krishna and Rādhā, Buddha and Tārā, and the power of lust thereby became the sustaining force for the cosmic urge. Sexual union came to represent the microcosm of the macrocosm of divine creation, and the sex act, a rite for spiritual enlightenment. To realize the state of absoluteness the man had to conceive of himself as the male deity; then by *nyāsa* ("worship") he transfigured his partner until she became the *śakti*, his divine female counterpart, the consecrated field for his operation. The pair then united, physically, mentally, and spiritually. Hindu cultism is most active in this aspect of sex, each sect or cult stipulating different ways of preparing for this union.

Though Śiva is the God of destruction, destruction is regarded as a necessary prelude to generation and construction. Nothing can be made out of nothing, and creating is the process of rebuilding. Thus Śiva is also a creator. In his image as a God of creation, Śiva is represented by the *linga* or phallus; in a number of *linga* shrines in India the principal idol is a phallus-shaped stone supported on a round base. The base and the phallus combined symbolize the divine sex act believed necessary to sustain the universe. There are many legends about the origin of *linga* worship. The Saivites attribute the origin of their belief from the primary day of creation, when both Brahmā and Vishnu sprang forth into being out of nonbeing. Both gods, bewildered by their sudden appearance, started questioning each other about their origin, to establish precedence and superiority, when they noticed beside them a resplendent *linga* of such huge dimensions that neither its top nor bottom could be seen, and so they investigated it. Vishnu assumed the form of a boar to dive into the primal ocean to get at the base, and Brahmā converted himself into a swan to fly to the top. Though Vishnu dove deep, he could find no base to the *linga* and reluctantly returned to the surface of the water to find Brahmā waiting for him with news of his success in reaching the top. On this basis Brahmā asked Vishnu to agree that he was the superior creation, but at that instant Śiva, the owner of the *Linga*, appeared. He questioned Brahmā about the top of the *Linga*, and when Brahmā proved ignorant, it was evident he had not reached the top. Both Brahmā and Vishnu were then forced to admit that the *Linga* was infinite, lower than the deep, and higher than the heavens, and both offered to do homage to the *Linga* and to urge man to do likewise.[37] In addition to the shrines where phallus-shaped images are worshipped, natural-sized *lingas* with symbolic devices carved on them are often used in religious sex rites. In several cult groups the male penis itself is worshipped. In this last case, the phallus of the guru is kissed and adored by his followers. In some areas and by certain peoples the penis of a naked *sadhu* ("ascetic" or "wonderworker") is regarded as a particular object of reverence, and women desirous of bearing children kiss the phallus of such holy ones to gain fertility.

Among the sects that worship the *linga* is the *Lingāyat* sect, founded or reformed by Basava in the twelfth century. The initiate is presented with a small phallus, which he or she wears around his or her neck; it represents the soul, and its loss is held to be equivalent to spiritual death. In spite of its symbolism, the sect in many ways is rather puritanical. Its members are strict vegetarians who abjure liquor and tobacco, abhor sorcery and magic, condemn child marriages, and have no caste lines. They believe the souls of the adherents find union with God on death, no rites or prayers for the dead being allowed among them. Gods dwell on earth where the *lingas* exist. Members of the cult today are found mostly in south India, where there are a couple of million adherents.[38]

At the opposite end of the spectrum from the *Lingāyats* are the *Śaktas*, Hindus who consider the Godhead to be essentially feminine. Śakti is the wife of Śiva, although she is also known under many different names. Her worshippers are broadly divided into two groups, "right-handed" adherents, who worship the god in public; and "left-handed" ones, who insist on complete secrecy. The sexual overtones are most rampant in the latter form. The *Śaktas* might also be classified as a form of Tantrism, so called because the adherents follow scriptures known as *Tantras*. Essentially, tantric cults are antinomians; that is, they hold that man is not bound by the moral law and can reach a state that takes him so far beyond its purview that he can cease to obey its precepts. Both in Hinduism and Buddhism these antinomian groups are known quite literally as "the left," although some scholars derive the term from *vāmā,* meaning "women." Within Hinduism the sects that follow the left-hand path are characterized by a disregard for the conventional *dharma* and a belief that a person is beyond good and evil. The tantric cults hold that spiritual union with the god can best be attained through sexual union in the flesh. During intercourse man is able to comtemplate reality face to face, and the supreme bliss that proceeds from ritual sexuality is the height of religious experience. In this stage of nonduality all differences vanish, and everything, high and low, good and bad, ugly and beautiful, becomes the same. In this pose the couple is able to comprehend the mystery of the whole cosmic process and taste the transcendent bliss of divine experience.

In such sects promiscuous intercourse is spoken of as an act of devotion to the deity and regarded as obligatory for all members. The best possible union occurs when the woman is as different as possible from the man. Thus the union of a man with his own wife is more or less devoid of merit for the true devotee and should be only temporary, for the duration of the rite. Beyond this union there are succeeding grades of sexual intercourse, each representing, so to speak, a higher stage: adultery, virgin taking, union with a high-caste woman, union with low caste-women and prostitutes, incest, union with a demoness, and ultimately, the seventh and highest grade, union with the goddess herself. The ideal union is the unconventional, perilous intimacy of a man with a woman with whom he can never unite, a union thus similar to Kṛishna's love for the milkmaid Rādhā, the wife of another cowherd. Since union with a low-caste woman, dancing girl, or prostitute marks the collapse of caste barriers, its spiritual merit is great. Even higher than this, however, is the total eradication of distinction between one woman and another so that one's sister, daughter, or even mother is the same as any other. Incestuous relationships are thus an advanced step on the pathway to adepthood. The final stages are purely magical, because in these sex acts the man must invoke demonesses to have intercourse with them until he eventually unites with the goddess. There is no good because there is no evil, there is no deed that cannot be done, and there is no woman who is not for enjoyment.[39]

Some tantric sects taught that a man could attain the highest bliss by concentrating his mind on the soul seated in the female organ, and some temples are dedicated to this, the most famous being that in Gauhāti in Assam, built in 1565 to the goddess of love, Kāmākhya. According to tradition it was on the hill of Kāmagiri just north of the modern town that the goddess Śakti used to meet the god Śiva in secret for prolonged lovemaking sessions. After her death, a distraught Śiva carried her dismembered body on his head, dropping parts of it all over India. Her genitals fell on Kāmagiri, the site of her lovemaking, whereupon the hill took on a bluish appearance. The temple contains no images, but in the depth of the shrine is a cleft in the rock adored as the *yoni* of Śakti, and a natural spring within the cave keeps the cleft moist. For a time the goddess Kāmākhyā was worshipped not only by sexual intercourse but also by human sacrifice. Under British rule the human sacrifice was replaced by sacrificial goats.[40]

Various forms of worship are associated with the cult of Śakti, the most common known as *Chakrapūjā* ("Circle Worship"), in which small groups gather for a ceremonial meal climaxed by sexual intercourse. The male members of the group are referred to as *vīra* ("heroes"), the female, as *śakti* ("potencies"). A person may or may not have intercourse with his or her spouse, depending on the sect. The *Mahānirvāṇa Tantra*, for example, insist that intercourse in such ceremonies be with the spouse, but there are other variations. There is an elaborate ritual involving the five *makāra,* ceremonies all starting with the Sanskrit letter *M,* including (1) intoxicants, representing fire; (2) flesh or meat, representing air; (3) fish, representing water; (4) grain, representing earth; and (5) sexual intercourse, representing ether. Intercourse is to be performed only when the female partner is sexually excited. In some cases the male does not achieve orgasm but, through coitus reservatus, preserves the essence of the semen, which is then believed to be transmitted to the brain.[41] The special rituals required to bring about the ascension are called *askanda* ("nonspilling"), its secrets zealously guarded by the various sex cults and used by adepts to gain supernatural essence.

According to Hindu occultism, semen or *bindu*, "the drop" or "globule," was the quintessence of all manifested things. The *Upanishads* stated;

> The earth, verily, is the essence of all these beings; of earth (the essence is) water; of water (the essence is) plants; of plants (the essence is) flowers; of flowers (the essence is) fruits; of fruits (the essence is) the man; of man (the essence is) semen.[42]

Semen existed throughout the body in subtle form, but only under the influence of the procreative will could it be withdrawn and concentrated in gross form in the sex organs. Thus he who knew the secret of sexual intercourse turned "the good deeds of woman to himself but he, who without knowing this, practices sexual intercourse, his good deeds women turn into themselves."[43] Similar ideas appeared in Chinese thought, although whether the Chinese originated it or imported it from India is a matter of some debate.

In engaging in sexual intercourse the man was to spread apart the thighs of the woman, saying:

> Spread youselves apart, Heaven and Earth. After having inserted the member in her, after having joined mouth to mouth, he strokes her three times as the hair lies, (saying) "Let Vishnu make the womb prepared. Let Tvastr shape the (various) forms. Let *Prajā-pati* pour in. Let Dhātr place the germ (the seed) for you. O *Sinīvāli, Asvins* crowned with lotus wreaths place the seed.[44]

Tantrism taught there were two kinds of semen, male and female. *Śukra,* "white," originally located behind the throat, contained the male seed and represented Śiva; *rakta,* "red," and possessing the fiery and magical potency of the female, was located in the genitals and represented Śakti.

These primordial male and female elements could be united into the non-dual state of Absolute Reality. Though the male element was centered in the head behind the throat, and the female in the pudenda, the right side of the body was also conceived of as male and the left as female.[45] These two elements could be brought together through a man's practicing either celibacy or coitus reservatus, which they believed drew the semen up the spinal column, although we know that it was actually voided with the urine. The technique of nonspilling (*askanda*) is represented symbolically in Hindu art by *nicha medhra* or "down penis." Such a penis is shown on the famous statue of the Jain saint Gomatésvara. Jainism, in fact, teaches that, though sex is a gateway to salvation, sexual indulgence itself is a weakness and an evil to overcome because it is the chief manifestation of lust. The most extreme form in Jainism is the Digambara or nude sect, whose members at one time went about nude. Today only the holy ones observe strict nudity. The adherents of this sect regard women as the greatest temptation in the world, the cause of all sinful acts, and prevent women from entering their temples.

Even within orthodox Hinduism, there is a double standard in the male–female relationship, which has traditionally appeared in many different ways. For example, though asceticism and abstinence were approved for men, virginity for women was not particularly esteemed. In fact, it was widely believed that a virgin could neither attain spiritual enlightenment in this world nor attain the abode of bliss in the next. Unmarried women also posed other dangers. A menstruating virgin, for example, was regarded as particularly dangerous, and a woman with her hymen intact at marriage would, it was believed, damage her husband's penis and perhaps ruin him forever. Thus defloration was widely practiced, usually when girls were very young. Mothers of girls, through a process known as deep cleaning, would penetrate deep into the vulva of their child, tearing the hymen and enlarging the vulva. Even when a woman married, menstruation was regarded as an unclean period, and a man who touched a menstruating woman became as impure as if he had touched a corpse.[46] A menstruating woman was regarded as impure for 3 days and nights, and during that time she was not to anoint her body, bathe in water, touch fire, clean her teeth, eat meat, or perform numerous other deeds.[47] The wisdom, energy, strength, sight, and vitality of a man who approached a woman covered with menstrual excretions utterly perished.[48] Among some Hindus a girl at her first menstruation was locked in a dark room and cautioned against touching anyone or using milk, oil, or meat, until she had undergone purification. Virgins who menstruated while still in their father's care, that is, who remained unmarried, drew calamity on all the household.[49]

All the varieties of sexual intercourse were tolerated by Hinduism, although some forms were regarded by some groups with greater hostility than others. Oral–genital contact, for example, was classed by some lawgivers as equivalent to the killing of a Brāhmin, and the sin involved could not be expiated in less than 100 incarnations. Nevertheless, the erotic manuals discussed it at length. Vātsyāyana devoted a chapter to mouth congress (*maukhyā*), beginning his analysis with a discussion of eunuchs who disguised themselves as females and used their mouths as women used their sexual parts to make a living as courtesans. He reported that eunuchs who lived the life of a male also tried to touch the *linga* of men, and if they found them erect, they engaged in oral–genital sex. Oral–genital sex (described from the male viewpoint) involved an eight-step process:

1. When, holding the man's lingam with his hand, and placing it between his lips, the eunuch moves his mouth about, it is called the "nominal congress."

2. When, covering the end of the lingam with his fingers collected together like the bud of a plant or flower, the eunuch presses the sides of it with his lips, using his teeth also, it is called "biting the sides."

3. When, being desired to proceed, the eunuch presses the end of the lingam with his lips closed together, and kisses it as if he were drawing it out, it is called the "outside pressing."

4. When, being asked to go on, he puts the lingam further into his mouth, and presses it with his lips and then takes it out, it is called the "inside pressing."

5. When, holding the lingam in his hand, the eunuch kisses it as if he were kissing the lower lip, it is called "pressing."

6. When, after kissing it, he touches it with his tongue everywhere, and passes his tongue over the end of it, it is called "rubbing."

7. When, in the same way, he puts the half of it into his mouth, and forcibly kisses and sucks it, this is called "sucking a mango fruit."

8. And, lastly, when with the consent of the man, the eunuch puts the whole lingam into his mouth, and presses it to the very end, as if he were going to swallow it up, it is called "swallowing up."[50]

Not only eunuchs engaged in such contact with men, but also "unchaste and wanton women," and it was not unknown, Vātsyāyana added, for male servants of some men to engage in mouth congress with their masters. Even some citizens who knew each other well performed it on each other. He also recognized that women, particularly those of the harem, also engaged in oral–genital sex with each other. He said that in such cases the act was similar to kissing the mouth, and some women became so addicted to this kind of sexual activity, called the "congress of a crow," that they sought out those who would do it to them, whether male or female. He felt fellatio was prevalent among the people of Lata, Sindu, Sākata, and Sūrasena, the eastern provinces of India.[51] In some areas it was apparently considered part of the foreplay. For example, the women of Bengal have traditionally been known for "beginning with their mouths the business of the vulva to excite a man's desire."[52]

As in other aspects of sexual practice, considerable sex magic is associated with the technique of oral congress, and many fiery powers are believed to be derived from its practice, particularly when done in conjunction with anal stimulation. According to legend, Śiva's seed was received into the mouth of Agni, god of fire, then transferred by him to the womb of Parvati, who thus gave birth to the great war god Kārttikeya. Tantric manuals cite between 6 to 12 stages in the maukhyā. The first stages involved the ritual ablution of the *linga,* then erection by manual massage by the worshipper, invocation of the deity to take possession, homage by the worshipper, then excitation by oral means until orgasm had been reached. This was followed by "putting to bed" and the dismissal of the deity. Before orgasm had been achieved, it is believed that the vital powers of the organ and of the activated seed became manifest, and these could be absorbed by a third party present during the ritual by introducing the left-hand ring finger into the worshipper's rectum throughout the performance. The same was true when cunnilingus was involved. In lesbianism, artificial phalluses were often used to attain culmination, after which the phallus was withdrawn and even worshipped. Kṛishṇa's more than 16,000 wives were said to make "little images" of him to ease their passion, and apparently it was believed that women isolated in groups often engaged in group lesbianism.[53]

The anus (*guda* or *payu*) is one of the most important *chakras* ("center of psychic energy") in the human body, its significance repeatedly emphasized in the tantric texts with what might be called homosexual overtones. In fact, anal intercourse or *adhorata* (literally, "under love"), either between males or between males and females, was one of the main expedients for using the potential of the rectal center, whose animation was believed to energize the artistic, poetic, and mystical faculties. Some medieval Indian writers regarded the practice as quite common and in no way perverse, but others claimed that men who engaged in it with other men were reborn as men incapable of begetting.[54] Manu said that men who engaged in such activities lost their caste.[55] Nevertheless, concentration on the anus, introduction of wooden plugs into the rectum during meditation, digital insertion *in ano* during certain rituals, constriction of the rectal sphincter, and stimulation of the region during certain mystical poses all give maximum psychic power. Such beliefs are common yogic disciplines based on the belief in a close correspondence between the anus and certain higher centers of the subtle body. With such beliefs anal intercourse could assume mystical meaning, and male homosexuality, at least under certain conditions, was tolerated if not encouraged. Even when regarded with some hostility, it was usually not considered with as great a hostility as some other sexual activities. Kautilya, who wrote his *Arthásátra* in the fourth century B.C., fined male participants in homosexual activity between 48 and 94 *panas,* and women who engaged in sexual relations with each other were fined 12 to 24 *panas,*[56] much less than participants in certain heterosexual activities were fined.

Part of the ambiguity surrounding oral and anal intercourse resulted from the belief that male seed was precious. This also led to considerable ambiguity about masturbation. The *Laws of Manu* stated:

Let him always sleep alone, let him never waste his manhood; for he who voluntarily wastes his manhood, breaks his vow. A twice-born student who has involuntarily wasted his manly strength during sleep, must bathe, worship the sun, and afterwards thrice mutter the *Rik*-verse (which begins), "Again let my strength return to me."[57]

Those who know the Veda declare that voluntary effusion of semen by a twice-born (youth) who fulfills the vow (of studentship constitutes) a breach of that vow. . . . When this sin has been committed, he shall go begging to seven houses, dressed in the hide of the (sacrificed) ass, proclaiming his deed.[58]

Such punishment was however, generally restricted to the discipline bound to chastity, and most other Hindus who engaged in such practices were required only to make a light penance.[59] In the antinomian cults masturbation became a religious ceremony associated with the god Kṛishṇa, who was believed to practice manual orgasm. The deep massage given by mothers to their daughters was recognized as a kind of pacifying gesture, and the same thing was true for male infants. The importance of self-stimulation is evident by the number of artificial aids, *apadravya*, literally "bad implements," or in the West what are known as *olisboi* or dildos. There were *apadravya* designed to take the place of the *yoni*, to take the place of the *linga*, and to heighten satisfaction in intercourse itself. The first category is not so numerous but included the *viyoni* ("without *yoni*") employed by men. It was made of wood and cloth and shaped like the female, with a *yoni*-shaped aperture of fruit, vegetables, and leaves. They were probably used more in fertility rites than for other purposes, since as a general rule, a punishment was prescribed for any man who availed himself of an idol of any kind for self-gratification. The second category, the *Kṛitrima-linga* or artificial phallus, was widely used by both men and women. In many temples a fixed stone *linga*, located in a secluded part of the premises, served for the ritual defloration of temple girls and virgins. They were made to sit on the stone, which penetrated the vagina and caused the rupture of the hymen. Barren wives also sat on such devices in the hope of becoming fertile. For more erotic purposes, whether for heterosexual intercourse, lesbianism, or self-masturbation among women, dildos were made from radishes or other tubers, eggplant, or even the banana. Phalluses of candle-wax, baked clay, wood, bone, or metal were also common. Many writers on erotics urged men to use such devices to stimulate their partners before intercourse.

Another aspect of the *apadravya* involved the attempt to change the shape of the genital organ, particularly by males. Special attachments were made for the penis, of gold, silver, copper, iron, zinc, lead, ivory, or wood, depending on the economic status of the individual. Usually made in two parts and fitting around the penis like a glove, these were designed so that, in theory, the man could satisfy his partner irrespective of old age or impotence. This is important, because in India the female was to achieve orgasm as well as the male. Those too poor to afford such fancy gadgets simply used a stalk, like the bamboo, coated with oil and tied with string around the waist. All were supposed to be rough on the outside. There were also rather painful prescriptions for enlarging the penis. Vātsyāyana, for example, recommended that the man periodically rub his *linga* with bristles of certain insects that live in trees, after which he should rub oil on it. Eventually, this would result in inflammation and swelling of the penis. When this happened, the man was advised to allow his penis to hang down through a hole in his cot. If he followed the correct procedures, his penis, after healing, would be much larger and remain so for the rest of his life. In some areas of India it was believed necessary to perforate the penis, just like the lobes of the ears for earrings, to enjoy the greatest pleasure.

> Now, when a young man perforates his lingam he should pierce it with a sharp instrument, and then stand in water as long as the blood continued to flow. At night he should engage in sexual intercourse, even with vigor, so as to clean the hole. After this he should continue to wash the hole with decoctions, and increase the size by putting into it small pieces of cane . . . thus gradually enlarging the orifice. . . . In the hole made in the lingam a man may put Apadravyas of various forms, such as the "round," the "round on one side," the "wooden mortar" . . .

to fit the mood of his sex partner. Others sewed tiny bells made of gold, silver, or bronze, depending on their income, into the skin of the penis. This also caused the penis to swell and supposedly heightened the pleasure of the female. Vātsyāyana also gave an overview of various parts of India where the inhabitants engaged in different kinds of sexual techniques, and of the type of olisboi or dildos used, and of whether they preferred anal, oral, or vaginal intercourse.[60]

Bestiality was also tolerated under certain conditions. In early legend Prajāpati was said to have cohabited with the dawn goddess Ushas, who tried to escape him by assuming hundreds of different animal shapes, and it was through such copulation that all the animal species were produced.[61] Later mythology attributed to Śiva the creation of various animal species through his coupling with prototypal female beasts engendered out of the primeval chaos. Kauṭilya fined a person who copulated with animals 12 *panas,* much less than for anal intercourse among humans.[62]

Portrayals of animal and human sexual contacts frequently appear in the temple sculpture, although it might oftentimes be more symbolic than representative of life. Tantrism often portrayed man as a rabbit, bull, or horse; the woman is represented as a doe, mare, or she elephant; and individuals with animal faces are often pictured copulating. Not all such representations are symbolic. Animals were believed to be much more voluptuous and sense filling than man, and among the supernatural powers promised to practitioners of various yogic disciplines are those by which a man could become a beast, to have sexual enjoyment with animals. Man could thus experience sex in its total range and sweep. There was also the belief that all desire is holy, and if the mind is pure, there is no sin. In Hindu mythology, Mallikā, wife of Prasenajit, gratified her lust with her pet dog, and Prasenajit sought satisfaction with a goat. Later, pet dogs and monkeys were kept in harems. In some bestiality the motive of the adept may have been to try to experience revulsion or, contrariwise, to demonstrate through bestiality his unconcern with the things of life. Perhaps the most vivid portrayals of bestiality are seen in the sculpture at the Black Pagoda at Konārak and in some of the temples at Bhuvanesvar.[63]

Necrophilia also played a part in some of the Tantric rituals, some disciplines emphasizing the *śavavāda* ("corpse way"), in which matters pertaining to death, corpses, decay, and putrefaction are meditated on. The sects are all Saivite, specifically Śakta, and some rituals associated with death have sexual overtones. This is particularly true when the practitioner sits in a graveyard or cremation ground with a skull pressed against his genitals. In other cases he lies prostrate or squats on a cadaver until the flesh decays, and then he eats the flesh. In the so-called black ritual (*nīlasādhana*) the adept sits astride a male and animates the body by occult means. The corpse twitches and struggles, its tongue protrudes, and the penis erects and ejaculates. The fluid was collected and used.[64]

The condition of hermaphroditism was, in some phases of Hindu esoteric belief, regarded as an ideal to be pursued. According to Tantric belief the Supreme Being is one complete sex, possessing both the male and female principle. Such a deity is said to be *ardhanārī* ("half female") with the qualities of both genders. Śiva is sometimes represented in hermaphroditic form in sculpture and painting with female elements on his left side, and male elements on his right side. Vishṇu and Krishṇa, as well as lesser deities, are also pictured in this way. There are also many legends about sex change in which the male god took a female form. Vishṇu himself set the example by taking the form of a ravishing beauty named Mohinī to settle a dispute between the gods and demons over who had precedent. So enchanted was Śiva with the charms of Mohinī that he begged Vishṇu to assume female form again, and when the god obliged, they engaged in intercourse, giving birth to Harihara, a hermaphroditic deity. The change of sex theme appears frequently in Hindu mythology, although in most cases it is from man to woman. An exceptions is Śikhaṇḍin, who was born a girl. Her father had, however, been told that she was destined to become a man, and so he brought her up as a boy and married her to the daughter of a powerful king. On the wedding night the bride discovered her husband's true sex and fled to her father's house, where she revealed the hoax played on her. The father, regarding this as an insult, declared war, and Śikhaṇḍin, disgraced by what happened, retired to the forest, determined to end her life. Here she encountered a kindhearted *yaksha* ("supernatural being"), who, when he found out the cause of the distress, offered to change sex with the princess temporarily. Śikhaṇḍin eagerly accepted the exchange and in return offered to give his sex back to the *yaksha* later. Śikhaṇḍin then returned to the palace to await the army of his father-in-law. When his father-in-law received word of his presence, he sent eunuchs and old women to examine him, and these, after a thorough examination, reported to the king that the youth really was a man and that his daughter was probably suffering from hallucinations. The war quickly ended, and a much-chastened wife returned to her husband's side. True to his word, Śikhaṇḍin returned to the forest, but the *yaksha* was no longer there, because a passing king, seeing him as a female, had taken him for a wife. As a result, Śikhaṇḍin kept his male sex until his death, when the *yaksha* was able to reclaim it.[65]

In addition to the mythical accounts of sex changes there are numerous instances of transvestism in Indian literature, usually of men donning the clothes of women. The god Sāmba, son of Kṛishṇa, was notorious for his drunkenness, venery, gluttony, and homosexuality. He seduced the wives of other men and then dressed as a female, usually as a pregnant woman, went about mocking the other gods. As Sāmbali his name became a synonym for eunuch.[66] Arjuna, the hero of the *Mahābhārata*, disguised himself as a eunuch in women's clothing and taught the young princess and her companions at the court of King Virāta the arts of dancing, singing, and music.[67] Kauṭilya regarded cross-dressing as a nonpunishable activity.[68]

In the real world of men and women, Hinduism taught that every man and woman contained within himself or herself both male and female principles. A man was a man only because of the excess of the principle of masculinity, and a woman had an excess of femininity. This maleness or femaleness remained in conflict within the individual and could be harmonized only for very brief periods during sexual intercourse, when the couple realized the Absolute. It was impossible to realize this union until one lost consciousness of his or her own sex and found the other, although within Hinduism, it was much more possible for the male to do this than the female, because by the nature of her additional orifices (*yoni* and breasts), she could not really achieve this except through sexual intercourse. As a result, male transvestism is often a part of some of the left-hand Hindu sects, but female transvestism is rare.

The Sakhībhāva, a form of Vaishnavism, held that only the Godhead, Kṛishṇa, was truly male, and every other creature in the world was female and subject to the pleasures of Kṛishṇa. They worshipped Rādhā, the favorite milk-maid of Kṛishṇa, and the object of their devotion was the attainment of the state of a female attendant upon Rādhā. Female followers of the sect granted sexual favors freely to anyone, since Kṛishṇa himself was believed to participate in all sexual acts with them. Male followers dressed like women, affecting the behavior, movements, and habits of women, even including menstruation. During their imitation menses they retired and abstained from worship. Many of them made themselves eunuchs, and all were supposed to permit the sexual act on their persons (playing the part of women) as an act of devotion. Usually, the male members did not show themselves much in public, in part because of public hostility.[69]

In some of the tantric sects of the Śaktás, particularly those which worshipped Durgā in the form of Tripurasundari, the male votaries had a religious exercise wherein they tried to accustom themselves to thinking they were women. Śakti implied to them female power and, to understand this power, the Sahajīyā ("worshipper"), at a certain stage of his spiritual development, believed that he must transform himself into a woman; only in this way could he realize the nature of the woman within himself, and only when this occurred could he experience true love.[70] Rāmakrishna, the founder of a nineteenth-century sectarian group, emphasizes the continuity of this belief, because, to achieve a vision of Krishna, he took to wearing women's clothes and imagining himself to be Rādhā. He is regarded as one of the modern reformers of Hinduism.[71]

Hinduism also taught that there was a third sex, divided into four categories: the male eunuch or *klība*, literally "the waterless," since he had desiccated testes; the *mūshka-sūnya* ("testicle voided"), one who had been castrated; the *shandha*, a neuter or hermaphrodite; and *nastrīkam*, "not woman," or female eunuch. Those decidedly male wear false beards and make advances like men; those decidedly female wear false breasts and imitate the voice, gestures, dress, delicacy, and timidity of women; and those in between assume either form. Their main function, which all shared, was to provide alternative techniques of sexual gratification.[72]

No discussion of the Indian subcontinent would be complete without some mention of Buddhism, for Buddha (Gautama Sākyamuni) came out of a Hindu environment, and his ideas were deeply influenced by Hinduism. Key to the teachings of the Buddha are two Hindu concepts, *karma* and rebirth. *Karma,* literally "the deed" or "act," is based on the belief that every act produces a result or fruit, and this fruit can be either good or evil. For the Buddha, *karma* involved not only the deed but also the intention behind the deed. If the deed was unintentional, even though it resulted in good, no *karma* was generated. On the other hand, if the right intention existed, even though the deed itself was not actually performed, *karma* was produced. In its fullest form, *karma* encompassed intention plus the bodily deed resulting from that intention. When a living being died, the *karma* he had accumulated determined the nature of his next rebirth, which could be either as a deity, a man, an animal, a hungry ghost, or a resident of hell. Man was subject to an endless cycle of rebirth. Life itself was suffering, and suffering was caused by a craving for existence and sensual pleasure. The followers of Buddha tried to suppress suffering, which could be done by the noble eightfold path: right view, right intention, right speech, right action, right livelihood, right effort, right mindfulness, and right concentration. This was condensed into the three categories of Buddhist discipline: moral conduct, mental discipline, and intuitive wisdom or insight. Individuals who followed the eightfold path faithfully and honorably could ultimately hope to escape the endless cycle of rebirths and thus achieve nirvana or cessation of suffering. Once craving had been extinguished, no more *karma* was generated, and there could be no further rebirths. This version of Buddhism would emphasize an ascetic life, but Buddhism, like Hinduism, has many paths. The view just described is that of the *Theravāda* Buddhists, literally "the doctrine of the elders." Knowledge of this comes from the *Pali* canon committed to writing during the first century B.C.

Many scholars, as well as the majority of Buddhists, hold that what is taught in the *Pali* canon does not constitute the original teachings of the Buddha but rather represents the view of the monastic community of the first century B.C. In simple terms *Theravāda,* or canonical Buddhism, is a discipline for personal salvation by the individual for himself or herself. Taking a different path is the *Mahāyāna* school of Buddhism, whose canon was first written in Sanskrit. *Mahāyāna,* or "Great Vehicle Buddhism," applies the term *Hīnāyana* or Lesser Vehicle" to the *Theravāda.* The difference between the two schools is quite radical.

The *Mahāyāna* teach that enlightenment is to be achieved mainly by faith, devotion to Buddha, and love for all fellowmen, and this is manifested by compassion, charity, and altruism. The religious ideal is the *bodhisattva,* a being destined for enlightenment. Though qualified to achieve nirvana as a result of merits accumulated in the past, the *bodhisattva* delays his final entry, choosing to remain in the world until he has brought every knowing being across the sea of misery to the shores of enlightenment. He accomplishes this by transferring some of his inexhaustible stock of merit to less fortunate creatures, who can then share in the rewards of these merits. The *bodhisattva* will vow to do anything, even to the extent of sacrificing himself, if this would be of assistance to others. Universal compassion, as manifested by self-sacrifice, might be described as the chief characteristic of the *mahāyāna bodhisattva,* and spiritual individualism could perhaps best describe that of the *Theravāda* or *Hīnayāna* school. There are other differences. The *Theravāda* regard Buddha as a human teacher who lived on earth, carried out his mission, and achieved nirvana. The *Mahāyāna* believe Buddha was an eternal being, the embodiment, so to speak, of universal and cosmic truth, who was neither born nor died but lives on from eternity to eternity. The Buddha was incarnated as the historical Sākyamuni to save mankind from evil. They believe that the Buddha had appeared at other times and will continue to do so in the future, although in reality such appearances must be classified as only illusory, for the Buddha could neither be born nor die.

Common to both groups is the *sangha* ("monastic community"), whose original intention was to provide the best possible conditions for the pursuit of the religious goals preached by the Buddha. In a community where the members no longer need worry about material sustenance or the care and anxieties of family and society, the Buddhist monk or nun could devote his or her whole mind and energy to the spiritual disciplines demanded by the Buddha. These rules were common to all groups of Buddhists. But entry into the monastery was and is an individual affair, dependent entirely on the wishes of the individual or his family.

We know little about Buddha's teachings about sex. One of the early surviving moral codes, the *Patimokka* is designed more for the monastic community than the general public, and carnal knowledge, for a Buddhist adept, was more serious than committing theft, participating in murder, or engaging in a falsehood, the other of the four major sins.[73] The *Kullavagga,* another of the *Pali* sources, condemned lust but insisted that a male was not to castrate himself to avoid such a sin.[74] The type of Buddhism in which sexuality is most openly discussed and the Indian background of Buddhism is most obvious is Buddhist Tantrism. Mircea Eliade believed that, originally, Tantrism was a separate pan-Indian movement, whose ideas were assimilated into all the great Indian religions, particularly Hinduism and Buddhism, but also Jainism, and various sectarian schools such as Saivism and Vaisnavism.[75] The term *tantra* derives from the root *tan,* meaning "succession," "unfolding," "continuous process," or perhaps best translated as "that which extends knowledge." Tantrism had become an important influence in Buddhism by the fourth century A.D. and reached its height in the eighth century. Usually, it is called *Mantrayāna* or *Vajrayāna* Buddhism. *Mantrayāna* comes from the term *mantra,* "a magic spell" or "incantation," the Tantrists believing these *mantras* represent the epitome of the *sutras,* a shortcut to enlightenment. When an individual who has gone through the proper discipline and training pronounces the *mantras,* he generates enormous power for good as well as evil. The most famous *mantra, "om mani padme hūm"* (literally, "O the Jewel and the Lotus"), as recited by the adept, is sufficient to stop the cycle of rebirth and convey one to paradise or deliverance. Closely associated with the *mantras* are the *mudras* or "signs," made by the particular position of the hands and fingers, which contain all the secrets of touch. A common custom is to touch the parts of the body (that is, heart, head, and so forth) with suitable gestures. There are also *mandalas,* a word originally meaning "circle" but in Tantric texts referring to images or symbols of groups of Buddhas and *bodhisattvas* painted in a kind of mystic circle, each deity being assigned a portion of space. There are essentially two kinds of *mandala* ("mystic circles"), one composed of 9 divisions and containing 1461 deities and the other made of 13 divisions with 405 deities. The latter form has the most sexual overtones and has to be included in any examination of sexual attitudes.[76]

The term *Vajrayāna* comes from the fact that the *vajra* ("thunderbolt") is the dominant symbol of the Tantric Buddhists. Originally, in Hindu iconography, it was portrayed as the weapon of Indra (also known as Vajrapāṇi), but in Buddhism it came to be associated with the male generative organ. In this sense *vajra* is called *mani*, the "indestructible jewel," which penetrates *padma*, the "lotus flower," and thus the mantra *"om mani padme hūm"* figuratively symbolizes the male penis in the female vulva. This interpretation emphasizes that Tantrism included a highly specialized sexual mysticism teaching complete unity with the deity could be achieved by a meditative process based on coitus reservatus. In simple terms, Tantrism, following Hinduism, held that every man has in him a feminine element, and every woman has a masculine element. The adept, aware of this fact, tried to effect a mystic marriage between his two genders and thus overcome duality and achieve oneness. To them, the hermaphrodite was the closest likeness to human deity. Giuseppe Tucci observed that, through the sexual act, the disciple reproduces the creative moment. But the act was not to be performed to its natural conclusion or orgasm, but rather, through *prāṇayāma* ("Yogic breath control") the semen was to be directed from its downward path upward until it reached the top of the head, hence to vanish into the uncreated source of the Whole.[77] Every Buddha or *bodhisattva* was said to have his female counterpart who was worshipped with him, and from the concept of the female consort, Tantrism went on to imply that nirvana lay in the female organ.[78]

Sexual dualism in the human body resided in two nerve channels that ran along the left and right sides of the spinal cord, named respectively *lalanā* and *rasanā*. *Lalanā*, the female part, represents the female creative energy, mother, ova, the vowel series, and corresponds to the moon; in final sublimation it is the void, the *gnosis* or spiritual truth. *Rasanā*, the male part, is male creative energy, father, semen, the consonant series, and corresponds to the sun. In final sublimation it is compassion and also praxis or practical truth. As long as this dualism exists in man, he remains caught in the chain of rebirths, separated from the deity.

To overcome this dualism, the practitioner must join in imagined or real sexual embrace with a female partner. He must then concentrate on the *bodhi–mind* (*bodhicitta*), which resides in germinal form in the *nirmana-chakra*, the nerve center around his navel. The female energy acquired from the woman stimulates the *bodhicitta* of the man, and it blends with his activated but unshed semen into a new, more powerful essence called *bindu* ("the drop" or "semen"). The *bindu* is built out of the essence of the five elements (earth, water, fire, air, and ether), just as the human embryo is, and in fact, the formation of the *bindu* in the practitioner's body is compared to the normal conception in the uterus. The *bindu* breaks through the separation of *lalanā* and *rasanā*, opening a new sexual nerve channel, *avadhutika*, "the cleansed one."

The *bindu* proceeds upward along this channel to the *dharmachakra,* the nerve center in the heart region, from whence it rises to the center of the throat, until finally, it reaches the "Lotus on top of the head." During its upward course the *bindu* has blended its five elements into one homogenous effulgence, and the male and female elements have also merged, completing the final identification of the practitioner with the deity and with the Void, that is, the state of eternal bliss called *nirvana.*[79]

The Tantric Buddhists claim that the revelation of their teachings did not take place on the earth but on Mount Sumeru or in Akanistha, the highest of Buddhist heavens. Thus, like the Mahāyāna, they shift the place of revelation to a sphere beyond the earth. Tantrists believe that man is sunk in ignorance, although a divine spark, his Buddha-nature, remains within him. For redemption from his prison of ignorance he needs to arouse this divine spark, something he can accomplish only by esoteric concentration and consecration. Much of the imagery is cast in sexual terms, but these can be interpreted in either a literal or esoteric meaning. The decisive stage is the formation of the *bindu,* effectuated through the stimulus received from the woman partner. Some texts imply that this is an image invoked by concentrated meditation, and union is, therefore, only spiritual, but the majority of texts imply that she must be a real woman, stating rather plainly that "Buddha-hood abides in the female organ." Some would imply that this woman should be the initiate's wife, but others imply that she can be any woman he chooses. In a sense, Tantrism advocates an extreme idealism; that is, the external world has no objective basis, since all phenomena are merely illusory appearances created by the mind. If such a view is carried to its logical conclusion, action by itself can be neither moral nor immoral but can be judged only by the effect it produces in the general scheme of life. By implication then, the motive behind the action can be the only criterion, and any action taken that can lead to salvation can be justified. The *bodhisattva* cannot, under such conditions, be judged by the ordinary moral standards of mankind. As soon as the initiate knows the truth; that is, when the world appears to him as a dream without any reality, there is no restriction for him. A stanza in one of the early tantric works states that the initiate should freely immolate animals, utter any number of falsehoods without ceremony, take things that do not belong to him, and even commit adultery.[80]

Sexual intercourse is not just a satisfaction of an instinct but the repetition of the primal copulation of the divine couple, the eternal principle of all things, and a means of ascending the spatial–temporal plane of life. Coitus, in Tantric Buddhism, becomes the achievement of the thought of illumination.[81] Since both sexes bear marks of their unitary existence in the primal androgynous state, they are always striving toward integration outside the bounds of time. In fact, they had become separate only to produce and guarantee the inexhaustible rhythm of cosmic life.[82] On earth the male seeks his counterpart, and the female hers, but both lie hidden within each other. Whenever the male comes into contact with his female counterpart, that is, the aspect of life not lived by the individual and excluded from his conscious attitude, his whole being will be enriched. This enrichment is of the utmost importance for the whole future life. Until this transcendental state has been realized, the relation between male and female, between masculinity and femininity, appears in two different aspects, and although the one cannot exist without the other, this is not always clear to the initiated, because the nature of femaleness is to obscure masculinity, and vice versa. This means the male feels subjectively as a male, and the female as a female, both unable to satisfy fully their desires. Only when an individual establishes a rapport with a member of the opposite sex through extrajection of himself or herself is he or she able to realize his or her true nature; that is, the male realizes his essential femininity and the female her masculinity.[83]

Logically then, it is important for the male to express his femininity and the female her masculinity, since otherwise, neither would be able to understand the specific nature of the opposite sex. Those males whose femininity is not sufficiently developed, or in whom it is repressed, will not be able to understand woman or her specific nature but instead will become more or less intolerant of the feminine. Instead of longing for the receptive, affectionate, and emotionally responsible being, a woman who recognizes her own masculinity, he will despise the feminine in himself by despising the weakness, emotionality, awkwardness, and whimsicality of women. When men concentrate their whole interest on women as sex, on the differences between the male and female, they do so at the expense of and understanding of their own feminine nature.[84] On the other hand, when a man and woman truly unite, when maleness and femaleness meet, both are altered. Each participant takes on himself or herself the qualities of the other, sharing with each other. When the sex act is "only" a consummation of a powerful drive to which the man or woman has succumbed, neither realizes the basic unity of maleness and femaleness but has only caused the conflict between these two forces to subside temporarily. The important thing in sexual experience is to experience basic union, to have the two make one, and then, having achieved this, not to lose it. No lasting experience can ever be achieved by the satiation of a sudden biological urge.[85]

Some people who have kindled the inner heat and raised it to the fontanelle,

Stroke the uvula with the tongue in a sort of coition and confuse
That which fetters with what gives release,
In pride will call themselves yogis.
As higher awareness they teach what they experience
Within. What fetters them they will call liberation.
A glass trinket colored green to them is a (priceless) emerald;
Deluded, they know not a gem from what they think it should be.[86]

There is obvious homosexual connotation in some tantric theory, although little direct evidence supports its widespread existence. Nevertheless, it seems clear that each partner in the sex act must reorient and refashion his personality, recognizing the elements of the opposite sex in himself or herself. There can be a profound personal relationship between a man and a woman, but there can also be an overpowering recognition of the opposite sex within an individual. In tantric cults a man can take on a feminine role in identifying with his mother or some other woman, and since his ego now feels as female, the woman as a love object is obliterated. He assumes the interests of a woman, is effeminate, and throws out his masculinity.[87] On the whole, however, the person who achieves true integration of his maleness and femaleness deepens the awareness of his emotional satisfaction, and those who have found enlightenment will live in the center of existence rather than be precariously situated on the periphery,[88] that is, neither male nor female.

Some scholars would hold that Tantrism enhanced the position of women, although there is little writing that teaches the sexual secrets of attaining nirvana for women. Obviously, Tantrism is primarily aimed at a male audience. Nonetheless, the *Kaulavālie-tantra* stated that

> One should bow to any female, be she a young girl, flushed with youth, or be she old, be she beautiful or ugly, good or wicked. One should never deceive, speak ill of, or do ill to, a woman and one should never strike her. All such acts prevent the attainment of siddhi (i.e., success in religious exercises).[89]

This new emphasis on women led to the introduction of a number of female deities in Buddhism, perhaps some of them originally fertility goddesses in the areas in which it spread. Women also became important as spiritual guides in Tantric Buddhism,[90] and in one of the most interesting cases of sexual transformation, Kuan-yin changes from a male figure to a female one. Whether this transformation was accidental or whether it might have come about because of tantric ideas is little explored. Because enlightenment is conceived as the union of male and female elements, Kuan-yin, the companion of the Buddha, may have come to be visualized in female form. At any rate, Kuan-yin represents an interesting case of scriptural transsexualism within the Buddhist tradition. Most Buddhist scholars believe that the character of Kuan-yin is derived from Avalokitesvara, the chief minister of Amitabha, the Buddha who presided over the Pure Land or Western Paradise. The Pure Land is portrayed as a rich, fertile land, filled with gods and men, lacking the evil modes of existence. Avalokitesvara, the always-compassionate *bodhisattva,* is always ready to go anywhere to lead the faithful to the land of purity and bliss. His name is composed of two different parts, *avalokta,* meaning "seen," and *isvara,* meaning "lord," and can be translated in any of a number of different ways: "the lord who looks down," "the lord who is seen," "the lord of compassionate glances," or "the lord whom one sees." The Tibetan term is *spyan-ras-gzigs*, literally "one who sees with eyes." In Chinese the *bodhisattva* was called Kuan-yin, "one who hears sounds," or Kuan-shih-yin, "one who hears the sounds (prayers) of the world." Later the expression *Kuan-tzu-tsai*, the "onlooking lord," was also used, which is a somewhat more accurate translation. In the *Lotus Sutra* he is given the epithet *Samntamukha*, "He who looks in every direction," and this develops the concept of the merciful character of Kuan-yin. He manifested himself everywhere in the world, saving people from suffering and assuming various forms to carry out his mission.

In the eighth century in parts of China, Kuan-yin, for the first time, is sometimes pictured as a female figure clad in white. By the tenth century this has become the dominant representation. The best explanation seems to come from the tantric belief that all Buddhas and *bodhisattvas* must have female consorts. In Tibetan Buddhism the consort of Avalokitesvara was called White Tārā, in Sanskrit, Pāṇḍarāvasinī, meaning "clad in white," and a literal translation of this in Chinese is Pai-i Kuan-yin. The white-clad Kuan-yin was introduced into China from Tibet and was soon adopted as a symbol by the popular or folk religion of China as Sung-tzu Kuan-yin or Kuan-yin the giver of children. Even before the introduction of the female consort Kuan-yin, the male Kuan-yin had been regarded as the person to pray to if a woman wanted a son. Pāṇḍarāvasinī, in Tantric Buddhism, was assigned to the *mandala* or cosmogram entitled *Garbhakoṣa dhatu,* the "World of the Womb treasury," which undoubtedly was interpreted literally by many, and thus Pāṇḍarāvasinī came to be regarded as a giver of children. At first, Buddhist theology preserved the maleness of Kuan-yin, but popular folk religion increasingly adopted the female. This was eventually accepted by the scholars on the grounds that a *bodhisattva* could assume any form and shape to assist mankind.[91]

Tantric Buddhism declined in China after a few short centuries, although it was briefly revived during the Mongol rule (1280–1367) in its Lamaistic forms. With the decline of the Mongols it again declined in China but managed to maintain its organization and teachings in Nepal and Tibet, which today furnish us most of the clues about what its teachings might once have been. In its later years, portrayals of the sex act in Tibetan Buddhism probably became more symbolic than representative of reality, at least in its Buddhist form.[92] In their Hindu form, such representations continued to have strong sexual connotations, as they do in Nepal.

In sum, the peoples of the Indian subcontinent embraced sex and gave it a mystical connotation, and, though sexual attitudes varied from sect to sect, almost anything in the sexual field received approval from some segment of Hindu society. These ideas, as incorporated in Tantrism and also in Buddhism, spread from India throughout much of the Far East, although one of the lesser controversies in dealing with sexual concepts is whether Tantric Buddhism carried new sexual concepts into China or whether the sex practices associated with Tantrism were indigenous to China. R. H. Van Gulik, who has written the classic works on Chinese sexual practices, held that the concepts of Tantrism were derived from Taoist sexual teachings.[93] In this he had the support of Joseph Needham, who has done the most extensive investigations into ancient Chinese science.[94] The question is not easily settled, for it is not clear how much the Taoist sexual alchemy was based on Indian concepts. Moreover, several investigators of the question, among them Chou Yi-Liang and H. Maspéro, felt that Tantric Buddhist sexual practices never gained any headway in China, because they ran counter to the Confucian ritualistic principles of the separation of the sexes and basic Chinese moral tenets.[95] Part of the difficulty with any definitive answer is that no translations of tantric texts dealing with sexual practices have been found to exist in Chinese, although it is possible that some that escaped destruction after the rise and dominance of Chu Hsi (1120–1200) were later translated into Japanese.[96] Even if the Chinese had a parallel tradition to that expressed in Tantrism, the ideas exported by India strengthened and enforced them. The male seed in India, as also in China, was recognized as sacred, something that should not be lost involuntarily but only when one had acquired the right techniques necessary to preserve virility; then anything was permissible. Women were quite clearly inferior to men and could not, therefore, learn the higher yogic disciplines about sex, but they were also more sexual. While chastity for males, at least of the special holy man, was permitted. virginity for women was viewed with disfavor. In effect, it seems as if the Indian subcontinent turned the ideas of the West almost totally around, and much of what was desirable in the West was undesirable in India and what was undesirable in the West was desirable, or at least tolerated, in India. This view lends added support to the belief that many of our Western ideas about sex have been based on Greek philosophical assumptions rather than on any moral absolutes indigenous to civilized humanity.

NOTES

1. Much of this appears in the introductory preface by Vātsyayāna to his *Kama Sutra,* translated by Richard Burton (reprinted, New York: Dutton, 1962), p. 55.

2. See the introduction to Kalyāṇamalla, *Anaṅga Raṅga,* translated with the introduction and comments by Tridibanth Ray (New York: Citadel Press, 1964). See also S. K. De, *Ancient Indian Erotics* (1938); and Edward Powys Mathers, *Eastern Anthology* (12 vols. in 4). A valuable summary can be found in Benjamin Walker, *The Hindu World* (New York: Praeger Publishers, 1968, 2 vols.), Vol. 1, pp. 517–519.

3. *Rig Veda,* X, 129, the "Hymn of Creation," as translated by Abinash Chandra Bose in *Hymns from the Vedas* (Bombay: Asia Publishing House, 1966), p. 305. Each translator renders the

verses slightly differently. Mulk Raj Anand, *Kama Kala* (Geneva: Nagel Publishers, 1963), p. 12, gives a slightly more erotic translation:

> *Desire, then, at first arose within it,*
> *Desire, which was the earliest seed of spirit.*
> *The bond of Being, in Non-Being sages,*
> *Discovered searchings in their hearts with wisdom.*

4. *Hymns of the Atharva Veda*, VI, 138, translated by Maurice Bloomfield in vol. 42, *The Sacred Books of the East*, F. Max Müller, ed. (reprinted, Delhi: Motilala Banarsidass, 1964), pp. 108–109. Other charms devoted to Kāma can be found on pp. 94–110.

5. *The Laws of Manu*, XI, 172, translated by G. Bühler, in Vol. 25, *The Sacred Books of the East*, p. 466. In essence this refers to bestiality (except with a cow, which involves special problems) and to homosexual activity. The term *unnatural* comes from the translator; this term does not appear in the original. A Sāmtapana Krikkhra is defined in Book XI, 213 (p. 474) as "(Subsisting on) the urine of cows, cowdung, milk, sour milk, clarified butter, and a decoction of Kusa-grass, and fasting during one (day and night)."

6. *Ibid.*, Book XI, 171, p. 465. The penalty is defined in Book XI, 104, as requiring confession, and then the individual is to "extend himself on a heated iron bed, or embrace the red hot image (of a woman)," or as alternative to "cut off his organs," or performing a hard penance for a year, or subsisting on sacrificial food or barley gruel for three months. Apparently, the first penalty is prescribed only for repeated intentional offenses.

7. *Ibid.*, Book XI, 175, p. 466. The twice-born man is the Brāhmin.

8. *Ibid.*, Book VIII, 364–365, p. 317.

9. *Ibid.*, Book VIII, 369–370, p. 318.

10. *Ibid.*, Book IV, 131, p. 150.

11. W. G. Archer, *The Loves of Krishna* (London: George Allen & Unwin, 1957), p. 60.

12. *Ibid.*, p. 118, n. 16.

13. *Ibid.*, P. 73.

14. *Bridhadaranyaka Upanishad*, IV, 3. 21 in the *Principal Upanishads,* introduction by S. Radhakrishana, ed. (London: George Allen & Unwin, 1953), p. 262.

15. This is the translation by the Ceylonese poet George Keyt and printed in Archer, *op. cit.*, p. 78.

16. *Ibid.*, p. 83.

17. *Ibid.*, p. 84.

18. Vātsyāyana, *op. cit.*, I, Chap. 5, pp. 81–84.

19. Walker, *op. cit.*, Vol. 1, pp. 433–437; and Kalyāṇamalla, *op. cit.*, Chap. 2, pp. 55–56.

20. Walker, *op. cit.*, Vol. 2, 618–619.

21. *Ibid.*, Vol., 594–597.

22. Kalyāṇamalla, *op. cit.*, Chap. 10, pp. 243–247.

23. *Ibid.*, Chap. 9, sec. 3, pp. 202–206 for nail marks; and sec. 4, pp. 206–210 for bites. Vātsyāyana, *op. cit.*, I, 4, pp. 104–107 for nail marks; 5, pp. 108–111 for bites.

24. *Ibid.*, II, 7, 116–119; and Kalyāṇamalla, *op. cit.*, Chap. 2, sec. 2, pp. 59–61.

25. *Ibid.*, Chap. 9, sec. 1, pp. 188–193; and Vātsyāyana, op. cit., II, 2, pp. 98–99.

26. *Ibid.*, II, 6, 7, 8, 9, 10, pp. 112–132; and Kalyāṇamalla, *op. cit.*, Chap. 10, secs. 1, 2, 3, 4, 5, pp. 217–243. See also Walker, *op. cit.*, Vol. 1, pp. 334–340.

27. Johann Jakob Meyer, *Sexual Life in Ancient India* (New York: Barnes and Noble, 1953), pp. 376–380. Meyer's work is essentially an analysis of the sexual practices found in the two Indian epics *Rāmāyaṇa* and *Mahābhārata* and includes long extracts from each.

28. *Ibid.*, p. 375.

29. There is a popular retelling of this story in Aubrey Menen, *The Ramayana* (New York: Scribner's, 1954), pp. 103–125.

30. Meyer, *op. cit.*, p. 380, n. 2.

31. *Rig Veda*, VIII, 31, 8–9, in Bose, *op. cit.*, p. 151.

32. *Ibid.*, X, 85, 42, 43, 45, pp. 138–139.

33. *Atharva Veda*, XIV, 2, 71, p. 12.

34. *Chandogya Upanishad*, V, 8. 1–2, in the *Principal Upanishads*, p. 431. Similar verses appear in the *Bridhadaranyaka Upanishad*, VI, 2, 13, VI, 4., 3, pp. 313, 321.

35. *Bridhadaranyaka Upanishad*, II, 7. 23, p. 230.

36. *The Bhagavadgītā*, XIV, translated by Kāshīnath Trimak Telan in Vol. 8, *The Sacred Books of the East*, p. 196.

37. P. Thomas, *Kāma Kalpa or the Hindu Ritual of Love*, (Bombay: D. B. Taraporevala Sons & Company, 1959), pp. 113–114.

38. *Ibid.*, pp. 114–116. See also R. B. Bhandarkar, *Vaiṣṇavism Śaivism and Minor Religious Systems* (Varanasi India: Indological Book House, 1965), pp. 131–140.

39. Walker, *op. cit.*, Vol. 1, pp. 51–54. See also John Woodroffe, *Śakti and Śakta*, 7th ed. (Madras: Ganesh & Company, 1969), pp. 376–412; and David N. Lorenzen, *The Kāpāmukhas* (Berkeley, Calif.: University of California Press, 1972); and Sashi Bhusan Dasgupta, *Obscure Religious Cults*, 2nd ed. (Calcutta: Firma K. L. Mukhopadhay, 1962).

40. Thomas, *op. cit.*, pp. 120–126; and K. R. Kankooij, *Worship of the Goddess according to the Kālikāpuāna* (Leiden, Netherlands: E. J. Brill, 1972); and Walker, *op. cit.*, Vol. 1, pp. 516–517.

41. Thomas, *op. cit.*, pp. 120–126; Walker, *op. cit.*, Vol. 1, p. 221. See also Pandurang Vaman Kane, *History of Dharmāstra* (Poona Bhandarka, India: Oriental Research Institute, 1962), Vol. 6, Part 2, pp. 1089–1090.

42. *Bridhadaranyaka Upanishad*, VI, 4. 1, p. 321.

43. *Ibid.*, VI, 4, p. 321.

44. *Ibid.*, VI, 4. 21, pp. 327–328.

45. Anand, *op. cit.*, p. 38.

46. *Laws of Manu*, V, 88, p. 183.

47. *The Institutes of Vishnu*, v. 5–6, translated by Julius Jolly in Vol. 7, *Sacred Books of the East*, p. 32.

48. *The Laws of Manu*, IV, 41, p. 135.

49. For a brief discussion of some of the customs in different parts of India, see Robert Briffault, *The Mothers* (New York: Macmillan, 1927, 3 vols.), Vol. 2, pp. 376–378.

50. Vātsyāyana, *op. cit.*, Part 2, Chap. 9, pp. 124–126.

51. *Ibid.*, pp. 126–127.

52. Meyer, *op. cit.*, p. 242.

53. Walker, *op. cit.*, Vol. 2, pp. 199–200, 432–433.

54. Meyer, *op. cit.*, p. 242.

55. *Laws of Manu,* XI, 68, p. 444.

56. Pratap Chandar Chunder, *Kauṭilya on Love and Morals* (Calcutta: Jayanti, 1970), p. 128.

57. *Laws of Manu,* II, 180–181, p. 63.

58. *Ibid.,* XI, 121, 123, pp. 454, 455.

59. Meyer, *op. cit.,* pp. 246–257 n.

60. Much of this is based on Vātsyāyana, *op. cit.,* VII, 2, pp. 247–252. The quotation is on p. 248. See also Walker, *op. cit.,* Vol. 2, pp. 154–155.

61. *Bridhadaranyaka Upanishad,* I, 4.5, p. 165.

62. Chunder, *op. cit.,* p. 131.

63. Kanwar Lal, *The Cult of Desire* (New Hyde Park, N. Y.: University Books, 1966), pp. 89–90, and the illustrations. He includes some photographs of the use of animals, notably illustrations 118 and 119 in Temple Ranakpur, and 41–46 at Tirupakesa Temple in Belgavi. Various other forms of sexual congress are also shown. See also Walker, *op. cit.,* Vol. 1, pp. 132–133. Anand, *op. cit.,* in his photographs of Konārak, does not include any animal representations.

64. Walker, *op. cit.,* Vol. 1, pp. 132–133.

65. Thomas, *op. cit.,* pp. 53–54.

66. Walker, *op. cit.,* Vol. 2, p. 343.

67. Meyer, *op. cit.,* p. 470.

68. Chunder, *op. cit.,* p. 129.

69. Bhandarkar, *op. cit.,* pp. 86–87.

70. *Ibid.,* pp. 146–147; Walker, *op. cit.,* Vol. 1, p. 44.

71. Walker, *op. cit.,* Vol. 2, pp. 282–284.

72. Walker, *op. cit.,* Vol. 1, pp. 44–45.

73. *The Patimokka,* translated by T. W. Rhys Davids and Hermann Oldenberg in *The Vinaya Texts* of the Sacred Books of the East Series, F. Max Müller ed. (reprinted, Delhi India: Motilala Banarsidass, 1966), pp. 3–4, 7, 16–17, 32. See also *The Mahavagga,* I, 52, 60, 61, 78, translated by T. W. Rhys Davids and Hermann Oldenberg in the *Vinaya Texts,* pp. 205–215, 235.

74. *The Kullavagga,* I, 32, 2, V, I, IV, 7, i, X, 10, i, translated by T. W. Rhys Davids and Hermann Oldenberg in the *Vinaya Texts,* pp. 378–379, 68, 77.

75. Mircea Eliade, *Yoga: Immortality and Freedom,* translated by Willard R. Task, Bollingen Series 56 (New York: Pantheon Books, 1958), pp. 200–273. This is the chapter on "Yoga and Tantrism."

76. Giuseppe Tucci, *The Theory and Practice of the Mandala,* translated by Alan Houghton Brodrick (London: Rider & Company, 1969).

77. Giuseppe Tucci, *Tibetan Painted Scrolls* (Rome: Libreria dell Stato, 1949, 3 vols.), Vol. 1, p. 242.

78. Giuseppi Tucci, *Rati Līla: An Interpretation of the Tantric Imagery of the Temples of Nepal,* translated into English by James Hogarth (Geneva: Nagel Publishers, 1966), passim.

79. R. H. Van Gulik, *Sexual Life in Ancient China* (Leiden, Netherlands: E. J. Brill, 1961), pp. 341–342.

80. B. Bhattacharyya, *Introduction to Guhyasamāja,* viii, quoted in Chou Yi-Liang, "Tantrism in China," *Harvard Journal of Asiatic Studies,* (1944–1945), pp. 241–332, appendix E, p. 313. Yi-Liang says this was not true of Chinese esoteric Buddhism, but final judgment must be reserved.

81. Tucci, *Rati Līla,* p. 73.

82. H. V. Guenther, *Yuganaddha: The Tantric View of Life,* 2nd ed. (Varanasi, India: The Chokhambra Sanskrit Series Studies, 1969), Vol. 3, pp. 9–28.

83. *Ibid.,* pp. 47–59.

84. *Ibid.,* pp. 50–51.

85. *Ibid.,* pp. 56–57.

86. *The Royal Song of Saraha,* translated and annotated by Herbert V. Guenther (Seattle: University of Washington Press, 1969), par. 24–25. Saraha was translated into Tibetan sometime in the eleventh century, and his poetry is known from the Tibetan version.

87. Guenther, *Yuganaddha,* pp. 58–59.

88. *Ibid.,* pp. 65–66.

89. Quoted by Van Gulik, *op. cit.,* p. 346.

90. Eliade, *op. cit.,* p. 261, n. 204.

91. Kenneth K. S. Ch'en, *Buddhism in China* (Princeton, N.J.: Princeton University Press, 1964).

92. This at least is the claim of Herbert V. Guenther, *Tibetan Buddhism without Mystification* (Leiden, Netherlands: E. J. Brill, 1966), p. 60. See also Guenther, *Treasures on the Tibetan Middle Way* (Leiden; Netherlands: E. J. Brill, 1969), p. 66. Many of the works were translated by Sir John Woodroof under the name of A. Avalon. The difficulty with his editions and translations is that he was the subject of a rather violent and unscholarly criticism, and this encouraged him to adopt the role of an apologist and elevate the philosophical aspects of the system while glossing over its more dubious tracts. Other translators have also been active. D. L. Snellgrove translated the *Hevajra Tantra* (London: Oxford University Press, 1939, 2 vols.). Snellgrove has also written on some of the sexual aspects of Tantrism. For his bibliography, see his own introduction, pp. 42–43 to the *Hevajra Tantra.* See also the works of D. N. Bose, such as *Tantras: Their Philosophy and Occult Secrets,* 3rd ed. (Calcutta: Oriental Publishing Company, 1956); and also the popular account by L. Austine Waddell, *Tibetan Buddhism* (reprinted, New York: Dover Books, 1972). The book was originally published in 1895, a period when it was difficult to deal publicly and openly with sex. For Nepal, see the numerous works by Tucci. There is also a good bibliography in Eliade, *op. cit.,*

93. Van Gulik, *op. cit.,* appendix 1 pp. 339–359.

94. Joseph Needham, *Science and Civilisation in China,* (Cambridge, England: University Press, 1956), Vol. 2, p. 248.

95. Chou Yi-Liang, *op. cit.,* pp. 241–332; and Henri Maspéro, "Les Procédés de 'nourir le principe vital' dans la religion taöiste ancienne, *Journal Asiatique,* CCXXVIII (1937), pp. 177–252, 353–430. See also H. Maspéro, *Le Taoisme,* (Paris: Musée Guimet, 1950).

96. Van Gulik, *op. cit.,* appendix 1, pp. 348–359.

11

SEXUAL THEORY AND
ATTITUDES IN ANCIENT CHINA

The ancient Chinese viewed man and society somewhat differently than did either the peoples of the West or of the Indian subcontinent. Like the Greeks, the Chinese saw the world in dualistic terms, but they did not concentrate on the conflict between the spiritual and the material; instead they looked to the inherent unity of the opposing forces. Similarly, though there were beliefs similar to Tantrism, these ideas received a unique Chinese formulation that now makes it difficult for scholars to determine whether they were derived from India or were uniquely Chinese. Sex was an integral part of the Chinese explanation of the universe. Man was a microcosmos functioning in the same ways as the macrocosmos, the sexual union of male and female a repetition of the interaction of heaven and earth. The *I Ching,* oldest of the Chinese classics, dating from the Chou dynasty (1150–249 B.C.), though revised during the Han dynasty (206 B.C.–220 A.D.), stated:

> There is an intermingling of the general influence of heaven and earth, and transformation in its various forms abundantly proceeds. There is an intercommunication of seeds between male and female, and transformation in its living types proceeds.[1]

As in Western thought, heaven was regarded as masculine and the earth feminine, but the simile was carried further. Clouds were the vaginal secretions or the lining of the womb necessary for allowing the heavenly sperm, the rain, into the earth womb, and from the union of these two forces all life came.

Various terms were used originally to describe these dual cosmic forces, but by the sixth century B.C., the words *yin* and *yang* had come to dominate. *Yang* is heaven, *yin* is earth; *yang* is the sun, *yin* is the moon; *yang* is male, *yin* is female. The two forces come together by intercourse, the principle of universal life. In the *I Ching* the hexagram symbolizing sexual union is a combination of the triagram *k'an* ("water," "clouds," or "woman") on top and the triagram *li* ("fire," "light," or "man") on the bottom.

The hexagram indicates that everything is in its proper place with the strong lines in the strong places and the weak lines in the weak places, stressing the combination of perfect harmony of man and woman complementing each other.[2]

Sexual union of man and woman is like the intermingling of heaven and earth and is essential to achieve harmony as well as a happy and healthy sex life. The operation of the two opposing forces produces universal phenomena and determines human conduct. Though male and female are dominated by different essences, within the human body there is both *yin* and *yang,* the *yin* essence more important in women, the *yang* more important in men. The body's surface is *yang,* the interior *yin; yang* is the back part, *yin* the front. *Yin* is in the liver, heart, spleen, lungs, and kidneys, and *yang* is in the gallbladder, stomach, large intestine, small intestine, and the "warmer," a term difficult to define but interpreted by some modern scholars to refer to the lymphatic system.[3]

The diseases of the winter and spring are localized in the *yin* area, those of summer and fall in the *yang.* The pulse is controlled by both *yin* and *yang,* although *yin* wants to turn inside and *yang* seeks to thrust to the outside. The aura of the *yang* nourishes the mind and simultaneously influences the muscles. If it does not succeed in opening and closing the pores properly, coldness sets in, swelling occurs, ulcers penetrate into the flesh, the blood vessels are weakened, and the patient is full of anxiety and fears. If the aura in the blood vessels is not brought into harmony with the condition of the flesh, ulcers and tumors result, perspiration is inhibited, the body begins to waste, and the "hollow points" (the terms used in acupuncture) close up. Eventually, the patient dies from this overaccumulation. The solution is to relieve the compression.

Conversely, if the *yin* essence becomes too strong, the patient perspires incessantly and appears nervous and apprehensive. In time, if nothing is done, the patient becomes rebellious and dies of overloading. Those who do not achieve a balance between *yin* and *yang* in their own bodies must die; only when the *yin* and *yang* aura are sound and sane, living in peaceful interaction, can man's body and mind be in proper order and life go on.[1] Sex is one of the major ways to regulate the body.

At birth the individual is filled with the principle of primordial *yang* and *yin*, although the *yang* content is comparable to the sun at its winter solstice. As the body matures, the *yang* increases until it reaches a peak as the sun does at the summer solstice, after which it begins to wane. The *yin* essence, on the other hand, continues to increase as the *yang* begins to decline unless positive steps are taken. Death is caused by the imbalance of *yin* and *yang*, which means that man's breath, spirit, and seminal essence are dissipated. To the Chinese, death is not a separation of the spirit from the body, as in Western thought, but rather, a separation of the *yang* and *yin* parts of man. If man could imitate the sun through its waxing and waning and hold on to the life-giving principle of the *yang*, then the process from life to death could be reversed. Instead of the *yang's* being outdistanced by the *yin*, the balance could be restored or maintained. The secret of long life was thus to try to retain as much *yang* as possible so that the pores would open and close properly; the key to this was sexual intercourse. Techniques for doing this were called "the method of nourishing the life by means of the yin and the yang (*yin yang yang sêng chih tao*)." The basic aim was to conserve as much of the seminal essence (*ching*) and the divine element (*shen*) by causing the *ching* to return (*huan ching*).

Chinese folk medicine taught that the male body operates on an eight-year cycle, the female on a 7-year one. It was believed that, at the age of eight, a boy's kidney aura grows strong, his hair becomes thick and long, and his first teeth fall out. At 2 times 8 his kidney aura is fully developed and he secretes semen. The more semen secreted within the body, the more the young man desires to free himself of some of it, the result being a desire to beget children. At 3 times 8 the kidney aura balances out, the man reaches his full height, and his muscle and bones are most powerful. At 4 times 8 he remains in splendid health with his flesh firm and full. At 5 times 8 his kidney aura begins to decline, his hair to fall out, and his teeth to decay. By 6 times 8 his masculine vigor slackens, his face wrinkles, and his hair turns grey at the temples. At 7 times 8 his liver aura is deteriorating, his muscles lose their agility, and his semen emanation falls off. By 8 times 8 he has lost his teeth and hair, and his decline is well advanced.

A girl's kidney aura grows strong at age 7 when her baby teeth fall out and her hair grows long. At 14, or twice 7, she has her menarche, when circulation starts in the *Jen* vessel and her *Ch'ung* vessel has grown strong. By the time she is 3 times 7, her kidney aura has become sturdy and she is fully grown. At 4 times 7 her muscles and bones are firm, her hair at its full length, and her body at its blossoming best. Her pulse begins to ebb at 5 times 7; then her face loses its moisture and her hair begins to fall; at 6 times 7 the pulses of all three yang regions in the upper body wane, her face begins to wrinkle, and her hair turns gray. Finally, by 7 times 7, her Jen vessel has run dry, the Ch'ung vessel begins to harden, menstruation is sparse, the blood ceases to circulate, and she can no longer bear children.[5]

Just when these physiological concepts first appeared in Chinese thought is debatable, but if the speculations of the French sinologist Marcel Granet are correct, some of these stages were symbolized in preliterate China by dances and games of young men and women. Some of the songs associated with the dances and ritual assemblies that took place in the spring and autumn have survived and are regarded as among the most ancient literary texts preserved in China.[6] Gradually, if Granet's view is valid, these folk beliefs were given metaphysical backing by the religious and philosophical leaders of ancient China, both Taoist and Confucianist. Sexual intercourse was an important part of the thought, serving two essential purposes, procreation and the strengthening of vitality.

The conception of children, particularly of male children, was believed to constitute not only a necessary part of the order of the universe but also a sacred duty to one's ancestors. In fact, the well-being of the dead in the Hereafter could be assured only by regular sacrifices made by their descendants here on earth. Intercourse also strengthened the male's vitality through absorption of the woman's yin essence, of which she had an abundant supply, and if a man knew the correct techniques, he could salvage some, if not all, his yang essence by forcing it to the brain, where it would open his pores and increase his health and well-being. Women also derived physical benefit from intercourse because it stirred up their latent yin nature, and if a woman knew the correct techniques, she might also draw up some yang essence from the male. The intellectual belief behind this was a part of the Taoist physiology.

Taoist writers, unlike the tantric ones, held that the seminal essence was located in the lower part of the male abdomen, the same place where menstrual blood (yin essence) accumulated in the female body. The purpose of the Taoist sexual techniques was to increase the amount of life-giving seminal essence (ching) by sexual stimulus, while at the same time avoiding possible loss. If the yang force in man was continually fed by the yin force from women, not only would it lead to health and longevity but also the resulting intensity of his maleness would ensure that, when emission did take place, the resulting child would be male. It was essential, therefore, that the woman reach orgasm in intercourse so that the man could receive her yin essence; the more yin essence he himself received without giving out his precious male substance, the greater his strength would grow. This could be done through coitus reservatus, keeping the penis in the female vagina but avoiding orgasm. Taoists also taught another method of preserving the male semen for those unable to practice coitus reservatus; it was called the *huan ching pu nao,* literally, "making the *ching* [semen] return to nourish the brain." At the moment of ejaculation, pressure was exerted on the urethra between the scrotum and anus, and this diverted the seminal secretion into the bladder, where it would later be voided with the excreted urine. The Taoists did not understand modern physiology, and since by observation the semen was no longer there, they held that by this method and positive thinking the seminal essence could be made to ascend and rejuvenate or revivify the upper parts of the body.[7]

To explain the secrets of intercourse there were a number of manuals, collectively called the *fang chung,* literally "inside the bedchamber" or *fang-chung-shu,* the "art of the bedchamber." The earliest listing of such works occurs in the Han dynasty, but the only reference to their existence that has survived in Chinese is the brief explanatory note:

> The Art of the Bedchamber constitutes the climax of human emotions, it encompasses the Supreme Way (Tao). Therefore, the Saint Kings of antiquity regulated man's outer pleasures in order to restrain his inner passions and made detailed rules for sexual intercourse. An old record says: "The ancients created sexual pleasure thereby to regulate all human affairs." If one regulates his sexual pleasure he will feel at peace and attain a high age. If, on the other hand, one abandons himself to its pleasure, disregarding the rules set forth in the above mentioned treatises one will fall ill and harm one's very life."[8]

All bedchamber books composed during the Sui dynasty (590–618 A.D.) have also disappeared, except for fragments mostly preserved in Japanese medical works from the tenth century onward. We know most about them from these Japanese versions. The most valuable is that made by Tamba Yasuyori, a Chinese physician living in Japan in the late tenth century. Tamba compiled a voluminous medical collection known as *The Essence of the Medical Prescriptions (Ishimpo)* in some 30 books, the oldest extant Japanese work on medicine. Its value is enhanced by its being an extremely valuable repository of ancient Chinese sources, many surviving only through redundant quotations in the *Ishimpo.* One of the books, the 28th, consists of extracts relating to the art of the bedchamber.[9]

In 1902 a Chinese scholar, Yeh Teh-hui, realizing the antiquity of the sources, published them as part of a compendium of rare Chinese sources under the title *Shuan mei ching an ts'ung shu ("The Double Plum-Tree Collection").* From the Japanese sources Yeh reconstructed some five handbooks on sex, four mentioned in a Sui bibliography, plus the *Tung-hsüan-tzu* or the "*Ars amatoria of Master Tung-hsüan.*" Van Gulik, the pioneer investigator in the field, identified Tung-hsüan as a seventh-century scholar and physician, although others have since argued that he was a Taoist writer, Chang Ting, who used the appellation *Tung-hsüan* for his work on the bedroom arts. One brief seventh-century portion of the sexual manuals was also preserved in the Chinese—*Yang-seng yen ming* (*"Delaying Life by Nourishing Body"*), a treatise on Taoism.[10]

In spite of the lack of any primary source from the Han period, most scholars feel that the Japanese versions represent a continuing Chinese tradition dating from that time and that they indicate the basic sexual philosophy of the learned classes in China. It has been postulated that perhaps the origin of such treatises was an attempt to instruct the upper-class males on how to deal with the numerous women in their polygamous households, a very real problem. Coitus reservatus in such situations was perhaps essential, the secrets of the method being passed on through the manuals. Tung-hsüan wrote:

> Of all things that make man prosper none can be compared to sexual intercourse. It is modeled after Heaven and takes its pattern by Earth, it regulates Yin and rules Yang. Those who understand its significance can nurture their nature and prolong their years; those who miss its true meaning will harm themselves and die before their time.[11]

Learning the art of love not only brought pleasure to the participants but also served as an act of piety, for heaven itself made love, overlying the earth, as the male lay upon the female, warming her with his heat and making her fruitful with his fluid. Likewise, the male above and the female below was part of the cosmic orientation in lovemaking, although the Chinese recognized that different positions were possible and acceptable; nothing was unnatural.

Some 30 positions were described in the *Ishimpo,* many named after animals, used as symbols because of the ways they moved or flew or swam on the earth, in the sky, or in the water. At least one position, the last one described and known as the Dog of Early Autumn, in which male and female connect rear to rear, seems to be a physical impossibility. This raises the question of how far the Chinese really followed the various postures. Three of the 30 positions include a third party, indicating the polygamous nature of Chinese royalty and aristocracy and the prevalence and availability of servants. In one instance, a woman uses two men, but mostly the manuals are written from a male point of view. The position known as the Winding, or in other translations as the Shifting Turning Dragon, requires the woman to lie

> down on her back, bending both legs. The man kneels within the woman's thighs and pushes both her legs forward with his left hand, causing them to go past her breasts. He takes the jade stalk (penis) with his right hand and inserts it into the jade gate.[12]

In the posture known as the Galloping Steed, the woman lies down, the man squats "with his left hand supporting the woman's neck and his right hand lifting up the woman's leg, he inserts his jade stalk into her womb."[13] In the Paired Dance of the Female Phoenixes:

> A man and (two) women, one lying on her back and one lying on her stomach. The one on her back raises her legs, and the one on her stomach rides on top. Their two vaginas face one another. The man sits cross-legged, displaying his jade thing, and attacks (the vaginas) above and below.[14]

Regardless of the positions he attempts, the male was always to try to bring the female to orgasm, and he should try to hold off his own. To do this, Tung-hsüan wrote, a man

> closes his eyes and concentrates his thoughts, he presses his tongue against the roof of his mouth, bends his back and stretches his neck. He opens his nostrils wide and squares his shoulders, closes his mouth and sucks in his breath. Then (he will not ejaculate and) the semen will ascend inwards on its own account. A man can completely regulate his ejaculations. When having intercourse with women he should only emit semen two or three times in ten.[15]

The leading character in the Chinese sex manual is the Yellow Emperor, Huang-ti, the mythological character believed to have taught man his various earthly skills. There are several woman participants with such names as Woman Plain, the Woman Selective, and the Woman Profound who are called in as arbiters on sexual matters. They were the women immortals who had reversed the process prescribed for males and had coitus with innumerable virgin boys until they reached the realm beyond old age and death. Men were particularly warned against such women. When the Yellow Emperor asked the Plain Woman why his life was deteriorating and out of harmony, she answered:

> The reason for the decline of men is only that they all abuse the ways of female–male element intercourse. Now woman's superiority to man (in this respect) is like water's extinguishing fire. If you understand this and carry it out, you will be like the cauldrons and the tripods, which harmonizes well the five flavors and thereby achieves a broth of meat and vegetables. Those who know well the ways of the female and male elements achieve the five joys, while those who are ignorant of them shorten their lives. What pleasures and joys to be gotten! Can you fail to be cautious?[16]

The Woman Profound taught that sexual intercourse was important because

> Between Heaven and Earth, movement must (accord with) the female and male elements. The male element gets the female one and and is converted; the female element gets the male one and is moved. The female element and the male element

must operate in mutuality. Therefore, if the male (penis) feels, firm and strong, and the female (vagina) moves, open and extended, two life forces exchange emissions and flowing liquids penetrate mutuality.[17]

Though a man could build up his *yang* essence through intercourse with one women, he could strengthen it even more through intercourse with a number of women.

> Those who practice the ways of sex and take in the life-force in order to cultivate longevity cannot do this through one woman (alone). If one gets three, nine, or eleven (women), there is much benefit and good, He elects that his semen liquid revert to the Upper Vast Stream (of the brain cavity). His oily skin is glossy, his body light, his eyes clear, and his life-force strong and flourishing. He can subdue all (feminine) adversaries. Old men are as young in years as they were at twenty, and their vigor is increased a hundredfold.[18]

To carry out the implications of such teachings, the upper-class Chinese developed a system whereby a male could satisfy his principal wives, a number of secondary wives, and a variety of concubines without destroying his *yang* essence. Each time a man had intercourse he was to try to absorb as much as possible of the woman's *yin* principle without giving up his own *yang*. This required that he remain within the woman's vagina while she achieved orgasm and then withdraw before ejaculation. This practice was called drinking at the "fountain of jade," and males were advised to drink frequently and to take long draughts at the jade fountain. After satisfying five or six concubines in this way without losing any of his male force, but in fact increasing his store of *yin* in the process, a man might then perform the pious duty of impregnating the wife from whom he desired a child.

> If a man performs the act once without emitting sperm he will give vigour to his vital inflow. If he performs it twice, his sight and hearing will become sharper. Three times, and all ailments will disappear. Four times, and his soul will find peace. Five times and his circulation will improve . . . (if ten times then he is) like unto the immortals.[19]

In a class-structured society such as China there was also a distinction between the rulers and the ruled in the art of intercourse. Though the life activity of all was governed by the life force *ch'i*, corresponding to the waning and waxing of the universe, those who adapted their life and thought to this order would live the longest and happiest, and those who deviated from it would expose themselves to grief and to untimely death. Living according to the nature of the cosmic forces resulted in the accumulation of a great amount of *ch'i* and an increase in *tê*, a sort of magical power or virtue. Some people, such as members of the ruling class, were born with greater amounts of *tê* than others because their ancestors had accumulated this and passed it on to them. They could preserve it by regular sacrifice to their ancestors and by observing the rules of intercourse. Inevitably, the king, as the most powerful individual, had the greatest amount of tê, and if he wanted to preserve its strength, he had to observe a set ritual with his wives, whose numbers were to correspond to magical theory. There was to be 1 queen or first wife, 3 consorts, 9 wives of the second rank, 27 of the third rank, and 81 concubines. These numbers had special significance because odd numbers stood for the positive force of nature, male, and male potency, and even numbers stood for the negative, female, and female fertility. Thus three stood for strong male potency, three times three for superabundant potency, and multiplying the result by three and then by three again resulted in truly royal potential. Special court women known as the *nü-shih* regulated and supervised the sexual relations of the king and his wives. The king had to engage in sex with each of his wives or concubines on the correct calendar days with the frequency established by the rites for each rank. As a general rule, he was to have sex with women of the lower ranks more frequently and before women of higher rank. The queen was to have intercourse with the king only once a month, at the time when his potency was at its height, a potency he had carefully nourished by not having orgasms with women of the lower rank.[20]

The ancient Chinese realized that women had fertility cycles, but their understanding of these was not particularly accurate, and this kind of misconception forces us to question just how far they followed the practices in the sex manuals. If they had followed them religiously, the possibility of conception would have been extremely low.

> If you have intercourse with a woman before menstruation has ended, you'll make her sick. If she has a child, it will have a red mark affixed to its face like a hand, or it may be on its body. Furthermore, a male child will get a white macular sickness (when he gets older).[21]

> When a woman's monthly (menstrual) event ends, she should cleanse and purify herself. If she has intercourse on the third and fifth days, the child she begets, if a boy, will be intelligent, talented, wise, long-lived and loftily eminent. If a girl, she will be pure and virtuous and shall wed a man of eminence.[22]

Because the sexual ritual was so involved, there were, of course, all kinds of taboos. A child was not to be conceived at midnight or at the winter or summer solstice; during an eclipse, a rainbow, thunder or lightning, or a crescent or full moon; or when the sun was at its height or when the parents were drunk or gorged with food.[23] The reward for observing all the taboos was long life.

Master Jung-ch'êng was adept at nurturing and controlling (his physical functions). He absorbed (new semen) from the Mysterious vagina. The main point of this art is to prevent the Spirit of the Vale (i.e., potency) from drying by preserving one's vital essence and by nurturing his vital force (ch'i). Then one's grey hair will turn black again and new teeth will replace those that have fallen out. This art of having sexual intercourse consists of restraining oneself so as not to ejaculate, thus making the semen return to strengthen the brain.[24]

Most sexual prescriptions were male oriented, emphasizing the necessity of the male's capturing some of the woman's *yin* essence. In theory, however, women could also achieve immortality, although there was an attempt to deny them the secrets of sexual practice. One woman, the Queen Mother of the West, was an immortal equal to the Yellow Emperor, who had ascended into heaven through union with more than a thousand women. She had duplicated his feat by taking the semen of innumerable youths and males who were ignorant of the art of sexual intercourse. Women could also strengthen their blood by gaining semen of young men without having orgasm themselves. Thus the woman who wanted to gain health and longevity had to turn the sexual tables on the male by getting him agitated while keeping herself under control. In effect, the Chinese taught there was a kind of war of the sexes that the woman failed to win only because most of them did not fully know the secrets. From fear that women would learn the secret ways the manuals as a whole kept silent about female techniques, but the masculine ones are carefully and minutely described. There are only a few suggestive hints to women:

In having intercourse with a man, (the woman) should tranquilize her heart and settle her intent. If, for example, the male is not yet excited, you must wait till he becomes agitated. Therefore, control your feelings somewhat so as to respond in concert with him. In any event, you must not shake and dance about, causing your female fluid to be exhausted first. If it is exhausted first, since your body is emptied, you therefore incur the illness of wind and cold. Or, hearing that the male has had intercourse with other women, you should repress and beware of the following, which are all (harmful manifestations): jealousy and grievous trouble; arousal of your female element life-force; rage, whether sitting or rising; emission of the fluid when you are alone; and becoming haggard and suddenly aging.[25]

In general, the sexual theories of *yin* and *yang* were most closely associated with Taoism, the religion founded by the sixth-century B.C. prophet Lao Tzu. Competing with and supplementing Taoism as a movement was Confucianism, based on the teachings of the fifth-century Confucius or, literally, K'ung Fu Tzû. Confucius, believing he had a mission to bring about peace and good government by reaffirming the virtues of the ancient sages, did this by training young men for political office, his students becoming disciples bound to him by affection, loyalty, and devotion. In the main, he accepted and approved the traditional religious teachings of his time, although we do not know specifically whether he accepted or rejected the sexual practices associated with Taoism. We do know that he thought women were troublesome.

> Of all people, girls and servants are the most difficult to behave to. If you are familiar with them, they lose their humility. If you maintain a reserve towards them, they are discontented.[26]

Later, the Confucianist school held that women were absolutely, unconditionally inferior to men. As to ethical values Confucius ascribed great importance to sincerity, loyalty to principles, and the cultivation of human warmheartedness and good character and taught that inward goodness found its fullest expression in all human relationships through cultivation of propriety and decorum and observance of the proper rites and rituals. True nobility was not inherited, but all men could become noble. The influence of Confucius gradually grew until, in the Han dynasty, it came to be dominant among the government circles, and since that time he has generally been recognized as China's greatest sage, although there have been periods when he has been denigrated.

One of the earliest indications, if not the earliest, of Confucianist attitudes toward the sexual alchemy appears in the *Po-hu-t'ung*, a record of discussions on the classics held in 79 A.D. under imperial auspices. The section devoted to marriage included the following paragraph:

> Why does a man after having reached his sixtieth year abstain from sexual intercourse? Because then he needs to nurture his growing weakness, and abstention then means that he treasures his life. . . . When a man has reached the age of seventy, this is the time of great debility. He can eat his fill only on meat, and if he sleeps alone he cannot be warm. Therefore at that age he again starts having sexual intercourse.[27]

A few Confucianist writers were more hostile to the Taoist sexual alchemy. The philosopher Wang Ch'ung (27–97 A.D.), for example, called the art of the bedchamber a perverse doctrine that not only harmed the body but also infringed on the nature of man and woman.[28] In general, however, though the Confucianists were upset at some of the more extreme claims of the Taoist sexual alchemy, they subscribed to the theory. This is evident even in the writings of Lady Pan Chao, the literate, intelligent woman who completed the history of the Han dynasty that her brother Pan Ku had left unfinished at his death. Lady Pan Chao was no feminist, and in fact, used her learning and education to justify the subordinate role of a woman in her most famous work the *Nü-chieh* or *"Woman's Precepts"* written at the beginning of the second century. Nevertheless, her sexual beliefs were influenced by Taoism. For her, the way of the husband and wife

> represents the harmonious blending of ying and yang, it establishes man's communication with the spirits, it reaffirms the vast significance of Heaven and Earth, and the great order of human relationships. It is therefore that the Book of Rites honours the relation of man and woman, and that the Book of Odes celebrates the sexual union of man and wife. . . . Strength is the virtue of yang, yielding constitutes the use of yin. Man is honoured for his power, woman is praised for her weakness.[29]

A similar view is expressed by Ko Hung, usually known by his pseudonym Pao-p'u-tzu. His chief work, the *Nei p'ien,* written about 320 A.D., is essentially Taoist, although his *Wai-p'ien,* its rival, is essentially Confucianist. His two works might be taken to represent the union of the two trains of thought. He wrote:

> The taking of medicines may be the first requirement for enjoying Fullness of Life, but the concomitant practice of breath circulation greatly enhances speedy attainment of the goal. Even if medicines are not attainable and only breath circulation is practiced, a few hundred years will be attained provided the scheme is carried out fully, but one must also know the art of sexual intercourse to achieve such extra years. If ignorance of the sexual art causes frequent losses of sperm to occur it will be difficult to have sufficient energy to circulate the breaths.[30]

Later on he added:

> The best of sexual recipes can cure the lesser illnesses, and those of a lower quality can prevent us from becoming empty; but that is all. There are very natural limits to what such recipes can accomplish. . . . It is inadmissible that man should sit and bring illness and anxieties upon himself by not engaging in sexual intercourse. But then again, if he wishes to indulge his lusts and cannot moderate his dispersals, he hacks away at his very life. Those knowing how to operate the sexual recipes can check ejaculation, thereby repairing the brain. . . . They can cause a man, even in old age, to have an excellent complexion, and terminate the full number of his allotted years.[31]

Though somewhat skeptical of the claim that the Yellow Emperor mounted to heaven because he had a harem of 1200, Ko Hung nevertheless believed that the emperor's mastery of the art of sexual intercourse was an important factor in his longevity.[32] On this subject, he added, at least ten other authors had written.

> The essential here lies solely in reverting the sperm to repair the brain. God's Men have transmitted this method orally without any writing. Though one were to take

all the famous medicines, without a full knowledge of this essential it would be impossible to attain Fullness of Life. Man may not, however, give up sexual intercourse entirely, for otherwise he would contract melancholia through inactivity, and die prematurely through the many illnesses resulting from depression and celibacy. On the other hand, overindulgence diminishes one's life, and it is only by harmonizing the two extremes that damage will be avoided. Unless the oral directions are available, not one man in ten thousand will fail to kill himself by attempting to undertake this art. . . . Personally, I had instructions along these lines from my teacher Cheng Yin, and I record them here as information for future believers in the divine process. It is not personal opinion that I am chatting. I must admit that I have not yet personally gotten all the directions involved in the art. Sometimes, narrow-minded processors try to observe solely the recipes regarding sexual intercourse in order to control the gods and genii without utilizing the great medicines of gold and cinnabar. This is the height of folly![33]

As the influence of Confucianism grew, female chastity became more and more emphasized as a prerequisite for orderly family life and the undisturbed continuation of the lineage. To ensure such chastity, the Confucianists advocated segregation of the sexes, carrying their belief through to its most absurd consequences. For example, a husband and wife were not to hang their garments on the same clothesrack. Still, the sexual ethic of the past continued to hold sway.

The amalgamation of the Taoist sexual ethic with Confucianism was comparatively short-lived. It reached its height in the writings of the Sung philosopher and statesman Chu Hsi (1130–1200), who combined Taoist alchemy with some of the concepts of Buddhism to form what is sometimes called neo-Confucianism. He stressed the inferiority of women and the strict separation of sexes and forbade all manifestations of heterosexual love outside the intimacy of the wedded couch.[34] The sex handbooks still had their readers, but increasingly, the Confucianists, essentially puritanical in their public conduct, condemned them, although they had nothing against sex itself. Typical of the condemnations was that of Wang Mou (1151–1213), who devoted a long discussion to the sexual habits of the ruler, condemning them because they did not meet Confucianist standards:

The princes and noblemen of to-day keep large numbers of consorts and concubines, they use them as a kind of medicine, in order to obtain the "true essence" and in order to strengthen their vital power. But this will not prove advantageous to them, on the contrary it will soon ruin their health. And even a superior man who understood (the Confucianist) Reason like (the famous T'ang Confucianist) Han Yü could not avoid succumbing to these teachings so difficult it is to control one's carnal desires. Thus countless members of the gentry harm their bodies and lose their lives through "those with the powdered faces and painted eyebrows," but they still persist in these practices and will not see reason.[35]

The eventual result of such condemnations was, however, to make the sexual teachings of Taoism more of a cult secret, and gradually the manuals themselves disappeared in China, only to survive in Japan.

Also influencing changing attitudes was the emergence of Buddhism, which in its Māhayāna form, entered China at the beginning of the Christian era. Because Taoist scholars assisted as translators of the Buddhist teachings, Taoist terms were used and the similarities between Buddhism and Taoism stressed. As Buddhism spread, this link with Taoism was increased as it became more adopted to the Chinese culture, incorporating both Confucian and Taoistic doctrines. Buddhism reached its height in the ninth century, when its influence was broken by the persecutions of the Emperor Wu-tsung, and neo-Confucianism emerged. Though Buddhism in its Indian form had given a prominent place to women, this aspect of Buddhism was considerably modified in translation, but there were always Buddhist nunneries that gave women a chance, within limits, to control their own destinies. Perhaps for this reason, nuns were regarded with disfavor in Chinese literature.

Although Buddhism was generally what might be called a sex-positive religion, it did regard certain sexual practices as sins, some more sinful than others, as appears in the description of the various hells, a concept Chinese Buddhism derived from Indian. The hells served as punishment for crimes in this world, although, unlike the Hell of the West, some of the Buddhist hells were hot, others cold. The first Chinese text to describe these hells dates from the sixth century, the *Cheng-fa nien-ch'u ching,* and it was soon followed by numerous others. In Chinese Buddhist thought a human being was held responsible for his own actions, at least in most instances, his every action, good or bad, known and recorded. If a person did not suffer punishment for his sins in this world, he most assuredly would in hell.[36]

Though the rank listing of the hells varied from period to period, as did the number, it is still possible to gain a rough estimate of sexual sins—most of them fairly minor—from the punishments prescribed. Incest with a mother was, however, so serious it required punishment in nine different hells, as well as the loss of wives, children, and grandchildren, who normally would have performed the ancestral sacrifices. Incest with a sister was regarded as much less serious. Wolfram Eberhard attempted a rough approximation of some of the sins based on a scale from one to nine. On such a scale unnatural ways of intercourse would be classified as a three, as would adultery, although if the adulterer talked about it so that the woman was caught and punished, his sins would fall into category five. Seduction or rape of women by monks, or of nuns by men, was classified in the eighth category, and the worst sexual sin was a sexual act with a Buddhist saint. Homosexuality was classified as a third-level sin, as was transvestism, which was regarded as a ritual impurity. In the earlier listings sexual sins comprise a larger part of the discussion than in the later ones.[37] Eberhard also analyzed Chinese short stories to find what was regarded as sinful conduct. He found that about a quarter of the sins listed fell into the sexual category; the rest fell into sins of violence, property, or religion. He felt that the Chinese authors ascribed fewer offenses of violence and more sexual sins to middle-class people, and fewer religious and more property sins to the lower classes.[38]

Chinese prudishness and sexual segregation apparently increased during the Mongol conquest that led to the Yüan dynasty (1279–1368). Perhaps in an effort to keep their women from falling prey to the conquerors—a more difficult task than it might seem on the surface, since Mongol soldiers were billeted among the people—sex segregation was increasingly emphasized. This tended to lead to greater and greater prudery in open discussions about sex, as is evident in the *Kung-kuo-ko* or *"Tables of Merits and Demerits,"* which began to appear at this time. Van Gulik translated two such tables, the *Shih-chieh-kung-kuo-lu* or *"Tables of Merits and Demerits Regarding the Ten Precepts"* and *Ching-shih-kung-kuo-ko* or *"Table of Merits and Demerits to Warn the World."* The latter is shorter but has more severe punishments. Producing an erotic book, song, or picture was regarded as deserving of 1000 demerits, and even joking about women deserved 50 demerits. Not keeping men and women separate in the household resulted in a comparatively minor three demerits, but having an affair with a prostitute or catamite caused 50 demerits. In the *Shih-chieh* sexual sins were spelled out in detail. Touching the hand of a woman in the house while handing things to her caused one demerit, but if it was done with lustful intent, it deserved 10 demerits. Entering the women's quarters without warning led to a demerit, and exciting lust in a woman cost 20. Showing nakedness while easing nature, even in the middle of the night, led to one demerit, and nocturnal emissions deserved five demerits.[39]

As Confucianism became more prominent, Taoism came to be centered in monasteries and nunneries patterned on Buddhist models. Increasingly, it was characterized by withdrawal from the world, asceticism, meditation, and religious study. From its earliest promotion of heterosexuality and intercourse, it came to favor the bachelor or unmarried state. Only in the country districts did a married secular clergy continue to exist. Perhaps because of this the Taoists, at the end of the T'ang dynasty (618–906), turned to training the adept to practice sexual discipline in the solitude of the "meditation chamber." Instead of focusing on the two sexes, they attended to the *yin* and *yang* element present in each person. According to this alchemical theory, the human body has two poles: the heart, corresponding to fire and the *yang*; and the loins or sexual parts, coinciding with water and the *yin*. The heart is not, however, merely *yang* but the summit of *yang*, and once something has reached the summit, it begins to decline, the same being true of the *yin* in the loins, which, after descending as far as it can, begins to climb. As the *yin* grows, the *yang* diminishes, and in what can only be called a reversal of form, the ascetic Taoists equated the heart with a young girl, since while it is *yang,* it is becoming *yin;* the loins are the dwelling place of the divine male child because, while they are in the midst of the *yin,* they are becoming *yang.* The union on which salvation and immortality depend consists in marrying the girl of the heart with the young man in the loins. The Taoist ascetics imagined that the area an inch and a half below the navel contained the seat of the Go-Between, without whose aid no marriage could take place. This area was termed the *Good Wife Yellow,* and like any go-between in a marriage situation, she had the task of bringing lovers together. The boy of the loins had to rise to the residence of the girl of the heart, the Red Residence or nuptial chamber. From this union an embryonic immortal would result, who, as he grew, would gradually replace the mortal frame.[40] In this form the full secrets of the Taoist sexual alchemy were kept alive in an increasingly prudish China,[41] although never in their greatest extremes of prudishness did the Chinese deny the joys of sex between husband and wife, still symbolizing the heavenly union.[42]

Reinforcing the mystical sexual alchemy of Taoism was the tantric concept associated with Lamaism, a Vajrayānic form of Buddhism that found its way into Mongolia from Tibet and thence into China. Sexual union was a prominent aspect both in actuality and in the imagery of tantric speculation. In Lamaist iconography, most deities are represented in sexual union with their female counterparts, a position known as the "Progenitors." Tantric adepts were supposed to attain salvation by practicing this divine pairing with female partners. Whereas some Chinese writers have argued that Tantrism was a foreign import that "perverted" sexual practices among married couples, others have claimed it was indigenously Chinese.[43]

Though the art of the bedchamber remained an important part of Chinese culture, sex was increasingly considered a private affair by the average Chinese. This prominence given to privacy resulted, not from a belief in the shamefulness of sex, but from the belief, even by the nonmystical, that sex was a sacred act, and, like other sacred acts, it should not be engaged in or talked about in front of those not members of the family or household. As Joseph Needham said:

> No sharp line of distinction can be drawn between arts specific to the Taoists and the general techniques of the lay bedchamber, which they, as well as others, taught and transmitted.[44]

From the surviving materials, short stories, pictures, poems, and novels, the Chinese evidently enjoyed sex. As indicated, the handbooks go into great detail about various positions, to suggest variety, perhaps a necessity if the male was to observe the restrictions imposed in reaching the orgasm. Foreplay was encouraged. Oral–genital contacts were permitted, although penilingus was never to result in a complete emission; any slight loss of semen and secretions incurred during such action was deemed to be compensated by the *yin* essence the man would obtain from the woman's saliva. Cunnilingus was approved because it prepared the woman for the act and simultaneously procured *yin* essence for the man. It is viewed with particular favor in Taoist-oriented texts. Anal intercourse with a wife was also permitted, for the man could obtain *yin* essence here as well as from the vagina or from the mouth. Intercourse with prostitutes was accepted; some writers stated that such intercourse did not imply a man's wanton spending of his semen, because prostitutes, through their frequent intercourse with a variety of men, had developed such a strong and abundant *yin* essence that the patron received back more than he gave. Such theories about prostitutes were abandoned as Chinese medical science, particularly after 1500, began to connect certain diseases with the sexual act. Voluntary abstention from sexual intercourse, and celibacy of either men or women were viewed with contempt and profound suspicion; perhaps for this reason Buddhist nuns and monks were the object of widespread contempt.[45] Both practices were also equated with homosexuality.

In general, it seems obvious that the Chinese would not encourage masturbation for males, if only because this would lead to a loss of vital essence. Masturbation was, in fact, condoned only in special circumstances, when males, particularly young ones at the height of their *yang,* were deprived of female company and when the devitalized semen (*pai ching*) was believed to be capable of blocking his system unless it was removed. Manipulation of the genitals without orgasm was, however, encouraged, being part of the practice of the adept. Involuntary emissions were likewise viewed with concern, for they would diminish a man's vital force unless compensated by acquiring an equivalent amount of *yin* essence from women. Moreover, involuntary emissions, since they represented such an unconscious loss of vital spirits, were popularly believed to be caused by fox spirits. According to Chinese mythology, these spirits were mysterious creatures who changed themselves from foxes into beautiful young women to bewitch men and steal their vital essence through having intercourse with them in their dreams. The Christian concept of witchcraft included a similar belief in their explanation of incubi and succubi.

If male masturbation was disapproved, female masturbation was more or less ignored if not encouraged. Since the *yin* supply of women (as evidenced by their menstrual periods) was almost unlimited, they would not suffer any permanent damage by masturbating. Probably the general indifference to female masturbation was a necessary adjunct to the existence of polygamy and concubinage in the more important households, and it is the literature written for this group that has survived. The imperial gynoecium in some periods contained at least a thousand women who had to look for sexual pleasures to themselves or

to other women or remain unsatisfied, a condition alien to Chinese thought. Women were, however, cautioned against excessive use of artificial devices because these might damage the lining of the womb.
womb.

> Women who insert powder into their vaginas or make a male stalk out of ivory and use it always injure their livers and quickly age and die.[46]

There was great concern that women who did not have intercourse with men or somehow satisfy themselves through masturbation might engage in intercourse with devils.

> Since this method of intercourse is superior to that of humans, when it is practiced for a long time the human partner becomes bewitched, avoids mention of it, conceals it, and is unwilling to report it (to others). Considering this beautiful, the person therefore dies without anyone ever having discovered it. If you get this illness, the way to cure it is to make a woman have intercourse with the male, who does not emit his semen.[47]

Nevertheless, there were a number of devices on the market to assist women. A description of one dates from the fourteenth century Ming writer T'ao Tsung-i, who described a plant for making *olisbos* and other instruments:

> In the pastures of the Tartars wild horses often copulate with dragons. Drops of the semen will fall down and enter the earth, and after some time put forth shoots resembling bamboo-shoots, of pointed shape and covered with small scales close together like the teeth of a comb, and with a network of veins, making them similar to the male member. They are called *so-yang* . . . lewd country-women insert these things into their vaginas; as soon as they meet the yin-essence they will suddenly swell and grow longer.[48]

There were *mien-ling,* "exertion bells" or "Burma bells," which were placed inside the vagina, either for masturbating or for heightening the pleasures of intercourse. These small, brass-like vases in the form of a conical bell were said to have the droppings of a mythical bird, the P'êng of Burma, enclosed within them; these droppings expanded or moved under heat, something like the larva in the Mexican jumping bean. The result was a soft pinging in the bell that the woman could sense after it was inserted.[49] Women also used small bags stuffed with dried mushrooms that swelled if they were soaked in water or put in the vagina for a period. There were also special instruments made of wood or ivory, with silk bands attached to the middle that two women could use together or one could use alone. Sometimes instruments were attached to the heel of one leg and moved in and out of the vagina. There are several surviving Chinese illustrations of just such masturbatory techniques.[50]

Inevitably, the same factors leading to toleration of masturbation among women also led to the acceptance of female homosexuality. Either the Chinese recognized that throwing a number of women together and denying them access to male companions could only lead to homosexuality, or, as in much of the Western world, the things women did were not considered important enough for men to be concerned. In fact, since the sources are generally silent about women's sex life, at least as compared to men's there is a tendency to read back into an earlier China from practices reported in later times. Though it can be debated whether Ming attitudes after 1500 actually reflect earlier practices, they do represent the same kinds of tolerant, bemused attitude toward female sexual practices that seem to be part of the Chinese psyche. Much of our information comes from the Chinese novels of the Ming period in which there was a deliberate attempt to write in an erotic manner.

The novel *Ko-lien-hua-ying* (*"Flower Shadows on a Window Blind"*) portrays two girlhood friends, Coral Tree and Scented Jewel, teaching each other how to kiss lip to lip and tongue to tongue. After a while they begin to explore more, and after hearing murmuring of lovemaking in a nearby room, they go to bed with each other, imitating the love play about which they have heard.[51] The whole thing is pictured as a more or less natural phenomenon. The classic of lesbianism is the *Lien-siang-pan* (*"Love for the Perfumed Companion"*) by Li Yü, a seventeenth-century pornographic novelist best known for his *Jou-pu-t'uan* or *"Prayer Cushion of the Flesh."* In the *Perfumed Companion*, Shih Yün-chien meets a beautiful young girl of 15, Yün-hua, while walking in the garden of a Buddhist convent. The two fall in love, and for a time Shih Yün-chien prays to be reborn as a man so that they can be married. Failing this miracle, Madame Shih decides to dress as a man and marries Yün-hua in this costume. The two are soon separated and Madam Shih marries. To be with Yün-hua, Madame Shih decides to have her husband take her loved one as his concubine. She tells Yün-hua

> Why don't you marry my husband? Between us, there would be no difference between wife and concubine, and we should be always together. We could all three live in delightful intimacy.

After many tribulations, Madame Shih's scheme succeeds, to the delight both of her husband and the two women.[52] A variant version appears in a short story "The Tale of a Fugitive Life" by Shen-fu, but the ending is not quite so happy. In Shen-fu's story, Yün, the wife of a scholar, falls in love with a young woman, Han-yüan, who is destined to become a prostitute. She encourages her husband to take the girl as a concubine, and as a sign of her indissoluble union with the girl, exchanges a jade bracelet. Her husband, not oblivious to what is taking place, tries to oblige his wife but lacks the necessary money to buy the girl. As a result, the girl is given to a rich and important person. Yün is so heartbroken at this turn of events that she soon wastes away and dies.[53]

In several of the Chinese descriptions of sexual intercourse two women are involved, and often a woman is a voyeur of the act itself. But these incidents probably cannot be regarded as female homosexuality but rather as efforts to give greater pleasure to the male, about whom and for whom the manuals were written.[54] Some fear of lesbianism might be evident in the writings of T'ao Tsung-i in the Yuan dynasty, who cautioned his readers against allowing any outside women visitors to the women's quarters because they might stir up trouble. He divided his troublesome visitors into nine groups, the three "aunts" and the six "crones."

> The three 'aunts' are the Buddhist nun, the Taoist nun, and the female fortune-teller. The six 'crones' are the procuress, the female go-between, the sorceress, the female thief, the female quack, and midwife. These are indeed like the three punishments and the six harmful cosmic influences. Few are the households which, having admitted one of them, will not be ravaged by fornication and robbery. The men who can guard against those, keeping them away as if they were snakes and scorpions, those men shall come near the method for keeping their household clean.[55]

In Chinese thinking the celibate Buddhist and Taoist nuns were always suspected of lesbianism, if not prostitution, and the passage just quoted may indicate real fear of contamination if such women were allowed free reign in the women's quarters. Still, it seems safe to conclude that the Chinese tolerated female homosexuality.

The same was true of male homosexuality, about which we have slightly more documentary evidence. Probably a factor in this toleration was the Confucianists' strict emphasis on sex segregation as well as the educational system's encouragement of close master–student relations. Chinese philosophers, as early as the sixth century B.C., had stressed the importance of the separation of the sexes and the necessity of observing the proper ceremonial behavior (li) between men and women.[56] Mo Ti, the fifth-century B.C. founder of the Mo'ist school of philosophy and the central figure in a number of anecdotes in the Mo Tzu, a book compiled by his disciples to preserve his teachings, went so far as to claim that a major reason people built houses was to separate men from women.[57]

Sex segregation was established fairly early in Chinese history, and so was the heirarchical position of each individual in the family, a fact tending to discourage intimacy. Chinese philosophers held that the ideal society should be based on five different kinds of human relationships: noble and humble, superior and inferior, elder and younger, near and remote, and finally, equality. Four of the relationships involve superordination and subordination, and in a family the relationship of superior to inferior, such as between a husband and a wife or a father and his son, was most important.[58] Marcel Granet has argued that the discipline inherent in such societal organization

> was a significant feature at first in the relations between husbands and wives, and between father and son. It appears to have become the rule for all family relations. Dominated by ideas of respect, domestic morality seems in the end to have become mixed up with a ceremonial of family life. . . . Civil morality, having gravitated toward an ideal of strained politeness, seems to tend solely to organizing among men, a regulated system of relations, in which the actions befitting each age are fixed by edict, as are also those for each sex, each social condition and each actual situation.[59]

The ultimate perhaps was sex segregation of clothing and a real lack of intimacy.

In such a situation, male friendships outside the family were particularly important, and the Chinese classics extol such relationships. Further intimacy, at least among the educated classes, was encouraged by the educational system, which, after Confucius, was primarily a private affair between scholar and student. In fact, before Confucius, the only literary reference to any schools are those established to teach archery.[60] Confucius said the purpose of education was to bring about better government and tried to make his students into gentlemen. Most of those he taught lived with him in his home, and though his method of instruction was fairly informal, later teachers established a much more rigid struggle. A disciple of Mo Ti, for example, complained that his teacher compelled him to wear short jackets and eat coarse vegetable soup.[61]

Confucianism was spread through the master–student relationships, and gradually it dominated much of the educational system. Such control is usually set as taking place during the reign of the Han dynasty ruler Wu Ti (141–87 B.C.), who collected the leading scholars of his empire into an advisory council. Tung Chung-shu acted as spokesman for the council:

> I beg your majesty to establish an imperial academy and bring great scholars to teach the people. Give examinations in order to select the best, and you will be able to secure learned men. The governor of a province and the magistrate are the teachers of their people, and they should encourage the spread of education . . .[62]

Increasingly, examination became the key to social mobility, and by the sixth century the scholars were uniting with the nobility to reunify China. These political parvenus, so to speak, owed their official position to their academic success, and inevitably, they developed a strong group solidarity. Advancement depended on being allowed access to schools, most of them private and expensive. The bright boy who attracted the attention of a sponsor could move ahead, but since he owed so much to a sponsor or to a teacher, he became fair game for those with homosexual desires who wanted to take advantage of him. Not until 1369, during the Ming dynasty, were schools established widely in every prefecture. Even during the Ming period, when advancement depended on examination, it was possible to advance somewhat faster with an important patron.[63] Perhaps because of this, homosexuality was tolerated, if not encouraged, much as it was among the English upper class in the so called public school. Most officials were probably not homosexually inclined, but there was a toleration of those who were.

Whether the Chinese system was as conductive to homosexuality as Greece of the Golden Age is perhaps debatable. Numerous recorded incidents of homosexuality are recorded, but on the other hand, there are records of intimate friendships between men in which there is no hint or thought of homosexuality. We know that some powerful ministers kept young boys as catamites (*lüan-tung*), and various rulers had favorites (*pi*), both male and female, who obtained favor by playing up to their masters and encouraging them in their vices. Some *pi* obviously served homosexual purposes, and one of them, Lung-yang Chün, made his name a euphemism for catamite.[64] According to the *Chan-Kuo ts'e*, a third-century B.C. compilation, Lung-yang Chün served the ruler of Wei as an intimate companion—so intimate, in fact, that the story of their adventures is translated as "The Catamite and the Fish." The King of Wei and Lung-yang were fishing together, and though they were very successful, Lung-yang began to weep. The king, distressed at his friend's grief, sought to find the trouble. After some hesitation, Lung-yang said that he wept because of the vast number of fish in the sea. When the king still looked puzzled, Lung-yang Chün went on to explain that when he caught his first fish he was delighted,

> But then I got one even bigger, so I wanted to throw the first one back. Then I thought: today, despite my bad auspices and offensive behavior I have the privilege of straightening and brushing your majesty's mat. My rank is that of a ruler. When I am in court men step aside for me. On the road men clear the way for me. But within the four seas, oh, how many beauties there must be! When they hear that the likes of me has gained the favor of the king, they will pick up their skirts and race to you. Then I will be the object of feelings such as I had toward the first fish I caught—I will be thrown back. How might I not weep at such thoughts?[65]

The king sought to assure his favorite, even going so far as to state he would post an order throughout his kingdom that no one was to speak of other beauties in his presence. The point of the story in this section is not the fears of Lung-yang but the general acceptance of such a relationship.

Chinese historians also recorded the existence of male homosexuality without any overt hostility or condemnation. Ssu-ma Ch'ien, who wrote in the second century B.C., devoted a section of his history of the Han dynasty to biographies of male favorites of the emperor.

> Those who served the ruler and succeeded in delighting his ears and eyes, those who caught their lord's fancy and won his favor and intimacy, did so not only through the power of lust and love; each had certain abilities.[66]

He listed the male favorites of some four emperors, Kao-tsu (206–195 B.C.), Hui-ti (194–188 B.C.), Wen-ti (179–157 B.C.), and Wu-ti (140–87 B.C.). The favorite of Kao-tsu was a young boy named Chi, and that of Hui-ti was named Hung.

> Neither Chi nor Hung had any particular talent or ability; both won prominence simply by their looks and graces. Day and night they were by the ruler's side, and all the high ministers were obliged to apply to them when they wished to speak to the emperor. As a result all the palace attendants at the court of the Emperor Hui took to wearing caps with gaudy feathers and sashes of seashells and to painting their faces, transforming themselves into a veritable hosts of Chis and Hungs.[67]

The most notorious of the emperors was Wen-Ti, whose intimate companions included Teng T'ung and the eunuchs Chao T'an and Pei-kung Po-tzu. Wen-ti had selected Teng as his companion from among the boatmen in the Imperial Palace after a dream in which a boatman had helped him reach the abode of the Immortals. When Wen-ti died, his successors moved against Teng and brought him to trial on the charge of smuggling, and he died in poverty. The favorite companion of the Emperor Wu-ti was his boyhood companion Han Yen, later executed for harem intrigue. Other favorites included an actor, Li Yen-nien, who had been castrated because of criminal activity before he moved into the imperial household.[68] The last emperor of the Former Han dynasty, Ai-ti (6 B.C.–2 A.D.), who lived after the time Ssu-ma Ch'ien wrote, had a number of boy lovers, the best known of whom was Tung Hsien, who figured in the so-called "cut sleeves" incident. According to the story, the emperor was sharing his bed with Tung, who fell asleep lying across the emperor's sleeve. When the emperor was forced to arise to attend to his imperial duties, he took his sword and cut off his sleeve rather than disturb the sleep of his favorite. Inevitably, the term *tuan-hsui*, "cut sleeve," became a euphemism for homosexuality in Chinese literature.[69]

Male favorites did not cease to exist with the breakup of the Han dynasty. One of the more incompetent of the later rulers was the boy emperor Liu Tzu-yen (449–465 A.D.), who ruled for only one year. He is remembered for his indiscriminate sexual orgies with both sexes as well as for his cruelty. He was put to death by his father's minister.[70] Several literary figures are grouped in pairs, such as Hsi K'ang (223–262 A.D.) and Yüan Chi (210–263 A.D.), Li Po (701–762) and Mêng Hao-jan (698–740), and Po Chü-i (772–846) and Yüan Chên (779–831), although in the majority of such groups the attachments were probably intellectual and not sexual. This was not the case with Hsi K'ang and Yüan Chi, who are generally regarded as homosexuals.[71]

During the Northern Sung Dynasty (960–1127), so many men were making a living as male prostitutes that a law was promulgated prescribing a hundred blows with the bamboo and a heavy fine for those engaging in prostitution. Such activity continued during the Southern Sung dynasty (1127–1279), when male prostitutes walked the streets dressed and made up like women and apparently even had their own guild.[72] This was probably the high point of overt homosexuality, after which, like most Chinese sexual practices, it became much more discreet. Men were still, however, accustomed to express their friendship in much more intimate terms than is customary in the West, and even as late as the nineteenth century, Western observers remarked on the Chinese tolerance:

> Public opinion remains completely indifferent to this type of distraction, paying no attention to it at all, except to say that, since it seems to please the dominant partner and the other is willing, no harm is done.[73]

Certain areas in China seem to be equated with homosexuality more than others, perhaps because of poverty or other social factors. One area that acquired a reputation for homosexuality was Fukien. This has been explained as resulting from the shipping industry there and the superstition among the residents and the sailors that, if women were taken aboard the ships, the ships would be cursed and overturned. In this area, older homosexuals were called *ch'i hsung* and the younger *ch'i ti*.

> When a *ch'i hsung* went to the home of a *ch'i ti*, he was welcomed by the whole family as if he were a bridegroom. If the *ch'i ti* were later to marry (a woman), the *ch'i hsung* would pay all the expenses. There was even a special word, *chi*, in Fukien that was used when a *ch'i ti* had illicit relations with another man.[74]

Only in a few of the cases dealing with either male or female homosexuality has the individual been exclusively homosexual. *Bisexual* might well be a better descriptive term. The Chinese insistence on the necessity for children encouraged all but the most dedicated homosexual to become married. For women there was actually no other alternative, except for Buddhist nuns. In some groups in society, however, marriage was discouraged or even impossible. Included in the first group would be the actors, who, like prostitutes, were outside the Confucian scheme of social relationships.[75]

Several factors in the Chinese theater probably encouraged homosexuality. During the beginning of the theater, actors as well as stage properties were owned by the rich or else the actors were vagabonds. Not until the T'ang Dynasty (618–907 A.D.) did the emperors begin to patronize actors and the theater. Later, formal schools were established, but descendants of actors to the third generation were regarded as pariahs.[76] As in much of the West during the ancient and medieval period, women were forbidden to appear on the stage, and so men played the female as well as male roles. Though at first there was undoubtedly an interchanging of roles, a hierarchy eventually developed in the Chinese theater. Those who regularly played the female roles, the *tan* actors, were regarded as subordinate to those who played the more important male roles, the *sheng* actors. Homosexuality was regarded as more or less a norm among the actors, just as it is among the female impersonators in the West today.[77] Some writers have even gone so far as to claim that anal intercourse was a norm for actors, since custom demanded that a master deflower his young disciple. The pseudonymous Wu Shan Shen has written that there were rigid procedures for preparing the student for anal intercourse. According to his account, pupils in the actors' classes sat on benches, the least experienced at the bottom of the class. Round wooden pegs, growing progressively larger as the student approached the master, lay on the benches, and as the pupil progressed, he inserted bigger and bigger pegs into his anus until he was ready to graduate and be initiated.[78] The account sounds apocryphal, although we do know that actors were rather brutally treated by their superiors on the stage and as a group were illiterate and subject to superstition. On the stage, the play often stressed the Confucian ethics, particularly the bond between two males, where the loyalty of pledged friendship seemingly offered great scope for the actor. We know such relationships were encouraged among the actors themselves, the long training the actors underwent to play the female roles tending to encourage them to adopt the feminine role offstage as well as on. Several actors became notorious for their homosexual affairs, particularly those who played *tan* roles. Among them was Chêng Ling-t'ao, a favorite of the fourth-century King of Chao, Shih Chi-lung. The last emperor of the Ch'en dynasty, Ch'ên Hou-chu (582–589), had a number of favored *tan* actors. The Sui emperor Yang Ti (605–612) gave a great part of his time to theatricals and actors and built a palace, to Lo King or "Palace of Joy" where he kept and supported several hundred actors. The T'ang emperor Ming Huang established a somewhat more refined atmosphere, the Pear Garden Palace, and also a park, *I Ch'un Yüan* or "Garden of Everlasting Springtime," an allusion to the beautiful youths who inhabited the park. Many of the rich officials during the Sung and Liao dynasties also bought good-looking boys and kept them in their establishment to play and sing.[79]

Actors also play a part in some of the homosexual novels in later Chinese history, and this might reflect earlier reality as well. One of the most famous homosexual novels is the *P'in-hua-pao-chien* (*"Precious Mirror for Gazing at Flowers"*), written in the middle of the nineteenth century by Ch'en Sen-shou. All the characters in the novel are men, most of them actors, and the relationships reflect the life of actors and their friends at the time.[80] In effect, it seems that acting and male homosexuality had a long association in China.

Other novels also included incidents of male homosexuality, including the most famous of Chinese novels, the *Dream of the Red Chamber,* by Tsao Hsueh-chin, although here it is more or less casual and not the main part of the story.[81] There are also homosexual incidents in the seventeenth century, for example, *Jou pu t'uan,* by Li Yu, whose lesbian novel has already been discussed. In the *Jou pu t'uan,* the hero Wei Yang-chêng became so ashamed of the inadequacy of his penis that he arranged to have a graft, to satisfy any female lover. Before he underwent the operation, he believed he had to relieve his pent-up desires, and since no women were available, he called on his male servants for assistance.

> He called in the younger servant and gave him to understand that he was to come into bed and play the role of a 'she'. . . . He knew how to take his master's hints and incline to his desires. He had learned to raise his 'rear audience chamber' just like a woman and to wriggle his belly muscles in such a way as to facilitate his esteemed visitor's entrance. He was also able to emit cries of pleasure and moans of bliss, which though simulated, were just like those of a woman.[82]

Obviously, if the novel has any validity, the widespread existence of servants totally dependent on their masters for favor could also lead to homosexual activity. Within the Chinese alchemical beliefs, two male partners who shared orgasms were in no danger of losing their *yang* essence, because the result was an exchange and not a loss.

In addition, homosexuality was probably tolerated, if not encouraged, by the power and influence of eunuchs. Those eunuchs who had lost both their testicles and their penis were believed still to have erotic feelings in their anus as well as in their mouths and also to have a highly developed sense of touch, which, if true, might make it pleasurable to engage in homosexual activity. It was also probably safer than attempts at heterosexual intercourse for many of them, particularly in the imperial palace, where they had access to the harem. Eunuchs date from fairly early in Chinese history. In the *Shih ching* or *"Book of Odes,"* dating from the fifth or sixth century B.C., there is a lament about women's and eunuchs' meddling in affairs of state.

> Those from whom come no lessons, no instruction, Are women and eunuchs.[83]

Undoubtedly, the hostility to the eunuchs, linked to hostility to women of the palace, came from the fact that they were in frequent and intimate contact with the emperor and were thus able to capitalize on his weaknesses or to play to his strengths.

Eunuchs fulfilled a valuable function in China, much as they did in the West—in the Byzantine empire, for example. As incomplete men they were technically unable to succeed to the Chinese throne and could thus be trusted as loyal servants. Whether this had been planned or developed accidentally is now difficult to ascertain. It probably developed accidentally, since at one time castration was a punishment, in the early listings regarded as the second most severe of the five punishments: branding on the forehead, cutting off the nose, cutting off the feet, castration, and execution. Castration remained as a punishment on the statute books until the sixth century A.D., when the five punishments were changed to beating with bamboo, beating with a cudgel, short banishment, long banishment, and execution.[84] Prisoners of war were also occasionally castrated, particularly if they came from important families. During the reign of the Emperor Wu in the former Han dynasty, a young prince of Lou Lan was taken hostage and made into a eunuch. Later, when his father died and his return was requested, it was refused because of his eunuchoid status.

Originally, the castration process must have been fairly brutal. During the T'ang dynasty a certain An Lu Shan (about 755), a rebel against the Emperor Hsuan Tsung, became angered with a hard-to-manage houseboy, Li Chu Erh, and in a fit of anger cut off his genitals with his sword. The boy bled profusely and lay in a half-dead condition before he was finally treated with hot ashes. He eventually recovered to become an inseparable companion of An Lu Shan.[85] The mortality rate with such methods must have been very great, although the Chinese gradually perfected a fairly safe method. We have several nineteenth-century Western descriptions of the operation, when both the penis and scrotum were removed with one cut. The eunuch makers at that time were specialists whose profession was hereditary, which might indicate they had perfected the operation long before. The operation was particularly expensive, and those who wanted to become an eunuch usually had to have a patron to help them pay for it. In preparation for the operation the patient's abdomen and upper thighs were tightly bound with white strings or bandages. The scrotum and penis were then washed three times in hot pepper water while the patient was seated in a semireclining position on a heated, couchlike affair known in Chinese as the k'ang. Before the operation, the eunuch maker (tao tzu chiang) approached the patient and asked him whether he would regret the operation or not. If the man showed the slightest uncertainty, the operation was not to be performed. If he gave his consent, his waist and legs were held firmly by assistants, and then, with one sweep of a razor-sharp sickle-shaped knife, the penis and scrotum were cut off. The urethra was plugged and blocked off, and the wound was covered by paper soaked in cold water, after which the patient was bound tightly. The assistants then had to walk the patient around the room for 2 or 3 hours before allowing him to lie down. He was forbidden to drink water for 3 days after the operation and, usually, toward the end of the period, the patient suffered almost as much from thirst as from the aftereffect of the operation. After 3 days, the urethra plug was removed, and if urine gushed out, the operation was regarded as a success. If no urine appeared, the prognosis was that the man would soon die an agonizing death. G. Carter Stent, a nineteenth-century observer, reported that over several years, he saw only one patient who had died, a 30-year-old man.[86] One aftereffect was the tendency to lack bladder control with the result that eunuchs often suffered from incontinence. The eunuch was supposed to preserve his genitals in a container, and immediately after amputation the penis and testicles went through a kind of pickling process before being returned to him for safe keeping. As he advanced up the ranks of the palace hierarchy or the civil service, he had to show them. They were also buried with him at death so that he would be restored to masculinity in the next world.

Stent felt there were three reasons males might become eunuchs: compulsion, poverty, and choice. Compulsion usually came from the family, who were also usually poor. Since a eunuch was a highly regarded individual, ambitious but poor parents might well risk one of their male children to the operation in expectation of considerable favor. Indicative of the homosexual overtones in the eunuch world, boys who became eunuchs were favored over those who became eunuchs at a later stage in life, since, it is said, their boyish features and high, clear voices made them particularly desirable sexual mates. Whether this was the case might actually be debatable, since in a sense, eunuchs would represent to some extent the transsexuals of today, and such individuals usually find themselves ostracized from the homosexual world. In a bisexual China, however, they might prove an interesting diversion. Why anyone would choose to become a eunuch is difficult to explain, but some of these might well fit into the modern diagnosis of transsexuality. Stent said that some of them he knew had been married and had had a family before undergoing the surgery. He said they chose to become eunuchs to avoid the tongue-lashings of their spouses—a rather simplistic answer—but the self-selection process that probably always existed would clearly fit in today's definition of transsexualism.

It might well be that the reason eunuchs have received such a hostile press among the intellectual class in China is that they were rivals for power to both the aristocracy and the Confucian literati, the opinion makers. The palace eunuchs usually came, moreover, from the lower classes, and they owed their influential position to their intimate day-to-day relationships with the emperor, a relationship that made them subject to the whims of those they served. If they remained close confidants or trusted servants, they could count on obtaining government posts and titles and making a fortune for themselves as well as their families. Many of them were able and dedicated servants, and several ended as virtual dictators, particularly during the fifteenth and sixteenth centuries. The most powerful of the eunuch dictators were Wang Chen (1440s), Wang Chih (1470s), Liu Chin (early 1500s), and Wei Chung-hsien (1620s). They remained an important force until November 5, 1924, when Hsuan T'ung Ti, the last emperor of the Ch'ing dynasty, was driven out of the Tzu Chin Palace, where he had been allowed to live with many of his eunuchs after the 1912 revolution. Some estimates place the number of eunuchs in China in 1912 as high 100,000.

Eunuchs were also known in other fields. The second-century B.C. Emperor Wu had the father of Chinese history, Ssu-ma Ch'ien, castrated. Only after his punishment, when he was palace secretary, did he begin his history.[87] The inventor of paper was a Chinese eunuch. In fact, the list of distinguished eunuchs is quite long. There are also occasional statements about men turning into women or women into men, and these are classified under the headings of "green misfortunes" (*ching hsiang*) and were thought to indicate the possibilities of serious harm to the rulers in whose dominions they occurred. Needham makes the point that the Chinese attitude to such changes, whether in animals of in humans, was quite different from Western attitudes.

> The Chinese were not so presumptuous as to suppose that they knew the laws laid down by God for non-human things so well that they could proceed to indict an animal at law for transgressing them. On the contrary, the Chinese reaction would undoubtedly have been to treat these rare and frightening phenomena as *chien kao* (reprimands from Heaven) . . ."[88]

Sexual intercourse with animals is not reported in Chinese annals or literature. Prince Chien, in the former Han dynasty (221 B.C.–24 A.D.), is said to have forced women to have intercourse with dogs, but he is regarded as a sadistic degenerate by Van Gulik.[89] The T'ang scholar Li Yin mentions a woman's having intercourse with a dog and giving birth to a monster,[90] but repetitions of this story are all that Van Gulik could find. It might well have been that bestiality, more a sexual act of rural dwellers, did not come to the attention of the Chinese literati, and they did not find it particularly interesting to discuss. At any rate, it never received the attention it did in the West.

Transvestism was institutionalized on the stage, and until fairly late in Chinese history it was always possible for an amateur, particularly the patron, to take part in the theatricals. How many of these played the *tan* roles is unknown. Women cross-dressed at times to lessen the dangers of traveling, and the *Tse-hiong-hiong-ti,* or *"Two Brothers of Different Sex,"*[91] is a short story on the theme. Here a young girl was dressed by her aged father as a boy for travel, and when he died, she was taken in by another couple, who raised her as a son. They also took in another boy the same way, and though both were in their teens and slept together, the girl remained undiscovered until she revealed herself to the man she loved. There was no condemnation of her cross-dressing, indicating that in China as in the West the hostility to transvestism was probably strongly influenced by status lines between the sexes. The story is interesting for another reason in that it indicates the growing prudishness of the Chinese, evident during the Yüan dynasty, and a desire never to expose oneself naked. The Confucianists opposed nudity as incompatible with their standards.

In short, the Chinese had a fairly open attitude toward sexual practices, although their public attitudes near the end of the Yüan dynasty came more and more to regard it as a private affair. Though homosexuality was accepted, exclusive homosexuality was condemned because then children would not be around to keep up the ancestor worship. To the adept, sex was a way of achieving immortality, and as a general rule we can say that anything in the sexual field was acceptable as long as it was not too wasteful of life's energy. In its Chinese setting, sex was not something to be feared, nor was it regarded as sinful, but rather, it was an act of worship, and increasingly a private matter.

NOTES

1. *I Ching,* translated by James Legge in *The Sacred Books of the East,* 2nd ed., F. Max Müller, ed. Vol. 16 (Oxford, England: Clarendon Press, 1899), The Great Appendix, sec. II, Chap. 5, par. 43, p. 393. The Chinese name for this section is the *Ta chuan* or the *Hsi tz'u chuan,* literally, the "Commentary on the Appended Judgments." There is a slightly different translation in the Cary F. Baynes English version of Richard Wilhelm's German translation in the Bollingen Series 19, 3rd. ed., (Princeton, N.J.: Princeton University Press, 1967), sec. II, Chaps. 5, 13, pp.342–343. There are numerous other translations.

2. *I Ching,* LXIII.

3. The warmer is difficult to define. The Chinese believed there were three of them in charge of the waterways and that they gave the necessary life warmth to the kidneys. The first warmer was said to be located in the front part of the body with its opening in the chest; the second started at the center of the chest and reached toward the abdomen; the third was situated in the adbominal area. Professor Franz Hübotter, *Chinesisch-Tibetische Pharmakologie* (Ulm, Germany: K. F. *Haug,* 1957), theorized that the warmer might well be interpreted as the lymphatic system, since the main trunk of the lymphatic vessels, the thoracic duct, extends up through the thorax and opens into the left subclavian vein.

4. See Heinrich Wallnöfer and Anna von Rottauscher, *Chinese Folk Medicine,* translated by Marion Palmedo (New York: Crown Publishers, 1965), pp.10–12.

5. *Ibid.,* pp. 93–94.

6. See Marcel Granet, *Festivals and Songs of Ancient China* (New York: Dutton, 1932), passim.

7.   Joseph Needham, assisted by Wang Ling, *Science and Civilization in China*, Vol. 2, (Cambridge, England: University Press, 1956), pp. 149–150.

8.   See R. H. Van Gulik, *Sexual Life in Ancient China* (Leiden, Netherlands: E. J. Brill, 1961), pp. 70–71. Without the work of Van Gulik this chapter could not have been written.

9.   This has been translated by Akira Ishihara and Howard S. Levy under the title of *The Tao of Sex* (Yokohama, Japan: Shibundö, 1968).

10.   For a discussion of the fragments, see Van Gulik, *op. cit.*, pp. 122–123; and Needham, *op. cit.*, p. 147.

11.   For a complete translation into English and Latin of the manual attributed to Tung-hsüan, see Van Gulik, *op. cit.*, pp. 125–134. The quotation is from sec. 1, p. 125.

12.   Ishihara and Levy, *op. cit.*, Chap. 13, position No. 6, p. 60.

13.   *Ibid.*, position No. 19, p. 74.

14.   *Ibid.*, position No. 15, p. 69.

15.   Van Gulik, *op. cit.*, Chap. 12, pp. 131–132.

16.   Ishihara and Levy, *op. cit.*, Chap. 1, p. 17.

17.   *Ibid.*, Chap. 1, pp. 19–20.

18.   *Ibid.*, Chap. 2, p. 24.

19.   [René] Étiemble, *Yun Yu: An Essay on Eroticism and Love in Ancient China (Illustrated)*, translated by James Hogarth (Geneva: Nagel Publishers, 1970), p. 49.

20.   Van Gulik, *op. cit.*, pp. 16–17. For other discussion, see Marcel Granet, *La Polygnie sorale et le sororat dans la Chine feodale* (Paris: Editions Ernest Leroux, 1920), pp. 39–40.

21.   Ishihara and Levy, *op. cit.*, Chap. 24, pp. 136–137.

22.   *Ibid.*, Chap. 21, p. 125.

23.   For these and other prohibitions, see *ibid.*, Chap. 21, pp. 120–130.

24.   Van Gulik, *op. cit.*, p. 71.

25.   Ishihara and Levy, *op. cit.*, Chap. 3, passim; the quotation is from p. 27.

26.   See the *Analects of Confucius*, translated by James Legge in *The Chinese Classics* (edition Hong Kong: Hong Kong University Press, 1960, 5 vols.), Book XVII, Chap. 25, Vol. 1, p. 330.

27.   Van Gulik, *op. cit.*, p. 78.

28.   *Ibid.*, p. 79.

29.   There are various translations of the brief Nü-chieh by Lady Pan. The one quoted is by Van Gulik, *op. cit.*, pp. 97–103, and is from Chap. 2, p. 99. For another version, see Nancy Lee Swann, *Pan Chao: Foremost Woman Scholar of China* (reprinted, New York: Russell and Russell, 1968). She translates the work on pp. 83 ff.

30.   Ko Hung (Pao-p'u-tzu), *Nei p'ien*, translated by James R. Ware under the title of *Alchemy, Medicine, Religion in the China of* A.D.*320* (Cambridge, Mass.: the MIT Press, 1966), Chap. 5, 5a, p. 105.

31.   *Ibid.*, Chap. 6, 8a–8b, p. 122.

32.   *Ibid.*, Chap. 6, 8b, p. 123.

33.   *Ibid.*, Chap. 8, 3b–4a, pp. 140–141.

34.   Van Gulik, *op. cit.*, p. 223.

35.   *Ibid.*, p. 224.

36.   Wolfram Eberhard, *Guilt and Sin in Traditional China* (Berkeley, Calif.: University of California Press, 1967), pp. 29–32.

37. *Ibid.*, pp. 61–63.

38. *Ibid.*, p. 84.

39. Van Gulik, *op. cit.*, pp. 248–250.

40. For a discussion of this, see the brief summary by Kristofer Schipper in Michel Beurdeley, Kristofer Schipper, Chang Fu-Jui, and Jacques Pimpaneau, *Chinese Erotic Art* translated by Diana Imber, (Rutland, Vt.: Charles E. Tuttle, 1969), pp. 34–38.

41. For an example of this, see Lu K'uan Yü, *Taoist Yoga: Alchemy and Immortality* (New York: Samuel Weiser, 1970). This is a translation of the *Hsin ming fa chueh ming chih* by the nineteenth-century Taoist master Chao Pi Ch'en.

42. See Eberhard, *op. cit.*, p. 77.

43. See Van Gulik, *op. cit.*, pp. 260–261, and appendix 1; Needham, *op. cit.*, pp. 428–429. For a recent version of Tantra sex practice, see Omar Garrison, *Tantra, The Yoga of Sex* (New York: Julian Press, 1964).

44. Needham, *op. cit.*, p. 147.

45. *Ibid.*, pp. 49–50.

46. Ishihara and Levy, *op. cit.*, Chap. 24, p. 134.

47. *Ibid.*, Chap. 25, pp. 139–140.

48. Van Gulik, *op. cit.*, p. 165.

49. *Ibid.*, pp. 165–166.

50. See, for example, Michel Beurdeley et al., *op. cit.*, p. 174.

51. There is a French version of this by Franz Kuhn, *Femmes derrière un voile* (Paris: Calman-Levy, 1962) a title that would be translated as "Women Behind a Veil."

52. For a brief synopsis, see Van Gulik, *op. cit.*, p. 302; and Michel Beurdeley et al., *op. cit.*, pp. 174–176.

53. *Ibid.*, p. 171.

54. Ishihara and Levy, *op. cit.*, pp. 69, 79.

55. Van Gulik, *op. cit.*, p. 254.

56. Fung Yu-lan, *A History of Chinese Philosophy*, translated by Derk Bodde (Princeton, N.J.: Princeton University Press, 1952), Vol. 1, p. 86.

57. Mo Ti, *The Ethical and Political Works of Motse*, translated by Ui-pao Mei (London: Arthur Probsthain, 1929), Chap. xlviii, p. 237.

58. See T'ung-tsu Ch'ü, *Law and Society in Traditional Society* (Paris: Mouton & Company, 1965), pp. 236–237, and Chap. 6, passim.

59. Marcel Granet, *Chinese Civilization*, translated by Kathleen E. Innes and Mabel R. Barilsford (New York: Barnes and Noble, 1951), p. 427.

60. H. G. Creel, *Confucius: The Man and the Myth* (London: Routledge & Kegan Paul, 1951), p. 84.

61. Mo Ti, *op. cit.*, Book 13, Chap. xlix, p. 252.

62. Translated in John K. Shyrock, *The Origin and Development of the State Cult of Confucius* (reprinted, New York: Paragon Book Reprint Corp., 1966), p. 55.

63. For a discussion, see Ping-ti Ho, *The Ladder of Success in Imperial China* (reprinted, New York: Wiley, 1964), pp. 168–203.

64. See Herbert A. Giles, *A Chinese Biographical Dictionary* (reprinted, Taipei, Formosa: Literature House, 1964), No. 1465, p. 564.

65. *Chan-kou ts'e*, translated by J. I. Crump, Jr., (Oxford, England: Clarendon Press, 1961), "The Book of Wei, or Liang," No. 376, pp. 449–450.

66. Ssu-ma Ch'ien, *Shih chi*, translated under the title of *Records of the Grand Historian of China* by Burton Watson (New York: Columbia University Press, 1961, 2 vols.), sec. 125, Vol. 2, p. 462. Ssu-ma Ch'ien was, however, a eunuch, and this might have helped his tolerant attitude.

67. *Ibid.*

68. *Ibid.*, Vol. 2, pp. 463–467. There is another incident in sec. 63 of *Shih chi* that Watson did not translate. This deals with the Lord of Wei and his favorite, Mi Tzu-hsia. See n. 2, p. 467.

69. See the section "Cut Sleeves," by Michel Beurdeley in Beurdeley et al., *op. cit.*, pp. 157–168. Van Gulik, *op. cit.*, p. 63, says there is a seventeenth-century treatise dealing with male homosexuality by an anonymous author entitled *Tuan-hsui-pien* or, literally, *Records of the Cut Sleeve.*" It was printed in the *Hsiang-yen-ts' ung-shu* or *Collected Writings of Fragrant Elegance,*" a comprehensive collection of reprints of old and later books, treatises, and essays relating to women and sexual relations and including many writings proscribed during later Chinese dynasties. It was published in 80 volumes (Shanghai: Kuo-Hsüeh-fu-lun-shê, 1909–1911). Volume 2 contains the treatise on homosexuality. I have not seen the work, but there is a copy in the Kinsey collection at the University of Indiana.

70. Giles, *op. cit.*, No. 1366, "Liu yeh," p. 526; and Van Gulik, *op. cit.*, p. 93.

71. Van Gulik, *op. cit.*, pp. 92–93.

72. *Ibid.*, p. 163.

73. J. J. Matignon, *La Chine hĕrmetique superstition, crime, et misère* (reprinted, Paris: Librairie orientaliste Paul Geuthner, 1936).

74. Taisuke Mitamura, *Chinese Eunuchs,* translated by Charles A. Pomeroy (Tokyo; Charles A Tuttle, 1970) p. 64.

75. T'ung-tsu Ch'ü, *op. cit.*, pp. 129 ff.

76. A. C. Scott, *The Classical Theatre of China* (London: George Allen & Unwin, 1957), pp. 28 ff.; Cecilia S. L. Zung, *Secrets of the Chinese Drama* (reprinted, New York: Benjamin Blom, 1964), passim; and L. C. Arlington, *The Chinese Drama* (reprinted, New York: Benjamin Blom, 1966), passim.

77. For this, see Esther Newton, *Mother Camp: Female Impersonators in America* (Englewood Cliffs, N.J.: Prentice-Hall, 1972).

78. This is reported by Wu Shan Sheng, *Erotologie de la Chine* (Paris: J. J. Pauvert, 1963). It is repeated by other authors, but the source is unknown to me.

79. Arlington, *op. cit.*, pp. 11–12.

80. A brief summary of this is in the essay by Michel Beurdeley, "Cut Sleeves," *op. cit.*, p. 160.

81. This has been translated and adapted into English by several translators. See, for example, Tsao Hsueh-chin, *Dream of the Red Chamber,* translated and adapted by Chi-chien Wang (New York: Doubleday, 1958), pp. 73 ff. 129, 215–216.

82. Li Yü, *Jou pu tuan,* translated by Richard Martin from the German version of Franz Kuhn (New York: Grove Press, 1967), pp. 106–107.

83. *The She King*, translated by James Legge, in Vol. 4 of the *Chinese Classics, op. cit.,* Part 3, Book III, Ode 10, stanza 3, pp. 561–562.

84. See the *Shoo King* [Shu ching], translated by James Legge, in Vol. 3 of the *Chinese Classics*, Part 2, Book I, Chaps. 3, 11, and p. 38, note.

85. Mitamura, *op. cit.*, p. 34.

86.   G. Carter Stent, "Chinese Eunuchs," *Journal of the Royal Asiatic Society,* North China Branch, No. XI (1877). See also the chapter in J. J. Matignon, *op. cit.*

87.   There is a good biography of Ssu-ma Ch'ien by Burton Watson, *Ssu-ma Ch'ien: Grand Historian of China* (New York: Columbia University Press, 1958).

88.   Needham, *op. cit.,* Vol. 2, pp. 574–575. It should be stated, however, that the first-century A.D. philosopher Wang Ch'ung wrote that a man could no more be transformed into a woman or a woman into a man than the heaven into earth or the sun into the moon. See Wang Ch'ung, *Lun-hêng,* 2nd. ed., translated by Alfred Forke (reprinted, New York: Paragon Book Gallery, 1962, 2 vols.), "Unfounded Assenrtions (Wu-hsing), " Book II, Chap. 3, Vol. 1, p. 325.

89.   Van Gulik, *op. cit.,* p. 61.

90.   *Ibid.,* p. 167.

91.   *Tse-hiong-hiong-ti,* translated from the French of Stanislas Julien into English by Frances Hume under the title of *The Two Brothers of Different Sex* (London: Rodale Press, 1955).

PART FOUR

THE CHRISTIAN WORLD

12

BYZANTIUM AND EASTERN ORTHODOX CHRISTIANITY

C hristian theory, as we have seen, was extremely hostile to human sexuality. But theory and practice do not always necessarily coincide. The potential for conflict between them was exacerbated when Christianity changed from being just one of a number of competing religious groups within the Roman Empire to being the official religion of the state. Their new position soon forced Christian thinkers to come to terms with new problems that they had previously been able to ignore. Since Christians came from disparate backgrounds and cultures, it is not surprising that they disagreed with each other. In general, common areas of agreement were hammered out in a series of Church Councils, but large numbers of Christians, refusing to accept such decisions, were labeled heretics. Though ostracized and even persecuted by the state, heretical groups continued to exist, usually on the fringes of the Roman Empire or outside it, many surviving until today.

Even Christians agreeing on the larger issues decided at the Councils often disagreed on lesser ones. Eventually these differences between the two major segments of orthodox Christianity (the Greek-oriented East and the Latin-oriented West) grew so great that they split into two separate communions in the eleventh century, excommunicating each other. The Western branch, Roman Catholicism, was united in looking to Rome for guidance, but the

Eastern orthodox Christians had several centers of authority based on liguistic and cultural differences, although they more or less agreed on basic dogma.

Part of the difficulty encountered by Christians in the fourth century was that, previous to this, they had regarded themselves more or less as temporary sojourners on earth, unconcerned with its problems. Some individuals and groups had regarded the imperial government at Rome as the work of Satan, although probably the majority had accepted it as ordained by God. All, however, had viewed it as an external power alien to themselves. When the government became Christian, or at least oriented to Christianity, as it did under the Emperor Constantine early in the fourth century, Christians found themselves in a dilemma as they attempted to reconcile the obligations imposed by governmental responsibility with their personal belief. This proved particularly painful to those who had to carry out official obligations contradicting basic Christian beliefs, such as those toward life itself. In general the Christian tradition had been pacifist, opposed to taking life, a stance hard to reconcile with the demands put on a Christian judge or soldier who had to kill as part of his official duties.

Some Christians still tried to insist that Christianity was incompatible with military service. St. Basil, for example, went so far as to claim that a soldier who killed a man in the course of duty had to abstain from communion for 3 years,[1] equivalent to excommunication. This perhaps represents an extreme view, but no Christian authority offered any positive message to soldiers other than urging them to refrain from extortion and be content with their pay. Siricius, the Bishop of Rome (384–399), debarred from holy orders anyone who, after baptism, had held administrative posts, had served in the army or the civil service, or had even been an attorney in the court. In the same spirit, those who had performed penance and received absolution were forbidden to return to their posts.[2] St. Ambrose was somewhat more lenient, for he reported that he did not excommunicate Christian judges who passed a death sentence, but he stated that officials would be praised if they did not order the death sentence.[3] Innocent I (401–417), Bishop of Rome, agreed, because "these powers had been granted by God and the sword had been permitted for the punishment of the guilty, those who wielded it were not blameworthy."[4] The implication seems to be that government service, if not sinful, was so perilous and so apt to lead to acts of extortion or cruelty that it made a man unfit for the service of God and was not to be risked by those who had no further opportunity of having their sins remitted. Perhaps for this reason, Paulinus, the fifth-century Bishop of Nola (died 431), urged his correspondents to resign from their posts and abandon their official careers, to take up a Christian life, since it was impossible to serve both Caesar and Christ.[5]

By the fifth century, however, the Roman Empire was officially Christian, and this left the Christians in a dilemma. They could regard secular laws and government as outside the purview of Christianity, cutting the Church and its members off from government altogether, or they could recognize the existence of government and try to draw a separate line between service to God and service to the state. In the East, where the state was stronger, the latter position was the only viable alternative. In the West, where centralized government was much weaker, the Church as an institution often had greater influence and at times regarded itself as independent from government altogether. Eventually it, too, adopted the Eastern position but only after a struggle. In both East and West the Church officials offered advice, often negative, continually warning officials not to pervert justice or oppress widows and orphans, but the political realities of power prevented the Church from acting as independently in the East as in the West. Those insisting on a purist position could retire to the monastery, where they could live with only a minimum of contact with the state.

Even in a monastery, however, man's animal urges could not be ignored. The most influential monastic rule for the Eastern Church was that promulgated by St. Basil in the fourth century. Basil emphasized obedience and organization to make certain that every waking moment of a monk's life was dedicated to God. For Basil, all sins were capital sins, and a single sin could provoke the wrath of God. Determined to make every monk perfect and realizing he could not prevent sin, he believed he could safeguard against it by providing a penalty for every sin. St. Basil regarded sex as particularly dangerous, inveighing against it in his various rules. He warned young monks not to approach too close to one another, to address each other with downcast eyes, and never to touch each other. Boys at the age of puberty were not to sleep beside each other, and if more than one boy slept in a bed, there was always to be an old monk between. The monk was always to be alert to sexual temptation, for the key to good life was absolute celibacy.[6]

Even for the ordinary laymen, standards were set so high in the early Church that many Christians despaired of leading a sinless life, even those not in political positions. In the fourth century many who had not been baptized in childhood remained catechumens (unbaptized) all their days, relying on a last-minute baptism to secure salvation. In this, the Emperor Constantine served as an example. As the Church moved to eliminate such practices by insisting on baptism in infancy or early adolescence, deathbed penance came to the fore. At the same time, the Christian Church began to pressure secular authorities, encouraging them to modify secular law to suit religious purposes, although on this there were differences among Christians themselves. And one area where Eastern and Western Churches disagreed, was on clerical celibacy.

One of the earliest councils to deal with the questions was the Council of Elvira, held in Spain in 305–306, which attempted to impose a rule of sexual abstinence on all bishops, presbyters, deacons, and others employed in the service of the altar.[7] Efforts to get a similar prohibition adopted at the Council of Nicaea, the first ecumenical council, held 325 A.D., failed because of the opposition of Paphnutius, an Egyptian bishop, who probably carried the day because his personal example was so admired by the delegates. A celibate himself, he had also suffered the loss of his right eye rather than recant his faith during a period of persecution prior to the reign of Constantine.[8] The rejection by the assembled delegates at Nicaea did not, however, end the matter; it was revived in the West by Siricius, Bishop of Rome, who issued a decretal on the subject in 385 A.D. in response to a request from Hermeius, Archbishop of Tarragona in Spain. Hermeius had appealed to Siricius for assistance in enforcing the ideal of celibacy set forth by the Council of Elvira, even though the Council of Nicaea had rejected it. As a result, Siricius threw his influence behind the necessity of clerical celibacy, prohibiting all coitus by presbyters and deacons, even if they were married.[9] Further reinforcement for clerical celibacy came from a succession of Western synods, held at Carthage in 390, at Toledo in 400, at Turin in 401, and at Rome in 402.[10] Leo I, Bishop of Rome (440–461) allowed married clergy to retain their wives but stipulated they should have wives as "though they had them not," extending the prohibition against sexual intercourse to subdeacons as well as presbyters and deacons.[11] In spite of such prohibitions, there was widespread lack of observance, for the clergy themselves did not view celibacy with any great enthusiasm, and in their support they could always cite the Council of Nicaea. Not until the thirteenth century was the West able to enforce the concept of clerical celibacy generally.[12]

Contrasting with the Western view was that of the Eastern Churches, which opposed celibacy for the ordinary priest but accepted it as essential for bishops. The most nearly complete statement on the matter was given in 692 at the Council of Constantinople, which stipulated that a lawfully married man might become a subdeacon, deacon, or priest, but only lectors and cantors (minor clerics) were permitted to marry after ordination. Bishops were supposed to be celibate, and if a married man was advanced to the episcopate, his wife was to be separated from him and retired to a monastery.[13] Generally, however, bishops were chosen from the celibate monks. There were also restrictions on clerical marriages. Clergy were forbidden to marry a second time, and ordination was prohibited to those men who had married widows. Clergy were also not supposed to marry after ordination.[14] The essential difference in outlook about clerical marriage is still reflected, not only in the Orthodox Churches, but also in the various Byzantine rite or uniate Churches, that is, non-Latin rite Churches that today recognize the authority of the Pope. In spite of papal insistence on clerical celibacy in Latin rite Churches, priests in the Byzantine rite Churches are permitted to be married, although this is no longer true of uniate priests now residing in the United States, where the double standard within Catholicism had led to serious internal controversy.

Though the Eastern and Western Churches differed on clerical celibacy, they held the same attitude towards *syneisaktism* or "spiritual marriage." In this relationship, persons of the opposite sex cohabitated under conditions of strict continence, sharing the same house, often the same room, and sometimes the same bed. Though the practice probably had pagan antecedents, it was also uniquely Christian.[15] Some of the early desert Fathers were accompanied by female hermits who acted as their maidservants, and it was not unusual for monks and nuns to live together in the same monastic establishment during the early Middle Ages. Women also shared the dwelling of celibate priests and bishops as housekeepers or spiritual companions, and some husbands and wives also tried to make their marriage a spiritual one by ignoring sex entirely. As the insistence on the necessity of celibacy grew, a number of married clerics tried to make their wives their celibate companions, but inevitably, many such unions of enforced chastity became obsessed with sex, and many of the faithful suspected that the soul bride of the ascetic was in fact a sexual companion as well.[16] Thus, even though the spiritual marriage had originally been viewed with approval,[17] it increasingly began to be seen as a source of open scandal. From the beginning of the fourth century onward, Church Councils condemned the custom, insisting that women be prohibited from residing in the house of clerics, unless they were mothers or others whose natural relationship with their protectors would disarm suspicion.[18] Bishops also spoke out against spiritual wives, taking action against those clergy who refused to part with their virginal companions. Finally, when none of these pronouncements proved effective in eliminating the practice, the Church turned to the secular authorities. In 420 a law was passed forbidding all so-called sisterly cohabitation and forbidding females to live with clerics of any grade unless they were the mother, sister, daughter, or other near relative.[19] Still the practice proved difficult to eradicate, and as late as the sixth century, the Emperor Justinian issued a similar edict.[20]

As to regular marriage, the Christian Church had taken over the Roman marriage rites with only slight changes. One of the earliest Christian attempts to regulate marriage was by the second-century Ignatius of Antioch, who held it fitting that "when men and women marry they should be united with the consent of the bishop, that the marriage may be according to the Lord, and not for the sake of lust."[21] Officially, the Church was slow to act on his recommendation, and episcopal approval was not essential nor were there any special ecclesiastical rites or blessings to confer validity upon marital unions. Traditional Roman ceremonies continued to be carried out, except that certain pagan aspects, such as the consultation of the auspices, were eliminated. The Eastern Church Orders contain no Christian marriage rite, nor is there any reference to any in the literature of the period. Even in the Western part of the empire, where the Church had somewhat greater say over marriage and morals than it

did in the East, there is no detailed account of a specifically Christian matrimonial ceremony until the ninth century, and even at that late date, it was the
same as the ceremony carried out in pagan Rome, except that the Eucharist
had been substituted for sacrifice and divination.[22]

This absence of specifically Christian ceremonies in the East implied that
marriage remained essentially a civil affair, a contractual relationship established by consent, and voidable like any other contract.[23] Divorce then was a
private act and not particularly a juridical one, although it did have to take
place in front of seven adult citizens. Divorce could be by mutual agreement
(*divortium ex consensu*), but it could also be by unilateral action (*repudium*). If
it was the latter, it could be for quite arbitrary reasons, or it could be justified
because of sterility, illness, or insanity of the spouse, but in any case no moral
stigma was attached to the repudiated partner.[24] Repudiation could also result
because a spouse had committed, or attempted to commit, a serious crime such
as murder. Usually, the decision to divorce was made by the wronged partner.
In only one case was a husband not allowed to use his own discretion, namely,
when his wife had committed adultery. A husband who knowingly retained an
adulterous wife and neglected to prosecute her paramour was guilty of pandering (*lenocinum*). Several Christian emperors, notably Constantine, Honorius,
Theodosius II, Valentinian III, and Justinian, attempted to restrict the grounds
on which a spouse could repudiate a partner, but considerable liberty remained
to both husband and wife.[25]

In this as in most other legislation, the Christian emperors acted as secular
magistrates, and though they might have been motivated by Christian ideals,
they did not impose the strict Christian rule upon the multitudes of their subjects, who were still influenced by the old customs. But dedicated Christians
could, and often did, observe a separate standard from the states, and perhaps
for this reason differences between the East and West began to appear in the
ecclesiastical handling of divorce and remarriage. Both Eastern and Western
Churches, for example, agreed that a husband could put away an adulterous
wife, or a wife an adulterous husband, and both disapproved remarriage for the
innocent party. In practice, however, the Eastern Church proved more lenient,
at least for males. St. Basil of Caesarea, for example, held that indulgence
ought to be shown toward male but not toward female immorality. Though he
was not particularly happy advocating such a double standard, he still believed
that, when a man who had separated from his wife cohabited with another
woman, neither he nor his mistress should incur the full ecclesiastical penance
for adultery but only that imposed for nonadulterous fornication. On the other
hand, if the husband had put away his wife to form an illicit connection, both
he and his paramour merited the full punishment for adultery.[26] St. Basil was
probably more concerned with the penance of those who entered into irregular

unions than with the problem of divorce, since the Eastern Church generally condemned those who remarried while the divorced partner was still alive.[27]

In spite of attempts by various Christian-oriented emperors to change the law on divorce, it was still possible in the fifth century to obtain a divorce by mutual consent, and this remained the law in the Byzantine state with only occasional modification.[28] Under Leo III, the Isaurian, whose *Ecloga* was issued about 740, marriage and divorce were temporarily regulated exclusively by the Church. For a brief period greater restrictions were put on divorce, it being allowed only for a wife's adultery, a husband's impotence, threat of murder, or leprosy. By the ninth century, however, Basil I had returned to the liberality of the early Justinian and Roman law.[29]

Legal restriction on the remarriage of a divorced or widowed person followed a similar development, although the restrictions were never as severe for the widowed as for the divorced. The inability of the Church to enforce restrictions on remarriage and the unwillingness of the state to do so are evident from the case of the Emperor Leo VI (886–912). Leo, at the request of his father Basil I, had married Theaphono, who turned out to be more of a saint than a wife. Once she had become empress, Theaphono became both more pious and more ascetic, eating nothing but dry bread and watery vegetables, clothing herself in sackcloth, and sleeping on the floor. Unhappy with his wife, yet unwilling to divorce such a saintly woman, Leo consoled himself by taking his childhood sweetheart Zoe as mistress, waiting for Theaphono to die. In 897, at the age of 29, she finally did so and quickly became recognized as a saint by the Greek Church. Leo almost immediately married Zoe, in spite of opposition from his confessor, who felt it wrong for a widower, particularly the widower of such an exceptionally holy woman, to marry. Part of his justification for the marriage was the necessity of begetting a male heir. Unfortunately matters did not end here, for Zoe died in 899 under somewhat mysterious circumstances, and the Emperor, at 32, still lacked an heir for his throne. Leo quickly took a third wife, Eudocia Baiana, in open violation of both Church regulations and state law prohibiting third marriages. Eudocia soon became pregnant but died in childbirth within the year, and the heir, a boy, perished with her. Leo then temporized by living with a mistress while trying to decide what to do. A fourth marriage would have been a severe violation of both the canons of the Church and the laws of the state, but in his mind the lack of an heir would have resulted in more serious consequences. When his mistress Zoe Carbonopsina gave birth to a son in 905, Leo felt it imperative to legalize his potential heir in spite of religious opposition. On January 6, 906, the baby was baptized and christened as Constantine in Santa Sophia by the Patriarch Nicholas Mysticus, but only on condition that his father separate from Zoe. In spite of his agreement to leave his mistress, Leo married Zoe 3 day later. Nicholas

Mysticus attempted to forbid the emperor from entering any consecrated building but proved unable to enforce any such prohibition. Eventually, when Leo
died, he was succeeded by Constantine. With such imperial examples, it proved
difficult for the Church to enforce an absolute prohibition on remarriage of a
divorced or widowed person.

Underlying the differences between the Eastern and Western Churches on
divorce and remarriage was probably an essential difference in attitudes toward
sexual intercourse, a difference implied in some of the writings of St. John
Chrysostom. Though Chrysostom, like St. Augustine, held that marriage had
been established to prevent fornication, he concluded from this that intercourse
was permissible with one's spouse, not only when procreation was possible, but
also in old age, by those who were sterile, and during pregnancy, when no conception was possible. Chrysostom had apparently arrived at this position because of his conviction that intercourse, in and of itself, was not what produced
children, but rather, that the word of God caused men to increase and multiply.
Chrysostom had undoubtedly observed that not all acts of intercourse led to
pregnancy; he offered as proof for the importance of God in procreation the fact
that many men entered into marriage but failed to become fathers.[30]

From looking upon God as the chief factor in procreation, it is not too difficult to look upon the generative act itself as sacred, and this view can perhaps
be read into some of the Eastern Christian writers on the subject.[31] Such a view
also had implications for contraception as well as celibacy. If taken literally,
any interference with the generative act was an attack on the work of God, and
thus refusal to engage in sexual intercourse was as much a sin as using artificial
contraceptives. Chrysostom did not, however, fully develop the implications of
his passing statement, and since he believed in continence, it is possible some
have read more into his statement than he intended. We do know that Chrysostom opposed artificial contraceptives as being worse than homicide.[32]

In spite of such opposition, many Eastern Christians still practiced
contraception for the subject is discussed in the medical literature. In fact, the
best discussion of the subject in medieval medical literature is by Aëtio of
Amida, a Byzantine court physician of the sixth century. Aëtio recognized a
safe period and urged those wishing to avoid pregnancy to engage in intercourse either at the beginning or end of menstruation. He also reported that
smearing the cervix with astringent, fatty, or cooling ointments would close the
orifice of the womb and prevent sperm from entering the uterus. Most effective,
in his mind, were those ointments that so irritated the womb that liquid came
from the uterus (infection?). He also advised males to wash their genitals with
vinegar or brine before coitus if they desired to avoid conception; this prescription probably proved somewhat effective, although not quite as effective as a
vaginal douche with the same materials.[33] No toleration whatever was extended
to abortion or infanticide; generally, the Eastern Church followed the policy

adopted by the Council of Ancyra, which provided for 10 years of penance for women who fornicated and then destroyed the product of their intercourse. Some of the Churches in the East apparently excluded such women "sinners" from communion the rest of their lives.[34]

Abortion was probably the aspect of sex and reproduction most affected by Christian teachings. In other areas, however, Christianity seemed to have little or no influence in changing sexual customs. This is particularly true for prostitution, which, in spite of laws against it and the severe penalties imposed on keepers of disorderly houses, was widespread in the Byzantine Empire. Apparently, innkeepers, tavern owners, and attendants at bathhouses regularly augmented their wages by prostitution or by procuring; widespread poverty provided an almost inexhaustible supply of prostitutes. The vast majority of them lived in abject squalor, providing their services for a mere pittance. Their numbers in Constantinople are difficult to compute with any accuracy, but at any one time they probably totaled into the thousands.[35] One street leading to the theater was called the Street of the Harlots, and certain occupations, particularly that of actress, were regarded as synonymous with prostitution. Perhaps the essential difference between Byzantine and pagan attitudes toward prostitution was the view of the prostitute herself. In Byzantine society the prostitute was generally considered a creature made after the "image and the likeness of God" and a human being deserving society's compassion. During the reign of the Emperor Justin (518–527), for example, prostitutes were regarded as the equal of manumitted slaves as far as marriage was concerned. Justin stated that, since ex-slaves could become full citizens after gaining their freedom, it was only right that women who had left the life of prostitution should at least have equal opportunity to become a full citizen.[36] The Emperor Justinian issued a special *novel* (that is, a law) against procuring and exploitating poor and minor girls. He, along with Empress Theodora, also erected a special convent named *Metanoia* or "Repentance" to provide for the needs of former prostitutes. A similar institution was established by the Emperor Michael IV in the eleventh century.[37]

Concubinage, another pagan custom, also continued in the Christian Byzantine Empire. The Emperor Constantine tried at first to prohibit the residence of a concubine in a married man's house, but by the time of Justinian in the sixth century, the right of natural children (as distinguished from legitimate children) to one-half of the father's possessions was recognized, and concubinage was accepted as a fact of life. In 539 A.D. the emperor went so far as to stipulate that a father could leave all his possessions to his natural children if he had none who were legitimate.[38] In short, in spite of the theoretical attitudes of Christianity toward sex, peoples in the Byzantine Empire continued to express their sexuality in traditional ways.

Christianity actually effected changes in individual sexual conduct only occasionally, although it did inhibit open discussion of such activities. Inevitably, Byzantine literature and law fails to give us the detailed description of sexual life that we have from the pagan classical world or even from the Jewish and Muslim writers. More or less official silence about sexual matters, did not, however, prevent individuals from thinking or talking about sex, as evidenced in the writings of the seventh-century physician, Paulus Aegineta. Paulus continued to believe that coition was the best remedy for melancholy and that it restored reason to those afflicted with mania. He did, however, advise moderation in frequency of sexual activities, since, like any other kind of labor, it was best not to overdo it. He also felt that certain times were better for sexual activity than others. He felt that the best time was after eating and before sleep, since this not only allowed the man to relieve his "lassitude" by sleep but also provided the best time for procreation, because the "woman falling asleep is more likely to retain the semen." Paulus' recommendation continued in the same vein as pagan Greek and Roman predecessors and his Arabic contemporaries and successors.[39]

One of the most glaring contradictions between Christian theory and Byzantine practice was in the use of eunuchs, who constituted an important sex variant. At the Council of Nicaea, Christianity itself had come out against self-castration. The first canon of the council stipulated that those who had voluntarily castrated themselves were not to be ordained clerics, and if they had already been ordained clerics, they were not to function as such any longer.[40] Though such a prohibition did not apply to those who had been involuntarily castrated by others, the intent and meaning seem clear. Involuntary castration had, moveover, been prohibited by Roman law. Traditionally, in fact, the Romans had a horror of castration. This attitude was still evident at the end of the first century A.D., when the Emperor Domitian prohibited the castration of slaves for commercial purposes. Those violating the imperial edict were to be fined half of their material wealth. To discourage such a practice further, he attempted to lower the market price of castrated slaves by fixing a low maximum price for eunuchs (spadones). But legislation was one thing, and reality another, for there is considerable evidence that the legislation was more or less ignored. In the fourth century under the Emperor Constantine and in the fifth century under Emperor Leo I, castration of slaves was again forbidden, although the purchase of eunuchs from barbarian peoples was not forbidden. The Emperor Justinian confirmed the prohibition against castration of slaves and provided for further punishment by giving freedom to all castrated slaves. In fact, he went so far as to stipulate that anyone castrated after a specific date should be regarded as free, regardless of whether or not the victim had given his consent, and even if the castration had been done for medical reasons.[41] Theoretically, a free man could be castrated at his own request without penalty, but Christianity was concerned to prevent this as well. Nonetheless in spite of all prohibitions, slaves continued to be castrated, probably before they arrived within the borders of Byzantium. Numerous individuals also submitted to voluntary castration. The major reason for this contradiction between Christian teaching and practice was that eunuchs held such powerful positions in the Byzantine state, and since society rewarded those who had the operation that the law prohibited, castration continued. One writer has gone so far as to call the Byzantine Empire the "eunuch's paradise."[42]

The position of eunuchs in Byzantium was entirely different from that in the Arab countries or in Persia, where eunuchs were primarily domestic servants who could be safely trusted with the harem. Their position was also far more powerful than in China, for in Byzantium they often ran the government. In the sixth century, one of the greatest of Byzantine generals was a eunuch. By the tenth century, eunuchs in the imperial court took precedence over non-eunuchs, and many of the most prominent men in both the state and the Church were eunuchs.[43] The key to their power lay in their being forbidden to serve as Prefect of Constantinople, quaestor, domestic of the four imperial regiments, or as emperor. Thus they could be appointed to powerful positions by emperors who knew they could never wear the imperial crown and could never have children to whom they could pass on their office. This made them the safest and most desirable of civil servants—so much so that they became the bulwark of a strong central bureaucracy as well as a counterfoil to the power of a hereditary nobility. Whereas a powerful eunuch could (and did) advance his favorites, even the most powerful had to be content with being the power behind the throne rather than take the thone himself.

The Emperor Diocletian had first institutionalized the eunuch system at the end of the third century. In the beginning, most of the eunuchs had been slaves or foreigners, but as the Byzantine system matured, even the noblest of parents at times castrated their sons to help advance him as well as themselves. Emperors also castrated boys who might grow up to become potential rivals or who might otherwise challenge the imperial power. Nicetas, the young son of Michael I (811–813) was castrated when his father fell, and then, no longer a threat to the usurper, he was free to express his ability in other directions. He eventually became Patriarch of Constantinople, taking the name of Ignatius (847–858, 867–878). The Emperor Romanus I (920–944) castrated his bastard son Basil, who, as *Parakoimomenus* (the Great Chamberlain) ruled the empire in everything but name for several decades. Romanus also castrated his younger legitimate son Theophylact, whom he intended to make patriarch. Not surprisingly, a significant number of Patriarchs of Constantinople were eunuchs.

Within the civil service, the castrated bearer of a title took precedence over his uncastrated compeer, many high ranks being reserved entirely for eunuchs.[44] Eunuchs also served in the armed forces. Narses in the sixth century and Nicephorus Uranus in the tenth century were brilliant examples of successful eunuch commanders. In the eleventh century, Nicephorus the Logothet, a eunuch, reformed the army after its disastrous defeat at the Battle of Manzikert (1071). A leading eunuch admiral during the same period was Eustathius Cymineanus.

Eunuchs were also important as palace servants, particularly those who controlled the bedchamber (*cubiculum*). Eunuchs served as keeper of the wardrobe, manager of imperial estates, captain of the bodyguard, keeper of the privy purse, and majordomo of the palace. Above the majordomo in the eunuch scale of ranking was the senior eunuch, and above him was the superintendent of the sacred bedchamber.[45] Since emperors, for the most part, lived in a rather secluded state, the eunuchs, by their access to his person, could not only give him advice but also control which outsiders he would see. As early as the fourth century, Constantius II (377–461) was reported to be entirely in the hands of his eunuchs, particularly his superintendent of the sacred bedchamber, a eunuch by the name of Eusebius. For a brief period during the reign of the Emperor Arcadius (395–408), the eunuch Eutropius was the virtual head of the government, and during the later years of the reign of Theodosius II (408–450), the eunuch Chrysaphius controlled affairs. In short, the power of the eunuchs coincided with the development of the Christian state, in spite of Christian hostility to eunuchs. Even when the eunuchs were not dominant, they exercised great influence, since anyone wishing a private audience with the emperor had to get their permission, and many used their position to become fabulously rich.

Because castration of slaves had been prohibited within the empire, eunuchs were often imported from Persia, Armenia, and other Caucasian lands. For the most part they were the victims of piracy, kidnapping, and tribal wars. In the sixth century, most eunuchs came from the pagan tribe of the Abasgi on the eastern shore of the Black Sea, where the local kings made a regular business of seizing the handsomest boys among their subjects and selling them to slave dealers. Often, the parents of such boys were killed, to avoid the danger of future vengeance.[46] Eunuchs were much more valuable than other slaves; as early as the reign of Justinian in the sixth century, a eunuch boy under 10 was priced at 30 *solidi* in certain legal cases, as compared with 10 *solidi* for the noneunuch boy of the same age. An untrained eunuch adult was worth 50 and a trained one 70, as compared with 20 and 30 *solidi* for the man with unimpaired masculinity.[47] Probably a major reason for the discrepancy in price was the mortality rate associated with castration. During Justinian's reign it was reported that only 3 of an original 90 survived castration.[48] These figures might have represented the mortality present in total castration, that is, when both the penis and testicles were removed, instead of only the testicles, which was the norm and much less dangerous. Paulus Aegineta, the seventh-century medical writer, implied that this second type of operation was rather simple and did not lead to high casualty rates.

> . . . Since we are sometimes compelled against our will by persons of high rank to perform the operation, we shall briefly describe the mode of doing it. There are two ways of performing it, the one by compression, and the other by excision. That by compression is thus performed: children, still of a tender age, are placed in a vessel of hot water, and then when the parts are softened in the bath, the testicles are to be squeezed with the fingers until they disappear, and, being dissolved, can no longer be felt. The method by excision is as follows: let the person to be castrated be placed upon a bench, and the scrotum with the testicles grasped by the fingers of the left hand, and stretched; two straight incisions are then to be made with a scalpel, one in each testicle; and when the testicles start up they are to be dissected around the cut out, having merely left the very thin bond of connexion between the vessels in their natural state. This method is preferred to that by compression; for those who have had them squeezed sometimes have venereal desires, a certain part, as it would appear, of the testicles having escaped the compression.[49]

As Paulus Aegineta implies, sexual desire was not always removed by castration. Success in this direction depended not only on the method of castration but also on the age of the person being castrated. If the testicles were removed after puberty, the eunuch could well have an erection, although he would be sterile, and in most cases eunuchs developed a feminine fat distribution, owing to the loss of male hormones. They were also usually beardless.

Even when it inhibited erection, castration did not necessarily remove sexual desire, although the palace eunuchs would have been executed if they had approached the women of the palace. By implication, if not always in actuality, Byzantine eunuchs were often equated with homosexuality. Under many of the Byzantine rulers, it was not unusual for eunuchs with "juvenile good looks" to be valued more highly than those lacking such assets, and many an emperor is said to have welcomed his eunuchs much as the "dwellers in Sodom" welcomed their "angelic" visitors.[50] Western-oriented historians have often expressed shock at the widespread existence of eunuchs, equating them with homosexuals, although in rather veiled terms. The pattern was set by Edward Gibbon in the eighteenth century, who claimed that Byzantines dishonor "the names both of Greeks and Romans, present a dead uniformity of abject vices, which are neither softened by the weakness of humanity nor animated by the vigour of memorable crimes."[51] In the nineteenth century, W. E. H. Lecky claimed that the Byzantine Empire constituted

> the most thoroughly base and despicable form that civilization has yet assumed. Though very cruel and very sensual, there have been times when cruelty assumed more ruthless, and sensuality more extravagant, aspects, but there has been no

other enduring civilization so absolutely destitute of all the forms and elements of greatness and none to which the epithet *mean* may be so emphatically applied. The Byzantine Empire was pre-eminently the age of treachery. Its vices were the vices of men who had ceased to be brave without learning to be virtuous . . . immersed in sensuality and in the most frivolous pleasures, the people only emerged from their listlessness when some theological subtilty, or some rivalry in the chariot races, stimulated them into frantic riots. . . . The history of the Empire is a monotonous story of the intrigues of priests, eunuchs, and women, of poisonings, of conspiracies, of uniform ingratitude, of perpetual fratricide.[52]

In the twentieth century Joseph McCabe summarized Byzantine history as full of "barbaric cruelty, gilded coarseness, unscrupulous ambition, and reckless lying and perjury."[53] Even a comparatively sympathetic observer said the Byzantine administration was "honeycombed with vices," that the Byzantines lacked moderation, and that "their character was not up to the level of their mentality."[54] Such characterizations seem, however, to be the result more of a Western prejudice than of an examination of what actually took place. In recent years, historians have begun to exercise more caution. One leader of the new Byzantine historiography was Steven Runciman, who wrote that

It has long been the custom to talk of eunuchs as always having a demoralizing influence all round, and historians that seem otherwise sane talk Gibbonesque cant about the intrigues and cowardice rampant in a life so full of eunuchs and women. When we read this, we should remember that, in the first half of the tenth century, the only period during which the Byzantine government pursued a bold and straightforward policy—a policy which failed largely through these "masculine" qualities—was that during which it was controlled by the Empress Zoe Carbonopsina and her eunuch minister Paracoemomene Constantine. Such generalizations are a disgrace to the historians that make them. You cannot interpret history if you create three inelastic types, man, woman, and eunuch.[55]

It was not only the widespread existence of eunuchs that gave many earlier interpreters of Byzantine culture the impression that homosexuality must have been widespread but also the availability of slave partners. Though *stuprum* with free men was condemned by public opinion, intercourse with slaves did not arouse any great legal objection, provided the slaves never engaged in prostitution for their masters' monetary benefit. Undoubtedly, when slavery existed on a widespread scale, a slave's lot would vary according to his or her ability to attract the master, and the darling of a wealthy citizen might well be in much better circumstances and entrusted with greater authority than many a free person. Slavery was widespread, slaves being plentiful until the twelfth century. Though ill treatment was common enough, there were always ways to advance one's position, and there are too many hints of affairs between masters and slaves, even on the imperial level, to deny that homosexuality existed.[56]

How widespread was homosexuality? Here we run into difficulty, for in spite of hints and some references early in Byzantine history, there is very little documented reference to homosexuality. Byzantine history abounds with references to mistresses, adultery, and even incest, and licentious heterosexual acts are given prominent play, but only rarely are sexual relations between two individuals of the same sex mentioned. Perhaps one reason that historians such as Gibbon or Lecky received their impressions about homosexuality was that some of the early Greek Fathers were particularly concerned about or fearful of such activities. St. John Chrysostom (died 407) condemned those pederasts who came to church to look with lustful curiosity upon handsome youths.[57] His concern might not reflect reality so much as it does his own inner tensions. "Vainglory is like the fruit of Sodom,"[58] he wrote. He cautioned parents not to let their sons' hair grow long: "And thou lettest his hair hang down behind, thereby at once making him look effeminate and like a girl and softening the ruggedness of his sex."[59] The reason long hair upset him was that he believed long-haired boys were particularly attractive to the sodomist, and long hair was inevitably a sign of corruption. "We must remove the chief part of his physical charm by clipping the locks on his head all around to attain severe simplicity."[60] He regarded any attempt to enhance a male's appearance as dangerously effeminate, warning against those males who attempted to imitate females in look, appearance, or dress.[61] So fearful was he of lurking pederasts that he felt it essential that young boys always be accompanied by an attendant who would shield them in the public squares and as they passed open alleys.[62]

His near contemporary St. Basil (died 379) was somewhat less concerned about the dangers of homosexuality, although he also wrote that men who committed indecencies with other men should be disciplined the same as those who committed adultery,[63] that is, excluded from the sacraments for 15 years. St. Gregory of Nyssa (died 398) agreed with this punishment, explaining that the reason homosexuals and adulterers were to be punished alike and much more severely than those engaging in fornication was that homosexuality involved unlawful pleasure and adultery involved treachery, the theft of something belonging to another.[64] Such concern by the fourth-and fifth-century Greek Fathers over the dangers of homosexuality led one scholar, M. L. W. Laistner, to conclude that there was a "prevalence of pederasty" in the Greek Christian Church.[65]

After the sixth century, however, there are comparatively few references to homosexuality in Byzantine literature. Does this lack of literary references indicate that homosexuality had disappeared or simply that it was a subject not considered worthy of discussion? Probably neither is the correct answer. Part of the difficulty is that most published sources are centered around the imperial court, where open accusations of homosexual conduct were dangerous. Usually, the closest a writer could come to the subject was to hint about it, but are such hints to be taken at face value or simply at attempts to blacken the character of the individual involved? Moreover, because most of our Byzantine records depend on copies made by others, even the hints can be made ambiguous. The term *stuprum*, for example, can mean "debauchery," "seduction," "violation," "wantonness," "lewdness," "rape," "dishonor," or "disgrace," covering a whole range of heterosexual, homosexual, and even asexual activities, and it is not always clear just what meaning was intended. The term *cinaedicus*, meaning "lustful" or "lewd," had no particular homosexual connotation, but the term *cinaedus* has exclusively homosexual connotations. It is far too easy to misread or mistranscribe the term for us to speak about homosexuality with any definitiveness as far as literary references are concerned.

No such ambiguity is, however, attached to the legal aspects of homosexuality, some scholars having argued that the Christian emperors launched a "veritable crusade" against homosexualtiy."[66] Like most such statements associated with homosexuality in history, this one is exaggerated. Probably pederasty, the corruption of young boys by an adult male, was regarded as a capital crime as early as the third century A.D. In 342 the Emperors Constantius and Constans apparently tried to extend this penalty to adults as well:

> When a man "marries" in the manner of a woman, a "woman" about to renounce men, what does he wish, when sex has lost it significance; when the crime is one which it is not profitable to know; when Venus is changed into another form; when love is sought and not found? We order the statutes to arise, the laws to be armed with an avenging sword, that these infamous persons who are now, or who hereafter may be, guilty, may be subjected to exquisite punishment.[67]

In spite of the awkward wording, this seems to apply to a kind of homosexual marriage,[68] but the difficulty is that there are no references to homosexual "marriages" elsewhere in literature. To get around this dilemma it has been suggested that the law was enacted in a "spirit of mocking complacency,"[69] but this also is doubtful. We are thus left with an ambiguous law.

No such ambiguity surrounds the law issued by the Emperors Theodosius, Valentinian II, and Arcadius in 390, which for the first time prescribed burning for those who engaged in anal intercourse.[70]

> All persons who have the shameful custom of condemning a man's body, acting the part of a woman's, to the sufferance of an alien sex (for they appear not to be different from women), shall expiate a crime of this kind by avenging flames in the sight of the people.[71]

Though the law was clearly directed against sodomists and homosexual prostitutes (*exsoleti*), it is not clear that the law was always enforced. Lack of enforcement is indicated by the fact that a tax was collected on male prostitutes until the Emperor Anastasius (491–518) abolished it.[72] But even abolition of a tax did not necessarily abolish homosexual prostitution. All we can safely conclude from his action is that revenue derived from what was regarded as a disreputable source was no longer collected.

John Addington Symonds, a pioneer investigator into homosexuality in history, believed that neither the law of Constantius nor of Theodosius was rigidly enforced. Instead, he dated rigid enforcement from the time of Justinian.[73] Whether Symonds is correct is a matter for debate, but Justinian's sponsorship of the collection of Roman law, the *Corpus juris civilis,* was probably the most important factor in setting not only the Byzantine legal attitude but also the Western Christian one in most matters concerning sexual conduct. The collection is divided into four separate parts, the *Codex,* a collection of valid imperial edicts issued since the time of Hadrian in the second century; the *Digest* (or *Pandects*), a collection of the writings of the classical Roman jurists; the *Institutes,* a handbook for use in law schools that also gives extracts from the other parts; and the *Novellae* or *Novels,* the new laws issued by Justinian and his successors. The *Codex, Digest,* and *Institutes* are in Latin, but most of the *Novels* are in Greek. Each of these four major sections of the *Corpus* includes references to homosexuality, although most references are to pederasty rather than to sexual activity between adults.[74] The most concise summarization of basic law is that in the *Institutes.* This stated that homosexual conduct was to be governed by the Lex Julia, a law that punished with death not only those guilty of adultery but also those who "give themselves up to works of lewdness with their own sex."[75] The Lex Julia had originally been passed under the Emperor Augustus (about 17 B.C.) and dealt with marriage, divorce, adultery, and *stuprum.* Whether it had originally included penalties for homosexual acts is at least debatable, although by the third century it was being interpreted to include homosexual offenses.[76] Justinian also made two significant additions to the subject. In 538 A.D. he issued *Novel 77,* calling for repentance and confession by homosexuals and warning that God would condemn the sinner.

> Since certain men, seized by diabolical incitement, practice among themselves the most disgraceful lusts, and act contrary to nature; we enjoin them to take to heart the fear of God and the judgment to come, and to abstain from such-like diabolical and unlawful lusts, so that they may not be visited by the just wrath of God on account of those impious acts with the results that cities perish with all their inhabitants. . . . For because of such crimes there are famines, earthquakes, and pestilences; wherefore we admonish man to abstain from the aforesaid unlawful acts, that they may not lose their souls. But if, after this our admonition, any are found persisting in such offences, first they render themselves unworthy of the mercy of God, and then they are subjected to the punishment enjoined by the law . . .[77]

This denunciation provides no new penalties and, in spite of its "stern and pious" language, is strongly hortatory. Quite clearly, however, homosexuality is regarded as a threat to the welfare of the state. This belief is even more clearly expressed in *Novel* 141, issued in Lent during the year 544 following a plague that hit Constantinople:

> . . . We have provoked Him to anger on account of the multitude of our sins. And though He has warned us and has shown us clearly what we deserve because of our offences, yet He has acted mercifully towards us, and, awaiting our penitence, has reserved His wrath for other times . . . we ought to abstain from all base concerns and acts—and especially does this apply to such as have gone to decay through that abominable and impious conduct deservedly hated by God. We speak of the defilement of males (*de stupro masculorum*) which some men sacrilegiously and impiously dare to attempt, perpetrating vile acts upon other men.

> For instructed by the Holy Scriptures, we know that God brought a just judgment upon those who lived in Sodom, on account of this very madness of intercourse, so that to this very day the land burns with inextinguishable fire. By this God teaches us, in order that by legislation we may avert such an untoward fate . . . And we . . . entreat God the merciful that those who have been contaminated by the filth of this impious conduct may strive for penitence, that we may not have to prosecute this crime on another occasion. Next, we proclaim to all who are conscious that they have committed any such sin, that unless they desist and, renouncing it before the blessed Patriarch, take care of their salvation, placating God during the holy season for such impious acts, they will bring upon themselves severer penalties, even though on other counts they are held guilty of no fault. . . . If, with eyes as it were blinded, we overlook such impious and forbidden conduct, we may provoke the good God to anger and bring ruin upon all—a fate which would be but deserved.[78]

With these edicts, homosexuality become a matter of not only legal concern but also of community concern, since homosexuals caused God to be wrathful and threatened everyone. Although the edict implied that the penalty for homosexual activities was death, in practice Justinian castrated those guilty of homosexual activities,[79] a practice that further gave eunuchs a reputation for homosexual activity. The death penalty not only remained on Byzantine law books but also was periodically restated. For example, in the tenth-century compilation known as the *Basilica* made under Basil I and his son Leo VI, it was reiterated that homosexual activity was to be punished by death.[80] In the fifteenth century, when the empire was near collapse, the writer George Gemistus Pletho continued to support the death penalty:

> Convinced that the reproduction of the species is a duty, we owe to God . . . we would visit with capital punishment and condemn to death by fire all who are

guilty of sexual aberration and misconduct. Those who are guilty of unnatural offences must be purified by fire: the offender and his accomplice must both be burned alive.[81]

How many individuals were actually burned alive because of their sexual practices? This is impossible to determine, although we do know that some died in a particularly gruesome fashion. In the year 521 two bishops, Isaiah of Rhodes and Alexander of Diospolis, were allegedly guilty of pederasty. Gibbon described their punishment in his inimitable fashion:

A painful death was inflicted by the amputation of the sinful instrument, or the insertion of sharp reeds into the pores and tubes of most exquisite sensibility; and Justinian defended the propriety of the execution, since the criminals would have lost their hands, had they been convicted of sacrilege. In this state of disgrace and agony, two bishops, Isaiah of Rhodes and Alexander of Diospolis, were dragged through the streets of Constantinople, while their brethren were admonished by the voice of a crier, to observe this awful lesson, and not to pollute the sanctity of their character. Perhaps these prelates were innocent. A sentence of death and infamy was often founded on the slight and suspicious evidence of a child or a servant . . . and pederasty became the crime of those to whom no crime could be imputed.[82]

Though Gibbon has his facts confused, since Justinian was not yet emperor, his willingness to associate Justinian with the event is understandable. This is because Justinian's character has been etched in historical memory by Procopius, a particularly difficult source to unravel. Procopius was the court historian during Justinian's reign (527–565), who, after he had finished his official histories, wrote an unofficial or secret one, recounting the scandals he said he had left out of his official one. In his unofficial history, Procopius alleged that homosexuality was the standard charge leveled against anyone who opposed the emperor politically or was too rich or too powerful for the emperor to abide.[83] Though this might well have been the case, Procopius is not particularly effective at documenting his charge. He alleged that prosecution against pederasts was:

conducted in the most irregular fashion, since the penalty was imposed even where there was no accuser, and the word of a single man or boy, even if he happened to be a slave forced to give evidence most unwillingly against his owner, was accepted as final proof. Men convicted in this way were castrated and exposed to public ribaldry.[84]

The only example of using a charge of homosexuality for political purposes that Procopius gave concerns a certain Vasianus, who made uncomplimentary remarks about the Empress Theodora, the wife of Justinian. Unable or unwilling to punish him for his statements about her, Theodora instead allegedly charged him with "offences against boys."

> The officer soon had the man out of the church and tortured him with an unendurable form of punishment. When the people saw a member of the upper classes who had been surrounded with luxury all his life overwhelmed with such agonies, they were immediately cut to the heart, and their groans and shrieks rose to high heaven as they pleaded for the young man. But Theodora made his punishment even worse; she had his privy member cut off and destroyed, although he had never been brought to trial, and finished by confiscating his estate for the Treasury.[85]

Since homosexuality was seemingly regarded in such a hostile fashion, it would appear logical that charges of homosexual activity would be made against various individuals in Byzantine history who fell out of imperial favor. This turns out not to be the case, and after Justinian's reign, in spite of hints about homosexual activity, it is spelled out only rarely. Perhaps it was just too dangerous a charge to make, since even the most hated figures are rarely accused of such activity, and when they are, the charge is made only in the most general way. The Byzantine Emperor Nicephorus I (802–811), for example, was called the "sink of all vices,"[86] by the chronicler Theophanes, who began writing at the end of his reign, but his portrait is not confirmed by other writers.[87] Usually regarded as the worst of emperors is Michael III, nicknamed the Drunkard (842–867). This "Byzantine Caligula," as he has been called, was known for his persistent drunkenness, impiety, scurrility, and sexual deviation. Contemporary chroniclers stated his behavior was due to the fact that his uncle Bardas had provided the young emperor with "every facility for gratifying his passions," to maintain his control over his nephew.[88] The veiled hints of homosexuality are not as important in proving that Michael was or was not a homosexual as they are an indication of how the Byzantines regarded homosexuality and of what kind of conduct they equated with a homosexual emperor. George Finlay, the nineteenth-century historian, described Michael's court with only thinly veiled allusions to homosexuality.

> The favorite parasite of Michael at this time was a man named Basil, who from a simple groom had risen to the rank of lord chamberlain. Basil attracted the attention of the emperor while still a stable-boy in the service of an officer of the court.[89]

Bardas allegedly became jealous of this new favorite of his nephew, and Basil, knowing this, determined to murder Bardas to retain his power. At any rate, after the death of his uncle, Michael adopted Basil and crowned him as his successor in May 866. Basil was, however, soon replaced as the imperial favorite by Basilicius (or Basiliscianus), a former galley slave. Basil, fearful that he might be superseded as heir, had Michael and his new favorite Basiliscianus, killed, ascending the throne himself as Basil I. Even though Basil might have secured the throne through being a catamite, no hint of homosexual behavior is reported about him during his rule. In fact, he went on to found one of the greatest dynasties in Byzantine history. Since this was the case, the historians of the time were careful how they described him or even how they detailed the reign of his predecessor Michael.

In the eleventh century, the chronicler Michael Psellus dropped hints about several other emperors, although for some, such as Basil II (976–1025), the allusion is highly debatable.[90] Of Basil's younger brother and successor, Constantine VIII (1025–1028) the statements are somewhat more explicit.[91] Still, the most that can be said about Constantine is that he was bisexual, since he was married and the father of three daughters.

In describing Constantine IX (1042–1055) Psellus is more cautious and much more hostile. Before beginning his description Psellus cautions his readers that he does not desire to be looked upon as a scandalmonger but only as a "lover of history."[92] Then, having warned his readers, he recounts the scandals of Constantine's reign and describes at length one episode involving a certain rascal afflicted "with just that kind of impediment in his speech." This is quite clearly an allusion to homosexuality, for the homosexual was often portrayed as a person with a lisp, although Psellus was hesitant to make any open accusation. Psellus wrote that the man often went to the emperor, kissing him on the breast and face, and addressing him before he was spoken to, all the while squeezing the emperor's hands. The affairs went on until:

The emperor refused to be parted from him at all. The clown, on the other hand, became bored with this constant attendance. He longed for freedom, to pass the time as he wished. Now, it chanced on a certain occasion that he lost a particularly good polo pony. At that time, he used to sleep beside the emperor. Suddenly, in the middle of the night, he got up, roused him (Constantine) from a deep sleep, and gave way to uncontrollable demonstrations of joy. The emperor asked him what was the matter and why he was so exultant. The clown put his arms around the emperor's neck and kissed him, over and over again on the face. "Sir," said he, "he's been found—the horse that I lost! A eunuch rides him now, a wrinkled old chap, too old for riding. Please let me take a horse for the palace now and bring him here to you, and the mount as well." At these words the emperor laughed gaily. "Ah well," he replied, "you have my permission to go—but mind you come back as soon as possible, and tell me all about it when you find him." So off he went, without wasting a moment, to enjoy the pleasures he had in mind. After his feasting was done, back he came in the evening, panting and puffing, trailing behind him a eunuch. "Here he is, Sir," he said, "the fellow who stole my horse. He has it for sure, but he won't give it up. What's more, he swears he never stole it in the first place." At this, the poor old man appeared to be weeping. . . . To settle the matter, he (the emperor) consoled the old one with a fresh horse, a better one too, while he dried the counterfeit tears of the eunuch with gifts that surpassed his wildest dreams. Actually, this eunuch was one of the comedian's most fervid admirers, and the object of his flattery and long desired him to benefit from the emperor's generosity. Since, however, he could hardly petition Constantine on behalf of a man unknown to him, he devised the playacting about his dream . . . if I had not promised to write on serious matters, and if I cared to record foolish trifles, my history could be augmented with a vast collection of such anecdotes.[93]

In effect, though Psellus hints and hints, he never makes an open accusation.

In the West, which in some ways was much more open about sex, there was considerable worry about homosexuality in the monasteries or among the clergy. In the East, where the clergy were married, there would probably be less grounds for such charges, but what is rather surprising is the lack of any accusation against the monks in the surviving sources. Perhaps this is because, as one historian has written, on "so delicate a matter as this one must not expect to find any precise information in our historical sources."[94] It is possible that many earlier references were simply destroyed, for monastic records were less likely to survive in the East than in the West, if only because the nature of Turkish rule tended to downgrade the intellectual level of monasteries. As a result, until fairly recently, both monastic libraries and manuscripts were in poor condition.[95] Gossip about homosexuality in the monasteries was and is common in the Greek East, even though it rarely appears in the extant sources. There is a humorous story on the subject dating from the eleventh century, when

Monks from Athos appeared at the Imperial Court to complain that the presence of Vlach shepherd-boys on the Holy Mountain was leading to unnatural vice, and Alexius discovered that they had invented the scandal to give them an excuse to visit Constantinople.[96]

The monks themselves were concerned about homosexuality, and probably for this reason the monasteries on Mount Athos, the area in Greece where there were numerous monasteries, established a rule that no male under 18 years of age could stay on the mountain or join a monastery.[97] Michael Choukas, a critic of the monks of Athos who visited the monasteries in the 1930s, hunted diligently for evidence of homosexual scandal but found only one document (Codex Number 328 at Iveron) that included even a veiled reference to the subject.[98] In spite of his lack of historical evidence, he concluded:

No greater obstacles have been erected throughout the years against possible deviation from proper monastic conduct than those related to the satisfaction of sexual desire. The exclusion of women, female animals and beardless youth has been the subject of legislation persistently. Women have been successfully kept away from the mountain, and female animals until recently. Beardless youth, however, have been a constant cause of disturbance, and methods had to be devised to prevent their arrival to Athos. Of these, the expulsion of the monk who had brought the boy to his skete or kellion before maturity; the confiscation of his property by the monastic house; and even whipping have been generally practiced.[99]

During his visit, Choukas found a widespread belief among Greek shopkeepers and workmen in homosexuality among the monks, but he offers little hard evidence. Nonetheless, he continued to speak of "saintly flesh merchants," "canonized paederasts," and "sellers and buyers of 'masculine flesh'."[100] Maryse Choisy, in an exposé of the monastic community on Athos, reported rampant homosexuality.[101] A more sympathetic writer, John Norwich, cautioned that for

> countless generations of Greeks, the sexual habits of Athonite monks have provided an unfailing source of ribald anecdote and lubricious speculation. How much homosexuality, in fact, exists on Athos it is clearly impossible to say. Certainly some—as in any community from which, for whatever reason it may be, one sex or the other is altogether excluded. In the idiorrhythmic monasteries especially, where opportunities are greater and where it is still the custom for a young novice to be attached to an older monk, and to live with him in joint capacity of servant and disciple, some suspicions are unavoidable. It should also be remembered that the existence of homosexuality has always been accepted in the Near East, where, thanks to Hellenistic broadmindedness and sense of proportion, public opinion has never failed—and so lamentably in the West—to see it in its proper perspective. On the other hand, the general atmosphere in the monasteries, as it strikes the normal visitor, is not such as to suggest an unbridled licentiousness.[102]

Probably this description would apply to Greek monasteries in the past. They were concerned with lust, as evidenced by the prohibitions against even mentioning women on Athos, and it would seem likely that many had to wrestle with their own homoerotic desires as well.

We know that the founders of monasticism in the East were conscious of what they felt to be the dangers of homosexuality, although probably the East was far less concerned about it than the West. St. Athanasius, in his *Typica*, for example, recommended two monks to a cell,[103] something frowned on in the West. To St. Athanasius the real dangers afflicted the solitary monk, not one with a cellmate. St. Basil, the regulator of Eastern monasticism, was more concerned, warning young monks to avoid the company of young men lest their desires be kindled and they be flung into the pit where the inhabitants of Sodom resided.

> At meals take a seat far from other young men. In lying down to sleep, let not their clothes be near thine, but rather have an old man between you. When a young man

converses with thee, or sings psalms facing thee, answer him with eyes cast down,
lest perhaps by gazing at his face thou receive a seed of desire sown by the enemy
and reap sheaves of corruption and ruin.[104]

Basil also cautioned monks against "polluting" themselves, but whether this
referred to masturbation, nocturnal emission, overt homosexuality, or simply
thinking lustful thoughts is unclear.[105] To protect the young monks, Basil
recommended that an older monk always be in charge of the youth but that, to
avoid further temptation, the apartments of the young and old also be
separate.[106]

St. Basil also felt that frivolous conversations were to be avoided, as were unnecessary travel or companions who might prove to be seductive.

> The Superior of the company has the power both to order those whom he thinks
> suitable to take necessary journeys and to bid those for whom it is best so to do to
> keep at home and abide within the house. For it often happens when men's bodies
> are young, however zealously the hardships of continence are embraced, that the
> beauty inseparable from youth blooms, so to speak, and becomes an occasion of sin
> to those that meet him. So if anyone is young in respect of bodily bloom, let him
> hide such beauty and keep it out of sight, until his appearance reaches a fitting
> state.[107]

Basil might have been fighting with his own homoerotic desires, for remarks
about the dangers of homosexuality appear only rarely afterward. At the
Council of Constantinople in 692, where various aspects of monastic life were
covered, there is no hint of a concern with homosexuality. Specific regulations
were passed requiring separate quarters for monks and nuns when both sexes
shared the same monastery;[108] the age for entering monastic life was set at 10
years,[109] and men were forbidden from dressing in the clothing of women[110]—a
passing unexplained reference to transvestism. There was also a decree against
"indecent pictures"[111] but nothing on homosexuality. The reference to indecent
pictures is probably not a reference to pornography but an indication of the
growing hostility to icons, which erupted in the iconoclastic controversy, when
all pictures were considered evil. Again in the ninth century, when monks
proved the bulwark of the opposition to the imperial policy of iconoclasm, their
opponents accused them of behaving lustfully with nuns, ignoring their vows of
poverty, selling gifts given to the monastery, and holding unintellectual attitudes,[112] but not of being homosexual.

Interestingly enough, the Byzantine Empire ended on a note that
demonstrated their hostility to homosexuality when the Turk Muhammad II
conquered Constantinople in 1453, capturing several ministers of the dead Emperor Constantine XI (1449–1453). Among them was Megadux (admiral)
Lucas Notaras, whom he considered making governor of the newly conquered

city. His advisers warned him, however, not to trust Notaras, and eventually the Megadux was executed. Steven Runciman described why Muhammad II acted as he did. During a banquet the conqueror gave celebrating the fall of the city,

> when he was well flushed with wine, someone whispered to him that Notaras's fourteen year old son was a boy of exceptional beauty. The Sultan at once sent a eunuch to the house of the Megadux to demand that the boy be sent to him for his pleasure. Notaras, whose two elder sons had been killed fighting, refused to sacrifice the boy to such a fate. Police were then sent to bring Notaras with his son and his young son-in-law, the son of the Grand Domestic Andronicus Cantacuzensus, into the Sultan's presence. When Notaras still defied the Sultan, orders were given for him and the two boys to be decapitated on the spot. Notaras merely asked that they should be slain before him, lest the sight of his death should make them waver. When they had both perished, he bared his neck to the executioner.[113]

Byzantium, although a Christian state, turns out upon investigation not to be so sex negative as the theoretical Christian attitudes would have indicated. In its attitudes on such matters as divorce and remarriage, it followed Roman tradition rather than Christian exhortations. For those who demanded stricter adherence to the ascetic standards of the Church Fathers, monasticism served as an answer. At the same time, the almost overwhelming concern with sexual matters evident in the early phases of the Byzantine state disappeared. Though there are veiled hints about homosexual activities, there is little actual documentation. The evidence seems to indicate that homosexuality was disapproved, even though there was general knowledge it existed. Few were severely punished. Some of the Byzantine customs, in fact, would tend to encourage homosexuality: the strict segregation of men and women, the prevalence of slavery, the existence of eunuchs, and in the case of the monks of Mount Athos and elsewhere, an almost pathological fear of the female. If we have little information about male homosexuality, we have next to nothing about women, regardless of their position. Perhaps the most interesting aspect of Byzantium is its taking separate paths from the West on a whole host of sexual attitudes. These Western attitudes will now be examined.

NOTES

1. St. Basil, *Letters*, No. CLXXXVIII, par. 3, translated by Agnes Clare Way in Vol. 28, *The Fathers of the Church* (New York: Fathers of the Church, 1955).

2. Siricius, *Epistolae et decreta, Epistola V, ad Episcopos Africae*, par. 2, in Vol. 13, J. P. Migne, *Patrologiae Latina* (Paris: Garnier frères, 1844–1864).

3. St. Ambrose, *Epistolae, XXV*, 3, in Vol. 8, *Opera omnia*, D. A. B. Caillau, ed. (Paris: Paul Mellier, 1842).

4. Innocent, *Epistolae et decreta, Epistola VI,* cap. iii. 8, in Vol. 20, Migne, *Patrologiae Latina.*

5. A. H. M. Jones, *The Later Roman Empire* (Norman, Okla.: University of Oklahoma Press, 1964, 2 vols.), Vol. 2, p. 984. The citation is from Paulinus, *Epistolae,* XXXV, 2–5, in Vol. 61, Migne, *Patrologiae Latina.*

6. St. Basil, *De renuntiatione saeculi (On the Renunciation of the World),* translated by Sister M. Monica Wagner in vol. 9, *The Fathers of the Church,* pp. 23–24.

7. *Concilium Eliberitanum,* Canon XXXIII in *Sacrorum conciliorum nova et amplissima collectio,* J. D. Mansi et al., eds. (Florence & Venice, 1795–1798, 31 vols.), Vol. 2, pp. 246–252.

8. Sozomen, *Ecclesiastical History,* I, 23 (London: Henry G. Bohn, 1855); and Socrates, *Ecclesiastical History,* I, ii (London: Henry G. Bohn, 1855).

9. Siricius, *op. cit., Epist. I, ad Himer,* passim.

10. See Derrick Sherwin Bailey, *Sexual Relation in Christian Thought* (New York: Harper and Brothers, 1959), p. 30.

11. Leo I, *Epistolae,* CLXVII, inquis., iv, v, vi, in Vol. 44, Migne, *Patrologiae Latina.*

12. For a comprehensive discussion, see Henry C. Lea, *History of Sacerdotal Celibacy in the Christian Church,* 4th ed. (revised and reprinted, London: Watts and Company, 1932).

13. This was at the Council in Trulo (692), Charles Joseph Hefele, *A History of the Councils of the Church* (Edinburgh: T. T. Clark, 1896), V, vi, and for episcopate, xlviii.

14. Bailey, *op. cit.,* p. 31.

15. H. Achelis, "Agapetae," in *Hastings Encyclopaedia of Religion and Ethics* (New York: Scribner and Sons, 1926), I, 177b–178a. See also Bailey, *op. cit.,* p. 33.

16. Achelis, *op. cit.,* p. 178a, and Joseph Bingham, *Origines Ecclesiasticae* (London: William Straker, 1843, 9 vols.), Vol. 2, pp. 133–137.

17. Tertullian, *De exhortatione castitatis,* xii, *De monogamia,* xvi, in Vol. 2, ser. 2, Migne, *Patrologiae Latina,* cols. 977–978, 1001.

18. See Bailey, *op. cit.,* p. 35, for a list of councils.

19. *Codex Theodosianus,* XVI, ii, 44 (Berlin: Weidmann, 1954); and *Codex,* I, iii (19) in *Corpus juris civilis* (Berlin: Weidmann, 1959, 3 vols.).

20. *Novella,* cxxiii, 29 (541), in *Corpus juris civilis.* See also *Roman State and Christian Church: A Collection of Legal Documents,* P. R. Coleman-Norton, ed. (London: SPCK, 1966, 3 vols.), Vol. 3, pp. 1032–1033.

21. Ignatius, *Epistle ad Polycarp,* V. 2, translated by Joseph Kleist (London: Longmans, Green and Company 1961).

22. Ernst H. Kantorowicz, "On the Golden Marriage Belt and the Marriage Rings in the Dumbarton Oaks Collection," *Dumbarton Oaks Papers,* No. 14 (1960), 1–16. See also Bailey, *op. cit.,* pp. 74–80.

23. *Digest,* L, xvii, 30 (*Nuptias non concubitus sed consensus facit*), in *Corpus juris civilis.*

24. *Digest,* XXIV, 60, 61, 62, ii, 4, 9, iii, 22, par. 7.

25. For details, see O. D. Watkins, *Holy Matrimony* (London: Rivington, Percival and Company, 1895), pp. 291–293.

26. St. Basil, *Letters,* clxxxviii, 9; ccxvii, 58, 59, 77; and ccxiv, 21.

27. Watkins, *op. cit.,* p. 418; Bailey, *op. cit.,* pp. 83–85.

28. Under Justinian, *Novella,* xxii (536), mutual consent still sufficed to effect divorce, although another *Novella,* cxxiv (556), prohibited divorce and allowed it only on specific grounds. *Novella,* cxvii (542), gave some of the grounds.

29. Bertha Diener, *Imperial Byzantium*, translated by Eden and Cedar Paul (Boston: Little Brown, 1938), pp. 182–193.

30. St. John Chrysostom, *On Those Words of the Apostle*, "On Account of Fornication," in Vol. 51, *Patrologiae Graeca*, J. P. Migne, ed. (Paris: Garnier frères, 1857–1886), col. 213, and "Messenger," II, col. 143–144.

31. See John T. Noonan, *Contraception* (Cambridge, Mass.: Harvard University Press, 1966), p. 79.

32. St. John Chrysostom, *On Those Words of the Apostle*, "On Account of Fornication," Migne, *Patrologiae Graeca*, Vol. 51, col. 213.

33. Norman E. Himes, *Medical History of Contraception* (reprinted, New York: Schocken Books, 1970), pp. 94–96. Himes gives a translation of the pertinent parts of Aëtius, *On Medicine in Sixteen Books*, XVI, xvi and xvii.

34. *Concilium Ancyra* (314), Canon XXI, Mansi, *op. cit.*, Vol. 2, p. 519. See also Roger John Huser, *The Crime of Abortion in Canon Law* (Washington, D.C.: Catholic University of America Press, 1943).

35. R. J. H. Jenkins, "Social Life in the Byzantine Empire," *Cambridge Medieval History*, new edition, Vol. 4, Part 2, J. M. Hussey, ed. (Cambridge, England: University Press, 1967), pp. 88–89. The most nearly complete account of prostitution in the Byzantine Empire can be found in P. Koukoules, *The Private Life of the Byzantines* (in Greek) (Athens. Institut Francais, 1947–1957, 8 vols.), Vol. 2, 2, pp. 117–162. There is no similar account in English.

36. A. A. Vasiliev, *Justin the First* (Cambridge, Mass.: Harvard University Press, 1950), p. 74. For translations of some of his legislation, see Coleman-Norton, *op. cit.*, Vol. 3, p. 1169.

37. Demetrios J. Constantelos, *Byzantine Philanthropy and Social Welfare* (New Brunswick, N. J.: Rutgers University Press, 1968), pp. 272–273.

38. Vasiliev, *op. cit.*, pp. 395–396.

39. Paulus Aegineta, *Seven Books of Medicine*, Book I, sec. xxxv, translated from the Greek with a commentary by Francis Adams (London: Sydenham Society, 1844–1847, 3 vols.), Vol. 1, pp. 44–45.

40. *Concilium Nicaenum*, (325), Canon I, Mansi, *op. cit.*, Vol. 2, p. 668.

41. William L. Westermann, *The Slave Systems of Greek and Roman Antiquity* (Philadelphia: American Philosophical Society, 1955), p. 113, No. 88. For an account of the various legislative enactments, see W. W. Buckland, *The Roman Law of Slavery* (reprinted, New York: AMS Press, 1969), pp. 37, 40–41, 80, n. 7, 602–603.

42. Steven Runciman, *Byzantine Civilization* (reprinted, New York: Meridian Books, 1956), p. 162.

43. Steven Runciman, *The Emperor Romanus Lecapenus and His Reign* (Cambridge, England: University Press, 1963), p. 30.

44. For a breakdown of the offices, see J. B. Bury, *The Imperial Administrative System in the Ninth Century* (reprinted, New York: Burt Franklin, 1958), pp. 120–129, the section entitled "Dignities and Offices of the Eunuchs." There were eight orders of eunuchs. Bury's account is based on the *Keltorologion* of Philotheos. See also Wilhelm Ensslin, "The Emperor and Imperial Administration," in *Byzantium*, Norman H. Baynes and H. St. L. B. Moss, eds. (Oxford, England: Clarendon Press, 1948), p. 286.

45. For references, see Jones, *op. cit.*, Vol. 2, pp. 1232–1233, n. 7.

46. *Ibid.*, Vol. 2, pp. 851–852.

47. For prices of eunuchs, see *Codex*, VII, vii, I, (530).

48. For casualties in castration, see *Novella*, cxlii (558).

49. Paulus Aegineta, Book VI, see lxviii, "On Castration," in Vol. 2, pp. 379–380. The description is similar to a description by Celsus for dealing with cirsocele or pneumatocele. Similar descriptions appear in various Arabic writers.

50. Diener, *op. cit.*, pp. 74–75.

51. Edward Gibbon, *The History of the Decline and Fall of the Roman Empire*, J. B. Bury, ed. (reprinted, New York: Heritage Press, 1946, 6 vols. in 3), Vol. 4, p. 1605 (Chap. 48).

52. W. E. H. Lecky, *History of European Morals* (reprinted, New York: George Braziller, 1955, 2 vols. in 1), Vol. 2, p. 13.

53. Joseph McCabe, *Morals in Early Medieval Europe*, Vol. 5 in *A History of Human Morals*, E. Haldeman-Julius, ed. (Girard, Kansas: Haldeman-Julius Publications, n.d.), p. 43.

54. Charles Diehl, "Byzantine Civilization," in *Cambridge Medieval History*, J. R. Tanner et al., eds., 1st ed. (New York: Macmillan, 1936), Vol. 4, p. 775. The revised second edition gives a quite different picture, indicating scholars' changing outlook about the whole field of study.

55. Runciman, *The Emperor Romanus Lecapenus and His Reign*, p. 31.

56. Westermann *op. cit.*, pp. 18–19; see also Buckland, *op. cit.*, pp. 8–9, n. 3; Jenkins, "Social Life in the Byzantine Empire," *op. cit.*, p. 89. In the twelfth century, as the slave trade declined, some free men sold themselves into slavery.

57. St. John Chrysostom, *Homilies*, LXXIII, 3, in Vol. 7, *Oeuvres completes* (Nantes and Mazear: Libraire-Editeur, 1865). For further discussion of Chrysostom, see Derrick Sherwin Bailey, *Homosexuality and the Western Christian Tradition* (London: Longmans, Green and Company, 1955), pp. 82–83.

58. M. L. Laistner, *Christianity and Pagan Culture in the Later Roman Empire* (Ithaca, N.Y.: Cornell University Press, 1951), p. 87, No. 3.

59. *Ibid.*, p. 94.

60. *Ibid.*, p. 111, No. 57.

61. *Ibid.*, p. 136, fn. 11.

62. *Ibid.*, p. 110, No. 56.

63. St. Basil, *Letters*, CCXVII, 62.

64. Gregory of Nyssa, *Epistula Canonica*, 4, in Migne, *Patrologiae Graeca*, Vol. 45, p. 227. I am indebted to Bailey, *Homosexuality and the Western Christian Tradition*, p. 89, for this reference.

65. Laistner, *op. cit.*, p. 81.

66. E. Westermarck, *Christianity and Morals* (reprinted, Freeport, N.Y.: Books for Libraries, 1969), pp. 371–372.

67. *The Theodosian Code*, translated by Clyde Pharr (Princeton, N.J.: Princeton University Press, 1952), pp. 231–232.

68. Bailey, *Homosexuality and the Western Christian Tradition*, p. 70.

69. W. G. Holmes, *The Age of Justinian and Theodora* (London: G. Bell and Company, 1912, 2 vols.), Vol. 1, p. 121.

70. Westermarck, *op. cit.*, p. 372, and n. 6. This became the common way of executing alleged sodomists in the Middle Ages and in some countries until recent times.

71. *The Theodosian Code*, p. 232.

72. Evagrius, *Ecclesiastical History*, III, 39–41 (London: Henry G. Bohn, 1854).

73. John Addington Symonds, *A Problem in Modern Ethics* (London: privately printed, 1896), p. 8.

74. See, for example, *Codex,* IX, ix, "Ad legem de adulteriis et de stupro"; Digest, XLVIII, v. 35.1, *"Stuprum . . . puero";* Digest, XLVIII, v. 9 *"Cum masculo";* Institutes, IV, xviii, 4; and *Novellae* LXXVII and CXLI, in the *Corpus juris civilis.*

75. *Institutes,* IV, xviii, 4. There are several English translations, including one by J. B. Moyle (Oxford, England: Clarendon Press, 1937); and by Thomas Collett Sandars (London: Longmans, Green and Company, 1910).

76. Bailey, *Homosexuality in the Western Christian Tradition,* pp. 66–67.

77. *Novel,* LXXVII. The translation is that made by Bailey, *Homosexuality and the Western Christian Tradition,* pp. 73–74.

78. *Novel,* CXLI, and Bailey, *Homosexuality and the Western Christian Tradition,* pp. 74–75.

79. Procopius, *Anecdota,* XI. 36, translated by H. B. Dewing (London: William Heinemann, 1940).

80. *Basilicorum,* LX, 36.46 (Amsterdam: A. M. Hakkert, 1962).

81. Ernest Barkert, *Social and Political Thought in Byzantium* (Oxford, England: Clarendon Press, 1957), p. 124. The source can be found in Pletho, *On Laws,* Book 3.

82. Gibbon, *op. cit.,* Vol. 4, p. 1476. For a description of the incident, see Theophanes, *Chronographia,* in Vol. 108, Migne, *Patrologae Graeca,* col. 407.

83. Procopius, *Anecdota,* XI, 36.

84. *Ibid.*

85. *Ibid.,* XVI, 20.

86. Joseph McCabe, *Empresses of Constantinople* (London: Methuen, 1913), p. 101.

87. For a brief summary of some modern studies, see A. A. Vasiliev, *History of the Byzantine Empire* (Madison, Wis.: University of Wisconsin Press, 1952), pp. 272–273; and George Ostrogorsky, *History of the Byzantine State,* rev. ed., translated by Joan Hussey (New Brunswick, N. J.: Rutgers University Press, 1969), pp. 223–224.

88. George Finlay, *A History of Greece* (Oxford, England: Clarendon Press, 1877), p. 171. Finlay reported that the Empress Theodora "countenanced the vices of her son," and that Bardas corrupted the young man in an "endeavor to secure a mastery over his mind." *Ibid.,* pp. 161, 171. McCabe, *Empresses of Constantinople,* p. 111, claimed that Michael was "deliberately educated in vice and sensuality."

89. Finlay, *op. cit.,* p. 198.

90. Michael Psellus, *The Chronographia,* I, 4, translated by E. R. A. Sewter (New Haven, Conn.: Yale University Press, 1953).

91. *Ibid.,* II, 1, 3.

92. *Ibid.,* VI, 22.

93. *Ibid.,* VI, 139–144.

94. Hippolyte Delehaye, "Byzantine Monasticism," in Baynes and Moss, *op. cit.,* p. 155.

95. Sir Robert Curzon, *Monasteries of the East* (New York: A. S. Barnes, 1854).

96. Runciman, *Byzantine Civilization,* p. 107.

97. Michael Choukas, *Black Angels of Athos* (Brattleboro, Vt.: Stephen Day Press, 1934), p. 293.

98. *Ibid.,* p. 304, n. 25.

99. *Ibid.,* pp. 248–249.

100. *Ibid.,* pp. 284–292.

101. Maryse Choisy, *A Month among the Men,* translated from the French by Lawrence G. Blochman (New York: Pyramid Books, 1962).

102. John Julius Norwich, Resby Sitwell, and A Costa, *Mount Athos* (New York: Harper and Row, 1966), p. 77.

103. Delehaye, *op. cit.,* p. 151.

104. St. Basil, *De renuntiatione saeculi,* translated by W. K. L. Clarke in *The Ascetic Works of Basil* (New York: Macmillan, 1925), p. 66.

105. *Ibid.,* p. 134.

106. *Ibid.,* p. 176.

107. *Ibid.,* p. 138.

108. See the regulations of the Council of Trullo in Hefele, *op. cit.,* V. p. 384.

109. See Canons, 3, 40, 62, in *Ibid.,* passim.

110. *Ibid.,* No. 62, p. 236.

111. *Ibid.*

112. Joan Hussey, *The Byzantine World* (New York: Harper, 1961), p. 129.

113. Steven Runciman, *The Fall of Constantinople 1453* (Cambridge, England: University Press, 1965), p. 151.

13

THE EARLY MIDDLE AGES
IN THE WEST

The period from the fifth to the tenth centuries has often erroneously been called the Dark Ages. Such a designation is misleading on two counts, for it implies both that we know nothing about the period and that there is nothing worth knowing. In fact, as modern historians have begun to examine these years in detail, we are discovering that, rather than a period of stagnation, this era was quite the reverse. Innovations of the period were in large measure responsible for the termination of what could be considered Roman civilization and the beginning of what can be called European. Where the Byzantine and Arab civilizations were more or less continuations of ancient ways and concepts with a Christian or Islamic overlay, European civilization grew to be quite different, even though it also owed much to Rome, Greece, and the ancient Near East.

By the end of the fifth century, the Roman Empire had disappeared in the Latin West in all but name. In its place there appeared various Germanic "nations." Urban life, so characteristic of the old Mediterranean civilization, had declined noticeably and in many places was almost nonexistent. This deterioration of the city was in part a result of the same economic circumstances that had led Constantine to transfer the imperial capital to Constantinople. Compounding the problem was the fact that the Germans were a rural people, hostile and suspicious of much of city life. Though Rome continued for a time to function as a Western capital after the center of the empire moved eastward, the government offices were gradually transferred to Milan, and ultimately to Ravenna, which remained an outpost of the Byzantine Empire for centuries. The chief reason that the cities continued to survive in the West, if only in name, stemmed from the Church practice of using them for administrative centers where the bishop of the diocese resided. The Church also took over many of the functions of the state in education and social welfare and increasingly regarded itself as dominant in all areas of human morality. Thus the history of sexual attitudes in the early Middle Ages is largely a record of what the Church officials thought and said, although the beliefs of the Germans as a people must also be taken into account.

The Middle Ages were not a stagnant period but, rather, underwent several changes in attitude, although the dominant beliefs might well have remained the same. This is important to emphasize, for it is often stated, as a result of the pioneering research of Edward Westermarck, that throughout the medieval period, only a painful death by burning could atone for homosexual acts.[1] Westermarck gave no evidence to support this generalization. Rather, he assumed that the Justinian Code was the basic law of the Latin West in the early medieval period, believing that the hostility of the Church Fathers to sexual activity had the force of law. This is simply not the case. Medieval men and women, like other people before and since, often said one thing and did another, and a person could and did regard himself or herself as a Christian without necessarily subscribing to all the rules of conduct defined by ecclesiastical authorities as essential for Christians. Moreover, whereas the Church officials condemned various forms of sexual activity, the penalties for engaging in such forbidden activities usually lay in the hands of the Church officials, not the secular, and they stressed spiritual rather than corporal punishment.

One of the best sources for German sexual attitudes is their law codes. Originally, these were the unwritten customs regarded as the inalienable possession of an individual German, which he carried with him. In this sense Germanic law was individual rather than territorial, and the accused individual, regardless of where he found himself, had a right to negotiate penalties according to his own law. The emphasis here is on the masculine pronoun, for women were originally not so much persons in the Germanic law codes as they were property. Female chastity and virtue had property value, and women were, to put it simply, the property of their menfolk. They were always under the protection of some male: father, brother, son, or other near male relatives. Theoretically, the justification for this was the female's physical inferiority. Since a woman was held to be constitutionally unable to bear arms, it was essential she be protected by a relative who wore a sword and could draw it, if necessary, to defend her. The laws of the Ripuarian Franks set the penalty for killing a free woman between puberty and her 40th year at 600 *solidi,* and the death of a young girl cost 200. The code estimated 600 *solidi* to be the equivalent of 300 cattle or 50 male horses, and so severe was the penalty that provisions were made to pay it in installments extending over three generations.[2]

As the Germans moved into the Roman Empire in greater and greater numbers, Germanic customs clashed more and more with Latin legal codes and led to the Germanic customs' being committed to writing and to being codified, usually in Latin. Visigothic laws, for example, were codified under King Euric (466–485), and his son Alaric II published a code in 506, the so-called *Breviarum*. This was designed to serve as regulations for the Romans under his jurisdiction, for the Visigothic rulers recognized that the Romans would have been accustomed to different laws. Later a new compilation was issued, setting up a common law for all Visigothic territory; this concept of territoriality, a fusion of Visigothic and Roman law, marked a new stage in the emergence of Germanic law. Eventually, all Germanic law became territorial. The Burgundian codes, compiled around 500, continued to be used into the ninth century. Anglo-Saxon law, one of the few to be written in the original German, was codified for the first time between 597 and 614. A Lombard code was published in the seventh century and modified a century later. The law of the Ripuarian Franks was codified in the early seventh century, and that of the Alemanni, Bavarians, and Saxons, between the seventh and ninth centuries. The law of the Salian Franks was probably set down at the instance of King Clovis in the sixth century, but the Thuringian, Alemanni, and Bavarian laws continued also to be valid in his territories. In only one set of these laws is there any reference to what could be regarded as variant sexual activity.[3]

This omission indicates that, in general, sexual morality was regarded as under the control of the family and not a matter for criminal law. When the law did enter these areas, its purpose was to replace individual acts of retaliatory violence with symbolic payments, to curtail blood feuds and secure peace. This was done by establishing a specific fine for an offense, part of which went to the family of the injured one and part to the king and his judicial officer. Every crime had its price. The price for murder, for example, was full payment of a man's *wergeld*, literally, "man-money." The codes only rarely recognized the right of the state to intervene directly and punish in some other fashion, such as death by war axe or sword or by hanging, or simply by outlawry, that is, putting the man beyond the protection of the law, an open invitation for anyone to kill him.

Wergeld varied according to the person's status. The *wergeld* of a pregnant woman was three times that of a woman too old to have children. A noblewoman was worth more than a peasant woman. The *wergeld* of a man was higher if he was in the service of the king than if not. For lesser crimes, fines were levied against the family, not the individual. Fines, varying according to the crime, were different for a person who stole a "bull which rules the herd and has never been yoked," than for stealing a bull "used for the cows of three villages in common," or a "bull belonging to the king." The sexually related crime most often mentioned in the various Germanic codes is adultery, but it was the adultery of the wife rather than the husband. This was not, however, so much a sex crime as a violation of property, and the husband in most cases had the right to kill his wife and her accomplices outright if he caught them in the act.[4] On the other hand, a husband was free to fornicate, although he had to be careful not to violate some other male's property rights, because female chastity had property value to a father, a brother, and a male guardian; anyone who caught a trespasser in carnal intimacy with a female relative was allowed to impose a physical punishment without fear of retribution.[5]

This toleration of most forms of sexual activity that did not damage property ran into conflict with the Christian sexual attitudes. The Church tended to regard incest, adultery, and numerous other sexual activities as offenses against God, as well as insults to the whole Christian community. In the mind of the Church, the persons guilty of such wrongs were impious and had to be isolated from the community of the faithful until they repented of their wrongdoings.[6] As Christianity became the official religion of the Germans, the Church hierarchy found itself dealing with peoples who saw nothing wrong in open and frank sexuality as long as sexual practices did not violate property rights.

How deeply these sexual beliefs were engrained in Germanic culture is still unclear, but if the Scandinavian sources are to be trusted as reflecting on Germanic customs before their conversion, they were very much a part of the German tradition. From the archaeological evidence we know the Germanic peoples gave prominence to the phallic nature of mankind, there being numerous representations of copulation in the surviving petroglyphs. Frey, the God whose name is still commemorated in the word *Friday,* was the god of fruitfulness and sexuality. He was usually portrayed with an exaggerated phallus and associated with stallions. His worship was apparently linked with the phallus; hints about its nature have been preseved in the *Edda,* surviving collections of Scandinavian folklore and history, written in Iceland in the thirteenth century. One of the stories in the *Elder Edda* tells how a peasant family had cut off the phallus of a dead stallion, wrapped it in linen with onions and herbs to prevent it from rotting, and stored it in a chest. Every evening it was taken out and worshipped, always being addressed with the dedicatory words, "the devil made it swell and become stiff, so that it could stand with the woman as often as she wanted it." At the evening meal it was passed around among members of the household.[7] Other rituals also had strong sexual overtones.

Inevitably, the Church spent much of its energies fighting such "immoral" beliefs, and though in the process much of pagan belief and ceremony (such as the Christmas tree and the Easter rabbit) were incorporated into Christianity, the overt sexuality was eliminated. The depth of this struggle is evident from what appears to be the obsession the Western Church had in regard to sex. G. Rattray Taylor, in his popular history of sex, wrote that it seemed to him the ideal Christians held out to non-Christians was primarily asexual. Christians laid down an elaborate system of regulations based

> upon the conviction that the sexual act was to be avoided like the plague, except for the bare minimum necessary to keep the race in existence. Even when performed for this purpose it remained a regrettable necessity.[8]

The easiest way the Church could impose its moral standards on its communicants was to attempt to give religious concepts the force of law. The provisions dealing with homosexuality in the Theodosian Code and later in the various edicts of Justinian and his successors reflect the initial success of such attempts. In general, however, Church leaders were less successful with the Germanic legal systems, and gradually a separate legal system, Canon Law, developed to deal with such matters; it was here that most matters of faith, morals, and sex were ultimately assigned in the West during the medieval period.

The chief exception to this generalization in the early Middle Ages occurred in Spain, where the Visigothic kings needed the support of the Church to retain and consolidate their power and ensure the succession of their chosen heirs. This fact probably gave the clergy somewhat more influence in the legislative process and led to a kind of intolerant royal orthodoxy that alienated many and ultimately was a factor in the Muslim conquest of the Spanish peninsula. It is also possible, however, that the legal enactments on sex matters in Spain demonstrate an effort to incorporate Roman law into Visigothic law and had comparatively little to do with attempts of Christianity to enforce sexual orthodoxy.[9] The former explanation seems to be more likely than the latter, but both have merit, and it is noteworthy that only homosexuality was singled out. The ordinance in question was issued in 650 A.D. by King Chindaswinth (642–653) and is quoted at length.

> The crime which ought always to be detested, and is regarded as an execrable moral depravity, ought not to be left unavenged. Therefore those who lie with males, or who consent to participate passively in such acts, ought to be smitten by the sentence of this law—namely, that as soon as an offence has been admitted, and the judge has publicly investigated it, he should forthwith take steps to have the offenders of both kinds castrated. Then he should hand them over to the bishop of the district where the offence happens to have been committed, so that by his authority those who are known to have perpetrated such unlawful acts voluntarily may be subjected to forcible expulsion if they show themselves reluctant to undergo punish-

ment for what they have done. Meanwhile, if anyone is known to have performed this horrible and disgraceful act unwillingly and not voluntarily, whether he was active (*inferens*) or passive (*patiens*), then he can be held free of guilt if he comes forward himself to reveal the base crime. But the man who is well known to have sunk to this madness of his own free will is undoubtedly liable to punishment. And if those who have consented to do such acts have wives, their sons or legitimate heirs can obtain possession of their property; while as for the wife, when she has received for her own portion sufficient for a dowry, and has retained her own belongings intact, she shall remain unquestionably and absolutely free to marry whom she wills.[10]

One reason that Church influence seems to be the dominating factor in such legislation is that the Church Councils held in Spain also paid considerable attention to sexual legislation. These councils, which included both clerical and lay representatives, issued a number of ordinances dealing with homosexual activity, although Church Councils in other areas were also concerned with various sexual matters.[11] The Visigothic King Egica (687–701), for example, in a special communication to the sixteenth Council of Toledo (693), urged the assembled clergy and distinguished men to concern themselves with curtailing homosexual activities:

> Among other matters, see that you determine to extirpate that obscene crime committed by those who lie with males, whose fearful conduct defiles the charm of honest living and provokes from heaven the wrath of the supreme Judge.[12]

The Council responded with a statement that probably reflected the official Church attitude

> . . . If any one of these males who commit this vile practice against nature with other males is a bishop, a priest, or a deacon, he shall be degraded from the dignity of his order, and shall remain in perpetual exile, struck down by damnation. Moreover, if any have been implicated in the evils of another's filthy doings, let them be punished nonetheless, without respect of order, rank, or person, by the sentence of the law [apparently the law of Chindaswinth mentioned above] which was enacted concerning such offences, and let them be excluded from all communion with Christians, and furthermore let them be punished with one hundred stipes of the lash, shorn of their hair, as a mark of disgrace, and banished in perpetual exile . . .[13]

When King Egica received the statement of the Council, he reinforced it with an edict of his own to eliminate and abolish the detestable outrages that lust had led men to do. He required not only castration but also the death penalty for all those found guilty.[14]

Why such hostility to homosexuality among the Visigothic rulers? Some historians, taking the statutes at face value, have suggested that the motivating factor was the rapid growth of homosexuality in Spain. They suggest this is what enabled the Muslims to conquer Spain so quickly, for the effeminacy and military decadence of the Visigoths made them unable to fight effectively.[15] There is no basis for such a charge of effeminacy in the records (other than the enactments against homosexuality), and even if homosexuality was widespread, it would not necessarily have weakened the fighting ability of the Visigothic army. The effect of such a charge is, however, to establish a circular process by which homosexuality is blamed for the fall of Spain without the least shred of evidence, except that the Visigothic rulers expressed hostility to homosexuality.

The only other set of secular enactments against "deviant" sexuality came in Western Europe during the reign of Charlemagne at the end of the eight century. These statutes seem, however to have been issued more as guides to clergy than as actual laws, since the statutes cite as authority the Council of Ancyra, which set ecclesiastical penances for sexual activities. Though Derrick Sherwin Bailey has expressed doubt whether the statutes of the Council of Ancyra had originally been directed against homosexual activity,[16] this was the way they were interpreted by various councils in the West. For example, Carolingian interpretations of the Council appear in an ordinance from Aachen in 789, which in turn was based on Latin interpretations of Canon 16 of the Council of Ancyra.[17] Three of the Carolingian enactments cite the Council of Ancyra in grouping three categories of sexual sins and assigning penances for them: those who fornicate with animals, those who engage in consanguineous marriages, and those who sin against nature, a rather ambiguous category needing some explanation.[18] Before defining the sin against nature, however, it might be well to finish a listing of Carolingian laws. A capitulary of 803 condemned those evildoers who committed acts of sodomy contrary to divine law,[19] and the prohibitions of this capitulary are repeated in three others.[20] Still another capitulary condemned sodomy among monks, pointing out that there have been reports of such sexual activity,[21] but the general tenor of the capitulary is hortatory rather then penalizing. Sodomy or other homosexual actions do not seem to have become part of the criminal law as they did in Visigothic Spain. Rather, sexual activities seem to be regarded as coming under the jurisdiction of the ecclesiastical courts; in England, for example, such activities were not regarded as part of the secular law until the sixteenth century.[22]

In the Church law the concept of sin against nature comes to be a euphemism for forbidden secular activity, although just what constitutes such a sin is not always clear. The key Biblical reference appears in the Pauline *Epistle to the Romans*, where it is reported that God had given up on some idolatrous pagans who in their lust had dishonored their own bodies:

> Who changed the truth of God into a lie, and worshipped and served the creature
> more than the Creator, who is blessed forever. Amen. For this cause God gave
> them up into vile affections: for even their women did change the natural use into
> that which is *against nature*; and likewise also the man, leaving the natural use of
> the woman; burned in their lust one toward another; men with men working that
> which is unseemly, and receiving in themselves that recompense of their error
> which was meet.[23]

Today Biblical scholars are not agreed over the meaning of the passage. Some
have contended that the exchange of "natural use" for "unnatural" was aimed
at anal intercourse within marriage, others that it included coitus interruptus,
and others that it was specifically aimed at homosexual activities.[24] Important
to emphasize is the use of nature as a criterion for right action. Such a usage
assumed that man could discover the basis for right conduct by observation of
the world around him, an essential concept in the teachings of the Stoic and
neo-Platonic philosophers contemporary with the emergence of Christianity.

Probably the original source of natural observations in the classical world
was Aristotle, who used his observations of nature to prove to his satisfaction
the female's biological inferiority.[25] Going a step further than Aristotle were
the Stoics, who turned to nature as a source for discovering what was right
conduct, assuming a natural law governed this that could be discovered through
reasoning. Closely tied into this Stoic belief was the belief that men should be
rationally self-sufficient, not dependent on the body, if only because bodily
activities were so irrational.[26] This Stoic concentration on nature, virtue, decorum, and freedom from excess proved, of course, attractive to the formulators
of Christian doctrine, who incorporated these concepts into their interpretation
of the ideal life style.

As to sex, the Stoics believed that marriage could be justified only on the
grounds that it propagated the race.[27] Obviously then, anything going beyond
this was contrary to the self-sufficiency and moderation dictated to mankind by
their nature, that is, was contrary to nature. This idea was picked up and amplified by the Jewish philosopher Philo, who has already been discussed. All
sexual activities not leading to procreation, he wrote, debased the "sterling coin
of their nature," and their perpetrators were bad husbandmen in that they let
the "deep-soiled and fruitful fields lie sterile, by taking steps to keep them from
bearing," while "they spent their labor on soils from which no growth at all"
could be expected.[28] When Christian writers came to deal with sex, they
adopted the philosophical concept of nature in several different ways, although
all of their beliefs were firmly rooted in the pagan writers who had preceded
them. One method was to compare the sexual process to the sowing of a field,

and thus any pattern uncontaminated by human sin or error could be regarded as natural. A second method was to compare sexual behavior in animals with that in humans; what animals did was considered natural, what they did not do was considered unnatural. Thirdly, there was an attempt to determine what nature intended by the functional structure of the organs. That is, eyes were to see with, ears to hear with, and in all cases the obvious function of the organ was a natural one, and what was natural was taken as self-evident. As John T. Noonan has emphasized:

> In each sense of the term, the "natural" was selectively chosen. An agricultural phenomenon was considered where human effort was completed by physical forces; the example of human beings damming a river to prevent a flow was not used as an example of "nature." Not all animal behavior was found appropriate to follow: the hyena, for instance, popularly supposed to have a set of organs serving a sexual but not a generative purpose, was an example to avoid. The human sexual organs function for a variety of purposes; some of them were "unnatural."[29]

In effect, in all cases the appeal to nature was used to reinforce theoretical positions already taken. It was not so much observation of what took place in nature, but rather an already adopted position that was then justified by observation. Though there was some debate on the subject among the Church Fathers, the final definition of what was against nature was given by St. Augustine in the fifth century. Augustine saw nothing rational, spiritual, or sacramental in the act of intercourse, although he recognized that Jesus has sanctioned marriage by blessing it. This meant that marriage, including sexual intercourse within it, must be good. He would however, accept this concept of sexual intercourse as a good only if it led to offspring.[30] Anything else went beyond the natural use, which he defined as using a member not granted for this purpose. His definition, then, would include using contraceptives of any kind, engaging in anal intercourse, masturbation, homosexual activity, coitus interruptus, bestiality, oral–genital contacts, and, in effect, anything not leading to conception.[31] Augustine established the intellectual basis for the belief in a sin against nature that much later entered the law codes as the crime against nature.

The concept of sexual activity as sin gave the Church officials a means of entering into the sexual practices of their parishioners. Since sex, after all, is basically a private matter, any secular legislation could be concerned only with the more flagrant and more notorious cases, but this was not enough for the Church authorities. Once sexual activity was equated with sin, it became a different matter, since sin involved penance. In the early Christian Church, penance, technically the reconciling of a sinner with God, had been a public affair, and open confession had been both a means of discipline and a method of probation whereby the Church sought to maintain its purity in the evils of the secular world. Almost from the beginning, penance had involved sexual purity; in the early Western Church, the three principal or capital sins were idolatry or reversion to paganism, sexual impurity, and homicide. Those who had committed any of these sins were excluded from communion and from the fellowship of the Church and could be restored only by submitting to a strict regimen of public penance for a set number of years.

As the Christian Church increased in numbers and influence, public penance fell into disuse, and more and more, a system of private penance and recurrent confession was used. Most scholars believe that the system of private penance and devotional confession for lesser or venial sins appeared originally in the Welsh and Irish monasteries. Monks from these monasteries introduced it into England, and from England it spread to the continent, eventually extending through both the regular (monastic) and the secular church. It did not, however, become established as the official practice of the Church until the Fourth Lateran Council in 1215.

Penance came to be regarded as a healing medicine for the soul, and the confessors, following the physicians' example, felt it essential to have their patients describe their diseases and their symptoms and probed ever deeper into what they felt were the festering sores of sinful activity. The clerical healers tried to distinguish various types of spiritual illness, classifying them by degrees of seriousness and describing all the symptoms. Idolatry, sexual impurity, and homicide were the general categories, but they had to be divided into specific categories. There were different levels of sexual sins, the more serious requiring a more drastic cure than the minor peccadillo. One of the earliest attempts to enumerate the sins in some detail was made by John Cassian (about 360–435), a monk from southern Gaul, credited also with introducing the rules of Eastern monasticism into the West. In his *Institutes,* John devoted several books to listing what he regarded as the principal vices, which he set as eight. Listed in order of seriousness, they included gluttony, fornication, avarice, anger, dejection (*tristitia*), languor (*accedia*), vainglory, and pride. Pride was the worst, since it was the germinal source of all the rest.[32] Several penitential writers followed John Cassian's listing, although, because the more influential Pope Gregory the Great (560–604) listed only seven vices in his *Moralia,* omitting languor, seven eventually came to be the accepted number.[33] By the ninth century, Gregory's seven sins had become accepted as almost canonical.

To describe a sin, the penitential writers had to be rather frank in their discussions, and we are thus able to get a fairly good idea of the types of sexual activity with which they were concerned. This very frankness has often been criticized, particularly by our Victorian predecessors, who were upset at the details they found. One of them, C. Plummer, an editor of the works of the

Venerable Bede, wrote that the

> Penitential literature is in truth a deplorable feature of the medieval Church. Evil deeds, the imagination of which may perhaps have dimly floated through our minds in our darkest moments, are here tabulated and reduced to a system. It is hard to see how anyone could busy himself with such literature and not be the worse for it.[34]

What repelled our Victorian forebears, however, turns out to be a gold mine of information. As the author of a ninth-century penitential wrote:

> For no one can raise up one who is falling beneath a weight unless he bends himself that he may reach out to him his hand; and no physician can treat the wounds of the sick unless he comes in contact with their foulness, so also no priest or pontiff can treat the wounds of sinners or take away the sins from their souls, except by intense solicitude and the prayers of tears. Therefore, it is needful for us, beloved brethren, to be solicitous on behalf of sinners, since we are "members one of another" and "if one member suffers anything, all the members suffer with it."[35]

The penitentials give us a picture of the attempts of the Christian Church to impose its will upon a society that, though nominally Christian, had not yet accepted Christian morality. Probably, in most of the newly Christianized territories, there were a few sincere ascetics and a small minority of dedicated clergy, but most people were comparatively untouched by Christian ethics. The Church set out to change such matters. The earliest penitentials to survive are those ascribed to two Welsh synods held under the influence of St. David (about 500), although the part David played is doubtful. These penitentials are known respectively as the *Synod of North Britian* (about 520) and the *Synod of the Grove of Victory* (about 567). Two other early Welsh penitentials have also been preserved, the *Preface of St. Gildas on Penance* (495–570) and *Excerpts from a Book of David* (sixth century). Two of these, that of Gildas and that of North Britain, are restricted to the sins of monks and clergy; the other two are more general.

The Preface of St. Gildas starts out:

> A presbyter or a deacon committing natural fornication or sodomy who has previously taken the monastic vow shall do penance for three years. He shall seek pardon every hour and keep a special fast once every week, except during the fifty days following the Passion. He shall have bread without limitation and a refection with some butter spread over it on Sunday. On the other days his allowance of bread shall be a loaf of dry bread and a dish enriched with a little fat, garden vegetables, a few eggs, British cheese, a Roman half-pint of milk in consideration of the weakness of the body.

From this quotation, it appears that sodomy (not defined) is no worse a sin than fornication and neither deserves any kind of death penalty. Later in the penitential, other sexual sins are spelled out. Bestiality, that is, "one who sins with a beast" required a year to expiate the sin, although if the man had been living by himself when it happened, three 40-day periods of fasting served as sufficient penance. Nocturnal emission was also a sin. It required three nights of an hour-long standing vigil, provided the sinner had been supplied with an adequate diet of beer and meat. If, however, he had been on a rigid diet, the sinner was required to sing 28 or 30 psalms or undertake extra work.[36] Apparently, it was assumed that a person who had been fasting would have less control over his bodily processes, and so involuntary nocturnal emissions by such persons were less serious.

The Synod of North Britain also provided a 3-year penance for fornication or sodomy but added the sin of masturbation to the list of sexual prohibitions, something not mentioned in St. Gildas. An adult masturbator (*Qui se ipsum quoinquinauerit*) had to do penance for a year; a boy of 12 years, either for 40 days or three 40-day periods.[37]

If the Welsh penitentials can serve as any criterion, the laity must have been far more inventive in their sexual activities than the monks or clergy, since the two penitentials written for their confessors include much more detail about sexual activity. *The Synod of the Grove of Victory* listed a 3-year penance for an adulterer, a 3-year pilgrimage for incest with one's mother, 2½ years of penance for those engaged in bestiality, a 4-penance for coitus *in ano*, 3 years for coitus *in femoribus,* and for those who had orgasms in their hands (masturbation), 2 years of penance were required.[38] The *Book of David* lists many of the same sins, but requires heavier penalties; bestiality, for example, requires a lifetime of penance, as does fornication with a nun. There were also variations in penance according to the office the sinner held in the Church. A bishop who committed any kind of fornication had to undergo 13 years of penance, but a presbyter was to serve 7 years for the same crime. Incidentally, the same penalties were required for bishops or clergy who had engaged in murder. Seminal emission, whether voluntary or involuntary, was regarded as polluting, and if one intentionally has such an emission while he was asleep, he was supposed to sing 7 psalms on arising and live on bread and water for a day. If he had intended to sin in his sleep but did not, he had to sing 15 psalms, and if he touched his genital organs but did not have an emission, he was to sing 24. Involuntary nocturnal emissions required the sinner to sing 15 psalms. Bestiality, incest, and adultery, all required a penance of 3 years.[39]

The Welsh penitentials seem in retrospect rather haphazard in their treatment of sins compared to the Irish ones, of which the earliest is that of Finnian (about 525–550). Interestingly, in spite of the greater detail in the early Irish penitentials, there is at first no reference to what could be interpreted as homosexual activity, although one of the manuscript sources of Finnian does have three paragraphs dealing with oral–genital contacts, the first time these are mentioned. Most scholars feel this is a later interpolation. Why such references are missing in the earlier penitentials is difficult to explain, unless the writers' experience was somewhat limited, and whenever they found some new variation, they added to it. This might explain the addition to Finnian stating that those "who satisfy their desire with their lips, 3 years (penance). If it has become a habit, 7 years."[40] The Irish penitentials include such added attractions as the consequences of engaging in sexual relations with a neighbor's virgin daughter. This was punished by a year-long penance, extended to 3 years if she became pregnant. If a male had intercourse with his female slave, the slave was to be sold, and he was forbidden to have intercourse with his wife for a year. If the female slave had a child by her master, she was to be set free.[41]

A sixth-century Irish penitential attributed to St. Columban, one of the Irish monks who acted as missionaries to the Germans, distinguished between clerical sodomy and sodomy committed by laymen. Clerics had to do penance for 10 years, but laymen had to do penance for only 7 years. For the first 3 years, the penitent was to be restricted to a diet of bread and water, salt, and dry produce from the garden. Simple fornication of laymen was punished only by a year's penance if it was with a widow, 2 years if with a virgin. Bestiality required a 1-year penance if the man had a wife, and if not, the penance was a year and a half. The same penalties were required for masturbation. Whether this implies that bestiality was as frequent or infrequent as masturbation is uncertain, but obviously both were regarded more lightly than sexual relations with a person of the same sex. A cleric who had intercourse with a woman had to do penance for 3 years, but if he was a bishop, the penance was extended to 12 years. Simple lust for a woman by cleric, even though unsatisfied, required a half-year's penance on bread and water, and clerical masturbators and those who committed bestiality were required to undergo 2 years' penance.[42] Most of the sexual sins were discussed in terms of males; only rarely are females mentioned except as objects of male sexual drives.

The most nearly comprehensive early listing of possible homosexual activity is found in the penitential of Cummean, believed to have been written by Cummean Fota (the Long), a seventh-century Irish Abbot. Those who engaged in oral–genital contacts (that is, "befoul their lips") were required to do penance for 4 years; if they were accustomed to the habit, they had to do penance for 7 years. Anal intercourse required a 7-year penance, but interfemoral intercourse (between the legs), only 2 years. Bestiality was punished with a year's penance, and incest with one's mother required a 3-year penance. A layman committing adultery with a neighbor's wife or daughter had to do penance for a year and forego intercourse with his own wife. Other provisions on fornication, nocturnal emissions, and so forth are in general the same as set forth in earlier penitentials, although Cummean also entered more deeply into the everyday sex life of his subjects than most writers. Married couples, for example, were to be continent during three 40-day periods of the year, plus every Saturday night and Sunday, and on Wednesday and Friday, during the wife's pregnancy, and during the menstrual period. After a wife gave birth, the husband was to continue to abstain from intercourse for 33 days if it was a son, 66 days if a daughter.[43]

Cummean also has a section entitled "Let us Now Set Forth the Decree of Our Fathers before Us on the (Sinful) Playing of Boys," (*Ponamus nunc de ludis puerilibus priorum statuta patrum nostrorum*). This section provided penances for kissing, licentious kissing, and kissing with seminal emission between boys under 20 years of age, and between men over 20. In general, his penances were light, since he believed such sinful activity could be corrected by special feasts. Boys who practiced mutual masturbation were to do 20 to 40 days of penance, and if they repeated it, 100 days. If they engaged in such practices frequently, they were to be separated and do penance for a year. Interfemoral intercourse among minors resulted in a penance of 100 days, or a year for a repeated offense. If a small boy was "misused" by an older one, the older one had to do penance for a week if he was under 10 years of age; if he consented to the act, he had to do penance for 20 days. Men guilty of such practices were to be given a year's penance for the first offense, 2 years if it was repeated, and 7 years if it had become a habit. Fellatio was punished with a penance of 4 years. Similar punishments were given for heterosexual intercourse.[44]

The penitential literature is obviously a valuable source of information about sexual attitudes, but how much do the penitentials reflect the actual sexual activities of the people? It is here that the historian must tread with caution, for the fact that a particular sexual act is given considerable attention in a penitential does not necessarily mean that such activity was widespread. Likewise, even though a particular sexual activity is not mentioned in one penitential or in one locality, it does not necessarily mean that that particular sexual activity is missing. In fact, the listing might express only the concern of the penitential writer. Derrick Sherwin Bailey, for example, surveyed three English penitentials and concluded that one attributed to Theodore devoted 3.5 percent of its content to homosexual practices; one attributed to Bede, 8 percent; and one attributed to Egbert, 5.5 percent. Each also mentioned bestiality in about the same ratio, Bede giving it the most attention.[45] Obviously, homosexuality and, to a lesser extent, bestiality were of concern to these penitential writers, but why did Bede emphasize these activities more than some of his contemporaries? Does this mean that Bede was a homosexual or that homosexuality was rampant in Bede's monastery? Probably not, although the temptation to homosexual activity in a sexually segregated institution such as a monastery was probably recognized. This is indicated by the fact that homosexual and homoerotic activity is often spelled out in more detail than heterosexual activity, and there are as many references to lusting after a woman as to engaging in actual fornication in many of the penitentials. There is also considerable attention to masturbation. This would fit in with what we know about life in a monastery, where the ascetic monks would probably be more troubled by lusting after a woman than by actual fornication, where masturbation was a real temptation in their solitude, where homoeroticism and homosexuality were possible alternatives, and where bestiality could be contemplated by those who were conscious of their sexual stirrings but saw no other way of expressing them. In short, the manuals written by the celibate monks tended to reflect their own anxieties, perhaps even their experiences, as much as or more than those who confessed to them. Some further evidence of this comes from the fact that female sexual activities are generally ignored. The first appearance of lesbianism, for example, is in the penitential of Theodore of Tarsus, Archbishop of Canterbury (668–690), edited after his death.

In general, Theodore repeats the material found in other penitentials but occasionally adds significant details. In Section 2, concerning fornication, he included as a sinner a woman "who practices vices with a woman," and required such women to undergo penance for 3 years. If the woman in question was married, she deserved a longer penance. Theodore held the "worst of evils" was receiving semen in one's mouth, and for such oral–genital contacts he required a penance of 7 years, although he also recognized that some required 12 years' penance for this sin. Though he regarded oral–genital contact as the worst of sins, he imposed longer penances for other activities. Incest with one's mother resulted in a 15-year penance, as did incest with a sister, and the same penalty was applied for a brother fornicating with a brother. Sodomites were to do penance for 7 years, and the effeminate man, apparently the passive partner, was to be regarded the same as an adultress. If a mother initiated acts of fornication with her little son, she was to do penance for 3 years.[46] The Venerable Bede also deals with lesbianism, although his penalties are usually lighter than those given by Theodore.[47] *The Bigotean Penitential,* an eighth-century Irish manual, also implies that homosexuality is a sin that "is not forgiven either in the present world or that which is to come."[48]

Some sexual activities are only rarely referred to in the penitentials, even though they have Biblical examples. This is the case with onanism, which in the mind of the penitential writers, was clearly distinguished from masturbation. Masturbation was usually regarded as a form of self-arousal, but onanism was seen as a form of contraception. This, at least, appears in what John T. Noonan regarded as the first definitely dated reference to onanism, that by Theodulphus, bishop of Orléans in the ninth century.[49] Penitential references quickly follow. One of the earliest is that in *St. Hubert's Penitential,* a

Frankish compilation dating from the middle of the ninth century, where it is described as the "spilling of the seed in coitus with a woman as the sons of Judah did to Tamar."[50]

Transvestism is also referred to only rarely in the penitentials. The first such reference apparently is found in the penitential of Silos, compiled in a monastery of that same name in the diocese of Burgos in Spain in the ninth century. Transvestism is not, however, regarded as a sexual act, nor does it seem to have any sexual connotations. Instead, it seems to be associated with paganism and witchcraft and is set off in a separate section dealing with dancing:

> Those who in the dance wear women's clothes and strangely devise them and employ jawbones and a bow and a spade and things like these shall do penance for one year.[51]

St. Hubert's Penitential, mentioned above, included a similar reference in a section dealing with dancing before the church, but the penance for a man "who dresses in women's clothing" or a woman "who dons the clothing of men" is 3 years, instead of the 1 year mentioned in Burgos.[52]

It should appear obvious that the penitential writers did not agree on the length or kinds of punishments for the sins they enumerated. Sometimes, different penalties were given in the same penitential; though in some cases this might represent careless copying, it is also possible that the writer himself was either trying to assemble divergent views about penalties or to leave as much latitude as possible to the confessor administering the discipline. The eighth-century *Penitential of Egbert,* Archbishop of York, for example, included sodomy among his listing of capital crimes, and in this section he equated it with adultery, homicide, perjury, idolatry, rape, false testimony, and so forth and stipulated a penance of 4 years for a layman, 5 for a *clericus,* 6 for subdeacons, 7 for deacons, 10 for priests, and 12 for bishops. He also listed sodomy among the minor sins and made the penalties more severe: laymen 5 years, and on up to 14 years for a bishop. Still later, in the same penitential he added to the confusion by stating that if one in orders committed sodomy, the penance could be as much as 10 years according to some authorities, 7 years according to others, and 1 year for some, particularly if the individual assumed the passive role.[53]

The contradictions did not go unnoticed by the medieval ecclesiastical authorities. Pope Gregory III (731–741) stated in a penitential regulation that if

> any ordained person has been defiled with the crime of sodomy, which is described as a vice so abominable in the sight of God that the cities in which its practitioners dwelt were appointed for destruction by fire and brimstone, let him do penance for

ten years, according to the ancient rule. Some, however, being more humanely disposed, have fixed the term at seven years. Those also who are ignorant of the gravity of this offence are assigned three years in which to do penance. As for boys who know that they are indulging in this practice, it behooves them to hasten to amend; let them do penance for 50 days, and in addition let them be beaten with rods; for it is necessary that the crop which has brought forth bad fruit be cut down.[54]

The confusion continued, and in the tenth century, Regino of Prum, in his work *Of Synodical Cases and Ecclesiastical Discipline,* wrote:

Some consider that he who commits fornication like a sodomist must do penance for ten years; others, for seven years; others again, for one year. Some hold that if the practice is habitual, a layman must do five years' penance; a *clericus,* seven years; one who is a subdeacon or a monk, eight years; a deacon, ten years; a priest, twelve years; and a bishop, 13 years.[55]

The person who brought things to a head was the eleventh-century reformer, St. Peter Damian (1007–1072). Damian was in the forefront of Church reform in the eleventh century and was closely associated with the movement known as the Hildebrandine reform, though Damian had died before Hildebrand had been selected as Pope Gregory VII. In the period prior to 1049, before the reform movement had begun in Rome, Damian voiced the need for vigorous action, and with the accession of Pope Leo IX (1049–1054), Damian came to the forefront. During this period he wrote two of his most important works, the *Liber Gomorrhianus,* a devastating treatise on the vices of the secular and regular clergy, and the *Liber Gratissmus,* which dealt with the validity of simoniacal ordinations.[56] In the *Liber Gomorrhianus,* Peter alleged that the higher clergy were not only failing to practice celibacy but also were indulging in various sexual vices. Peter addressed his treatise to Pope Leo IX, since he felt that only the Apostolic See, as the source of heavenly wisdom and ecclesiastical discipline, could deal with the problems he wrote about. He stated that he felt he should be ashamed to mention so foul a sin but did so because "if the physician shrinks from the plague poison, who will take in hand to apply the remedy?" Peter was particularly upset at what he believed to be the practice of homosexual offenders' confessing to persons with whom they committed the acts and thereby ensuring that the matter would go no further and that the penance would be trivial.[57] He felt this was wrong, since every kind of sin "*contra naturam*" deserved the maximum penalty without admitting the least mitigation. Moreover, he added, we know that the sodomites committed numerous other sins besides sodomy, since the Bible stated that, impelled by their lusts, they performed all sorts of vile acts.[58] He felt that sodomists should be degraded from their orders, even if they had committed only one of the lesser sodomitical sins.[59] He urged the Pope to set standards for penitentials, for unless there was a single author for all penalties, the punishment would lose all authority.[60]

Pope Leo accepted the dedication of Peter's work to him[61] and commended Peter, his beloved hermit, for raising the arm of the spirit against obscene license but noted that it was necessary for him as Pope to season justice with mercy. As a result, he felt he could not go as far as Peter urged him to go but would depose only those clerics found guilty of the most serious criminal offenses. Leo stated that not all sexual acts were equally sinful, nor did they all merit the same ecclesiastical censure. He stated an unwillingness to expel anyone from their order unless they had long engaged in homosexual activities with many men.[62] The result of the Pope's refusal to go along with Peter was a break between them, although other factors might have been involved, and some have even claimed that no break took place.[62] Still, Peter's work aroused a storm of protest, much of it justified, since he had maligned the clergy as a whole, and any such blanket charge is likely to be met with hostility. Sexual regulations came, however, to be more and more the subject for canon law as the Church struggled to find a consistent system of penalties. This is discussed in a later chapter.

Though the ecclesiastical writers believed sexual sins were rampant, only occasionally do we get documentation of actual practices, and often even these references are not clear. The Venerable Bede, for example, in his *Ecclesiastical History*, reported the destruction of a monastery at Coldingham by a great fire that, he stated, resulted from the evil lives of the inmates, who continually visited each other in their cells. On the surface this sounds like rampant homosexuality, but we know from other sources that the monastery was a mixed one, that it included both men and women. In fact, it is not even clear that the visits implied sexual activities. Bede listed among the monks of this wicked monastery a certain Scot, Adamnan, who took food or drink only on Sundays and Thursdays and fasted the rest of the days to atone for a sin he had committed in his youth.[63] Wickedness is a relative thing, and a monkish chronicler might regard certain conduct as wicked that others, less judgmental, might find praiseworthy.

Interestingly enough, the kind of sexual behavior best documented in the monasteries is transvestism, which, when practiced by female saints, was not necessarily regarded as deviant behavior at all. Though Christians accepted the Biblical prohibition against wearing clothes of the opposite sex (Deuteronomy 22:5), Christianity through much of its history was not particularly hostile to women's wearing men's clothing. Perhaps this attitude derives from the general medieval Christian attitude toward women, which, following the example of the Greeks, held that women were to be subordinate to men.[64] Tied in with this general overall view was a kind of mystic view of the inferiority of the female, which entered into Christianity through the writings of the Alexandrian Jewish philosopher Philo. As indicated earlier, he taught that the male was superior, because the male represented the more rational parts of the soul, the female representing the less rational. The easiest way for women to approach the male level of rationality was to deny their sexuality and remain virgins, and the words *virgin, virginity,* and *ever-virginal,* occur continually in Philo's references to the best kind of women.[65]

From such an assumption, it would almost logically follow that the female who wore male clothes and adopted the male role would be trying to imitate the superior sex, to become more rational, but the man who wore women's clothes, who tried to take on female gender attributes, would be losing status and becoming less rational. This seems to be implied in the writings of St. Jerome, who wrote in the fourth century that as

> long as woman is for birth and children, she is different from man as body is from soul. But when she wishes to serve Christ more than the world, she will cease to be a woman and will be called man.[66]

A similar concept was expressed by St. Ambrose, also in the fourth century:

> She who does not believe is a woman and should be designated by the name of her sex, whereas she who believes progresses to perfect manhood, to the measure of the adulthood of Christ. She then dispenses with the name of her sex, the seductiveness of youth, the garrulousness of old age.[67]

The list of similar statements could be much expanded, but the result undoubtedly was to encourage women to adopt the guise of men and live like men to attain the higher level of spirituality normally reserved for males. Whether this was the actual intention of these saintly Church Fathers is doubtful, but regardless of the intentions there are numerous stories about saintly women who lived and worked as men. Scholars today might argue that many, if not all, of these saints were legendary rather than real,[68] but since these fictitious creations were believed to be real, the result was to encourage women to act like men and to discourage and punish men who acted like women. Thus, there are no male transvestite saints. A cross-dressing male would not only have lost status but probably also would have been associated with heresy. The hostility that greeted male cross-dressing is exemplified by a study taken from Gregory of Tours, a Frankish writer, who wrote in the sixth century A.D.

According to Gregory, the Abbess of the Convent of Radegunde was accused by a group of rebellious nuns with keeping a man clothed in female garb and pretending he was a woman. Everyone knew, they claimed, that he "was most plainly of the male sex; and that this person regularly served the Abbess." The charges resulted in an investigation that confirmed that there was indeed a male nun. The Abbess was, however, found innocent because a physician appeared who said that he had operated on the male nun when he was a little boy for a disease of the groin and cut out his testicles and that the boy had then adopted feminine garb. As a result of this testimony, the charges against the Abbess were finally dropped.[69] The implication remains, however, that there either had to be something wrong with a man who donned female garb or that the person who did so had other than devotional objectives in mind.

No such implication can be drawn about women who dressed as men, particularly if they assumed the garb of a monk. Probably the archetype for the female transvestite saints is Pelagia. Her story is confused and contradictory, probably because it is a composite of several conflicting legends. She is known both as Pelagia and as Margarito and is also confused with another saint, Margarita, also known as Pelagius. According to the most common version of the story, Pelagia was a beautiful dancing girl and prostitute in Antioch, who was also called Margarito because of the spendor of her pearls. She became converted to Christianity through the efforts of the saintly Bishop Nonus of Antioch, who acted as her patron and sponsor. Not wishing to be identified with her past, Pelagia left Antioch dressed as a male, and under her outer clothes she wore, with the permission of Nonus himself, a hair cloth undershirt. After much travel she found refuge on Mount Olivet, where she lived as a man known as Pelagius, who was admired throughout the Holy Land for his asceticism and holiness. Not until after her death was her true sex revealed. Then her mourners cried out: "Glory be to thee, Lord Jesus, for thou has many hidden treasures on earth, as well female as male."[70]

The other Saint Margarita–Pelagius has a slightly different story. In the more or less standardized version, a girl named Margarita held marriage in such horror that, after her betrothal, she fled the nuptial chamber in male dress, cut her hair, and took refuge in a monastery under the name of Pelagius. Such were her qualities of devotion that she was elected prior of a monastery that had both monks and nuns. She acted the part of a man so well that when the portress (doorkeeper) became pregnant and accused Margarita–Pelagius of being the father, the charge was believed. After being expelled from the convent, Margarita–Pelagius found refuge as a hermit in a cave, and only at her death, when her true sex was discovered, was she proclaimed innocent of the crime of which she had been accused.[71]

A somewhat similar story is told about Marina, the daughter of a Bithynian called Eugenius. After being left a widower, Eugenius decided to enter a monastery. No sooner had he done so than he began to worry about his little daughter Marina, whom he had left in the care of a relative. He went to his abbot with his worries, but, certain that the abbot would not allow him to bring his daughter into the monastery, he changed her into a son, Marinus by name.

The abbot gave his permission for little Marinus to join the monastery, and she continued to live there long after her father's death. One of her jobs was to drive a cart down to the harbor to fetch supplies, a job necessitating an overnight stay at an inn. After one such visit, a pregnant girl accused Marinus of seducing her, and Marinus, true to the code of the transvestite saints, suffered ostracism from the monastery rather than admit to her true sex. After her expulsion, she and the infant son lived as beggars at the gate of the monastery pleading to be readmitted. After some 5 years of this, the monks at the monastery pleaded with the abbot to readmit her, and Marinus and "his son" both entered the monastery. The austerities Marina imposed on herself led to her death shortly after her readmission, and when the monks came to prepare her body for burial, they naturally discovered her true sex. Inevitably, the abbot of the monastery was overcome with remorse, and the woman who had falsely accused her became possessed by demons. The demons were driven away only when the woman confessed her sin and called on St. Marinus for intercession in heaven.[72]

Though all these stories are different, there is enough similarity that some scholars believe they are Christian survivals of the legend of Aphrodite, wherein women sacrificed to the goddess in men's clothing and men in women's.[73] Other scholars refuse, however, to accept this explanation.[74] Important to emphasize is, not the origin of the custom, but the fact that female transvestism was given sanction in the West through such stories and that such stories helped stereotype female–male roles. The stories also have women don male clothing at a time when they are undergoing a crisis in their lives; transvestism then seems to denote a breaking with a former existence. Some of the saints go to such extremes as burning their old clothes and even visualizing themselves as males. St. Perpetua, for example, saw herself in a dream being carried into an amphitheatre, stripped of her clothes, and changed into a man.[75] The mere fact that such women became saints indicates that women were encouraged to visualize themselves as attaining the merits of maleness.

There are numerous other variants of the standard story of the transvestite saints. St. Athanasia lived her male role so well that even her husband did not know his fellow monk was his wife.[76] Other variations recount the adventures of St. Apollinaris or Dorotheus,[77] St. Eugenia,[78] St. Euphrosyne,[79] St. Anastasia Patricia,[80] and still others.[81] An interesting variation of the transvestite saints is that of the bearded female saints, the most famous of which is Uncumber or Wilgefortis. According to tradition, Wilgefortis was one of septuplets born to a non-Christian ruler of Portugal and his Christian wife. Through the influence of her mother, Wilgefortis early decided to devote herself to the contemplative life and to remain a virgin, but her pagan father had different ideas. A crisis erupted when her father announced her betrothal to the King of Sicily. Wilgefortis protested, but her father ordered her to marry him anyway.

In desperation, Wilgefortis prayed for help, and her prayer was anwered by the sudden growth of a long, drooping mustache and a silky, curling beard. In spite of this masculine disfigurement, her father pushed on with the marriage plans, but when Wilgefortis managed to move her veil so that the King of Sicily saw his bride, he refused to marry her. In a fit of rage her father then had her crucified.

The story has been described as having the "unenviable distinction of being one of the most obviously false and preposterous of the pseudo-pious romances by which simple Christians have been deceived or regaled."[82] In spite of this, Wilgefortis, much venerated by the people, is known by a variety of names throughout Europe, many of them based on the term *Liberata*, the "deliverer." In northern France she was known as *Livrade*, in Spain as *Librada*, and in southern France as *Debarras*. In German-speaking Europe her name was quite different: *Ohnkummer* in Germany, *Ontcommer* in Flanders, and *Uncumber* in England, probably based on the German *kummer*, meaning "trouble." In England she became the patron saint of married women who wanted to rid themselves of their husbands.[83] Uncumber is not alone in the bearded-saint category. There are at least two others, a St. Galla and St. Paula, both of whom also grew beards to avoid marriage.[84]

The most famous transvestite in the early medieval period, and the one who perhaps has caused the greatest anguish to Catholic historians, is the legendary Pope Joan, who supposedly ruled under the name of John Anglicus.[85] Several thirteenth-century chroniclers wrote about her life in great detail, and during much of the later medieval period her existence was accepted as fact. A statue of her was included among the popes in the Cathedral of Siena in the fourteenth century, and in the fifteenth century, John Hus, the Bohemian heretic, reproached the delegates at the Council of Constance (1415) for allowing a woman to be pope. It was not until the sixteenth century, when her existence was seriously disputed, that she became relegated to legend rather than to history. She still has an occasional supporter, although few members of the scholarly world now accept her existence.

The legend is fairly complicated, and today it seems difficult to believe that medieval people were convinced of her authenticity, but believe they did. Though there are various forms of the legend, Joan is usually said to have been born in England early in the ninth century, and hence, the title *Anglicus* by which she is usually known. As a child she was taken by her father, a learned man, to Mainz, where she was taught to read and write and where she fell in love with a monk, Ulfilias by name. At his urging, she disguised herself as a man and entered the same monastery at Fulda to which he belonged. Later, she and her beloved Ulfilias traveled as pilgrims together, and after a series of adventures, found themselves in Athens. The two, with Joan still in male clothing, studied philosophy, theology, and holy and humane letters for some 10 years and acquired reputations as great scholars. Tragedy struck with the unexpected death of Ulfilias, and Joan, anxious and heartbroken, decided to return to Mainz. When she stopped off in Rome on her way home, still in her male role, she found her reputation as a scholar had preceded her. At the urging of some of her former pupils, she began to lecture in Rome. As her reputation grew she rose rapidly in the Church hierarchy, becoming first a notary, then a cardinal, and on Pope Leo's death in the 850s, pope under the name of John VIII, Anglicus. Unfortunately, she still had a woman's sex drives, and she fell easy prey to a Benedictine monk from Spain, who was said to look very much like her beloved Ulfilias. She became pregnant, although this phenomenon remained unnoticed until, in the midst of a papal procession, she entered into labor and gave birth to a child. Both she and the child died shortly after, although there are conflicting versions. One version has her child becoming pope later under the name of Adrian III. The importance of the story for the purposes of any history of sex is, not whether or not a woman actually sat on the papal throne, but that the Church, which was opposed to transvestism, tolerated it in a woman because a higher value was placed on other factors. According to the medieval belief, the male was a higher status individual, and it was understandable and permissible for a woman to try to achieve this status, provided she was not too overtly threatening to males. This attitude remained throughout the medieval period, although some limitations on the idea will be discussed in the next chapter.

One other source of information about sexual customs is in the literature of the period. Some scholars have implied that there is a strong homosexual theme in the clerical medieval literature, but how much this is a literary device is uncertain. One of the earliest medieval poems that touched the subject of homosexuality is by Paulinus of Nola, a friend and pupil of Ausonius, the Roman rhetorician and poet who died about 410. Paulinus, after his conversion to Christianity, sold his estates, retired to a chapel in Spain, and tried to sever his relations with his old master. Ausonius made several attempts to renew contact and wrote many letters that were unanswered. At last, Paulinus replied in a poem which included the lines:

> *I hold you mine, entwined in every part—*
> *not dim, with distant face.*
> *Clasping you close, I see you in my heart,*
> *here and in every place . . .*[86]

Some have regarded the poem as an expression of love, and on the surface it seems very homoerotic, but in early medieval literature, this often seems to be more a literary device than a sign of homosexual love.[87] There are, however, poems that clearly seem to go beyond literary convention and express erotic feeling. This would seem to be the case with a poem by Walafrid Strabo (809–849), Abbot of Reichenau, who wrote a poem "To His Friend in Absence."[88]

Philip Schuyler Allen, who edited and translated several such poems, came to believe that the Germans, particularly the Franks,

> attached as high a value as did Socrates to the association of friends, an older and a younger, in a comradeship intense enough to merit the name of love. With due regard to the difference between the plastic ideal of ancient religion in the stream of neo-Platonism and the romantic ideal of early medieval Christianity, this Platonic conception of *Paiderastia* is a close analogue to the chivalrous devotion to women. This love of man and boy (and no less of woman and girl), judged by its ideal, is a fine and noble thing, no more apt to sink in the mire of phallicism than modern love itself.[89]

Usually, it is only through indirection that we can find any direct allusions to sexual activity in the Middle Ages, and though we know there was great concern with various forms of sexuality, most of the recorded incidents of sexual misbehavior are heterosexual.[90] Still, pederasty, if not homosexuality, by the very nature of the concepts of women, and the seclusion into segregated male groupings, could have been a great temptation to many monks. A very strong overtone of this appears in the *Ecologue of Theodolus,* which Gottschalk (about 805–870), a heretic priest, wrote in exile:

O young my lad, you would have me sing—
  Why, O why?
What song, my boy, do you seek to wring
  From such as I?
Singing is sweet, but not from me
Who am exiled deep in the distant sea—
  Why will you make me sing?

O little my son, it were better far
  I weep my wrongs—
Tears from a broken heart, they are
  More than songs.
And O beloved, it cannot be
You seek such singing as this from me—
  Why will you make me sing?

You must know, little brother, that I desire
  Your sympathy;
Child, let not the help of you tire—
  Pity me!

A generous heart and a soul brought low,
Yours and mine—I would have it so—
   Why will you make me sing?

You are young, and hard are the words of youth!
   Little you know,
Though you give yourself to heaven's high truth,
   This is my woe—
Exile is long and a weary way,
And I suffer by night and endure by day—
   Why will you make me sing?

But since you desire that I sing to you,
   Comrade mine,
And whatever manner I use will do:
   A theme divine,
I choose, and the Father I sing, and the Son
And the Spirit proceeding from both as from one—
   Why will you make me sing?

Thou art the Blessed One, O Lord,
   Paraclete,
Born of the Father, Incarnate Word,
   O Thou complete,
Thou God that is one, Thou God that is three,
Thou art holy and just, Thou wilt pity me—
   From a full heart now I sing.

Sweetly I sing of my accord:
   Hear me, boy,
What time I sing of our gracious Lord
   A song of joy.
A song of the soul, a song of the lips,
A song by day and at night's eclipse—
   He is a merciful King.[91]

Occasionally there are hints of more overt homosexual activity. Marbod, Bishop of Rennes (about 1035–1123), for example, regretting the follies of his youth, proclaimed his moral reformation with the words: "Unpleasing to me now the embrace of either sex," and stated that he is no longer glowing with love.[92] Baudri of Meung-sur-Loire, Archbishop of Dol in Brittany (1046–1130), stated that he had written of love to both boys and to maids.[93] A wandering scholar by the name of Hilary carried on a series of flirtations with both nuns and young monks and very much desired the reappearance of the pagan past with fair Ganymedes everywhere.[94]

In a tenth-century poem, "To the Fleeing Boy," the homoerotic content seems even more obvious:

> *O thou eidolon of Venus adorable,*
> *Perfect thy body and nowhere deplorable!*
> *The sun and the stars and the sea and the firmament,*
> *These are like thee, and the Lord made them permanent.*
> *Treacherous death shall not injure one hair of thee,*
> *Clotho the thread-spinner, she shall take care of thee*
>
> *Heartily, lad, I implore her and prayerfully*
> *Ask that Lachesis shall treasure thee carefully . . . .*
> *Joy that was mine is my rival's tomorrow,*
> *While I for my fawn like a stricken deer sorrow!*[95]

In sum, the early Middle Ages was a period very much concerned with modifying ways and forms of sexual behavior. It advanced the ideal of celibacy but encouraged marriage and procreation of children for those who could not abide by the ideal of celibacy. Great hostility was expressed toward those who engaged in intercourse for purposes other than procreative, regardless of whether it was heterosexual, homosexual, or autosexual. All were sins against nature, and the concept that certain forms of sex were against nature became institutionalized in Western thought. The church officials not only condemned overt sexuality but also took care to make the cloistered life as asexual as possible, trying to eliminate monasteries where both females and males were housed together. For the segregated monastery they adopted strict rules to avoid overt homoerotic contact. The rule of St. Benedict, for example, stipulated that two people should be prohibited from sleeping in one bed, that lamps in the dormitories be kept burning throughout the night, and that monks sleep with clothes on.[96]

In spite of such efforts, life in the monastery did not eliminate sexual thoughts, even homoerotic ones. The penitential literature is one indication of this, so are some of the surviving poems. Though the charges of Peter Damian are exaggerated, homosexuality was recognized by the Church as a problem. This ultimately led to harsher treatment in the later medieval period as the Church more directly influenced secular legislation and as it standardized penalties in ecclesiastical courts. Transvestism for women, somewhat surprisingly, was tolerated and accepted in the early Church, and it was in part this denial of the female's importance, symbolized by the transvestite saints, that forced a reassessment of the importance of the Virgin Mary in the twelfth and thirteenth centuries. Still, the acceptance of female transvestism, within limits, resulted in a distinction between male and female cross-dressing that might well have influenced transvestism in the West.

NOTES

1. Edward Westermarck, *Christianity and Morals* (reprinted, Freeport, N.Y.: Books for Libraries Press, 1969), pp. 362–373.

2. *Lex Ribuaria,* Rudolph Sohm, ed. *Monumenta Germaniae historica, Leges* (Hannover, Germany: Hahn, 1875–1879), V. 216, 231. Henceforth abbreviated *MGH, Leges.*

3. The texts of the Visigothic law are in *MGH, Leges,* Karl Zeumer, ed., I (Hannover and Leipzig: Hahn, 1902). See also *Leges Alamanorum, Lex Baiwariorum,* K. Lehmann and Ernst de Schwind, eds., *MGH, Leges,* sectio I, V, pars. 1 and 2 (Hannover, Germany: Hahn, 1888); *Ancient Laws and Institutes of England,* B. Thorpe, ed. (London: The Commissioners of the Public Records, 1840), pp. 1–189; *Lex Salica,* Karl A. Eckhardt, ed., *MGH, Leges,* sectio VIII, IV, par. II (Hannover, Germany: Hahn, 1969); *Pactus legis Saliciae,* Karl A. Eckhardt, ed., *MGH, Leges,* sectio VIII, IV, par. 1 (Hannover, Germany: Hahn, 1962); *Lex Ribuaria,* Franz Beyerle and Rudolf Buchner, eds., *MGH, Leges,* sectio VIII, II, par. 2 (Hannover, Germany: Hahn, 1965); *Lex Frisonum,* Karl von Richthofen, ed., and *Lex Burgundionum,* Fredrico Bluhme, ed., in *MGH, Leges,* III (Hannover, Germany: Hahn, 1863); *Leges Saxonum,* Karl Richthofen and Karl Frederic von Richthofen, eds., and *Lex Thuringorum,* Karl Frederic von Richthofen, ed., *MGH, Leges,* V (Hannover, Germany: Hahn, 1875).

4. Jean Brissaud, *A History of French Private Law,* translated by Rapelje Howell (Boston: Little, Brown, 1912), p. 136.

5. See, for example, the Laws of King Alfred, cap. 42, in *Ancient Laws and Institutes of England,* p. 40. A man who finds another man with his daughter, sister, mother, or other female relative is given the right to deal with the intruder.

6. See J. R. Reinhard, "Burning at the Stake in Medieval Law and Literature," *Speculum,* XVI (1941), p. 190.

7. Some discussions of this appear in Gwyn Jones, *A History of the Vikings* (New York: Oxford University Press, 1968), 322–323. See also Thorkil Vanggard, *Phallos: A Symbol and Its History in the Male World* (London: Jonathan Cape, 1972), pp. 84–85.

8. G. Rattray Taylor, *Sex in History* (New York: Vanguard Press, 1954), p. 51.

9. Rafael Altamira, "Spain Under the Visigoths," in *Cambridge Medieval History,* (reprinted, Cambridge, England: University Press, 1964), Vol. 2, pp. 159–193.

10. See *Lex Visigoth,* Book III, titulus V, cap. 4, "De masculorum stupris," in *MGH, Leges,* sectio I, *Legum nat. Germ.,* I, p 163. Though this is my translation, it is essentially the same as that of Derrick Sherwin Bailey, *Homosexuality and the Western Christian Tradition* (London: Longmans, Green and Company, 1955), p. 92.

11. For a list and summary of some of the sexual legislation of other councils, see Derrick Sherwin Bailey, *Sexual Relation in Christian Thought* (New York: Harper & Brothers, 1959), pp. 71–72, text and notes.

12. *Concilium Toletanum XVI, tomus Egicani regis concilio oblatus Concilium XVI,* cap. III, in *MGH, Legum,* sectio I, *Legum nat. Germn.,* I, p. 483.

13. *Concilium Toletanum XVI,* in J. Mansi, *Sacrorum Concilorum* (Florence: 1766), XII, col. 71.

14. "De sodomitis, qua debeant ultionis sententia perculi," Book III, titulus V. cap. 7, in *MGH, Legum,* sectio I, *Legum nat. Germ.,* I, p. 165.

15. Altamira, *op. cit.,* p. 187.

16. Bailey, *Homosexuality and the Western Christian Tradition,* pp. 86–87, 95.

17. *Capitulare Aquisgran,* XLVII, in Mansi, *op. cit.,* XVII B, col. 230. Vols. XVII B and XVIII B are separate volumes of Mansi dealing with Carolingian councils and edicts.

18. See *Capitularium Karoli M. et Ludovici pii libri VII,* Book V, cap. LXXXII, in Mansi, *op. cit.,* XVII B, col. 839, "De his qui contra naturam peccant"; Book VII, cap. CCCLVI, in *ibid.,* XVII B, col. 1107; and *Canones Isaac Episcopi Linonensis,* titulis IV, "De incestis," cap. XI, in *ibid.,* XVII B, col. 1529.

19. *Capitulare octarum anni* in *ibid.,* XVII B., col. 412. This capitulary is concerned primarily with the immunity of bishops and others from military service but also refers to sodomites, fornicators, adulterers, and others.

21. *Capitulare tertium,* cap. II, in *ibid.,* XVII B, col. 526; *Capitularium Karoli et Ludovici pii libri VII,* Liber VII, titulus 143, in *ibid.,* XVII B, col. 1055; and in the "additio secunda," of the same collection, cap. XXI, "De diversis malorum flagitis," in *ibid.,* XVII B, col. 1143.

22. Sir Frederick Pollock and F. W. Maitland, *History of English Law,* 2nd ed. (reprinted, Cambridge, England: University Press, 1952, 2 vols.), Vol. 2, pp. 556–557.

23. Romans, 1:24–47. The translation is from the Authorized Version. The Douay translation differs only slightly. Both use the term *against nature,* which appears also in the Vulgate. The italics are mine.

24. Matthew Black and H. H. Rowley, *Peake's Commentary on the Bible* (London: Thomas Nelson, 1962), par. 817b, holds that the passage refers to homosexuality, as does Otto Michel, *Der Brief an die Romer* (Gottingen, Germany: Van de Hoeck & Ruprecht, 1955), p. 59. A much broader interpretation that includes all sexual activities not leading to procreation is given by Herman L. Strack and Paul Billerbeck, *Kommentar zum Neuen Testament auf Talmud und Midrash,* 3rd ed. (Munich: Beck, 1961) III, *Die Brief des Neuen Testament und die Offenbarun Johannis,* pp. 68–69.

25. For Aristotle's ideas about this, see Aristotle, *Historia animalium,* 608B, translated by D'Arcy Thompson in *The Works of Aristotle,* IV (Oxford, England: Clarendon Press, 1910): *Politics,* I, 2 (1252B), 7, translated by H. Rackham, ed. (London: William Heinemann, 1944).

26. For Stoic ideas, see Epictetus, *Encheiridion,* 41, in *Discourses,* translated by W. A. Oldfather, ed. (London: William Heinemann, 1956, 1959, 2 vols.).

27. See John T. Noonan, *Contraception: A History of Its Treatment by the Catholic Theologians and Canonists* (Cambridge, Mass.: The Belknap Press of Harvard University, 1966), p. 46.

28. Philo, *On the Special Laws,* translated by F. H. Colson, ed. (London: William Heinemann, 1958), VII, 37–42. See also Richare A. Baer, Jr., *Philo's Use of the Categories Male and Female* (Leiden, Netherlands: E. J. Bill, 1970), p. 46.

29. Noonan, *op. cit.,* p. 75.

30. St. Augustine, *Soliloquies,* I, 10 (17), translated by Thomas F. Gilligan, in Vol. 1, *Fathers of the Church* (New York: Cima Publishing Company, 1948).

31. See St. Augustine, *The Good of Marriage* 11:12, translated by Charles T. Wilcox in *Fathers of the Church,* Vol. 15 (New York: Fathers of the Church, 1955); and St. Augustine, *Confessions,* III, cap. viii, translated by William Watts, ed. (London: William Heinemann, 1950, 2 vols.).

32.   John Cassian, *De coenobiorum institutis,* v, I, and *Consolationes,* v, 2, *Corpus scriptorum ecclesiasticorum Latinorum* (Leipzig: Akademische Verlagsgesellschaft, G. Foch, 1866), XVII, p. 81; XIII, p. 121.

33.   Gregory, *Moralia,* xxvi, 28, in J. P. Migne, *Patrologiae Latina* (Paris: Garnier frères, 1844–1864), LXXVI, 364. See also F. H. Dudden, *Gregory the Great* (London: Longmans, Green and Company, 1905, 2 vols.), Vol. 2, pp. 384 ff.

34.   C. Plummer in his edition of Bede, *Historia Ecclesiastica gentis Anglorum* (Oxford, England: Clarendon Press, 1896, 2 vols), Vol. 1, pp. cclvii f.

35.   The quotation is from the *Pseudo-Roman Penitential,* collected by Halitgar, Bishop of Cambria. The pertinent section, part of the prologue, is translated in John T. McNeill and Helena M. Gamer, editors and translators of *Medieval Handbooks of Penance* (New York: Columbia University Press, 1938), p. 297. Many of the penitentials included in this section can be found in this collection.

36.   *Ibid.,* pp. 174–178, Nos. 1, 11, 22. The penitential can also be found in Ludwig Beiler, editor and translator, *The Irish Penitentials* (Dublin: Dublin Institute for Advanced Studies, 1963), pp. 60–62. Beiler gives the Latin version as well as the English translation. McNeill and Gamer give only the English translation.

37.   Beiler, *op. cit.,* pp. 66–67; and McNeill and Gamer, *op. cit.,* p. 170, No. 1 (sodomy and fornication); No. 2 (masturbation).

38.   *Ibid.,* pp. 171–172; and Beiler, *op. cit.,* pp. 68–69, Nos, 3, 6, 7, 8.

39.   *Ibid.,* pp. 70–71; and McNeill and Gamer, *op. cit.,* pp. 172–174, Nos. 5, 6, 7, 8, 9, 11. Beiler, following a different MSS tradition, lists the punishment for unintentional pollution (No. 9) as 16 rather than 15 days.

40.   Beiler, *op. cit.,* pp. 74–75.

41.   *Ibid.,* pp. 86–89; and McNeill and Gamer, *op. cit.,* pp. 94–95, Nos. 36–40.

42.   *Ibid.,* pp. 250–257; and Beiler, *op. cit.,* pp. 96–107, Nos. 2, 4, 10, 11, 15, 16, 17.

43.   *Ibid.,* pp. 112–117; and McNeill and Gamer, *op. cit.,* pp. 102–105, sec. 2, Nos. 1, 2.

44.   *Ibid.,* pp. 12–114; and Beiler, *op. cit.,* pp. 126–129.

45.   Bailey, *op. cit.,* p. 101.

46.   McNeill and Gamer, *op. cit.,* pp. 184–186, sec. 2.

47.   See F. W. H. Wasserschleben, *Die Bussordnungen der abendläischen Kirche* (reprinted, Graz, Austria: Akademische Druck-U. Verlagsanstal, 1958), pp. 221–224, sec. III, 21, 22, 23, 24, 31, 32. There are at least two penitentials attributed to Bede. Portions of a second one are reproduced in McNeill and Gamer, *op. cit.,* pp. 217–221.

48.   Beiler, *op. cit.,* pp. 200–201, lines 20–23. Italics mine.

49.   John T. Noonan, Jr., *op. cit.,* pp. 161–162.

50.   Wasserschleben, *op. cit.,* p. 385, cap. lvi.

51.   McNeill and Gamer, *op. cit.,* p. 289, XI.

52.   Wasserschleben, *op. cit.,* p. 383, cap. 42.

53.   *Ibid.,* pp. 233 (cap. I), 234 (cap. 2), 237 (caps. 17, 18, 19).

54.   Mansi, *op. cit., Excerptum a Beato Gregorio, Papae III, incipiunt Judica congrua poentibus,* cap. xxi, "De sodomistis," in Vol. 12, cols. 293. Basically I have followed the translation given by Bailey, *Homosexuality,* p. 106.

55.   F. W. H. Wasserschleben, *Regionis abbatis Prumiensis, libri duo de synodalibus et disciplinis ecclesiasticis* (Leipzig: B. Tauchnitz, June, 1840), 254. Book 2, 254 in *Beitrage zur geschichte der vorgratianischen Kirchenrechtsquellen.*

56.   For a discussion of Peter Damian, see J. Joseph Ryan, *Saint Peter Damian and His Canonical Sources* (Toronto: Pontifical Institute of Mediaeval Studies, 1956); Owen Blum, *St. Peter Damian: His Teachings on the Spiritual Life* (Washington, D.C.: The Catholic University of America Press, 1947); and Patricia McNulty, *St. Peter Damian* (London: Faber and Faber, 1959).

57.   Peter Damian, *Liber Gomorrhianus,* cap. vii, in *Opera omnia,* Constantini Cajetan, ed., in J. P. Migne, *PL,* CXLV, col. 167.

58.   *Ibid.,* cap. xxii, col. 183.

59.   *Ibid.,* cap. ii, col. 162.

60.   *Ibid.,* col. 172, and translated in McNeill and Gamer, *op. cit.,* p. 411.

61.   See Horace K. Mann, *The Lives of the Popes in the Middle Ages* (London: Kegan Paul, Trench, Trubner & Company, 1925), Vol. 6, pp. 49–53.

62.   Ryan, *op. cit.,* pp. 154–155.

63.   Venerable Bede, *Ecclesiastical History,* IV, xxv (xxiii), translated by Bertram Colgrave and R. A. B. Mynors, eds. (Oxford, England: Clarendon Press, 1969), pp. 421–427.

64.   Vern L. Bullough, *The Subordinate Sex* (Urbana, Ill.: University of Illinois Press, 1973), pp. 97–120.

65.   Philo, *On the Creation,* 69–70, 151, 162, translated by F. H. Colson and G. H. Whittaker, eds. (London: Willian Heinemann, 1963); and *Questions and Answers on Genesis,* I, 40, translated by Ralph Marcus, ed. (London: E. J. Brill, 1970), pp. 46–51.

66.   Jerome, *Commentarius in Epistolam ad Ephesios,* III, v (658), in J. P. Migne, *PL,* XXVI, 567.

67.   Ambrose, *Expositionis in Evangelius secundum Lucam libri X,* 161 (1539) in Migne, *PL,* XV, 1938.

68.   H. Delehaye, *The Legends of the Saints,* translated by V. M. Crawford (South Bend, Ind.: University of Notre Dame Press, 1961), p. 189.

69.   Gregory of Tours, *History of the Franks,* Book 10, cap. 16, translated with an introduction by O. M. Dalton (Oxford, England: Clarendon Press, 1927, 2 vols.).

70.   Where possible I have used *Butler's Lives of the Saints,* revised and supplemented by Herbert Thurston and Donald Attwater, eds. (New York: P. J. Kennedy & Sons, 1956, 4 vols.), for references, since it is readily available to most readers. For more scholarly readers I have referred to the massive collection of saints' lives in their original languages published under the title of *Acta Sanctorum* (Antwerp: 1643, in progress), which is arranged according to saints' days. The story of St. Pelagia can be found in *Butler's Lives of the Saints,* Vol. 4, pp. 59–61, *Acta Sanctorum,* October IV, 248, and there is also an interesting account in Helen Waddell, *The Desert Fathers* (reprinted, Ann Arbor, Mich.: University of Michigan Press, 1957), pp. 177–188.

71.   *Butler's Lives of the Saints,* Vol. 4, pp. 59–61; Delehaye, *op. cit.,* pp. 197–199; and *Acta Sanctorum,* July IV, 287; October IV, 24.

72.   *Butler's Lives of the Saints,* Vol. 1, pp. 313–314; *Acta Sanctorum,* July IV, 149.

73.   See Herman Usener's edition of Jacob the Deacon, *Legenden der heiligen Pelagia* (Bonn: n.p., 1879), p. 20.

74.   Delehaye, *op. cit.,* pp. 204–206.

75.   Marie Delcourt, *Hermaphrodite,* translated from the French by Jennifer Nicholson (London: Studio Books, 1956), pp. 90–99.

76.   *Butler's Lives of the Saints,* Vol. 4, pp. 60–70; *Acta Sanctorum,* October IV, 99.

77.   *Ibid.,* January I, 258; *Butler's Lives of the Saints,* Vol. 1, p. 33.

78.   *Ibid.,* Vol. 4, p. 612.

79. *Ibid.,* Vol. 1, pp. 4–5; *Acta Sanctorum,* February II, 535.

80. Ibid., March, II, *Butler's Lives of the Saints,* Vol. 2, pp. 546–547.

81. See Vern L. Bullough, "Transvestites in the Middle Ages," *American Journal of Sociology,* LXXIX (1974), pp. 1381–1394.

82. *Butler's Lives of the Saints,* Vol. 3, pp. 151–152; *Acta Sanctorum,* July IV, 50.

83. For a popular discussion of the saint, see Gillian Edward, *Uncumber and Pantaloon* (New York: Dutton, 1969).

84. *Butler's Lives of the Saints,* Vol. 4, pp. 36–37; *Acta Sanctorum,* February III, 174; October III, 162.

85. There is a massive literature on Pope Joan, divided into pro-Joan, anti-Joan, and scholarly. Among the pro-Joan advocates were Alexander Cooke, *Pope Joan* (London: Blunt and Barin 1610), which is also anti-Catholic; and more recently, Clement Wood, *The Woman Who Was Pope* (New York: William Faro, 1931). A tongue-in-cheek pro-Joan appears in the semifictionalized retelling of her story of Ira Glackens, *Pope Joan* (New York: Coleridge Press, 1965). A good brief summary of the scholarship and sources of the legend can be found in *The New Catholic Encyclopedia,* which is scholarly and to the point. Horace K. Mann, *The Lives of the Popes* (London: Kegan Paul, 1925), Vol. 2, p. 325, includes a brief summary of the coinage evidence against her existence. Perhaps the most nearly complete scholarly examination was by Johann Dollinger, *Papstfabeln des Mittelalters,* 2nd ed. (Stuttgart: J. G. Cotta, 1890). She has been the subject of considerable fiction, from Giovanni Boccaccio to Lawrence Durrell.

86. Paulinus of Nola, *To Ausonius,* translated by Jack Lindsay, and reprinted in *Eros: An Anthology of Friendship,* Alistair Sutherland and Patrick Anderson, eds. (London: Anthony Blond, 1961) p. 109. There is a prose translation of this in the *Epistles of Ausonius,* I, xxx, 50 ff., translated by Hugh G. E. White (London: William Heinemann, 1961).

87. A good example is a poem written by Colman the Irishman, which is translated by Helen Waddell, *Medieval Latin Lyrics,* 5th ed. (London: Constable and Company, 1948), p. 75.

88. *Ibid.,* p. 117. There is a slightly different translation by Howard Mumford Jones in Philip Schuyler Allen and Howard Mumford Jones, *The Romanesque Lyric* (Chapel Hill, N.C.: The University of North Carolina Press, 1928), p. 150. This last includes the Latin text as well.

89. Allen and Jones, *op. cit.,* p. 148.

90. See, for example, Henry Hart Milman, *History of Latin Christianity* (New York: A. C. Armstrong and Son, 1886, 8 vols. in 4), Vol. 1, pp. 394–397.

91. Allen and Jones, *op. cit.,* pp. 150–151. Latin text is included. Reprinted by permission of University of North Carolina Press.

92. E. R. Curtius, *European Literature and the Latin Middle Ages,* translated by Willard R. Trask, Bollingen Series 36 (New York: Pantheon Books, 1953), pp. 115–116.

93. *Ibid.,* p. 115.

94. *Ibid.,* p. 116.

95. Allen and Jones, *op. cit.,* p. 285. Latin text is included.

96. Dom Paul Delatte, *The Rule of St. Benedict,* cap. 22, translated by Dom Justin McCann, (reprinted, Latrobe, Pa.: The Archabbey Press, 1950).

14

THE LATER MIDDLE AGES

B y the middle of the eleventh century, Europe had recovered from the inva-
sions and anarchy that had plagued it for several hundred years. Wealth
was increasing, population was growing, new institutions were developing, and
both the ecclesiastical and secular institutions were attempting to centralize
their control. The key to centralization was the renewed attention given to
Roman law, which began to be studied with a new intensity. The result was
the replacement of German tribal law with new centralized codes based on
Roman law both in the Church and the states. Canon or religious law became
the cement that bound the Church together, and civil or secular law served a
similar function for the state. Even in countries such as England, where
Germanic law continued dominant, Roman law exercised considerable in-
fluence in molding the common law. As to sex, canon law, the law of the
Church, was most important until the end of the medieval period, for the
Church claimed that all matters of sex and morals fell within its purview.

Canon law was not, however, Roman law, even though it was derived from
it, since underlying canon law (and civil law for that matter) were certain
Christian assumptions, and these were also being subjected to rigorous
analysis. One reason was that European intellectuals were becoming more sophisticated and educated. Inevitably, they had found contradictions in the
teachings and assumptions of the Church Fathers that could be answered only
by turning to the source materials, not only to the Scriptures, but also to pagan

philosophers, such as Aristotle, whose logical formulations proved particularly attractive to medieval Christians. In ferreting out the teachings of Aristotle, the medieval theologians also found support in Muslim and Jewish philosophers who had been concerned with some of the same questions. The result was the growth of scholasticism, which in simple terms, is the reconciliation of Aristotelian philosophy with Christian theology providing a new logical basis for belief in the Christian teachings.

Strengthened administratively by canon law and fortified intellectually by scholasticism, the Church rose to new positions of power in the twelfth and thirteenth centuries. In these two centuries Western assumptions about sexuality that existed in early Christian theology were reset in legal and ecclesiastical thought and continued to dominate Western thinking on the subject down to the twentieth century with only slight modification. During this period also celibacy was officially set as a requirement for clerical ordination.

Basic to these developments of the twelfth and thirteenth centuries was the theological belief in the sin against nature, which, as explained in the last chapter, was based on the teachings of St. Augustine. One of the more influential theological writers of the twelfth century was Peter Lombard (about 1100–1160), who held that the sin against nature, which he defined as any sexual activity not leading to procreation, was worse than fornication, adultery, or incest, presumably because these others could possibly lead to offspring.[1] Taking a rather different tack was St. Albertus Magnus (1206–1280), who in many ways was more tolerant of sexual activity than most of the medieval theological writers. St. Albert, the only person in history to be called great for his intellectual achievement, held that there could be no sin at all in matrimonial copulation, although just exactly how this should be interpreted is unclear.[2] Part of the difficulty is that he never bothered to amplify what he meant by this statement. Elsewhere he tends to contradict it. For example, he stated that there were two basic justifications for sexual intercourse. Nature had formed the sex organs for the procreation of offspring, and this was the natural end of intercourse. In addition, there was the human end of intercourse, the "end of medicine and of fidelity to bed and of the sacrament." Intercourse within marriage could be both one of nature and one of man, but there were also some types of intercourse that might serve man's purpose but were against nature and against reason.[3] The worst of these was sodomy, which he defined as outside the marital relationship and as constituting male with male or female with female. Sodomy, Albert held, deserved special condemnation for at least four reasons: (1) It proceeded from a burning frenzy that subverted the order of nature; (2) the sin was distinguished by its disgusting foulness but yet was likely to be found more often among persons of high degree than of low; (3) those who became addicted to such vices seldom succeeded in freeing themselves; and (4) such vices were as contagious as a disease and spread rapidly from one person to another.[4] This last view will be amplified later in this chapter.

More important in forming Western ideas was St. Thomas Aquinas (1225–1274), the pupil of St. Albert. St. Thomas concentrated his discussion about sex under the general heading of lust, which he regarded as a vice because it exceeded the order and mode of reason.[5] Sins against nature were a species of lust, since such acts were directed solely to the pursuit of venereal pleasure and excluded procreation. Sexual acts against nature were different from other sins of lust, such as fornication, adultery, seduction, rape, and incest, not only because they were contrary to right reason, but also because they were contrary to "the natural order of the venereal act as becoming to the human race."[6] For Aquinas, the sin against nature included four different activities: (1) procuring ejaculation (*pollutio*) without coitus, that is, masturbation, something that Aquinas equated with effeminacy; (2) copulation with nonhuman creatures, that is, bestiality; (3) copulation with an undue sex (*concubitus ad non debitum sexum*), which could be equated with homosexuality; and (4) deviation from the natural manner of coitus, which according to Aquinas, was limited to face-to-face contact with the female on her back. The most grievous of the sins against nature was bestiality, followed by homosexuality, then intercourse in an unnatural position, and last of all, masturbation.[7]

Aquinas was willing to grant that in many ways the sexual activities he classified as sins against nature did not seem to be as serious as adultery, seduction, and rape—sexual activities that injured others and were contrary to the virtue of charity. Nonetheless, Aquinas held that, since the order of nature was derived from God, its contravention was always an injury to God and thus a more serious offense than those committed against one's neighbor or other people. Even sexual acts against nature entered into by mutual agreement were to be regarded as injurious to God and a transgression of the Divine law by which man's sexual nature was governed.[8] Minor actions, such as touches, caresses, and kisses, between persons of the same sex were not reckoned as mortally sinful but could become so by reason of the motive behind them. According to St. Thomas, when such actions were undertaken for enjoying forbidden pleasure, they become lustful and therefore gravely sinful, for consent to the pleasure of a lustful act was not less than consent to the act itself. Only those acts between persons of the same sex that did not arouse venereal excitement were to be permitted.[9]

The definitions of St. Thomas tended to dominate all thinking on sexual subjects to the end of the Middle Ages, with the result that any kind of sexual activity not leading to procreation could be classed as deviant whether it took place inside or outside marriage. As late as the fifteenth century, St. Bernardine of Siena (died 1444) wrote that the sin against nature included any act of semination committed "wherever" and in "whatever way" that made it impossible to generate.[10] All such acts were to be regarded as against nature because they were against the nature of the individual, the rational species, and the animal genus.[11]

The term *sodomy* was frequently used interchangeably with the sin against nature and, occasionally, all such sins were classed as onanism. In the twelfth century Peter Cantor classified sodomy with the sin of Onan, because the sodomites, like Onan, spilled their "seed on the earth."[12] John Gerson (1363–1429), Chancellor of the University of Paris, used the term *sodomy* to refer to sexual acts between persons of the same sex and semination in a vessel not "ordained for it."[13] St. Antoninus (1381–1451), in his book for confessors, defined sodomy as "man with man, a woman with a woman, or a man with a woman outside of the fit vessel."[14] This tendency to use euphemisms such as sodomy, onanism, and even the sin against nature to describe numerous different forms of sexual activities eventually resulted in great ambiguity about just what constituted a sexual sin. It was probably assumed that those who had to deal with sexual activities would trace the meaning back to the sources. In the meantime, it was better not to spell out sexual activities in any detail where the ordinary person might learn about them, because they would then want to experiment with forms of sexual activity about which they knew very little. When the concept of sin was transformed into a legal prohibition, the confusion remained, for many were ignorant of the original sources.

Legal collections generally followed the theological assumptions, becoming more ambiguous as time went on. One of the earliest collections of canon laws was the *Decretum* of Burchard of Worms, made in the eleventh century. Burchard attempted to gather authoritative materials on penance, including those dealing with sex. Though he compiled a rather detailed listing of sexual activities, his penances were not particularly severe until he came to sodomy. A sodomite who had a wife was to do 10 years' penance, and one with whom sodomy was habitual was to do 12 years.[15] More important, in terms of the legal tradition, was Ivo of Chartres (1091–1116), who avoided the detailed listing of Burchard but incorporated the concept of unnatural intercourse into the law. His definition of what constituted unnatural was based on the Augustinian formula of using a "member not granted for this."[16] Though Ivo amplified this definition somewhat, nowhere did he become very precise.

> A use which is natural and lawful in marriage is unlawful in adultery. To act against nature is always unlawful and beyond doubt more flagrant and shameful than to sin by a natural use in fornication or adultery, as the Holy Apostle contends as to both men and women.[17]

The effect of the passage was to condemn all intercourse in which the possibility of conception did not exist[18] and to encourage the grouping of all forbidden sexual activities into one category, those against nature.

A general category formulated by Ivo was carried over into Gratian, the Camaldolese monk who completed his *Concordia discordantium canonum* in about 1140 and to whom historians have given the title of "Father of the Science of Canon Law."[19] Gratian had conceived his work as a universal treatise on the institutions and problems of canon law, basing it on his researches into Roman law; canons of the Church Councils, particularly the ecumenical ones of the fourth and fifth centuries; papal and royal ordinances; Biblical, liturgical, patristic, and penitential texts; and contemporary theological discussion. When he came to the question of sexual intercourse, Gratian, following the example of Ivo as well as the theological writers, relied on concepts formulated by St. Augustine. He equated the acts against nature committed in Sodom with a transgression of the commandment to love God and one's neighbor.[20] In a partial compilation of sexual sins, he placed fornication as the least, followed by adultery and then incest, since it was worse to sleep with one's mother than with another man's wife. The worst sin of all, however, was what was done contrary to nature, defined as using a member not conceded for this purpose.[21] In addition to using the broad categories of sexual sins, Gratian also included a specific reference to the sins of boys, probably based on the Justinian legislation on the subject, and included in his description both abduction and corruption of boys. He said the sin against boys (*stuprum pueri*) merited capital punishment if the offense was *perfectus* but only banishment if it was *imperfectus*. This might be an attempt to distinguish between acts that were performed and completed as against those that were attempted, but this is by no means certain.[22]

In many ways, Gratian raised more problems about sexual sins than he answered. He listed the crime against nature as the most serious of sexual sins but defined it only in general terms. In one section, he equated it with the sins of Sodom, but in another he indicated it could take place between a husband and a wife. He referred specifically to sins of boys but without any real definition of what this constituted. Gratian's hesitation to define what he meant might have been motivated by a desire to avoid spelling out sexual activites for fear that some might find new sins to commit. It might also have been motivated by a desire to lump sexual sins into large categories without detailing what constituted each category, for fear that one particular sin might be overlooked and thus not be subject to penalty. Regardless of his reason, with Gratian, the law came increasingly to use euphemisms to deal with forbidden sexual activities, and though Gratian himself was certain about which sex acts he classified in which categories, later writers were not at all certain about which activities should be included. The general rule was, however, that any departure from the assumed normal position of female on her back or any attempt to avoid conception, regardless of the sex of the partner, was a sin against nature. This is important to emphasize, for many casual investigators into sexual behavior have assumed that all references to sin against nature referred to homosexuality. This is simply not the case.

Even when the term *sodomy* is specifically used, it is not clear that this should be interpreted as coitus *in ano*. This can be illustrated by the action of a Church Council in England in 1102 summoned by King Henry I. The purpose of the council was to deal with alleged moral abuses in the kingdom; among the canons enacted by this Council of London were two mentioning sodomy but never defining it. The first canon stated that:

> Those who commit the shameful sin of sodomy, and especially those who of their own free will take pleasure in doing so, were condemned by weighty anathema, until by penitence and confession they should show themselves worthy of absolution.[23]

If the person found guilty was an ecclesiastic, he was to be deposed, and if a layman, deprived of his legal status and dignity. Only a bishop was entitled to give absolution, unless the guilty person was a member of a monastic order, and then his superior was permitted give dispensation. The second canon ordered that the news of the excommunication of the guilty be published in all the churches in the realm so that no one be ignorant of the censure passed by the leaders of the Church and state upon the vices of the last reign,[24] that is, that of William Rufus. Nowhere, however, is sodomy defined, and whether we should regard this as a veiled reference to homosexuality in the court of William Rufus is something on which scholars are not agreed.

The Church Councils occasionally went into detail about sexual activities. The most extensive series of enactments against sodomy in the late medieval period were passed at the Council of Napolouse, held on the site of ancient Sichem in the Holy Land in 1120. The council was under the direction of Baldwin II, King of Jerusalem, and Garmund, patriarch of the city. The Crusaders had captured Jerusalem in 1099, but the hold of the Christians on the city was still regarded as tenuous, and both the king and patriarch felt it essential that the Crusaders and other inhabitants maintain a high moral standard. To do so the council passed some 25 canons designed to raise the level of morality to the expected standard. Most of the canons dealt with the sins of the flesh, four of them specifically with homosexuality. These laws are important, since, for the first time in medieval law, the punishment for sodomy is listed as burning. There were, however, extenuating circumstances, since if any

> sodomist, before he is accused, shall come to his senses, and having been brought to penitence, shall renounce that abominable vice by the swearing of an oath, let him be received into the Church and dealt with according to the provisions of the canons. But if he falls a second time into such practices and wishes again to do

penance, he may be admitted to penance, but let him be expelled from the
kingdom.[25]

The fact that the death penalty is prescribed indicates that the legislation was
more secular than religious and that the Justinian enactments on sex activities,
had a growing influence.

As to general ecclesiastical enactment about sexual activity, the actions taken
by the Council of Napolouse were ignored. Instead, the most important enactment was that taken by the Third Lateran Council, held in Rome in 1179
under the direction of Pope Alexander III. Included in the enactments was a
canon directed against that "incontinence which is against nature" and by
reason of which the anger of God "came upon the children of disobedience, and
consumed five cities by fire."[26] Obviously, the sin against nature and the sins of
Sodom are equated, but nowhere are they defined. This phraseology is repeated
in other conciliar enactments. The Council of Paris in 1212, for example,
repeated the statement from the Third Lateran Council almost verbatim,[27] although it added a special provision about nuns. This might indicate a growing
concern about female homosexuality. Nuns were prohibited from sleeping two
to a bed, and it was stipulated that a lamp should burn in the convent dormi-
tory at night, provisions long a part of the regulations for Benedictine
monasteries.[28]

The growing influence of the enactments of the Third Lateran Council appears also from the fact that similarly worded proposals were enacted at the
Council of Rouen in 1214.[29] The influential Fourth Lateran Council, held in
1215 under the leadership of Pope Innocent III, also repeated the wording of
the Third Lateran on incontinence.[30] The importance of sexual rulings in these
councils might be indicated from the fact that the Third and Fourth Lateran
Councils finally established clerical celibacy as the rule for the Western church,
although it had been an ideal for most of its history.

Synodical legislation for the next century or so is essentially repetitious of the
actions taken at these councils. Almost always, the sin against nature was a euphemism for most sexual activities not leading to conception. It was also
regarded as a reserved sin, that is, one that had to be referred to a higher authority, such as a bishop, for final decision.[31] The wordings of the Third and
Fourth Lateran Councils were incorporated into the Decretals issued by Pope
Gregory IX in 1234 as the official and authoritative collections of rulings on
questions of canon law decided since Gratian,[32] and in this form they remained
the final legal word of the Church on the subject until the sixteenth century,
when the Protestant movement led to further amplification. Quite clearly the
Church was opposed to the sin against nature, but this included a broad range
of sexual activities and was not confined to homosexuality.

Laws or even ecclesiastical opinion are one thing, reality another. How did
sexual practices in the later Middle Ages conform to what the Church taught

and tried to enforce? From the evidence it appears that the Church was increasingly effective in asserting its control. A good example of this success is in the changing nature of marriage. From being a ceremony with no ecclesiastical or canonical implications, it became a matter of greater and greater Church concern. Between the fourth century and the middle of the tenth century the Church worked hard to establish the custom of having the newly wedded pair attend religious service in the church to partake of the sacrament and receive a priestly benediction for their future. An elaborate and imposing ritual gradually developed, and by the thirteenth century, ecclesiastical marriage was fully established within the Church and was celebrated by the priest.[33] Marriage was urged for all those unable to bear the superior state of virginity or continence and not restrained from doing so by solemn vows. In general, the medieval canonists distinguished between two degrees of marriage, the *conjugium initiatum,* arising from the simple consent of the espoused, and the *conjugium ratum,* resulting from carnal intercourse and perfecting the marriage. A marriage in the first stage might be dissolved, but one in the second stage was indissoluble. In effect, once a man and woman had become one flesh, separation was almost impossible. There was no requirement for parental consent, and a private or even secret agreement was sufficient for a valid contract.[34]

Control of marriage was one way of regulating sexual conduct, particularly since marriage had become a sacrament, but the Church also continued to enforce its concept of sin through confession, a practice encouraged for all Christians. Here general categories were used in the latter Middle Ages rather than the more specific ones of the earlier Middle Ages, for fear that the confessor might reveal to the penitent new ways by which he or she could sin. The thirteenth century Henry of Susa (Hostiensis), in his *Golden Summa,* set the pattern for penitentials by defining the sin against nature as any semination "outside the vessel" for which it was intended and any departure from the normal mode.[35] Though Henry indicated some of the ways in which this sin could take place, in the vernacular penitentials, that is, those written in the vernacular languages, which the laymen might read for themselves, the ambiguity remains. These penitentials indicate the growing literacy of the laity, and it is from such penitentials that the idea of sin against nature enters into the vernacular literature. In a penitential work attributed to John Myrc and written before 1450, it is stated that the wise priest would refrain from preaching or teaching to his congregation what the sin against nature (*kynde*) would be:

> *Also written will I find*
> *That of sin against Kynde*
> *Thou shalt to thy parish no thing teach,*
> *Nor of that sin no thing preach;*
> *But say thus by good advice*

That too great sin forsooth it is,
For any man that beateth life
To forsake his wedded wife
And do his kynde another way,
That is great sin without nay.[36]

Generally, in these popular penitentials, the sexual sins are included under lechery, of which there are five stages; from foolish looks, to foul words, to foul touchings, then foul kissings, and finally "cometh a man to do the deed."[37] There are various ways of performing the deed, some more foul than others, and the worst of these is the sin against nature, a

sin so foul and so hideous that it should not be named, that is, sin against kynde, that the devil teacheth to a man or to a woman in many vices that more not be spoken, for the matter is so foul that it is abomination to speak it; but nevertheless be man or woman that be guilty thereof he must tell it openly in his confession to the priest as it was done.[38]

In fact, the mere confession of such a shameful sin was regarded as part of the penance for committing such a sin.

For in that sin is fouler and more shameful, insomuch is the confession more worth, for the same that he hath in confessing it, that is great part of his penance.

So serious was the sin that it could not be named except by allusions:

This sin is so misliking to God that he made rain, fire and stinking brimstone upon the cities of Sodom and Gomorra, and sunk into hell five cities. The devil that purchaseth that sin is squeamish thereof when anyone does it.[39]

The writer pointed out that a married couple could commit the sin against nature "when that one draweth the other to do this thing against kynde and in other wise than the nature of man asketh or law of marriage granteth."[40]

Many of the popular confessionals compared men unfavorably to animals, since beasts copulated but once a year, but men were at it almost anytime, everywhere.[41] Sex itself was painted in rather sordid terms. Young girls were warned of the sorrows of wedlock, since when they married, they would descend from their high virginal estate to a far lower one:

Into the filth of the flesh, into the manner of life of a beast, into thralldom of a man, and into the sorrows of the world . . . to cool thy lust with filth of thy body, to have delight of thy fleshy will from man's intercourse; before God, it is a nauseous thing to think thereon, and to speak thereof is yet more nauseous. Consider of what sort is that thing itself, and that deed to be done. All that foul delight is in filth ended, as thou turnest thine hand. But that loathsome beast remains and lasts on: and the disgust at long after. . . . Scorn to do what it seems to thee evil and pain to hear of. For when it is such, and by far more loathsome than any well conditioned mouth for shame may tell of, what maketh it love among beastly man, except their great immorality.[42]

Not only the confessional and corrective literature included such discussions but more secular literature also. William Langland (about 1322–1400), in his *Piers Plowman,* for example, compared men with beasts and gave beasts the advantage since "reason controlled all beasts in eating, in drinking, in engendering their kind. And after conception, none took heed of the other as they did in mating-time; in the time following males went with males."[43] Sexual sins were also a form of gluttony:

Moderation is precious, no price too high for it. For the awful catastrophe that came on the Sodomites was due to overplenty and to pure sloth. Laziness and abundant bread fostered the worst sin, for they used no restraint in eating and drinking and did deadly sins that pleased the devil.[44]

Langland felt that it was the rich rather than the poor who engaged in the greatest number of sins. Lechery, he wrote, was particularly expensive, and only the richest could afford to engage in the sin against nature, in which he included homosexuality and which he regarded as a particular failing of monks:

There's one word they skip over every time they preach . . . Holy Writ bid men beware (I won't write this here in English for fear it be repeated too often and scandalize good men, but scholars should read it): *"Let everyone beware of friars, for there is peril in false brethren."*[45]

Since there was no need for nuns to draw out confessions from penitents, they were kept even more in the dark about what the sexual sins were than the priests, or even than the general public. They were to arrive at an understanding of what the unnameable sin was by reflecting on their "own accursed devices when tempted by concupiscence." Regardless of how the flesh was satisfied, with the exception of certain activities that could take place only in wedlock, nuns were to realize it was a deadly sin.[46]

The Scorpion of Lechery—that is, of lustfulness—hath such a progeny, that it doth not become a modest mouth to name the names of some of them; for the name alone might offend all modest ears, and defile all clean hearts.[47]

Masturbation must have proved particularly troublesome to nuns. This is indicated by the story of a nun whom the devil rode day and night for 20 years.

On the night that the devil first climbed on her back she had committed "one particular sin, on the same night, through his instigation, and though she would, on the morrow, make confession of it, but she committed it again and again, and fell into such an evil habit that she lay and rotted in it . . ."[48]

Some writers regarded the sexual sins as both unclean and unnameable. The *Pearl Poet* stated that the descendants of Adam and Eve had been turned filthy by fleshly deeds:

> Contriving practices contrary to nature, using them basely, each on the other, harming one another by their bad habits. They fouled their flesh strangely, till the fiends saw that the daughters of noblemen were delightfully fair, and formed fellowships with them in human fashion, thus engendering giants by their evil jesting.[49]

As a result, God had destroyed mankind through the flood, but He remained troubled by the continuation of "indecent harlotry, and self-degradation." Self-degradation, for the *Pearl Poet,* was homosexuality, since man had learned a lust of the flesh where each man took for a mate "a man like himself and they join filthily, in the female way," and thereby established an unclean custom.[50]

Geoffrey Chaucer (about 1343–1400) recognized many sexual sins against nature but classified relations between members of the same sex as one of the primary ones.[51] Though Chaucer recognized that any discussion of the sins against nature was venturing into a forbidden area, he argued that, since the Bible spoke about it, then men should also be able to discuss it.

> The cursedness doon men and women in diverse entente and diverse manere; but though that hooly write speke of horrible synne, certes hooly write nat been defouled namoore than the soone that shyneth on the misne (dunghill).[52]

In his "Parson's Tale," he defined the sin against nature (literally, *unkyndely synne*) as an act by which a "man or woman shedeth hire nature in amere or in place ther as child may nat be conceived."[53] He used a similar reference in the "Merchant's Tale."[54]

Dante Alighieri (1265–1321), the great Italian poet, put all those guilty of unnatural offenses among the violent in the seventh level of Hell, but those who had expiated their offenses were raised to Purgatory, where they lodged with those guilty of various other kinds of lust. Nowhere did he spell out exactly what constituted either violence against nature or unnatural lust, although he implied that it was a crime limited to males, and many of those who committed it were clerks and great men of letters.[55] Grouped in Purgatory are those whose transgression was "hermaphrodite" along with those who acted like brute beasts in indulging their appetites, and included in his listing are two troubadours, Arnaut Daniel and Guido Gunicellis, indicating the possibility that heterosexual activities were included.[56]

If the literary evidence and the popular confessional literature can be taken as evidence, it seems that most sexual activities were regarded as deviant in the later Middle Ages and classified under the category of sins against nature, a catch-all grouping for all kinds of sexual activity that tended to inhibit impregnation or to use a vessel not regarded as proper for sexual purposes. Those who engaged in such activities were often, as the selections quoted indicate, regarded as the servants of the devil, and increasingly, in the later medieval period, there was a tendency to identify those individuals who refused to conform sexually with those who practiced heresy and witchcraft.

Social scientists have long been intrigued by the phenomenon known as scapegoating, in which aggression and hostility are displaced from the real sources of frustration to a group or individual defined by society as a legitimate object of hostility. Increasingly, in the later Middle Ages, both heretics and witches served as scapegoats, and the dangers of contamination from them became one of the favorite sermon topics. Since St. Albertus Magnus had also considered certain kinds of sexual conduct contagious, various forms of forbidden behavior inevitably came to be associated with heretics, and later with witchcraft. Undoubtedly, much of the deviant sexuality associated with heresy and witchcraft was the product of fervid imagination, but even so, the accounts have value to the historian as an indicator of the types of sexual behavior most feared.

Why sexuality became associated with deviant religious conduct is a difficult question to answer. It might well be, as Gerhart Ladner has argued, that the results of the cultural revolution of the twelfth and thirteenth century encouraged a desire for material pleasure that hastened a conflict with traditional Christian values, leading to psychological dissonance and widespread alienation. To some extent the new forces unleashed by the cultural revolution could be sublimated in orthodox reform movements such as the Franciscans, but they also frequently found refuge in unorthodox religious movements that took on almost revolutionary fervor.[57] If this argument has any value, it would seem logical that the repressed desire for material pleasure characteristic of the orthodox might also have encouraged them to attribute to the heretics enjoyment of the very materialistic pleasures they were denying themselves. Sex was one such pleasure.

The only alternative hypothesis presenting itself is that the heretics did in fact engage in many of the sexual activities with which they were charged. From what we can reconstruct of the times, there is undoubtedly a grain of truth in such a statement. Many of the heresies of the twelfth and thirteenth centuries can be traced to the dualistic concepts of the ancient Manichaeans discussed earlier, but others seem to have strong pantheistic tendencies. The

German Marxist Ernst Werner has argued that both dualism and pantheism have the same basic religious motivation, namely, an attempt to escape the bonds of worldly uprighteousness and inadequacy, an escape also coupled with a quest for godly purity. To his mind, libertinism could be regarded as a decisive way of taking a stand against the hypocrisy of the world and thus dramatically asserting the holiness of the believers. We find expressions of this in some of the sixteenth-century anabaptist movements, and probably also in the medieval heresies. The break of the committed with the established order could even be highlighted by an act of desecration, since it implied conduct that the establishment would regard as blasphemous.[58] Sexual deviation became then a way of denying the validity of current societal standards. Probably the explanation for the association of sexuality with heresy is a combination of the two; the heretic was both more sexual than the orthodox, and the orthodox attributed greater sexuality to the heretic than he or she had. This was because, in the minds of the establishment, the heretic was not only wrong but also sinful; it was only a small step to attribute other forms of evil and sinful conduct to him or her, since a sinner had many sins. If someone adopted one kind of forbidden behavior or was thought to have done so, it was considered perfectly correct to attribute all other forms, including sexual, to him.

Once social and sexual deviation were equated in Western culture, the correlation became deeply engrained in Western thinking and belief. The truth of this proposition can nowhere be better illustrated than by use of the term *buggery* to imply deviant sexual behavior. Originally, the term was used to describe Albigensianism, a renewed form of the Manichaeanism of Augustinian times, that appeared in western Europe in the thirteenth and fourteenth centuries. The term is a corruption of the term *Bulgar,* another name for the Albigensians, who were believed to have originated in Bulgaria. Just when the term lost its strictly religious connotation and acquired a sexual connotation is debatable but nonetheless important. One of the earliest uses of the term in English appears in the writings of Robert Mannyng of Brunne (1288–1388), who has one of the characters in his *Langtoft's Chronicle* state that the Pope was a heretic who "lyved in bugerie."[59] Some, including the compilers of the *Oxford English Dictionary* have given this a sexual meaning when no such meaning was intended. With such authorities behind him, Havelock Ellis, the pioneering investigator into sexual habits at the beginning of this century, might be forgiven for equating the word *bougerie* with sodomy wherever and whenever he found it. Ellis erroneously wrote that Louis IX (1226–1370), the saintly king of France, handed sodomists over to the Church to be burned, when there is no real evidence to back up such an assertion.[60] First, the medieval Church never burned anyone; those people who were burned in the medieval period were burned by the state, although the Church might well have found them guilty and turned them over to the state for punishment. This pious hypocrisy of allowing the state to execute the condemned kept the Church officially from shedding blood or executing anyone. More importantly, Ellis confused buggery with sodomy. The statute in question reads:

> If anyone is suspected of bouggerie, the magistrate must seize him and send him to the Bishop; and if he is convicted, he must be burnt and all his goods confiscated to the Baron. And the heretic ought to be dealt with in the same way, when his offence has been proven, and all his goods confiscated to the Baron.[61]

Though there is a distinction in the statute between *bouggerie* and the *l'ome herité*, the distinction is not between a sexual crime and a religious one, but between the Albigensian heretics (*bouggerie*) and other forms of heresy. In effect, the purpose of the royal edict was, not to list the sexual sins,[62] but to stamp out heresy.[63] This is verified by an examination of the contemporary documents, none of which ever use the word *buggery* to describe sexual acts. A legal collection made about 1260 at Orleans includes several passages dealing with *bogrerie* (the word is spelled in various ways) in the sense of heresy and one passage dealing specifically with sodomy. This last statute requires burning for a person found guilty of committing an offense for the third time.[64] In spite of this statute, however, there is no evidence that sodomists were in fact burned.[65] Rather, the statutory provision for burning was probably a *pro forma* one based on the provisions of late Roman law codes and transmitted into Europe through the Carolingian legislation of the ninth century.

An early more or less standard association of heresy and sexual deviation appears in the description of the Waldensians by the twelfth-century writer, Alan of Lille:

> . . . in their assemblies they indulge in gluttony, and devote themselves to excesses, as those who have ceased to consort with them testify . . . lovers of pleasures, putting carnal delights before the spiritual. These are they who creep into the house of widows and lead them astray.[66]

In spite of such charges, we know that the Waldensians were a reformist-minded ascetic group who were somewhat on the order of later Baptists. Obviously, if such charges could be made against an ascetic group like the Waldensians, it does not take much imagination to realize that most of the charges of sexual deviation in the Middle Ages were made out of whole cloth. In fact, most of the stories about sexual promiscuity and deviation fail the basic historical test of corroboration. Upon close examination, only a handful are based on eyewitness accounts, and only rarely is there an independent corroborating witness. Moreover, stories of sexual promiscuity become part of the folklore about deviant religious groups, and the same story is repeated about different groups.[67]

Some heretical groups are, however, associated more with deviant sexuality than others, perhaps because their teachings were more likely to be misunderstood. This is particularly true of the Albigensians or Cathars or Bulgars, who had such a horror of procreation that those who fully accepted the Cathar way of life, the *perfecti,* were taught to avoid procreation. So hostile were the Cathars to sexual procreation that they refused to eat any food engendered by the sex act, such as meat, eggs, cheese, and milk. Such a teaching followed naturally from their belief that the act of insemination led to the continued imprisonments of spirits in the material flesh. Salvation thus implied the removal of the material. Typical of the charges against the Cathars is that made by Guibert of Nogent in the twelfth century.

> They condemn marriage and the begetting of offspring through intercourse. And surely, wherever they are scattered throughout the Latin world, you may see men living with women but not under the name of husband and wife, and in such fashion that man does not dwell with woman, male with female, but *men are known to lie with men, women with women*; for among them it is unlawful for men to approach women. They reject foods of all sorts which are the product of coition.

> They hold meetings in cellars and secret places, the sexes mingling freely. When candles have been lighted in the sight of all, light women with bare buttocks (it is said) offer themselves to a certain one lying behind them. Directly the candles are extinguished, they all cry out together "Chaos!" and each one lies with her who first comes to hand.

> Now it so happens that a woman has there been gotten with child, as soon as the offspring is delivered, it is brought back to the same place. A great fire is lit, and the child is thrown from hand to hand through the flames by those sitting around the fire until it is dead. It is then reduced to ashes; from the ashes, bread is made, of which a morsel is given to each as a sacrament. Once that has been eaten, it is very rarely that one is brought back to his sense from that heresy.[68]

Guibert's list of sexual and other crimes attributed to the heretics is a more or less standard listing of all the sexual charges against heretics: homosexuality, intercourse in the wrong position, coitus interruptus, and infanticide. Guibert is not alone in his listing; similar accounts are reported by Henry of Le Mans[69] and Walter Map,[70] both in the twelfth century.

Different charges were made against the Amalricans. They allegedly taught that, since all men were God, there could be no evil. Evil things perforce became good, since they were from God and were God. The faithful need not obey the law and could follow their urges to sex, lust, greed, and other activities because these urges came from God.[71] The thirteenth-century pseudo-

Apostles, led by Gerard Segarelli and Colcino of Novaro, allegedly taught that holy poverty was the only perfect state, and to point up this poverty, their followers shed all their clothing, donned a special garb, and went out preaching. Segarelli was accused by one chronicler of recruiting a horde of boys who submitted to sodomy. Salimbene, the chronicler who made such a charge, saw homosexuality everywhere else, too, and commented on its widespread existence among scholars, clerks, and nuns.[72]

As long as heresy was regarded as a minor threat, efforts at control were left in the hands of the local bishops. Heretics were frequently ignored or tolerated as harmless. As the number of dissenters grew, however, there was a demand for more positive action against them, and the same trend toward centralization that appeared in other aspects of ecclesiastical organization appeared in this area as well. By the thirteenth century the papacy itself attempted to take over control of the operations to root out heresy through establishment of the Inquisition. The newly founded Dominicans became the papal agents for ferreting out heretics. By the middle of the thirteenth century, inquisitors were authorized to seize the goods of suspected heretics, imprison and torture them, and upon conviction, turn them over to secular officials for execution. Once heresy hunting became institutionalized, the charges against the heretics assumed a uniformity in which sexual deviation remained an important part.

Sometimes, in fact, it seems that everything that medieval people feared came to have sexual overtones. Leprosy is a good example; inevitably in the Middle Ages its victims were linked with moral and sexual impurity. Even the medical writers regarded leprosy as a punishment for carnality and the leper as sexually inflamed.[73] The leper was a person afflicted with coarse sexual needs, and his leprosy was symbolic of his depravity. The leper not only suffered but was also ostracized by a society that felt he deserved to suffer for his sexual sins.[74] Later, in the sixteenth century, when syphilis came to be recognized as a separate disease, the same connotations associated with leprosy came to be associated with syphilis and in part have continued to be associated with it to our own time.

Witchcraft was also, of course, associated with sexual deviance, although not so much in the medieval as in later periods. Male transvestism, for example, was regarded as witchcraft; one of the earliest references to this association came in the tenth century, when bishops were requested to be on the lookout for a throng of demons transformed into women.[75] Apparently, the concept of change of sex was unusual but not regarded as impossible, and both transvestism and transsexualism were regarded as symptomatic of witchcraft. In the thirteenth century, a group of men went around impersonating women, claiming to be the spirits of the good people, although the chroniclers regarded them as impersonations of evil.[76] Female transvestites were still, however, tolerated, but there were some limitations. Perhaps the most famous transvestite saint of the later medieval period is St. Hildegund, who died in 1188 and whose feast day is celebrated on April 20. According to the romanticized story of her life, she was the daughter of a knight from Neuss on the Rhine, who, after his wife's death, decided to make a pilgrimage to the Holy Land. Concerned over the fate of his daughter Hildegund, then a girl of 12, the knight dressed her as a boy, renamed her Joseph, and took her with him. The two traveled together to Jerusalem, happy and content. On the way home the knight fell ill, and just before he died, he commended his "son" to a fellow knight. Her new guardian robbed Joseph and deserted him–her at Tyre. Somehow, still passing as Joseph, Hildegund managed to find her way back to Europe through a series of exciting adventures that vary according to the chronicler. Back in Europe, Hildegund, still passing as a man, became a servant to a cleric at Cologne and decided to travel with him on a visit to the Pope. On this trip she again had an exciting series of adventures, including being condemned to death as a supposed robber. She saved herself by undergoing the ordeal of the red-hot iron to prove her innocence, but in retaliation for her betrayal, she was hanged by her former criminal confederates. Their technique proved so slipshod that Joseph managed to survive the hanging, and after being cut down, she continued her journey to Rome. Returning to Germany she entered the monastery at Schönau, where she stayed until her death, although she never took formal vows. Only after her death was she discovered to be a woman.[77] Though much romanticized, her story probably contains more elements of truth than those of some of the early transvestite saints.

In spite of her adventures, St. Hildegund did not threaten men in what could be regarded as any masculine task. But when women attempted to meet men on their own terms, they did suffer trouble; this is most obvious in the trial of Joan of Arc (about 1412–1431). Though Joan also eventually achieved sainthood, she did so only after being executed, and one major reason for her execution was her transvestism. In the original complaint against her, she was charged with having a male costume made for herself with weapons to match and with abandoning women's clothes. Later, the various charges against her were summarized in 12 articles, 2 of which dealt with her impersonating a male, as did 2 of the 6 admonitions directed against her. Joan eventually recanted, and as part of her recantation, she promised to don female clothing. It was her resumption of male dress that led to her execution. When asked why she had resumed her male garb, she supposedly said that she preferred it to women's dress and that she never meant to take an oath not to wear male clothes.[78] In the postmortem trial that led to her rehabilitation, a quite different explanation was advanced for her resumption of male dress, one that proved more acceptable than her earlier testimony. It was claimed that, when she had arisen on the morning in question, she had found that her jailers had removed all of her women's clothes, leaving only men's garments behind. Knowing that male garb was forbidden to her, she asked for the return of her female ones, but the guards refused. Rather than put on male clothing, she returned to her bed, where she stayed until noon, when physical necessity finally forced her to put on the forbidden male garments to answer the call of nature. Though, politically, the English probably found it expedient, if not essential, to execute her, it is an indication of the thinking of the period that they used the resumption of male dress as a justification and even went so far as to force her to wear male clothes.[79] For a woman to assume a male guise for holy purposes was permitted, but to compete with men on such masculine grounds as warfare was simply not permitted, and a woman who was successful at such efforts must have been a witch.

One type of symbolic activity associated with both heresy and witchcraft was the *osculum infame,* the infamous kiss in which participants in heretical or witchcraft ceremonies were reported to kiss the buttock or anus of an animal. Though the first mention of this activity does not appear until early in the thirteenth century, official sanction was given the association of such practices with witchcraft by Pope Gregory IX in a bull issued in 1233. This bull, an official document of the pope, was reportedly based on the statement of an inquisitor.[80] Numerous variations of the obscene kiss were recorded. Some observers reported that the bishops of the heretics bared their buttocks, which were then kissed by the congregation. At times the "bishop" inserted a silver spoon into his anus, upon which he then offered an oblation. Closely associated with such ceremonies was a black cat.[81]

Probably the most notorious attempt to equate deviant sexuality with heretical conduct, including the obscene kiss, was in the trial of the Knights Templar, a military crusading order founded at the beginning of the twelfth century to protect pilgrims visiting the holy places in Jerusalem. Like other monastic orders, the Templars adopted vows of poverty and chastity. They differed from regular orders in that only knights of noble birth were admitted to full membership, and their duty was to fight for Christianity rather than to pray. Over the years the Templars built up a network of houses that also served as banking institutions, since pilgrims would deposit money or goods in France and be able to cash the chits they received at other Templar houses on the way to the Holy Land. The Templars were also the favorite recipients of many donations, and the Order became very rich in its own right. Their wealth, their chain of treasure houses, and their reputation for honesty caused them to be looked to as a source of loans. Various people, particularly the kings of France, borrowed large sums of money from them. Inevitably, such a rich Order came to wield great financial power throughout much of Christian Europe, and some rulers were fearful that the Templars had more power than they did. It was probably this fear as much as anything else that led to their downfall. On the order of the French King Philip IV, who was heavily in debt to them, all the Templars in France, including the Grand Master Jacques de Molay, were arrested on the night of October 13, 1307, and charged with heresy and sodomy. How much the charge of sodomy was justified and how much it represented part of the standard arsenal of charges against any accused group has been a matter of debate. Gershon Legman has argued that the Templars in fact practiced homosexuality and that Jacques de Molay was a homosexual.[82] At the opposite pole of thought is Julius Gmelin, who held that the Templars were as "pure as the Holy Father himself."[83] Probably the truth lies somewhere between these two extremes.

Historians have long been fascinated by the sudden fall of the Templars, who, until the massive arrests of 1307 and their ultimate dissolution in 1312, were the most colorful, most powerful, and most widely known of the crusading orders.[84] Henry C. Lea, the nineteenth-century collector of information on witchcraft and the Inquisition, felt that the condemnation of the Templars was the "great crime of the Middle Ages."[85] Though probably the real reason for moving against the Templars was the greed of others for their wealth, greed in itself is something that cannot be adjudicated in court. Instead, heresy and sexual irregularity became the main charges. The reality of these charges is in doubt, in part because the original accusations were made by a certain Esquiu de Floyran, a former member of the Order who had been charged by the Order with murdering a Templar official. It is widely believed that Esquiu, to save himself, accused the Templars of heinous crimes, charges that were more or less ignored by King James II of Aragon, to whom he first confessed, but were eventually accepted by Philip of France. Philip requested Pope Clement V to investigate the charges, but before the Pope decided what action he would take, Philip denounced the Templars to the Inquisition. Two of the eight charges against them were sexual, namely, that they took part in a mock ceremonial involving the *osculum infame* and that they were addicted to immorality and sodomy. It was alleged that during the initiation the Templars had to kiss the official receiving them on the buttocks, on the navel, and on the mouth and that they were also instructed they might have carnal copulation one with another. It was also alleged that the novices were instructed to submit to copulation passively if requested to do so by another Templar.[86]

The most important trial was that involving the leader Jacques de Molay, and the results of that trial are instructive both for what de Molay admitted and for what he denied. The grand master confessed that he had denied Christ depicted on the cross when he was accepted into the Order, and he also admitted that he had even spat on the cross as part of his initiation. He denied, however, that he had ever been told to unite himself carnally with another brother and claimed that he had never done such a thing. Since he continued to maintain his innocence on such charges even under torture, most historians are inclined to dismiss the charges of homosexuality and claim that they were politically motivated. Since de Molay never confessed to sodomy, the question centers on why he so willingly confessed to desecrating the cross, an admission he had made even before he was tortured. One historian has written:

> If the confession is genuine, and doubt has been thrown on it—the only expression consistent with his innocence is fear of the consequences for himself and the Templars if he denied the charges. He is said to have especially feared the charge of homosexuality brought against him and had been promised that this part of the indictment would not be pressed if he acknowledged other charges.[87]

The only difficulty with this explanation is trying to determine why de Molay would have such a fear of admitting homosexuality. Sodomy, as has been indicated, was an extremely ambiguous term in the Middle Ages and could include anything from masturbation to anal intercourse; it was, moreover, a much less serious accusation than some of the others against him. The desecration of the cross was probably a symbolic part of the initiation, an indication of the novice's willingness to put the Order above everything else. If this is true, then the charge of homosexuality clearly appears to be manufactured, even though a certain Hugh de Narsac also claimed that de Molay had engaged in sodomy with his own valet. De Molay never admitted this charge, nor did most of the other Templars. In fact, only three of the thousands who were examined over the 7-year period confessed to engaging in any kind of sexual act, although several hundred confessed that they had heard homosexuality had been permitted, even though they swore they had not practiced it themselves. Most of this later group confessed, however, only after some of the implications of the Templars' oath were pointed out to them. Since the torture was severe and many knights died under the torture, it would seem on the whole that the charges of sodomy were based more on fiction than reality.[88] The only other possible answer is that the inquisitors did not pursue the question of sodomy with the same eagerness they devoted to other charges. Perhaps they themselves were fearful of allegations of homosexuality about those in religious orders, and rather than probe deeper, they were content to secure confessions about the possible existence of such practices.[89] Whether homosexual acts took place or not cannot now be proved, but it does seem that the case of the Templars documents a willingness to attribute sexual deviation to those accused of heresy, as well as to monks in general. One author wrote:

> The insistence that the fighting monks were to shun women even more stringently than most other religious fraternities lent added fuel to the train of thought; it was seriously submitted that the injunction to sodomy had been designed to clinch the Templar's aversion to all feminine contact. So the train of thought sped on to the final point of arrival; for a group of men obviously more sinful than the generality

to be more privileged than anyone else, could not be just. Envy and greed call themselves righteous.[90]

A label of being sexually deviant was not confined to the ecclesiastical arena or limited to superstition. A good example appears in the *Divine Comedy* of Dante Alighieri, already mentioned. Interestingly, many of the contemporary Italians whom Dante assigned to the seventh level of the *Inferno* for their sodomitical activities turn out on examination to have been his political opponents. Guido Guerra, Jacopo Rusticucci, Tegghiaio Aldrobandi, Brunetto Latini, and quite possibly, Guilielmo Brosiere were Guelphs, a political party associated with the Pope and responsible for the exile of Dante from Florence, a member of the Ghibelline party supporting the emperor. The only contemporary he places in Hell about whom the charge of homosexuality might have some basis is Andrea de Mozzi, the Bishop of Florence, who was transferred by the pope in 1266 from Florence to another city, allegedly because of his "unseemly" conduct. Dante also held that bachelor clergy and men of letters were particularly addicted to sodomitical activity, a statement that would fit into the general rationalization for charging the Templars with sexual deviation.[91]

The equation of religious heresy or political opposition with sexual deviation does not necessarily mean that the sexual activities were homosexual. This is important to emphasize, because the controversy over the introduction of Aristotle and Averroës at the University of Paris in the thirteenth century has sometimes been interpreted as a hidden struggle over homosexuality.[92] Though the Averroists (and the Aristotelians) were condemned at the University of Paris in 1210 and charged with encouraging sexual vices, the charges, on close reading, have nothing at all to do with homosexuality. Rather, the Averroists were charged with teaching that continence was not a virtue, that total abstinence from sexual acts corrupted virtue, that delights in the act of sex did not impede intellectual development, and that simple fornication among unmarried people was not sinful.[93] Arguments over sexuality probably lay beneath the surface of many medieval controversies, but in this period deviance was very broadly defined. Toward the end of the Middle Ages the earlier concern with heresy became secondary to a growing concern over sorcery and witchcraft, but this will be examined in somewhat more detail in the next chapter, where it more properly belongs.

Not all charges of sexual deviation were politically motivated, and though it is difficult to prove or disprove charges, it does seem that in the twelfth and thirteenth centuries there is increasing reference to homosexuality in the surviving records. Two sons of William the Conqueror, William Rufus, who ruled England as William II (1087–1100), and his brother Robert, Duke of Normandy, were both charged by a contemporary chronicler with engaging in sexual relations with other males. Ordericus Vitalis stated that, when William was king, the "effeminate predominated everywhere and revelled without restraint," while "filthy catamites," fit only to "perish in the flames," abandoned themselves "shamefully to the foulest practices of Sodom."[94] William Malmesbury, another writer, reported much the same thing.[95] The great nineteenth-century historian of the Anglo–Norman period, E. A. Freeman, wrote that it was well not to investigate too closely the private life of William Rufus, since in him "England might see on her own soil the habits of ancient Greek and the modern Turk. His sins were of a kind from which his brother, Henry, no model of moral perfection, was deemed to be wholly free, and which he was believed to look upon with loathing."[96] Earlier in this chapter the results of a council called by William's successor, Henry I, to deal with the shameful vice of sodomy were reported, and this might well have been a political use of sodomy charges to consolidate Henry's own hold on the throne at the expense of other claimants. Still, the accusations are not entirely political by any means. A whole series of rulers have been identified as being homosexual, although not always with any supporting evidence. Richard I, better known as the Lion Hearted (1157–1199) was allegedly involved with Raife de Clermon, a young knight freed by him from Saracen captivity. Edward II (1284–1327) was allegedly so enamored of Piers Gaveston that his father banned the older boy from the court; Piers was immediately returned to favor when Edward himself succeeded to the throne. Later, Edward was supposedly involved with Hugh Despenser. Other rulers alleged to have had homosexual affairs include Richard II (1367–1400), the Emperor Frederick II (1194–1250), King Conradin of Sicily (1252–1268), who was also a claimant to the imperial throne, and several lesser nobles.[97] Though it would be difficult to prove or disprove such charges, except perhaps in the case of Edward II,[98] some explanation other than political hostility might also have validity in explaining such charges. Generally, the explanation, following Ordericus Vitalis, is that the "infection" was imported from the Arabs by the Crusaders. This is much too simple. Sexual deviation is not a contagious disease. Rather, cultural conditioning would seem to be a more satisfactory answer. Earlier we saw how the Greek educational system tended to encourage homosexuality. Later we will see how the English public (that is, private) school system did the same thing.

In the later Middle Ages, the training for knighthood might well have led to hostility to the female, and a close bonding pattern between males, particularly between a would-be knight and an older man, might have led to toleration of, if it did not encourage, homosexuality. Usually, the young noble youth was incorporated into a group of friends who were taught to love one another as brothers, who were led by an older man, and whose every waking moment was spent in each other's company. Sometimes these groups stayed together for as long as 20 years, from age 11 or 12 until 30 or so, when they were then supposed to marry. Sometimes marriage was further delayed, for eligible women were not particularly plentiful, if only because the older nobles often went through several periods of being widowers as their wives predeceased them. They then often took the younger eligible women as their wives, leaving their younger rivals with little choice for a mate. Excluded from official adult society, tossed into long-term companionships with each other, unable to establish any stable relationships with females, it is quite possible that they turned to each other for friendship, encouragement, and even sexual relief.[99] Under such conditions, though ultimately the eligible male would marry, if only because social convention demanded he do so, homosexuality, or at least bisexuality, was encouraged.

Sometimes the socializing patterns must have led to rather perverted value systems, although it is difficult from our vantage point to determine whether it was the social system or the individual's own inability to adjust that gave rise to such troubled figures as Gilles de Rais (or Retz) (1404–1440). Gilles, orphaned when he was 11, was raised by his maternal grandfather. Unlike most of his contemporaries, he was married young, when he was 16, to a rich heiress, and the combination of his fortune and that of his bride made him one of the wealthiest men in France. In the struggle of the French king Charles VII against the English claimants to the French throne, Gilles sided with Charles VII and was made responsible for the safety of Joan of Arc, who first appeared on the French political scene in 1428. Gilles twice saved her life, and in gratitude for his services, he was made a marshal of France by Charles VII. After Joan's execution, Gilles returned to his castle in Brittany, where he set up a court that temporarily rivaled that of the French king. This effort nearly bankrupted him and led to legal action by his family, designed to prevent him from selling any of his estates to keep up his standard of living. In desperate need of money, Gilles turned to magic and alchemy, and he became convinced that human sacrifice to Satan would restore his wealth. With the assistance of a number of disciples, most particularly an Italian priest and alchemist, François Prelati, he began scouring the countryside for suitable subjects, mostly young boys. Though his original motive for enticing his subjects might have been for sacrifice, Gilles became interested in the children as sexual objects as well. Many were sexually assaulted before they died, and even after death he abused the cadavers. Although the disappearance of so many boys around the castle aroused suspicions and rumors, as did Gilles' demands for boy servants, his activities went unchecked until 1440. Then, in a fit of anger, he stormed into a church during the celebration of Mass, sword in hand, to seize a minor cleric who had antagonized him. This led to a break with his protector, the Duke of Brittany, and to an investigation of his activities by the Bishop of Nantes. His arrest soon followed. During his trial on heresy Gilles broke down and confessed; later, a more detailed confession was given under torture. He confessed to murdering large numbers of victims—so many he could not remember but estimated today at between 150 to 200—and engaging in sexual activities with his victims, both before and after their deaths. He was executed by hanging at Nantes on October 26, 1440, and his confession, repentance, and resignation at his execution were acclaimed at the time as an example of Christian penitence.[100] Whether Gilles served as the model for Bluebeard, a story that made its appearance in a collection of stories by Charles Perrault in 1697, is debatable. Both stories were set in Brittany, and while there are similarities, Gilles mostly killed young boys rather than wives. In fact, he had only one wife, from whom he kept apart as much as possible. It might well be that Perrault, if he did use the story of Gilles, decided that public sensibility would not tolerate the homosexual version and changed it to a heterosexual one.

Obviously, Gilles was no more representative of the fifteenth-century noble than the Charles Manson family was representative of the culture of Los Angeles in the twentieth century, but there is little doubt that the medieval system at the least, encouraged the nobility to turn to their own sex for support. In the earliest feudal literature, such as the *Song of Roland,* the portrayals of the deepest affections are those between males, particularly the mutual love of warriors who die together fighting against odds, or between the would-be knights and their leaders or lords.[101] The noble male was chiefly absorbed in war and the chase. His wife bore him sons and his mistresses satisfied his momentary lusts, but beyond this, women had no particular place, and often he was not particularly interested in them as individuals. Prior to the twelfth century, women were pictured in literature in one of two ways, either as sex objects or as noble and virtuous wives and mothers, nursing their children, mourning their slain husbands, and exhorting their sons to do brave, and sometimes cruel, deeds. A change in this stereotype came only with the development of romantic love. Scholars have spent a good deal of time and energy in trying to trace the sources of romantic love to Islamic lyric poerty, to Greek Platonism, to Ovid, to the patronage of women—all contributory factors—but the fear of homosexuality should be added to the list.

Some parts of this hypothesis are easier to document than others. Literature, for example, is molded by the type of audience it has. In much of the past, the audience that counted most was male. Men had the money to hire poets to sing their praises and recount epic stories of war. When prose developed, it was men who were usually literate, since so many obstacles were put in the paths of women who wanted to be educated. During much of the medieval period, the most literate group was the clergy, but the rich laymen, even though not particularly literate, were interested in a good story, and storytellers emerged to keep them entertained. The patron of the storyteller exercised great influence on the subject matter and the outcome of the stories told him, and since women could also act as patrons, it might well have been their influence as patrons that proved such an important factor in the development of romantic love.

The historian Sidney Painter speculated that the genesis of the whole movement occurred one day when a hungry minstrel who was wandering about the duchy of Aquitaine came to a castle where he hoped that his tales of battles and his tumbling tricks would earn him a good dinner. The lord of the castle, much to his misfortune, was absent, and the lady who acted as his hostess found his endless stories of battles both tiring and boring and did not even care for his tumbling. Since this was a particularly sensitive poet, it occurred to him that his stay in the castle would be neither pleasant nor lengthy unless he managed to gain the lady's attention and give her pleasure. Being inventive, he composed a song in praise of the lady's beauty and virtue, describing their effect on him in rather glowing terms. Naturally, he found the lady was quite pleased, and she rewarded him with a better bed and more ample food. Soon other wandering minstrels followed his example, and it was not long before the baronial halls of southern France were ringing with songs in praise of ladies who were able to dispense lavish hospitality, and any lady who did not have a minstrel singing her virtues felt definitely out of fashion. On this scene came William IX, Count of Poitou and Duke of Aquitaine, who thought such songs might prove a pleasant accompaniment to his numerous triumphs over feminine virtue and an entertainment to his companions. The Duke's accounts of his amorous adventures, not so surprisingly, proved as interesting to his friends as his stories of battles, and with the example of a powerful prince who ruled a third of France as a spur, the fashion grew and expanded. Those barons unable to sing or write hired someone to do so for them.[102]

Romantic love is, however, more complicated than a singer's entertaining a lady at her home or his male companions around the campfire. Though based in literature aimed at the nobility and associated with knighthood and chivalry, it was a despairing and tragic emotion that drove a lover to accomplish great deeds of derring-do for his beloved and the Christian God. In theory, true love was unattainable love; that is, it was not to be consummated by sexual intercourse. The theory undoubtedly reflected the real situation of noble ladies who acted as patrons, since they were usually married and could be portrayed only as unattainable. Adultery probably occurred in some cases where reality coincided with theory, but the medieval poet usually condemned any such amorous interludes. The theory of romantic love first espoused by the eleventh-century French poets and given backing by the Church eventually spread throughout Europe, gradually becoming embedded in the European psyche, where it "effected a change which has left no corner of our ethics, our imagination, or our daily life untouched." In the process, it "erected impassable barriers between us and the classical past or the Oriental present."[103] The Western code of etiquette with its rules that women always have precedence is based on the concepts of romantic love, as is the concept of the gentle, courteous male. In an important sense, also, romantic love represented a break from the Christian tradition, which held that all love, or at least any such thing as passionate love, was more or less wicked unless directed to God.

In the chivalric literature, love was the emotion produced by the unrestrained adoration of a lady. It might be rewarded by smiles, kisses, or still other, more intimate favors, but the presence or absence of these was not supposed to have any effect on the love itself. The male in love lost interest in food and drink, scarcely noticed whether it was hot or cold outside, and concentrated every fiber of his being on his love for his lady. Love encouraged the development of *preux,* skill, and knightly honor; made a cowardly man act valiant; and made a brave man braver. It came to be doubted whether a man who did not adore a lady could ever be a true knight.

As troubadour poetry moved northward, sexual intercourse became an integral and sometimes necessary part of the conception of love; knights also felt called upon to make themselves attractive to ladies. How often did the love end in ultimate consummation? The answer probably depended on the poet's or hero's status. When the poet was a great lord, he was occasionally rewarded by sharing the bed with his lady love; if he was just a humble knight praising the wife of a great baron, he kept his distance. As romantic love developed, it also bred its own philosophers; among the most important of these was Andreas Capellanus, who wrote *The Art of Courtly Love* toward the end of the twelfth and the beginning of the thirteenth century.

To Andreas, love was a passion that came from looking at and thinking too much about the body of a person of the opposite sex; it could be satisfied only by embracing and fulfilling love's commands, in other words, by sexual intercourse. Love was, however, separate from marriage, since marriage was a contractual obligation, but love was entirely voluntary. True love might well become adulterous, but it need not end up that way. The fact that he might really be sanctioning adultery, or at the very least, fornication, troubled Andreas, and his book is full of ambiguities. He resolved his doubts in his last chapter, "The Rejection of Love," a diatribe against women. Why he wrote the book if he felt this way is unclear, but he cleansed his hands of all blame by concluding that it was all woman's fault that she was so sexual, and she, not man, was to blame.[104]

Coinciding with the development of romantic love was the growth and influence of the Virgin Mary, perhaps also encouraged by a repressed fear of homosexuality. In the early Middle Ages there had been a tendency to frighten men into heaven, and in the process, God became almost a relentless prosecutor, and Jesus became Christ the Judge. There was an obvious need for a mediator, for a feminine influence on this all-male Godhead, and increasingly, this position was filled by Mary. She was the grieving, sorrowful mother, sorry that her children had strayed but loving them, regardless of what they had done. In the eyes of most men, Jesus was too sublime, too terrible, too just, to deal with effectively, but even the weakest of humans could approach his mother, and she could exercise her influence on her son.

Mary remained essentially feminine, being conceived very much as a noble-woman with womanly moods and caprices. She loved grace, beauty, ornament, her toilette, robes, and jewels, and she demanded attention. She protected her friends and punished her enemies. Mary had always been important in medieval Christendom but was more of a fringe figure than a central one until the eleventh and twelfth centuries. Some see her originally as a Christian counterpart to the pagan Isis, and the statutes of Mary and Jesus have been shown by archaeologists to have been originally the same ones representing Isis and Horus. In the renewed attention given her in the later Middle Ages, however, Mary came to be particularly revered by men, especially celibate monks and fighting nobles. The Cistercian Order, founded in 1098, put all its churches under the special protection of the Virgin, and the result was a vast number of cathedrals dedicated to her, including Notre Dame de Paris ("Our Lady of Paris"). She protected warriors, and the favorite battle cry of each side in the various wars of the later Middle Ages was to Our Lady, Notre Dame. The "Fighting Irish" of Notre Dame emphasize this contradiction on the football field today. Not only was the Son absorbed into the Mother, or represented as under her guardianship, but also the Father fared no better, and the Holy Spirit nearly disappeared. Some of the poets regarded her as the temple of the Trinity, the Church itself, and in the building of a church, the Trinity, as represented by the triple aisle, was absorbed in her. Undoubtedly, part of this elevation was due to a masculine tendency to feminize things such as ships, institutions such as the church, and buildings such as cathedrals. The priest was married to the church, and it was much easier to visualize this in feminine form than in masculine.[105] By so doing, the emphasis becomes heterosexual rather than homosexual.

Though perhaps motivated by a fear of homosexuality, there is no evidence that the cult of the Virgin or romantic love led to any rise in the status of women. In fact, the focus on virginity tended to create in many minds an almost hysterical aversion to the state of matrimony. In the devotional literature, it was Mary as the Virgin who was elevated, and though she was a mother figure, she was an immaculate mother figure who not only remained a virgin but also had herself been conceived without sin, which, in medieval terminology, meant without intercourse. Women might be of the same sex as Mary, but they were also the same as Eve, and it was as Eve that women kept reminding a religious man of his sinfulness, of his desire to have sex. Moreover, the concentration on unattainable love in the chivalric literature ultimately led to the same thing, since though it might well lead to adultery, it also could lead to a turning away from women, to homosexuality rather than heterosexuality.

Obviously, the later Middle Ages were caught up in contradictions, which are perhaps nowhere better summarized than in the medieval attitudes toward nudity. Medieval Christianity in general adopted the ancient Jewish idea of nudity, that any kind of public display of nakedness was a barbarity of the most abhorrent kind, and nothing was so hateful or abominable to the almighty.[106] Hand in hand with this view, however, was the recognition that man, in his original state of innocence, the Garden of Eden, had obviously been nude. It was also believed that man would appear nude for his final judgment before God. Thus, in spite of the hostility to nudism, medieval art usually portrays figures going nude, though they were most often undergoing humiliation, martyrdom, or torture or suffering expulsion from Paradise.[107] A fascinating example of this appears in the Bayeux tapestry, the famed tapestry woven to commemorate the conquest of England by William the Conqueror in 1066. Nude figures appear frequently in the border of this, some perhaps even engaged in sexual activity.[108]

The belief in a nudity of innocence also led to periodic outbursts among millennial cults, such as the Adamites of the fourteenth century, who went naked to symbolize their association with Adam. To them nakedness was essential to purity, because only by going nude could man's innocence be restored.[109] At the same time, the public bath, where individuals had to undress, was regarded as a place of lewdness, and the synonyms for it, such as stews or bagnios, still retain this association today as euphemisms for brothels.[110] That the medieval people regarded public nudity as something extraordinary is best indicated by the famous story of Lady Godiva. This is one of the best known incidents of nudism in history, although the story is probably more legend than fact. The story was first told by Roger of Wendover in the thirteenth century, some 200 years after the event is supposed to have taken place. According to Roger, Godiva had implored her husband Leforic to reduce the heavy taxes he had imposed on Coventry. Her ceaseless pleading led him to declare in exasperation that he would lower the taxes if she would ride naked through the crowded marketplace. Godiva undertook the ride, accompanied by two soldiers, although there was little to be seen of her, since her long, golden hair covered all her body, except for the lower part of her legs. On her return from the ride her husband issued a charter freeing Coventry from all servitude. As the story was repeated by later mythmakers, new elements were added, including the legend of Peeping Tom, which became part of the story in the seventeenth century. In this revised version, all the citizens locked their doors and shutters, except a young man by the name of Tom, who managed to peep from behind the shutters. He was either struck blind or fell dead, according to which version one reads. Some scholars feel that the whole story was derived from the long continuation at Coventry of some pagan or semipagan fertility rite, but this bit of debunking has not stopped the ride of Lady Godiva from being reenacted at periodical intervals as part of the Coventry Fair.[111]

Still, medieval people in some ways did not have the aversion to nudity that the Jews had, and most people slept in the nude. This was true even in hospitals, where there were often several patients in the same bed. Nudity in such conditions was accepted as a fact of life and not regarded as any kind of indecent exposure. There are also several recorded incidents of public nudity. In 1461, when Louis XI entered Paris, three very beautiful naked maidens, representing the Sirens, greeted him, declaiming poems for his edification. In 1468, when Charles the Bold entered Lille, he was pleased to note that, among the various festivities arranged for his edification, was a representation of the judgment of Paris in which the three goddesses were nude.[112] Still, nudity, other than in bed or in the hospital, must have been only an occasional thing because of the notice given it when it does appear.

The men (and women) of the later Middle Ages worked hard to institutionalize and regulate attitudes and concepts about sexuality and to punish deviant attitudes, but there were surprising contradictions, and it would seem that in the later Middle Ages these contradictions were accepted and justified for much the same reasons as they were in other cultures. Another indication of this is the attitude toward female impersonators when they appeared on the stage. In Greek times most women's roles had been acted by men, but the Romans were much more open-minded on the subject, allowing women to portray themselves. But actresses received a bad name, as did the theater in general, the early Church Fathers strongly condemning it. Though such condemnation did not entirely eliminate drama, professional acting more or less disappeared, at least temporarily.[113]

Important in reviving drama, and ultimately a key factor in the development of modern drama, were the medieval mystery play, depicting the passion of Jesus, and the morality play, portraying the lives of the saints. Since these plays were performed in the church, most of the actors were drawn from the ranks of priests or minor clerics. This tradition continued well beyond the medieval period and, occasionally, we even get glimpses of some of the actors. This is the case with a young barber's apprentice at Metz, who is said to have performed the role of St. Barbara so

thoughtfully and reverently that several persons wept for pity; for he showed such fluency of elocution and such polite manners, and his countenance and gestures were so expressive when among his maidens, that there was not a nobleman or priest or layman who did not wish to receive this youth into his house to feed and educate him; among whom there was a rich widow . . . who wanted to adopt him as her heir.[114]

The youth's reputation as a female impersonator proved short-lived, for the next year, when he acted another woman's part, that of St. Catherine, his voice had changed, and the audience was not so impressed. The young man then abandoned his acting career and went off to Paris to study for the priesthood.

Obviously, the Church encouraged the transvestism inherent in such role playing because they put greater value on keeping women away from the altar of the Church than they did on the Biblical prohibition against wearing clothes of the opposite sex. Even in the secular drama, most of the female roles were played by men, since the actors, for the most part, were vagabonds traveling around the country and regarded as outcasts.[115] In sum, the medieval attitudes toward sex are full of contradictions. Officially, at least, the concept that sex was bad and the work of the devil was accepted at the same time that the cult of courtly love, emphasizing the erotic, was being proclaimed. Women were praised on the one hand and condemned on the other. Sexual deviation was feared, associated with heresy, and punished, and yet many institutions in society encouraged the very practices condemned. In a sense, the medieval people found themselves in exactly the same situation as twentieth-century man—a contradiction between moral theory and actual practice.

NOTES

1. Peter Lombard, *Libri IV sententiarum,* 2nd ed., Libri IV, Distinctio XXXVII, cap. ii, Fathers of the College of St. Bonaventura eds. (Florence: College of St. Bonaventura, 1916, 2 vols.), Vol. 2, p. 970.

2. Albertus Magnus, *Summa Theologiae,* Liber II, Tractatus XVIII, Questio 122, Membrum I, Articulus iv, in *Opera omnia,* S. C. A. Bornet, ed., Vols. 31–34 (Paris: Ludovicum vives, 1895).

3. Albertus Magnus, *Commentarii in IV sententarium,* Distinctio III, 27, in *Opera omnia,* Vol. 29.

4. Albertus Magnus, *Evangelium Lucam,* XVII, 29, in *Opera omnia,* Vols. 22, 23.

5. St. Thomas Aquinas, *Summa Theologica,* II–II, Q. cliv, 1, as translated by the Fathers of the English Dominican Province (New York: Benzinger Brothers, 1947). See also the section on virginity, II–II, q. clii, 2, 3.

6. *Ibid.,* II–II, Q. cliv, 11.

7. *Ibid.,* II–II, Q. cliv, 11 and 12.

8. *Ibid.,* II–II, Q. cliv, 12.

9. *Ibid.,* II–II, Q. cliv, 4.

10. Bernardine of Siena, *Quadragesimale de Evangelio aeterno, Sermo* XIX, *Articulus* II, cap, 4, ii, 3, in *Opera omnia,* Fathers of the College of St. Bonaventura eds. (Florence: College of St. Bonaventura, 1956), Vol. 3, pp. 334, 337–338. See also *Contra soddomian* in *Selecta ex autographo Budapestmensi,* cap. 27, in *op. cit.,* Vol. 9, pp. 427–430.

11. Bernardine, Sermo XV, *"De horren peccato contra naturam,"* I, 1, in *Quadragesimale, op. cit.,* Vol. 3, pp. 267–284.

12. Peter Cantor, *Verbum abbreviatum,* cap. CXXXVIII, *De vito sodomitico,* in J. P. Migne, *Patrologiae Latina,* (Paris: Garnier frêres, 1844–1900, 221 vols.), Vol. 205, col. 333–335, esp. 335. Henceforth abbreviated *PL.*

13. John Gerson, *Regulae morales*, XCIX, *"De luxuria,"* in *Opera omnia*, L. Eliss du Pin, ed. (Antwerp, 1706), Vol. 3, col. 95.

14. St. Antonino, *Confessionale*, cap. 57 (Venice: 1514), pp. 57–58.

15. F. W. H. Wasserschleben, *Die Bussordnungen der abendlaischen Kirche* (reprinted, Graz, Austria: Akademische Druck-U Verlagsanstal, 1958), p. 653, c. cvii, and passim. See also Burchard, *Decretum libri* XX, xix, cap. v, "Interrogatory," in Migne, *PL*, Vol. 140, cols. 951–976, esp. 967–968, "item de fornication."

16. Ivo, *Decretum*, par. IX, caps. 110, 128, in Migne, *PL*, Vol. 141, cols. 686, 699. This section deals with activities *contra naturam*. He has another section dealing with the sins of boys, cap. 109, col. 686.

17. *Ibid.*, IX, 106, cols. 685–686.

18. A much more thorough exposition of this can be found in John T. Noonan, *Contraception: A History of Its Treatment by Catholic Theologians and Canonists* (Cambridge, Mass.: The Belknap Press of Harvard University, 1966), p. 173, and passim.

19. For a brief popular discussion of the origins of canon law, see Stephen G. Kuttner, *Harmony from Dissonance*, Wimmer Lecture X, Saint Vincent College (Latrobe, Pa.: Archabbey Press, 1960).

20. Gratian, *Decretum, pars secunda*, Causa XXXII, Questio vii, c. 13, in *Corpus juris canonica*, Emil Friedberg, ed. (Leipzig: Bernard Tauchnitz, 1879–1881, 2 vols.), Vol. 1, col. 1143.

21. *Ibid.*, Causa XXXII, Questio vii, c. 11 and 14, in Vol. 1, cols. 1143–1144.

22. *Ibid.*, Causa, XXXIII, Questio iii, distinctio cap. xv, in Vol. 2, col. 1161.

23. *Concilium Londoniense*, cap. XXVII, in J. Mansi, *Sacrorum Conciliorum* (Florence, 1766), Vol. 20, 1152.

24. *Ibid.*, cap. XXIX.

25. *Concilium Neapolitanum*, cap. XI, in Mansi, *op. cit.*, Vol. 21, col. 624. Canons 8, 9, and 10 deal with sodomy and spontaneous pollution. Mansi has some discussion on the subject in his introduction, *ibid.*, cols. 261–262. The translation is based on that of Derrick Sherwin Bailey, *Homosexuality and the Western Christian Tradition* (London: Longmans, Green and Company, 1955), p. 96.

26. *Concilium Lateranense III*, cap. xi, in Mansi, *op. cit.*, Vol. 22, cols. 224–225.

27. *Concilium Parisiense*, par. II, xxi, in Mansi, *op. cit.*, Vol. 22, col. 831.

28. *Ibid.*, par. III, ii, col. 849.

29. *Concilium Magistri Roberti apud Rotomagum* (1214), xxiii, xxiv, xxii, in Mansi, *op. cit.*, Vol. 22, col. 1003.

30. *Concilium Lateranense IV*, XIV, in Mansi, *op. cit.*, Vol. 22, col. 1003.

31. For example, see the actions taken at the Second Council of Rouen in 1235, Bezier in 1246, Le Mans in 1247, Clermont in 1268, *Concilium Ramense*, XL, in Mansi, *op. cit.*, Vol. 23, col. 379; *Concilium Biterrense*, XIX, in Mansi, *op. cit.*, Vol. 23, col. 379; *Concilium Biterrense*, XIX, in Mansi, Vol. 23, col. 696; *Statuta Sinodalia Ecclesiae canomanensis*, par. III (i), in Mansi, Vol. 23, col. 755; and *Incipiunt statuta Synodalia Clarmontensis Ecclesiae*, par. II, i, in Mansi, Vol. 23, col. 1203. The Council of Paris in 1196 reserved the sin for dispensation to pope or bishop, *Odonis Episcopi Parisiensis Synodicae constitutiones*, cap. VI, 4, 5, in Mansi, Vol. 23, col. 678. Three other councils referred it to the bishop or his penitentiaries, namely, *Concilium provinciale Fritzlariae*, IV, in Mansi, Vol. 23, col.726; the *Statuta Synodalia Johannis Episcopi Leodiensis*, IV, xi, Mansi, Vol. 24, col. 891; and *Ad Remense Concilium*, Mansi, Vol. 26, col. 1073. There are no numbered paragraphs in this last.

32. *Decretales Gregory IX,* Liber quintus, titulus XXXI, cap. iv. in *Corpus juris canonici,* Vol. 2, col. 836.

33. A discussion of this can be found in George Elliott Howard, *A History of Matrimonial Institutions* (reprinted, New York: Humanities Press, 1964, 3 vols.), Vol. 1, pp. 308–314.

34. *Ibid.,* Vol. 1, pp. 334–338.

35. Henrici de Seguso, Cardinal Hostiensis, *Summa aurea,* (Venice, 1574, reprinted, Turin: Bottega d'Erasmo, 1963), Liber V, cap. 49, col. 1808.

36. John Myrc, *Instructions for Parish Priests,* Edward Peacock, ed. *Early English Text Society,* Vol. 31 (reprinted, New York: Greenwood Press, 1969), lines 222–231, p. 7. The spelling has been modernized.

37. *The Book of Vices and Virtues,* W. Nelson Francis, ed. *Early English Text Society,* Vol. 227 (London: Oxford University Press, 1942), p. 43a. This book was edited from three extant texts of a translation from the French of Lorens d'Orleans, *Somme le Roi.*

38. *Ibid.,* p. 46.

39. *Ibid.,* p. 244.

40. *Ibid.,* p. 248.

41. *Hali Maidenhad,* F. J. Furnivall, ed., revised from the edition of Oswald Cockayne, *Early English Text Society,* Vol. 17 (reprinted, New York: Greenwood Press, 1969), p. 35.

42. *Ibid.,* pp. 34–35. Translation is by Furnivall.

43. William Langland, *Piers the Plowman,* translated by Margaret Williams (New York: Random House, 1971), Passus XI, lines 326–330, p. 195.

44. *Ibid.,* Passus XIV, lines 74–78.

45. *Ibid.,* Passus XIII, lines 68–72, pp. 212–213. Langland put the italicized line in Latin.

46. *The Ancren Riwle,* James Morton, ed. (reprinted, New York: Cooper Square Publishers, 1966), pp. 154 155.

47. *Ibid.,* p. 153.

48. *Ibid.,* pp. 199–200.

49. "Cleanness," in the *Pearl Poet,* translated by Margaret Williams (New York: Random House, 1967), p. 131.

50. *Ibid.,* pp. 147–152.

51. The subject of sexuality and sin against nature in the writings of Chaucer has received some attention. See Paul F. Baum, "Chaucer's Puns," *PMLA,* LXXI (1956), p. 232; P. J. C. Field, "Chaucer's Merchant and the Sin Against Nature," *Notes and Queries,* March, 1970, p. 84; George Williams, *A New View of Chaucer* (Durham, N. C.: Duke University Press, 1965), Chap. 8, "Chaucer's Best Joke—The Tale of Sir Thopas"; and Helen Storm Corsa, *Chaucer, Poet of Mirth and Morality* (South Bend, Ind.: University of Notre Dame Press, 1964).

52. Geoffrey Chaucer, "The Parson's Tale," in *The Canterbury Tales,* 2nd ed., F. N. Robinson, ed. (Boston: Houghton Mifflin, 1961), pp. 909–910.

53. *Ibid.,* line 577.

54. *Ibid.,* "The Merchant's Tale," pp. 1839–1840.

55. Dante Alighieri, *Divine Comedy, Inferno,* Canto XV, 106–108. There are many editions and translations. A widely sold translation by Dorothy L. Sayers (New York: Basic Books, 1962, 3 vols.).

56. *Ibid., Purgatory,* Canto XXVI, 40–42, 76–93.

57. Gerhart Ladner, "Homo Viator: Medieval Ideas of Alienation and Order," *Speculum,* XLII (1967), pp. 233–259.

58. Ernst Werner, in Theodora Büttner and Ernst Werner, *Circumcellionen und Adamiten: Zwei Form mittealterlich Haeresie* (Berlin: Akademia Verlag, 1959), pp. 93–116.

59. For references to early use of the term, including that of Robert de Brunne, see the discussion in the *Oxford English Dictionary,* (corrected, Oxford, England: Clarendon Press, 1933, 12 vols.).

60. Havelock Ellis, *The Nature of Sexual Inversion,* in *Studies in the Psychology of Sex* (New York: Random House, 1936, 2 vols.), Vol. 1, Part 4, p. 347.

61. P. Viollet, *Les etablissment de St. Louis,* Livre I, xc (Paris: Renouard, 1881–1886, 4 vols.), Vol. 2, pp. 147–148. It is also found in *Ordonnances de Roys de France,* Eusèbe Jacob de Lauriére, Denis François Secousse, et al., eds. (Paris: 1723–1849, 21 vols.), Vol. 1, Chap. 85, 175, (1279). My translation is essentially that of Derrick Sherwin Bailey, *Homosexuality and the Western Christian Tradition* (London: Longmans, Green and Company, 1955), pp. 141–142.

62. Viollet, *op. cit.,* introduction, "Sodomie," Vol. 1, p. 254, n. 1.

63. See *Coutume de Touraine-Anjou,* 78, in Viollet, *op. cit.,* Vol. 3, p. 50.

64. P. N. Rapetti, *Li livres de jostice et de plet* (Paris: Typographic de firmin Didot fréres, 1850), XVIII, xxiv. 22, pp. 279–280.

65. For example, of the 1500 judgments pronounced in the French parlement during the reign of St. Louis, only one refers to sodomists, and this concerns a disputed jurisdiction between the Bishop of Amiens and the town of Amiens over who was to judge sodomists. A. A. Beugnot, *Les olims, ou registres des arrêts* (Paris: Imprimerie Royale, 1849–1868, 3 vols.), Vol. 1, v, p. 136, (1261). Other references to sodomy come under King Philippe IV in 1310, LXVII, *ibid.,* III, 3A, p. 572, where an unjust accusation is made, and under Philippe V in 1317, VIII, *ibid.,* III, 3B, p. 1212, where the man is found innocent.

66. Alan of Lille, *De fide catholica contra haereticos sui temporis,* II, 1, in Migne, *PL,* Vol. 210, col. 80. A translation of this can be found in Walter Wakefield and Austin P. Evans, *Heresies of the High Middle Ages* (New York: Columbia University Press, 1969), pp. 219–220.

67. See Robert E. Lerner, *The Heresy of the Free Spirit in the Middle Ages* (Berkeley and Los Angeles: University of California Press, 1972), especially his first chapter entitled "Heresy and Fornication," pp. 10–34. See also Gordon Leff, *Heresy in the Later Middle Ages* (Manchester, England: Manchester University Press, 1967, 2 vols.); Norman Cohn *The Pursuit of the Millennium* (Fairlawn, N.J.: Essential Books, 1957); and I. von Döllinger, *Geschichte der gnostisch-manichaischen Sekten in Beitrage zur Sektengeschichte des Mittelalters* (reprinted, New York: Burton Franklin, 1970, 2 vols.). A background study that is also valuable is Jeffrey Burton Russell, *Dissent and Reform in the Early Middle Ages* (Berkeley, Calif.: University of California Press, 1965).

68. Guibert de Nogent *Histoire de sa vie,* George Bourgin, ed. (Paris: A. Picard et fils, 1907), pp. 212–215. There is a translation in Wakefield and Evans, *op. cit.,* p. 103, on which this is based. Italics are mine.

69. Henry of Le Mans, *Actus pontificium cenomannis in urbe degentium,* G. Busson and A. Ledru, eds., *Archives historiques du Maine,* II (Le Mans: Société-historique de la province du Mans, 1901), pp. 407–415. See Wakefield and Evans, *op. cit.,* p. 109 for a pertinent extract.

70. Walter Map, *De nugis curialium,* I, xx, Montague R. James, ed. (Oxford, England: Clarendon Press, 1914), pp. 57–59. See Wakefield and Evans, *op. cit.,* pp. 254–255, for a pertinent extract.

71. A primary-source description of them appears in Caesarius of Heisterbach, *Dialogus mi-*

raculorum, v, xxi, Joseph Strange, ed. (Cologne: H. Lempertz & Company, 1851, 2 vols.), Vol. 1, pp. 304–307. A pertinent extract is translated in Wakefield and Evans, *op. cit.,* p. 259.

72.   See Salimbene, *Chronica fratris Salimbene de Adam,* Oswald Holder-Egger, ed., *Monumenta Germaniae Historica, Scriptores,* XXXII, pt. 1. (1248) 255–294, (1274) 489, (1284) 563, (1286) 619–620. There is an English summary of the chronicle in G. G. Coulton, *From St. Francis to Dante* (London: David Nutt, 1906).

73.   See, for example, Charles Singer, ed. and trans., "A Thirteenth Century Clinical Description of Leprosy," *Journal of the History of Medicine,* IV (1949), pp. 237–239.

74.   For a more nearly complete discussion of the association of sexuality with leprosy, see Saul Nathaniel Brody, *The Disease of the Soul* (Ithaca, N.Y.: Cornell University Press, 1974), passim.

75.   This appears in the *Canon episcopi* of Regino of Prüm, of which there are two versions, a shorter and a longer one. They can be found in his *De Synodalibus causis et disciplinis ecclesiasticis libri duo,* II, 45, 364, in Migne, *PL,* Vol. 132; and in Burchard of Worms, *Decretorium libri viginti,* I, 94, X, 1, 29; and XIX, 70, 90 in Migne, *PL,* Vol. 140. The documents in question can also be found in Jeffrey Burton Russell, *Witchcraft in the Middle Ages* (Ithaca, N.Y.: Cornell University Press, 1972), appendix I, p. 292.

76.   This is reported in Stephen of Bourgon, *Anecdotes historiques,* Albert Lecoy de Marche, ed. (Paris: Librairie Renouard, 1877), pp. 319–325; and see also Russell, *Witchcraft,* p. 157.

77.   Alban Butler, *Lives of the Saints,* revised and supplemented by Herbert Thurston and Donald Attwater, eds. (New York: P. J. Kennedy, 1956, 4 vols.), Vol. 2, p. 135.

78.   W. P. Barrett, *Trial of Jeanne d'Arc* (London: George Routledge and Sons, 1931), pp 152–158.

79.   W. S. Scott, *The Trial of Joan of Arc* (Westport, Conn.: Associated Booksellers, 1956), p. 14.

80.   Gregory IX, *Vox in Rama,* titulus vii, par. 363–369, in *Monumenta Germaniae Historica, Epp. saec.,* XIII, I, 413.

81.   Döllinger, *op. cit.,* Vol. 2, pp. 369–373; Russell, *Witchcraft,* pp. 162–163.

82.   Gershon Legman, *The Guilt of the Templars* (New York: Basic Books, 1966).

83.   Julius Gmelin, *Schuld oder Unschuld des Templerordens: Kritischer Versuch zur Lösung der Frage* (Stuttgart: W. Kohlhammer, 1893).

84.   Thomas Parker, *The Knights Templars in England* (Tucson, Ariz.: University of Arizona Press, 1963), p. 1.

85.   Henry C. Lea, *History of the Inquisition of the Middle Ages* (reprinted, New York: S. A. Russell, 1955, 3 vols.), Vol. 3, p. 238.

86.   The charges are summarized in Edith Simon, *The Piebald Standard: A Biography of the Knights Templars* (Boston: Little, Brown, 1959), pp. 284–285.

87.   G. A. Campbell, *The Knights Templars, Their Rise and Fall* (New York: Robert McBride, 1937), p. 258.

88.   Simon, *op. cit.,* p. 286.

89.   For a statistical breakdown of some of the confessions, see Edward J. Martin, *The Trial of the Templars* (London: George Allen & Unwin, 1928), p. 65. In one sample of 138, he found that 11 confessed to the renunciation of Jesus, 109 to kissing in some abnormal form, 121 to spitting or other insults to the cross, 99 to licence to vice, 8 to having an idolatrous head that they worshipped, and 1 to omissions in the canon; 6 denied all charges.

90.   Simon, *op. cit.,* p. 336.

91.   Dante, *op. cit., Inferno,* Canto XV, 106–108. Biographical and other information on the in-

dividuals concerned is summarized in Paget Toynbee, *A Dictionary of Proper Names and Notable Matters in the Works of Dante,* revised by Charles S. Singleton (Oxford, England: Clarendon Press, 1968). The revised edition includes a list of recent periodical articles about the individuals.

92.   D. Stanley-Jones, "Sexual Inversion and the English Law," *The Medical Press and Circular,* CCXV, No. 5588 (June 12, 1946), pp. 391–398.

93.   *Chartularium Universitatis Parisiensis,* Henricus Denifle and Aemelio Chatelain, eds. (Paris: reprinted, Brussels: Culture et Civilization, 1964, 4 vols.), Vol. 1, No. 473, pp. 543–558, pars. 166, 169, 170, 172, 176, 177, 183.

94.   Ordericus Vitalis, *The Ecclesiastical History,* VIII, 10, translated by Marjorie Chibnall, ed. (Oxford, England: Clarendon Press, 1969—in progress, 4 vols.).

95.   William of Malmesbury, *Chronicle,* IV, 1, translated by J. A. Giles (London: Henry Bohn, 1847), p. 337.

96.   E. A. Freeman, *The Reign of William Rufus* (Oxford, England: Clarendon Press, 1882, 2 vols.), Vol. 1, pp. 147, 157–158; Vol. 2, pp. 340, 502–503; and also E. A. Freeman, *The History of the Norman Conquest* (Oxford, England: Clarendon Press, 1876, 6 vols.), Vol. 5, p. 72, and n. 1.

97.   This listing is taken from Noel I. Garde, *Jonathan to Gide: The Homosexual in History* (New York: Vantage Press, 1964), passim. Some are better documented than others; many are identified as homosexuals on only the flimsiest of evidence.

98.   T. F. Tou, "The Captivity and Death of Edward of Carnarvon," *Bulletin of the John Rylands Library,* VI (1920), No. 1.

99.   I put forth this idea with some hesitation, since it is still nebulous, but I think it will be borne out by further research. I am indebted to the research of Georges Duby, whose article "The 'Youth' in Twelfth Century Aristocratic Society," was translated and published in Frederic L. Cheyette, *Lordship and Community in Medieval Europe* (New York: Holt, Rinehart, and Winston, 1968), pp. 198–209.

100.   See Thomas Wilson, *Blue-Beard: A Contribution to History and Folk-lore* (New York: G. P. Putnam's Sons, 1899); D. B. Wyndham Lewis, *The Soul of Marshal Gilles de Raiz* (London: Eyre and Spottiswoode, 1952). J. K. Huysmans wrote a novel on the subject, *La Bas* in 1891, which was translated into English by Keene Wallis under the title of *Down There* (New Hyde Park, N.Y.: University Books, 1958).

101.   See *Song of Roland,* of which there are numerous translations. A helpful one is by Patricia Terry (Indianapolis, Ind.: Bobbs-Merrill, 1965).

102.   Sidney Painter, *French Chivalry* (Baltimore: Johns Hopkins Press, 1957), pp. 111–112.

103.   C. S. Lewis, *The Allegory of Love* (New York: Oxford University Press, 1958), p. 4.

104.   Andreas Capellanus, *The Art of Courtly Love,* Book 1, Chaps. 1–4, and final section, translated by J. J. Parry (New York: Columbia University Press, 1941). There is a vast literature on this whole topic. So far scholars are not in agreement about Andreas and his work. For a classic work on the subject, see C. S. Lewis, *The Allegory of Love* (reprinted, New York: Oxford University Press, 1958).

105.   For a discussion of this, see the classic work by Henry Adams, *Mont Saint-Michel and Chartres* (reprinted, Boston: Houghton Mifflin, 1933).

106.   Louis M. Epstein, *Sex Laws and Customs in Judaism* (reprinted, New York: Ktav Publishing House, Inc., 1967), pp. 27, 32–34.

107.   Kenneth Clark, *The Nude: A Study in Ideal Form* (Bollingen Series, 35, 2, New York: Pantheon Books, 1956), pp. 310–319.

108.   See Simone Bertrad, *La tapisserie de Bayeux* (Paris: Zodiaque, 1966), panels 13, 15, 48,

58; and various other editions, such as Frank Rede Fowke, *The Bayeux Tapestry* (London: G. Bell and Sons, 1913).

109.   Jeffrey Burton Russell, *Witchcraft,* pp. 224–225.

110.   See Vern L. Bullough, *History of Prostitution* (New Hyde Park, N.Y.: University Books, 1964), p. 115.

111.   For a discussion, see Frederick R. Burbide, *Old Coventry and Lady Godiva* (Birmingham, England: Cornish Brothers, 1952).

112.   Quoted in Havelock Ellis, *The Evolution of Modesty,* in *Studies in the Psychology of Sex* (republished, New York: Random House, 1936, 2 vols.), Vol. 1., Part 1, p. 29.

113.   Joseph Tunison, *Dramatic Traditions of the Dark Ages,* (reprinted, Folcroft, Pa.: Folcroft Press, 1969).

114.   Karl Mantzuis, *A History of Theatrical Art,* translated by Louise von Cossell (New York: Peter Smith, 1937), Vol. 2, p. 89.

115.   See J. J. Jusserand, *English Wayfaring Life in the Middle Ages,* translated by Lucy Toulmin Smith (London: T. Fisher Unwin, n.d.), pp. 177–218.

15

A REEVALUATION AND REAFFIRMATION

A persistent theme throughout the history of Western thought has been the influence of Greek ideas, however modified or reinterpreted. This Greek tradition becomes more important in the fifteenth century, when there was a renewed interest in the classical past as a source of ideas, particularly Plato. In a sense, this movement, known as humanism, was a reaction to ongoing scholastic thought based on Aristotle, the difference being one both of aim and of audience. Humanism tended to appeal to the new urban-oriented middle class and its scholars, as opposed to the scholasticism of the cleric or the chivalric ideal of the noble. Humanism was not, however, paganism. One of its chief patrons was the pope, and other churchmen joined in. Humanism appealed initially to the Italians, who, deprived of much of their glory by the shifting economic and political interests of Europe, looked to their ancient past. Soon their ideas were disseminated to all of Europe. Inevitably, the humanist ideal had some effect on sexuality, if only because the humanists became conscious of the Greeks' positive attitudes and justifications for homosexuality, but the challenge to the established sexual standards of the West, if Platonic love can be regarded as a challenge, was fairly short-lived.

To some of the people of the time, it seemed a more serious challenge. Giorgio Vasari, an Italian painter of the sixteenth century best known for his biographies of famous artists, wrote that it seemed to him that Christianity might prove to be "a mere interlude in the history of Hellenic religion."[1]

Among the later scholars picking up these ideas, one historian, accepting the charges of sexual deviation as fact, wondered whether a civilization that "carried refinement to too high a pitch," did not always suffer from the "imprint of vice."[2] John Addington Symonds, a nineteenth-century historian of Italy and a secret admirer and fervent advocate of Greek homoerotic concepts, publicly complained that the "decay of liberty, relaxation of morals, and the corruption of the Church, had brought the Italians to the point that their literature is stained with flattery, contaminated with licentiousness, and enfeebled with levity."[3] Jacob Burckhardt, another nineteenth-century admirer of Italian culture, who popularized the term *Renaissance* for this period, stated that the end of the fifteenth century found Italy in the "midst of a grave moral crisis, out of which the best men saw hardly any escape."[4]

Platonic love became a frequent theme of Italian literary endeavor, particularly after the translation of several Platonic dialogues in the first half of the fifteenth century. In the cinquecento, Platonic love generally was viewed as an intellectual, nonsexual, or even antisexual phenomenon. One of the most influential writers in this vein was Baldesar Castiglione, whose *The Book of the Courtier* was published in 1528. The popularity and influence of the work are highlighted by the fact that 100 different printings were made in the sixteenth century; it was translated from Italian into Latin, German, Spanish, English, and French. For Castiglione, sexual love was on a level with animal love.[5] The purpose of true love was to raise men upward, and the spiritual love of a man toward women could do this. About the only intimate contact Castiglione would allow was the kiss; this was given, not to awaken "unchaste desires," but to bring about a union of the souls, since, though the mouth was a part of the body, it was also an exit place for the soul.[6] Other writers wrote along similar lines.[7]

Underlying many discussions of Platonic love was a realization that Plato was idealizing homoerotic attachments. Marsilio Ficino (1443–1499), citing Plato, wrote that those best suited for soul love loved males rather than females and adolescents rather than children.[8] In the sixteenth century, Flaminio Nobili wrote that Plato and other worthy men had judged a youth's beauty more fit than a young lady's to excite the amorous desires of the intellect and had considered those who loved women to be fecund and gravid in the body rather than in the soul.[9] John Charles Nelson, discussing Renaissance theories of love, pointed out that the treatise writers avoided the implications of homosexuality by two devices: first, by attributing only an intellectual or moral fervor to men who loved youths and, second, by attributing to females, not males, the personal beauty that excited men to love and impelled the lover to seek ever higher forms of beauty.[10]

Ficino stressed the first alternative in the so-called Platonic Academy, which he ran in Florence under the patronage of the Medici princes. Never an organized institution, it was a group of men, under the direction of Ficino, who shared an interest in and discussed Platonic love. Seeking more or less successfully to reconcile Platonism and neo-platonism with Christianity, Ficino sought to make Platonic love the basis of personal relationships. To him, love was the power enabling men to change and become ennobled, and it arose from the body of shared participation in the contemplative life. Souls joined by their love and contemplation of God would raise men above the beasts, for without love, men would be little different than beasts, who simply copulated without thought of love.[11]

The transition to the female love object from the earlier male one was more or less complete by the beginning of the sixteenth century with Pietro Bembo (1470–1547), whose *Gli asolani* is dedicated to Lucrezia Borgia. To him, love was infinitely good and could never be fully known. Excited by feminine beauty, it incited the courtly virtues and a desire for beauty. It was not the same as desire, although desire was impossible without loving. Unerring nature gave man the willpower to descend through the senses to animals and to rise by reason to the superior species; through love man could either remain a dirty beast or become a god. Beyond the material world of love there is a divine, illuminated, changeless world, the soul's true satisfaction being found in this divine love inspired by woman.[12]

The problem with Platonic love, whether heterosexual or homosexual, was that it was difficult to maintain on a spiritual level. In the sixteenth century, Flaminio Nobili reported that, owing to the nature of things, beauty in a male was not as apt to awaken carnal desire as beauty in a woman, since women were ordained to rouse in males the desire of corporal generation. For this reason, he said, Plato and his imitators had urged love of males by males, because they had not "let themselves be carried away by that dishonest appetite, altogether repugnant to nature," and thereby demonstrated that they "ardently desired to help them and to make them valorous and learned."[13] Perhaps for this reason Ariosto, author of the sixteenth-century classic *Orlando Furioso,* could write that all humanists engaged in homosexual activity. Others made similar charges. Inevitably, those seeking to identify persons as homosexual have found a number of distinguished individuals to claim, including Leonardo da Vinci, Machiavelli, Erasmus, Michelangelo, Raphael, Politian, Cellini, and others.[14]

Many such claims of homosexuality are based on the slimmest evidence, and yet contemporaries were also concerned about the growth of "unnatural" sex, one result being the establishment of so-called sodomy courts in Florence, Venice, and perhaps other Italian cities in the fifteenth century. In Florence, about which we have the most information, the *Ufficiali di notte* was established in 1432 and continued at least until 1502 if not longer. Holders of the office were charged with eradicating sodomy from Florence and its environs and with maintaining the purity of Florentine convents. To carry out this task, the officials set up boxes (*tamburi*) in various prominent locations around the city and encouraged citizens to drop anonymous accusations in these drums. Over the period of 70 years for which records are extant, there were often several hundred accusations in one year, the total being a record of thousands of names, although little research has been done so far into the records of such complaints or into exactly what activity was implied by sodomy. The accused were brought before the officials, testimony was given, and a verdict was rendered. Technically, the ultimate penalty was execution, but this was rarely if ever applied. Instead, those found guilty were fined, some lightly, others fairly heavily. Officials also issued licenses allowing male inspectors to enter convents and to look for dishonest or immoral women living in or near convents.[15] Venice also had an office to ferret out sodomites, but efforts were apparently not as well organized.[16]

One of those charged in Florence was Leonardo da Vinci. An anonymous charge was placed in the *tamburo* located near the Palazzo vecchio on April 8, 1476, that a certain Leonardo da Vinci was engaging in unnatural activities with a 17-year-old boy named Jacopo Saltarelli. The accusation of "sodomy" was forwarded to the *Ufficiali di notte,* and Leonardo was held for trial. His father refusing aid, Leonardo turned to his uncle Francesco, who enlisted the help of Bernardo di Simone Cortigiani, an important figure in Florence.[17] Two months later, the charges were dropped. Apparently, Leonardo spent part of those 2 months in jail, since he later wrote about being put in jail because he used as a model a boy with a bad reputation and wondered that, if he used the same model, now a man, worse things might not happen to him.[18] One result of the incident was to make Leonardo rather wary of any sexual desires. He wrote in a later letter: "The act of coitus and the members that serve it are so hideous that if it were not for the beauty and craftsmen's ornamentation and the liberation of the soul, the human species would lose its humanity."[19] Sigmund Freud, examining the scanty evidence, concluded that Leonardo was the kind of person who would "pursue research with the same passionate devotion another would give to his love" and that Leonardo turned to investigation of phenomena instead of sex.[20] Perhaps the matter is not so simple. Others would argue that Leonardo remained a homosexual and that Jacopo Saltarelli was replaced by a series of other favorites, including Andrea Salaino, Francesco Melzi, Cesare da Sesto, and Giuliano Boltraffio. He was apparently charged a second time with sodomy, but few details are known about this latter case.

Elsewhere in this book we have stressed the importance of eduation and training in inculcating sexual ideas; going hand in hand with the emphasis on Platonism by the humanists was a renewed attention to the education of children. A number of educational theorists wrote in the last part of the fourteenth and first part of the fifteenth centuries, one result being the development of a new kind of school, the forerunner of the grammer school, or what the English came to call the public school. One of the most important theorists was Vittorino da Feltre (died 1446), who opened his school, *La Casa Ciocosa* ("The Happy House") in Mantua under its rulers' sponsorship. Vittorino advocated education for both boys and girls, but most of the new schools were for boys and were often boarding schools. In England, Eton, Winchester, St. Paul's, and a number of others were founded, mostly teaching the new humanistic curriculum.[21] Though no hard evidence can be deduced to prove these schools encouraged homosexuality, it would seem logical that throwing a number of boys together in such schools without strong female figures and with a curriculum featuring the study of some of the Greek and Latin classics tended to make them aware of homosexuality and of their own sexual urges. Undoubtedly, there must have been some sexual experimentation in such schools, just as in the nineteenth century.

There is, however, a danger in reading too much into the humanistic dialogues on love or in attributing new kinds of sexual awareness to the new boarding schools of this time simply because there are numerous references to homosexuality. A factor to be taken into account is the invention of printing, one of the most revolutionary developments in history and one that encouraged publication and dissemination of information previously known only to a few. Books printed from movable type date from the second quarter of the fifteenth century, and the method spread rapidly. By the end of the fifteenth century, the beginning of a small-scale mass production of books opened new worlds of learning and thought. Part of the explanation for the humanists' success lies in their access to printing presses. By the sixteenth century, reformers, radicals, and dissenters could turn to the press to disseminate their ideas, the age of mass communication having made its first tentative appearance, as had a new market for pornography and sexual information. Thus, much of the sexuality, whether open or repressed, that we read into the period may simply be due to the demand on behalf of a rising literate readership for more information. Scandal could be disseminated much more widely also, and one of the first to make a career of spreading gossip and innuendo was Pietro Aretino (1492–1556), who made his living by his wits and his pen. His writings could make a person or ruin him or her; only those paying tribute, financial or otherwise, to his talents, were spared his scurrilous pen. He turned out reams of material, sending it off to the press almost as fast as he could write. He was quick to play up a suspected sexual peccadillo, to blacken the reputation of those who did not cater to him.[22]

How much should be read into Aretino's sexual charges? He once wrote to Michelangelo Buonarroti (1475–1564), the great painter, sculptor, and poet, complaining about his failure to send something Aretino had requested. He then got in his sexual dig:

> Yet the truth is that if you had sent me what you had promised, you would have done what it was in your own best interest to do, since by so doing, you would have silenced all those spiteful tongues, who say that only certain Gherardos and Tommasos can obtain them.[23]

Should Michelangelo be regarded as homosexual on the basis of this charge? Magnus Hirschfeld asserted that the artist's homosexual relationships with these boys and others were well known during his lifetime, but the position of the painter of the Sistine Chapel in society prevented them from being mentioned, except by Aretino.[24] Yet a contemporary of Michelangelo, Scipione Ammirati, wrote in 1564 that there was never found, in all the 90 years Michelangelo lived, any imputation of stain or ugliness of manners by anyone who knew him.[25] Perhaps this was too sweeping a defense, for doubts about Michelangelo's sexual life have continued to be a subject of interest, fanned by Aretino's charge and fueled by his own sonnets, which sometimes discuss love in terms of a male object and other times in female form.[26] Those addressed to Tommaso Cavalieri (mentioned by Aretino) seem to suggest physical contact:

> Nay, it were easier to forget the feed which only nourishes my body miserably, than your name, which nourishes my body and my soul, filling the one and the other with such sweetness that neither weariness nor fear of death is felt by men while memory preserves you in my mind.[27]

How much this is an expression of the Platonic ideal, the love that ascends, depends on which interpreter one reads. Perhaps the ambiguity was deliberate, since Michelangelo feared that his noble thoughts would be misunderstood by future generations. We know that his grand-nephew, when he came to publish his ancestor's poems in 1623, chose to edit out some of the more direct references to homoerotic feelings. Still, we have nothing to suggest that Michelangelo's activities went so far as physical intercourse, although perhaps if Aretino had not made the charges he did, the whole subject might have been ignored.

Sometimes the charge of homosexual acts was made by more respected authority, and it seems clear that at least one artist of the time was homosexual. This is Giovanni Antonio Bazzi (1477–1549), given the name "il Sodoma" by Vasari, the name he is known by today. Vasari described his life style:

> His manner of life was licentious and dishonorable, and as he was always keeping boys and beardless youths around him of whom he was inordinately fond, thus

earning him the name of Sodoma; but instead of feeling shame, he gloried in it, writing stanzas and verses on it, and singing them to the accompaniment of the lute.[28]

Vasari implied that Bazzi's sexual proclivities affected his artistic life and that he was replaced on a painting in Rome because he spent too much time on such things. Magnus Hirschfeld who regarded Sodoma as a homoerotic person with bisexual tendencies, used him to symbolize the homoerotic tendencies of the age.[29] Certainly there was an undercurrent of literature favoring homoerotic love. Among the earliest poems written in support of homosexuality supposedly was the *In laudem sodomiae* (*"In Praise of Sodomy"*), now lost, by Giovanni della Casa (1503–1556).[30] The poem was allegedly dedicated to Pope Julius III (Giovanni Maria Ciocchi, 1487–1555), who himself has been suspected of homerotic tendencies, largely on the basis of rather gossipy stories preserved in the letters of Cardinal Jean du Bellay.[31] The combination of the letters and the association of Julius III with della Casa have kept allegations of sexual "deviation" alive, although there is no evidence that Julius engaged in any overt sexual activity, homosexual or otherwise.

Focusing further attention on the undercurrent of forbidden sexuality in this period is the growth in witchcraft, a phenomenon reaching epidemic proportions in the sixteenth and seventeenth centuries. Though fear of witches had existed in the later Middle Ages, the real medieval fear had been of heresy. In the fifteenth century the fear of witches increased, probably encouraged by the same neo-Platonic beliefs that had so affected the literary world. Neo-Platonism featured a magical world view, this in turn encouraging a belief in magic and evil powers. Undoubtedly also serving as a major contributing factor was the disastrous effects of the Black Death, which had swept Europe in the fourteenth century and continued to devastate Europe for several centuries. Inevitably, the Inquisition, originally established to deal with heresy, became active against magicians and diviners.

Increasingly also, withcraft came to be associated with various kinds of stigmatized sexual behavior. Leading the struggle against witchcraft was the papacy itself. Pope Eugenius IV (1431–1447), in a number of bulls, ordered the Inquisition to proceed against magicians and diviners, whose crimes he defined in terms of classical witchcraft. Pope Nicholas V (1447–1455), his successor, urged the Inquisition to prosecute sorcerers even when a connection with heresy was dubious.[32] Finally Pope Innocent VIII (1484–1495), in his bull entitled *Summis desiderantes affectibus,* issued on December 5, 1484, equated certain forms of sexual activity with witchcraft:

It has come to our ears that members of both sexes do not avoid having intercourse with demons, incubi and succubi; and that by their sorceries and by their incantations, charms and conjurations, they suffocate, extinguish and cause to perish the births of women, the increase of animals, the corn of the ground, the grapes of the vineyard and the fruit of the trees, as well as men, women, flocks, herds and other various kinds of animals, vines and apple trees, corn and other fruits of the earth; making and procuring that men and women, flocks and herds and other animals shall suffer and be tormented both from within and without so that men beget not nor women conceive; and they impede the conjugal action of men and women.[33]

This papal bull had been issued at the request of Heinrich Institor (Kramer) (1403–1505) and Jakob Sprenger (1436–1495), who needed the support of the pope to overcome German opposition to their witch-hunting activities. The two used the bull as a prefatory justification in their *Malleus maleficarum,* a manual that became the handbook for all witch-hunters. The *Malleus maleficarum* or "*Hammer of Witches,*" written in 1485–1486, was printed in 1486; it immediately achieved broad popularity. The authors' purpose was to refute systematically all arguments against the reality of witchcraft; in the process they gathered into a stringent code all the previous folklore about black magic, summarizing in popular form Church dogma on the matter. Witchcraft, defined as the most abominable of heresies, involved four essentials: (1) renunciation of the Christian faith, (2) the sacrifice of unbaptized infants to Satan, (3) the devotion of body and soul to evil, and (4) sexual relations with incubi or succubi.[34] Usually, the sexual activities associated with witchcraft were either autoerotic or heterosexual and only occasionally homosexual.[35]

The sexual activity most often described is intercourse with demons, either incubi or succubi. Incubi and succubi were not so much real demons in themselves as the manifestation of demons, who assumed the forms of a male (incubus) or female (succubus) for intercourse. Technically they were angels who had fallen from their status because of their lust, and this meant that intercourse with them raised several problems, not the least of which was a kind of transsexual change, for the demons appeared first as females, then as males. Moreover, since the incubus or succubus could be defined as a member of a species different from men, intercourse with them was also condemned as bestiality or buggery. One ecclesiastical authority wrote that to sin with a succubus or incubus was bestiality, "to which sin is added also malice against religion, sodomy, adultery, and incest." To bolster such theoretical assumptions, the witch-hunters gathered many accounts of monsters, half human and half animal, born of such unions.[36]

One theological problem involved in intercourse with demons was to explain how the demons, particularly the incubi, could have human-like sexual organs and give forth semen. Some authorities, such as Caesarius of Hesiterbach, who wrote in the thirteenth century, had argued that these devils collected the human semen emitted during nocturnal emissions or as a result of masturbation and then used this to create new bodies for themselves.[37] This belief gave an added fear to the dangers of involuntary emissions or masturbation, and although this remained a popular belief, most authorities preferred to adopt the logic of St. Thomas Aquinas. Aquinas had argued that devils in the form of succubi seduced males and thereby received their semen, and then, assuming the role of incubi, poured this semen into female repositories.[38] This last was the view of the authors of the *Malleus maleficarum*.[39]

The sexual practices equated with witchcraft are usually described in the most generalized ways, although occasionally terms such as *sodomy* or statements such as "intercourse after the manner of beasts" are used. Sometimes the demons appeared in animal form, particularly that of a bull, a fox, or occasionally a hare, but the most likely form was as an incubus. Demons were far more likely to seek intercourse with women than with men, for women were regarded as far more licentious than men. One authority has estimated that the male incubus appeared approximately nine times more frequently in the works on demonology than the female succubus.[40]

Witchcraft and sorcery were also believed to be responsible for impotence, infertility, and a whole series of other sex-connected activities. One of the supposed powers of a witch was her ability to make the penis disappear by casting a "glamour" over it. Once this happened, only the witch herself could restore normal sexual activity by making it reappear. A witch was also regarded as the main cause of the male failure to achieve an erection, and witchcraft prevented women from conceiving or caused them to miscarry. Impotence was believed to be caused by a ligature; that is, the witch, by tying knots in threads or hanks of leather, would cause impotence until the hidden knot was discovered or untied or until the witch lifted her spell. Generally, however, the believers in witchcraft held that the devil wished to encourage, not discourage, fornication, and so ligature was believed to be less common than the other forms of *malefica* or "evils" that a witch might impose.[41]

The witch craze, after reaching its height about 1600, ended in the eighteenth century. It was mainly confined to Christianized western Europe, both Catholic and Protestant. It was encouraged by Catholic popes and Protestant reformers, by saints and by scholars, and most particularly by lawyers. The last legal execution was in Glarus in Switzerland in 1782, although there was illegal witch-burning in Poland in 1793. It is impossible to state how many persons were executed as witches in Europe during the period of witchcraft persecution from 1450 to 1750. Witches were beheaded, hanged, whipped to death, and burned alive, but the records are incomplete. An Inquisitor at Como in Italy is quoted as saying that he burned 1000 witches in one year (probably 1523), and records from three little villages totaling 300 households under the jurisdiction of the Archbishop of Cologne show that between 125 and 150 persons were executed in the years 1631–1636. Probably the *minimum* number executed in Europe would total about a quarter of a million, but some estimates range into the millions. Certainly millions were accused, but fortunately most were not executed.[42]

Women were particularly susceptible to sexual enticement by the devil, no women being more vulnerable than nuns. At a convent in Cologne the devil, in the form of a dog, was said to lift up the robes of nuns to abuse them. In another convent supposedly possessed by demons, an investigator saw dogs lying on the nuns' cots:

> Shamelessly awaiting those suspected of having been assaulted and having committed the sin called the secret sin [i.e., sodomy, since the word was too shocking for honest ears.] At Toulouse, he found a woman who abused herself in this manner; and in front of everybody the dog wanted to mount her. She confessed to the truth and was burned.[43]

An eyewitness to such activities swore that:

> The devil in the form of a goat, having his member in the rear, had intercourse with women by joggling and shoving the thing against their belly. Marie de Marigrane, aged fifteen years, a resident of Biarritz, affirmed that she had often seen the devil couple with a multitude of women, who she knew by name and surname, and that it was the devil's custom to have intercourse with the beautiful women from the front, and with the ugly from the rear.[44]

Another witness reported that the devil appeared either as man or goat, but he always had:

> A member like a mule's, having chosen to imitate that animal as being best endowed by nature; that it was as long and as thick as an arm . . . and that he always exposed his instrument, of such beautiful shape and measurements.[45]

One of the most notorious cases took place in the seventeenth century among the Loudun Nuns; this was clearly a trumped-up charge, as were perhaps vast numbers of witchcraft persecutions. Opponents of a priest, Urbain Grandier, who had openly ignored his vows of celibacy with considerable impunity because of his political connections, hatched a plan to entrap him. They persuaded a few sisters of the Ursuline convent at Loudun in France to swear that they were possessed because they had been bewitched by Father Grandier. The Mother Superior, Sister Jeanne des Anges, and a nun cooperated by going into convulsions, holding their breath until their bodies swelled, and altering their looks and voices. When the initial efforts failed to limit Father Grandier's activities, the plot was extended. Under exorcism some 60 witnesses deposed to adultery, incest, sacrilege, and other sexual crimes, committed by him even in the most secret places of the Church. A whole series of trumped-up evidence against Grandier was manufactured, and even though several nuns later tried to retract their confessions, the courts refused to allow this, on the grounds that their retractions had been arranged by the Devil to save his servant. Father Grandier was convicted of causing demoniacal possession of several Ursuline nuns; He died a particularly horrible death, being tortured even as he was burned to death in 1634. Typical of the nuns' conduct under exorcism was the behavior of a young nun, Sister Claire:

> She fell on the ground, blaspheming, in convulsions, lifting up her petticoats and chemise, displaying her privy parts without any shame, and uttering filthy words. Her gestures became so indecent that the audience averted its eyes. She cried out again and again, abusing herself with her hands, "Come on, then, *foutez-moi* [screw me]."[46]

Underlying the fear of witches was the fear, not only of sex and of sexual deviance, but also of women themselves. Obviously, women were sexual creatures, and evidence for the need to control their sexuality is the growth in use of chastity belts in the fifteenth century. How widespread such contraptions were is debatable, but the first authenticated picture of one dates from 1405. If it was the virtuous woman who was going to be admired, some husbands and fathers were going to make every effort to ensure the chastity of their wives and daughters, even if it meant putting them into chastity belts. The custom began in Italy, the home of the Renaissance, and continued in that country and elsewhere for several hundred years.[47]

Though female sexuality was feared, it was also exploited. An indication of this is the belief in the *jus primae noctis* or *droit du seigneur,* stories of which have intrigued the male imagination since medieval times. In popular theory, the *jus primae noctis* was the right of the noble landlord to spend the first night with the brides on his estates. Known under various terms, *culagium, jambage, gambada, cuissage, derecho de pernada, jus cunnagii, jus cunni, jux coxae locandae, jus coxae luxandae,* it has often been the topic of popular literature from Voltaire to Sir Walter Scott to George Bernard Shaw. The stories were probably derived from references to *culagium,* which was a request for permission to marry. This required that a fine called a *marchet* or *merchet* (also *marchetta* or *marquetta*) be paid. The fine had originated from the fact that a woman moved into her husband's house, leaving the jurisdiction of one landowner for another. Since such a move technically deprived the lord of part of his property, his human stock, he required indemnification for this loss. Even if the marriage took place among his own tenants or serfs, it was customary to request the lord's permission to marry, and this often also entailed a fine. In addition, in some dioceses the husband had to pay his bishop or the supervisory ecclesiastical authority for the privilege of sleeping with his wife on the first night or first few nights of their marriage. This was not regarded as a compensation for the relinquishment of the right of such authorities to sleep with the girl first, as some have argued, but rather a payment for a dispensation to sin, since the Church urged newly married couples to observe chastity on their wedding night and actually advocated that the first 3 days and nights of marriage be observed in chastity. The fine then served as a penance for not observing the rules. Kings Philip VI and Charles VI of France, in the fourteenth century, tried to induce the Bishop of Amiens to give up his right of demanding a fine for granting every newly married couple permission to have conjugal intercourse during the first 3 nights of their marriage.[48]

This explanation would mean that there was no implication of sexual right to the bride by either the bishop or the secular lord, but some authorities believe that in some areas there is some justification for belief in sexual rights to the bride and that this was a holdover custom from pre-Christian Europe. The controversy centers around the Celtic populations of Europe, particularly Scotland, where the Chronicle of Boecus reported that King Ewen III (about 875 A.D.) established the right of *jus primae noctis*: "Ane othir law he maid, that wiffis of the commonis sal be fre to the nobilis; and the lord of the ground sal have the madinheid of all virginis dwelling on the same." Boecus wrote, however, at the beginning of the sixteenth century, and his history included many fabulous narratives, of which this was probably one. One Scottish authority, nevertheless, concluded that

> After weighing all the evidence, it is difficult to avoid the conclusion that the *Jus primae noctis* was the custom, at any rate in some parts of Scotland, in early times. There is no authority to the contrary, nor have any facts inconsistent with such a right ever been advanced by those who challenge it."[49]

Whether such a legal right ever existed in western Europe is doubtful, although it was customary in many areas to allow the lord free access to the women on his estates, since opposition to such a powerful person was difficult. In the fifteenth and early sixteenth centuries, various kings tried to limit such rights, and ecclesiastical authorities encouraged them in their efforts.

Though the *jus primae noctis*, at least in Western culture, is more legend than fact, the sixteenth century saw a real growth in the fear of venereal disease. How much this fear was responsible for reassessing sexual practices is not clear, but it is an important undercurrent in much of the sixteenth-century discussions of sex and has continued to be an important factor to the present day. The reasons for this new focus on venereal disease boil down to the fact that an epidemic of syphilis began sweeping Europe, although the reasons for it have been the subject of controversy centering around arguments of whether syphilis was a new disease introduced into Europe from the Americas or whether it existed in Europe before and suddenly became epidemic. In support of the American origin is the fact that no unequivocal description of syphilis has ever been discovered in any literature of the Old World before the time of Columbus. Though we have descriptions of disease that might have been syphilis, they might also be of leprosy, scabies, or any number of other diseases. Giving impetus to the American origin is the fact that the Chinese, who revered the ancients and quoted from their classics whenever possible, have no description of syphilis until after it appears in Europe. Galen in the Latin and Avicenna in the Arabic, both accomplished clinicians, failed to describe the disease, and on the other hand, most of the sixteenth-century physicians, surgeons, and laymen who wrote about venereal disease in the sixteenth century felt it was a new disease.[50] Until recently those arguing for its existence in the Old World have brushed aside most of these arguments and hypothesized that syphilis had existed in Europe and the Old World in a mild form prior to the 1490s, after which the causative organism had mutated into the *Treponema pallidum,* and syphilis began to affect the deep body structures and became a killer.

The earliest mention of the disease in connection with Europeans in the New World appears in a biography of Columbus by his son Ferdinand. This book's value as a source is somewhat diminished by its existing only in an Italian translation, for the Spanish original was lost. Nevertheless, for what it is worth, Ferdinand recounted that in his 1498 vogage Columbus found that some of the people he had left behind in Espanola were dead and that more than 160 of the survivors were "sick with the French sickness." By itself, this statement might indicate that the European brought syphilis to America, but the euphemism "French disease" is believed to be a later interpolation. Giving some indication of the prevalence of syphilis in America is an account of a certain Friar Ramon, who, on order of Columbus, had learned the language of the Indians and compiled an account of their history and customs. In his biography of his father, Ferdinand stated that Ramon had observed venereal disease among the Indians. In fact he reported that there was a legend about an Arawak folk hero who had "great pleasure" with women but then had to "look for many bathhouses in which to wash himself because he was full of those sores that we call the French sickness."[51] If Friar Ramon was an accurate observer and his information has passed down correctly, then it might seem there is some proof that the indigenous Americans did have some form of syphilis.

The two most important historians of the early Spanish empire, Bartolomé de las Casas and Gonzalo Fernandez de Oviedo y Valdés, agreed that Columbus brought syphilis back from America, though their accounts differ somewhat in detail. Las Casas was in a good position to observe, for he was in Seville in 1493 when Columbus came to that city with his report on his discoveries and accompanied by his Indian prisoners. Both his father and uncle sailed with Columbus on his 1493 voyage, and las Casas probably knew many other participants in the early voyages. He himself came to the New World in 1502 and spent most of the rest of his life working for and with Indians. Fernandez was also in a position to make accurate observations. He had been attached to the Spanish court in the 1490s and had met with Columbus before his 1492 voyage. He was friendly with the sons of Columbus, as well as with members of the Pinzón family, one of whom, Martin Alonso Pinzón, commander of the *Pinta,* is believed to have died from syphilis.[52] The third person to point to the American origin was another Spaniard, the physician Ruy Diaz de Isla. He recalled in his book, written before 1539, how he had treated many of the sailors accompanying Columbus for the disease while practicing in Barcelona.[53] Diaz was a remarkable clinician; one of his beliefs, that a high fever, such as that caused by malaria, tended to arrest syphilis, was finally confirmed in the twentieth century.[54] If contemporaries had been inclined to doubt such testimonials about the origin of syphilis, their doubts were shaken by the fact that guaiacum, a decoction of a West Indian wood, was believed to be a certain cure for syphilis. Since the medical logic of the time held that God would have arranged for a cure of a disease to originate in the same locality as the disease itself, this was taken to be the definitive clinching argument for a New World origin. Perhaps because of such a belief some historians who have doubted the New World origins of syphilis have argued that the source of the Columbian theory lay in the fact that guaiacum came from the New World rather than syphilis itself.[55]

The first recorded European reference to what has been diagnosed as syphilis occurred in the winter of 1494–1495 in Naples, when French soldiers garrisoned in the city reported tumors on the genitals. No sooner had these sores healed than they were followed by a series of eruptions, such as sores inside the mouth or festering, malignant ulcers on the legs or other parts of the body. Since the disease was first reported among soldiers in the French army, it was inevitably called *morbus Gallicus* or the "French sickness." The French in turn called it the Neapolitan disease. Seemingly, no one country or group wanted to be associated with the disease. The Turks called it the Christian disease, the Chinese knew it as the Portugese disease, and it has also been called the German, American, Spanish, Syrian, Egyptian, and English disease. Of the non-national names the best remembered is the Great Pox, after which the other pox, smallpox, seemed to be so minor.[56] Whatever the name, the disease soon reached epidemic proportion. The name *syphilis* by which it is now known was given to the disease by Girolamo Fracastoro (or Fracastorius) of Verona, a physician, poet, physicist, and geologist, whose poem on the disease, *Syphilis sive morbus Gallicus,* was published in 1530. Fracastorius recounted how a dreadful drought had afflicted the island of Haiti, killing animals as well as human beings. A shepherd, known as Syphilis, angered at what he felt was unjust treatment by the gods, led a rebellion against the god and switched allegiance to King Alcithous, an earthly mortal. Alcithous, intoxicated by the implications of the sudden allegiance, decreed that while the gods could have the heavens, he was king of the earth. In retaliation for this impiety, Sirius, the Sun God, sent a new scourge to the earth that claimed Syphilis as its first victim.[57] Inevitably, the new disease infecting Europe came to be called syphilis, a fact also pointing to the European belief that it came from America.

Most of the early accounts attributing the origin of the disease discussed the subject only incidentally and more or less dispassionately. If the discussion had remained at this level, it might never have become controversial. It became a matter of polemics in the eighteenth century, when a Frenchman, Jean Astruc, determined to remove the stigma of having syphilis called the French disease, launched an offensive to prove its American origin.[58] Much of the difficulty associated with any dispassionate discussion of the disease is that it has often been regarded in Christian culture as proof of sinfulness, as a curse, and thus, whereas we can look more dispassionately at the origin and transmission of other diseases, syphilis has proved far more controversial.[59]

Perhaps the most difficult obstacle to overcome for those believing in the non-American origins of the disease is its rapid spread and extreme virulence in sixteenth-century Europe, followed by a gradual lessening of malignancy, all of which are the classic characteristics of a new disease. This is because, when a new disease appears (or reappears after a long absence), the most susceptible members are eliminated by death, as are the most virulent strains of the germ, if only because they kill off their hosts before transmission to other hosts occurs. Gradually, some kind of immunity is built up that might not prevent the disease but lessens the mortality rate. We know that syphilis spread rapidly in Europe. It was first mentioned officially in an August 1495 edict of the Emperor Maximilian, who viewed it as sent by God to punish the ungodly. His edict was followed by a whole series of other references as the disease spread. It was mentioned in Paris in 1496, in Nuremberg in 1496–1497, and in Glasgow, Scotland, about the same time. The disease also began to receive attention in he writings of various physicians, where there had been no mention before. Some 10 different accounts are known to have been published in Germany, Italy, Spain, and Austria between 1495 and 1498.[60]

Theoretically, since third-stage syphilis (as well as congenital syphilis) often leaves scarring in the bones, it ought to be possible to determine whether syphilis existed outside the Americas before 1492. In fairly exhaustive surveys of ancient bones, including some 25,000 ancient Egyptian skeletons, no trace of syphilis has been found. On the other hand, quantities of syphilitic bones have been found in Peru and elsewhere. Whereas this was once regarded as proving the American origin, it is now recognized that much of the dating of the American bones was invalid and that most might well not date before Columbus at all.[61]

An alternative to the American origin is the unitary theory. This hypothesis is based on the assumption that syphilis has always been worldwide but has been known by different names in different societies. Various explanations have been put forward in the past to justify such a hypothesis, but the one with the most current support is that of E. Herndon Hudson, who held that a number of closely related infections are caused by treponemal organisms, including yaws, bejel, pinta, and irkinja, all of which develop similar clinical syndromes under different environmental conditions. It is possible, Hudson believes, that the organism causing treponematosis has undergone various mutational changes. He theorized that man had first acquired the *Treponema* causing these maladies in moist, hot sub-Saharan Africa, where the climate originally allowed the organism to live on the surface of the body. This original *Treponema* manifested itself as yaws, an infection that, initially at least, affected only the surface layers of the body. As the disease spread into the hot, drier areas, the organism retreated into the bodies of the host, becoming a kind of nonvenereal syphilis, a disease of childhood transmitted by close contact under very unhygienic conditions. This manifestation was and is called bejel in the Middle East. In other areas, with more careful personal hygiene or less favorable climate conditions, the treponemas were deprived of most of their avenues of transmission from one human being to another. Inevitably, they retreated ever deeper into the human body, into the bones, arteries, and nervous system, adjusting themselves to changed conditions. Eventually, the only means of transmission left open to them was the one extremely intimate contact with another human being that modern man still endorsed, sexual intercourse. Thus venereal syphilis appeared.[62] Though Hudson's theory still leaves a lot unexplained, it has raised the controversy over the American origin of syphilis to a new level, since there is some evidence to support it, at least at the present stage of scientific development. One kind of evidence is the fact that the different treponemas, *Treponema pallidum, Treponema pertenue,* and *Treponema carateum,* in spite of their different names, cannot yet be differentiated under a microscope. Moreover, the antibodies created within the body of the host by one *Treponema* immobilize others, that is, give the host immunity to all. For these reasons, some scholars, though disagreeing in detail with Hudson, are willing to believe that syphilis existed in Europe in a nonvenereal form before it assumed a venereal form of transmission.[63]

The evidence is not, however, conclusive, and the debate has not ended. Simply because there is a close relationship between the various treponemas does not mean they are the same. Smallpox and cowpox, for example, are closely related symptomatically, and immunity to one gives immunity to both, but no one would claim the diseases are the same, even though the organisms appear nearly identical under the electron microscope. In fact, the discovery that cowpox gave immunity to smallpox led to modern vaccination. It is also possible that our current means of distinguishing organisms are too crude.

Until a more discriminating test is invented, all we can now say is that, regardless of its origin, venereal syphilis reached epidemic proportions in the sixteenth century.

But perhaps we make too much over the possible New World origin of syphilis, for the Europeans themselves long remained unsure about the nature of the disease, often confusing it with other forms of venereal disease long known to have existed in Europe and associated with sexual intercourse. In fact, the term *venereal* comes from the word *venery,* that is, the pursuit of Venus, goddess of love. We also know that gonorrhea, derived from a Greek word meaning "a flow of seed," existed long before Galen invented the descriptive name in the second century A.D. Other forms of venereal disease, such as chancroid (*ulcus molle*), *lymphogranuloma venereum,* and *lymphogranuloma inguinale,* also have an old history, although they were often confused with other diseases, such as leprosy and elephantiasis. As late as the eighteenth century there was an attempt to prove that gonorrhea and syphilis were the same. The great eighteenth-century surgeon John Hunter felt he had proved conclusively that they were the same when he inoculated his penis with pus from a man known to have gonorrhea and found that he had contracted syphilis as well. Obviously, Hunter's patient had an unsuspected case of syphilis to match his gonorrhea, but for a time Hunter's experiments seemed to prove the two were one. Hunter himself announced that "matter from gonorrhea will produce chancres."[64] In a sense, Hunter might be called a martyr to science, since he ultimately died of an aortic aneurysm resulting from syphilis.

Coupled with the new fears of syphilis was a disillusion with the papacy, the traditional enforcer of sexual standards. This resulted from several factors. Papal power had been undermined by the so-called Babylonian Captivity, when the papacy had moved its headquarters to Avignon in what is today southern France; this had been followed by the Great Schism, in which two or more popes claimed to rule at the same time, and then by papal involvement in a political struggle to control Italy. During this same period popes themselves seemed less committed to traditional medieval views of sexuality, particularly to clerical celibacy, with the result that the sexual peccadilloes of the pope and lesser ecclesiastical dignitaries became notorious. Pope Innocent VIII, elected in 1484, has facetiously been called the "honest" pope because he was the first to acknowledge publicly his own illegitimate children. He was followed by the even more notorious Rodrigo Borgia, better known as Pope Alexander VI. Borgia had bought the papal crown when the cardinals had auctioned it off to the highest bidder and then had tried to recoup his investment as pope by giving key offices to his relatives, the most notorious of whom was his son Cesare Borgia. Cesare was appointed a cardinal while still in his teens, and later, when a favorable marriage opportunity opened up, was allowed to resign. Alexander's daughter Lucrezia served as a pawn in her father's plans for family aggrandizement. Inevitably, with the example of the popes before them, it was difficult for Church officials to reprimand lesser believers for sexual sins. Nevertheless, there was a strong persistence of belief in traditional Christian values, as is indicated by the rise of a number of preachers of repentance in various parts of Italy and elsewhere. Such preachers started revivals aimed at reform that were marked by mass conversions, hysteria, and extreme austerity. The most famous was the Dominican Jerome Savonarola, who attained a position of power at Florence. He began preaching in 1482 and so stirred his audience that many wept and others were petrified with horror. He succeeded in driving out the Medici and in introducing a government that he believed was directly sanctioned by God. He attacked the morals of the clergy as well as of the people and attempted to suppress all evidence of public immorality and frivolity. People burned their playing cards, false hair, and indecent pictures; gamblers were tortured; and blasphemers had their tongues pierced. Ultimately, he moved in opposition to the pope, who excommunicated him. By 1498, however, there was sufficient decline in his popular support for his enemies to move against him, and he was seized, tortured, and forced to confess that he was not a prophet. On May 22, 1498, he was condemned, and he and two companions were speedily executed.[65] Other Italian cities had similar reformers who in the long run were no more successful than he.

One result of the difficulty in enforcing clerical celibacy was a questioning of the basic concept of celibacy. As the interest in reform grew stronger, many reformers even began to question the necessity for a pope. Inevitably one demand for change was the elimination of clerical celibacy, a change advocated almost unanimously by the Protestants. This was probably the greatest difference between Protestants and Catholics in sexual matters, since the Protestants otherwise kept to the tradition set forth by the early Church Fathers, particularly St. Augustine. In fact, St. Augustine exercised great influence on one of the major Protestant figures, Martin Luther (1438–1546). Luther had not started out questioning celibacy but only gradually became convinced that clerical celibacy was wrong because it originated from what he regarded as a false belief that divine favor could be won by performing self-imposed tasks. The key to his religious thought was that salvation came from faith, not good works, and by implication, chastity, which had been regarded as a good work, could no longer be so regarded. He believed that sex in and of itself did not involve man in any more sinful conduct than other potentially sinful acts. Wedlock, in fact, was God's gift to mankind, a state of life approved by God and possessing the authority of his sanctions. Marriage, inherent in the very nature of man, had been instituted in Paradise, confirmed by the Fifth Commandment, and safeguarded by the Seventh. It was a true, heavenly, spiritual, and divine estate. Luther was not opposed to celibacy but regarded continence as a gift from God and not all had received this gift; this belief led him to oppose compulsory lifelong celibacy. As he wrote to his fellow reformer Philip Melancthon in 1521: "God's Word clearly established that the prohibition [of marriage] originates with the devil."[66] Marriage was also an effective way of curing the sin of lust, and marriage and family were the mainstays of society:

> Many good things may be perceived in a wife. First, there is the Lord's blessing, namely offspring. There then is community of property. These are some of the pre-eminently good things that can overwhelm a man.

> Imagine what life would be like without this sex. The home, cities, economic life, and government would virtually disappear. Men cannot do without women. Even if it were possible for men to beget and bear children, they still could not do without women.[67]

In attempting to deal with the Augustinian concentration on celibacy, he believed that the early Church Fathers had observed celibacy freely "without coercion by any law." Only later, when celibacy had become a matter of Church discipline, had it become a bad thing, and in his mind nothing could have been more monstrous than a law requiring celibacy.[68] He believed that most Christians found it difficult to observe celibacy and that often only an appearance of the celibate life had been achieved rather than actual celibacy. The Archbishop of Mainz, he reported, had two wives, and the pope had "as many concubines as Solomon had."[69] When he dealt with the Biblical injunction about celibacy, he wrote that:

> This is Christ's way. When the disciples praised continence and said, "If such is the case of a man with his wife, it is expedient not to marry," he at once set their minds straight on the matter and said. "Not all men can receive this precept." This must be accepted, but it was Christ's will that only a few should understand it.[70]

Who were these few? Luther agonized over this question in several of his tracts. In one he said that each man had to find out what is conducive to chastity in his own case. In another he felt that a general Church Council might be called to settle the matter, but eventually he arrived at the conclusion that celibacy had to be a gift from God and that only a few individuals had ever been granted the power to resist all sexual desires.[71] In his mind, sex, when undertaken with the precepts of God in mind, was good:

> Just as a gold vessel is ennobled when it is used as a container of a noble wine, and degraded when it is used as a container of excrement and filth, so our body (in this respect) is ordained to an honorable marriage and to chastity which is still more honorable.[72]

Giving impetus to his belief in the nearly impossible difficulty of observing celibacy was his experience as a monk. He wrote that, even as a monk, he had known the temptations of the flesh, and many of his fellow monks had suffered nightly pollutions:

> Almost every night the brothers were bothered by them, so that they don't dare celebrate Mass the next day. But when a large number of Masses that had been imposed on us and appointed for us had to be omitted on account of our refusal, it became public, and the Prior conceded that anybody at all could and should celebrate Mass, even if he had had nocturnal pollutions.[73]

Eventually Luther distinguished between those emissions brought about by man's own efforts and those that occurred naturally, accepting the latter and condemning the former unless they took place in marriage. Those attempting to prevent the body from acting naturally would endanger themselves, since sex was a natural function ordained by God. "This is the Word of God, through whose power procreative seed is planted in man's body and a natural, ardent desire for women is kindled and kept alive."[74] He advised one of his correspondents to stop thinking so much about sex and get on with it, since the body demanded it.[75] Another time he wrote: "You are just as foolish if you do not take a wife when passion stirs and you remain continent to the danger of your soul."[76]

Most of Luther's statements about sex reflect a male point of view, but he also recognized that women had sexual feelings and had problems in living in lifelong celibacy. In his view, however, women were to be helpmates to men, and few were ever in complete mastery of themselves. In fact, God had so created the female body that "she should be with a man and bear and raise children."[77]

> Men have broad shoulders and narrow hips, and accordingly they possess intelligence. Women have narrow shoulders and broad hips. Women ought to stay at home; the way they were created indicates this, for they have broad hips and a wide fundament to sit upon (to keep house and bear and raise children).[78]

Women, he believed, were physically and emotionally weaker than males, easily frightened, easily angered, easily made suspicious, and always in need of a male.[79]

Sex was to be confined to marriage. Luther was particularly hostile to prostitution, which had been tolerated by the medieval Christian Church as a lesser of two evils. How much the new antagonism to prostitution was due to the growing fear of syphilis is perhaps debatable, but Luther was adamant.

> Through special enemies of our faith the devil has sent some whores here to ruin our poor young men. As an old and faithful preacher I ask you in fatherly fashion, dear children, that you believe assuredly that the evil spirit sent these whores here and they are dreadful, shabby, stinking, loathsome, and syphilitic, as daily experience unfortunately demonstrates.[80]

In dealing with prostitution, Luther and most of the other reformers also departed once again from the medieval church. Punishment for such activities was not in the hands of the Church but in the hands of the state and ultimately, of course, of God. Luther believed that preachers should speak powerfully against such activities and should mount public campaigns to pressure the good consciences of public officials so that they enact the laws to deal with them, but the Church itself was not to take it upon itself to punish such activities.

> Let the government, if it wishes to be Christian, punish whoredom, rape, and adultery, at least when they occur openly; if they still occur in secret, the government is not to be blamed."[81]

The result of such beliefs was to bring sexual regulations increasingly into the purview of secular laws in Protestant countries and even in some Catholic ones.

In spite of his focus on marriage, Luther was fairly tolerant of some sexual activities. When his political ally Philip of Hesse entered into bigamy rather than commit adultery, Luther consoled him with the statement that bigamy had many "well-known examples in the Scriptures." When Philip's bigamy became widely known, Luther expressed sorrow that it could not have been kept secret and advised Philip to remain calm, since the storm would soon blow over or perhaps one of his wives would die.[82] Elsewhere, he wrote that, though a Christian man should normally have only one wife, if for various reasons he needed another sexual companion, he might keep a girl as a concubine rather than marry her.[83] He was opposed to adultery but believed that, unless it was flagrant and frequent, there should always be an attempt to save the marriage.[84]

When it came to sexual activity other than that intended to bring about procreation, Luther was not so tolerant. He made his attitute quite clear in his commentary on Genesis:

> The heinous conduct of the people of Sodom is extraordinary, in as much as they departed from the natural passion and longing of the male for the female, which was implanted by God, and desired what is altogether contrary to nature. Whence comes this perversity? Undoubtedly from Satan, who, after people have once turned away from the fear of God, so powerfully suppresses nature that he beats out the natural desire and stirs up a desire that is contrary to nature.[85]

Fornication, for Luther, was a far less serious sin than sodomy or the sin against nature, however, broadly defined.[86] His solution for those tempted with such sins was to get the soul of the sinner back to God and his body into bed with a good wife. A good summary of his views appears in a letter he wrote to a newly married priest:

> You lucky man, that you have by an honorable marriage conquered that unclear celibacy which is reprehensible because it causes either a constant burning or unclean pollutions. Suffer whatever this way of life brings, since it is instituted by God, and be grateful to Him. That most miserable celibacy of young men and women daily presents such great horrors to me that even now nothing sounds worse to my ears than the words "nuns," "monk," and "priest." I consider marriage to be a paradise, even if it has to endure greatest poverty.[87]

Most of the Protestant reformers followed Luther's example. John Calvin (1509–1564), the major theologican of the Protestant cause, was usually more cautious than Luther but essentially agreed with him. Calvin held that celibacy was superior to marriage,[88] and if given by God as a virtue and not embraced under compulsion, it was not to be despised.[89] Like Luther, however, he disapproved of those acts of celibacy regarded as acts of religious service that had been undertaken rashly by those who could not keep their commitment.[90] Celibacy and continence, Calvin felt, were not in everyone's power, but he believed it was possible for a normal person to be continent with God's help, since God aided those who obeyed His call, and nothing was impossible with God's help.[91] He agreed with Luther that the imposition of celibacy upon the clergy was contrary to Scripture, since man had no right to forbid what God had left free for each person to decide.[92]

As to sexual intercourse, Calvin was even more positive about it than Luther. For him, coitus was undefiled, honorable, and holy because it was a pure institution of God.[93] The only reason it sometimes had not been viewed in such a way was that Satan had dazzled man with an appearance of what was right so that men would imagine that they had been "polluted by intercourse" with their wives.[94] Calvin was, however, uneasy about the pleasure element in sexual intercourse, feeling that this must be attended by a certain element of evil, owing to immoderate desire, which had resulted from the corruption of human nature. Yet God would not treat this pleasure as sinful when it was sought or accepted as incidental to procreation and the building of society. In effect, a husband and wife should feel free to enjoy their sexual activity,[95] as long as they did so with modesty and propriety and kept their behavior sober and appropriate to the dignity of their state.[96] To Calvin, the primary purpose of marriage was social, not generative, and God had not created women simply to be man's assistant in procreation nor as a remedy for his sexual needs caused by the corruption of human nature brought on by the Fall. Instead, woman was man's inseparable associate in life as well as in the bedchamber.[97]

Calvin was far more harsh toward polygamy and concubinage than Luther, and he even went so far as to argue that the plural unions of the Biblical patriarchs were indefensible.[98] Calvin recognized adultery as grounds for divorce[99] and was equally hostile to other forms of sexual behavior. To practice coitus interruptus was doubly monstrous, for it extinguished the hope of the race and killed the hopes for a son before he was born.[100] Though Calvin did not quite equate the Biblical story of Sodom with homosexuality,[101] he in general adopted the now standard Western attitude of condemning as unnatural all forms of intercourse not leading to procreation. On other aspects of sex he followed the general teachings of the Old Testament, which he believed to be based on natural laws.[102]

In England, influenced by both Lutheranism and Calvinism but not quite following either, the major difference with the continental reformers was that spiritual courts remained and continued to deal with questions of marriage and divorce until the nineteenth century. Though the English reformers agreed with the continental ones that marriage was not a sacrament, they continued to regard it as a holy symbol. The purpose of marriage was procreation, to serve as a remedy for carnal desires, and to furnish mutual friendship and society. As to sexual relations, the Anglicans adopted the traditional Western attitudes that sex was unlawful unless sanctioned by wedlock. Within marriage, temperance in coitus should be observed, and so should the order of nature: the purpose of coition was procreation. Onanism, which separated the act of sex from its proper end, was condemned. Some Anglicans even condemned sexual intercourse during menstruation as a transgression of the Seventh Commandment; others, however, saw no reason to prohibit it. The most detailed of the Anglican theological writers on sexual matters was Jeremy Taylor (1613–1667), who also proved fairly tolerant toward what had traditionally been regarded as the sin against nature. To Taylor, the sins against nature were not intrinsically worse than other sins, for all alike were committed against God, and there could be no rating scale fixing gravity of different acts. Rather, the factors to be considered were motive, occasion, and consequences of the act. Though this represents some modification of the traditional Christian position, it is not a radical departure from what was written and thought at this time.[103]

Catholicism, under attack from outside by Protestantism and urged to change by reformers from within, was reinvigorated by decisions taken at the Council of Trent (1545–1564), finally called to deal with the problems that had been plaguing the Catholic Church for a century or so. As to sexual matters, the delegates in the council reaffirmed the traditional views that virginity was a higher state than marriage, continued to hold that jurisdiction in matrimonial cases belonged to ecclesiastical authority, and reasserted traditional ideas of sexual morality. As John T. Noonan, a Catholic specialist in canon law and sexuality, wrote:

> The Catholic moralists were not eager to appear to abandon a moral doctrine of the Fathers if the Protestants still held it. With particular force this feeling held as to sexual sins.[104]

One consequence of the reaffirmation of traditional Catholic ideas about sexuality was an endeavor to clean house, to enforce high moral standards for the clergy, and to make the Church far less tolerant of the sexual abuses that earlier might have been ignored.

In both Protestant and Catholic countries the state began to intervene more directly in matters of faith and morals previously delegated to the Church. One result was to transform such concepts as the sin against nature into the crime against nature. In England, the first legal enactments took place in 1533 under King Henry VIII, when buggery, now equated with the sin against nature, was made a crime. This original statute had a rather checkered history, indicating the hesitation and ambiguity with which the state initially entered the sex field. The statute was reenacted in 1536, 1539, and 1541, and then in 1547, it and other statutes dealing with felonies established during the reign of Henry were repealed by the first parliament of Edward VI, his successor. In 1548 buggery was again made a crime, but that law was abolished in 1553 under Queen Mary and finally reestablished in the English law in 1563 under Queen Elizabeth.[105] One result of such legislative history was to confuse the issue of sex and the law and to make uncertain exactly what constituted buggery or the crime against nature. Sir Edward Coke made some effort to remove the confusion. Publishing his famous study of English law in 1625, he wrote that:

> Buggery is a detestable, and abominable sin, against Christians not to be named, committed by carnal knowledge against the ordinance of the Creator, and order of nature, by mankind with mankind or with brute beast, or by womankind with brute beast.[106]

Coke made, however, an additional qualification to his definition that other commentators did not make, since he claimed that, without penetration, there could be no buggery. This interpretation put some limitations on the general medieval notion of sin against nature and limited it to coitus *in ano,* whether heterosexual or homosexual, and to bestiality. Other commentators did not, however, necessarily accept this definition, and in general the English law has been as ambiguous about the "Crime Against Nature" as the canon law was about the "Sin Against Nature."

Similar laws were enacted in the Holy Roman Empire during the sixteenth century. Emperor Charles V decreed that

> If a man should lie with a beast, or a man with a man, or a woman with a woman, both shall forfeit their lives, and it should be the common custom that they should meet their deaths through the means of fire.[107]

The laws of Prussia provided for the same punishment for males and for bestiality but ignored the whole topic of women.[108] In most of the West, in fact, sexual relations between women did not arouse the same kind of hostility, legal or otherwise, that relations with men or beasts did. For males, however, there was a tendency to provide the death penalty, although it was enforced only rarely.

If legal definitions of the crime against nature proved contradictory to the people of the time, so did the growth of pornography. Several factors seem important in explaining this new concern, not the least of which were the changes taking place in art itself. So great did these changes appear to some cultural historians of the nineteenth century that the term Renaissance was coined to describe them. Though we now know that the change was more gradual than it seemed to Jacob Burckhardt, who popularized the concept, there was a change in both materials and subject matter. One factor most responsible for this was the change in the nature of patronage as private patrons began to exercise greater influence than the ecclesiastical institutions, and secular art developed to meet the demand. At first, these new patrons hired artists to decorate churches, content to have themselves portrayed as a Biblical character in one of the scenes. Later, the secular patrons asserted more control, demanding portraits of themselves, as well as paintings with themes not quite so religious. Classical mythology became a favorite subject matter, and several themes, such as the rape of Lucretia or the birth of Venus, could give the artist some opportunity to touch on sex.

Coinciding with this were new media for artistic expression: the development of an oil base for mixing pigments that would allow realistic colors; the development of more naturalistic settings; a new concentration on light, shade, color, and composition; and, perhaps most importantly, the discovery of perspective. The result was a new realism that the artist could use to convey kinds of meaning.

There was also a new interest in the body, an interest appearing not only in art but also in costume. This new style appears toward the end of the medieval period, perhaps encouraged by the invention of the button, which allowed costumes to be fitted more closely. Soon, instead of following the body contours, there was a tendency to exaggerate, particularly with female costumes. By the end of the fifteenth century, the "busc" and the "farthingale" had appeared to give more erotic connotations to the female form. The "busc" was an early form of corset, made from two pieces of linen stiffened by paste, stitched together, and shaped to the waist at the sides. To keep the front part really rigid, a piece of wood, horn, whalebone, metal, or ivory (*busc* was the technical term) was inserted between the layers, thick at the top and tapering toward a point at the waist. Shoulder straps were attached to hold these "pair of bodys" or stays in place, since they were not shaped to the breasts but were laced together. The effect must have been like a tight waistcincher that also held the breasts in, since illustrations and literary references indicate that the ideal woman in the last part of the sixteenth and first part of the seventeenth centuries was one with a small waist.

To accentuate the waist further, farthingales were developed. The term comes from the Spanish *verdugos* ("saplings"). They were basically a kind of hooped petticoat, probably originally made from saplings. At the beginning of the sixteenth century, the farthingale was cone shaped by a series of graduated hoops, giving the required shape, but they were bolstered by adding extra padding at the hips to give more rounded shape. Some required enormous amounts of material to complete and as much as 50 yards of whalebone and buckram to construct. The Venetian ambassador to the court of France described the French women in 1577 as having

> inconceivably narrow waists: they swell out their gowns which increases the elegance of their figures. Over the chemise they wear a corset or bodice, that they call a *'corps pique'* which makes their shape delicate and more slender. It is fastened behind which helps to show off the form of the bust.[109]

By the seventeenth century, the French-type farthingale had replaced the Spanish. The hooped petticoat remained tub shaped, but it was stretched out from the sides by means of a thick bolsterlike bustle commonly known as a "bum roll," a sort of donut open at one end and tied around the waist. Anne, the wife of King James I, wore one so expansive that she was 4 feet wide at the hips.[110] In male costumes similar exaggeration took place. The point of the shoe was extended until sometimes the shoe was two or three times the length of the foot. Shoulders and the upper part of the sleeve were padded, and the codpiece changed from a practical to an ornamental part of the costume; occasionally stiffening devices were used to imply a permanent erection.

As women donned more clothes, the female nude came in for renewed attention in art. Though there had always been nude figures in medieval art, a new sensuousness appears. Some of this can be seen in the paintings of Alessandro di Botticelli (1445–1510), whose *The Birth of Venus* and *Minerva and the Centaur* were probably commissioned by the Medicis of Florence. According to tradition, Botticelli later fell under the sway of Savonarola's sermons, repented of his pagan pictures, and gave up painting altogether. Since he continued to paint after the death of Savonarola, the validity of both statements has been questioned, but the subject matter of his painting became increasingly mystical.

Raphael (1483–1520) also painted several nudes, using both Biblical and classical themes as an excuse for eroticism. Some of his figures, such as his *Leda and the Swan,* are really very sexual, highlighting the sensuousness of the female form, but others are more chaste. Entering into the spirit, most artists of the sixteenth century painted female nudes, giving a renewed interest in the female form. Some paintings included specifically sexual scenes, most notably those by Giulio Romano (1499–1546), a former pupil and later assistant to Raphael. Romano undertook to portray 16 different postures of coitus, in a series he called *Posizione,* completed in 1524; he then turned to the new technique of engraving to have copies made. Probably other artists of the time made drawings for their own edification, but Romano seems to have been the first to attempt to distribute his efforts on such a scale. Within a few days of publication of the prints in Rome, notice was taken by Pope Clement VII, who was shocked that such pictures would be published in Rome and painted by an artist often employed by the Church. Vasari wrote that the pictures dealt with the various "attitudes and postures in which lewd men have intercourse with lewd women." The engraver Marcantonio Raimondi was arrested and Romano himself was in fear of arrest. Both were defended by Pietro Aretino, who at that time was in the good graces of the pope and managed to persuade the pontiff to intervene and release Marcantonio.

Aretino, whose power of flattery or vituperation we have already mentioned, was soon found out himself, since either Romano's pictures had been meant to illustrate some verses of Aretino on the same subject, or else Aretino, hearing of the pictures, had written sonnets to amplify them, including the following, from Sonnet III.

> *Let him who hath it small play sodomite.*
> *But one like mine, both pitiless and proud,*
> *should never leave the female nest of joy.*

His partner replied

> *Ay, but we girls, boy,*
> *so greedy are of what we hold so glad*
> *a thruster that we'd take him whole behind.*[111]

When Aretino's association came out, he had to flee Rome along with Romano and Raimondi. Apparently, Romano's original drawings were seized and destroyed, although some of the engravings survived. One supposedly exists in the *Biblioteca Corsiniana* in Rome. Aretino's verses were preserved and have often been published. Aretino continued to be interested in erotic portrayals, his most famous being his *Dialogues*. Some see the *Dialogues* as an account of what men and women do to and with each other in the pursuit of their pleasure, but others have seen the work as an anguished cry of a stifled moralist and preacher who uses the image of mercenary love to express his deepest feelings about the greed and bestiality of his times. One of Aretino's recent translators concluded that neither view was particularly accurate.

If anything, simply the tone of his work as a whole, which, being plebian, is per force crude and frank. As for pleasure, enjoyment? These things Aretino hardly ever associated with sex; on the contrary, when feelings of tenderness or peace manage to steal onto the scene—in the interludes that suddenly, inexplicably crop up between the bouts of raging invective and scorn—they are most often produced or evoked by some conscious piece of artistry or fabrication, such as a musical concert, a dancer's performance, a beautiful dinner table set by two devoted nuns, a hermitage built by an eccentric monk. Aretino is much too conscious an opponent of the reigning Humanist conception of Platonic love promulgated by the philosophers and the poet Petrarch to allow his sexual partners even a modicum of tenderness and affection . . . (the work) is a satire . . . Aretino is an improviser of genius, but still only an improviser. Out of this genius comes a verbal exuberance, a talent for malign observation, a gift for piling up sarcastic details—an innocence of eye and spirit, so improbably conjoined with sophistication and cynicism, that produces the astonishing profusion which . . . typifies satire in one of its most characteristic moods.[112]

As the reformers increased their attack on the Church, there was a reaction to open sexuality both in literature and in art. In literature the result was the *Index,* technically the *Index of Prohibited Books,* officially established by the Council of Trent in 1562, although the germ of such a list had been adopted earlier. A list of books was drawn up and published under the direction of a commission established by Pope Paul IV in 1564. Though most of the condemned books dealt with theology, also listed were obscene books, books written by heretics, and books on witchcraft and necromancy. To keep the *Index* up to date, a special Congregation of the Index was established that lasted until the twentieth century. Among authors included on the *Index* were Boccaccio, whose *Decameron* was listed, not for its indecency, but for its satire of ecclesiastics. An expurgated version was allowed that changed most of the clerics into laymen. Also banned were the *Gargantua and Pantagruel* of Rabelais. The eventual effect was to drive much of the pornography underground.

Another result of the new morality evidenced in the sixteenth century were the so-called breeches makers. First to fall to the new view of sexuality was Michelangelo, whose paintings on the ceiling of the Sistine Chapel were called obscene by Aretino, apparently in an attempt to blackmail Michelangelo for his alleged homosexual activities. When Michelangelo had ignored Aretino's efforts at blackmail, Aretino attacked the painting in the Sistine Chapel for its obscenity. The charges were ignored until 1555, when Paul IV mounted the papal throne; the new pope, convinced of the obscenity of the paintings, ordered them to be removed from the chapel, in effect destroying them, since they were frescoes. When his decision leaked out, a storm of protest arose, and though he retracted his decision to remove the paintings, he ordered clothes to be put on the heavenly hosts in *The Last Judgment,* on the Virgin Mary and the angels surrounding her, and on all other figures. A pupil of Michelangelo, Daniele Volterra (1509–1566) was commissioned to clothe the figures. Other painters made fun of him by nicknaming him *Il Braghettone,* the Breeches Maker. The reaction was not confined to the papacy. Michelangelo's picture *Leda and the Swan,* which he had painted for the Duke of Ferrara, was burned by the French, who had been charged with its safekeeping. Others also had to clothe their pictures or put fig leaves on their statues, but the period of reaction was comparatively short, and throughout much of Europe nudes could still be painted and were painted. Only in Spain was the nude more or less perpetually banned.[113]

The new prudery indicated by the antinudity campaign was marked by a number of contradictions; one of the most obvious was the continued use of female impersonators on the stage. Though drama took on new luster in the sixteenth century, men continued to play the heroines. Actors were formed into companies, each under the patronage of a wealthy member of the aristocracy, and younger boys were apprenticed to leading actors from whom they learned their art. Many would start out playing female roles as well as smaller male parts. Some became quite famous for their impersonations.[114]

Though it might seem difficult for some to imagine males playing female roles in some of Shakespeare's plays, this was the custom, and the playwrights adjusted to it. It might well be that some of the female roles were written more masculine than they might otherwise have been. The modern drama critic Kenneth Tynan has suggested, for example, that Lady Macbeth was basically a man's role and that it would be a mistake a cast a woman in the role. This might well be an example of male chauvinism, which denies that women could be or should be as dominating a personality as Lady Macbeth, but it might also be Shakespeare's own way of coping with the customs of his day. We know the names of some of the men and boys who played the Shakespearean roles. The first Ophelia is thought to have been Nathaniel Field; the first Desdemona, the famous Richard or "Dickie" Robinson. Lady Macbeth was probably originally played by Alexander Cooke, and the ambitious role of Rosalind was played by Willie Ostler. Robert Gough or Goffe was the first Juliet and possibly the first Cleopatra. Perhaps the difficulty boys and men had in impersonating women in their early 20's and 30's was a major reason that Shakespeare's female roles were written either for older women or young girls. The French included actresses in their dramas somewhat earlier than the English, and when a French troop with women actresses ventured onto the English stage in 1632, the women were jeered and pelted with apples. Only in the last part of the seventeenth century did female actresses make their appearance in England. Women were banned on the stage at Rome to the end of the eighteenth century.

If the use of males as actresses allowed an out for the would-be transvestites, in spite of prohibitions against cross-dressing, an even more flagrant contradiction of Christian morality was the use of *castrati,* eunuchs deliberately castrated to preserve their singing voices. In spite of Church prohibitions against castration, the Church itself used the *castrati* in choirs. This was because the Catholic Church held that women were not to sing in churches, and when high voices were required, boys, falsettists, and eunuchs were employed. When opera appeared as a new musical form at the end of the fifteenth century, the demand for eunuchs to portray females increased. This placed the Church officials in a rather uncomfortable position, because, though they prohibited castration, they also discouraged the appearance of women on the stage and as singers in the church. The obvious alternative was the use of *castrati.* Some popes spoke against the *castrati,* but they did not quite come out and forbid their use. Though everyone connected with the operation of castration was subject to excommunication, once a person was castrated, no punishment was imposed on him. Since the financial rewards were very great if a poor boy had a good voice, his family might well have him castrated. Unfortunately, not all those castrated proved to have good voices as they matured. One contemporary remarked that the

> cruel operation is but too frequently performed without trial, or at least without sufficient proofs of an improvable voice; otherwise such numbers could never be found in every great town throughout Italy, without any voice at all, or at least without one sufficient to compensate such a loss.[115]

Obviously, any male with transsexual tendencies was probably able to satisfy his need by castration and was able to adopt a woman's life, at least on stage, if not sometimes off stage. Once again, prohibitions about sexual activities turned out to be relative and not the absolutes they sometimes seem.

Though the influence of venereal disease on sixteenth-century sexual mores is not fully understood, one documented result of the fears of venereal disease was an attempt to design or uncover ways of giving protection. One such invention was the condom, the first published description of which is in the works of the great Italian anatomist Gabriele Falloppio (1523–1562), whose name is most closely associated with the description of the fallopian tubes. In his work on venereal disease, *De morbo Gallico*, first published in 1564, some 2 years after his death, Falloppio described a linen sheath cut to shape and designed to fit over the glans and claimed to have invented it.

In his chapter dealing with ways of preventing the spread of the so-called French disease, Falloppio stated:

> As often as a man has intercourse, he should (if possible) wash the genitals, or wipe them with a cloth; afterward he should use a small linen cloth made to fit the glans, and draw forward the prepuce over the glans; if he can do so, it is well to moisten it with saliva or with a lotion. However, it does not matter; if you fear lest caries (syphilis) be produced (in the midst of) the canal, take the sheath of linen cloth and place it in the canal; I tried the experiment on eleven hundred men, and I call immortal God to witness that not one of them was infected.[116]

Whether Falloppio invented the condom is debatable. Several scholars have believed that the condom originated in the medieval slaughterhouses, where membranes of animals were used to form sheaths for the penis, probably more for prophylactic purposes than as a contraceptive. Even the name *condom* is a matter of controversy. According to legend, the term was named after a certain Dr. Condom or Conton, a physician at the court of Charles II (reigned 1660–1685). A variant version has it that he was a physician living at the time but not attached to the court. Still another version declares that Charles II, unhappy over the growing number of his illegitimate children, turned to Dr. Condom for advice, and the result was the condom, for which the good doctor was knighted. Others have claimed that Condom was not a physician but a mere courtier of Charles II, but unfortunately for historical accuracy, so far no Dr. Condom who was active in the court of Charles II has been identified.[117] One of the earliest printed uses of the term is spelled cundum. This is *A Panegyric upon Cundum* attributed to John Wilmot, Earl of Rochester (1647–1680),[118] a work I have not been able to examine. If this is the case, then the work would seem to be derived from the term *cunnus,* the Latin term for the female pudenda, and *dum* or *dumb,* a term that can imply an inability to function. In military terms a cundum was a false scabbard worn over a sword or the oil skin case for holding the colors of a regiment, and this might also indicate its derivation. The first medical work to use the term *condom* is a work on syphilis by Daniel Turner in 1717.[119]

Whereas some of the writings about prophylactics were fairly open, discussion of female homosexuality was not. Though there are a number of possible references to lesbianism, all are ambiguous. One of the earliest appears in the *Orlando furioso* of Ariosto (1474–1533). Orlando is the Italian name of Roland, the mythical Carolingian hero who made his first appearance in the medieval poem *Chanson de Roland*. Women had played no part in the original poem, but they do in Ariosto's version. One of the leading feminine figures is Bradamante, a young Amazon whose exploits equaled if they did not excel those of the male knights. In Canto 25, Ariosto tells how Bradamante, suffering from a head wound, is shorn of her hair and thereafter is mistaken for her twin brother. Sleeping one day in the forest, she is passionately kissed by a young Spanish princess. Immediately Bradamante confesses her true sex, but the princess ignores this and takes her home, showering her with gifts and women's clothes, lamenting that she should be cursed with love for a woman. Bradamante herself is not so afflicted. When the women go to bed

> One sleeps, one moans and weeps in piteous plight
> Because her wild desire more fiercely glows.
> And on her wearied lids should slumber light,
> All is deceitful that brief dreaming shows:
> To her it seems as if relenting heaven
> A better sex to Bradamante has given.[120]

Upon awakening, Bradamante departs, and when she gets home, she tells her twin brother of her adventures, and he, recognizing in the princess a beauty he had long admired, makes off in secret in his sister's knightly clothes and visits the Spanish castle in her place. The princess welcomes him with rapture, supplies him with women's dress, and only at night discovers his sex, which the boy, still posing as his sister, attributes to a timely bit of magic. The two live together for several weeks before the truth is learned by anyone else. Whether this can be regarded as a lesbian tale is questionable, but at least one of the participants is depicted as regarding it as such.

A slightly different version of a similar story appears in Sir Philip Sidney's *Arcadia*, published in 1590. Here the hero masquerades as an Amazon to gain access to a princess whose family is living in pastoral seclusion for political reasons. He is more successful than he had anticipated, because the heroine's father conceives a passion for what he believes to be a young woman. His wife is not deceived but holds her peace, since she is also smitten by the handsome stranger, and both work to prevent the hero from revealing his secret to his true love. The girl herself, however, realizing the passion Zelmane, the "Amazon," has for her, worries about her own willingness to respond. Eventually, her agony over her homosexual love is ended by the discovery that Zelmane is really a male.[121] There is another scene in the *Arcadia* wherein the princess and her sister retire to bed together, both aching with unrequited love, and some have regarded this as an instance of lesbianism, perhaps the first in English literature. But Jeanette Foster, in her study of female homosexuality, felt that it was an exaggeration to view this scene as actual lesbian love. At most, what we have is picture of the anxieties the princess went through when she thought her love was lesbian, and in her mind the sisterly affection some-times looked upon as lesbianism was only a chaste consolation.[122] Stories of im-personation with the attendant difficulties appear in several other writers of this time, but the love that seems to be lesbian always turns out to be heterosexual in the end.[123] Shakespeare included several incidents of mas-querading in his plays, but only in one case (Rosalind in *As You Like It*) does it become very involved. One recent commentator on Shakespeare has said that Rosalind's sexual experience anticipated the vagaries of our own age closely, and her capacity for bisexuality seemed to "impress" Shakespeare.[124] Yet, ulti-mately, she achieves a proper heterosexual attachment, and nothing comes of the incipient lesbianism. The other major case of sex impersonation is that of Viola in *Twelfth Night,* but Viola is never a particularly convincing male.

The tolerance shown toward incipient lesbian attachments, perhaps an effec-tive indicator of the male belief that what women could do by themselves did not amount to much, did not exist with regard to male homosexuality. Here, though references to the subject are much more frequent, they are only hu-morously treated when the situation is ambiguous. In English literature, one of the most open expressions of a homosexual theme is by Christopher Marlowe (1564–1593) in his poem *Hero and Leander.* Marlowe also uses a homosexual theme in this play *Edward the Second,* as well as in his *Dido.* The fragments of his play about Henry III of France, *The Massacre at Paris,* also carry strong overtones of homosexuality. Obviously, Marlowe seems to have been attracted by homosexual themes, and some have said that Marlowe himself was a ho-mosexual, although the only concrete evidence for this derives from testimony after his death given by Richard Baines, a government informer who also ac-cused him of atheism and blasphemy and hinted at his treason—in effect heresy, treason, and sexual deviance remained the standard grouping of libels associated with scapegoating.[125]

Part of the accusation against Marlowe might well have been due to his association with the theater, which in the eyes of many Englishmen, particu-larly in the seventeenth century, was regarded as the center of immorality. For a time all theaters were closed, and actors and their patrons were lambasted for sodomy and other immoral conduct, a charge probably encouraged by the use of female impersonators. Even Shakespeare has been labeled a homosexual, usually on the basis of his *Sonnets,* although also because of his general associa-tion with the theater. Evidence for any such belief is at best dubious.[126]

Several other writers wrote seriously about Platonic friendship, many inves-tigators having found it easy to read homosexual connotations into such writ-ings. The French writer Michel de Montaigne (1533–1592) thought perfect sympathy between men brings the greatest happiness,[127] but this does not necessarily make him homosexual. The only support for such a beleif is his close friendship with Estienne de la Boëtie. There is much less doubt about

Francis Bacon (1561–1626), who also wrote an essay on friendship and in his utopian society of *New Atlantis* made his society as asexual as possible. Bacon was called a pederast by John Aubrey, whose *Brief Lives* is usually reliable. Aubrey wrote:

> His Ganimeds and Favourites tooke Bribes; but his Lordship (Bacon) always gave Judgment *secundum aequum et bonum* (according as was just and good). His Decrees in Chancery stand firme, i.e., there are fewer of his Decrees reverst than of any other Chancellor.[128]

A letter from Bacon's mother has survived in which she accused him of keeping his male servants as his lovers. Apparently also there was a brief period when it seemed possible that Bacon would be brought to trial for his sexual activities, but this powerful patrons, particularly the homosexual King James I, saved him. Bacon's public life was always circumspect. The only hint of homosexuality in his writings appears in his essay on friendship and in a second essay on beauty where male beauty is praised.[129]

Also clearly homosexual was Nicholas Udall, known for his *Ralph Roister Doister,* the earliest extant English comedy. Udall had been headmaster of Eton from 1534 to 1541, where he gained a reputation for inflicting corporal punishment. In 1541 he was accused of committing an "unnatural crime" with two students and a servant, confessed his crime to the Privy Council, and wrote them a letter of repentance in which he promised to reform. Though he lost his post at Eton and was briefly imprisoned, he eventually ended up as headmaster at another school, Westminster.[130] Obviously, if individuals had powerful patrons, the English penalties against homosexuality were not usually enforced. This is also evidence in the case of Richard Barnfield (1574–1627), whose first poetic work, *The Affectionate Shephard,* published in 1574, was addressed to a youth to whom the poet declared:

> *If it be sin to love a lovely lad,*
> *O then sin I.*

Even the *Dictionary of National Biography,* not usually known for candor about the sexual lives of its subjects, included the statement: "All his best early pieces," but most particularly "his sonnets, are dedicated to a sentiment of friendship so exaggerated as to remove them beyond all wholesome sympathy."[131] *The Affectionate Shepherd* has been called the most "blatantly homosexual poem" published in English during the period.[132] Later in his life he retired to his estate, married, and reared a family, and so it appears that even the most amorous of homosexuals often conformed to the customs of the day.

Several figures prominent in literature and the arts in France were also charged with homosexuality. Perhaps the most prominent was Theodore de Bèze, but his homosexuality is most doubtful. The charge derives from the fact that de Bèze published a book of poems entitled *Juvenilia* in 1548. Among the poems is one describing his affection for his friend Audebert and a woman, Candide. He called both of them his *mignons,* saying he loved each dearly, but if he had to choose, he would take Audebert. Probably the poem is only another example of neo-platonic convention praising deep soul companionship, but in the same year that he published his poems, de Bèze underwent conversion and became a leader of the Protestant cause in France. He later succeeded Calvin as the religious leader of Geneva. Catholic polemicists used the verses of de Bèze to claim that he had followed Calvin because he could substitute a spiritual male for a carnal one and still remain a sodomite at heart. After his conversion, de Bèze married and lived a most conventional and respected life. On the evidence it would seem that the charge of homosexuality was used to discredit de Bèze, to equate heresy with sexual deviation. Nevertheless, he has been claimed as one of the great homosexuals.[133]

Similar charges of homosexuality were made against Marc Antoine Muret, a contemporary of de Bèze, who in 1553 was arrested and imprisoned at Chatelet on a charge of sodomy. When he was released after intervention of friends, he went to Toulouse, where again he was accused of sodomy and of being a Protestant as well. He fled, was tried *in absentia,* found guilty, and burned in effigy. Again in 1558, this time in Padua, he was charged with sodomy; he fled to Venice, where he faced the same charge. Soon after, he came under the protection of Cardinal d'Este, prominent in the Catholic hierarchy in Rome and France, and with such patronage he returned to France and spent the rest of his life there, becoming, if he had not been before, a person of eminent respectability. Though his letters reveal evidence of strong emotional friendships with men, they also contain harsh disapproval of homosexuality; in his youth he also wrote erotic poems to women.[134] Though some of the charges might have been political, there might have been some basis for them. Only later in life, with the backing of a powerful patron and through the exercise of considerable caution, did Muret's reputation became rehabilitated. Individuals with homosexual leanings, who lacked powerful patrons, had to be *cautious.* Giving proof to the dangers of too careless an avowal of homosexuality is the case of the Flemish sculptor Jerome Duquesnoy, brother of François Duquesnoy, who made the famous statue *Mannekin pis* in Brussels. Jerome was burned in 1654 for allegedly seducing into sodomy two acolytes who had modeled for him.[135]

Even kings and powerful nobles had to be somewhat cautious in expressing their sexual preferences, for fear of reaction. This is best indicated by the case of Henry III of France and James I of England. Henry III (1551–1589) was, without doubt, the most notorious royal homosexual. Though for a brief period in his adolescence he gained a reputation as a woman chaser, by the time he had reached his 20's, his interests had shifted to males. He liked to dress up in women's clothes, and in many ways his is a first-class royal example of the classical drag queen. He had a series of homosexual favorites, whose names and descriptions have survived. A diarist in his court, Pierre de L'Estoile, wrote in 1576:

> At this time the word *mignons* began to be heard in the mouths of the people, to whom they were quite odious, as much for their ways, which were waggish and haughty, as for their effeminate and indecent paint and apparel, but especially for the king's boundless gifts and generosity to them, which the people thought were the cause of their ruin, even though the truth was that such gifts could not stay in their savings for one moment, and were immediately transmitted to the people as is water in a pipe.

> These pretty *mignons* wore their hair pomaded, artificially curled and recurled, flowing back over their little velvet bonnets, like those of whores in a bordello, and the ruffs of their starched linen shirts were a half foot long, so that seeing their heads above their ruffs was like seeing Saint John's head upon a platter. The rest of their clothes were made the same way. Their exercises were playing, blaspheming, jumping, dancing, fencing, fighting and whoring and following their king everywhere.[136]

During this time France was involved in religious struggles between the Catholics and the Huguenots, and when it became apparent that Henry was not going to have any heirs, the struggle exploded into the so-called War of the Three Henrys (1585–1589), which ended with the murder of the king and victory for the Protestant Henry of Navarre, who renounced his religion to become Henry IV. During much of the crisis Henry III appeared at parties and tourneys dressed as an Amazon or wearing a ball gown, makeup, earrings, and extravagant jewelry, attended by groups of boys and men whose behavior outraged an already contemptuous public. Protestants publicized the king's behavior, and it so infuriated the Catholics that they, led by Henry of Guise, the third Henry in the war, attempted to replace the king. Henry of Guise was murdered by the king's agents. One of the most devastating portraits of the court was given by the Huguenot poet Agrippa d'Aubigné in his work *The Princes*. He accused the royal family of being false to nature, false to their country, and false to Christianity, using charges of sexual deviation to cement his case. He placed the blame for the sexual problems of the French king on Henry's mother Catherine de Medici. Catherine has the unique distinction of having three sons sit on the French throne—Francis II, Charles IX, and Henry III. All died without begetting an heir. D'Aubigné accused Catherine of encouraging her children to be depraved and feminized so that she could rule

France in her own right.[137] Though scholars now disagree with such a portrait of Catherine, it seems clear that Henry III was a deeply troubled person, that he was also homosexual, and that this fact added to his political difficulties.

Another ruler with homoerotic tendencies was James VI of Scotland, who became James I, king of England in 1603. His homosexual activity was, however, much more discreet, and though it gave him some troubled moments, he proved to be an effective king. He was also able to meet the essential requirement of a king, producing a male heir. Among his lovers was Robert Carr, whom he advanced from being a page to Earl of Somerset. Once he had achieved this rank, Carr married, much to the king's chagrin. Somerset was later arrested on orders of the weeping king, but eventually he was pardoned. Carr was succeeded in his position by George Villiers, who was eventually made Marquess of Buckingham and became one of the richest noblemen in England. Buckingham was executed after the death of James, but James' willingness to support some of Buckingham's scatter-brained schemes caused him considerable political difficulty.[138]

In summing up the period, it would seem that, though Europeans briefly began to question old concepts about sexuality, there was little change in the long run. For a time, it was permissible to speak of bisexuality, of even a lover of the same sex, but for males to put words into action was dangerous. Females did not yet speak of such activities themselves, but when males looked at lesbianism, they did so with a condescending eye. Several important figures were associated, either properly or improperly, with various forms of variant sexual behavior, but few were particularly open, and those who were, suffered. This was true even of a king such as Henry III, a rather emotionally troubled individual whose homosexuality probably compounded his difficulties. King James I was far more cautious, but he also faced difficulties with a rising tide of Puritanism, which eventually resulted in the execution of his son and successor. Neither Protestanism nor Catholicism departed from the standard Western hostility to nonprocreative sexuality, although the Protestants were somewhat more radical in their denial of the virtue of celibacy and insistence on the importance of marriage. Increasingly also, the state regulated sexual expression, encouraged by the attitudes of Protestants and by a rising nationalism. The effect was to change a sin into a crime, and though successful prosecutions were not particularly numerous, many people were accused and many more threatened. Probably contributing to the continuing hostility to sex was the epidemic of syphilis that hit Europe in the sixteenth century. Protestantism took a forward step in putting less stress on celibacy and emphasizing the importance of marital intercourse, but its thrust, like that of Catholicism, was toward reaffirming procreative sex. In short, Europe, after some hesitant steps toward a relaxation of sexual mores, officially reaffirmed its traditional attitudes.

NOTES

1. Giorgio Vasari, *Lives of the Painters, Sculptors and Architects* (London: J. M. Dent & Sons Ltd., n.d.), III, 116. See also Nesca A. Robb, *Neoplatonism of the Italian Renaissance* (London: George Allen & Unwin, 1935).

2. Pompeo Molmenti, *Venice, Its Individual Growth from the Earliest Beginnings to the Fall of the Republic,* translated by Horatio F. Brown, Part 2 (Chicago: A. C. McClurg & Company, 1907), p. 218.

3. John Addington Symonds, *The Renaissance in Italy* (*reprinted,* New York: Modern Library, 1935, 2 vols.), Vol. 2, p. 174.

4. Jacob Burckhardt, *The Civilization of the Renaissance in Italy* (*reprinted,* New York: Modern Library, 1954), p. 320.

5. Baldesar Castiglione, *The Book of the Courtier,* translated by Leonard Eckstin Opdycke (New York: Scribner's, 1903), IV, liii.

6. *Ibid.,* IV, lxiii–lxiv.

7. See Nicholas James Perella, *The Kiss Sacred and Profane* (Berkeley and Los Angeles: University of California Press, 1969), pp. 158–188.

8. Marsilio Ficino, *Sopra lo amore o veri convito di Platone* (Florence, 1544), p. 182. There is a copy of this in the British Museum. A translation of the pertinent passage can be found in John Charles Nelson, *Renaissance Theory of Love* (New York: Columbia University Press, 1958), pp. 70–71. Professor Nelson has a much fuller discussion of the whole topic, and the interested reader should consult his work.

9. Flaminio Nobili, *Il trattato dell'amore humano* (Lucca, Italy: 1567; republished, Rome: 1895) p. 16 v, and translated in Nelson, *op. cit.,* p. 71. There is a copy in the British Museum.

10. Nelson, *op. cit.,* p. 72.

11. Ficino, *op. cit.,* passim.

12. Pietro Bembo, *Gli asolani e le rime* (Venice: 1505). There are several copies in the British Museum. There is an English translation by Rudolf B. Gottfried (Bloomington, Ind.: Indiana University Press).

13. Flaminio Nobili, *op. cit.,* p. 16, translated in Nelson *op. cit.,* p. 72.

14. See Noel Garde, *Jonathan to Gide* (New York: Vantage Press, 1964).

15. See the records in the *Archivio de Stato* of Florence, *Ufficiali di notte,* 1432–1502.

16. See *Leggi e memorie Venete sulla prostituzione,* Conte di Orford, ed. (Venice: 1870–1872).

17. Antonio Vallentine, *Leonardo da Vinci* (New York: Viking, 1953).

18. Leonardo da Vinci, *The Literary Works,* compiled by Jean Paul Richter, ed. (London: Phaidon Press, 1970), vol. 2, p. 342.

19. Vallentine, *op. cit.,* p. 39.

20. Sigmund Freud, *Leonardo da Vinci and a Memory of His Childhood* (New York: W. W. Norton, 1964), pp. 21, 27.

21. See William Harrison Woodward, *Studies in Education during the Age of the Renaissance 1400–1600* (Cambridge, England: University Press, 1906); and Woodward, *Vittorino da Feltre and Other Humanists* (Cambridge, England: University Press, 1905).

22. See James Cleugh, *The Divine Aretino* (New York: Stein and Day, 1966).

23. See Pietro Aretino, *Letters of Pietro Aretino,* translated by Thomas Caldecott Chubb, (Hamden, Conn.: The Shoe-String press, 1967), p. 224.

24. See Magnus Hirschfeld, in *Jahrbuch für sexuelle Zwischenstufen,* IX (1909), pp. 73–165.

25. John Addington Symonds, *The Life of Michelangelo Buonarroti* (London: John C. Nimmo, 1893, 2 vols.), Vol. 1, p. 164.

26. See the article by Numa Praetorius in *Jahrbuch für sexuelle Zwischenstufen,* I, pp. 118–119; and Symonds, *op. cit.,* p. 160. Numa Praetorius was one of the pseudonyms used by Hirschfeld.

27. *Ibid.,* pp. 136–137. See also Michelangelo, *The Complete Poems of Michelangelo* (New York: Noonday Press, 1960), pp. 39, 91, and passim. For a discussion of the issue of homosexuality by his early biographers, see Francis Haskel, "Michelangelo and some of this Biographers," *Times Literary Supplement,* No. 3,828 (25 July, 1975) pp. 842–843.

29. Magnus Hirschfeld, *op. cit.,* pp. 94–95.

30. See Magnus Hirschfeld, *Die Homosexualität des Mannes und des Weibes* (Berlin: Louis Marcus, 1925), p. 660. I have been unable to locate della Casa's book and believe it probably never existed. He did write a poem *Il capitolo del forno* metaphorically describing the sex act as similar to baking bread in an oven, and this included some stanzas referring to pederasty. It is believed these were seized upon by Protestant writers for attacks on the Church. See Gilles Ménage, *Anti-Baillet ou critique du livre de M. Baillet,* . . . (The Hague: Estienne Foulque et Louis van Dole, 1688), vol 2, pp. 88–153. See also J. Z. Eglinton, *Greek Love* (New York: Oliver Layton Press, 1964), pp. 469–470, n. 265.

31. The references to Pope Julius III are cited in Pisanus Fraxi, *Index librorum prohibitorum* (*Bibliography of Prohibited Books*), (republished, London: Jack Brussel, 1962), p. xxxiii (introduction), n. 42. See also Hirschfeld, *Die Homosexualität,* p. 665.

32. Jeffrey Burton Russell, *Witchcraft in the Middle Ages* (Ithaca, N.Y.: Cornell University Press, 1972), pp. 227–229.

33. For the sources, see Joseph Hansen, *Quellen und Unterrushungen zur Geschichte des Hexenwahns und Hexenverfolgung im Mittelalter* (Bonn: 1901, reprinted, Ulm, Hildesheim, Germany: 1963), pp. 24–30; and Hansen, *Zauberwahn, Inquisition, und Hexenprozess im Mittelalter und die Entstehung der grossen Hexenverfolgung* (Munich: R. Oldenbourgh, 1900), pp. 467–475; Henry C. Lea, *Materials toward a History of Witchcraft,* Arthur Howland, ed. (reprinted, New York: Thomas Yoseloff, 1957, 3 vols.), pp. 304–305. A translation of the bull appears in the introduction to Henrich Kramer (Institor) and James Sprenger, *The Malleus maleficarum,* translated by Montagu Summers (New York: Dover Publications, 1971).

34. Kramer and Sprenger, *op. cit.,* passim. See also Russell, *op. cit.,* pp. 226–264.

35. *Ibid.,* pp. 219–238.

36. Rossell Hope Robbins, *The Encyclopedia of Witchcraft and Demonology* (New York: Crown, 1959), p. 258.

37. For this and other beliefs, see Lea, *op. cit.,* Vol. 1, p. 152 and passim. He includes an extract from Caesarius.

38. St. Thomas Aquinas, *Summa Theologica* (New York: Benziger Brothers, 1947) I.1, q. 51, 3; 6. See Lea, *op. cit.,* Vol. 1, pp. 155–156. St. Bonaventura and Duns Scotus follow Aquinas on this.

39. Kramer and Sprenger, *op. cit.,* Part 2, Q. 1, Chap. 4, p. 112.

40. *Ibid.,* Part 1, Q. 6, pp. 41–48.

41. For some examples, see Lea, *Materials,* Vol. 1, pp. 162–170.

42. See Robbins, *op. cit.,* pp. 178–180. See also H. R. Trevor Roper, *The European Witch-Craze* (New York: Harper Torchbooks, 1969), pp. 90–192.

43. Robbins, *op. cit.,* p. 463.

44. *Ibid.*, pp. 463–464.

45. *Ibid.*, p. 465.

46. *Ibid.*, P. 316. See also Aldous Huxley, *The Devils of Loudun* (reprinted, New York: Harper, 1959).

47. The subject is somewhat controversial, but probably the best account in English is by Eric John Dingwal, *The Girdle of Chastity* (reprinted, New York: Macauley Co., n.d.). There has been some attempt to find evidence of the introduction of the custom during the crusades, and though this is the legendary tradition of its beginning, there is no hard evidence for such an assumption.

48. For a discussion of it, see Edward Westermarck, *The History of Human Marriage*, 5th ed. New York: Allerton Books, 3 vols.), Vol. 1, pp. 177–179.

49. Hector MacKechnie, in an article on the "Ius primal noctis, "*Judicial Review,* XLIII (1930), pp. 303–311.

50. See Bruce Barrack, "Syphilis and Yaws," *Archives of Dermatology,* LXXIII (1956), pp. 510–515; Folke Henschen, *The History and Geography of Diseases,* translated by Joan Tate (New York: Delacorte Press, 1966), pp. 124–126. The book that has argued most forcibly for the American origin of the disease is that by Iwan Bloch, *Der Ursprung des Syphilis* (Jena, Germany: Verlag von Gustav Fischer, 1901, 2 vols.). The person most associated with argument for the Old World origin of the disease is Karl Sudhoff, whose arguments are summed up in English in "The Origins of Syphilis," in his *Essays in the History of Medicine* (New York: Medical File Press, 1926). See also Charles Dennie, *A History of Syphilis* (Springfield, Ill.: Charles C Thomas, 1962).

51. Ferdinand Columbus, *The Life of Admiral Christopher Columbus by his Son Ferdinand,* translated from the Italian by Benjamin Keen (New Brunswick, N.J.: Rutgers University Press, 1959), pp. 155, 191.

52. Bartolomé de Las Casas, *Historia de las Indias,* A. Millares Carlo, ed., estudio preliminary de Lewis Hanke (Mexico City: Fondo de cultura económica, 1951), Vol. I, and Gonzalo Fernández Oviedo y Valdés, *Natural History of the West Indies,* translated by Sterling A. Stoudemire (Chapel Hill, N.C.: University of North Carolina Press, 1959), xi, xii, pp. 88–90. For a more nearly complete discussion of this, see Alfred Crosby, *The Columbian Exchange: Biological and Cultural Consequences of 1492* (Westport, Conn.: Greenwood Press, 1972), pp. 138–139. See also Theodor Rosebury, *Microbes and Morals: The Strange Story of Venereal Disease* (New York: Viking, 1971), pp. 24–25. Crosby is inclined to credit their testimony, but Rosebury is not.

53. Ruy Diaz de Isla, *Tractado ilamado fructo de todos sanctos contra el mal serpentino* (Seville: 1542), iii.

54. For further discussion, see Richmond C. Holcomb, "Ruiz Diaz de Isla and the Haitian Myth of European Syphilis," *Medical Life,* XLIII (1936), pp. 270–316, 318–364, 415–470, 487–514. From the title it is obvious that Holcomb did not accept Diaz's explanations.

55. For a discussion, see Crosby, *op. cit.,* p. 127.

56. Bloch, *op. cit.,* Vol. 1, pp. 297–305, reported a number of these names.

57. There are several translations of this poem. I have used an anonymous one. Hieronymus Fracastro, *Syphilis* (Saint Louis: The Philmar Company, 1911).

58. Jean Astruc, *De morbus Veneris* (Paris: 1736). Astruc's treatise was in Latin, and there were several translations, including an anonymous one in English entitled *A Treatise of Venereal Diseases in Nine Books,* (London: W. Innys and J. Richardson, C. Davis, J. Clarke, R. Manby, and H. S. Cox, 1754).

59. For transmission of some other diseases, see Crosby, *op. cit.,* passim; and P. M. Ashburn, *The Ranks of Death: A Medical History of the Conquest of America* (New York: Coward-Mc-

Cann, 1947). See also André Siegfried, *Routes of Contagion*, translated by Jean Henderson and Mercedes Clarasó (New York: Harcourt Brace Javanovich, 1965).

60. See Karl Sudhoff, *Der Ursprung der Syphilis* (Leipzig: F. C. W. Vogel, 1913). His collection of tracts was reedited and in part translated by Charles Singer, *The Earliest Printed Literature on Syphilis* (Florence: R. Lier & Company, 1925).

61. Henry E. Sigerist, *A History of Medicine* (New York: Oxford University Press, 1951), Vol. 1, pp. 55–56.

62. See E. H. Hudson, *Non-Venereal Syphilis* (Edinburgh: E & S Livingston, 1958); and E. H. Hudson, *Treponematosis* (New York: Oxford University Press, 1946). He has written numerous articles on the subject.

63. See C. J. Hackett, "On the Origin of the Human Treponematoses," in *Bulletin of the World Health Organization*, XXIX (1963), pp. 7–41. See also Rosebury, *op. cit.*, pp. 67–82.

64. For a brief description of this, see the short biography of Hunter by Henry E. Sigerist, *The Great Doctors*, translated by Eden and Cedar Paul (New York: W. W. Norton, 1933).

65. See Michael de la Dedeyenne, *The Meddlesome Friar* (London: Collins, Collins, 1958).

66. Martin Luther, *Works*, American edition, Jaroslav Pelikan and Helmut Lehmann, eds., and translated by various individuals (Philadelphia and St. Louis, 55 vols.: Muhlenberg and Concordia, 1955–1967), *Letters to Philip Melancthon*, Vol. 48 p. 278. The English edition includes most of the material in the German edition, tracts, letters, and table talk. The standard German edition is *Werke: kritische Gesamtsgabe* (Wiemar: Böhlau, 1883, 58 vols.). In the footnotes the English edition is cited as *Works*, The german as *Werke*.

67. This is from Luther's *Table Talk*, No. 1658, in *Works*, Vol. 54, pp. 160–161.

68. Luther, *Lectures on Titus, Works*, Vol. 29, p. 18.

69. *Ibid.*

70. Luther, *Letter to Hans Luther*, Nov. 21, 1521, in *Works*, Vol. 48, p. 334.

71. Luther, *Treatise on Good Works* in *Works*, Vol. 44, p. 105.

72. See Luther, *Lectures on Romans*, William Pauck, ed. (Philadelphia: Westminster Press, 1961, Vol. 15, Library of Chistian Classics), p. 32.

73. Luther, *Letters of Spiritual Counsel*, Theodore G. Tappert, ed. (Philadelphia: Westminster Press, 1955, Vol. 18, Library of Christian Classics), p. 273.

75. *Ibid.*, p. 274.

76. Luther, *On Monastic Vows, Works*, Vol. 44, p. 391.

77. Luther, *Letters of Spiritual Counsel*, p. 271.

78. Luther, *Table Talk*, No. 1658, in *Works*, Vol. 54, p. 8.

79. Luther, *Lectures on Titus, Works*, Vol. 29, p. 57.

80. Luther, *Letters of Spiritual Counsel*, p. 293. See also *Lectures on Genesis, Works*, Vol. 3, p. 259.

81. *Ibid.*, p. 293. In his tract about brothels published in 1539, he said the earlier Christian practice of allowing brothels as a method of curbing greater sins was no longer justified, since St. Augustine and others who had done so had lived under a pagan regime. Luther, *Werke, Table Talk*, Vol. 5, p. 297.

82. Luther, *Table Talk, Works*, Vol. 54, p. 382.

83. Luther, *Correspondence, Werke*, Vol. 4, p. 140.

84. Luther, *Letters of Spiritual Counsel*, p. 251.

85. Luther, *Lectures on Genesis*, in *Works*, Vol. 3, p. 255.

86.   *Ibid.*, Vol. 3, p. 259.

87.   Luther, *Letter to Nicholas Gerbel,* Nov. 1, 1521, in *Works,* Vol. 48, pp. 321–322.

88.   John Calvin, *Commentaries on the First Epistle to the Corinthians,* VII, 7–8, in *Calvin's Commentaries,* David W. Torrance and Thomas W. Torrance, eds. (Grand Rapids, Mich.: William B. Eerdmans, 1960), Vol. 9, pp. 141–142. See also the *Second Helvetic Confession,* XXIX, in Arthur C. Cochrane, *Reformed Confessions of the Sixteenth Century* (Philadelphia: Westminster Press, 1966), pp. 208–209. He includes several confessions of faith.

89.   John Calvin, *Institutes of the Christian Religion,* Book 2, Chap. 7, p. 42, translated by Henry Beveridge (Grand Rapids, Mich.: William B. Eerdmans, 1962, 2 vols.).

90.   *Ibid.,* IV, xiii, pp. 18–19.

91.   *Ibid.,* II, vii, pp. 42–43.

92.   *Ibid.,* IV, xiii, p. 21.

93.   Calvin, *Commentary on the First Epistle to Corinthians,* VII, 6–8, in *Commentaries,* IV.

94.   *Ibid.,* VII, 5.

95.   Calvin, *Commentaries on the Last Four Books of Moses, Deuteronomy,* XXIV, 5, translated by Charles William Bingham, ed. (reprinted, Grand Rapids, Mich.: William B. Eerdmans, n.d., 3 vols.), Vol. 3, p. 84.

96.   *Ibid., Leviticus,* XX, 18, in Vol. 3, p. 95.

97.   Calvin, *Commentaries on the First Book of Moses Called Genesis,* II, 18, translated by John King, ed (reprinted, Grand Rapids: William B. Eerdmans, 1948, 2 vols.), Vol. 1, pp. 128–130.

98.   *Ibid.,* XVI, 1, in Vol. 1, pp. 422–425.

99.   See Derrick Sherwin Bailey, *Sexual Relation in Christian Thought* (New York: Harper, 1959), pp. 176–177.

100.   Calvin, *Commentaries on . . . Genesis,* XXXVIII, 8–10, in Vol. 2, p. 285. It is worthy of comment that this particular English translation neglects to translate Calvin's commentary completely for fear of offending readers. The interested reader will have to consult the Latin edition.

101.   See Derrick Sherwin Bailey, *Homosexuality and the Western Christian Tradition* (London: Longmans, Green and Company, 1955), p. 5. n. 1.

102.   Calvin, *Commentaries on . . . Four Books of Moses, Leviticus,* XVIII, 1–18, in Vol. 3, pp. 97–106.

103.   See Bailey, *Sexual Relation,* pp. 182–210.

104.   John T. Noonan, *Contraception: A History of Its Treatment by the Catholic Theologians and Canonists* (Cambridge, Mass.: Harvard University Press, 1966), p. 353.

105.   A good brief background of the history can be found in Alex K. Gigeroff, *Sexual Deviations in the Criminal Law* (Toronto: University of Toronto Press for the Clarke Institute of Psychiatry, 1968), pp. 1–7.

106.   Edward Coke, *Institutes of the Laws of England,* Part 3 (reprinted London: E. and R. Brooke, 1797), cap. x, "Of Buggery, or Sodomy," pp. 58–59.

107.   Magnus Hirschfeld, *Die Homosexualität,* pp. 822–823.

108.   *Ibid.,* p. 284.

109.   Quoted in Norah Waugh, *Corsets and Crinolines* (London: B. T. Batsford, 1954), p. 27.

110.   See C. Willett Cunnington and Phyllis Cunnington, *The History of Underclothes* (London: Michael Joseph, 1951), pp. 48–51.

111.   This is the translation by James Cleugh, *op. cit.,* pp. 69–70. Some of the illustrations at-

tributed to Romano can be found in Vol. 2 of Ove Brusendorff & Poul Henningsen, *A History of Eroticism* (New York: Lyle Stuart, 1965). Unfortunately, the source of these illustrations is not identified, and I am inclined to believe that they are not copies of the originals but later French paintings based on the verses of Aretino and not the actual paintings.

112. Aretino, *Dialogues,* translated with an introduction by Raymond Rosenthal (New York: Stein and Day, 1971), pp. 7–8. See also Aretino, *The Works of Aretino,* translated by Samuel Putnam (New York: Covici-Friede, 1926). This is basically a selection of his letters and sonnets and includes several of his more pornographic endeavors.

113. See Kenneth Clark, *The Nude: A Study in Ideal Form,* Vol. 35.2 in the Bollingen Series (Princeton, N.J.: Princeton University Press, 1956).

114. Roger Baker, *Drag: A History of Female Impersonation on the Stage* (London: Triton Books, 1968); and C. J. Bulliet, *Venus Castina: Famous Female Impersonators* (reprinted, New York: Bonanza Books, 1956).

115. See Angus Heriot, *The Castrati in Opera* (London: Secker and Warburg, 1956), pp. 45–46.

116. Gabriele Falloppio, *De morbo Gallico liber absolutismus* (Patavii, 1564), Chap. 89, p. 52. There is a copy in the British Museum.

117. For discussion, see Norman E. Himes, *Medical History of Contraception* (reprinted, New York: Schocken Books, 1970), pp. 189–194.

118. See Eric Partridge, *A Dictionary of Slang and Unconventional English,* 7th ed. (New York: Macmillan, 1970), p. 197.

119. Daniel Turner, *Syphilis, A Practical Dissertation on Venereal Disease* (London: 1717), p. 74. A much more amplified edition was published in 1732.

120. Ludovico Ariosto, *Orlando furioso,* translated by W. S. Rose (reprinted, London: Bell, 1907, 2 vols,) Vol. 2, v. 2–9. There are many other translations.

121. Philip Sidney, *The Countess of Pembroke's Arcadia* (Cambridge, England: University Press, 1912), 174–175.

122. Jeanette Foster, *Sex Variant Women in Literature* (London: Frederick Muller, 1958), p. 38.

123. *Ibid.,* pp. 38–39.

124. Hugh M. Richmond, *Shakespeare's Sexual Comedy* (Indianapolis, Ind.: Bobbs-Merrill, 1971), p. 137.

125. See A. L. Rowse, *Christopher Marlowe* (New York: Harper and Row, 1964); and F. S. Boas, *Christopher Marlowe: A Biographical and Critical Study* (Oxford, England: Clarendon Press, 1940).

126. The subject was much debated with the appearance of some of the works of A. L. Rowse, including *William Shakespeare: A Biography* (New York: Harper and Row, 1963); and Rowse's edition of *Shakespeare's Sonnets* (New York: Harper and Row, 1964), but I think the general scholarly opinion is that he was heterosexual.

127. Michel de Montaigne, *The Essays of Montaigne,* translated by John Florio (reprinted, New York: Modern Library, n.d.), Book 1, Chap. 27.

128. John Aubrey, *Brief Lives,* Oliver Lawson Dick, ed. (Ann Arbor, Mich.: University of Michigan Press, 1957), p. 11.

129. Havelock Ellis, *Sexual Inversion,* in *Studies in the Psychology of Sex* (New York: Random House, 1936, 2 vols.), Vol. 1, Part 4, p. 44–45.

130. See "Nicholas Udall," *Dictionary of National Biography* (London: 1885–1901), Vol. 20, pp. 6–9.

131. See "Richard Barnfield," *DNB*, Vol. 1, pp. 1182–1183. The author of the article was Edmund Gosse, himself a repressed homosexual.

132. Noel Garde, *op. cit.*, pp. 329–330.

133. As does Garde, *ibid.*, pp. 297–298.

134. *Ibid.*, pp. 300–302.

135. *Ibid.*, p. 361.

136. Pierre de L'Estoile, *Journal des choses memorables advenues durant le regne de Henry III*, (originally published in 1621, republished, Paris: Gallimard, 1943), pp. 143, 225. The translation of this passage follows that given by Arno Karlen, *Sexuality and Homosexuality* (New York: W. W. Norton, 1971), p. 110, who has some interesting statements about this period.

137. Agrippa d'Aubigne, *Les tragiques, livre 2, les princes* (Baltimore: Johns Hopkins Press, 1953).

138. See William McElwee, *The Wisest Fool in Christendom* (London: Faber & Faber, 1958), p. 230; David Harris Wilson, *King James VI and I* (New York: Oxford University Press, 1967).

PART FIVE

NEW HORIZONS
AND THE NEW WORLD

16

FROM RELIGION TO SCIENCE

Throughout this study the importance of religion in defining and reinforcing sexual concepts has been stressed. By the end of the seventeenth
century traditional religious influence over sex mores seemed to be declining,
and Europeans began to question traditional sexual attitudes. Just as it seemed
that the new sexuality would undermine the Western hostility to sex, science
came up with new justifications for sexual repression. These ideas appeared
first in the medical literature at the beginning of the eighteenth century but
gradually became elaborated and more formalized, until by the end of the
century they began percolating into the general consciousness. Eventually, they
were seized upon by the conservative moralists and became the dominant theme
of the nineteenth century, providing the intellectual basis for what we regard as
Victorian morality, which tended to drive sex underground, where it remained
until well into the twentieth century.

The changes in outlooks can be viewed best in England, and this chapter
concentrates on that country but includes substantiation from other areas of
Europe. At the beginning of the seventeenth century most intellectual discussion was still dominated by religion, and though men and women thought
about all aspects of life, their conceptions were likely to be formulated in traditional religious terms. In England, much of the religious discussion centered
around Puritanism, a movement that had grown up during the last part of the

reign of Queen Elizabeth and that made a particularly strong appeal to those
who felt that the Elizabethan religious settlement remained far too Catholic in
tone. In simple terms, the Puritans felt that the English Church (what Americans sometimes call the Episcopal Church) had not been sufficiently purified of
"heathenish" Catholic practices, even though it no longer required clerical celibacy and had denied the supremacy of the pope. Since they wanted to purify
the Church further, these individuals came to be called Puritans. Puritanism
was, however, more than an attempt to modify the English Church; it was a
way of life and a philosophic system derived in large part from the teachings of
John Calvin.

Calvin's sexual views have already been examined; as to clerical celibacy and
the powers of the state over morals, Calvin was in general agreement with the
other Protestant reformers. Calvin went further, however, than most would-be
reformers in his attempt to provide a logical and systematic world view. His *Institutes* did for Protestantism what St. Thomas Aquinas had done for Catholicism in the thirteenth century; that is, it established a logical system of belief—
a Protestant dogmatics. Calvin's general system had great influence on sexual
morality, more so than his actual ideas about sex.

Calvin believed that man had been sinless and immortal in his pristine state,
a condition that changed drastically after expulsion from the Garden of Eden.
This expulsion, the so-called Fall of Man, had made men and women so totally
depraved that their only hope of salvation lay in the grace of God, Who had
created them in His own image. Not all individuals would, however, be saved,
God having predetermined those who would and would not. Those God had
marked for salvation were the elect, the new Israelites, so called because God
had earlier chosen the ancient Israelites as his people. But after the advent of
Christianity God no longer selected whole nations or peoples to be saved, only
individuals. Calvin was uncertain about who had been elected by God for salvation, but he believed that those so designated could realize their own elect
status and would act accordingly. A necessary corollary was the assumption
that the chosen would do the right things in life, since the spiritual part of man,
his soul, could and ought to control the fleshy component, the body, which
tended to do wrong things. In simple terms, Calvin, with modifications, held
the concepts of Greek dualism. Inevitably, the damned would do ethically
wrong things. Thus, the new Israelites could best be identified by their
profession of faith, their upright life, and their participation in the sacrament.
For the truly saved, however, it was simply not enough to be saved; it was
essential that the chosen people establish a theocracy, a holy community in
which every member would make the glory of God his sole concern. Calvin
found his opportunity to establish such a community in Geneva.

The underlying principle of the community of the elect was Calvin's belief
that God's plan for salvation had been set forth in the Bible, whose every

phrase and sentence was infallible. Unfortunately, much of the Bible remained obscure to the uninitiated, and so Scripture and the meaning of God's plan could best be interpreted by ministers appointed by the congregation of the faithful; final authority rested in their hands, provided they were guided by the Holy Spirit. When Calvin began to transform Geneva into the theocracy he envisioned, he insisted that taverns be abolished (but not alcoholic beverages); that the Sabbath be kept inviolate; that cardplaying, dancing, and the theater be prohibited; and that all opponents of God's plan either conform or be removed. The thoroughness of his attempted reforms caused so much unrest that in 1539 he was expelled from the city, but when he was recalled in 1541, he was given a free hand. Most of his opponents went into exile, and those who remained were largely excluded from the affairs of the Church and the city. Calvin soon ruled Geneva almost as if he were an absolute monarch, although he was always careful to point out that his authority lay in the support of the believers. Perhaps one reason for the lack of overt opposition was that his power was cemented by threat of execution. In the 4-year period between 1542 and 1546 some 48 persons were executed, 34 of them for witchcraft. After this period the number of executions declined rapidly, since those who did not conform left the city. In spite of this, Geneva, gained population, the exiles being replaced by others seeking refuge from persecution in England, France, Italy, Spain, the Low Countries, and elsewhere. The result was a community whose dedication to the Christian Gospel as visualized by Calvin spread the fame of Calvin and Calvinism throughout Christendom and led to many imitators. Though the model commonwealth of Geneva could not be installed everywhere, the ideal was most nearly achieved in Scotland and in New England, and for a brief time, in England. In the rest of Europe, where Protestantism was tolerated, the Calvinists remained a minority, regarding themselves as a spiritual aristocracy. Since the Calvinistic concepts had such an important part in forming American attitudes, it is important to examine them in some detail.

The Puritans were strict Sabbatarians because they felt that the Catholics had profaned the Sabbath by letting all sorts of worldly activities take place, changing the day into a holiday instead of keeping it a holy day. They took the commandment against adultery literally, but as indicated, accepted marriage as good and a spouse as essential for the good life. In general, the Puritans set the rigid standards for the community of believers that the Catholics had left to the monks, namely, dedication to an ascetic, hard-working life. The result was an achievement-oriented society, for almost everyone would work to demonstrate that he or she was among the saved. In England, the Puritans became increasingly disenchanted either with royal indifference or outright opposition to what they regarded as essential reforms, and increasingly, they either left England or went into opposition. Since opposition to the monarch was centered in Parliament in the seventeenth century, they became leading advocates of the Parliamentary cause. One result was Parliamentary concern with morals, particularly sexual morals.

Even under Elizabeth, however, the state had been trying to deal with morals, establishing a quasi-royal–ecclesiastical court known as the Court of the High Commission that had jurisdiction over ecclesiastical and spiritual offenses. Established on a temporary basis in 1558 and on a permanent basis in 1583, the court, among other things, was charged with punishing incest, adultery, fornication, "outrages," "misbehaviors," and "disorders" in marriage.[1] The court proved unsatisfactory to all concerned because it was inefficient, inconsistent, and generally ineffective. Cases ran on for years without resolution.[2] Puritans were also unhappy with the court because one of its effects was seemingly to inhibit the ecclesiastical reforms they felt essential, if only because departure from the established ritual was also grounds for punishment.

In spite of such criticism, the court survived until Charles I was forced to summon Parliament in 1640, the famous Long Parliament, which found Puritans in a position to assert themselves. One of the first acts of that Parliament was to repeal the statute of Elizabeth establishing the Court of the High Commission. No immediate alternative took its place, because of the growing antagonism between the king and Parliament, antagonism that in 1642 led to civil war and ended only with the beheading of Charles in 1649. The leader of the military forces of Parliament, usually known as the Roundheads, to distinguish them from the Cavaliers or royal forces, was Oliver Cromwell; his control of the army gave him control of the country after the king's execution. Once the king was executed and the country more or less at peace, Parliament, or rather the remnants of Parliament, turned to the state's regulation of morals. The result was the Act of May 1, 1650, which made adultery a felony punishable by death, and fornication a crime punishable by 3 months' imprisonment and the posting of a bond to guarantee good behavior. Sodomy was punished by death.[3] How effective the law was is debatable. Generally, there was a reluctance to convict those charged with simple fornication, but prosecutions for adultery were likely to be more successful, at least at first. Within a few years, however, it was difficult to get even an indictment. On sodomy and the sin against nature, the Puritans were in agreement with the generally accepted morality, this type of sexual activity not being an issue. But Cromwell, increasingly unhappy over what he felt was the continuation of sexual immorality, tried to order speedier execution of the laws against adultery, fornication, and other acts of uncleanness, though few listened to him. In fact, Geoffrey May has written that "drunkenness and immorality seem to have been looked upon as a pleasant method of showing contempt and defiance of authority, civil and ecclesiastical."[4]

The Puritans were not opposed to sexual intercourse taking place within the marriage bed, only outside. This aspect of Puritanism is highlighted by that most literate of Puritans, John Milton (1608–1674), who at age 33 in 1642 married 16-year-old Mary Powell after only a brief courtship. Emotionally and sexually, the marriage was a mistake, and within a few weeks Mary returned to her family for an extended visit and refused to leave. Milton, who wanted love, could not seek love outside marriage and, upset at the rebuffs of his adolescent young wife, decided the only solution was divorce. He wrote a 42-page pamphlet on the subject, *The Doctrine and Discipline of Divorce*, in 1643, and later wrote three similar tracts. In them Milton distinguished between two kinds of married sexual expression, the noble and the vulgar. Noble sex feeling grew out of beautiful and natural desire, and the vulgar came from a venomous burning, from illicit love or lustful connection between a husband and wife who did not love each other.[5] This inevitably led Milton to conclude that divorce should be granted where there was a deep-seated inability for the man and wife to be happy together.

Eventually, Milton and his wife Mary were reconciled, though in spite of their having four children, they seem ill suited to each other. After Mary's death, Milton remarried, and when his second wife died, he married for a third time, although by this time he was blind and somewhat helpless. Still, he maintained the importance of sexuality in marriage, as witnessed by his masterpiece *Paradise Lost*, which had great influence on pious Puritans. Milton portrayed Adam and Eve as enjoying beautiful and pure conjugal love:

> . . . *Into thir inmost bowere*
> *Handed they went; and eas'd the putting off*
> *These troublesome disquises which wee wear,*
> *Strait side by side were laid; nor turned, I weene*
> *Adam from his fair spouse, nor Eve the rites*
> *Mysterious of connubial love refus'd*
>
> . . .
>
> *Haile wedded Love, mysterious Law, true source*
> *Of human offspring, sole proprietie,*
> *In Paradise of all things common else.*
> *By thee adulterous lust was drivin from men . . .*[6]

In fact, according to Milton, Adam had eaten the forbidden fruit simply for love of Eve, since

> *How can I live without thee, how foregoe*
> *Thy sweet Converse and Love so dearly joyn'd,*
> *To live again in these wilde woods forlorn?*[7]

In any conflict, revolutionary or not, it is not the virtue of the enemy that count for much, but rather their vices and excesses, and in the minds of their opponents, the Puritans went to excess in their attempt to regulate sexual conduct. With the restoration of King Charles II in 1660 and the ending of the Puritan experiment, all sex laws except those dealing with sodomy were repealed. William Blackstone, the great English legal commentator summed up the result:

> ... at the Restoration, when men, from an abhorrence of the hypocrisy of the late times, fell into a contrary extreme of licentiousness, it was not thought proper to renew a law of such unfashionable rigour. And these offences have been ever since left to the feeble coercion of the spiritual court, according to the rules of the canon law—a law which has treated the offence of incontinence, nay even adultery itself, with a great degree of tenderness of lenity, owing, perhaps, to the constrained celibacy of its first compilers. The temporal courts, therefore, take no cognizance of the crime of adultery, otherwise than as a private injury.[8]

Symbolic of the change in moral standards was the court of Charles II, although other areas of Europe, particularly France, seem to have also entered into a period of similar toleration of sexual activity. Charles II (reigned 1660–1685) set, however, an example hard to match. He had a number of mistresses: Barbara Palmer, née Villiers, who became the Duchess of Cleveland; Louise de Keroualle, who became Countess of Fareham and Duchess of Portsmouth; and Nell Gwyn, the popular favorite, affectionately known as the Protestant whore, whose illegitimate son was made Duke of St. Albans. A succession of more casual bedmates was also secured by William Chiffinch, keeper of the privy closet and page of the bedchamber. Most of these temporary visitors came by boat from London and docked just below the king's bedchamber, which conveniently overlooked the Thames River.[9]

In surveying the history of royalty from the last part of the seventeenth until almost the end of the eighteenth century, it seems as if kings had to have mistresses as part of the mark of their royalty, even if they were not particularly sexually enterprising. The example for the rest of Europe was set by the kings of France, from the time of Henry IV (reigned 1589–1610) to Louis XV (reigned 1715–1774). Henry IV, who had managed to bring some sort of stability to France by converting to Catholicism, was alleged to have had some 56 mistresses during his lifetime, 3 of them nuns. His most famous bedmate was Gabrielle d'Estrées. Perhaps in reaction to his father, Henry's successor, Louis XIII, lived more or less monogamously, but his successor, Louis XIV, revived the custom of keeping royal mistresses. Louise de la Vallière was the official mistress from 1662 to 1670; she was then ousted from the royal bed by the Marquise de Montespan, who some 9 years later was supplanted by Madame de Maintenon. Madame de Maintenon was so successful that she eventually became queen. In his old age, the king grew increasingly religious and moralistic, almost a model of moral rectitude.[10] The French court, and royalty in general, reached new heights under Louis XV, who succeeded his great-grandfather, Louis XIV, as a 5-year-old boy and who spent much of his reign hunting and fornicating. His wife, Queen Maria Leczinska, daughter of the exiled king of Poland, after giving birth to several children, denied the king access to her bedchamber, and he turned to other sources for sexual relief. As the king's promiscuity increased, the queen grew more angry, and rather than carry on his affairs at the official residence in Versailles, the king purchased a separate chateau for his mistresses. Three of them came from the same family, the Neslé family. The most famous, however, was Jeanne-Antionette d'Etoiles, née Poisson, who deserted her husband for the king and the title of Marquise de Pompadour. Madame de Pompadour realized quite early in her career as royal mistress (she was 24 when she first met the king) that, to maintain her position, she had to keep the king continually distracted, dreaming up new ways to satisfy his physical desires, to satisfy and feed his ego. She also set out to ease the tensions between the king and queen, and in spite of her position, managed to ingratiate herself with the queen. As she grew older, she brought in younger girls to satisfy the king's needs, and to accommodate these the king purchased a house in the Deer Park (*Parc aux cerfs*) district of Versailles. Each woman resident in the house had her own private room, a maidservant, and a footman, but she was never allowed to go out unchaperoned. They were led to believe that their lover was a Polish nobleman, a relative of the queen, who held a high position at court. One of the women who did discover the true identity of their patron was committed to a madhouse. After the death of Madame de Pompadour, the mantle of chief mistress eventually settled on Jeanne Comtesse du Barry, the daughter of a woman innkeeper, who first came to royal attention as the mistress of Jean, Comte du Barry. To make her background more respectable, more suitable for a king, she was married to a younger brother of the Comte du Barry, and a fortune in diamonds was lavished upon her. With her ascension as royal mistress, the Deer Park became less important, and the king increasingly spent his time with Jeanne at the Petit trianon, a small chateau set in a rural scene. When Louis died in 1774, after some 59 years of misrule, he is reported to have said on his deathbed: "I have governed and administered badly, because I have little talent and I have been badly advised."[11] Within a few short years, monarchy itself in France fell victim to the French Revolution.

The figure who fathered the most royal bastards, however, was neither an English nor French king, but Augustus the Strong (1670–1733), King of Poland and Elector of Saxony. His nickname of the Strong came, not from his military abilities, not particularly notable, but from his ability in the bedchamber. He is the known father of some 365 children, only one of whom was legitimate, his successor Augustus III. Among the most famous of his illegitimate children was Maurice de Saxe, who became marshal of France.[12]

The sexual morals of the kings were, at best, a poor measure of the period, but there is other evidence for changing sexual mores. For example, the literature of the time, both fiction and nonfiction, tends to support the belief that there was a marked change in outlooks. In the seventeenth century the dominant fictional figure in the sexual field might be said to be Don Juan, a character given literary personality in the tragic drama *El burlador de Sevilla* (*The Rake of Seville*), attributed to Tirso de Molina (Gabriel Telléz). There probably always have been stories of seducers, but now the seducer was exalted and admired, the figure's popularity being magnified by his entering French literature with Molière, *Don Juan, ou le festin de Pierre* (1665). Don Juan was elaborated upon by Molière's contemporary, Pierre Corneille; was dramatized in English by Thomas Shadwell (1642–1692) as *The Libertine* and in German by Christian Dietrich Grabbe (1829); was worked into a libretto by Lorenzo da Ponte for the opera by Mozart (*Don Giovanni*); and eventually became a staple of Western culture. In the standardized version, although each author added variants, Don Juan, after seducing several women, is hunting for another victim. At the height of his licentious career, he seduces Doña Ana, kills her father, throws suspicion on others, and mocks the stone image of the murdered man. Though Don Juan is eventually punished for his evil deeds, his name came to be associated with libertinism, especially in Lord Byron's *Don Juan*, which still remained incomplete at Byron's death in 1824.

In spite of attempts to identify Don Juan with real-life individuals, particularly a certain Miguel de Manara, he is a fictional creation who obviously has struck deep into the Western psyche. How typical is he of the period? Edmond and Jules de Goncourt, in their study of women undertaken over a hundred years ago, implied that the eighteenth century was marked not only by sensuality but also by a desire to seduce and desert for malicious sport.[13] If this was the case, the Don Juan was symbolic of the age, and fiction recreated reality. Providing some verification of this is the career of Giovanni Jacopo Casanova de Seingalt (1725–1798). An Italian of Spanish descent, Casanova was abandoned by his actor parents when he was a year old and handed over to a grandmother to rear. He was expelled from the University of Padua at age 15 for gambling and from a seminary at age 16 for immoral and scandalous conduct. Widely traveled, well read, and with an ingratiating personality, he met most of the prominent men and women of his age, served as secretary to an ambassador, acted as a spy, and worked as a director of state lotteries. In his old age he wrote his *Memoirs,* which are tinged with a kind of wishful thinking of a man who had only memories of a few precious moments with beautiful women left to comfort him. His first recorded sexual experience consisted of coitus with two young sisters in one bed, and ever after that he felt that he achieved his best results when he dealt with novices in sexual matters. He mentions some 116 mistresses by name and claims to have possessed hundreds more, ranging from chambermaids to noblewomen, making love to them standing, sitting, and lying down, in coaches, on boats, in beds, and even in alleys. Usually, after he had intercourse, his interest in the lady was gone, and he happily moved on to other conquests. He made love to at least one of his own illegitimate daughters, to a 9-year-old girl, and to a 70-year-old woman. His judgment of his life was contained in the words, "I regret nothing," although on his deathbed he reportedly said, "I have lived a philosopher and die a Christian." In his old age his chief regret seemed to be that he no longer retained his youthful vigor and potency. Though some of his stories might well have been his own fantasy running wild, most are accepted as genuine.[14]

In England the new eroticism was reflected in the pornographic novel *Memoirs of a Woman of Pleasure,* or *Fanny Hill,* by John Cleland, which recounts the adventures of a young innocent in London using only the most modest of language. In France Pierre Ambroise Laclos (1741–1803) achieved similar fame with his more realistic novel, *Les Liaisons dangereuses,* which tells how two young men seduced an innocent girl, who then became a whore, and how a religious matron was systematically driven to infidelity and finally to death. Even Denis Diderot, most famous for his compiling of an *Encyclopedia,* supposedly wrote in a similar vein in his *Bijoux indiscrets.* Many other examples of this new pornographic literature tended to point out the sensuous and unstable female nature and probably reached its ultimate in the Marquis de Sade (1740–1814). De Sade believed that, because a woman's sensation of pleasure in sex could be shammed but pain could not, pain rather than pleasure was the highest form of sexual activity for women. Though de Sade wrote to his wife that his sole wrong in life was to love women too much, and though he gave them some wickedly triumphant roles in his novels, the opposite seems to have been true. Simone de Beauvoir, for example, has written that de Sade's novels demonstrate the contempt and disgust he felt for servile, tearful, mystified, and passive women. She wondered whether de Sade might not have hated women so much because he saw in them his double rather than his complement and because there was nothing he could get from them.

> De Sade felt himself to be feminine and he resented the fact that women were not the males he desired. He endows Durand, the greatest and most extravagant of them all, with a huge clitoris which enables her to behave sexually like a man.[15]

De Sade, from whose name we have coined the word *sadism,* was a particularly troubled individual. As a young officer in Paris he had enticed a young girl into his summer house, threatened her with a knife, and inflicted wounds upon her for the thrill of watching her fear. The girl managed to escape and denouced de Sade, who served a brief period of detention. Later he visited a house of prostitution, treating the prostitutes to wines and liquors, after which he gave them bonbons containing cantharides, an aphrodisiac that also caused blistering and burning. Two women succumbed to internal burns, and another in her agony threw herself out the window and suffered severe injuries. Though the marquis was condemned to death *in absentia,* the death sentence was soon quashed by his powerful friends, as were most other serious charges. Instead, he was accused of excessive debauchery and fined. He was put into custody temporarily, and though his imprisonment was to be for only a brief period, his enemies managed to keep him confined for some 17 years before he was released. While in prison he began to work on a novel purporting to describe all imaginable forms of perversion, and though this project was apparently never completed, he did achieve notoriety with two of his novels, *Justine, ou les malheurs de la vertu* (published in 1791) and *Juliette ou les prospérités du vice* (1797). In the first he describes the careers of two girls left to make their own way after the death of their father, a banker. Juliette, the elder, entered a high-class brothel, married one of her customers, encouraged him to change his will in her favor, and then poisoned him. Once started on such a career, she continued and ended up as mistress of one of the highest dignitaries of France. On the other hand, her younger sister, moved to defend her virtue at all costs, was violated, unjustly accused, thrown into prison, and rescued only through the arson of a fellow prisoner. She soon fell victim to other horrors, including being bound hand and foot, spanned between four trees, set upon by blood-hounds, and so forth. Eventually she found a refuge with a surgeon, who tried to vivisect her. When she escaped, fleeing to a cloister for safety, the monks assaulted her. She then fell into the hands of a sex murderer, who specialized in cutting off women's heads with a saber. She escaped this fate but was suspected of being the murderer's accomplice and was unjustly condemned to death.

The second novel, a reworking of his earlier work, portrays the further adventures of Juliette, the embodiment of evil. The greater the crime, the more depraved the debauchery, the more monstrous the deed, the more exquisite was Juliette's pleasure. She set fire to a peasant cottage, to gloat over the death of its inmates; encouraged the pope to perform a black mass, to engage in sex with her; robbed the King of Naples; engaged in a homosexual act; committed incest with her real father when she found that the banker whom she thought was her father was not; and engaged in a plan to enslave children sexually. She concluded:

Such is the happy position you see me in, my friends: I have a furious fondness for crime, I would not dream of pretending otherwise; crime, and nothing else, irritates my senses, I shall go on professing its maxims down to my dying hour.

Exempt from all religious dreads, able, by discreet procedures and by wealth, to avoid difficulties with the law, what is the power, human or divine, that could impose a check upon my desires? The past encourages me, the present electrifies me, and I have little fear for the future; and my hope is that the rest of my life shall by far surpass the extravagances of my youth. Nature created human beings to no other end than that they amuse themselves on earth, and make it their playground, its inhabitants their toys; pleasure is the universal motor and law, it shall always be mine. Too bad for the victims, victims there must be; all the world would fly to pieces were it not for the sublime economy that assures equilibrium; only through acts of wickedness is the natural balance maintained, only thereby does Nature recover ground lost to the incursion of virtue. Thus, we are obeying her when we deliver ourselves unto evil; our resistance thereto is the sole crime she can never pardon in us. Oh, my friends! let us take these principles well to heart; in their exercise lie all the sources of human happiness.[16]

In his *Philosophy in the Boudoir*, de Sade argued that punishing pederasty was a barbarity because no "abnormality of taste" could be a crime. Lesbianism should also not be a crime, and both pederasty and lesbianism had been highly regarded by the ancients because they enhanced courage and bravery. Sodomy, according to Dolmance, one of the characters in the book, was universal and desired.

It divides into two classes, active and passive: the man who embuggers, be it a boy, be it a woman, acquits himself of an active sodomization; he is a passive sodomite who was himself buggered. The question has often been raised which of the two fashions of sodomistic behavior is the more voluptuous? Assuredly, 'tis the passive, since one enjoys at a single stroke the sensations of before and behind; it is so sweet to change sex, so delicious to counterfeit the whore, to give oneself to a man who treats us as if we were a woman, to call that man one's paramour, to avow oneself his mistress! Ah! my friends, what voluptuousness![17]

De Sade was again arrested, in part because of a thinly disguised romance he wrote about Joséphine de Beauharnais, the wife of Napoleon. He was never brought to trial but dragged from prison to prison until, eventually, he was put into a lunatic asylum, where he died in 1814. Though posterity has made a monster of him, the only documented evidence of any acts of sadism took place early in his life, and later he seems quite harmless. In a sense, he could be called a moralist, at least in a perverse sort of way, showing that virtue was not its own reward but instead that those who lied and cheated to get ahead often became famous and respectable. Perhaps his perverted imagination saw life as it all too often was and is.

Though the Marquis de Sade was not published until the end of the eighteenth century, and Casanova had to wait for the nineteenth century, they are symbolic of the growing concern about and interest in all aspects of sexual behavior that were evident in the eighteenth century. Also symbolic is the appearance of sex manuals, the most popular one in the English-speaking world being that usually going by the name of *Aristotle's Masterpiece* and, occasionally, *Aristotle's Experienced Midwife*. Though on first impression this seems a curious title for a sex guide, on further consideration there is considerable logic behind the title, since Aristotle had been regarded for centuries as the standard authority on the generation of animals. Moreover, his name was equated with science by both laymen and their more learned brethren until well beyond the end of the eighteenth century.[18] As the introduction to the pseudonymous Aristotle stated:

> To say that Aristotle, the learned Author of the following sheets, was reported to be the most learned philosopher in the world, is no more than what every intelligent person already knows. . . . Though Aristotle applied himself to the investigation of the secrets of nature, yet he was pleased to bring into a fuller and more true light those secrets with respect to the generation of man. This he stiled his Masterpiece, and in this he has made so thorough a search that he has as it were turned nature inside out.[19]

Before *Aristotle's Masterpiece* was produced in an English edition, some parts had circulated in Latin versions, some of which can be traced to the early medieval period. Other parts seem, however, to have been gathered in the seventeenth century.[20] One of the earliest editions, if not the earliest edition, to be published was one entitled *Aristotle's Masterpiece or the Secrets of Generation Displayed in All Parts Thereof*, printed in London in 1684. This was soon followed by other editions, since success brought imitators. One of the imitators, *Aristotle's Last Legacy*, was later incorporated into most editions of the book. The book was read not only in England but also throughout the English-speaking world, and numerous American editions of the work were also printed as late as the nineteenth century.

Because the manual was compiled in the seventeenth century, it was perhaps inevitable that the authors justified their subject matter by putting it into a worthwhile moral category, citing Biblical precedents as a guide.

> Divine records assure us that the secrets of nature have been the study of diverse illustrious persons, equally renowned for wisdom and goodness, the first of whom Job, has made it sufficiently evident by the excellent philosophical account of the generation of man, in the tenth chapter of the books which bear his name.

Also quoted are portions of the 139th Psalm (King James Version):

> Thou hast covered me in my mother's womb. I will praise thee; for I am fearfully and wonderfully made: marvellous are thy works, and that my soul knoweth right

well. My substance was not hid from thee when I was in secret, and curiously
wrought in the lower parts of the earth: thine eyes did see my substance, yet being
imperfect; and in thy book all my members were written, which in continence were
fashioned, when as yet there was none of them.

With the Bible as justification, the anonymous compiler felt secure in
disseminating the secrets of nature to a wider world.

The author or authors were apparently aware of the seventeenth-century debate between the spermaticists and ovists mentioned at the beginning of this
book and tried to straddle a middle ground while still preserving the male's superior status. Since both the male and female had "seminal vessels," and nature "doth nothing in vain," both must contribute to the process of conception.
In fact, the book advanced the notion, at least as old as the Greeks, that unless
women have periodic intercourse after maturity, which would allow them to
expel their seed, they would fall into strange diseases, that is, hysteria. Having
thus argued that women do have seed, the authors then explained that the
ovaries were receptacles for eggs and said these could be seen and boiled. As to
coitus, the manual stressed the importance of the clitoris, claiming that this is
what gives women pleasure in copulation. Several editions advised the male
lover to pay particular attention to the clitoris, since "blowing the coals of these
amorous fires" would lead to greater satisfaction. The penis is called the
"yard" because it hung "from the belly," and the male seed came from the
"stones," whose purpose was to convert "blood and spirit into the seed for the
procreation of man." The testicles also gave "strength, heat and courage to
man," as was evident from examination of eunuchs, who were "neither so hot,
strong, nor valiant as other men."

Though the emphasis throughout the various sections of the manual is on
marital sex, partners were encouraged to engage in foreplay. To help them
better "delineate the scene," poetry, which at least in this context had a double
meaning, is often cited. Thomas Carew's (1594 or 1595–1639) poem *Rapture*
was quoted in several editions:

> *I will enjoy thee, now, my fairest; come,*
> *And fly with me to love's Elysium:*
> *Now my infranchis'd hand on every side*
> *Shall o'er thy naked polish'd iv'ry slide.*
> *Now free as th' ambient air I will behold*
> *Thy bearded snow, and thy unbraided gold.*
> *No curtain, though of transparent lawn,*
> *Shall be before thy virgin treasure drawn.*
> *No, thy rich mine to my inquiring eye*
> *Expos'd, shall ready for my mintage by*
> *My rudder with thy bold hand, like a try'd*
> *And skillful pilot, thou shalt steer and guide*

My bark into love's chamber, where it shall
Dance as the bounding waves do rise and fall
And my tall pinnace in the Cyprian streight,
Shall ride at anchor and unlade her freight.

Once the male achieved orgasm, he was to take heed of how he retreated from the field of love, since if he withdrew too soon, he might leave the entrance too open, and "some cold" might "strike into the womb." Only after he had allowed sufficient time for the matrix "to close up, and made all sure, he may withdraw," and leave his partner to her repose. On his honeymoon the male was cautioned about engaging in sex too frequently, since he was to remember that he had all his life to enjoy, and he should take care of spending his energy too lavishly. Though sex was to be enjoyed, its ultimate aim was procreation, and there are lengthy sections on the problems of barren and unfruitful women. In spite of considerable misconceptions, the work attributed to Aristotle maintains that sex was good, a necessary part of life, a gift from God, to be enjoyed and accepted, and this more than anything else indicates the changing Western concepts about sex, at least of the marital variety.

Though there was still a horror of sexual deviation throughout much of the seveteenth and eighteenth centuries, among certain classes and groups, variant sexuality was likely to be tolerated, if not too openly practiced. If, however, an individual was indiscreet or exceeded the bounds of what was regarded as good taste, the results could be fatal. This was particularly true of homosexuality, and in the seventeenth century several people were executed for such activities. The first person to be executed under the Tudor legislation establishing death for the crime against nature was Mervyn Touchet, the second Earl of Castlehaven. He was found guilty of sodomy and rape (upon his own wife) and executed on July 6, 1631, although one reason for the death penalty's being applied was that he encouraged his servants to have intercourse with his wife while he watched, and such a social lapse was almost as serious as the act itself. The Earl's trouble began with his second wife, Lady Anne Stanley, whom he married after the death of his first. She was apparently an amorous woman, and Castlehaven soon came to believe he could not satisfy her. Without getting her consent, he ordered one of his servants to get in bed together with him and his wife and then encouraged the servant to have intercourse with his unwilling wife. Lord Castlehaven also engaged in mutual masturbation with his male attendants, insisting that his wife join in. Still, his wife tolerated his activities, until he arranged for her daughter by a previous marriage, a girl of only 12, whom Castlehaven had married to his own young son, to be impregnated by one of his male attendants while Castlehaven looked on. Apparently, the marriage had not yet been consummated, and the servant used considerable force to complete the sex act. This was the last straw. Lady Castlehaven initiated suit against her husband, and in the trial, two of his male companions testified against him. One reported that Castlehaven had used his "body as a woman, but never pierced it, only spent his seed betwixt my thighs," and the second stated that he often lay in bed with his master. His daughter-in-law testified that she had to submit to intercourse with one of his minions, and his treatment of his wife also came out. Castlehaven and two of the servants were executed. As indicated, the status differences seemed as important to the officials as the actual act, one official stating that "having honour and fortune to leave behind you, you should have the impious and spurious offspring of a harlot to inherit." His voyeurism was not looked upon as a sexual deviation but only as evidence that he had given himself over to lust.[21]

The Castlehaven case became a landmark case in more ways than one. It was used by the pious to point out that such actions had been rare in England in the past and to prove that the increasing prevalence of overt sexuality, heterosexual and homosexual, that they witnessed around them was a sign of growing degeneration. In 1699, for example, an account of the Castlehaven case was published with an anonymous preface claiming that

> *Ravishing Women* was a crime rarely heard of among our ancestors . . . yet now this sin is grown so common, that scarce a *Sessions* passes, wherein there is not one or more Convicted of Rape, and that in the most scandalous manner, too, upon the Bodies of Mere Children. . . . Another abomination that shocks our Natures, and puts our Modesty to the Blush, to see it so common perpetrated, is the *Devilish and Unnatural Sin of Buggery*, a Crime that sinks a Man below the *Basest* Epithet, is so Foul that it admits of no Aggravation, and cannot be expressed in its Horror, but by the Doleful Shrieks and Groans of the Damned.[22]

As Caroline Bingham remarked in her study of the Castlehaven trial, such statements were simply exaggerations. Ravishing women had never been a rare crime, and homosexuality had never been that uncommon.[23] In fact, as indicated elsewhere in this book, homosexuality might well have been encouraged in the court of James I, and it was common enough in London society in 1590 for the poet John Donne to write:

> *Why should'st thou (that dost not onely approve*
> *But in ranke itchy lust, desire, and love*
> *the nakedness and barnesse to enjoy*
> *Of thy plump muddy whore, or prostitute boy)*
> *Hate virtue, though she be naked and bare?*[24]

Though the prosecution in the Castlehaven case made much of the rarity of homosexual acts, the real rarity was the prosecution, not the acts.

Others were also charged and convicted in the seventeenth century. In 1640 John Atherton, the Right Reverend Lord Bishop of Waterford and Lismore in Ireland, was convicted of buggery with a certain John Childe, who testified against him. Though the bishop denied the charge at his trial and repeated the denial as he mounted the scaffold, he apparently admitted his guilt to a fellow divine. John Childe, who accused the bishop, was also hanged and on the scaffold confessed that he had given false evidence.[25] Obviously, if both partners were going to be executed, it would seem there would be a reluctance for one participant to accuse another. Usually, however, those found guilty were not executed. The Reverend John Wilson, Vicar of Arlington, was deprived of his benefices for committing buggery with several of his parishioners, to avoid, he said, the begetting of bastards. He also engaged in sex contacts with a mare.[26] There are occasional references to other instances of homosexual intercourse and to bestiality. A certain Major Thomas Weir, who commanded the town guard of Edinburgh, confessed that he had dealth "carnally" with a mare, a cow, and three other kinds of animals and had had incestuous relations with his sister. He was strangled at the stake in 1670, after which his remains were burned to ashes. His sister was hanged.[27]

Probably the most notorious literary work devoted to the homosexual theme during this period is the short play *Sodom or The Quintessence of Debauchery*, attributed to John Wilmot, the Earl of Rochester, and published in 1684. Son of a royalist general who supported the Stuart cause, Wilmot never knew his father, who had gone into exile with the future Charles II, where he was rewarded with the title of Earl of Rochester. When his father died in 1658, John Wilmot, then a boy of 11, inherited his father's title and only a limited estate, but shortly after the return of the royalists, his station in life changed radically. He was later closely connected with the royal court. Though Rochester denied authorship of *Sodom*, the general scholarly opinion seems inclined to identify him as the author of the play, one that his biographer, in the prim-minded *Dictionary of National Biography*, calls a play of "intolerable foulness."[28] Supposedly, the play was performed before Charles II and his court, and though it was probably printed in 1684, no printed copy survived, and it was known only in manuscript to the famed bibliographer Henry Spencer Ashbee, who wrote under the name of Pisanus Fraxi.[29] It has since been printed, however.

The plot recounts the happenings resulting from a proclamation issued by Bolloxinon, King of Sodom, to Borastus, his "Buggermaster-general" and to his companion Buggeranthos, that in the future buggery would be the order of the day for his subjects. Other characters include Cuntigratia, the queen; Pricket, the prince; Swivia, the princess; and four maids of honor named Fuckadilla, Officina, Cunticula, and Clytoris. All kinds of misfortunes fall on the Kingdom of Sodom, supposedly as a result of the edict, leading the royal physician Flux to request the King

> *To Love and nature all their rights restore—*
> *Fuck women and let buggery be no more:*
> *It doth the procreative End destroy,*
> *Which nature gave with pleasure to enjoy.*
> *Please her, and she'll be kind; if you displease,*
> *She turns into corruption and disease.*

The king refused, however, stating that he would rather die and proclaiming

> *Let heaven descend, and set the world on fire—*
> *We to some darker cavern will retire.*

Then, fire and brimstone and a cloud of smoke appear as the curtain descends. This is followed by an epilogue in which Cuntilla, the maid of honor, argues that women's vaginas are far better suited to men than the alternative of buggery, a sentiment with which Fuckadilla agrees. Princess Swivia then concludes that her vagina

> *Here is a mine or ocean full of treasure,*
> *'tis we alone enjoy the chiefest pleasure*
> *Whilst men do toil and moil to spend their strength,*
> *The pleasures does to us rebound at length.*
> *Men when they've spent are like some piece of wood*
> *Or an insipid thing, tho flesh and blood,*
> *Whilst we are still desirous of more*
> *And valiantly dare challenge half a score,*
> *Nay canthes like we'll swive with forty men;*
> *Then home to our husbands and there swive again.*[30]

Rochester himself was apparently bisexual, and if his poetry is an expression of his personality, he felt that everyone was fair game. In one of his poems entitled the *Debauchée*, he wrote:

> *I rise at Eleven, I dine about Two*
> *I get drunk before Sev'n; and the next Thing I do,*
> *I send for my whore, when for fear of a Clap*
> *I fuck in her hand, and I spew in her Lap;*
> *Then we quarrel and scold, 'till I fall asleep,*
> *When the Bitch growing bold, to my Picket does creep;*
> *Then slily she leaves me, and t'revenge the Affront*

> *At once she bereaves me of Money and Cunt.*
> *If by Chance then I wake, hot-headed and drunk*
> *What a Coil do I make for the Loss of my Punk?*
> *I storm, and I roar, and I fall in Rage,*
> *And missing my Whore, I bugger my Page.*
> *Then Crop-sick all Morning, I rail at my Men,*
> *And in Bed I lie yawning 'till Eleven again.*[31]

Other of his poems also make reference to his love of both boys and wenches.[32]

Rochester was in and out of the king's favor, since he and his "merry Gang," as they were called, seemed marked by a great lack of discretion. Anxious to secure a better economic status than the king's bounty, Rochester became interested in a rich heiress, Elisabeth Malet, but she rejected his suit because of pressure from relatives, who thought the young rakehell would not make a good husband. Rochester, certain that Miss Malet was interested in him, abducted her.[33] Her relatives appealed to the king, who had Rochester committed to the tower for "high misdemeanors," but after Elisabeth Malet was released, Rochester was also released. He left England briefly to serve in the Royal Navy, then engaged in fighting the Dutch in the North Sea. He distinguished himself enough to be rewarded with a pension from the king, and soon after this he married the same Elisabeth Malet, since either she had recovered from her abduction or her relatives now accepted him. Though the couple had four children, and with Elisabeth Malet's fortune were very rich, Rochester never quite settled down. He enjoyed court life, remaining a favorite of Charles II in spite of the king's often being the victim of Rochester's escapades. On his deathbed in 1680 he repented and ordered the burning of his "profane and lewd writings" and his "obscene and filthy pictures." Apparently many of his pornographic writings were destroyed, but not *Sodom* or some of his poetry, perhaps because others had copies.

Rochester's plays, even though they might have been performed for the king, were not meant for the commercial playhouse. Here homosexuality was approached more gingerly by John Vanbrugh in his comedy *The Relapse*. The first public performance was at the Theatre Royal in Drury Lane in 1696, and some believe the homosexual allusions are veiled references to the feelings of King William III, husband of Mary II, for some of his courtiers.[34] The chief source for such an accusation is the Duchess of Orleans, who angered at her husband's homosexuality, was willing to regard the phenomenon as universal. Her information on England was second hand, based on information she said she had received from an attendant of William Bentinck, Earl of Portland, the ambassador to France. This attendant informed her that Portland had been lover to William III and had been shipped away because his place had been taken by a former page boy, who had been made Earl of Albemarle for his services. She wrote that the king was said to have been with Albemarle as with a woman, and added that "nothing is more ordinary in England than this unnatural vice." According to her gossip, several members of Portland's entourage joined in the homosexual circle around the Duc d'Orleans.[35] Such open discussion of variant sex among the upper classes indicated a considerable change in attitude, since no matter how much such conduct might have been deplored, it was also being publicized.

During the eighteenth century England underwent a further revolution in manners and morals, as the disparity between the rich and the powerful and the poor and the helpless increased by almost geometric ratios. T. H. White has called the period *The Age of Scandal,* and it was a period in which aristocratic and privileged eccentrics flourished. The lords knew one another, gossiped about one another, and recorded the latest scandals in their letters and memoirs.[36] As the turmoil between classes increased, and disorder seemed to threaten, the ruling class increased the harshness of punishments until more than 200 offenses were penalized by the death penalty. In an age of violence, violence was also used for discipline of the young, and flogging became a standard part of the school curriculum, a practice that apparently had erotic connotations. Evidence for this comes as early as the seventeenth century, when the dramatist Thomas Otway (1652–1685) included a masochistic scene in his tragedy *Venice Preserv'd.* Thomas Shadwell (1642–1692) has a character in his *The Virtuoso* (1676) demand to be flagellated, saying that he had acquired the taste at Westminister School. The first overtly pornographic work on the subject, *A Treatise on the Use of Flogging,* was published in 1718. Edward ("Ned") Ward gave a sketch of a flogging incident in *The London Spy* at the beginning of the eighteenth century. He reported visiting a brothel where a certain sober citizen asked the "Mother of the Maids" if there were any rods in the house. When she replied there were, the prostitutes retired from the room, and Ward reported he found a new vice that he had not yet heard of:

> That Sober-seeming Saint, says he, is one of that Classis of the Black School of *Sodomy,* who are call'd by Learned Students in the Science of Debauchery, *Flogging Cullies.* This Unnatural beast gives Money to those Strumpets which you see, and they down with his Breeches and Scourge his Privities till they have laid his *Leachery.* He all the time begs their Mercy, like an Offender at a *Whipping-Post,* and beseeches their forbearance; but the more importunate he seems for their favorable usage, the severer Vapulation they are to exercise upon him, till they find by his Beastly Extasie, when to with-hold their Weapons.[37]

The learned Dr. Samuel Johnson was an ardent advocate of the birch, writing that he owed his knowledge of Latin to the plentiful flogging by his master. The headmaster of Eton was accustomed to flog 80 boys a day and only regretted his inability to flog more.[38] Since a large proportion of English pornography of the nineteenth century is devoted to flagellation, it is evident the custom continued to attract many converts.

When the graduates of the English schools grew up, they continued to meet in their clubs to drink, whore, and in the eighteenth century, play sadistic pranks. Ward wrote in his *Secret History of the London Clubs* in 1709 of the existence of such groups as the Mohocks, who went out nightly to beat up on people, stand women and girls on their heads so that their skirts would fall down, roll other people down hills inside casks, and other such boisterous activities. The Bold Bucks specialized in rape, the Sweaters in slashing people with swords, the Blasters in exposing themselves to passing women, and the Fun Club in practical jokes. All the clubs had sexual overtones, and their bulletin boards listed famous madams and noted prostitutes.

One club that Ward described was known as the Mollies, whose members met in women's clothes to drink and party.

> They adopt all the small vanities natural to the feminine sex to such an extent that they try to speak, walk, chatter, shriek and scold as women do, aping them as well in other aspects. In a certain tavern in the City, the name of which I will not mention, not wishing to bring the house into disrepute, they hold parties and regular gatherings. As soon as they arrive, they begin to behave exactly as women do, carrying on light gossip, as is the custom of a merry company of real women.[39]

This particular club, regarded by some as the first organized homosexual club, was broken up through the efforts of some zealous "agents of the Reform Society"; several frequenters of the club were "publicly punished." Such "punishment" was infrequent; most club members were regarded as above the law because of their powerful and influential positions in society. Even the Mollies, after they disappeared as an organized club, continued to exist informally; the term *Molly,* the familiar form of Mary, came to be applied to particularly effeminate types of males during this period. Such usage is still implied through the term *mollycoddle.* The most notorious of the clubs in the middle of the eighteenth century was the Hell Fire Club, sometimes known as the Mad Monks of Medmenham Abbey, who allegedly practiced black masses as well as promiscuous copulation. Among its members were Lord Sandwich (after whom the sandwich is named); Sir Francis Dashwood; William Whitehead, a poet laureate; and Charles Churchill.

If the sexual activities in the clubs were not satisfying, there were plenty of opportunities for outside activity. Special brothels devoted to flagellation existed, and there were also houses specializing in homosexual prostitution, usually called "molly" houses. A record of one such house has survived because the proprietress, Margaret Clap, popularly known as Mother Clap, was indicted in 1726 for keeping a house where she procured and encouraged persons to commit sodomy. In her trial, a police constable gave evidence that he had visited the house on a Sunday evening and found between 40 and 50 men "making love to one another as they called it." Some, he reported, sat on another man's lap, kissing, and using their "hands indecently," others would dance, curtsy, and mimic the voices of women. After settling on a partner for the evening, they would go to another room on the same floor "to be married, as they called it." Since no one came forward to defend Mother Clap, the judge asked her whether she had anything to state in her defense. She replied that, since she was a woman, "it cannot be thought that I would ever be concerned in such practices." In spite of such a plea, she was found guilty, sentenced to stand in the pillory, pay a fine of 20 marks, and go to prison for 2 years.[40]

Conviction of an occasional madam did not end the houses of homosexual prostitution; they continued to exist. One of the most famous brothels was that associated with the Vere Street Cottery, which existed until it was raided in 1810. Some of the individuals involved assumed women's names when they entered the house, and among the members or patrons identified were people from all walks of life, including a coal merchant, a police officer, a butcher, a grocer, and several members of the nobility. Some 23 patrons were arrested and exposed in the pillory, where the onlookers covered them with mud and excrement and even threw dead cats at them.[41] Tobias Smollett, in his *Roderick Random*, had his character Lord Struwell declare that sodomy has gained so much ground in recent times that, if it continued, it would soon be a "more fashionable device than simple fornication."[42]

Associated with homosexuality in the popular mind was the general growth of dandyism and foppery. As the gaps between the classes in English society widened in the eighteenth century, class divisions were emphasized, particularly by the younger members of the upper classes, through the adoption of a new kind of formalism, of "dandyism" in dress. Many of the older, more conservative English worried about the changes. One book with a section subtitled *Reasons for the Growth of Sodomy* (1749) denounced the new fashions, particularly that of men's kissing each other.

This *Fashion* was brought over from *Italy*, (the *Mother* and *Nurse* of Sodomy); where the Master is oftner *Intriguing* with his Page, than a fair lady. And not only in that country, but in *France*, which copies from them, the *Contagion* is diversify'd, and the Ladies (in the *Nunneries*) are criminally amorous of each other, in a *Method* too gross for Expression. . . . Under this Pretext vile *Catamites* make their preposterous *Addresses*, even in the very *Streets;* nor can any thing be more shocking, than to see a Couple of *Creatures*, who wear the shapes of *Men*, *Kiss* and *Slaver* each other, to that Degree, as is daily practised even in our most publick places; and (generally speaking) without Reproof; because they plead in

Excuse, *That it is the Fashion.* Damn'd Fashion! Imported from *Italy* amids't a Train of other *unnatural* Vices.[43]

Such tracts lumped all kinds of conduct under the rubric of unnatural, and in reading them the impression remains that homosexuality, however defined, was on the rampage. It might well have been merely a change in public morals rather than a change in sexual proclivities, since people were still executed for sodomy, and the public at large remained hostile to any openly effeminate man. The best indication of this is that charges of homosexuality against an individual were enough to cause him to lose public respect, if not to lead him into greater difficulty. This is indicated by the case of Samuel Foote (1720–1777), a poet and actor and author of many farcical comedies, whose lampooning of his contemporaries so angered some that they sough to discredit him by having a discharged servant accuse him of making a homosexual assault on a young man. Even though Foote was acquitted of such charges in court, he lost much of his support with the public.[44] Somewhat similar was the case of Thady ("Fribble") Fitzpatrick, who after a quarrel with the actor David Garrick (1716–1779), was satirized by Garrick in a poem called the "Fribbleriad."

> *A* Man *it seems—'tis hard to say—*
> *A* Woman *then? A moment pray—*
> *Unknown as yet be sex or feature,*
> *Suppose we try to guess the creature:*
> *Whether a* wit, *or a* pretender?
> *Of* masculine *or* feminine *gender?*
> *Nor male? Nor female? then on oath*
> *We safely may pronounce it* Both . . .
> *At which, ONE larger than the rest*
> *With visage sleek, and swelling chest,*
> *With stretch'd out fingers, and a thumb*
> *Stuck to his hips, and jutting bum,*
> *Rose up!—All knew his smirking air—*
> *They clap'd, and cry'd—the* chair, *the* chair!
> *He smil'd—and to the honour'd seat,*
> *Padle'd away on mincing feet.*[45]

The poet's nickname became so popular that Dr. Samuel Johnson included the verb "to fribble" in his *Dictionary*, quoting from the magazine *Spectator* the explanation that "a fribbler is one who professes rapture for a woman, and dreads her consent."[46] Other poets picked up the attack.[47]

England was not the only country in which the eighteenth century was the age of scandal. The French royal family set the standard not only for mistresses but also for other forms of sexual behavior. Louis XIV allegedly despised homosexuality[48] so much that he wanted to drive all such individuals from his kingdom but was unable or unwilling to do so because his brother Philip, Duc d'Orleans (1640–1701) was a publicly admitted transvestite and homosexual. Popularly known as Monsieur, Philip rode into battle wearing makeup, powder, ribbons, and jewelry but no hat, allegedly for fear of messing up his hairdo. We have rather detailed accounts of his activities from his second wife, Princess Elizabeth Charlotte of the Palatinate, a not unbiased witness, since she was hostile to her husband's homosexual friends. She wrote that her husband

> had the manners of a woman rather than those of a man. He likes to play, chat, eat well, dance and perform his toilet—in short, everything that women love . . . He loves finery and he takes care of his complexion. He dances well, but he dances like a woman. Except in time of war, he could never be prevailed upon to mount a horse. The soldiers said of him that he was more afraid of the sun, or the black smoke of gunpowder, than he was of musket bullets.[49]

Monsieur liked to appear in public dressed in women's clothes, wearing bracelets, rings, perfume, rouge, and very high heels, this last a custom introduced into court society by his brother Louis XIV. Various explanations have been advanced for his impersonation. Some have argued that he was deliberately feminized as a child so that he would not challenge his older brother's right to rule. Others claim his homosexuality was due to an early seduction by the homosexual Duc de Nevers. Whatever the cause, he apparently surrounded himself with sympathetic and likeminded people, many of whom were also homosexual, although we have only his wife's word for the homosexuality of many of them. Included in his entourage were Prince Eugene of Savoy, General Duc Claude de Villiars, and Louis, Prince of Condé, known as the Grand Condé. Since other evidence tends to indicate that Eugene of Savoy (1663–1736), the great Franco–Italian–Austrian general, was homosexual, perhaps the allegations about the others might have some merit.

It is claimed that a number of French nobility formed an Order of Sodomites known as the *La Sainte congregation des glorieux pédérastes* (Sacred Fraternity of Glorious Pederasts), which allegedly included the Prince of Condé, the Duc de Grammont, and the great court composer Jean-Baptiste Lully. The Order of Sodomites swore their members to avoid women, except for the need to produce an heir, and they all wore beneath their coats a cross carrying a picture of a man trampling a woman. Distinguished guests to the meetings of the society had fellatio performed on them.[50] How much the reported details of the organization reflect the truth is perhaps debatable, but we do know that many of the persons associated with the alleged society were bisexual, if not homosexual.

Undoubtedly, there was considerable experimentation with homosexuality among certain groups, particularly the upper classes, during this period. Frederick the Great (1712–1786) of Prussia, for example, may have had a homosexual experience as a young man, but one affair does not make a homosexual, even though some histories claim him as one of the great homosexuals.[51] The basis for the story lies in his close friendship with a young man, a friendship so provoking to his father that the young man was beheaded in front of Frederick. Though Frederick was never particularly hostile to variant sexual behavior, this might have been because of the avowed homosexuality of his younger brother, Prince Henry of Prussia (1726–1802). Honoré Gabriel Victor Riqueti, better known as the Comte de Mirabeau (1749–1791), the special French envoy at the Prussian court, wrote of Henry's *mignons* in his *The Secret History of the Court of Berlin*.[52] Henry is of particular interest to Americans, since in the aftermath of the American Revolution, some influential Americans, discouraged by the weakness of the American government, for a time gave some thought to the possibility of establishing a constitutional monarch. Among the names suggested for possible candidates as king was Prince Henry, whose name had been presented by Baron von Steuben, former Inspector General of the Continental Army. A letter was sent to the prince in November 1786 asking whether he was interested, but by the time he got around to responding in a decidedly ambiguous way, the decision had been made by the group, including Alexander Hamilton, James Monroe, and Nathaniel Gorham, President of the Continental Congress, to have an elected president. The matter was then dropped.[53]

Just how far were homosexuals tolerated in society? This is a difficult question, since all we can depend on are the legal and literary sources. Some indication of its prevalence is given by the philosopher Jean Jacques Rousseau (1712–1778) in his *Confessions,* one of the more candid of autobiographies. Rousseau for a time considered converting to Catholicism, and preparatory to receiving instruction, he stayed in a Catholic hospice. One of the brothers attempted to seduce him. When he mentioned the incident to one of the administrators, instead of being greeted with sympathy, he heard a lecture on impugning the honor of a sacred establishment and of making much out of nothing. In the process his preceptor explained that, while homosexual intercourse

> was a forbidden act, like lechery, but yet that its intention was not to offend the person who was its object, and that I had no reason to be so vexed at having been found lovable. He told me straightforwardly that in his own youth he had the same honor, and, having been surprised in a state where he could make no resistance, he had found nothing so dreadful about it. He pushed his impudence so far as to use plain language, and, imagining that the cause of my resistance had been fear of pain, assured me that such fear was vain, and that there was nothing to be alarmed at.[54]

A number of houses were devoted to homosexual prostitution in Paris. Restif de la Bretonne (1734–1806) included many vignettes of homosexuality in his *Les Nuits de Paris,* as well as in his other works. Though undoubtedly fictionalized, his accounts also bear the stamp of his own observation:

> Since coming to Paris I had heard much talk of effeminate men, but either these people never go out, like the drones of a beehive, or they go in disguise. It was at the ball that I saw them, for the first time in all their depravity. Five or six gallants came to the ball at Coulon's ten times more womanly than women. They were immediately surrounded but they made the most of themselves: the swarm of brazen coquettes sought them out, teased them, even pursued them . . .[55]

He recorded how a young man, whom he at first thought was a sweet young girl, by whom he was enchanted, and whose career he followed, became a well-known "effeminate male."[56]

Lesbianism was also recorded, particularly in the works of Pierre de Bourdeilles, Seigneur Brantôme (1535?–1614), whose *Lives of Fair and Gallant Ladies* was originally published in 1665. In his first discourse he questioned whether two women sleeping together in one bed and doing what is called *donna con donna,* imitating Sappho of Lesbos, could commit adultery. He gave examples of several women lovers, although the women involved would seem to be regarded as bisexual rather than exclusively homosexual.

> Still excuse may be made for maids and widows for loving these frivolous and empty pleasures, preferring to devote themselves to these than to go with men and come to dishonour, or else to lose their pains altogether, as some have done and do every day. Moreover, they deem they do not so much offend God, and are not such great harlots, as if they had to do with the men, maintaining that there is a great difference betwixt throwing water in a vessel and merely watering about it and round the rim . . . 'tis much better for a woman to be masculine and a very Amazon and lewd after this fashion, than for a man to be feminine.[57]

A few women seem to have been rather aggressive in their homosexual activity and ran great danger of hostility from their contemporaries, both male and female. In the court of Charles II, the Earl of Rochester, already mentioned, and a certain Miss Hobart, a maid of honor to the Duchess of York, competed for the affections of a young court beauty, Anne Temple. When Lady Hobart attempted to embrace her favorite, the girl screamed, the other waiting women came running, and Miss Hobart was banished from court, her reputation ruined.[58] Casanova gave several examples of lesbian activity, some involving nuns, in his memoirs, but the most detailed accounts appear in two novels of the last part of the eighteenth century, one in French, the other in English. It is not surprising that novels would be more instructive about possible lesbianism than memoirs, since, for the most part, men wrote the memoirs and letters and in general paid little attention to the doings of women, except as they dealt with men. In the novel, the authors were freer to examine the female psyche, although since one of the authors is male, his account might well be entirely lacking in verisimilitude or authenticity. The French book is *La Religieuse* by Denis Didêrot (1713–1784), compiler of the famous *L'Encyclopédie*. Diderot's concern was with the physical and psychological effects of celibacy on women, particularly when such celibacy had not been a matter of choice but imposed by Church and family. His novel purports to be the autobiography of a girl who had escaped from a convent and is recounting her experiences with various abbesses, one of whom was an overt lesbian. The efforts of this abbess to seduce the young girl encompass about a third of the book.[59] Havelock Ellis believed the model for the abbess was drawn from the real-life figure of the Abbess of Chelles, a daughter of Philip, Duc d'Orleans, and from a family that for several generations demonstrated a marked tendency toward sexual experimentation.[60] Jeanette Foster, in her study of lesbianism, believed that Diderot's picture of "fevered intrigue, jealousy, skilled seduction, and finally of the frustrated Superior's decline into acute neurosis, was unparalleled in fiction before the present century."[61] She regarded it as a landmark in the literature of female sex variance.

The second fictional account of lesbianism was the novel *Mary, A Fiction,* by Mary Wollstonecraft (1759–1797), best known for her famous tract *Vindication of the Rights of Woman.* It is generally regarded as the first novel dealing with lesbianism to be written by a woman. Though married, the mother of a daughter named Mary, who married the poet Percy Bysshe Shelley and known in her own right as the author of the famous Frankenstein, Mary Wollstonecraft was deeply attached to a woman friend, Fanny Blood. Mary Wollstonecraft's husband, William Godwin, wrote that the affection between Mary and Fanny was so fervent as "to have constituted the ruling passion in her mind."[62] If this is the case, her novel might have some basis in her own experience. In the novel, the heroine, Mary, submits to a marriage to a man she does not love, at the urging of her dying mother. When her young husband left for a grand tour of the continent without consummating the marriage, her girlhood friend Ann moved in to keep her company. "Her friendship with Ann had occupied her whole heart and resembled a passion."[63] When Ann fell sick, Mary took her to Lisbon for the beneficial change of climate, but Ann died, and Mary was forced to return to England, where, refusing to live with her husband, she retired to the country, devoting herself to good works and waiting for death, which would reunite her with Ann in that place "where there is neither marrying nor giving in marriage."[64] What we have here is the opposite extreme of Diderot's novel, rather, a chaste homoerotic friendship that looks upon friendship between women as the highest form of emotional experience.

An earlier work in English, Henry Fielding's (1707–1754) *The Female Husband,* was based on a true account of lesbian love, although he fictionalized the incident. In his account, the heroine fell in love with a young female neighbor and engaged in sex activities with her until the neighbor proved to be more interested in males than females. She then donned the garb of a man to live and work as a man. For a time she served as a physician; while in this role she married a young woman who took some time to discover that her husband lacked the "essentials" of a man. Eventually, after her impersonation was exposed, she was sentenced to be publicly whipped and imprisoned. Later, after serving her sentence, she set up practice as a midwife, still seducing women, with whom she allegedly engaged in sex with some "diabolical machines."[65]

Male transvestism was also common during this period, some of it among homosexual groups, but others among groups who would seem to fit the modern definition of a transvestite, that is, one who receives pleasure from cross-dressing and role impersonation and who might well be heterosexual. From one of the individuals in this period Havelock Ellis coined the term *eonism* to describe the phenomenon that Magnus Hirschfeld called transvestism.[66] Hirschfeld's term has been favored over that of Ellis, probably justifiably, since the Chevalier d'Eon is a somewhat ambiguous case.

Much less ambiguous is the case of François Timolcon de Choisy, better known as the Abbé de Choisy (1644–1724), the boyhood friend of Philip, Duc d'Orleans. Young Choisy, according to tradition, was dressed in girl's clothes in an effort to ingratiate him with the queen regent of France, Anne of Austria, who was dressing her own younger son Philip similarly. Since Choisy's father was an adviser to the young Philip, some 4 years older than his own son, the story probably has some elements of truth. Other reasons also seem to be present. Choisy was the youngest of his mother's three sons, and she had very much desired a daughter, as evidenced by her encouraging him in his feminine role. He was put in corsets just like a young girl and was kept so tightly laced that his body developed a somewhat feminine contour. His mother closely supervised his dressing, and for a time (after the death of his father) she had him live as a girl. Together mother and "daughter" attended theaters, receptions, and dances, and so well was the impersonation carried off that among the uninitiated he was assumed to be a young lady. This period of his life ended in 1662, at age 18, when his mother died.

The young Choisy then resumed his masculine garb, but he reported that he was so often mistaken for a girl that he decided to revert to his corsets and assume the life of a woman. For a time he used the pseudonym of Madame de Sancy, although, like so many transvestites, he delighted in letting people know he really was a male in skirts. He took into his house a girl companion, whom he dressed as a boy and whom he pretended to marry. When he tired of this charade, he married the girl off to someone else. After being reprimanded by an old family friend for his continual impersonation, he left Paris for the provinces, where no one would know his true sex. He settled down near Bourges, where, under the name of the Comtesse de Barres, he prentended to be a widow. Since he was the richest woman in the area, he could do more or less as he pleased, and he delighted in taking young neighborhood girls under his wing to train them in the proper ways for a lady to act. He loved to take them to bed to fondle them; he also engaged in sexual intercourse with at least two of them, one of whom became pregnant. This fact forced Choisy to return to Paris, where family pressure was so great that he publicly resumed a male role, took to travel, and gambled away much of his initial inheritance. He was saved from bankruptcy when he inherited the title and income of the Abbey de Saint Seine in Burgundy, to where he moved. Although the title *Abbé* is translated into English as Abbot, François was neither a monk nor a clergyman but a holder of a benefice. Although he continued to appear in public dressed as a man, he wore dresses in private, and regardless of costume always wore corsets. In his old age he wrote an account of his life as a woman, recording his clothes and his experiences in great detail.[67] In short, the abbé seems to fit the classic definition of transvestism.

Much more tragic is the figure of the Chevalier d'Eon de Beaumont (1728–1810), mentioned above. Unlike the Abbé de Choisy, he did not leave an autobiographical account to guide us, the facts of his life having been complicated by considerable fictionalizing by some of his biographers, a fictionalizing that has also penetrated the psychological literature. As far as is known, he had a normal boyhood. In his late teens he joined the secret service of King Louis XV of France and was sent to serve in the court of the Csarina Elizabeth of Russia. Though some of the fictionalized accounts of his life indicate that he served part of his mission in female guise, there is no evidence to support this and no reason to believe he did. After his return from Russia, he served as an officer in the dragoons during the Seven Years War, at the end of which, in 1763, he was attached to the Frency embassy in London as an agent for the French secret service. While in England, he became involved in a disastrous quarrel with the French ambassador, which reached such heat that the chevalier believed the French ambassador had hired assassins to kill him. This in turn led d'Eon to threaten to publish secret correspondence dealing with French plans for England, an action that made him *persona non grata* to the French and resulted in his discharge.

As indicated elsewhere in this chapter, England at this time was a country of great contrasts, a few people having great wealth and the masses having almost nothing. To while away their time, many English aristocrats engaged in gambling, and few were willing to bet on almost anything. Some 5000 pounds, for example, was bet on a race between two woodlice. When the French ambassador during his quarrel with d'Eon denounced him as a hermaphrodite, his sex immediately became the subject of debate and wagers. Apparently, the chevalier had a somewhat effeminate appearance, contemporaries describing him as being short and plump and having a soft, pleasing voice. The betting mounted when it was pointed out that d'Eon seemed to avoid the company of women. Soon the amounts had so escalated that the chevalier found himself in some personal danger, because plans were made to kidnap him to settle the question of his sex.

It seems possible that at this crisis in his life, the chevalier realized that he might get back into the good graces of the French king by claiming to be a woman. The king could then pardon his excesses without losing face, award him a pension, and welcome him back to France. D'Eon apparently took a fellow Frenchman into his confidence, Pierre Augustin Caron (1732–1799), better known as Beaumarchais, a Rabelasian character with a joy for living and an interest in both sex and controversy. The author of *The Barber of Seville* and *The Marriage of Figaro,* Beaumarchais saw an opportunity not only to help his countryman but also to have some fun with the English and win some money. The upshot was that d'Eon confessed he was a woman, the English victors collected their winnings, and d'Eon returned to France. The French king stipulated, however, that d'Eon had to wear female dress. Apparently, d'Eon had not anticipated this condition, and he was reluctant to put himself in female garb, but the king would not finance him unless he did. Once back in France he was warned that he would lose his newly won pension and be subject to charges of treason if he was not a woman, and the chevalier found himself in a quandary—remain a man and lose a pension or don women's clothes and gain a sinecure. As a result he went into hibernation for a period to get used to feminine clothing, and we have some surviving correspondence describing his difficulty in adapting to the feminine role:

> In the seclusion of my apartment I am forcing myself to become accustomed to my melancholy fate. Since leaving off my uniform and my sword, I am foolish as a fox who has lost his tail! I am trying to walk in pointed shoes with high heels, but have nearly broken my neck more than once; it has happened that, instead of making a courtesy, I have taken off my wig and three tiered headdress, taking them for my hat or my helmet.[68]

D'Eon was briefly the sensation of Paris, where he delighted in burlesquing the gestures and activities of women, but he grew increasingly unhappy at the restrictions of the woman's role. Using the excuse that he had business to complete in England, the chevalier was given permission in 1785 to return to that country and still receive his pension, provided he remained in his woman's clothes. He remained the rest of his life in England, although he found himself in increasingly distressing circumstances as the Revolutionary government in France confiscated his estates and cut off his pension. Reduced to penury, he

still kept to his women's clothes, supporting himself by giving fencing lessons
and exhibitions as a woman, since he was an excellent swordsman, whether in
pants or in skirts. In 1796, however, he was seriously wounded in an exhibition and unable to support himself, he fell on the charity of some of his friends.
He died in poverty in 1810, and while his body was being prepared for burial,
it was conclusively proved that the chevalier was a perfectly formed male, a fact
that proved somewhat shocking to the woman who had taken care of him and
lived with him for the last 14 years of his life.[69] Though Havelock Ellis used
the term *eonism* to describe transvestism, it is perhaps fortunate that the term
did not catch on, for the chevalier's case is full of ambiguities. It is possible that
he had characteristics associated with the pseudohermaphrodite, and there is
some indication that he himself felt ambiguous about his own physiognomy:

> I am sufficiently mortified at being what nature has made me, and that the coolness
> of my natural temperament, having never led me into pleasure-seeking, should in-
> duce my friends to imagine in their innocence, in France as much as in Russia and
> in England, that I am of the female sex. The malice of my enemies has confirmed
> all this. . . . If the Great Master of the Universe has not endowed me with all the
> exterior vigour of manhood, He has amply made amends by giving me head and
> heart. . . . I am what the hands of God have made me; satisfied with my weakness,
> I would not change it . . . even if that were in my power.[70]

There were also female transvestites. One of the most famous was Charlotte
Charke, daughter of the English actor and playwright Colley Cibber (1671–
1757). She spent much of her life in male clothes. Her father, who controlled
the Drury Lane Theater, was famous for his role as Lord Foppington, a
character in his own play, *The Careless Husband*. When her marriage failed,
Charlotte took to acting the role of Lord Foppington, and this so antagonized
her father that he not only cut off her funds but also tried to use his influence to
prevent her from getting acting parts. She continued to live as a man, for a time
running a grocer shop in London while living with a young widow. At least
two women allegedly fell in love with her, forcing her to reveal her true sex to
them, but one still refused to believe her. Eventually she wrote up her
experiences.[71] Similarly, there was the case of Mary Frith, commonly known as
Moll Cutpurse, who lived in London at the beginning of the seventeenth
century.[72] In neither case is there any evidence of homosexual activity; Mary
Frith seemed to shy away from women entirely. Her only companion was her
dog, a large mastiff. How common such impersonation was can only be conjec-
tured, but the *Annual Register,* a review of events founded in 1758, recorded a
number of cases in their surveys for the years 1761, 1766, 1769, 1771, 1773,
1777, 1779, 1782, 1793, and so forth. In the 1777 case, the woman had
married three different women who thought she was a man. One of the women,

Mary Ann Talbot, served as a cabin boy on a man-of-war, and another, Hannah Snell, was wounded in battle and suffered some 500 lashes without revealing her sex.[73]

Impersonation continued to be an important part of the stage, but as women became more prominent, the role of the female impersonator went into a decline, and instead the new fad came to be actresses' playing breeches parts. Between 1660 and 1700 nearly a quarter of the plays produced in London contained one or more roles for actresses to play in boys' parts (some 89 plays), and women played parts originally written for men in at least 14 others. Almost every actress appeared at one time or another dressed like a man, although few continued to impersonate men as Charlotte Charke had done. In effect, the wheel had come almost full circle as the "boys who impersonated women in Shakespeare's time were replaced in the Restoration wonderland by raffish hoydens, breeched and periwigged with swords at their sides and masculine oaths on their lips."[74] The effect was noted by Bernard Mandeville in his *The Fable of the Bees* (1714):

> If a woman at a merrymaking dresses in Man's clothes, it is reckon'd a Frolick amongst Friends, and he that finds too much Fault with it is counted censorious: Upon the Stage it is done without Reproach, and the most Virtuous Ladies will dispense with it in an Actress, tho' every Body has a full view of her Legs and Thighs; but if the same Woman, as soon as she has Petticoats on again, should show her Leg to a Man as high as her Knee, it would be a very immodest Action, and every Body will call her impudent for it.[75]

Female impersonation remained in the opera, where the *castrati* still held sway. In fact, if anything, throughout much of the period the *castrati* were more important than they had been earlier, owing to the growth of a star system in Italy and Germany. Some *castrati* who achieved European-wide reputations, were possibly motivated by the same desires that afflict transsexuals today, although it is difficult if not impossible to document this without much more evidence than we have. One of the most famous was Carlo Broschi, best known by his pseudonym of Farinelli (1705–1782), who exercised great influence on Philip V of Spain and for many years sang nightly for that monarch. Another famous *castrati* was Girolamo Crescentini (1762–1846), who so enchanted the Emperor Napoleon Bonaparte that he was invited to Paris to sing. Still a third singer was Gaetano Majorano, better known as Caffarelli or Cafariello (1710–1783), who might well have insisted on his own castration. Though some of the *castrati* lived more or less normal lives, and some even took wives, others were said to have liked to play the part of women offstage as well as on. Reasons for the popularity of the *castrati*, especially as women also entered the musical stage, are hard to come by, but among them was their better training, their greater endurance, and most importantly, the cultivated musical taste of the period. It has been estimated that 70 percent of all male opera singers in the eighteenth century were *castrati,* a ratio that began to change only in the last two decades of the century, owing both to the intellectual and attitudinal changes resulting from the French Revolution as well as to changes it brought on in musical tastes. Many of the *castrati* had male patrons, the illusion of femaleness that the *castrati* gave leading Casanova to remark that Rome, "the holy city," forces every man to become a pederast, but "will not admit it, nor believe in the effects of an illusion" which it "does its best to arouse."[76] Female impersonation itself was much admired, many men delighting in their ability to portray females, and many impersonators apparently delighted in their male conquests.

Why these changes in sexual outlook occurred in the late seventeenth century is difficult to explain. The change was not just in one aspect of sexual behavior but in many and can be documented in references to homosexuality, transvestism, prostitution, and even to pornography, although until the eighteenth century most of the pornography popular in England came from France.[77] Obviously, part of the change in England was due to a reaction against the restrictions of Puritanism, but it was more than a simple reaction against religion. Sexuality might have served as a safety valve for society during a period of rapid change. It was a return to the known, nature, against the unknown future, but it was also an appeal to the senses as against authorities.[78] Adding to these factors was the realization of the wide variety of sex activities taking place throughout the world. Travelers, explorers, and settlers reported on sex customs in India, China, and the colonies. India, in particular, held great fascination for the English, many visitors to that country seeming to revel in the sexuality they found there. Many former residents of India turn up as active members in the various sex clubs in England.[79]

Also important in effecting change was the growth of secularism, a turning away from organized religion, and the growth of a literate and leisured middle class. Ultimately, however, the most effective in temporarily undermining traditional Western sexual attitudes were new scientific assumptions seized upon by the middle classes as a foundation stone for their beliefs. Key to much of the scientific thought of the late seventeenth and much of the eighteenth centuries was the concept of a great chain of being, a theory that life existed in descending steps from God to the smallest and most inanimate of substances. Nature prescribed a place for everything, each level having its own laws. Man stood midway in this chain, a middle link in that he was lower than the lowest of angels but higher than all other earthly creatures. Within mankind there were various levels, the Caucasian being the highest, followed by the Oriental, Indian, Negro, and Hottentot races, and then by various forms of apes, some of which were believed to be near human by observers of the time. Within the sphere reserved for men, women were at the lower end, since they were more animal-like and had a simpler mind than men. The universe, it was assumed, was the best of all systems; any other system would be good only insofar as it was constructed on the same principles and was the object of the same infinite wisdom that had fashioned it. Clearly then, human society was constituted on principles of inequality, and each individual should labor truly to do his duty in that state of life to which God had called him.[80]

Though there were challenges to this system, challenges that ultimately proved successful, for a time it gave importance to the belief that man should follow his nature. God himself was perfect, but man was imperfect, and some more imperfect than others. Imperfect beings resulted from God's goodness, for there must be various degrees of perfection. It could therefore be argued that a homosexual might be somewhat less perfect than the normal well-adjusted man because he had more of the feminine in him, or a lesbian could be somewhat better than ordinary women because she had more of the masculine in her. Still, this was God's doing, and men and women had to make do with what God had given them. That these ideas were taken seriously is evidenced from the concern that many had over woman's lower place in the chain of being, a concept leading to the question whether woman had a soul or was merely a translation from the unisexual to bisexual creatures higher on the chain. This was because women were specialized creatures whose purpose was mainly procreative, a function not needing to be fulfilled in heaven, and therefore there was no need for her to have an immortal soul. Few went quite so far as to deny her soul, although some believed the feminine soul was different from the male and would occupy a different place in heaven. Others believed that the original soul was nonsexed and became male or female only during embryonic development; thus man and woman were equally important in the great chain of being and would have equality in the next life. Others argued that the soul itself had a sexual nature, the person pushing this to its ultimate extreme being Emanuel Swedenborg (1688–1772), a Swedish philosopher, inventor, and visionary, who devoted much of the last part of his life to attempts to explain what God meant. For Swedenborg the soul had no sex, but man and woman retained different natures in the hereafter—man was masculine and woman feminine, and by implication some were in between. None could exchange their original nature for that of the other. The earthly marriages remained in force after death to stimulate heavenly marriage, the position of women in heaven being much the same as on earth, except the tyranny of the male and the disobedience of the female would be missing. The offspring of heavenly marriage would not be children but "love" and "wisdom."[81]

Attempting to put traditional ideas and concepts into their place in the new learning were the *philosophes,* men (and women) who desired to bring about social and political changes in the movement known as the Enlightenment.

Mankind was to be raised to a new height of intellectual civilization through the illumination of every phase of life with the dominant principle of reason. Denis Diderot, for example, wrote that "religious institutions have attached the labels 'vice' and 'virtue' to actions that are completely independent of morality." He believed that once upon a time there had been a natural man, "then an artificial man was built up inside him. Since then a civil war had been raging continuously within his breast," and the natural man always had the "moral man's foot on his neck."[82]

Though superficially this focus on the natural might be seen as encouraging libertinism, the *philosophes* as a group were suspicious of passion. The most influential writer and critic of the period was François Marie Arouet, better known as Voltaire (1694–1778). Voltaire believed that passion was a prime source of human folly, and the surest way to love forever was not to love too much. He had a long affair (some 16 years) with the Marquise du Châtelet, his "divine Emilie," which ended only with her death. Though Emilie was married, the affair was carried on with her husband's tolerant consent. Voltaire wrote that his meeting with Emilie was the turning point in his life and that when he found "a young woman who thought as I did, and who decided to spend several years in the country, cultivating her mind," he decided she was the woman for him. When the affair began, Voltaire was 39, Madame du Châtelet, 27 and the mother of three children. Interestingly, when Emilie began to tire of the affair, Voltaire would not let her break with him, for reasons of propriety,[83] an indication of the mixed emotions that even the *philosophes* had.

Though the affair reveals the contradictions even in the free love of the time and the hold of traditional institutions, Voltaire tried to approach human sexuality with the same rationality that he did the rest of his life. When a literary acquaintance, the Abbé Desfontaines, was arrested and charged with sodomy, Voltaire sympathized with his sexual needs and pulled strings to rescue him from the death penalty that might have been decreed. He later wrote about homosexuality in his *Philosophical Dictionary* under the title of "Socratic Love."

> How can it be that a vice, one which would destroy the human race if it became general, an infamous assault upon nature, can nevertheless be so natural? It looks like the last degree of thought-out corruption, and at the same time, it is the usual possession of those who haven't had the time to be corrupted yet. It has entered hearts still new, that haven't known either ambition, nor fraud, nor the thirst of riches; it is a blind youth that, by a poorly straightened-out instinct, throws itself into the confusion upon leaving childhood.

> The attraction of the two sexes for each other is welcomed; but regardless of whatever has been said about the women of Africa and Southern Asia, this attraction is usually much stronger in men than in women; it is a law that nature has es-

tablished for all animals. It is always the male that attracts the female. The young males of our species, reared together, feeling this force that nature begins to develop in them and not finding the natural object of their instinct, throw themselves upon that which resembles it. A young boy will often, by the freshness of his complexion, by the intensity of his coloration and by the sweetness of his eyes, resemble a beautiful girl for the space of two or three years; if he is loved, it is because nature is misunderstood: on becoming attached to the one who has these beauties, one renders homage to sex, and when age has made this resemblance vanish, the errors cease. . . . Socratic love was not an infamous love at all: it is this word *Love* that has confused people. Those who were called the lovers of a young man were precisely those who, among us, are the companions of our princes, the elite: these people attended to the education of a distinguished child, partaking of the same education, the same military life: warring and holy institutions, in which some abuses entered, turning it into nocturnal feasts and orgies. . . . In conclusion, I do not believe that there has ever been an organized nation which has made laws against morals.[84]

Voltaire's acceptance of pederasty, if not approval, is indicative of the new wave of toleration based on what was regarded as in accord with reason and nature; the resemblance of boys to women explained variance in a natural way. Sex was recognized as a necessity. One of the most remarkable confessions in literary history is that of Jean Jacques Rousseau (1712–1778), who satisfied his sexual desires by masturbation. He later wrote that his desire for masturbation was always associated in his mind with the spankings he received from the hand of Mlle Lambercier, who temporarily acted as his mother. But the various English translations sometimes make it difficult to understand his meaning:

At the very time my senses were fired, my desires took so opposite a turn, that, confined to what they had experienced, they sought no farther. With blood boiling with sensuality almost from my birth, I preserved my purity from every blemish, even until the age when the coldest and backwardest constitutions discover themselves. Long tormented without knowing by what, I devoured with an ardent eye every fine woman; my imagination recalled them incessantly to my memory, solely to submit them to my manner, and transform them into so many Mlles Lambercier. Even after the marriageable age, this odd taste, always increasing, carried even to depravity, even to folly, preserved my morals good, the very reverse of which might have been expected.[85]

Throughout his life Rousseau had difficulty having intercourse with women. When he engaged in heterosexual sex for the first time, he reported that he felt he had committed incest. His ambiguous feelings appear in his life with his mistress, a laundress, Thérèse le Vasseur, by whom he had five children, all of whom were put in a foundling home. Rousseau himself admitted his reluctance to discuss his own sex life but felt that, unless he recorded what was ridiculous and shameful in his own life, his memoirs would not be truthful, and once he had recorded his own pettiness, he had nothing else to fear.[86] Rousseau set out to establish a better understanding of sex. In the process, he distinguished between males and females, to the disadvantage of women.

> The consequences of sex are wholly unlike for man and woman. The male is only a male now and again, the female always a female, or at least all her youth; everything reminds her of her sex; the performance of her functions requires a special constitution. She needs care during pregnancy and freedom from work when her child is born; she must have a quiet, easy life while she nurses her children. . . . The mutual duties of the two sexes are not, and cannot be, equally binding on both.[87]

Sex was to be indulged in only in moderation. According to Rousseau the virtuous man was the one who conquered his affections, followed reason and conscience, and did his duty. Passion had to be controlled, and though passion was born of honor and nursed in innocence, it made a slave and was good only so long as one was master.[88] The key to success was education, and the educated man knew moderation. Rousseau's ideas were widely disseminated in his romance *Émile* (1762). Though the *philosophes* wanted to remove barriers to marriage and divorce, secularize marriage, and eliminate old restrictions on moral behavior, they were very much opposed to excess. This new tolerance was reflected in the laws of the French Revolutionary Councils and in the Napoleonic Code. It was comparatively short-lived, however, not just because of the reaction following the defeat of Napoleon but also because of the changes in the very science on which the *philosophes* had based their concepts, changes well under way by the end of the eighteenth century.

Underlying the more restrictive views of sex that began again to appear was a changing concept of what constituted sickness and treatment. Eventually, the new apostle of a reinvigorated sexual code came to be S. A. D. Tissot, but Tissot was only like the tip of an iceberg going back to the beginnings of the eighteenth century, if not before. Early in the eighteenth century the great clinician Hermann Boerhaave (1668–1738), a dominant figure in medical thought, had written in his *Institutiones medicae* that the "rash expenditure of semen brings on a lassitude, a feebleness, a weakening of motion, fits, wasting, dryness, fevers, aching of the cerebral membranes, obscuring of the senses and above all the eyes, a decay of the spinal chord, a fatuity, and other like evils."[89] Though his statement was undoubtedly influenced by traditional Christian prejudices, it was also based on observations of the general lassitude usually afflicting men after orgasm. His observations also fitted into the new medical theory known as Vitalism, a theory based on the works of Georg Ernst Stahl (1660–1734) as well as others. Stahl had taught that there was a unity of the soul and body, a unity symbolized by the *anima,* which protected the body from the deterioration to which it tended. When the movements representing normal life were altered by the body or its organs, disease supervened. Disease was thus little more than the tendency of the *anima* (or of nature) to reestablish the normal order of tonic movements as quickly and efficiently as possible. A contemporary of Stahl, Frederick Hoffman (1660–1742), equated life with movement and death with cessation of movement. The living organism was composed of fibers having a special characteristic *tonus,* the ability to contract and dilate being regulated by the nervous system, seated in the brain. When the *tonus* was normal, the body was healthy, but every modification of the *tonus* brought with it a disturbance of health. For him an individual who gave way to masturbation gradually damaged his memory because of the strain on the nervous system.[90]

Building on this foundation were two other physicians, John Brown (1753–1788) and Théophile de Bordeu (1722–1776). Brown's medical philosophy was summarized in his *The Elements of Medicine* (1780), the basis of his philosophy being his own experience with gout. Brown had started to suffer from gout while still a young man, and after failing to cure himself with the traditional treatment, he sought other remedies. Eventually, he arrived at the conclusion that "debility was the cause of his disorders; and that the remedy was to be sought in strengthening measures." To banish his gout he had to strengthen himself, avoiding debilitating foods, and to treat himself with wine and opium. Whether his gout was cured or not remains debatable, but from his experience he erected a medical philosophy known as Brunonianism. Basic to his teachings was the notion of excitability, defined as the essential distinction between the living and dead. The seat of excitability was in the nervous system, and all bodily states were explained by the relationship between excitability and excitement. Too little stimulation was bad, but excessive stimulation could be worse because it could lead to debility by exhausting the excitability. Excitability was compared to fire: if there was not enough air (insufficient excitement), the fire would smolder and go out, but under a forced draft (too much excitement), the fire would burn excessively, become exhausted, and go out. Following this logic he claimed there were two kinds of diseases, those arising from excessive excitement (sthenic) and those from deficient excitement (asthenic). Too much stimulation carried an asthenic ailment into a sthenic one. Mutual contact of the sexes, as it took place in kissing and being in each other's presence, gave an impetuosity to the nerves, but intercourse itself, while it gave temporary relief, could also release too much turbulent energy if carried to excess and could cause difficulty. Taking a somewhat different tack but with a similar conclusion was Théophile de Bordeu, who maintained that the lymphatic glands as well as the muscular nervous system had vital activity. Secretion then also drained the vital essences residing in every part of the body.[91]

Trying these disparate ideas together for masturbation was Tissot, who published his monograph on masturbation in 1758. Tissot believed that physical bodies suffered a continual waste, and unless this was periodically restored, death would result. Much of this wastage was restored through nutrition, but even with an adequate diet the body could waste away through diarrhea, loss of blood, and most importantly for our purposes, seminal emission. Evidence of the importance of semen to the male was the effect it had on physiognomy, for it caused the beard to grow and the muscles to thicken. These masculine changes could, however, be prevented by destroying the organ producing them, as through the amputation of the testicles. Sometimes, however, semen is involuntarily lost, and this too weakened the male; the only acceptable loss was that through intercourse, which aimed at replenishing the human race. Frequent intercourse in itself was dangerous, but the most dangerous loss of semen occurred when the individual lost it through unnatural means, the most dangerous of which was masturbation. Masturbation was, however, defined in broader terms as onanism, that is, all seminal emissions not intended for procreation. Such waste of semen would lead to (1) cloudiness of ideas and sometimes even madness; (2) a decay of bodily powers, resulting in coughs, fevers, and consumption; (3) acute pains in the head, rheumatic pains, and an aching numbness; (4) pimples of the face, suppurating blisters on the nose, breast, and thighs, and painful itchings; (5) eventual weakness of the power of generation, as indicated by impotence, premature ejaculation, gonorrhea, priapism, and tumors in the bladder; and (6) disordering of the intestines, resulting in constipation, hemorrhoids, and so forth. Though Tissot recognized that not everyone addicted to onanism was so cruelly punished, he felt most were to some degree or another so afflicted.

Onanism affected females in the same ways as males but in addition caused them to be subject to hysterical fits, incurable jaundice, violent cramps in the stomach, pains in the nose, ulceration of the matrix, and uterine tremors, which deprived them of decency and reason and lowered them to the level of the most lascivious, vicious brutes. Even worse than masturbation in the female was mutual clitoral manipulation, something causing women to love other women with as much fondness and jealousy as they did men. Onanism was far more pernicious than excesses in simple fornication, although this was also dangerous. Onanism was particularly debilitating to those who had not yet attained puberty, because it tended to destroy the mental faculties by putting too great a strain on the nervous system.[92]

Essentially, Tissot gave a new scientific basis for the Western hostility to sex at the very time when the earlier foundations of this hostility were being undermined. Sex was still natural, but obviously, many forms were unnatural. Giving added force to this new formulation was the reaction that set in as an aftermath of the French Revolution. Thought libertarianism was by no means dead, it was going underground, and the emerging middle classes of the nineteenth century seized upon sexual purity as a way of distinguishing themselves from the sexual promiscuity of the noble and the lower classes, or at least this is how they viewed these classes. The intellectual community that for a time seemed to favor fewer inhibitions on sexuality found itself faced with a science emphasizing the dangers of sex. Not only was onanism dangerous, but even marital sex had to be carefully regulated lest one be forever weakened and waste away and go insane. The age of masturbatory insanity was upon the Western world.

NOTES

1. See R. G. Usher, *The Rise and Fall of the High Commission* (Oxford, England: Clarendon Press, 1913).

2. A brief survey of some of the sex cases handled by the court and the results can be found in Geoffrey May, *Social Control of Sex Expression* (New York: William Morrow, 1931), pp. 175–191.

3. See C. H. Firth and R. S. Rait, *Acts and Ordinances of the Interregnum, 1642–1660* (London: H. M. Stationery Office, 1911, 3 vols.), Vol. 2, pp. 387–389.

4. May, *op. cit.*, p. 199.

5. John Milton, *The Doctrine and Discipline of Divorce,* in *The Works of John Milton* (New York: Columbia University Press, 1931, 13 vols.). The *Tetrachordon* is the most important of his other treatises on divorce. See Vol. 4 for other divorce tracts.

6. John Milton, *Paradise Lost,* IV, 738–753 in *The Works,* Vol. 2, pp. 132–133.

7. *Ibid.,* IX, 908–910 in *The Works,* Vol. 2, Part 2, p. 292.

8. William Blackstone, *Commentaries on the Laws of England* (Philadelphia: Robert Bell, 1771) IV, 65.

9. This period is well covered by historians. Among the most important of primary sources is the *Diary of Samuel Pepys,* which has been published in numerous editions, as have several other diarists of the period. Many of the women involved with the king have been the subject of biographies: John H. Wilson, *Nell Gwyn: Royal Mistress* (New York: Pellegrini and Cudahy, 1952); Gordon Goodwin, *The Story of Nell Gwyn* (Edinburgh: John Grant, 1908); Allen Andrews, *The Royal Whore: Barbara Villiers, Countess of Castlemaine* (Philadelphia: Chilton Books, 1970); and for a general account, Maurice Petherick, *Restoration Rogues* (London: Hillis and Carter, 1951).

10. See Vern L. Bullough, *History of Prostitution* (New Hyde Park, N.Y.: University Books, 1954), pp. 145–160, for a brief general account of this period. For the reign of Louis XIV, see W. H. Lewis, *The Splendid Century* (New York: William Sloane, 1953). Joan Sanders, *La Petite: The Life of Louise de la Vallière* (Boston: Houghton Mifflin, 1959), is an account of one of the mistresses. There are numerous accounts of Madame de Maintenon. See J. Cordelier, *Madame de Maintenon* (Paris: Editions du Seuil, 1955); and Louis Hastier, *Louis XIV et Madame de Maintenon* (Paris: Librarie A. Frayard, 1957).

11. For the court of Louis XV, see Iain D. B. Pilkington, *The King's Pleasures* (London: Jarrolds, 1957); Nancy Mitford, *Madame de Pompadour* (London: Reprint Society, 1954); H. Noel Williams, *Memoirs of Madame Du Barry* (New York: Collier, 1910); but especially Stanley Loomis, *Du Barry* (Philadelphia: J. B. Lippincott, 1959).

12. John B. Wolf, *The Emergence of the Great Powers* (New York: Harper, 1951), p. 76.

13. Edmond and Jules de Goncourt, *The Woman of the Eighteenth Century,* translated by Jacques le Clercq and Ralph Roeder (New York: Minton, Blach, 1927), pp. 97–140.

14. See Jacques Casanova, *The Memoirs of Jacques Casanova de Seingalt,* translated by Arthur Machen (New York: A. & C. Bon, 1932).

15. Simone de Beauvoir, *Must We Burn de Sade?* translated by Annette Michelson (London: Peter Nevill, 1953), p. 38.

16. Quoted from The Marquis de Sade, *Juliette,* translated by Austryn Wainhouse (New York: Grove Press, 1968, 6 vols. in 1), pp. 1188–1189. See also the other volume in the Grove Press series, *Justine,* translated by Richard Seaver and Austryn Wainhouse (New York: Grove Press, 1965). See also Iwan Bloch, *Marquis de Sade: His Life and Works* (New York: Brittany Press, 1948); and Geoffrey Gorer, *The Revolutionary Ideas of the Marquis de Sade* (London: Wishart and Co., 1934).

17. This is from Marquis de Sade, *Philosophy in the Bedroom,* published in the Grove press volume *Justine, op. cit.,* pp. 247–248.

18. For a discussion of this, see Richard Harrison Shryock, *The Development of Modern Medicine,* 2nd ed. (New York: Knopf, 1947).

19. There are numerous editions, and this wording of the introduction is more or less standard. Most of my analysis is based on editions found in the Huntington and UCLA libraries. The Huntington has an edition published in 1711 and various later ones. UCLA has editions published as early as 1808. My own edition was published in 1845.

20. For a more nearly complete analysis of this, see Vern L. Bullough, "An Early American Sex Manual, Or Aristotle Who?" *Early American Literature,* 1973, pp. 236–246. See also Otho T. Beall, Jr., "Aristotle's Masterpiece in America," *William and Mary Quarterly,* 3rd series, XX (1963), pp. 207–221; and Sir D'Arcy Power, "Aristotle's Masterpiece," in *The Foundations of Medical History* (Baltimore: Williams and Wilkins, 1931), 147–188.

21. See Caroline Bingham, "Seventeenth-Century Attitudes toward Deviant Sex," *The Journal of Interdisciplinary History,* I (1971), pp. 447–472.

22. From *The Trial and Condemnation,* an account of Lord Castlehaven's trial quoted in Bingham, *op. cit.,* pp. 466–467.

23. *Ibid.,* p. 467.

24. John Donne, "Satyre I," 37–41 in *John Donne, The Satires, Epigrams, and Verse Letters,* W. Milgate, ed. (Oxford, England: Clarendon Press, 1967), p. 4.

25. See Nicholas Bernard, *Penitent Death of John Atherton* (London, 1641); and his biographical sketch in the *Dictionary of National Biography* (reprint, London: Oxford University Press, 1949–1950, 22 vols.) Vol. 1, p. 689. See also H. Montgomery Hyde, *The Love That Dared Not Speak Its Name* (Boston: Little, Brown, 1970), pp. 58–59.

26. This is included in W. Benbow, *The Crimes of the Clergy* (London: Benbow, 1823), and cited in Pisanus Fraxi (W. S. Ashbee) *Bibliography of Prohibited Books,* Vol. 2, *Centuria librorum absconditorum* (reprinted, New York: Jack Brussell, 1962, 3 vols.), pp. 40–41.

27. The trial is included in Ravillar Redivibus, *Being a Narrative of the Late Tryal of Mr. James Mitchell, a Conventicle Preacher* (London: Henry Mills, 1678), and summarized in Pisanus Fraxi, *op. cit.,* Vol. 2, pp. 51–61.

28. See his biography in the *Dictionary of National Biography,* Vol. 21, pp. 534–538; the quote is from p. 538.

29. Fraxi, *Centuria,* in Vol. 2, *op. cit.,* pp. 326–345.

30. The quotations are from John Wilmot, Earl of Rochester, *Sodom or The Quintessence of Debauchery Written for the Royall Company of Whoremasters* (Paris: Taveller's Companion Series published by The Olympia Press, n.d.), Act V, Scene 2, pp. 113–116.

31. *Ibid.,* pp. xiii–xiv.

32. John Wilmot, Earl of Rochester, *Poems on Several Occasions,* James Thorpe, ed. (Princeton, N.J.: Princeton University Press, 1950), Nos. 17, 20, 74.

33. Samuel Pepys, *The Diary of Samuel Pepys,* Henry B. Wheatley, ed. (New York: Random House, n.d., 2 vols.), Vol. 1, p. 1091 (May 28, 1665); Vol. 2, p. 414, (Feb. 4, 1666–1667).

34. Hyde, *op. cit.,* p. 61.

35. Elizabeth Charlotte, Duchesse d'Orleans, *The Letters of Madame,* Gertrude Scott Stevenson, ed. (London: Chapman & Dodd, 1924, 2 vols.), Vol. 1, pp. 217, 156–157.

36. T. H. White, *The Age of Scandal* (New York: Putnam's, 1950).

37. Pisanus Fraxi, *op. cit.,* Vol. 2, pp. 449–450.

38. White, *op. cit.,* Vol. 2, pp. 449–450.

39. Ned (Edward) Ward, *The London Spy,* Arthur Hayward, ed. (New York: George H. Doran Company, 1927). See also Daniel P. Mannix, *The Hell Fire Club* (New York: Ballantine Books, 1959); and Jack Loudan, *The Hell Rakers* (Letchworth, England, Books for You, 1967).

40. *Select Trials for Murders, Robberies, Rapes, Sodomy, Coining, Frauds and Other Offences 1720–1732, 1733–1740, 1741–1764* (London: J. Wilkie, 1734–1735, 1764); III, 37–38 (1742); and also I, 105–108 (1721), for earlier cases.

41. See *The Phoenix of Sodom, or the Vere Street Coterie* (London: J. Cook, 1813) authored by a person signing himself as Holloway, who describes these events. It is summarized in Pisanus Fraxi, *op. cit.,* Vol. 1, pp. 328–342.

42. Tobias Smollett, *The Adventures of Roderick Random* (reprinted, London: Oxford University Press, 1930).

43. *Satan's Harvest Home: or the Present State of Whorecraft, Adultery, Fornication, Procuring, Pimping, Sodomy, And the Game at Flatts . . . Collected from the Memoirs of an Intimate Comrade of the Hon. Jack S**n**r* (London: 1749), and cited and summarized in Pisanus Fraxi, *op. cit.,* Vol. 1, pp. 357–367. The second part has a separate title, *Reasons for the Growth of Sodomy.*

44. See the article in the *Dictionary of National Biography,* Vol. 7, pp. 37–375.

45. David Garrick, *Poetical Works* (London: George Kearsley, 1785, 2 vol.), Vol. 1, pp. 21–34, lines 11–15.

46. Samuel Johnson, *A Dictionary of the English Language* (London: Knapton, Longman et al., 1755, 2 vols.).

47. W. H. Lewis, *The Splendid Century* (Garden City, N.Y.: Doubleday, 1957), p. 398.

48. Arno Karlen, *Sexuality and Homosexuality* (New York: W. W. Norton, 1971), pp. 143–144.

49. Duchesse d'Orleans, *op. cit.*

50. Roger de Rabutin, Comte de Bussy, *Histoire amoureuse des Gaules* (Paris: Grange, 1754, 5 vols.), in a chapter entitled "France turned Italian," See also Allen Edwardes, *The Rape of India: A Biography of Robert Clive* (New York: Julian Press, 1966), p. 301. Clive was a member.

51. Noel Garde, *Jonathan to Gide* (New York: Vantage Press, 1964), pp. 442–448.

52. Honore Gabriel Requeti, Comte de Mirabeau, *The Secret History of the Court of Berlin* (Washington, D.C.: M. Walter Dienne, 1901). Unfortunately, many editions are expurgated,

including this one. References can be found in Letters 33, 39, 45, and 48, among others. See also *Zeitschrift fur sexual wissenschaft*, XV (1928-1929) pp. 465-476.

53.   See Richard Krauel, "Prince Henry and the Regency of the United States, 1786," *American Historical Review*, XVII, (October 1911).

54.   Jean Jacques Rousseau, *Confessions*, anonymous translation 1783 and 1790 (revised, reprinted, New York: Heritage Press, 1955), Part 1, Book 2, p. 61.

55.   Nicolas-Edme Restif de la Bretonne, *Les nuits de Paris*, translated by Linda Asher and Ellen Fertig (New York: Random House, 1964), pp. 29-30, "The Dance Hall."

56.   *Ibid.*, pp. 30-31, "The Boy in Girl's Clothing."

57.   Seigneur de Brantôme, *Lives of Fair and Gallant Ladies*, translated by A. R. Allinson (New York: Liveright, 1933), First Discourse, Chap. 15, pp. 128-136. The quote is from pp. 133-134.

58.   Anthony Hamilton, *Count de Grammont* (London: Grolier Society, n.d.), Vol. 2, p. 89.

59.   Denis Diderot, *La Religieuse* (Paris: Editions de Cluny, 1938).

60.   Havelock Ellis, *Studies in the Psychology of Sex* (New York: Random House, 1936, 2 vols.), Vol. 1, Part 4, *Sexual Inversion*, p. 199, n.

61.   Jeanette H. Foster, *Sex Variant Women in Literature* (London: Frederick Muller, Ltd., 1958), p. 55.

62.   William Godwin, *Memoirs of Mary Wollstonecraft* (New York: Richard Smith, 1930), p. 18.

63.   Mary Wollstonecraft, *Mary, A Fiction* (London: Johnson, 1788), p. 51.

64.   *Ibid.*, p. 187.

65.   Henry Fielding, *The Female Husband* (reprinted, Liverpool: Liverpool University Press, 1960).

66.   Ellis, *op. cit.*, Vol. 2, Part 2, *Eonism and Other Supplementary Studies*.

67.   See Abbé de Choisy, *Mémoires de l'Abbé de Choisy habillé en femme*, Georges Mongredien, ed., in his volume *Mémoires de l'Abbé de Choisy: Mémoires pour sevir à l'histoire de Louis XIV* (Paris: Mercure de France, 1966). This particular account has gone under various names, including *Histoire de Madame la comtesse des Barres, à Madame la marquise de Lambert, Histoire de Madame de Sancy, Histoire de la marquise-marquis de Banneville*, et al.

68.   Cynthia Cox, *The Enigma of the Age: The Strange Story of the Chevalier d'Eon* (London: Longmans, Green and Company, 1966), p. 166.

69.   In addition to the Cox biography of the chevalier, the reader might also consult Edna Nixon, *Royal Spy: The Strange Case of the Chevalier d'Eon* (New York: Reynal & Company, 1965), which is also based on primary source material. Some of the other biographies are less accurate. See, for example, M. Coryn, *The Chevalier d'Eon* (London: Thornton Butterworth, 1932); J. B. Telfer, *The Strange Career of the Chevalier d'Eon de Beaumont* (London: Longmans, Green and Company, 1885); E. A. Vizetelly, *The True Story of the Chevalier d'Eon* (London: Tylston & Edwards, 1895). D'Eon himself was somewhat of a literary figure, and several volumes of his works were published. See *Les Loisirs du Chevalier d'Eon de Beaumont* (Amsterdam, 1774, 13 vols.), and particularly his *Lettres, mémoires et négociations particulières du Chevalier d'Eon* (London: Jacques Dixwell, 1764).

70.   Cox, *op. cit.*, p. 140.

71.   Charlotte Charke, *Narrative of the Life of Charlotte Charke Written by Herself* (London: W. Reeve, 1755).

72.   *The Life and Death of Mrs. Mary Frith* (1662). Also Thomas Middleton and William

Rowley, *The Roaring Girl* (London: Vizetelly & Company, 1887–1890, 2 vols.), Mermaid Series, Vol. 2.

73. Gordon Rattray Taylor, *The Angel-Makers* (London: William Heinemann, 1958), p. 290.

74. John H. Wilson, *All the King's Ladies: Actresses of the Restoration* (Chicago: University of Chicago Press, 1958), p. 73.

75. Bernard Mandeville, *The Fable of the Bees*, F. B. Kaye, ed. (Oxford, England: Clarendon Press, 1924, 2 vols.), Remark P, Vol. 1, pp. 172–173.

76. Angus Heriot, *The Castrati in Opera* (London: Secker & Warburg, 1956), passim. Casanova is quoted on p. 55, but I am unable to find the exact quote elsewhere.

77. David Foxon, *Libertine Literature in England 1660–1745* (New Hyde Park, N.Y.: University Books, 1965), passim.

78. A few works discuss this theme. See Dale Underwood, *Etherege and the Seventeenth Century Comedy of Manners* (New Haven, Conn.: Yale University Press, 1957). See also René Pintard, *Le Libertinage erudit dans la première motié du xvii siècle* (Paris: Boivin, 1943); and G. Spini, *Ricerca dei libertini* (Rome: Editrice universale di Roma, 1950).

79. Allen Edwardes, *op. cit.*, passim.

80. For a summary of this, see Arthur O. Lovejoy, *The Great Chain of Being* (reprinted, New York: Harper and Row, 1960), pp. 186–207.

81. See Emanuel Swedenborg, *The Delights of Wisdom concerning Conjugal Love after Which Follow the Pleasures of Insanity concerning Scortatory Love*, translated from the Latin (Philadelphia: Francis and Robert Bailey, 1796), passim. There are numerous editions.

82. Denis Diderot, *Supplement to Bougainville's Voyage* in *Oeuvres philosophiques* (Paris: Garnier frères, 1956).

83. For a delightful description of the affair, see Nancy Mitford, *Voltaire in Love* (New York: Harper, 1957).

84. Voltaire, *Philosophical Dictionary*, translated by William Fleming (London: E. R. du Mont, 1901, 10 vols.), Vol. 7, pp. 147–153. This translation is different from the one I have used, which is essentially that of Donald Webster Cory, *Homosexuality: A Cross Cultural Approach* (New York: Julian Press, 1956), pp. 350–352.

85. Rousseau, *op. cit.*, Book 1, Part 1, p. 13.

86. *Ibid.*, p. 15.

87. Jean Jacques Rousseau, *Émile*, translated by Barbara Foxley (London: J. M. Dent & Sons, Ltd., 1911), p. 324 (Book 5, "Sophy or the Woman").

88. *Ibid.*, pp. 408–409 (Book 5).

89. This quotation of Boerhaave is cited in S. A. D. Tissot, *Onanism: or a Treatise upon the Disorders of Masturbation*, translated by A. Hume, (London: J. Pridden, 1766), p. 15.

90. Cited in *ibid.*, p. 17.

91. See John Brown, *The Elements of Medicine*, translated from the Latin by the author, new edition revised by Thomas Beddoes (Portsmouth, N.H.: William & Daniel Treadwell, 1803, 2 vols. in 1). For a brief discussion of some of these ideas, see Lester S. King, *The Medical World of the Eighteenth Century* (Chicago: University of Chicago Press, 1958), pp. 143–147.

92. S. A. D. Tissot, *Dissertatio de febribue bibliosis . . . tentamen de morbis ex manusturpatione* (Lausanne, Switzerland: Marci-Mic Bousquet, 1758). His work was rapidly translated into various languages, including the 1776 edition mentioned in footnote 89. The English translation, however, contains additional material inserted by Hume from his own practice, and I have cited it in preference to the Latin.

17

EUROPEANS IN A NEW SETTING: COLONIAL AMERICA

Colonial America included a diversity of occupations, ethnic and linguistic groups, and religious identities, though they all shared the same general sexual attitudes. What little differences there were soon gave way to what could be called an American outlook. Encouraging a growing uniformity were the legal attitudes brought from England, strongly influenced by John Calvin, and the very nature of the early American settlements, marked as they were by a scarcity of women, a shortage of material possessions, and a concentration on agriculture. Also important were the presence of large numbers of Indians and, by the middle of the seventeenth century, an increasing number of Negro slaves. Americans stressed marriage, almost all kinds of sex outside marriage being condemned. Homosexuality and various other nonprocreative activities came in for particular condemnation, perhaps more so than they did in Europe during the same period.

Probably the dominant influence in forming early American outlooks was that of the Puritans. In America this is a somewhat loosely defined grouping of people, including Presbyterians and Congregationalists at least, and perhaps Quakers and all those groups in England who were dissatisfied with the established Church. The essence of Puritanism, regardless of which groups one includes, was an experience of conversion separating the believer from the mass of mankind and endowing him or her with the privileges and duties of the elect. The new birth brought with it not only a conviction of salvation but also a dedication to warfare against sin.[1] Though American Puritanism had strong affinity to Calvinism, it was also closely related to Rhineland Protestantism. John T. McNeill, for example, connected Puritanism with continental Protestantism through the influence of Martin Bucer of Strasbourg and Jan Laski, the Polish reformer (both of whom lived for some time in England); Zwingli, and Calvin.[2] Also influential on the American scene was Pietism, a movement originating in Germany that was more concerned about the inner life of the individual Christian than Puritanism was. Puritanism, by focusing on people's outward behavior, tended to stress the moral law, but Pietism concentrated on the inner light and left the issues of public morality to secular control. Both were, however, strongly influenced by the teaching of Calvin.

Since Calvin has been examined elsewhere, this will not be repeated, but it is necessary to put his ideas into the American scene. Generally, the early Americans agreed that there were no areas of human conduct for which the Bible did not serve as the norm after which all men were to pattern their conduct for the greater glory of God.[3] The Puritans taught and believed that God had given man the Bible to direct his thinking and conduct in science, culture, business, society, home, and politics, and some went so far as to hestitate to codify any secular laws, since Christians would find all truth in the Bible.[4]

As to sex in particular, the American Puritans held that it was a fact of creation. God had created woman so that men and women together could "cultivate mutual society between themselves," but this was permissible only within the marriage and family. Sex was part of the divine plan, but it was to be confined to the bounds of monogamous marriage, subservient to the community's needs. It was neither to be abhorred nor exalted. Satan tempted the faithful into believing they were polluted by intercourse in marriage and led them to abandon coitus. The marriage act could not pollute nor corrupt, since marriage itself had been ordained by God as a means of producing offspring and avoiding fornication. Within the confines of the conjugal bed, the wife was equal to the husband and had the same rights he had.

Outside marriage, sex, regardless of its nature, was condemned. Calvin had set the example. He had admitted that Jewish law had not forbidden simple fornication but argued—and the Puritans agreed with him—that it would be unthinkable for God to condone what mankind condemned. History was seen to provide massive evidence that human society in general had regarded fornication as a scandal and sin. Thus, the Seventh Commandment was regarded as an exhortation to sexual purity in general and as a prohibition against engaging in any sexual activity outside marriage.

Adultery was worse than fornication because it not only violated the sanctity of marriage but also was a breach of the covenant consecrated by God. Calvin had argued that the Old Testament writers had been justified in urging the death penalty for adultery, and he tried unsuccessfully to win the civil authorities of Geneva over to his position. As might be expected, the American settlers regarded sodomy as a particularly heinous crime, a perversion of nature. Bestiality was equally repugnant. Intercourse during menstruation was a sin. Masturbation and oral–genital contacts were immodest as well as wrong.[5]

Since the Puritans believed that true Christians would indicate their state of grace by dedicated activities, they became activists in enforcing their beliefs upon the societies in which they lived. True believers and societies of true believers stressed people's outward behavior and urged the necessity for the enforcement of morals. Allowing only what the Bible expressly permitted, the Puritans developed a rigidly prescribed code of moral behavior. They frowned on excessive sexual expression, whether in or out of marriage, but they also looked askance at celibacy and unnatural continence.[6]

Giving support to these Puritan ideas were the Pietists, although they generally did not leave the established churches but instead attempted to influence others from within to achieve a greater piety. Pietism emphasized austerity, since only those avoiding the world's practices and pleasures were regarded as giving proof that they were regenerate. The purpose of marriage was threefold: procreation, a remedy against sin, and companionship in fidelity and love. The Pietists were, however, more troubled by the pleasures associated with the sex act than the Puritans. The Puritans felt that marriage tended to launder sex, to make it clean and wholesome, but some Pietists, such as Nicholas Ludwig Zinzendorf, held that there should be no more enjoyment of sex in marriage than there was in taking the wine in the eucharist.[7] A few Pietists avoided marriage altogether, and married couples were encouraged to refrain from cohabitation for extended periods of time because it was believed that sexual intercourse was worldly and wicked. The ascetic ideals of the Pietists blended with the religious concepts of the Puritans as the two groups met on the Western frontier.[8] Other factors also encouraged such an amalgam. William Penn, the proprietor of Pennsylvania, had close contacts with German Pietists,[9] and the Quakers themselves drew from both the Pietist and Calvinist traditions. The result was a fairly standardized code of sexual conduct to which most of the early Americans subscribed.

Other forces also contributed to uniformity. V. F. Calverton held that Puritan sexual ideals were primarily those of the middle class. He wrote that, when we understand.

the Puritan's attitude toward love or sex, we can understand the social basis of his life. If we would know why he could not and did not indulge in the sentiments of the aristocracy, why his poetry was chastened, his churches barren of ornament and filigree, his theaters banned, his music subdued, we must turn to the economics of his existence. If we would know why his life was ascetic, his family strictly monogamous, his sex impulse religiously repressed, his simplicity severely cultivated, we must turn again to the same source.[10]

Carnality, according to Calverton, was contrary to the Puritan ethic because it threatened the very economic basis of life; it was condemned as a defense mechanism "unconsciously designed to protect the private property upon which it has thrived."[11]

There is a strong kernel of truth in this, but it still remains an exaggerated oversimplification. Puritanism never offered itself as anything but a doctrine of salvation addressing itself neither directly nor indirectly to social classes but to man as man. It made converts in all classes, although some classes were more attracted than others. Members of neither high society nor slum society were particularly plentiful among converts; neither, for that matter, were fieldworkers. The lack of appeal to the ordinary worker might be due to Puritanism's being a religion of the Book, and without opportunity or capacity to read and master the Book, it was not particularly attractive. Weavers at their looms, tradesmen in their shops, and yeomen farmers in their homes could be organized to discuss and engage in mutual criticism and edification about doctrine, but the peasant in the field was a different matter. Calverton is right in believing that Puritanism appealed to an upwardly mobile group willing to sacrifice to get ahead, and it would seem logical to them that sex and other forms of recreation and enjoyment had boundaries. Large numbers of early (and later) Americans came here to better themselves, the result being a reenforcement of the sexual ethic that originally had been established here. Moreover, many emigrants were, for one reason or another, out of sympathy with official policy in England (or elsewhere), and this too had its effect on America, since, in part, America was to be established as a corrective to society in Europe, to be a more perfect state. This tended to make the colonial Americans more concerned with any straying from the path of righteousness than their contemporaries in Europe.

Since this was the case, the early colonists predictably reacted harshly to any sexual deviance. The laws promulgated at Jamestown in 1607 provided the death penalty for sodomy, adultery, and rape.[12] The so-called Dale's law, issued by Sir Thomas Dale, Governor of Virginia from 1611 to 1616, made it clear that chastity was a "vertue much commended in a souldier;" any sexual contacts outside marriage were discouraged.[13] In New England, the death penalty was provided for sodomy, bestiality, and adultery,[14] although not for rape, since there were no scriptural injunctions about it.

The lack of marital partners complicated enforcement of such laws. Colonial documents offer a constant refrain that single women would find America a paradise of bachelors eager to wed. It was implied that a woman would have several proposals the minute she arrived, no matter what her physical or financial status. To a society hungry for sexual companionship, the alternative to marriage was sexual activity with prostitutes, Indian women, or Negro slaves or other forms of "forbidden" sexual activity. Even after 9 years (1616), 285 of the 350 making up the European population were men, the rest, women and children. In 1620 there were more than 30 adult English males for every adult English female in Virginia. Yet in spite of this, there was only one example of intermarriage, that of Pocahontas with John Rolfe. Under such conditions prostitution was profitable, and a few women engaged in such activities, enough that the Great Charter of 1619 set up machinery to search out such "skandalous offences as suspicions of whoredomes, dishonest keeping with women, and such like."[15]

New England also had a woman shortage, particularly in some of the trading posts, the most notorious of which was Merry Mount, established within the limits of what is modern Quincy. The settlement was made by the Wollaston Company in 1624 but came under the control of Sir Thomas Morton in 1626, when Wollaston and most of the settlers moved on to Virginia. Morton had little sympathy for his nearby Pilgrim and Puritan neighbors and made little effort to disguise his antipathy. He erected a maypole, encouraged conviviality and merriment, wrote bawdy verse, poked fun at the Plymouth settlers, used nearby Indians for sexual relations, and traded firearms with them for furs and other commodities. As Governor Bradford of Plymouth Plantation put it, Morton and his followers invited

> Indian women, for their consorts, dancing and frisking together, (Like to many fairies, or furies, rather), and worse practices. As if they had anew revived and celebrated the feasts of ye Roman Goddes Flora, and ye beastly practices of ye madd Bacchinalians."[16]

The men of Plymouth eventually put an end to Merry Mount on the grounds that Morton insisted in trading in guns and other armaments with the Indians, although his ability to attract settlers from Plymouth to engage in his revels must have been a motivating cause as well.

A major factor in maintaining the sexual imbalance beyond the early years was the practice of importing indentured servants who served for fixed periods of time. It has been estimated that the sex ratio for such servants was 75 percent male and 25 percent female.[17] Some of the female bondservants were purchased directly as wives by farmers or planters; others were hired as maids, although they soon married, usually within the year.

It would seem predictable that the continued scarcity of women might have led some men to turn to various disapproved forms of sexuality. Even if this did not actually happen, the Puritans believed it was always a possibility, for they held that enforced continence in itself was dangerous.[18] Hence, the early

Americans were ever on the lookout for disapproved sexual activity, with the result that seventeenth-century records seem to be full of incidents of sexual transgression, although most seem to have been heterosexual. Plymouth colony leads the list of "deviant" sex crimes in percentages with between one-fifth and one-fourth or all prosecutions for sex offenses labeled as sodomy. Since sodomy was a catchall category including coitus *in ano,* mutual masturbation, and bestiality, it cannot necessarily be equated with homosexuality. In the Massachusetts Bay Colony, where the records are not quite so descriptive, there are numerous cases of "defiling," of "uncleanness," of "unclean practices," and similar offenses, some of which may have been euphemistic expressions for the same activities categorized as sodomy in Plymouth.[19] In spite of the shortage of women, Americans seemed nevertheless to have remained strongly heterosexual. Since it is often pointed out today that men confined in institutions, such as prisons, without access to women often resort to homosexuality, it is perhaps important to try to explain why heterosexuality remained so firmly entrenched.

Most of the early settlers came to America as adults, when their sexual orientation was well established. In America this basic heterosexual orientation plus the religious and legal emphasis put on heterosexual activities would tend to make any homosexual relations furtive and hidden. Moreover, even though there was a shortage a women, the shortage did not extend equally through all levels of society. Usually, it was the upper classes who had wives and who also set the moral tone of the community. This meant that not only religion and law but also class structure itself tended to disparage homosexual relations in colonial America, a different situation than might have existed in England. Still, the comparative absence of homosexual activities does not necessarily mean that homosexuals did not exist in the same ratios as in Europe, whatever that might be. It could be that community pressure forced those with homoerotic inclinations to suppress them with greater fervor than in Europe, but there are also other possible explanations. Obviously, those engaging in homosexual activities were more conscious that they were doing something society disapproved of and took considerable care not to be discovered. The very absence of women encouraged, moreover, a general camaraderie in the masculine world that camouflaged discreet sexual contacts between men and permitted them to go undiscovered. On the other hand women with homosexual inclinations were put at a distinct disadvantage because of their desirability as wives and because of their lives' being much more circumscribed than males'.

A major factor throughout history in making homosexual activities less obvious than heterosexual ones has been the fact that pregnancy did not result. This difference is obvious in the colonies, where premarital intercourse was frequent. In fact the church records are full of confessions of such relations, confessions usually brought on when the young woman became pregnant. If the male involved failed to confess, the colonists had what they felt was a foolproof method of identifying him. They simply asked the young woman his name while she was in labor; under such circumstances it was believed that no woman could lie. Even individuals who engaged in adultery would have been more likely to be found out than those engaged in homoerotic affairs, simply because of the greater difficulty in arranging places of assignation.

Another reason variant activities must have remained furtive and undercover is that women and children were an economic asset if not a necessity. Without a wife and a family a man had a difficult time moving ahead in colonial society. Settlers in New England and in large parts of Virginia or Carolina established farms based on family labor. A wife was a full-time employee who spun and wove, churned, and made sausages, beer, and cheese, and without such a helpmate a man was severely handicapped. Children were crucial as workers, for in a labor-short farm economy, a larger family was important. The colonists were also conscious that they had a vast area to conquer and tame, and large families were the norm, even though the mortality rate was high. Even in the plantation society that developed in Virginia and elsewhere, women continued to hold an important economic role, since as mistresses of the manors, they were superintendents of all household activities from housecleaning to butchering; in fact the profitability of the housekeeping operations depended on their administrative and business abilities. Probably one of the major reasons there was not greater intermarriage with Indians was that the male colonists felt Indian women could not fulfill such wifely obligations.

The law itself encouraged a man to marry by allowing him to assert authority over his wife. Holding or willing of property by women was restricted, and what a woman might say, do, or learn without her husband's consent were delineated by social customs as strong as or stronger than statutes. Even a wife's clothing belonged to her husband, and she had no jurisdiction over her children. Two men who settled down to running a farm would have to be in a position of master and servant or of a partnership and would be at an economic disadvantage because so many of the tasks were held to be women's duties. In sum, though a man could live without a wife and children, his economic position was seriously undermined without their contributions.[20]

The rigid demarcation of sex roles tending to prevent men from doing women's tasks and vice versa is illustrated in the poems of Anne Bradstreet (1612–1672), America's first woman poet, who wrote:

> *I am obnoxious to each carping tongue*
> *Who says my hand a needle better fits.*
> *A Poets pen all scorn I should thus wrong,*
> *For such despite they caste on Female wits:*
> *If what I do prove well, it won't advance,*
> *They'd say it's stoln, or else it was by chance.*[21]

Since Puritanism (and Protestantism in general) emphasized the Bible, women were taught to read, write, and do basic arithmetic, but little else. Anne Bradstreet, in her poem entitled "In Honour of Queen Elizabeth," attempted to show the mistakes in generalizing about female inferiority. After reporting the accomplishments of Elizabeth's reign, Anne asked:

> *Now say, have women worth? or have they none?*
> *Or have they some, but with our Queen is't gone?*
> *Nay Masculine, you have thus taxt us long,*
> *But she, though dead, will vindicate our wrong.*
> *Let such as say our Sex is void of Reason,*
> *Know tis a Slander now, but once was treason.*[22]

The charge that she had exceeded "woman's place" was one of the difficulties Anne Hutchinson had to face. Mrs. Hutchinson, one of the early rebels against the Puritan dominance in Massachusetts Colony, taught at meetings in her home, "a thing not tolerable nor comely in the sight of God nor fitting" for a woman. When Anne was able to find scriptural justification for her efforts in Titus 2:3–5, which indicates that the aged women should teach the young, the court held that this was to be restricted to teaching younger women "about their business to love their husbands," not religious views that differed from the majority's.[23]

The colonists, perhaps as a safety valve for their restricted lives, provided for greater opportunities for the unmarried of both sexes to meet together than was common in Europe. The American custom of "dating" extends back to the chaperonless times of early settlement, when in many areas groups of young men and women set off for pleasure by themselves. One early observer of customs in Albany, New York, reported that the adolescents of that area went picnicking in mixed groups on the river islands, the young women conscientiously carrying their sewing baskets, the young men their rifles.[24] Another observer, Dr. Alexander Hamilton, found that a public house outside Newport, Rhode Island, was the goal of evening walks for young couples. In company with two other couples he and a woman friend made the hike, enjoying, he noted, "all the pleasures of gallantry without transgressing the rules of modesty or good manners."[25] Europeans often remarked on the amazing innocence of such ventures, but some of the American guardians of morals were not so sure. Jonathan Edwards, for example, condemned those kinds of frolics where mixed groups were out at night.[26] Not all excursions were innocent, and what was permissible between young Americans often shocked visitors. The French traveler François de Chastellux observed a young man and woman who, in the presence of her family, held hands and kissed. He assumed they were betrothed. When he later found out this was not the case, he marveled that it was not a crime "for a girl to kiss a young man."[27] Kissing, pinching, and fondling were to the American women of the eighteenth century, if not the seventeenth, merely flirtations, not to be regarded seriously.[28] American women were frank and open in their opinions.[29] Even the "last slip," according to Chastellux, was no real "blemish in the character of the frail fair one."

> Both sexes arrive early at puberty, their constitutions are warm, there are few restraints, and they lose no time in completing the great object, the population of the country.[30]

Americans were also fairly open about sex. Anglo-Saxonisms were not replaced by Victorian euphemisms or scientific terms until after the end of the colonial period, when a more restrictive stance toward the body and its functions developed, especially among the upper classes. The Scottish Dr. Alexander Hamilton, already mentioned, was not a little embarrassed at the bawdy conversation of a New Yorker whose cure for female hysterics was "a good mowing." Hamilton felt the presence of women made such language an inexcusable piece of rudeness

> especially when it is practised before wifes and daughters whose ears should never receive anything from husbands and fathers but what is quite modest and clean.[31]

Americans also early faced a generation gap that helped weaken the strictness of enforcement. Thomas Cobbet, who wrote an early *Discourse on the Raising of Children* (1656), complained that in New England

> many of the youth grow so rude and profane, so regardless of superiors in the family as master, in the State as Magistrates, in the Church as Elders: where many of them are so vainly given, so loose in their company, so proud and supercilious in their carrriages, so new-fangled in their fashions and ruffianly in their hair . . .

and are drawn to vices learned from "loose and lewd companions."[32]

Bundling was also a safety valve. Though it usually has been described only in terms of heterosexual relationships, sharing of a bed by members of the same sex was widespread and not much commented on. Bundling technically consisted in two persons' of the opposite sex, generally completely dressed, occupying the same bed. Bundling was generally of two sorts, either between strangers or between lovers. In the first, it was a simple domestic, makeshift arrangement arising from the necessities of a new country where early bedtimes were the custom, if only because there was little to do in the evening, and there were few beds, cold rooms, and no hotels. Where a married couple had but one bed, it was a mark of hospitality for the host to allow the visitor, male or female, to use his half of the bed while the host himself slept on the floor.

Lieutenant Thomas Anburey, in his travels through America, reported that he once stopped in a storm at a Massachusetts cabin. Anburey was prepared to sit up all night, but instead his host had him share a bed with the host's teenaged daughter. Anburey was somewhat surprised, but the father laughed and said that he was not the first man Jemima had bundled with, although Jemima volunteered that he was the first Britisher.[33]

Bundling between lovers also had economic and social implications. To save firewood, courting couples often went to bed, which in itself would have implications. Although from the earliest colonial records there appear attempts by some to stamp out the custom, the practice continued through the eighteenth century, for it was a recognized concomitant of courtship.[34] In part, the "immorality" that undoubtedly resulted from bundling was fostered by Puritan laws about marriage. Throughout New England the custom of a precontract or formal betrothal was adopted. Under the system the betrothed woman was, by law and social custom, put in a position midway between that of a single woman and a married woman. In several of the New England colonies, for example, sexual intercourse of an espoused woman with another man was punishable, not as fornication, but as adultery. The betrothed couple, like the married couple, was recognized as a unit apart, not to be violated by outsiders. Conversely, within the safety of formal betrothal, greater intimacy was allowed. A couple guilty of incontinence with each other after betrothal was generally punished only half as severely as an uncontracted couple for the same offense.[35]

One reason there are so many recorded incidents of sexual crimes was that privacy was not highly valued among colonial Americans. Even punishment was public; those caught were often publicly whipped or had to proclaim their guilt publicly or wear some distinctive mark on their clothing.[36] In most cases the secret sin was discovered when the girl became pregnant, but this was not true in all cases, and it might be wondered how the courts managed to charge so many people with the crime of fornication. A clue to the possible answer comes from the case of John Pearce and the widow who later became his wife, both of whom were sentenced to be whipped or fined "for uncleanness before marriage." Conviction had been based on evidence submitted by a neighbor, who swore that having heard that

> John Pearce was accustomed to take widow Stanard to his house at night and she was seen to go away in the morning, [he] went to Pearce's house and looked in the window, etc. He called Anthony Dey and Deacon Steevens, and they saw enough to warrant a complaint against the said Pearce . . .[37]

It was difficult for a courting man and woman to be entirely unobserved, even in their own homes.

If the laws are any indication, indentured servants, particularly women, were often punished for engaging in sexual activities. Several colonies, such as Virginia, made laws to protect the planter's investment in a female servant who became pregnant; such a woman could be flogged, as could the father, if he was known. Sometimes the father of an illegitimate child was permitted to build a public works project instead of being flogged. During the 1630s, for example, John Pope built a ferry boat for Plantation Creek as punishment for "illegal" intimacies, and an unwed father in Lower Norfolk built a bridge across a creek.[38] In addition to being flogged a servant who had a child out of wedlock had her term of service extended for a year,[39] a punishment extended to 2 years in the 1660s. Any servant girl made pregnant by her master had to be sold into service for another 2 years by the churchwardens to pay for the support of her child.[40]

Matters were no different in New England than in Virginia. A wife of a New England minister complained that her husband was so unable to control his sexual desires that she could keep no maids because he was always "meddling with them." Complaints continued to mount in the eighteenth century. A servant girl, Elizabeth Dickerman, complained to Middlesex County Court that her master forced her to have coitus and threatened to kill her if she told her mistress. The man was sentenced to 20 stripes. Sarah Lepingwell, of the same county, when brought to court on fornication charges because she was pregnant, charged her master's brother with being the father. When questioned about why she had not cried out for rescue when he had "forced" her to engage in sex, Miss Lepingwell replied:

> I was posesed [sic] with fear of my master least my master shold think I did it only to bring scandall on his brother and thinking they wold all bears witnes agaynst me.[41]

Earlier, the citizens of Massachusetts had acted to prevent such abuse of their servants. For example the *Body of Liberties,* issued in 1641, stipulated

> If any servant shall flee from the Tiranny and crueltie of their masters to the howse of any freeman of the same Towne, they shall be there protected and susteyened till due order be taken for their relief.[42]

In spite of all efforts, however, servant girls continued to become pregnant, and fornication, to be widespread, if only because of the sexual imbalance. John Cotton, Jr., a Plymouth paster, blamed King Philip's War (1675–1676) on God's displeasure with the dissolute youth of New England. Cotton's authority on the subject was considerably diminished when it was discovered that he had exceeded his pastoral duties with the families of his congregation. He had long been fond of lecturing women on their sins of pride and sexuality, and his cure allegedly turned out to be private prayer sessions ending in purifying sexual intercourse with the pastor.[43]

There were other, even less acceptable means of seeking sexual gratification, such as prostitution. Prostitutes, as indicated, were mentioned in the Great Charter of Virginia in 1619, and to prevent an influx, authorities kept close watch on all women arriving in the colony. Two who arrived pregnant in 1611 were returned to England. A visitor to Carolina in 1686 reported that 12 of the 60 bound for the New World with him were prostitutes.[44] In 1672 in Massachusetts Bay Colony, Alice Thomas was found guilty of

> giving frequent secret and unseasonable Entertainment in her house to Lewd Lascivious and Notorious persons of both Sexes, giving them opportunity to commit carnall wickedness, and that by common fame she is a common Baud.[45]

Her case led to stern measures to curb prostitution. The General Court, meeting in Boston in 1672, declared:

> Whereas by sad experience: It is too obvious to all our people and others, that the sin of Whoredome and uncleanness grows amongst us, notwithstanding all the wholesome Laws made for punishing and suppressing such lands Defiling Evils; And whereas there is of late, too just ground to suspect a greater Evil growing upon us, by the bold and audacious Presumption of some, to erect a Stews, Whore-House, or Brothel-House. . . . It is therefore ordered by this Court . . . That if any Person, Male of Female, shall presume to set up or keep any such House, wherein such wicked lusts may be nourished, and Whoredome committed, every such Baud, Whore, or Vile Person . . . shall be severely whipt at the Carts-tayle, through the Streets, . . . and thence to be commited to the House of Correction . . .[46]

In New York by 1680 a small path beyond Wall Street had acquired the name Maiden Lane, apparently because so many maidens lost their maidenhood there. In 1695 a visitor to New York spoke of the "wandering liberties" there.[47] In 1744 Alexander Hamilton reported that the New York Battery was a rendezvous point for the city's prostitutes and that patrons had a "good choice of pritty lasses among them, both Dutch and English." Newport, Rhode Island, had streetwalkers in 1744; one observer described one "in a flaunting dress" who raised such blushes upon his companion that it was determined he was one of her patrons.[48]

Indians had different sexual attitudes than the European colonists, and illicit sexual contacts between Indians and Europeans came early in the colonizing of America. The law of adultery in Massachusetts, in fact, grew out of a sentence of whipping to which the court had condemned a man for enticing an Indian squaw to lie with him. Both the squaw and her Indian mate were present at the execution of the sentence and were reported as "very well satisfied."[49] Sir Thomas Morton, a seventeenth-century English-born American adventurer, whose difficulties with the Pilgrims have already been recounted, reported seeing an Indian infant with gray eyes. The Indian father said the child had the eyes of an Englishman, and when Morton

> tould the father that his sonne was . . . (a) bastard, he replied . . . hee could not tell; his wife might play the whore and his child the father desired might have an English name, because of the likeness of his eies which his father had in admiration, because of novelty amongst their nation.[50]

One dedicated Protestant observer of the colonies, in fact, felt that the big advantage the English colonists had over the French was the ability of the English clergy to marry:

> Our young missionaries may procure a perpetual alliance and commercial advantage with the Indians, which the Roman Catholic clergy cannot do, because they are forbid to marry. I mean our missionaries may intermarry with the daughters of the sachems and other considerable Indians, and their progeny will forever be a certain cement between us and the Indians.[51]

William Byrd, the early historian of the Virginia colony, had similar ideas feeling it a pity there was not more intermarriage between Europeans and Indians.[52]

In contrast, marriage rarely took place. Instead, Indian girls served as temporary sexual companions. In fact, the marriage between John Rolfe and Pocahontas was one of the few official ones between Europeans and Indians. Though this marriage was an important factor in preserving peace between the Indians and Europeans, Rolfe's own attitude about his wife and offspring is indicated by his failure to provide in his will for his child by Pocahontas.[53] Virginia colonists, in fact, before they set out, had been warned about intermarriage in a sermon preached in White Chapel in 1609:

> [Abraham's] posteritie (must) keepe to themselves. They may not marry nor give in marriage to the heathen, that are uncircumcised. . . . The breaking of this rule, may breake the neck of all good success of this voyage.[54]

If few colonist married Indians, many a male had sexual intercourse with them. In Virginia, in 1655, for example, Alice Clawson, of Northampton County, secured a divorce on the grounds that her husband had for many years lived among the Indians and refused to give up his Indian concubine.[55] An Indian girl, Molly Brant, served as mistress to William Johnson and bore him eight children before he died.[56] Ususally, however, the Indian women served as temporary mistresses, to be cast aside when a suitable wife appeared. Dr. J. Brickell, who wrote a *Natural History of North Carolina* in the eighteenth century, reported a case that perhaps might be regarded as typical:

> I knew an European man that lived many years amongst the Indians and had a child by one of their women, having bought her as they do their wives, and afterwards married a Christian. Some time after, he came to the Indian town (and wanted) to pass away a night with his former mistress as usual, but she made answer, that she then had forgot that she ever knew him, and that she never lay with another woman's husband; so full a crying, took up the child she had by him, and went out of the cabin in greater disorder, altho he used all possible means to pacify her. . . . She would never see him afterwards, or be reconciled.[57]

Brickell added that there were several Europeans who travel among the Indians and who have Indian wives or mistresses, and besides

> having the satisfaction they have of a bed-fellow, they find these girls very serviceable to them upon several occasions; especially in dressing their victuals, and instructing them in the affairs and customs of the country. . . . One great misfortune that generally attend the Christians that converse with these women as husbands, is that they get children by them which are seldome otherwise brought up or educated than in the wretched state of infidelity . . .[58]

Another observer, John Lawson, reported that the

> English trader is seldom without an Indian female for his bedfellow, alleging these reasons as sufficient to allow for such familiarity. First, they being remote from any white people, that it preserves their friendship with the heathens, they esteeming a white man's child much above one of their own getting. . . . And lastly, this correspondence makes them learn the Indian tongue much the sooner.[59]

In general the colonist looked with more favor on temporary Indian wives than Negro ones, and Massachusetts, for example, did not prohibit the marriage of whites to Indians until 1786. Sometimes the colonists did not even bother to consult with the Indian woman about her willingness; there are numerous cases where a male colonist was accused of either seduction of an Indian, attempted seduction, or rape.[60]

Sexual relations with Negroes eventually became much more common than with Indians, if only because the Negroes were less able to resist because of their slave status. In the southern colonies especially, which during much of the colonial period were also frontier areas, there was a continuing fear of collusion between Indians and Negroes, which led to a tendency of

> every planter to regard himself as the supreme source of law in his own bailiwick
> and the creator of his own slave code. With little or no regard for the law that was
> created in the colonial assembly or in London, the planter made of the institution of
> slavery whatever he desired it to be.[61]

Not the least of the desires of both the planters and slaves was sex. Evidence of
the extent of interracial sexual relationship appears most obviously in the
existence of mixed-race children. Peter Fontaine claimed that in 1757 the
country swarmed "with mullattoe bastards."[62] Thomas Anburey noticed many
mulattoes of varied shades on a southern plantation, commenting that many of
the young women

> are really beautiful, being extremely well made, and with pretty delicate features;
> all of which, I was informed, were the colonel's own. . . . It is a pleasant method to
> procure slaves at a cheap rate.[63]

Fornication was one thing, marriage another, and while one was tolerated,
the other was usually prohibited. Laws against marrying Negroes were enacted
earlier and stayed longer on the books than those dealing with intermarriage
with Indians. A Massachusetts law of 1705 not only prohibited intermarriage
but also provided that any Negro or mulatto found guilty of improper intercourse with whites was to be sold out of the province.[64] Pennsylvania, in 1725–
1726, stipulated that no Negro could marry a European under any circumstances.[65] Most colonies had similar laws. Laws did not, however, stop men
from having Negro mistresses or concubines or prevent other forms of what was
regarded as illicit sexual activity. John Woolman wrote in his *Journal*, after a
1757 trip through Maryland and Virginia, that

> Men and women have many times scarcely clothes sufficient to hide their naked-
> ness, and boys and girls ten and twelve years old are often quite naked amongst
> their master's children. Some of our society, and some of the society called New-
> lights, use some endeavors to instruct those they have in reading; but in common
> this is not only neglected, but disapproved.[66]

The inevitable results, according to another writer, was a debilitating effect on
sexual morals.

> A sad consequence of this practice, is that their children's morals are debauched by
> the frequency of such sights, as only fit them to become the masters of slaves.[67]

Some slave owners discouraged heterosexual intercourse among their slaves
on the grounds that children would result, an unwanted commodity in some

areas. Under such conditions, as well as the general condition of slavery, it is possible there was a toleration of homosexual activity among slaves, many of whom did not have the same attitudes on the subject as their masters. Evidence for such an assumption is, however, almost nonexistent. In fact what little evidence there is tends to contradict it. A Pennsylvania law of 1700, for example, provided that buggery among Negroes be punished by the death penalty, the same penalty given for the rape of a white women.[68] Generally, however, the sexual activities of the slave, or of the slaves and the masters, were ignored, as long as not too many interracial pregnancies resulted. If a master or mistress had a homosexual orientation, slavery probably proved to be an opportune way of satisfying sexual desires. Many sexual relationships between the races were more than mere sexual exercises, and there are not a few cases of genuine affection; there are also numerous incidents of slavemasters' providing for their bastard children.

It should be apparent from this discussion that homosexual activity in colonial America could result from a host of factors, ranging from what today we would regard as an individual's being inclined to homosexuality, to one's seeking sexual release with a person of the same sex because no other means was available, to someone's simply experimenting. In light of the condemnation in both law and religion, however, the latter was less likely to take place than the two former activities. Regardless of the cause, whenever any kind of homosexual activity was officially recorded, the treatment was likely to be harsh, although not all reported incidents were punished. The first conviction for a homosexual offense was recorded in Virginia in 1624. Richard Cornish (alias Williams) was executed for forcing a young man into sexual relations. In spite of the execution there is considerable doubt about whether Cornish was guilty as charged, since two men were pilloried, lost their ears, and were indentured for protesting that Cornish "was put to death through a scurvie boys meanes, & no other came against him."[69] All we can determine today is that there was some talk that his conviction had been engineered by the authorities, who had some interest in getting rid of him.

The Cornish case raises all kinds of problems, because so many interpretations can be drawn. It could well be argued that the authorities moved against those engaging in homosexual activity only when they wanted to get rid of them for some reason or when they were forced to do so by a complaint forcing the matter on public attention. Either reason seems possible. It is also possible that there was very little sexual activity of any kind, which would mean that the charge of homosexuality was a convenient way of eliminating potential troublemakers.

The first record of a conviction for a homosexual crime in the Pilgrim colony at Plymouth took place in 1637, 17 years after settlement. In that year John Alexander and Thomas Roberts were found "guilty of lude behavior and uncleane carriage one with another, by often spending their seed one upon another. . ."[70] It is not clear from the record how Alexander and Roberts were found out. Very early in the settlement of the Massachusetts Colony, the Puritans also were faced with a case of alleged sodomy. The Reverend Francis Higgeson, making his way westward on the ship *Talbot,* was concerned about what would happen to "five beastly Sodomiticall boyes" whose sins were so horrible that he said they were "not to bee named." Sodomy itself was a capital offense in the Bay Colony, but whether colony law applied was debatable, since the boys engaged in such practices on the high seas. The matter was decided by sending them back to England.

> The fact was so fowle wee reserved them to bee punished by the governor when he came to New England, who afterward sent them backe to the company to bee punished in ould England, as the crime deserved.[71]

Exactly what kind of sexual activity was involved is unclear, since sodomy was a catchall category in America, just as it traditionally had been in Europe. The ambiguity is evident in a 1641 case involving a middle-aged farmer and two young girls. The authorities were certain he had sinned "by agitation and effusion of seed," and "by entering the body of the elder" of the two girls, but there was confusion in the General Court about whether this was sodomy, rape, or something different altogether. Part of the difficulty was that the Bible had not mentioned rape, and though most agreed this is exactly what had taken place, there "was no express law in the word of God" for giving the death sentence for rape, and so they were willing to charge sodomy.[72] Eventually, the authorities of Massachusetts Bay established penalties for rape and in the process at least distinguished statutory rape from sodomy.

No such clear distinction was ever made between sodomy and bestiality. Buggery included sexual relations not only with members of the same sex but with animals as well. William Hackett, a servant, engaged in the first act of bestiality to be recorded in the Massachusetts Colony. As a young man of 18 or 20, he was discovered on Sunday by

> a women, who being detained from the public assembly by some infirmity that day, and by occasion looking out at her window, espied him in the very act.[73]

Governor Richard Bellingham felt the evidence of one witness was insufficient for the death penalty, but the lieutenant governor, who felt no such qualms, ordered the execution. After several church members had spoken with him, Hackett confessed to the crime and admitted he had done such things before. The cow was burned before his eyes, after which he was hanged.

Soon after, Plymouth became involved in a case of homosexual activity. Two men involved in an intimate relationship allegedly invited a third to join with them. This third person went to the authorities with the result that

> Edward Preston, for his lude practices tending to sodomye with Edward Michell, and pressing John Keene thereunto, (if he would have yielded,) is also censured to be forthwith whipt at Plymouth, and once more at Barnestable, (when Edward Michell is whipt), in the p'sence of Mr Freeman & the committee of the same town . . . John Keene, because he resisted the temtacon, & vsed meanes to discouer it, is appoynted to stand by whilst Michell and Preston are whipt, though in some thing he was faulty.[74]

They were not, however, executed.

The following September, in the same colony, a servant residing in Dusbery, Thomas Granger by name, about 16 or 17, confessed and was found guilty of buggery with a mare, a cow, two goats, five sheep, two calves, and a turkey. Though there was some difficulty in identifying the sheep so unnaturally used, mixed as they were in the flock, somehow five were selected to be executed along with the other animals, and they were burned in a great pit. Granger himself was executed on September 8, 1642.[75]

Two incidents of such unusual sexual activity sent the clergy of New England into spasms of self-questioning. Granger and one of the men accused of homosexual activity were examined about how they had come to the knowledge of such practices. The homosexual said he had been so inclined while living in Old England. Granger said also that he had learned to appreciate a cow while a herd boy in England. This information somewhat relieved the mind of the clerics, who still looked upon their colonizing efforts as an attempt to create a more perfect state where such things would not happen.

But any feeling of security the colonists had about their new society was shaken to its foundations when a prominent church member was found guilty of having intercourse with his farm animals. Cotton Mather, in particular, was upset, for the man had been "devout in worship, gifted in prayer, forward in edifying discourse among the religious . . . (and) zealous in reproving the sins of the other people." At the same time he had regularly been mounting his animals, even though he had witnessed the hanging of a bugger in 1660. His wife was aware of his sexual eccentricity, having seen him in intercourse with a bitch some 10 years before his arrest, but his undoing came when his son found him with a sow. Mather sadly pointed out the errors possible in human judgments about sanctity.[76]

In spite of the shortage of women and the difficulties women faced in isolating themselves from their nosey townspeople, there was also at least one case of

suspected lesbianism in Plymouth. In 1649 Mary Hammon and Goodwife
Norman, wife of Hugh Norman, were brought before the court "for leude
behauior each with the other upon a bed." Mary Hammon was cleared, but
Goodwife Norman was sentenced "to make publick acknowlidgement . . . of
her unchaste behavior."[77] How one woman could be cleared and the other
found guilty is not explained.

There were various other cases of alleged improper sexual conduct. In 1666
there was a suspected "bugger" in the Plymouth Jail, but there was insufficient
evidence against him, and he was set free.[78] In 1668 a resident of Salem named
George Emery was convicted of an "unnatural crime" and made to sit upon the
gallows with the rope about his neck in symbolic execution, though what
precisely he had done is unknown.[79] Buggery, which following Sir Edward
Coke's definition, probably implied that penetration had taken place, was
theoretically punished with the death sentence throughout the seventeenth
century, but such a harsh penalty was often ignored. Instead those adjudged
guilty were often whipped and sent into exile. This clemency upset the
Reverend Samuel Danforth, who in 1674 felt called upon to justify the death
penalty in a sermon entitled "The Cry of Sodom Enquired into, upon the Occasion of the Arraignment and Condemnation of Benjamin Goad, for His Pro-
digious Villany,"[80] Increasingly, however, hanging for sexual crimes was
abandoned. Perhaps, as Edmund Morgan claimed, New Englanders had become "inured to sexual offenses because there were so many."[81]

Contributing to this attitude were the famous witch trials at Salem Village,
which, like those in Europe, often had a connotation of sexuality associated
with them. One of the opponents of the Mathers brought this out in the open.
Robert Calef, in his "More Wonders of the Invisible World, 1700" reported
that the Mathers, father and son, treated Margaret Rule for possession by rubbing her breast and stomach and found that this soothed her. They allegedly
continued the practice until even Margaret began to be concerned about its appearance. This charge upset the Mathers, who denied that they ever rubbed
Margaret's stomach or her uncovered breast; the younger Cotton denied that
his father's hand was ever near her.[82] Whether the accusation or denial should
hold more weight is debatable, but the accusation emphasizes that even contemporaries saw sexual connotations in demonic possession.

Of moral but not legal concern was the "solitary vice," that is, masturbation.
The Mosaic Code was interpreted to designate any ejaculation as unclean (Leviticus 15:16–17), although the Bible failed to stipulate any punishment for
self-procured ejaculations. Emphasizing the sinfulness of such acts was the
Reverend Samuel Danforth, who included self-pollution or onanism in the list
of sexual acts proscribed by divine decree.[83] The author of the first American
child-rearing manual, Thomas Cobbet, was so concerned about masturbation
and other "filthy practices in secret" that he urged early marriage as a remedy.

Cotton Mather summed up the general attitude about sex in his medical work *The Angel of Bethesda:*

The Sins of *Unchastity* are Such Violations of the *Good Order,* which the GOD of Nature has praescribed unto the Children of Men, wisely to govern the *Appetites of Generation;* Such Trespasses on the Rules, to be observed for the Comfort and Beauty of *Humane Society;* such Pollutions of a *Body,* the Maker where of has *desired* it for an *Holy Temple* to Himself; that we have no cause to wonder at what the Divine Oracles have told us: *The unjust Shall be Punished; but CHIEFLY they that walk after the Flesh in the Lust of UNCLEANNESS.* . . . Among other *Judgments* which even in This World overtake the Vicious, who *being past all Feelings, have given themselves over unto Lasciviousness, to Work all Uncleanness with Greediness;* there is of Later time, inflicted a *Foul* Disease; the Description whereof, and of the Symptoms that attend it, would be such a *Nasty Discourse,* that Civility to the Readers will supersede it. . . .[84]

In short, those who engaged in extramarital, premarital, or unapproved sex in marriage were likely to be cursed with veneral disease, and everyone would know that they had sinned. Mather felt those so inflicted deserved to go through the torment; if they were eventually cured, they would ever be reminded not to sin anymore.

Still, in spite of such hostility to unapproved sexual activity, the colonials seem to have had as wide a variety of sexual activity as modern Americans. There was even occasional transvestism. One of the earliest incidents reported is the case of Edward Hyde, Lord Cornbury, who served as governor of New York and New Jersey from 1702 to 1708. Cornbury headed a rather corrupt administration; moreover his personal life so shocked his subjects that they denounced him for drunkeness, vanity, and oppression. His enemies also claimed that he dressed himself in women's clothing and, thus attired, paraded "on the ramparts of the fort, the most conspicuous place in New York." The facts are ambiguous, and investigators have had a field day in trying to explain such alleged behavior. One writer attempted to explain this conduct because of his likeness to his cousin Anne, which led him to impersonate her by dressing "in elaborate and sumptuous female attire like a lady of the court." Another author suggested that overindulgence in liquor resulted in this strange behavior and that it was after one drinking bout that "he dressed himself in his wife's clothes and paraded up and down" in such a manner he was arrested as an intoxicated vagrant by the officers of the watch. Another writer said that Cornbury impersonated a woman to show the people what the queen looked like. Quite clearly, the early reporters of his activities were puzzled by a case of what apparently might have been genuine transvestism. Doubts remain, however, since it is quite possible that the charges were made against him to get him removed as governor, something that eventually occurred.[85]

There are other occasional references to transvestites in colonial America,[86] including many involving the theater. One incident in New York received some attention in the *New York Gazette* of March 1749. According to the newspaper, several young men attempted to trick a local "stuffed shirt" by having him fall for one of them disguised as a woman. The impersonation worked too well. The unnamed stuffed shirt was so attracted to the "lady" that "her" only escape was to ask her fellow conspirators to dance. "She" even went into a corner and pretended to hug and kiss with one of her companions, but the enamored lover followed her, and in the struggle the "lady" lost her temper and was arrested for assault and battery.[87] Undoubtedly, there were other such incidents, but few made the newspapers of the day.

The most famous case of transvestism took place at the end of the colonial period, namely that of Deborah Sampson, who fought in the Continental Army under the name of Robert Shirtliff. Deborah served some 17 months in the Fourth Massachusetts Regiment of Foot between 1782 and 1783 without being discovered, although her beardless, healthy cheeks caused her to be nicknamed "our blooming soldier." Deborah, whose father had died when she was young and whose mother had been unable to raise her, had been an indentured servant for a time. When she completed her term of service, she wanted to travel and see the world, but realizing the difficulties of traveling as a woman, decided to impersonate a man. To get financial backing she enlisted in the army, since in spite of Cornwallis' surrender at Yorktown, the army still needed recruits. She first enlisted under the name of Timothy Thayer, and after receiving a bounty for enlisting, she became so drunk that she did not show up for duty. Shortly after, denounced by an "old woman," Deborah had to return the unspent portion of the bounty. She also agreed to stay out of sight, lest punishment overtake her, and was disfellowshipped from the First Baptist Church of Middleboro for her escapade.

Apparently, the Timothy Thayer episode had been something of an experiment, for on May 20, 1782, Deborah joined the army again under the name of Robert Shirtliff. She wore a bandage about her breasts during her enlistment to disguise herself and reportedly augmented her waist, although how is unknown. She engaged in combat with several scattered units of British troops and Tory bandits during the summer of 1782, receiving a superficial head wound and a much more severe wound in the right thigh below the groin. She permitted the head wound to be dressed by a French Army doctor but kept secret her thigh wound and cleansed it with rum, extracting the bullet with a penknife during a moment of privacy.

In the summer of 1783 in Philadelphia she was stricken with fever, taken to a hospital, and sank into a coma, whereupon her true sex was uncovered, although the doctor and nurse temporarily kept this fact to themselves. During her service, Deborah had apparently flirted with several women, some of whom visited her in the hospital. After she was released, she spent some time with a woman friend in Baltimore who had sent letters and fruits to her in the hospital. She then went to the Ohio frontier, where she saved the life of a white slave girl held by the Indians by purchasing her as a wife. "Robert" then returned to Baltimore, and after settling the former Indian captive with her long-lost family, she broke off her affair with the woman in Baltimore. By the time she returned to Philadelphia, the physician who had treated her had written to her commanding general, John Patterson, in West Point, indicating that his soldier was really a woman. General Patterson at first thought the matter was a great joke, but after satisfying himself that the physician was telling the truth, issued Deborah an honorable discharge on October 25, 1783. For a brief time she passed herself off as her brother, but in April 1784, she married Benjamin Gannett and apparently spent the rest of her life in female clothes. She gave birth to three children, two girls and one boy. For her wartime services she received a pension and thus can be regarded as one of the first women, if not the first woman, to serve in the U.S. Army. As her story got out, she was an object of considerable curiosity and gossip, but eventually she came to be regarded as a heroine. She died in 1827 in her 67th year.[88]

Colonial America had at least its share of sexual adventures. Though the only proper sex was within marriage, the colonials no more observed this provision as a group than their predecessors or successors. In general, except for premarital fornication, which was widespread, the colonists used discretion. Homosexuality, in spite of the shortage of women, does not seem to have been particularly prevalent. In fact, there were as many cases of bestiality recorded in New England as what we would now class as homosexual conduct. In their attempts to establish a more perfect society the colonists kept stricter surveillance on residents in the seventeenth century than probably was possible in the eighteenth century, and in general the reported incidents of "deviant" sex declined in the eighteenth.[89] At the same time the lessening disparity in the sex ratio probably allowed larger numbers of men to seek heterosexual relations in marriage or otherwise. Whereas all sex activities outside marriage were punishable, some were punished more severely than others, particularly those condemned in the Bible. Americans favored early marriage and fecundity, and this ethic of large families tended to reinforce official hostility to nonprocreative sex. In short, homosexuality in particular, and nonprocreative sex in general, was disapproved in colonial America, and this hostility carried over into the post-Revolutionary stage.

NOTES

1. Alan Simpson, *Puritanism in Old and New England* (Chicago: University of Chicago Press, 1955), pp. 1–3.

2.   John T. McNeill, *Modern Christian Movements* (Philadelphia: Westminster Press, 1954), pp. 25–26. See also L. J. Trinterud, "Origins of Puritanism," *Church History*, XX (1951), pp. 35–57.

3.   John Calvin, *Institutes of the Christian Religion,* I, xviii, 4 translated by John Allen (Grand Rapids, Mich.: Eerdmans, 1949).

4.   Perry Miller, *Orthodoxy in Massachusetts, 1630–1650* (reprinted, Boston: Beacon, 1959), pp. 148–149. They also did not want to make too great a break with England.

5.   William Graham Cole, *Sex in Christianity and Psychoanalysis* (New York: Oxford University Press, 1966), pp. 126–128.

6.   Chard Powers Smith, *Yankess and God* (New York: Hermitage House, 1954), p. 122.

7.   Roland H. Bainton, *What Christianity Says About Sex, Love, and Marriage* (New York: Association Press, 1957), p. 104.

8.   Carl E. Schneider, *The German Church on the American Frontier* (Saint Louis: Eden Publishing, 1939), p. 215.

9.   See *Sex and the Church,* Oscar E. Feucht, Harry G. Coiner, and other members of the Family Life Committee, eds., Lutheran Church, Missouri Synod (Saint Louis: Concordia Publishing, 1961), pp. 115–118.

10.   V. F. Calverton, "Sex and Social Struggle," in *Sex in Civilization,* V. F. Calverton and S. D. Schmalhausen, eds. (New York: Macaulay Company, 1929), p. 265.

11.   *Ibid.,* p. 271.

12.   George F. Willison, *Behold Virginia!* (New York: Harcourt Brace Jovanovich, 1951), p. 121.

13.   *Ibid.,* p. 136.

14.   George Lee Haskins, *Law and Authority in Early Massachusetts* (New York: Macmillan, 1960), pp. 146–149. There were, however, few executions, and most of these were for contacts with animals.

15.   Willison, *op. cit.,* p. 200.

16.   William Bradford, *History of Plimouth Plantation* (Boston: Wright and Potter, 1898), Book 2 (1628), pp. 285–286.

17.   Mildred Campbell, "Social Origins of Some Early Americans," in *Seventeenth Century America* (Chapel Hill, N.C.: University of North Carolina, 1959), p. 71.

18.   Edmund S. Morgan, "The Puritans and Sex," *New England Quarterly,* XV (1942), p. 600.

19.   Geoffrey May, *Social Control of Sex Expression* (New York: William Morrow, 1931), p. 247.

20.   Arthur M. Schlesinger, *The Birth of the Nation* (New York: Knopf, 1968), pp. 18–25.

21.   Anne Bradstreet, *The Works of Anne Bradstreet,* John Harvard Ellis, ed. (New York: Peter Smith, 1932), p. 101.

22.   *Ibid.,* p. 361.

23.   David D. Hall, ed., *The Antinomian Controversy, 1636–1638* (Middleton, Conn: Wesleyan University Press, 1968), pp. 312–315.

24.   Anne Grant, *Memoirs of an American Lady* (New York: Dodd, Mead, 1903), pp. 114–116.

25.   Alexander Hamilton, *Gentleman's Progress: The Itinerarium of Dr. Alexander Hamilton, 1744* (Chapel Hill, N.C.: University of North Carolina Press, 1948), p. 155.

26.   Mary Sumner Benson, *Women in Eighteenth-Century America* (New York: Columbia University Press, 1935), p. 276.

27. François Jean de Chastellux, *Travels in North America in the Years 1780, 1781, and 1782* (London: Robinson, 1787, 2 vols.), Vol. 1, p. 120.

28. Benson, *op. cit.*, p. 279.

29. George Francis Dow, *Everyday Life in the Massachusetts Bay Colony* (New York: Benjamin Blom, 1967), p. 118.

30. Chastellux, *op. cit.*, Vol. 1, p. 288.

31. Hamilton, *op. cit.*, p. 177.

32. Thomas Cobbet, *Discourse on the Raising of Children* (London: 1656, written in Lynn, Mass., 1654–1655).

33. Thomas Anburey, *Travels through the Interior Parts of America* (Boston: Houghton Mifflin, 1923, 2 vols.), Vol. 2, pp. 25–26.

34. There are several accounts of bundling in America. The most famous and widely quoted is that by Henry Reed Stiles, originally written in 1871. It has gone through innumerable editions, as, for example, *Bundling: Its Origin, Progress and Decline in America* (reprinted, New York: Book Collectors Association, 1934). See also C. F. Adams, *Some Phases of Sexual Morality and Church Discipline in Colonial New England*, in Massachusetts Historical Society, *Proceedings*, 2d s., VI (June, 1891), pp. 503–510; and Arthur W. Calhoun, *A Social History of the American Family* (reprinted in 1 vol., New York: Barnes and Noble, 1945, 3 vols.), pp. 129–132.

35. May, *op. cit.*, pp. 248–249.

36. The first case in Massachusetts of a distinctive mark on clothing was in 1634 when Robert Coles, the town drunkard, was required to wear a red letter *D*. The first sexual offenses was in 1639, when John Davies was required to wear the letter *V* for venery. See Edwin Powers, *Crime and Punishment in Early Massachusetts, 1620–1692* (Boston: Beacon Press, 1966), pp. 198– 201.

37. *Ibid.*, p. 173.

38. Philip Alexander Bruce, *Institutional History of Virginia in the Seventeenth Century* (New York: Putnam's, 1910, 2 vols.), Vol. 1, pp. 47, 48.

39. William Waller Hening, compiler, *The Statutes at Large: Being a Collection of All the Laws of Virginia From the First session of the Legislature in the Year 1619* (New York: R. & W. and G. Barton, 1823), Vol. 1, p. 438.

40. *Ibid.*, Vol. 2, pp. 167–168.

41. Morgan, *op. cit.*, p. 600.

42. *The Body of Liberties of 1641* are reprinted in Powers, *op. cit.*, appendix 1, par. 85, p. 543.

43. George F. Willison, *Saints and Strangers, Being the Lives of the Pilgrim Fathers and Their Families, with Their Friends and Foes* (New York: Reynal and Hitchcock, 1945), pp. 368, 371– 372.

44. See Vern L. Bullough, *History of Prostitution* (New Hyde Park, N.Y.: University Books, 1964), pp. 188–189. See also Durane De Deuphine, *A Huguenot Exile in Virginia, or Voyages of a Frenchman Exiled for His Religion* (New York: Press of the Pioneers, 1934), p. 93.

45. Powers, *op. cit.*, p. 179.

46. *Ibid.*, pp. 179–180.

47. The eminent historian John Fiske, *The Dutch and Quaker Colonies in America* (Boston: Houghton Mifflin, 1899, 2 vols.), Vol. 2, p. 65, say the lane received its name because women did their washing there. This explanation seems to be more an attempt of historians to ignore sex than face reality.

48. Hamilton, *op. cit.*, pp. 46, 151.

49. John Winthrop, *The History of New England from 1630–1649,* James Savage, ed. (Boston: Little, Brown, 1853, 2 vols.), Vol. 1, p. 60.

50. Quoted from Morton's book, *New English Canaan* by Calhoun, *op. cit.,* Vol. 1, p. 149.

51. *Ibid.,* Vol. 1, p. 166.

52. *Ibid.,* Vol. 1, p. 215. The passage occurs in his Letters from Virginia.

53. *Ibid.,* Vol. 1, p. 324.

54. Quoted by Calhoun, *Ibid.,* Vol. 1, p. 323.

55. *Ibid.,* Vol. 1, p. 304.

56. *Ibid.,* Vol. 1, p. 166.

57. J. Brickell, *Natural History of North Carolina* (Dublin, 1737), quoted by Calhoun, *op. cit.,* Vol. 1, pp. 324–325.

58. *Ibid.,* Vol. 1, p. 323.

59. John Lawson, *History of Carolina* (London, 1709), quoted in Thomas Gossett, *Race: The History of an Idea in America* (Dallas: Southern Methodist Press, 1963), p. 27.

60. Alden T. Vaughan, *New England Frontier: Puritans and Indians 1620–1675* (Boston: Little, Brown, 1965), p. 215.

61. John Hope Franklin, *From Slavery to Freedom* (New York: Knopf, 1967), pp. 87–88.

62. Robert E. and B. Katherine Brown, *Virginia, 1705–1786* (East Lansing, Mich: Michigan State University Press, 1964), p. 68.

63. Anburey, *op. cit.,* Vol. 2, pp. 342–343.

64. *Ibid.,* Vol. 1, p. 211.

65. Adolph Niemoeller, *Sexual Slavery in America* (New York: Panurage Press, 1935), pp. 54–55.

66. John Woolman, *Journal,* introduction by John G. Whittier (Boston: James R. Osgood, 1871), pp. 109–110.

67. Quoted by Calhoun, *op. cit.,* Vol. 1, p. 328.

68. *Ibid.,* Vol. 1, pp. 210–211.

69. *Minutes of the Council and General Court of Colonial Virginia,* 1622–1632, 1670–1676, H. R. McIlwaine, ed. (Richmond, Va.: Virginia State Library, 1924), pp. 85, 93.

70. *Records of the Colony of New Plymouth in New England* (Boston: William White, 1855), Vol. 1, p. 64.

71. Powers, *op. cit.,* p. 43.

72. John Winthrop, *op. cit.,* II Vol. 2, pp. 45–48.

73. *Ibid.,* Vol. 2, pp. 48–49.

74. *Records of the Colony of New Plymouth,* Nathaniel B. Shurtleff, ed. (Boston: Published by order of the General Court, William White, Printer to the Commonwealth, 1855–1861), Vol. 2, p. 35.

75. *Ibid.,* Vol. 2, p. 44; and Bradford, *op. cit.,* pp. 474–475.

76. Cotton Mather, *Magnalia Christi Americana* (Hartford, Conn.: Silas Andrus, 1820, 2 vols.), Vol. 2, p. 349.

77. *Records of the Colony of New Plymouth,* Vol. 2, p. 137.

78. Emil Oberholzer, *Delinquent Saints* (New York: Columbia University Press, 1956), p. 149.

79. George Francis Dow, *Every Day Life in the Massachusetts Bay Colony* (reprinted, New York: Benjamin Blom, 1967), p. 179.

80. Samuel Danforth, *The Cry of Sodom Enquired Into* (Cambridge, Mass., 1674).

81. Morgan, "The Puritans and Sex," p. 595.

82. Robert Calef, "More Wonders of the Invisible World, 1700," reprinted in *Narratives of the Witchcraft Cases,* George Lincoln Burr, ed. (reprinted, New York: Barnes and Noble, 1966), pp. 289–393.

83. Danforth, *op. cit.*

84. Cotton Mather, *The Angel of Bethesda,* introduction by Gordon W. Jones, ed. (Barre, Mass.: American Antiquarian Society, 1972), cap. XXI, pp. 116–120.

85. For an account of his administration in New York and in New Jersey, see Herbert L. Osgood, *The American Colonies in the Eighteenth Century* (New York: Columbia University Press, 1924, 4 vols.), Vol. 2, pp. 61–94. The charge of female impersonation was first made in 1707. Philip H. Stanhope, *History of England Comprising the Reign of Queen Anne,* 5th ed. (London: J. Murray, 1889, 2 vols.), Vol. 1, p. 79, said that Cornbury hoped to represent Queen Anne through his impersonations. John Fiske, *op. cit.,* Vol. 2, p. 238, noted Cornbury's strong likeness to his cousin Anne, which led him to dress in elaborate and sumptuous female attire. Edward Robins, *Romances of Early America* (Philadelphia: G. W. Jacobs and Company, 1902), stated that his overindulgence in liquor was responsible. See also John Burns, *Controversies between Royal Governors and Their Assemblies* (Boston: privately printed, 1923); Charles Worthen Spencer, "The Cornbury Legend," *Proceedings New York State Historical Association,* XIII (1914), pp. 309 ff. Most scholars regard him as an extremely weak governor. Edwin Platt Turner in the *Dictionary of Modern biography* (reprinted, New York: Scribner's, 1957–1958, 22 vols. in 11), Vol. 2, Part 2 (Vol. 4 in original edition), pp. 441–443, held that New York (and New Jersey) never had a governor so universally detested. When Cornbury was recalled, he was arrested and held in New York for his creditors. The death of his father and the subsequent inheritance allowed him to pay his debts. On his return to England, however, he was raised to the Privy Council and served as Envoy Extraordinary on the continent. The brief biography of him in *The National Cyclopaedia of American Biography* (New York: James T. White, 1907), Vol. 5, p. 407, says he was so weak a governor that he sometimes dressed in the "garb of a woman and thus made his appearance publicly." It added that he was universally detested.

86. Henry B. Parkes, "Morals and Law Enforcement in Colonial New England," *The New England Quarterly,* V (1932), p. 451. See also Parkes, "Sexual Morality and the Great Awakening," *The New England Quarterly,* III (1930), p. 133–135.

87. Richardson Wright, *American Wags and Eccentrics* (reprinted, New York: F. Ungar, 1965), p. 67.

88. An early account of her escapades appeared under the title of *The Female Review: or Memoirs of an American Young Lady* (Dedham, Mass.: Nathaniel and Benjamin Heaton, 1797). The anonymous author was Herman Mann. This was republished with Introduction and Notes by John Adams Vinton (Boston: J. K. Wiggin and Wm. Parsons Lunt, 1866). Vinton's work was republished as *Extra Number 47 of the Magazine of History with Notes and Queries,* 1916. The most recent and most scholarly investigation was by W. F. Norwood, "Deborah Sampson, alias Robert Shirtliff, Fighting Female of the Continental Line," *Bulletin of the History of Medicine,* XXXI (1957), pp. 147–161.

89. For tabular representations, see the appendix in Oberholzer, *op. cit.,* pp. 251 ff. There is no consistency, however, Some churches record an increase in cases during the Great Awakening, others do not. He does not deal with sodomy.

18

NINETEENTH CENTURY
ATTITUDES TOWARD SEX

American ideas about sex in the colonial period, as evidenced in the last chapter, were much the same as those of Europe during the same time span, although the American living conditions undoubtedly imposed some special problems. In the nineteenth century, European concepts about sex continued to influence American thinking on sexual matters, but Americans also contributed ideas of their own. This chapter deals with these generalized Western attitudes with illustrations from both Europe and America.

Sexual concepts of the Enlightenment, for example, were carried to the United States by English writers such as William Wollaston, Mary Wollstonecraft, and William Godwin, Mary's husband. Wollaston's *The Religion of Nature Delineated,* which went through seven editions between 1724 and 1750, included a section devoted to "Truth concerning Families and Relations," stating that marriage involved not only the propagation of the species but also the mutual happiness of the couple. Mary Wollstonecraft argued for the equality of women in sex and in other areas of life in her *Vindication of the Rights of Woman* (1792), and Godwin's *Enquiry concerning Political Justice and Its Influence on Morals and Happiness,* published in the United States in 1796, held that monogamous marriages were inconsistent with man's psychological makeup. Marriage was then little more than a romantic deception, entered into with haste, confirmed irrevocably by law, and opposed to common reason. Removing the unnecessary bindings of law and property would allow man to apply reasonable virtue and moderation to his sex life.[1]

Americans as diverse as Benjamin Franklin, Tom Paine, and the Reverend John Witherspoon (president of Princeton), picked up and modified the ideas of the *philosophes* for their American readers. Of these leaders, Franklin remains by far the best known. One of his earliest efforts, based in part on the concepts of William Wollaston, was his *Reflections on Courtship and Marriage,* published originally at Philadelphia in 1746. Franklin, as Ben Jonson did earlier, held that love might come by chance, but that it was kept only by art. In his *Autobiography,* Franklin explained that the "hard-to-be governed passions of youth" hurried him frequently into "intrigues with low women" who fell in his way, although these affairs caused him "some expense and great inconvenience, besides a continual riseque" to his health. His solution to such problems was to get married, a remedy he later proposed in his pamphlet *Advice to a Young Man on the Choice of a Mistress.* After first advising his fictional young friend to seek out marriage as the proper remedy for the "violent natural inclinations," Franklin added that if the young man

> could not take such advice and persisted in "thinking a commerce with sex inevitable," he should choose a mistress but an older one rather than a young one, since the older women likely would be more prudent, knowledgeable, and would be unable to have children. A young man could also make an old woman much more happy than a young one, and besides all mares looked the same in the dark.[2]

The Enlightenment attitudes also entered into fiction, particularly into the writings of Charles Brockden Brown, usually regarded as the first professional author in the United States. In his *Alcuin: A Dialogue* (1798), a Utopian treatise proclaiming the rights of women, Brown created a paradise where sexual equality was the norm. Women in the actual world, he felt, were regarded more or less as animals existing only for the convenience of the more dignified sex, the male. This condition should change, and he wrote a series of "gothic" romances propounding his ideas on sexual equality, including *Wieland* (1798), *Arthur Mervyn* (1799), *Ormand* (1799), *Edgar Huntly* (1799), *Clara Howard* (1801), and *Jan Talbot* (1801). He also edited several magazines carrying the new ideas on love, marriage, and society.

Rationalism and its religious component Deism were, however, soon challenged by other forces. David Hume and Immanuel Kant, among others, pointed out the limitations of reason, and Frederick Schleiermacher argued that religion was not so much a matter of intellectual belief or moral conduct as a feeling of absolute dependence on God. Moreover, even when rationalist influence was at its height, the weight of custom and tradition caused the inherited conceptions of marriage and family to remain dominant among the great majority of Americans and Europeans. There were always critics of the slightest deviation to keep people conscious of their sinfulness. Henry Muhlenberg, the great American Lutheran leader of the eighteenth century, wrote in 1743:

> There are not wanting here atheists, deists, naturalists, and freemasons. In short, there is not a sect in the world which is not cherished here. The most scandalous things are heard freely and publicly spoken against God and His holy Word. In the whole land there are many thousands, who according to their baptism, education and confirmation, should be Lutherans, but they are in part scattered. There is such a pitiable condition and ruin among our poor Lutheran people that it cannot be sufficiently wept for with tears of blood.[3]

The attempts of the American *philosophes* to establish a new sexual morality became a political issue, and some of the Federalist opponents of Thomas Jefferson attempted to link his ideas of democracy with threats to property, religion, marriage, and the family, represented by the ideas of Godwin and others. A poem in the *Columbian Centinel* in 1801 exemplified this line of attack:

> *When Godwin can prove that thieving is just,*
> *That virtue is pleasure, and pleasure is lust,*
> *That marriage is folly, and wh-r-ng is wise,*
> *And Wollstonecraft pure in philosophy's eyes.*[4]

One leader of the opposition was Timothy Dwight, grandson of Jonathan Edwards and the president of Yale University. Dwight lashed out at what he felt was the growing immorality of Americans, an immorality he equated with sexual activities. Dwight felt that the cause of America's moral descent had been a failure of the clergy to speak out against lewd thoughts and practices, since every social influence, including art, literature, and business, was working to stimulate the latent but easily reached passions of the people.[5]

Giving ammunition to the controversy was the French Revolution and the Napoleonic Wars (1789–1815), often regarded as a watershed of modern history. The Revolution itself has been studied more extensively than almost any other movement in history, in large part because it has served as an object lesson of what to do or what not to do to preserve the status quo or bring about radical change. Karl Marx was a keen student of the French Revolution, as were many other would-be revolutionaries. For most such students the Revolution was incomplete, since it did not go far enough. Though the special influence and privileges of the aristocrats had been curtailed, at least somewhat, they had not been replaced by the values of the workingman or the peasant, but instead, by those of the bourgeois, lawyers, accountants, businessmen, and so forth.

Intellectually, these bourgeois ideas are usually called liberalism, and the nonrevolutionary prophet of the new movement was the economic philosopher Adam Smith (1723–1790), whose ideas were employed to free the middle classes from what they believed hampered them in their exercise of initiative. Based on his and similar ideas, nineteenth-century liberals believed they had the answers to all types of situations and could offer a remedy for every problem. Basic to a society founded on liberalism was the absence of control, although not all the "liberals" would carry this lack of control to the sexual field. Most effective in so doing were the utilitarians, centered around Jeremy Bentham (1748–1832), who evolved a simple criterion for deciding public policy in virtually any area—that program should be pursued that would ensure the greatest happiness or good to the greatest number. This principle of utility was to be the guiding principle in formulating laws regarding sexual conduct as well, and Bentham and his disciples, particularly John Stuart Mill (1806–1873), had strong ideas about this.

Wherever there are liberals in today's world, there are also conservatives, although neither the term *liberal* nor *conservative* any longer has the meaning it once did. For a time, especially after Napoleon's defeat and the restoration of the French monarchy, conservatism was dominant, and it, like liberalism, had a strong English tinge. Edmund Burke (1729–1797), an opponent of the French Revolution, was a major prophet of conservatism, but it was more fully developed on the European continent through the efforts of Joseph de Maistre (1753–1821) and the Vicomte de Bonald (1754–1840), who started out as simple reactionaries, striking out with fury at the *philosophes,* whom they held had introduced the poison of revolution. Eventually, however, both men saw the need for reconstructing society and put this reconstruction in terms of the need for discipline, since without the discipline of monarchy, the Church, nobility, and morality, they felt disorder, corruption, and decay would result. For them individualism and democracy were diseases resulting in social anarchy and immorality, and by implication any lessening of the sexual code would increase the possibility of infection.

Modifying the harshness of the conservatives toward sex was the movement known as romanticism, which started out as a reaction to the rationalism of the enlightened philosophers and liberals, who held that man and his needs in life could be objectified. Instead, the romantic believed that man represented something more than the sum of his parts and that to ignore this was to overlook essential elements of man and his world. Romanticism, which can be traced to some of the writings of Jean Jacques Rousseau and Johann Wolfgang von Goethe (1749–1832), reached its greatest influence in nineteenth-century Germany, from whence it spread outward. In many ways romanticism was sexually liberating, particularly in its emphasis on passion and emotion as distinct from the rational intellect; the critical spirit was to be replaced by an imaginative one. The true romantic was encouraged to go against social conventions, to emphasize physical passion, to recognize the fact of sexual inconstancy, and to cultivate emotion and sensation for their own sake. Put in this way, the sexual beliefs of the romantics turned out to be not so different from those of the *philosophes*, although the thought processes by which they arrived at conclusions were different; in fact, romantic ideas served as an antidote to the nineteenth-century rationalists, who adopted an antisex policy because science had pointed out its dangers.

Adherents of romanticism revived Plato's theory that every individual was but one-half of a complete entity, so that somewhere there was to be found the twin-soul, the missing half, the only person in the world who provided the full complement for one's own personality. For the romantic, sex had a positive value, but only if it took place within this intense psychological relationship. In fact, for many, sexual union was illegitimate unless the lovers were joined by emotional and intellectual ties as well as physical ones. Sex was possible only with the beloved, and its purpose was to link together two individuals motivated by the highest emotions. In Percy Bysshe Shelley's terms, the female partner should be "as perfect and beautiful as possible, both in body and in mind, so that all sympathies may be harmoniously blended, and the moment of abandonment be prepared by the entire consent of all the conscious portions of our being."[6]

Marriage relationships that were loveless and oppressive ought to be dissolved, and the German Johann Fichte (1762–1814) went so far as to state that marriage without love was to be regarded as grounds for an automatic divorce.[7] Generally, the romantics believed that, once a true love was found, the lovers became so perfectly united in body and soul that true love was identical with fidelity.[8] Not all agreed, however, that love was eternal and immutable; Shelley, for one, held that, in the normal course of life, one could fall in love more than once.

> A husband and wife ought to continue so long united as they love each other: any law which should bind them to cohabitation for one moment after the decay of their affection would be most intolerable tyranny. . . . The connection of the sexes is so long sacred as it contributes to the comfort of the parties, and is naturally dissolved when its evils are greater than its benefits.[9]

According to the romantics, woman had been denied her humanity in a world ruled by men; she needed to be liberated from masculine tyranny, although they were ambivalent about how far woman should be allowed to go. Their contradictory feelings were at least partially a result of the fact that, while they recognized the disabilities under which women lived, they still stressed the nature of the opposite in the male and female psychology. Marriage was the union of opposites, the female complementing the male, and thus if he was aggressive, she was passive; if he was rational, she was emotional.

Increasingly, as the nineteenth century developed, the free-love aspects of romanticism were modified and marriage came to be looked on as the natural result of romantic love. Those romantics conscious of the inherent masculine bias in their characterizations of maleness and femaleness attempted to soften the demarcation between male and female by preferring "delicate and dreamy men, free and daring girls." The German Friedrich von Schlegel (1772–1829) wondered what

> is uglier than overemphasized womanliness, what is more repulsive than the exaggerated manliness which prevails in our mores, our opinions, yes, even in our art? . . . Only self-reliant womanliness, only gentle manliness, is good and beautiful.[10]

In his novel *Lucinda* the male protagonist stated to his mistress:

> We exchange roles and with childish delight try to see who can best imitate the other; whether you succeed best with the tender vehemence of a man, or I with the yielding devotion of a woman. . . . This sweet game has for me quite other charms than its own. . . . I see in it a wonderful and profoundly significant allegory of the development of man and woman into complete humanity.[11]

Since, in most cases, sexual roles were not blurred but only intellectually exchanged, men generally continued to be portrayed as aggressively masculine and women as femininely yielding. Theoretically, however, it was possible for a woman to have the volatile and spontaneous qualities of the male and for a man to have the patient and receptive qualities of the female, and occasionally such individuals entered into heterosexual relationships, as George Sand (Amandine Aurore Lucie née Dupin, 1804–1876) did with her various lovers. The result was often, however, an idealization of homoerotic attachments.

Such a theme appears in the work of Goethe, the giant of German literature during this period. In his novel *Wilhelm Meisters Wanderjahre,* Goethe described a scene in which Wilhelm Meister observed his friend swimming in the water.

> It was so warm and damp that one wanted to go into the shade, and from the shade into the cooler water. Therefore, it was easy for him to entice me into the water. I found his invitation irresistable . . . (he) returned, and when he emerged and stood up in the bright sunlight to dry himself, I felt as if my eyes were blinded by a triple sun, so beautiful was the human body. I had had no idea. He seemed to observe me with the same attention. . . . Our souls attracted each other, and with the most passionate kisses we swore eternal friendship. . . . My friend accompanied me; we seemed inseparable already. When I timidly requested permission to take him into the official's house with me, the minister's wife denied it, quietly commenting on the impropriety of it. . . . The boy departed, but promised with hand and mouth to wait for me this evening in the near corner of the woods.[12]

Similar themes appear in several of his poems and plays.[13]

Other romantic poets also dealt with homoerotic attachments. Johann Christoph Friedrich von Schiller (1759–1805), in his trilogy on *Wallenstein*, included this passage in the section *Wallensteins Tod*. Wallenstein is speaking:

> *Max! Stay with me—don't leave me, Max!*
> *Remember when you, a tender boy, were brought to me in my*
> *tent in winter quarters at Prague,*
> *Unused to the German winter, your hand*
> *Benumbed on the heavy flag,*
> *You dutifully clung to it, then I took*
> *You in, covered you with my coat,*
> *I alone was your nursemaid, no service*
> *Was too petty for me, I cared*
> *For you with careful womanly zeal,*
> *Until you, warmed by me, on my heart,*
> *Happily felt young life again.*
> *Has my feeling changed since then?*
> *I have made thousands rich,*
> *Given them estates, rewarded*
> *Them with positions of honor—I've loved you,*
> *Given you my heart, my self.*
> *They were all strangers, you were*
> *The child of the house—Max! you can't leave me!*
> *It cannot be, I can't and won't believe*
> *That Max can leave me.*

> Max.   *O God!*
> Wallenstein.   *I have guided and protected you*
> *Since childhood—What did your father*
> *Do for you that I didn't do abundantly?*
> *I've spun a love-net around you,*
> *Tear it if you can—you are*
> *Linked to me with the most tender spiritual bond,*
> *With the holiest fetters of nature*
> *That can join humans together.*
> *Go, leave me, serve your Kaiser,*
> *Be rewarded a little golden chain*
> *Grace, a ram's skin, (order of the Golden Fleece)*
> *Because your buddy, the father of your youth,*
> *The holiest sentiment, doesn't count for anything.*

> . . .

> *You are part of me, I am your Kaiser,*
> *Your honor; your law of nature*
> *Is that you belong to me, you obey me.*[14]

Sometimes we might read more into these passages than the author intended, since the meaning often remains ambiguous. Johann Christian Friedrich Hol-derlin's (1770–1843) poem *Sokrates und Alcibiades,* for example, is often considered an example of homoerotic love, but it can also be interpreted to describe close, intimate friendships without any erotic connotations:

> *Why do you, holy Socrates, so*
> *Constantly honor this youth? Don't you know anything greater?*
> *Why do you look on him with love,*
> *As on a god?*
> *He who has thought profoundly loves the liveliest,*
> *Understands youth when he's seen the world,*
> *And often, the wise are finally attracted to beauty.*[15]

Less ambiguous is the poem *Ghaselen* by the homophile August Graf von Platen-Hallermünde (1796–1835), dedicated to the German poet Friedrich Rückert.

> *I am as body to soul, as soul to body for you;*
> *I am as wife to husband, as husband to wife for you,*
> *Who else do you dare love, since I drove death*
> *From your lips with eternal kisses for you?*
> *I am your scent of roses, your nightingale's son,*
> *I am a ray of sunlight, the new moon for you;*
> *What more do you want? Why do you look with desire?*
> *Throw everything away; you know, I exist for you!*[16]

Such ardent expressions of homoerotic affection did not go unchallenged. Hein-rich Heine (1797–1856), for example, included comments on the poetic efforts of Count Platen in his writings:

As a man I feel somewhat flattered that Count Platen places us above women, but as a friend of women, I find I am an opponent of such a man. People are like that! One likes onions, another warm friendship. As an honest man, I must admit I like onions, and find a cockeyed housekeeper preferable to the most beautiful comrade. Honestly, I really can't find so much beauty in the male sex that I should fall in love with it.[17]

Praise of homoerotic attachments was not limited to the German romantics but was an underlying theme among many writers. George Gordon Byron, Lord Byron (1788–1824), for example, made reference to homoerotic attach-ments in some of his writings,[18] although the long *Don Leon* poems in which boy love is praised are now believed to be by George Colman the younger (1762–1836).[19] Unavoidably, though the romantics had caught the fancy of the middle class, their attacks on long-cherished institutions made them unaccepta-ble in the long run to the powerful bourgeoisie, whose code proclaimed personal responsibility, respect for parents, and formal adherence to religion, if not enthusiastic response. Writers such as Stendhal (Marie Henri Beyle, 1783–1842) led an offensive against the romantics by noting that passion was a subjective experience leading to distortion. Stendhal noted that a bare bough of a tree that fell into a saltpit and lay there for some time acquired a covering of brilliant crystals, and as a result, when it was extracted, the shabby branch appeared to be a priceless *objet d'art,* although in reality it was worthless. From this, he drew an analogy to the experience of love, which he called crystallization. Love was a fantasy, a projection of the individual's ego-ideal onto the often undeserved object, but when reality intruded, crystallization ended, as did love.[20] Gustave Flaubert (1821–1880), ridiculed romanticism further in his *Madame Bovary,* the heroine of which dreamed of being a romantic figure, although she was married to a dull country doctor. Her aspirations were soon jarred by the reality of being seduced by a frayed roué and a simple clerk. Eventually, her love fantasies gone, she poisoned herself.[21]

Even when the romantics were under attack, they could not be ignored, if only because they represented a mood of sexual freedom that had strong support, particularly among the young, for whom the bourgeois code was regarded as preventing excitement and freedom of action. Even conservative writers criticized marriages of convenience as morally wrong, damning their participants to perpetual unhappiness. Large segments of the reading public identified with Jane Eyre in Charlotte Brontë's novel of the same name, when she refused the suit of St. John Rivers, whom she liked but did not love. To receive the bridal ring from such a man, most readers probably agreed, would make for a monstrous martyrdom.[22]

In America the most clearly defined romantic literary movement was transcendentalism, which included such authors as Henry Thoreau, Ralph Waldo Emerson, Louisa May Alcott, and Margaret Fuller at the center, with most other major American writers of the period on the fringe. Though the romantics often emphasized natural beauty, the common man uncorrupted by civilization, and the picturesque past or remote places, they were also of this world, and in their concern with humanitarianism took the lead in such things as abolitionism and feminism, as well as in the communal living experiments at Brook Farm and New Harmony. Many of their communal experiments were designed to remove the sexual inhibitions of outer society.

Increasingly, however, the romantic notions about sex came to be diluted by an elevation of the woman, the angel who purified the passions, at least when they were expressed in the confines of holy matrimony.[23] As the medical writers and the Victorian handbooks of sexuality ever emphasized in the period after 1830, marriage transformed and purified lust. No longer was the inherent bisexuality of the two sexes stressed, but rather the female's duty to keep the male beast in control. Charles Kingsley (1819–1875), in his novel *Yeast* (1850), had his hero Lancelot Smith bemoan the peccadilloes that had led him not only to sin against God but also to face the prospect of bringing a soiled body to the wedding bed:

> The contact of her stainless innocence . . . made him shrink from her whenever he remembered his own guilty career. . . . She would cast him from her with abhorrance if she once really (knew) . . . that she would bring to him what he could never, never bring to her! . . . he would have welcomed centuries of a material Hell . . . to buy back that pearl of innocence, which he had cast recklessly to be trampled under the feet of his own swinish passions![24]

Ultimately, the attempt to fuse romanticism and conventional marriage failed. Often, in fact, it led to serious difficulties, as evidenced by the author, critic, and social reformer, John Ruskin (1819–1900). Ruskin refused to consummate his own marriage with his 19-year-old bride Effie because he found Effie had pubic hair. As Effie later wrote, "he had imagined women were quite different to what he saw I was and . . . the reason why he did not make me his wife was because he was disgusted with my person the first evening."[25] She endured this state of affairs for some 6 years before having the marriage annulled, whereupon she married the painter John Millais and bore him eight children.

Ruskin later fell in love with a 10-year-old child whom he was tutoring, Rose La Touche. Their courtship waned as Rose became a woman, but they maintained some contact until her death in her 20's.[26] The difficulty with this mid-Victorian concept of love was that it left men and women in constant turmoil and conflict.

> It was difficult enough to suppress sexual behavior, but to excite oneself by talking constantly about passion and then forego the sensual pleasures was doubly frustrating. The *Westminster Review* could extol the virtue of 'repressed . . . hallowed and elevated passion', but few living examples could be found. . . . Ruskin's madness probably stemmed, in part, from his guilt over masturbation and his inability to fulfill his interest in sex with adult women. It proved most difficult to be preoccupied with sex, to sublimate, and still remain well adjusted.[27]

The mid-nineteenth-century Englishman perceived his fellowmen as weak and base physical animals, who through thrift, self-control, and perseverance, could rise to the pinnacle of success, namely, a successful Christian businessman. Horatio Alger stories were an American reflection of the ideal. Only a respectable and well-established man could afford to marry and have a family, and so marriage was delayed for men until they had achieved some modicum of success; then they married a woman much younger than themselves. Though this proved to be an effective method of birth control, it caused difficulty for the

male who delayed marriage so long, and prostitution, pornography, and homosexuality were concomitants of such practices.

Sexual misconceptions were probably more prevalent in the nineteenth
century than in an earlier age because of the growing concept of privacy, a concept encouraged by the change in living conditions. Until almost the
seventeenth century it was rarely possible for anyone to be left alone. People
lived closely together, and the density of social life made isolation virtually impossible; even children were aware of the nature of sex. People who shut
themselves up in a room for some time were regarded as exceptionally eccentric. In the eighteenth century, owing in part to increased prosperity, the
style of living changed, and houses themselves were altered to establish new
means of achieving privacy. Rooms, for example, were made independent of
each other, opening on a hallway instead of passing from one to another. Beds
were confined to the bedroom, which was furnished with cupboards of alcoves,
often fitted out with the new toilet and hygienic equipment. In France and Italy
the word *chambre* began to be used to denote the room in which one slept, as
distinct from *salle,* the room where one received visitors and ate. In England,
though the word *room* was kept for all functions, a prefix was added to give
precision, the dining room, the bedroom, and so forth. Privacy became even
more valued in the nineteenth century.

At the same time, there was a great concentration on family life, particularly
among the middle class. It was recognized that the child was not ready for life,
that he or she had to be subject to special treatment, a sort of quarantine before
being allowed to join the adults. Since the child was to be isolated from society,
it seemed obvious that women also, the natural guardians of the children,
should be isolated. Motherhood became a special calling, demanding equal
time with other occupations, and the tendency to put a woman on a pedestal
reached a new height. Collectively, this led to a set of attitudes going by the
name of Victorianism, although Victorianism is much more than prudery. In a
sense it represents a compromise between the heroic and the Utopian aspects of
the new ethics and the real life of ordinary people who strove to follow conventional Christianity. The term *Victorian* is also associated with the self-satisfaction engendered by the great increase of wealth taking place in the nineteenth
century that led the middle class in particular to adopt conscious rectitude and
an unquestioning acceptance of authority and to believe that their society was
more moral than those of the past. Victorianism, as the term implies, originated in Great Britain, which, as the most powerful nation of the time, set the
tone in many matters of morals, manners, and even taste. Although it was primarily associated with the attitudes of the middle class, it had marked implications for attitudes toward both women and sex.

Victorianism was in part also a result of industrialization, since the industrial revolution of the late eighteenth and early nineteenth centuries had

forced women to alter their styles of life and inevitably brought them into conflict with customs and institutions based on more or less obsolete economic factors. Though there is nothing inherent in the industrial revolution itself to fix
how the family would be organized or what attitudes toward women would be,
it did give further emphasis to the nuclear family. Inevitably women, particularly
of the middle class, found themselves confined to a home that had lost much of its
economic importance. To compensate for this the Victorians moved, consciously
or unconsciously, to make the home the center of social life revolving around the
family, paying great reverence to woman's role in raising children and in providing a haven for the male to retreat to from the outside world. A new concept of
motherhood developed, enveloping the woman into a mystique that asserted their
special status but at the same time kept them confined. Common women went to
work in the factories, neglecting their families, and aristocratic women remained
outside the bounds of middle-class morality, but the good woman, the true middle-class woman, as befitted her newfound moral purity and spiritual genius, had
to devote herself to the task of homemaking, something that in the past had not
been regarded as particularly important. Chastity was the mark of the new
gentility, and though chastity or its lack might be difficult to prove, the assumptions of chastity were not. Thus there were many things a proper lady could not
or would not do. If a girl's dress was too revealing, her ornaments too provocative, her speech and gestures too bold, then some people would assume that she
had lost her chastity. Appearance counted for more than reality. It was
absolutely essential that a proper girl look and behave with a respectable
"modesty."

The burden put on women by such an attitude was one that many of them
did not want and could not bear, but often the only outlet for their discontent
was in church work or in literary pursuits. Religion in a sense became a justification for what they wanted to do but otherwise could not do, and even
women's suffrage became overlaid with the concepts of raising the standards of
morality by allowing the purer and finer species, the woman, to vote. Victorianism taught women to think of themselves as a special class, and having become conscious of their unique sexual identity, they could no longer accept
uncritically the role definitions drawn up for them. Denied liberty, they sought
power, and not infrequently the way to gain power was through their children.
Motherhood came to be elevated into a mystique, which Sigmund Freud made
into a pseudoscientific basis of existence. Though the Victorian conception of
women as wan, ethereal, spiritualized creatures bore little relation to the real
world, where women operated machines, worked the fields, handwashed clothing, and toiled over great kitchen stoves, it was endorsed by both science and
religion. Even fashion conspired to the same end, for the bustles and hoops, the
corsets and trailing skirts in which women were encased throughout much of
the nineteenth century, seem, in retrospect, to have been designed to prevent

them from entering the vigorous world of men. Feminine delicacy, which might well have been encouraged by their constricting corsets, was considered visible evidence of their superior sensibilities, the "finer clay" out of which they were supposedly made. Since it was expected that women demonstrate a meticulous personal daintiness, their gestures were to be void of signs of vigorous masculinity, and their clothes and hairdress were to have an unfunctional fragility. Women who were not delicate by nature became so by design, since women themselves believed in their special calling, their special genius, and those women who failed to conform were usually ostracized by other women. The world was regarded as being made up of good girls and bad girls. The bad girls represented sexuality, the good girls, purity of mind and spirit, unclouded by the shadow of any gross or vulgar thought. The largest collection of bad girls were the prostitutes, and they were thought to have poor moral inheritance. Even the creative activities for women had to be restricted to certain fields. They could paint or sketch but not too creatively and not in oils; they could play a musical instrument but not professionally, and their instruments were restricted to those that could be played without spreading their legs, pursing their lips, viscerally demonstrating their muscles, or mussing their dress or coiffure. This meant that primarily they played the piano. The list of restrictions could be extended for several pages, but the point is that proper women became by design and training wan, ethereal, sedentary, passive persons, symbols of chastity and delicacy.[28]

The Victorian hostility to sex was not, however, without foundation, and large segments of nineteenth-century Europe and America came to be more and more influenced by the medical concepts featuring the dangers of masturbation, articulated earlier by Tissot. Though Tissot's work was not printed in America until 1832, his influence appears much earlier and is evident in the writings of Benjamin Rush (1745–1813), the dominant medical figure in America at the end of the eighteenth century. Rush was not only a signer of the Declaration of Independence but also a crusader for the emancipation of slaves, abolition of the death penalty, temperance, and in the context of this chapter, sexual reform. Rush, who had studied in Edinburgh, returned to his native country to introduce a variation of John Brown's medical idea. All disease could be reduced to one basic causal model, either the diminution or increase of nervous energy. One led to direct debility, the other to indirect debility, but in either case, the body was left in such a poor condition that it was unable to resist the external forces that attacked it and made it susceptible to illness and disease.[29]

Since all disease could be reduced to the single causal factor of the debility of the nervous system, the physician's duty was to relieve the strains on the nervous system, and this would then permit the underlying debility to disappear. Sexual intercourse was a major cause of excitement; Rush taught that careless indulgence in sex would lead to "seminal weakness, impotence, dysury, tabes dorsalis, pulmonary consumptions, dyspepsia, dimness of sight, vertigo, epilepsy, hypochondriasis, loss of memory, manalgia, fatuity, and death." Rush did not entirely discount the positive aspects of sex, stressing also that abnormal restraint in sexual matters was dangerous, since it might produce "tremors, a flushing of the face, sighing, nocturnal pollution, hysteria, hypochondriasis, and in women, the furor uterinus."[30]

Even more fearful of the dangers of sexuality than Rush was Sylvester Graham (1794–1851), perhaps best remembered for his advocacy of unbolted wheat or Graham flour and commemorated today by the Graham cracker. Graham believed that his contemporaries suffered from an increasing incidence of debility, skin and lung diseases, headaches, nervousness, and weakness of the brain, much of which resulted from sexual excess. He taught that the body had both organic and animal life. Animal life was represented by the organs and powers of sensation, voluntary motion, and volition, and organic life included those organs and powers concerned with the function of nutrition, particularly those pertaining to digestion, respiration, circulation, secretion, absorption, and excretion. Both the animal and organic aspects of the body were controlled by networks of nerves. Those pertaining to animal life were connected with the brain and the spinal marrow and from there were distributed to the muscles of voluntary motion and to the "sensitive surface of the body, or external skin." Organic life was controlled within the organs themselves by a kind of rudimentary brain or bulbous enlargement of the nervous substance that he called a ganglion or knob, of which there was "a large number in different parts of the body."[31]

Reproduction, almost alone of the body's functions, was related to the organs associated with both animal and organic life, and thus sex put a particularly unique strain on the body. Graham went further claiming it was not only an orgasm that posed dangers to the body but also lascivious thought and imagination; by exciting and stimulating the genital organs, these also posed dangers. Similarly, since sex involved both forms of life in the body, there was reciprocity between it and the condition of the stomach, heart, lungs, skin, and brain—all of which could be greatly influenced by the abuse or misuse of the sexual organs.[32] From such assumptions Graham concluded that one result of excessive sexual desire was insanity, and insanity itself incited excessive sexual desire. Desire was also affected by eating stimulating substances such as "high seasoned food, rich dishes, the free use of flesh," and so forth.[33] The influence of sexual desire was so all pervasive that a heat of passion disturbed and disordered "all the functions of the system," causing a general debility. Husbands and wives who overindulged in sex would soon be afflicted with

languor, lassitude, muscular relaxation, general debility and heaviness, depression of spirits, loss of appetite, indigestion, faintness and sinking at the pit of the stomach, increased susceptibilities of the skin and lungs to all the atmospheric changes, feebleness of circulation, chilliness, headache, melancholy, hypochondria, hysterics, feebleness of all the senses, impaired vision, loss of sight, weakness of the lungs, nervous cough, pulmonary consumption, disorders of the liver and kidneys, urinary difficulties, disorders of the genital organs, spinal diseases, weakness of the brain, loss of memory, epilepsy, insanity, apoplexy, abortions, premature births, and extreme feebleness, morbid predispositions, and early death of offspring.[34]

Graham taught that the loss of an ounce of semen was equivalent to the loss of several ounces of blood, with the result that, every time a man ejaculated, he lowered his life force and thereby exposed his system to diseases and premature death. Graham wanted his readers to change their diet to include foods such as unbolted wheat flour (hence Graham flour), rye meal, and hominy, which foods he felt would cut down on their sexual desires. He also urged married individuals to limit their sexual indulgence to not more than 12 times a year.[35] Graham's work went through 10 editions between 1834 and 1848, was translated into several foreign languages, and obviously added to the growing fears about untrammeled sexuality.[36]

Fears of sex were not confined to the English-speaking world; one of the influential forces in highlighting the dangers of sex was the French surgeon Claude-Francois Lallemand, whose book received an American edition in 1839. Lallemand was primarily concerned with the involuntary loss of male semen, spermatorrhea, something he felt would lead to insanity. Since spermatorrhea in adults was a natural consequence of youthful masturbation, parents had to be ever vigilant. Equally dangerous was the inflammation of youthful minds through reading lascivious books; even daydreaming was dangerous, for young people either began to masturbate to gratify their "morbid" thoughts or had involuntary emissions (wet dreams) at night. Lallemand's American translator added to the evidence produced by the French writer by pointing out that the reports of the Massachusetts State Lunatic Hospital at Worcester indicated that 55 of the 407 patients had become insane from the effects of masturbation, 43 of the males and 12 of the females. Thus, even though a person ceased masturbating in his adult life, he might still become insane because of spermatorrhea, or he could suffer other serious consequences.[37]

William Acton (1814–1875), an English physician, was equally worried about the loss of vital energy through sexual activity. He taught that the emission of semen imposed such a great drain on the nervous system that the only way the male could avoid damage was to engage in sex infrequently and then without prolonging the sex act. Males were able to do this because God had created females indifferent to sex to prevent the male's vital energy from being overly expended. Only out of fear that their husbands would desert them for courtesans or prostitutes did most women waive their own natural inclinations and submit to their husband's ardent embraces. But woman's reluctance forced the husband to perform his necessary biological function of impregnation in as expeditious a way as possible without severe damage to the nervous system.[38] Still, there were dangers if the act was repeated too frequently, and any kind of seminal emission, even that aimed at procreation, posed dangers. The worst kind of seminal emission was masturbation. The only way to keep biological man and women under control was to insist that their sexual energy be used almost totally for procreation.[39]

Motherhood was woman's normal destiny, and though women were not particularly sexual, it was dangerous for them to thwart nature's purpose. The maiden lady was thus fated to have a greater incidence of physical and emotional disturbances and a much shorter life span.[40] The medical literature is, however, inconsistent, since sex was natural and yet unnatural, natural because God had ordained it but unnatural if used for any other purpose than procreation. Children were innocent, yet they had to be zealously guarded because of the risk of a suddenly appearing sexual appetite.

Masturbation was a sin against nature, equal to sodomy, but far more dangerous because it was the most extensively practiced, and there were no "bounds to its indulgence."[41] The American John Harvey Kellogg, whose Battle Creek Sanitarium introduced new breakfast foods to the world, wrote that there were many suspicious signs of the masturbator, including a general debility, consumption-like symptoms, premature and defective development, sudden changes in disposition, lassitude, sleeplessness, failure of mental capacity, fickleness, untrustworthiness, love of solitude, bashfulness, unnatural boldness, mock piety, being easily frightened, confusion of ideas, aversion to girls in boys but a decided liking for boys in girls, round shoulders, weak backs and stiffness of joints, paralysis of the lower extremities, unnatural gait, bad position in bed, lack of breast development in females, capricious appetite, fondness for unnatural and hurtful or irritating articles (such as salt, pepper, spices, vinegar, mustard, clay, slate pencils, plaster, and chalk), disgust of simple food, use of tobacco, unnatural paleness, acne or pimples, biting of fingernails, shifty eyes, moist cold hands, palpitation of the heart, hysteria in females, chlorosis or green sickness, epileptic fits, bed-wetting, and the use of obscene words and phrases. The dangers were terrible to behold, since genital excitement produced intense congestion and led to urethral irritation, inflammation of the urethra, enlarged prostate, bladder and kidney infection, priapism, piles and prolapsus of the rectum, atrophy of the testes, varicocele, nocturnal emissions, and general exhaustion. Kellogg believed that the nervous shock accompanying the exercise of the sexual organs was the most profound to which the nervous system was subject, and even those who engaged in procreation would have to limit their activities strongly or else insanity would result.[42]

But why, if sexual activity was so harmful, had not generations of individuals become insane in the past? Those concerned with the new "scientific

findings" about sex had an answer to that question, namely, the growing com-
plexities of modern civilization and the higher evolutionary development of humanity. One popularizer of this idea was the physician George M. Beard, who
argued that "modern" civilization had put such increased stress on mankind
that larger and larger numbers of people were suffering from nervous exhaustion. Such exhaustion, he held, was particularly great among the educated,
brainy workers in society, who represented a higher stage on the evolutionary
scale than the less advanced social classes, and thus as man advanced, it became
more and more necessary to save his nervous energy. According to Beard, the
human body was a reservoir of "force constantly escaping, constantly being
renewed" but frequently in danger of imbalance. A chief cause of nervous
exhaustion was sexual intercourse; unless the nervous energy that went into it
was carefully regulated and guarded, nervous exhaustion would result.[43]

Predictably, the result of these theories was a renewed hostility to sex, the
reinforcing of traditional Western hostility to sex with a scientific foundation.
Writers of most popular sex manuals, whether physicians, clergy, or teachers,
mounted a crusade against sex, hitting with sledgehammer force the dangers of
unnatural sex, which came to be interpreted as any kind of sex activity not
leading to procreation. One reason masturbation was viewed with such horror
was that the term itself became a catchword for all "unnatural" sex, from the
use of contraceptives to homosexuality.[44] It was regarded as 10 times worse
than simple illicit intercourse between an unmarried man and woman, since at
least children might result from the latter activities.[45] It was described as the
most criminal, most pernicious, and most "unnatural"[46] and eventually came
to be described consistently as a disease and sometimes a contagious one at
that.[47] Moreover, masturbation was worse than most other diseases, for it continually drained off the vital body fluids and gradually took away life itself.[48]
Every loss of semen was regarded as equivalent to the loss of 4 ounces of
blood,[49] and though the body could eventually replace this loss, it took time for
it to recuperate. Even worse than seminal loss in the male was masturbation in
the female. Women masturbators not only suffered from the consequences that
males did but also were afflicted with rickets, hysteria, jaundice, stomach
cramps, womb ulcers, elongation and eruption of the clitoris, *furor uterinus,*
loss of interest in the opposite sex, hermaphroditism, leucorrhea, painful
menstruation, falling of the womb, loss of pleasures in the sex act, painful
childbirth, and obstinate sterility.[50]

Those physicians who hesitated to warn patients of the danger of sex activity
were chastised by other physicians, since it was alleged that their silence led to
wasted lives.[51] The famed Abraham Jacobi, considered the founder of pediatrics
in the United States, was reflecting the best medical opinion when he blamed
infantile paralysis and infantile rheumatism on masturbation.[52] Though
medical practitioners recognized that occasionally the dangers of sex were

overexaggerated, this was felt not to be as dangerous in the long run as ignoring them.[53]

In some of the medical literature, onanism or masturbation was also a euphemism for homosexuality. Kellogg, already mentioned, pointed to the dangers of a "hired man" in communicating sex knowledge about masturbation and other evils to young boys, just as hired girls did to young girls. Parents had to be ever vigilant.[54] A description of a typical insane masturbator featured his effeminate manners, and masturbation was believed to encourage the formation of "morbid attachments" for persons of the same sex.[55] Some writers went so far as to claim that pederasts were diseased individuals who had started on their path by masturbating.[56]

Just how far the term *masturbation* had replaced the old concept of sin against nature is indicated by the physician James Foster Scott, who described masturbation as including coitus interruptus, coitus *in os,* coitus *interfemora,* pederasty, bestiality, mutual masturbation, and "self pollution," the same breakdown that the early confessional manuals had made for the sin against nature. According to Scott, once a young person began to manipulate his or her genitals, he or she went further and further down the road to unnatural relationships, eventually forming attractions for persons of the same sex.[57] This danger existed for girls as well as boys,[58] and homosexuality remained a strong undercurrent, even in early twentieth-century fears of masturbation. This is best exemplified by the writings of G. Stanley Hall, a pioneer of American psychology and an early writer on adolescence. Hall held that onanism was caused by seduction of "younger by older" children, and once established, it was the major cause of "one or more of the morbid forms of sex perversion."[59]

Any unusual position in intercourse or any action outside that designed to impregnate the female was cause for trouble. One manual reported the case history of a young woman whose husband "had the fatal habit of applying the tongue and lips to his wife's genitals to provoke in her a venereal orgasm." The unavoidable result was "gastralgia" and "constant exhaustion" in the woman, until the physician treating her felt called upon to warn her that her very life would be in danger unless her husband ceased this foul practice. The physician warned that cunnilingus and fellatio would cause a cancer of the tongue, and anal intercourse would result in even greater afflictions.[60] The worst danger of all was that if anyone engaging in such "perversions" had offspring, the child itself would be born with perverted instincts.[61]

Most writers were careful to point out that they were not against procreative intercourse, provided the participants observed moderation and temperance. Those able to preserve marital continence would be rewarded "by a sound constitution, an approving mind, and the applause of the deserving and considerate,"[62] but those who engaged only moderately would elevate the noblest faculties of their minds,[63] and in no case was it ever possible that chastity could be excessive.[64] Married couples interested in procreation were to limit their attempts at coition to "one indulgence to each lunar month." This was all "the best health of the parties can require."[65] The concept of once a month was widely advocated, provided it was tempered by God's wish, and couples were urged not to engage in sex at all when the female was pregnant or otherwise incapable of procreation. Moreover, it was the law of God that no animal, let alone a human, should "use the reproductive powers and organs for any other purpose than simple procreation."[66] The more individuals were able to confine their sexual indulgence to the generation and development of offspring, the nearer they came to fulfilling the "supreme law" of being and the nearer they came to being true Christians.[67] Medical writers increasingly assured their readers that the only reason God had designed the "intercourse of the sexes" was for the production of offspring.[68] Though the pleasure, at least for the male, in doing his duty to beget children could not be denied, parents were warned about seeking or prolonging pleasure, since there were "undeniable instances where children begotten in the moment of intoxication remained stupid and idiots during their whole life." Logic was marshaled to demonstrate that conception during time of ill humor, bodily indisposition, or too much nervous strain would affect the child that resulted.[69] Licentious indulgence could result only in some degree of mental inactivity and imbecility,[70] and intercourse during pregnancy reduced the constitutional vigor of the fetus and predisposed it to debilitating diseases.[71] Some believed that a woman would not get pregnant unless she had an orgasm, and others said that, if she participated in the enjoyment when she was pregnant, her role as a mother would be endangered, and it would cause miscarriage.[72] Intercourse should cease when the woman entered her menopause, since this was nature's way of putting a "cessation" to the female's sexual functions.[73] Those who did engage in sexual pleasures after the age of 50 would find themselves exhausted and dangerously prone to illness.[74] Thus, in "well-regulated lives," the sexual passions became less and less imperious, diminishing gradually, until at an average age of 45 in the woman and 55 in the man, they were but rarely awakened and seldom satisfied.[75]

Even at the height of their powers of procreation, women were warned not to enjoy sex, since women were maternal rather than sexual creatures. Only the diseased female had an "excessive animal passion."[76] For many writers, the woman who enjoyed sex was a sick creature, and women themselves often tended to agree, perhaps because they saw that the only way they could liberate themselves from the continual burdens of pregnancy and lactation was to deemphasize their sexuality. Some of the strongest advocates of women's maternal nature were other women. A certain Mrs. E. B. Duffy wrote that real women regarded all men, not as lovers, but as stepsons for whom they had a mother's "tenderness."[77] Perhaps the best summation of these ideas was by Mrs. Eliza-

beth Osgood Goodrich Willard, who held that the sexual orgasm was more debilitating to the system than a day's work. She regarded sex as more or less a
loathsome thing and was unhappy that people were generated under a system
so easily abused. She argued that mankind must stop the waste of energy

> through the sexual organs, if we would have health and strength of body. Just as
> sure as that the excessive abuse of the sexual organs destroy their power and use,
> producing inflammation, disease, and corruption, just so sure is it that a less
> amount of abuse in the same relative proportion, injures the parental function of
> the organs, and impairs the health and strength of the whole system. Abnormal ac-
> tion is abuse.[78]

With such attitudes toward the dangers of sexual abuse, there was a determined effort to find preventatives for those unable to control their own
sexuality. Some doctors perforated the foreskin of the penis and inserted a ring
or cut the foreskin with jagged scissors. Others applied ointments that would
make the genitals tender to touch, and others applied hot irons to girls' thighs.
In some cases clitoridectomies were performed, and in a few cases actual
amputation of the penis was attempted to prevent masturbation. Castration
was not unusual. Most popular, however, were mechanical devices that the
interested could purchase; large numbers of these are listed under the category
of medical appliances in the U.S. Patent Office records. There were various
kinds of devices with metal teeth designed to prevent erection in the male, or
various kinds of guards to be worn around the pudenda of the female. There
were special devices for patients in mental institutions, including a unique pair
of gloves that prevented the patient from touching his or her genitals. There
was even a device to prevent bed covers from coming into contact with sensitive
areas.[79]

There were, of course, countercurrents within nineteenth-century culture, as
indicated by the widespread distribution and continual reprinting of *Aristotle's
Masterpiece,* discussed in an earlier chapter. There were also a number of
treatises on contraception, although medical writers as a whole avoided discussing the subject. This was most unfortunate, for many people were interested in
limiting population, if only because of the writings of Thomas Malthus (1766–
1834) whose *An Essay on the Principle of Population,* first published in 1798,
argued that human beings were possessed by a sexual urge that led them to
multiply faster than their food supply. The results, he held, were misery, wars,
and vice. In fact, without such checks, population would increase at a geometric
rate, but the food supply would increase at an arithmetic rate. Unless man
could bridle his sexual instincts, misery was unavoidable. Malthus himself was
opposed to any mechanical restraints to conception, but instead urged men to
restrain their sex instincts and marry as late as possible. For Malthus, all pro-

miscuous intercourse, unnatural passions, violations of the marriage bed, or irregular sexual connections were classed as vice.[80]

Those believers in the theories of Malthus who saw a solution through the
adoption of contraceptives were known as neo-Malthusians. One of the earliest
neo-Malthusians in the English-speaking world was Francis Place, whose
Illustrations and Proofs of the Principle of Population was published in 1822.
In his treatise Place had advocated the use of "precautionary means" by married couples but had not explained what he meant. To remedy this, he made up
handbills addressed "To The Married of Both Sexes," describing ways to
avoid pregnancy. Place favored the use of a "piece of sponge, about an inch
square," which was to be placed in the "vagina previous to coition" and afterwards withdrawn by means of a double twisted thread or bobbin attached to
it. He advised his users to dampen and warm the sponge before insertion.[81]

Place's pamphlets and similar works by his disciples, such as Richard
Carlile, were allowed to circulate without interference in England, but since so
few seemed interested in what they were attempting to do, Place and Carlile
turned to other subjects, and no one bothered to carry on their work. The next
phase of the birth control movement emerged in America with the appearance
of a booklet, *Moral Physiology,* by Robert Dale Owen. Much of this booklet
was devoted to social and eugenic arguments for family limitations, although
Owen also discussed three methods of birth control: coitus interruptus, the
vaginal sponge, and the *baudruche* or condom. Owen favored coitus interruptus
because in his mind the vaginal sponge was not always successful, and the
condom was both much too expensive and very disagreeable. He reported that
a good condom cost about a "dollar" and could be used only once. He did,
however, recognize the effectiveness of the condom in preventing venereal
disease.[82]

More controversial was the booklet by the Massachusetts physician Charles
Knowlton. His *Fruits of Philosophy,* originally published in 1832, was the
most influential tract of its kind, although, unfortunately, his methods were not
equal to his influence. Knowlton relied chiefly on douching, which consisted of

> syringing the vagina, soon after the male emission into it, with some liquid, which
> will not merely dislodge nearly all the semen, as simple water would do—the fe-
> male being in the most proper position for the operation—but which will destroy
> the fecundating property of any portion of semen that may remain.[83]

For a douching he recommended a solution of alum with infusions of almost
any astringent vegetables, such as white oak or hemlock bark, green tea, or
raspberry leaves, although alum itself would do. For some cases he recommended the use of sulfate of zinc in combination with alum salts. Actually,
alum would have been fairly effective as a spermaticide, but the same cannot be

said for zinc sulfate. For even alum to be effective, however, it had to be used almost immediately after intercourse, and is doubtful that even then it would be entirely successful.

Knowlton had some difficulty in disseminating his book. He was fined in 1832 at Taunton, Massachusetts, and in 1833 he was jailed at Cambridge for 3 months for attempting to distribute it. A third attempt to convict him in Greenfield, Massachusetts, led to disagreement between the two different juries and the dropping of the case. As in many other cases of attempted censorship, the effect of his trial was to so publicize his work that, by 1839, it had sold more than 10,000 copies.

The spread of contraceptive information sexual mores brought about by the shifting attitudes of both the medical profession and the public itself. This is symbolized by the case of Edward Bliss Foote, who might well have been the inventor of the rubber cervical cap or diaphragm. Foote, as early as 1858, had advocated the right of women to decide when to have children,[84] but he ran afoul of the new sexual repression with an inexpensive pamphlet *Words in Pearl for the Married*. Foote sent a copy to Anthony Comstock, who had requested it (albeit under a pseudonym), and for this action Foote was fined $3000 and had to pay $5000 in costs.[85] Though Foote counterattacked with a pamphlet assailing the so-called Comstock Law as imposing a "Roman asceticism" on free America, contraceptive information had to go underground for much of the rest of the nineteenth century. A growing number of medical writers condemned condoms or even douches as nothing more than onanism[86] and agreed with those who said their use would lead to uterine cancer and sterility. Since excitation without release was dangerous and damaging, the best solution for any married couple was to be chaste and to think chaste thoughts.[87]

There were still occasional advocates of greater sexuality for all, most notoriously, Victoria Woodhull, and even Anthony Comstock was unable to silence her. Increasingly, however, her sister feminists ignored her. Ms. Woodhull called herself and her movement spiritualistic, although it later came to be renowned as the Free Love movement. Central to her belief was the importance of sex, which she felt the Christian tradition had tried to make out to be filthy, obscene, and indecent, when in truth it was "the chiefest jewel in our crown in brilliants." Contrary to what many of the medical writers taught, Ms. Woodhull held that sexual activity was basic to one's health and vital strength. "Show me a man or woman who is a picture of physical strength and health and I will show you a person who has healthy sexual relations," she wrote. While never condoning overt promiscuity, she remained hostile to marriage as an institution, since it led only to sexual starvation and slavery for women and too often produced unloved and unwanted children. The way to combat such evils in her mind was to give people the freedom to love, "love wrought of mutual consent based upon desire." When her opponents called her plan

"Woodhullism," she replied that they could "slime" it with any perjorative they wanted, but she could only "rejoice that this ism is affixed to my name."[88]

Many who might have favored the "free love" notions of Ms. Woodhull were reluctant to do so publicly because of new anxieties being raised about veneral disease, particularly syphilis. Though syphilis, as indicated earlier, had wreaked havoc in the sixteenth and succeeding centuries, the nineteenth century saw an increase in fears as the implications of third-stage syphilis finally began to be understood. Because third-stage syphilis might appear as late as 20 years after the disappearance of the second stage and has many different kinds of symptoms, the difficulty in connecting the three stages with the one infection is understandable. Probably the most noticeable sign, and the easiest to connect, is the skin lesions type consisting of gummata and group nodules that heal with considerable scarring and occur all over the body. At the same time, bones, joints, eyes, and most organs become painfully and chronically inflamed. It is this aspect of third-stage syphilis that leaves the so-called syphilitic mark on bones. Syphilis also attacks the cardiovascular system, where it often results in inflammation of the aorta and a weakening of the aorta wall. Ultimately, there is an outpocketing known as aneurysm that causes death when it ruptures. Neurosyphilis is syphilis of the brain and spinal cord leading to general paralysis or tabes dorsalis, an inability to coordinate muscular movement. Before this was recognized as syphilis, many nineteenth-century physicians associated it with masturbation. This was true of some other aspects of third-stage syphilis, such as cerebral hemorrhage, deafness, blindness, mental disturbance, and epilepsy, although other things besides syphilis can also cause these afflictions. Syphilis can also be passed from the mother to the fetus, with the result that children are born with the disease.

Many of the discoveries about third-stage syphilis were made by Philip Ricord (1799–1889), an American-born Frenchman, who also proved through a series of experiments involving some 2500 innoculations that gonorrheal pus could not cause syphilis chancres. Conclusive proof of the existence of third-stage syphilis came with the discovery that microorganisms caused disease, a discovery made by Ricord's fellow Frenchman, Louis Pasteur. Following Pasteur's discovery, other researchers were able to demonstrate the existence of several types of veneral diseases: Albert Neisser in 1879 discovered the diplococcus of gonorrhea; Augusto Ducrey and Paul Unnas found the bacillus causing soft chancre in 1889; and in 1905 Fritz Shaudinn and Eric Hofman found the *Spirochaeta pallida,* the cause of syphilis. With these discoveries, August von Wasserman, Neisser, and C. Bruck were able, through a blood test, to document the existence of the syphilis *spirochete.*[89]

As the full implications of the havoc wrought by syphilis were publicized, sexual promiscuity came under even greater condemnation. Syphilis was viewed as God's punishment for the evildoer; a few physicians even refused to treat its victims. Others, however, sought for more effective treatment, for it was realized that the traditional mercury treatment had only brought on a false cure and caused other difficulties. The pioneering investigator in a search for a successful cure was Paul Ehrlich, who, with the help of Sahachira Hata, experimented with a number of compounds to attack the spirochete without killing the patient. His 606th compound, an arsenic derivative he called salvarsan, proved moderately successful in both respects, although it seemed a race whether the spirochete or the patient would be killed first. Ehrlich continued his experiments until his 914th compound, which he called neosalvarsan, proved to be more effective in treating the disease. Not until the development of penicillin and the sulfonamides in the middle of the twentieth century, however, was a really effective cure found. With veneral disease under control, some of the inhibitions about sexuality were removed, and men and woman could engage in sexual activity without the anxieties and fears present in the late nineteenth century, especially when coupled with more effective contraceptives.

Before this new freedom resulted, however, all kinds of distorted views existed, either consciously or unconsciously disseminated to cut down on sexual promiscuity. Ruskin, as indicated earlier in this chapter, was shocked to find that his wife had pubic hair, and instead of the wan, ethereal, asexual creature he imagined, his wife turned out to be human, more or less like him. Ruskin was not alone in imagining women as different, somehow better than men. Leopold von Sacher-Masoch (1836–1895), the historian, dramatist, and novelist from whose name the term *masochist* was coined, held that women had been created to subdue man's animal passions. With such attitudes all kinds of masochistic punishment were justified. He himself was attracted to women older and stronger than himself, to whom he could submit and who would maltreat him physically for expressing his "animal" passions. Increasingly, his fictional writings became stereotyped, almost always featuring a woman in furs (he had a fetish for furs), who, with a whip, symbolic of lust, scourged her male lover for his "animal" lusts.[90] Though the plot in his novels varied slightly, invariably all included a whip scene.

> I enter. She stands in the middle of the room, in a white satin robe which flows about her like light, a jacket of scarlet satin richly trimmed in sumptuous ermine, with a small diamond in her powdered snow-white hair, her arms folded across her breast, her brows knotted together. . . . I bow down and kiss the hem of her garment. . . . Her lower lip twiched contemptuously and she looked at me mockingly with half-closed eyes.
> "Give me the whip."
> I looked about the room.
> "No," she cried, "stay on your knees." She stepped to the fireplace, took the whip

from the mantle, looked at me with a grin as she let the whip whistle through the
air, and then slowly rolled up the sleeves of her fur jacket.
"Wonderful, woman!" I cried . . .
"Whip me," I begged, "whip me without pity."[91]

Though the phenomenon of whipping and erotic torture is usually associated
with Sacher-Masoch, whipping, spanking, and other physical punishments
given for erotic satisfaction are peculiarly associated with England and the
English, much more so than the continent, and demonstrate how deeply engrained were the anxieties over sex.

Books innumerable in the English language are devoted to this subject alone; no
English bawdy book is free from descriptions of flagellation, and numerous
separate plates exist, depicting whipping scenes; it has caused the separation of
man and wife; the genteelest female schools have been made subservient to the
passions of its votaries; and formerly it was spoken of without reserve on the public
stage.

In the early part of the nineteenth century

very sumptuously fitted up establishments, exclusively devoted to the administration of the birch, were not uncommon in London; and women of the town served,
as it were, an apprenticeship in order to acquire the art of gracefully and effectively
administering the rod.[92]

Women, the "less animal" and "more controlled" of humankind, were visualized as punishing men for expressing their animal nature. Among the
underground pornographic works circulating in nineteenth-century England
about the subject were *The Order of St. Bridget: Personal Recollections of the
Use of the Rod*,[93] *The Romance of Chastisement: or, The Revelation of Miss
Darcy*,[94] *Sublime of Flagellation*,[95] *Venus School Mistress*,[96] and many others.
There are numerous erotic histories of spanking.[97]

Closely allied to spanking and whipping were the underground Victorian
epics about bondage that usually recount how recalcitrant and unmanageable
boys were put into tight corsets and educated to be docile and feminine and
lived more or less happily ever after as women. Two such works are *Miss High
Heels* and *Gynecocracy*, whose themes are similar. In the first, Dennis Evelyn
Beryl is transformed under the supervision of his step-sister Helen into a
properly trained young woman. As part of his corset discipline he was sent to a
girl's school, where he was punished with canes, riding whips, birch rods, and
ever more restrictive corsets, always totally subject to the whims of Helen and
her lady friends.[98]

In the second novel, Julian Robinson, Viscount Ladywood, like Dennis, had showed too much energy as a boy, and so his parents shipped him to a secret and select private school to be "disciplined," a discipline including birching and the wearing of corsets. The novel concluded:

> The petticoat, as administered by Mademoiselle and then by Beatrice, after all is said and done, I consider extremely beneficial. . . . A woman can make a man. In the first place she has the monopoly of the making, for she alone can conceive and give birth to him, and in the next place she can make him by discipline, by instilling her common sense into him and by keeping him rigidly under thumb. . . . I confess . . . that I love my bondage and I love my tyrant. . . . There is a wonderful luxuriousness and sensuality in being made to bow down before a woman, and to perform her behests. . . . My lady's stockings and drawers upon me give me, whenever I am reminded that I wear them, an electrifying thrill through and through. And as for the management of affairs, well, they are much better managed by my wife than they could be by me. . . . This world is woman's earth, and it is petticoated all over. Theirs is the dominion, turn and twist the matter as you will.[99]

By far the most numerous of underground books and submerged or repressed verses are those dealing with homosexuality, particularly male homosexuality. If some of the recent anthologies are representative, a large segment of the English literary fraternity had either covert or overt homosexual tendencies.[100] The question this vast literature raises is why homosexuality was so widespread, and undoubtedly part of the answer is tied in with the fear of sex described earlier in this chapter, into the distinction between female goodness and male badness, and with bondage, spanking, and the whole outward aspect of middle-class respectability. Also contributing, at least in England, is the English public school system, which inculcated such misconceptions. These schools wrenched boys away from family and parents, tossing them into crowds of other boys in which peer group pressure forced them to conform to the norms set by older boys at school, which invariably included a great deal of homoerotic play. Earlier in this book the school system of classical Greece and of Renaissance Italy have been depicted as perhaps being one causal factor in encouraging more overt homosexual expression, and this was probably true of nineteenth-century England. This does not imply that all schoolboys became practicing homosexuals, most probably they were not, but large numbers prided themselves on sublimating and suppressing their homoerotic desires, and not a few become more overt.[101]

These homoerotic attachments were, however, primarily associated with the upper or upper middle classes, who went to the public schools, and were not necessarily a part of the educational background of the lower economic classes, who did not. Thus homosexuality in England had, and still has, more of an upper-class orientation that it might have in America. In England a boy born in the upper classes, or one whose parents were striving to put him into the upper classes, was sent away at 8 or 9 years of age to board in a prep school. At 12 or 13 he went on to a public school, a school that in American terms would be called a private boarding school, and he lived at this school until he went on to university from whence he finally graduated at about 21. These schools were almost entirely male establishments, and the growing male lived in them for two-thirds of the year and most of his young manhood. In the school there was little possibility of seeing or meeting girls in any but a passing way, and when he went home on school holiday, unless he had sisters near his own age, he found it difficult to relate to any peer group of females. Even sisters were not necessarily a help, for the male culture in which he moved tended to frown upon them and put them down as silly creatures.

At Oxford or Cambridge, the socially correct universities, the don or tutor was unmarried, and in fact, married faculty were not allowed until 1882. Only a few took advantage of this opportunity to change their status, for married faculty were at a distinct disadvantage to the unmarried ones in terms of perquisites. Students were not permitted to marry at all, and those who were ambitious saw that success lay with those who remained bachelors until fairly late in life. When the student left the university, he often moved into an all-male club in London or elsewhere. Oxford and Cambridge remained citadels of bachelordom until almost the Second World War, and the clubs still remain all-male sanctuaries. Under such conditions male friendships were intense and considered the norm, although actual intimacies between boys or men were rarely reported except in private letters, which are only now beginning to appear. One of the masterpieces of such homoerotic attachment is Alfred Lord Tennyson's *In Memoriam,* written after the death of his friend Arthur Hallam. It included the following verses:

> *Dear friend, far off, my lost desire,*
> *So far, so near in woe and weal;*
> *O loved the most, when most I feel*
> *There is a lower and a higher;*
> *Known and unknown; human, divine;*
> *Sweet human hand and lips and eye;*
> *Dear heavenly friend that canst not die,*
> *Mine, mine, for ever, ever mine;*
> *Strange friend, past, present, and to be;*
> *Loved deeplier, darklier understood;*
> *Behold, I dream a dream of good,*
> *And mingle all the world with thee.*[102]

As might be expected, the whole nineteenth-century intellectual and religious life of England is undercut with repressed homoerotic feelings, from Henry Cardinal Newman, a leading convert to Roman Catholicism, to Charles Kingsley, one of the founders of muscular Christianity. Kingsley reveled in finding a successor to the old tales of David and Jonathan, Socrates and Alcibiades, and others whose love for each other passed "the love of woman." Even after a number of scandals and criminal actions had been brought against individuals such as Oscar Wilde, it was "perfectly possible for entirely upright, and even uptight, men to ignore tendencies at which others sneered or reared up in horror. The reason it was possible was because although Tennyson had the strongest empathy for Hallam, no one doubted that his love for him was platonic."[103]

Platonic was a word that went well with the English public school curriculum, since classical languages and literature, along with the Bible and Christianity wre emphasized. Greek notions of friendship were taught at every level. The ideal was the spiritual love of man for man, since the love of man for woman was flawed by the possibility of being carnal. Ineluctably, when individuals raised under such conditions turned to women, they felt their erotic thoughts were sinful. They had to be punished, dominated, and made slaves, at least in their own fervid imaginings, so that the sexless, spiritual woman could lead them to new heights. Many eventually married only because they felt it was their Christian duty to propagate the race.

Lust was evil, dangerous to health, and had to be controlled, and so, though the proper Englishman wrote extensively of homoerotic friendships, read pornographic classics sold under the counter rather than openly, and took his heterosexual sex from prostitutes, he outwardly conformed to respectability. Even divorcées were banished from proper society, and divorce itself was a costly and expensive procedure that institutionalized the double standard, for men were allowed to divorce adulterous wives, but wives could not divorce adulterous husbands. The English horror of divorce was no better indicated than in the twentieth-century forced abdication of a king because he married a divorced woman. Similarly, by denying the existence of youthful sexuality, the English allowed homoerotic attachments to go unchallenged in the schools, although there were some attempts to control too overt expressions through an emphasis on exercise, athletics, and cold baths. Standing behind the public morals was a harshly punitive law about sex, a subject to be discussed in the next chapter.

NOTES

1. For a discussion of these works and their influence on America, see Sidney Ditzion, *Marriage, Morals, and Sex in America* (New York: Bookman Associates, 1953), pp. 22–48.

2. There are many editions of Franklin's *Autobiography*. The original MS is in the Huntington Library and has been edited and annotated by Max Farrand (Berkeley: University of California Press, 1949). Franklin's advice on mistresses can also be found in various editions, including Benjamin Franklin, *Satires and Bagatelles,* Paul McPharlin, ed. (Detroit: Fine Book Circle, 1937). His *Reflections on courtship and Marriage* was first published anonymously, and it was not until the third edition was published in 1758 that he was referred to as the author. Franklin emphasized his own teachings by entering into a common-law marriage and having at least two illegitimate children. Other founding fathers also had unusual liaisons. Thomas Jefferson, for example, had a Negro mistress, the half-sister of his own dead wife.

3. Theodore Schmauk, *A History of the Lutheran Church in Pennsylvania (1638-1820)* (Philadelphia: General Council Publication House, 1903), Vol. 1, p. 225.

4. Quoted by Ditzion, *op. cit.,* p. 54.

5. *Ibid.,* pp. 54–56.

6. Percy Bysshe Shelley, "A Discourse on the Manners of the Ancient Greeks Relative to the Subject of Love," in *Shelley's Prose,* David Lee Clark, ed. (Albuquerque, N. Mex.: University of New Mexico Press, 1954), p. 222.

7. Johann Fichte, *Grundlage des Naturrechts nach Principien der Wissenschaftslehre von Johann Gottlieb Fichte's sammtliche Werke,* J. H. Fichte ed. (Berlin: Veit, 1845), Vol. 3, p. 336.

8. For a discussion of this, see the unpublished paper by Paul A. Robinson, "Romantic Sexual Theory," presented at the American Historical Association, Boston, 1970, passim, but especially pp. 16–17. Professor Robinson is presently at work on a book-length study.

9. Shelley, "Notes of Queen Mab," *Works,* p. 806.

10. Friedrich von Schlegel, "Über die Diotima," in *Fredrich von Schlegel: Seine prosaischen Jugendschrifiten,* J. Minor, ed. (Wein, Austria: Verlagsbuchhandlung Carl Konegen, 1906), Vol. 1, p. 59.

11. Schlegel, *Lucinda,* translated by Bernard Thomas, in *The German Classics* (Albany, N.Y.: J. B. Lyon, n.d.), Vol. 4, p. 131.

12. Johann Wolfgang von Goethe, *Wilhelm Meisters Wanderjahre,* Zweiter Tiel (Munich: Deutscher Taschenbüch Verlag, 1962), Book 2, Chap. 2, pp. 29–30, and also passim.

13. In his *Achilleis,* and *West-Östlicher Diwan,* Book 9.

14. Johann Christoph Friedrich von Schiller, *Wallensteins Tod* (Stuttgart: Deutsche Schiller Gesellschaft, E. Schrieber Graphische Kunstanstalten, 1955), Vol. 3, p. 18.

15. Johann Christian Friedrich Holderlin, *Sokrates und Alcibiades* in *Samtliche Werke,* (Potsdam: Gustav Kiepenheuer Verlag, 1921, 4 vols.), Vol. 1, p. 27.

16. August Graf von Platen-Hallermünde, *Ghaselen,* 2nd Collection, 1821 (Leipzig: Hesse & Becker, 1909), Vol. 8, p. 41. There are numerous other poems with a homoerotic theme in the *Mirror of Hafiz.* Technically, Platten is an archenemy of the romantics, but his material is included here anyway. He was apparently a homosexual, and in a series of sonnets he attempted to justify homosexual love. Hence Heine's criticism of him was probably based on reality and not fiction.

17. Heinrich Heine, *Reise von München nach Genua* (Munich: Carl Hanswer Verlag, 1969), Vol. 2, pp. 444–445. There are several other references to Platen.

18. See G. Wilson Knight, *Lord Byron's Marriage* (London: Routlege & Kegan Paul, 1957). For some of his homoerotic poems, see Alistair Sutherland and Patrick Anderson, *Eros: An Anthology of Friendship* (London: Anthony Blond, 1961), pp. 212–227. The homophile poems are "The Carnelian" in *House of Idleness,* "To Thyrza," "Away, Away, Ye Notes to Woe!," "One Struggle More, and I am Free," "And Thou Art Dead, As Young and Fair," "If Sometimes in the

Haunts of Men," and "On a Carnelian Heart Which Was Broken," in *Occasional Pieces*, plus several of the poems dealing with Loukas Chalan Chalandritsanos.

19. "Don Leon," which consists of 1455 lines, is a defense of sodomy, and in it Byron is represented as describing his various affairs with males. He also indicates that he preferred anal intercourse with his wife. This preference in also hinted at in "Leon to Annabell," allegedly an epistle from Lord Byron to Lady Byron that was printed with the "Don Leon." Pisanus Fraxi, *Bibliography of Prohibited Books* (reprinted, New York: Jack Brussell, 1962, 3 vols.), Vol. 1, pp. 189–193, discusses this work. It was privately printed in London in 1866. Byron was also accused of incest with his half-sister by Harriet Beecher Stowe, "Lady Byron Vindicated" (London: Samson Low, 1870). The identification of the author of "Don Leon" as George Colman was not by Pisanus Fraxi but by J. Z. Eglinton, *Greek Love* (New York: Oliver Layton Press, 1964), p. 360.

20. M. H. Beyle (Stendahl), *On Love*, translated by H. B. V. under the direction of C. K. Scott-Moncrieff (reprinted, New York: Doubleday Anchor Books, 1957), p. 6–9.

21. Gustave Flaubert, *Madame Bovary* (New York: Boni & Liveright, n.d.). It was originally published in 1857.

22. Charlotte Brontë, *Jane Eyre* (reprinted, New York: Random House, 1943). The novel was originally written in 1847.

23. For a further discussion, see Bernard K. Murstein, *Love, Sex, and Marriage* (New York: Springer, 1974), Chap. 12.

24. Charles Kingsley, *Yeast* (New York: Harper, 1851), pp. 146–147.

25. Mary Lutyens, ed. *Effie in Venice* (London: J. Murray, 1965), p. 20.

26. Joan Evans, *John Ruskin* (reprinted, New York: Haskell, 1970).

27. Murstein, *op. cit.,* Chap. 12 (sheet 188 in MSS).

28. I have developed this at some length in Vern L. Bullough, *The Subordinate Sex* (Urbana, Ill.: University of Illinois press, 1973), pp. 285–289.

29. Benjamin Rush, *Medical Inquiries and Observations* (Philadelphia: Thomas Dobson, 1794–1798, 5 vols.), Vol. 4, pp. 123–129.

30. Rush, *Medical Inquiries and Observations upon the Diseases of the Mind* (Philadelphia: Kimber and Richardson, 1812), p. 347.

31. Sylvester Graham, *A Lecture on Epidemic Diseases Generally, and Particularly the Spasmodic Cholera* (Boston: D. Campbell, 1838), pp. 5–7.

32. Sylvester Graham, *A Lecture to Young Men, on Chastity, Intended Also for the Serious Consideration of Parents and Guardians,* 10th ed. (Boston: C. H. Pierce, 1848), pp. 42–44. The book was first published in 1834.

33. *Ibid.,* pp. 45–57, 79–86.

34. *Ibid.,* pp. 78–79.

35. For a discussion of Graham, see Stephen Willner Nissenbaum, *Careful Love: Sylvester Graham and the Emergence of Victorian Sexual Theory in America, 1830–1840* (an unpublished Ph.D. dissertation, University of Wisconsin, Madison, 1968), passim.

36. For a general discussion of American sexual thinking during the period, see John S. and Robin M. Haller, *The Physician and Sexuality in Victorian America* (Urbana Ill.: University of Illinois Press, 1974). See also Charles E. Rosenberg, "Sexuality, Class and Role in 19th-Century America," *American Quarterly,* XXV (1973), pp. 131–153; and Carroll Smith-Rosenberg and Charles Rosenberg, "The Female Animal: Medical and Biological Views of Women and Her Role in Nineteenth-Century America," *Journal of American History,* LX (1973), pp. 332–356. For a

specific contemporary example, see (Anon.), "Excessive Venergy, Softening of the Brain," *New England Journal of Medicine*, XXXVI (1847), pp. 41–42.

37.   M. [Claude-Francois] Lallemand, *On Involuntary Seminal Discharges*, translated by William Wood (Philadelphia: A. Waldier, 1839). The original French edition had been published in 1836. There were several American and English editions.

38.   William Acton, *The Functions and Disorders of the Reproductive Organs in Childhood, Youth, Adult Age, and Advanced Life Considered in their Physiological, Social, and Moral Relations*, 5th ed. (London: J. & A. Churchill, 1871), pp. 135–140.

39.   For a discussion of Acton, see Steven Marcus, *The Other Victorians: A Study of Sexuality and Pornography in Mid-Nineteenth Century England* (New York: Basic Books, 1966), pp. 1–33.

40.   [Dr. Porter], *Book of Men, Women and Babies. The Laws of God Applied to Obtaining, Rearing, and Developing the Natural, Healthful, and Beautiful in Humanity* (New York: 1855), p. 56.

41.   J. H. Kellogg, *Plain Facts for Old and Young* (Burlington, Iowa: I. F. Senger, 1882), pp. 315.

42.   *Ibid.*, pp. 332–344.

43.   George M. Beard, *Sexual Neurasthenia, Its Hygiene, Causes, Symptoms, and Treatment with a Chapter on Diet for the Nervous*, posthumously edited by A. D. Rockwell (New York: E. B. Treat and Company, 1884), pp. 58, 134–207. See also his article, "Neurasthenia or Nervous Exhaustion," *Boston Medical and Surgical Journal*, III (1869); and the book by George M. Beard, *American Nervousness, Its Causes and Consequences* (New York: Putnam's, 1881). For a discussion, see Charles E. Rosenberg, "The Place of George M. Beard in Nineteenth Century Psychiatry," *Bulletin of the History of Medicine*, XXVI (1962), pp. 245–259; and Philip P. Weiner, "G. M. Beard and Freud on 'American Nervousness,'" *Journal of the History of Ideas*, XVII (1956), pp. 269–274.

44.   In this interpretation I differ somewhat from E. H. Hare, "Masturbatory Insanity: The History of an Idea," *Journal of Mental Sciences*, CVIII (1962); as well as R. H. MacDonald, "The Frightful Consequences of Onanism," *Journal of the History of Ideas*, XXVIII (1967), pp. 1–25; and René A. Spitz, "Authority and Masturbation," *The Psychoanalytic Quarterly*, XXI (1952), pp. 490–527. See also Vern L. Bullough and Martha Voght, "Homosexuality and Its Confusion with the 'Secret Sin,' in Pre-Freudian America," *Journal of the History of Medicine*, XXVIII (1973), pp. 143–155. See also Tristam Engelhardt, "The Disease of Masturbation: Values and the Concept of Disease," *Bulletin of the History of Medicine*, XLVIII (1974), pp. 234–248.

45.   Henry Thomas Kitchener, *Letters on Marriage* (London: C. Chapple, 1812, 2 vols.), Vol. 1, p. 24.

46.   Samuel Solomon, *A Guide to Health*, 64th ed. (printed for the author at West-Derby, n.d.), pp. 189–193.

47.   L. T. Nichols, *Esoteric Anthropology* (London: Nichols & Company, 1853), p. 84.

48.   W. J. Hunter, *Manhood Wrecked and Rescued* (New York: Health Culture Company, 1900), p. 118.

49.   Kitchener, *op. cit.*, Vol. 1, p. 26.

50.   *Ibid.*, Vol. 1, p. 49.

51.   Alfred Hitchcock, "Insanity and Death from Masturbation," *Boston Medical and Surgical Journal*, XXVI (1842), pp. 283–286.

52.   A. Jacobi, "On Masturbation and Hysteria in Young Children," *American Journal of Obstetrics*, VIII (1876), pp. 595–596.

53. Allen W. Hagenbach, "Masturbation as a Cause of Insanity," *Journal of Nervous and Mental Diseases,* VI (1879), pp. 603–612.

54. Kellogg, *op. cit.,* p. 325.

55. Hagenbach, *op. cit.,* passim.

56. Joseph W. Howe, *Excessive Venery, Masturbation, and Continence* (New York: E. B. Treat and Company, 1899), pp. 419–427.

57. James Foster Scott, *The Sexual Instinct* (New York: E. B. Treat and Company, 1899), pp. 419–427.

58. Mary Wood-Allen, *What a Young Woman Ought to Know* (Philadelphia: VIR Publishing Company, 1898), pp. 148–149, 173–176.

59. G. Stanley Hall, *Adolescence* (New York: D. Appleton and Company, 1904), Vol. 1, pp. 435, 445.

60. L. F. E. Bergeret, *The Preventive Obstacle or Conjugal Onanism* (New York: Turner and Mignard, 1897), p. 125.

61. James Foster Scott, *Heredity and Morals* (New York: E. B. Treat and Company, 1899), p. 434.

62. Kitchener, *op. cit.,* Vol. 2, pp. 247–258.

63. Solomon, *op. cit.,* p. 213.

64. Hunter, *op. cit.,* p. 126.

65. William Alcott, *The Physiology of Marriage* (Boston: Dinsmor and Company, 1866), p. 118.

66. Dio Lewis, *Chastity or Our Secret Sins* (New York: George Maclean and Company, 1875), p. 111.

67. E. P. Miller, *Abuses of the Sexual Function* (New York: John A. Gray and Green, 1867), pp. 32 33.

68. Edward Dixon, *Treatises on the Diseases of the Sexual System* (New York: O. A. Rorback, 1855).

69. Kitchener, *op. cit.,* Vol. 2, p. 318.

70. Alcott, *op. cit.,* p. 94.

71. *Ibid.,* p. 155.

72. Nichols, *op. cit.,* p. 98.

73. Bergeret, *op. cit.,* p. 105.

74. Nichols, *op. cit.,* passim.

75. (Anonymous) *Satin in Society* (Cincinnati: C. F. Vent, 1871), p. 168.

76. Dio Lewis, *op. cit.,* p. 117.

77. Mrs. E. B. Duffy, *Relations of the Sexes* (New York: Wood and Holbrook, 1876), p. 219.

78. Mrs. Elizabeth Osgood Goodrich Willard, *Sexology as the Philosophy of Life* (Chicago: published for the author by J. R. Walsh, 1867), pp. 306–308.

79. Similar devices can be found in Great Britain and on the continent. Among the American inventors listed, their patent numbers, and the dates for their inventions are:
1856, J. D. Sibley, No. 14,739; 1859, Dwight Gibbons, No. 22,796; 1861, Herman H. Reynolds, No. 32,842; 1862, LeRoy Sunderland, No. 37,116; 1870, Daniel P. Cooke, No. 104,117; 1876, Harvey A. Stephenson, No. 177,971, and another device in 1877, No. 232,858; 1887, James H. Bowen, No. 256,862; 1892, Frank Orth, No. 494,436; 1897, Michael McCormick; No. 587,994; 1898, George E. Duley, No. 698,497; 1900, Joseph Lees, No. 641,979; 1901, John C. Davis, No.

678,043; 1904, Willard F. Main, No. 789,826; 1905, Raphael A. Sonn, No. 826,377; 1907, Clarence W. Fraser, No. 879,534; 1908, Ellen E. Perkins, No. 875,845; 1910, Henry A. Wood, No. 973,330; 1911, Jonas Edward Heyser, No. 995,600; 1917, I. Edward Roody, No. 1,243,629; 1932, Allan P. Risley, No. 1,865,280. Both the descriptions and the drawings are fascinating.

80.   Thomas Robert Malthus, *An Essay On the Principle of Population*, 2nd ed. (London: J. Johnson, 1803), p. 11. This second edition is the first to which Malthus signed his own name.

81.   For a discussion of *Place* and a biographical sketch, see Peter Fryer, *The Birth Controllers* (London: Secker and Warburg, 1965), pp. 43–57, 72–74; a reproduction of his handbill can be found in Norman E. Himes, *Medical History of Contraception* (reprinted, New York: Schocken Books, 1970), pp. 216–217.

82.   Robert Owen, *Moral Physiology* (New York: Wright & Owen, 1831). See also Fryer, *op. cit.*, pp. 92–93; Himes, *op. cit.*, pp. 224–225. There is a copy of the first edition in the Boston Medical Library. The booklet went through several editions and had sold approximately 60,000 copies up to 1874.

83.   Charles Knowlton, *Fruits of Philosophy*, commentary by Norman E. Himes and Robert Latou Dickinson (reprinted, Mount Vernon, N.Y.: Peter Pauper Press, 1937), p. 60. Himes used the 10th edition of Knowlton's work. There are many unauthorized editions of Knowlton's work; some include discussion of methods he did not favor.

84.   Edward B. Foote, *Medical Common Sense* (revised, New York: published by the author, 1863), p. 338.

85.   Fryer, *op. cit.*, p. 118.

86.   Carl Capellman, *Pastoral Medicine* (Cincinnati: F. Pustat, 1879), p. 92.

87.   Bergeret, *op. cit.*; and Augustus Gardner, *Conjugal Sins* (New York: J. S. Redfield, 1870), pp. 107–109; or Edward Dixon, *Abnormal Conditions of the Sexual and Pelvic Organs* (New York: Brinckerhoof and Company, 1870) p. 23. There are many others.

88.   The quotes are from a speech, "The Elixir of Life; or Why Do We Die," which she gave at the 10th annual convention of the American Association of Spiritualists on September 18, 1873, in Chicago. The speech was printed in tract form, a few copies of which have survived, including one in my own library.

89.   See W. E. Pusey, *The History and Epidemiology of Syphilis* (Springfield, Ill.: Charles C Thomas, 1933); and also Theodor Rosebury, *Microbes and Morals* (New York: Viking Press, 1971).

90.   James Cleugh, *The First Masochist: A Biography of Leopold von Sacher-Masoch* (London: Anthony Blond, 1967), p. 8.

91.   Leopold von Sacher-Masoch, *Venus in Pelz* (*Venus in Furs*) (Munich: Lichtenberg Verlag, 1967), pp. 61–64.

92.   Pisanus Fraxi, *Bibliography of Prohibited Books* (reprinted, London: Jack Brussell, 1962, 3 vols), Vol. 1, pp.

93.   Margaret Anson, *The Merry Order of St. Bridget: Personal Recollections of the use of the Rod* (York, England: printed for the author's friends, 1857). Though the author adopts a female pseudonym, it was undoubtedly written by a man.

94.   *The Romance of Chastisement; or, The Revelations of Miss Darcy* (London: n.p., 1866,) and other editions.

95.   *Sublime of Flagellation: In Letters from Lady Termagant Flaybum, of Birch-Grove, to Lady Harriet Tickletail of Bumfiddle-Hall* (London: George Peacock, n.d.).

96.   *Venus School Mistress: or Birch Sports* by R. Birch. Several editions, including some done in the last few years. Most of these books are discussed in Fraxi, *op. cit.*, passim.

97. See William H. Cooper, *A History of the Rod in All Countries* (revised, London: William Reeves, 1896). Fraxi, *op. cit.*, Vol. 1, p. 460, says Cooper was a pseudonym for James G. Bertram.

98. *Miss High Heels* (reprinted, New York: Grove Press, 1969). I am not certain when the original of this first appeared, probably toward the end of the nineteenth century.

99. *Gynecocracy: A Narrative of the Adventures and Psychological Experiences of Julian Robinson (afterwards Viscount Ladywood) Under Petticoat-Rule Written by Himself* (republished, New York: Grove Press, 1971), pp. 405–406.

100. See, for example, Timothy d'Arch Smith, *Love in Earnest: Some Notes on the Lives and Writings of English Uranian Poets from 1889–1930* (London: Routledge and Kegan Paul, 1970); and most particularly, Brian Reade, ed., *Sexual Heretics: Male Homosexuality in English Literature from 1850 to 1900* (New York: Coward-McCann, 1970).

101. I am indebted to Noel Gilroy, Lord Annan, for permission to quote and cite from his paper on "The Rise of the Cult of Homosexuality," given at the conference on the *Victorian Counter Culture* at the University of South Florida, Tampa, February 27–March 2, 1974. Proceedings of the conference are being gathered by Willie D. Reader, Chairman of the Conference, and Professor of English at the University.

102. Alfred Lord Tennyson, *In Memoriam* (published 1850), sec. 129. A readily available copy is in Christopher Ricks, ed., *A Collection of Poems by Alfred Tennyson* (New York: Doubleday, 1972).

103. Annan, *op. cit.*

19

THE LAW AND IT ENFORCEMENT

Official stances, as indicated by the law and its enforcement, reflected many of the same ambiguities and contradictions toward sex as the currents and countercurrents of intellectual and political thought. For example, the French Revolutionaries, on September 20, 1792, made divorce dependent on the mutual consent of the parties, subject only to a short period of delay so that the couple might appear before a family council to try to settle their dispute. Twelve years later, in 1804, incompatibility was removed as a ground for divorce, divorce in general being made more difficult, although marriages could still be dissolved by mutual consent. In 1816, after the monarch's restoration, divorce was abolished and not permitted again in France until 1884.[1]

In other areas where changes had come slower, there were not quite the same contradictions, most notably in the laws dealing with nonprocreative sex. Up to the time of the Revolution in France, sodomy, however ambiguously defined, could be punished by burning. Although the ultimate penalty was only rarely given, some three individuals had been burned to death in France between 1750 and 1789. The revolutionaries early eliminated the death penalty for "sex crimes," but not until 1810 was work finally completed on revision of the criminal code. This new code, usually known as the Napoleonic code, recognized equality before the law and provided the same penalties for all crimes, regardless of social class. In general, penalties were harsh, including life imprisonment and the death penalty, but torture was forbidden. Sexually, the most important innovation in the laws was to leave unpunished any sexual behavior in private between consenting adult parties, whether this took place between women, men, or men and women. "Deviant" sexual acts were treated as a crime only when they implied an outrage on public decency, when there was violence or absence of consent, or when one of the parties was underage or regarded as unable to give valid consent.[2] In short, the law was not to be used to deter certain forms of sexual behavior nor to change the participants' sexual orientation. Changing the laws did not however, necessarily change public opinion; one unanticipated effect of the law was to encourage blackmail against individuals not violating any law but holding sensitive public positions. Invariably, homosexuals or other whose sexual activity was legally permitted kept their sexual life secret and hidden.

Because the legal codes of continental Europe followed the traditions of Roman law and because much of Europe was under French dominance and influence when the code was enacted, many countries adopted similar laws. Belgium, much of Italy, Spain, Portugal, Rumania, and Russia, as well as several Latin American countries followed the French lead on "sexual" crimes, as did some of the German states. Prussia was, however, an exception; when Germany was united under Prussian leadership in 1871, the more punitive Prussian law received attention.[3] In the Scandinavian states, change was also slow, many sex offenses still being punished by death until 1866, when capital punishment was abolished in Denmark. But the harshness of some of the penalties, when coupled with the lack of such penalties in other nearby countries, led to a reluctance of Danish and other officials to prosecute, and usually in the nineteenth century only sexual contact with animals was punished by execution. Once the death penalty was abolished for sex crimes, however, there was a greater willingness to prosecute.[4] Other countries also modified their laws, but England and the common-law countries such as the United States remained exceptions.[5]

The English law, harshly punitive about sex, had been most effectively enunciated by Sir William Blackstone (1723–1780), an eighteenth-century man with nineteenth-century sexual ideas. Part of the reason for Blackstone's popularity was his general common sense as well as his literary ability, but both failed him when he came to sex. Here he was suitably ambiguous, failing to spell out in detail what sex crimes entailed, so as not to rouse lustful desires. He classed mayhem, forcible abduction, rape, and "crime against nature" in the same general categories as those other crimes and misdemeanors "as more particularly affect the security of his person, while living."[6] His influence, coupled with the general prudery of the late nineteenth-century Englishman, discouraged the adopting of Napoleonic code provisions about consenting adults. Blackstone believed that, even though both parties might consent to a sex act "against nature," both should be liable to prosecution. Participation in the act alone implied danger, although his definition of what constituted the crime against nature is never quite clear. He mentions it following his discussion on rape, stating:

> What has been here observed, especially with regard to manner of proof, which ought to be the more clear in proportion as the crime is the more detestable, may be applied to another offense, of a still deeper malignity: the infamous *crime against nature,* committed either with man or beast. A crime which ought to be strictly and impartially proved, and then as strictly and impartially punished. But it is an offence of so dark a nature, so easily charged, and the negative so difficult to be proved that the accusation should be clearly made out: for, if false, it deserves a punishment inferior only to that of the crime itself.

> I will not act so disagreeable a part, to my readers as well as myself, as to dwell any longer upon a subject, the very mention of which is a disgrace to human nature. It will be more eligible to imitate in this respect the delicacy of our English law, which treats it, in its very indictments, as a crime not fit to be named.[7]

Unfortunately, Blackstone's discussion left unclear just what the "crime against nature" constituted, and although he cited Biblical statements and English statutes for his reader to consult, this ambiguity continued to plague discussion and enforcement of sex laws in both nineteenth-century England and America. Blackstone also included "unnatural" crimes under the general category of assault, to provide penalties where proof of the actual act was difficult to obtain.[8] In addition, he listed various sexual activities under the category of "Offences Against God and Religion," since such activities openly transgressed the precepts of religion "both natural and revealed."[9]

Coupled with Blackstone's reticence were the ambiguities inherent in the common law. The testimony of a person consenting to act, as Blackstone implied, was not sufficient to convict, because such a person was an accomplice. This meant that sexual activity, even involving children and adults, had to have a third party as witness for successful prosecution,[10] and this was most difficult to get, for mere solicitation to commit a sexual act was not a criminal offense.[11] What was needed was an entirely new rethinking of the sex laws, and this was one subject the utilitarian Jeremy Bentham turned his mind to. Unfortunately, his ideas have never been published in their entirety; although they could have provided a breakthrough in English legal thinking, they never received the hearing they deserved in the nineteenth century. Bentham recognized the inherent problem of dealing with sex offenses in the criminal law when many regarded any kind of sex as evil; he resolved this difficulty by attempting to neutralize all the terms involved. For him, any "act having for its object the immediate gratification of the sexual appetite may be termed an *act of sexuality.*"[12] Having defined acts in this broad sense, he proposed a further division of two categories—those regularly engaged in that conform to public opinion and those that do not. In the first category, he distinguished between sex acts that took place between persons of the same sex, persons of different sex but underage, unmarried persons, married persons but with different partners, and so forth.[13] Then, using the principle of utility, Bentham argued that there can be only one source of reference, namely, the act's effect on the sum of happiness. An act is noxious (hurtful, harmful, injurious in a moral sense) or it is not. Until it can be proved noxious, it must be acknowledged as beneficial (for unless attended with pleasure it is never performed), and not simply as innocuous. To give further guidance, Benthem set out five classifications:

1. Noxiousness to the operator himself and him alone on the score of health.

2. Noxiousness to the operator himself and him alone on the score of reputation.

3. Noxiousness to one of two or more parties, the party or parties being actually repugnant or at least not consenting.

4. Noxiousness with reference to a third person or determinate individual.

5. Noxiousness with reference to third persons at large, i.e., to individuals indeterminate in respect of identity or number.[14]

Bentham concentrated on the first two categories, holding that in such cases the legislature and the law should not interfere. In effect, an attending evil must be spelled out before sanction was to be imposed. As to so-called unnatural sex, Bentham held that the imputation of unnatural sex was senseless.

> The truth is that by the epithet *unnatural*, when applied to any human act or thought, the only matter of which it affords any indication that can be depended upon is the existence of a sentiment of disapprobation, accompanied with passion in the breast of the person by whom it is employed: a degree of passion by which without staying to inquire whether the practice be or be not noxious to society, he endeavours by the use thus made of this inflammatory word to kindle and point towards the object of this ill-will the same passion in other breasts for the purpose of inducing them to join with him in producing pain in the breast of him by whom the passion has been excited.

Similarly, on odiousness, Bentham wrote that the man who

> on the ground of the odiousness of the practice—i.e., the disgust excited in his mind and that of others by the idea of it—calls for punishment to be inflicted on those by

whom the unpleasant emotion is produced, sets up a principle of which, if adopted, nothing less than the extirpation of the human race would be the result. That without any other ground the bare existence of the affection of hatred should affored a sufficient justification for the gratification of it—did any notion more atrocious than this, or more universally destructive, ever gain entrance into the human breast.[15]

He then argued that

Irregular—unnatural—call them by what names of reproach you will, of these gratifications nothing but good, pure good, if pleasure without pain be a pure good (mischief from excess being implied out of the case), will be found. But when the act be pure good, punishment for whatsoever *purpose,* from whatever *source,* in whatsoever *name* and in whatsoever *degree* applied in consideration of it, will be not only evil, but so much pure evil.[16]

He added that the English looked with abhorrence upon men's being burnt alive by the Spanish *auto-da-fe,* but the English, on a subject of far less importance, since it was not a divergence of opinion but of taste, still relished with indefensible satisfaction the same punishment's being inflicted on a fellow countryman. Changing the law on sex acts would then bring pleasure to many, prevent injury, decrease the dangers of conception out of wedlock, lesson abortion and infanticide, and lead to a diminution of prostitution.[17] None of Bentham's disciples carried on his efforts to reform the sex laws, although his most famous successor, John Stuart Mill, did urge the reformation of laws on marriage and divorce, arguing for greater equality of women in his famous essay on *The Subjection of Women.*[18]

The English hostility toward and fear of sex ran too deep for Bentham even to publish his work, and it was the more conservative Sir James Fitzjames Stephen (1829–1894) who intellectually dominated efforts to deal with sex in much of the English-speaking world. Stephen's *General View of the Criminal Law of England,* published in 1863, is essentially the first published scholarly and literary introduction to the history of the English criminal law, and this pioneering effort was followed by several other influential works on the subject, capped by his *A History of the Criminal Law of England.*[19] Though Stephen wanted to codify the law, to reduce it to an explicit, systematic shape and remove the other defects disfiguring it,[20] he also felt that all of society rested on the two pillars of religion and law, and if one was weakened, the other was also weakened.

A man may disbelieve in God, heaven, and hell, he may care little for mankind, or society, or for the nation to which he belongs—let him at least be plainly told what are the acts which will stamp him in infamy, hold him up to public execration and bring him to the gallows, the gaol, or the lash.[21]

Backed by the nineteenth century's erroneous medical and scientific views of sex, Stephen provided legal justifications in his works for repressive sex laws that outweighed the arguments of the eighteenth-century liberals, of the emotional romantics, and the rationalist utilitarians, at least in the minds of many nineteenth-century lawmakers. Though the English never accepted Stephen's draft code, its influence was still deeply felt, and it exercised more direct influence on the laws of Canada, Australia, and other emerging English areas, and on the United States as well, for he wrote at a time when most American states were codifying their laws.

Even before Stephen wrote, the English had begun trying to reform their criminal laws, a hodgepodge of contradictions. Though the effort for reform came from the Whigs, a Tory conservative, Robert Peel, was in a position as home secretary between 1823 and 1830 to do the reforming. Peel (1788–1850), who later became a prime minister, succeeded in abolishing the death penalty for more than a hundred offenses but retained it for several crimes, including buggery, rape, and carnal knowledge of girls below the age of consent (then 13). Peel also eliminated the requirement that emission of seed had to be proved in addtion to penetration, since he felt this was next to impossible to prove in rape cases and would be extremely difficult in all other cases.[22] There were a few executions for alleged sex crimes after the bill's enactment but none after 1836. In 1861, the death penalty for any sex activity was eliminated. The result of the imposition of lesser penalties was a rapid increase in prosecutions, almost as if to demonstrate that few felt that sexual activities deserved the death penalty.

The most publicized sex scandal of the mid-Victorian period involved Lord Arthur Clinton and two transvestite homosexuals, Ernest Boulton and Frederick William Park. Boulton and Park both enjoyed playing female parts in amateur theatricals and frequently appeared in public dressed as women. *Drag* was the slang term used then, as now. All three men lived in the same place, a servant alleging that she thought Boulton was Lord Arthur's wife, and in fact Boulton, who went by the name of Stella, had engraved visiting cards with the name "Lady Arthur Clinton" printed on them. Park was known as Fanny. Both men were arrested in April 1870, after leaving the theater dressed in woman's clothes and wearing wigs and padded bosoms. Letters found in their rooms implicated Clinton as well as others, and the prosecutor, rather than charge them with committing a felony, something that would have been difficult to prove, charged them with conspiracy to commit a felony. The lord chief justice, Lord Cockburn, strongly disapproved of such indictments, asserting the defendants were charged with conspiracy when the only proof of such a conspiracy would be evidence of the commission of such crime, but his strictures were ignored, and though the men were acquitted (Clinton died before the trial), the charge of conspiracy became a favorite of prosecuting attorneys.[23]

The change in English laws regarding homosexuality resulted, not from a crusade against homosexuality, but from a campaign against prostitution; particularly the so-called "white slave" trade. It was widely believed that large numbers of young girls were unknowingly recruited into prostitution and, once involved, found it difficult to find their way back into respectable society. There was considerable truth in such beliefs, in part because of the hostility society expressed toward unmarried girls who were not virgins and in part because of the difficulty many women had in finding alternative occupations. We also know a more or less a standard price was paid to those who brought young girls into the field, and some were sold by their parents, others by professional procurers. The going rate for a working-class girl between 14 and 18 years of age was 20 pounds; a middle-class girl of the same age group would sell for 100 pounds; and a beautiful child, particularly one from the upper classes and under 12 years of age, would sell for 400 pounds, in part because girls of this class often had to be kidnapped. Only a small minority of girls were, however, actually kidnapped, since the great majority could be recruited as more or less willing victims. Usually, such girls volunteered for some sort of job that entailed going abroad and did not realize, or at least claimed they did not realize, until much later that they were in fact entering a brothel. Even if they were entirely innocent and refused to go along with the schemes of their would-be promoters, they found themselves in difficulty, for they were usually stranded in a strange country or area, with no way of earning their way back home. The newspapers of the day themselves connived at the traffic by running advertisements that were ill-disguised appeals for young girls.[24] Obviously, such traffic could not exist without considerable public indifference and covert protection by law enforcement officials. Belgium became the center of the European market, allegedly because the Belgian police did not disguise their willingness to accept bribes.[25]

Though there had been occasional protests about the white slave trade, there had been no organized movement until Mrs. Josephine Butler appeared on the scene. Mrs. Butler had become interested in the welfare of lower-class women, particularly of prostitutes, as a way of salving her grief at the loss of her daughter Eva, who died at age 7. One of her first projects was to repeal the Contagious Disease Act passed by Parliament in 1864, which, in the interest of preventing venereal disease, had established an official register of prostitutes and compulsory medical inspection in certain areas.[26] In large part through her efforts the act was repealed in 1886. She also succeeded in publicizing the Belgian markets for young girls and forced an investigation of these.[27]

A growing number of influential citizens and groups aided Mrs. Butler, forming "The London Committee for the Exposure and Suppression of the Traffic in English Girls for the Purposes of Continental Prostitution." To curtail some of what was felt to be the worst abuse of child prostitution, the committee attempted to raise the age of consent to 16, to give police the right to initiate proceedings before a justice of the peace in obtaining search warrants for investigating places where girls were believed to be detained for immoral purposes, and to provide summary powers for suppressing brothels and clearinghouses engaged in the so-called white slave traffic. The bill passed the House of Lords in 1883, 1884, and in modified form in 1885, but on each occasion, the House of Commons refused to pass it.[28]

This legislative impasse was broken largely through the efforts of W. T. Stead, editor of the *Pall Mall Gazette*. Conscious of the need to document effectively any charges of "white slavery," Stead organized a "Secret Commission," composed of regular reporters of the *Gazette,* plus three outsiders, two of whom were women—one a trainee reporter and the other an officer in the Salvation Army. One of the women managed to have herself decoyed into a clearinghouse for prostitutes, where she took notes and then escaped to report her findings. The other lived in a brothel for some 10 days, allegedly without having to sell her services. To prove his case, Stead felt he had to demonstrate that a child could actually be bought in England for immoral purposes and spirited away to the Continent without any official protest. For this purpose he decided to enter the "white slave" market himself. He hired a "repentant" procuress to hunt a "pure child" as a sexual companion for an older man. The woman quickly found a child who expressed a wish to serve in a "nice" house. The mother was initially paid 1 pound for her daughter, an intermediary was give 2 pounds, and an additional 2 pounds was given after the child's virginity had been certified by a competent authority. Stead staged a mock seduction, turned the girl over to the Salvation Army, who took her off to France, and then began publishing a series of articles exposing the traffic, the first of which appeared on July 6, 1885. The public reaction to the series on "The Maiden Tribute of Modern Babylon" was instantaneous. Even before the 5-day series concluded on July 10, Parliament had resumed debate on the previously unpassed bill. Before it passed, however, the bill was amended to include an additional clause.

> Any male person who, in public or private, commits, or is a party to the commission of, or procures or attempts to procure the commission by any male person of, any act of gross indencency with another male person, shall be guilty of a misdemeanor, and being convicted thereof, shall be liable, at the discretion of the court, to be imprisoned for any term not exceeding one year with or without hard labour.

The bill was further amended to increase the penalty from 1 year to 2 years, and then without much discussion, the bill passed Parliament with this provision and raising the age of consent to 16.[29]

Though it is believed that Henry Labouchere, a Liberal Radical M. P. who introduced the amendment, had primarily minors in mind, a considerable number of members of Parliament were also incensed over what they feared was a growing incidence of homosexuality, and this factor also has to be considered. Regardless of intent, the effect of the amendment was to punish acts between adult males (not females), even if these took place in private. It also opened up the possibility of blackmail, for those engaging in voluntary homoerotic activities could later be threatened with criminal penalties if the fact was ever made public.

Havelock Ellis wrote:

> Even "gross indecency" between males, however, privately committed, has been since 1885 a penal offense. The clause is open to critisim. With the omission of the words "or private," it would be sound and in harmony with the most enlightened European legislation; but it must be pointed out that an act only becomes indecent when those who perform it or witness it regard it as indecent. The act which brought each of us into the world is not indecent; it would become so if carried on in public. If two male persons, who have reached years of discretion, consent together to perform some act of sexual intimacy in private, no indecency has been committed. If one of the consenting parties subsequently proclaims the act, indecency may doubtless be created, as may happen also in the case of normal sexual intercourse, but it seems contrary to good policy that such proclamation should convert the act itself into a penal offense.[30]

Stead and his allies, who had enough trouble on their hands, had not contemplated the inclusion of homosexual activities. Stead's exposé had roused powerful enemies, including the London police, who were determined to punish him for putting them in a bad light. They found their opportunity when the parents of Eliza Armstrong, the girl whom Stead had purchased, sued to get her back and charged him with abducting the child. Stead was arrested, tried, and convicted for the abduction, and sentenced to 3 months in prison, some of his assistants also being imprisoned. The conviction only generating more publicity for the case, Stead, upon his release from prison, took to traveling and lecturing, in the process influencing legislation throughout much of the world. Two of his books dealt with vice and crime in America, one an exposé of New York, the other of Chicago, and he helped publicize the moral reform in these cities.[31] Regardless of intention, in many cities, homosexuality came to be associated with prostitutes, an exposé of one leading to action against the other. In fact the very term *gay*, originally applied to prostitutes in the last part of the nineteenth century, also came to be applied to homosexuals.

The most publicized victim of the new act was, not the child procurers, for whom it was theoretically designed, but the writer Oscar Wilde (1854–1900). A devotee of "art for art's sake," Wilde, while at Oxford, tried to practice a different life-style that involved speaking contemptuously of sports; decorating his rooms with peacock's feathers, lilies, sunflowers, and the like; and wearing his hair long. For this, Wilde's fellow students wrecked his rooms, but his persistence in his affectations won him adherents. A superb self-publicist, Wilde was soon invited to lecture in America. He did not, however, become a practicing homosexual until after his return from America. Apparently, his first affair was with Robert Ross. About this time also Wilde began to enjoy some literary success with *The Picture of Dorian Gray* (1890) and a book of fairy tales *The Happy Prince* (1888). As he became more successful, he also became bolder in his homosexual liaisons, Robert Ross being followed by John Gray, and in 1891, by Lord Alfred Douglas, the handsome son of the Marquess of Queensberry, now noted for his boxing rules. Douglas was already a homosexual, at least he so reported much later in his autobiography, having discovered this fact at public school.[32] How deeply the two men were involved is debatable, since Bosie, as Douglas was known, was more interested in young boys than older men.[33] Nonetheless, he apparently delighted in causing discomfort to his father and shocking others by implying that he was Wilde's minion. Douglas did, however, introduce Wilde into the homosexual underworld of London, although Bosie's father preferred to believe that his son had been enticed into homosexuality by Oscar Wilde, and he finally brought matters to a head in February 1895 by leaving his card for Wilde at The Albemarle Club, to which both belonged, with the notation, "To Oscar Wilde, Posing as a Somdomite!" This misspelled missive led Oscar Wilde to sue Queensberry for criminal libel.

Three trials followed. In the first trial, *Regina* v. *Queensberry,* the defendants seemingly gathered enough evidence that Wilde deemed it wise to withdraw his suit. On the strength of this evidence Wilde was then arrested under terms of the amended criminal law put on the books to outlaw white slavery. Arrested along with Wilde was Alfred Taylor, who had previously been arrested but not charged, because there was no one willing to give evidence against him. Taylor, who had inherited and spent a fortune, shared his rooms and bed with a succession of homosexual friends and acquaintances, some of whom he introduced to Wilde. Taylor also liked to dress in women's clothes, the police finding a considerable collection in his room. When the jury disagreed about guilt or innocence of Wilde and Taylor in the second trial, Wilde was tried again a third time, separately from Taylor, found guilty of several acts of gross indecency, and sentenced to 2 years at hard labor.[34]

Wilde spent much of his time in jail writing *De profundis,* a confessional essay in the form of a long letter to Lord Alfred Douglas, on whom he blamed most of his troubles. He entrusted it to his disciple Robert Ross, who published it in expurgated form in 1905 and in more nearly complete form later on. After his release from jail (Reading Gaol) he moved to France, where he took up residence under the name of Sebastian Melmoth. While there, he wrote *The Ballad of Reading Gaol,* published in 1898. Impressed by his attempt at recovery, his wife, née Constance Lloyd, whom he had married in 1884, attempted a reconciliation, but Bosie also invited him to join him in Naples. After some hesitation, Wilde went to visit Bosie, who was broke, a condition made worse by the fact the Wilde's wife, angered at his desertion, cut off the annuity she had arranged for him. When Bosie left him, Wilde returned to Paris, where his wife again helped provide for him. His demands for money mounted beyond what she gave him, and his continued importuning irritated his friends. His health declined, in part because of his heavy drinking, and he died on November 30, 1900, after being received into the Catholic Church. Bosie, by then married, publicly renounced his youthful indiscretions and also became a Roman Catholic. In 1912 he became involved in a libel suit against the author of a study of Oscar Wilde, but he lost not only the case in court but his wife as well. Much of the last part of his life was spent in writing a defense of his actions with Wilde, painting himself in glowing terms and Wilde in less glowing ones. Some of his attempts to deny his homoerotic interests now appear pathetic rather than hostile, but they are undoubtedly indicative of the fear many homosexuals felt and many still have about coming out of the closet.[35]

It has often been hypothesized that one reason the government prosecuted Wilde so vigorously was that the Liberal party, then in power, was fearful that it would be tarred with the brush of homosexuality. Though it is impossible to determine how many members of the Liberal party were homosexual or who had homoerotic contacts, two prominent young Liberals were later involved in homosexual affairs, Lewis Harcourt, later Viscount Harcourt, and William Earl Beauchamp. One of the few public figures who had anything to say on Wilde's behalf was W. T. Stead, who wrote:

The heinousness of the crime of Oscar Wilde and his associates does not lie, as is usually supposed, in its being unnatural. It would be unnatural for seventynine out of eighty persons. It is natural for the abnormal person. . . . At the same time it is impossible to deny that the trial and the sentence bring into very clear relief the ridiculous disparity there is between the punishment meted out to those who corrupt girls and those who corrupt boys. If Oscar Wilde, instead of indulging in dirty tricks of indecent familiarity with boys and men, had ruined the lives of half a dozen innocent simpletons of girls, or had broken up the home of his friend by corrupting his friend's wife, no one could have laid a finger upon him. . . . Another contrast . . . is that between the universal execration heaped upon Oscar Wilde and the tacit universal acquiescence of the very same public in the same kind of vice in our public schools. If all persons guilty of Oscar Wilde's offences were to be clapped into gaol, there would be a very surprising exodus from Eton and Harrow, Rugby and Winchester. . . .[36]

Frank Harris, Wilde's friend and one of his biographers, said that the Wilde trial forced many homosexuals to leave England:

> Never was Paris so crowded with members of the English governing classes; here was to be seen a famous ex-Minister; there the fine face of the president of a Royal society; at one table on the Café de la Paix, a millionaire recently ennobled and celebrated for his exquisite taste in art; opposite to him a famous general. It was even said that a celebrated English actor took a return ticket to Paris for three or four days just to be in fashion. The mummer returned quickly; but the majority of the migrants stayed abroad for some time. The wind of terror which had swept them across the Channel opposed their return, and they scattered over the Continent from Naples to Monte Carlo and from Palermo to Seville under all sorts of pretexts.[37]

In spite of the alleged flight, a number of other homosexuals were prosecuted or threatened with prosecution in the last part of the nineteenth and first part of the twentieth century.[38] Still, the trial brought homosexuality out into the open, and in spite of the tragedy to those involved, it encouraged study and discussion of sexuality and deviance.

In a united Germany, laws as oppressive as the English ones were enacted. In 1871 the new German Reichstag enacted a new penal code for the Reich, including Paragraph 175 which was directed against homosexuals. Inevitably charges or rumors of homoerotic affairs were used to blackmail opponents. Moreover, the German police, like the American FBI at a later date, had a secret file about the sexual characteristics of various powerful individuals and allegedly included dossiers on the homosexuality of the armament king Friedrich Krupp, a brother of the kaiser, the kaiser's aide Prince Eulenberg, and the secretary to the empress, Count Kuno von Moltke, and others. The secret files were brought into the open in 1902 by the Krupp scandal. Friedrich Krupp (1854–1902) had succeeded to the head of the Krupp empire at age 33 when his father died, and though he was married, he and his wife lived separately so that he could engage in his homosexual affairs. At his grotto on the island of Capri he created a private pleasure palace where he allegedly brought young fishermen, mule drivers, and others. Through the complaints of local clerics, details of his life on Capri leaked to the Italian press, and his indiscretions were documented by photographs. Though homosexual activities in themselves were not against the law in Italy, corruption of minors was, and Krupp was declared *persona non grata* and had to leave Italy. A German newspaper picked up the story, and Krupp's sexual indiscretions hit the German public in much the same way that the Wilde trial had hit England. The government attempted to cover up for Krupp, but newspapers, especially opposition ones, obtained and printed considerable evidence. When Krupp's wife requested the kaiser to help in handling the scandal, she was silenced by being locked away in an asylum. In an attempt to clear his name Krupp brought suit against the German newspaper that had first printed the scandal, but soon afterward he was found dead, almost surely by suicide. The kaiser tried to quell the public uproar and defend the house of Krupp by giving a state funeral, but the reverberations continued. Krupp family control went to his daughter Bertha (who gave her name to the Big Bertha cannon in the First World War) and to her husband, von Bohlen, who adopted the name of Krupp von Bohlen.[39]

The Krupp case differed from the Wilde case in that the government never stooped to prosecute Krupp; instead it tried to defend him. This action was taken by some to mean that the court around Kaiser Wilhelm II was riddled with homosexuality. Such charges were used by opponents of Wilhelm's policies to try to remove those they regarded as responsible for them. Though the intrigue at the court was rather complex, it centered around the person of Philip, Prince zu Eulenburg–Hertefeld (1847–1921), a friend and adviser to Kaiser Wilhelm. Eulenburg was opposed by Friedrich von Holstein, who had been forced to resign from the foreign office over the debacle of the so-called Moroccan criticism in 1906. Charges of homosexuality were brought against Eulenburg by Maximilian Harden, publisher of the Berlin periodical *Die Zukunst,* who allegedly had been told of Eulenburg's homosexuality by Bismarck when he had been dismissed by the kaiser in 1890, but if this was the case, Harden had done nothing about it until 1906, when von Holstein gave him more ammunition. In that year he began publishing a series of articles about alleged homosexual influence at the court. Harden charged that the kaiser was surrounded by a group of catamites who were perverting German policy. These homosexually inclined men formed a comradeship stronger than that of a monastic order or than any band of Freemasons, and he held that they were found everywhere in high position, not only in Germany but elsewhere. Since they were so united in a sort of international fraternity, treason was always a possibility.

According to Harden, a certain Count Günther von der Schulenburg in 1901 had sent to a select number of noble sypathizers a letter attempting to organize a union of noble "urnings," a term then often used for homosexuals. This was indicative of a trend that had reached the imperial court, where the Kaiser was under the influence of men who shunned women. When the government did nothing, Harden mentioned Eulenburg and the Count von Moltke by name. The kaiser wanted to put Harden in jail, but instead it was decided that Eulenburg and von Moltke should bring suit to clear their names. In October 1907, von Moltke launched a libel suit against Harden, but Harden produced extensive data about the homoerotic tendencies of von Moltke, and a number of experts were called to testify, including Magnus Hirschfeld, who testified von Moltke was a homosexual. Harden was acquitted, but von Moltke appealed his case to a higher court. In the second trial in 1908 much of the evidence produced against von Moltke was found to be fraudulent, and Harden was convicted and sentenced to 4 months in jail. Eulenburg's case, which had been delayed until the von Moltke case was decided, then came to trial, by now complicated by several additional factors. It was alleged, for example, that Eulenburg had bribed Harden with a million marks to lose his case, and Chancellor Bernhard von Bülow, one of those who had urged Eulenburg to go to trial, had himself been accused of being a homosexual by Paul Brandt, who had written about ancient sexual life under the pseudonym of Hans Licht. Brandt was tried and imprisoned for this accusation.

Harden's lawyer produced two witnesses who alleged that Eulenburg had seduced them some 25 years earlier. Since Eulenburg had denied under oath that he had violated Article 175 of the penal code (the article dealing with homosexual relations), he was charged with perjury, but he was too sick to appear before the court, and his trial was delayed until the defeat of Germany in World War I ended the proceedings against him. Since both von Moltke and Eulenburg were opposed to the more extremist military schemes of the kaiser, their removal from positions of power left the more aggressive faction in control. In retrospect the trials might well have had considerable influence on the direction Germany took in the events leading up to World War I.[40]

Highlighting the dangers of blackmail in an even more tragic way is the case of Alfred Redl (1864–1913), a member of the intelligence staff of the general staff of the Austrian–Hugarian Empire. Here he did a brilliant job at the Russian desk—so effective that the Russians concentrated their efforts on finding chinks in his armor. During their investigation the Russians found that Redl was a homosexual with transvestite tendencies, and in 1901 with the threat of blackmail and the payment of additional sums of money, they turned Redl into a double agent. Though the Austrians received information that a high-ranking Austrian officer was in the pay of the Russians, Redl was not suspected. For a time it seemed that Redl would become chief of the Intelligence Bureau, but when August von Osyrmiecz Urbanski was appointed instead, Redl was transferred to the command of an infantry battalion. In 1913 German intelligence intercepted a Russian letter to him, a trap was laid, and when Redl was confronted with the evidence, he confessed and was permitted to shoot himself. Though a number of Austrian disasters in World War I were attributed to the consequences of Redl's treachery, it would be hard to place the blame on Redl, for his death and homosexuality were widely reported in the world press in 1913, and the Austrians had every opportunity to change their plans. Nonetheless, the Redl case became the classic example to "prove" that homosexuals were security risks in any position involving confidential knowledge.[41]

The United States had no similar scandal during the nineteenth century, but

Americans were well informed about what was taking place in England and Europe, and American laws about sex were modeled on those of England. After the American Revolution, most states had generally adopted the ambiguous statements about "deviant" sex expressed by Blackstone. Massachusetts, for example, had a statute reading:

> Every person who shall commit the abominable and detestable crime against na-
> ture, either with mankind or with any beast, shall be punished by imprisonment in
> the State Prison, for not more than twenty years.

New York cut the sentence to 10 years but in other respects was similar. Pennsylvania was somewhat more specific, mentioning sodomy or buggery and distinguishing between a first and second offense. A first offender received 5 years, a second, 10 years. Virginia, with its background of slavery, added a further distinction between slave and freemen and stipulated that such punishment be limited to freemen.[42]

When cases were brought under the provisions of such statutes, the court usually relied upon common-law precedents to determine exactly what constituted the abominable and detestable crime. In a Maryland case, *Davis* v. *the State,* in 1810, the Maryland Court of Appeals held that the ambiguous Maryland statute had to be interpreted in the light of common law.[43] This meant that, in general, prosecutions in nineteenth-century America were not too frequent, since both persons involved were treated as accomplices, and if one was convicted, so would the other one be. The effect was to exclude sexual activities between consenting adults in private from prosecution, whether homosexual or heterosexual. Agitation for change of this came in America as in England, primarily because, even where children were involved, it was difficult to prosecute,[44] especially since solicitation to commit a sex act was not an offense.[45]

There were other difficulties in enforcement, if only because the ambiguity of the statutes and the common law made it difficult to determine exactly what constituted a crime against nature. This ambiguity is easier to document in Texas than in many other states, for Texas has separate reports on criminal cases, and these give more information about such activities. In two cases dating from the last part of the nineteenth century (*Fennel* v. *State,* 1869, and *Frazier* v. *State,* 1873), the courts held that the Texas code did not describe or define what constituted the "crime against nature," and the judges refused to look to common law for what might have been meant. As a result, they found sodomy was not punishable because it was not clear that this was the crime against nature. In 1883 (*Ex parte Bergen*), the Supreme Court of Texas, said, however, that it was not necessary to define an offense in great detail and held that sodomy could be punished under the penal code. This did not, however, end the matter. In 1893 (*Prindle* v. *State*) the same Texas court held that, since common law did not classify oral copulation as sodomy this could not be regarded as a crime. Texas' difficulties with exactly what constituted a sexual crime continued until 1943, when the state code was revised to cover almost every sexual act.[46]

Other states also had difficulty. Iowa courts in 1860 (*Estes* v. *Carter*) held that, even though sodomy was a crime punishable at common law, it was not a crime in Iowa, because it was not included and specified by name in the Iowa criminal code. It did not become a crime in Iowa until 1897, when the legislature acted to cover what was regarded as a legal loophole.[47] Many states refused to spell out what was meant by the crime against nature, or even sodomy, and by necessity judges turned to the common law for definition, but even this was unclear. Edward Livingston, in his *A System of Penal Law for the United States of America* (1828), for example, mentioned the keeping of brothels, printing of obscene materials, adultery, abduction, rape, procuring, and abortion as criminal activities but did not deal with any kind of voluntary sexual intercourse.[48] Joel Prentiss Bishop's *Commentaries on the Law of Statutory Crimes* (1883), discussed adultery, fornication, incest, miscegenation, seduction, and rape in some detail but only mentiond sodomy and bestiality without definition. It is apparent that he considered sodomy a heinous crime because in his *New Commentaries on Marriage* he stated that it was a "high matrimonial crime" and a better grounds for divorce than adultery, but probably here he was equating it with anal intercourse between husband and wife.[49] The various editions of Wharton include discussion of the criminal penalties for sodomy, but not until the eighth edition (1880) did he finally define it as sexual connection *per anum*. Before that he had merely stated that sodomy must be committed in that part where sodomy is "usually committed" to be so classified as sodomy.[50] This ambiguity must have left many of his legal readers uncertain of exactly what constituted sodomy or if such a thing as homosexual sodomy existed. Sir William Oldnall Russell summed up the English and American legal attitudes when he ambiguously stated:

> In treating of the offence of sodomy, *peccatum, illud horrible, inter Christiani non nominadum,* a sin, most horrible, and among Christians not named, it is not intended to depart from the reserved and concise mode of statement which has been adopted by other writers.[51]

In this setting the writings of Sir James Fitzjames Stephen exercised their great influence. Though it is easier to document his influence in Canada than in the United States, it seems clear that his efforts led to somewhat greater precision in the law, with the consequences of more severe punishments for those engaged in sexual activities that society disapproved. In California, for example, penal code 287 was enacted, which defined the crime against nature to include "any sexual penetration, however slight," and soon after, prohibitions were added against fellatio, cunnilingus, and other sexual activities.[52] Most states adopted similar specific laws in the first part of the twentieth century.

In sum, it seems as if the English-speaking world did not participate in the emancipating sex legislation of the French Revolution, but in the nineteenth century, in spite of the propaganda efforts of some of the romantics and the logical arguments of the utilitarians, chose to adopt more restrictive sex laws, in part to protect children and women and also as part of the general Victorian belief in the evils of sex propounded by the scientific writers of the nineteenth century.

As in other areas of sex legislation, however, there were contradictions, and there were no laws in English common-law countries against lesbianism. Efforts to change this were made in England in 1921, when a new Criminal Law Amendement Bill was introduced. A Scottish conservative lawyer, Frederick Macquisten, moved to amend the act by inserting a clause dealing with "Acts of indecency by females." He would have inserted:

> Any act of gross indecency between female persons shall be a misdemeanour and punishable in the same manner as any such act committed by male persons under section eleven of the Criminal Law Amendment Act, 1885.

The clause was passed by the House of Commons in August by 143 to 53 but was removed in the House of Lords.[53] In the United States, whereas most of the state statutes could be interpreted as applying to lesbianism, prosecution was almost nonexistent. Thus any discussion of lesbianism has to be based on literary and other references rather than legal ones. At the beginning of the nineteenth century Samuel Taylor Coleridge (1772–1834) left an unfinished narrative poem *Christabel*,[54] which includes numerous references to female bisexuality, if not homosexuality. One critic, Roy Basler, has argued that the reason Coleridge left the poem unfinished was that, if he had carried it to its logical conclusion, he would have been forced to be more specific about the sexual relationships between Christabel and Geraldine, and his audience would not have tolerated such a discussion. Such a hesitation is understandable, since the publication of the first part led to charges of obscenity against him.[55]

Obviously, when lesbianism was a subject of fictional treatment, the relations were better hinted at than spelled out. This was the course of action that Christina Georgina Rossetti (1830–1894) seems to have followed in her description of the homoerotic affair between the two sisters Laura and Lizzie in the *Goblin Market*.[56] Algernon Charles Swinburne (1837–1909) was somewhat more overt in his description of lesbianism in his writings but was also unfriendly, if not hostile, to the women he described. His *Anactoria* is a

10-page complaint from Sappho to a girl who no longer reciprocated her love; his *Sapphics* describes life on Mitylene as being full of music and fruitless women; his *Dolores, Faustine,* and *Masque of Queen Bersabe*[57] include references to lesbianism, as does his novel *Lesbia Brandon.*[58] Since the novel was supposedly based on the real-life character of Jane Faulkner, who had rejected Swinburne's advances, some critics have suggested that Jane herself had lesbian tendencies,[59] although it might well be that Swinburne was rationalizing his own rejection in terms of his fiancée's failure to appreciate a "real" man.

Toward the end of the nineteenth century, just when the law was becoming most severe against male homosexuality, the references to lesbianism increase. Lesbianism is a possibility in Thomas Hardy's description of the relationship between Cytherea and Miss Aldclyffe in *Desperate Remedies* (1871).[60] It is much more overt in Olive Schreiner's *Story of An African Farm* (1883), which has been described as a female protest against the brutalities and violence of masculine frontier society. In the novel the pregnant heroine turned against all men. She refused to marry the man who impregnated her, choosing to bear her child secretly and alone. When she became ill, she was nursed by an effeminate boy, long in love with her, who disguised himself as a woman to care for her[61] and overcome her hostility to men.

The only actual sexual descriptions of lesbianism occur in the pornographic writings, where it is described as the Game of Flats or other similar expressions. The anonymous author of *My Secret Life,* printed during the last two decades of the nineteenth century, recounts his anticipatory enjoyment in observing women engaged in "flat" intercourse with each other, perhaps content in the belief that he as a man could do things better.[62] Various houses of prostitution also staged exhibitions of lesbian lovemaking, but we know little about the actual women involved. Much of the bondage and discipline literature, described in an earlier chapter, has lesbian overtones.[63]

As the public became more aware of lesbianism, it became somewhat more hostile. The change in attitudes can be documented by examining three suspected lesbian couples and the treatment accorded them. The first couple is the famous Ladies of Llangollen, who died just before the onset of the Victorian period. The two women known by this title were Lady Eleanor Butler (died 1829) and Sarah Posonby (died 1831), both members of Irish noble families who conceived a passionate friendship for each other while students at a school in Kilkenny. Though the two girls were forbidden to see each other, they managed to carry on their affair through the connivance of Sarah's servant Mary Caryll, also known as Molly the Bruiser. Eventually, the families bowed to the inevitable and gave both women small allowances, provided they left Ireland. They settled in Llangollen, Wales, with Mary as their servant, where they established a sort of literary haven visited by the great and near great of

the time, who admired them for their powerful personalities and ardent Platonism. Though comparatively poor, they apparently did not suffer any ostracism
from either their local community or the world at large.[64]

The late ninteenth-century counterpart to the Ladies of Llangollen were
Katherine Bradley (1846–1914) and Edith Cooper (1862–1913), who
published poetry together under the collective name of Michael Field. Aunt and
niece respectively, with some 14 year's difference in age, the two became
lifelong companions. They published their first book of verse in 1881 under the
names of Arrand and Isla Leigh, and it was not until their second volume 1883
that they used the pseudonym Michael Field. This collection was initially given
a favorable reception until the identity of the two authors came out, whereupon
the critics proved more hostile. Though the two women were not particulary
persecuted, there was no tendency to idealize their friendship, and their reception by the critics was increasingly hostile. Included in their works were poems
based on fragments from Sappho.[65]

Too overt a lesbianism, however, only ran into hostility, as indicated by the
case of Radclyffe Hall (died 1943), who wrote *The Well of Loneliness* in 1928.
The original edition of the book had an introduction by Havelock Ellis, who
stated that he regarded it as the first English novel to present lesbianism in
faithful and uncompromising form. In spite of the support of Ellis, the novel
soon ran into opposition.[66] A few literary figures such as Arnold Bennett
initially praised it, but a review by a certain James Douglas attacking it as a
sensational piece of special pleading designed to display perverted decadence led
to demands that the book be withdrawn.[67] On the advice of the home secretary
the publishers withdrew the book from the English market, although it
continued to be published in Paris and was also published in the United States.
To prevent its further dissemination a prosecution was mounted, and in a
public trial the book was found obscene as well as dangerous and corrupting.
The real difficulty with the novel was that the lesbians were pictured as more
or less healthy people leading more or less normal lives. Since Radclyffe Hall
herself was a lesbian, a long-time companion and friend of Una, Lady
Troubridge, her picture of lesbian relationship has sometimes been regarded as
more or less accurate.[68] That it was the favorable portrayal of lesbian life that
got the book into trouble is indicated by the fact that Compton Mackenzie's
satire on lesbian love, *Extraordinary Women,*[69] published in that same year,
never came under the same kind of attack.

In sum, though lesbianism in England never resulted in the same kind of
prosecution as against male homosexuals, there was considerable hostility to it,
enough even to generate an effort to change the law on the subject. One reason
it was not prosecuted was that the male establishment was convinced that most
women knew nothing at all about the subject, and to pass a law against lesbianism would make women feel guilty about their own gregariousness. The

male establishment was willing to tolerate lesbianism, convinced of their own superiority; only when it threatened their status or position in society did they move against it.

NOTES

1. For a discussion of this, see Edward Westermarck, *The History of Human Marriage* 5th ed. (New York: Allerton Books, 1922, 3 vols.), Vol. 3, pp. 339–342.

2. For various revisions in the French sexual code, see Gerhard O. W. Maller, *The French Penal Code* (South Hackensack, N.J.: Fred B. Rothman, n.d.), articles 330–340, pp. 113–117.

3. Havelock Ellis, *Sexual Inversion,* pp. 348–349, in *Psychology of Sex* New York: Random House, 1936, 7 vols. in 2), Vol. 1 Part 4.

4. Thorkil Vanggaard, *Phallos: A Symbol and Its History in the Male World* (London: Jonathan Cape, 1972), pp. 173–176.

5. For an analysis and chart of laws regarding homosexual activity, see Magnus Hirschfeld, *Die Homosexualität des Mannes und des Weibes* (Berlin: Louis Marcus Verlagsbuchhandlung, 1920), pp. 841–870.

6. William Blackstone, *Commentaries on the Laws of England*, new ed. with notes by John Frederick Archibold (London: William Reed, 1811), Book 4, p. 205.

7. *Ibid.*, p. 215.

8. For a more nearly complete discussion of this, see Alex K. Gigeroff, *Sexual Deviation in the Criminal Law* (Toronto: University of Toronto Press for the Clark Institute of Psychiatry, 1968). This discussion is invaluable, and I am greatly indebted to Gigeroff.

9. Blackstone, *op. cit.,* Book 4, pp. 64–65.

10. Francis Wharton, *A Treatise on the Criminal Law of the U.S.,* 4th ed. (revised, Philadelphia: Kay and Brothers, 1857), p. 591.

11. *People* v. *Wilson,* 119 *Cal.* 384 (December 1897), *Reports of Cases Determined in the Supreme Court of the State of California,* C. P. Pomeroy, reporter (San Francisco: Bancroft-Whitney, 1906).

12. Jeremy Bentham, *The Theory of Legislation*, C. K. Ogden, ed. (London: Kegan Paul, French, Trubner, 1931), pp. 473–497. This is an appendix entitled "Bentham on Sex," but it is only an extract of Bentham's ideas on the subject.

13. The full treatise on sexual activities is contained in Portfolio 74b, University College, London.

14. Gigeroff, *op. cit.,* pp. 21–22.

15. *Ibid.,* pp. 22–23.

16. *Ibid.,* pp. 24–25.

17. *Ibid.,* pp. 25–27.

18. John Stuart Mill, *The Subjection of Women,* introduction by Wendell Robert Carr (Cambridge, Mass.: MIT Press, 1970). There are many other editions.

19. James Fitzjames Stephen, *A History of the Criminal Law of England* (reprinted, New York: Burt Franklin, 1967).

20. *Ibid.,* Vol. 3, pp. 347, 366.

21. *Ibid.,* Vol. 3, p. 367.

22. Great Britain, *The Parliamentary Debates* (published under the superintendence of T. C. Hansard, 1820–1830 n.s., 2 vols.), IX, pp. 350–360, (May 5, 1828).

23. See William Roughhead, *Bad Companions* (Edinburgh: W. Green & Son, 1930), pp. 149–183. See also H. Montgomery Hyde, *The Love That Dared Not Speak Its Name* (Boston: Little, Brown, 1970), pp. 93–98, 123–124.

24. Charles Terrot, *Traffic in Innocents* (New York: Dutton, 1960), pp. 22–40.

25. For a more nearly complete discussion of this, see Vern Bullough and Bonnie Bullough, *Women, Sex, and Prostitution* (in press).

26. Benjamin Scott, *A State Iniquity: Its Rise, Extension and Overthrow* (London: Horace Marshall & Sons, 1896), passim.

27. A. S. G. Butler, *Portrait of Josephine Butler* (London: Faber and Faber Ltd., 1954), esp. pp. 137–141; E. M. Turner, *Josephine Butler: An Appreciation* (London: The Association for Moral and Social Hygiene, 1927), passim; and Glen Petrie, *A Singular Iniquity* (New York: Viking Press, 1971).

28. Terrot, *op. cit.,* pp. 117–131.

29. Hansard, *Parliamentary Debates,* 3rd series (1830–1891) (Aug. 6, 1885), pp. 1397–1398. *Criminal Law Amendment Act, 1885,* 48 & 49 Vct. c. 69.

30. Ellis, *Sexual Inversion* Part 4, in *op. cit.,* Vol. 1, p. 349.

31. See W. T. Stead, *Satan's Invisible World Displayed* (New York: R. F. Fenno, 1897); and *If Christ Came to Chicago* (Chicago: Laird and Lee, 1894).

32. Lord Alfred Douglas, *Autobiography* (London: Martin Secker, 1929).

33. This fact, though denied by Douglas in his *Autobiography,* is attested to by the Marquess of Queensberry, *Oscar Wilde and the Black Douglas* (London: Hutchinson, 1949), p. 29. This biography is by the nephew of Alfred Douglas. See also André Gide, *If It Die,* translated by D. Bussy (New York: Random House, 1935), pp. 297, 300–301.

34. There are many accounts of the trials, including *The Three Trials of Oscar Wilde,* verbatim transcripts and introduction by H. Montgomery Hyde (New York: University Books, 1956).

35. There are literally bookcases of studies about Oscar Wilde. An interesting account is by Vyvyan Holland, *Son of Oscar Wilde* (London: Rupert Hart-Davis, 1954). Holland, the second son, gives considerable insight into his father and defends his reputation. See also *The Letters of Oscar Wilde,* Rupert Hart-Davis, ed. (London: Hart-Davis, 1962).

36. This is from *The Review of Reviews,* a journal founded by Stead, and quoted in Hyde, *op. cit.,* pp. 149–150.

37. Frank Harris, *Oscar Wilde* (New York: Covici Freed, 1930), pp. 171–172.

38. Hyde, *op. cit.,* pp. 155–170, and passim, includes several such incidents.

39. Ellis, *op. cit.* Vol. 1, Part 4, p. 39. For a fictionalized treatment of some of this, see Roger Peyrefitte, *The Exile of Capri* (London: Secker & Warburg, 1961), pp. 42–45, 57–59. This is a novelized biography of Jacques d'Adelsward-Fersen, a minor French poet and novelist who was a major figure in Capri's homosexual colony. See also Xavier Mayne, *The Intersexes: A History of Similisexualism as a Problem in Social Life* ([Florence], privately printed, 1908), p. 227. This was republished (New York: Arno Press, 1975) Mayne is a pseudonym for Edward I. Stevenson. See also William Manchester, *The Arms of Krupp 1587–1968* (Boston: Little, Brown, 1968).

40. Maximilian Harden, "Furst Eulenburg," in *Prozesse, Kopfe, Dritter Teil* (Berlin: 1913), pp. 182–183. See also Lyn Pedersen, "The Ordeal of Prince Eulenburg," *One* (Oct.–Nov., and Dec.1956). See also Magnus Hirschfeld, *op. cit.,* passim.

41. For a detailed account of this, see Robert Asprey, *The Panther's Feast* (New York: Putnam's, 1959).

42. Francis Wharton, *A Treatise on the Criminal Law of the U.S.*, 4th ed. (revised, Philadelphia: Kay and Brothers, 1857,) p. 591.

43. *Davis vs. the State*, in Thomas Harris and Reverdy Johnson, *Reports of Cases Argued and Determined in the Court of Appeals of Maryland in 1810, 1812, 1813, 1814, and 1815* (Annapolis, Md.: Jonas Green, 1826), Vol. 3, pp. 154–156.

44. Wharton, *op. cit.*, p. 591.

45. *People v. Wilson*, 119 *Cal.* 384 (December 1897), *Reports of Cases Determined in the Supreme Court of the State of California*, C. P. Pomeroy, reporter (San Francisco: Bancroft-Whitney, 1906).

46. See *Fennel v. State*, 32 *Texas* 378 (1869); *Supreme Court of Texas: Frazier v. State*, 39, *Texas* 390 (1873); *Supreme Court of State of Texas: Ex Parte ed. Bergen*, 14 *Texas Criminal Reports* 52 (1883); *Charles Prindle v. the State*, 31 *Texas Criminal Reports* 551 (1893); *Alex Lewis v. the State*, 36 *Texas Criminal Reports* 37 (1896); *Algie Adams v. the State*, 48 *Texas Criminal Reports* 90 (1905). See also *Vernon's Penal Code of the State of Texas* (annotated, Kansas City, Mo.: Vernon Law Books Company, n.d.), Vol. 1.

47. *Estes v. Carter*, 10 *Iowa* 400 (1860), *Reports of Cases in Law and Equity Determined in the Supreme Court of the State of Iowa*, T. F. Withrow, reporter (Des Moines, Iowa: Mill Brothers, 1861), Vol. 10.

48. Edward Livingstone, *A System of Penal Law for the United States of America* (Washington, D.C.: Gale and Seaton, 1828), pp. 86–87, 104–105.

49. Joel Prentiss Bishop, *Commentaries on the Law of Statutory Crimes* (Boston: Little, Brown, 1883), pp. 369, 411–414, 437–438; and *New Commentaries on Marriage, Divorce, and Separation* (Chicago: T. H. Flood and Company, 1891, 2 vols.), Vol. 1, pp. 754–756.

50. See the Wharton editions of 1857, 1874, and 1880 for comparison.

51. Sir William Oldnall Russell and Charles Greaves, *A Treatise on Crimes and Misdemeanors*, 9th American from the 4th London ed., 1877.

52. West's Annotated California Codes, *Penal Code Sections 211 to 446* (Official) *California Penal Code Classification* (St. Paul, Minn.: West Publishing Company, 1970), sec. 287, p. 554, and sec. 288a, p. 624.

53. See Hansard, *House of Commons Debates*, CXLV, cols. 1799–1807 (August 4, 1921) *House of Lords Debates*, XLVI, cols. 567–577 (August 15, 1921).

54. Samuel Taylor Coleridge, *Christabel*, in C. H. Page, *British Poets of the Nineteenth Century* (New York: Sanborn, 1917).

55. Roy Basler, *Sex, Symbolism and Psychology in Literature* (New Brunswick, N.J.: Rutgers University Press, 1948), pp. 24–51.

56. See G. H. Bell, *The Hamwood Papers of the Ladies of Llangollen and Lady Caroline Hamilton* (London: Macmillan, 1931); Blanche C. Harcy, *The Princesse de Lamballe* (New York: Appleton, 1904); H. C. V. Morton, *In Search of Wales* (New York: Dodd, 1932); and Jeanette Foster, *Sex Variant Women in Literature* (London: Frederick Muller, 1958), pp. 122–125.

57. A. C. Swinburne, *Poems and Balads*, Ser. 1 (London: Chatto, 1893).

58. A. C. Swinburne, *Lesbia Brandon*, Randolph Huges, ed. (London: Falcon Press, 1952).

59. George Lafourcade, *La jeunesse de Swinburne* (Oxford, England: Humphrey Milford, 1928), Vol. 1, p. 307.

60. Thomas Hardy, *Desperate Remedies* (New York: Harper, 1896).

61. Olive Schreiner, *Story of An African Farm* (Boston: Little, Brown, 1920).

62. Anonymous, *My Secret Life* (reprinted, New York: Grove Press, 1966, 11 vols.), Vol. 5, Chap. 1, pp. 858–867; Chap. 3, pp. 882–895.

63.   There are numerous titles listed in Pisanus Fraxi, *Bibliography of Prohibited Books* (reprinted, London: Jack Brussell, 1962, 3 vols.).

64.   See G. H. Bell, ed., *op. cit.;* Sidonie Gabriella Colette, *Ces Plaisiris* (Paris: Ferenczi, 1932), pp. 155–161; and H. C. V. Morton, *op. cit.;* Foster, *op. cit.,* pp. 122–125.

65.   See Michael Field, *Works and Days,* a compilation from the journal kept by the two women, T. and D. C. Surge Moore, eds. (London: Murray, 1933); and Foster, *op. cit.,* pp. 141–145.

66.   Radclyffe Hall, *The Well of Loneliness* (New York: Covici, Friede, 1929). The London edition with the introduction by Havelock Ellis was published by Jonathan Cape.

67.   *Sunday Express,* August 19, 1928.

68.   Una, Lady Troubride, *Life of Radclyffe Hall* (New York: Citadel Press, 1963).

69.   Compton Mackenzie, *Extraordinary Women* (London: Secker, 1932). The first edition was in 1928.

20

STIGMATIZED SEXUAL BEHAVIOR
IN NINETEENTH-CENTURY AMERICA

American investigation into nonprocreative sexual behavior, beginning in the last few decades of the nineteenth century, was heavily influenced by continental investigators. A distinguished psychologist, G. Alder Blumer, for example, reported a case of "perverted sexual instinct" in 1882, which he noted was similar to the cases reported by Professor C. Westphal of Berlin in 1869. Blumer viewed his patient, a sometime transvestite who abhorred females but did not practice sodomy, as insane, possibly epileptic, a description frequently applied in the medical literature to all those departing from the accepted norms in sexual behavior.[1] A year later, in 1883, the physician J. C. Shaw described a patient who had come to him for treatment of what would now be called homosexual tendencies. Shaw reported that the existing literature on the subject was mostly in German or French, although he said he managed to find two articles on the topic in other languages, one in English and one in Italian. Since no American journal had dealt with the subject, he and a fellow physician, G. N. Ferris, tried to educate members of American professional groups. In their description of homosexuality, they made no conclusions of their own and, more to the point, failed to refer to the existence of homosexuals in the United States. In fact, they implied that such cases were not often seen on the North American continent.[2] Challenging such innocence was

an article by A. B. Holder on the custom of *berdache* among the Crow Indians
in Montana, where he had lived and practiced; it also included comments on
homosexual behavior in groups outside the Indian community.[3] Gradually, a
few other American physicians began to be conscious of the existence of homosexuality, a growth in consciousness that led the editor of the *Medical
Record* in 1884 to remark:

> Science had indeed discovered that, amid the lowest forms of bestiality and
> sensuousness exhibited by debased men, there are phenomena which are truly
> pathological and which deserve the considerate attention and help of the physician.[4]

In the subsequent years a few American medical practitioners, encouraged
by researchers on the continent, began to contribute case histories and discussions of various "deviant" practices, including homosexual behavior. Sometimes wider public attention was focused on the "deviant" sexual practices.
Probably the best informed American medical writer on the subject was G.
Frank Lydston of Chicago. He recognized the complexity of the phenomenon of
"perversity" and the difficulty in determining its cause. Like the continental
writers, he stressed the impulse to "sexual gratification in an abnormal manner," noting that the "perverts" showed "partial or complete apathy toward
the normal method" of intercourse. Though uncertain of the cause, he believed
it was possible a person might be born with a tendency toward perversion because of physical deformity of either the brain (idiots, for example) or genitalia
(such as hermaphrodites), or because of congenitally misdirected impulses. He
remained a believer in the dangers of masturbation, holding out the possibility
that homosexuality was a result of the "overt stimulation of sexual sensibility
and the receptive sexual centers, incidental to sexual excesses and masturbation." Lydston, nevertheless, was one of the first Americans to look for
psychological causes, although in general other nineteenth-century physicians
did not repeat his kind of analysis.[5]

The reluctance of Americans to search for psychological factors is exemplified by an anonymous American medical reviewer in 1902, who after com-
plimenting Havelock Ellis for pursuing his studies of sex on a scientific level,
felt that the volumes in too many instances were

> filled with the pornographic imaginings of perverted minds rather than cold facts,
> and the data which are collected are seemingly of little value. Whether any
> practical results can come from such labor is doubtful.[6]

Earlier, William Noyes had reviewed the first German edition of Ellis' work by
protesting

against the appearance of such a work as this in a library (series) intended primarily for popular reading. Even Krafft Ebing [sic], although writing solely for the medical profession, has been severely and justly criticized for the unnecessary emphasis and importance he has given this subject by his articles on the perversions of the sexual sense, and nothing but harm can follow if popular scientific literature is to suffer a similar deluge.

Noyes claimed that publicity given various kinds of alternative sexual activity only allowed "perverts" to recognize their condition, and since understanding failed to lead to any amelioration, it was best if it had not been mentioned at all.[7]

Medical writers continuing to investigate homosexuality confined themselves to reporting isolated cases in the hope that the gathering of as many facts as possible might lead to scientific conclusions. By and large, they believed that "degeneration" was congenital and probably caused by hereditary physical weaknesses of some sort. Case reports highlight the peculiarities of the brain and genitals, both before and after death, this kind of reporting undoubtedly confirming others' tendency to think of the individuals involved as "perverts," as isolated, physically handicapped persons. Even when social aspects of homosexuality were discussed, American medical commentators ignored the possibility that such matters had any relevance to American life as ordinarily encountered.

Unlike bestiality or even masturbation, homoerotic activity was a form of group socialization. Americans were slow to realize the implications of this for institutions. One of the earliest incidents of institutional homosexuality to gain publicity in medical journals occurred in a boy's corrective institution in Baltimore in 1886. The matter came to medical attention because of an outbreak of gonorrhea spread by rectal coition. The physician in charge, Randolph Winslow, believed that, though other observers had probably "seen urethral inflammation arise from this unnatural and filthy practice," they had not publicized it, and he personally was "unaware of any such observation." He found anal intercourse common in the institution, adding that, even after it was discovered, it could not be stamped out. He reported that younger boys sold their favors for economic gain, and when questioned about it, they justified their conduct by the existence of prostitution in the outside world.[8] Though Winslow and others knew that European investigators had reported a tendency among homosexuals to group together, American observers generally ignored the real life around them and only rarely went beyond the facts of a particular case before them. G. Alder Blumer asserted that his homosexual patients told him they were "able to recognize each other," but he did not add any detail about how.[9] Lydston again was the exception, writing:

> There is in every community of any size a colony of male sexual perverts; they are usually known to each other, and are likely to congregate together. At times they operate in accordance with some definite and concerted plan in quest of subject wherewith to gratify their abnormal sexual impulses. . . . The physician rarely has his attention called to these things, and when evidence of their existence is placed before him, he is apt to receive it with skepticism. . . . The man about town is very often *au fait* in these matters and can give very valuable information. Indeed, witnesses enough can be found to convince the most skeptical.[10]

Whether he was repeating what European investigators said or whether he based his statement on his own investigations in the United States is unclear, since he failed to provide any evidence.

Nevertheless, there was a slowly growing awareness among the medical community of homosexuality and other nonprocreative sexual activities. Some of the reference works on medical forensics included references to homosexuality. A widely reprinted one by Johann Ludwig Casper stated that, though such relations were called "paederastia," this term was a misnomer because such sexual appetites existed in "individuals far more advanced in life." He included references to lesbianism and to sodomy, although he defined the latter in terms of bestiality.[11] One reason for the reluctance to accept such things as homosexuality was that it seemed so morally wrong. A member of the Philadelphia Bar told J. Richardson Parke that he would refuse to defend anyone accused of sexual "inversion," on the grounds of social and professional decency. Parke himself had no such qualms. He explained that sexual inversion had

> been perceptibly stimulated in our larger cities, and by our native born population, particularly, by the ever-growing desire to escape having children.[12]

This association of city life and "perversion" was not unique to Parke. Many physicians of the time believed that modern city living imposed such terrible strains on the nervous system that sexual crimes and deviations would be an expected result for persons with weak nervous systems, for they could not stand the pace and would resort to degenerate behavior. The medical historian John Burnham has argued that

> these environmental but somatic explanations had the additional advantage of letting their proponents avoid confronting a purely social level—or even psychological level—of explanation for 'contrary sexual feelings,' as the rather clumsy contemporaneous translation from the German delicately characterized the phenomenon. Widespread recognition of the social aspects of homoerotic behavior was therefore a prerequisite to social analysis.[13]

Until that happened, homosexuality remained merely a series of case studies.

Because of this reluctance, as Allan M'Lane Hamilton, a leading forensic psychiatrist, pointed out, courts would be ill prepared to deal with the cases of inversion coming to their attention. If such matters did come to trial, homosexuals were usually regarded as "instances of mental unsoundness" and classed with the insane. As demonstration Hamilton reported the case of Henry B. Palmer of New Brunswick, New Jersey, whose brother had taken steps to have him declared a lunatic to get control of his wealth. While defending Palmer, Hamilton found that his client had paid out some $70,000 in blackmail over a period of years. Years earlier, Palmer, a homosexual, had taken a young boy to the Centennial Exposition at Philadelphia in 1876. While there, the two had occupied the same room and engaged in sexual relations. Later, when the boy threatened to expose him, Palmer, who confessed to Hamilton that he had the "contrary sexual instinct," paid rather than suffer exposure. Only through such payment of blackmail was Palmer, a bachelor, able to remain a respected member of society and an officer of his church. At the time of his trial for incompetence he was president of an insurance company.

During the commitment proceedings Hamilton tried to distinguish three varieties of homosexuality

namely, those which were connected with or are the result of insanity, where loss of restraint exists, and where there is a conspicuous defect in intellectual power, and where, of course, responsibility is lost; secondly, a form which is simply an ordinary result of depravity and libidinous curiosity and gratification in which responsibility is not lost; and a third form existed as an index of defective organization, to which class I believe Palmer belonged. How far he was criminally responsible was a matter for the court and jury to decide, but whatever their verdict might be, I did not regard Palmer as being insane, so far as it presupposed any inability to care for himself or his property.

In spite of Hamilton's efforts, Palmer was adjudged insane, the court holding that such a "depth of depravity could not be anything else but a mark of insanity." Hamilton concluded

The attitude of the law so far is very harsh regarding the punishment of offenders of this kind when detected, when they happen to be distinctly responsible, and it rarely recognizes any extenuating circumstances, and while possibly this restriction is best for society, there is no doubt that in cases where a congenital taint exists, some degree of protection should be afforded the possessors of developed mental weakness who are apt to be the prey of designing persons of their own sex.[14]

With such confusion about sex, it becomes very difficult to describe "deviant"

sex practices in any detail in nineteenth-century America. There are some hints
in private correspondence or diaries about sexual deviance, but exactly what
the writer was referring to is sometimes debatable. Some friendships between
women, for example, regarded as innocent at the time, might today have deeper
meaning. Innocence in the unmarried woman was widely believed in by a society that portrayed the male as sensual and animal and the female as pure and
chaste. As might be expected intense friendships between women were accepted
without question, as indicated by the failure of the British Parliament to deal
with lesbianism. Though it is possible to speculate that some of these
friendships had sexual overtones, the evidence is never quite definitive. All we
can gather from the surviving references is that homosexuality was probably
not as scarce on the American scene as some writers would have one believe.
Moreau de St. Méry, for example, a West Indian lawyer who became a
bookseller in Philadelphia in the 1790s, reported on the liaisons he observed
among certain women.

> I am going to say something that is almost unbelievable. These women, without
> real love and without passions, give themselves up at an early age to the enjoyment
> of themselves; and they are not at all strangers to being willing to seek unnatural
> pleasures with persons of their own sex.[15]

Unfortunately, we do not know what grounds St. Méry had for making such a
statement nor how true his observations were. It might be that St. Méry was
only giving vent to a general hostility about women in general.

A somewhat less debatable report was that given by Margaret Fuller, who
was fascinated by instances in history and literature of intimate relationships—
some of them undoubtedly sexual—between members of the same sex. She
wrote:

> It is true that a woman may be in love with a woman, and a man with a man. . . .
> It is regulated by the same laws as that of love between persons of different sexes,
> and it is purely intellectual and spiritual, unprofaned by any mixture of lower in-
> stincts. . . . Why did Socrates love Alcibiades? Why did the Kaiser so love
> Schneider? How natural is the love of Wallenstein for Max, that of Madame de
> Staël for Recamier, mine for _____? I loved _____ for a time with as much
> passion as I was then strong enough to feel. . . . She loved me, for I well remember
> her suffering when she first could feel my faults . . .[16]

There are other hints about Fuller's own homoerotic inclinations. For a time
she served as a headmistress of a school in Providence, and though she parted
from the boys without emotion, she wept when she left her girl students. Not
until age 34 did she experience her first romantic love for a man, James
Nathan, and when he expressed passion for her, she was deeply disturbed, even

shocked, although he soon returned to Europe, supposedly to escape her "platonic" hold on him. She later lived with Marchese d'Ossoli, whom she married after discovering she was pregnant. Her heterosexual memories in general were permitted to survive, but her friends who edited her work, in regard for her memory, are said to have "inked out, scissored or pasted over a third of the never-to-be duplicated mass of material they had before them."[17] Jeanette Foster, in her study of sex-variant women, however, is careful to point out that, considering

> her emotional inhibitions as shown in her affair with Nathan, and, more particularly in view of the rigorous prudery of Boston at the time, it is unlikely that any of her numerous feminine attachments reached the point of overt expression. But the student of variance must forever regret the loss of those confessional passages obliterated by the three moral vigilantes (Ralph Waldo Emerson, William Ellery Channing, and James Freeman Clarke) who edited them.[18]

This investigation into sexual attitudes is not concerned with trying to pinpoint who was or was not homosexual, for this is almost impossible to document and of doubtful historical validity. Occasionally, however, the two subjects get mixed into one, and nowhere is this more true than in the case of Emily Dickinson. At about 30 she cloistered herself in the family house in Amherst, Massachusetts, and communicated, even with old friends, only through the open door of a room in which she remained invisible. Later, her surviving sister and sister-in-law successfully suppressed publication of much of her poetry. The result has been, of course, to excite scholarly curiosity, if not public interest, in the enigma of Emily's character, and both heterosexual and homosexual explanations have been advanced. She apparently had crushes on various male tutors, including Benjamin F. Newton, who died young, and the Reverend Charles Wadsworth, who moved to San Francisco in 1862, but she was also emotionally involved with women. One of her biographers, Rebecca Patterson, believes that the key to Emily's life was, not her disappointed idealistic love for her tutors, but a homoerotic attachment to Kate Scott Anthon, an attachment that marked Emily for the rest of her life. To authenticate her hypothesis, Patterson compared the available versions of Dickinson's poems and letters, demonstrating how various editors either deliberately falsified or wishfully confused sex and gender to support the version of a male lover. Though the association between the two women lasted for only 2 years and was confined to Kate's semiannual visits to Sue Gilbert Dickinson, who lived next door to Emily, Patterson believed the affair went deep. She feels, however, that it was marked by little more than some demonstrative caresses; when Kate wanted more intimacy, Emily reacted with shock and withdrawal. The two women corresponded briefly thereafter, but as Emily grew increasingly troubled about the relationship, Mrs. Anthon, a widow, broke off correspondence. Emily thereupon withdrew from social contacts and refused to see anyone who might mention Kate's name. Whether Patterson's reconstruction can be accepted or not is at least debatable;[19] it is of interest, however, in that it might indicate the great fear that proper young women had of forming attachments to members of their own sex. Platonic love was permissible, but anything beyond this was enough to cause severe censure, and fear of censure may have contributed to the aberrant behavior that today would have resulted in institutionalization.

The psychologically oriented writer of today could probably have a field day in examining the lives of many nineteenth-century feminists, particularly those who, in their resentment of what they regarded as male subjugation, had rather hostile attitudes to men. In their own times, however, they were free from public speculation about possible lesbianism, if only because it was considered much too vulgar to talk about. One exception was the outspoken Victoria C. Woodhull, who was once accused of lesbianism in conjuction with Isabella Beecher Hooker. The obvious heterosexuality of Mrs. Woodhull, who, as indicated earlier, was notorious for her attitudes on free love, made it little remarked upon at that time and more or less ignored today.[20] Others, whose sexual activity once went unnoticed, now seem to arouse questions about possible homoerotic activity. This is particularly true of Susan B. Anthony, longtime leader of the woman's rights movement. Miss Anthony seemed to have had some erotic interests in some of her young protégés, most notably Anna Dickinson, regarded in the Civil War period as America's Joan of Arc.

Miss Anthony's letters to Anna have such endearments as "Dicky darling Anna" and "Dear Chick-a-dee," and she is constantly wanting to give Anna "one awful long squeeze." She attempted to make Anna promise never to marry a man and encouraged her to visit her in New York, where, though the quarters were plain, there was a double bed, "big enough and good enough to take you in." She wrote that she could hardly wait for Anna, "for the scolding and pinched ears and everything I know awaits me. . . . What worlds of experience since I last snuggled the wee child in my long arms." Is this a homosexual attachment or is it simply a spinster expressing her need for affection? Andrew Sinclair held the latter view and stated that Miss Anthony

never asserted that her desperate love was more than a maternal feeling. She could not think in other terms, nor give her passion a modern name. "Anna," she wrote in a scrawled hand in 1869, with tears blotting the ink, "My soul goes out to you in real mother yearnings—I don't believe you have believed the depths thereof." When time abated her passion, and Anna Dickinson aged and grew a little mad, Anthony did not forget her. In 1895, she wrote a letter of fond reminiscence. "I have had several lovely Anna girls—'nieces'—they call themselves now-a-day—

since my first Anna—but none of them—ever has or ever can fill the niche in my heart that you did."[21]

Still, these affairs do have homoerotic overtones, even if there was never any overt sexual activity. Antoinette Brown, for example, fell in love with Lucy Stone, "with all the passion and sentimental licence possible between women of the time, before they learned to question their subconscious motives." Lucy Stone was older, more aggressive, unorthodox, and determined, but Antoinette Brown was a gushing, lonely, dependent personality. For the decade of her adoration of Lucy Stone she wrote endless letters to her friend.

I have never been happier in the world for the last few months but it is a new kind of happiness and I have kept it all buried up in my heart. If you had been here it would not have been so and it shall not be so now.

She later begged Lucy, her "dearest little cow boy" to come and visit her.

I love you Lucy any way, and if you would only come and take a nap with me here on my bed my head would get rested a great deal faster for it is aching now.[22]

Women obviously turned to each other for affection and support, but whether there was more involved is beyond our ability to determine.

Occasionally, particularly in the last part of the nineteenth century, some women were much more obvious in their homosexual behavior. Havelock Ellis recorded several such American women in his *Psychology of Sex,* revised and published at the turn of the century. Some of these women lived, dressed, and married as men. One of the most notorious was Murray Hall, neé Mary Anderson, who died in New York in 1901. Born in Scotland, Mary was left an orphan at an early age. Shortly after, following the death of her only brother, she put on his clothes and went to Edinburgh, where she gained employment as a man. When her true sex was revealed there as a result of an illness, she left for the United States, where she lived as a man for 30 years, made some money, was active in politics, and had a reputation as a man-about-town. She married twice, and though the first marriage ended in separation, the second lasted for 20 years, until the "wife" died. She liked to associate with pretty girls, being jealously protective of them. She seems to have been slight, not particularly masculine in build, and squeaky voiced, but her ways, attitudes, and habits were all masculine. She smoked, chewed tobacco, drank, and could sing a ribald song with the best of them. To disguise her figure, she wore clothes somewhat large for her, baggy trousers and an overcoat, even in summer. She is said to have died of cancer of the breast, and when her sex was finally disclosed, it was said to have been a revelation, particularly to her adopted daughter.[23]

Another American woman who lived as a man was a Carolina Hall of Boston, a watercolor painter who had resided for a long period in Milan, Italy. Some time prior to 1901 she had discarded female dress and lived as a husband to an Italian woman somewhat her junior. She called herself "Mr. Hall" and appeared to be a thoroughly normal young man, able to shoot with a rifle and fond of manly sports. As a man she traveled on a ship with her wife. The officers of the ship reported that she smoked and drank heartily, joked with the other male passengers, and was hail-fellow-well-met with everyone. Death was due to advanced tuberculosis of the lungs, hastened, according to the diagnosis of the time, by excessive drinking and smoking.[24]

Still another case was that of Ellen Glenn, alias Ellis Glenn, a Chicago swindler who preferred to dress as a man and had many love escapades with women.[25] Nicholai de Raylay, the confidential secretary to the Russian consul, was found, on "his" death in Chicago in 1906, to be a woman. The twice-married Nicholai had been divorced by "his" first wife after 10 years of marriage because of misconduct with chorus girls. His second wife, a chorus girl, who had a child from a previous marriage, was devoted to him. Both wives were firmly convinced that their husband had been a man and ridiculed the idea that "he" could have been a woman, although "he" was small and slight in build and not particularly masculine in appearance. Nicholai always wore a long-waisted coat to disguise the lines of "his" figure. Careful arrangement had been made in "his" will to avoid detection, but these plans were frustrated when "he" died in a hospital.[26] Cora Anderson of Milwaukee posed for 13 years as a man and during that time lived with two different women without her disguise's being penetrated.[27]

Lucy Ann Slater, alias the Reverend Joseph Lobdell, alias the "Female Hunter of Long Eddy," was eventually arrested when she was recognized by another person. On petition of her "wife" she was released. Some time later she was institutionalized and eventually died of "progressive dementia."[28] One observer of the American scene, impressed by the number of women who dressed and acted as men, was moved to comment that the practice was

a matter of very general observation, in large cities particularly; and I have little doubt that a fair proportion of cases reported by the newspapers, in which young girls suddenly disappear from their homes, for a longer or shorter period of time, may be thus accounted for. To show, however, that these manifestations of viraginity [sic] are in most cases purely psychical, though we frequently find associated with them a certain masculinity of physical texture, and coarseness of feature, there is seldom any trace of the more distinctive masculine appendages, such as hairy legs, beard, and mustache.[29]

That these women homosexuals were reported by Ellis and others is due in part to their being discovered as women during illness or at death. Their living as men was also due to the fact that economic conditions and sexual prejudices were such that a woman living as a man was better able to support herself and her partner than if she lived as a woman. Large numbers of women lived together in the last part of the nineteenth century, most probably without any overtones of lesbianism, but even if some were lesbian couples, questions were raised only rarely, and then usually by the family. One such case of family interference was reported at the end of the century by a lawyer consulted by the family of a rich young heiress. According to the story the family told, the young woman, while visiting New York City, had become an intimate friend with a woman doctor to whom she had gone for a uterine disorder. Allan M'Lane Hamilton, the forensic psychiatrist, reported:

> The doctor was a large-framed, masculine-looking woman of about forty, with short, black hair, a raucous, deep voice, and a manner of talking which was in marked contrast to her patient, who was gentle and refined. When it pleased her she did not hesitate to emphasize her conversation with oaths, and affected the carriage and manner of an energetic and coarse man. Her attire even was affected, and was in harmony with her other peculiarities.

The stay in New York was prolonged, and eventually she went to live with her medical adviser. The family, particularly after she had withdrawn large amounts of money, entered the case, and Hamilton interviewed her. The young woman remained loyal to her doctor friend, Hamilton remarking that he was "impressed with the peculiarity of manner and the intensity of feeling" exhibited by the woman who was defending her lover. A detective was hired, evidence was gathered, and it was revealed that the doctor "had debauched several young girls, one of whom eventually committed suicide." The two women continued to live together, however, since the family was unwilling to bring criminal action or to have their relative declared insane.[30] For more discreet women there was probably never any question raised.

In addition to the women living as men and marrying other women, a number of women, apparently without any homosexual motivation, spent at least part of their lives as men. Whether this phenomenon was what we would regard today as transvestism or whether women were forced to don such clothes to make their way in a man's world is not clear from the sources. There are a few incidents in which the transvestite made no attempt to deny her sex, the most interesting case being that of Dr. Mary Walker. The daughter of a teacher, she had studied medicine, and considering that bustles, pads, and heavy skirts were a menace to women's health, she early rebelled against female clothing. After receiving an M.D. degree from Syracuse Medical College in 1855, she married a classmate, Albert E. Miller. She insisted on being married in her reform dress of long trousers, over which she wore a short dress. When the couple separated on the grounds of incompatibility, Dr. Walker moved to Iowa, where her divorce was finalized in 1860. At the outbreak of the Civil War she joined with Elizabeth Blackwell in organizing and training nurses for the Northern Army, after which she applied for a commission as an assistant surgeon. She was not commissioned a First Lieutenant until October 1864, and in January 1865 she was assigned to the 52nd Ohio Volunteer Infantry Regiment then in Chattanooga, Tennessee. In this capacity she also traveled behind the lines to administer medical care, was arrested as a spy, and later exchanged for a Confederate officer. After resigning from the army in June 1865, she stayed briefly in New York City before moving to Washington, D.C., where she set up practice. According to her public statements, President Andrew Johnson, on November 11, 1865, awarded her a Congressional Medal of Honor. This later became a disputed point. On February 15, 1917, her name was stricken from the list of holders of the medal when the War Department archives failed to disclose any record of such an award.

Dr. Walker aroused considerable antagonism by her dress. Her medical expertise was also questioned by many of her contemporaries, her practice never being very large. Dr. Walker ignored such criticisms, preferring to spend her time and energy lecturing on women's rights and dress reform, supplementing her income with a wartime disability pension. During the 1870s she abandoned her so-called reform dress in favor of full masculine apparel consisting of striped trousers, a stiff-bosomed white shirt, frock coat, and a high silk hat. Her one concession to feminiinity was her long curls, which she claimed she wore so that everyone would know she was a woman. Her insistence on wearing male clothing made her the butt of many jokes, exposing her to considerable indignities, including arrests, and eventually overshadowing her championship of women's rights. She died at the age of 87 in an army hospital at Oswego, New York, on February 21, 1919, from injuries suffered in a fall from the Capital steps in 1917. Whether she should be classified as a transvestite, a mere crank, or perhaps as a transsexual is debatable. James A. Brussel felt she was a transsexual, his hostile study concluding that

> Mary Walker's history clearly indicates a well-established diagnosis of paranoia, representing a compromise with reality unwelcomingly thrust upon a militant and determined ego that revolted against its sex, rebelling—not in a mere turn to homosexuality—but in an open, and as complete as possible, switch to the opposite sex. At best, Mary Walker was a poorly adjusted and chronically unhappy wretch of a woman.

There is no doubt she was eccentric. For example, she battled the "nicotine evil" by stepping up to any smoking male she happened to see and knocking the cigar or pipe from his mouth with a tightly rolled umbrella. She also had touches of genius. She is regarded as the inventor of the return receipt for registered mail and of the removable collar.[31] Her diagnosis, if one is needed, must remain the subject of conjecture.

Mary Walker was not the only woman who served in the Civil War; following the example of Deborah Sampson in the Revolutionary War, several women impersonated men to go on active duty. Private Frank Fuller, alias Frances Hook, of the 90th Illinois, carried a rifle and served until wounded and captured at the Battle of Chattanooga. A private of the 25th Michigan Cavalry turned out to be Elizabeth Compton. Mathilda Joslyn Gage, a suffrage leader in the post–Civil War period, collected incidents of at least 10 other females with similar experience.[32]

One such woman, Loretta Janeta Velazquez, wrote a book about her adventures. According to her almost unbelievable story, she was born in Cuba of a Spanish father and a French–American mother. She was sent to the United States to be educated in a convent in the South, where she met and married a young army officer who resigned from the U.S. Army and joined the Confederate forces when the war broke out. Since her three children had all died shortly after birth, the childless Loretta determined to follow her husband. When he refused to allow her to do so, she set out alone for New Orleans. There she had a tailor make her a half-dozen wire net shields that she wore next to her skin to disguise her true form, since a

woman's waist, as a general thing, is tapering, and her hips are very large in comparison with those of a man, so that if I had undertaken to wear pantaloons without some such contrivance, they would have drawn in at the waist and revealed my true form. . . . So many men have weak and feminine voices that, provided the clothing is properly constructed and put on right, and the disguise in other respects is well arranged, a woman with even a very high-pitched voice need have very little to fear on that score.

Over her wire net shield she wore a tight-fitting undershirt of silk or lisle thread, held in place by straps across the chest and shoulders. Around her waist she had a band with eyelet holes arranged so that the pantaloons would stand out. She felt that her eventual detection was due to the fact that her "apparatus got out of order." After recruiting some troops in her new disguise, she presented herself and her troops to her husband. Seeing the futility of arguing with her, her amazed husband helped her train the men but was accidentally killed in the process. Then, according to her story, she took part in the Battle of Bull Run, after which she specialized in spying, passing sometimes as a woman and sometimes as a man. When her disguise was finally penetrated in New Orleans, she was sentenced to 10 days in jail and fined 10 dollars. No sooner was she released than she joined a different company, where upon being wounded, she was discharged. She then enlisted as a spy, this time in woman's garb.[33]

How much truth there is in the story told by Loretta Velazquez is difficult to verify, but there is little doubt about the case of Sarah Emma Edmonds, who served in the war as Franklin Thomson. As a girl in New Brunswick, Canada, Emma, the name by which she was known, read a novel by M. M. Ballou, *Fanny Campbell: or, the Female Pirate Captain,* published in 1844 and reprinted in 1852. The heroine of the novel, Fanny, set out to rescue her lover, who had been captured by pirates. To do so she cut her curls and stepped into "the freedom and glorious independence of masculinity." Starting as Seaman Channing, Fanny somehow ended up as Captain Channing and in the process rescued her lover. How much the story influenced her is debatable, but young Emma developed a strong dislike for marriage and objected violently when her father tried to marry her off at 15. To escape she went to live with a friend of her mother's. When her father traced her, she escaped by disguising herself as a man and soon went to work as a Bible salesman. For a time she dated a girl. By her own statement she came near "marrying a pretty little girl," but to avoid such a disaster she moved to Flint, Michigan, where she became a book agent. After the outbreak of the Civil War, she, still in men's guise, tried to enlist, but her first attempt was unsuccessful, because she failed to meet the minimum height requirement. Standards changed rapidly, however, and by May 1861, she was allowed to enlist in the Second Michigan Volunteer Infantry as a male nurse with the rank of private. "He" served as a nurse, spy, and general's aid for the next 2 years, but in 1863, sick from malaria and on the verge of being unmasked, she deserted and resumed female attire. She later published her memoirs under the title of *Nurse and Spy* (Hartford, Conn., 1864), a book republished in 1866 and also appearing under the title of *Unsexed or the Female Soldier.* In later years she became a housewife, a mother, and in 1897, she was mustered into the George B. McClellan Post, Grand Army of the Republic and thus became the only woman member of the GAR.[34]

The popularity of such stories in nineteenth-century America must be indicative of a strong feminine wish to escape the limitations imposed on females and of a general willingness of males to tolerate such escapades. Apparently, there were large numbers of women who had brief intervals of transvestism, most of whom were discovered only accidentally. A Mary Smith served for 5 years in the 24th Iowa Infantry, carefully saving her wages. When she was mustered out, she used part of her savings to buy land in northern Iowa and went to school on the rest. Her story became known only when she revealed her past to her would-be husband, who then authenticated it. Much more colorful was the story of Emma Barner of Maine, who served as an able-bodied seaman for 18 years before being discovered. She had signed on the whaling ship *James Rae* when she was 15. Her sex was discovered during a storm when she inadvertently answered a command in her natural voice instead of the gruff tone she usually used. After the discovery of her femininity the captain refused to pay her wages. Emma, undaunted, took her case to the alderman's office in Philadelphia, where news of it reached the public through a story in the *Philadelphia Ledger* in 1865. The newspaper reported that Emma was a tall, fine-looking woman who claimed to have served under the name of George Stewart. At that time, she was 5 feet 9¼ inches and weighed 180 pounds. Among the questions asked her was whether she was afraid to trust herself with sailors.

> God knows I was not. They are easily managed and generally speaking they are the warmest-hearted beings in the world. I drank and smoked with the men at all times. George Stewart hasn't any enemy among men.

She was awarded the pay due her, whereupon she disappeared, perhaps to go to sea again.[35]

One of the first women to vote in California was Charles Durkee Parkhurst, of Santa Cruz County, who cast her ballot in 1867 as a man. A stagecoach driver in various California mining towns, "Charley," on "his" death in 1879, was discovered to be a woman, although her true name and identity were unknown.[36] Several women seemed to have combined into the legendary figure of Mountain Charley, a woman who lived as a man in the western territories in the 1850s, since at least three women later claimed the title. One of them, Mrs. E. J. Guerin, published her autobiography in Dubuque, Iowa, under the title of *Mountain Charley: An Autobiography Comprising a Period of Thirteen Years in the States, California, and Pike's Peak*. Married at 12, widowed at 15, Mrs. Guerin said she donned male clothing both to make an honest living and to avenge her husband's murder. She made two trips to California, one in 1855 and one in 1857, the second as head of a wagon train that included 15 men and a herd of cattle as well as horses and mules. Her true sex was discovered twice, both times after gunfights. She also claimed to have served in the Civil War in the Iowa Cavalry under the name of Charles Hatfield. One of the other claimants to the title of Mountain Charley later married and had four children, but another remained a spinster–bachelor and became a real estate speculator in Cheyenne in the Wyoming Territory.[37] Occasionally, other cases come to light, such as Mary Hollingsworth, who can be classed as a transvestite or a homosexual or both. She was a southern women who, to recoup the family fortunes after the Civil War, set out for the West as a man. She was successful in both financial and social matters until she became engaged to a girl. Before the wedding was to take place, Mary, perhaps frightened at the implications, left town. She returned to her southern home, but the jilted bride and her mother followed right after her. A local lawyer, to whom they showed a picture of Mary as a young man, recognized Mary, filed a suit against her for jilting the girl, and won.[38]

As in Europe, women also took to playing men's parts on the stage, although often as juveniles. There are occasional hints about possible homosexuality, but the evidence should not be stretched too far. One possible case is the famous nineteenth-century actress Adah Isaacs Menken. The much-married Adah became famous as Mazeppa, the character of the same name in the poem by Lord Byron, first published in 1819. In the poem, Ivan Mazeppa, a page in the court of Casimir V, King of Poland, is detected in an intrigue with a lady of the court and bound naked on the back of a wild horse, which is then loosed and lashed into madness. The horse gallops until it drops dead in the Ukraine, where Mazeppa, near death, is not only rescued but also becomes a prince of the Ukraine. In the play, Adah was bound to the neck of a horse, her feet in his mane, her head hanging from the crupper, and in this fashion became famous throughout America and Europe. Her career aroused considerable literary curiosity, particularly since it was so fiery and short-lived. After she died in 1868 at the age of 33 there were references to her not only as Mazeppa but also as a modern Sappho who had a virile soul in a feminine body. Several of her poems were addressed to women, but what this means is known only to Adah herself.[39]

Obviously, there were many women in nineteenth-century America who were unhappy with their confined role, but only a few used impersonation to escape. In most areas of America women remained in short supply, and any woman, except one disguised as a man, was almost immediate marriage bait. In the more settled Eastern seaboard areas, however, and in parts of the South, women outnumbered men. This changing sexual rate, owing to the mortality of the Civil War and mass migration westward and to the cities, not only affected attitudes toward woman's place and toward sex but probably also gave impetus to the organization of women on a national scale. In the aftermath of the war there were rapid development of large industrial centers and major population shifts as rural and village youths went to the new commercial and industrial centers to find their fortunes, large numbers of immigrants from all parts of the world following their example. Women often predominated in certain older settled areas and small towns, men predominating in the large cities and on the frontier. The rise of industry also created a greater imbalance of wealth that further heightened the social class barriers. Increasing numbers of women were denied the security and satisfactions of marriage and family life. Undoubtedly, some women deliberately chose to remain unmarried, but society continued to regard the unmarried woman as a failure. In the process the word *spinster,* originally meaning a woman who spins, came to be synonymous with old maid, and the old maid increasingly became a character in American fiction.[40]

Though almost never mentioned in the literature of the nineteenth century, it would appear that many single women might turn to members of their own sex for the affection and comfort that others might have sought in their husbands. This might have been particularly true of those women who, to get ahead and develop their own intellectual abilities, deliberately refused marriage. Some twentieth-century studies tend to indicate that such was the case at least as early as the 1920s,[41] but the only open discussion we have about such matters is in the case notes kept by Robert Latou Dickinson.[42] Dickinson began his own practice in 1893, although he had assisted another physician in gynecology as early as 1884. His notes include data on only 46 patients for the period before 1900, some of whom reported having had a homoerotic experience. At that time Dickinson himself was more concerned with masturbation, and so other sexual information is incidental. He did note that the younger generation of women in the last part of the century were demanding somewhat more from sex than their husband's satisfaction, and the older women were so fearful of discussing or showing pelvic trouble to a male physician that they often delayed diagnosis until the sickness was acute, chronic, or serious. The fact that under such conditions a few women admitted lesbian experiences is significant, although whether the incidences increased or decreased is unclear. Obviously, there were more opportunities for women to come together in groups without male chaperons at the end of the century than before. Women congregated in the girls colleges and in the factory dormitories and even lived together, since, if a spinster did not live with her family, it was considered most proper for her to live with another woman. More notice was being taken of the possible existence of lesbianism at the end of the nineteenth century than at the beginning, but that is about all that can be said with scholarly certitude.

One other source of information about women's erotic attraction is found in fiction, where there are occasional references to female homosexuality. An early reference is in Charles Brockden Brown's *Ormond* (1799). The narrator, Sophia Westwyn, abandoned as a child by her profligate mother, had been brought up by the Dudley family, in whose home she learned to love their daughter Constantia. Later, as Sophia was about to marry an American in Italy, she heard that Constantia had been left destitute. After only a week of marriage she rushed back to the United States to seek out Constantia. The next 3 days were spent, Sophia writes,

> ... in a state of dizziness and intoxication. ... The appetite for sleep and food were ... lost within the impetuosities of a master passion. To look and to talk to each other afforded enchanting occupation for every moment. I would not part from her side, but ate and slept, walked and mused and read, with my arm locked in hers, and with her breath fanning my cheek.[43]

This in 1799. Brown was apparently hinting at a homoerotic affair, but there was no indication that the affair went beyond this stage.

No similar instance of homoerotic affection appears in American works until
the writings of Oliver Wendell Holmes, the physician and man of letters who
wrote three psychologically oriented novels. One modern psychiatrist, in commenting on them, wrote:

> The theory of bisexuality and the importance of bisexual components in influencing
> the character of individuals is more than implied in each one of his abnormal per-
> sonalities. The masculine traits in childhood of both Elsie Venner and Myrtle
> Hazard (in the *Guardian Angel,* 1867), something of a tomboy, are unmistakable.
> The bisexual theme becomes even clearer in *A Mortal Antipathy* (1885), where
> Holmes repeatedly contrasts the femininity of Euthemia Tower with the
> masculinity of Lurida Vincent, and it is apparent that he has but little sympathy
> with the latter.[44]

Elsie Venner is the most homoerotic. Shunned by other children, she tested
herself with various kinds of dangerous "masculine" activity. In adolescence
she developed a crush on a teacher in the female academy so intense that it
frightened the woman. Holmes, who ascribed hypnotic power to the girl, implied that the crush was more an attempt to test Elsie's power than love, but
hypnotic power is another euphemism for what Holmes regarded as "unnatural" desire. The teacher became half hysterical but eventually consented to
act as nurse and companion to Elsie, who was dying. Elsie also expressed love
for a young male instructor who also failed to respond; the implication is that
she died almost as a result of subduing the innate desire to overpower those
whom she loved.

Henry James also dealt with female homosexuality in *The Bostonians,*
published originally in 1885. The story first ran as a serial in *Century
Magazine,* whose editor wrote James that he had never published anything
quite "so unpopular." When the novel was published as a book in 1886, it still
proved unpopular—so unpopular that it was not reprinted until 1945. Philip
Rahv, in the preface to this later edition, set forth several reasons for its
unpopularity, but in his mind the "most disquieting" one was its keen analysis
of "the emotional economy of the Lesbian woman."[45] The story was basically a
triangle, as Olive Chancellor, Boston intellectual and feminist spinster, and
Basil Ransom, Olive's cousin, attempted to win over Verena Tarrant,
ultrafeminine, passive, and suggestible. Olive encouraged Verena to throw
herself into the feminist movement, where by degrees she separated her from
her family and previous suitors. The two women became wholly absorbed in
the feminine cause for several years, and Olive also became increasingly
obsessed by her love for Verena. As James stated, her "share in the union" was
not long passive, "purely appreciative; it was passionate too, and it put forth a
beautiful energy."[46] The story recounted in ambiguous terms the rivalry for

Verena. Eventually, Basil won out, and Verena settled down in marriage in preference to public triumph and a brilliant career. There were as many hints as possible at the time about the relationship. James stated it "was a very peculiar thing, their friendship; it had elements which made it probably as complete as any (between women) that had ever existed."[47] James also used the theme of lesbianism in *The Turn of the Screw* (1898), stating in one of his letters that his intention was to give the impression of "the most infernal imaginable evil and danger."[48] One investigator has said that the novel marks the "first literary appearance of lesbian corruption of a child by an adult," and added that this was probably attributable to the increasing publicity of clinical case studies.[49] If this statement is true, it nonetheless seems clear that James, as well as other turn-of-the-century writers, took care, in their portrayals of strong-willed women with lesbian tendencies, to make them responsible for murder, suicide, and ruin; in short, such women were pictured as a menace to society. Lesbianism might have been becoming more obvious at the end of the nineteenth century, but when it became obvious, it was regarded with great hostility.

What about homosexual activities between males? There is somewhat more literary material than for females but not much more actual documentation. Occasional references might be interpreted in homoerotic terms. James Thome, a young music student at Oberlin, became a passionate disciple of the abolitionist Theodore Weld. He wrote to his idol in 1838:

> Pardon my frankness when I say that I have never been able, hitherto, to satisfy myself that you reciprocated even a little of that affection which I . . . cherished for you, but which I have been restrained from expressing as it might appear to your masculine Roman nature girlish and sickly . . . and often when the gushings of my soul have prompted me to throw my arms around your neck and kiss you, I have violently quelled these impulses and affected a *manly* bearing . . ."[50]

Both Thome and Weld later married, but marriage in and of itself, of course, does not preclude the existence of homoerotic feelings.

Similar affections existed between Theodore Tilton and Henry Ward Beecher, who, in the post–Civil War period, were antagonists in a famous adultery case. At first, Tilton and Beecher were almost inseparable, and every Wednesday, after reading the first proofs of the *Independent,* which Tilton edited, the two men would walk together through Manhattan. Tilton later looked back on these evenings with gratitude, and when Beecher was on a brief visit to England, Tilton wrote to him:

> My friend, from my boyhood you have been to me what no other man has been, what no other man can be. . . . The intimacy with which you have honored me for

twelve years has been, next to my wife and family, the chief affection of my life. . . .
You are my minister, teacher, father, brother, friend, companion. The debt I owe
you I can never pay. . . . Whether you have been high or low, great or common, I
believe that my heart knowing its mate, would have loved you exactly the same. . . .
Our friendship is yet of this earth, earthy; but it shall one day stand uplifted
above mortality, safe, without scar or flaw, without a breath to blot or a suspicion
to endanger it.[51]

Though some might regard the letter as evidence of a homoerotic friendship, it
can also be regarded simply as an example of the breast-heaving literary style
of the day. When Beecher was accused of committing adultery with Tilton's
wife, the two temporarily patched up the scandal by kissing each other on the
mouth. How much can we read into this?

George Templeton Strong, who regarded himself as a pillar of respectability
and who kept a diary of his times, wrote:

Plymouth Church is a nest of 'psychological phenomena,' *vulgo vacato* lunatics,
and its chief Brahmin is as moonstruck as his devotees. Verily, they are a peculiar
people. They all call each other by their first names and perpetually kiss one
another. The Rev. Beecher seduced Mrs. Tilton and then kisses her husband, and
he seems to acquiesce in the osculation. . . . They all seem, on their showing, to
have been afflicted with moral and mental insanity.[52]

Obviously, not all contemporaries regarded such activities as harmless pastimes, but there is no evidence to go further.

Henry James, in his letters to Hendrik Andersen, used similar language, but
in his case we know he had strong homosexual tendencies that he struggled to
keep under control. James wrote to Andersen on the death of Andersen's
brother:

The sense that I can't help you, see you, talk to you, touch you, hold you close and
long, or do anything to make you rest on me and feel my participation—this tor-
ments me, dearest boy, makes me ache for you. . . . I wish I could go to Rome and
put my hands on you (oh, how lovingly I should lay them!), but that, alas, is
odiously impossible.[53]

If James was a homosexual, did all American homosexuals take such care to
disguise their true inclination? Most probably they did exercise great discretion. Did any American homosexuals come out into the open during this period? Probably not, since the penalties of social ostracism were so great.

The care they took to remain inconspicuous to the noninitiated is indicated
by Magnus Hirschfeld, an experienced investigator of homosexuality and a homosexual himself. As part of his studies, Hirschfeld visited Philadelphia and

Boston, reporting that he could scarcely detect any outward evidence of homosexuality; only much later did he become aware that both cities had homosexual communities of considerable size. In fact, his later informant said that homosexuality was "*kolossal viel los*," or extremely widespread.[54] In 1906, a New York neurologist, Edward Spitzka, reported to the editor of the *Archiv für kriminelle Anthropologie and Kriminalist* that, after a special yearlong search, he had been able to find only two "personal" advertisements that might refer to homosexuality. The two advertisements, in the *New York Herald*, were as follows:

SIR—Would you appreciate faithful, genteel companionship; refined, trustworthy gentleman. Address CONVERSATION, 270 Herald.

FRIENDSHIP CLUB CORRESPONDENCE EVERYWHERE: PARTICULARS FREE. BOX 24. CLEVELAND, OHIO.

The editor, P. Näcke, was incredulous, since such advertisements were a common occurrence in Europe. Since Americans were so open about advertising everything else, Näcke concluded that homosexuals found each other so easily that they did not have to advertise. He added that he knew there were homosexuals in the United States because the emigrant groups bound for the United States contained a high proportion of deviates, many well-known homosexuals having gone to America.[55] Without necessarily agreeing with Näcke, it would seem that homosexuals had indeed adopted methods of meeting each other different from those existing in Europe, and until one caught on to the methods, even an expert like Hirschfeld could be misled.

That this was the case is evident from an earlier correspondence of two German investigators, J. L. Casper and Carl Liman, who reported that a German who visited America in 1871–1872, wrote that

the unnatural vice in question is more ordinary that it is here; and I was able to indulge my passions with less fear of punishment or persecution. The American's tastes in this matter resemble my own: and I discovered in the United States, that I was always immediately recognized as a member of the confraternity.[56]

An American authority on hygiene who knew his way around the larger cities would have seconded the unknown German visitor. In 1870, George Napheys reported that every unnatural lust recorded in Juvenal, Martial, and Petronius was practiced in America, a roundabout way of referring to various "deviant" sexual practices without mentioning them. He added that such vices existed, not just rarely and accidentally, but deliberately and habitually and that there were even restaurants frequented by men in women's dress who indulged in indescribable lewdness.[57]

One of the more obvious meetingplaces for homosexuals was the male brothel. The existence of these is documented in various sources, although there are far fewer references to them than to regular houses of prostitution. In the 1879s, for example, a Saint Louis newspaper reported in the most casual manner that an obnoxious house of ill fame had been raided and eight prostitutes arrested, half of them men.[58] The crusading Reverend Charles Parkhurst, who led a campaign to clean up New York City's brothels in the 1890s, was shocked to find that homosexual prostitutes existed. His testimony is firsthand, coming about from thorough investigation. Parkhurst got into the subject because he had alleged in a sermon that brothels, gambling houses, and saloons were protected by police in return for carefully graded and regulated payments. City officials, antagonistic to his statements, summoned him before a grand jury to prove his charge, whereupon he was forced to admit that his allegations had been based on newspaper accounts that he believed to be true. The grand jury rebuked him for his intemperate outbursts based on sensational stories. Parkhurst, angered at what he felt was a deliberate attempt to discredit him and backed by a group of wealthy citizens, made a detailed investigation of vice in the city. He hired a detective to take him and an associate into the worst dens of the city. Disguised in shabby clothes, the trio spent 3 weeks visiting brothels, Chinese opium dens, saloons, and various assorted other places. As part of his tour he was taken to the Golden Rule Pleasure Club on West Third Street, which was divided into cubicles, in each of which sat a youth with his face painted who assumed the airs of a young girl, calling the other youths by girls' names and talking in a high falsetto voice. When the Reverend Parkhurst was told by the guide what the boys were there for, he fled in horror. The Golden Rule Pleasure Club was not the only such club in New York City. Others were the Manila Hall, The Black Rabbit, The Palm, and Paresis Hall. This last offered the services of "old Dr. Gray" and "old Dr. Grindle."[59]

Other cities had similar institutions. During a vice crusade in Philadelphia investigators reported a number of homosexual houses of prostitution. The males lived precisely as the female prostitutes did, being visited by their male patrons or lovers "and indulging their homosexual passions." The observer added, however, that these homosexual affairs were carried on in "a far more idealistic and less venal basis than that found in the average female brothel." The police are said to have reported that social disorders such as alcoholic intoxication, profanity, brawling, and nocturnal orgies were less matters of public complaint in these houses than in other types of bawdy houses. The observer also noted that the prostitutes were known to their patrons by their different abilities, with names such as "tasters," "fruit," and "lady men." "Dolly Vardens" were prostitutes who specialized in intercourse by "orastupration," and "brownies" preferred the "rectal method."[60] Other cities had similar institutions. Hirschfeld, for example, reported several such institutions, and they are known to have existed in San Francisco, New Orleans, Chicago, and other places.

Certain occupations, then as now, seem to have been more accepting of homosexuals, or at least of the more obvious homosexuals. Apparently, many found employment as "counter-jumpers," a slang word for those engaged in the dry goods trade, then thought to be an occupation particularly suitable for the most effete man. In 1860 *Vanity Fair* ran a parody of some of Walt Whitman's poetry under the title of "Counter-Jumps."

> *I am the counter-jumper, weak and effeminate.*
> *I love to loaf and lie about dry-goods.*
> *I loaf and invite the Buyer.*
> *I am the essence of retail. . . .*
> *I am the crate, and the hamper, and the yard-wand,*
> *And the box of silks fresh from France,*
> *And when I came into the world I paid duty,*
> *And I never did my duty,*
> *And never intend to do it,*
> *For I am the creature of weak depravities;*
> *I am the counter-jumper;*
> *I sound my feeble yelp over the woofs of the World.*[61]

The counter-jumpers were the subject of considerable investigation by the Chicago Vice Commission in 1909. The commission had originally been established to investigate prostitution, but during its inquiries, several members also became concerned over what they believed to be a striking increase in homosexuality. Since the members had always pictured Chicago as a virile western city, the idea that homosexuality might be prevalent came as a great shock. After investigation, the commission concluded that there were apparently 10,000 homosexuals living in Chicago, most of them employed as "counter-jumpers." Supposedly, homosexuals recognized each other by wearing a red necktie, and when one of the investigators put on a red tie and went into certain areas of the Loop, he was shocked at the number of approaches made to him.

The medical section of the report stated that the commission's investigator became acquainted

with whole groups and colonies of these men who are sex perverts, but who do not fall in the hands of the police on account of their practices, and who are not known in their true character to any extent by physicians because of the fact that their habits do not, as a rule, produce bodily disease . . .

It appears that in this community there is a large number of men who are thoroughly gregarious in habit; who mostly affect the carriage, mannerisms, and speech of women; who are fond of many articles ordinarily dear to the feminine heart; who are often people of a good deal of talent; who lean to the fantastic in dress and other modes of expression, and who have a definite cult with regard to sexual life. They preach the value of non-association with women from various standpoints and yet with one another have practices which are nauseous and repulsive. Many of them speak of themselves or each other with the adoption of feminine terms, and go by girl's names or fantastic application of women's titles. They have a vocabulary and signs of recognition of their own, which serve as an introduction into their own society. The cult has produced some literature, much of which is uncomprehensible to one who cannot read between the lines, and there is considerable distribution among them of pernicious photographs.

In one of the large music halls recently, a much applauded act was that of a man who by facial expression and bodily contortion represented sex perversion, a most disgusting performance. It was evidently not at all understood by many of the audience, but others widely applauded. Then, one of the songs recently ruled off the stage by the police department was inoffensive to innocent ears, but was really written by a member of the cult, and replete with suggestiveness to those who understood the language of this group.

Some of these men impersonate women on the cheap vaudeville stage, in connection with disorderly saloons. Their disguise is so perfect, they are enabled to sit at tables with men between the acts, and solicit for drinks the same as prostitutes.

Two of these 'female impersonators' were recently seen in one of the most notorious saloons on [code number] street. These 'supposed' women solicited for drinks, and afterward invited the men to rooms over the saloon for pervert practices.[62]

The claim of the Chicago Commission that homosexuals identified each other by wearing a red tie had been earlier commented upon by Havelock Ellis. He stated that

In recent years there has been a fashion for a red tie to be adopted by inverts as their badge. This is especially marked among the 'fairies' (as a *fellator* is there termed) in New York. "It is red," writes an American correspondent, himself inverted, "that has become almost a synonym for sexual inversion, not only in the minds of inverts themselves, but in the popular mind. To wear a red necktie on the street is to invite remarks from newsboys and others—remarks that have the practices of inverts for their theme. A friend told me once that when a group of streetboys caught sight of the red necktie he was wearing, they sucked their fingers in imitation of *fellatio*. Male prostitutes who walk the streets of Philadelphia and New York almost invariably wear red neckties. It is the badge of all their tribe. The rooms of many of my inverted friends have red as the prevailing color in decorations. Among my classmates, at the medical school, few ever had the courage to wear a red tie; those who did never repeated the experiment."[63]

This leads to the question of whether homosexuals had earlier adopted red as a color in Chicago or whether they wore red because Havelock Ellis told them it was the thing to do.

In addition to the homosexual houses of prostitution, homosexual bars, and saloons, there were also numerous streetwalkers, particularly among the swarms of adolescent boys who ran homelessly throughout the larger cities. James Huneker, who later served as a literary critic for the *New York Sun,* reported that he and Stephen Crane were propositioned by a boy with painted purple eyes in 1894 on the sidewalks of New York. Crane immediately took an interest in the boy, fed him, and when the lad said he needed treatment for a disease, Crane borrowed 50 dollars to give him. The experience led Crane to begin a novel tentatively entitled *Flowers of Asphalt* about an innocent country boy who came to the city and turned prostitute. When he read a part of it to Hamlin Garland, Garland was so horrified that Crane decided to abandon the work.[64] Interestingly, some observers, then and more recently, attributed the increase in homosexual streetwalkers to the influx of Italians into the United States, which demonstrates most effectively how Americans held stereotypes about immigrant groups whose customs differed from their own. As one twentieth-century commentator stated:

Some of the Italians took up the occupation of bringing boys and girls into the United States and receiving the pennies that were flung to them as they fiddled and begged on the streets. The *padroni* also set up brothels, in which 'fresh girls' aged ten or twelve were usually the principal attractions. Sometimes boys were substituted.

Apparently the immigration from Italy and the other countries of southern Europe increased pederasty in the United States. . . .[65]

The author of such statements obviously subscribed to Burton's view about a geographic concentration of sotadical practices a view that undoubtedly fitted his own prejudices about immigrants. His attitude also expresses a kind of class hostility about homosexuality that for a time marked much of the American writing on the subject.

Havelock Ellis indicated that there were numerous "criminal cases and scandals" in the United States in which homosexuality had come to the surface, and he also believed that in the United States, if not elsewhere, transvestism was closely related to homosexuality.[66] The difficulty lies, however, in documenting such a statement. There seems to have been a homosexual incident at West Point that aroused the authorities in the 1880s,[67] but generally the newspapers and the public media tried to avoid discussion of the subject. Ellis gave only one example to back up his statement, that of Guy T. Olmstead, a former mail carrier in Chicago who in 1894 fired a revolver at another letter carrier,

William Clifford, a former lover. At one time Clifford seemed to have been interested in Olmstead, but he ended the relationship and urged his friend to undergo medical treatment. Olmstead continued, however, to pester Clifford, who complained to the postmaster, an action resulting in the forced resignation of Olmstead from the postal service. Olmstead also entered a hospital for treatment, where, following the custom of the day in such cases, he had his testicles removed. Not so surprisingly, this treatment did not work, and he commented that, after emasculation, it was possible "to have erections, commit masturbation, and have the same passions as before." In fact, his passion for William Clifford became more intense. In desperation, after writing a letter "To Him Who Cares to Read," he tried to kill Clifford. Olmstead was tried and sentenced to the criminal insane asylum. On his discharge, he demanded his testicles from the city postmaster, whom he accused to being part of a plot against him. He was then committed to the Cook County Insane Hospital.[68]

Ellis recounted the cases of other homosexuals in the last part of the nineteenth century who were either Americans or spent some time in America, but none of them seemed to have achieved great notoriety.[69] A correspondent wrote:

> The great prevalence of sexual inversion in American cities is shown by the wide knowledge of its existence. Ninety nine normal men out of a hundred have been accosted on the streets by inverts, or have among their acquaintences men whom they know to be sexually inverted. Everyone has seen inverts and knows what they are. The public attitude toward them is generally a negative one—indifference, amusement and contempt.

> The world of sexual inverts is, indeed, a large one in any American city, and it is a community distinctly organized—words, customs traditions of its own; and every city has its numerous meeting places: certain churches where inverts congregate; certain cafes well known for the inverted character of their patrons; certain streets where, at night, every fifth man is an invert. The inverts have their own 'clubs,' with nightly meetings. These 'clubs' are, really, dance halls, attached to saloons, and presided over by the proprietor of the saloon, himself almost invariably an invert, as are all the waiters and musicians. The frequenters of these places are male sexual inverts (usually ranging from seventeen to thirty years of age); sightseers find no difficulty in gaining entrance; truly they are welcomed for the drinks they buy for the company—and other reasons. Singing and dancing turns by certain favorite performers are the features of these gatherings, with much gossip and drinking at the small tables ranged along the four walls of the room. The habitués of these places are, generally, inverts of the most pronounced types, i.e., the completely feminine in voice and manners, with the characteristic hip motion in their walk, though I have never seen any approach to feminine dress there, doubtless the desire for it is not wanting and only police regulations relegate it to other occasions and places. You will rightly infer that the police know of these places and endure

their existence for a consideration; it is not unusual for the inquiring stranger to be directed there by a policeman.[70]

Josiah Flynt, a hobo, indicated another face of homosexuality when he sketched its existence among the hoboes in the 1890s. He wrote that every

> hobo in the United States knows what 'unnatural intercourse' means, talking about it freely, and according to my finding, every tenth man practices it, and defends his conduct. Boys are the victims of this passion. . . . On the road the lad is called a 'prushun,' and his protector a 'jocker.' The majority of prushuns are between ten and fifteen years of age, but I have known some under ten and a few over fifteen. Each is compelled by hobo law to let his jocker to do with him as he will, and many, I fear, learn to enjoy his treatment of them. . . . How the act of unnatural intercourse takes place is not entirely clear; the hoboes are not agreed. From what I have personally observed I should say that it is usually what they called 'leg work' (intercrural), but sometimes *immissio penis in anum*, the boy, in either case, lying on his stomach. I have heard terrible stories of the physical results to the boy of anal intercourse. . . . Among the men the practice is decidedly one of passion. The majority of them prefer a prushun to a woman and nothing is more severely judged than rape. . . . I believe, however, that there are a few hoboes who have taken to boys because women are so scarce 'on the road.' For every woman in hoboland there are a hundred men.[71]

He estimated that there were 50,000 to 60,000 genuine hoboes in the United States, including boys, and that between 5000 and 6000 of them were sexually inverted. He also added that tramps are looked upon by other men, nontramps, as legitimate, complacent, and purchaseable objects of homosexual lust.

Then as now, ghetto areas were often more tolerant of homosexual activities than other sections of the cities. This tendency to live and let live led some late nineteenth-century observers to equate a tendency toward homosexuality with belonging to racial minorities and thus allowed them to emphasize further the biological degeneracy of Blacks. For example, in 1893, C. H. Hughes, a St. Louis nervous and mental disease specialist, published a brief description of "An Organization of Colored Erotopaths":

> I am credibly informed that there is, in the city of Washington, D.C., an annual convocation of negro men called the drag dance, which is an orgie of lascivious debauchery beyond pen power of description. I am likewise informed that a similar organization is lately suppressed by the policy of New York City.

> In this sable performance of sexual perversion, all of these men are lasciviously dressed in womanly attire, short sleeves, low-necked dresses and the usual ballroom decorations and ornaments of women, feathered and ribboned head-dresses, garters, frills, flowers, ruffles, etc., and deport themselves as women. Standing or seated on

a pedestal, but accessible to all the rest, is the naked queen (a male), whose phallic member, decorated with a ribbon, is subject to the gaze and osculations in turn, of all the members of this lecherous gang of sexual perverts and phallic fornicators.

Among those who annually assemble in this strange libidinous display are cooks, barbers, waiters, and other employees of Washington families, some even higher in the social scale—some being employed as subordinates in the Government departments.[72]

John Burnham, who originally noted this comment, held that what was most significant about it was the absence of any reference to a white community. He compared it to discussions of narcotic abuse in the middle twentieth century, which, for a long time, was primarily viewed as a ghetto problem. Only later did authorities realize that what was obvious in the black ghettoes also existed less obviously among white groups as well as various social classes. Hughes himself, some 14 years later, began to realize that "erotomania" was not confined to the Negro community.

Male negroes masquerading in woman's garb and carousing and dancing with white men is the latest St. Louis record of neurotic and psychopathic sexual perversion. Some of them drove to the levee dive and dance hall at which they were arrested in their master's cars. All were gowned as women at the miscegenation dance and the negroes called each other feminine names. They were all arrested . . . and freed on bonds put up by whites. The detectives say that the levee resort at which these black perverts were arrested is a rendezvous for scores of West End butlers, cooks, and chauffeurs. Apartments in the house are handsomely furnished and white men are met there. The names of these negro perverts, their feminine aliases and addresses appear in the press notices of their arrest, but the names of the white degenerates consorting with them are not given.

Social reverse complexion homosexual affinities are rarer than non-reverse color affinities, yet even white women sometimes prefer colored men to white men and *vice versa*. Homosexuality may be found among blacks, though this phase of sexual perversion is not so common or at least has not been so recorded, as between white males or white females. I have recorded but one male instance in my own personal observation, vis: that of gentleman George, for a time a valet and later a cook who loved to masquerade in woman's attire. . . . A Moll, Krafft-Ebing, Havelock Ellis or Kiernan might find material in St. Louis for further contributions to their studies of reverse sexual instinct. . . . These perverted creatures appear to be features of million peopled cities and they come into the light, if the people are vigilant . . .[73]

In a strong-minded but brilliant essay, Leslie Fiedler tied in the concept of the Negro and homosexuality in American literature. Fiedler held that mythic

America centered around boyhood and that, in many of the past classics associated with innocent boyhood, from *Moby Dick* to *Huckleberry Finn,* almost everything could be included except the frank description of adult heterosexual love. The authors of these classics preferred a chaste male love as the ultimate emotional experience, invariably between a white and a Negro or an Indian. In James Fenimore Cooper's *Leather-Stocking Tales* it is the lifelong affection of Natty Bumppo and Chingachgook; in Melville it is Ishmael's love for Queequeg; in Twain, Huck's feeling for Nigger Jim; and in Richard Henry Dana's *Two Years Before the Mast* it is the love of the narrator for the *kanaka,* Hope. Though the beloved in the books might be Polynesian or Indian, primarily he was a person of color, and for Americans the Negro or Black was most significant.

> Just as the pure love of man and man is in general set off against the ignoble passion of man for woman, so more specifically (and more vividly) the dark desire which leads to miscegenation is contrasted with the ennobling love of a white man for a colored one. . . . Nature undefiled—this is the inevitable setting of the Sacred Marriage of males. Ishmael and Queequeg, arm in arm, about to ship out, Huck and Jim swimming beside the raft in the peaceful flux of the Mississippi. . . . In the myth, one notes finally, it is typically in the role of outcast, ragged woodsman, or despised sailor . . . or unregenerate boy . . . that we turn to the love of a colored man. . . . The dread recedes; the immaculate passion and the astonishing reconciliation become a memory, and less, a regret, at last the unrecognized motifs of a child's book. "It's too good to be true, Honey," Jim says to Huck. "It's too good to be true."[74]

Fiedler wondered if Americans could ever really forget their guilt when their literary heritage kept dramatizing the colored man as the victim and emphasizing the love–hate relationship between the white and black. If his thesis has merit, it is possible that the love–hate relationship between American Blacks and whites is also tied in with our anxieties about sex.

Not all literary allusions to man–boy relationships, however, were between Negroes and whites; some were between whites themselves. Henry David Thoreau, for example, in his poem *Sympathy,* wrote:

> *Lately, alas. I knew a gentle boy,*
> *Whose features all were cast in Virtue's mould,*
> *As one she had designed for Beauty's boy,*
> *But after manned him for her own stronghold . . .*
>
> *. . .*
>
> *I quite forgot my homage to confess;*

Yet now am forced to know, though hard it is,
I might have loved him, and I loved him less.

Each moment as we dearer drew to each,
A stern respect withheld us farther yet,
So that we seemed beyond each other's reach,
And less acquainted than when first we met . . .[75]

In his *A Week on the Concord and Merrimac Rivers* Thoreau discussed friendship in what could be called homoerotic terms,[76] but it is difficult again to draw any implications from this.

Can we go so far as to claim that such references had any homosexual meaning to their authors? In some cases it seems obvious they did. This would seem particularly true of the stories of Herman Melville, who is his own experiences at sea, would have been aware of the attachments that might spring up in the womanless society of a ship long at sea. In *Moby Dick* Ishmael tells us:

> I found Queequeg's arm thrown over me in the most loving and affectionate manner. You had almost thought I had been his wife . . . he still hugged me tightly, as though naught but death should part us twain. . . . Thus, then in our heart's honeymoon, lay I and Queequeg—a cosy, loving pair . . . he pressed his forehead against mine, clasped me around the waist, and said that henceforth we were married.

The ambiguous relationship is almost explicitly rendered, in perhaps as frank a passage as the nineteenth-century publisher could tolerate. There are numerous other examples in Melville. In *Billy Budd,* which Melville wrote just before his death but which was not published until 1924, the fair-haired, trusting, virginal Billy fascinated both the satanic Master-at-Arms Claggart and the noble Captain Vere. Claggart gained a deep sadistic pleasure from hurting Billy, and eventually Vere had to see the young boy killed. In *Pierre* there is a love affair between Pierre and his cousin Glen that fell short only by "one degree, of the sweetest sentiments entertained between the sexes." Even if it had gone beyond this, or if Melville had visualized it as such, he probably would not have been able to go further in explaining the meaning to his readers. Jack Chase in *White Jacket* is the ideal man, sailor, and father image who won Melville's "best love." Other allusions to homosexuality occur in *Typee* and *Omoo*, but none are such that they could not pass the censors of the time.

Often the minor writers of a period serve as a better guide to what society actually feels than the major ones, since the ability of the major writers to universalize, to go beyond their time period, makes them great. Some of the most open expressions of homosexuality, for example, are found in the poems of Bayard Taylor (1825–1878), a roving journalist for Horace Greeley, the

Saturday Evening Post, and the *U.S. Gazette.* He is best remembered today for his popular essays, lectures, and travel accounts, but not for his sentimental poems. Taylor, as a result of travel throughout the Middle East, became interested in the different kinds of sexual behavior he observed. In his *The Poet's Journal* (1862) he speaks of loneliness of a king that could be relieved by "man, woman, young or old," "the fisherman's baby" or "the sunburnt sailor," whom he could take "like a brother, to my breast." His journal also included a poem called "Love Returned," which begins:

> *He was a boy when first we met;*
> *His eyes were mixed of dew and fire,*
> *And on his candid brow was set*
> *The sweetness of a chaste desire:*
> *But in his veins the pulses beat*
> *Of passion waiting for its wing,*
> *As ardent veins of summer heat,*
> *Throb through the innocence of spring.*

Often he left the gender of his beloved carefully ambiguous, but in "To a Persian Boy," this is not the case.

> *In the Bazaar at Smyrna*
> *The gorgeous of that magic tree*
> *Beneath whose shade I sat a thousand nights*
> *Breathed from their opening petals all delights*
> *Embalmed in spice of Orient poesy.*
> *When first, young Persian, I beheld thine eyes*
> *And felt the wonder of the beauty grow*
> *Within my brain, as some fair planet's glow*
> *Deepens, and fills the summer's evening skies:*
> *From under thy dark lashes shone on me*
> *The rich voluptuous soul of Eastern land,*
> *Impassioned, tender, calm, serenely sad—*
> *Such as immortal Hafiz felt when he*
> *Sang by the fountain stream of Rochabad*
> *Or in the bowers of blissful Samarcand!*

There are other poems that also seem to imply a love theme that could be homosexual.[77]

The most overt discussion of homosexuality appears in two minor American novels, Alfred J. Cohen's *A Marriage below Zero* (1889), and Robert Hichens' *The Green Carnation* (1895). Though both Cohen (who published under the pseudonym of Alan Dale) and Hichens were English, their novels were originally published in America, perhaps to avoid the problems of English censorship, which, were even more severe than in the United States. Cohen, moreover, also lived for a time in the United States. *A Marriage below Zero* recounts the growing homosexual involvement of Arthur Ravener, described as a delicate, good-looking young man, member of English ,high society, and Captain Jack Dillington, a "coarse and vulgar person." College classmates, their intimacy had continued to grow "since those days." In an effort to overcome his growing homosexuality, Revener married Elsie Bouverie. Elsie in turn had married him because of his lack of "demonstrative devotion," and when he tried to consummate the marriage, she ran from him. The author implied, however, that she was just being coquettish, since women were not supposed to be too forward. At any rate, Elsie soon began to worry about the lack of physical contact, and fearing another woman was involved, set out to investigate her husband. To her relief she found that his absences were spent, not with a woman, but with his old college chum Captain Jack Dillington. She was much too innocent to suspect anything.

Encouraged by a physician to travel together, Elsie and Arthur made a trip to America. Here they listened to a sermon by a sensational preacher on sodomy. Both were much shaken by this open and frank discussion, and Arthur seemed, on the road, to reform, when Dillington turned up and took him back to London with him. Elsie was still rather naive, but her concern was aroused when Dillington's name was mentioned in connection with a Parisian scandal in which a group of "men of high standing" were engaged in activities that were "the most disgraceful revelations that Paris had known in many years." She immediately set out to reclaim her husband from such a fate, but when she arrived at Dillington's, she found that Dillington had been arrested and her husband had committed suicide.[78] How much of the story reflected real life is uncertain. Cohen lived in New York when the novel was written and served for a time as a journalist. It was more or less standard practice to regard the English aristocracy as effeminate. The emphasis of the sermon on sodomy and Revener's growing awareness of his condition make it fairly obvious that the author is trying to highlight the homosexuality of his characters without coming out openly and saying what the trouble with Ravener might be.

Robert Hichens' *The Green Carnation* is usually regarded as an obvious satire on Oscar Wilde's *The Picture of Dorian Gray*. The chief character Esme Amarinth is portrayed as effeminate and affected, and though he briefly courted a widow, she rejected him as "unnatural" as the green carnation that he and his followers wore.[79] The term *unnatural* is obviously used to refer to his homosexuality, but the novel is nowhere near as clear on this as the work of Cohen is.

The works of Cohen and Hichens remained consigned to obscurity, but this is not true of Walt Whitman, whose case seems central to any discussion of homosexuality. Not only the writings of Whitman have been much analyzed but his sexuality as well. The key to the sexual controversy is the "Calamus" section of the *Leaves of Grass,* first issued in 1860. The theme of this group of 45

poems has usually been interpreted to focus on the spiritual love of man for
man. The calamus is a plant, sometimes known as the sweet flag, whose fasci-
cles, clinging together for support, supposedly represented the "adhesive love"
of friendship. Many readers of the poems have seen something more than
spiritual love, the question of what Whitman intended having been the subject
of considerable debate. John Addington Symonds, a homosexual himself, felt
that no modern man had expressed so strong a conviction of the "manly attachment," "athletic love," "the high towering love of comrades."

> The language of "Calamus" ... has a passionate glow, a warmth of emotional
> tone, beyond anything to which the modern world is used in the celebration of the
> love of friends. It recalls to our mind the early Greek enthusiasm—that fellowship
> in arms which flourished among Dorian tribes, and made a chivalry for prehistoric
> Hellas. Nor does the poet himself appear to be unconscious that there are dangers
> and difficulties involved in the highly-pitched emotions he is praising . . .[80]

To remove all doubts about Whitman's own intentions, Symonds, the author
of a biography of Whitman, wrote to him posing the "questions which per-
plexed my mind" about his homosexuality. Whitman delayed several years in
answering but finally replied:

> About the question on "Calamus," &, they quite daze me. "Leaves of Grass" is
> only to be rightly construed by and within its own atmosphere and essential
> character—all its pages and pieces so coming strictly under. That the Calamus part
> has ever allowed the possibility of such construction as mentioned is terrible. I am
> fain to hope the pages themselves are not to be even mentioned for such gratuitous
> and quite at the the time undreamed and unwished possibility of morbid in-
> ferences—which are disavowed by me and seem damnable.[81]

Symonds concluded that Whitman must have had feelings at least as hostile to
sexual inversions as any law-abiding humdrum Anglo–Saxon could desire. "It
is obvious that he has not even taken the phenomena of abnormal instinct into
account." Still, Symonds feeling there were strong points of contact between
sexual inversion and his doctrine of comradeship, concluded that Whitman had
founded comradeship, as he would call it, on a natural basis.

Whitman's answer should, of course, have ended the matter, but things are
not always so simple as they appear, and Whitman lived in the nineteenth
century, not in post–World War II America. Homosexuality was disapproved,
and he was nothing if not cautious. The nature of his reticence is obvious even
in his notebooks. In the summer of 1870, for example, certain mysterious
entries appear in them:

> It is IMPERATIVE that I obviate and remove myself (and my orbit) *at all
> hazards* from this incessant enormous and PERTURBATION . . . TO GIVE UP

ABSOLUTELY & *for good, from this present hour,* this Feverish, FLUCTUAT-
ING, useless undignified pursuit of 164—*too long, (much too long)* persevered in—
so humiliating—*It must come at last* & had better come now—*(It cannot possibly
be a success)* LET THERE FROM THIS HOUR BE NO FALTERING, NO
GETTING—all henceforth, (NOT ONCE, *under any circumstance—avoid seeing
her, or meeting her, or any talk or explanations—or* ANY MEETING
WHATEVER, FROM THIS HOUR FORTH, FOR LIFE.

Who is the mysterious woman? Or is it a woman? A long-time friend of the
poet declared many years later that he never "knew a case of Walt's being
bothered by a woman." Some have tried to decipher 164 by referring to a
phrenological chart, where it stood for Hope, personified by a woman. Others
have thought it was a simple code for letters of the alphabet with 16 standing
for P and 4 for D, the initials of a certain Peter Doyle. This seems to fit, since
Doyle was a young streetcar conductor from whom Whitman had become es-
tranged because he found that his own strong feelings were reciprocated.
Whitman wrote: "I never dreamed that you made so much of having me with
you, nor that you could feel so downcast at losing me. I foolishly thought it was
all on the other side."[82] Their correspondence was posthumously published
under the title of "Calamus," although Whitman had nothing to do with the
title. This was the work of his editor, Richard Maurice Bucke, M.D., a Ca-
nadian alienist and long-time admirer of Whitman, who had been one of his
literary executors. The "Calamus" title might have been psychologically correct, but it was not literarily correct, since Whitman had written all the "Calamus" poems before he met Peter Doyle. Nevertheless, as A. E. Smith had
pointed out, probably "no man in all history has had the question of his hetero-
or homosexuality so publicly, hotly, and continuously fought over as Whitman.
It is a unique distinction."[83]
    The scholarly world's division over the question of whether Whitman was an
overt homosexual or an unconscious one is in a sense, like arguing over how
many angels can stand on the head of a pin, but it also had important implications, even today. This was evident in the furor that arose over the Delaware
River Port Authority's decision in July 1955 to name the new bridge connecting South Philadelphia and Camden, New Jersey (where Whitman died), after
the poet. The Reverend Edward B. Lucitt of the Camden diocese sent a letter
on behalf of Roman Catholics in Camden and surrounding counties protesting
the name of Walt Whitman Bridge because Whitman's life and works were
"personally objectionable," as evidenced by the fact that G. W. Allen's
biography had called him "homoerotic." His letter was followed by a series of
letters from the 58 Catholic schools in the Camden diocese asking to find a less
objectionable man from New Jersey for whom the bridge could be named. The
chairman of the Delaware River Authority issued a bulletin stating that they
had asked three historical societies (never named), and they could find no evi-

dence that Whitman was homosexual. G. W. Allen himself, on December 16, 1955, issued a bulletin to the press:

> I used the term 'homoerotic' rather than 'homosexual' because the latter suggests sex perversion. There is absolutely no evidence that Whitman engaged in any perverted practice.

That apparently ended the matter, since later the officials confirmed the name of Walt Whitman Bridge,[84] even though *homoerotic* was defined in the second edition of *Webster's New International Dictionary* as homosexual. Whitman himself apparently consciously wanted to write homosexual poems; he indicated that his poems the "Children of Adam," dealing with heterosexual love, were conceived as a counterbalance to his "Calamus" poems. Malcolm Cowley, in two articles published in the *New Republic,* gave considerable evidence for Whitman's active homosexuality. Reproducing a page of a Whitman notebook showing Whitman's listing of the men whom he accosted in New York streets and beer cellars during 4 days of July 1862, he concluded that Whitman played the passive role in such relations and was a member of the homosexual group that met at Pfaff's and other beer cellars.[85]

Whitman himself stated his ideas:

> Intense and loving comradeship, the personal and passionate attachment of man to man—which hard to define, underlies the lessons and ideals of the profound saviors of every land and age, and which seems to promise, when thoroughly develop'd, cultivated and recognized in manners and literature, the most substantial hope and safety of the future of these States, will then be fully express'd.
>
> It is to the development, identification, and general prevalence of that fervid comradeship, (The adhesive love, at least rivaling the amative love hitherto possessing imaginative literature, if not going beyond it,) that I look for the counterbalance, and offset of our materialistic and vulgar American democracy, and for the spiritualization thereof. Many will say it is a dream, and will not follow my inferences: but I confidently expect a time when there will be seen, running like a half-hid warp through all the myriad audible and visible wordly interests of America, threads of manly friendship, fond and loving, pure and sweet, strong and life-long, carried to degrees hitherto unknown—not only giving tone to individual character, and making it unprecedentedly emotional, muscular, heroic, and refined, but having the deepest relations to general politics. I say democracy infers such loving comradeship, as its most inevitable twin or counterpart, without which it will be incomplete, in vain, and incapable of penetrating itself.[86]

The theme repeats itself in the *Calamus* section of his poems:

> *Come, I will make the continent indissoluble,*
> *I will make the most splendid race the sun ever shone upon,*

I will make divine magnetic lands,
With the love of comrades,
   With the life-long love of comrades.

We two boys together clinging,
On the other never leaving,
Up and down the roads going, North and South excursions
   making,
Power enjoying, elbows stretching, fingers clutching,
Arm'd and fearless, eating, drinking, sleeping, loving
No law less than ourselves owning, sailing, soldiering,
   thieving, threatening,
Misers, menials, priests alarming, air breathing, water
   drinking, on the turf or the sea-beach dancing,
Cities wrenching, ease scorning, statutes mocking,
   feebleness, chasing,
Fulfilling our foray.[87]

If Whitman was a homosexual, and it is possible he was, his life's activities give us some indication of what such a person might do in nineteenth-century America. Whitman went daily to a public bath in Brooklyn as a young man, which reinforces the ideas that such baths, then as now, were meetingplaces for homosexuals or, at least for homoerotic individuals; he served as a male nurse and had a coterie of uneducated workingmen around him. In fact, Whitman seemed to be attracted to people in the transportation industry. He even used some of the words now frequently used by homosexuals, such as "mild orgie" and "gay" in speaking of the "gayest Party" of young, handsome men and going to "the gay places." From Whitman's case, it seems obvious that, as early as the Civil War period, major cities such as New York had places where homosexually inclined individuals could congregate and that the law would interfere only rarely. After the war, Whitman was hired as a clerk in the Indian Bureau of the Department of the Interior but was later fired by his supervisor for pornographic writing, mainly on the basis of his poems "Children of Adam" in the *Leaves of Grass.*

Whitman himself said that he often kissed other men. In a letter he said "I put my arm around him and we gave each other a long kiss half a minute long. . . . I go around some . . . to the gay places." Probably Americans at that time would have been shocked if they had known the kind of activities that really went on in their rapidly growing cities, but Victorianism had either the defect or merit of closing its eyes to some of the disapproved activities. If certain practices were never spoken or written about, then they did not exist. Americans in the late nineteenth century became increasingly prudish, witness the indirection with which Herman Melville approaches the activity of men aboard ship. Taylor and Whitman were much more open in their expressiveness, but apparently their message reached only such people as Symonds or Edward Carpenter, admitted homosexuals, who immediately boosted Whitman's reputation overseas.

A number of individuals dressed in drag in the nineteenth century, as the references previously cited in the chapter indicated, but there were occasional instances of heterosexual transvestism. From the literature, it would seem female transvestism was more common than male, but this might be only because it was more tolerated and therefore more likely to be reported. Still, there were isolated cases. Havelock Ellis recorded the case of Commander James Robbins, of Cooper's Mills in Maine, who managed to gain notoriety through the newspapers. Robbins, a jeweler, was said to have a "startling picturesque" hobby, namely, the wearing of petticoats, although, when he went down to do his marketing, he slipped on "masculine pantaloons." He also wore women's shoes.

> Mr Robbins isn't squeamish about showing himself in petticoats. He enjoys wearing them; he has worn them when opportunity presented itself all his life long, and he wears them scientifically, too. In the first place, there's no halfway business about it. Every detail of feminine attire is there, and Mr. Robbins is rightly fussy about the details.

> There is no woman in Cooper's Mills who owns so many dresses of such excellent material as does the commander of the Cooper's Mills Post. He takes pride in having only the best. His lingerie is elaborately tucked and ruffled, edged with lace and fashioned according to the most approved models of any lady's wardrobe. The material is of the finest quality, and when Mr. Robbins lifts his skirts the eye gets a vision of ruffles, lace and 'all such like' of dazzling whiteness and immaculate smoothness."

Apparently, however, he left the washing and ironing for his wife to do, although he was very insistent things be correctly ironed. Robbins was also said to wear corsets continually and to change gowns several times during the day. In the morning he wore print gowns because he assisted with the housework. In the afternoon he wore somewhat more elaborate garb. He did his jewelry work at home, and his bench, lathe, and tools were in the front hallways of his house.[88]

The reportorial attitude here is surprisingly tolerant, although the "hobby" is regarded as highly unusual. Though impersonation of females does not appear as frequently in the nineteenth-century sources as impersonation of males, several incidents are recorded in Mark Twain's novels. Huck Finn, for example, dresses briefly as a girl but is recognized. Mrs. Loftus stated:

> You do a girl tolerable poor, but you might fool men maybe. Bless you child . . .

when you throw at a rat or anything, hitch yourself up on tiptoe and fetch your
hand up over your head as awkward as you can, and miss your rat by six or seven
feet. Throw stiff-armed from the shoulder, like there was a pivot there for it to turn
on, like a girl; not from the wrist and elbow with your arms out to one side, like a
boy. And, mind you, when a girl tries to catch anything in her lap she throws her
knees apart; she don't clap them together.

The most famous case in nineteenth-century American literature is, however,
that taking place in *Pudd'nhead Wilson*, which ties the stereotype of the Negro
and the sexual deviant together. Pudd'nhead ran onto a mystery when he was
up early one morning and happened to look out to the Driscoll house. He
found the room contained a young woman

where properly no young woman belonged; for she was in Judge Driscoll's house,
and in the bedroom over the Judge's private study or sitting-room. This was young
Tom Driscoll's bedroom. He and the Judge, the Judge's widowed sister, Mrs.
Pratt, and three Negro servants were the only people who belonged in the house.
Who, then, might this young lady be? . . . Wilson was able to see the girl very
well, the windowshades of the room she was in being up, and the widow also. The
girl had on a neat and trim summer dress, patterned in broad stripes of pink and
white, and her bonnet was equipped with a pink veil. She was practicing steps,
gaits, and attitudes, apparently; she was doing the thing gracefully, and very much
absorbed in her work. Who could she be, and how come she to be in young Tom
Driscoll's room?[89]

Young Driscoll was using his girl's outfit as a disguise to rob houses, but
Twain paints him with other characteristics to imply that a person who would
enjoy putting on woman's clothes was a dissolute character. He had Driscoll
actually born a slave whose mother (who was only one-sixteenth Negro)
switched babies with the master. He described the growing ex-slave as dissolute
and used several other hateful adjectives, to stress further the association of
Negroes with "deviancy." Driscoll eventually murdered his imagined uncle.
Quite clearly, transvestites were dissolute, immoral people, unless they indulged in the activity as a lark, as Huck Finn did.

Female impersonation began, however, to be popular on the American stage,
particularly in burlesque. George Holland, who played Ophelia in a travesty of
Hamlet in 1828, has been called the forerunner of what might be styled "legitimate burlesque" in the United States. Others soon followed his lead. In 1839
William Mitchell played a female part in a burlesque ballet:

First time in this or any other country, a new comic burlesque ballet, entitled "La
Mosquito," in which Monsieur Mitchell will make his first appearance as *une
premiere danseuse,* and show his ability in a variety of terpsichorean efforts of all

sorts in the genuine Blerocachucacacavonienne style. . . . The ballet is founded on the well-known properties of the mosquito, whose bites render the patient exceedingly impatient, and throw him into a fit of slapping and scratching and swearing delirium commonly called "Cacoethes Scratchende," causing the unfortunate being to cut capers enough for a considerable number of legs of mutton. The scene lies in Hoboken.

Mitchell performed his dance in an exaggerated makeup of Miss Fanny Elssler and burlesqued the graceful ballerina with comic humor, according to contemporary writers.

As Mitchell's popularity began to wane, he was replaced in public esteem by William E. Burton. Burton played several female leads, including Lady Macbeth and a gypsy woman in a piece entitled *St. Cupid.* Mark Smith, another actor, was well known for his part of Mrs. Normer in a play of the same name. Harry Beckett played the female lead in several plays by Lydia Thompson, including Minerva in her *Ixion,* Widow Twankey in her *Aladdin,* Maid Marian in *Robin Hood,* and Queen Elizabeth in her *Kenilworth.* Another female impersonator on the burlesque circuit was James Lewis, who played the part of Lucrezia Borgia, as well as that of Rebecca in *Ivanhoe.* Daniel Setchell was another, known for his portrayal of "Leah the Foresaken." The most popular duo in the last part of the nineteenth century, however, was Edward Harrigan and Tony Hart, who impersonated various types of characters on the American scene. In nationality skits, Harrigan depicted a typical stage Irishman and Hart a stage German, but they also played various kinds of married couples, Hart playing the female role. Clyde Fitch, a popular songwriter whose most popular farce, *Captain Jinks of the Horse Marines,* was later revised as a musical comedy, *The Girl with the Green Eyes,* also wrote several plays in which men played women's parts. He himself, at least in college, played the parts of several women. The Lambs Club, the private club founded in 1874 as a society for theater people in New York, periodically put on plays in which female impersonation, more or less serious, was an important part of the action.[90]

In effect, transvestism on stage and in real life was regarded as a lark, but anyone who would engage seriously in it was thought to be somewhat deficient, as in the case of Tom Driscoll, or just wonderfully eccentric, as with Robbins. There was as yet no real understanding of the sexual implications of impersonation of either men or women, although some scholars in the field might have begun to have some inkling of the psychological factors present.

Though in retrospect Americans seem to have been rather naive about sexuality, such naiveté was encouraged by official policy, and underneath the surface there was considerable ferment. It was not only dangerous to be unmasked as sexually "deviant" but also dangerous to write publicly or talk

about it, since any discussion might fall into the category of obscenity. The
height of the censorship movement came in the post–Civil War period and
coincided in the United States and in Great Britian with the movement we call
Victorianism. In the United States the person most identified with the new
prudery was Anthony Comstock, who, with his supporters in 1873, managed to
lobby through both houses of Congress a law governing the depositing of obscene materials in the mail. To make certain that the law was enforced
Comstock managed to get himself appointed a special agent of the post office.
Though "Comstockery" put serious difficulties in the path of any open discussion of sex, the United States remained more liberal in its publication
policies than England.

Comstockery is, however, more a symptom than a major causal factor in the
fears about the hidden dangers lurking beneath the surface of American life. In
fact, Comstock himself was probably unaware of many forms of this sexuality,
and his innocence in the matter probably allowed homosexual communities to
exist on the fringe of society, provided not too much was published about them.
Underlying Comstockery, both in America and in parts of Europe, were deep-
seated fears about the drift of urban life as society in much of the Western
world rapidly changed from rural to an urban one. The growing cities offered
considerable opportunities for economic advancement to ambitious and restless
young men, and many went to the cities to seek their fortunes or to find more
freedom to express themselves. As they arrived, they left behind them the traditional sources of guidance and support, the family, the church, and a close-knit
community that tended to watch their every move. The result was not only a
new freedom but also alienation and rootlessness, most noticeable among many
of the immigrants to the United States and elsewhere, who had to adjust to
radically changed living conditions and to different customs and even languages. The growing cities also offered the possibility of anonymity for individuals to engage in activities, including sexual activities, that would have been
severely reprimanded in their villages or rural communities. The cities also offered an opportunity for individuals of like mind to come together, and for homosexuals to belong to a "gay" community. Moral reformers of the time,
consious of changing attitudes, tried to preserve the "old values" by putting
restraints on what could be openly expressed. An 1866 YMCA survey of New
York's young workingmen described the rootless anonymity of those who once
would have lived "directly under the eye" of their employers but who now
resided in rented rooms and boardinghouses, devoid of restraint or guidance.
Since to change conditions would have required a massive reorganization of society, the establishment in New York City and other cities sought to combat
symptoms, in the process ignoring root causes. The YMCA, for example,
launched a campaign for stricter state obscenity laws and, in 1872, created a
committee for the suppression of vice, conceived as consisting of prostitution,

"dirty books, and various associated sexual evils." This committee became an independent organization in 1873 with a charter from the New York State legislature. Later that year a group of ministers organized the New England Society for the Suppression of Vice, centered in Boston, which achieved notoriety under the name of the New England Watch and Ward Society. Similar groups appeared in Chicago, Saint Louis, Louisville, Cincinnati, San Francisco, and other places not quite so large.[91]

These societies represented the establishment of the time, and to read their names today is like reading a *Who's Who* of the past. Most of the leaders had been bred in the pious atmosphere of a small town or farm, and when, after making their fortunes, they faced the apparent lack of cohesiveness in the rootless urban society, what today sociologists call alienation or anomie, they thought to control things by imposing the moral influence of their past on the growing urban areas. In their campaign they invariably had the support of newspapers and other official and semiofficial weapons of the establishment, since these reflected the same background as the crusaders against vice. Though the vice societies often became notorious for their lawsuits and actions, particularly those of Comstock, most of their influence was exercised informally. The vice societies became laughable, as they did in the twentieth century, only when they lost their influential supporters, and the ideas they were working to achieve no longer seemed so desirable to more sophisticated Americans, who had adjusted to urban life and whose ideas about sex were changing. Inevitably, for a time, sex went underground, and any kind of "deviant" sex behavior that came into the open was condemned. Though there was much concern with prostitution, homosexuality was something the average American was reticent to acknowledge openly, and homosexuals themselves were cautious. That homosexuality existed in America seems obvious, and discerning observers knew of such practices but were careful to keep their reader's susceptibilities in mind. If the observer was homosexual, as Walt Whitman probably was, or at least knew very many homosexuals, as Whitman clearly did, they were particularly discreet and, if questioned, even denied knowledge. The nineteenth-century American might well have been Victorian in his attitudes, but beneath the sea of respectability there was a wide range of human sexual conduct. Some of it, such as transvestism, could be made fun of, but mostly there was a tendency to deny that it existed.

NOTES

1. G. Alder Blumer, "A Case of Perverted Sexual Instinct," *American Journal of Insanity,* XXXIX (1882), pp. 22–35.

2. J. C. Shaw and G. N. Ferris, "Perverted Sexual Instinct," *Journal of Nervous and Mental Disease,* X (1883), pp. 185–204.

3.   A. B. Holder, "The Bote: Description of a Peculiar Sexual Perversion Found Among North American Indians," *New York Medical Journal,* I (1889), pp. 623–625.

4.   *Medical Record* (New York), 1884, ?.

5.   G. Frank Lydston, *Lecture on Sexual Perversion, Satyriasis and Nymphomania,* a 22-page reprint from the *Philadelphia Medical and Surgical Reporter* (Chicago, about 1889).

6.   Anonymous review of Havelock Ellis, *Sexual Inversion,* which appeared in the *American Journal of Insanity,* LIX (1902), p. 182.

7.   William Noyes' review of the German edition of the first volume of Havelock Ellis, which listed J. A. Symonds as coauthor. The review appeared in *Psychological Review,* IV (1897), p. 447.

8.   Randolph Winslow, "Report of an Epidemic of Gonorrhea Contracted from Rectal Coition," *Medical News,* XLIX (August 14, 1886), pp. 180–182.

9.   Blumer, *op. cit.,* pp. 22–35.

10.   Lydston, *op. cit.*

11.   Johann Ludwig Casper, *A Handbook of the Practice of Forensic Medicine,* translated from the 3rd ed. by George William Balfour (London: New Sydenham Society, 1864, 4 vols.,), Vol. 3, pp. 330–346.

12.   J. Richardson Parke, *Human Sexuality: Medico-Literary Treatise* (Philadelphia: Professional Publishing Company, 1906), p. 251.

13.   John Burnham, "The Physicians' Discovery of a Deviate Community in America," *Medical Aspects of Human Sexuality,* 1973.

14.   Allan M'Lane Hamilton, "The Civil Responsibility of Sexual Perverts," *American Journal of Insanity,* LII (1895–1896), pp. 503–511.

15.   *Moreau de St. Méry's American Journey,* 1793–1798, translated by Kenneth Roberts and Anna M. Roberts, eds. (Garden City, N.Y.: Doubleday, 1947), p. 286.

16.   Mason Wade, *Margaret Fuller: Whetstone of Genius* (New York: Viking Press, 1940), p. 90.

17.   *Ibid.,* p. xv.

18.   Jeanette Foster, *Sex Variant Women in Literature* (London: Frederick Muller, Ltd., 1958), p. 138. This book was in galley when the study of Carroll Smith-Rosenberg, "The Female World of Love and Ritual: Relations between Women in Nineteenth-Century America," *Signs,* I (1975), pp. 1–30, appeared.

19.   Rebecca Patterson, *The Riddle of Emily Dickinson* (Boston: Houghton Mifflin, 1951). See also John E. Walsh, *The Hidden Life of Emily Dickinson* (New York: Simon and Schuster, 1971); and John Cody, *After Great Pain, The Inner Life of Emily Dickinson* (Cambridge, Mass: Harvard University Press, 1971).

20.   M.M. Marberry, *Vicky* (New York: Funk and Wagnalls, 1967), p. 171.

21.   Andrew Sinclair, *The Better Half: The Emancipation of the American Women* (New York: Harper and Row, 1965), pp. 75–76.

22.   *Ibid.,* p. 156.

23.   Havelock Ellis, "Sexual Inversion in Women," in *Psychology of Sex,* Part 4, *Sexual Inversion* (reprinted, New York: Random House, 1936, 7 parts in 2 vols.), Vol. 1, iv, pp. 246–247.

24.   *Ibid.,* p. 247.

25.   *Ibid.*

26.   *Ibid.,* p. 248.

27. *Ibid.*, p. 249.

28. *Ibid.*, p. 246.

29. Parke, *op. cit.*, pp. 267–268.

30. Hamilton, *op. cit.*, pp. 505–507.

31. The only full-length biography of Mary Walker is by Charles McCool Snyder, *Dr. Mary Walker* (reprinted New York: Arno Press, 1974). She has also often been the subject of popular study. See Lidya Poynter, "Dr. Mary Walker—Pioneer Woman Physician," *Medical Woman's Journal,* LIII (October 1946), p. 10; James A. Brussel, "Pants, Postage, and Physic," *Psychiatric Quarterly Supplement,* XXXV (1961), pp. 332–345; Linden F. Edwards, "Dr. Mary Edwards Walker (1832–1919): Charlatan or Martyr," *The Ohio State Medical Journal,* LIV (1958), pp. 1296–1298. Descriptions of her activities can be found in the *New York Medical Journal,* IV (1867), pp. 314–316; and V (1867), pp. 167–170. See also "Dr. Mary Walker's Eccentric Dress Drew Attention from Her Real Achievements," *The Literary Digest* (March 15, 1919).

32. Cited in Stewart H. Holbook, *Dreamers of the American Dream* (Garden City, N.Y.: Doubleday, 1957), p. 187.

33. Loretta Janeta Valezquez, *The Woman in Battle,* C. J. Wothington, ed. (Hartford, Conn.: T. Belknap, 1876). See also C. J. S. Thompson, *Mysteries of Sex: Women Who Posed as Men and Men Who Impersonated Women* (London: Hutchinson and Company, n.d.), pp. 139–152.

34. The full story is recounted by Sylvia Dannett, *She Rode with the General: The True and Incredible Story of Sarah Emma Seelye, Alias Franklin Thompson* (New York: Thomas Nelson, 1960).

35. Rosanne Smith, "Women Who Wanted to be Men," *Coronet* (Sept. 1957), pp. 62–64.

36. Mary Chaney Hoffman, "Whips of the Old West," *American Mercury,* LXXXIV (April 1957), pp. 107–110.

37. For a discussion of the various Mountain Charlies and the biographical account of two of them, see Mrs. E. J. Guerin, *Mountain Charley or the Adventures of Mrs. E. J. Guerin, Who Was Thirteen Years in Male Attire,* introduction by Fred W. Marzulla and William Kostka (Norman, Okla: University of Oklahoma Press, 1968).

38. Dannett, *op. cit.*, p. 43.

39. Foster, *op. cit.*, pp. 138–141; and Clement Wood, *Poets of America* (New York: Dutton, 1925), Chap. 4; S. J. Kunitz and Howard Haycraft, eds., *American Authors 1600–1900* (New York: H. W. Wilson, 1938); and J. G. Huneker, *Steeplejack* (New York: Scribner's, 1928), v. pp. 1–278.

40. See Dorothy Yost Deegan, *The Stereotype of the Single Woman in American Novels* (New York: King's Crown Press, Columbia University, 1951).

41. Katherine Bement Davis, *Factors in the Sex Life of 2200 Women* (New York: Harper, 1929); and Frances M. Strakosch, *Factors in the Sex Life of 700 Psychopathic Women* (Utica, N.Y.: State Hospitals Press, 1934).

42. Robert Latou Dickinson and Lura Beam, *The Single Woman: A Medical Study of Sex Education* (Baltimore: Williams and Wilkins, 1934); and *A Thousand Marriages: A Medical Study of Sex Adjustments* (Baltimore: Williams and Wilkins, 1931). The latter was regarded as the first volume of a three-volume study on medical aspects of human fertility sponsored by the National Committee on Maternal Health. The study of the single woman was Vol. 2, and the third was to explore sex patterns fully. It was never published.

43. Charles Brockden Brown, *Ormond,* Ernest Marchant, ed. (New York: American Book Company, 1937), pp. 185 ff.

44.   Clarence P. Oberndorf, *The Psychiatric Novels of Oliver Wendell Holmes* (New York: Columbia University Press, 1943), pp. 221 ff.

45.   Henry James, *The Bostonians*, introduction by Philip Rahv (New York: Dial Press, 1945), pp. vi, ix.

46.   *Ibid.*, p. 144.

47.   *Ibid.*, p. 325.

48.   Van Wyck Brooks, *The Pilgrimage of Henry James* (New York: Dutton, 1925), p. 150; and Henry James, *The Letters of Henry James,* Percy Lubbock, ed. (New York: Scribner's, 1920, 2 vols.), Vol. 1, p. 301.

49.   Foster, *op. cit.,* pp. 111–112. For another novel with a possible lesbian theme, see Nathaniel Hawthorne, *The Birthedale Romance.*

50.   *Letters of Theodore Dwight Weld, Angelica Grimke Weld and Sarah Grimke, 1822–1844,* G. H. Barnes and D. L. Dumond, eds. (New York: Appleton Century, 1934), ii, p. 642.

51.   Robert Shaplen, *Free Love and Heavenly Sinners* (New York: Knopf, 1954), pp. 30–31.

52.   George Templeton Strong, *Diary of George Templeton Strong,* Allan Nevins and Milton Halsey Thomas, eds. (New York: Macmillan, 1952), Vol. 4, p. 552.

53.   Leon Edel, *Henry James,* Vol. 4, *The Treacherous Years: 1895–1901* (Philadelphia: Lippincott, 1969), pp. 306–316.

54.   Magnus Hirschfeld, *Die Homosexualität* (Berlin: Louis Marcus, 1920), p. 550.

55.   P. Näcke in *Archiv für kriminelle Anthropologie und Kriminalist,* XXII (1906), p. 277. It is possible that the high incidence of mental illness among immigrants might have been partly due to the classifying of different sex standards as mental illness.

56.   J. L. Casper and Carl Liman, *Handbuch der gerichtlichen Medicin* (Berlin: Hirschwald, 1889), Vol. 1, p. 173, and translated and quoted in John Addington Symonds, *A Problem in Modern Ethics* (London, 1896), privately printed, p. 116, note.

57.   George H. Napheys, *The Transmission of Life,* 2nd ed. (Philadelphia: J. G. Fergus, 1897), passim.

58.   Burnham, *op. cit.*

59.   See Charles W. Gardner, *The Doctor and the Devil or the Midnight Adventures of Dr. Parkhurst* (reprinted, New York: Vanguard Press, 1931). Gardner was the guide for Dr. Parkhurst.

60.   Parke, *op. cit.,* p. 310.

61.   Quoted in Mary Cable, et al., *American Manners and Morals* (New York: American Heritage Press, 1969), p. 236.

62.   Chicago Vice Commission, *The Social Evil in Chicago* (Chicago: Gunthorp-Warren Printing Company, 1911).

63.   Ellis, *op. cit.,* Vol. 1, pp. 299–300.

64.   John Berryman, *Stephen Crane* (New York: William Sloane Associates, 1950), p. 86.

65.   Leo Markun, *Mrs. Grundy* (New York: Appleton, 1930), p. 547.

66.   Ellis, *op. cit.,* Vol. 1, iv, p. 63.

67.   Holder, *op. cit.,* Vol. 1, p. 625.

68.   Ellis, *op. cit.,* Vol. 1, iv, pp. 169–173, case 26.

69.   *Ibid.,* case 5, p. 98; case 9, pp. 111–115; case 14, p. 133 had a lover who was an American; case 27, pp. 173–179.

70.   *Ibid.,* pp. 351–353.

71. Josiah Flynt, "Homosexuality among Tramps," in Ellis, *op. cit.,* Vol. 1, iv, appendix A, pp. 359–367.

72. C. H. Hughes, "Postscript to Paper on 'Erotopathia,'" in *The Alienist and Neurologist,* XIV (October 1893), pp. 731–732.

73. C. H. Hughes, "Homo Sexual Complexion Perverts in St. Louis," *The Alienist and Neurologist,* XXVIII (1907), pp. 487–488.

74. Leslie A. Fiedler, "Come Back to the Raft Ag'in, Huck Honey!", reprinted in *An End to Innocence* (Boston: Beacon Press, 1952), pp. 142–151. The essay originally appeared in the *Partisan Review* (June 1948).

75. Henry David Thoreau, *Letters to Various Persons* (Boston: Ticknor and Fields, 1865).

76. At least this is the claim of Alistair Sutherland and Patrick Anderson, *Eros: An Anthology of Friendship* (London: Anthony Blond, 1961), p. 308.

77. Bayard Taylor, *Collected Poems* (Boston: Household Edition, 1880). The first poem is from his *Poet's Journal,* the second from *Poems of the Orient.* In the same cycle there is the "Nilotic Drinking Song" and one called "The Bath," which is a plea to walk naked and unashamed. See also J. Z. Eglinton, *Greek Love* (New York: Oliver Layton Press, 1964), pp. 364–366.

78. Alfred J. Cohen (pseud. Alan Dale), *A Marriage below Zero* (New York: G. W. Dillingham, 1889).

79. Robert Hichens, *The Green Carnation* (New York: Appleton, 1895). This novel was reprinted in 1929 by Argus Books, Chicago, and in 1949 in London. Dover Books has also published it.

80. Symonds, *op. cit.,* pp. 116–117.

81. *Ibid.,* pp. 118–119.

82. See G. W. Allen, *The Solitary Singer* (New York: Macmillan, 1955), pp. 421–424; and Sutherland and Anderson, *op. cit.,* p. 290.

83. A. E. Smith, "The Curious Controversy Over Whitman's Sexuality," *One Institute Quarterly,* IV (Winter 1959), p. 6.

84. *Ibid.,* p. 21.

85. Malcolm Cowley, "Walt Whitman: The Miracle," and "Walt Whitman: The Secret" in *New Republic* (March 18 and April 8, 1946).

86. Walt Whitman, *Democratic Vistas* in *Leaves of Grass and Selected Prose,* John A. Kouwenhoven, ed. (New York: Modern Library, 1950), p. 505, and fn.

87. *Ibid.,* "Calamus" section. The poems are "For You O Democracy," and "We Two Boys Together Clinging."

88. Ellis, *Eonism and Other Supplementary Studies,* in *op. cit.,* Vol. 2, ii, pp. 30–32.

89. Mark Twain, *Pudd'nHead Wilson* (New York: Mark Twain, 1899), pp. 53–54. See also his *Huckleberry Finn* for the other incident of transvestism.

90. C. J. Bulliet, *Venus Castina* (reprinted, New York: Bonanza Books, 1956), pp. 274–278.

91. Paul S. Boyer, *Purity in Print* (New York: Scribner's, 1968), pp. 3–7.

PART SIX

THE TWENTIETH CENTURY:
TRENDS AND ASSUMPTIONS

21

PROBLEMS AND PROSPECTS

At the beginning of the twentieth century, Western sexual attitudes remained essentially as they had been for the past 2000 years. Although the influence of religion in enforcing traditional sex-negative attitudes had been somewhat undermined, reinforcement had come through medical and scientific assumptions, and in the English-speaking world sex hostility remained a part of the law. Though several continental and Latin American countries had followed the French example in removing legal penalties for sexual activity between consenting adults, public opinion still ostracized those it stigmatized as deviant, and this left such individuals open to blackmail. In the first decades of the twentieth century, some changes in attitude began to come about, gradually increasing in momentum until they reached almost flood tide in the decades of the fifties, sixties, and seventies. Such changes were more than a reaction to past beliefs; rather, they were due to basic breakthroughs in understanding sexuality, to the discovery of cures for venereal diseases, to the development of effective contraceptives, to the growing emancipation of women, and ultimately also to more effective organization and lobbying on behalf of those whose sexual behavior had previously been stigmatized.

Some of these changes, derived from a better understanding of reproduction, were detailed at the beginning of this book, but many were also due to a realization of the basic sexual nature of man. Researchers into this aspect of human behavior were, however, generally cautious in drawing sweeping conclusions about sexual mores, since they faced, or believed they faced, considerable public hostility. Many researchers continued, of course, to condemn certain forms of sexual behavior at the same time they offered new insights into them, and almost all researchers until well past the midcentury continued to stress the dangers of premarital, extramarital, or unusual sexual activity. Nevertheless, research progressed, particularly into some of the varieties of human sexual behavior, for many researchers believed that, before men and women could come to grips with their own sexuality, the full spectrum of sexual behavior had to be understood. Adding to this "scientific" reason for interest in stigmatized sexual behavior were a number of individuals labeled as sexual deviates by society who tried to come to a better understanding of themselves, to find a rationalization for their behavior that would enable society to accept them as they were. Equally important was the scientific community's desire to define terms and behavior, to engage in better diagnosis and cure. Because much of sexual behavior had come to be classified as pathological, there was an attempt, in studying sexual behavior, as there was in studying other diseases, to isolate symptoms, to break down the generalized concept of sexual "perversion" into smaller and smaller areas. There were also some researchers, initially few but growing more plentiful by the midcentury, who were concerned with showing that sex was good and that the attitudes adopted by Western society toward sex were only choices among many possible alternatives.

Sex researchers, like other researchers, also reflected the generalized outlooks of their time; thus a researcher in the late nineteenth century looked at sex differently than one did who wrote in the early years of the twentieth century, and those who did their investigations in the 1920s had different assumptions than those who did their research in the 1970s. A good example of this difference is the English physician George Drysdale (1825–1904), who in many ways had ideas reminiscent of the middle half of the twentieth century and yet in others remained very much part of the nineteenth. In his *The Elements of Social Science: or Physical, Sexual and Natural Religion* (1854), Drysdale took as his mission the importance of pointing out that sexual intercourse could and should be a delightful thing. Preventing it from being delightful was the ever-present possibility of children, and since he believed that overpopulation was a major cause of poverty and that fear of having more children encouraged men to turn to prostitutes and to inhibit female sexuality, Drysdale urged the use of contraceptives. On the other hand Drysdale also believed that immoderate amounts of sexual activity were dangerous, and he had a horror of variant forms of sexuality.[1]

One of the earliest investigators into nonprocreative sex was Karl Heinrichs Ulrichs (1825–1895). Both under his own name and under the pseudonym of Numa Numantius, Ulrichs poured out a series of polemical, analytical, and theoretical pamphlets about homosexuality in the years between 1865 and

1875. A homosexual himself, Ulrichs tried to demonstrate that the "abnormal" instincts were inborn and therefore natural, and he was also concerned with finding nonderogatory terms to describe individuals born with certain kinds of sexual inclinations. Ulrichs coined the term *urning* to describe homosexual individuals, a term he derived from an allusion to Uranus in Plato's *Symposium.* Ulrichs also invented a number of other words to describe different kinds of individuals with possible homosexual inclinations, but most were not adopted by others.[2] Ulrichs argued that, up to a certain stage of development, the sexes were the same, after which a threefold division took place: male, female, and urning (or uringin), this last group being made up of individuals who had the physical features of one sex but whose sexual instinct failed to correspond to their sexual organs. The result was an inversion of sexual desires. Ulrichs also believed that the line of differentiation between males and females had been overemphasized; as proof he pointed out that normal males had rudimentary breasts and normal females a rudimentary penis. Many people failed to develop along expected lines, and it was easily understandable why a body might have one sex and the soul another.[3]

Havelock Ellis (1859–1939), the great English sexologist, held that, because of the special pleading inherent in Ulrichs' writing, he held no marked influence on scientific thought. In a sense this is true, but such a statement ignores the fact that Ulrichs' belief that "urnings" were born that way was an influential factor in medical and scientific thinking on "deviant" sexuality until well into the twentieth century. His nomenclature of a third sex was also picked up by many of the apologetic writers for homosexuality,[4] though his term *urning* was eventually disregarded by the scientific community and replaced by the word *homosexual,* a philologically awkward hybrid combining both Greek and Latin elements. Coiner of the word was a Hungarian physician, Karoly Maria Benkert, who, under the pseudonym of Kertbeny in 1869, published a pamphlet on the subject.[5] He wrote:

> In addition to the normal sexual urge in men and women, Nature in her sovereign mood had endowed at birth certain male and female individuals with the homosexual urge, thus placing them in a sexual bondage which renders them physically and psychically incapable—even with the best intention—of normal erection. This urge creates in advance a direct horror of the opposite sex, and the victim of this passion finds it impossible to suppress the feeling which individuals of his own sex exercise upon him.[6]

Gradually, but not without opposition, the term *homosexual* came to be used by scholars in the field, in spite of attempts to make it more philologically pure by using terms such as *homogenic* or *homophile.*[7]

The necessity for defining and narrowing terms is evident from the hostility greeting any form of sexual deviation in the various medical forensic books. One standard French work, that by A. Tardieu, devoted a large section to describing the active and passive signs of immorality in individuals addicted to engaging in sins against nature. All kinds of misinformation were perpetuated, such as Tardieu's belief that the active pederast had a slender, underdeveloped penis tapered like a dog's and that those assuming the passive position in anal intercourse had smooth rectums.[8] Somewhat less judgmental was the work by the German J. L. Casper as edited by Carl Liman. The later editions of Casper's work recognized that greater precision in terminology was needed, the authors attempting to distinguished between congenital or innate deviants and those who acquired their deviance later in life because of a satiety with other, more normal pleasures.[9]

Before any generalizations could be made on such a subject as homosexuality, it was necessary to gather quantities of data, and few medical practitioners, even those writing about the subject, had contact with any large numbers of individuals. The first quantitative study of homosexuality was made by F. Carlier, a police official in Paris, who concentrated on male prostitutes. Carlier complained that, previous to his own writing, the whole subject of male prostitution had been ignored or omitted, and this had forced the police to develop their own methods of combating homosexuality. French police, he felt, were further handicapped because prostitution was legal in France, homosexual activity between consenting adults was not punishable, and male prostitution could become a matter of police concern only when it was an affront to public decency or when minors were seduced. In spite of these difficulties Carlier reported that there were 6242 homosexuals (he called them pederasts) in Paris who had come to the attention of the police: 2049 native-born Parisians, 3709 provincials, and 484 foreigners, of whom less than half, in his opinion, could be convicted of illegal acts. He devoted most of his attention to the "professionals," who dressed and acted like women, perhaps because they were the most noticeable and most likely to be a cause of complaint to the police.[10]

Gradually, and with some reluctance, the medical and scientific community came to be involved in specialized studies of sexual deviation, although their reluctance to do so on any scale is understandable. Earlier, for example, Franz Anton Mesmer (1734–1815), the discoverer of a treatment called mesmerism, the forerunner of modern hypnotism, had come in for considerable criticism for dealing with hysteria, a subject often associated with female sexuality. The Lancet, a British medical journal, in 1864 had felt it necessary to caution its readers about the evils and dangers of mesmerism (also sometimes called animal magnetism), particularly when women were patients:

Can we wonder at all this, when we know that the magnetiser—independently of making the *passes,* and of fixing his eye upon her—often takes her hands between his and then draws his fingers over various parts of her body, now over her face, and then over her body and legs, pressing, perhaps, his knees against hers, and sometimes applying (we have seen this done) his lips to her stomach, and making insufflations upon it. Have we said enough to show that—in some cases at least— the use of animal magnetism is morally dangerous? We have heard it acknowledged by a most zealous practitioner of the art, that he has, more than once, witnessed all the excitement of actual coition thus produced in a woman.[11]

Understandably then, when the medical community began to investigate sexuality, they entered with caution and in general were even more reluctant to deal openly with sexuality in the female than in the male. The first physician to put the study of stigmatized sexual expression on a scientific basis was Carl Westphal (1833-1890), professor of psychiatry at Berlin. In 1869 he published the case history of a young woman who, from her earliest years, liked to dress as a boy, cared for boys' games, and found herself attracted only to women. Sympathetic to his patient and interested in the phenomenon, Westphal came to the conclusion, similar to Ulrichs', that the abnormality was congenital, not acquired, and that it could not be termed a vice. Whereas he insisted on the presence of neurotic elements, he felt there was nothing present that could be called insanity. He called the phenomenon "contrary sexual feeling," (konträre Sexualempfindung) and in the process opened the discussion of such phenomena to the medical community.[12] Westphal went on to study more than 200 cases of homosexuality as well as related behavior; within a few years there was a flood of literature. Some indication of this is that, between 1898 and 1908, there were more than 1000 published titles devoted to homosexuality in German alone.[13] For a time the term konträre or "inverted sexual instinct," as it was translated into English, was widely used. Not until well into the twentieth century did the term homosexuality win out, mainly because "inverted sex instinct" turned out to be not precise enough.[14]

If inversion was inborn, could it be cured? The famous French neurologist Jean Martin Charcot (1825-1893), the director of the Saltpetrière asylum, and his colleague Valentin Magnan (1835-1916) tried to cure several cases of "sexual inversion" with hypnosis. Since they had only modest success, they came to believe that "inversion" was a constitutional nervous weakness due to hereditary degeneration.[15] In trying to explain the causes of this constitutional weakness, the French physician Paul Moreau argued that, in addition to the usual senses of sight, hearing, touch, taste, and feeling, man had a sixth sense, a genital sense that, like the others, could also suffer physical or psychical injury without damaging the other mental functions. Such propensity to injury was due to hereditary taint, a sort of predisposition to perversion that certain environmental factors provoked. These factors included age, poverty, constitution, temperament, seasons of the year, climate, and food, and the result could be sexual inversion, nymphomania, satyriasis, bestiality, rape, or profanation of corpses. The only real solution other than imprisonment, which he opposed, was to turn the individuals, the victims of the bad heredity, over to asylums, where they could be cared for. There was little hope they could be cured, since this intermediate class lacked the real genital sense but constituted a mixed class midway between reason and madness, forever being pulled close to madness. One factor most likely to set them off was masturbation,[16] an explanation that did nothing to lessen fears about masturbatory insanity.

In effect, what had started as a defense of homosexuality by individuals such as Ulrichs had now become a reason for institutionalizing people departing from the sexual norms, since they were born with congenitally inadequate sixth senses. Ultimately, this led to the concept of degeneracy, a concept affecting thinking about sexual matters for generations. Degeneracy was held to be a defect in an individual's heredity, often equated with atavism, that is, the sudden reappearance of primitive tendencies in civilized human beings. Each new scientific theory was, however, seized upon to bolster further the evidence for psychic or physical degeneration. The theories of Charles Darwin, for example, were brought forth to explain degeneracy as a variant reversal of progressive evolution. The degenerate strains—for the defect was believed to be both progressive and inherent—involved nervous illness, physical weakness, and deviant behavior. Ineluctably, any departure from conventional behavior, whether sexual or social, was regarded as a sign of degeneracy. The popular fear of a "sexual degenerate" was thus based on the idea of an uncontrolled, primitive, animal-like person who might do anything. In no way could such a person be regarded as a solid member of the community who happened to be deviant only in some of his sexual inclinations.

Even "authorities" sympathetic to some forms of sexual inversion saw no alternative to institutionalization. Benjamin Tarnowski, a Saint Petersburg physician sympathetic to his homosexual patients, tried to distinguish between those who had been born "perverted" and those who had acquired it. These born "perverted" were probably the children of individuals suffering from hysteria, epilepsy, alcoholism, anemia, typhus, "debauchery," or similar illnesses or had been affected by the soil or climate of their birthplace. Others had acquired their "perversion" by reading dirty books, keeping bad company, living in luxuriousness, or masturbating. He believed that epilepsy and sexual perversion had much in common, since both were indications of psychic degeneration. Mothers who were hysterical were also likely to pass on traits of sexual perversion to their children.[17] The only solution was institutionalization.

Cesar Lombroso, used Darwinian assumptions to bolster his argument that sexual deviates were on a lower stage of the evolutionary ladder than normal heterosexual individuals. Lombroso and his allies accepted the belief that animal life had evolved from lower forms, but they went further, arguing that life had progressed sexually from a hermaphroditic or self-fertilizing stage to a higher monosexual stage. Just as life itself had evolved, so did species, and as man had progressed from primitive society to higher levels of civilization, mankind had outgrown robbery, murder, promiscuity, and perversion, or at least the most civilized among mankind had done so. Because, however, a child had to repeat the progression of the species to become civilized, it was understandable that those with defective heredity would become criminals, deviants, or mental defectives. It was also understandable why sexual behavior common among primitive groups or observed among animals would be unacceptable in higher, civilized societies. Thus, innate crime and sexual deviation were equivalent to moral insanity. Lombroso measured the skulls, bodies, sexual organs, and features of criminals, prostitutes, idiots, arsonists, and the "sexually perverted," in the process proving, at least to his own satisfaction, that such individuals had a large number of primitive characteristics such as jutting jaws, malformed craniums, and close-set eyes. Lombroso agreed, however, that those who were born criminally or "morally insane" should not be punished but rather sequestered in asylums and prevented from perpetuating their species.[18] The medical model of stigmatized behavior had replaced the criminal one.

By far the most important of these early researchers in influencing public opinion was Richard von Krafft-Ebing (1840–1902), whose *Psychopathia sexualis* is still in print. He combined several prevailing nineteenth-century theories to explain sexual "perversion": (1) the idea that disease was caused by the physical nervous system, (2) the idea that there were often hereditary defects in this system, and (3) the concept of degeneracy. He also, like Drysdale before him, attached great importance to man's sexual drive. He wrote that sexuality was the

> most important factor in social existence, the strongest incentive to the exertion of strength and acquisition of property, to the foundation of a home, and the awakening of altruistic feeling, first for a person of the opposite sex, then for the offspring, and in a wider sense for all humanity.[19]

He was, however, very much a man of the nineteenth century, stressing that civilization had been made possible only by the tempering of lust through altruism and restraint and teaching that sexual excess weakened the body. The purpose of sex was reproduction, and sexual activities not undertaken with this ultimate purpose in mind were "unnatural practices," a perversion of the sexual instinct. Though religion, law, education, and morality all gave civilized man the aids by which he could bridle his passion, man was still always in danger of sinking from the clear height of pure, chaste love into the mire of common sensuality. To retain his morality man had to fight a constant struggle with natural impulses.

Only characters endowed with strong wills are able to completely emancipate themselves from sensuality and share in that pure love from which springs the noblest joys of human life.[20]

To demonstrate the dangers of excessive sexuality, Krafft-Ebing collected a number of cases, more than 200 by the 11th edition of his work, of "abnormal" or "pathological" individuals. He firmly believed that the abnormality he reported resulted either from frequent abuses of the sexual organs (masturbation) or from an inherited abnormal constitution of the nervous system. Each case began with an evaluation of the subject's heredity, noting the presence of insanity, epilepsy, hysteria, convulsions, alcoholism, and severe physical disorders in his family. Though he distinguished between innate and acquired perversion, he argued that even the acquired perversions could exist only when there were hereditary weaknesses in the nervous system. Krafft-Ebing coined the term *masochism*, based on the novels of Sacher-Masoch, and popularized the term *sadism*, based on de Sade, although sadism had been used by others to describe the association of cruelty and violence with lust. He also popularized such terms as *fetishism* and *exhibitionism,* which had been defined as separate perversions earlier by Binet[21] and Lasegue,[22] respectively. He was generally concerned with the broad categories of fetishism, homosexuality (which he also called "the contrary sexual instinct" and "urning"), sadism, and masochism, but also included are sections on satyriasis, nymphomania, exhibitionism, voyeurism, zoophilia, sexual arousal with young girls, and others. Though his cases document the wide range of human sexuality, his moral judgments are ever-present through references to things such as "hereditary taint" and "moral degeneracy" and his willingness to consider masturbation a causal factor for anything he regarded as deviant or unpleasant. As his title would indicate, he also classified almost every kind of sex activity except those leading to procreation as psychopathic acts. In the same grouping with lust murderers and cannibals, he includes such harmless phenomena as the collector of violet-striped handkerchiefs, a man's loving to smell roses, and a girl's longing to kiss and embrace other girls. Inevitably, the reader who might find some of his or her own sexual proclivities somewhere in the book would be fearful that he or she might become a sex murderer unless strong control was exercised.[23]

One recent investigator, Edward Brecher, has gone so far as to state that Krafft-Ebing made sex a loathsome disease,[24] but this is much too strong an indictment, since sex had already been viewed as a loathsome activity by much of the Western world. The great importance of Krafft-Ebing, as the numerous editions of his work would testify, lay in his bringing all forms of sexual activity out into the open, the subject for public discussion, even though this might not have been his original intention. When Krafft-Ebing found that the general public as well as the professionals for whom he was writing read his book, he tried to make it ever more obscure by using more technical language, putting the more specific descriptions of sexual acts into Latin. In a sense, this was only a matter of self-defense, to save him from severe criticism for bringing "sexual anomalies" to public attention. Even this did not always save him. The *British Medical Journal* in 1893, for example, editorialized about his book:

> We have considered at length whether we should notice this book or not, but we deem the importance of the subject and the position of the author make it necessary to refer to it in consideration of the feelings with which it has been discussed by the public. We have questioned whether it should have been translated into English at all. Those concerned could have gone to the original. Better if it had been written entirely in Latin, and thus veiled in the decent obscurity of a dead language.[25]

Krafft-Ebing, through his focus on heredity, felt that the penal laws should be repealed and asked for the repeal of some of the harsher provisions of the German law. This led to a controversy over the nature versus nurture theory, in part between Krafft-Ebing and his followers and those who opposed him. For a time, Krafft-Ebing dominated, and a number of important investigators such as Charles Féré,[26] Albert Moll,[27] and L. Thoinot[28] agreed with him, and even many of his opponents, particularly P. Näcke[29] and Iwan Bloch,[30] eventually came to agree with him. Modifying but accepting the basic premise was one of the truly major sexologists of the first part of the twentieth century, Havelock Ellis (1859–1939), who probably more than anyone else, popularized the concept of individual and cultural relativism in sex. The result of his studies were published in a monumental series of volumes. *Studies in the Psychology of Sex,* originally issued and revised betwen 1896 and 1938. Like Krafft-Ebing, Ellis covered most of the variations in sexual behavior, but unlike his predecessor, he exhibited a far more sympathetic understanding of the individuals involved. In a sense, Ellis was a naturalist, observing and collecting information about human sexuality instead of judging it, and as such can be considered the forerunner of the sex researchers of today. Being cautious, when he turned to questions such as whether homosexuality was inborn or acquired, physical or psychic, he felt there was perhaps some truth in all the views. He tended to believe that sexual differences were inborn and nonpathological, although he granted that perhaps there was a higher number of neurotics among deviants than among other groups. Essentially, Ellis' work was a plea for tolerance and for acceptance that deviations from the norm were harmless and occasionally perhaps even valuable. He was a sex reformer who urged society to recognize and accept sexual manifestations during infancy, to realize that there was sexual experimentation during adolescence, and to take steps to repeal its bans on contraception and its laws dealing with sexual activity between consenting adults in private.[31] In spite of this, the medical community continued to regard most nonprocreative sexual activities as signs of illness.

The first volume of Ellis' work had been conceived as a collaboration between himself and John Addington Symonds (1840–1893), best known for his studies of Renaissance Italy. Symonds, a homosexual who was married and the father of four children, had dealt with homosexuality in two earlier works, *A Problem in Greek Ethics* (1883) and *A Problem in Modern Ethics* (1891).[32] Symonds preferred the term *inversion* to describe homosexuality, and for a time the term enjoyed some popularity but was eventually discarded because it was not precise enough. In his books on homosexuality Symonds denied both that masturbation was a cause of homosexuality and that it might be hereditary but offered no satisfactory explanation of his own. To investigate this problem further he joined forces with Ellis, but before their work appeared in 1896 in German in Germany (to avoid problems of English censorship), Symonds had died. When an English version was published in 1897 his family immediately sought to remove his name from the publication; failing to do so, they bought up most of the edition, destroyed it, and secured an agreement with Ellis that, if any further editions were published, Symonds' name would be removed from the title page. Ellis then turned to American publishers.

One of the first Englishmen to write about homosexuality under his own name was Edward Carpenter (1844–1929), who was much more a publicist for homosexuality than Symonds was. In his pamphlet *Homogenic Love* (1894) and in his book *The Intermediate Sex* (1908) he argued that the bisexually endowed were specially fitted for progressive leadership in a democratic society. To document the nature of homosexual genius he gathered a collection of literary references to homoerotic friendships, *Iolaus* (1902), and followed this with *Intermediate Types among Primitive Folk* (1914), in which he highlighted the privileged and honored status of the homosexual in primitive societies.[33]

Also more of a propagandist than researcher was the American Edward Irenaeus Stevenson (1868–1942), who wrote about homosexuality under the pseudonym of Xavier Mayne. Stevenson wrote several novels under his real name that he later claimed had disguised homoerotic themes. Later, in 1908, he published a more openly homosexual novel under the Xavier Mayne pseudonym and a more specialized kind of work, *The Intersexes, a History of Similisexualism as a Problem in Social Life*. Mayne or Stevenson held that homosexual relations were natural, necessary, and legitimate and that homosexuals constituted a third sex between the extreme male and extreme female.[34]

Being homosexual did not, however, necessarily preclude individuals from doing valuable research into sexuality, and one of the more important figures was Magnus Hirschfeld (1868–1935), who was both a homosexual and a transvestite. Undoubtedly, his own sexual inclinations helped convince Hirschfeld that homosexuality was not a perversion, but his explanation that it was the result of certain inborn characteristics influenced by internal secretions of the glands has failed to win many converts. His value is not so much in his theory as in the information he compiled about homosexuality, transvestism, and other forms of sexual activity. He founded the first journal devoted to the study of sex and the first Institute of Sexual Science and gathered an important library of more than 20,000 volumes and 35,000 pictures to assist his research. In effect he founded the first sex research institute. To do the first widescale study of sexual habits he devised what he called a "psychobiological questionnaire" containing some 130 questions that he had some 10,000 men and women fill out. Unfortunately, much of his library, along with the questionnaires and other information, was destroyed by Nazi hoodlums shortly after Hitler came to power. Interested in areas of sex other than homosexuality and transvestism, Hirschfeld established a marriage counseling service, worked for legal reforms, and gave advice on contraception and sex problems. Independently wealthy, highly educated, and an effective propagandist, he should be recognized as the first great entrepreneur in sexual studies. In addition, he wrote, under his own name or one of his pseudomys, particularly Numa Praetovius, a number of monographs and longer studies on various aspects of sex, including a study on transvestism (he coined the term), a study of homosexuality, a textbook for physicians and students on sexual pathology, a summary of his research, and a survey of sex practices throughout the world.[35]

Among his more important organizing efforts was the foundation of the Wissenschaftlich-humanitäre Komittee (usually translated as the "Scientific-Humanitarian Committee") in 1897. In 1899 the comittee, with Hirschfeld as editor, began publishing a journal, *Jahrbuch für sexuelle Zwischenstufen,*[36] devoted primarily to the study of homosexuality. Though he believed that homosexuality had a constitutional basis, Hirschfeld was also convinced that physiological and psychological differences could be found between homosexuals and heterosexuals and that homosexuals constituted a group born with a destiny to live "between the sexes," that is, to be *zwischen* or in an intermediate state. Hirschfeld also claimed that homosexuals had special virtues and were more democratic and more altruistic than heterosexuals, a belief leading many later investigators to downgrade his research in spite of the vast amounts of data he collected and published.

In a sense, the comittee, the group behind the clinic, journal, and research center, came close to being an association of homosexuals, and it has sometimes been regarded as the first effective organization of homosexuals. The difficulty with such a claim is that it was never a membership organization but rather a steering committee that was self-perpetuating. The comittee was, however, an effective propagandizer for changes in laws regarding sexual activity, and Hirschfeld never confined his efforts to homosexuality. He was a convener of the first International Congress for Sexual Reform, held in Berlin in 1921, out of which came the World League for Sexual Reform. Subsequent congresses were held in Copenhagen, London, Vienna, and Brno (Czechoslovakia), before the league ran into difficulty, in part because of political disputes among its members. For a time many of the league officials had been favorably impressed with sexual reforms in Russia following the revolution, and though members of the league regarded themselves as liberal, if not radicals, on matters of sex, sexual reform and political outlook are not necessarily related. With the destruction of the Hirschfeld Institute in 1933, the key element in the league, and the deaths shortly afterward of Havelock Ellis, August Forel, and Hirschfeld himself, all of whom had been past presidents of the World League for Sexual Reform, the two surviving presidents, Norman Haire and J. H. Leunbach, took different paths. Leunbach wanted the league to join the revolutionary workers' movements, but Haire was determined to keep all revolutionary activity out of the league, to concentrate on educational projects. The result was the dissolution of the league and a setback, although temporary, to sexual reform.[37]

Many others viewed sexual behavior as more or less congenital,[38] but challenging and modifying these assumptions were Sigmund Freud and his followers. Freud agreed with Krafft-Ebing on the necessity of redirecting sexual energies, but where Krafft-Ebing had held that variant sexual behavior came from sexual drives that had been misdirected in their aim or object, Freud held the cause of the misdirection lay in the nervous system and the mind through which the instinctual drive operated. Though Freud paid comparatively little attention to most forms of variant sexual behavior, his followers seized upon his concepts to emphasize the environmental and accidental causes of variant impulses far more than Freud himself did. Though later behaviorists, stressing learning and conditioning of animals and man, carried this type of environmental and accidental determination to an extreme, the practical result of both Freudianism and learning psychologies was to suggest that everyone had the potential to channel his drives toward any form of gratification and use any object. Unavoidably, this undermined the assumption that certain forms of sex were against nature, for nature itself, the instinctual drive, was visualized as being able to express itself in many ways.

Freud regarded homoerotic behavior as a normal part of growing up. Most individuals moved beyond this stage into adult heterosexuality, and so, by implication, adult homosexuality was a distortion of natural development. His explanations for the failure of certain individuals to move beyond the homoerotic phase centered around the relationship of a child to its parents, most particularly to the parent of the opposite sex. Homosexuality was conceived by Freud and his followers also as a flight from incest. In the absence of a father or in the presence of a weak one, a boy child who fell in love with his mother and sought to become her lover repressed his desire most effectively by suppressing sexual feelings toward all women. In other instances the child fell in love with the parent of the same sex and replaced or attempted to oust the parent of the other sex. The boy, suppressing his desires for his father, sought to be like the woman who accepted his father, but unable to reconcile the incestuous sin of a father love, sought the father in other males. Such a boy might become effeminate, play the female role in the sex act, and become attracted to older men.[39] Although each psychoanalytic investigator tends to point up different factors in his diagnosis, most, following Freud, have agreed that homosexuality is environmentally rather than constitutionally caused and, by implication, curable.[40]

Freud's belief in the underlying biological forces involved in forming sex-specific behavior also contributed to the concept of latent homosexuality. For example, he equated femininity with passivity, gentleness, and timidity and implied that females who were ambitious, athletic, aggressive, or in other ways "masculine" were showing latent homosexuality and losing their femininity. Such assumptions have been criticized by leaders of the women's movement, most notably and uncharitably by Kate Millet,[41] but the difficulty with criticizing Freud is that he said different things at different times. In his later life, he modified some of his earlier views about sex,[42] seemed more relaxed about the topic, and toward the end of his life, expressed doubts about the possibilities for the cure of homosexuality. This is best illustrated by his 1935 letter to a mother whose son was homosexual.

Dear Mrs. _____:

I gather from your letter that your son is a homosexual. I am most impressed by the fact that you do not mention this term yourself in your information about him. May I question, why you avoid it? Homosexuality is assuredly no advantage, but it is nothing to be classified as an illness; we consider it to be a variation of the sexual development. Many highly respectable individuals of ancient and modern times have been homosexuals, several of the greatest men among them (Plato, Michelangelo, Leonardo da Vinci, etc.). It is a great injustice to persecute homosexuality as a crime and cruelty, too. If you do not believe me, read the books of Havelock Ellis.

By asking me if I can help, you mean, I suppose, if I can abolish homosexuality and make normal heterosexuality take its place. The answer is, in a general way, we cannot promise to achieve it. In a certain number of cases we succeed in developing the blighted germs of heterosexual tendencies which are present in every homosexual; in the majority of cases it is no more possible. It is a question of the quality and the age of the individual. The result of treatment cannot be predicted.

What analysis can do for your son runs in a different line. If he is unhappy, neurotic, torn by conflicts, inhibited in his coital life, analysis may bring him harmony,

peace of mind, full efficiency, whether he remains a homosexual or gets changed. If
you make up your mind he should have analysis with me—I don't expect you
will—he has to come over to Vienna. I have no intention of leaving here. However,
don't neglect to give me your answer.[43]

For a time Freud's influence and attitudes seemed all pervasive. Though his
research was based on case studies and not subject to the statistical sampling
concepts that social and behavioral scientists have since begun to apply to
human activities, it was not without some strong underpinnings. One factor undermining the assumptions of those arguing for the congenital origins of sexual
behavior were observations reported by those studying animals. G. V.
Hamilton, influenced by Freudian theories, studied monkeys and baboons in
conditions approaching their normal environment,[44] and Edward J. Kempf
studied the sexual behavior of monkeys in laboratories.[45] Though both investigators demonstrated that homosexuality was natural among animals, they saw
it as a stage in the development of the animal to heterosexuality. Success in
moving from a homosexual to a heterosexual stage was due to the animal's
ability to manipulate its environment. Submission as a homosexual object was
a sign of inferior social status among the infrahuman primates. But later researchers challenged some of the Freudian assumptions of these early animal
investigators,[46] and the question is by no means clear. In recent years sex research has split into two conflicting schools, clinical case research (primarily
psychoanalytical) on the one hand and all other research on the other, the
psychoanalytic school coming under increasing attack.[47] Martin Weinberg and
Colin Williams, in their 1974 study of homosexuality, summed up the basis of
the attack. Their complaint was that the psychoanalysts, by their emphasis on
cure, hinder theoretical progress and prevent a better understanding of variations in sexual behavior. They also criticized the methodological deficiencies in
such studies:

> First, the samples used have been extremely small. This in itself need not always be
> a serious defect, even if it does limit more complex analysis of the data. A much
> more important problem is that such samples are usually made up of persons who
> are patients of the clinicians doing research and cannot provide much knowledge
> about homosexuals in toto. While a representative sample of homosexuals may be
> impossible to achieve, certainly less biased groups can be obtained. . . . Another
> major defect of such studies has been that control groups are rarely used. Com-
> parison groups are crucial if, for example, one is concerned with determining the
> degree to which homosexuals are maladjusted (instead of claiming it by fiat). A
> heterosexual control group is essential to answer this question as well as etiological
> questions. Finally most studies of homosexuality have been culture bound.[48]

Weinberg and Williams are criticizing not only the methodology used by
many of the psychiatrists but also the validity of the medical model. Though in

the past the medical model undoubtedly proved useful, many have now questioned its continual application to problems of sexual orientation. One advantage the medical model afforded the researcher was that of investigating sexual behavior without suffering the public condemnation that faced the nonphysician.[49] The medical model also offered an opportunity for the investigator to examine sexual behavior, even if his only sample was his patients. In fact, until the last few decades, one major problem that researchers into sexuality had to face was getting information. Krafft-Ebing solved this problem by collecting court and medical cases. Others went to prison populations. Ellis compiled individual case histories of friends and others, gathered historical examples, reported on primitive tribes, and consulted literary sources. Hirschfeld tried to examine the general population, one of the pioneering efforts to do so. For this he was brought to trial and charged with disseminating indecent information. Though fined 200 marks, Hirschfeld continued his researches. Understandably, Freud returned again to the patient, a safer and easier, if not a more accurate, solution.

The difficulty with case histories is that they are selective, self-selective in fact, and it is difficult to see how a patient with a sex problem reflects the sexual attitudes of those who do not feel they have a problem. One solution to this dilemma is to gather sexual data from a number of subjects through interviews or questionnaires, and there were several pioneering attempts in this direction,[50] but the man who, more than anyone else, set the stage for current sex research and who brought about a radical change in attitudes was Alfred C. Kinsey with his associates. The Kinsey studies were based on the detailed sexual behavior of 12,000 Americans of both sexes and all ages, unmarried, married, and formerly married, drawn from every state and from every educational and socioeconomic status. Kinsey originally planned to interview some 100,000 individuals, but death intervened, and his successors at the institute he founded have since chosen other paths. In terms of sample statistics, 12,000 individuals ought to have given an effective indication of American sexual behavior, but Kinsey's sampling techniques have often been criticized by social scientists because his interviewees tended to be self-selected or to belong to groups to which Kinsey had an entrée. But even those who criticized his sampling techniques have been impressed by the size of his sample and the results he obtained.

Kinsey examined sex from the point of view of a scientist whose purpose was to find what kind of sexual activities people engaged in, not to condemn or even to define what was natural or unnatural. In compiling his data he upset many existing stereotypes. For example, Kinsey found a higher percentage of his male sample to be homosexually inclined than previously estimated, although in part the results he obtained depended on what is defined as homosexual.[51] Kinsey reported that 37 percent of the total male population had at least some overt homosexual experience to the point of orgasm between adolescence and old age, and 50 percent of males who remained single until age 35 had overt homosexual experience. Some 13 percent of the population had more homosexual than heterosexual experiences between the ages of 16 and 55, and 4 percent of the male population were labeled by Kinsey as exclusively homosexual,[52] a figure corresponding to some of Hirschfeld's estimates. Kinsey also reported on animal contacts. He found that such contacts constituted only a fraction of 1 percent of the total number of orgasms.

Women in his sample reported considerably fewer homosexual contacts than the men. Some 28 percent had reported homosexual arousal by age 45, but only 13 percent had actually reached orgasm. Less than 3 percent could be regarded as exclusively homosexual.[53] The majority of the women in the Kinsey survey had experienced orgasm in heterosexual intercourse at least once, although 10 percent of his sample who had been married at least 15 years had never had an orgasm. He also reported cases in which women failed to reach orgasm until after 20 years of marital intercourse. On the other hand Kinsey also documented what some had long suspected, namely, the female ability to achieve multiple orgasm. Some 14 percent of the females in his sample responded that they had multiple orgasms. Several managed to have a dozen or more orgasms while their husbands ejaculated only once.[54]

Anthropologists also contributed to helping change sexual attitudes by bringing to public attention the wide variety of sexual practices extant in the world. Many of these findings were reported on earlier in this book, but particularly important in concentrating on sexual observation was Bronislaw Malinowski, a major founder of functionalism. Functionalism is the belief that institutions survive only if they serve a purpose and that all institutions of a society interact to help individuals adapt to their environment. Malinowski concentrated on the family, determined to find out whether the conflicts, passions, and attachments within the family varied with its constitutions or whether these remained the same throughout humanity. He investigated a matrilineal society, the Trobriand Islanders, trying to live and experience as they did. His example of participant observation had great influence on other anthropologists, as did his frankness about the sex life of the peoples among whom he lived. Other anthropologists soon followed his example, some concentrating on deviant sexual behavior. George Devereux's study of the *berdaches* among the Mohave Indians is an example of such studies, a pioneering effort to study institutionalized homosexuality in a non-Western culture.[55]

Helping to disseminate the new kinds of information (as well as misinformation) were a number of popularizers and apologists of sexual behavior,[56] who also made the public more receptive to information about sexual behavior. Equally, if not more important, were basic breakthroughs in contraception, for effective contraceptives, by their nature, implied that nonprocreative sex was good. In the long run contraceptives probably undermined much of the hostility to sex. Some of the pioneers in contraception have been mentioned previously, but a key breakthrough came with the development of the cervical diaphragm by the German W. P. J. Mensinga. Designed to fit in the vagina with the forward end under the pubic bone and back end in the posterior fornix, it proved easier to handle than the cervical cap, for it could be made in fewer sizes and was easier to fit. Mensinga, professor of anatomy at Breslau, perfected his rubber diaphragm in the middle of the nineteenth century, but its use spread only slowly through northern Europe, and widespread knowledge of it did not reach the United States until after the end of World War I. Mensinga strongly believed that women should have equal rights with men and saw no reason why their lives should be made either shorter or more painful through bearing too many children. His discussion of birth control was both cautious and enlightening, his influence as a physician helping to persuade other physicians to adopt his recommendations.[57] Rubber condoms also began to be manufactured in great quantities at the end of the nineteenth century and the process became cheaper and more available for use as contraceptives, although they were not so effective as the diaphragm and depended on the male's willingness to use them.

A number of effective spermicides also appeared on the market at the end of the nineteenth century. Usually regarded as the first person to become active in manufacturing and selling spermicidal suppositories is the English chemist W. J. Rendell, who in about 1880 first put his quinine and cacao butter pessaries on the market. Cacao or coco butter, a yellowish, hard, and brittle vegetable fat obtained from the seeds of the *Theobroma cacao* plant, contains about 30 percent oleic acid, 40 percent stearic acid, and various other fatty acids. It is a fairly effective material for a suppository because of its low melting point, and it probably worked as a spermicide by blocking the cervix with an oily film. The quinine used by Rendell added to its effectiveness as a spermicide because it is a general proptoplasmic poison, although many individuals might also have a toxic reaction to it. Other chemicals also began to appear on the market.[58]

We know that various intrauterine devices (IUDs) were used in the nineteenth century, although it is not easy to determine just what they were. Most of the comments about them made by physicians were not particularly informative, when not actually hostile. Women, still, however, inserted various devices, one physician reporting to his shock that a device designed to alleviate uterine disorders was being used by women to prevent conception.[59] Though IUDs are probably as old as woman, it was not until massive experiments conducted on them in Israel and Japan were reported in 1959 that their use became widespread. Further encouraging their use was the development of new plastic materials that proved far less irritating than earlier ones. Foams and jellies were also introduced during the twentieth century, but the most effective device to appear were the oral contraceptives.

Research on them began in 1950 after a meeting between Margaret Sanger, the long-time outspoken advocate of birth control, and Gregory Pincus, the director of the Worcester Foundation for Experimental Biology. Pincus, attracted by Mrs. Sanger's passionate conviction, began to search for means of preventing conception by oral means through the use of progesterone. In experiments carried out with Min-Chueh Chang, also of the Worcester Foundation, he found that progesterone given orally was often effective in hindering ovulation in rats and rabbits. Deciding to experiment further, they teamed up with John Rock, a gynecologist at Harvard University doing studies on ovulation. They found that the same results they obtained in rats and rabbits could be obtained in a majority of women. The trio then turned to synthetic compounds of progesterone known as gestagens, of which there were then some 200. Three of these proved to be particularly suitable in hindering ovulation but posed other difficulties, for bleeding tended to be irregular and sometimes would occur unexpectedly during the middle of the cycle. This difficulty was finally overcome by combining one of the gestagens with a synthetic estrogen. This estrogen–gestagen combination was tested on a large scale in Puerto Rico, beginning in 1956, and was then marketed under the name of Enovid. Since that time other oral contraceptives have appeared on the market, and the dosage has been lowered.

With the means of effective family planning available, the problem was to disseminate the information, this proving at least as difficult as developing the effective means. In previous chapters we have touched upon some of the difficulties of disseminating this information, but the problem became both easier and more complicated at the end of the nineteenth century and the beginning of the twentieth century through the growth of the Eugenics movement. The word *eugenic* was coined by Francis Galton in 1885; he defined it as an applied biological science concerned with increasing from one generation to another the proportion of persons with better than average eugenic, that is, intellectual endowment. Galton, a cousin of Charles Darwin and a major figure in nineteenth-century science, was a great believer in heredity as a means of improving the "race" and thus in the importance of sexual selection. Galton did not take into account the importance of contraceptives, a subject about which he knew little, but concentrated on urging judicious marriages and large families for the wealthy and gifted, terms he sometimes used as more or less synonymous. To advance research in the area, Galton endowed first a fellowship and later a chair at University College, University of London, the first holder of both being Karl Pearson, a brilliant mathematician. Pearson was convinced that environment had little to do with the development of mental or emotional qualities and that both were the result of heredity. From this assumption he concluded that the high birth rate of the poor was a threat to civilization and that the "higher races" must supplant the "lower." Though the English Eugenic Society, founded by Galton, eventually opposed Pearson's racist views, large sections of the Eugenics movement had racist overtones, and the American Eugenics movement, founded in 1905, adopted Pearson's view wholeheartedly.

As a group, the American eugenicists believed that the white race was superior to other races and that within the "white race" the Nordic "white was superior to other whites." It was also assumed that upper-class people had superior hereditary qualities justifying their being the ruling class. To document this assumption they gathered any evidence supporting their interpretation. Intelligence tests, introduced in the early 1900s by Alfred Binet, for example, in spite of opposition by Binet himself, were held to be measures of innate, genetic intelligence. On the basis of such tests, the eugenicists classified all people whose IQs gave them a mental age of 12 as feebleminded or morons, without regard to the educational background or deprived environment that might have led to such test results. Criminality was considered a concomitant of feeblemindedness. Insane, idiotic, imbecilic, feebleminded, and epileptic persons were often sterilized, either voluntarily or involuntarily; so in some areas were habitual criminals, "moral perverts," and others deemed socially undesirable. Studies by some of the American eugenicists, such as R. L. Dugdale and Lothrop Stoddard on the pseudonymous Jukes and Kallikaks, were taken to prove that hundreds of persons in each of these families became feebleminded or criminal types because of the inheritance they had received from a single ancestor five or six generations back.[60] Later much of the data were found to have been fabricated.

The eugenicists also mounted campaigns to have the "better people" reproduce more, while the "lower elements," that is, the poor, black, immigrant, and so forth, were to be encouraged not to produce so much. Much of the early contraceptive movement inevitably became involved with the eugenicist movement, although most of the racial and class overtones have since been removed from most of the Planned Parenthood programs. In the long run, the Eugenics movement, in spite of much of its fallacious thinking, encouraged numbers of influential people to support dissemination of contraceptives; this in itself helped bring about new sexual attitudes.

Many radicals were also for contraception, if only because they felt that one of the burdens from which the poor suffered most was large families. This group first tried to disseminate contraceptive information on a mass scale. A few of the early feminist leaders were also concerned with helping the poor, overburdened mother who did not want to have additional children. To disseminate their message they had to come to grips with the laws against pornography, since these laws were used to prohibit dissemination of contraceptive information. The first laws against pornography in England, passed in 1853, had been supplemented in 1857 by Lord Campbell's Act, which gave magistrates the power to order the destruction of books and prints if, in their opinion, publication would amount to a "misdemeanor proper to be prosecuted as such."[61] The meaning of what constituted pornography was further extended by the so-called Hicklin decision in 1868, in which Sir Alexander Cockburn wrote that the test of obscenity was whether "the tendency of the matter as obscenity is to deprive and corrupt those whose minds are open to such immoral influences and into whose hands a publication of this sort may fall."[62]

Almost immediately, pamphlets giving birth control information came under attack, even those that had long been circulating. One of the first items seized was Charles Knowlton's *Fruits of Philosophy,* a work discussed earlier in this book. A local court found the bookseller guilty of selling obscene literature. With this decision before them, Charles Bradlaugh and Annie Besant, two English freethinkers who had established the Free Thought Publishing Company, decided to republish the book in London but without the illustrations, which they thought might have prompted prosecution. Their purpose, at least in part, was to publicize birth control information. As a result they announced that they would publicly sell the book themselves on March 23, 1877, an action that more or less invited arrest. The police obliged, and though Sir Alexander Cockburn, the trial judge, held that there had never been a more ill-advised or injudicious prosecution, since the book had been sold for more than 40 years without interference, he carefully explained the law to the jury. The jury returned a rather unusual verdict, in that they found the book was "calculated to corrupt public morals," but exonerated the "defendants from any corrupt motives in publishing it." Cockburn held that this was a verdict of guilty, a decision causing some consternation among the jury, for at least a few of them had thought they were acquitting the defendants. In spite of his finding, Cockburn decided to discharge the two without sentence, a decision he apparently soon regretted when Mrs. Besant, with Bradlaugh at her side, mentioned at a public meeting that the judge was on their side and that they would continue to publish the book. This remark leading Cockburn to reconsider his decision, he sentenced the two to 6 months' imprisonment plus a fine of 200 pounds each. On appeal, however, the conviction was quashed on the grounds that the indictment itself was erroneous. The immediate result was a rapid rise in the circulation of the *Fruits of Philosophy* and considerable publicity for the birth control movement.[63]

Following the example of Mrs. Besant, women entered into the fight for birth control in increasing numbers; this act in itself helped bring sex out into the open, since much of the prudery had ostensibly been to protect women. Mrs. Besant, encouraged by her success, organized the Malthusian League, a militant body that set out to achieve complete freedom of discussion on birth control and, incidentally, on sexual matters. During the following decades, similar leagues appeared in Holland, Germany, and much of the rest of the Western world.[64] In America, however, obstacles still remained because of some of the same factors that had prevailed in England and that were discussed in an earlier chapter. Anthony Comstock, as a special postal agent, considered contraceptive information pornographic; he had moved against Edward Bliss Foote and others for disseminating pamphlets discussing birth control.

The effective challenge to Comstock in this area is associated with the name of Margaret Sanger, a radical nurse. In 1914 she began to publish a magazine called *The Woman Rebel,* whose aim was to stimulate working women to think for themselves. In an effort to attract attention she announced in the magazine that she would defy the laws pertaining to the dissemination of contraceptive information. In 1914 she published a small pamphlet on *Family Limitation,* for which she was arrested. Though she attended the preliminary hearing, she fled to Europe before her formal trial. During her absence, her husband, William Sanger, who had little to do with his wife's publishing activities, was arrested and convicted after being tricked into giving a copy of the pamphlet to a Comstock agent.

Upset at the infringement of their right to know, a group of women, among them Mary Ware Dennett, organized the National Birth Control League in 1915 to demand a change in the law. In the meantime, Mrs. Sanger, angered at what she felt was unjust punishment of her husband, returned to America to stand trial, but the government, after several delays, refused to prosecute. Undoubtedly, one reason for the reluctance to prosecute was the death of Anthony Comstock. Another reason was that prominent people from all over the United States had come to Mrs. Sanger's defense, some because they believed in eugenics, others because they were feminists, and others because they thought she was unjustly persecuted. In the aftermath of the Sanger case, birth control information could be more widely disseminated, although Mrs. Sanger felt she was still not reaching the workingwomen, the group about whom she was most concerned. To do more in this direction, she, her sister Ethel Byrne, who was also a nurse, and two social workers, Fania Mindell and Elizabeth Stuyvesant, opened a birth control clinic in the Brownsville section of Brooklyn in October 1916. Since the opening had been widely publicized, there were long queues of women waiting along with several vice officers. Not until some 10 days later, however, were Ethel Byrne, Fania Mindell, and Mrs. Sanger arrested. Ethel Byrne was tried first, found guilty, and sentenced to 30 days in jail, whereupon she promptly went on a hunger strike that attracted national attention. After 11 days, she was pardoned by the governor of New York. Fania Mindell was next, but she was fined only 50 dollars. By this time the courts were willing to drop charges against Mrs. Sanger, provided she would close down her clinic, but she refused. As a result, she was sentenced to 30 days in jail, but she immediately appealed her case. The Court of Appeals eventually held that contraceptive information could be disseminated for the "cure and prevention of disease" but did not specify the disease. Defining pregnancy as a disease, the militants used this loophole to continue to disseminate information.[65] New York was just one state, and there were numerous other state laws to be overcome. Even when contraceptive clinics were allowed, public agencies made it difficult to give out information to those people economically most in need of it. It was, in fact, not until 1965 that the U.S. Supreme Court removed the last obstacle, in the case of *Griswold* v. *Conn,* and birth control information could be given out freely in all 50 states. At about that time the U.S. Government also began to initiate positive programs in this regard as part of a massive program to educate the public, incidentally imparting a great amount of sexual information at the same time. Most countries in Europe had also established contraceptive centers, although some, such as Ireland, allowed free dissemination of information only in the 1970s. In Great Britain the first birth control clinic was opened in 1921 by Dr. Marie Stopes and her husband H. V. Roe.

Tied in with contraception was a new attitude toward abortion. Abortion is obviously one form of birth control, one way of eliminating the penalties for sexuality, albeit a much less desirable form. Here there were greater moral and legal obstacles than with birth control, although most dated from the nineteenth century and had been designed to protect the mother from unskilled abortionists. This same argument about protecting mothers provided some of the rationale for legalizing abortions, for it was widely believed that illegal abortions were a significant factor in maternal deaths. The first British statute against abortion was enacted in 1803, New York State put its first law on the books in 1828, and most other states had acted by the end of the nineteenth century. Even when abortions were technically illegal, therapeutic abortions were permitted, these being defined as necessary to preserve the life or health of the mother. During the early 1960s, it was estimated that in the United States approximately 8000 legal therapeutic abortions were performed every year, and 50 to 80 times that many illegal ones. As medicine perfected aseptic techniques and antibiotics were developed to prevent infection, abortions had potentially become, by the middle of the twentieth century, a far safer procedure than they had been in the nineteenth century, when abortions had been made illegal.

The first European country to legalize abortion was the Soviet Union, a step it took in 1920 as part of the revolutionary changes introduced into that country. During the twenties the Russians used abortion in lieu of effective contraceptives, and, as might be expected, the number of abortions escalated rapidly, although this is more a surmise than something based on hard data, for the Soviets never gave any meaningful statistics. In 1936, the Soviet government, for reasons not yet clear, banned legalized abortion, a ban that remained in effect until 1955, when abortion was again legalized. Though the Soviet Union, as of this writing, still does not release abortion statistics on any regular basis, estimates of the number range from 2 million to 6 million annually, and in the larger cities it is believed that the number of abortions approximates the number of live births.[66]

Other Communist bloc countries have not been so reticent in reporting statistics, the growing safety of abortions having been demonstrated in several Eastern European countries. In Czechoslovakia, for example, not a single death had been reported for the 140,000 abortions performed during the years 1963–1964, and only 2 for the 358,000 abortions reported in Hungary during the same period. Outside the Soviet bloc, Yugoslavia had somewhat higher rates with 5 deaths per 100,000 reported in 1961. Estimates for abortion deaths in the Scandinavian countries ranged somewhat higher, from 14 to 18 per 100,000 the difference being in part blamed on the cumbersome process of getting approval, which sometimes pushed the abortion past the 3-month limit imposed in most of the Eastern European countries.[67]

Japan was the first country to use abortions to deal with what was felt to be a population emergency. The original law, passed in May 1948, legalized abortion only for those women whose health might be impaired from either the physical or economic point of view. Within the next few years the law was extended to include abortion at a woman's request. The result was a steep climb in abortions, from 246,000 in 1949 to 1,128,000 in 1958. These figures are probably conservative, for it is believed that many physicians failed to report significant numbers of office abortions, to lower their taxable incomes. The result of the Japanese policy was a rapid drop in birth rates from 34.3 per 1,000 in 1947 to 16.0 in 1961.[68] In recent years the number of abortions has declined somewhat as other means of birth control have been used.

In the United States, the initial impetus for abortion law reform came from the recommendations of the model penal code adopted in 1962 by the American Law Institute. The code provided for termination of pregnancy when the physical or mental health of the mother was greatly impaired, when the child might be born with a grave physical or mental defect, or when pregnancy was a result of rape, incest, or other felonious intercourse, including illicit intercourse with a girl under the age of 16.[69] Little action was taken on these rather mild proposals until the thalidomide controversy burst on the scene. Dramatizing the case for abortion was Mrs. Sherri Finkbine, a Phoenix, Arizona, mother of four, who found that she had taken the drug thalidomide during the first few months of her fifth pregnancy. As news of the thalidomide deformities began to reach the United States, she became interested in seeking an abortion. Thalidomide, which had been introduced as a tranquilizer, resulted in damage to the embryo if a woman took the drug during the early months of her pregnancy. Such damage often resulted in phomelia, a congenital malformation in which the infants are born with flaps instead of arms or no arms at all. In more severe cases, infants are born with shortened thigh bones, twisted legs, missing ears, flattened nose, and a paralyzed face. In West Germany, where the drug had originally been developed and manufactured, some 4000 to 6000 infants had been born deformed as a result of mothers' taking the drug, and an additional 1000 others were reported elsewhere in Britain and on the continent. Since the U.S. Food and Drug Administration had prevented its manufacture in this country pending further tests, only a handful of samples of the drug from abroad, including that taken by Mrs. Finkbine, had reached the United States, and as a result only a few thalidomide-deformed children were born in the United States.

When Mrs. Finkbine reported to her physician that she had taken thalidomide, he, after studying the odds on deformity, which he estimated to be at least 50 percent, recommended a therapeutic abortion. He wrote a formal letter to the abortion committee of the hospital, which routinely approved the abortion, scheduling it for the following week. In the meantime, through Mrs. Finkbine's conversation with a close friend, the wife of a newspaper editor, the Phoenix newspapers became aware of the upcoming abortion and, in a front-page feature story, reported that the "Drug Causing Deformed Infants May Cost Woman Her Baby Here." Though Mrs. Finkbine's identity was thoroughly disguised, the Maricopa County attorney, after some public pressure, announced that he would prosecute any hospital performing such an operation if a complaint was filed. Fearful that such a complaint would be filed, the hospital's executive board called an emergency meeting that resulted in a decision to postpone the operation temporarily. To protect itself, the hospital filed a suit in court trying to get a declaratory judgment on the legality of a therapeutic abortion that its staff felt was medically desirable. The legal brief disclosed, however, the identity of the woman in question. Since Mrs. Finkbine was well known in Phoenix as the hostess of a local children's television program she soon found herself besieged by the press. To escape national publicity and to get an abortion as rapidly as possible, the Finkbines flew to Los Angeles, planning to go to either Japan or Sweden for an abortion. When the Japanese consul, fearful of possible harmful publicity, refused to give her a visa until he could obtain approval from Tokyo, the couple went to Sweden, where she had her abortion. The fetus was deformed.

Encouraged by the Finkbine case, many individuals and disparate groups working on abortion law reform thereupon began to pull together. One weapon was a book by Lawrence Lader urging abortion reform, on which some of the information in this section is based. In California, a Committee for Therapeutic Abortion was formed in 1965 representing a coalition of several groups working for abortion reform. Among them was the American Civil Liberties Union

(ACLU) of southern California, which had adopted a statement urging abortion as a woman's right; the American Association of University Women, which had studied the problem for several years; the Episcopal diocese of northern California; and various members of the medical profession, who felt that the existing laws prevented them from practicing good medicine. At the same time, in New York, a group formed the Association for the Study of Abortion, and in 1967 the Reverend Howard Moody started the Clergy Consultation Service by gathering a group of clergymen throughout the nation to offer advice on all aspects of abortion. In essence it was an abortion referral service, an action that could be taken by clerics at that time because of the law's unwillingness to interfere in the clergy's counseling and pastoral functions. The clergymen gathered lists of physicians willing to perform abortions from around the country as well as in places such as Tijuana, Mexico. At the same time Colorado liberalized its abortion statutes, followed by California, and then, between 1967 and 1970, by some 18 other states. Opponents of abortion were not idle, and California became a test case. A physician prominent in forming the Californians for Therapeutic Abortion was arrested for referring a woman to an "illegal" abortionist in the period before the law was changed. He was convicted in the local court, but upon appeal to the California Supreme Court by the southern California ACLU, his conviction was reversed in 1969. The California court not only reversed the conviction but also held that abortion was a fundamental right of privacy. Other courts followed suit, aided by the lobbying efforts of the National Association for the Repeal of Abortion Laws, formed in 1969. Opposition grouped around the Right to Life League. The result was a series of contradictory court decisions until the U.S. Supreme Court decided, on January 22, 1973, that abortions were a constitutional right. State law prohibiting them were null and void, although the court recognized the state's right to regulate abortions under certain conditions. For the first 3 months of pregnancy, however, the matter of abortion was to be decided by a woman and her physician. During the next 6 months the state could regulate abortion procedures in ways reasonably related to maternal health. Only in the last 10 weeks could a state ban abortions, and even then, they could not be banned if they were necessary to preserve a woman's life or health.

Free from fears of pregnancy, and with a new awareness of their bodies, women also became more conscious of their own sexuality. Giving further encouragement to changes in sexual outlook was the growth of vasectomies and tubal ligations. By 1973 vasectomies had passed the million mark in the United States, and the numbers desiring the minor operation were rapidly growing. Tubal ligations, in part because until the 1970s they have been more difficult to perform, have not been as popular, but with the development of the laparoscopic tubal cauterization procedures, the number has increased. Also encouraging the new sexuality has been the growing ability to control most of the dangers associated with venereal disease. Following the success of Ehrlich's neosalvarsan came the discovery of the sulfa drugs and of penicillin, which lessened the horrors of venereal disease and promised cures for those who had contracted it.

Research into sex kept up with the opportunities for new freedom. Kinsey had begun some research into the physiology of intercourse, and there are several long chapters on the subject in his book on females, but his studies in this area had only touched the surface. Moreover, Kinsey, at least in this area of sexuality, was not so much a pioneer as a follower. In fact, the first studies had been done by Felix Roubaud in the nineteenth century.[70] Other studies had followed, the most important of which were those undertaken in the thirties by Robert Latou Dickinson.[71] Dickinson, along with W. F. Robie and LeMon Clark, was responsible for the introduction into American gynecological practice of the electrical vibrator or massager, a device producing intense erotic stimulation and even orgasm in some women who previously had been unable to reach a climax. It was Dickinson's theory, as well as his collaborators', that a woman who had once achieved orgasm, even with a vibrator applied to the mons veneris near the clitoris, was more likely to proceed to orgasm during coitus or through masturbation. Dickinson used a glass tube resembling an erect penis in size and shape to observe the behavior of the vaginal lining and cervix during orgasm; in the process he proved once and for all that women did have orgasms involving physiological changes.[72] Other physicians recorded heart rates, blood pressure, and even brain waves during coitus.

In this setting William H. Masters and Virginia Johnson began their studies into sexual physiology. Masters had begun his study with prostitutes (both female and male) but soon found he was able to extend it to nonprostitutes. For his initial study 382 women and 312 men, a total of 694 individuals, participated and all told, they experienced a total of 10,000 orgasms under laboratory conditions. Volunteers masturbated either with their hands or with mechanical vibrators, had artificial coition with a transparent probe similar to that used by Dickinson except that it was electronically controlled, and engaged in various types of sexual intercourse with each other. In the process Masters, and Johnson, who soon had become his collaborator, were able to answer many of the previously unanswered questions associated with the physiology of the sex act. They found that the clitoral orgasm and the vaginal orgasm were physiologically indistinguishable, something that Freud and others had misunderstood. They also found that, whereas the clitoris played a major role in orgasm during intercourse, the penis rarely if ever made contact with the clitoris. Instead, the movement during intercourse stimulated movement of the clitoral hood, which moved with the labia. Masters and Johnson also developed ways to bring effective help to men suffering from premature ejaculation or impotence and to women unable to have an orgasm.[73] They set up a counseling center to help couples with their sexual problems, and their example was soon followed by numerous others, some of whom were trained by them.

In reassessing past misconceptions about sex, pornography also came in for study. The most important step in this direction was a study sponsored by the U.S. Government, and although neither the U.S. Congress nor the Supreme Court has fully accepted the findings, The President's Commission on Obscenity and Pornography concluded that pornography was not particularly dangerous or harmful. The final report stated:

> When people are exposed to erotic materials, some persons increase masturbatory or coital behavior, a smaller proportion decrease it, but the majority of persons report no change in these behaviors. Increases in either of these behaviors are short lived and generally disappear within 48 hours. . . . In general, established patterns of sexual behavior were found to be very stable and not altered substantially by exposure to erotica. When sexual activity occurred following the viewing or reading of these materials, it constituted a temporary activation of the individual's preexisting patterns of sexual behavior.[74]

Though the report and subsequent appendix noted that young persons are more likely to be aroused than older persons, and persons who first view pornography more than those who have seen it before, the commission felt that many of the problems with pornography came from the fact that people had been unable or reluctant in the past to be open and direct in dealing with sexual matters. Though the basic institutions of marriage and family have been built upon sexual attraction, love, and sexual expression, so much so that society depends on healthy sexual attitudes, the commission wrote that there has been great difficulty in obtaining such information, and the result has been a distorted and warped understanding. The commission felt that massive sex education programs should be launched and that legislation prohibiting the sale, exhibition, or distribution of sexual materials to consenting adults should be repealed, although members emphasized that some protective legislation might be necessary for young people. The commission's report also stated that individuals who did not want to see or receive pornography should be protected in their rights as well.[75]

Though a U.S. government commission might not be the best agency to decide the merits or demerits of pornography, the backing of the U.S. government allowed members to consult a variety of experts whose reports were filed as an addendum to the main report. In a sense the report on obscenity was another indication of the rapidly changing public opinion as well as of the growing scientific knowledge about sex. Another, similar indication was the report of the task force on homosexuality, established by the National Institute of Mental Health (NIMH). This commission was chaired by Evelyn Hooker, a psychologist who had done research on male homosexuals. Though the purpose of the task force was to recommend directions for future programs of the NIMH in homosexuality, it also urged that sexual behavior between consenting adults be decriminalized and that discrimination in employment against those labeled homosexual or deviant be eliminated.[76] In this the task force was following the recommendations made by the Wolfenden Commission in Great Britain,[77] by the model penal code of the American Law Institute, by the Ninth International Congress on Criminal Law, by the American Civil Liberties Union, by the Quakers and other religious groups, and by numerous other agencies. One important result of the study was the successful movement by the American Psychiatric Association to remove homosexuality from the category of pathological illness.

Perhaps the most remarkable indicator of change has been the public acceptance of sex reversal operations. The term *transsexual,* as used to describe individuals wanting to change their anatomical sex, was coined by D. O. Cauldwell in *Sexology* magazine in 1949 and amplified in two pamphlets. Cauldwell wrote:

> If the term transsexual gives you an itch to turn to your dictionary save the scratch and I'll serve the balm. You'll find the trans, the prefix, defined as meaning through, beyond, or across. The combination is mine so far as I know but I hereby give it freely to all who desire to use it.[78]

Harry Benjamin, who used the term soon after, at first believed he had invented it but later recognized Cauldwell's earlier usage.[79]

Though Westphal, Hirschfeld, Krafft-Ebing, and Havelock Ellis, among others, had described individuals who might or might not have been what today would be called transsexuals, such a person could not technically exist until the development of modern surgical techniques and modern hormonal therapy. In a sense the transsexual is the ultimate extension of the medical model of sexuality, since once a diagnosis of transsexualism is made, a surgical cure can be provided. One of the earliest recorded cases of sex change by surgical means was that of Sophia Hedwig in 1882, who, with medical cooperation, began to masculinize her appearance (it is not explained how). The article describing her case stated that she managed to grow a beard, and surgeons made efforts to give her genitals and the appearance of male testicles and scrotum, and they also fashioned a penis. At the completion of the surgery her name was changed to Herman Karl.[80] Whether this was an actual early attempt at surgical transformation of a female to a male or whether Sophia Hedwig was in reality a pseudohermaphrodite is difficult to determine at this point in time. As surgery improved, however, there were a number of attempts to change the sex organs of individuals,[81] the most famous case being that of the Danish artist

Einar Wagener, who became Lili Elbe.[82] Before the sex change surgery was a medical possibility, some individuals might have lived a dual existence, claiming to be a woman in a male body or vice versa. One of the more interesting of these cases was the English writer William Sharp (1855–1905), who created a female personality for himself in which he increasingly found refuge, that of Fiona MacLeod, and as Fiona MacLeod he became one of the leading literary figures in the Scottish Celtic movement. Toward the end of his life Sharp came to identify so much as Fiona that he neglected his identity as Sharp.[83]

One of the earliest transsexuals to gain some notoriety was Robert Marshall Cowell, who became Roberta Elizabeth Cowell, on May 17, 1951.[84] Gaining far more publicity, however, was Christine Jorgensen, born George Jorgensen, whose case first came to public notice in December 1952.[85] Dr. Christian Hamburger, the surgeon in charge of the Jorgensen case, later reported that, when news of the sex change became public, he was flooded with communications requesting sex change.[86] Other cases soon followed, not all of them achieving the publicity accorded Ms. Jorgensen, including those of a number of females who were surgically transformed into males.[87] In the United States, as of this writing, there are an estimated 2000 transsexuals and many more waiting to complete the surgery. Many of those who have been operated upon have become highly successful in their new role; others have, however, found that they have just exchanged one set of problems for another.

Transsexuals, are, however, only a small minority of those regarded by the medical profession as having a sexual identity or gender identity problem, although most of those identified by the medical groups as being sick did not regard themselves as in need of treatment. Many of these individuals began to band together, to publicize their existence, first under pseudonyms but then more openly, and as they organized and publicized their existence, they proved a significant factor in changing attitudes toward stigmatized behavior. The process was, however, circular, since individuals were fearful of identifying themselves as belonging to a "deviant" group unless the public, or at least a portion of the public, was willing to accept them. Usually, organization had been preceded by a journal or some other publication, as with Hirschfeld in Germany, and then when members of a particular group realized there were others like them, some form of organization followed.

The best organized group today are the homosexuals, followed by the transvestites. Transsexuals have also received massive publicity, and there are some organized groups of transsexuals, although many seek to submerge their past in a new identity. As of this writing there is no group arguing for the rights of individuals to engage in sexual activity with animals, although there are some individuals urging the recognition of pedophilia.[88] Sadomasochism also has its adherents, but most of the clubs remain underground.[89] Wife swapping or "swinging" is fairly common in certain levels of American society, and most of the "underground" newspapers run columns or advertisements dealing with this.[90] There are, in fact, advertisements appealing to almost every kind of sexual taste.

Since homosexuals are, in their own terms, "coming out of the closet" in increasing numbers, the growth of organized homosexual groups might be taken as illustrative of what happens. One of the first major figures to declare himself a homosexual during his own lifetime was André Gide (1869–1951). He did so first in an autobiographical novel published in 1924, *Si le grain ne meurt* (translated into English as *If It Die*), and to make certain that the implications of the novel were fully understood, he published his dialogues on homosexuality, *Corydon,* that same year.[91]

Gide's was a relatively isolated case until after the end of the Second World War, when homosexual organizations began to become more open and more vocal, homosexuality became institutionalized, and homosexuals could speak from a position of strength. Although several groups had existed before the Second World War, most such groups and publications had disappeared as a result of either the Nazi occupation or the strains of the war and only began to reemerge at the end of the war. An exception is the oldest continuously existing homosexual publication *Der Kreis,* which has been published since 1932 in Zurich, although not always under its present name. At first published entirely in German, it began in 1941 to publish articles in French, and articles in English appeared in 1952. The magazine now regards itself as trilingual. From 1938 a club was also affiliated with the magazine, and this has also continued to exist. In the Netherlands, a group affiliated with Hirschfeld's group in Berlin continued to exist after the destruction of Hirschfeld's institute, but it disappeared during the Nazi occupation of that country. Immediately after the end of the war, in 1945 in fact, a group began publishing a homosexual magazine, *Vriendschap,* and this was soon followed by an organized group. The Dutch group also began publishing *Lesbos,* a lesbian-oriented publication, one of the earliest to deal with problems of interest to the female homosexual. Much more notorious in the United States, at least for a time, was another Dutch group, the International Committee for Sexual Equality (ICSE), founded in 1951. Its notoriety stemmed from the fact that an American writer, R. E. L. Masters, denounced the ICSE as "by far the most powerful body in the history of homosexual organization and may control to an extent of which few even dream the policies and organizational activities of homosexual groups throughout the world."[92] For a time the ICSE was a center of correspondence, a sort of clearinghouse for the exchange of opinion and information, but it has not been very effective in organizing any international group of homosexuals.

In fact no homosexual organization takes orders from other organizations, although all have gone through revolutions and counterrevolutions and through periods of greater or lesser activity. This is evident in postwar Germany, where many homosexual publications sprang up between 1946 and 1955, most of them lasting for only a few issues, some of them affiliated with the organization of German homosexuals Gesellschaft für Menschenrechte (Society for Human Rights), others in revolt against its policies. For a time the German society published *Die Insel,* which soon changed its name to *Der Weg,* but any list of other publications would include *Die Gefährten, Humanitas, Hellas, Freond, Dein Freund, Pan, Vox, Jungline, Der Ring,* and *Zwischen den Andern.* France was somewhat slower to have its own homosexual magazine, *Arcadie* not appearing until 1954. *Arcadie* soon also sponsored a private club. Most other countries in Western Europe had magazines aimed at homosexual groups and either nebulous or more organized groups of homosexuals. Somewhat unique is the Homosexual Law Reform Society of England and its related Albany Trust, which came into being to change the English law.

In the United States most of the early homosexual organizations started under innocuous sounding titles, and the members used pseudonyms to protect themselves. Even then they often suffered difficulties. Some of the groups included only a few members, many being simply paper organizations. In 1925 a Chicago group formed and published a few issues of a paper called *Friendship and Freedom,* but they were denounced to the police, and four of them were arrested and dragged off to jail. Though charges against three of the four were dismissed (the fourth had to pay a $10 fine), the dangers of such activities are indicated by the fact that one of the group who worked in the post office was dismissed. Inevitably, there was a tendency to remain underground. One group called the Sons of Hamidy, which might have dated from as early as 1934, claimed thousands of members, but from what can now be determined it seems to have been mostly a paper organization with an ambitious program that never got off the ground.

Initial organization, in fact, seems to have come from without the homosexual community rather than from within. Among those agitating for change at the end of the nineteenth century were Social Democrats such as August Bebel, and the tradition of left-wing agitation was continued in the United States by Emma Goldman. Religous groups were also active—particularly the Society of Friends. In 1945 a group of New York City Quakers approached the New York psychiatrist George W. Henry to head up a Quaker Emergency Committee to deal with the problems of young people arrested on charges of homosexuality in New York City. To this end an executive committee was established (with Alfred Gross as executive officer), and a network committee of physicians, educators, and clergymen set to work. When differences developed between Dr. Henry and the Quakers, the Quakers withdrew and set up another group under the title of the Quaker Readjustment Center. This necessitated the reorganization of the Quaker Emergency Committee, which then became the George W. Henry Foundation and concerned itself with giving aid, advice, and encouragement to youths troubled with problems of homosexuality, although the foundation also had other concerns. Though not technically a part of the organized homosexual movement, many of the directors later became active in homosexual groups. Following the death of Dr. Henry on May 23, 1964, the foundation was reorganized, and it remains the oldest social work agency dealing with the problems of homosexuality. The new Quaker organization, the Quaker Readjustment Center, concentrated its activities on court cases involving sex offenders, most of which were cases of homosexuality. Its activities became closely identified with another psychiatrist, Frederic Wertham.

The first homosexual membership organization in New York was the Veteran's Benevolent Association, which existed primarily as a social club. It started in 1945 and lasted until 1954. The earliest American magazine devoted to homosexuality was the Los Angeles-based *Vice Versa,* some nine issues of which were published in 1947 and 1948. Edited by lesbians, it aimed to reach the lesbian community, and though it soon disappeared, many of the people associated with it were instrumental in the publication of *One,* a homosexual magazine, and later in the *Ladder,* a lesbian publication. Los Angeles rivaled New York as a center of homosexual activity, the nucleus of most subsequent homosexual groups in Los Angeles being a nebulous group organized in 1948 as American Bachelors for Wallace to back the Progressive party's presidential candidate Henry A. Wallace. From this group came a second, the Citizens' Committee to Outlaw Entrapment, organized to fight for the rights of homosexuals in the courts. Also active in Los Angeles was the Knights of the Clock, organized in 1950 to fight for the rights of homosexuals as well as the civil rights of Blacks and interracial couples.

The Citizens' Committee to Outlaw Entrapment, encouraged by the dismissal of a sex charge against an admitted homosexual (who had denied the specific charge against him), decided to broaden its activities. The result was the formation of the Mattachine Foundation, a name chosen to commemorate the medieval jesters who "spoke the truth" to authoritarian rulers. The Mattachine Foundation soon spawned another group, the Mattachine Society, overlapping it in membership and leadership. Edward Sagarin, in his study of the organized homosexual movements in the United States, compared the early Mattachine Society to Alcoholics Anonymous in its aims and purposes. Secrecy was a byword, and the society aimed at helping its members live a well-oriented and socially productive life in spite of their being homosexual. The Los Angeles organization ran, however, into difficulty in 1952, when it circulated a political questionnaire to candidates in a city election. A local newspaper columnist denounced the activities of the group, and much of its support evaporated. In a 1953 reorganization convention the Mattachine Foundation was terminated, and the reorganized association moved its headquarters to San Francisco. For several years thereafter the Mattachine Society made efforts to become a national organization with branches in various cities, but many of the groups, while adopting the name Mattachine, had little connection with the national organization. About the only tie-in was a journal, the *Mattachine Review,* which was published for several years.

Taking a different, and for a time a more successful, tack was a group of Los Angeles homosexuals, some of them members of the Mattachine Society, who wanted to have a journal independent of the society. the result was the appearance of *One* magazine in January 1953, probably the first widely circulated homosexual publication in the United States. *One* had its difficulties with the law, and for a time the U.S. Post Office tried to prevent its circulation, a right it finally won in 1958.[93] Giving further encouragement to organizations of homosexuals was a book by Donald Webster Cory (that is, Edward Sagarin) on *The Homosexual in America,* the first semi-objective survey of homosexual life-style in the United States.[94] Following the success of the book Cory established a book service, soon taken over by others, which, by promising publishers an audience, encouraged the publication of more books, both fiction and nonfiction, dealing with homosexuality.

Female homosexuals, at first content to work together with the men, established their own organization, the Daughters of Bilitis, in 1955. The organization took its name from Bilitis, the sometime lesbian poet in Pierre Louys' *Song of Bilitis.* It also published a magazine, *The Ladder,* containing fiction and nonfiction of interest to the female homosexual.

As more and more groups appeared, the innocuous sounding names were dropped to be replaced with more descriptive ones, such as the Homosexual Information Center and the Gay Counseling Center, until by 1975 almost every American city of any size had an organized homosexual group. Giving further courage to gays to organize was the Stonewall demonstrations in New York City in 1969. Homosexuals, angered at police harassment fought back, giving official notice to the birth of Gay Liberation. Stonewall was not an isolated incident, however, but part of the changing picture. One of the more successful of the homosexual-oriented groups has been the Metropolitan Community Church, a Pentecostal Christian Church originally organized in 1968 specifically to serve the needs of the "gay" community. Founded by the Reverend Troy Perry in Los Angeles, the church soon had branches throughout the United States as well as an active missionary program in Africa, although this last is not necessarily oriented toward homosexuals. Following the success of the Metropolitan Community Church other churches began to pay special attention to their gay members, and the Unitarians, Episcopalians, and others set up special programs to serve them. Judaism followed suit, and in 1972 a Jewish homosexual congregation, Congregation Beth Chayim Chadishim, was organized in Los Angeles.

Indicative of the changing image of homosexuality has been the appearance of openly homosexual newspapers such as the *Advocate* or *Gay Sunshine*, sold openly on the newsstands and sent through the mail. Also indicative of the change is the public discussion of homosexuality at meetings of professional societies, such as the American Sociological Association or the American Historical Association, often with participants identified as being homosexuals. *College English*, the official journal of the National Council of Teachers of English, devoted a special issue to the homosexual imagination, and two scholarly journals are specifically devoted to research and discussion of homosexuality, the *Journal of Homosexual Counseling* and the *Journal of Homosexuality*.[95]

Transvestites followed a path similar to that of homosexuals, although they were several years behind. A Los Angeles transvestite, Charles (Virginia) Prince, began publishing *Transvestia* in January 1960. The success of the magazine soon resulted in the organization of a sorority of transvestites, Phi Pi Epsilon, which served as a meetingplace for men who gained pleasure through dressing and impersonating women. Mr. Prince also established a correspondence club and took to traveling around the country meeting subscribers, and within a few years, there were groups of organized transvestites in most of the major cities of the United States, Canada, and Western Europe. As the transvestites came out of the closet and met each other, conflicts soon developed between them and Virginia Prince, just as similar conflicts had developed in homosexual organizations. Other groups and publications sprang up, many of them short-lived, including the Street Transvestite Action Revolutionaries, Empathy Club, Transvestite Action Organization, and a group calling itself the Transexuals and Transvestites. Such opposition to particular groups or spokesmen among groups usually stigmatized as being deviant must be regarded as more or less predictable. About the only thing most homosexuals have in common is that they are homosexual, and when some of the pressures of being homosexual are lessened, they feel freer to express the other aspects of their personalities. Homosexual groups today range from those who call themselves Gay Nazis, an antisemitic right-wing group, to the Gay Radicals (Lavender Reds). The transvestites include both heterosexual and homosexual individuals, and an undercurrent in much of the transvestite literature (although not that issued by Virginia Prince) is masochistic bondage.

In short, by 1975, there seems to have been a radical change in sex attitudes. Sex seems to be no longer regarded as an evil but rather is looked upon by large segments of the public as something to be enjoyed, a way of seeking pleasure. Debate in the religious communities is often no longer centered around the evils of sex but around where and when one should engage in sexual intercourse and how far one should express his or her sexual being. Science, which at one time had bolstered sex-negative attitudes, is now being used to justify the new sexual freedom. Medicine has not only been involved in sex change but also, in doing various kinds of corrective surgery and therapy, has helped individuals better enjoy their sex life. Many individuals who once would have disguised their sexual orientation have publicly proclaimed it, and there are societies and public meetings devoted to such subjects as the glories of gay liberation or the joy of being a transvestite. The sex revolution, in fact, has come on so fast that traditional institutions have been caught unprepared. Other institutions and organizations have moved into the gap. Sexual counselors, many of them with no more qualification than having read a book by Masters and Johnson, have sprung up. Group sex has become a way of life for a significant number of individuals, and all varieties of sexual expression are being given a hearing. One result of the new sexual freedom has been a drop in the number of children, a drop encouraged by the recognition of the population crisis as well as by the new sexual freedom, but a result that will have long-term consequences. Women have also become freer in expressing their sexuality, and fortified by women's liberation, they are working to eliminate many of the vestiges of the double standard. The new sexual freedom has in turn fueled the women's liberation movement. The implication of some of these changes will be examined in the final chapter.

NOTES

1. [George Drysdale], *Physical, Sexual and Natural Religion, by a Student of Medicine* (London: [Edward Truelove], "1855" (1854)). Later editions were published under the title of *The Elements of Social Science*. Some 35 English editions had appeared by 1905. It was translated into some 10 European languages.

2. Other terms included *urningin* for the female homosexual, *dioning* for a heterosexual male, *zwitter* for a hermaphrodite, *mannling* for urnings who preferred effeminate males as mates, *weiblings* for those who preferred powerful and masculine males, *zwischen-urning* for those who looked to adolescents, and so forth. All possible categories were included. In the *Symposium* Pausanius referred to homosexual love as belonging to the Muse Urania.

3. Ulrichs wrote a number of works, but probably the most important was *Memnon: Die Geschlechtsnatur des mannliebenden Urnings* (Schleiz, Germany: M. Heyn, 1868). He recounted some of his own personal experience in this work in sec. 73, p. 54 f.

4. See, for example, John Addington Symonds, *A Problem in Modern Ethics* (London: privately printed, 1891), who uses the term frequently. He also has a rather lengthy discussion and bibliography of Ulrichs' writing.

5. Benkert's pamphlet on the subject was more or less forgotten until it was republished and widely disseminated by Magnus Hirschfeld in *Jahrbuch für sexuelle Zwischenstufen,* VI (1905), i–iv, pp. 3–66. The title here was "Section 143 des preuszischen Strafgesetzbuches vom 14 April 1851 und seine Aufrechterhaltung als section 152 im Entwurfe eines Strafgesetzbuches für den norddeuschen Bund. Ofene, fachwissenschaftliche Zurschrift an Seine Excellenz Hern Dr. Leonhardt, königl. preuszischen Staats- und Justizminster." Benkert's prime concern was with the Prussian legal code which was then being adopted by the North German Confederation.

6. *Ibid.,* pp. 36 ff.

7. Both Magnus Hirschfeld and Havelock Ellis used the term *homosexual,* and probably their acceptance was critical in winning acceptance. See Magnus Hirschfeld, *Die Homosexualität des Mannes und des Weibes,* 2nd ed. (Berlin: Louis Marcus Verlagsbuchhandlung, 1920); and Havelock Ellis, *Sexual Inversion* in *Studies in the Psychology of Sex* New York: Random House, 1936, 2 vols. Vol. 1, Part 4.

8. A. Tardieu, *Etude medico-légale sur less attendent aux moeurs* (Paris: J. B. Bailliere, 1857), pp. 213-255.

9. J. L. Casper and Carl Liman, *Handbuch der Gerichtlichen Medicin* (Berlin: Hirschwald, 1889). An earlier edition by Johann Ludwig Casper alone was translated into English under the title of *A Handbook of the Practice of Medicine* (London: New Sydenham Society, 1964, 4 vols.). Translator was George William Balfour.

10. F. Carlier, *Lex deux prostitutions* (Paris: Dentu, 1889). Carlier's title is given as Ancien chef du service actif des moeurs a la prefecture de police.

11. *Lancet,* II (1846), p. 646.

12. C. Von Westphal, "Die konträre Sexualempfinding," *Archiven für Psychiatrie & Nervenkrankheiten,* II (1869), pp. 73-108.

13. See Hirschfeld, *op. cit.,* p. 6, note 19.

14. This is the claim of Hirschfeld in his article on "Homosexuality," in the *Encyclopaedia Sexualis: A Comprehensive Encyclopaedia-Dictionary of the Sexual Sciences,* Victor Robinson, ed. (New York: Dingwall-Rock, 1936), p. 322. Since Hirschfeld published an annual bibliography in his journal, he was in a position to know, but in checking his references he counted works with only the most casual mention of homosexuality.

15. Jean Martin Charcot and Valentin Magnan, "Inversion du sens génital et autres perversions sexuelles," *Archives de neurologie,* III and IV (1882).

16. P. Moreau, *Des aberrations du sens génétique* (Paris: Asselin et Houzeau 1887), pp. 149, 301, and passim.

17. Benjamin Tarnowsky, *Anthropological, Legal, and Medical Studies on Pederasty in Europe* translated by Paul Gardner (New York: Falstaff Press, 1933), pp. 9-13, 46, 70, 88.

18. Cesare Lombroso, *Criminal Man* (reprinted, Montclair, N.J.: Patterson Smith, 1972); and the *Female Offender* (New York: Appleton, 1899).

19. Richard von Krafft-Ebing, *Psychopathia sexualis,* translated from the 7th enlarged and revised German edition by Charles Gilbert Chaddock (Philadelphia: F. A. Davis, 1894), p. 1.

20. *Ibid.,* p. 5.

21. A. Binet, "Le féticisme dans l'amour," *Revue philosophique,* XXIV (1887), p. 143.

22. Charles Lasegue, *Union médicale,* (May 1877).

23. Krafft-Ebing, *op. cit.,* passim. There are other translations of different editions. A more recent one was by Franklin S. Klaff (New York: Bell Publishing Company, 1965).

24. Edward M. Brecher, *The Sex Researchers* (Boston: Little, Brown, 1969), p. 50.

25. This is quoted in the introduction to the translation of the 12th German edition of *Psychopathis sexualis* by Franklin S. Klaff, *op. cit.,* p. xi.

26. Charles Féré, *Sexual Degeneration in Mankind and in Animals,* translated by Ulrich van der Horst (New York: Anthropological Press, 1932). This was also printed under the title of *The Sexual Urge: How It Grows and Wanes* (New York: Falstaff Press, 1932).

27. See Albert Moll, *Perversions of the Sexual Instinct* (Newark, N.J.: Julian Press, 1931); and *The Sexual Life of the Child* (New York: Macmillan, 1913). He wrote many other works.

28. L. Thoinot, *Medicolegal Aspects of Moral Offenses,* translated from the French by Arthur W. Weysse (Philadelphia: F. A. Davis, 1911).

29. P. Näcke, "Le monde homosexual de Paris," *Archives d'anthropologie criminelle,* IV, 1905. He wrote on homosexuality in several cities.

30. Iwan Bloch, *The Sexual Life of Our Time,* translated from the 6th German edition by M. Eden Paul (New York: Allied Book Company, n.d.). Anyone who uses the work of Bloch, of which this is one, has to do so with caution. His studies of prostitution, the Marquis de Sade, various sexual practices, and so forth, contain much valuable data, but his references and citations are often not to be trusted, and his data are often suspect.

31. See *Studies in the Psychology of Sex* (reprinted, New York: Random House, 1936, 2 vols.). Ellis is a fascinating case himself, since he apparently suffered from premature ejaculation throughout much of his life. He also had a fascination with the act of urination, what he called urolagnia, resulting from the fact that his mother once urinated in his presence. We know a great deal about him from his autobiography, Havelock Ellis, *My Life* (Boston: Houghton Mifflin, 1939). After a few years of marriage he and his wife (who had lesbian tendencies) agreed not to engage in sexual intercourse, although both embarked on extramarital affairs. His mistress, Françoise Delisle, with whom he finally found himself potent, wrote an account of her relationship with him under the title of *Friendship Odyssey* (London: William Heinemann, 1946). There are numerous other biographies or accounts of Ellis, including Houston Peterson, *Havelock Ellis: Philosopher of Love* (Boston: Houghton Mifflin, 1928); Arthur Calder Marshall, *The Sage of Sex* (New York: Putnam's 1959); and John Stewart Collis, *Havelock Ellis* (New York: William Sloane, 1959).

32. John Addington Symonds, *A Study in Greek Ethics* (reprinted, n.p., 1928); and Symonds, *A Problem in Modern Ethics* (London: 1891). Both of the original editions were limited to 10 copies. Symonds also wrote an autobiography, but this was never published. It was used as a basis for a biography of him by Phyllis Grosskurth, *The Woeful Victorian: A Biography of John Addington Symonds* (New York: Holt, Rhinehart, and Winston, 1964).

33. Edward Carpenter, *Homogenic Love* (Manchester, England: Labour Press Society Limited, 1894); Edward Carpenter, *The Intermediate Sex: A Study of Some Transitional Types of Men and Women* (reprinted, New York: Mitchell Kennerley, 1912); Edward Carpenter, *Iolaus: An Anthology of Friendship* (reprinted, New York: Albert & Charles Boni, 1935); and Edward Carpenter, *Intermediate Types among Primitive Folk* (London: George Allen, 1914). Michael Davidson, *The World, The Flesh and Myself* (London: Barker, 1962), an autobiography of a homosexual journalist, includes a discussion of Carpenter and of Davidson's personal encounter with him.

34. Xavier Mayne, *The Intersexes, a History of Similisexualism as a Problem in Social Life* (n.p. 1908?). There is a discussion of Mayne by Noel I. Garde (pseud. i.e., Edgar Leoni) in the *One Institute Quarterly,* III (1958), pp. 94–98; and IX (1960), pp. 185–189. Stevenson sometimes listed himself as Prime-Stevenson.

35. There is a brief autobiography of Hirschfeld in the *Encyclopaedia sexualis,* pp. 317–332. His two major works are *Die Homosexualität des Mannes und des Weibes,* cited above, and *Die Transvestiten* (Berlin: Alfred Pulvermachier & Company, 1910). Neither has ever been translated, although several of his lesser works have been, including *Sexual Anomalies* (New York: Emerson Books, 1948); *Sexual Pathology,* translated by Jerome Gibbs (New York: Emerson Books, 1945); and *Men and Women: The World Journey of a Sexologist* (New York: Putnam's, 1935).

36. The full title was *Jahrbuch für sexuelle Zwischenstufen unter besonderer Beruchsichtigung der Homosexualität. Krsg. unter mitwirkung namhafter Autoren von Wissenschaftlich-hu-*

manitären Komittee or Yearbook for Sexual Intermediate States with Special Consideration for Homosexuality. Published in Cooperation with the Well-Known Authors of the Scientific-Humanitarian Committee.

37. See Hedwig Lesser, "The Hirschfeld Institute for Sexology," and Robert Wood, "Sex Reform Movement," in the *Encylopedia of Sexual Behavior,* Albert Ellis and Albert Abarbanel, eds. (New York: Hawthorn Books, 1961, 2 vols.), Vol. 2, pp. 956–970; see also *Sexual Reform Congress,* Norman Haire, ed. (London: Kegan Paul, Trench, Trubner & Company, 1930), for examples of the proceedings.

38. Some of those who held these views included W. H. Robinson, "My Views on Homosexuality," *American Journal of Urology,* X (1914), p. 550; A. Abrams, "Homosexuality," *Medical Review of Reviews,* XXIV (1918), p. 528; J. Bauer, "Homosexuality as an Endocrinological, Psychological, and Genetic Problem," *Journal of Criminal Psychopathology,* II (1940), p. 188; S. J. Glass and B. J. McKennon, "The Hormonal Aspects of Sex Reversals," *Western Journal of Surgery,* XLV (1937), pp. 467–473; R. Neustadt and A. Myerson, "Quantitative Sex Hormone Studies in Homosexuality," *American Journal of Psychiatry,* CXVII (1940), p. 524; H. H. Newman, "Twins and Sex," in *Encylopedia sexualis,* pp. 802–880; A. J. Rosanoff, *Manual of Psychiatry* (New York: Wiley, 1938); J. Sanders, "Homosexual Twins," *Encyclopedia sexualis,* pp. 342–343; E. Steinach, *Sex and Life* (New York: Viking Press, 1940). There are many others.

39. Freud actually wrote comparatively little about homosexuality *per se,* and it is necessary to examine his general works as well as some of his disciples to see his view in detail. See Freud, *Three Contributions to Sexual Theory* (New York: Journal of Nervous and Mental Diseases Publishing Company, 1910); *Leonardo da Vinci,* translated A. A. Brill (London: Kegan Paul, Trench, Trubner and Co., 1922), and some of his general writings, particularly his *Collected Papers* (London: Imago Publishers, 1924–1950); *Basic Writings* (New York: Modern Library, 1938); and *Letters* (New York: Basic Books, 1960). For some of the early Freudian influenced analyses of homosexuality, see "Die drei Grundform der Homosexualität," *Jahrbuch für sexuelle Zwischenstufen* 15 (1913), Parts 2, 3, 4. Among the early Freudians listed in the article are Hans Bluher, Isodor Corio, A. Sadger, and Max Rudolf Senf, most of whom were writing in 1912 and 1913.

40. For some of those in the psychoanalytic movement who argued that homosexuality is environmentally caused, see A. Adler, "The Homosexual Problem," *Alienist & Neurologist,* XXXVIII (1917), p. 285; Irving Bieber, et al., *Homosexuality* (New York: Basic Books, 1962); Edmund Bergler, *Homosexuality* (New York: Hill and Wang, 1956); A. A. Brill, "Conception of Homosexuality," *Journal of the American Medical Association,* LX (1913), p. 336; S. Ferenczi, *Contributions to Psychoanalysis: Sex in Psychoanalysis* (Boston: Badger, 1916); L. S. London, "Analysis of a Homosexual Neurosis," *Urology and Cutaneous Review,* XXXVII (1933), p. 93; L. S. London, *Mental Therapy* (New York: Liveright, 1937); R. E. Money-Kryle, *Development of the Sexual Impulses* (London: Kegan, Paul, Trench, Trubner, and Company 1932); W. Stekel, *Bisexual Love* (Boston: Badger, 1922); and F. Wittels, *Critique of Love* (New York: Macauley, 1929). Nonpsychoanalytic psychiatrists have also advanced the view that homosexuality is the result of psychological or environmental influences, including C. Allen, *The Sexual Perversions and Abnormalities* (London: Oxford University Press, 1949); F. S. Caprio, *The Sexually Adequate Male* (New York: Citadel Press, 1952); G. V. Hamilton, "Defensive Homosexuality," in *Encylopedia sexualis,* pp. 334–342; G. W. Henry, *Sex Variants* (New York: Hoeber, 1941); and *All the Sexes* (New York: Holt, Rinehart, and Winston, 1955); and D. J. West, *The Other Man* (New York: William Morrow, 1955). For a more nearly complete discussion, see Albert Ellis, *Homosexuality: Its Causes and Cure* (New York: Lyle Stuart, 1965).

41. Kate Millet, *Sexual Politics* (Garden City, N.Y.: Doubleday, 1970).

42. In some of his works Freud appears quite prudish, for example, in his *Civilization and Its Discontents* (London: Hogarth Press, 1930). Criticizing Freud for some of his inconsistencies in the

sex field was his disciple Wilhelm Reich, who broke with him and later wrote *The Functions of the Orgasm* (New York: Farrar, Straus and Giroux, 1961); and *The Sexual Revolution* (New York: Farrar, Straus and Giroux, 1962). See Paul A. Robinson, *The Freudian Left* (New York: Harper and Row, 1969); and Vern L. Bullough, "Sex in History, A Virgin Field," *The Journal of Sex Research*, VIII (1972), pp. 101–116.

43.   "Historical Notes: A Letter from Freud," *American Journal of Psychiatry*, CVII (April 1955), pp. 786–787. The letter was uncovered by Alfred Kinsey.

44.   G. V. Hamilton, "A Study of Sexual Tendencies in Monkeys and Baboons," *Journal of Animal Behavior*, IV (1914) pp. 295–318.

45.   Edward J. Kempf, "The Social and Sexual Behavior of Infra-Human Primates with Some Comparable Facts in Human Behavior," *The Psychoanalytic Review* IV (April, 1917), pp. 127–154.

46.   For some later animal research, see Frank A. Beach, "A Review of Physiological and Psychological Studies of Sexual Behavior in Mammals," *Physiology Review*, XXVII (1947), pp. 240–307. See also J. P. Scott, *Animal Behavior* (Chicago: University of Chicago Press, 1958).

47.   For a survey of some of the recent research into sexuality, see Arno Karlen, *Sexuality and Homosexuality* (New York: W. W. Norton, 1971), Part 2.

48.   Martin S. Weinberg and Colin J. Williams, *Male Homosexuals: Their Problems and Adaptations* (New York: Oxford University Press, 1974), p. 6. Though much of their criticism is probably justified, it might be that they are reflecting the bias of sociologists toward psychoanalytic thought. The same criticism they render against the psychiatric and psychological view can be leveled against their own historical view. In their brief four-page summary of sexual history they make more mistakes and erroneous assumptions than any similar four pages that I have read.

49.   For an account of some of the barriers to sex research in the past, see Sophie D. Aberle and George W. Corner, *Twenty-Five Years of Sex Research: History of the National Research Council Committee for Research in Problems of Sex 1922–1947* (Philadelphia: W. B. Saunders, 1953). See also Edward Sagarin, "Sex Research and Sociology: Retrospective and Prospective," in James M. Henslin, ed., *Studies in the Sociology of Sex* (New York: Meredith Corporation, 1971), pp. 377–408; and Winston Ehrmann, "Marital and Non-Marital Sexual Behavior," in Harold Christensen, ed., *Handbook of Marriage and the Family* (New York: Rand McNally, 1964).

50.   A good survey of these pre-Kinsey studies can be found in Alfred Kinsey, Wardell B. Pomeroy, Clyde E. Martin, *Sexual Behavior in the Human Male* (Philadelphia: W. B. Saunders, 1948), pp. 23–31. Kinsey was careful to cite those upon whom he relied or with whom he differed. Among the more valuable of the pre-Kinsey statistical studies, in addition to those of Hirschfeld, were Katharine B. Davis, *Factors in the Sex Life of Twenty-Two Hundred Women* (New York: Harper, 1929); G. V. Hamilton, *A Research in Marriage* (New York: A. & C. Boni, 1929); Robert Latou Dickinson and Laura Beam, *A Thousand Marriages* (Baltimore: Williams and Wilkins, 1931); Dorothy Dunbar Bromley and F. H. Britten, *Youth and Sex: A Study of 1300 College Students* (New York: Harper, 1930); L. M. Terman et al., *Psychological Factors in Marital Happiness* (New York: McGraw-Hill, 1938); and L. B. Hohman and B. Schaffner, "The Sex Lives of Unmarried Men," *American Journal of Sociology*, LII (1947), pp. 501–507.

51.   Kinsey, *op. cit.*, pp. 627–628.

52.   *Ibid.*, pp. 650–651.

53.   Alfred C. Kinsey, Wardell B. Pomeroy, Clyde E. Martin, Paul H. Gebhard, *Sexual Behavior in the Human Female* (Philadelphia: W. B. Saunders, 1953), pp. 474–475.

54.   *Ibid.*, pp. 377, 383.

55.   See Bronislaw Malinowski, *The Sexual Life of Savages* (London: George Routledge & Sons, 1932, 3rd ed.); also Malinowski, *Sex and Repression in Savage Society* (reprinted, New

York: Meridian Books, 1955). See also George Devereux, "Institutionalized Homosexuality of the Mohave Indians," in *The Problem of Homosexuality,* Hendrik Ruitenbeek, ed. (New York: Dutton, 1963). I have excluded the earlier anthropological studies of Carpenter, *op. cit.,* since he was not a professional anthropologist. Another early anthropological study was by Ferdinand Karsch-Haack, *Das Gleichgeschlechtliche Leben der Naturvölker* (Munich: 1911, reprinted, New York: Arno Press, 1975).

56.   There is a whole series of semischolarly works on sex, including such works as Paolo Mantegazze, *Sexual Relations of Mankind,* originally published in the 1880s and translated into English by Samuel Putnam (New York: Eugenics Publishing Company, 1935); and even the works of Iwan Bloch, cited above. Some-what more literary are the various works by Edward Carpenter as well as the writings of John Addington Symonds, cited above. Included in this category might be Richard Burton, some of whose ideas are summarized in *The Erotic Traveler,* Edward Leigh, ed. (New York: Putnam's, 1967); and in one of his Terminal Essays to his edition of *The Book of the Thousand Nights and a Night,* discussed earlier in this book. Also included in this category would be a number of contraceptive manuals that began to appear in greater quantities in the twentieth century.

57.   See W. P. J. Mensinga, *Über facultative Steriltät. I. Beleuchet vom prophylactischen und hygenischen Stanpunkte für practische Aerzte. II. Das Pessarium occusium und dessen Application,* 4th ed. (Neuweid und Leipzig, L. Heuser, 1885). The second part discusses the diaphragm. The best discussion of the whole subject is in Norman E. Himes, *Medical History of Contraception* (reprinted, New York: Schocken Books, 1970).

58.   A good discussion of the chemical contraceptives from the viewpoint of the 1930s can be found in Cecil I. B. Voge, *The Chemistry and Physics of Contraceptives* (London: Jonathan Cape, 1933). The discussion of cocoa butter and quinine can be found on pp. 146–149, 153–154.

59.   Clive Wood and Beryl Suitters, *The Flight for Acceptance* (Aylesbury, England: Medical and Technical Publishing Company, 1970), p. 107.

60.   For some of these works, see Lothrop Stoddard, *The Rising Tide of Color* (New York: Scribner's, 1922); and the *Revolt Against Civilization* (New York: Scribner's, 1923); or Alfred P. Schulz, *Race or Mongrel* (Boston: L. C. Page & Company, 1908). For a continuation of such views in somewhat more gentlemanly form, see Carleton Putnam, *Race and Reason* (Washington, D.C.: Public Affairs Press, 1961).

61.   Norman St. John-Stevas, *Obscenity and the Law* (London: Secker & Warburg, 1956), pp. 66–67.

62.   *Ibid.,* pp. 71, 126–127.

63.   *Ibid.,* pp. 70–74.

64.   Himes, *op. cit.,* pp. 243–250.

65.   For a discussion of Ms. Sanger's work, see her own autobiography written in 1938, published under the title *Margaret Sanger: An Autobiography* (republished, New York: Dover Books, 1971). There are several other biographies of her and her work, but recommended is that by Lawrence Lader, *The Margart Sanger Story* (N.Y. Garden City, Doubleday 1955).

66.   Lawrence Lader, *Abortion* (Indianapolis: Bobbs-Merrill, 1966), p. 123.

67.   *Ibid.*

68.   *Ibid.,* p. 133.

69.   *Ibid.,* p. 145.

70.   Felix Roubaud, *Traité de l'impuissance et de la stérilité chez l'homme et chez la femme,* (Paris: J. B. Bailliere et Fils, 1876) 2nd ed.

71. Robert Latou Dickinson, *Human Sex Anatomy* (Baltimore: Williams and Wilkins, 1933, republished in a 2nd ed., 1949).

72. *Ibid.*, Chap. 7, 2nd ed.

73. See William E. Masters and Virginia E. Johnson, *Human Sexual Response* (Boston: Little, Brown, 1966); and Masters and Johnson, *Human Sexual Inadequacy* (Boston: Little, Brown, 1970). For an example of sex counseling, see Mr. and Mrs. K., *The Couple,* as told to Monte Ghertle and Alfred Palca (New York: Coward, McCann and Geohegan, 1971).

74. See *The Report of the Commission on Obscenity and Pornography,* William B. Lockhard, chairman (Washington, D.C.: U.S. Government Printing Office, 1970), p. 25. There were also a number of technical reports dealing with all aspects of pornography and obscenity published as separate volumes.

75. *Ibid.,* pp. 51–64.

76. *National Institute of Mental Health Task Force on Homosexuality: Final Report and Background Papers,* John M. Livingood, ed. (Rockville, Md. National Institute of Mental Health, 1972).

77. *Report of the Committee on Homosexual Offences and Prostitution,* Sir John Wolfenden, chairman (London: Her Majesty's Stationary Office, 1957).

78. D. O. Cauldwell, *Questions and Answers on the Sex Life and Sexual Problems of Trans-Sexuals* (Girard, Kans.: Haldeman-Julius Publications, 1950), p. 3. See also his *Sex Transmutation—Can One's Sex Be Changed?* (Girard, Kans.: Haldeman-Julius Publications, 1951).

79. Harry Benjamin, "Transsexualism and Transvestism as Psychosomatic and Sinatipsychich Syndromes," *American Journal of Psychotherapy,* VIII, (1954), p. 219; "Clinical Aspects of Transsexualism in the Male and Female," *American Journal of Psychotherapy,* XVIII (1964), p. 458; *The Transsexual Phenomenon* (New York: Julian Press, 1966); and Benjamin's introduction to Richard Green and John Money, *Transsexualism and Sex Reassignment* (Baltimore: Johns Hopkins Press, 1969).

80. Hans Houstein, "Transvestism and the State at the End of the Eighteenth and Nineteenth Centuries," *Zeitschrift für sexual Wissenschaft,* XV (1928–1929), p. 353.

81. See *Zeitschrift für sexual Wissenschaft,* XVI (1929–1930), p. 145, for the case of Toni Claus Hans F. den Antrag, who attempted to change his birth record from male to female. His application was denied because he had all the biological characteristics of the male, although he wore female clothing, looked completely feminine, and thought of himself as female.

82. Nels Hoyer, *Man into Woman* (London: Jarrold's 1933).

83. See Flavia Alaya, *William Sharp—"Fiona Macleod"* (Cambridge, Mass.: Harvard University Press, 1970).

84. Roberta Cowell, *Roberta Cowell's Story* (New York, British Book Centre, 1954).

85. Christine Jorgensen, *A Personal Autobiography* (New York: Paul S. Eriksson, 1967).

86. Christian Hamburger, "Desire for Change of Sex as Shown by Personal Letters from 465 Men and Women," *Acta endocrinologica,* VIII (1954), pp. 231–242. See also C. Hamburger, G. K. Stürup, and E. Dahl-Iversen, "Transvestism: Hormonal, Psychiatric and Surgical Treatment," *Journal of the American Medical Association,* CLII, p. 391.

87. There have been a number of biographies of individuals. Among the most recent is Jan Morris, *Conundrum* (New York: Harcourt, Brace, Jovanovich, 1974). Since Morris was a well-known writer before the sex change, his book perhaps received more publicity than some. See also Gilbert Oakley, *Man into Woman* (London: Walton Press, 1964); and Robert Allen, *But for the Grace* (London: W. H. Allen, 1954).

88.   J. Z. Eglinton, *Greek Love* (New York: Oliver Layton Press, 1964), argues that the acceptance of boy love is needed today. The Guyon Society propagates these ideals in an organized way, although the membership seems to be confined to a few people in Los Angeles.

89.   There have been some studies that would indicate that it is coming more out into the open. There are also a number of leather bars and speciality houses catering to possible SM (as it is called) individuals. See Michael Leigh, *The Velvet Underground* (New York: MacFadden Books, 1963); and *The Velvet Underground Revisited* (New York: MacFadden Books, 1968); Gerald and Caroline Greene, *S-M, The Last Taboo* (New York: Grove Press, 1973).

90.   For some recent studies as well as exposés, see Gilbert Bartell, *Group Sex* (New York: Peter H. Wyden, 1971); William and Jerrye Breedlove, *Swap Clubs* (Los Angeles: Sherbourne Press, 1963); and Stuart Barton, *The Human Swop Shop* (Worthing, England: Lyle Publications, 1972). See also the *Village Voice*, the *Los Angeles Free Press*, et al.

91.   André Gide, *If It Die*, translated by Dorothy Bussy (New York: Modern Library, 1957); and *Corydon*, translated by Hugh Gibb (New York: Farrar, Straus, 1950).

92.   R. E. L. Masters, *The Homosexual Revolution* (New York: Julian Press, 1962), p. 39. Masters' book is a mishmash of information and sensationalism. Much more accurate is the doctoral dissertation of Edward Sagarin, *Structure and ideology in an Association of Deviants* (Unpublished Ph.D. dissertation, New York University, 1966). Also helpful is *Homosexuals Today: A Handbook of Organizations and Publications*, Marvin Cutler, ed. (Los Angeles: One, Inc., 1956). See also Don Teal, *The Gay Militants* (New York: Stein and Day, 1971), and John Lauritsen and David Thorstad, *The Early Homosexual Rights Movement* (1869–1935) (Albion, Calif.: Times-Change Press, 1974).

93.   *One, Inc. v. Olesen*, 241 f, 2nd 772. 9th Gr (1957), and 355 U.S. 271 (1958). See also *One Institute Quarterly*, II (1958).

94.   Donald Webster Cory, *The Homosexual in America: A Subjective Approach* (New York: Greenberg, 1951).

95.   *College English*, XXXVI (Nov. 1974), No. 3. One of the first attempts to be scholarly was the *One Institute Quarterly*, which still publishes an occasional issue. Among the periodicals in addition to the *Advocate* and *Gay Sunshine* are *Amazon Quarterly*, *The Body Politic*, *Fag Rag*, *Focus*, *The Gay Alternative*, *Gay News*, *Integrity*, *Lesbian Tide*, *Manroot Poetry Journal*, *Mouth of the Dragon*, and *Out Sappho*. For a directory to gay organizations, see *International List of Gay Organizations*, published by the Gay Activists Alliance, Box 2, Village Station, New York, N.Y. 10014. There is also *Gay Yellow Pages*, Box 292, Village Station, New York, N.Y. 10014, as well as many others. In Los Angeles the Homosexual Information Center also publishes listings.

22

WHERE WE ARE GOING
AND HOW WE GET THERE

Western society is in a period of rapidly changing attitudes about sex. As with any radical change, people are anxious and uncertain. The future seems to hold dangers, and in spite of the difficulties and horrors of the past, we have come to be comfortable with the knowledge that we have lived through it. The future can perhaps be made to seem less threatening if we attempt to come to grips with some of the issues facing us, and if this book has a message, it is that, for the first time in Western culture, we have the potential of coming to terms with human sexuality. It is essential we do so, for it is impossible to ignore or repress the whole subject of sexuality as we have so often done in the past. Conditions have changed much too radically, and though there are several reasons for this, four might be emphasized, since they are a result of historical forces.

1. Perhaps the major change from the past is the acceptance by women of their own sexuality. Though women have always been the sexual partners of men, and humanity would not have survied if they had not served their generative function, generation and sexuality are not necessarily the same thing. Usually in the past, even in cultures such as China and India, where sexuality was more likely to be accepted, women were looked at in terms of male needs or in terms of their potential for progeny, and not in terms of their own needs.

677

The *Yin-Yang* theory stressed the male's need to gain the female essence, and though this might have encouraged the male to bring about orgasm in the female, his purpose was strictly selfish. In India, women, in spite of their satisfaction in the sex act, were conceived of as nothing without men. In the West, those women who enjoyed sex usually did not make it public, since the penalties for so doing were severe. Proper women, the good wives and mothers, were not supposed to enjoy sex, and if they admitted they did, they were suspect, looked upon as nymphomaniacs or prostitutes, and regarded as not proper company for other women. Even the women who enjoyed sex in the privacy of their bedchambers had anxieties because it so often resulted in pregnancy. Though this meant that the male partner was also made a father, fatherhood in most societies has never been the confining task that motherhood was. Most frequently in the past the female's willingness to engage in sex has implied the concomitant of pregnancy, childbirth, and the long period of infant care.

It is estimated that a woman engaged in sexual intercourse on a random basis would become pregnant about once in every 33 or 34 times she had sex. This incidence would decrease with the age of her partner; if he was an older man, the incidence might fall to once in every 65 or 70 acts of intercourse. In a normal life of sex activity, a woman who married at 15 and lived past 45, and whose husband was roughly the same age, might have become pregnant every other year or approximately 15 times, unless other factors intervened. If she had several early spontaneous abortions, the numbers of pregnancies would increase. Other factors would, however, tend to decrease the pregnancy factor, and few ever achieved the maximum. Some indication of this is the total maternity ratio, defined as the average number of live births (excluding spontaneous and induced abortions) per woman aged 45 or over. For the Ashanti of Africa, the ratio has been estimated at about 6, for the Sioux Indians at 8, and for certain groups of Eskimo at less than 5. The highest ratio of 10.6 recorded today is among the Hutterites, a religious communal group in the United States and Canada who are well nourished and who also believe in large families.[1]

One way in the past that women avoided getting pregnant so often was to marry men considerably older than themselves or to delay their own marriages and introductions to sexuality. Another way was for women to deny their sexuality, to emphasize that they engaged in sex only reluctantly to have children, and, as their pregnancies became burdens, to force their husbands, whose sexuality was always recognized, to find alternative means of satisfying themselves, through prostitution, polygamy, concubinage; in short, through the adoption of a double standard. Sex was usually regarded as a good for the male, but for the female it has always been a mixed pleasure.

In a sense, women could play down their sexuality because in the past there have been fewer women in the desirable marriage ages than men,[2] and this has meant that the man she married was usually not at the height of his sexuality, but an older man. Though we have little data on the frequency of intercourse among men in the past, Kinsey and his associates found that the highest rate of sexual outlet for males under optimum conditions took place between the ages of 16 and 20, after which the male tended to decrease his frequency over each succeeding 5-year period.[3] Other ways of lessening a woman's sexuality, and therefore her reproductivity, was through polygamy or concubinage. As compensation for her denial of sexuality, a woman's procreative abilities were admired, and motherhood was the badge of honor, sometimes her only honor in those societies that regarded a woman as a piece of property.

In most societies, if a woman committed adultery, was raped, or lost her virginity, she was damaged property, and her husband or father could expect to gain compensation for this damage and, in the case of adultery, kill her and her paramour if she was caught. The safest thing for a woman to do was to keep a careful check on her sexuality, to deny it in public, since if she did not, she was seen as inviting rape or encouraging adultery. Understanding of female physiology was also lacking. The male sex organs are open and exposed, but the female's are hidden, and the whole process of female orgasm is difficult to observe and much easier to fake than in the male. Undoubtedly, women talked to other women about their own sexual problems, but officially at least, this kind of information was communicated primarily by males, since it was the males who wrote or who were educated. In fact, almost everything we know about women before the eighteenth century is something we know through male eyes and male writers.[4] The result has been a great distortion of the female, a distortion believed and accepted by the female herself, since this is what she was taught. In male eyes, the female was nothing without a male. Evidence for this is that female homosexuality has never been as severely punished as male homosexuality, and in many areas, even in Western culture, it has not been proscribed at all. Though there has long been a recognition of the importance of the clitoris in arousing the female, perhaps because it was visible, most of the other sexual aspects of the female were ignored until fairly recently.

As women's sexuality has gradually come to be recognized, it has also been more possible for her to express it without being anxious about pregnancy, and even when pregnancy accidentally resulted, abortion has come to be an accepted solution. In the process female virginity has become less prized in many areas, although in still other areas of the world it is still so highly prized that girls about to be married often take the precaution of having their labia sewn together so that their virginity would never be questioned by their bridegrooms. Almost inevitably, however, as women became more liberated, better able to express themselves, they have mounted a challenge to the continued existence of the double standard. Probably males today are no more sexually oriented than they were in the past, but where previously they turned to prostitution or similar outlets for relief, they now find sexual satisfaction with their girl friends and other nonprofessionals. This trend will continue, and as the vestiges of the double standard crumble, women more and more will demand sexual equality with men, and if the past is any indication, this will lead to greater rather than less incidence of heterosexual intercourse.

2.   Second only to the emancipation of women as a factor in the changing sexual scene is the growth of the antinatal philosophy, a philosophy that, at least by implication if not stated purpose, holds that the main purpose of sex is no longer procreation but enjoyment. Encouraging this have been a whole series of economic, political, and environmental factors. In the past, children were an economic necessity, and one of the main purposes in life was to have children, particularly sons, who would take care of their parents in this life and perform the necessary rituals when the parents died. An old person without a family had no one to take care of him or her, and even eunuchs were allowed to adopt in many societies. An agricultural economy could always put another hand to work, and someone from a person's own family costs less than an outsider. In many less urbanized societies today, kinship is still more important than friendship. Inevitably, the political structure of the past encouraged children; when population began to level off, as it did in nineteenth-century France, the government made efforts to encourage more children.

In an urban society where childhood has been prolonged to keep children off the job market, where education goes on for longer and longer periods, and where children have come to be recognized as special individuals with special needs instead of someone who could serve his or her parents, children are no longer an economic asset but a financial liability. In the past, this was rarely the case, and in fact, without children, a person who became sick or disabled or grew old was helpless. Relatives, particularly children, were the eventual sources of succor and assistance, an assistance no longer so important as the state and governmental units intervene to provide income insurance, medical care, and old age security.

Adding to the burdens of parenthood is the emergence of the concept of childhood, in large part through the decline in infant mortality, but also through the process of redefining parenthood. When perhaps half of one's children might die before reaching adulthood, it was difficult to become emotionally involved with them. Though infant mortality figures of the past are notoriously unreliable, there is a kind of consensus among experts that probably between 30 and 40 percent of the infants born prior to the nineteenth century failed to live beyond their first year. There were periods of variation, and in England during the decade 1730–1740, probably as many as 437 infants out of every 1000 born alive died before reaching their first year, but in the decade 1791–1800 the number had dropped to 240 per 1000 live births. These are probably the extremes, with the mean lying fairly close to 30 percent.[5] As infant and child mortality has declined, parents have been encouraged to invest more and more of themselves in their children, deemphasizing large families and emphasizing the duties of parents to each individual child.

Giving a further impetus to smaller families has been the growing consciousness of the dangers of overpopulation. Though the concept of over-population has been around at least since the time of Thomas Malthus, it has gained more backing in the past few decades as the cost of child rearing has risen and the world's resources seemed to diminish. Though Malthus advocated abstinence and self-control, few of his supporters, even in the early nineteenth century, accepted this solution to the problem he posed. Instead, as has been pointed out earlier in this book, the neo-Malthusians accepted the necessity of contraception, of nonprocreative sex, if you will. In short, a combination of economic, political, and environmental forces has led to an antinatalist position that recognizes the importance of sex but attempts to limit offspring. If this is carried to its logical conclusion, it is difficult to justify traditional Western attitudes toward marriage or even toward sex, since progeny is no longer the end purpose. In fact, one effect of the antinatalist position has been a willingness to experiment with nonprocreative sex, including not only the use of contraception but also body touching, body awareness, group sex, and eroticism in general. Predictably, homosexuality, transvestism, masturbation, and even sadomashochism became permissible, if only because they give pleasure (at least to some) and do not result in progeny. Probably one reason the Greeks tolerated and encouraged homosexuality was as a population control measure, and though the Christians did not put forth celibacy in any such terms, the special reward accorded to those who remained chaste had the same effect. If progeny are no longer so important and sex itself is recognized as a good, then it becomes difficult to deny others the right to engage in the nonprocreative sex they want.

3. A third major factor in changing attitudes has been the growing recognition of the variety possible in human sexuality. Some of the reasons for this growing consciousness have been discussed in previous chapters, and there is no need to repeat here. It is important to point out, however, that it has not only been scientific discoveries that have changed Western outlook but also contact with other cultures and peoples through their literature, through travel, and through histories such as this. Not only have Western sexual attitudes been influenced by other cultures but we have been influenced by them. The Christian missionaries to the Hawaiian Islands encouraged the native women to cover their breasts, and the muumuu was invented, but it was not only missionaries who visited other cultures. The native women of Bali went barebreasted and seemed to American advertisers to represent such a desirable state that a brand of women's brassieres was named after them. Many of the homophile poets of the nineteenth century were deeply influenced by the Muslim Sufi

poets. Pornography began to be studied as a scholarly subject by first examining classical writings on the subject,[6] and a whole series of early studies on sex were devoted to what the Greeks or Romans did.[7] Primitive cultures were also examined, and the results were used to indicate the possibilities of different attitudes in sex.[8] Sex life in India apparently had considerable influence on British attitudes, and India provided a haven for those unable to conform to staid British practices. In fact, the whole relationship of colonial countries to western European masters is comparatively unexplored, and when it is explored, I believe it will be demonstrated that the alternative sexual styles available were a source of attraction to many.[9]

Often, the contact with different cultural norms was unintentional, as was the case of the American presence in the Far East, particularly in Japan following World War II. Japan, which had inherited and modified traditional Chinese sexual attitudes, proved a cultural shock to many Americans. American military authorities were in a quandary about what to do with the warehouses of sex and pornographic materials, which at that time were banned in America. Though they eventually destroyed much of the material, many an American G.I. came back to this country with a changed attitude. Japanese pillow books (or sex advice for young brides) found their way into the United States, and so did samples of Japanese pornography.[10] Many of the sexual aids and devices that shocked Americans in 1945 and 1946 were standard material in American sex stores by 1974.

4.   Last, but no less important, has been the organized propaganda for new forms of sexuality. Though there have always been individuals who advocated variety in sexual behavior, organized groups are fairly new. In the past, when sex was a forbidden subject or when many forms of sex behavior were socially ostracized, those who had certain sexual tastes attempted to find others who agreed with them. Often, certain bars or baths or other places came to be congregating places, but few organized and came out into the open. Probably the first of the organized groups to do so were the nudists, and since the history of this group parallels other groups, it is worth some attention, even though many nudists would deny a sexual connotation to nudity. Organized nudism usually traces its appearance to a book by Richard Ungewitter, *Die Nacktheit* ("Nudity"), which appeared in 1905. Unable to find a commercial publisher, Ungewitter issued the book himself to foster the formation of a sort of Utopian society where all persons would go without clothing, observe strict vegetarianism, and abstain from using tobacco and alcohol.[11] His book was quickly followed by a similar one by Heinrich Pudor,[12] and by the organization of a nudist spa by Paul Zimmerman, The Freilichtpark at Klingberg am See near Lübeck, Germany.

From Germany the movement spread into France and the Scandinavian countries and slowly into other areas. Growth was slow until after the end of

World War I, when the movement was introduced into both England and America. The first organized nudist activities in the United States took place in 1929, and the movement was not discovered by the newspapers until the 1930s, when it became the center of sensational headlines.[13] Some of the early nudists were arrested, but they thrived on publicity, and every time the newspapers ran a story, the idea of nudism was brought into "thousands of American homes, where it had never been dreamed of before."[14]

A number of nudist groups formed across the country, but the movement ran into difficulty when, in 1939, both the Los Angeles City Council and the Los Angeles County Board of Supervisors passed ordinances prohibiting heterosexual nudity of more than two people. The ordinance was widely imitated and almost brought the movement to an end in this country, but it managed to stay alive, largely through the publication of the magazine *Sunshine and Health,* which made its appearance in 1933. In spite of continuing efforts at censorship, the magazine managed to survive by the willingness of the publisher to paint out pubic areas on all subjects, but in 1947, when there was a refusal to do this any longer, the magazine was banned from the mails. In a series of court cases challenging some of the basic issues of sex censorship that lasted until 1958, *Sunshine and Health* had a checkered career. Though the publishers of *Sunshine and Health* emerged victorious, the magazine itself rapidly declined as other, more stylishly produced, and less prudish magazines, taking advantage of the freedom it won, replaced it on the newsstands.[15]

Nudists also won several other court cases. The most important occurred in Michigan, where a 1956 police raid on a resort known as Sunshine Gardens resulted in the arrest of four persons who were charged with indecent exposure. One of those arrested was an elderly woman nudist who was recuperating from a severe illness and who died shortly after the raid. Her death was explained as in part due to the effects of the raid. On appeal in 1958 the Michigan Supreme Court reversed the conviction of those arrested, and Justice John D. Voelker, better known as the novelist Robert Traver, wrote that the major "indecency in the whole case was the raid and the actions of the police officers in descending on the camp like storm troopers, herding them (the nudists) before clicking cameras and then hauling them off in police cars."[16] Equally important as the Michigan case was the final overturn of the Los Angeles ordinance prohibiting organized nudism. To test the law, a group of individuals organized as the Elysium Institute and set up a nudist camp known as Elysium Field, which was soon raided by three helicopter loads of officials, plus a detachment of police cars. Some 24 people were rounded up, but in the 1968 trial, the ordinance outlawing nudist camps was declared unconstitutional on the grounds that it violated the rights of free association and expression, privacy, due process, and equal protection, all rights guaranteed under the Constitution and the Bill of Rights.[17] The change in public mores was not better indicated than by the fact that, in 1975, only 7 years later, several southern California cities had established certain beaches as nude beaches.

Organized homosexuality, as was indicated in the last chapter, followed a pattern similar to that of the nudists, as did various other sexually oriented groups. Side by side with the special interest groups are others, such as the Sex Information and Education Council of the United States (SIECUS), a nonprofit group formed in 1964 to act as a resource center and catalyst for change in sexual attitudes. Its purposes were to prevent the flagrantly exploitive aspects of sexuality and to offer children and young adults an opportunity to understand sexuality in terms of integrity, dignity, and the spirituality it deserves. More scholarly is the Society for the Scientific Study of Sex, which publishes a journal, the *Journal of Sex Research,* to understand human sexuality better. Perhaps the ultimate in current society is the organization of a surrogate society, a group of women and men (mostly women) who undertake to engage in sexual intercourse with individuals who have sexual problems. The members consider themselves professionals in the field and stress that intercourse is the culmination of treatment, not the beginning.

As sex has come to stage center, instead of being relegated to the prop room or the nether recesses under the stage, mainstream American groups have also begun to come to grips with the problem of sexuality. The American Civil Liberties Union, for example, has argued that sexual behavior between consenting adults in private is a constitutional right. The Society of Friends, or at least some elements among them, have argued that the quality of human relationships matters more than the kind of sexual activity.[18] The Unitarians and other groups have appointed ministers to deal with homosexuals and with the divorced and have tried to come to terms with sexuality by including a base unit on sexuality in their Sunday school curriculum. Many ministers, rabbis, and priests have set up as sexual and marital counselors, and sexual therapy is a rapidly growing field.

With these kinds of historical forces working for change, it becomes more and more important that we come to terms with sexuality, even though some might find this a painful and threatening thing to do. Here, perhaps, history can offer some assistance. As should be evident from this book, every type of current sexual behavior has been recorded in the past, although undoubtedly the modern penchant for analytical description has provided for more categories than once existed and perhaps even created treatments that have made new definitions possible, as is the case with the operation for transsexuals. Although every culture has defined some types of sexual behavior as deviant, what constituted deviance has varied from culture to culture, and even such innocent pastimes as kissing have been regarded as pornographic in some cultures. Where certain forms of sexual behavior have been repressed or punished, they have not necessarily disappeared but generally have gone underground.

Those who fear the new sexuality are, however, probably correct in assuming that toleration will increase the incidence of what previously has been disapproved sexual behavior. Many people will feel freer to experiment with variant forms of sexuality, and though variant sexuality is not contagious, many in the past who made painful efforts to conform will be less likely to do so now. This makes it more important than ever that society understand sexual behavior and realize that some cultural conditioning probably encourages certain forms of sexual behavior, although there are still a lot of unknown factors. Even in such sexually repressive societies as nineteenth-century England or sixteenth-century Italy, homosexuality was probably more widely prevalent than it might otherwise have been because of the institutionalization of homosexuality within the educational system. Though this book has not attempted to label individuals homosexual or deviant, any investigator into the products of the English public school in the nineteenth and twentieth centuries is struck by the number of individuals who were homoerotic. How many other unconscious decisions that society makes that have similarly encouraged what society has regarded as deviant is still unknown.[19]

Even though homosexuality furnished a strong undercurrent in British literary and government circles, it was rarely mentioned, and when it was, it was often used in a negative way. For example, when Roger Casement, the Irish patriot, was convicted of high treason in 1916, the British government publicized his homosexuality, supposedly in an effort to make his execution more publicly acceptable.[20] André Gide was passed over for the Nobel prize for many years because he was an admitted homosexual who had written on the subject. Somerset Maugham was denied any official British honor until he was in his 80's, in part because he was a homosexual. Many others carefully repressed their homosexuality, including John Maynard Keynes, Hugh Walpole, Lytton Strachey, E. M. Forster, and Virginia Woolf, or only expressed their complete personality to a few intimates. They were forever conscious of the cloud hanging over their heads. It was not just homosexuality that proved dangerous; even individuals like Bertrand Russell got into difficulty because of their expressed approval of sexuality in general.

By denying sex so vehemently, Western culture has probably tended to make us more conscious of sexuality than those cultures that have accepted it with little question. Even if this was the case, to deny and repress sex in the past was probably not as harmful as today, since most people grew up with animal life around them and with a lack of privacy in which all ages were tossed into one room, and everyone was early acquainted with the sexual aspects of life. With the growth of the concept of privacy in the nineteenth century, with the appearance of special rooms, and the more sheltered life-style made possible by middle-class wealth and protection, large numbers of people were either ignorant about sexual matters or had acquired the haziest of notions about what to do. An indication of this lack of knowledge is the fact that one of the problems that sexual and marital counselors have is showing people how to engage in the sex act.

This denial of sexuality has given us only a partial view of mankind, and historians have added to the problem by refusing to deal with the subject at all. We have failed to realize that the basis of Western sex hostility lies deep in Greek mythology, if not earlier, a mythology long ago rejected by Western culture. Because the Christians accepted the notions of Greek mythology and reinterpreted them to meet their needs and because eighteenth- and nineteenth-century medical writers accepted these same concepts and reinterpreted them to meet their prejudice, we have never really come to grips with our own sexuality. Unavoidably, there has been an interaction between mythology, religion, science, and law, and as one was challenged, it was reinforced by the other. In today's world we need a new mythology, if you will, and a growing number of Christian clergymen and theologians have argued that the Western hostility to sex is not necessarily Christian, that alternative Christian views are possible. Certainly contemporary science no longer accepts the assumptions of the nineteenth-century advocates of sexual repression. The law has, however, only just begun to change in the United States, although most of Europe long ago modified their laws, even including England, after whose laws our own are modeled. If history shows anything about sex, it demonstrates that human sexuality has been extremely varied; that, in spite of the restrictions, people have always found ways to express themselves sexually, often contrary to accepted norms; and that there are alternative views to the monolithic hostility we have usually advocated in the West. I hope, if I may be personal, that we as a society can come to terms with sexuality, and I firmly believe that, as far as an individual is concerned, it is essential to understand his or her own sexuality, and to the extent that the person understands himself or herself, it will be possible to understand better those with whom he or she interacts. I hope that this book will aid in this understanding. With this note I close, hopeful that I have brought some understanding, even though I have only touched the surface of the vast, untapped storehouse of information about sex in history.

NOTES

1. See the discussion by Clive Wood and Beryl Suitters, *The Fight for Acceptance* (Aylesbury, England: Medical and Technical Publishing Company, 1970), p. 10.

2. Gy Acsadi and J. Nemeskeri, *History of Human Life Span and Mortality* (Budapest: Akadémai Kaidó, 1970), p. 221.

3. See Alfred C. Kinsey, Wardell B. Pomeroy, Clyde E. Martin, *Sexual Behavior in the Human Male* (Philadelphia: W. B. Saunders, 1948), pp. 336, 356, Tables 81 and 88.

4. I have amplified on this at great length in Vern L. Bullough, *The Subordinate Sex: A History of Attitudes Towards Women* (Urbana, Ill.: University of Illinois, 1974).

5. See Richard Harrison Shryock, *The Development of Modern Medicine,* 2nd ed. (revised, New York: Knopf, 1947), p. 102.

6. Charles Forberg, *De figuris veneris* (reprinted, New York: Medical Press of New York, 1964). The original came out early in the nineteenth century.

7. See Julius Rosenbaum, *The Plague of Lust* (Paris: Charles Carrington, 1901, and originally published in 1882); John Addington Symonds, *A Study in Greek Ethics* (reprinted, private publisher, 1928); M. H. F. Meier, "Paederastie," *Allgemeine Encyclopädie und Kunsten,* (Leipzig: Brockhaus, 1837, 167 vols.); the various studies by Paul Brandt, who under the pseudonym of Hans Licht, issued a 3-volume *Sittengeschichte Griechenlands,* a 1-volume condensation of which was translated by J. H. Freese under the title of *Sexual Life in Ancient Greece* (London: Routledge & Kegan Paul), 1932). The number could be added to greatly. See the chapters on Greece and Rome for other examples.

8. One of the early studies was the terminal assay by Richard Burton in his translation of *The Books of the Thousand Nights and a Night* (reprinted, New York: Heritage Press, 1934, 6 vols.) Vol. 6, pp. 3748–3782. Another early example was Edward Carpenter, *Intermediate Types among Primitive Folk* (London: George Allen & Company, 1914). More recently there were the studies by Clellan S. Ford and Frank A. Beach, *Patterns of Sexual Behavior* (New York: Harper and Paul B. Hoeber, 1951). See appropriate chapters for others.

9. One of the few attempts to do so was Allen Edwardes, *The Rape of India: A Biography of Robert Clive and a Sexual History of the Conquest of Hindustan* (New York: Julian Press, 1966). There is also some discussion of this topic in Fawn M. Brodie, *The Devil Drives: Life of Sir Richard Burton* (New York: W. W. Norton, 1967).

10. See, for example, *Shunga: Images of Spring,* Charles Grosbois, ed. (Geneva: Nagel Publishers, 1965), for some examples.

11. Richard Ungewitter, *Die Nackheit* (Stuttgart: Strecker & Schröder, 1907).

12. Heinrich Pudor, *Nackkultur* (Berlin: Steglitz, 1906).

13. For a discussion, see Donald Johnson, *The Nudists* (New York: Duell, Sloan and Pearce, 1959); Fred Ilfeld, Jr., and Roger Lauer, *Social Nudism in America* (New Haven, Conn.: College and University Press, 1964); and especially William E. Hartman, Marilyn Fithian, and Donald Johnson, *Nudist Society* (New York: Crown Publishers, 1970). One of the first books to be printed in English was Joseph Michael Setiz, *Die Nacktkulturbewegung,* which was translated by Clifford Coudray as *Back to Nature: An Exposition of Nude Culture* (Dresden, Germany: R. A. Gieseck, 1923). Interestingly enough it was never published in England or America. The first published in England, I think, was Hans Suren, *Der Mensch und die Sonne,* which was translated by David Arthur Jones as *Man and Sunlight* (Slough, England: Sollux Publishing Company, 1927). In America one of the earliest books was Frances and Mason Merrill, *Among the Nudists* (New York: Knopf, 1931), and they followed this up with *Nudism Comes to America* (New York: Knopf, 1932). An early history of nudism in America is a privately printed pamphlet, published in August 1952, by one of the founders of American nudism, Kurt Barthel, *Facts about the Origin of Nudism Abroad and in the United States.*

14. Barthel, *op. cit.*

15. Hartman, Fithian, and Johnson, *op. cit.,* pp. 216–224.

16. *Ibid.,* p. 232.

17. *Los Angeles Times,* March 30, 31, 1972.

18. This is expressed in *Towards a Quaker View of Sex* (London: Friends Home Service Committee, 1964).

19. See, for example, some of the research by John Money, some of which was summarized in John Money and Anke A. Ehrhardt, *Man & Woman, Boy & Girl* (Baltimore: Johns Hopkins University Press, 1972). See also Richard Green, *Sexual Identity Conflict in Children and Adults* (New York: Basic Books, 1974).

20. See, among other works, Alfred Noyes, *The Accusing Ghost or Justice for Casement* (London: Victor Gollancz, 1957); René MacColl, *Roger Casement* (London: Hamish Hamilton, 1956); and Peter Singleton-Gates and Maurice Girodias, *The Black Diaries of Roger Casement* (New York: Grove Press, 1959).

SUGGESTIONS FOR
FURTHER READING

Though homosexuality and other forms of stigmatized sexual behavior have been almost a taboo topic for the professional historian, there is a vast amount of source material, and great quantities of medical, legal, and other monographic literature available to the reader who wants to pursue the matter further. Some of this material is indicated in the footnotes, and the interested reader would be advised to pursue the leads suggested there, although some words of caution are in order. One difficulty with investigating the source material is identifying the euphemisms used to discuss any sexual question. There is also a danger of trying to read more into the euphemisms than the writer originally intended.

As to early cultures, the greatest number of references to sexual behavior are found in the mythological writing, in the philosophical and religious speculation, and in the law codes. Later, both literary and scientific writings contain numerous references, although most of the monographic material will be found in the medical literature, particularly during the last hundred years. Beginning about 1870 and through to the present day, there has been a massive outpouring of medical and psychiatric literature about homosexuality, transvestism, and other forms of stigmatized sexual behavior. During my research I have collected literally thousands of references, and the reader who is interested in pursuing these can turn to a bibliography I and several colleagues have compiled, Vern Bullough, Dorr Legg, Barry Elcano, et al., *An Annotated Bibliography of Homosexuality and Other Stigmatized Behavior* (New York: Garland Publishers, 1976). The bibliography includes more than 10,000 titles, including an estimated 4000 in medical and allied literature written between 1870 and the present. Whereas many of these medical articles are valuable, the majority offer no new insights, and most could be dismissed as pseudoscience. For the period between 1940 and 1968 there is a more detailed bibliographical listing of medical and scientific literature in English, M. S. Weinberg and A. B. Bell, *Homosexuality: An Annotated Bibliography* (New York: Harper & Row, 1972). Barry Elcano and Vern Bullough have also compiled an *Annotated Bibliography of Prostitution* (New York: Garland, 1976). Over 3,000 titles are included.

Medical and psychiatric monographs about stigmatized sexual behavior, though the largest part of catalogued writings on the subject, are not the only studies available. Sociologists, anthropologists, biologists, lawyers, and psychologists have also added to the growing literature, and a fairly comprehensive listing of their works can also be found in the Bullough–Legg–Elcano bibliography. Long before the researcher entered the field of human sexuality, the creative writer was exploring the topic, many of them with remarkable insight. A listing of most of the poems, novels, dramas, and other similar material can be found in the above-listed bibliography. Another valuable guide is William Parker, *Homosexuality: A Selective Bibliography* (Metuchen, N. J.: Scarecrow Press, 1971). Somewhat more specialized but no less valuable is Jeannette H. Foster, *Sex Variant Women in Literature* (London: Frederick Muller, 1958), particularly when used with Gene Damon and Lee Stuart, *The Lesbian in Literature* (San Francisco: Daughters of Bilitis, 1967).

There are other bibliographies that should prove helpful. One of the more comprehensive is the bibliography of the Kinsey Library at the University of Indiana (G. K. Hall, publishers). A good general survey is by Flora C. Seruya, Susan Losher, and Albert Ellis, *Sex and Sex Education: A Bibliography* (New York: Bowker, 1972). Also helpful is Roger Goodland, *A Bibliography of Sex Rites and Customs* (London: George Routledge & Sons, 1931). For a generalized survey of sexual information, see *The Encyclopedia of Sexual Behavior,* Albert Ellis and Albert Abarbanel, eds. New York: Hawthorn Books, 1961, 2 vols.); and the *Encyclopaedia Sexualis,* Victor Robinson, ed. (New York: Dingwall-Rock, 1936). To keep current in the field it is important to examine the reviews and bibliographies published in the *Journal of Sex Research* or in the *Archives of Sexual Behavior.* Both are American publications, and similar research journals are available in several different countries. *Index Medicus* lists the current medical literature about sex, but the best guide to current historical studies of sexual behavior is the quarterly *Current Work in the*

History of Medicine, published by the Wellcome Institute for the History of Medicine in London. Somewhat less current but no less valuable is the *Bibliography of the History of Medicine,* issued annually by the U.S. Government Printing Office. Though both bibliographies are devoted to medical history, they include most aspects of research on sexual behavior under their purview.

One of the best ways of gaining some understanding of the vast amounts of published material devoted to homosexuality and associated behavior is to go through the *Jahrbuch für sexuelle Zwischenstufen,* a German yearbook devoted to homosexuality, first published in 1899 and continued in various forms up to the Nazi era. The force behind the journal was Magnus Hirschfeld; he and his collaborators made research into the subject almost an industry. They ferreted out any reference to homosexuality, transvestism, transsexualism, and similar sexual activities in whatever culture or period it appeared. Obviously, any study of stigmatized sexual behavior has to begin with the researches of Hirschfeld and his associates, although they must be used with caution, for the writers did not always exercise the critical examination of sources required by historians. Some results of Hirschfeld's researches appeared in his large-scale studies of homosexuality and transvestism: *Die Homosexualität,* 2nd ed. (Berlin: Louis Marcus, 1914, 1920), and *Die Transvestiten* (Berlin: Alfred Pulvermacher, 1910). These studies were historical as well as medical and legal and are the beginnings of serious historical studies, in spite of their occasionally casual scholarship. Equally important are the researches of Havelock Ellis, whose writings are probably more readily available to the English-speaking world. A good start are his *Studies in the Psychology of Sex* (reprinted, New York: Random House, 1940, 2 vols.). Ellis had originally collaborated with John Addington Symonds on a study of homosexuality, which because of difficulties with English publishers, was originally published in German under the title of *Das konträre Geschlechtsgefuhl* (Leipzig: George Wigand, 1896). Symonds had also written more specialized studies on homoerotic love that were published anonymously, namely, *A Problem in Greek Ethics* and *A Problem in Modern Ethics,* both often reprinted.

The fact that Symonds had first approached the subject through a discussion of the Greeks was no accident, since most of the research into what we now call homosexuality was, until Hirschfeld began his investigations, done in terms of Greek love. The fact that the Greeks emphasized boy love and that there were Greek figures who were homosexuals, lesbians, or transvestites made it both possible and necessary for classical scholars to come to terms with such behavior. As a result there is a vast literature on homosexuality and similar behavior in Greece. The most important of the early studies was by M. H. E. Meier, who wrote on "Paderastie" in the *Allgemeine Encyclopädie und Kunsten* (Leipzig: Brockhaus, 1837, 167 vols.), IV, 149–188. His research has since been updated and amplified by L. R. de Pogey-Castries, *Histoire de l'amour Grec dans l'antiquité* (Paris: Stenhal et Cie, 1930). No similar studies exist in such detail for any other period of history, nor have historians devoted as much time to sexual behavior in general in other periods or cultures. Most valuable for the medieval period is John T. Noonan, *Contraception: A History of Its Treatment by the Catholic Theologians and Canonists* (Cambridge, Mass.: Belknap Press of Harvard University, 1966). Though this study concentrates on contraception, Noonan also includes a discussion of all non-procreative sex. Also important is Derrick Sherwin Bailey, *Homosexuality and the Western Christian Tradition* (London: Longmans, Green and Company, 1955). Other generalized studies preceding this book and published in English include Arno Karlen, *Sexuality and Homosexuality* (New York: W. W. Norton, 1971); Thorkil Vangard, *Phallós* (London: Jonathan Cape, 1969); and Wainwright Churchill, *Homosexual Behavior among Males* (New York: Hawthorn Books, 1967). For anthropological sources, the Human Relations Area Files has collected and translated many of the reports of missionaries, travelers, and investigators dealing with various forms of sexual behavior.

In the last decade or so the study of homosexuality and other stigmatized sexual behavior has expanded almost at a geometric ratio. Most scholarly journals are now willing to carry articles on the topic, and inevitably, the nature of research on the top has been improving. One of the first attempts to encourage scholarly research in this country was by One, Inc., of Los Angeles, which published the *One Quarterly* for several years in the fifties and sixties and which is still issued sporadically. As of this writing, two scholarly journals are devoted specifically to homosexuality in the United States, the *Journal of Homosexual Counseling* and the *Journal of Homosexuality*. Transvestism and transsexualism, as yet, do not have their own journals, but as they are more and more recognized as separate and distinct from homosexuality and from each other, the research on them also increases. Some indication of this is the increase in the number of organizations and specialized magazines appealing to transvestites and transsexuals. Some discussion of this phenomenon was contained in the last chapter of this book.

In sum, there is still a vast amount of material about stigmatized sexual behavior to be investigated. The sources of history offer a vast, untapped storehouse of information, and this book, detailed as it is, has only touched the surface.

INDEX